IMPROVED EDITION

THE HOLY
QUR'ÂN

Transliteration in Roman Script with
Arabic Text and English Translation

English Translation By
Abdullah Yusuf Ali

Transliteration By
M. Abdul Haleem Eliyasee

Islamic Book Service

THE HOLY QUR'ÂN

Transliteration in Roman Script with
Arabic Text and English Translation

English Translation By
Abdullah Yusuf Ali

Transliteration By
M. Abdul Haleem Eliyasee

ISBN 81-7231-570-8

First Edition: 2004
Improved Edition: 2007

Published by *Abdul Naeem* **for**

 Islamic Book Service

**2872-74, Kucha Chelan, Darya Ganj,
New Delhi 110 002 (INDIA)**
Ph.: 011-23253514, 23286551, 23244556
Fax: 011-23277913, 23247899
E-mail: islamic@eth.net / ibsdelhi@del2.vsnl.net.in
Website: www.islamic-india.com

OUR ASSOCIATES:

- **Al-Munna Book Shop Ltd., (U.A.E.)**
  Sharjah *Tel.:* 06-561-5483, 06-561-4650 Dubai *Tel.:* 04-352-9294

- **Azhar Academy Ltd., London (United Kingdom)**
  Tel.: 020 8911 9797

- **I.B. Publisher Inc., New York (U.S.A.)**
  Tel.: 91-73328008, 6312540909

- **Husami Book Depot, Hyderabad (India)**
  Tel.: 040-6680-6285

Printed in India

Contents

Page No.

1. Important Disclosure .... *iv*
2. Transliteration Key of Arabic Letters .... *viii*
3. Arabic Words Explained .... *x*
4. List of Prostration Places in The Qur'ân .... *xi*
5. Symbols Denoting Pause .... *xii*
6. Index of Sûras – Chapters .... *xiii*

Important Disclosure

Praise be to Allah, the Cherisher and Sustainer of the worlds, Who has said in His Noble Book:
> There has come to you from Allah
> Light and a Perspicuous Book. (1)

And may peace and blessings be upon the Seal of the Prophets, Mohammad, who has said that:
> The best among you is he who learned
> The Qur'ân and then taught it. (2)

May the peace and blessings of Allah be upon him, his family and all his Companions.

The Glorious Qur'ân is the Book of Allah, the Wise and Worthy of all Praise, Who has promised to safeguard it from any violations in its purity. It becomes incumbent upon each and every person who seeks the dignity of this world and the bliss of the Hereafter to regulate his life according to it, to implement its commandments and to pay homage to the magnificence of the One Who revealed it. This can be an easy task for those favoured with guidance from Allah, especially those blessed by a understanding of Arabic, the language of the divine communication. But for those not acquainted with Arabic, their ignorance is a barrier between them and this source of guidance and illumination. A translation of the message of Allah is thus a task not to be taken lightly or performed superficially.

Before the reader begins to study the Qur'ân he must realise that unlike all other writings, this is a unique book with a supreme author, an eternal message and a universal relevance. Its contents are not confined to a particular theme or style, but contain the foundations for an entire system of life, covering a whole spectrum of issues, which range from specific articles of faith and commandments to general moral teachings, rights and obligations, crime and punishment, personal and public law, and a host of other private and social concerns. These issues are discussed in a variety of ways, such as direct stipulations, reminders of Allah's favours of His creation, admonitions and rebukes. Stories of past communities are narrated, followed by the lessons to be learned from their actions and subsequent fates.

The Qur'ân enjoys a number of characteristics unique to it alone, some of which are as follows:

1. It is the actual Word of Allah; not created but revealed for the benefit of all mankind.
   > Blessed is He Who sent down the Criterion
   > To His servant, that it may be
   > An admonition to all creatures. (3)

2. It is complete and comprehensive. The Almighty says:
   > Nothing have We omitted from the Book. (4)

   In another place we read,
   > And We have sent down to thee
   > The Book explaining all things. (5)

3. It is a theoretical and a practical Book, not only moralising but also defining specifically the permissible and the forbidden. The importance of understanding the message of the

---

(1) Sûrat al-Mâ'idah: 15.   (2) Narrated by the six ones except Muslim.   (3) Sûrat al-Furqân: 1.
(4) Sûrat al-An'âm: 38.   (5) Surat an-Naḥl: 89.

Qur'ân is undeniable, but simply reciting it with the intention of seeking Allah's pleasure and reward is also an act of worship and meritorious in itself. Allah Almighty says:

> So take what the Prophet gives you
> And refrain from what he prohibits you. (6)

4. Allah has perfected His religion for all mankind with the revelation of this Book. He say:

> This day have I perfected your religion for you,
> Completed my favour upon you and have chosen
> For you Islam as your religion. (7)

5. It is Allah's eternal miracle revealed to the Prophet Muhammad for all succeeding generations. In response to those who doubt the authorship of the Qur'ân, Allah Almighty has challenged the most articulate Arabs to produce a whole book, ten chapters or even one solitary chapter which can be remotely comparable to the Qur'ân. But to this day, no one has succeeded in meeting the challenge of the Almighty. The critics of the Qur'ân have been struck dumb by its ineffable eloquence and surpassing beauty.

> Say, if the whole of mankind and jinns
> Were to gather together to produce the
> Like of this Qur'ân, they could not
> Produce the like thereof; even if they
> Backed up each other with help and support. (8)

The Almighty also says:

> Or they may say: he forged it.
> Say: Bring ye then ten chapters
> Forged, like unto it and call
> (To your aid) whomsoever ye can
> Other than Allah, if ye speak
> The truth. (9)

And again:

> Or do they say: he forged it?
> Say: Bring then a chapter like
> Unto it and call (to your aid)
> Anyone ye can besides Allah,
> If it be ye speak the truth. (10)

6. It has been revealed to re-establish the sincere worship of Allah alone, without association of any partners with Him.

> This is a Book with verses basic or
> Fundamental (of established meaning),
> Further explained in detail,-
> From One who is Wise and Well-Aware.
> (It teaches) that you should worship
> None but Allah. (11)
> And they have been commanded no more
> Than this: to worship Allah,
> Offering Him sincere devotion, being true

---

(6) Sûrat al-Ḥashr: 7.   (7) Sûrat al-Mâ'idah: 3.   (8) Sûrat Banî Isrâ'îl: 88.

(9) Sûrat Hûd: 13   (10) Sûrat Yûnus: 38   (11) Sûrat Hûd: 1-2.

> In faith, to establish regular prayer
> And to give Zakat, and that is
> The religion Right and Straight. (12)

7. It contains a complete code which provides for all areas of life, whether spiritual, intellectual, political, social or economic. It is a code which has no boundaries of time, place or nation.

> Verily this Qur'ân doth guide
> To that which is most right. (13)

8. Allah Almighty has taken upon Himself the duty of preserving the Qur'ân for ever in its entirety, as He says:

> We have without doubt sent down
> The Message, and We will assuredly
> Guard it (from corruption). (14)

So well has it been preserved, both in memory and in writing, that the Arabic text we have today is identical to the text as it was revealed to the Prophet. Not even a single letter has yielded for corruption during the passage of the centuries. And so it will remain for ever, by the consent of Allah.

Given the depth as well as the sublimity of the Qur'ânic text, a faithful translation of it into another language is virtually impossible. The various translations that exist today, however accurate they may be, cannot be designated as the Qur'ân, since they can never hope to imitate the diction or the style of the Book of Allah. But as translation is one of the few ways to export the message of the Qur'ân to allow those lacking in knowledge of Arabic to share this priceless gift, it becomes a duty for those in a position to fulfil this task.

A number of individuals have in the past ventured to translate the Qur'ân, but their works have generally been private attempts, greatly influenced by their own prejudices. In order to produce a reliable translation free from personal bias, a Royal decree (No. 19888, dated 16/8/1400 AH) was issued by the Custodian of the Two Holy Mosques, King Fahd ibn Abdul Aziz, at that time the deputy prime minister, authorising the General Presidency of the Departments of Islamic Researches, Ifta, Call and Guidance to undertake the responsibility of revising and correcting a particular translation which would be selected for this purpose and made publicly available later.

To accomplish this enormous task, a number of committees were formed, comprising scholars well-qualified both in Islamic Shari'a and the English language. Some of these scholars were associated with the General Presidency of the Departments of Islamic Researches, Ifta, Call and Guidance.

The first committee was given the task of examining the existing translations and choosing the most suitable one from among them. The committee discovered that there was no translation free from defects and so there were two options open for consideration: the first was to select the best translation available and then adopt it as a base for further works as well as a source of reference, with the objective of revising its contents and correcting any faults in view of the objections raised against it; the second was to prepare a fresh and independent translation, starting from scratch.

It became obvious from studying these translations that the second option demanded much time and efforts, neither of which were available at the time.

---

(12) Sûrat al-Bayyinah: 5.   (13) Sûrat Banî Isrâ'îl: 9.   (14) Sûrat al-Ḥijr: 9.

The first option was therefore considered to be more practical, since it met the existing urgent requirements and helped to achieve the desired goal in a comparatively short period of time. The translation by the late Ustadh ABDULLAH YUSUF ALI was consequently chosen for its distinguishing characteristics, such as highly elegant style, a choice of words close to the meaning of the original text, accompanied by scholarly notes and commentaries.

The committee began revising and correcting this translation with the aid of other translations available, by comparing and then adopting best expressions as well as by introducing fresh expressions where necessary. The committee was fully aware of all the criticisms that had been directed against this translation and which had been carefully brought to the notice of the presidency by a number of academic bodies and other involved parties. In the second stage, the entire work of this committee was referred to a number of individuals and organizations who then augmented any deficiencies in the work of the committee.

A third committee was set up to collate all their suggestions. It then compared all such views regarding specific issues, selected the appropriate one (s) and arrived at a text as authentic and defect-free as was humanly possible.

Finally, a fourth committee was formed to look into the findings of the second and third committees and to implement the recommendations made by them. Furthermore, this committee had to finalise the text by adopting the most accurate expression where needed, besides checking the notes vigilantly so as to clear any misconceptions regarding the articles of faith, varying juristic opinions and thoughts not in conformity with the sound Islamic point of view.

According to the Royal decree (No.12412, dated 27/10/1405 AH), this translation is printed at King Fahd Holy Qur'ân Printing Complex in Al-Madinah Al-Munawarah and also with coordination of the General Presidency of the Departments of Islamic Researches, Ifta, Call and Guidance.

To implement the directions of the Custodian of the Two Holy Mosques (May Allah preserve him) concerning the Propagation of the Book of Allah, its distribution and translation into every language spoken by Muslims the worldwide, and due to the cooperation between the General Secretariat of King Fahd Holy Qur'ân Printing Complex and the Presidency of Islamic Researches, Ifta, Call and Guidance regarding a faithful, specific and scholarly translation of the meanings of the Holy Qur'ân, we are pleased to present to all Muslims and those seeking spiritual light among English-speaking people this translation which comes as one of the Series of the translations of the meanings of the Holy Qur'ân into various languages printed by the Complex in Al-Madinah Al-Munawarah.

May Allah reward bounteously those who were behind this blessed work.

Transliteration Key of Arabic Letters

The following table shows the system which I have followed in transliterating the letters of the Arabic alphabet:

1. Alphabet

No.	Name of Arabic Letters	Arabic Letters	Latin Characters	Pronunciation
1	Hamzah	ء	’	Pronounced as *a*, *i*, *u* preceded by a very slight aspiration.
2	Bâ’	ب	b	In English like the 'big'.
3	Tâ’	ت	t	A soft dental, as in Italian *t*.
4	Thâ’	ث	s̲	A nearly sound between *th* and *s*.
5	Jîm	ج	j	In English like the 'judge'.
6	Ḥâ’	ح	ḥ	A strong and sustained expulsion of breath.
7	Khâ’	خ	kh	Guttural, as similar to the German 'ach'.
8	Dâl	د	d	A soft dental, as in English 'the'.
9	Dhâl	ذ	z̲	A sound between *d* and *z*.
10	Râ’	ر	r	In English like the 'roll'.
11	Zâ’	ز	z	In English like the 'zone'.
12	Sîn	س	s	In English like the 'sea'.
13	Shîn	ش	sh	In English like the 'sheet'.
14	Ṣâd	ص	ṣ	A strongly articulated *sw*, as in English 'swallow'.
15	Ḍâd	ض	ḍ	A strong sound between *d* and *z*, articulated as letter 'Ṣâd'.
16	Ṭâ’	ط	ṭ	A strongly articulated palatal *t*.
17	Ẓâ’	ظ	ẓ	A strongly articulated *z*.
18	‘Ayn	ع	‘	A guttural an, the pronunciation must be learnt by an Arabic teacher.
19	Ghayn	غ	gh	A strong guttural *gh*.
20	Fâ’	ف	f	In English like the 'foot'.
21	Qâf	ق	q	A strongly articulated semi guttural *k*.
22	Kâf	ك	k	In English like the 'king'.
23	Lâm	ل	l	In English like the 'love'.
24	Mîm	م	m	In English like the 'mat'.

25	Nûn	ن	n	In English like the 'never'.
26	Hâ'	ه	h	In English like the 'happy'.
27	Wâw	و	w	In English like the 'work'.
28	Yâ'	ى	y	In English like the 'yet'.

2. Short Vowels

ـَ	Fatḥa	a	كَتَبَ	kataba
ـِ	Kasra	i	سُئِلَ	su'ila
ـُ	Ḍamma	u	يَذْهَبُ	yaẕhabu

3. Long Vowels

اَ	aa	قَالَ	qaala
اِى	ee	قِيلَ	qeela
اُوْ	oo	يَقُوْلُ	yaqoolu

4. Diphthong

| اَى | ay | كَيْفَ | kayfa |
| اَوْ | aw | حَوْلَ | ḥawla |

5. Points to Remember

- Alif (ا) is not be confused with Hamza (ء). If it has diacritical marks (as ـَ , ـِ , ـُ) it is hamza. Alif is always followed by another letter as بَ = ba بَا = baa.

- Alif Jaazim (اْ) = å. It gives a glottal stop while reading the letter 'Alif' above which it is placed, *e.g.*, تَأْتِيَهُمْ = taåtiyahum.

- Gunna = ñ (nasal sound), as *n* is pronounced in 'uncle'.

- When silent ن =n or Tanween (nunation) were followed by ب =b. They are pronounced like م = m with a gunna, *e.g.*, اَنْبَا = 'ambaa / خَبِيرٌ بِمَا =khabeerum bimaa.

- Shaddah (ـّ) (double letter). It is pronounced with a sustained emphasis on that letter, *e.g.*, دَلَّ =dalla.

- For Madd (ـٓ) (elongation of vowels) three symbols have been introduced: *a, i, u,* as in بَ =ba بَا =baa بَآ =baaa, بِ =bi بِى =bee بِىٓ =beee, بُ =bu بُوْ =boo بُوٓ =booo.

- There is only 'Mâ'roof' (known) sound in the Qur'ân as بِ =bi, بُ = bu. There is no 'Majhool' (unknown) sound in the Qur'ân except in one word: مَجْرٰىهَا 'Majrayhaa' (as in English 'ray') (P. 12, S. 11:41).

Arabic Words Explained

A comprehensive list of names, places and topics appears as an index at the end of the book. Here some oft-repeated Arabic words occurring in the translation are given with brief explanation.

ALLAH: The proper name of God in Arabic.

HAJJ: The pilgrimage to Makkah which takes place in the last month of the Islamic calendar.

IBLÎS: Satan.

ISLÂM: Literally, to submit.
The Religion of all the Prophets of Allah confirmed finally by the mission of the Prophet Muhammad ﷺ.

JINN: Invisible beings constituting a whole race like mankind.

MUHAJIR: Literally, the emigrant.
One who leaves the home town to join a Muslim community.

MUSLIM: One who professes the faith of Islam or born to a Muslim family.

QIBLA: The Ka'ba. The direction for the daily prayers of a Muslim.

QUR'ÂN: Literally, the recital.
The final revelation given to the Prophet Muhammad ﷺ in Arabic.

RAMADAN: The ninth month of the Islamic calendar during which the Muslims fast.

SÛRAH: A chapter of the Qur'ân.

ṬAGUT: Literally, a tyrant, oppresser, false god, temper to error.
Tagut is applied to any object which is worshipped besides Allah.

UMRAH: A minor form of pilgrimage to Makkah.

UMMAH: Literally, a nation but is usually applied to the Muslim Brother-hood.

YATHRIB: The name by which Madinah was known before the Prophet's migration to that city.

ZAKAT: Literally, to grow, to purify.
The third pillar of Islam.
It is a definite portion of wealth which is given to needy at the turn of the year.

List of Prostration Places in The Qur'ân

It is a good practice to prostrate at the following places while reciting the Qur'ân.

No.	Part No.	Name of Sûrah	Sûrah No.	Verse No.
1	9	Al-A'râf	7	206
2.	13	Ar-Ra'd	13	15
3.	14	An-Naḥl	16	50
4.	15	Banî Isrâ'îl	17	109
5.	16	Maryam	19	58
6.	17	Al-Ḥajj	22	18
7.	17	Al-Ḥajj	22	77*
8.	19	Al-Furqân	25	60
9.	19	An-Naml	27	26
10.	21	As-Sajdah	32	15
11.	23	Ṣâd	38	24
12.	24	Ḥâ-Mîm Sajdah	41	38
13.	27	An-Najm	53	62
14.	30	Al-Inshiqâq	84	21
15.	30	Al-'Alaq	96	19

* In all, fourteen places of prostration are agreed upon by all Muslim religious scholars and 'Ulama, while Imâm Shâf'i (R.A) suggests prostration at this place also.

The following invocation is usually recited during the prostration:

(سَجَدَ وَجْهِيَ لِلَّذِي خَلَقَهُ وَصَوَّرَهُ وَشَقَّ سَمْعَهُ وَبَصَرَهُ تَبَارَكَ اللهُ أَحْسَنُ الْخَالِقِينَ)

Sajada wajhiya lillazee khalaqahoo wa ṣawwarahoo, wa shaqqa sam'ahoo wa baṣarahoo, tabaarak-Allaahu Aḥsanul-Khaaliqeen.

[*Sahih Muslim*, Vol.4, *Hadîth* No.201].

Symbols Denoting Pauses

Symbol	Extract from Verse	Sûrah Number	Verse Number
Compulsory stop			
مـ	وَاذْكُرْ فِي الْكِتٰبِ مَرْيَمَ ۚ اِذِ انْتَبَذَتْ	19	16
Necessary stop			
ط	عَلَيْهَا صَعِيْدًا جُرُزًا ۚ	18	8
Stop vocal sound for a moment without breaking the breath			
وقفة	وَاعْفُ عَنَّا ۗ وَاغْفِرْ لَنَا ۗ وَارْحَمْنَا ۗ اَنْتَ	2	286
سكتة	كَلَّا بَلْ ۜ رَانَ	83	14
Necessary to continue, do not pause			
لا	فَاعْبُدْنِيْ ۙ وَاَقِمِ الصَّلٰوةَ لِذِكْرِيْ	20	14
Desirable to continue, do not pause			
ز	اِلَّا اَنْ يَّشَاءَ اللّٰهُ ۚ وَاذْكُرْ رَّبَّكَ	18	24
ص	حِجَابًا ۙ فَاَرْسَلْنَاۤ اِلَيْهَا رُوْحَنَا	19	17
ق	قَالُوا اتَّخَذَ اللّٰهُ وَلَدًا ۚ مَا لَهُمْ بِه	18	4/5
صلى	وَزِدْنٰهُمْ هُدًى ۖ وَّرَبَطْنَا	18	13/14
Recommended pause			
قف	وَمَلٰئِكَتِه وَكُتُبِه وَرُسُلِه ۖ لَا نُفَرِّقُ	2	285
Optional to pause or to continue			
ج	رَبِّكَ ۚ لَا مُبَدِّلَ لِكَلِمٰتِه ۚ وَلَنْ	18	27
Any two of the three verses may be read in continuity			
∴	وَقَالَ الَّذِيْنَ كَفَرُوْا لَوْلَا نُزِّلَ عَلَيْهِ الْقُرْاٰنُ جُمْلَةً وَّاحِدَةً ۚ كَذٰلِكَ ۚ لِنُثَبِّتَ بِه فُؤَادَكَ وَرَتَّلْنٰهُ تَرْتِيْلًا	25	32

﴿ فهرس بأسماء السُّوَر ﴾ وبيان المكّى والمدنى منها ﴿

Index of Sûras – Chapters
(Showing The Makki and The Madani ones)

Sûrah	No.	Page No.	Makki/Madani	مكّية/مدنيّة	رقم الصفحة	رقم السورة	اسم السورة
Al-Fâtiḥah	1	2	Madani	مكّية	٢	١	الفاتحة
Al-Baqarah	2	4	Madani	مدنيّة	٤	٢	البقرة
Âl-'Imrân	3	53	Madani	مدنيّة	٥٣	٣	ال عمران
An-Nisâ'	4	83	Madani	مدنيّة	٨٣	٤	النّساء
Al-Mâ'idah	5	113	Madani	مدنيّة	١١٣	٥	المائدة
Al-An'âm	6	135	Makki	مكّية	١٣٥	٦	الانعام
Al-A'râf	7	160	Makki	مكّية	١٦٠	٧	الاعراف
Al-Anfâl	8	188	Madani	مدنيّة	١٨٨	٨	الانفال
At-Tawbah	9	199	Madani	مدنيّة	١٩٩	٩	التّوبة
Yûnus	10	220	Makki	مكّية	٢٢٠	١٠	يونس
Hûd	11	235	Makki	مكّية	٢٣٥	١١	هود
Yûsuf	12	250	Makki	مكّية	٢٥٠	١٢	يوسف
Ar-Ra'd	13	265	Makki	مكّية	٢٦٥	١٣	الرّعد
Ibrâhîm	14	272	Makki	مكّية	٢٧٢	١٤	ابراهيم
Al-Ḥijr	15	279	Makki	مكّية	٢٧٩	١٥	الحجر
An-Naḥl	16	286	Makki	مكّية	٢٨٦	١٦	النّحل
Banî Isrâ'îl	17	302	Makki	مكّية	٣٠٢	١٧	بنى اسرائيل
Al-Kahf	18	315	Makki	مكّية	٣١٥	١٨	الكهف
Maryam	19	329	Makki	مكّية	٣٢٩	١٩	مريم
Ṭâ-Hâ	20	337	Makki	مكّية	٣٣٧	٢٠	طه
Al-Anbiyâ'	21	349	Makki	مكّية	٣٤٩	٢١	الانبياء
Al-Ḥajj	22	360	Madani	مدنيّة	٣٦٠	٢٢	الحج
Al-Mu'minûn	23	370	Makki	مكّية	٣٧٠	٢٣	المؤمنون
An-Nûr	24	380	Madani	مدنيّة	٣٨٠	٢٤	النّور
Al-Furqân	25	391	Makki	مكّية	٣٩١	٢٥	الفرقان
Ash-Shu'arâ'	26	399	Makki	مكّية	٣٩٩	٢٦	الشّعراء

Sûrah	No.	Page No.	Makki/Madani	مكّة/مدنية	رقم الصفحة	رقم السورة	اسم السورة
An-Naml	27	411	Makki	مكّية	٤١١	٢٧	النّمل
Al-Qaṣaṣ	28	421	Makki	مكّية	٤٢١	٢٨	القصص
Al-'Ankabût	29	433	Makki	مكّية	٤٣٣	٢٩	العنكبوت
Ar-Rûm	30	442	Makki	مكّية	٤٤٢	٣٠	الرّوم
Luqmân	31	449	Makki	مكّية	٤٤٩	٣١	لقمان
As-Sajdah	32	454	Makki	مكّية	٤٥٤	٣٢	السّجدة
Al-Aḥzâb	33	457	Madani	مدنيّة	٤٥٧	٣٣	الاحزاب
Saba'	34	468	Makki	مكّية	٤٦٨	٣٤	سبا
Fâṭir	35	476	Makki	مكّية	٤٧٦	٣٥	فاطر
Yâ-Sîn	36	482	Makki	مكّية	٤٨٢	٣٦	يس
Aṣ-Ṣâffât	37	488	Makki	مكّية	٤٨٨	٣٧	الصّافات
Ṣâd	38	497	Makki	مكّية	٤٩٧	٣٨	ص
Az-Zumar	39	504	Makki	مكّية	٥٠٤	٣٩	الزّمر
Al-Mu'min	40	513	Makki	مكّية	٥١٣	٤٠	المؤمن
Ḥâ-Mîm Sajdah	41	524	Makki	مكّية	٥٢٤	٤١	حم السّجدة
Ash-Shûra	42	531	Makki	مكّية	٥٣١	٤٢	الشّورى
Az-Zukhruf	43	538	Makki	مكّية	٥٣٨	٤٣	الزّخرف
Ad-Dukhân	44	546	Makki	مكّية	٥٤٦	٤٤	الدّخان
Al-Jâs̱iyah	45	550	Makki	مكّية	٥٥٠	٤٥	الجاثية
Al-Aḥqâf	46	554	Makki	مكّية	٥٥٤	٤٦	الاحقاف
Muḥammad	47	559	Madani	مدنية	٥٥٩	٤٧	محمّد
Al-Fat-ḥ	48	564	Madani	مدنيّة	٥٦٤	٤٨	الفتح
Al-Ḥujurât	49	569	Madani	مدنيّة	٥٦٩	٤٩	الحجرات
Qâf	50	572	Makki	مكّية	٥٧٢	٥٠	ق
Aẕ-Ẕâriyât	51	576	Makki	مكّية	٥٧٦	٥١	الذّاريات
Aṭ-Ṭûr	52	580	Makki	مكّية	٥٨٠	٥٢	الطّور
An-Najm	53	583	Makki	مكّية	٥٨٣	٥٣	النّجم
Al-Qamar	54	586	Makki	مكّية	٥٨٦	٥٤	القمر

Sûrah	No.	Page No.	Makki/ Madani	مكّية/مدنيّة	رقم الصفحة	رقم السورة	اسم السورة
Ar-Raḥmân	55	590	Madani	مدنيّة	٥٩٠	٥٥	الرّحمن
Al-Wâqi'ah	56	593	Makki	مكّية	٥٩٣	٥٦	الواقعة
Al-Ḥadîd	57	598	Madani	مدنيّة	٥٩٨	٥٧	الحديد
Al-Mujâdilah	58	603	Madani	مدنيّة	٦٠٣	٥٨	المجادلة
Al-Ḥashr	59	607	Madani	مدنيّة	٦٠٧	٥٩	الحشر
Al-Mumtaḥanah	60	610	Madani	مدنيّة	٦١٠	٦٠	الممتحنة
Aṣ-Ṣaff	61	613	Madani	مدنيّة	٦١٣	٦١	الصّف
Al-Jumu'ah	62	615	Madani	مدنيّة	٦١٥	٦٢	الجمعة
Al-Munâfiqûn	63	617	Madani	مدنيّة	٦١٧	٦٣	المنافقون
At-Taghâbun	64	618	Madani	مدنيّة	٦١٨	٦٤	التّغابن
Aṭ-Ṭalâq	65	620	Madani	مدنيّة	٦٢٠	٦٥	الطّلاق
At-Taḥrîm	66	623	Madani	مدنيّة	٦٢٣	٦٦	التّحريم
Al-Mulk	67	625	Makki	مكّية	٦٢٥	٦٧	الملك
Al-Qalam	68	628	Makki	مكّية	٦٢٨	٦٨	القلم
Al-Ḥâqqah	69	631	Makki	مكّية	٦٣١	٦٩	الحاقّة
Al-Ma'ârij	70	634	Makki	مكّية	٦٣٤	٧٠	المعارج
Nûḥ	71	636	Makki	مكّية	٦٣٦	٧١	نوح
Al-Jinn	72	638	Makki	مكّية	٦٣٨	٧٢	الجن
Al-Muzzammil	73	641	Makki	مكّية	٦٤١	٧٣	المزّمّل
Al-Muddassir	74	643	Makki	مكّية	٦٤٣	٧٤	المدّثّر
Al-Qiyâmah	75	646	Makki	مكّية	٦٤٦	٧٥	القيامة
Ad-Dahr	76	647	Madani	مدنيّة	٦٤٧	٧٦	الدّهر
Al-Mursalât	77	650	Makki	مكّية	٦٥٠	٧٧	المرسلات
An-Naba'	78	652	Makki	مكّية	٦٥٢	٧٨	النّبا
An-Nâzi'ât	79	654	Makki	مكّية	٦٥٤	٧٩	النّازعات
'Abasa	80	656	Makki	مكّية	٦٥٦	٨٠	عبس
At-Takwîr	81	658	Makki	مكّية	٦٥٨	٨١	التّكوير
Al-Infiṭâr	82	659	Makki	مكّية	٦٥٩	٨٢	الانفطار
Al-Muṭaffifîn	83	660	Makki	مكّية	٦٦٠	٨٣	المطفّفين
Al-Inshiqâq	84	661	Makki	مكّية	٦٦١	٨٤	الانشقاق

Sûrah	No.	Page No.	Makki/ Madani	مكيّة/مدنيّة	رقم الصفحة	رقم السورة	اسم السورة
Al-Burûj	85	663	Makki	مكيّة	٦٦٣	٨٥	البروج
Aṭ-Ṭâriq	86	664	Makki	مكيّة	٦٦٤	٨٦	الطّارق
Al-A'lâ	87	665	Makki	مكيّة	٦٦٥	٨٧	الاعلى
Al-Ghâshiyah	88	665	Makki	مكيّة	٦٦٥	٨٨	الغاشية
Al-Fajr	89	667	Makki	مكيّة	٦٦٧	٨٩	الفجر
Al-Balad	90	668	Makki	مكيّة	٦٦٨	٩٠	البلد
Ash-Shams	91	669	Makki	مكيّة	٦٦٩	٩١	الشّمس
Al-Layl	92	670	Makki	مكيّة	٦٧٠	٩٢	الّيل
Aḍ-Ḍuḥâ	93	670	Makki	مكيّة	٦٧٠	٩٣	الضّحى
Al-Inshirâḥ	94	671	Makki	مكيّة	٦٧١	٩٤	الانشراح
At-Tîn	95	671	Makki	مكيّة	٦٧١	٩٥	التين
Al-'Alaq	96	672	Makki	مكيّة	٦٧٢	٩٦	العلق
Al-Qadr	97	673	Makki	مكيّة	٦٧٣	٩٧	القدر
Al-Bayyinah	98	673	Madani	مدنيّة	٦٧٣	٩٨	البيّنة
Az-Zilzâl	99	674	Madani	مدنيّة	٦٧٤	٩٩	الزلزال
Al-'Âdiyât	100	674	Makki	مكيّة	٦٧٤	١٠٠	العاديات
Al-Qâri'ah	101	675	Makki	مكيّة	٦٧٥	١٠١	القارعة
At-Takâṣur	102	675	Makki	مكيّة	٦٧٥	١٠٢	التّكاثر
Al-'Aṣr	103	676	Makki	مكيّة	٦٧٦	١٠٣	العصر
Al-Humazah	104	676	Makki	مكيّة	٦٧٦	١٠٤	الهمزة
Al-Fîl	105	676	Makki	مكيّة	٦٧٦	١٠٥	الفيل
Quraysh	106	677	Makki	مكيّة	٦٧٧	١٠٦	قريش
Al-Mâ'ûn	107	677	Makki	مكيّة	٦٧٧	١٠٧	الماعون
Al-Kawṯar	108	677	Makki	مكيّة	٦٧٧	١٠٨	الكوثر
Al-Kâfirûn	109	677	Makki	مكيّة	٦٧٧	١٠٩	الكافرون
An-Naṣr	110	678	Madani	مدنيّة	٦٧٨	١١٠	النّصر
Al-Lahab	111	678	Makki	مكيّة	٦٧٨	١١١	اللّهب
Al-Ikhlâṣ	112	678	Makki	مكيّة	٦٧٨	١١٢	الاخلاص
Al-Falaq	113	678	Makki	مكيّة	٦٧٨	١١٣	الفلق
An-Nâs	114	679	Makki	مكيّة	٦٧٨	١١٤	النّاس

تَنْزِيلُ الْكِتَابِ الْعَزِيزِ

الْقُرْآنُ الْكَرِيمُ

أَحْكَامُ التَّجْوِيدِ الْمُدَوَّنِ بِالْأَلْوَان

وَتَرْجَمَةُ مَعَانِيهِ مَعَ الْحُرُوفِ الْمَنْقُولَةِ إِلَى اللُّغَةِ الْإِنْجِلِيزِيَّة

الترجمة

عبد الله يوسف علي

اسلامك بك سروس

1. The Opening

In the name of Allah, Most Gracious, Most Merciful.

1. Praise be to Allah, the Cherisher and Sustainer of the Worlds;

2. Most Gracious, Most Merciful;

3. Master of the Day of Judgment.

4. You do we worship, and Your aid do we seek.

5. Show us the straight way,

6. The way of those on whom You have bestowed Your Grace, those whose (portion) is not wrath, and who do not go astray.　　　**(Section 1)**

Sûrat al-Fâtiḥa–1

(Revealed at Makkah)

Bismillaahir Raḥmaanir Raḥeem

1. Alḥamdu lillaahi Rabbil-'aalameen;

2. Ar-Raḥmaanir-Raḥeem;

3. Maaliki Yawmid-Deen.

4. Iyyaaka na'budu wa Iyyaaka nasta'een.

5. Ihdinaṣ-Ṣiraaṭal-Mus-taqeem,

6. Ṣiraaṭal-lazeena an'amta 'alayhim ghayril-maghḍoobi 'alayhim wa laḍ-ḍaalleen.

2. The Cow

In the name of Allah, Most Gracious, Most Merciful.

1. *Alif-Lum-Mim.*

2. This is the Book; in it is guidance sure, without doubt, to those who fear God;

3. Who believe in the Unseen, are steadfast in prayer, and spend out of what We have provided for them;

4. And who believe in the Revelation sent to you, and sent before thy time, and (in their hearts) have the assurance of the Hereafter.

5. They are on (true) guidance, from their Lord, and it is these who will prosper.

6. As to those who reject Faith, it is the same to them whether you warn them or do not warn them; they will not believe.

7. God hath set a seal on their hearts and on their hearing, and on their eyes is a veil; great is the penalty they (incur).

8. Of the people there are some who say: "We believe in God and the Last Day;" but they do not (really) believe.

9. Fain would they deceive Allah and those who believe, but they only deceive themselves, and realise (it) not!

10. In their hearts is a disease; and Allah has increased their disease: And grievous is the penaltey they (incur), because they are false (to themselves).

11. When it is said to them: "Make not mischief on the earth," they say: "Why, we only want to make peace!"

Sûrat al-Baqarah–2

(Revealed at Madinah)

Bismillaahir Rahmaanir Raheem

1. Alif-Laaam-Meeem.

2. Zaalikal-Kitaabu laa rayba feeh; hudal-lilmuttaqeen.

3. Allazeena yu'minoona bilghaybi wa yuqeemoonas-Salaata wa mimmaa razaq-naahum yunfiqoon.

4. Wallazeena yu'minoona bimaaa unzila ilayka wa maaa unzila min qablika wa bil-Aakhirati hum yooqinoon.

5. Ulaaa'ika 'alaa hudam-mir-Rabbihim wa ulaaa'ika humul-muflihoon.

6. Innal-lazeena kafaroo sawaaa'un 'alayhim 'a-anzar-tahum am hlam tunzirhum laa yu'minoon.

7. Khatamal-laahu 'alaa quloobihim wa 'alaa sam'i-him wa 'alaaa absaarihim ghishaa-watuñw-wa lahum 'azaabun 'azeem.   **(Section 1)**

8. Wa minan-naasi mañy-yaqoolu aamannaa billaahi wa bil-Yawmil-Aakhiri wa maa hum bimu'mineen.

9. Yukhaadi'oonal-laaha wallazeena aamanoo wa maa yakhda'oona illaaa anfusahum wa maa yash'uroon.

10. Fee quloobihim mara-dun fazaadahumul-laahu maradan wa lahum 'azaabun aleemum bimaa kaanoo yakziboon.

11. Wa izaa qeela lahum laa tufsidoo fil-ardi qaalooo innamaa nahnu muslihoon.

12. Of a surety, they are the ones who make mischief, but they realise (it) not.

13. When it is said to them: "Believe as the others believe:" They say: "Shall we believe as the fools believe?" No, of a surety they are the fools, but they do not know.

14. When they meet those who believe, they say: "We believe;" but when they are alone with their evil ones, they say: "We are really with you: We (were) only jesting."

15. Allah will throw back their mockery on them, and give them rope in their wrong-doing; so they will wander like blind ones (to and fro).

16. These are they who have bartered guidance for error: But their traffic is profitless, and they have lost true direction.

17. Their similitude is that of a man who kindled a fire; when it lighted all around him, Allah took away their light and left them in utter darkness. So they could not see.

18. Deaf, dumb, and blind, they hwill not return (to the path).

19. Or (another similitude) is that of a rain-laden cloud from the sky: In it are zones of darkness, and thunder and lightning: They press their fingers in their ears to keep out the stunning thunder-clap, the while they are in terror of death. But Allah is ever round the rejecters of Faith!

20. The lightning all but snatches away their sight; every time the light (helps) them, they walk therein, and when the darkness grows on them, they stand still. And if Allah willed,

12. Alaaa innahum humul-mufsidoona wa laakil-laa yash'uroon.

13. Wa izaa qeela lahum aaminoo kamaaa aamanan-naasu qaalooo anu'minu kamaaa aamanas-sufahaaa'; alaaa innahum humus-sufahaaa'u wa laakil-laa ya'lamoon.

14. Wa izaa laqul-lazeena aamanoo qaalooo aamannaa wa izaa khalaw ilaa shayaateenihim qaalooo innaa ma'akum innamaa naḥnu mustahzi'oon.

15. Allaahu yastahzi'u bihim wa yamudduhum fee ṭughyaanihim ya'mahoon.

16. Ulaaa'ikal-lazeenash-tara-wuḍ-ḍalaalata bilhudaa famaa rabiḥat-tijaaratuhum wa maa kaanoo muhtadeen.

17. Maṣaluhum kamaṣalillazis-tawqada naaran falammaaa aḍaaa'at maa ḥawlahoo zahabal-laahu binoorihim wa tarakahum fee zulumaatil-laa yubṣiroon.

18. Ṣummum bukmun 'umyun fahum laa yarji'oon.

19. Aw kaṣayyibim-minas-samaaa'i feehi zulumaatuñw-wa ra'duñw-wa barq, yaj'aloona aṣaabi'ahum feee aazaanihim minaṣ-ṣawaa'iqi ḥazaral-mawt; wallaahu muḥeeṭum bilkaafireen.

20. Yakaadul-barqu yakhṭafu abṣaarahum kullamaaa aḍaaa'a lahum mashaw feehi wa izaa azlama 'alayhim qaamoo; wa law shaaa'al-laahu

He could take away their faculty of hearing and seeing; for Allah has power over all things.

21. O you people! Adore your Guardian-Lord, who created you and those who came before you, that you may have the chance to learn righteousness;

22. Who has made the earth your couch, and the heavens your canopy; and sent down rain from the heavens; and brought forth therewith Fruits for your sustenance; then set not up rivals unto Allah when you know (the truth).

23. And if you are in doubt as to what We have revealed from time to time to Our servant, then produce a Sura like thereof; and call your witnesses or helpers (if there are any) besides Allah, if your (doubts) are true.

24. But if you cannot- and of a surety you cannot- then fear the Fire whose fuel is men and stones,- which is prepared for those who reject Faith.

25. But give glad tidings to those who believe and work righteousness, that their portion is Gardens beneath which rivers flow. Every time they are fed with fruits therefrom, they say: "Why, this is what we were fed with before," for they are given things in similitude; and they have therein companions pure (and holy); and they abide therein (for ever).

26. Allah disdains not to use the similitude of things, lowest as well as highest. Those who

lazahaba bisam'ihim wa abṣaarihim; innal-laaha 'alaa kulli shay'in Qadeer. **(Section 2)**

21. Yaaa ayyuhan-naasu'budoo Rabbakumul-lazee khalaqakum wallazeena min qablikum la'allakum tattaqoon.

22. Allazee ja'ala lakumul-arḍa firaashaňw-wassamaaa'a binaaa-'aňw-wa anzala minassamaaa'i maaa'an fa-akhraja bihee minas-samaraati rizqal-lakum falaa taj'aloo lillaahi andaadaňw-wa antum ta'lamoon.

23. Wa in kuntum fee raybim-mimmaa nazzalnaa 'alaa 'abdinaa fa-too bi-Sooratim-mim-mislihee wad'oo shu-hadaaa'akum min doonil-laahi in kuntum ṣaadiqeen.

24. Fail-lam taf'aloo wa lan taf'aloo fattaqun-Naaral-latee waqooduhan-naasu walḥijaaratu u'iddat lilkaafireen.

25. Wa bashshiril-lazeena aamanoo wa 'amiluṣ-ṣaaliḥaati anna lahum Jannaatin tajree min taḥtihal-anhaaru kullamaa ruziqoo minhaa min samaratir-rizqan qaaloo haazal-lazee ruziqnaa min qablu wa utoo bihee mutashaabihaa, wa lahum feehaaa azwaajum-muṭahhara-tuňw-wa hum feehaa khaalidoon.

26. Innal-laaha laa yastaḥyeee aňy-yaḍriba masalam-maa ba'oodatan famaa fawqahaa; fa-ammal-lazeena

believe know that it is truth from their Lord; but those who reject Faith say: "What means Allah by this similitude?" By it He causes many to stray, and many He leads into the right path; but He causes not to stray, except those who forsake (the path),-

aamanoo faya'lamoona anna-hul-ḥaqqu mir-Rabbihim wa ammal-laẕeena kafaroo faya-qooloona maaẕaa araadal-laahu bihaaẕaa maṣalaa; yuḍillu bihee kaṣeeranw-wa yahdee bihee kaṣeeraa; wa maa yuḍillu biheee illal-faasiqeen.

27. Those who break Allah's Covenant after it is ratified, and who sunder what Allah Has ordered to be joined, and do mischief on earth: there cause loss (only) to themselves.

27. Allaẕeena yanquḍoona 'Ahdal-laahi mim ba'di meesaaqihee wa yaqta'oona maaa amaral-laahu biheee añy-yooṣala wa yufsidoona fil-arḍ; ulaaa'ika humul-khaasiroon.

28. How can you reject the faith in Allah?- seeing that you were without life, and He gave you life; then will He cause you to die, and will again bring you to life; and again to Him will you return.

28. Kayfa takfuroona billaahi wa kuntum amwaatan fa-aḥyaakum ṣumma yumeetukum ṣumma yuḥyeekum ṣumma ilayhi turja'oon.

29. It is He Who has created for you all things that are on earth; moreover His design comprehended the heavens, for He gave order and perfection to the seven firmaments; and of all things He has perfect knowledge.

29. Huwal-laẕee khalaqa lakum-maa fil-arḍi jamee'an ṣummas-tawaaa ilas-samaaa'i fasaw-waahunna sab'a samaa-waat; wa Huwa bikulli shay'in 'Aleem. **(Section 3)**

30. Behold, your Lord said to the angels: "I will create a vicegerent on earth." They said: "Will you place therein one who will make mischief therein and shed blood?- while we do celebrate your praises and glorify your holy (name)?" He said: "I know what you know not."

30. Wa iz qaala Rabbuka lil-malaaa'ikati innee jaa'ilun fil-arḍi khaleefatan qaalooo ataj'alu feehaa mañy-yufsidu feehaa wa yasfikud-dimaaa'a wa naḥnu nusabbiḥu biḥamdika wa nuqaddisu laka qaala inneee a'lamu maa laa ta'lamoon.

31. And He taught Adam the nature of all things; then He placed them before the angels, and said: "Tell me the nature of these if you are right."

31. Wa 'allama Aadamal-asmaaa'a kullahaa ṣumma 'araḍahum 'alal-malaaa'ikati faqaala ambi'oonee bias-maaa'i haaa'ulaaa'i in kuntum ṣaadi-qeen.

32. They said: "Glory to You, of knowledge we have none, save what You have taught us: in truth it is You Who are perfect in know-ledge and wisdom."

32. Qaaloo subḥaanaka laa 'ilma lanaaa illaa maa 'allamtanaaa innaka Antal-'Aleemul-Ḥakeem.

33. He said: "O Adam! tell them their natures." When

33. Qaala yaaa Aadamu ambi'-hum biasmaaa'ihim falammaaa

he had told them, Allah said: "Did I not tell you that I know the secrets of heaven and earth, and I know what you reveal and what you conceal?"

34. And behold, We said to the angels: "Bow down to Adam" and they bowed down: not so Iblis: he refused and was haughty: he was of those who reject Faith.

35. We said: "O Adam! dwell you and your wife in the Garden; and eat of the bountiful things therein as (where and when) you will; but approach not this tree, or you run into harm and transgression."

36. Then did Satan make them slip from the (Garden), and get them out of the state (of felicity) in which they had been. We said: "Get you down, all (you people), with enmity between yourselves. On earth will be your dwelling-place and your means of livelihood for a time."

37. Then learnt Adam from his Lord words (of repentance), and his Lord turned towards him; for He is Oft-Returning, Most Merciful.

38. We said: "Get you down all from here; and if, as is sure, there comes to you guidance from Me, whosoever follows My guidance, on them shall be no fear, nor shall they grieve.

39. "But those who reject Faith and belie Our Signs, they shall be Companions of the Fire; they shall abide therein."

40. O Children of Israel! call to mind the (special) favour which I bestowed upon you, and fulfil your covenant with Me as I fulfil My Covenant with you, and fear none but Me.

41. And believe in what I reveal, confirming the revelation which is

amba-ahum bi-asmaaa'ihim qaala alam aqul lakum inneee a'lamu ghaybas-samaawaati wal-ardi wa a'lamu maa tubdoona wa maa kuntum taktumoon.

34. Wa iz qulnaa lilmalaaa'i-katis-judoo li-Aadama fasaja-dooo illaa Ibleesa abaa wastak-bara wa kaana minal-kaafireen.

35. Wa qulnaa yaaa Aadamus-kun anta wa zawjukal-Jannata wa kulaa minhaa raghadan haysu shi'tumaa wa laa taqrabaa haazihish-shajarata fatakoonaa minaz-zaalimeen.

36. Fa-azallahumash-Shay-taanu 'anhaa fa-akhrajahumaa mimmaa kaanaa feehi wa qulnah-bitoo ba'dukum liba'din 'aduwwuñw-wa lakum fil-ardi mustaqarruñw-wa mataa'un ilaa heen.

37. Fatalaqqaaa Aadamu mir-Rabbihee Kalimaatin fataaba 'alayh; innahoo Huwat-Taw-waabur-Raheem.

38. Qulnah-bitoo minhaa jamee-'an fa-immaa yaåtiyannakum minnee hudan faman tabi'a hudaaya falaa khawfun 'alayhim wa laa hum yahza-noon.

39. Wallazeena kafaroo wa kaz zaboo bi-Aayaatinaaa ulaaa'ika Ashaabun-Naari hum feehaa khaalidoon. **(Section 4)**

40. Yaa Baneee Israaa'eelaz kuroo ni'matiyal-lateee an'amtu 'alaykum wa awfoo bi-'Ahdeee oofi bi'ahdikum wa iyyaaya farhaboon.

41. Wa aaminoo bimaaa anzaltu musaddiqal-limaa

with you, and be not the first to reject Faith therein, nor sell My Signs for a small price; and fear Me, and Me alone.

42. And cover not Truth with falsehood, nor conceal the Truth when you know (what it is).

43. And be steadfast in prayer; practise regular charity; and bow down your heads with those who bow down (in worship).

44. Do you enjoin right conduct on the people, and forget (to practise it) yourselves, and yet you study the Scripture? Will you not understand?

45. Nay, seek (Allah's) help with patient perseverance and prayer: it is indeed hard, except to those who bring a lowly spirit,-

46. Who bear in mind the certainty that they are to meet their Lord, and that they are to return to Him.

47. O, Children of Israel! call to mind the (special) favour which I bestowed upon you, and that I preferred you to all others (for My Message).

48. Then guard yourselves against a day when one soul shall not avail another nor shall intercession be accepted for her, nor shall compensation be taken from her, nor shall anyone be helped (from outside).

49. And remember, We delivered you from the people of Pharaoh: they set you hard tasks and punishments, slaughtered your sons and let your women-folk live; therein was a tremendous trial from your Lord.

ma'akum wa laa takoonooo awwala kaafirim bihee wa laa tashtaroo bi-Aayaatee ṣamanan qaleelanw- wa iyyaaya fattaqoon.

42. Wa laa talbisul-ḥaqqa bilbaaṭili wa taktumul-ḥaqqa wa antum ta'lamoon.

43. Wa aqeemuṣ-Ṣalaata wa aatuz-Zakaata warka'oo ma'ar-raaki'een.

44. Ataåmuroonan-naasa bilbirri wa tansawna anfusakum wa antum tatloonal-Kitaab; afalaa ta'qiloon.

45. Wasta'eenoo biṣṣabri waṣ-Ṣalaah; wa innahaa lakabee-ratun illaa alal-khaashi'een.

46. Allażeena yaẓunnoona annahum mulaaqoo Rabbihim wa annahum ilayhi raaji'oon.
(Section 5)

47. Yaa Baneee Israaa'eelaż-kuroo ni'matiyal-lateee an'amtu 'alaykum wa annee faḍḍaltukum 'alal-'aalameen.

48. Wattaqoo Yawmal-laa tajzee nafsun 'an nafsin shay'anw-wa laa yuqbalu minhaa shafaa'atunw-wa laa yu'khażu minhaa 'adlunw-wa laa hum yunṣaroon.

49. Wa iz najjaynaakum min Aali Fir'awna yasoomoonakum sooo'al-'azaabi yuzabbiḥoona abnaaa'akum wa yastaḥyoona nisaaa'akum; wa fee zaalikum balaaa'um mir-Rabbikum 'aẓeem.

50. And remember, We divided the sea for you and saved you and drowned Pharaoh's people within your very sight.

51. And remember We appointed forty nights for Moses, and in his absence, you took the calf (for worship), and you did grievous wrong.

52. Even then We did forgive you; there was a chance for you to be grateful.

53. And remember We gave Moses the Scripture and the Criterion (between right and wrong): there was a chance for you to be guided aright.

54. And remember, Moses said to his people: "O my people! you have indeed wronged yourselves by your worship of the calf: So turn (in repentance) to your Maker, and slay yourselves (the wrong-doers); that will be better for you in the sight of your Maker." Then He turned towards you (in forgiveness): for He is Oft-Returning, Most Merciful.

55. And remember, you said: "O Moses! we shall never believe in you until we see Allah manifestly," but you were dazed with thunder and lightning even as you looked on.

56. Then We raised you up after your death: you had the chance to be grateful.

57. And We gave you the shade of clouds and sent down to you manna and quails, saying: "Eat of the good things We have provided for you:" (But they rebelled); to us they did not harm, but they harmed their own souls.

58. And remember, We said: "Enter this town, and eat of the plenty therein as you wish;

---

50. Wa iz faraqnaa bikumul-baḥra fa-anjaynaakum wa-aghraqnaaa Aala Fir'awna wa antum tanzuroon.

51. Wa iz waa'adnaa Moosaaa arba'eena laylatan summat-takhaztumul-'ijla mim ba'dihee wa antum zaalimoon.

52. Summa 'afawnaa 'ankum mim ba'di zaalika la'allakum tashkuroon.

53. Wa iz aataynaa Moosal Kitaaba wal-Furqaana la'allakum tahtadoon.

54. Wa iz qaala Moosaa liqawmihee yaa qawmi innakum zalamtum anfusakum bittikhaazikumul-'ijla fatoobooo ilaa Baari'ikum faqtulooo anfusakum zaalikum khayrul-lakum 'inda Baari'ikum fataaba 'alaykum; innahoo Huwat-Tawwaabur-Raheem.

55. Wa iz qultum yaa Moosaa lan nu'mina laka ḥattaa naral-laaha jahratan fa-akhazat-kumuṣ-ṣaa'iqatu wa antum tanzuroon.

56. Summa ba'asnaakum mim ba'di mawtikum la'allakum tashkuroon.

57. Wa zallalnaa 'alaykumul-ghamaama wa anzalnaa 'alaykumul-Manna was-Salwaa kuloo min ṭayyibaati maa razaqnaakum wa maa zalamoonaa wa laakin kaanooo anfusahum yazlimoon.

58 Wa iz qulnad-khuloo haazihil-qaryata fakuloo minhaa haysu shi'tum raghadañw-

---

وَإِذْ فَرَقْنَا بِكُمُ الْبَحْرَ فَأَنجَيْنَاكُمْ وَأَغْرَقْنَا آلَ فِرْعَوْنَ وَأَنتُمْ تَنظُرُونَ ۝

وَإِذْ وَاعَدْنَا مُوسَىٰ أَرْبَعِينَ لَيْلَةً ثُمَّ اتَّخَذْتُمُ الْعِجْلَ مِن بَعْدِهِ وَأَنتُمْ ظَالِمُونَ ۝

ثُمَّ عَفَوْنَا عَنكُم مِّن بَعْدِ ذَٰلِكَ لَعَلَّكُمْ تَشْكُرُونَ ۝

وَإِذْ آتَيْنَا مُوسَى الْكِتَابَ وَالْفُرْقَانَ لَعَلَّكُمْ تَهْتَدُونَ ۝

وَإِذْ قَالَ مُوسَىٰ لِقَوْمِهِ يَا قَوْمِ إِنَّكُمْ ظَلَمْتُمْ أَنفُسَكُم بِاتِّخَاذِكُمُ الْعِجْلَ فَتُوبُوا إِلَىٰ بَارِئِكُمْ فَاقْتُلُوا أَنفُسَكُمْ ذَٰلِكُمْ خَيْرٌ لَّكُمْ عِندَ بَارِئِكُمْ فَتَابَ عَلَيْكُمْ إِنَّهُ هُوَ التَّوَّابُ الرَّحِيمُ ۝

وَإِذْ قُلْتُمْ يَا مُوسَىٰ لَن نُّؤْمِنَ لَكَ حَتَّىٰ نَرَى اللَّهَ جَهْرَةً فَأَخَذَتْكُمُ الصَّاعِقَةُ وَأَنتُمْ تَنظُرُونَ ۝

ثُمَّ بَعَثْنَاكُم مِّن بَعْدِ مَوْتِكُمْ لَعَلَّكُمْ تَشْكُرُونَ ۝

وَظَلَّلْنَا عَلَيْكُمُ الْغَمَامَ وَأَنزَلْنَا عَلَيْكُمُ الْمَنَّ وَالسَّلْوَىٰ كُلُوا مِن طَيِّبَاتِ مَا رَزَقْنَاكُمْ وَمَا ظَلَمُونَا وَلَٰكِن كَانُوا أَنفُسَهُمْ يَظْلِمُونَ ۝

وَإِذْ قُلْنَا ادْخُلُوا هَٰذِهِ الْقَرْيَةَ فَكُلُوا مِنْهَا حَيْثُ شِئْتُمْ رَغَدًا

but enter the gate with humility, in posture and in words, and We shall forgive you your faults and increase (the portion of) those who do good."

59. But the transgressors changed the word from that which had been given them; so We sent on the transgressors a plague from heaven, for that they infringed (Our command) repeatedly.

60. And remember, Moses prayed for water for his people; We said: "Strike the rock with your staff." Then gushed forth therefrom twelve springs. Each group knew its own place for water. So eat and drink of the sustenance provided by Allah, and do no evil nor mischief on the (face of the) earth.

61. And remember, you said: "O Moses! we cannot endure one kind of food (always); so beseech your Lord for us to produce for us of what the earth grows, - its pot-herbs, and cucumbers, its garlic, lentils, and onions." He said: "Will you exchange the better for the worse? You go down to any town, and you shall find what you want!" They were covered with humiliation and misery; they drew on themselves the wrath of Allah. This because they went on rejecting the Signs of Allah and slaying His Messengers without just cause. This because they rebelled and went on transgressing.

62. Those who believe (in the Qur'an), and those who follow the Jewish (scriptures),

wadkhulul-baaba sujjadañw-wa qooloo ḥiṭṭatun naghfir lakum khaṭaayaakum; wa sanazeedul-muḥsineen.

59. Fabaddalal-lazeena ẓalamoo qawlan ghayral-lazee qeela lahum fa-anzalnaa 'alal-lazeena ẓalamoo rijzam-minas-samaaa'i bimaa kaanoo yafsuqoon. **(Section 6)**

60. Wa iẕis-tasqaa Moosaa liqawmihee faqulnaḍ-rib bi'aṣaakal-ḥajara fanfajarat minhuṣnataa 'ashrata 'aynan qad 'alima kullu unaasim-mash-rabahum kuloo washraboo mir-rizqil-laahi wa laa ta'saw fil-arḍi mufsideen.

61. Wa iẕ qultum yaa Moosaa lan naṣbira 'alaa ṭa'aaminw-waaḥidin fad'u lanaa Rabbaka yukhrij lanaa mimmaa tumbitul-arḍu mimbaqlihaa wa qiṣ-ṣaaa'ihaa wa foomihaa wa 'adasihaa wa baṣalihaa qaala atastabdiloonal-lazee huwa adnaa billazee huwa khayr; ihbiṭoo miṣran fa-inna lakum maa sa-altum; wa ḍuribat 'alayhimuẕ-zillatu walmaska-natu wa baaa'oo bighaḍabim-minal-laah; zaalika bi-annahum kaanoo yakfuroona bi-Aayaatil-laahi wa yaqtuloonan-Nabiy-yeena bighayril-ḥaqq; zaalika bimaa 'aṣaw wa kaanoo ya'tadoon. **(Section 7)**

62. Innal-lazeena aamanoo wallazeena haadoo

وَادْخُلُوا الْبَابَ سُجَّدًا وَّقُوْلُوْا حِطَّةٌ نَّغْفِرْ لَكُمْ خَطٰيٰكُمْ ۖ وَسَنَزِيْدُ الْمُحْسِنِيْنَ ۞

فَبَدَّلَ الَّذِيْنَ ظَلَمُوْا قَوْلًا غَيْرَ الَّذِيْ قِيْلَ لَهُمْ فَاَنْزَلْنَا عَلَى الَّذِيْنَ ظَلَمُوْا رِجْزًا مِّنَ السَّمَاءِ بِمَا كَانُوْا يَفْسُقُوْنَ ۞

وَاِذِ اسْتَسْقٰى مُوْسٰى لِقَوْمِهٖ فَقُلْنَا اضْرِبْ بِّعَصَاكَ الْحَجَرَ ۖ فَانْفَجَرَتْ مِنْهُ اثْنَتَا عَشْرَةَ عَيْنًا ۖ قَدْ عَلِمَ كُلُّ اُنَاسٍ مَّشْرَبَهُمْ ۖ كُلُوْا وَاشْرَبُوْا مِنْ رِّزْقِ اللّٰهِ وَلَا تَعْثَوْا فِى الْاَرْضِ مُفْسِدِيْنَ ۞

وَاِذْ قُلْتُمْ يٰمُوْسٰى لَنْ نَّصْبِرَ عَلٰى طَعَامٍ وَّاحِدٍ فَادْعُ لَنَا رَبَّكَ يُخْرِجْ لَنَا مِمَّا تُنْۢبِتُ الْاَرْضُ مِنْ بَقْلِهَا وَقِثَّائِهَا وَفُوْمِهَا وَعَدَسِهَا وَبَصَلِهَا ۖ قَالَ اَتَسْتَبْدِلُوْنَ الَّذِيْ هُوَ اَدْنٰى بِالَّذِيْ هُوَ خَيْرٌ ۚ اِهْبِطُوْا مِصْرًا فَاِنَّ لَكُمْ مَّا سَاَلْتُمْ ۗ وَضُرِبَتْ عَلَيْهِمُ الذِّلَّةُ وَالْمَسْكَنَةُ ۖ وَبَاءُوْ بِغَضَبٍ مِّنَ اللّٰهِ ۗ ذٰلِكَ بِاَنَّهُمْ كَانُوْا يَكْفُرُوْنَ بِاٰيٰتِ اللّٰهِ وَيَقْتُلُوْنَ النَّبِيّٖنَ بِغَيْرِ الْحَقِّ ۗ ذٰلِكَ بِمَا عَصَوْا وَّكَانُوْا يَعْتَدُوْنَ ۞

اِنَّ الَّذِيْنَ اٰمَنُوْا وَالَّذِيْنَ هَادُوْا

and the Christians and the Sabians, - and who believe in Allah and the Last Day, and work righteousness, shall have their reward with their Lord; on them shall be no fear, nor shall they grieve.

63. And remember, We took your covenant and We raised above you (the towering height) of Mount (Sinai): (saying): "Hold firmly to what We have given you and bring (ever) to remembrance what is therein: perchance you may fear Allah."

64. But you turned back thereafter: had it not been for the Grace and Mercy of Allah to you, you had surely been among the lost.

65. And well you knew those amongst you who transgressed in the matter of the Sabbath: We said to them: "Be you apes, despised and rejected."

66. So We made it an example to their own time and to their posterity, and a lesson to those who fear Allah.

67. And remember, Moses said to his people: "Allah commands that you sacrifice a heifer". They said: "Makes you a laughing-stock of us?" He said: "Allah save me from being an ignorant (fool)!"

68. They said: "Beseech on our behalf your Lord to make plain to us what (heifer) it is!" He said; "He says: the heifer should be neither too old nor too young, but of middling age: now do what you are commanded!"

69. They said: "Beseech on our behalf your Lord to make plain to us her colour." He said: "He says: a fawn-coloured heifer, pure and rich in tone, the admiration of beholders!"

wan-Naṣaaraa waṣ-Ṣaabi'eena man aamana billaahi wal-Yawmil-Aakhiri wa 'amila ṣaaliḥan falahum ajruhum 'inda Rabbihim wa laa khawfun 'alayhim wa laa hum yaḥzanoon.

63. Wa iz akhaznaa meesaaqakum wa rafa'naa fawqakumuṭ-Ṭoora khuzoo maaa aataynaakum biquwwatiñw-wazkuroo maa feehi la'allakum tattaqoon.

64. Summa tawallaytum mim ba'di zaalika falawlaa faḍlullaahi 'alaykum wa raḥmatuhoo lakuntum minal-khaasireen.

65. Wa laqad 'alimtumullazeena'-tadaw minkum fis-Sabti faqulnaa lahum koonoo qiradatan khaasi'een.

66. Faja'alnaahaa nakaalallimaa bayna yadayhaa wa maa khalfahaa wa maw'izatallilmuttaqeen.

67. Wa iz qaala Moosaa liqawmiheee innal-laaha yaamurukum an tazbaḥoo baqaratan qaalooo atattakhizunaa huzuwan qaala a'oozu billaahi an akoona minaljaahileen.

68. Qaalud-'u lanaa Rabbaka yubayyil-lanaa maa hee; qaala innahoo yaqoolu innahaa baqaratul-laa faariḍuñw-wa laa bikrun 'awaanum bayna zaalika faf'aloo maa tu'maroon.

69. Qaalud-'u lanaa Rabbaka yubayyil-lanaa maa lawnuhaa; qaala innahoo yaqoolu innahaa baqaratun ṣafraaa'u faaqi'ullawnuhaa tasurrunnaazireen.

70. They said: "Beseech on our behalf your Lord to make plain to us what she is: to us all heifers are alike: we wish indeed for guidance, if Allah wills."

71. He said: "He says: a heifer not trained to till the soil or water the fields; sound and without blemish". They said: "Now you has brought the truth." Then they offered her in sacrifice, but not with good-will.

72. Remember, you slew a man and fell into a dispute among yourselves as to the crime: but Allah was to bring forth what you did hide.

73. So We said: "Strike the (body) with a piece of the (heifer)." Thus Allah brings the dead to life and shows you His Signs: perchance you may understand.

74. Thenceforth your hearts were hardened: they became like a rock and even worse in hardness. For among rocks there are some from which rivers gush forth; others there are which when split asunder send forth water; and others which sink for fear of Allah. And Allah is not unmindful of what you do.

75. Can you (O you men of Faith) entertain the hope that they will believe in you?- seeing that a party of them heard the Word of Allah, and perverted it knowingly after they understood it.

76. Behold! when they meet the men of Faith, they say: "We believe": but when they meet each other in private,

70. Qaalud-'u lanaa Rabbaka yubayyil-lanaa maa hiya innal-baqara tashaabaha 'alaynaa wa innaaa in-shaaa'al-laahu lamuhtadoon.

71. Qaala innahoo yaqoolu innahaa baqaratul-laa zaloolun tuseerul-arda wa laa tasqil-harsa musallamatullaa shiyata feehaa; qaalul 'aana ji'ta bilhaqq; fazabahoohaa wa maa kaadoo yaf'aloon. **(Section 8)**

72. Wa iz qataltum nafsan faddaara'tum feehaa wallaahu mukhrijum-maa kuntum taktu-moon.

73. Faqulnad-riboohu biba'di-haa; kazaalika yuhyil-laa hul-mawtaa wa yureekum Aayaatihee la'allakum ta'qi-loon.

74. Summa qasat quloobukum mim ba'di zaalika fahiya kalhijaarati aw-ashaddu qaswah; wa inna minal-hijaarati lamaa yatafajjaru minhul-anhaar; wa-inna minhaa lamaa yash-shaqqaqu fayakhruju minhul-maaa'; wa inna minhaa lamaa yahbitu min khashyatil-laah; wa mal-laahu bighaafilin 'ammaa ta'maloon.

75. Afatatma'oona añy-yu'mi-noo lakum wa qad kaana fareequm-minhum yasma'oona Kalaamal-laahi summa yuharri-foonahoo mim ba'di maa 'aqa-loohu wa hum ya'lamoon.

76. Wa izaa laqul-lazeena aamanoo qaalooo aamannaa wa izaa khalaa ba'duhum ilaa ba'din

they say: "Shall you tell them what Allah has revealed to you, that they may engage you in argument about it before your Lord?"- do you not understand (their aim)?

qaalooo atuḥaddisoonahum bimaa fataḥal-laahu 'alaykum liyuḥaajjookum bihee 'inda Rabbikum; afalaa ta'qiloon.

77. Do they not know that Allah knows what they conceal and what they reveal?

77. Awalaa ya'lamoona annal-laaha ya'lamu maa yusirroona wa maa yu'linoon.

78. And there are among them illiterates, who know not the Book, but (see therein their own) desires, and they do nothing but conjecture.

78. Wa minhum ummiyyoona laa ya'lamoonal-Kitaaba illaaa amaaniyya wa in hum illaa yazunnoon.

79. Then woe to those who write the Book with their own hands, and then say:"This is from Allah," to traffic with it for miserable price!- Woe to them for what their hands do write, and for the gain they make thereby.

79. Fawaylul-lillazeena yaktu-boonal-kitaaba bi-aydeehim summa yaqooloona haazaa min 'indil-laahi liyashtaroo bihee samanan qaleelan fawaylul-lahum mimmaa katabat aydeehim wa waylul-lahum mimmaa yaksiboon.

80. And they say: "The Fire shall not touch us but for a few numbered days:" Say: "Have you taken a promise from Allah, for He never breaks His promise? or is it that you say of Allah what you do not know?"

80. Wa qaaloo lan tamassanan-Naaru illaaa ayyaamam-ma'doo-dah; qul attakhaztum 'indal-laahi 'ahdan falañy-yukhlifal-laahu 'ahdahooo am taqooloona 'alal-laahi maa laa ta'lamoon.

81. No, those who seek gain in evil, and are girt round by their sins,- they are companions of the Fire: therein shall they abide (Forever).

81. Balaa man kasaba sayyi'atañw-wa aḥaaṭat bihee khatee'atuhoo fa-ulaaa'ika Aṣḥaabun-Naari hum feehaa khaalidoon.

82. But those who have faith and work righteousness, they are companions of the Garden: therein shall they abide (Forever).

82. Wallazeena aamanoo wa 'amiluṣ-ṣaaliḥaati ulaaa'ika Aṣḥaabul-Jannati hum feehaa khaalidoon. **(Section 9)**

83. And remember, We took a covenant from the Children of Israel (to this effect): worship none but Allah; treat with kindness your parents and kindred, and orphans and those in need; speak fair to the people;

83. Wa iz akhaznaa meesaaqa Baneee Israaa'eela laa ta'bu-doona illal-laaha wa bil-waali-dayni iḥsaanañw-wa zil-qurbaa walyataamaa walmasaakeeni wa qooloo linnaasi ḥusnañw-

قَالُوٓا اَتُحَدِّثُوۡنَهُمۡ بِمَا فَتَحَ اللّٰهُ عَلَيۡكُمۡ لِيُحَاۤجُّوۡكُمۡ بِهٖ عِنۡدَ رَبِّكُمۡ ؕ اَفَلَا تَعۡقِلُوۡنَ ۞

اَوَلَا يَعۡلَمُوۡنَ اَنَّ اللّٰهَ يَعۡلَمُ مَا يُسِرُّوۡنَ وَمَا يُعۡلِنُوۡنَ ۞

وَمِنۡهُمۡ اُمِّيُّوۡنَ لَا يَعۡلَمُوۡنَ الۡكِتٰبَ اِلَّاۤ اَمَانِىَّ وَاِنۡ هُمۡ اِلَّا يَظُنُّوۡنَ ۞

فَوَيۡلٌ لِّلَّذِيۡنَ يَكۡتُبُوۡنَ الۡكِتٰبَ بِاَيۡدِيۡهِمۡ ۖ ثُمَّ يَقُوۡلُوۡنَ هٰذَا مِنۡ عِنۡدِ اللّٰهِ لِيَشۡتَرُوۡا بِهٖ ثَمَنًا قَلِيۡلًا ؕ فَوَيۡلٌ لَّهُمۡ مِّمَّا كَتَبَتۡ اَيۡدِيۡهِمۡ وَوَيۡلٌ لَّهُمۡ مِّمَّا يَكۡسِبُوۡنَ ۞

وَقَالُوۡا لَنۡ تَمَسَّنَا النَّارُ اِلَّاۤ اَيَّامًا مَّعۡدُوۡدَةً ؕ قُلۡ اَتَّخَذۡتُمۡ عِنۡدَ اللّٰهِ عَهۡدًا فَلَنۡ يُّخۡلِفَ اللّٰهُ عَهۡدَهٗۤ اَمۡ تَقُوۡلُوۡنَ عَلَى اللّٰهِ مَا لَا تَعۡلَمُوۡنَ ۞

بَلٰى مَنۡ كَسَبَ سَيِّئَةً وَّاَحَاطَتۡ بِهٖ خَطِيۡٓئَتُهٗ فَاُولٰٓئِكَ اَصۡحٰبُ النَّارِ ۚ هُمۡ فِيۡهَا خٰلِدُوۡنَ ۞

وَالَّذِيۡنَ اٰمَنُوۡا وَعَمِلُوا الصّٰلِحٰتِ اُولٰٓئِكَ اَصۡحٰبُ الۡجَنَّةِ ۚ هُمۡ فِيۡهَا خٰلِدُوۡنَ ۞

وَاِذۡ اَخَذۡنَا مِيۡثَاقَ بَنِىۡٓ اِسۡرَآءِيۡلَ لَا تَعۡبُدُوۡنَ اِلَّا اللّٰهَ ۖ وَبِالۡوَالِدَيۡنِ اِحۡسَانًا وَّذِى الۡقُرۡبٰى وَالۡيَتٰمٰى وَالۡمَسٰكِيۡنِ وَقُوۡلُوۡا لِلنَّاسِ حُسۡنًا

be steadfast in prayer; and practise regular charity. Then you turned back, except a few among you, and you backslide (even now).

84. And remember We took your Covenant (to this effect): shed no blood amongst you, nor turn out your own people from your homes: and this you solemnly ratified, and to this you can bear witness.

85. After this it is you, the same people, who slay among yourselves, and banish a party of you from their homes; assist (their enemies) against them, in guilt and rancour; and if they come to you as captives, you ransom them, though it was not lawful for you to banish them. Then is it only a part of the Book that you believe in, and do you reject the rest? But what is the reward for those among you who behave like this but disgrace in this life?- and on the Day of Judgment they shall be consigned to the most grievous Chastisement. For Allah is not unmindful of what you do.

86. These are the people who buy the life of this world at the price of the Hereafter: their Chastisement shall not be lightened nor shall they be helped.

87. We gave Moses the Book and followed him up with a succession of Apostles; We gave Jesus the son of Mary, clear (Signs) and strengthened him with the holy spirit. Is it that whenever there comes to you an Apostle with what you yourselves desire not, you are puffed hup with pride?-

wa aqeemuṣ-Ṣalaata wa aatuz-Zakaata ṣumma tawallaytum illaa qaleelam-minkum wa antum mu'riḍoon.

84. Wa iz akhaznaa meesaaqakum laa tasfikoona dimaa-a'akum wa laa tukhrijoona anfusakum min diyaarikum ṣumma aqrartum wa antum tashhadoon.

85. Ṣumma antum haaa'ulaaa'i taqtuloona anfusakum wa tukhrijoona fareeqam-minkum min diyaarihim taẓaaharoona 'alayhim bil-iṣmi wal'udwaani wa iñy-yaåtookum usaaraa tufaadoohum wahuwa muḥarramun 'alaykum ikhraajuhum; afatu'mi-noona biba'ḍil-Kitaabi wa takfuroona biba'ḍ; famaa jazaaa'u mañy-yaf'alu zaalika minkum illaa khizyun fil-ḥayaatid-dunyaa wa Yawmal-Qiyaamati yuraddoona ilaaa ashaddil-'azaab; wa mal-laahu bighaafilin 'ammaa ta'maloon.

86. Ulaaa'ikal-lazeenash-tarawul ḥayaatad-dunyaa bil-Aakhirati falaa yukhaffafu 'anhumul-'azaabu wa laa hum yunṣaroon.   **(Section 10)**

87. Wa laqad aataynaa Moosal-Kitaaba wa qaffaynaa mim ba'dihee bir-Rusuli wa aataynaa 'Eesab-na-Maryamal-bayyinaati wa ayyadnaahu bi-Rooḥil Qudus; afakullamaa jaaa'akum Rasoolum bimaa laa tahwaaa anfusukumus-takbartum

some you called impostors, and others you slay!

88. They say, "Our hearts are the wrappings (which preserve Allah's Word: we need no more)." Nay, Allah's curse is on them for their blasphemy: little is it they believe.

89. And when there comes to them a Book from Allah, confirming what is with them,- although from of old they had prayed for victory against those without Faith,- when there comes to them that which they (should) have recognised, they refuse to believe in it but the curse of Allah is on those without Faith.

90. Miserable is the price for which they have sold their souls, in that they deny (the revelation) which Allah has sent down, in insolent envy that Allah of His Grace should send it to any of His servants He pleases: thus they have drawn on themselves Wrath upon Wrath. And humiliating is the punishment of those who reject Faith.

91. When it is said to them, "Believe in what Allah has sent down," they say, "We believe in what was sent down to us:" yet they reject all besides, even if it be Truth confirming what is with them. Say: "Why then have you slain the prophets of Allah in times gone by, if you did indeed believe?"

92. There came to you Moses with clear (Signs); yet you worshipped the Calf (even) after that, and you did behave wrongfully.

93. And remember, We took your Covenant and We raised above you (the towering height) of Mount (Sinai): (saying): "Hold firmly to what We have given you and hear ken (to the Law)": they said: "We hear, and we disobey:" and they had to drink into their hearts (of the taint) of the Calf

fafareeqan kazzabtum wa fareeqan taqtuloon.

88. Wa qaaloo quloobunaa ghulf; bal la'anahumul-laahu bikufrihim faqaleelam-maa yu'minoon.

89. Wa lammaa jaaa'ahum Kitaabum-min 'indil-laahi muşaddiqul-limaa ma'ahum wa kaanoo min qablu yastaftiḥoona 'alal-lazeena kafaroo falammaa jaaa'ahum maa 'arafoo kafaroo bih; fala'natul-laahi 'alal-kaafireen.

90. Bi'samash-taraw biheee anfusahum añy-yakfuroo bimaaa anzalal-laahu baghyan añy-yunazzilal-laahu min fadlihee 'alaa mañy-yashaaa'u min 'ibaadihee fabaaa'oo bighadabin 'alaa ghadab; wa lilkaafireena 'azaabum-muheen.

91. Wa izaa qeela lahum aaminoo bimaa anzalal-laahu qaaloo nu'minu bimaaa unzila 'alaynaa wa yakfuroona bimaa waraaa'ahoo wa huwal-ḥaqqu muşaddiqal-limaa ma'ahum; qul falima taqtuloona Ambiyaaa'al-laahi min qablu in kuntum mu'mineen.

92. Wa laqad jaaa'akum Moosaa bilbayyinaati summat-takhaztumul-'ijla mim ba'dihee wa antum zaalimoon.

93. Wa iz akhaznaa meesaa-qakum wa rafa'naa fawqa-kumut-Țoora khuzoo maaa aataynaakum biquwwatiñw-wasma'oo qaaloo sami'naa wa 'aşaynaa wa ushriboo fee quloobihimul 'ijla

فَفَرِيقًا كَذَّبْتُمْ وَفَرِيقًا تَقْتُلُوْنَ ۞

وَقَالُوْا قُلُوْبُنَا غُلْفٌ ۚ بَلْ لَّعَنَهُمُ اللهُ بِكُفْرِهِمْ فَقَلِيْلًا مَّا يُؤْمِنُوْنَ ۞

وَلَمَّا جَآءَهُمْ كِتَابٌ مِّنْ عِنْدِ اللهِ مُصَدِّقٌ لِّمَا مَعَهُمْ ۙ وَكَانُوْا مِنْ قَبْلُ يَسْتَفْتِحُوْنَ عَلَى الَّذِيْنَ كَفَرُوْا ۚ فَلَمَّا جَآءَهُمْ مَّا عَرَفُوْا كَفَرُوْا بِهٖ ۚ فَلَعْنَةُ اللهِ عَلَى الْكٰفِرِيْنَ ۞

بِئْسَمَا اشْتَرَوْا بِهٖٓ أَنْفُسَهُمْ أَنْ يَّكْفُرُوْا بِمَآ أَنْزَلَ اللهُ بَغْيًا أَنْ يُّنَزِّلَ اللهُ مِنْ فَضْلِهٖ عَلٰى مَنْ يَّشَآءُ مِنْ عِبَادِهٖ ۚ فَبَآءُوْ بِغَضَبٍ عَلٰى غَضَبٍ ۚ وَلِلْكٰفِرِيْنَ عَذَابٌ مُّهِيْنٌ ۞

وَإِذَا قِيْلَ لَهُمْ اٰمِنُوْا بِمَآ أَنْزَلَ اللهُ قَالُوْا نُؤْمِنُ بِمَآ أُنْزِلَ عَلَيْنَا وَيَكْفُرُوْنَ بِمَا وَرَآءَهٗ وَهُوَ الْحَقُّ مُصَدِّقًا لِّمَا مَعَهُمْ ۗ قُلْ فَلِمَ تَقْتُلُوْنَ أَنْبِيَآءَ اللهِ مِنْ قَبْلُ إِنْ كُنْتُمْ مُّؤْمِنِيْنَ ۞

وَلَقَدْ جَآءَكُمْ مُّوْسٰى بِالْبَيِّنٰتِ ثُمَّ اتَّخَذْتُمُ الْعِجْلَ مِنْ بَعْدِهٖ وَأَنْتُمْ ظٰلِمُوْنَ ۞

وَإِذْ أَخَذْنَا مِيْثَاقَكُمْ وَرَفَعْنَا فَوْقَكُمُ الطُّوْرَ ۚ خُذُوْا مَآ اٰتَيْنٰكُمْ بِقُوَّةٍ وَّاسْمَعُوْا ۗ قَالُوْا سَمِعْنَا وَعَصَيْنَا وَأُشْرِبُوْا فِيْ قُلُوْبِهِمُ الْعِجْلَ

because of their Faithlessness. Say: "Vile indeed are the behests of your Faith if you have any **faith!**"

94. Say: "If the last Home, with Allah, be for you specially, and not for anyone else, then seek you for death, if you are sincere."

95. But they will never seek for death, on account of the (sins) which their hands have sent on before them. And Allah is well-acquainted with the wrong-doers.

96. You will indeed find them, of all people, most greedy of life,- even more than the idolators: each one of them wishes he could be given a life of a thousand years: but the grant of such life will not save him from (due) punishment. For Allah sees well all that they do.

97. Say: Whoever is an enemy to Gabriel - he has brought down the (revelation) to your heart by Allah's will, a confirmation of what went before, and guidance and glad tidings for those who believe,

98. Whoever is an enemy to Allah and His Angels and Apostles, to Gabriel and Michael,- certainly Allah is an enemy to those who reject Faith.

99. We have sent down to you Manifest Signs (ayaat); and none reject them but those who are perverse.

100. Is it not (the case) that every time they make Covenant, some party among them throw it aside?- Nay, most of them are faithless.

101. And when there came to them an Apostle from Allah, confirming what was with them, a party of the People of the Book threw away the Book of Allah

bikufrihim; qul bi'samaa yaåmu-rukum biheee eemaanukum in kuntum mu'mineen.

94. Qul in kaanat lakumud-Daarul-Aakhiratu 'indal-laahi khaalişatam-min doonin-naasi fatamannawul-mawta in kuntum şaadiqeen.

95. Wa lañy-yatamannawhu abadam bimaa qaddamat aydeehim; wallaahu 'aleemum bizzaalimeen.

96. Wa latajidannahum ahraşan-naasi 'alaa hayaatiñw wa minal-lazeena ashrakoo; yawaddu ahaduhum law yu'ammaru alfa sanatiñw wa maa huwa bi muzaḥziḥihee minal-'azaabi añy-yu'ammar; wallaahu başeerum bimaa ya'maloon.
(Section 11)

97. Qul man kaana 'aduwwal-li-Jibreela fainnahoo nazzalahoo 'alaa qalbika bi-iznil-laahi muşaddiqal-limaa bayna yadayhi wa hudañw-wa bushraa lilmu'mineen.

98. Man kaana 'aduwwal-lillaahi wa malaaa'ikatihee wa Rusulihee wa Jibreela wa Meekaala fa-innal-laaha 'aduw-wul-lilkaafireen.

99. Wa laqad anzalnaaa ilayka Aayaatim bayyinaatiñw wa maa yakfuru bihaaa illalfaasiqoon.

100. Awa kullamaa 'aahadoo 'ahdan nabazahoo fareequm-minhum; bal aksaruhum laa yu'minoon.

101.Wa lammaa jaaa'ahum Rasoolum min 'indil-laahi muşaddiqul-limaa ma'ahum nabaza fareequm-minal-lazeena ootul-Kitaaba Kitaabal-laahi

behind their backs, as if (it had been something) they did not know!

102. They followed what the evil ones gave out (falsely) against the power of Solomon: the blasphemers were, and not Solomon, but the evil ones, teaching men magic, and such things as came down at Babylon to the angels Harut and Marut. But neither of these taught anyone (such things) without saying: "We are only for trial; so do not blaspheme." They learned from them the means to sow discord between man and wife. But they could not thus harm anyone except by Allah's permission. And they learned what harmed them, not what profited them. And they knew that the buyers of (magic) would have no share in the happiness of the Hereafter. And vile was the price for which they did sell their souls, if they but knew!

103. If they had kept their Faith and guarded themselves from evil, far better had been the reward from their Lord, if they but knew!

104. O you who believe! say not (to the Apostle) words of ambiguous import, but words of respect; and listen (to him): to those without Faith is a grievous punishment.

105. It is never the wish of those without Faith among the People of the Book, nor of the Pagans, that anything good should come down to you from your Lord. But Allah will choose for His special Mercy whom He will - for Allah is Lord of grace abounding.

waraaa'a zuhoorihim ka-annahum laa ya'lamoon.

102. Wattaba'oo maa tatlush-Shayaateenu 'alaa mulki Sulaymaana wa maa kafara Sulaymaanu wa laakinnash-Shayaateena kafaroo yu'al-limoonan-naasas-sihra wa maaa unzila 'alal-malakayni bi-Baabila Haaroota wa Maaroot; wa maa yu'allimaani min aḥadin ḥattaa yaqoolaaa innamaa naḥnu fitnatun falaa takfur fayata'al-lamoona minhumaa maa yufarriqoona bihee baynal-mar'i wa zawjih; wa maa hum biḍaaarreena bihee min aḥadin illaa bi-iznillaah; wa yata'al-lamoona maa yaḍurruhum wa laa yanfa'uhum; wa laqad 'alimoo lamanish-taraahu maa lahoo fil-Aakhirati min khalaaq; wa labi'sa maa sharaw biheee anfusahum; law kaanoo ya'lamoon.

103. Wa law annahum aamanoo wattaqaw lamasoobatum-min 'indillaahi khayrun law kaanoo ya'lamoon. **(Section 12)**

104. Yaaa ayyuhal-lazeena aamanoo laa taqooloo raa'inaa wa qoolun-zurnaa wasma'oo; wa lilkaafireena 'azaabun aleem.

105. Maa yawaddul-lazeena kafaroo min Ahlil-Kitaabi wa lal-mushrikeena añy-yunazzala 'alaykum min khayrim-mir-Rabbikum; wallaahu yakhtaṣṣu biraḥmatihee mañy-yashaaa'; wallaahu zul-faḍlil-'azeem.

106. None of Our revelations do We abrogate or cause to be forgotten, but We substitute something better or similar: do you not know that Allah has power over all things?

107. Do you not know that to Allah belongs the dominion of the heavens and the earth? And besides Him you have neither patron nor helper.

108. Would you question your Apostle as Moses was questioned of old? But whoever changes from Faith to Unbelief, has strayed without doubt from the even way.

109. Quite a number of the People of the Book wish they could turn you (people) back to infidelity after you have believed, from selfish envy, after the Truth has become Manifest to them: but forgive and overlook, till Allah accomplish His purpose; for Allah has power over all things.

110. And be steadfast in prayer and regular in charity: and whatever good you send forth for your souls before you, you shall find it with Allah: for Allah sees well all that you do.

111. And they say: "None shall enter Paradise unless he be a Jew or a Christian." Those are their (vain) desires. Say: "Produce your proof if you are truthful."

112. Nay,- whoever submits his whole self to Allah and is a doer of good,- he will get his reward with his Lord;

---

106. Maa nansakh min Aayatin aw nunsihaa na-ti bikhayrim-minhaaa aw mislihaaa; alam ta'lam annal-laaha 'alaa kulli shay'in Qadeer.

107. Alam ta'lam annallaaha lahoo mulkus-samaawaati wal-arḍ; wa maa lakum min doonil-laahi miñw-waliyyiñw-wa laa naṣeer.

108. Am tureedoona an tas'aloo Rasoolakum kamaa su'ila Moosaa min qabl; wa mañy-yatabaddalil-kufra bil-eemaani faqad ḍalla sawaaa'as-Sabeel.

109. Wadda kaseerum-min Ahlil-Kitaabi law yaruddoo-nakum mim-ba'di eemaanikum kuffaaran ḥasadam-min 'indi anfusihim mim ba'di maa tabayyana lahumul-ḥaqqu fa'foo waṣfaḥoo ḥattaa yaa-tiyallaahu bi-amrih; innal-laahu 'alaa kulli shay'in Qadeer.

110. Wa aqeemuṣ-Ṣalaata wa aatuz-Zakaah; wa maa tuqad-dimoo li-anfusikum min khayrin tajidoohu 'indal-laah; innal-laaha bimaa ta'maloona Baṣeer.

111. Wa qaaloo lañy-yadkhulal-Jannata illaa man kaana Hoodan aw Naṣaaraa; tilka amaaniy-yuhum; qul haatoo burhaa-nakum in kuntum ṣaadiqeen.

112. Balaa man aslama wajhahoo lillaahi wa huwa muḥsinun falahooo ajruhoo 'inda Rabbihee wa laa

---

مَا نَنسَخْ مِنْ ءَايَةٍ أَوْ نُنسِهَا نَأْتِ بِخَيْرٍ مِّنْهَا أَوْ مِثْلِهَا ۗ أَلَمْ تَعْلَمْ أَنَّ اللّٰهَ عَلَىٰ كُلِّ شَىْءٍ قَدِيرٌ ۝

أَلَمْ تَعْلَمْ أَنَّ اللّٰهَ لَهُۥ مُلْكُ السَّمَٰوَٰتِ وَالْأَرْضِ ۗ وَمَا لَكُم مِّن دُونِ اللّٰهِ مِن وَلِىٍّ وَّلَا نَصِيرٍ ۝

أَمْ تُرِيدُونَ أَن تَسْـَٔلُوا۟ رَسُولَكُمْ كَمَا سُئِلَ مُوسَىٰ مِن قَبْلُ ۗ وَمَن يَتَبَدَّلِ الْكُفْرَ بِالْإِيمَٰنِ فَقَدْ ضَلَّ سَوَآءَ السَّبِيلِ ۝

وَدَّ كَثِيرٌ مِّنْ أَهْلِ الْكِتَٰبِ لَوْ يَرُدُّونَكُم مِّنۢ بَعْدِ إِيمَٰنِكُمْ كُفَّارًا حَسَدًا مِّنْ عِنْدِ أَنفُسِهِم مِّنۢ بَعْدِ مَا تَبَيَّنَ لَهُمُ الْحَقُّ ۖ فَاعْفُوا۟ وَاصْفَحُوا۟ حَتَّىٰ يَأْتِىَ اللّٰهُ بِأَمْرِهِۦٓ ۗ إِنَّ اللّٰهَ عَلَىٰ كُلِّ شَىْءٍ قَدِيرٌ ۝

وَأَقِيمُوا۟ الصَّلَوٰةَ وَءَاتُوا۟ الزَّكَوٰةَ ۚ وَمَا تُقَدِّمُوا۟ لِأَنفُسِكُم مِّنْ خَيْرٍ تَجِدُوهُ عِندَ اللّٰهِ ۗ إِنَّ اللّٰهَ بِمَا تَعْمَلُونَ بَصِيرٌ ۝

وَقَالُوا۟ لَن يَدْخُلَ الْجَنَّةَ إِلَّا مَن كَانَ هُودًا أَوْ نَصَٰرَىٰ ۗ تِلْكَ أَمَانِيُّهُمْ ۗ قُلْ هَاتُوا۟ بُرْهَٰنَكُمْ إِن كُنتُمْ صَٰدِقِينَ ۝

بَلَىٰ مَنْ أَسْلَمَ وَجْهَهُۥ لِلّٰهِ وَهُوَ مُحْسِنٌ فَلَهُۥٓ أَجْرُهُۥ عِندَ رَبِّهِۦ وَلَا

on such shall be no fear, nor shall they grieve.

113. The Jews say: "The Christians have nothing (to stand) upon"; and the Christians say: "The Jews have nothing (to stand) upon." Yet they (profess to) study the (same) Book. Like unto their word is what those say who know not; but Allah will judge between them in their dispute on the Day of Judgment.

114. And who is more unjust than he who forbids that in places for the worship of Allah, Allah's name should be celebrated?- whose zeal is (in fact) to ruin them? It was not fitting that such should themselves enter them except in fear. For them there is nothing but disgrace in this world, and in the world to come, an exceeding torment.

115. To Allah belong the East and the West: whithersoever you turn, there is the presence of Allah. For Allah is All-Pervading, All-Knowing.

116. They say: "Allah has begotten a son": glory be to Him.-Nay, to Him belongs all that is in the heavens and on earth: everything renders worship to Him.

117. To Him is due the primal origin of the heavens and the earth: when He decrees a matter, He says to it: "Be," and it is.

118. Those without knowledge say: "Why does not Allah speak to us? Or why does a Sign not come to us?" So said the people before them words of similar import. Their hearts are alike. We have indeed made clear the Signs for any people who hold firmly to Faith (in their hearts).

khawfun 'alayhim wa laa hum yaḥzanoon.   **(Section 13)**

113. Wa qaalatil-Yahoodu laysatin-Naṣaaraa 'alaa shay' iñw-wa qaalatin-Naṣaaraa laysatil-Yahoodu 'alaa shay-iñw-wa hum yatloonal-Kitaab; kazaalika qaalal-lazeena laa ya'lamoona miṣla qawlihim; fallaahu yaḥkumu baynahum Yawmal-Qiyaamati feemaa kaanoo feehi yakhtalifoon.

114. Wa man-aẓlamu mimmam-mana'a masaajidal-laahi añy-yuzkara feehas-muhoo wa sa'aa fee kharaabihaaa; ulaaa'ika maa kaana lahum añy-yadkhuloohaaa illaa khaaa'ifeen; lahum fiddunyaa khizyuñw-wa lahum fil-Aakhirati 'azaabun 'aẓeem.

115. Wa lillaahil - mashriqu walmaghrib; fa-aynamaa tuwalloo faṣamma Wajhullaah; innal-laaha Waasi'un 'Aleem.

116. Wa qaalut-takhazal-laahu waladan Subḥaanahoo bal lahoo maa fis-samaawaati wal-arḍi kullul-lahoo qaanitoon.

117. Badee'us-samaawaati wal-arḍi wa izaa qaḍaaa amran fa-innamaa yaqoolu lahoo kun fayakoon.

118. Wa qaalal-lazeena laa ya'lamoona law laa yukalli-munal-laahu aw taåteenaaa Aayah; kazaalika qaalal-lazeena min qablihim miṣla qawlihim; tashaabahat quloobuhum; qad bayyannal-Aayaati liqawmiñy-yooqinoon.

اَلْقِيَامَةِ فِيْمَا كَانُوْا فِيْهِ يَخْتَلِفُوْنَ ۝

وَمَنْ اَظْلَمُ مِمَّنْ مَّنَعَ مَسٰجِدَ اللّٰهِ اَنْ يُّذْكَرَ فِيْهَا اسْمُهٗ وَسَعٰى فِيْ خَرَابِهَا ۭ اُولٰٓئِكَ مَا كَانَ لَهُمْ اَنْ يَّدْخُلُوْهَآ اِلَّا خَآئِفِيْنَ ۬ لَهُمْ فِي الدُّنْيَا خِزْيٌ وَّلَهُمْ فِي الْاٰخِرَةِ عَذَابٌ عَظِيْمٌ ۝

وَلِلّٰهِ الْمَشْرِقُ وَالْمَغْرِبُ ۡ فَاَيْنَمَا تُوَلُّوْا فَثَمَّ وَجْهُ اللّٰهِ ۭ اِنَّ اللّٰهَ وَاسِعٌ عَلِيْمٌ ۝

وَقَالُوا اتَّخَذَ اللّٰهُ وَلَدًا ۙ سُبْحٰنَهٗ ۭ بَلْ لَّهٗ مَا فِي السَّمٰوٰتِ وَالْاَرْضِ ۭ كُلٌّ لَّهٗ قٰنِتُوْنَ ۝

بَدِيْعُ السَّمٰوٰتِ وَالْاَرْضِ ۭ وَاِذَا قَضٰٓى اَمْرًا فَاِنَّمَا يَقُوْلُ لَهٗ كُنْ فَيَكُوْنُ ۝

وَقَالَ الَّذِيْنَ لَا يَعْلَمُوْنَ لَوْلَا يُكَلِّمُنَا اللّٰهُ اَوْ تَاْتِيْنَآ اٰيَةٌ ۭ كَذٰلِكَ قَالَ الَّذِيْنَ مِنْ قَبْلِهِمْ مِّثْلَ قَوْلِهِمْ ۭ تَشَابَهَتْ قُلُوْبُهُمْ ۭ قَدْ بَيَّنَّا الْاٰيٰتِ لِقَوْمٍ يُّوْقِنُوْنَ ۝

119. Surely We have sent you in truth as a bearer of glad tidings and a warner: but of you no question shall be asked of the Companions of the Blazing Fire.

120. Never will the Jews or the Christians be satisfied with you unless you follow their form of religion. Say: "The Guidance of Allah,- that is the (only) Guidance." If you were to follow their desires after the knowledge which has reached you, then would you find neither Protector nor Helper against Allah.

121. Those to whom We have sent the Book study it as it should be studied: they are the ones that believe therein: those who reject faith therein, - the loss is their own.

122. O Children of Israel! call to mind the special favour which I bestowed upon you, and that I preferred you to all others (for My Message).

123. Then guard yourselves against a Day when one soul shall not avail another, nor shall compensation be accepted from her nor shall intercession profit her nor shall anyone be helped (from outside).

124. And remember that Abraham was tried by his Lord with certain commands, which he fulfilled: He said: "I will make you an Imam to the Nations." He pleaded: "And also (Imams) from my offspring!" He answered: "But My Promise is not within the reach of evil-doers."

125. And remember, We made the House a place of assembly for men and a place of safety; and take you the station of Abraham as a place of prayer; and We covenanted with Abraham and Isma'il, that they should sanctify My House for those who compass it round,

119. Innaaa arsalnaaka bilḥaqqi basheeranw-wa naẕeeranw-wa laa tus'alu 'an Aṣḥaabil-Jaḥeem.

120. Wa lan tarḍaa 'ankal-Yahoodu wa lan-Naṣaaraa ḥattaa tattabi'a millatahum; qul inna hudal-laahi ₒ huwalhudaa; wa la'init-taba'ta ahwaaa'ahum ba'dal-laẕee jaaa'aka minal-'ilmi maa laka minal-laahi miñw-waliyyiñw-wa laa naṣeer.

121. Allaẕeena aataynaahumul-Kitaaba yatloonahoo ḥaqqa tilaawatiheee ulaaa'ika yu'minoona bih; wa mañy-yakfur bihee fa-ulaaa'ika humul-khaasiroon. **(Section 14)**

122. Yaa Baneee-Israaa'eelaẕ-kuroo ni'matiyal-lateee an'amtu 'alaykum wa annee faḍḍaltukum 'alal-'aalameen.

123. Wattaqoo Yawmal-laa tajzee nafsun 'an nafsin shay-'añw-wa laa yuqbalu minhaa 'adluñw-wa laa tanfa'uhaa shafaa'atuñw-wa laa hum yunṣaroon.

124. Wa iẕib-talaaa Ibraaheema Rabbuhoo bi-Kalimaatin fa-atammahunna qaala Innee jaa'iluka linnaasi Imaaman qaala wa min ẕurriyyatee qaala laa yanaalu 'Ahdiẓ-ẓaalimeen.

125. Wa iz ja'alnal-Bayta maṣaabatal-linnaasi wa amnañw wattakhiẕoo mim-Maqaami Ibraaheema muṣallaa; wa 'ahidnaaa ilaaa Ibraaheema wa Ismaa'eela an ṭahhiraa Baytiya littaaa'ifeena

or use it as a retreat, or bow, or prostrate themselves (therein in prayer).

126. And remember, Abraham said: "My Lord, make this a City of Peace, and feed its people with fruits,- such of them as believe in Allah and the Last Day." He said: "(Yes), and such as reject Faith,- for a while will I grant them their pleasure, but will soon drive them to the torment of Fire, - an evil destination (indeed)!"

127. And remember, Abraham and Isma'il raised the foundations of the House (with this prayer): "Our Lord! accept (this service) from us: for You are the All-Hearing, the All-Knowing.

128. "Our Lord! make of us Muslims, bowing to Your (Will), and of our progeny a people Muslim, bowing to Your (Will); and show us our place for the celebration of (due) rites; and turn unto us (in Mercy); for You are the Oft-Returning, Most Merciful.

129. "Our Lord! send among them an Apostle of their own, who shall rehearse Your Signs to them and instruct them in scripture and wisdom, and sanctify them: for You are the Exalted in Might, the Wise."

130. And who turns away from the religion of Abraham but such as debase their souls with folly? Him We chose and rendered pure in this world: and he will be in the Hereafter in the ranks of the Righteous.

131. Behold! his Lord said to him: "Bow (your will to Me):" he said: "I bow (my will) to the Lord and Cherisher of the Universe."

132. And this was the legacy that Abraham left to his sons, and so did Jacob; "Oh my sons! Allah has chosen the Faith for you;

wal'aakifeena warrukka'is-sujood.

126. Wa iz qaala Ibraaheemu Rabbij-'al haazaa baladan aaminaňw-warzuq ahlahoo minas-samaraati man aamana minhum billaahi wal-Yawmil Aakhiri qaala wa man kafara fa-umatti'uhoo qaleelan summa adtarruhooo ilaa 'azaabin-Naari wa bi'salmaseer.

127. Wa iz yarfa'u Ibraaheemul-qawaa'ida minal-Bayti wa Ismaa'eelu Rabbanaa taqabbal minnaa innaka Antas-Samee'ul-'Aleem.

128. Rabbanaa waj'alnaa muslimayni laka wa min zurriyyatinaaa ummatam-muslimatal-laka wa arinaa manaasikanaa wa tub 'alaynaa innaka Antat-Tawwaabur-Raheem.

129. Rabbanaa wab'as feehim Rasoolam-minhum yatloo 'alayhim Aayaatika wa yu'allimuhumul-Kitaaba wal-Hikmata wa yuzakkeehim; innaka Antal-'Azeezul-Hakeem. **(Section 15)**

130. Wa maňy-yarghabu 'am-Millati Ibraaheema illaa man safiha nafsah; wa laqadis-tafaynaahu fid-dunyaa wa innahoo fil-Aakhirati laminas-saaliheen.

131. Iz qaala lahoo Rabbuhooo aslim qaala aslamtu li-Rabbil-'aalameen.

132. Wa wassaa bihaaa Ibraa-heemu baneehi wa Ya'qoob, yaa baniyya innal laahas-tafaa lakumud-deena

then die not except in the Faith of Islam."

133. Were you witnesses when Death appeared before Jacob? Be-hold, he said to his sons: "What will you worship after me?" They said: "We shall worship your God (Allah) and the God (Allah) of your fathers, of Abraham, Isma'il and Isaac, - the One (True) God (Allah): to Him we bow (in Islam)."

134. That was a people that has passed away. They shall reap the fruit of what they did, and you of what you do! Of their merits there is no question in your case!

135. They say: "Become Jews or Christians if any would be guided (to salvation)." You say: "Nay! (I would rather) the Religion of Abraham the True, and he joined not gods with Allah."

136. You say: "We believe in Allah, and the revelation given to us, and to Abraham, Isma'il, Isaac, Jacob, and the Tribes, and that given to Moses and Jesus, and that given to (all) prophets from their Lord: we make no difference between one and another of them: and we bow to Allah (in Islam)."

137. So if they believe as you believe, they are indeed on the right path; but if they turn back, it is they who are in schism; but Allah will suffice you as against them, and He is the All-Hearing, the All-Knowing.

138. (Our religion is) the Baptism of Allah: and who can beptize better than Allah? And it is He Whom we worship.

139. Say: Will you dispute with us about Allah, seeing that He is our Lord and your Lord; that we are responsible for our doings and you for

---

falaa tamootunna illaa wa antum muslimoon.

133. Am kuntum shuhadaaa'a iz haḍara Ya'qoobal-mawtu iz qaala libaneehi maa ta'budoona mim ba'dee qaaloo na'budu ilaahaka wa ilaaha aabaaa'ika Ibraaheema wa Ismaa'eela wa Ishaaqa Ilaahañw-waahidañw-wa nahnu lahoo muslimoon.

134. Tilka ummatun qad khalat lahaa maa kasabat wa lakum maa kasabtum wa laa tus'aloona 'ammaa kaanoo ya'maloon.

135. Wa qaaloo koonoo Hoodan aw Naṣaaraa tahtadoo; qul bal Millata Ibraaheema Ḥaneefañw-wa maa kaana minal mush-rikeen.

136. Qoolooo aamannaa bil-laahi wa maaa unzila ilaynaa wa maaa unzila ilaa Ibraaheema wa Ismaa'eela wa Ishaaqa wa Ya'qooba wal-Asbaaṭi wa maaa ootiya Moosaa wa 'Eesaa wa maaa ootiyan Nabiyyoona mir-Rabbihim laa nufarriqu bayna ahadim-minhum wa nahnu lahoo muslimoon.

137. Fa-in aamanoo bimisli maaa aamantum bihee faqadih-tadaw wa-in tawallaw fa-innamaa hum fee shiqaaq; fasayakfeekahumul-laah; wa Huwas-Samee'ul-'Aleem.

138. Ṣibghatal-laahi wa man ahsanu minal-laahi ṣibghatañw-wa nahnu lahoo 'aabidoon.

139. Qul atuḥaaajjoonanaa fil-laahi wa Huwa Rabbunaa wa Rabbukum wa lanaaa a'maa-lunaa wa lakum

---

فَلَا تَمُوتُنَّ إِلَّا وَأَنْتُمْ مُّسْلِمُونَ ۞

أَمْ كُنْتُمْ شُهَدَآءَ إِذْ حَضَرَ يَعْقُوبَ الْمَوْتُ ۚ إِذْ قَالَ لِبَنِيهِ مَا تَعْبُدُونَ مِنْ بَعْدِيْ ۖ قَالُوا نَعْبُدُ إِلَهَكَ وَإِلَهَ اٰبَآئِكَ إِبْرٰهِمَ وَإِسْمٰعِيلَ وَإِسْحٰقَ إِلٰهًا وَّاحِدًا ۖ وَّنَحْنُ لَهُ مُسْلِمُونَ ۞

تِلْكَ أُمَّةٌ قَدْ خَلَتْ ۚ لَهَا مَا كَسَبَتْ وَلَكُمْ مَّا كَسَبْتُمْ ۖ وَلَا تُسْئَلُونَ عَمَّا كَانُوا يَعْمَلُونَ ۞

وَقَالُوا كُونُوا هُودًا أَوْ نَصٰرَى تَهْتَدُوا ۗ قُلْ بَلْ مِلَّةَ إِبْرٰهِمَ حَنِيفًا ۖ وَمَا كَانَ مِنَ الْمُشْرِكِينَ ۞

قُولُوا اٰمَنَّا بِاللّٰهِ وَمَا أُنْزِلَ إِلَيْنَا وَمَا أُنْزِلَ إِلَى إِبْرٰهِمَ وَإِسْمٰعِيلَ وَإِسْحٰقَ وَيَعْقُوبَ وَالْأَسْبَاطِ وَمَا أُوتِيَ مُوسٰى وَعِيسٰى وَمَا أُوتِيَ النَّبِيُّونَ مِنْ رَّبِّهِمْ ۖ لَا نُفَرِّقُ بَيْنَ أَحَدٍ مِّنْهُمْ ۖ وَنَحْنُ لَهُ مُسْلِمُونَ ۞

فَإِنْ اٰمَنُوا بِمِثْلِ مَا أٰمَنْتُمْ بِهِ فَقَدِ اهْتَدَوْا ۖ وَّإِنْ تَوَلَّوْا فَإِنَّمَا هُمْ فِيْ شِقَاقٍ ۖ فَسَيَكْفِيكَهُمُ اللّٰهُ ۚ وَهُوَ السَّمِيعُ الْعَلِيمُ ۞

صِبْغَةَ اللّٰهِ ۖ وَمَنْ أَحْسَنُ مِنَ اللّٰهِ صِبْغَةً ۖ وَّنَحْنُ لَهُ عٰبِدُونَ ۞

قُلْ أَتُحَاجُّونَنَا فِي اللّٰهِ وَهُوَ رَبُّنَا وَرَبُّكُمْ ۖ وَلَنَا أَعْمَالُنَا وَلَكُمْ

yours; and that we are sincere (in our faith) in Him?

140. Or do you say that Abraham, Isma'il, Isaac, Jacob and the Tribes were Jews or Christians? Say: Do you know better than Allah? Ah! who is more unjust than those who conceal the testimony they have from Allah? But Allah is not unmindful of what you do!

141. That was a people that have passed away. They shall reap the fruit of what they did, and you of what you do! Of their merits there is no question in your case:

142. The fools among the people will say: "What has turned them from the Qibla to which they were used?" Say: To Allah belong both East and West: He guides whom He will to a Way that is straight.

143. Thus, have We made of you an Ummat justly balanced, that you might be witnesses over the nations, and the Apostle a witness over yourselves; and We appointed the Qibla to which you were used, only to test those who followed the Apostle from those who would turn on their heels (from the Faith). Indeed it was (a change) momentous, except to those guided by Allah. And never would Allah make your faith of no effect. For Allah is to all people most surely full of kindness, Most Merciful.

144. We see the turning of your face (for guidance) to the heavens: now shall We turn you to a Qibla that shall please you. Turn then

a'maalukum wa naḥnu lahoo mukhliṣoon.

140. Am taqooloona-inna Ibraaheema wa Ismaa'eela wa Isḥaaqa wa Ya'qooba wal Asbaaṭa kaanoo Hoodan aw Naṣaaraa; qul 'a-antum a'lamu amil-laah; wa man aẓlamu mimman katama shahaadatan 'indahoo minallaah; wa mal-laahu bighaafilin 'ammaa ta'maloon.

141. Tilka ummatun qad khalat lahaa maa kasabat wa lakum maa kasabtum wa laa tus'aloona 'ammaa kaanoo ya'maloon.

(Section 16)

142. Sayaqoolus-sufahaaa'u minan-naasi maa wallaahum 'an Qiblatihimul-latee kaanoo 'alayhaa; qul lillaahil mashriqu walmaghrib; yahdee many-yashaaa'u ilaa Ṣiraaṭim-Mustaqeem.

143. Wa kazaalika ja'alnaakum ummataňw-wasaṭal-litakoonoo shuhadaaa'a 'alan-naasi wa yakoonar-Rasoolu 'alaykum shaheedaa; wa maa ja'alnal-Qiblatal-latee kunta 'alayhaaa illaa lina'lama many-yattabi'ur-Rasoola mimmaňy-yanqalibu 'alaa 'aqibayh; wa in kaanat lakabeeratan illaa 'alal-lazeena hadal-laah; wa maa kaanal-laahu liyuḍee'a eemaanakum; innal-laaha binnaasi la-Ra'oofur-Raḥeem.

144. Qad naraa taqalluba wajhika fis-samaaa'i fala-nuwalliyannaka Qiblatan tarḍaahaa; fawalli

your face in the direction of the sacred Mosque: wherever you are, turn your faces in that direction. The people of the Book know well that that is the truth from their Lord. Nor is Allah unmindful of what they do.

145. Even if you were to bring to the people of the Book all the Signs (together), they would not follow your Qibla; nor are you going to follow their Qibla; nor indeed will they follow each other's Qibla. If you after the knowledge has reached you were to follow their (vain) desires,- then you were indeed (clearly) in the wrong.

146. The people of the Book know this as they know their own sons; but some of them conceal the truth which they themselves know.

147. The Truth is from your Lord; so be not at all in doubt.

148. To each is a goal to which Allah turns him; then strive together (as in a race) toward all that is good. Wheresoever you are, Allah will bring you together. For Allah has power over all things.

149. From wheresoever you start forth, turn your face in the direction of the Sacred Mosque; that is indeed the truth from the Lord. And Allah is not unmindful of what you do.

150. So from wheresoever you start forth, turn your face in the direction of the Sacred Mosque; and wheresoever

wajhaka shaṭral-Masjidil-Ḥaraam; wa ḥaysu maa kuntum fawalloo wujoohakum shaṭrah; wa innal-lazeena ootul-Kitaaba laya'lamoona annahul-ḥaqqu mir-Rabbihim; wa mal-laahu bighaafilin 'ammaa ya'maloon.

145. Wa la'in ataytal-lazeena ootul-Kitaaba bikulli Aayatim-maa tabi'oo Qiblatak; wa maaa anta bitaabi'in-Qiblatahum; wa maa ba'ḍuhum bitaabi'in Qiblata ba'ḍ; wa la'init-taba'ta ahwaaa'ahum mim ba'di maa jaaa'aka minal-'ilmi innaka izal-laminaz-zaalimeen.

146. Allazeena-aataynaahumul Kitaaba ya'rifoonahoo kamaa ya'rifoona abnaaa'ahum wa inna fareeqam-minhum layaktumoonal-ḥaqqa wa hum ya'lamoon.

147. Alḥaqqu mir-Rabbika falaa takoonanna minal-mumtareen. **(Section 17)**

148. Wa likulliñw-wijhatun huwa muwalleehaa fastabiqul-khayraat; ayna maa takoonoo ya- āti bikumullaahu jamee'aa; innal-laaha 'alaa kulli shay'in Qadeer.

149. Wa min ḥaysu kharajta fawalli wajhaka shaṭral-Masjidil-Ḥaraami wa innahoo lalḥaqqu mir-Rabbik; wa mallaahu bighaafilin 'ammaa ta'maloon.

150. Wa min ḥaysu kharajta fawalli wajhaka shaṭral-Masjidil-Ḥaraam; wa ḥaysu maa

you are, turn your face to it: that there be no ground of dispute against you among the people, except those of them that are bent on wickedness; so fear them not, but fear Me; and that I may complete My favours on you, and you May (consent to) be guided;

151. A similar (favour have you already received) in that We have sent among you an Apostle of your own, rehearsing to you Our Signs, and sanctifying you, and instructing you in Scripture and Wisdom, and in new Knowledge.

152. Then you remember Me; I will remember you. Be grateful to Me, and reject not Faith.

153. O you who believe! seek help with patient perseverance and prayer; for Allah is with those who patiently persevere.

154. And say not of those who are slain in the way of Allah: "They are dead." Nay, they are living, though you perceive (it) not.

155. Be sure We shall test you with something of fear and hunger, some loss in goods or lives or the fruits (of your toil), but give glad tidings to those who patiently persevere,

156. Who say, when afflicted with calamity: "To Allah we belong, and to Him is our return":-

157. They are those on whom (descend) blessings from Allah, and Mercy, and they are the ones that receive guidance.

158. Behold! Safa and Marwa are among the Symbols of Allah. So if those who visit the House in the Season or at other times, should compass them round, it is no sin in them. And if any one obeys his own impulse to Good,- be sure that Allah is He Who recognises and knows.

---

kuntum fawalloo wujoohakum shatrahoo li'allaa yakoona linnaasi 'alaykum ḥujjatun illal-lazeena ẓalamoo minhum falaa takhshawhum wakhshawnee wa liutimma ni'matee 'alaykum wa la'allakum tahtadoon.

151. Kamaaa arsalnaa feekum Rasoolam-minkum yatloo 'alaykum Aayaatinaa wa yuzakkeekum wa yu'alli-mukumul-Kitaaba wal-Ḥikmata wa yu'allimukum maa lam takoonoo ta'lamoon.

152. Fazkurooneee azkurkum washkuroo lee wa laa takfuroon.

(Section 18)

153. Yaaa ayyuhal-lazeena aamanus-ta'eenoo biṣṣabri waṣ-Ṣalaah; innal-laaha ma'aṣ-ṣaabireen.

154. Wa laa taqooloo limañy-yuqtalu fee sabeelil-laahi amwaat; bal aḥyaaa'uñw-wa laakil-laa tash'uroon.

155. Wa lanablu-wannakum bishay'im-minal-khawfi waljoo'i wa naqṣim-minal-amwaali wal-anfusi waṣ-ṣamaraat; wa bashshiriṣ-ṣaabireen.

156. Allazeena izaaa aṣaabat-hum muṣeebatun qaalooo innaa lillaahi wa innaaa ilayhi raaji'oon.

157. Ulaaa'ika 'alayhim ṣala-waatum-mir-Rabbihim wa raḥmah; wa ulaaa'ika humul-muhtadoon.

158. Innaṣ-Ṣafaa wal-Marwata min sha'aaa'iril-laahi faman ḥajjal-Bayta awi'-tamara falaa junaaḥa 'alayhi añy-yaṭṭawwafa bihimaa; wa man taṭawwa'a khayran fa-innal-laaha Shaakirun 'Aleem.

159. Those who conceal the clear (Signs) We have sent down, and the Guidance, after We have made it clear for the People in the Book,- on them shall be Allah's curse, and the curse of those entitled to curse,-

160. Except those who repent and make amends and openly declare (the Truth): to them I turn; for I am Oft-returning, Most Merciful.

161. Those who reject Faith, and die rejecting,- on them is Allah's curse, and the curse of angels, and of all mankind.

162. They will abide therein: their Chastisement will not be lightened, nor will respite be their (lot).

163. And your God (Allah) is One God (Allah): There is no god but He, Most Gracious, Most Merciful.

164. Behold! in the creation of the heavens and the earth; in the alternation of the night and the day; in the sailing of the ships through the ocean for the profit of mankind; in the rain which Allah sends down from the skies, and the life which He gives therewith to an earth that is dead; in the beasts of all kinds that He scatters through the earth; in the change of the winds, and the clouds which trail like their slaves between the sky and the earth;- (here) indeed are Signs for a people that are wise.

165. Yet there are men who take (for worship) others besides Allah, as equal (with Allah): they love them as they should love Allah. But those of Faith are overflowing in their love for Allah. If

159. Innal-lazeena yaktumoona maaa anzalnaa minal-bayyinaati walhudaa mim ba'di maa bayyannaahu linnaasi fil-Kitaabi ulaaa'ika yal'anuhumul-laahu wa yal'anuhumul-laa'inoon.

160. Illal-lazeena taaboo wa aṣlaḥoo wa bayyanoo fa-ulaaa'ika atoobu 'alayhim; wa Anat-Tawwaabur-Raḥeem.

161. Innal-lazeena kafaroo wamaa-too wa hum kuffaarun ulaaa'ika 'alayhim la'natul-laahi walmalaaa'ikati wannaasi ajma'een.

162. Khaalideena feehaa laa yukhaffafu 'anhumul-'azaabu wa laa hum yunzaroon.

163. Wa ilaahukum Ilaahuñw-waaḥid, laaa ilaaha illaa Huwar-Raḥmaanur-Raḥeem. **(Section 19)**

164. Inna fee khalqis-samaa-waati wal-arḍi wakhtilaafil-layli wannahaari walfulkil-latee tajree fil-baḥri bimaa yanfa'un-naasa wa maaa anzalal-laahu minas-samaaa'i mim-maaa'in fa-aḥyaa bihil-arḍa ba'da mawtihaa wa bas̱s̱a feehaa min kulli daaabbatiñw-wa taṣreefir-riyaaḥi wassaḥaabil-musakh-khari baynas-samaaa'i wal-arḍi la-Aayaatil-liqawmiñy-ya'qiloon.

165. Wa minan-naasi mañy-yattakhizu min doonil-laahi andaadañy-yuḥibboonahum kaḥubbil-laahi wallazeena aamanooo ashaddu ḥubbal-lillaah; wa law yaral-

إِنَّ الَّذِينَ يَكْتُمُونَ مَا أَنْزَلْنَا مِنَ الْبَيِّنَتِ وَالْهُدَى مِنْ بَعْدِ مَا بَيَّنَّهُ لِلنَّاسِ فِي الْكِتَبِ أُولَٰٓئِكَ يَلْعَنُهُمُ اللَّهُ وَيَلْعَنُهُمُ اللَّعِنُونَ ۝

إِلَّا الَّذِينَ تَابُوا وَأَصْلَحُوا وَبَيَّنُوا فَأُولَٰٓئِكَ أَتُوبُ عَلَيْهِمْ ۚ وَأَنَا التَّوَّابُ الرَّحِيمُ ۝

إِنَّ الَّذِينَ كَفَرُوا وَمَاتُوا وَهُمْ كُفَّارٌ أُولَٰٓئِكَ عَلَيْهِمْ لَعْنَةُ اللَّهِ وَالْمَلَٰٓئِكَةِ وَالنَّاسِ أَجْمَعِينَ ۝

خَلِدِينَ فِيهَا ۖ لَا يُخَفَّفُ عَنْهُمُ الْعَذَابُ وَلَا هُمْ يُنْظَرُونَ ۝

وَإِلَٰهُكُمْ إِلَٰهٌ وَاحِدٌ ۖ لَا إِلَٰهَ إِلَّا هُوَ الرَّحْمَٰنُ الرَّحِيمُ ۝

إِنَّ فِي خَلْقِ السَّمَٰوَٰتِ وَالْأَرْضِ وَاخْتِلَافِ الَّيْلِ وَالنَّهَارِ وَالْفُلْكِ الَّتِي تَجْرِي فِي الْبَحْرِ بِمَا يَنْفَعُ النَّاسَ وَمَا أَنْزَلَ اللَّهُ مِنَ السَّمَاءِ مِنْ مَاءٍ فَأَحْيَا بِهِ الْأَرْضَ بَعْدَ مَوْتِهَا وَبَثَّ فِيهَا مِنْ كُلِّ دَابَّةٍ وَتَصْرِيفِ الرِّيَحِ وَالسَّحَابِ الْمُسَخَّرِ بَيْنَ السَّمَاءِ وَالْأَرْضِ لَأَيَتٍ لِقَوْمٍ يَعْقِلُونَ ۝

وَمِنَ النَّاسِ مَنْ يَتَّخِذُ مِنْ دُونِ اللَّهِ أَنْدَادًا يُحِبُّونَهُمْ كَحُبِّ اللَّهِ ۖ وَالَّذِينَ ءَامَنُوا أَشَدُّ حُبًّا لِلَّهِ ۗ وَلَوْ يَرَى

only the unrighteous could see, behold, they would see the Chastisement: that to Allah belongs all power, and Allah will strongly enforce the Chastisement.

166. Then would those who are followed clear themselves of those who follow (them): they would see the Chastisement, and all relations between them would be cut off.

167. And those who followed would say: "If only we had one more chance, we would clear ourselves of them, as they have cleared themselves of us." Thus will Allah show them (the fruits of) their deeds as (nothing but) regrets. Nor will there be a way for them out of the Fire.

168. O you people! Eat of what is on earth, lawful and good; and do not follow the footsteps of the Satan, for he is to you an avowed enemy.

169. For he commands you what is evil and shameful, and that you should say of Allah that of which you have no knowledge.

170. When it is said to them: "Follow what Allah has revealed:" they say: "Nay! we shall follow the ways of our fathers." What! even though their fathers were void of wisdom and guidance?

171. The parable of those who reject Faith is as if one were to shout like a goat-herd, to things that listen to nothing but calls and cries: deaf, dumb, and blind, they are void of wisdom.

172. O you who believe! Eat of the good things that We have provided for you and be grateful

lazeena zalamooo iz yarawnal 'azaaba annal-quwwata lillaahi jamee'anw-wa annallaaha shadeedul-'azaab.

166. Iz tabarra-al-lazeenat-tubi'oo minal-lazeenattaba'oo wa ra-awul-'azaaba wa taqatta'at bihimul asbaab.

167. Wa qaalal-lazeenat-taba'oo law anna lanaa karratan fanatabarra-a minhum kamaa tabarra'oo minnaa; kazaalika yureehimullaahu a'maalahum hasaraatin 'alayhim wa maa hum bikhaarijeena minan-Naar.
(Section 20)

168. Yaaa ayyuhan-naasu kuloo mimmaa fil-ardi halaalan tayyibanw-wa laa tattabi'oo khutu-waatish-Shaytaan; innahoo lakum 'aduwwum-mubeen.

169. Innamaa yaamurukum bissooo'i walfahshaaa'i wa an taqooloo 'alal-laahi maa laa ta'lamoon.

170. Wa izaa qeela lahumut-tabi'oo maaa-anzalal-laahu qaaloo bal nattabi'u maaa alfaynaa 'alayhi aabaaa'anaaa; awalaw kaana aabaaa'uhum laa ya'qiloona shay'anw-wa laa yahtadoon.

171. Wa masalul-lazeena kafaroo kamasalil-lazee yan'iqu bimaa laa yasma'u illaa du'aaa'anw-wa nidaaa'aa; summum-bukmun 'umyun fahum laa ya'qiloon.

172. Yaaa ayyuhal-lazeena aamanoo kuloo min tayyibaati maa razaqnaakum washkuroo

الَّذِينَ ظَلَمُوٓاْ إِذْ يَرَوْنَ الْعَذَابَ ۙ أَنَّ الْقُوَّةَ لِلَّهِ جَمِيعًا ۙ وَّأَنَّ اللَّهَ شَدِيدُ الْعَذَابِ ۝

إِذْ تَبَرَّأَ الَّذِينَ اتُّبِعُوا مِنَ الَّذِينَ اتَّبَعُوا وَرَأَوُا الْعَذَابَ وَتَقَطَّعَتْ بِهِمُ الْأَسْبَابُ ۝

وَقَالَ الَّذِينَ اتَّبَعُوا لَوْ أَنَّ لَنَا كَرَّةً فَنَتَبَرَّأَ مِنْهُمْ كَمَا تَبَرَّءُوا مِنَّا ۗ كَذَٰلِكَ يُرِيهِمُ اللَّهُ أَعْمَالَهُمْ حَسَرَاتٍ عَلَيْهِمْ ۖ وَمَا هُم بِخَارِجِينَ مِنَ النَّارِ ۝

يَا أَيُّهَا النَّاسُ كُلُوا مِمَّا فِي الْأَرْضِ حَلَالًا طَيِّبًا ۖ وَّلَا تَتَّبِعُوا خُطُوَاتِ الشَّيْطَانِ ۚ إِنَّهُ لَكُمْ عَدُوٌّ مُّبِينٌ ۝

إِنَّمَا يَأْمُرُكُم بِالسُّوٓءِ وَالْفَحْشَاءِ وَأَن تَقُولُوا عَلَى اللَّهِ مَا لَا تَعْلَمُونَ ۝

وَإِذَا قِيلَ لَهُمُ اتَّبِعُوا مَا أَنزَلَ اللَّهُ قَالُوا بَلْ نَتَّبِعُ مَا أَلْفَيْنَا عَلَيْهِ آبَاءَنَا ۗ أَوَلَوْ كَانَ آبَاؤُهُمْ لَا يَعْقِلُونَ شَيْئًا وَّلَا يَهْتَدُونَ ۝

وَمَثَلُ الَّذِينَ كَفَرُوا كَمَثَلِ الَّذِي يَنْعِقُ بِمَا لَا يَسْمَعُ إِلَّا دُعَاءً وَّنِدَاءً ۚ صُمٌّ بُكْمٌ عُمْيٌ فَهُمْ لَا يَعْقِلُونَ ۝

يَا أَيُّهَا الَّذِينَ آمَنُوا كُلُوا مِن طَيِّبَاتِ مَا رَزَقْنَاكُمْ وَاشْكُرُوا

to allah, if it is Him you worship.

173. He has only forbidden you dead meat, and blood, and the flesh of swine, and that on which any other name has been invoked besides that of Allah. But if one is forced by necessity, without wilful disobedience, nor transgressing due limits,- then is he guiltless, for Allah is Oft-Forgiving, Most Merciful.

174. Those who conceal Allah's revelations in the Book, and purchase for them a miserable profit,- they swallow into themselves nothing but ꞌFire; Allah will not address them on the Day of Resurrection, nor purify them: grievous will be their Chastisement.

175. They are the ones who buy Error in place of Guidance and Torment in place of Forgiveness. Ah! what boldness (they show) for the Fire!

176. (Their doom is) because Allah sent down the Book in truth but those who seek causes of dispute in the Book are in a schism far (from the purpose).

177. It is not righteousness that you turn your faces toward East or West; but it is righteousness - to believe in Allah and the Last Day, and the Angels, and the Book, and the Messengers; to spend of your substance, out of love for Him, for your kin, for orphans, for the needy, for the wayfarer, for those who ask, and for the ransom of slaves; to be steadfast in prayer, and practice regular charity; to fulfil the

lillaahi in kuntum iyyaahu ta'budoon.

173. Innamaa ḥarrama 'alay-kumul-maytata waddama wa laḥmal-khinzeeri wa maaa uhilla bihee lighayril-laahi famaniḍ-ṭurra ghayra baaghiñw-wa laa 'aadin falaaa iṣma 'alayh; innal-laaha Ghafoorur-Raḥeem.

174. Innal-lazeena yaktu-moona maaa anzalal laahu minal-Kitaabi wa yashtaroona bihee ṣamanan qaleelan ulaaa'ika maa yaåkuloona fee buṭoonihim illan-Naara wa laa yukallimu-humul-laahu Yawmal Qiyaamati wa laa yuzakkeehim wa lahum 'azaabun aleem.

175. Ulaaa'ikal-lazeenash-tarawuḍ-ḍalaalata bilhudaa wal'azaaba bilmaghfirah; famaaa asbarahum 'alan-Naar.

176. Zaalika bi-annal-laaha nazzalal-Kitaaba Bilḥaqq; wa innal-lazeenakh-talafoo fil-Kitaabi lafee shiqaaqim ba'eed.
(Section 21)

177. Laysal-birra an tuwalloo wujoohakum qibalal-mashriqi walmaghribi wa laakinnal birra man aamana billaahi wal-Yawmil-Aakhiri walmalaaa-'ikati wal-Kitaabi wan-Nabiy-yeena wa aatalmaala 'alaa ḥubbihee zawilqurbaa walyataa-maa walmasaakeena wabnas-sabeeli wassaaa'ileena wa firriqaabi wa aqaamaṣ-Ṣalaata wa aataz-Zakaata walmoofoona

بِٱللّٰهِ إِن كُنتُمۡ إِيَّاهُ تَعۡبُدُونَ ۝

إِنَّمَا حَرَّمَ عَلَيۡكُمُ ٱلۡمَيۡتَةَ وَٱلدَّمَ وَلَحۡمَ ٱلۡخِنزِيرِ وَمَآ أُهِلَّ بِهِۦ لِغَيۡرِ ٱللّٰهِ ۖ فَمَنِ ٱضۡطُرَّ غَيۡرَ بَاغٍ وَلَا عَادٍ فَلَآ إِثۡمَ عَلَيۡهِ ۚ إِنَّ ٱللّٰهَ غَفُورٌ رَّحِيمٌ ۝

إِنَّ ٱلَّذِينَ يَكۡتُمُونَ مَآ أَنزَلَ ٱللّٰهُ مِنَ ٱلۡكِتَٰبِ وَيَشۡتَرُونَ بِهِۦ ثَمَنًا قَلِيلًا ۙ أُولَٰٓئِكَ مَا يَأۡكُلُونَ فِي بُطُونِهِمۡ إِلَّا ٱلنَّارَ وَلَا يُكَلِّمُهُمُ ٱللّٰهُ يَوۡمَ ٱلۡقِيَٰمَةِ وَلَا يُزَكِّيهِمۡ وَلَهُمۡ عَذَابٌ أَلِيمٌ ۝

أُولَٰٓئِكَ ٱلَّذِينَ ٱشۡتَرَوُاْ ٱلضَّلَٰلَةَ بِٱلۡهُدَىٰ وَٱلۡعَذَابَ بِٱلۡمَغۡفِرَةِ ۚ فَمَآ أَصۡبَرَهُمۡ عَلَى ٱلنَّارِ ۝

ذَٰلِكَ بِأَنَّ ٱللّٰهَ نَزَّلَ ٱلۡكِتَٰبَ بِٱلۡحَقِّ ۗ وَإِنَّ ٱلَّذِينَ ٱخۡتَلَفُواْ فِي ٱلۡكِتَٰبِ لَفِي شِقَاقٍ بَعِيدٍ ۝

لَّيۡسَ ٱلۡبِرَّ أَن تُوَلُّواْ وُجُوهَكُمۡ قِبَلَ ٱلۡمَشۡرِقِ وَٱلۡمَغۡرِبِ وَلَٰكِنَّ ٱلۡبِرَّ مَنۡ ءَامَنَ بِٱللّٰهِ وَٱلۡيَوۡمِ ٱلۡأَخِرِ وَٱلۡمَلَٰٓئِكَةِ وَٱلۡكِتَٰبِ وَٱلنَّبِيِّۦنَ وَءَاتَى ٱلۡمَالَ عَلَىٰ حُبِّهِۦ ذَوِي ٱلۡقُرۡبَىٰ وَٱلۡيَتَٰمَىٰ وَٱلۡمَسَٰكِينَ وَٱبۡنَ ٱلسَّبِيلِ وَٱلسَّآئِلِينَ وَفِي ٱلرِّقَابِ وَأَقَامَ ٱلصَّلَوٰةَ وَءَاتَى ٱلزَّكَوٰةَ وَٱلۡمُوفُونَ

contracts which you have made; and to be firm and patient, in pain (or suffering) and adversity, and throughout all periods of panic. Such are the people of truth, those who fear Allah.

178. O you who believe! The law of equality is prescribed to you in cases of murder: the free for the free, the slave for the slave, the woman for the woman. But if any remission is made by the brother of the slain, then grant any reasonable demand, and compensate him with handsome gratitude, this is a concession and a Mercy from your Lord. After this whoever exceeds the limits shall be in grave Chastisement.

179. In the Law of Equality there is (saving of) Life to you, O you men of understanding; that you may restrain yourselves.

180. It is prescribed, when death approaches any of you, if he leave any goods that he make a bequest to parents and next of kin, according to reasonable usage; this is due from those who fear Allah.

181. If anyone changes the bequest after hearing it, the guilt shall be on those who make the change. For Allah hears and knows (all things).

182. But if anyone fears partiality or wrong-doing on the part of the testator, and makes peace between (the parties concerned), there is no wrong in him: for Allah is Oft-Forgiving, Most Merciful!

183. O you who believe! Fasting is prescribed to you as it was prescribed to those

178. Yaaa ayyuhal-lazeena aamanoo kutiba 'alaykumul-qisaasu fil-qatlaa alhurru bilhurri wal'abdu bil'abdi wal-unsaa bil-unsaa; faman 'ufiya lahoo min akheehi shay'un fattibaa'um-bilma'roofi wa adaaa'un ilayhi bi-ihsaan; zaalika takhfeefum-mir-Rahbikum wa-rahmah; famani'-tadaa ba'da zaalika falahoo 'azaabun aleem.

179. Wa lakum fil-qisaasi hayaatuny-yaaa-ulil-albaabi la-'allakum tattaqoon.

180. Kutiba 'alaykum izaa hadara ahadakumul-mawtu in taraka khayranil-wasiyyatu lilwaalidayni wal-aqrabeena bilma'roofi haqqan 'alalmut-taqeen.

181. Famam-baddalahoo ba'da maa sami'ahoo fa-innamaaa ismuhoo 'alallazeena yubaddi-loonah; innallaaha Samee'un 'Aleem.

182. Faman khaafa mim-moosin janafan aw isman fa-aslaha baynahum falaaa isma 'alayh; innal-laaha Ghafoorur-Raheem.   **(Section 22)**

183. Yaaa ayyuhal-lazeena aamanoo kutiba 'alaykumus-Siyaamu kamaa kutiba 'alal lazeena

before you, that you may (learn) self-restraint,-

184. (Fasting is) for a fixed number of days; but if any of you is ill, or on a journey, the prescribed number (should be made up) from days later. For those who can do it (with hardship), is a ransom, the feeding of one that is indigent. But he that will give more, of his own free will,- it is better for him. And it is better for you that you fast, if you only knew.

185. Ramadhan is the (month) in which was sent down the Qur'an, as a guide to mankind, also clear (Signs) for guidance and judgment (between right and wrong). So every one of you who is present (at his home) during that month should spend it in fasting, but if any one is ill, or on a journey, the prescribed period (should be made up) by days later. Allah intends every facility for you; He does not want to put you to difficulties. (He wants you) to complete the prescribed period, and to glorify Him in that He has guided you; and perchance you shall be grateful.

186. When My servants ask you concerning Me, I am indeed close (to them): I listen to the prayer of every suppliant when he calls on Me: let them also, with a will, listen to My call, and believe in Me: that they may walk in the right way.

187. Permitted to you, on the night of the fasts, is the approach to your wives. They are your garments and you are their garments. Allah knows what you used to do secretly among yourselves; but He turned to you and forgave you; so now associate with them, and seek what Allah has ordained

min qablikum la-'allakum tattaqoon.

184. Ayyaamam-ma'doodaat; faman kaana minkum mareeḍan aw 'alaa safarin fa'iddatum-min ayyaamin ukhar; wa 'alal-lazeena yuṭeeqoonahoo fidyatun ṭa'aamu miskeenin faman taṭawwa'a khayran fahuwa khayrul-lahoo wa an taṣoomoo khayrul-lakum in kuntum ta'lamoon.

185. Shahru Ramaḍaanallazeee unzila feehil-Qur'aanu hudal-linnaasi wa bayyinaatim-minal-hudaa wal-furqaan; faman shahida minkumush-shahra falyaṣumhu wa man kaana mareeḍan aw 'alaa safarin fa'iddatum-min ayyaamin ukhar; yureedul-laahu bikumul-yusra wa laa yureedu bikumul-'usra wa litukmilul'iddata wa litukabbirul-laaha 'alaa maa hadaakum wa la'allakum tashkuroon.

186 Wa izaa sa-alaka 'ibaadee 'annee fa-innee qareebun ujeebu da'wataddaa'i izaa da'aani falyastajeeboo lee walyu'minoo bee la'allahum yarshudoon.

187. Uḥilla lakum laylataṣ Ṣiyaamir-rafaṣu ilaa nisaaa'i-kum; hunna libaasullakum wa antum libaasullahunn; 'alimal-laahu annakum kuntum takhtaanoona anfusakum fataaba 'alaykum wa 'afaa 'ankum fal'aana baashiroo-hunna wabtaghoo maa katabal-laahoo

for you, and eat and drink, until the white thread of dawn appear to you distinct from its black thread; then complete your fast till the night appears; but do not associate with your wives while you are in retreat in the mosques. Those are limits (set by) Allah: do not go near to those. Thus Allah makes clear His Signs to men: that they may learn self-restraint.

لَكُمْ وَكُلُوا وَاشْرَبُوا حَتّٰى يَتَبَيَّنَ لَكُمُ الْخَيْطُ الْأَبْيَضُ مِنَ الْخَيْطِ الْأَسْوَدِ مِنَ الْفَجْرِ ثُمَّ أَتِمُّوا الصِّيَامَ إِلَى الَّيْلِ وَلَا تُبَاشِرُوهُنَّ وَأَنْتُمْ عَاكِفُونَ فِي الْمَسَاجِدِ تِلْكَ حُدُودُ اللهِ فَلَا تَقْرَبُوهَا كَذٰلِكَ يُبَيِّنُ اللهُ أيٰتِهِ لِلنَّاسِ لَعَلَّهُمْ يَتَّقُونَ ۝

lakum; wa kuloo washraboo ḥattaa yatabayyana lakumul-khayṭul abyaḍu minal-khayṭil-aswadi minal-fajri ṣumma atimmuṣ-Ṣiyaama ilal-layl; wa laa tubaashiroo-hunna wa antum 'aakifoona fil-masaajid; tilka ḥudoodul-laahi falaa taqraboo-haa; kazaalika yubayyinul-laahu Aayaatihee linnaasi la'allahum yattaqoon.

188. And do not eat up your property among yourselves for vanities, nor use it as bait for the judges, with intent that you may eat up wrongfully and knowingly a little of (other) people's property.

188. Wa laa taåkulooo amwaa-lakum baynakum bilbaaṭili wa tudloo bihaaa ilal-ḥukkaami litaåkuloo fareeqam min amwaalin-naasi bil-iṣmi wa antum ta'lamoon. **(Section 23)**

وَلَا تَأْكُلُوا أَمْوَالَكُمْ بَيْنَكُمْ بِالْبَاطِلِ وَتُدْلُوا بِهَا إِلَى الْحُكَّامِ لِتَأْكُلُوا فَرِيقًا مِّنْ أَمْوَالِ النَّاسِ بِالْإِثْمِ وَأَنْتُمْ تَعْلَمُونَ ۝

189. They ask you concerning the New Moons. Say: They are but signs to mark fixed periods of time in (the affairs of) men, and for Pilgrimage. It is no virtue if you enter your houses from the back: it is virtue if you fear Allah. Enter houses through the proper doors: and fear Allah: that you may achieve success.

189. Yas'aloonaka 'anil-ahillati qul hiya mawaaqeetu linnaasi wal-Ḥajj; wa laysal-birru bi-an taåtul-buyoota min ẓuhoorihaa wa laakinnal-birra manit-taqaa; waåtul-buyoota min abwaa-bihaa; wattaqullaaha la'allakum tufliḥoon.

يَسْأَلُونَكَ عَنِ الْأَهِلَّةِ قُلْ هِيَ مَوَاقِيتُ لِلنَّاسِ وَالْحَجِّ وَلَيْسَ الْبِرُّ بِأَنْ تَأْتُوا الْبُيُوتَ مِنْ ظُهُورِهَا وَلٰكِنَّ الْبِرَّ مَنِ اتَّقٰى وَأْتُوا الْبُيُوتَ مِنْ أَبْوَابِهَا وَاتَّقُوا اللهَ لَعَلَّكُمْ تُفْلِحُونَ ۝

190. Fight in the cause of Allah those who fight you, but do not transgress limits; for Allah love not transgressors.

190. Wa qaatiloo fee sabeelil-laahil-lazeena yuqaatiloonakum wa laa ta'tadooo; innal-laaha laa yuḥibbul-mu'tadeen.

وَقَاتِلُوا فِي سَبِيلِ اللهِ الَّذِينَ يُقَاتِلُونَكُمْ وَلَا تَعْتَدُوا إِنَّ اللهَ لَا يُحِبُّ الْمُعْتَدِينَ ۝

191. And slay them wherever you catch them, and turn them out from where they have turned you out; for tumult and oppression are worse than slaughter; but fight them not at the Sacred Mosque, unless they (first) fight you there; but if they fight you,

191. Waqtuloohum ḥaysu saqif-tumoohum wa akhrijoohum min ḥaysu akhrajookum; walfitnatu ashaddu minal-qatl; wa laa tuqaatiloohum 'indal-Masjidil-Ḥaraami ḥattaa yuqaatilookum feehi fa-in qaatalookum

وَاقْتُلُوهُمْ حَيْثُ ثَقِفْتُمُوهُمْ وَأَخْرِجُوهُمْ مِّنْ حَيْثُ أَخْرَجُوكُمْ وَالْفِتْنَةُ أَشَدُّ مِنَ الْقَتْلِ وَلَا تُقَاتِلُوهُمْ عِنْدَ الْمَسْجِدِ الْحَرَامِ حَتّٰى يُقَاتِلُوكُمْ فِيهِ فَإِنْ قَاتَلُوكُمْ

slay them. Such is the reward of those who suppress faith.

192. But if they cease, Allah is Oft-Forgiving, Most Merciful.

193. And fight them on until there is no more tumult or oppression, and there prevail justice and faith in Allah; but if they cease, let there be no hostility except to those who practise oppression.

194. The prohibited month for the prohibited month,- and so for all things prohibited,- there is the law of equality. If then any one transgresses the prohibition against you, transgress you like-wise against him. But fear Allah, and know that Allah is with those who restrain themselves.

195. And spend of your substance in the cause of Allah, and make not your own hands contribute to (your) destruction; but do good; for Allah loves those who do good.

196. And complete the Hajj or 'umra in the service of Allah. But if you are prevented (from completing it), send an offering for sacrifice, such as you may find, and do not shave your heads until the offering reaches the place of sacrifice. And if any of you is ill, or has an ailment in his scalp, (necessitating shaving), (he should) in compensation either fast, or feed the poor, or offer sacrifice; and when you are in peaceful conditions (again), if any one wishes to continue the 'Umra or the Hajj, he must make an offering, such as he can afford, but if he cannot afford it, he should fast three days during the Hajj and seven days on his return, making ten days in all. This is for those whose household is not in (the precincts of) the Sacred Mosque. And fear Allah,

faqtuloohum; kazaalika jazaaa'ul-kaafireen.

192. Fa-ini-ntahaw fa-innal-laaha Ghafoorur-Raheem.

193. Wa qaatiloohum hattaa laa takoona fitnatuñw-wa yakoonad-deenu lillaahi fa-inin-tahaw falaa 'udwaana illaa 'alaz-zaalimeen.

194. Ash-Shahrul-Haraamu bish-Shahril-Haraami wal-hurumaatu qisaas; famani'tadaa 'alaykum fa'tadoo 'alayhi bimisli ma'-tadaa 'alaykum; wattaqul-laaha wa'lamooo annal-laaha ma'al-muttaqeen.

195. Wa anfiqoo fee sabeelil-laahi wa laa tulqoo bi-aydeekum ilat-tahlukati wa ahsinoo; innal-laaha yuhibbul-muhsi-neen.

196. Wa atimmul-Hajja wal-'Umrata lillaah; fain uhsirtum famas-taysara minal-hadyi walaa tahliqoo ru'oosakum hattaa yablughal-hadyu mahil-lah; faman kaana minkum mareedan aw biheee azam-mir-raåsihee fafidyatum-min Siyaamin aw sadaqatin aw nusuk; fa-izaa amintum faman tamatta'a bil-'Umrati ilal-Hajji famastaysara minal-hady; famal-lam yajid fa-Siyaamu salaasati ayyaamin fil-Hajji wa sab'atin izaa raja'tum; tilka 'asharatun kaamilah; zaalika limal-lam yakun ahluhoo haadiril-Masjidil-Haraam; wattaqul-laaha

and know that Allah is strict in punishment.

197. For Hajj are the months well known. If any one undertakes that duty therein, let there be no obscenity, nor wickedness, nor wrangling in the Hajj. And whatever good you do, (be sure) Allah knows it. And take a provision (with you) for the journey, but the best of provisions is right conduct. So fear Me, O you that are wise.

198. It is no crime in you if you seek of the bounty of your Lord (during pilgrimage). Then when you pour down from (Mount) 'Arafat, celebrate the praises of Allah at the Sacred Monument, and celebrate His praises as He has directed you, even though, before this, you went astray.

199. Then pass on at a quick pace from the place whence it is usual for the multitude so to do, and ask for Allah's forgiveness. For Allah is Oft-Forgiving, Most Merciful.

200. So when you have accomplished your holy rites, celebrate the praises of Allah, as you used to celebrate the praises of your fathers,- yes, with far more heart and soul. There are men who say: "Our Lord! Give us (Your bounties) in this world!" but they will have no portion in the Hereafter.

201. And there are men who say: "Our Lord! Give us good in this world and good in the Hereafter, and save us from the torment of the Fire!"

202. To these will be allotted what they have earned; and Allah is quick in account.

203. Celebrate the praises of Allah during the Appointed Days.

wa'lamoo annal-laaha shadee-dul-'iqaab. **(Section 24)**

197. Al-Hajju ashhurum ma'-loomaat; faman farada feehinnal-Hajja falaa rafasa wa laa fusooqa wa laa jidaala fil-Hajj; wa maa taf'aloo min khayriñy-ya'lamhul-laah; wa tazawwadoo fa-inna khayraz-zaadit-taqwaa; wattaqooni yaaa ulil-albaab.

198. Laysa 'alaykum junaahun an tabtaghoo fadlam-mir-Rabbikum; fa-izaaa afadtum min 'Arafaatin fazkurul-laaha 'indal-Mash'aril-Haraami waz-kuroohu kamaa hadaakum wa in kuntum min qablihee laminad-daaalleen.

199. Summa afeedoo min haysu afaadan-naasu wastagh-firul-laah; innal-laaha Ghafoo-rur-Raheem.

200. Fa-izaa qadaytum manaa-sikakum fazkurul-laaha kazikrikum aabaaa'akum aw ashadda zikraa; faminannaasi mañy-yaqoolu Rabbanaaa aatinaa fiddunyaa wa maa lahoo fil-Aakhirati min khalaaq.

201. Wa minhum mañy-yaqoolu Rabbanaaa aatinaa fid-dunyaa hasanatañw-wa fil-Aakhirati hasanatañw-wa qinaa 'azaaban-Naar.

202. Ulaaa'ika lahum nasee-bum-mimmaa kasaboo; wal-laahu saree'ul-hisaab.

203. Wazkurul-laaha feee ayyaamim-ma'doodaat;

But if any one hastens to leave in two days, there is no blame on him, and if any one stays on, there is no blame on him, if his aim is to do right. Then fear Allah, and know that you will surely be gathered unto Him.

204. There is the type of man whose speech about this world's life may dazzle you, and he calls Allah to witness about what is in his heart; yet he is the most contentious of enemies.

205. When he turns his back, his aim everywhere is to spread mischief through the earth and destroy crops and cattle. But Allah loves not mischief.

206. When it is said to him, "Fear Allah", he is led by arrogance to (more) crime. Enough for him is Hell;- an evil bed indeed (to lie on)!

207. And there is the type of man who gives his life to earn the pleasure of Allah: and Allah is full of kindness to (His) devotees.

208. O you who believe! Enter into Islam whole-heartedly; and follow not the footsteps of the Satan; for he is to you an avowed enemy.

209. If you backslide after the clear (Signs) have come to you, then know that Allah is Exalted in Power, Wise.

210. Will they wait until Allah comes to them in canopies of clouds, with Angels (in His train) and the question is (thus) settled? but to Allah do all questions go back (for decision).

211. Ask the Children of Israel how many clear (Signs) We have sent them. But if any one,

faman ta'ajjala fee yawmayni falaaa isma 'alayhi wa man ta-akhkhara falaaa isma 'alayh; limanit-taqaa; wattaqul-laaha wa'lamoo annakum ilayhi tuḥsharoon.

204. Wa minan-naasi mañy-yu'jibuka qawluhoo fil ḥayaatid-dunyaa wa yushhidul-laaha 'alaa maa fee qalbihee wa huwa aladdulkhiṣaam.

205. Wa izaa tawallaa sa'aa fil-arḍi liyufsida feehaa wa yuhlikal-ḥarsa wannasl; wallaahu laa yuḥibbul-fasaad.

206. Wa izaa qeela lahuttaqil-laaha akhazathul-izzatu bil-ism; faḥasbuhoo Jahannam; wa labi'sal-mihaad.

207. Wa minan-naasi mañy-yashree nafsahub-tighaaa'a marḍaatil-laah; wallaahu ra'oofum-bil'ibaad.

208. Yaaa ayyuhal-lazeena aamanud-khuloo fis-silmi kaaaffatañw-wa laa tattabi'oo khuṭuwaatish-Shayṭaan; innahoo lakum 'aduwwum-mubeen.

209. Fa-in zalaltum mimba'di maa jaaa'atkumul-bayyinaatu fa'lamoo annallaaha 'Azeezun-Ḥakeem.

210. Hal yanẓuroona illaaa añy-yaåtiyahumul-laahu fee zulalim-minal-ghamaami walmalaaa'ikatu wa quḍiyal-amr; wa ilal-laahi turja'ul-umoor. **(Section 25)**

211. Sal Baneee Israaa'eela kam aataynaahum min Aayatim-bayyinah; wa mañy-yubaddil

after Allah's favour has come to him, substitutes (something else), Allah is strict in punishment.

212. The life of this world is alluring to those who reject faith, and they scoff at those who believe. But the righteous will be above them on the Day of Resurrection; for Allah bestows His abundance without measure on whom He will.

213. Mankind was one single nation, and Allah sent Messengers with glad tidings and warnings; and with them He sent the Book in truth, to judge between people in matters wherein they differed; but the People of the Book, after the clear signs came to them, did not differ among themselves, except through selfish contumacy. Allah by His Grace Guided the believers to the Truth, concerning that wherein they differed. For Allah guided whom He will to a path that is straight.

214. Or do you think that you shall enter the Garden (of Bliss) without such (trials) as came to those who passed away before you? They encountered suffering and adversity, and were so shaken in spirit that even the Apostle and those of faith who were with him cried: "When (will come) the help of Allah?" Ah! Verily, the help of Allah is (always) near!

215. They ask you what they should spend (in charity). Say: Whatever you spend that is good, is for parents and kindred and orphans and those in want and for wayfarers. And whatever you do that is

ni'matal-laahi mim ba'di maa jaaa'athu fa-innallaaha shadeedul-'iqaab.

212. Zuyyina lillazeena kafa-rul-ḥayaatud-dunyaa wa yaskharoona minal-lazeena aamanoo; wallazeenat-taqaw fawqahum YawmalQiyaamah; wallaahu yarzuqu mañy-yashaaa'u bighayri ḥisaab.

213. Kaanan-naasu ummatañw-waaḥidatan faba'aṣal-laahun-Nabiyyeena mubashshireena wa munzireena wa anzala ma'ahumul-Kitaaba bilḥaqqi liyaḥkuma baynan-naasi feemakh-talafoo feeh; wa makh-talafa feehi 'illallazeena ootoohu mim-ba'di maa jaaa'athumul-bayyinaatu baghyam baynahum fahadal-laahul-lazeena aamanoo limakh-talafoo feehi minal-ḥaqqi bi-iznih; wallaahu yahdee mañy-yashaaa'u ilaa Şiraaṭim-Mustaqeem.

214. Am ḥasibtum an tad-khulul-Jannata wa lammaa yaåtikum maṣalul-lazeena khalaw min qablikum massathumul-baåsaaa'u waḍḍarraaa'u wa zulziloo ḥattaa yaqoolar-Rasoolu wallazeena aamanoo ma'ahoo mataa naṣrul-laah; alaaa inna naṣral-laahiqareeb.

215. Yas'aloonaka maazaa yunfiqoona qul maaa anfaqtum min khayrin falilwaalidayni wal-aqrabeena walyataamaa walmasaakeeni wabnis-sabeel; wa maa taf'aloo min

good, - Allah knows it well.

216. Fighting is prescribed for you, and you dislike it. But it is possible that you dislike a thing which is good for you, and that you love a thing which is bad for you. But Allah knows, and you know not.

217. They ask you concerning fighting in the Prohibited Month. Say: "Fighting therein is a grave (offence); but graver is still in the sight of Allah to prevent access to the path of Allah, to deny Him, to prevent access to the Sacred Mosque, and drive out its members." Tumult and oppression are worse than slaughter. Nor will they cease fighting you until they turn you back from your faith if they can. And if any of you turn back from their faith and die in unbelief, their works will bear no fruit in this life and in the Hereafter; they will be companions of the Fire and will abide therein.

218. Those who believed and those who suffered exile and fought (and strove and struggled) in the path of Allah,- they have the hope of the Mercy of Allah: and Allah is Oft-Forgiving, Most Merciful.

219. They ask you concerning wine and gambling. Say: "In them is great sin, and some profit, for men; but the sin is greater than the profit." They ask you how much they are to spend; Say: "What is beyond your needs." Thus does Allah make Clear to you

khayrin fa-innal-laaha bihee 'Aleem

216. Kutiba 'alaykumulqitaalu wa huwa kurhullakum wa 'asaaa an takrahoo shay'añw-wa huwa khayrullakum wa 'asaaa an tuḥibboo shay'añw-wa huwa sharrullakum; wallaahu ya'lamu wa-antum laa ta'lamoon.

(Section 26)

217. Yas'aloonaka 'anish-Shahril-Ḥaraami qitaalin feehi qul qitaalun feehi kabeeruñw-wa ṣaddun 'an sabeelil-laahi wa kufrum-bihee wal-Masjidil-Ḥaraami wa ikhraaju ahlihee minhu akbaru 'indal-laah; walfitnatu akbaru minal-qatl; wa laa yazaaloona yuqaati-loonakum ḥattaa yaruddookum 'an deenikum inis-taṭaa'oo; wa mañy-yartadid minkum 'an deenihee fayamut wahuwa kaafirun fa-ulaaa'ika ḥabiṭat a'maaluhum fid-dunyaa wal-Aakhirati wa ulaaa'ika Aṣḥaabun-Naari hum feehaa khaalidoon.

218. Innal-lazeena aamanoo wallazeena haajaroo wa jaahadoo fee sabeelil-laahi ulaaa'ika yarjoona raḥmatal-laah; wallaahu Ghafoorur-Raḥeem.

219. Yas'aloonaka 'anilkhamri walmaysiri qul feehimaaa ismun kabeeruñw-wa manaafi'u linnaasi wa ismuhumaaa akbaru min naf'ihimaa; wa yas'aloonaka maazaa yunfiqoona qulil-'afw; kazaalika yubayyinul-laahu lakumul-

His Signs: in order that you may consider-

220. (Their bearings) on this life and the Hereafter. They ask you concerning orphans. Say: "The best thing to do is what is for their good; if you mix their affairs with yours, they are your brethren; but Allah knows the man who means mischief from the man who means good. And if Allah had wished, He could have put you into difficulties: He is indeed Exalted in Power, Wise."

221. Do not marry unbelieving women (idolators), until they believe: a slave woman who believes is better than an unbelieving woman, even though she allures you. Nor marry (your girls) to unbelievers until they believe: a man slave who believes is better than an unbeliever, even though he allures you. Unbelievers do (but) beckon you to the Fire. But Allah beckons by His Grace to the Garden (of Bliss) and forgiveness, and makes His Signs clear to mankind so that they may celebrate His praise.

222. They ask you concerning women's courses. Say: They are a hurt and a pollution: so keep away from women in their courses, and do not approach them until they are clean. But when they have purified themselves, you may approach them in any manner, time, or place ordained for you by Allah. For Allah loves those who turn to Him constantly and He loves those who keep themselves pure and clean.

223. Your wives are as a tilth unto you; so approach your tilth when or how you will; but do some good act for your souls beforehand; and fear Allah. And know that you are to meet Him (in the Hereafter), and give (these) good tidings to those who believe.

224. And make not Allah's (name) an excuse in your oaths

aayaati la'allakum tatafak-karoon.

220. Fid-dunyaa wal-Aakhirah; wa yas'aloonaka 'anil-yataamaa qul işlaaḥullahum khayr, wa in tukhaaliţoohum fa-ikhwaanu-kum; wallaahu ya'lamul-mufsida minalmuşliḥ; wa law shaaa'al-laahu la-a'natakum; innal-laaha 'Azeezun Ḥakeem.

221. Wa laa tankiḥul-mushri-kaati ḥattaa yu'minn; wa la-amatum mu'minatun khayrum-mim-mushrikatiñw-wa law a'jabatkum; wa laa tunkiḥul-mushrikeena ḥattaa yu'minoo; wa la'abdummu'minun khay-rum-mimmushrikiñw-wa law 'ajabakum; ulaaa'ika yad'oona ilan-Naari wallaahu yad'ooo ilal-Jannati walmaghfirati bi-iznihee wa yubayyinu Aayaa-tihee linnaasi la'allahum yataẕakkaroon.   **(Section 27)**

222. Wa yas'aloonaka 'anil maheeḍi qul huwa aẕan fa'ta-zilun-nisaaa'a fil-maheeḍi wa laa taqraboo-hunna ḥattaa yaṭhurna fa-iẕaa taṭahharna faå-toohunna min ḥaysu amara-kumul-laah; innallaaha yuḥibbut-Tawwaabeena wa yuḥibbul-mutaṭahhireen.

223. Nisaaa'ukum ḥarsullakum faåtoo ḥarsakum annaa shi'tum wa qaddimoo li-anfusikum; wattaqul-laaha wa'lamooo annakum mulaaqooh;wa bash-shirilmu'mineen.

224. Wa laa taj'alul-laaha 'urdatal-li-aymaanikum

against doing good, or acting rightly, or making peace between persons; for Allah is One Who hears and knows all things.

225. Allah will not call you to account for thoughtlessness in your oaths, but for the intention in your hearts; and He is Oft-Forgiving, Most Forbearing.

226. For those who take an oath for abstention from their wives, a waiting for four months is ordained; if then they return, Allah is Oft-Forgiving, Most Merciful.

227. But if their intention is firm for divorce, Allah hears and knows all things.

228. Divorced women shall wait concerning themselves for three monthly periods. Nor is it lawful for them to hide what Allah has created in their wombs, if they have faith in Allah and the Last Day. And their husbands have the better right to take them back in that period, if they wish for reconciliation. And women shall have rights similar to the rights against them, according to what is equitable; but men have a degree (of advantage) over them. And Allah is Exalted in Power, Wise.

229. A divorce is only permissible twice: after that, the parties should either hold together on equitable terms, or separate with kindness. It is not lawful for you, (men), to take back any of your gifts (from your wives), except when both parties fear that they would be unable to keep the limits ordained by Allah. If you (judges) do indeed fear that they would be unable to keep the limits ordained by Allah, there is no blame on either of them if she give something for her freedom. These are the limits ordained by Allah; so do not

an tabarroo wa tattaqoo wa tuslihoo baynan-naas; wallaahu Samee'un-'Aleem.

225. Laa yu'aakhi-zukumul-laahu billaghwi feee aymaa-nikum wa laakiny-yu'aakhi-zukum bimaa kasabat quloo-bukum; wallaahu Ghafoorun Haleem.

226. Lillazeena yu'loona min nisaaa'ihim tarabbusu arba'ati ashhurin fain faaa'oo fa-innal-laaha Ghafoorur-Raheem.

227. Wa in 'azamut-talaaqa fa-innal-laaha Samee'un 'Aleem

228. Walmutallaqaatu yatarab-basna bi-anfusihinna salaasata qurooo'; wa laa yahillu lahunna añy-yaktumna maa khalaqal-laahu feee arhaamihinna in kunna yu'minna billaahi wal-Yawmil-Aakhir; wa bu'oola-tuhunna ahaqqu biraddihinna fee zaalika in araadooo islaahaa; wa lahunna mislul-lazee 'alayhinna bilma'roof; wa lirrijaali 'alayhinna darajah; wallaahu 'Azeezun Hakeem.
(Section 28)

229. Attalaaqu marrataani fa-imsaakum bima'roofin aw tasreehum bi-ihsaan; wa laa yahillu lakum an taakhuzoo mimmaaa aataytumoohunna shay'an illaaa añy-yakhaafaaa allaa yuqeemaa hudoodallaahi fa-in khiftum allaa yuqeemaa hudoodal-laahi falaa Junaaha 'Alaihimaa feemaf-tadat bihee tilka Hudoodul-laahi falaa

transgress them, if any do transgress the limits ordained by Allah, such persons wrong (themselves as well as others).

230. So if a husband divorces his wife (irrevocably), he cannot, after that, re-marry her until after she has married another husband and he has divorced her. In that case there is no blame on either of them if they re-unite, provided they feel that they can keep the limits ordained by Allah. Such are the limits ordained by Allah, which He makes plain to those who understand.

231. When you divorce women, and they fulfil the term of their ('Iddat), either take them back on equitable terms or set them free on equitable terms; but do not take them back to injure them, (or) to take undue advantage; if any one does that; he wrongs his own soul. Do not treat Allah's Signs as a jest, but solemnly rehearse Allah's favours on you, and the fact that He sent down to you the Book and Wisdom, for your instruction. And fear Allah, and know that Allah is well acquainted with all things.

232. When you divorce women, and they fulfil the term of their ('Iddat), do not prevent them from marrying their (former) husbands, if they mutually agree on equitable terms. This instruction is for all among you, who believe in Allah and the Last Day. That is (the course making for) most virtue and purity among you and Allah knows, and you know not.

233. The mothers shall give suck to their offspring

ta'adoohaa; wa many-yata'adda ḥudoodal-laahi fa-ulaaa'ika humuẓẓaa-limoon.

230. Fa-in ṭallaqahaa falaa taḥillu lahoo mim ba'du ḥattaa tankiḥa zawjan ghayrah; fa-in ṭallaqahaa falaa junaaḥa 'alayhimaaa any-yataraaja'aaa in ẓannaaa any-yuqeemaa ḥudoodal-laah; wa tilka ḥudoodul-laahi yubayyinuhaa liqawminy-ya'lamoon.

231. Wa izaa ṭallaqtumun-nisaaa'a fabalaghna ajala-hunna fa-amsikoohunna bima'roofin law sarriḥoo-hunna bima'roof; wa laa tumsikoo-hunna ḍiraa-rallita'tadoo; wa many-yaf'al zaalika faqad ẓalama nafsah; wa laa tattakhizooo Aayaatillaahi huzuwaa; waẕkuroo ni'matal-laahi 'alaykum wa maaa anzala 'alaykum minal-Kitaabi wal-Ḥikmati ya'iẓukum bih; wattaqul-laaha wa'lamooo annal-laaha bikulli shay'i 'Aleem. **(Section 29)**

232. Wa izaa ṭallaqtumun-nisaaa'a fabalaghna ajalahunna falaa ta'ḍuloo-hunna any-yankiḥna azwaaja-hunna izaa taraaḍaw baynahum bilma'-roof; zaalika yoo'aẓu bihee man kaana minkum yu'minu billaahi walYawmil-Aakhir; zaalikum azkaa lakum wa aṭhar; wallaahu ya'lamu wa antum laa ta'lamoon.

233. Walwaalidaatu yurḍi'na awlaada hunna

تَعْتَدُوهَا ۚ وَمَن يَتَعَدَّ حُدُودَ ٱللَّهِ فَأُولَٰٓئِكَ هُمُ ٱلظَّٰلِمُونَ ۝

فَإِن طَلَّقَهَا فَلَا تَحِلُّ لَهُۥ مِنۢ بَعْدُ حَتَّىٰ تَنكِحَ زَوْجًا غَيْرَهُۥ ۗ فَإِن طَلَّقَهَا فَلَا جُنَاحَ عَلَيْهِمَآ أَن يَتَرَاجَعَآ إِن ظَنَّآ أَن يُقِيمَا حُدُودَ ٱللَّهِ ۗ وَتِلْكَ حُدُودُ ٱللَّهِ يُبَيِّنُهَا لِقَوْمٍ يَعْلَمُونَ ۝

وَإِذَا طَلَّقْتُمُ ٱلنِّسَآءَ فَبَلَغْنَ أَجَلَهُنَّ فَأَمْسِكُوهُنَّ بِمَعْرُوفٍ أَوْ سَرِّحُوهُنَّ بِمَعْرُوفٍ ۚ وَلَا تُمْسِكُوهُنَّ ضِرَارًا لِّتَعْتَدُوا۟ ۚ وَمَن يَفْعَلْ ذَٰلِكَ فَقَدْ ظَلَمَ نَفْسَهُۥ ۚ وَلَا تَتَّخِذُوٓا۟ ءَايَٰتِ ٱللَّهِ هُزُوًا ۚ وَٱذْكُرُوا۟ نِعْمَتَ ٱللَّهِ عَلَيْكُمْ وَمَآ أَنزَلَ عَلَيْكُم مِّنَ ٱلْكِتَٰبِ وَٱلْحِكْمَةِ يَعِظُكُم بِهِۦ ۚ وَٱتَّقُوا۟ ٱللَّهَ وَٱعْلَمُوٓا۟ أَنَّ ٱللَّهَ بِكُلِّ شَىْءٍ عَلِيمٌ ۝

وَإِذَا طَلَّقْتُمُ ٱلنِّسَآءَ فَبَلَغْنَ أَجَلَهُنَّ فَلَا تَعْضُلُوهُنَّ أَن يَنكِحْنَ أَزْوَٰجَهُنَّ إِذَا تَرَٰضَوْا۟ بَيْنَهُم بِٱلْمَعْرُوفِ ۗ ذَٰلِكَ يُوعَظُ بِهِۦ مَن كَانَ مِنكُمْ يُؤْمِنُ بِٱللَّهِ وَٱلْيَوْمِ ٱلْءَاخِرِ ۗ ذَٰلِكُمْ أَزْكَىٰ لَكُمْ وَأَطْهَرُ ۗ وَٱللَّهُ يَعْلَمُ وَأَنتُمْ لَا تَعْلَمُونَ ۝

وَٱلْوَٰلِدَٰتُ يُرْضِعْنَ أَوْلَٰدَهُنَّ

for two whole years, if the father desires to complete the term. But he shall bear the cost of their food and clothing on equitable terms. No soul shall have a burden laid on it greater than it can bear. No mother shall be treated unfairly on account of her child. Nor father on account of his child, an heir shall be chargeable in the same way. If they both decide on weaning, by mutual consent, and after due consultation, there is no blame on them. If you decide on a foster-mother for your offspring, there is no blame on you, provided you pay (the mother) what you offered, on equitable terms. But fear Allah and know that Allah sees well what you do.

234. If any of you die and leave widows behind, they shall wait concerning themselves four months and ten days: when they have fulfilled their term, there is no blame on you if they dispose of themselves in a just and reasonable manner. And Allah is well acquainted with what you do.

235. There is no blame on you if you make an offer of betrothal or hold it in your hearts. Allah knows that you cherish them in your hearts: but do not make a secret contract with them except in terms honourable, nor resolve on the tie of marriage till the term prescribed is fulfilled. And know that Allah Knows what is

ḥawlayni kaamilayni liman araada añy-yutimmar-raḍaa'ah; wa 'alalmawloodi lahoo rizquhunna wa kiswatuhunna bilma'roof; laa tukallafu nafsun illaa wus'ahaa; laa tuḍaaarra waalidatum-biwaladihaa wa laa mawloodul-lahoo biwa-ladih;Wa 'alal-waariṣi miṣlu zaalik; fa-in araadaa Fiṣaalan 'an taraaḍim-minhumaa wa tashaawurin falaa junaaḥa 'alayhimaa; wa in arattum an tastarḍi'ooo awlaadakum falaa junaaḥa 'alaykum iẓaa sallamtum maaa aataytum bilma'roof; wattaqul-laaha wa'lamooo annal-laaha bimaa ta'maloona Baṣeer.

234. Wallaẓeena yutawaffawna minkum wa yaẓaroona azwaajañy-yatarabbaṣna bi-anfusihinna arba'ata ashhuriñw-wa 'ashran fa-iẓaa balaghna ajalahunna falaa junaaḥa 'alaykum feemaa fa'alna feee anfusihinna bilma'roof; wallaahu bimaa ta'maloona Khabeer.

235. Wa laa junaaḥa 'alaykum feemaa 'arraḍtum bihee min khiṭbatin-nisaaa'i aw aknantum feee anfusikum; 'alimal-laahu annakum satazkuroonahunna wa laakil-laa tuwaa'idoohunna sirran illaaa an taqooloo qawlamma'roofaa; wa laa ta'zimoo 'uqdatan-nikaaḥi ḥattaa yablughal-kitaabu ajalah; wa'lamooo annal-laaha ya'lamu maa

in your hearts, and take heed of Him; and know that Allah is Oft-Forgiving, Most Forbearing.

236. There is no blame on you if you divorce women before consummation or the fixation of their dower; but bestow on them (a suitable gift), the wealthy according to his means, and the poor according to his means;- a gift of a reasonable amount is due from those who wish to do the right thing.

237. And if you divorce them before consummation, but after the fixation of a dower for them, then the half of the dower (is due to them), unless they remit it or (the man's half) is remitted by him in whose hands is the marriage tie; and the remission (of the man's half) is the nearest to righteousness. And do not forget liberality between yourselves. For Allah sees well all that you do.

238. Guard strictly your (habit of) prayers, especially the Middle Prayer; and stand before Allah in a devout (frame of mind).

239. If you fear (an enemy), pray on foot, or riding, (as may be most convenient), but when you are in security, celebrate Allah's praises in the manner He has taught you, which you knew not (before).

240. Those of you who die and leave widows should bequeath for their widows a year's maintenance and residence; but if they leave (the residence), there is no blame on you for what they do with themselves, provided it is

feee anfusikum faḥzarooh; wa'lamooo annallaaha Ghafoorun Ḥaleem **(Section 30)**

236. Laa junaaḥa 'alaykum in ṭallaqtumun-nisaaa'a maa lam tamassoohunna aw tafriḍoo lahunna fareeḍah; wa matti'oohunna 'alal-moosi'i qadaruhoo wa 'alal-muqtiri qadaruhoo mattaa 'am-bilma'roofi ḥaqqan 'alalmuḥsineen.

237. Wa in tallaqtumoohunna min qabli an tamassoohunna wa qad faraḍtum lahunna fareeḍatan faniṣfu maa faraḍtum illaaa añy-ya'foona aw ya'fuwallazee biyadihee 'uqdatunnikaaḥ; wa an ta'fooo aqrabu liittaqwaa; wa laa tansawulfaḍla baynakum; innal-laaha bimaa ta'maloona Baṣeer.

238. Ḥaafiẓoo 'alaṣ-Ṣalawaati waṣ-Ṣalaatil-Wusṭaa wa qoomoo lillaahi qaaniteen.

239. Fa-in khiftum farijaalan aw rukbaanan fa-izaaa amintum fazkurul-laaha kamaa 'allamakum maa lam takoonoo ta'lamoon.

240. Wallazeena yutawaffawna minkum wa yazaroona azwaajañw-waṣiyyatal-li-azwaajihim mataa'an ilal-ḥawli ghayra ikhraaj; fa-in kharajna falaa junaaḥa 'alaykum fee maa fa'alna feee anfusihinna mim

reasonable. And Allah is Exalted in Power, Wise.

241. For divorced women Maintenance (should be provided) on a reasonable (scale). This is a duty on the righteous.

242. Thus Allah Makes clear His Signs to you: in order that you may understand.

243. Did you not Turn by vision to those who abandoned their homes, though they were thousands (in number), for fear of death? Allah said to them: "Die"! Then He restored them to life. For Allah is full of bounty to mankind, but Most of them are ungrateful.

244. Then fight in the cause of Allah, and know that Allah hears and knows all things.

245. Who is he that will loan to Allah a beautiful loan, which Allah will double unto his credit and multiply many times? It is Allah that gives (you) Want or Plenty, and to Him shall be your return.

246. Have you not turned you vision to the Chiefs of the Children of Israel after (the time of) Moses? They said to a prophet (that was) among them: "Appoint for us a king, that we may fight in the cause of Allah." He said: "Is it not possible, if you were commanded to fight, that you will not fight?" They said: "How could we refuse to fight in the cause of Allah, seeing that we were turned out of our homes and our families?" But when they were commanded to fight, they turned back, except a small band among them. But Allah has full knowledge of those who do wrong.

ma'roof; wallaahu 'Azeezun Hakeem.

241. Wa lilmuṭallaqaati mataa-'um-bilma'roofi ḥaqqan 'alal-muttaqeen.

242. Kazaalika yubayyinul-laahu lakum Aayaatihee la'allakum ta'qiloon. **(Section 31)**

243. Alam tara ilal-lazeena kharajoo min diyaarihim wa hum uloofun ḥazaral-mawti faqaala lahumul-laahu mootoo ṣumma aḥyaahum; innal-laaha lazoo faḍlin 'alannaasi wa laakinna aksarannaasi laa yashkuroon

244. Wa qaatiloo fee sabeelil-laahi wa'lamooo annal-laaha Samee'un 'Aleem.

245. Man zal-lazee yuqriḍul-laaha qarḍan ḥasanan fayuḍaa-'ifahoo lahooo aḍ'aafan kaseerah; wallaahu yaqbiḍu wa yabsuṭ(u) wa ilayhi turja'oon.

246. Alam tara ilal-malai mim-Baneee Israaa'eela mim ba'di Moosaaa iz qaaloo li-Nabiyyil-lahumub-'as lanaa malikan nuqaatil fee sabeelillaahi qaala hal 'asaytum in kutiba 'alaykumul-qitaalu allaa tuqaatiloo qaaloo wa maa lanaaa allaa nuqaatila fee sabeelil-laahi wa qad ukhrijnaa min diyaarinaa wa abnaaa'inaa falammaa kutiba 'alayhimul-qitaalu tawallaw illaa qaleelam-minhum; wallaahu 'aleemum-biẓẓaalimeen.

247. Their Prophet said to them: "Allah has appointed Talut as king over you." They said: "How can he exercise authority over us when we are better fitted than he to exercise authority, and he is not even gifted, with wealth in abundance?" He said: "Allah has chosen him above you, and has gifted him abundantly with knowledge and bodily prowess: Allah grants His authority to whom He pleases. Allah cares for all, and He knows all things."

248. And (further) their Prophet said to them: "A Sign of his authority is that there shall come to you the Ark of the Covenant, with (an assurance) therein of security from your Lord, and the relics left by the family of Moses and the family of Aaron, carried by Angels. In this is a symbol for you if you indeed have faith."

249. When Talut set forth with the armies, he said: "Allah will test you at the stream: if any drinks of its water, he goes not with my army: only those who taste not of it go with me: a mere sip out of the hand is excused." But they all drank of it, except a few. When they crossed the river,- He and the faithful ones with him,- they said: "This day We cannot cope with Goliath and his forces." But those who were convinced that they must meet Allah, said: "How oft, by Allah's will, has a small force vanquished a big one? Allah is with those who steadfastly persevere."

247. Wa qaala lahum Nabiyyuhum innal-laaha qad ba'aṣa lakum Ṭaaloota malikaa; qaalooo annaa yakoonu lahul-mulku 'alaynaa wa naḥnu aḥaqqu bilmulki minhu wa lam yu'ta sa'atamminal-maal; qaala innallaahaṣ-ṭafaahu 'alaykum wa zaadahoo basṭatan fil-'ilmi waljismi wallaahu yu'tee mulkahoo mañy-yashaaa'; wallaahu Waasi'un 'Aleem.

248. Wa qaala lahum Nabiyyuhum inna Aayata mulkiheee añy-yaåtiyakumut-Taabootu feehi sakeenatummir-Rabbikum wa baqiyyatummimmaa taraka Aalu Moosaa wa Aalu Haaroona taḥmiluhulmalaaa'ikah; inna fee zaalika la-Aayatal-lakum in kuntum mu'mineen. **(Section 32)**

249. Falammaa faṣala Ṭaalootu biljunoodi qaala innal-laaha mubtaleekum binaharin faman shariba minhu falaysa minnee wa mallam yaṭ'amhu fa-innahoo minneee illaa manightarafa ghurfatam biyadih; fashariboo minhu illaa qaleelamminhum; falammaa jaawazahoo huwa wallazeena aamanoo ma'ahoo qaaloo laa ṭaaqata lanal-yawma bi-Jaaloota wa junoodih; qaalallazeena yaẓunnoona annahum mulaaqul-laahi kam min fi'atin qaleelatin ghalabat fi'atan kaseeratam bi-iznil-laah; wallaahu ma'aṣ-ṣaabireen.

وَقَالَ لَهُمْ نَبِيُّهُمْ إِنَّ اللّٰهَ قَدْ بَعَثَ لَكُمْ طَالُوْتَ مَلِكًا ۚ قَالُوْۤا اَنّٰى يَكُوْنُ لَهُ الْمُلْكُ عَلَيْنَا وَنَحْنُ اَحَقُّ بِالْمُلْكِ مِنْهُ وَلَمْ يُؤْتَ سَعَةً مِّنَ الْمَالِ ؕ قَالَ اِنَّ اللّٰهَ اصْطَفٰهُ عَلَيْكُمْ وَزَادَهٗ بَسْطَةً فِى الْعِلْمِ وَالْجِسْمِ ؕ وَاللّٰهُ يُؤْتِىْ مُلْكَهٗ مَنْ يَّشَآءُ ؕ وَاللّٰهُ وَاسِعٌ عَلِيْمٌ ۝

وَقَالَ لَهُمْ نَبِيُّهُمْ اِنَّ اٰيَةَ مُلْكِهٖۤ اَنْ يَّاْتِيَكُمُ التَّابُوْتُ فِيْهِ سَكِيْنَةٌ مِّنْ رَّبِّكُمْ وَبَقِيَّةٌ مِّمَّا تَرَكَ اٰلُ مُوْسٰى وَاٰلُ هٰرُوْنَ تَحْمِلُهُ الْمَلٰٓئِكَةُ ؕ اِنَّ فِىْ ذٰلِكَ لَاٰيَةً لَّكُمْ اِنْ كُنْتُمْ مُّؤْمِنِيْنَ ۝

فَلَمَّا فَصَلَ طَالُوْتُ بِالْجُنُوْدِ ۙ قَالَ اِنَّ اللّٰهَ مُبْتَلِيْكُمْ بِنَهَرٍ ۚ فَمَنْ شَرِبَ مِنْهُ فَلَيْسَ مِنِّىْ ۚ وَمَنْ لَّمْ يَطْعَمْهُ فَاِنَّهٗ مِنِّىْۤ اِلَّا مَنِ اغْتَرَفَ غُرْفَةً بِيَدِهٖ ۚ فَشَرِبُوْا مِنْهُ اِلَّا قَلِيْلًا مِّنْهُمْ ؕ فَلَمَّا جَاوَزَهٗ هُوَ وَالَّذِيْنَ اٰمَنُوْا مَعَهٗ ۙ قَالُوْا لَا طَاقَةَ لَنَا الْيَوْمَ بِجَالُوْتَ وَجُنُوْدِهٖ ؕ قَالَ الَّذِيْنَ يَظُنُّوْنَ اَنَّهُمْ مُّلٰقُوا اللّٰهِ ۙ كَمْ مِّنْ فِئَةٍ قَلِيْلَةٍ غَلَبَتْ فِئَةً كَثِيْرَةً بِاِذْنِ اللّٰهِ ؕ وَاللّٰهُ مَعَ الصّٰبِرِيْنَ ۝

250. When they advanced to meet Goliath and his forces, they prayed: "Our Lord! Pour out constancy on us and make our steps firm: Help us against those that reject faith."

250. Wa lammaa barazoo liJaaloota wa junoodihee qaaloo Rabbanaaa afrigh 'alaynaa ṣabrañw-wa ṣabbit aqdaamanaa wanṣurnaa 'alal-qawmil-kaafireen.

251. By Allah's will they routed them; and David slew Goliath; and Allah gave him power and wisdom and taught him whatever (else) He willed. And had not Allah checked one set of people by means of another, the earth would indeed be full of mischief: But Allah is full of bounty to all the worlds.

251. Fahazamoohum bi-iznillaahi wa qatala Daawoodu Jaaloota wa aataahul-laahulmulka wal-Ḥikmata wa 'allamahoo mimmaa yashaaa'; wa law laa daf'ullaahin-naasa ba'ḍahum biba'ḍil-lafasadatil-arḍu wa laakinnal-laaha zoo faḍlin 'alal-'aalameen.

252. These are the Signs of Allah: we rehearse them to you in truth: verily you are one of the apostles.

252. Tilka Aayaatul-laahi natloohaa 'alayka bilḥaqq; wa innaka laminal-mursaleen.

253. Those Messengers We endowed with gifts, some above others: to one of them Allah spoke; others He raised to degrees (of honour); to Jesus the son of Mary We gave Clear (Signs), and strengthened him with the holy spirit. If Allah had so willed, succeeding gene- rations would not have fought among each other, after Clear (Signs) had come to them, but they (chose) to wrangle, some believing and others rejecting. If Allah had so willed, they would not have fought each other; but Allah fulfills His plan.

253. Tilkar-Rusulu faḍḍalnaa ba'ḍahum 'alaa ba'ḍ; minhum man kallamal-laahu wa rafa'a ba'ḍahum darajaat; wa aataynaa 'Eesab-na Maryamal-bayyinaati wa ayyadnaahu bi-Rooḥil-Qudus; wa law shaaa'al-laahu maqtatalal-lazeena mim-ba'dihim mim ba'di maa jaaa'athumul-bayyinaatu wa laakinikh-talafoo faminhum man aamana wa minhum man kafar; wa law shaaa'al-laahu maq-tataloo wa laakinnallaaha yaf'alu maa yureed.   (Section 33)

254. O you who believe! Spend out of (the bounties) We have provided for you, before the Day comes when no bargaining (will avail), nor friendship nor intercession. Those who reject Faith- they are the wrong-doers.

254. Yaaa ayyuhal-lazeena aamanooo anfiqoo mimmaa razaqnaakum min qabli añy-yaå-tiya Yawmul-laa bay'un feehi wa laa khullatuñw-wa laa shafaa'ah; walkaafiroona humuz-zaalimoon.

وَلَمَّا بَرَزُوْا لِجَالُوْتَ وَجُنُوْدِهٖ

قَالُوْا رَبَّنَاۤ اَفْرِغْ عَلَيْنَا صَبْرًا وَّثَبِّتْ

اَقْدَامَنَا وَانْصُرْنَا عَلَى الْقَوْمِ

الْكٰفِرِيْنَ ۟

فَهَزَمُوْهُمْ بِاِذْنِ اللّٰهِ ۟ وَقَتَلَ

دَاوُدُ جَالُوْتَ وَاٰتٰهُ اللّٰهُ الْمُلْكَ

وَالْحِكْمَةَ وَعَلَّمَهٗ مِمَّا يَشَآءُ ؕ

وَلَوْلَا دَفْعُ اللّٰهِ النَّاسَ بَعْضَهُمْ

بِبَعْضٍ لَّفَسَدَتِ الْاَرْضُ وَلٰكِنَّ

اللّٰهَ ذُوْ فَضْلٍ عَلَى الْعٰلَمِيْنَ ۟

تِلْكَ اٰيٰتُ اللّٰهِ نَتْلُوْهَا عَلَيْكَ

بِالْحَقِّ ؕ وَاِنَّكَ لَمِنَ الْمُرْسَلِيْنَ ۟

تِلْكَ الرُّسُلُ فَضَّلْنَا بَعْضَهُمْ

عَلٰى بَعْضٍ ۘ مِنْهُمْ مَّنْ كَلَّمَ اللّٰهُ

وَرَفَعَ بَعْضَهُمْ دَرَجٰتٍ ؕ وَاٰتَيْنَا

عِيْسَى ابْنَ مَرْيَمَ الْبَيِّنٰتِ وَاَيَّدْنٰهُ

بِرُوْحِ الْقُدُسِ ؕ وَلَوْ شَآءَ اللّٰهُ مَا

اقْتَتَلَ الَّذِيْنَ مِنْ بَعْدِهِمْ مِّنْ

بَعْدِ مَا جَآءَتْهُمُ الْبَيِّنٰتُ وَلٰكِنِ

اخْتَلَفُوْا فَمِنْهُمْ مَّنْ اٰمَنَ وَمِنْهُمْ

مَّنْ كَفَرَ ؕ وَلَوْ شَآءَ اللّٰهُ مَا اقْتَتَلُوْا

وَلٰكِنَّ اللّٰهَ يَفْعَلُ مَا يُرِيْدُ ۟

يٰۤاَيُّهَا الَّذِيْنَ اٰمَنُوْۤا اَنْفِقُوْا مِمَّا

رَزَقْنٰكُمْ مِّنْ قَبْلِ اَنْ يَّاْتِيَ يَوْمٌ

لَّا بَيْعٌ فِيْهِ وَلَا خُلَّةٌ وَّلَا شَفَاعَةٌ ؕ

وَالْكٰفِرُوْنَ هُمُ الظّٰلِمُوْنَ ۟

255. Allah! There is no god but He,-the Living, the Self-subsisting, Eternal. No slumber can seize Him nor sleep. His are all things in the heavens and on earth. Who is there can intercede in His presence except as He permits? He knows what (appears to His creatures as) Before or After or Behind them. Nor shall they compass of His knowledge except as He wills. His Throne does extend over the heavens and the earth, and He feels no fatigue in guarding and preserving them for He is the Most High, the Supreme (in glory).

256. Let there be no compulsion in religion: Truth stands out clear from Error: whoever rejects evil and believes in Allah has grasped the most trustworthy hand-hold, that never breaks. And Allah hears and knows all things.

257. Allah is the Protector of those who have faith: from the depths of darkness He will lead them forth into light. Of those who reject faith the patrons are the Evil Ones: from light they will lead them forth into the depths of darkness. They will be companions of the fire, to dwell therein (For ever).

258. Have you not turned your vision to one who disputed with Abraham about his Lord, because Allah had granted him power? Abraham said: "My Lord is He Who gives life and death."He said: "I give life and death". Said Abraham: "But it is Allah that causes the sun to rise from the east: Do you then cause him to rise from the West."

255. Allaahu laaa ilaaha illaa Huwal-Ḥayyul-Qay-yoom; laa taåkhuzuhoo sinatuñw-wa laa nawm; lahoo maa fissamaa-waati wa maa fil-arḍ; man zal-lazee yashfa'u 'indahooo illaa bi-iznih; ya'lamu maa bayna aydeehim wa maa khalfahum wa laa yuḥeeṭoona bishay'im-min 'ilmihee illaa bimaa shaaa'; wasi'a Kursiyyuhus-samaa-waati wal-arḍa wa laa ya'oo-duhoo ḥifẓuhumaa; wa Huwal-Aliyyul-'Aẓeem.

256. Laaa ikraaha fid-deeni qat-tabayyanar-rushdu minal-ghayy; famañy-yakfur biṭ-Ṭaaghooti wa yu'mim-billaahi faqadis-tamsaka bil'urwatil-wusqaa lan-fiṣaama lahaa; wallaahu Samee'un-'Aleem.

257. Allaahu waliyyul-lazeena aamanoo yukhrijuhum-minaz-zulumaati ilan-noori walla-zeena kafarooo awli-yaaa'uhumuṭ-Ṭaaghootu yukhrijoonahum-minan-noori ilaz-zulumaat; ulaaa'ika Aṣḥaabun-Naari hum feehaa khaalidoon.　　**(Section 34)**

258. Alam tara ilal-lazee Ḥaaajja Ibraaheema fee Rabbiheee an aataahullaahul-mulka iz qaala Ibraaheemu Rabbiyal-lazee yuḥyee wa yumeetu qaala ana uḥyee wa umeetu qaala-Ibraaheemu fa-innal-laaha yaå-tee bishshamsi minal-mashriqi faåti bihaa minal-maghribi

اللّٰهُ لَاۤ اِلٰهَ اِلَّا هُوَ ۚ اَلْحَیُّ الْقَیُّوْمُ ۚ۬ لَا تَاْخُذُهٗ سِنَةٌ وَّلَا نَوْمٌ ؕ لَهٗ مَا فِی السَّمٰوٰتِ وَمَا فِی الْاَرْضِ ؕ مَنْ ذَا الَّذِیْ یَشْفَعُ عِنْدَهٗۤ اِلَّا بِاِذْنِهٖ ؕ یَعْلَمُ مَا بَیْنَ اَیْدِیْهِمْ وَمَا خَلْفَهُمْ ۚ وَلَا یُحِیْطُوْنَ بِشَیْءٍ مِّنْ عِلْمِهٖۤ اِلَّا بِمَا شَآءَ ۚ وَسِعَ كُرْسِیُّهُ السَّمٰوٰتِ وَالْاَرْضَ ۚ وَلَا یَـُٔوْدُهٗ حِفْظُهُمَا ۚ وَهُوَ الْعَلِیُّ الْعَظِیْمُ ۞

لَاۤ اِكْرَاهَ فِی الدِّیْنِ ۟ قَدْ تَّبَیَّنَ الرُّشْدُ مِنَ الْغَیِّ ۚ فَمَنْ یَّكْفُرْ بِالطَّاغُوْتِ وَیُؤْمِنْ بِاللّٰهِ فَقَدِ اسْتَمْسَكَ بِالْعُرْوَةِ الْوُثْقٰی ۙ لَا انْفِصَامَ لَهَا ؕ وَاللّٰهُ سَمِیْعٌ عَلِیْمٌ ۞

اللّٰهُ وَلِیُّ الَّذِیْنَ اٰمَنُوْا ۙ یُخْرِجُهُمْ مِّنَ الظُّلُمٰتِ اِلَی النُّوْرِ ۙ۬ وَالَّذِیْنَ كَفَرُوْۤا اَوْلِیَآؤُهُمُ الطَّاغُوْتُ ۙ یُخْرِجُوْنَهُمْ مِّنَ النُّوْرِ اِلَی الظُّلُمٰتِ ؕ اُولٰٓئِكَ اَصْحٰبُ النَّارِ ۚ هُمْ فِیْهَا خٰلِدُوْنَ ۞

اَلَمْ تَرَ اِلَی الَّذِیْ حَآجَّ اِبْرٰهٖمَ فِیْ رَبِّهٖۤ اَنْ اٰتٰىهُ اللّٰهُ الْمُلْكَ ۘ اِذْ قَالَ اِبْرٰهٖمُ رَبِّیَ الَّذِیْ یُحْیٖ وَیُمِیْتُ ۙ قَالَ اَنَا اُحْیٖ وَاُمِیْتُ ؕ قَالَ اِبْرٰهٖمُ فَاِنَّ اللّٰهَ یَاْتِیْ بِالشَّمْسِ مِنَ الْمَشْرِقِ فَاْتِ بِهَا مِنَ الْمَغْرِبِ

Thus was he confounded who (in arrogance) rejected faith. Nor does Allah Give guidance to a people unjust.

259. Or (take) the similitude of one who passed by a hamlet, all in ruins to its roofs. He said: "Oh! how shall Allah bring it (ever) to life, after (this) its death?" but Allah caused him to die for a hundred years, then raised him up (again). He said: "How long did you tarry (thus)?" He said: (Perhaps) a day or part of a day." He said: "No you hast tarried thus a hundred years; but look at your food and your drink; they show no signs of age; and look at your donkey: And that We may make of you a sign for the people, Look further at the bones, how We bring them together and clothe them with flesh." When this was shown clearly to him, he said: "I know that Allah has power over all things."

260. Behold! Abraham said: "My Lord! Show me how You give life to the dead." He said: "Do you not then believe?" He said: "Yes! but to satisfy my own understanding." He said: "Take four birds; Tame them to turn to you; put a portion of them on every hill and call to them: They will come to you (Flying) with speed. Then know that Allah is Exalted in Power, Wise."

261. The parable of those who spend their substance in the way of Allah is that of a grain of corn: it grows seven ears, and each ear has a hundred grains. Allah gives manifold increase to whom He pleases:

fabuhital-lazee kafar; wallaahu laa yahdil-qawmaz-zaalimeen.

259. Aw kallazee marra 'alaa qaryatiñw-wa hiya khaawiyatun 'alaa 'urooshihaa qaala annaa yuhyee haazihil-laahu ba'da mawtihaa fa-amaatahul-laahu mi'ata 'aamin summa ba'asahoo qaala kam labista qaala labistu yawman aw ba'da yawmin qaala bal labista mi'ata 'aamin fanzur ilaa ta'aamika wa sharaabika lam yatasannah wanzur ilaa himaarika wa linaj'alaka Aayatal-linnaasi wanzur ilal'izaami kayfa nunshizuhaa summa naksoohaa lahmaa; falammaa tabayyana lahoo qaala a'lamu annal-laaha 'alaa kulli shay'in Qadeer.

260. Wa iz qaala Ibraaheemu Rabbi arinee kayfa tuhyil-mawtaa qaala-awa lam tu'min qaala balaa wa laakil-liyatma'inna qalbee qaala fakhuz arba'atam-minat-tayri fasurhunna ilayka summaj-'al 'alaa kulli jabalim-minhunna juz'an summad-'uhunna yaå-teenaka sa'yaa; wa'lam annal-laaha 'Azeezun Hakeem.

(Section 35)

261. Masalul-lazeena yunfi-qoona amwaalahum fee sabeelil-laahi kamasali habbatin ambatat sab'a sanaabila fee kulli sumbulatim-mi'atu habbah; wallaahu yudaa'ifu limañy-yashaaa';

فَبُهِتَ الَّذِى كَفَرَ ۗ وَاللّٰهُ لَا يَهْدِى الْقَوْمَ الظّٰلِمِيْنَ ۝

اَوْ كَالَّذِى مَرَّ عَلٰى قَرْيَةٍ وَّهِىَ خَاوِيَةٌ عَلٰى عُرُوْشِهَا ۚ قَالَ اَنّٰى يُحْىٖ هٰذِهِ اللّٰهُ بَعْدَ مَوْتِهَا ۚ فَاَمَاتَهُ اللّٰهُ مِائَةَ عَامٍ ثُمَّ بَعَثَهٗ ۗ قَالَ كَمْ لَبِثْتَ ۗ قَالَ لَبِثْتُ يَوْمًا اَوْ بَعْضَ يَوْمٍ ۗ قَالَ بَلْ لَّبِثْتَ مِائَةَ عَامٍ فَانْظُرْ اِلٰى طَعَامِكَ وَشَرَابِكَ لَمْ يَتَسَنَّهْ ۚ وَانْظُرْ اِلٰى حِمَارِكَ وَلِنَجْعَلَكَ اٰيَةً لِّلنَّاسِ وَانْظُرْ اِلَى الْعِظَامِ كَيْفَ نُنْشِزُهَا ثُمَّ نَكْسُوْهَا لَحْمًا ۚ فَلَمَّا تَبَيَّنَ لَهٗ قَالَ اَعْلَمُ اَنَّ اللّٰهَ عَلٰى كُلِّ شَىْءٍ قَدِيْرٌ ۝

وَاِذْ قَالَ اِبْرٰهٖمُ رَبِّ اَرِنِىْ كَيْفَ تُحْىِ الْمَوْتٰى ۗ قَالَ اَوَلَمْ تُؤْمِنْ ۗ قَالَ بَلٰى وَلٰكِنْ لِّيَطْمَئِنَّ قَلْبِىْ ۗ قَالَ فَخُذْ اَرْبَعَةً مِّنَ الطَّيْرِ فَصُرْهُنَّ اِلَيْكَ ثُمَّ اجْعَلْ عَلٰى كُلِّ جَبَلٍ مِّنْهُنَّ جُزْءًا ثُمَّ ادْعُهُنَّ يَأْتِيْنَكَ سَعْيًا ۗ وَاعْلَمْ اَنَّ اللّٰهَ عَزِيْزٌ حَكِيْمٌ ۝

مَثَلُ الَّذِيْنَ يُنْفِقُوْنَ اَمْوَالَهُمْ فِىْ سَبِيْلِ اللّٰهِ كَمَثَلِ حَبَّةٍ اَنْبَتَتْ سَبْعَ سَنَابِلَ فِىْ كُلِّ سُنْبُلَةٍ مِّائَةُ حَبَّةٍ ۗ وَاللّٰهُ يُضٰعِفُ لِمَنْ يَّشَاءُ ۗ

and Allah cares for all and He knows all things.

262. Those who spend their substance in the cause of Allah, and follow not up their gifts with reminders of their generosity or with injury,-for them their reward is with their Lord: on them shall be no fear, nor shall they grieve.

263. Kind words and the covering of faults are better than charity followed by injury. Allah is free of all wants, and He is Most Forbearing.

264. O you who believe! waste not your charity by reminders of your generosity or by injury,-like those who spend their substance to be seen of men, but believe neither in Allah nor in the Last Day. They are in parable like a hard, barren rock, on which is a little soil: on it falls heavy rain, which leaves it (Just) a bare stone. They will be able to do nothing with anything they have earned. And Allah does not guide those who reject faith.

265. And the likeness of those who spend their substance, seeking to please Allah and to strengthen their souls, is as a garden, high and fertile: heavy rain falls on it but makes it yield a double increase of harvest, and if it does not receives heavy rain, light moisture suffice it. Allah sees well whatever you do.

266. Does any of you wish that he should have a garden with date-palms and vines and streams flowing underneath, and

---

wallaahu Waasi'un-'Aleem.

262. Allazeena yunfiqoona amwaalahum fee sabeelillaahi summa laa yutbi'oona maaa anfaqoo mannanw-wa laaa azallahum ajruhum 'inda Rabbihim; wa laa khawfun 'alayhim wa laa hum yahzanoon.

263. Qawlum-ma'roofunw-wa maghfiratun khayrum-min sadaqatiny-yatba'uhaaa azaa; wallaahu Ghaniyyun Haleem.

264. Yaaa ayyuhal-lazeena aamanoo laa tubtiloo sadaqaatikum bilmanni walazaa kallazee yunfiqu maalahoo ri'aaa'an-naasi wa laa yu'minu billaahi wal-Yawmil-Aakhiri famasaluhoo kamasali safwaanin 'alayhi turaabun faasaabahoo waabilun fatarakahoo saldaa: laa yaqdiroona 'alaa shay'im mimmaa kasaboo; wallaahu laa yahdil-qawmal-kaafireen.

265. Wa masalul-lazeena yunfiqoona amwaalahumub-tighaaa'a mardaatil-laahi wa tasbeetam-min anfusihim kamasali jannatim birabwatin asaabahaa waabilun fa-aatat ukulahaa di'fayni fa-il-lam yusibhaa waabilun fatall; wallaahu bimaa ta'maloona Baseer.

266. Ayawaddu ahadukum an takoona lahoo jannatum-min nakheelinw-wa a'naabin tajree min tahtihal-anhaaru lahoo feehaa min

---

all kinds of fruit, while he is stricken with old age, and his children are not strong (enough to look after themselves)- that it should be caught in a whirlwind, with fire therein, and be burnt up? Thus does Allah make clear to you (His) Signs; that you may consider.

267. O you who believe! Give of the good things which you have (honourably) earned, and of the fruits of the earth which We have produced for you, and do not ever aim at getting anything which is bad, in order that out of it you may give away something, when you yourselves would not receive it except with closed eyes. And know that Allah is Free of all wants, and Worthy of all praise.

268. Satan threatens you with poverty and bids you to conduct unseemly. Allah promises you His forgiveness and bounties. And Allah cares for all and He knows all things.

269. He grants wisdom to whom He pleases; and he to whom wisdom is granted receives indeed a benefit overflowing; but none will grasp the Message but men of understanding.

270. And whatever you spend in charity or devotion, be sure Allah knows it all. But the wrong-doers have no helpers.

271. If you disclose (acts of) charity, even so it is well, but if you conceal them, and make them reach those (really) in need, that is best for you: It will remove from you some of your (stains of) evil. And Allah is well acquainted with what you do.

272. It is not required of you (O Apostle), to set them on the right path, but Allah sets on the right path whom He pleases. Whatever of

kullis-samaraati wa aṣaabahul-kibaru wa lahoo zurriyyatun ḍu'afaaa'u fa-aṣaabahaaa i'ṣaa-run feehi naarun faḥtaraqat; kazaalika yubayyinul-laahu lakumul-Aayaati la'allakum tatafakkaroon. **(Section 36)**

267. Yaaa 'ayyuhal-lazeena aamanooo anfiqoo min ṭayyi-baati maa kasabtum wa mimmaaa akhrajnaa lakum minal-arḍi wa laa tayammamul-khabeeṣa minhu tunfiqoona wa lastum bi-aakhizeehi illaaa an tughmiḍoo feeh; wa'alamooo annal-laaha Ghaniyyun Ḥameed.

268. Ash-Shayṭaanu ya'idu-kumul-faqra wa yaåmurukum bilfaḥshaaa'i wallaahu ya'idu-kum maghfiratam-minhu wa faḍlaa; wallaahu Waasi'un 'Aleem.

269. Yu'til-Ḥikmata mañy-yashaaa'; wa mañy-yu'tal-Ḥikmata faqad ootiya khayran kaseeraa; wa maa yazzakkaru illaaa ulul-albaab.

270. Wa maaa anfaqtum min nafaqatin aw nazartum min nazrin fa-innal-laaha ya'lamuh; wa maa lizzaalimeena min anṣaar.

271. In tubduṣ-ṣadaqaati fani-'immaa hiya wa in tukhfoohaa wa tu'toohal-fuqaraaa'a fahuwa khayrul-lakum; wa yukaffiru 'ankum min sayyi-aatikum; wallaahu bimaa ta'maloona Khabeer.

272. Laysa 'alayka hudaahum wa laakinnal-laaha yahdee mañy-yashaaa'; wa maa tunfiqoo

good you give benefits your own souls, and you shall only do so seeking the "Face" of Allah. Whatever good you give, shall be rendered back to you, and you shall not be dealt with unjustly.

273. (Charity is) for those in need, who, in Allah's cause are restricted (from travel), and cannot move about in the land, seeking (For trade or work): the ignorant man thinks, because of their modesty, that they are free from want. You shall know them by their (Unfailing) mark: They beg not importunately from all the sundry. And whatever of good you give, be assured Allah knows it well.

274. Those who (in charity) spend of their goods by night and by day, in secret and in public, have their reward with their Lord: on them shall be no fear, nor shall they grieve.

275. Those who devour interest will not stand except as stand one whom the Satan one by his touch has driven to madness. That is because they say: "Trade is like interest," but Allah has permitted trade and forbidden interest. Those who after receiving direction from their Lord, desist, shall be pardoned for the past; their case is for Allah (to judge); but those who repeat (the offence) are companions of the Fire: They will abide therein (for ever).

276. Allah will deprive usury of all blessing, but will give increase for deeds of charity: for He does not love ungrateful and wicked creatures.

277. Those who believe, and do deeds of righteousness,

min khayrin fali-anfusikum; wa maa tunfiqoona illab-tighaaa'a Wajhil-laah; wa maa tunfiqoo min khayriñy-yuwaffa ilaykum wa antum laa tuẓlamoon.

273. Lilfuqaraaa'il-lazeena uḥṣiroo fee sabeelil-laahi laa yastatee'oona ḍarban fil-arḍi yaḥsabuhumul-jaahilu aghniyaaa'a minat-ta'affufi ta'rifuhum biseemaahum laa yas'aloonan-naasa ilḥaafaa; wa maa tunfiqoo min khayrin fa-innal-laaha bihee 'Aleem.

(Section 37)

274. Allazeena yunfiqoona amwaalahum billayli wan-nahaari sirrañw-wa 'alaaniyatan falahum ajruhum 'inda Rabbihim wa laa khawfun 'alayhim wa laa hum yaḥzanoon.

275. Allazeena yaåkuloonar-ribaa laa yaqoomoona illaa kamaa yaqoomul-lazee yatakhabbaṭuhush-Shayṭaanu minal-mass; zaalika bi-annahum qaalooo innamal-bay'u mislur-ribaa; wa aḥallal-laahul-bay'a wa ḥarmar-ribaa; faman jaaa'ahoo maw'izatum-mir-Rabbihee fantahaa falahoo maa salafa wa amruhooo ilal-laahi wa man 'aada fa-ulaaa'ika Aṣḥaabun-Naari hum feehaa khaalidoon.

276. Yamḥaqul-laahur-ribaa wa yurbiṣ-ṣadaqaat; wallaahu laa yuḥibbu kulla kaffaarin aseem.

277. Innal-lazeena aamanoo wa 'amiluṣ-ṣaaliḥaati

مِنْ خَيْرٍ فَلِأَنْفُسِكُمْ ۚ وَمَا تُنْفِقُونَ اِلَّا ابْتِغَاءَ وَجْهِ اللّٰهِ ۚ وَمَا تُنْفِقُوا مِنْ خَيْرٍ يُّوَفَّ اِلَيْكُمْ وَاَنْتُمْ لَا تُظْلَمُوْنَ ۝

لِلْفُقَرَاءِ الَّذِيْنَ اُحْصِرُوْا فِيْ سَبِيْلِ اللّٰهِ لَا يَسْتَطِيْعُوْنَ ضَرْبًا فِي الْاَرْضِ ۖ يَحْسَبُهُمُ الْجَاهِلُ اَغْنِيَاءَ مِنَ التَّعَفُّفِ ۚ تَعْرِفُهُمْ بِسِيْمَاهُمْ ۚ لَا يَسْـَٔلُوْنَ النَّاسَ اِلْحَافًا ۗ وَمَا تُنْفِقُوْا مِنْ خَيْرٍ فَاِنَّ اللّٰهَ بِهٖ عَلِيْمٌ ۝

اَلَّذِيْنَ يُنْفِقُوْنَ اَمْوَالَهُمْ بِالَّيْلِ وَالنَّهَارِ سِرًّا وَّعَلَانِيَةً فَلَهُمْ اَجْرُهُمْ عِنْدَ رَبِّهِمْ ۚ وَلَا خَوْفٌ عَلَيْهِمْ وَلَا هُمْ يَحْزَنُوْنَ ۝

اَلَّذِيْنَ يَاْكُلُوْنَ الرِّبٰوا لَا يَقُوْمُوْنَ اِلَّا كَمَا يَقُوْمُ الَّذِيْ يَتَخَبَّطُهُ الشَّيْطٰنُ مِنَ الْمَسِّ ۚ ذٰلِكَ بِاَنَّهُمْ قَالُوْۤا اِنَّمَا الْبَيْعُ مِثْلُ الرِّبٰوا ۘ وَاَحَلَّ اللّٰهُ الْبَيْعَ وَحَرَّمَ الرِّبٰوا ۚ فَمَنْ جَاءَهٗ مَوْعِظَةٌ مِّنْ رَّبِّهٖ فَانْتَهٰى فَلَهٗ مَا سَلَفَ ۗ وَاَمْرُهٗۤ اِلَى اللّٰهِ ۗ وَمَنْ عَادَ فَاُولٰٓئِكَ اَصْحٰبُ النَّارِ ۚ هُمْ فِيْهَا خٰلِدُوْنَ ۝

يَمْحَقُ اللّٰهُ الرِّبٰوا وَيُرْبِي الصَّدَقٰتِ ۗ وَاللّٰهُ لَا يُحِبُّ كُلَّ كَفَّارٍ اَثِيْمٍ ۝

اِنَّ الَّذِيْنَ اٰمَنُوْا وَعَمِلُوا الصّٰلِحٰتِ

and establish regular prayers and regular charity, will have their reward with their Lord: on them shall be no fear, nor shall they grieve.

278. O you who believe! Fear Allah, and give up what remains of your demand for usury, if you are indeed believers.

279. If you do it not, take notice of war from Allah and His Apostle: But if you turn back, you shall have your capital sums: deal not unjustly, and you shall not be dealt with unjustly.

280. If the debtor is in a difficulty, grant him time till it is easy for him to repay. But if you remit it by way of charity, that is best for you if you only knew.

281. And fear the Day when you shall be brought back to Allah. Then shall every soul be paid what it earned, and none shall be dealt with unjustly.

282. O you who believe! When you deal with each other, in transactions involving future obligations in a fixed period of time, reduce them to writing. Let a scribe write down faithfully as between the parties: let not the scribe refuse to write: as Allah has taught him, so let him write. Let him who incurs the liability dictate, but let him fear His Lord Allah, and not diminish anything of what he owes. If the party liable is mentally deficient, or weak, or unable himself to dictate, Let his guardian dictate faithfully, and get

wa aqaamuṣ-Ṣalaata wa aatawuz-Zakaata lahum ajruhum 'inda Rabbihim wa laa khawfun 'alayhim wa laa hum yaḥzanoon.

278. Yaaa ayyuhal-lazeena aamanut-taqul-laaha wa zaroo maa baqiya minar-ribaaa in kuntum mu'mineen.

279. Fail-lam taf'aloo faażanoo biḥarbim-minal-laahi wa Rasoolihee wa in tubtum falakum ru'oosu amwaalikum laa tażlimoona wa laa tuẓlamoon.

280. Wa in kaana zoo 'usratin fanaẓiratun ilaa maysarah; wa an taṣaddaqoo khayrul-lakum in kuntum ta'lamoon.

281. Wattaqoo Yawman turja'oona feehi ilal-laahi ṣumma tuwaffaa kullu nafsim-maa kasabat wa hum laa yuẓlamoon.   **(Section 38)**

282. Yaaa ayyuhal-lazeena aamanooo izaa tadaayantum bidaynin ilaaa ajalimmusam-man faktubooh; walyaktub baynakum kaatibum bil'adl; wa laa yaaba kaatibun añy-yaktuba kamaa 'allamahul-laah; falyaktub walyumlilil-lazee 'alayhil-ḥaqqu walyattaqil-laaha rabbahoo wa laa yabkhas minhu shay'aa; fa-in kaanal-lazee 'alayhil-ḥaqqu safeehan aw ḍa'eefan aw laa yastaṭee'u añy-yumilla huwa falyumlil waliyyuhoo bil'adl; wastash-hidoo

two witnesses, out of your own men, and if there are not two men, then a man and two women, such as you choose, for witnesses, so that if one of them errs, the other can remind her. The witnesses should not refuse when they are called on (for evidence). Disdain not to reduce to writing (your contract) for a future period, whether it be small or big: it is juster in the sight of Allah, more suitable as evidence, and more convenient to prevent doubts among yourselves but if it be a transaction which you carry out on the spot among your-selves, there is no blame on you if you reduce it not to writing. But take witness whenever you make a commercial contract; and let neither scribe nor witness suffer harm. If you do (such harm), it would be wickedness in you. So fear Allah; for it is Allah that teaches you. And Allah is well acquainted with all things.

shaheedayni mir-rijaalikum fa-il-lam yakoonaa rajulayni farajuluñw-wamra-ataani mimman tarḍawna minash-shuhadaaa'i an taḍilla iḥdaahumaa fatuẕakkira iḥdaahumal-ukhraa; wa laa yaåbash-shuhadaaa'u iẕaa maa du'oo; wa laa tas'amooo an taktuboohu ṣagheeran aw kabeeran ilaaa ajalih; ẕaalikum aqsaṭu 'indal-laahi wa aqwamu lishshahaadati wa adnaaa allaa tartaabooo illaaa an takoona tijaaratan ḥaaḍiratan-tudeeroonahaa baynakum falaysa 'alaykum junaaḥun allaa taktuboohaa; wa ashhidooo iẕaa tabaaya'tum; wa laa yuḍaaarra kaatibuñw-wa laa shaheed; wa in taf'aloo fa-innahoo fusooqum-bikum; wattaqul-laaha wa yu'allimu-kumul-laah; wallaahu bikulli shay'in 'Aleem.

283. If you are on a journey, and cannot find a scribe, a pledge with possession (may serve the purpose). And if one of you deposits a thing on trust with another, Let the trustee (faithfully) discharge His trust, and let him fear his Lord. Conceal not evidence; for whoever conceals it,- his heart is tainted with sin. And Allah knows all that you do.

283. Wa in kuntum 'alaa safa-riñw-wa lam tajidoo kaatiban farihaanum-maqbooḍatun fa-in amina ba'ḍukum ba'ḍan falyu'addil-lazi'-tumina amaa-natahoo walyattaqil-laaha Rabbah; wa laa taktumush-shahaadah; wa mañy-yaktumhaa fa-innahooo aasimun qalbuh; wallaahu bimaa ta'maloona 'Aleem. **(Section 39)**

284. To Allah belongs all that is in the heavens and on earth. Whether you show what is in your minds or conceal it, Allah calls you to account for it.

284. Lillaahi maa fissamaa-waati wa maa fil-arḍ; wa in tubdoo maa feee anfusikum aw tukhfoohu yuḥaasibkum bihil-laahu

شَهِيدَيْنِ مِن رِّجَالِكُمْ فَإِن لَّمْ يَكُونَا رَجُلَيْنِ فَرَجُلٌ وَّامْرَأَتَانِ مِمَّن تَرْضَوْنَ مِنَ الشُّهَدَاءِ أَن تَضِلَّ إِحْدَاهُمَا فَتُذَكِّرَ إِحْدَاهُمَا الْأُخْرَىٰ وَلَا يَأْبَ الشُّهَدَاءُ إِذَا مَا دُعُوا وَلَا تَسْئَمُوا أَن تَكْتُبُوهُ صَغِيرًا أَوْ كَبِيرًا إِلَىٰ أَجَلِهِ ذَٰلِكُمْ أَقْسَطُ عِندَ اللَّهِ وَأَقْوَمُ لِلشَّهَادَةِ وَأَدْنَىٰ أَلَّا تَرْتَابُوا إِلَّا أَن تَكُونَ تِجَارَةً حَاضِرَةً تُدِيرُونَهَا بَيْنَكُمْ فَلَيْسَ عَلَيْكُمْ جُنَاحٌ أَلَّا تَكْتُبُوهَا وَأَشْهِدُوا إِذَا تَبَايَعْتُمْ وَلَا يُضَارَّ كَاتِبٌ وَلَا شَهِيدٌ وَإِن تَفْعَلُوا فَإِنَّهُ فُسُوقٌ بِكُمْ وَاتَّقُوا اللَّهَ وَيُعَلِّمُكُمُ اللَّهُ وَاللَّهُ بِكُلِّ شَيْءٍ عَلِيمٌ ۝

وَإِن كُنتُمْ عَلَىٰ سَفَرٍ وَّلَمْ تَجِدُوا كَاتِبًا فَرِهَانٌ مَّقْبُوضَةٌ فَإِنْ أَمِنَ بَعْضُكُم بَعْضًا فَلْيُؤَدِّ الَّذِي اؤْتُمِنَ أَمَانَتَهُ وَلْيَتَّقِ اللَّهَ رَبَّهُ وَلَا تَكْتُمُوا الشَّهَادَةَ وَمَن يَكْتُمْهَا فَإِنَّهُ آثِمٌ قَلْبُهُ وَاللَّهُ بِمَا تَعْمَلُونَ عَلِيمٌ ۝

لِلَّهِ مَا فِي السَّمَاوَاتِ وَمَا فِي الْأَرْضِ وَإِن تُبْدُوا مَا فِي أَنفُسِكُمْ أَوْ تُخْفُوهُ يُحَاسِبْكُم بِهِ اللَّهُ

He forgives whom He pleases, and punishes whom He pleases, for Allah has power over all things.

285. The Apostle believes in what has been revealed to him from his Lord, as do the men of faith. Each one (of them) believes in Allah, His Angels, His Books, and His Apostles. "We make no distinction (they say) between one and another of His Apostles." And they say: "We hear, and we obey: (We seek) your forgive-ness, our Lord, and to you is the end of all journeys."

286. On no soul Allah places a burden greater than it can bear. It gets every good that it earns, and it suffers every ill that it earns. (Pray:) "Our Lord! condemn us not if we forget or fall into error; Our Lord! lay not on us a burden like that which you did lay on those before us; Our Lord! lay not on us a burden greater than we have strength to bear. Blot out our sins, and grant us forgiveness. Have mercy on us. You are our Protector; help us against those who stand against Faith.

fayaghfiru limañy-yashaaa'u wa yu'azzibu mañy-yashaaa'; wallaahu 'alaa kulli shay'in Qadeer.

285. Aamanar-Rasoolu bimaaa unzila ilayhi mir-Rabbihee walmu'minoon; kullun aamana billaahi wa Malaaa'ikatihee wa Kutubihee wa Rusulihee laa nufarriqu bayna aḥadim-mir-Rusulih; wa qaaloo sami'naa wa aṭa'naa ghufraanaka Rabbanaa wa ilaykal-maṣeer.

286. Laa yukalliful-laahu nafsan illaa wus'ahaa; lahaa maa kasabat wa 'alayhaa maktasabat; Rabbanaa laa tu'aakhiznaaa in naseenaaa aw akhṭaånaa; Rabbanaa wa laa taḥmil-'alaynaaa iṣran kamaa ḥamaltahoo 'alal-lazeena min qablinaa; Rabbanaa wa laa tuḥammilnaa maa laa ṭaaqata lanaa bihee wa'fu 'annaa waghfir lanaa warḥamnaa; Anta mawlaanaa fanṣurnaa 'alal-qawmil-kaafireen. **(Section 40)**

3. The Family of 'Imran
In the name of Allah, Most Gracious, Most Merciful.

1. *Alif-Lam-Mim*
2. Allah! There is no Allah but He,-the Living, the Self-Subsisting, Eternal.
3. It is He Who sent down to you (step by step), in truth, the Book, confirming what went before it; and He sent down the Law (of Moses) and the Gospel (of Jesus) before this, as a guide to mankind, and He sent down the criterion (of judgment between right and wrong).
4. Then those who reject Faith in the Signs of

Sûrat Âl 'Imrân–3
(Revealed at Madinah)
Bismillaahir Raḥmaanir Raheem

1. Alif-Laaam-Meeem.

2. Allaahu laaa ilaaha illaa Huwal-Ḥayyul-Qayyoom.

3. Nazzala 'alaykal-Kitaaba bilhaqqi muṣaddiqal-limaa bayna yadayhi wa anzalat-Tawraata wal-Injeel.

4. Min qablu hudal-linnaasi wa anzalal-Furqaan; innallazeena kafaroo bi-Aayaatil-

Allah will suffer the severest chastisement, and Allah is Exalted in Might, Lord of Retribution.

5.   From Allah, verily nothing is hidden on earth or in the heavens.

6.   He it is Who shapes you in the wombs as He pleases. There is no Allah but He, the Exalted in Might, the Wise.

7.   He it is Who has sent down to you the Book: In it are verses basic or fundamental (of established meaning); they are the foundation of the Book: others are allegorical. But those in whose hearts is perversity follow the part thereof that is allegorical, seeking discord, and searching for its hidden meanings, but no one knows its hidden meanings except Allah. And those who are firmly grounded in knowledge say: "We believe in the Book; the whole of it is from our Lord:" and none will grasp the Message except men of understanding.

8.   "Our Lord!" (they say), "Let not our hearts deviate now after You have guided us, but grant us mercy from Your own Presence; for You are the Grantor of bounties without measure.

9.   "Our Lord! You are He that will gather mankind together against a day about which there is no doubt; for Allah never fails in His promise."

10.   Those who reject Faith,- neither their possessions nor their (numerous) progeny will avail them nothing against Allah: They are themselves but fuel for the Fire.

laahi lahum 'azaabun shadeed; wallaahu 'Azeezun zun-tiqaam.

5. Innal-laaha laa yakhfaa 'alayhi shay'un fil-ardi wa laa fis-samaaa'.

6. Huwal-lazee yusawwiru-kum fil-arhaami kayfa yashaaa'; laaa ilaaha illaa Huwal-'Azeezul-Hakeem.

7. Huwal-lazeee anzala 'alaykal-Kitaaba minhu Aayaatum-Muhkamaatun hunna Ummul-Kitaabi wa ukharu Mutashaabihaatun fa-ammal-lazeena fee quloobihim zayghun fa-yattabi'oona maa tashaabaha minhubtighaaa'al-fitnati wabtighaaa'a taåweelih; wa maa ya'lamu taåweelahooo illal-laah; warraasikhoona fil-'ilmi yaqooloona aamannaa bihee kullum-min 'indi Rabbinaa; wa maa yazzakkaru illaaa ulul-albaab.

8. Rabbanaa laa tuzigh quloobanaa ba'da iz hadaytanaa wa hab lanaa mil-ladunka rahmah; innaka Antal-Wahhaab.

9. Rabbanaaa innaka jaami-'un-naasi li-Yawmil-laa rayba feeh; innal-laaha laa yukhfilul-mee'aad.   (Section 1)

10. Innal-lazeena kafaroo lan tughniya 'anhum amwaaluhum wa laaa awlaaduhum minal-laahi shay'añw-wa ulaaa'ika hum waqoodun-Naar.

الله لَهُمْ عَذَابٌ شَدِيدٌ ۗ وَاللَّهُ عَزِيزٌ ذُو انْتِقَامٍ ۞

إِنَّ اللَّهَ لَا يَخْفَى عَلَيْهِ شَيْءٌ فِي الْأَرْضِ وَلَا فِي السَّمَاءِ ۗ

هُوَ الَّذِي يُصَوِّرُكُمْ فِي الْأَرْحَامِ كَيْفَ يَشَاءُ ۚ لَا إِلَهَ إِلَّا هُوَ الْعَزِيزُ الْحَكِيمُ ۞

هُوَ الَّذِي أَنْزَلَ عَلَيْكَ الْكِتَابَ مِنْهُ آيَاتٌ مُحْكَمَاتٌ هُنَّ أُمُّ الْكِتَابِ وَأُخَرُ مُتَشَابِهَاتٌ ۖ فَأَمَّا الَّذِينَ فِي قُلُوبِهِمْ زَيْغٌ فَيَتَّبِعُونَ مَا تَشَابَهَ مِنْهُ ابْتِغَاءَ الْفِتْنَةِ وَابْتِغَاءَ تَأْوِيلِهِ ۗ وَمَا يَعْلَمُ تَأْوِيلَهُ إِلَّا اللَّهُ ۗ وَالرَّاسِخُونَ فِي الْعِلْمِ يَقُولُونَ آمَنَّا بِهِ كُلٌّ مِنْ عِنْدِ رَبِّنَا ۗ وَمَا يَذَّكَّرُ إِلَّا أُولُو الْأَلْبَابِ ۞

رَبَّنَا لَا تُزِغْ قُلُوبَنَا بَعْدَ إِذْ هَدَيْتَنَا وَهَبْ لَنَا مِنْ لَدُنْكَ رَحْمَةً ۚ إِنَّكَ أَنْتَ الْوَهَّابُ ۞

رَبَّنَا إِنَّكَ جَامِعُ النَّاسِ لِيَوْمٍ لَا رَيْبَ فِيهِ ۚ إِنَّ اللَّهَ لَا يُخْلِفُ الْمِيعَادَ ۞

إِنَّ الَّذِينَ كَفَرُوا لَنْ تُغْنِيَ عَنْهُمْ أَمْوَالُهُمْ وَلَا أَوْلَادُهُمْ مِنَ اللَّهِ شَيْئًا ۖ وَأُولَئِكَ هُمْ وَقُودُ النَّارِ ۞

11. (Their plight will be) no better than that of the people of Pharaoh, and their pre-decessors: They denied our Signs, and Allah called them to account for their sins. For Allah is strict in punishment.

12. Say to those who reject Faith: "Soon will you be vanquished and gathered together to Hell,-an evil bed indeed (to lie on)!

13. "There has already been for you a Sign in the two armies that met (in combat): One was fighting in the cause of Allah, the other resisting Allah; these saw with their own eyes twice their number. But Allah does support with His aid whom He pleases. In this is a warning for such as have eyes to see."

14. Fair in the eyes of men is the love of things they covet: Women and sons; heaped-up hoards of gold and silver; horses branded (for breed and excellence); and (wealth of) cattle and well-tilled land. Such are the possessions of this world's life; but in nearness to Allah is the best of the goals (to return to).

15. Say: Shall I give you glad tidings of things for better than those? For the righteous are Gardens in nearness to their Lord, with rivers flowing beneath; therein is their eternal home; with companions pure (and holy); and the good pleasure of Allah. For in Allah's sight are (all) His servants,-

16. (Namely), those who say: "Our Lord! we have indeed believed: forgive us, then, our sins, and save us from the agony of the Fire;"-

11. Kadaåbi Aali Fir'awna wallazeena min qablihim; kaz-zaboo bi-Aayaatinaa faakhazahumul-laahu bizunoobihim; wallaahu shadeedul-'iqaab.

12. Qul lillazeena kafaroo satughlaboona wa tuhsharoona ilaa Jahannam; wa bi'sal-mihaad.

13. Qad kaana lakum Aayatun fee fi'ataynil-taqataa fi'atun tuqaatilu fee sabeelil-laahi wa ukhraa kaafiratuñy-yarawnahum mislayhim raåyal-'ayn; wallaahu yu'ayyidu bi-nasrihee mañy-yashaaa'; inna fee zaalika la-'ibratal-li-ulil-absaar.

14. Zuyyina linnaasi hubbush-shahawaati minannisaaa'i wal-baneena walqanaateeril-muqantarati minaz-zahabi walfiddati walkhaylil-musawwamati wal-an'aami walhars; zaalika mataa'ul-hayaatid-dunyaa wallaahu 'indahoo husnul-ma-aab.

15. Qul a'unabbi'ukum bikhayrim-min zaalikum; lillazeenat-taqaw 'inda Rabbihim Jannaatun tajree min tahtihal-anhaaru khaalideena feehaa wa azwaajum-mutahharatuñw-wa ridwaanum-minal-laah; wallaahu baseerum bil-'ibaad.

16. Allazeena yaqooloona Rabbanaaa innanaaa aamannaa faghfir lanaa zunoobanaa wa qinaa 'azaaban-Naar.

كَدَأْبِ اٰلِ فِرْعَوْنَ ۙ وَالَّذِيْنَ مِنْ قَبْلِهِمْ ۚ كَذَّبُوْا بِاٰيٰتِنَا ۚ فَاَخَذَهُمُ اللّٰهُ بِذُنُوْبِهِمْ ۗ وَاللّٰهُ شَدِيْدُ الْعِقَابِ ۝

قُلْ لِّلَّذِيْنَ كَفَرُوْا سَتُغْلَبُوْنَ وَتُحْشَرُوْنَ اِلٰى جَهَنَّمَ ۚ وَبِئْسَ الْمِهَادُ ۝

قَدْ كَانَ لَكُمْ اٰيَةٌ فِيْ فِئَتَيْنِ الْتَقَتَا ۚ فِئَةٌ تُقَاتِلُ فِيْ سَبِيْلِ اللّٰهِ وَاُخْرٰى كَافِرَةٌ يَّرَوْنَهُمْ مِّثْلَيْهِمْ رَأْيَ الْعَيْنِ ۗ وَاللّٰهُ يُؤَيِّدُ بِنَصْرِهٖ مَنْ يَّشَاۤءُ ۗ اِنَّ فِيْ ذٰلِكَ لَعِبْرَةً لِّاُولِى الْاَبْصَارِ ۝

زُيِّنَ لِلنَّاسِ حُبُّ الشَّهَوٰتِ مِنَ النِّسَاۤءِ وَالْبَنِيْنَ وَالْقَنَاطِيْرِ الْمُقَنْطَرَةِ مِنَ الذَّهَبِ وَالْفِضَّةِ وَالْخَيْلِ الْمُسَوَّمَةِ وَالْاَنْعَامِ وَالْحَرْثِ ۗ ذٰلِكَ مَتَاعُ الْحَيٰوةِ الدُّنْيَا ۚ وَاللّٰهُ عِنْدَهٗ حُسْنُ الْمَاٰبِ ۝

قُلْ اَؤُنَبِّئُكُمْ بِخَيْرٍ مِّنْ ذٰلِكُمْ ۗ لِلَّذِيْنَ اتَّقَوْا عِنْدَ رَبِّهِمْ جَنّٰتٌ تَجْرِيْ مِنْ تَحْتِهَا الْاَنْهٰرُ خٰلِدِيْنَ فِيْهَا وَاَزْوَاجٌ مُّطَهَّرَةٌ وَّرِضْوَانٌ مِّنَ اللّٰهِ ۗ وَاللّٰهُ بَصِيْرٌ بِالْعِبَادِ ۝

اَلَّذِيْنَ يَقُوْلُوْنَ رَبَّنَاۤ اِنَّنَاۤ اٰمَنَّا فَاغْفِرْ لَنَا ذُنُوْبَنَا وَقِنَا عَذَابَ النَّارِ ۝

17. Those who show patience, firmness and self-control; who are true (in word and deed); who worship devoutly; who spend (in the way of Allah); and who pray for forgiveness in the early hours of the morning.

18. There is no Allah but He: that is the witness of Allah, His angels, and those endued with knowledge, standing firm on justice. There is no Allah but He, the Exalted in Power, the Wise.

19. The Religion before Allah is Islam (submission to His Will): nor did the People of the Book dissent therefrom except through envy of each other, after knowledge had come to them. But if any deny the Signs of Allah, Allah is swift in calling to account.

20. So if they dispute with you, say: "I have submitted my whole self to Allah and so have those who follow me." And say to the People of the Book and to those who are unlearned: "Do you (also) submit yourselves?" If they do, they are in right guidance, but if they turn back, your duty is to convey the Message; and in Allah's sight are (all) His servants.

21. As to those who deny the Signs of Allah and in defiance of right, slay the prophets, and slay those who teach just dealing with mankind, announce to them a grievous chastisement.

22. They are those whose works will bear no fruit in this world and in the Hereafter nor will they have anyone to help.

23. Has you not turned your vision to those who have been given a portion of the Book? They are invited to the Book of Allah, to settle their dispute, but a party of them turn back and decline (The arbitration).

17. Aṣṣaabireena waṣṣaa-diqeena walqaaniteena walmunfiqeena walmus-taghfireena bil-ashaar.

18. Shahidal-laahu annahoo laaa ilaaha illa Huwa walmalaaa'ikatu wa ulul-'ilmi qaaa'imam bilqiṣṭ; laaa ilaaha illaa Huwal-'Azeezul-Ḥakeem.

19. Innad-deena 'indal-laahil-Islaam; wa makhtalafal-lazeena ootul-Kitaaba illaa mim ba'di maa jaaa'ahumul-'ilmu baghyam baynahum; wa mañy-yakfur bi-Aayaatil-laahi fa-innal-laaha saree'ul-ḥisaab.

20. Fa-in ḥaaajjooka faqul aslamtu wajhiya lillaahi wa manit-taba'an; wa qul lillazeena ootul-Kitaaba wal-ummiyyeena 'a-aslamtum; fa-in aslamoo faqadih-tadaw wa in tawallaw fa-innamaa 'alaykal-balaagh; wallaahu baṣeerum bil-'ibaad.
(Section 2)

21. Innal-lazeena yakfuroona bi-Aayaatil-laahi wa yaqtu-loonan-Nabiyyeena bighayri ḥaqqiñw-wa yaqtuloonal-lazeena yaamuroona bilqiṣṭi minannaasi fabashshirhum bi'azaabin aleem.

22. Ulaaa'ikal-lazeena ḥabiṭat a'maaluhum fid-dunyaa wal-Aakhirati wa maa lahum min naaṣireen.

23. Alam tara ilal-lazeena ootoo naṣeebam-minal-Kitaabi yud'awna ilaa Kitaabil-laahi liyaḥkuma baynahum summa yatawallaa fareequm-minhum wa hum mu'riḍoon.

24. This because they say: "The Fire shall not touch us but for a few numbered days": their forgeries deceive them as to their own religion.

25. But how (will they fare) when we gather them together against a day about which there is no doubt, and each soul will be paid out just what it has earned, without (favour or) injustice?

26. Say: "O Allah! Lord of Power (And Rule), You give power to whom You please, and You strip off power from whom You please: You endow with honour whom You please, and you bring low whom You please: In Your hand is all good. Verily, over all things You have power.

27. "You cause the Night to gain on the Day, and You cause the Day to gain on the night; You bring the living out of the Dead, and You bring the Dead out of the Living; and You give sustenance to whom You please, without measure ."

28. Let not the believers take for friends or helpers Unbelievers rather than believers: if any do that, in nothing will there be help from Allah: except by way of precaution, that you may guard yourselves from them. But Allah cautions you (to remember) Himself; for the final goal is to Allah.

29. Say: "Whether you hide what is in your hearts or reveal it, Allah knows it all: He knows what is in the heavens, and what is on earth. And Allah has power over all things.

30. "On the Day when every soul will be confronted with all

24. Zaalika bi-annahum qaaloo lan tamassanan-Naaru-illaaa ayyaamam ma'doodaatiñw-wa gharrahum fee deenihim maa kaanoo yaftaroon.

25. Fakayfa izaa jama'naahum li-Yawmil-laa rayba feehi wa wuffiyat kullu nafsim-maa kasabat wa hum laa yuzlamoon.

26. Qulil-laahumma Maalikal-Mulki tu'til-mulka man tashaaa'u wa tanzi'ulmulka mimman tashaaa'u wa tu'izzu man tashaaa'u wa tuzillu man tashaaa'u biyadikal-khayru innaka 'alaa kulli shay'in Qadeer.

27. Toolijul-layla fin-nahaari wa toolijun-nahaara fil-layli wa tukhrijul-hayya minalmayyiti wa tukhrijul-mayyita minal-hayyi wa tarzuqu man tashaaa'u bighayri hisaab.

28. Laa yattakhizil-mu'minoonal-kaafireena awliyaaa'a min doonil-mu'mineena wa mañy-yaf'al zaalika falaysa minal-laahi fee shay'in illaaa an tattaqoo minhum tuqaah; wa yuhazzirukumul-laahu nafsah; wa ilal-laahil-maseer.

29. Qul in tukhfoo maa fee sudoorikum aw tubdoohu ya'lamhul-laah; wa ya'lamu maa fis-samaawaati wa maa fil-ard; wallaahu 'alaa kulli shay'in Qadeer.

30. Yawma tajidu kullu nafsim-maa 'amilat min

the good it has done, and all the evil it has done, it will wish there were a great distance between it and its evil. But Allah cautions you (to remember) Himself. And Allah is full of kindness to those that serve Him."

31. Say: "If you do love Allah, Follow me: Allah will love you and forgive you your sins: For Allah is Oft-Forgiving, Most Merciful."

32. Say: "Obey Allah and His Apostle": But if they turn back, Allah loves not those who reject Faith.

33. Allah did choose Adam and Noah, the family of Abraham, and the family of 'Imran above all people,-

34. Offspring, one of the other: And Allah hears and knows all things.

35. Behold! a woman of 'Imran said: "O my Lord! I do dedicate unto You what is in my womb for your special service: So accept this of me: For You hears and knows all things."

36. When she delivered (the baby girl) she said: "O my Lord! Behold! I am delivered of a female child!"- and Allah knew best what she brought forth- "And no wise is the male like the female. I have named her Mary, and I commend her and her offspring to Your protection from Satan, the Rejected."

37. Right graciously did her Lord accept her: He made her grow in purity and beauty: To the care of Zakariya was she assigned. Every time that he entered (Her) chamber to see her, He found her supplied with sustenance. He said:

khayrim muḥdaranw-wa maa 'amilat min sooo'in tawaddu law anna baynahaa wa baynahooo amadam ba'eedaa; wa yuḥazzirukumul-laahu nafsah; wallaahu ra'oofum bil'ibaad. **(Section 3)**

31. Qul in kuntum tuḥibboonal-laaha fattabi'oonee yuḥbibkumul-laahu wa yaghfir lakum zunoobakum; wallaahu Ghafoorur-Raḥeem.

32. Qul aṭee'ul-laaha war-Rasoola fa-in tawallaw fa-innal-laaha laa yuḥibbul-kaafireen.

33. Innal-laahaṣ-ṭafaaa Aadama wa Nooḥanw-wa Aala Ibraaheema wa Aala 'Imraana 'alal-'aalameen.

34 Zurriyyatam ba'ḍuhaa mim-ba'ḍ, wallaahu Samee'un 'Aleem.

35. Iz qaalatim-ra-atu 'Imraana Rabbi innee nazartu laka maa fee baṭnee muḥar-raran fataqabbal minnee innaka Antas-Samee'ul-'Aleem.

36. Falammaa waḍa'athaa qaalat Rabbi innee waḍa'tuhaaa unsaa wallaahu a'lamu bimaa waḍa'at wa laysaz-zakaru kal-unsaa wa innee sammaytuhaa Maryama wa inneee u'eezuhaa bika wa zurriyyatahaa minash-Shayṭaanir-Rajeem.

37. Fataqabbalahaa Rabbuhaa biqaboolin ḥasaniñw-wa ambatahaa nabaatan ḥasanañw-wa kaffalahaa Zakariyyaa kullamaa dakhala 'alayhaa Zakariyyal-Miḥraaba wajada 'indahaa rizqan qaala

خَيْرًا مُّحْضَرًا ۛ وَّمَا عَمِلَتْ مِن سُوٓءٍ ۛ

تَوَدُّ لَوْ أَنَّ بَيْنَهَا وَبَيْنَهُۥٓ أَمَدًۢا بَعِيدًا ۗ

وَيُحَذِّرُكُمُ ٱللَّهُ نَفْسَهُۥ ۗ وَٱللَّهُ رَءُوفٌۢ

بِٱلْعِبَادِ ۝

قُلْ إِن كُنتُمْ تُحِبُّونَ ٱللَّهَ فَٱتَّبِعُونِى

يُحْبِبْكُمُ ٱللَّهُ وَيَغْفِرْ لَكُمْ ذُنُوبَكُمْ ۗ

وَٱللَّهُ غَفُورٌ رَّحِيمٌ ۝

قُلْ أَطِيعُوا۟ ٱللَّهَ وَٱلرَّسُولَ ۖ فَإِن تَوَلَّوْا۟

فَإِنَّ ٱللَّهَ لَا يُحِبُّ ٱلْكَٰفِرِينَ ۝

إِنَّ ٱللَّهَ ٱصْطَفَىٰٓ ءَادَمَ وَنُوحًا وَءَالَ

إِبْرَٰهِيمَ وَءَالَ عِمْرَٰنَ عَلَى ٱلْعَٰلَمِينَ ۝

ذُرِّيَّةًۢ بَعْضُهَا مِنۢ بَعْضٍ ۗ وَٱللَّهُ

سَمِيعٌ عَلِيمٌ ۝

إِذْ قَالَتِ ٱمْرَأَتُ عِمْرَٰنَ رَبِّ إِنِّى

نَذَرْتُ لَكَ مَا فِى بَطْنِى مُحَرَّرًا

فَتَقَبَّلْ مِنِّىٓ ۖ إِنَّكَ أَنتَ ٱلسَّمِيعُ

ٱلْعَلِيمُ ۝

فَلَمَّا وَضَعَتْهَا قَالَتْ رَبِّ إِنِّى

وَضَعْتُهَآ أُنثَىٰ وَٱللَّهُ أَعْلَمُ بِمَا

وَضَعَتْ وَلَيْسَ ٱلذَّكَرُ كَٱلْأُنثَىٰ ۖ

وَإِنِّى سَمَّيْتُهَا مَرْيَمَ وَإِنِّىٓ أُعِيذُهَا

بِكَ وَذُرِّيَّتَهَا مِنَ ٱلشَّيْطَٰنِ ٱلرَّجِيمِ ۝

فَتَقَبَّلَهَا رَبُّهَا بِقَبُولٍ حَسَنٍ

وَأَنۢبَتَهَا نَبَاتًا حَسَنًا وَكَفَّلَهَا

زَكَرِيَّا ۖ كُلَّمَا دَخَلَ عَلَيْهَا زَكَرِيَّا

ٱلْمِحْرَابَ وَجَدَ عِندَهَا رِزْقًا ۖ قَالَ

"O Mary! Wherefrom (comes) this to you?" She said: "From Allah: for Allah provides sustenance to whom He pleases without measure."

38. Zakariya prayed there to his Lord, saying: "O my Lord! Grant for me from You a progeny that is pure: for You are He that hears prayer!

39. While he was standing in prayer in the chamber, the angels called to him: "Allah does give you glad tidings of Yahya, confirming the truth of a Word from Allah, and be (besides) noble, chaste, and a prophet,- of the (goodly) company of the righteous."

40. He said: "O my Lord! How shall I have son, seeing I am very old, and my wife is barren?" "Thus," was the answer, "Does Allah accomplish what He wills."

41. He said: "O my Lord! Give me a Sign!" "Your Sign," was the answer, "Shall be that you shall speak to no man for three days but with signals. Then celebrate the praises of your Lord again and again, and glorify Him in the evening and in the morning."

42. Behold! the angels said: "O Mary! Allah has chosen you and purified you- chosen you above the women of all nations.

43. "O Mary! Worship your Lord devoutly: Prostrate yourself and bow down (in prayer) with those who bow down."

44. This is part of the tidings of the things unseen, which We reveal unto you (O Apostle!) by inspiration: You were not with them when they cast lots with arrows, as to which of them should be charged with the care of Marry;

yaa Maryamu annaa laki haazaa qaalat huwa min 'indil-laahi innal-laaha yarzuqu mañy-yashaaa'u bighayri ḥisaab.

38. Hunaaalika da'aa Zakariyyaa Rabbahoo qaala Rabbi hab lee mil-ladunka zurriyyatan ṭayyibatan innaka samee'ud-du'aaa'.

39. Fanaadat-hul-malaaa'ikatu wa huwa qaaa'imuñy-yuṣallee fil-Miḥraabi annal-laaha yubashshiruka bi-Yaḥyaa muṣaddiqam bi-Kalimatim-minal-laahi wa sayyidañw-wa ḥaṣoorañw-wa Nabiyyam minaṣ-ṣaaliheen.

40. Qaala Rabbi annaa yakoonu lee ghulaamuñw-wa qad balaghaniyal-kibaru wamra-atee 'aaqirun qaala kazaalikal-laahu yaf'alu maa yashaaa'

41. Qaala Rabbij-'al-leee Aayatan qaala Aayatuka allaa tukalliman-naasa salaasata ayyaamin illaa ramzaa; wazkur Rabbaka kaseerañw-wa sabbiḥ bil'ashiyyi wal-ibkaar. **(Section 4)**

42. Wa iz qaalatil-malaaa'ikatu yaa Maryamu innal-laahaṣ-ṭafaaki wa ṭahharaki waṣṭafaaki 'alaa nisaaa'il-'aalameen.

43. Yaa Maryamuq-nutee li-Rabbiki wasjudee warka'ee ma'ar-raaki'een.

44. Zaalika min ambaaa'il-ghaybi nooḥeehi ilayk; wa maa kunta ladayhim iz yulqoona aqlaamahum ayyuhum yakfulu Maryama

nor were you with them when they disputed (the point).

wa maa kunta ladayhim iz yakhtaşimoon.

وَمَا كُنْتَ لَدَيْهِمْ اِذْ يَخْتَصِمُوْنَ ۞

45. Behold! the angels said: "O Mary! Allah gives you glad tidings of a Word from Him: his name will be Christ Jesus, the son of Mary, held in honour in this world and the Hereafter and of (the company of) those nearest to Allah;

45. Iz qaalatil-malaaa'ikatu yaa Maryamu innal-laaha yubashshiruki bi-Kalimatim-minhus-muhul-Maseehu 'Eesab-nu-Maryama wajeehan fid-dunyaa wal-Aakhirati wa minal-muqarrabeen.

اِذْ قَالَتِ الْمَلَـٰئِكَةُ يَا مَرْيَمُ اِنَّ اللّٰهَ يُبَشِّرُكِ بِكَلِمَةٍ مِّنْهُ ۖ اسْمُهُ الْمَسِيْحُ عِيْسَى ابْنُ مَرْيَمَ وَجِيْهًا فِي الدُّنْيَا وَالْاٰخِرَةِ وَمِنَ الْمُقَرَّبِيْنَ ۞

46. "He shall speak to the people in infancy and in maturity. And he shall be (of the company) of the righteous."

46. Wa yukallimun-naasa filmahdi wa kahlaňw-wa minaşsaaliheen

وَيُكَلِّمُ النَّاسَ فِي الْمَهْدِ وَكَهْلًا وَّمِنَ الصَّالِحِيْنَ ۞

47. She said: "O my Lord! how shall I have a son when no man has touched me?" He said: "Even so: Allah creates what He wills: When He has decreed a Plan, He but says to it, 'Be,' and it is!

47. Qaalat Rabbi annaa yakoonu lee waladuňw-wa lam yamsasnee basharun qaala kazaalikil-laahu yakhluqu maa yashaaa'; izaa qadaaa amran fa-innamaa yaqoolu lahoo kun fa-yakoon.

قَالَتْ رَبِّ اَنّٰى يَكُوْنُ لِيْ وَلَدٌ وَّلَمْ يَمْسَسْنِيْ بَشَرٌ ۖ قَالَ كَذٰلِكِ اللّٰهُ يَخْلُقُ مَا يَشَاءُ ۚ اِذَا قَضٰى اَمْرًا فَاِنَّمَا يَقُوْلُ لَهٗ كُنْ فَيَكُوْنُ ۞

48. "And Allah will teach him the Book and Wisdom, the Torah and the Gospel,?

48. Wa yu'allimuhul-Kitaaba wal-Hikmata wat-Tawraata wal-Injeel.

وَيُعَلِّمُهُ الْكِتٰبَ وَالْحِكْمَةَ وَالتَّوْرٰةَ وَالْاِنْجِيْلَ ۞

49. "And (appoint him) an apostle to the Children of Israel, (with this message): "'I have come to you, with a Sign from your Lord, in that I make for you out of clay, as it were, the figure of a bird, and breathe into it, and it becomes a bird by Allah's leave: And I heal those born blind, and the lepers, and I quicken the dead, by Allah's leave; and I declare to you what you eat, and what you store in your houses. Surely therein is a Sign for you if you did believe;

49. Wa Rasoolan-ilaa Baneee Israaa'eela annee qad ji'tukum bi-Aayatim-mir-Rabbikum anneee akhluqu lakum minaţ-ţeeni kahay'atittayri fa-anfukhu feehi fayakoonu ţayram bi-iznil-laahi wa ubri'ul-akmaha wal-abraşa wa-uhyil-mawtaa bi-iznil-laahi wa unabbi'ukum bimaa taåkuloona wa maa taddakhiroona fee buyootikum; inna fee zaalika la-Aayatal-lakum in kuntum mu'mineen.

وَرَسُوْلًا اِلٰى بَنِيْ اِسْرَاءِيْلَ ۙ اَنِّيْ قَدْ جِئْتُكُمْ بِاٰيَةٍ مِّنْ رَّبِّكُمْ ۙ اَنِّيْ اَخْلُقُ لَكُمْ مِّنَ الطِّيْنِ كَهَيْئَةِ الطَّيْرِ فَاَنْفُخُ فِيْهِ فَيَكُوْنُ طَيْرًا بِاِذْنِ اللّٰهِ ۖ وَاُبْرِئُ الْاَكْمَهَ وَالْاَبْرَصَ وَاُحْيِ الْمَوْتٰى بِاِذْنِ اللّٰهِ ۖ وَاُنَبِّئُكُمْ بِمَا تَاْكُلُوْنَ وَمَا تَدَّخِرُوْنَ فِيْ بُيُوْتِكُمْ ۚ اِنَّ فِيْ ذٰلِكَ لَاٰيَةً لَّكُمْ اِنْ كُنْتُمْ مُّؤْمِنِيْنَ ۞

50. "'(I have come to you), to attest the Torah which was before me. And to make lawful to you part of what was (Before) forbidden to you; I have come to you with a Sign from

50. Wa muşaddiqal-limaa bayna yadayya minat-Tawraati wa li-uhilla lakum ba'dal-lazee hurrima 'alaykum; wa ji'tukum bi-Aayatim-mir-

وَمُصَدِّقًا لِّمَا بَيْنَ يَدَيَّ مِنَ التَّوْرٰةِ وَلِاُحِلَّ لَكُمْ بَعْضَ الَّذِيْ حُرِّمَ عَلَيْكُمْ ۚ وَجِئْتُكُمْ بِاٰيَةٍ مِّنْ

your Lord. So fear Allah, and obey me.

51. "'It is Allah Who is my Lord and your Lord; then worship Him. This is a Way that is straight.'"

52. When Jesus found unbelief on their part He said: "Who will be My helpers to (the work of) Allah?" Said the disciples: "We are Allah's helpers: We believe in Allah, and you bear witness that we are Muslims.

53. "Our Lord! we believe in what You have revealed, and we follow the Apostle; then write us down among those who bear witness."

54. And (the unbelievers) plotted and planned, and Allah too planned, and the best of planners is Allah.

55. Behold! Allah said: "O Jesus! I will take you and raise you to Myself and clear you (of the falsehoods) of those who blaspheme; I will make those who follow you superior to those who reject faith, to the Day of Resurrection: then shall you all return unto me, and I will judge between you of the matters wherein you dispute.

56. "As to those who reject faith, I will punish them with terrible agony in this world and in the Hereafter, nor will they have anyone to help."

57. "As to those who believe and work righteousness, Allah will pay them (in full) their reward; but Allah loves not those who do wrong."

58. "This is what we rehearse unto you of the Signs and the Message of Wisdom."

Rabbikum fattaqul-laaha wa ațee'oon.

51. Innal-laaha Rabbee wa Rabbukum fa'budooh; haazaa Şiraațum-Mustaqeem.

52. Falammaaa aḥassa 'Eesaa minhumul-kufra qaala man anṣaareee ilal-laahi qaalal-Ḥawaariyyoona naḥnu anṣaarul-laahi aamannaa billaahi washhad bi-annaa muslimoon.

53. Rabbanaaa aamannaa bimaaa anzalta wattaba'nar-Rasoola faktubnaa ma'ash-shaahideen.

54. Wa makaroo wa makaral-laahu wallaahu khayrul-maaki-reen.   (Section 5)

55. Iz qaalal-laahu yaa 'Eesaaa innee mutawaffeeka wa raafi'uka ilayya wa muṭah-hiruka minal-lazeena kafaroo wa jaa'ilul-lazeenattaba'ooka fawqal-lazeena kafarooo ilaa Yawmil-Qiyaamati şumma ilayya marji'ukum fa-aḥkumu baynakum feemaa kuntum feehi takhtalifoon.

56. Fa-ammal-lazeena kafaroo fa-u'az zibuhum 'azaaban shadeedan fiddunyaa wal-Aakhirati wa maa lahum min naaşireen.

57. Wa ammal-lazeena aamanoo wa 'amiluş-şaaliḥaati fa-yuwaffeehim ujoorahum; wallaahu laa yuḥibbuz-zaalimeen

58. Zaalika natloohu 'alayka minal-Aayaati waz-Zikril-Ḥakeem.

59. The similitude of Jesus before Allah is as that of Adam; He created him from dust, then said to him: "Be". And he was.

60. The Truth (comes) from Allah alone; so be not of those who doubt.

61. If any one disputes in this matter with you, now after (full) knowledge has come to you, say: "Come! let us gather together,- our sons and your sons, our women and your women, ourselves and yourselves: Then let us earnestly pray, and invoke the curse of Allah on those who lie!"

62. This is the true account: there is no god except Allah; and Allah-He is indeed the Exalted in Power, the Wise.

63. But if they turn back, Allah has full knowledge of those who do mischief.

64. Say: "O People of the Book! come to common terms as between us and you: That we worship none but Allah; that we associate no partners with him; that we erect not, from among ourselves, Lords and patrons other than Allah." If then they turn back, say you: "Bear witness that we (at least) are Muslims (bowing to Allah's Will).

65. You People of the Book! Why dispute you about Abraham, when the Torah and the Gospel Were not revealed till after him? Have you no understanding?

---

59. Inna maṣala 'Eesaa 'indal-laahi kamaṣali Aadama khalaqahoo min turaabin ṣumma qaala lahoo kun fa-yakoon.

60. Alḥaqqu mir-Rabbika falaa takum-minal-mumtareen.

61. Faman ḥaaajjaka feehi mim ba'di maa jaaa'aka minal-'ilmi faqul ta'aalaw nad'u abnaaa'anaa wa abnaaa'akum wa nisaaa'anaa wa nisaaa'akum wa anfusanaa wa anfusakum ṣumma nabtahil fanaj'al la'natal-laahi 'alal-kaaẕibeen.

62. Inna haaẕaa lahuwal-qaṣaṣul-ḥaqq; wa maa min ilaahin illal-laah; wa innal-laaha la-Huwal-'Azeezul-Ḥakeem.

63. Fa-in tawallaw fa-innal-laaha 'aleemum bil-mufsideen.
         (Section 6)

64. Qul yaaa Ahlal-Kitaabi ta'aalaw ilaa Kalimatin sawaaa'im baynanaa wa baynakum allaa na'buda illal-laaha wa laa nushrika bihee shay'añw-wa laa yattakhiẕa ba'ḍunaa ba'ḍan arbaabam-min doonil-laah; fa-in tawallaw faqoolush-hadoo bi-annaa muslimoon.

65. Yaaa Ahlal-Kitaabi lima tuhaaaajjoona feee Ibraaheema wa maaa unzilatit-Tawraatu wal-Injeelu illaa mim ba'dih; afalaa ta'qiloon.

اِنَّ مَثَلَ عِيْسٰى عِنْدَ اللّٰهِ كَمَثَلِ اٰدَمَ خَلَقَهٗ مِنْ تُرَابٍ ثُمَّ قَالَ لَهٗ كُنْ فَيَكُوْنُ ۝

اَلْحَقُّ مِنْ رَّبِّكَ فَلَا تَكُنْ مِّنَ الْمُمْتَرِيْنَ ۝

فَمَنْ حَاجَّكَ فِيْهِ مِنْ بَعْدِ مَا جَآءَكَ مِنَ الْعِلْمِ فَقُلْ تَعَالَوْا نَدْعُ اَبْنَآءَنَا وَاَبْنَآءَكُمْ وَنِسَآءَنَا وَنِسَآءَكُمْ وَاَنْفُسَنَا وَاَنْفُسَكُمْ ثُمَّ نَبْتَهِلْ فَنَجْعَلْ لَّعْنَتَ اللّٰهِ عَلَى الْكٰذِبِيْنَ ۝

اِنَّ هٰذَا لَهُوَ الْقَصَصُ الْحَقُّ وَمَا مِنْ اِلٰهٍ اِلَّا اللّٰهُ وَاِنَّ اللّٰهَ لَهُوَ الْعَزِيْزُ الْحَكِيْمُ ۝

فَاِنْ تَوَلَّوْا فَاِنَّ اللّٰهَ عَلِيْمٌ بِالْمُفْسِدِيْنَ ۝

قُلْ يٰاَهْلَ الْكِتٰبِ تَعَالَوْا اِلٰى كَلِمَةٍ سَوَآءٍ بَيْنَنَا وَبَيْنَكُمْ اَلَّا نَعْبُدَ اِلَّا اللّٰهَ وَلَا نُشْرِكَ بِهٖ شَيْئًا وَّلَا يَتَّخِذَ بَعْضُنَا بَعْضًا اَرْبَابًا مِّنْ دُوْنِ اللّٰهِ فَاِنْ تَوَلَّوْا فَقُوْلُوا اشْهَدُوْا بِاَنَّا مُسْلِمُوْنَ ۝

يٰاَهْلَ الْكِتٰبِ لِمَ تُحَآجُّوْنَ فِيْ اِبْرٰهِيْمَ وَمَا اُنْزِلَتِ التَّوْرٰىةُ وَالْاِنْجِيْلُ اِلَّا مِنْ بَعْدِهٖ اَفَلَا تَعْقِلُوْنَ ۝

66. Ah! You are those who fell to disputing (Even) in matters of which you had some knowledge! but why dispute you in matters of which you have no knowledge? It is Allah Who knows, and you who know not!

66. Haaa-antum haaa'ulaaa'i ḥaajagtum feemaa lakum bihee 'ilmun falima tuḥaaajjoona feemaa laysa lakum bihee 'ilm; wallaahu ya'lamu wa antum laa ta'lamoon.

67. Abraham was not a Jew nor yet a Christian; but he was true in Faith, and bowed his will to Allah's (Which is Islam), and he joined not gods with Allah.

67. Maa kaana Ibraaheemu Yahoodiyyañw-wa laa Naṣraaniyyañw-wa laakin kaana Ḥaneefam-Muslimañw wa maa kaana minal-mushrikeen.

68. Without doubt, among men, the nearest of kin to Abraham, are those who follow him, as are also this Apostle and those who believe: And Allah is the Protector of those who have Faith.

68. Inna awlan-naasi bi-Ibraaheema lallazeenat-taba-'oohu wa haazan-Nabiyyu wallazeena aamanoo; wallaahu waliyyul-mu'mineen.

69. It is the wish of a section of the People of the Book to lead you astray. But they shall lead astray (not you), but themselves, and they do not perceive!

69. Waddat-ṭaaa'ifatum-min Ahlil-Kitaabi law yuḍilloonakum wa maa yuḍilloona illaaa anfusahum wa maa yash'uroon.

70. You People of the Book! Why do you reject the Signs of Allah, of which you are (Yourselves) witnesses?

70. Yaaa Ahlal-Kitaabi lima takfuroona bi-Aayaatil-laahi wa antum tashhadoon.

71. You People of the Book! Why do you clothe Truth with falsehood, and conceal the Truth, while you have knowledge?

71. Yaaa Ahlal-Kitaabi lima talbisoonal-ḥaqqa bilbaaṭili wa taktumoonal-ḥaqqa wa antum ta'lamoon. **(Section 7)**

72. A section of the People of the Book say: "Believe in the morning what is revealed to the believers, but reject it at the end of the day; perchance they may (themselves) turn back;

72. Wa qaalat-ṭaaa'ifatum-min Ahlil-Kitaabi aaminoo billazeee unzila 'alal-lazeena aamanoo wajhan-nahaari wakfurooo aakhirahoo la'allahum yarji'oon.

73. "And believe no one unless he follows your religion." Say: "True guidance is the Guidance of Allah: (Fear you) lest a revelation be sent to someone (else) Like that which was sent unto you? or that those (receiving such revelation) should engage you in argument before your Lord?"

73. Wa laa tu'minooo illaa liman tabi'a deenakum qul innal-hudaa hudal-laahi añy-yu'taaa aḥadum-misla maaa ooteetum aw yuḥaaajjookum 'inda Rabbikum, qul innal-

Say: "All bounties are in the hand of Allah: He grants them to whom He pleases: And Allah cares for all, and He knows all things."

74. For His Mercy He specially chooses whom He pleases; for Allah is the Lord of bounties unbounded.

75. Among the People of the Book are some who, if entrusted with a hoard of gold, will (readily) pay it back; others, who, if entrusted with a single silver coin, will not repay it unless you constantly stood demanding, because, they say, "there is no call on us (to keep faith) with these ignorant (Pagans)." But they tell a lie against Allah, and (well) they know it.

76. Nay, those that keep their plighted faith and act aright, verily Allah loves those who act aright.

77. As for those who sell the faith they owe to Allah and their own plighted word for a small price, they shall have no portion in the Hereafter: nor will Allah speak to them or look at them on the Day of Judgment, nor will He cleans them (of sin): They shall have a grievous Chastisement.

78. There is among them a section who distort the Book with their tongues: (As they read) you would think it is a part of the Book, but it is no part of the Book; and they say, "That is from Allah," but it is not from Allah: It is they who tell a lie against Allah, and (well) they know it!

79. It is not (possible) that a man, to whom is given

faḍla biyadil-laah; yu'teehi mañy-yashaaa'; wallaahu Waasi'un 'Aleem.

74. Yakhtaṣṣu biraḥmatihee mañy-yashaaa'; wallaahu zulfaḍlil-'aẓeem.

75. Wa min Ahlil-Kitaabi man in taåmanhu biqinṭaariñy-yu'addiheee ilayka wa minhum man in taåmanhu bideenaaril-laa yu'addiheee ilayka illaa maa dumta 'alayhi qaaa'imaa; zaalika biannahum qaaloo laysa 'alaynaa fil-ummiyyeena sabeeluñw wa yaqooloona 'alal-laahil-kaziba wa hum ya'la-moon.

76. Balaa man awfaa bi'ahdihee wattaqaa fainnal-laaha yuḥibbul-muttaqeen.

77. Innal-laẓeena yashtaroona bi-'Ahdil-laahi wa aymaanihim samanan qaleelan ulaaa'ika laa khalaaqa lahum fil-Aakhirati wa laa yukallimuhumul-laahu wa laa yanẓuru ilayhim Yawmal-Qiyaamati wa laa yuzakkeehim wa lahum 'azaabun 'aleem.

78. Wa inna minhum lafaree-qañy-yalwoona alsinatahum bil-Kitaabi litaḥsaboohu minal-Kitaab, wa maa huwa minal-Kitaabi wa yaqooloona huwa min 'indillaahi wa maa huwa min 'indillaahi wa yaqooloona 'alal-laahil-kaziba wa hum ya'lamoon.

79. Maa kaana libasharin añy-yu'tiyahul-laahul-

the Book, and Wisdom, and the prophetic office, should say to people: "Be you my worshippers rather than Allah's": on the contrary (He would say) "Be you worshippers of Him Who is truly the Cherisher of all: for you had been taught by the Book, and as you read it still."	Kitaaba walḥukma wan-Nubuwwata summa yaqoola linnaasi koonoo 'ibaadal-lee min doonil-laahi wa laakin koonoo rabbaaniy-yeena bimaa kuntum tu'allimoonal-Kitaaba wa bimaa kuntum tadrusoon.	الْكِتٰبَ وَالْحُكْمَ وَالنَّبُوَّةَ ثُمَّ يَقُوْلَ لِلنَّاسِ كُوْنُوْا عِبَادًا لِّىْ مِنْ دُوْنِ اللّٰهِ وَلٰكِنْ كُوْنُوْا رَبَّانِيِّيْنَ بِمَا كُنْتُمْ تُعَلِّمُوْنَ الْكِتٰبَ وَبِمَا كُنْتُمْ تَدْرُسُوْنَۙ

80. Nor would he instruct you to take angels and prophets for Lords and patrons. What! would he bid you to unbelief after you have bowed your will (to Allah in Islam)?

80. Wa laa yaåmurakum an tattakhizul-malaaa'ikata wan-Nabiyyeena arbaabaa; a-yaå-murukum bilkufri ba'da iz antum muslimoon. (Section 8)

وَلَا يَاْمُرَكُمْ اَنْ تَتَّخِذُوا الْمَلٰٓئِكَةَ وَالنَّبِيّٖنَ اَرْبَابًا ؕ اَيَاْمُرُكُمْ بِالْكُفْرِ بَعْدَ اِذْ اَنْتُمْ مُّسْلِمُوْنَۧ

81. Behold! Allah took the Covenant of the Prophets, saying: "I give you a Book and Wisdom; then comes to you an Apostle, confirming what is with you; do you believe in him and render him help." Allah said: "Do you agree, and take this my Covenant as binding on you?" They said: "We agree." He said: "Then bear witness, and I am with you among the witnesses."

81. Wa iz akhazal-laahu meesaaqan-Nabiyyeena lamaaa aataytukum min Kitaabiñw-wa Ḥikmatin summa jaaa'akum Rasoolum-muṣaddiqul-limaa ma'akum latu'minunna bihee wa latanṣurunnah; qaala 'a-aqrartum wa akhaztum alaa zaalikum isree qaalooo aqrarnaa; qaala fashhadoo wa ana ma'akum minash-shaahideen.

وَاِذْ اَخَذَ اللّٰهُ مِيْثَاقَ النَّبِيّٖنَ لَمَاۤ اٰتَيْتُكُمْ مِّنْ كِتٰبٍ وَّحِكْمَةٍ ثُمَّ جَآءَكُمْ رَسُوْلٌ مُّصَدِّقٌ لِّمَا مَعَكُمْ لَتُؤْمِنُنَّ بِهٖ وَلَتَنْصُرُنَّهٗ ؕ قَالَ ءَاَقْرَرْتُمْ وَاَخَذْتُمْ عَلٰى ذٰلِكُمْ اِصْرِىْ ؕ قَالُوْۤا اَقْرَرْنَا ؕ قَالَ فَاشْهَدُوْا وَاَنَا مَعَكُمْ مِّنَ الشّٰهِدِيْنَ

82. If any turn back after this, they are perverted trans-gressors.

82. Faman tawallaa ba'da zaalika fa ulaaa'ika humul-faasiqoon.

فَمَنْ تَوَلّٰى بَعْدَ ذٰلِكَ فَاُولٰٓئِكَ هُمُ الْفٰسِقُوْنَ

83. Do they seek for other than the Religion of Allah?- While all creatures in the heavens and on the earth have, willingly or unwillingly, bowed to His Will (accepted Islam), and to Him shall they all be brought back.

83. Afaghayra deenil-laahi yabghoona wa lahooo aslama man fis-samaawaati wal-arḍi ṭaw'añw-wa karhañw-wa ilayhi yurja'oon.

اَفَغَيْرَ دِيْنِ اللّٰهِ يَبْغُوْنَ وَلَهٗۤ اَسْلَمَ مَنْ فِى السَّمٰوٰتِ وَالْاَرْضِ طَوْعًا وَّكَرْهًا وَّاِلَيْهِ يُرْجَعُوْنَ

84. Say: "We believe in Allah, and in what has been revealed to us and what was revealed to Abraham, Isma'il, Isaac, Jacob, and the Tribes, and in (the Books) given to Moses, Jesus, and the Prophets, from their Lord: we make no distinction between one and another among them, and to Allah do we bow our will (in Islam)."

84. Qul aamannaa billaahi wa maaa unzila 'alaynaa wa maaa unzila 'alaaa Ibraaheema wa Ismaa'eela wa Isḥaaqa wa Ya'qooba wal-Asbaaṭi wa maaa ootiya Moosaa wa 'Eesaa wan-Nabiyyoona mir-Rabbihim laa nufarriqu bayna aḥadim-minhum wa naḥnu lahoo muslimoon.

قُلْ اٰمَنَّا بِاللّٰهِ وَمَاۤ اُنْزِلَ عَلَيْنَا وَمَاۤ اُنْزِلَ عَلٰۤى اِبْرٰهِيْمَ وَاِسْمٰعِيْلَ وَاِسْحٰقَ وَيَعْقُوْبَ وَالْاَسْبَاطِ وَمَاۤ اُوْتِىَ مُوْسٰى وَعِيْسٰى وَالنَّبِيُّوْنَ مِنْ رَّبِّهِمْ ۖ لَا نُفَرِّقُ بَيْنَ اَحَدٍ مِّنْهُمْ ۖ وَنَحْنُ لَهٗ مُسْلِمُوْنَ

85. If anyone desires a religion other than Islam (submission to Allah), never will it be accepted of him; and in the Hereafter he will be in the ranks of those who have lost (All spiritual good).

86. How shall Allah guide those who reject Faith after they accepted it and bore witness that the Apostle was true and that Clear Signs had come unto them? But Allah guides not a people unjust.

87. Of such the reward is that on them (rests) the curse of Allah, of His angels, and of all mankind;-

88. In that will they dwell; nor will their Chastisement be lightened, nor respite be (their lot);-

89. Except for those that repent (even) after that, and make amends; for verily Allah is Oft-Forgiving, Most Merciful.

90. But those who reject Faith after they accepted it, and then go on adding to their defiance of Faith, - never will their repentance be accepted; for they are those who have (of set purpose) gone astray.

91. As to those who reject Faith, and die rejecting, - never would be accepted from any such as much gold as the earth contains, though they should offer it for ransom. For such is (in store) a Chastisement grievous, and they will find no helpers.

92. By no means shall you attain righteousness unless you give (freely) of that which you love; and whatever you give, of a truth Allah knows it well.

93. All food was lawful to the Children of Israel, except what Israel made unlawful for itself,

85. Wa mañy-yabtaghi ghayral-Islaami deenan falañy-yuqbala minhu wa huwa fil-Aakhirati minal-khaasireen.

86. Kayfa yahdil-laahu qawman kafaroo ba'da eemaanihim wa shahidooo annar-Rasoola ḥaqquñw-wa jaaa'ahumul-bayyinaat; wallaahu laa yahdil-qawmaz̧-z̧aalimeen.

87. Ulaaa'ika jazaaa'uhum anna 'alayhim la'natal-laahi walmalaaa'ikati wannaasi ajma'een.

88. Khaalideena feehaa laa yukhaffafu 'anhumul-'az̧aabu wa laa hum yunz̧aroon.

89. Illal-laz̧eena taaboo mim ba'di z̧aalika wa aṣlaḥoo fa-innal-laaha Ghafoorur-Raḥeem.

90. Innal-laz̧eena kafaroo ba'da eemaanihim s̱ummaz-daadoo kufral-lan tuqbala tawbatuhum wa ulaaa'ika humuḍ-ḍaalloon.

91. Innal-laz̧eena kafaroo wa maatoo wa hum kuffaarun falañy-yuqbala min aḥadihim mil'ul-arḍi z̧ahabañw-wa lawiftadaa bih; ulaaa'ika lahum 'az̧aabun aleemuñw-wa maa lahum min naaṣireen. (Section 9)

92. Lan tanaalul-birra ḥattaa tunfiqoo mimmaa tuḥibboon; wa maa tunfiqoo min shay'in fa-innal-laaha bihee 'Aleem.

93. Kulluṭ-ṭa'aami kaana ḥillal-li-Baneee Israaa'eela illaa maa ḥarrama Israaa'eelu 'alaa nafsihee min

before the Law (of Moses) was revealed. Say: "Bring you the Law and study it, if you be men of truth."

94. If any, after this, invent a lie and attribute it to Allah, they are indeed unjust wrong-doers.

95. Say: "Allah speaks the Truth: follow the religion of Abraham, the sane in faith; he was not of the Pagans."

96. The first House (of worship) appointed for men was that at Bakka (Makkah); full of blessing and of guidance for all kinds of beings:

97. In it are Signs manifest; (for example), the Station of Abraham; whoever enters it attains security; pilgrimage thereto is a duty men owe to Allah,- those who can afford the journey; but if any deny faith, Allah stands not in need of any of His creatures.

98. Say: "O People of the Book! Why do you reject the Signs of Allah, when Allah is Himself witness to all you do?"

99. Say: "O you People of the Book! Why do you obstruct those who believe, from the path of Allah, seeking to make it crooked, while you were yourselves witnesses (to Allah's Covenant)? But Allah is not unmindful of all that you do."

100. O you who believe! If you listen to a faction among the People of the Book, they would (indeed) render you apostates after you have believed!

101. And how would you deny Faith while unto you are rehearsed the Signs of Allah, and among you lives the Apostle? Whoever holds firmly to Allah will be shown

qabli an tunazzalat-Tawraah; qul faâtoo bit-Tawraati fatloohaaa in kuntum şaadiqeen.

94. Famanif-taraa 'alallaahilkaziba mim ba'di zaalika fa-ulaaa'ika humuz-zaalimoon.

95. Qul şadaqal-laah; fattabi'oo Millata Ibraaheema Ḥaneefañw wa maa kaana minal-mushrikeen.

96. Inna awwala Baytiñw-wuḍi'a linnaasi lallazee bi-Bakkata mubaarakañw-wa hudal-lil-'aalameen.

97. Feehi Aayaatum-bayyinaatum-Maqaamu Ibraaheema wa man dakhalahoo kaana aaminaa; wa lillaahi 'alan-naasi Hijjul-Bayti manis-taṭaa'a ilayhi sabeelaa; wa man kafara fa-innal-laaha ghaniyyun 'anil-'aalameen.

98. Qul yaaa Ahlal-Kitaabi lima takfuroona bi-Aayaatillaahi wallaahu shaheedun 'alaa maa ta'maloon.

99. Qul yaaa Ahlal-Kitaabi lima taşuddoona 'an sabeelil-laahi man aamana tabghoonahaa 'iwajañw-wa antum shuhadaaa'; wa mallaahu bighaafilin 'ammaa ta'maloon.

100. Yaaa-ayyuhal-lazeena aamanooo in tuṭee'oo faree-qam-minal-lazeena ootul-Kitaaba yaruddookum ba'da eemaanikum kaafireen.

101. Wa kayfa takfuroona wa antum tutlaa 'alaykum Aayaatul-laahi wa feekum Rasooluh; wa mañy-ya'taşim billaahi faqad hudiya

a Way that is straight.

102. O you who believe! Fear Allah as He should be feared, and die not except in a state of Islam.

103. And hold fast, all together, by the rope which Allah (stretches out for you), and be not divided among yourselves; and remember with gratitude Allah's favour on you; for you were enemies and He joined your hearts in love, so that by His Grace, you became brethren; and you were on the brink of the Pit of Fire, and He saved you from it. Thus Allah makes His Signs clear to you: that you may be guided.

104. Let there arise out of you a band of people inviting to all that is good, enjoining what is right, and forbidding what is wrong: they are the ones to attain felicity.

105. Be not like those who are divided amongst themselves and fall into disputations after receiving Clear Signs: for them is a dreadful Chastisement,-

106. On the Day when some faces will be (lit up with) white, and some faces will be (in the gloom of) black: to those whose faces will be black, (will be said): "Did you reject Faith after accepting it? Taste then the Chastisement for rejecting Faith."

107. But those whose faces will be (lit with) white,- they will be in (the light of) Allah's mercy: therein to dwell (for ever).

108. These are the Signs of Allah: We rehearse them to you in Truth: And Allah means no injustice to any of His creatures.

109. To Allah belongs all that is in the heavens and on earth: to Him do all questions go back (for decision).

---

ilaa Ṣiraaṭim-Mustaqeem.
(Section 10)

102. Yaaa ayyuhal-lazeena aamanut-taqul-laaha ḥaqqa tuqaatihee wa laa tamootunna illaa wa antum muslimoon.

103. Wa'taṣimoo bi-Ḥablil-laahi jamee'añw-wa laa tafarraqoo; wazkuroo ni'matal-laahi 'alaykum iz kuntum a'daaa'an fa-allafa bayna quloobikum fa-aṣbaḥtum bini'matihee ikhwaanañw wa kuntum 'alaa shafaa ḥufratim-minan-Naari fa-anqazakum minhaa; kazaalika yubayyinul-laahu lakum Aayaatihee la'allakum tahtadoon.

104. Waltakum-minkum ummatuñy-yad'oona ilal-khayri wa yaåmuroona bilma'roofi wa yanhawna 'anil-munkar; wa ulaaa'ika humul-mufliḥoon.

105. Wa laa takoonoo kalla-zeena tafarraqoo wakhtalafoo mim ba'di maa jaaa'ahumul-bayyinaat; wa ulaaa'ika lahum 'azaabun 'azeem.

106. Yawma tabyaḍḍu wujoo-huñw-wa taswaddu wujooh; fa-ammal-lazeenas-waddat wujoohuhum akafartum ba'da eemaanikum fazooqul-'azaaba bimaa kuntum takfuroon.

107. Wa ammal-lazeenabyaḍ-ḍat wujoohuhum fafee raḥmatil-laahi hum feehaa khaalidoon.

108. Tilka Aayaatul-laahi natloohaa 'alayka bilḥaqq; wa mal-laahu yureedu ẓulmallil-'aalameen.

109. Wa lillaahi maa fissamaa-waati wa maa fil-arḍ; wa ilal-laahi turja'ul-umoor.
(Section 11)

110. You are the best of peoples, evolved for mankind, enjoining what is right, forbidding what is wrong, and believing in Allah. If only the People of the Book had faith, it were best for them: among them are some who have faith, but most of them are perverted transgressors.

111. They will do you no harm, barring a trifling annoyance; if they come out to fight you, they will show you their backs, and no help shall they get.

112. Shame is pitched over them (like a tent) wherever they are found, except when under a covenant (of protection) from Allah and from men; they draw on themselves wrath from Allah, and pitched over them is (the tent of) destitution. This because they rejected the Signs of Allah, and slew the Prophets in defiance of right; this because they rebelled and transgressed beyond bounds.

113. Not all of them are alike: of the People of the Book are a portion that stand (for the right): they rehearse the Signs of Allah all night long, and they prostrate themselves in adoration.

114. They believe in Allah and the Last Day; they enjoin what is right, and forbid what is wrong; and they hasten (in emulation) in (all) good works: they are in the ranks of the righteous.

115. Of the good that they do, nothing will be rejected of them; for Allah knows well those that do right.

116. Those who reject Faith,- neither their possessions nor their (numerous) progeny will avail them anything against Allah:

---

110. Kuntum khayra ummatin ukhrijat linnaasi taâmuroona bilma'roofi wa tanhawna 'anil-munkari wa tu'minoona billaah; wa law aamana Ahlul-Kitaabi lakaana khayral-lahum; minhumul-mu'minoona wa aksaruhumul-faasiqoon.

111. Lañy-yaḍurrookum 'illaaa azañw wa iñy-yuqaatilookum yuwallookumul-adbaara ṣumma laa yunṣaroon.

112. Ḍuribat 'alayhimuz zillatu ayna maa ṣuqifooo illaa biḥablim-minal-laahi wa ḥab-lim-minan-naasi wa baaa'oo bighaḍabim-minallaahi wa ḍuribat 'alayhimul-maskanah; ẕaalika bi-annahum kaanoo yakfuroona bi-Aayaatil-laahi wa yaqtuloonal-Ambiyaaa'a bighayri ḥaqq; ẕaalika bimaa 'aṣaw wa kaanoo ya'tadoon.

113. Laysoo sawaaa'a; min Ahlil-Kitaabi ummatun qaaa'imatuñy-yatloona Aayaatil-laahi aanaaa'al-layli wa hum yasjudoon.

114. Yu'minoona billaahi wal-Yawmil-Aakhiri wa yaâ-muroona bilma'roofi wa yanhawna 'anil-munkari wa yusaari'oona fil-khayraati wa ulaaa'ika minaṣ-ṣaaliheen.

115. Wa maa yaf'aloo min khayrin falañy-yukfarooh; wallaahu 'aleemum bilmut-taqeen.

116. Innal-laẕeena kafaroo lan tughniya 'anhum amwaaluhum wa laaa awlaaduhum minal-laahi

---

كُنتُمْ خَيْرَ أُمَّةٍ أُخْرِجَتْ لِلنَّاسِ
تَأْمُرُونَ بِٱلْمَعْرُوفِ وَتَنْهَوْنَ عَنِ
ٱلْمُنكَرِ وَتُؤْمِنُونَ بِٱللَّهِ ۗ وَلَوْ ءَامَنَ
أَهْلُ ٱلْكِتَٰبِ لَكَانَ خَيْرًا لَّهُم ۚ مِّنْهُمُ
ٱلْمُؤْمِنُونَ وَأَكْثَرُهُمُ ٱلْفَٰسِقُونَ ۝
لَن يَضُرُّوكُمْ إِلَّآ أَذًى ۖ وَإِن
يُقَٰتِلُوكُمْ يُوَلُّوكُمُ ٱلْأَدْبَارَ
ثُمَّ لَا يُنصَرُونَ ۝
ضُرِبَتْ عَلَيْهِمُ ٱلذِّلَّةُ أَيْنَ مَا
ثُقِفُوٓا۟ إِلَّا بِحَبْلٍ مِّنَ ٱللَّهِ وَحَبْلٍ
مِّنَ ٱلنَّاسِ وَبَآءُو بِغَضَبٍ مِّنَ ٱللَّهِ
وَضُرِبَتْ عَلَيْهِمُ ٱلْمَسْكَنَةُ ۚ ذَٰلِكَ
بِأَنَّهُمْ كَانُوا۟ يَكْفُرُونَ بِـَٔايَٰتِ ٱللَّهِ
وَيَقْتُلُونَ ٱلْأَنۢبِيَآءَ بِغَيْرِ حَقٍّ ۚ ذَٰلِكَ
بِمَا عَصَوا۟ وَّكَانُوا۟ يَعْتَدُونَ ۝
لَيْسُوا۟ سَوَآءً ۗ مِّنْ أَهْلِ ٱلْكِتَٰبِ أُمَّةٌ
قَآئِمَةٌ يَتْلُونَ ءَايَٰتِ ٱللَّهِ ءَانَآءَ ٱلَّيْلِ
وَهُمْ يَسْجُدُونَ ۝
يُؤْمِنُونَ بِٱللَّهِ وَٱلْيَوْمِ ٱلْءَاخِرِ
وَيَأْمُرُونَ بِٱلْمَعْرُوفِ وَيَنْهَوْنَ
عَنِ ٱلْمُنكَرِ وَيُسَٰرِعُونَ فِى ٱلْخَيْرَٰتِ
وَأُو۟لَٰٓئِكَ مِنَ ٱلصَّٰلِحِينَ ۝
وَمَا يَفْعَلُوا۟ مِنْ خَيْرٍ فَلَن يُكْفَرُوهُ ۗ
وَٱللَّهُ عَلِيمٌۢ بِٱلْمُتَّقِينَ ۝
إِنَّ ٱلَّذِينَ كَفَرُوا۟ لَن تُغْنِىَ عَنْهُمْ
أَمْوَٰلُهُمْ وَلَآ أَوْلَٰدُهُم مِّنَ ٱللَّهِ

they will be companions of the Fire,- dwelling therein (for ever).

117. What they spend in the life of this (material) world may be likened to a wind which brings a nipping frost: it strikes and destroys the harvest of men who have wronged their own souls:it is not Allah that has wronged them, but they wrong themselves.

118. O you who believe! take not into your intimacy those outside your ranks: they will not fail to corrupt you. They only desire your ruin: rank hatred has already appeared from their mouths: what their hearts conceal is far worse. We have made plain to you the Signs, if you have wisdom.

119. Ah! you are those who love them, but they love you not,- though you believe in the whole of the Book. When they meet you, they say, "We believe": but when they are alone, they bite off the very tips of their fingers at you in their rage. Say: "Perish in you rage; Allah knows well all the secrets of the heart."

120. If anything that is good befalls you, it grieves them; but if some misfortune overtakes you, they rejoice at it. But if you are constant and do right, not the least harm will their cunning do to you; for Allah compasses round about all that they do.

121. Remember that morning you left your household (early) to post the faithful at their stations for battle: and Allah hears and knows all things:

shay'añw wa ulaaa'ika Aṣḥaabun-Naar; hum feehaa khaalidoon.

117. Maṣalu maa yunfiqoona fee haazihil-ḥayaatid-dunyaa kamaṣali reeḥin feehaa ṣirrun aṣaabat ḥarsa qawmin ẓalamooo anfusahum fa-ahlakath; wa maa ẓalamahumul-laahu wa laakin anfusahum yaẓlimoon.

118. Yaaa ayyuhal-lazeena aamanoo laa tattakhizoo biṭaanatam-min doonikum laa yaåloonakum khabaalañw waddoo maa 'anittum qad badatil-baghḍaaa'u min afwaahihim; wa maa tukhfee ṣudooruhum akbar; qad bayyannaa lakumul-Aayaati in kuntum ta'qiloon.

119. Haaa-antum ulaaa'i tuḥib-boonahum wa laa yuḥibboo-nakum wa tu'minoona bil-Kitaabi kullihee wa izaa laqookum qaalooo aamannaa wa izaa khalaw 'addoo 'alaykumul-anaamila minal-ghayẓ; qul mootoo bighay-ẓikum; innal-laaha 'aleemum bizaatiṣ-ṣudoor.

120. In tamsaskum ḥasanatun tasu'hum wa in tuṣibkum sayyi'atuñy-yafraḥoo bihaa wa in taṣbiroo wa tattaqoo laa yaḍurrukum kayduhum shay'aa; innal-laaha bimaa ya'maloona muḥeet. **(Section 12)**

121. Wa iz ghadawta min ahlika tubawwi'ul-mu'mineena maqaa'ida lilqitaal; wallaahu Samee'un 'Aleem.

122. Remember two of your parties meditated cowardice; but Allah was their Protector, and in Allah the faithful should (ever) put their trust.

123. Allah had helped you at Badr, when you were a insignificant little force; then fear Allah; thus you may show your gratitude.

124. Remember you said to the Faithful: "Is it not enough for you that Allah should help you with three thousand angels (Specially) sent down?

125. "Yes, - if you remain firm, and act aright, even if the enemy should rush here on you in hot haste, your Lord would help you with five thousand angels making a terrific onslaught.

126. Allah made it but a message of hope for you, and an assurance to your hearts: (in any case) there is no help except from Allah, the Exalted, the Wise:

127. That He might cut off a fringe of the Unbelievers or expose them to infamy, and they should then be turned back, frustrated of their purpose.

128. Not for you, (but for Allah), is the decision: whether He turn in mercy to them, or punish them; for they are indeed wrong-doers.

129. To Allah belongs all that is in the heavens and on earth. He forgives whom He pleases and punishes whom He pleases; but Allah is Oft-Forgiving, Most Merciful.

130. O you who believe! Devour not interest, doubled and multiplied; but fear Allah; that you may (really) prosper.

---

122. Iz hammaṭ-ṭaaa'ifataani minkum an tafshalaa wallaahu waliyyuhumaa; wa 'alal-laahi falyatawakkalil-mu'minoon.

123. Wa laqad naṣarakumullaahu bi-Badriñw-wa antum azillatun fattaqul-laaha la'allakum tashkuroon.

124. Iz taqoolu lilmu'mineena alañy-yakfiyakum añy-yumiddakum Rabbukum bisalaasati aaalaafim-minal-malaaa'ikati munzaleen.

125. Balaaa; in taṣbiroo wa tattaqoo wa yaaatookum min fawrihim haazaa yumdidkum Rabbukum bikhamsati aaalaafim-minal-malaaa'ikati musawwimeen.

126. Wa maa ja'alahul-laahu illaa bushraa lakum wa litaṭma'inna quloobukum bih; wa man-naṣru illaa min 'indillaahil-'Azeezil-Ḥakeem.

127. Liyaqṭa'a ṭarafam-minallazeena kafarooo aw yakbitahum fayanqaliboo khaaa'ibeen.

128. Laysa laka minal-amri shay'un aw yatooba 'alayhim aw yu'az-zi-bahum fa innahum zaalimoon.

129. Wa lillaahi maa fissamaawaati wa maa fil-arḍ; yaghfiru limañy-yashaaa'u wa yu'azzibu mañy-yashaaa'; wallaahu Ghafoorur-Raḥeem. **(Section 13)**

130. Yaaa ayyuhal-lazeena aamanoo laa taaakulur-ribaaa aḍ'aafam-muḍaa'afatañw wattaqul-laaha la'allakum tufliḥoon.

131. Fear the Fire, which is prepared for those who reject Faith:

132. And obey Allah and the Apostle; that you may obtain mercy.

133. Be quick in the race for seeking forgiveness from your Lord, and for a Garden whose width is that (of the whole) of the heavens and of the earth, prepared for the righteous,-

134. Those who spend (freely), whether in prosperity, or in adversity; who restrain anger, and pardon (all) men; - for Allah loves those who do good,-

135. And those who, having done something to be ashamed of, or wronged their own souls, earnestly bring Allah to mind, and ask for forgiveness for their sins, - and who can forgive sins except Allah? - and are never obstinate in persisting knowingly in (the wrong) they have done.

136. For such the reward is forgiveness from their Lord, and Gardens with rivers flowing underneath,- an eternal dwelling: how excellent a recompense for those who work (and strive)!

137. Many were the Ways of Life that have passed away before you: travel through the earth, and see what was the end of those who rejected Truth.

138. Here is a plain statement to men, a guidance and instruction to those who fear Allah.

139. So lose not heart, nor fall into despair: for you must gain mastery if you are true in Faith.

131. Wattaqun-Naaral-lateee u'iddat lilkaafireen.

132. Wa atee'ul-laaha war-Rasoola la'allakum turhamoon.

133. Wa saari'ooo ilaa maghfiratim-mir-Rabbikum wa-Jannatin arduhassamaawaatu wal-ardu u'iddat lilmuttaqeen.

134. Allazeena yunfiqoona fis-sarraa'i waddarraaa'i wal-kaazimeenal-ghayza wal-aafeena 'anin-naas; wallaahu yuhibbul-muhsineen.

135. Wallazeena izaa fa'aloo faahishatan aw zalamooo anfusahum zakarul-laaha fastaghfaroo lizunoobihim; wa many-yaghfiruz-zunooba illal-laahu wa lam yusirroo 'alaa maa fa'aloo wa hum ya'lamoon.

136. Ulaaa'ika jazaaa'uhum maghfiratum-mir-Rabbihim wa Jannaatun tajree min tahtihal-anhaaru khaalideena feehaa; wa ni'ma ajrul-'aamileen.

137. Qad khalat min qablikum sunanun faseeroo fil-ardi fanzuroo kayfa kaana 'aaqibatul-mukazzibeen

138. Haazaa bayaanul-linnaasi wa hudanw-wa maw'izatul-lilmuttaqeen.

139. Wa laa tahinoo wa laa tahzanoo wa antumul-a'lawna in kuntum mu'mineen.

140. If a wound has touched you, be sure a similar wound has touched the others. Such days (of varying fortunes) We give to men and men by turns: that Allah may know those that believe, and that He may take to Himself from your ranks Martyr-witnesses (to Truth). And Allah loves not those that do wrong.

141. Allah's object also is to purge those that are true in Faith and to deprive of blessing those that resist Faith.

142. Did you think that you would enter Heaven without Allah testing those of you who fought hard (in His Cause) and remained steadfast?

143. You did indeed wish for death before you met him: now you have seen him with your own eyes, (and you flinch!)

144. Muhammad is no more than an Apostle: many were the Apostles that passed away before him. If he died or were slain, will you then turn back on your heels? If any did turn back on his heels, not the least harm will he do to Allah; but Allah (on the other hand) will swiftly reward those who (serve Him) with gratitude.

145. Nor can a soul die except by Allah's leave, the term being fixed as by writing. If any do desire a reward in this life, We shall give it to him; and if any do desire a reward in the Hereafter, We shall give it to him. And swiftly shall We reward those that (serve Us with) gratitude.

146. How many of the prophets fought (in Allah's way), and with them (fought) large bands of godly men? But they never lost heart if they

140. Iñy-yamsaskum qarḥun faqad massal-qawma qarḥum misluh; wa tilkal-ayyaamu nudaawiluhaa baynan-naasi wa liya'lamal-laahul-lazeena aamanoo wa yattakhiza minkum shuhadaaa'; wallaahu laa yuḥibbuz-zaalimeen.

141. Wa liyumaḥḥiṣal-laahul-lazeena aamanoo wa yamḥaqal-kaafireen.

142. Am ḥasibtum an tadkhulul-Jannata wa lammaa ya'lamil-laahul-lazeena jaahadoo minkum wa ya'lamaṣ-ṣaabireen.

143. Wa laqad kuntum tamannawnal-mawta min qabli an talqawhu faqad ra-aytumoohu wa antum tanzuroon. (Section 14)

144. Wa maa Muḥammadun illaa Rasoolun qad khalat min qablihir-Rusul; afa'im-maata aw qutilan-qalabtum 'alaaa a'qaabikum; wa mañy-yanqalib 'alaa-aqibayhi falañy-yaḍurral-laaha shay'aa; wa sayajzil-laahush-shaakireen.

145. Wa maa kaana linafsin an tamoota illaa bi-iznillaahi kitaabam-mu'ajjalaa; wa mañy-yurid sawaabad-dunyaa nu'tihee minhaa wa mañy-yurid sawaabal-Aakhirati nu'tihee minhaa; wa sanajzish-shaakireen.

146. Wa ka-ayyim-min Nabiyyin qaatala ma'ahoo ribbiyyoona kaseerun famaa wahanoo limaaa

met with disaster in Allah's way, nor did they weaken (in will) nor give in. And Allah loves those who are firm and steadfast.

147. All that they said was: "Our Lord! forgive us our sins and anything we may have done that transgressed our duty: establish our feet firmly, and help us against those that resist Faith."

148. And Allah gave them a reward in this world, and the excellent reward of the Hereafter. For Allah loves those who do good.

149. O you who believe! If you obey the Unbelievers, they will drive you back on your heels, and you will turn back (from Faith) to your own loss.

150. No, Allah is your protector, and He is the best of helpers.

151. Soon shall We cast terror into the hearts of the Unbelievers, for that they joined companions with Allah, for which He had sent no authority: their abode will be the Fire: and evil is the home of the wrong-doers!

152. Allah did indeed fulfil His promise to you when you with His permission were about to annihilate your enemy, - until you flinched and fell to disputing about the order, and disobeyed it after He brought you in sight (of the booty) which you covet. Among you are some that hanker after this world and some that desire the Hereafter. Then He diverted you from your foes in order to test you. But

Aṣaabahum fee sabeelil-laahi wa maa ḍa'ufoo wa mas-takaanoo; wallaahu yuḥibbuṣ-ṣaabireen.

147. Wa maa kaana qawlahum illaaa an qaaloo Rabbanagh-fir lanaa zunoobanaa wa israafanaa feee amrinaa wa sabbit aqdaamanaa wanṣurnaa 'alal-qawmil-kaafireen.

148. Fa-aataahumul-laahu sawaabad-dunyaa wa ḥusna sawaabil-Aakhirah; wallaahu yuḥibbul-muḥsineen. **(Section 15)**

149. Yaaa ayyuhal-lazeena aamanooo in tuṭee'ullazeena kafaroo yaruddookum 'alaaa a'qaabikum fatanqaliboo khaasireen.

150. Balil-laahu mawlaakum wa Huwa khayrun-naaṣireen.

151. Sanulqee fee quloobil-lazeena kafarur-ru'ba bimaaa ashrakoo billaahi maa lam yunazzil bihee sulṭaana(ñw)wa maaawaahumun-Naar; wa bi'sa maswaz-zaalimeen.

152. Wa laqad ṣadaqakumul-laahu wa'dahooo iz taḥussoo-nahum bi-iznihee ḥattaaa-izaa fashiltum wa tanaaza'tum fil-amri wa 'aṣaytum mim ba'di maaa araakum maa tuḥibboon; minkum mañy-yureedud-dunyaa wa minkum mañy-yureedul-Aakhirah; summa sarafakum 'anhum liyabtaliyakum wa laqad

He forgave you: for Allah is full of grace to those who believe.

153. Behold! you were climbing up the high ground, without even casting a side glance at any one, and the Apostle in your rear was calling you back. There did Allah give you one distress after another by way of requital, to teach you not to grieve for (the booty) that had escaped you and for (the ill) that had befallen you. For Allah is well aware of all that you do.

154. After (the excitement) of the distress, He sent down calm on a band of you overcome with slumber, while another band was stirred to anxiety by their own feelings, moved by wrong suspicions of Allah-suspicions due to ignorance. They said: "What affair is this of ours?" Say you: "Indeed, this affair is wholly Allah's." They hide in their minds what they dare not reveal to you. They say (to themselves): "If we had had anything to do with this affair, We should not have been in the slaughter here ." Say: "Even if you had remained in your homes, those for whom death was decreed would certainly have gone forth to the place of their death"; but (all this was) that Allah might test what is in your breasts and purge what is in your hearts. For Allah knows well the secrets of your hearts.

155. Those of you who turned back on the day the two hosts met - it was Satan who caused them to fail, because of some (evil) they had done. But Allah has blotted out (their fault): for Allah is

'afaa 'ankum; wallaahu zoo fadlin 'alal-mu'mineen.

153. Iz tuṣ'idoona wa laa talwoona 'alaaa aḥadiñw-war-Rasoolu yad'ookum feee ukhraakum fa-aṣaabakum ghammam bighammil-likaylaa taḥzanoo 'alaa maa faatakum wa laa maaa aṣaabakum; wallaahu khabeerum bimaa ta'maloon.

154. Summa anzala 'alaykum mim ba'dil-ghammi-amanatan nu'aasañy-yaghshaa ṭaaa'ifatam-minkum wa ṭaaa'ifatun qad ahammathum anfusuhum yaẓunnoona billaahi ghayral-ḥaqqi ẓannal-Jaahiliyyati yaqooloona hal lanaa minal-amri min shay'; qul-innal-amra kullahoo lillaah; yukhfoona feee anfusihim-maa laa yubdoona laka yaqooloona law kaana lanaa minal-amri shay'ummaa qutilnaa haahunaa; qul law kuntum fee buyootikum labarazal-lazeena kutiba 'alayhimul-qatlu ilaa maḍaaji'ihim wa liyabtaliyal-laahu maa fee ṣudoorikum wa liyumaḥḥiṣa maa fee quloobikum; wallaahu 'alee-mum biẓaatiṣ-ṣudoor.

155. Innal-lazeena tawallaw minkum yawmal-taqal jam'aani innamas tazallahumush-Shayṭaanu biba'ḍi maa kasaboo wa laqad 'afal-laahu 'anhum; innal-laaha

Oft-Forgiving, Most Forbearing.

156. O you who believe! Be not like the Unbelievers, who say of their brethren, when they are travelling through the Earth or engaged in fighting: "If they had stayed with us, they would not have died, or been slain." This that Allah may make it a cause of sighs and regrets in their hearts. It is Allah that gives Life and Death, and Allah sees well all that you do.

157. And if you are slain, or die, in the way of Allah, forgiveness and mercy from Allah are far better than all they could amass.

158. And if you die, or are slain, Lo! it is unto Allah that you are brought together.

159. It is part of the Mercy of Allah that you deal gently with them. If you were severe or harsh-hearted, they would have broken away from about you: so pass over (their faults), and ask for (Allah's) forgiveness for them; and consult them in affairs (of moment). Then, when you has taken a decision put your trust in Allah. For Allah loves those who put their trust (in Him).

160. If Allah helps you, none can overcome you: If He forsakes you, who is there, after that, that can help you? In Allah, then, let Believers put their trust.

161. No prophet could (ever) be false to his trust. If any person is so false, he shall, on the Day of Judgment, restore what he misappropriated; then shall every soul receive its due, whatever it earned,-

---

Ghafoorun Ḥaleem. (Section 16)

156. Yaaa-ayyuhal-lazeena aamanoo laa takoonoo kallazeena kafaroo wa qaaloo li-ikhwaanihim-izaa ḍaraboo fil-arḍi aw kaanoo ghuzzal-law kaanoo 'indanaa maa maatoo wa maa qutiloo liyaj'alal-laahu zaalika ḥasratan fee quloobihim; wallaahu yuḥyee wa yumeet; wallaahu bimaa ta'maloona Baṣeer.

157. Wa la'in qutiltum fee sabeelil-laahi aw muttum lamaghfiratum-minal-laahi wa raḥmatun khayrum-mimmaa yajma'oon.

158. Wa la'im-muttum 'aw qutiltumla-ilal-laahi tuḥsharoon.

159. Fabimaa raḥmatim-minal-laahi linta lahum wa law kunta fazzan ghaleezal-qalbi lanfaḍḍoo min ḥawlika fa'fu 'anhum wastaghfir lahum wa shaawirhum fil-amri fa-izaa 'azamta fatawakkal 'alal-laah; innallaaha yuḥibbul-mutawakkileen.

160. Iñy-yanṣurkumul-laahu falaa ghaaliba lakum wa iñy-yakhzulkum faman zal-lazee yanṣurukum mim ba'dih; wa 'alal-laahi falyatawakkalil-mu'minoon.

161. Wa maa kaana li-Nabiyyin añy-yaghull; wa mañy-yaghlul ya`ti bimaa ghalla Yawmal-Qiyaamah; ṣumma tuwaffaa kullu nafsim-maa kasabat

---

غَفُوْرٌ حَلِيْمٌ ۝

يٰٓاَيُّهَا الَّذِيْنَ اٰمَنُوْا لَا تَكُوْنُوْا كَالَّذِيْنَ كَفَرُوْا وَقَالُوْا لِاِخْوَانِهِمْ اِذَا ضَرَبُوْا فِي الْاَرْضِ اَوْ كَانُوْا غُزًّى لَّوْ كَانُوْا عِنْدَنَا مَا مَاتُوْا وَمَا قُتِلُوْا ۚ لِيَجْعَلَ اللّٰهُ ذٰلِكَ حَسْرَةً فِيْ قُلُوْبِهِمْ ۗ وَاللّٰهُ يُحْيٖ وَيُمِيْتُ ۗ وَاللّٰهُ بِمَا تَعْمَلُوْنَ بَصِيْرٌ ۝

وَلَئِنْ قُتِلْتُمْ فِيْ سَبِيْلِ اللّٰهِ اَوْ مُتُّمْ لَمَغْفِرَةٌ مِّنَ اللّٰهِ وَرَحْمَةٌ خَيْرٌ مِّمَّا يَجْمَعُوْنَ ۝

وَلَئِنْ مُّتُّمْ اَوْ قُتِلْتُمْ لَاِلَى اللّٰهِ تُحْشَرُوْنَ ۝

فَبِمَا رَحْمَةٍ مِّنَ اللّٰهِ لِنْتَ لَهُمْ ۚ وَلَوْ كُنْتَ فَظًّا غَلِيْظَ الْقَلْبِ لَانْفَضُّوْا مِنْ حَوْلِكَ ۖ فَاعْفُ عَنْهُمْ وَاسْتَغْفِرْ لَهُمْ وَشَاوِرْهُمْ فِي الْاَمْرِ ۚ فَاِذَا عَزَمْتَ فَتَوَكَّلْ عَلَى اللّٰهِ ۗ اِنَّ اللّٰهَ يُحِبُّ الْمُتَوَكِّلِيْنَ ۝

اِنْ يَّنْصُرْكُمُ اللّٰهُ فَلَا غَالِبَ لَكُمْ ۚ وَاِنْ يَّخْذُلْكُمْ فَمَنْ ذَا الَّذِيْ يَنْصُرُكُمْ مِّنْ بَعْدِهٖ ۗ وَعَلَى اللّٰهِ فَلْيَتَوَكَّلِ الْمُؤْمِنُوْنَ ۝

وَمَا كَانَ لِنَبِيٍّ اَنْ يَّغُلَّ ۚ وَمَنْ يَّغْلُلْ يَأْتِ بِمَا غَلَّ يَوْمَ الْقِيٰمَةِ ۚ ثُمَّ تُوَفّٰى كُلُّ نَفْسٍ مَّا كَسَبَتْ

and none shall be dealt with unjustly.

162. Is the man who follows the good pleasure of Allah like the man who draws on himself the wrath of Allah, and whose abode is in Hell?- A woeful refuge!

163. They are in varying grades in the sight of Allah, and Allah sees well all that they do.

164. Allah did confer a great favour on the believers when He sent among them an Apostle from among themselves, rehearsing unto them the Signs of Allah, sanctifying them, and instructing them in Scripture and Wisdom, while, before that, they had been in manifest error.

165. What! When a single disaster smites you, although you smote (your enemies) with one twice as great, do you say?- "Wherefrom is this?" Say (to them): "It is from yourselves: for Allah has power over all things."

166. What you suffered on the day the two armies met, was with the leave of Allah, in order that He might test the Believers,

167. And the Hypocrites also. These were told: "Come, fight in the way of Allah, or (at least) drive (the foe from your city)." They said: "Had we known there would be a fight, we should certainly have followed you." They were that day nearer to Unbelief than to Faith, saying with their lips what was not in their hearts. But Allah has full knowledge of all they conceal.

168. (They are) the ones that say, (of their brethren slain), while they themselves sit (at ease): "If only they had listened to us they would not have been slain." Say: "Avert

---

wa hum laa yuẓlamoon.

162. Afamanit-taba'a Riḍwaa-nal-laahi kamam baaa'a bisakhaṭim-minal-laahi wa maa-waahu Jahannam; wa bi'sal-maṣeer.

63. Hum darajaatun 'indal-laah; wallaahu baṣeerum bimaa ya'maloon.

164. Laqad mannal-laahu 'alal-mu'mineena iz ba'asa feehim Rasoolam-min anfusihim yatloo 'alayhim Aayaatihee wa yuzakkeehim wa yu'allimu-humul-Kitaaba walḤikmata wa in kaanoo min qablu lafee ḍalaalim mubeen.

165. Awa lammaaa aṣaabat-kum muṣeebatun qad aṣabtum mislayhaa qultum annaa haazaa qul huwa min 'indi anfusikum; innal-laaha 'alaa kulli shay'in Qadeer.

166. Wa maaa aṣaabakum yawmal-taqal-jam'aani fabi-iznil-laahi wa liya'lamal-mu'mineen.

167. Wa liya'lamal-lazeena naafaqoo; wa qeela lahum ta'aalaw qaatiloo fee sabeelil-laahi awid-fa'oo qaaloo law na'lamu qitaalallat-taba'naa-kum; hum lilkufri yawma'izin aqrabu minhum lil-eemaan; yaqooloona bi-afwaahihim maa laysa fee quloobihim; wallaahu a'lamu bimaa yaktumoon.

168. Allazeena qaaloo li-ikhwaanihim wa qa'adoo law aṭaa'oonaa maa qutiloo; qul fadra'oo 'an

---

وَهُمْ لَا يُظْلَمُونَ ۝

أَفَمَنِ اتَّبَعَ رِضْوَانَ اللهِ كَمَنۢ بَآءَ بِسَخَطٍ مِّنَ اللهِ وَمَأْوَاهُ جَهَنَّمُ ۖ وَبِئْسَ الْمَصِيرُ ۝

هُمْ دَرَجَاتٌ عِنْدَ اللهِ ۗ وَاللهُ بَصِيرٌۢ بِمَا يَعْمَلُونَ ۝

لَقَدْ مَنَّ اللهُ عَلَى الْمُؤْمِنِينَ إِذْ بَعَثَ فِيهِمْ رَسُولًا مِّنْ أَنْفُسِهِمْ يَتْلُوا عَلَيْهِمْ آيَاتِهِ وَيُزَكِّيهِمْ وَيُعَلِّمُهُمُ الْكِتَابَ وَالْحِكْمَةَ ۚ وَإِنْ كَانُوا مِنْ قَبْلُ لَفِي ضَلَالٍ مُّبِينٍ ۝

أَوَلَمَّا أَصَابَتْكُمْ مُّصِيبَةٌ قَدْ أَصَبْتُمْ مِّثْلَيْهَا ۙ قُلْتُمْ أَنَّىٰ هَٰذَا ۖ قُلْ هُوَ مِنْ عِنْدِ أَنْفُسِكُمْ ۗ إِنَّ اللهَ عَلَىٰ كُلِّ شَيْءٍ قَدِيرٌ ۝

وَمَا أَصَابَكُمْ يَوْمَ الْتَقَى الْجَمْعَانِ فَبِإِذْنِ اللهِ وَلِيَعْلَمَ الْمُؤْمِنِينَ ۝

وَلِيَعْلَمَ الَّذِينَ نَافَقُوا ۚ وَقِيلَ لَهُمْ تَعَالَوْا قَاتِلُوا فِي سَبِيلِ اللهِ أَوِ ادْفَعُوا ۖ قَالُوا لَوْ نَعْلَمُ قِتَالًا لَّاتَّبَعْنَاكُمْ ۗ هُمْ لِلْكُفْرِ يَوْمَئِذٍ أَقْرَبُ مِنْهُمْ لِلْإِيمَانِ ۚ يَقُولُونَ بِأَفْوَاهِهِمْ مَّا لَيْسَ فِي قُلُوبِهِمْ ۗ وَاللهُ أَعْلَمُ بِمَا يَكْتُمُونَ ۝

الَّذِينَ قَالُوا لِإِخْوَانِهِمْ وَقَعَدُوا لَوْ أَطَاعُونَا مَا قُتِلُوا ۗ قُلْ فَادْرَءُوا عَنْ

death from your own selves, if you speak the truth."

169. Think not of those who are slain in Allah's way as dead. Nay, they live, finding their sustenance in the presence of their Lord;

170. They rejoice in the bounty provided by Allah: and with regard to those left behind, who have not yet joined them (in their bliss), the (martyrs) glory in the fact that on them is no fear, nor have they (cause to) grieve.

171. They glory in the Grace and the bounty from Allah, and in the fact that Allah lets not the reward of the Faithful to be lost (in the least).

172. Of those who answered the call of Allah and the Apostle, even after being wounded, those who do right and refrain from wrong have a great reward;-

173. Men said to them: "A great army is gathering against you": and frightened them: but it (only) increased their Faith: they said: "For us Allah sufficient, and He is the best Disposer of affairs."

174. And they returned with Grace and Bounty from Allah: no harm ever touched them: for they followed the good pleasure of Allah: and Allah is the Lord of bounties unbounded.

175. It is only the Satan that suggests to you the fear of his votaries: be you not afraid of them, but fear Me, if you have Faith.

176. Let not those grieve you who rush headlong into

anfusikumul-mawta in kuntum ṣaadiqeen.

169. Wa laa taḥsabannal-lazeena qutiloo fee sabeelillaahi amwaataa; bal aḥyaaa'un 'inda Rabbihim yurzaqoon.

170. Fariḥeena bimaaa aataahumul-laahu min faḍlihee wa yastabshiroona billazeena lam yalḥaqoo bihim min khalfihim allaa khawfun 'alay-him wa laa hum yaḥzanoon.

171. Yastabshiroona bini-'matim-minal-laahi wa faḍ liñw-wa annal-laaha laa yuḍee'u ajral-mu'mineen.
(Section 17)

172. Allazeenas-tajaaboo lil-laahi war-Rasooli mim ba'di maaa aṣ aabahumulqarḥ; lillazeena aḥsanoo minhum wattaqaw ajrun 'azeem.

173. Allazeena qaala lahumun-naasu innan-naasa qad jama'oo lakum fakhshawhum fazaada-hum eemaanañw-wa qaaloo ḥasbunal-laahu wa ni'mal-wakeel.

174. Fanqalaboo bini'matim-minal-laahi wa faḍlil-lam yam-sashum sooo'uñw-wattaba'oo riḍwaanal-laah; wallaahu zoo faḍlin 'azeem.

175. Innamaa zaalikumush-Shayṭaanu yukhawwifu awli-yaaa'ahoo falaa takhaafoohum wa khaafooni in kuntum mu'mineen.

176. Wa laa yaḥzunkal-lazeena yusaari'oona fil-

Unbelief: not the least harm will they do to Allah: Allah's plan is that He will give them no portion in the Hereafter, but a severe punishment.

177. Those who purchase Unbelief at the price of faith,- not the least harm will they do to Allah, but they will have a grievous punishment.

178. Let not the Unbelievers think that our respite to them is good for themselves: We grant them respite that they may grow in their iniquity: but they will have a shameful punishment.

179. Allah will not leave the Believers in the state in which you are now, until He separates what is evil from what is good. Nor will He disclose to you the secrets of the Unseen, but He chooses of His Apostles (for the purpose) whom He pleases. So believe in Allah and His Apostles: and if you believe and do right, you have a reward without measure.

180. And let not those who covetously withhold of the gifts which Allah has given them of His Grace, think that it is good for them: Nay, it will be the worse for them: soon shall the things which they covetously withheld be tied to their necks like a twisted collar, on the Day of Judgment. To Allah belongs the heritage of the heavens and the earth; and Allah is well-acquainted with all that you do.

181. Allah has heard the taunt of those who say: "Truly, Allah is indigent and we are rich!"-We shall certainly record their word and (their act) of slaying the Prophets

Kufr; innahum lañy-yaḍurrul-laaha shay'aa; yureedul-laahu allaa yaj'ala lahum ḥazzan fil-Aakhirati wa lahum 'azaabun 'azeem.

177. Innal-lazeenash-tarawul-kufra bil-eemaani lañy-yaḍurrul-laaha shay'añw-wa lahum-'azdaabun aleem.

178. Wa laa yaḥsabannal-lazeena kafarooo annamaa numlee lahum khayrulli-anfusihim; innamaa numlee lahum liyazdaadooo ismaa wa lahum 'azaabum-muheen.

179. Maa kaanal-laahu liyazaral-mu'mineena 'alaa maaa antum 'alayhi ḥattaa yameezal-khabeesa minat-ṭayyib; wa maa kaanal-laahu liyuṭli'akum 'alal-ghaybi wa laakinnal-laaha yajtabee mir-Rusulihee mañy-yashaaa'u fa-aaminoo billaahi wa Rusulih; wa in tu'minoo wa tattaqoo falakum ajrun 'azeem.

180. Wa laa yaḥsabannal-lazeena yabkhaloona bimaaa aataahumul-laahu min faḍlihee huwa khayral-lahum bal huwa sharrul-lahum sayuṭaw-waqoona maa bakhiloo bihee Yawmal-Qiyaamah; wa lillaahi meeraasus-samaawaati wal-arḍ; wallaahu bimaa ta'maloona Khabeer.   **(Section 18)**

181. Laqad sami'al-laahu qawlal-lazeena qaalooo innal-laaha faqeeruñw-wa nahnu aghniyaaa'; sanaktubu maa qaaloo wa qatlahumul-Ambiyaaa'a

in defiance of right, and We shall say: "Taste the Chastise-ment of the Scorching Fire!

182. "This is because of the (unrighteous deeds) which your hands sent on before you: for Allah never harms those who serve Him."

183. They (also) said: "Allah took our promise not to believe in an Apostle unless he showed us a sacrifice consumed by fire (from heaven)." Say: "There came to you Apostles before me, with Clear Signs and even with what you ask for: why then did you slay them, if you speak the truth?"

184. Then if they reject you, so were rejected Apostles before you, who came with Clear Signs, Books of dark prophe-cies, and the Book of Enlighten-ment.

185. Every soul shall have a taste of death: and only on the Day of Judgment shall you be paid your full recompense. Only he who is saved far from the Fire and admitted to the Garden will have attained the object (of Life): for the life of this world is but goods and chattels of deception.

186. You shall certainly be tried and tested in your possessions and in your personal selves; and you shall certainly hear much that will grieve you, from those who received the Book before you and from those who worship many gods. But if you persevere patiently, and guard against evil,- then that will be a determining factor in all affairs.

187. And remember Allah took a Covenant from the People of the Book, to make it known and clear to mankind, and not to hide it; but they threw it away behind their backs,

bighayri ḥaqqiñw-wa naqoolu zooqoo 'azaaba-lḥareeq.

182. Zaalika bimaa qaddamat aydeekum wa annal-laaha laysa biẓallaamil-lil'abeed.

183. Allazeena qaalooo innal-laaha 'ahida ilaynaaa allaa nu'mina li-Rasoolin ḥattaa yaâti-yanaa biqurbaanin taâ-kuluhun-naar; qul qad jaaa'akum Rusulum-min qablee bilbayyinaati wa billazee qultum falima qataltumoohum in kuntum ṣaadiqeen.

184. Fa-in kaz-zabooka faqad kuz ziba Rusulum-min qablika jaaa'oo bilbayyinaati waz-Zuburi wal-Kitaabil-Muneer.

185 Kullu nafsin zaaa'iqatul-mawt; wa innamaa tuwaffawna ujoorakum Yawmal-Qiyaamati faman zuḥziḥa 'anin-Naari waudkhilal-Jannata faqad faaz; wa mal-ḥayaatud-dunyaaa illaa mataa'ul-ghuroor.

186. Latublawunna feee amwaalikum wa anfusikum wa latasma'unna minal-lazeena ootul-Kitaaba min qablikum wa minal-lazeena ashrakooo azan kaseeraa; wa in taṣbiroo wa tattaqoo fa-inna zaalika min 'azmil-umoor.

187. Wa-iz-akhazal-laahu meesaaqal -lazeena ootul-Kitaaba latubayyinunnahoo linnaasi wa laa taktumoona-hoo fanabazoohu waraaa'a ẓuhoorihim

بِغَيْرِ حَقٍّ ۚ وَنَقُولُ ذُوقُوا عَذَابَ الْحَرِيقِ ۞

الَّذِينَ قَالُوٓا إِنَّ اللَّهَ عَهِدَ إِلَيْنَآ أَلَّا نُؤْمِنَ لِرَسُولٍ حَتَّىٰ يَأْتِيَنَا بِقُرْبَانٍ تَأْكُلُهُ النَّارُ ۗ قُلْ قَدْ جَآءَكُمْ رُسُلٌ مِّن قَبْلِي بِالْبَيِّنَٰتِ وَبِالَّذِي قُلْتُمْ فَلِمَ قَتَلْتُمُوهُمْ إِن كُنتُمْ صَٰدِقِينَ ۞

فَإِن كَذَّبُوكَ فَقَدْ كُذِّبَ رُسُلٌ مِّن قَبْلِكَ جَآءُو بِالْبَيِّنَٰتِ وَالزُّبُرِ وَالْكِتَٰبِ الْمُنِيرِ ۞

كُلُّ نَفْسٍ ذَآئِقَةُ الْمَوْتِ ۗ وَإِنَّمَا تُوَفَّوْنَ أُجُورَكُمْ يَوْمَ الْقِيَٰمَةِ ۖ فَمَن زُحْزِحَ عَنِ النَّارِ وَأُدْخِلَ الْجَنَّةَ فَقَدْ فَازَ ۗ وَمَا الْحَيَوٰةُ الدُّنْيَآ إِلَّا مَتَٰعُ الْغُرُورِ ۞

لَتُبْلَوُنَّ فِىٓ أَمْوَٰلِكُمْ وَأَنفُسِكُمْ وَلَتَسْمَعُنَّ مِنَ الَّذِينَ أُوتُوا الْكِتَٰبَ مِن قَبْلِكُمْ وَمِنَ الَّذِينَ أَشْرَكُوٓا أَذًى كَثِيرًا ۚ وَإِن تَصْبِرُوا وَتَتَّقُوا فَإِنَّ ذَٰلِكَ مِنْ عَزْمِ الْأُمُورِ ۞

وَإِذْ أَخَذَ اللَّهُ مِيثَٰقَ الَّذِينَ أُوتُوا الْكِتَٰبَ لَتُبَيِّنُنَّهُ لِلنَّاسِ وَلَا تَكْتُمُونَهُ فَنَبَذُوهُ وَرَآءَ ظُهُورِهِمْ

and purchased with it some miserable gain! and vile was the bargain they made!

188. Think not that those who exult in what they have brought about, and love to be praised for what they have not done,- think not that they can escape the Chastisement. For them is a Chastisement grievous indeed.

189. To Allah belongeth the dominion of the heavens and the earth; and Allah has power over all things.

190. Behold! In the creation of the heavens and the earth, and the alternation of Night and Day,- there are indeed Signs for men of understanding,-

191. Men who celebrate the praises of Allah, standing, sitting, and lying down on their sides, and contemplate the (wonders of) creation in the heavens and the earth, (with the thought): "Our Lord! You have created (all) this not for nothing! Glory to You! Give us salvation from the Chastisement of the Fire.

192. "Our Lord! any whom You admit to the Fire, Truly You have covered with shame, and never will wrong-doers find any helpers!

193. "Our Lord! we have heard the call of one calling (us) to Faith, 'Believe you in the Lord,' and we have believed. Our Lord! Forgive us our sins, blot out from us our iniquities, and take to yourself our souls in the company of the righteous.

194. "Our Lord! Grant us what you promised unto us through Your Apostles, and save us from shame on the Day of Judgment: for You never break Your promise."

195. And their Lord has accepted of them, and answered them: "Never will I

washtaraw bihee samanan qaleelan fabi'sa maa yash-taroon.

188. Laa taḥsabannal-lazeena yafraḥoona bimaaa ataw wa yuḥibboona añy-yuḥmadoo bimaa lam yaf'aloo falaa taḥsabannahum bimafaazatim-minal-'azaabi wa lahum 'azaabun aleem.

189. Wa lillaahi mulkus-samaawaati wal-arḍ; wallaahu 'alaa kulli shay'in Qadeer.
(Section 19)

190. Inna fee khalqis-samaa-waati wal-arḍi wakhtilaafil-layli wannahaari la-Aayaatil-li-ulil-albaab.

191. Allazeena yazkuroonal-laaha qiyaamañw-wa qu'oodañ w-wa 'alaa juno-obihim wa yatafakkaroona fee khalqis-samaawaati wal-arḍi Rabbanaa maa khalaqta haazaa baaṭilan Subḥaanaka-faqinaa 'azaaban-Naar.

192. Rabbanaaa innaka man tudkhilin-Naara faqad akhzay-tahoo wa maa liẓẓaalimeena min anṣaar.

193. Rabbanaaa innanaa sami'naa munaadiyañy-yunaadee lil-eemaani an aaminoo bi-Rabbikum fa-aamannaa; Rab-banaa faghfir lanaa zunoobanaa wa kaffir 'annaa sayyi-aatinaa wa tawaffanaa ma'al-abraar.

194. Rabbanaa wa aatinaa maa wa'attanaa 'alaa Rusulika wa laa tukhzinaa Yawmal-Qiyaamah; innaka laa tukhliful-mee'aad.

195. Fastajaaba lahum Rabbu-hum annee laaa

واشْتَرَوْا بِهٖ ثَمَنًا قَلِيلًا ۗ فَبِئْسَ مَا يَشْتَرُوْنَ ۝

لَا تَحْسَبَنَّ الَّذِيْنَ يَفْرَحُوْنَ بِمَاۤ اَتَوْا وَّيُحِبُّوْنَ اَنْ يُّحْمَدُوْا بِمَا لَمْ يَفْعَلُوْا فَلَا تَحْسَبَنَّهُمْ بِمَفَازَةٍ مِّنَ الْعَذَابِ ۚ وَلَهُمْ عَذَابٌ اَلِيْمٌ ۝

وَلِلّٰهِ مُلْكُ السَّمٰوٰتِ وَالْاَرْضِ ۗ وَاللّٰهُ عَلٰى كُلِّ شَيْءٍ قَدِيْرٌ ۝

اِنَّ فِيْ خَلْقِ السَّمٰوٰتِ وَالْاَرْضِ وَاخْتِلَافِ الَّيْلِ وَالنَّهَارِ لَاٰيٰتٍ لِّاُولِي الْاَلْبَابِ ۝

الَّذِيْنَ يَذْكُرُوْنَ اللّٰهَ قِيٰمًا وَّقُعُوْدًا وَّعَلٰى جُنُوْبِهِمْ وَيَتَفَكَّرُوْنَ فِيْ خَلْقِ السَّمٰوٰتِ وَالْاَرْضِ ۚ رَبَّنَا مَا خَلَقْتَ هٰذَا بَاطِلًا ۚ سُبْحٰنَكَ فَقِنَا عَذَابَ النَّارِ ۝

رَبَّنَاۤ اِنَّكَ مَنْ تُدْخِلِ النَّارَ فَقَدْ اَخْزَيْتَهٗ ۗ وَمَا لِلظّٰلِمِيْنَ مِنْ اَنْصَارٍ ۝

رَبَّنَاۤ اِنَّنَا سَمِعْنَا مُنَادِيًا يُّنَادِيْ لِلْاِيْمَانِ اَنْ اٰمِنُوْا بِرَبِّكُمْ فَاٰمَنَّا ۖ رَبَّنَا فَاغْفِرْ لَنَا ذُنُوْبَنَا وَكَفِّرْ عَنَّا سَيِّاٰتِنَا وَتَوَفَّنَا مَعَ الْاَبْرَارِ ۝

رَبَّنَا وَاٰتِنَا مَا وَعَدْتَّنَا عَلٰى رُسُلِكَ وَلَا تُخْزِنَا يَوْمَ الْقِيٰمَةِ ۗ اِنَّكَ لَا تُخْلِفُ الْمِيْعَادَ ۝

فَاسْتَجَابَ لَهُمْ رَبُّهُمْ اَنِّيْ لَاۤ

suffer to be lost the work of any of you, be he male or female: you are members, one of another: those who have left their homes, or been driven out therefrom, or suffered harm in My Cause, or fought or been slain,- verily, I will blot out from them their iniquities, and admit them into Gardens with rivers flowing beneath; - A reward from the Presence of Allah, and from His Presence is the best of rewards."

Udee'u 'amala 'aamilim-minkum min zakarin aw unsaa ba'dukum mim-ba'din fal-lazeena haajaroo wa ukhrijoo min diyaarihim wa oozoo fee sabeelee wa qaataloo wa qutiloo la-ukaffiranna 'anhum sayyi-aatihim wa la-udkhilanna-hum Jannaatin tajree min tahtihal-anhaaru sawaabam-min 'indil-laah; wallaahu 'indahoo husnus-sawaab.

196. Let not the strutting about of the Unbelievers through the land deceive you:

196. Laa yaghurrannaka taqal-lubul-lazeena kafaroo fil-bilaad.

197. Little is it for enjoyment: their ultimate abode is Hell: what an evil bed (to lie on)!

197. Mataa'un qaleelun summa maåwaahum Jahannam; wa bi'sal-mihaad.

198. On the other hand, for those who fear their Lord, are Gardens, with rivers flowing beneath; therein are they to dwell (for ever),- a gift from the presence of Allah; and that which is in the Presence of Allah is the best (bliss) for the righteous.

198. Laakinil-lazeenat-taqaw Rabbahum lahum Jannaatun tajree min tahtihal-anhaaru khaalideena feehaa nuzulam-min 'indil-laah; wa maa 'indal-laahi khayrul-lil-abraar.

199. And there are, certainly, among the People of the Book, those who believe in Allah, in the revelation to you, and in the revelation to them, bowing in humility to Allah: they will not sell the Signs of Allah for a miserable gain! for them is a reward with their Lord, and Allah is swift in account.

199. Wa inna min Ahlil-Kitaabi lamany-yu'minu billaahi wa maaa unzila ilaykum wa maaa unzila ilayhim khaashi'eena lillaahi laa yashtaroona bi-Aayaatil-laahi samanan qaleelaa; ulaaa'ika lahum ajruhum 'inda Rabbihim; innal-laaha saree'ul-hisaab.

200. O you who believe! Persevere in patience and constancy; vie in such perseverance; strengthen each other; and fear Allah; that you may prosper.

200. Yaaa ayyuhal-lazeena aamanus-biroo wa saabiroo wa raabitoo wattaqul-laaha la'allakum tuflihoon. (Section 20)

4. The Women

In the name of Allah, Most Gracious, Most Merciful.

Sûrat an-Nisâ'–4

(Revealed at Madinah)

Bismillaahir Rahmaanir Raheem

(٤) سُوْرَةُ النِّسَاءِ مَدَنِيَّةٌ (٩٢)

بِسْمِ اللهِ الرَّحْمٰنِ الرَّحِيْمِ

1. O mankind! reverence your Guardian-Lord, Who created you from a single Person, created, of like nature, his mate, and from them twain scattered (like seeds) countless men and women;- reverence Allah, through Whom you demand your mutual (rights), and (reverence) the wombs (that bore you): for Allah ever watches over you.

1. Yaaa ayyuhan-naasuttaqoo Rabbakumul-lazee khalaqakum min nafsiñw-waahidatiñw-wa khalaqa minhaa zawjahaa wa bas-sa minhumaa rijaalan kaseerañw-wa nisaaa'aa; wattaqullaahallazee tasaaa-'aloona bihee wal-arhaam; innal-laaha kaana 'alaykum Raqeebaa.

2. To orphans restore their property (when they reach their age), nor substitute (your) worthless things for (their) good ones; and devour not their substance (by mixing it up) with your own. For this is indeed a great sin.

2. Wa aatul-yataamaaa amwaalahum wa laa tatabaddalul-khabeesa bittayyibi wa laa taåkulooo amwaalahum ilaaa amwaalikum; innahoo kaana hooban kabeeraa.

3. If you fear that you shall not be able to deal justly with the orphans, marry women of your choice, two or three or four; but if you fear that you shall not be able to deal justly (with them), then only one, or (a captive) that your right hands possess, that will be more suitable, to prevent you from doing injustice.

3. Wa-in khiftum allaa tuqsitoo fil-yataamaa fankihoo maa taaba lakum minannisaaa'i masnaa wa sulaasa wa rubaa'a fa-in khiftum allaa ta'diloo fawaahidatan aw maa malakat aymaanukum; zaalika adnaaa allaa ta'ooloo.

4. And give the women (on marriage) their dower as a free gift; but if they, of their own good pleasure, remit any part of it to you, take it and enjoy it with right good cheer.'

4. Wa aatun-nisaaa'a saduqaatihinna nihlah; fa-in tibna lakum 'an shay'im minhu nafsan fakuloohu haneee'ammareee'aa.

5. To those weak of understanding make not over your property, which Allah has made a means of support for you, but feed and clothe them therewith, and speak to them words of kindness and justice.

5. Wa laa tu'tus-sufahaaa'a amwaalakumul-latee ja'alal,-laahu lakum qiyaamañw-warzuqoohum feehaa waksoohum wa qooloo lahum qawlam-ma'roofaa.

6. Make trial of orphans until they reach the age of marriage; if then you find sound judgment in them, release

6. Wabtalul-yataamaa hattaaa izaa balaghun-nikaaha fa-in aanastum minhum rushdan fadfa'ooo

يَا أَيُّهَا النَّاسُ اتَّقُوْا رَبَّكُمُ الَّذِيْ خَلَقَكُمْ مِّنْ نَّفْسٍ وَّاحِدَةٍ وَّ خَلَقَ مِنْهَا زَوْجَهَا وَبَثَّ مِنْهُمَا رِجَالًا كَثِيْرًا وَّنِسَاءً وَاتَّقُوا اللهَ الَّذِيْ تَسَاءَلُوْنَ بِهِ وَالْأَرْحَامَ إِنَّ اللهَ كَانَ عَلَيْكُمْ رَقِيْبًا ۝

وَآتُوا الْيَتٰمٰى أَمْوَالَهُمْ وَلَا تَتَبَدَّلُوا الْخَبِيْثَ بِالطَّيِّبِ وَلَا تَأْكُلُوْا أَمْوَالَهُمْ إِلٰى أَمْوَالِكُمْ إِنَّهُ كَانَ حُوْبًا كَبِيْرًا ۝

وَإِنْ خِفْتُمْ أَلَّا تُقْسِطُوْا فِي الْيَتٰمٰى فَانْكِحُوْا مَا طَابَ لَكُمْ مِّنَ النِّسَاءِ مَثْنٰى وَثُلٰثَ وَرُبٰعَ فَإِنْ خِفْتُمْ أَلَّا تَعْدِلُوْا فَوَاحِدَةً أَوْ مَا مَلَكَتْ أَيْمَانُكُمْ ذٰلِكَ أَدْنٰى أَلَّا تَعُوْلُوْا ۝

وَآتُوا النِّسَاءَ صَدُقٰتِهِنَّ نِحْلَةً فَإِنْ طِبْنَ لَكُمْ عَنْ شَيْءٍ مِّنْهُ نَفْسًا فَكُلُوْهُ هَنِيْئًا مَّرِيْئًا ۝

وَلَا تُؤْتُوا السُّفَهَاءَ أَمْوَالَكُمُ الَّتِيْ جَعَلَ اللهُ لَكُمْ قِيٰمًا وَّارْزُقُوْهُمْ فِيْهَا وَاكْسُوْهُمْ وَقُوْلُوْا لَهُمْ قَوْلًا مَّعْرُوْفًا ۝

وَابْتَلُوا الْيَتٰمٰى حَتّٰى إِذَا بَلَغُوا النِّكَاحَ فَإِنْ آنَسْتُمْ مِّنْهُمْ رُشْدًا فَادْفَعُوْا

their property to but consume it not wastefully, nor in haste against their growing up. If the guardian is well-off, let him claim no remuneration, but if he is poor, let him have for himself what is just and reasonable. When you release their property to them, take witnesses in their presence: but all-sufficient is Allah in taking account.

7. From what is left by parents and those nearest related there is a share for men and a share for women, whether the property be small or large,- a determinate share.

8. But if at the time of division other relatives, or orphans or poor, are present, feed them out of the (property), and speak to them words of kindness and justice.

9. Let those (disposing of an estate) have the same fear in their minds as they would have for their own if they had left a helpless family behind: let them fear Allah, and speak words of appropriate (comfort).

10. Those who unjustly eat up the property of orphans, eat up a Fire into their own bodies: they will soon be enduring a blazing Fire!

11. Allah (thus) directs you as regards your Children's (inheritance): to the male, a portion equal to that of two females: if only daughters, two or more, their share is two-thirds of the inheritance; if only one, her share is a half. For parents, a sixth share of the inheritance to each, if the deceased left children; if no children, and the parents are the (only) heirs, the mother has a third;

ilayhim amwaalahum wa laa taâkuloohaaa israafañw-wa bidaaran añy-yakbaroo; wa man kaana ghaniyyan falyasta'fif wa man kaana faqeeran falyaâkul bilma'roof; fa-izaa dafa'tum ilayhim amwaalahum fa-ashhidoo 'alayhim; wa kafaa billaahi Haseebaa.

7. Lirrijaali naseebum-mimmaa tarakal-waalidaani wal-aqraboona wa lin-nisaaa'i naseebum-mimmaa tarakal-waalidaani wal-aqraboona mimmaa qalla minhu aw kasur; naseebam-mafroodaa.

8. Wa izaa hadaral-qismata ulul-qurbaa walyataamaa walmasaakeenu farzuqoohum minhu wa qooloo lahum qawlam-ma'roofaa.

9. Walyakhshal-lazeena law tarakoo min khalfihim zurriyyatan di'aafan khaafoo 'alayhim falyattaqul-laaha walyaqooloo qawlan sadeedaa.

10. Innal-lazeena yaâkuloona amwaalal-yataamaa zulman innamaa yaâkuloona fee butoonihim Naarañw-wa sayaslawna sa'eeraa. (Section 1)

11. Yooseekumul-laahu feee awlaadikum liz-zakari mislu hazzil-unsayayn; fa-in kunna nisaaa'an fawqas-natayni falahunna sulusaa maa taraka wa in kaanat waahidatan falahan-nisf; wa li-abawayhi likulli waahidim-minhumas-sudusu mimmaa taraka in kaana lahoo walad; fa-il-lam yakul-lahoowaladuñw-wa warisahooo abawaahu fali-ummihis-sulus;

if the deceased left brothers (or sister) the mother has a sixth. (The distribution in all cases is) after the payment of legacies and debts. You know not whether your parents or your children are nearest to you in benefit. These are settled portions ordained by Allah; and Allah is All-knowing, All-wise.

12. In what your wives leave, your share is a half, if they leave no child; but if they leave a child, you get a fourth; after payment of legacies and debts. In what you leave, their share is a fourth, if you leave no child; but if you leave a child, they get one eighth; after payment of legacies and debts. If the man or woman whose inheritance is in question, has left neither ascendants nor descendants, but has left a brother or a sister, each one of the two gets a sixth; but if more than two, they share in a third; after payment of legacies and debts; so that no loss is caused (to any one). Thus is it ordained by Allah; and Allah is All-knowing, Most Forbearing.

13. Those are limits set by Allah: those who obey Allah and His Apostle will be admitted to Gardens with rivers flowing beneath, to abide therein (for ever) and that will be the supreme achievement.

14. But those who disobey Allah and His Apostle and transgress His limits will be admitted to a Fire, to abide therein:

fa-in kaana lahooo ikhwatun fali-ummihis-sudus; mim ba'di waşiyyatiñy-yooşee bihaaa aw dayn; aabaaa'ukum wa abnaaa'ukum laa tadroona ayyuhum aqrabu lakum naf'aa; fareeḍatam-minallaah; innallaaha kaana 'Aleeman Ḥakeemaa.

12. Wa lakum niṣfu maa taraka azwaajukum il-lam yakullahunna walad; fa-in kaana lahunna waladun falakumurrubu'u mimmaa tarakna mim ba'di waşiyyatiñy-yooşeena bihaaa aw dayn; wa lahunnarrubu'u mimmaa taraktum il-lam yakul-lakum walad; fa-in kaana lakum waladun falahunnassumunu mimmaa taraktum; mim ba'di waşiyyatin tooşoona bihaaa aw dayn; wa in kaana rajuluñy-yooraşu kalaalatan awim-ra-atuñw-wa lahooo akhun aw ukhtun falikulli waaḥidim-minhumas-sudus; fa-in kaanooo aksara min zaalika fahum shurakaaa'u fiṣ-suluṣi mim ba'di waşiyyatiñy-yooşaa bihaaa aw daynin ghayra muḍaarr; waşiyyatam-minallaah; wallaahu 'Aleemun Ḥaleem.

13. Tilka ḥudoodul-laah; wa mañy-yuṭi'il-laaha wa Rasoolahoo yudkhilhu Jannaatin tajree min taḥtihal-anhaaru khaalideena feehaa; wa zaalikal-fawzul-'aẓeem.

14. Wa mañy-ya'ṣil-laaha wa Rasoolahoo wa yata'adda ḥudoodahoo yudkhilhu Naaran khaalidan feehaa

فَإِنْ كَانَ لَهُ إِخْوَةٌ فَلِأُمِّهِ السُّدُسُ مِنْ بَعْدِ وَصِيَّةٍ يُوصِي بِهَا أَوْ دَيْنٍ ۚ ابَاؤُكُمْ وَأَبْنَاؤُكُمْ لَا تَدْرُونَ أَيُّهُمْ أَقْرَبُ لَكُمْ نَفْعًا ۚ فَرِيضَةً مِّنَ اللَّهِ ۗ إِنَّ اللَّهَ كَانَ عَلِيمًا حَكِيمًا ۞

وَلَكُمْ نِصْفُ مَا تَرَكَ أَزْوَاجُكُمْ إِنْ لَمْ يَكُنْ لَهُنَّ وَلَدٌ ۚ فَإِنْ كَانَ لَهُنَّ وَلَدٌ فَلَكُمُ الرُّبُعُ مِمَّا تَرَكْنَ مِنْ بَعْدِ وَصِيَّةٍ يُوصِينَ بِهَا أَوْ دَيْنٍ ۚ وَلَهُنَّ الرُّبُعُ مِمَّا تَرَكْتُمْ إِنْ لَمْ يَكُنْ لَكُمْ وَلَدٌ ۚ فَإِنْ كَانَ لَكُمْ وَلَدٌ فَلَهُنَّ الثُّمُنُ مِمَّا تَرَكْتُمْ مِنْ بَعْدِ وَصِيَّةٍ تُوصُونَ بِهَا أَوْ دَيْنٍ ۗ وَإِنْ كَانَ رَجُلٌ يُورَثُ كَلَالَةً أَوِ امْرَأَةٌ وَلَهُ أَخٌ أَوْ أُخْتٌ فَلِكُلِّ وَاحِدٍ مِّنْهُمَا السُّدُسُ ۚ فَإِنْ كَانُوا أَكْثَرَ مِنْ ذَٰلِكَ فَهُمْ شُرَكَاءُ فِي الثُّلُثِ مِنْ بَعْدِ وَصِيَّةٍ يُوصَىٰ بِهَا أَوْ دَيْنٍ غَيْرَ مُضَارٍّ ۚ وَصِيَّةً مِّنَ اللَّهِ ۗ وَاللَّهُ عَلِيمٌ حَلِيمٌ ۞

تِلْكَ حُدُودُ اللَّهِ ۚ وَمَنْ يُطِعِ اللَّهَ وَرَسُولَهُ يُدْخِلْهُ جَنَّاتٍ تَجْرِي مِنْ تَحْتِهَا الْأَنْهَارُ خَالِدِينَ فِيهَا ۚ وَذَٰلِكَ الْفَوْزُ الْعَظِيمُ ۞

وَمَنْ يَعْصِ اللَّهَ وَرَسُولَهُ وَيَتَعَدَّ حُدُودَهُ يُدْخِلْهُ نَارًا خَالِدًا فِيهَا

and they shall have a humiliating punishment.

15. If any of your women are guilty of lewdness, take the evidence of four (reliable) witnesses from amongst you against them; and if they testify, confine them to houses until death do claim them, or Allah ordain for them some (other) way.

16. If two men among you are guilty of lewdness, punish them both. If they repent and amend, leave them alone; for Allah is Oft-returning, Most Merciful.

17. Allah accepts the repentance of those who do evil in ignorance and repent soon afterwards; to them will Allah turn in mercy: for Allah is full of knowledge and wisdom.

18. Of no effect is the repentance of those who continue to do evil, until death faces one of them, and he says, "Now have I repented indeed;" nor of those who die rejecting Faith: for them have We prepared a punishment most grievous.

19. O you who believe! you are forbidden to inherit women against their will. Nor should you treat them with harshness, that you may take away part of the dower you have given them,- except where they have been guilty of open lewdness; on the contrary live with them on a footing of kindness and equity. If you take a dislike to them it may be that you dislike a thing, and

wa lahoo 'azaabum-muheen.
(Section 2)

15. Wallaatee yaåteenal-faahishata min nisaaa'ikum fastashhidoo 'alayhinna arba'atam-minkum fa-in shahidoo fa-amsikoohunna fil-buyooti hattaa yatawaffaa-hunnal-mawtu aw yaj'alal-laahu lahunna sabeelaa.

16. Wallazaani yaåtiyaanihaa minkum fa-aazoohumaa fa-in taabaa wa aslahaa fa-a'riḍoo 'anhumaaa; innal-laaha kaana Tawwaabar-Raheemaa.

17. Innamat-tawbatu 'alallaahi lillazeena ya'maloonas-sooo'a bijahaalatin summa yatooboona min qareebin faulaaa'ika yatoobul-laahu 'alayhim; wa kaanal-laahu 'Aleeman Hakeemaa.

18. Wa laysatit-tawbatu lillazeena ya'maloonas-sayyi-aati hattaaa izaa hadara ahadahumul-mawtu qaala innee tubtul-'aana wa lallazeena yamootoona wa hum kuffaar; ulaaa'ika a'tadnaa lahum 'azaaban aleemaa.

19. Yaaa ayyuhal-lazeena aamanoo laa yahillu lakum an tarisun-nisaaa'a karhan wa laa ta'duloohunna litazhaboo biba'ḍi maaa aataytumoohunna illaaa añy-yaåteena bifaahisha-tim-mubayyinah; wa 'aashiroo-hunna bilma'roof; fa-in karihtumoohunna fa-asaaa an takrahoo shay'añ w-wa yaj'alal-

وَلَهُ عَذَابٌ مُّهِيْنٌ ۞

وَالّٰتِىْ يَأْتِيْنَ الْفَاحِشَةَ مِنْ نِّسَآىِٕكُمْ فَاسْتَشْهِدُوْا عَلَيْهِنَّ اَرْبَعَةً مِّنْكُمْ فَاِنْ شَهِدُوْا فَاَمْسِكُوْهُنَّ فِى الْبُيُوْتِ حَتّٰى يَتَوَفّٰهُنَّ الْمَوْتُ اَوْ يَجْعَلَ اللّٰهُ لَهُنَّ سَبِيْلًا ۞

وَالَّذٰنِ يَأْتِيٰنِهَا مِنْكُمْ فَاٰذُوْهُمَا فَاِنْ تَابَا وَاَصْلَحَا فَاَعْرِضُوْا عَنْهُمَا اِنَّ اللّٰهَ كَانَ تَوَّابًا رَّحِيْمًا ۞

اِنَّمَا التَّوْبَةُ عَلَى اللّٰهِ لِلَّذِيْنَ يَعْمَلُوْنَ السُّوْٓءَ بِجَهَالَةٍ ثُمَّ يَتُوْبُوْنَ مِنْ قَرِيْبٍ فَاُولٰٓئِكَ يَتُوْبُ اللّٰهُ عَلَيْهِمْ ۚ وَكَانَ اللّٰهُ عَلِيْمًا حَكِيْمًا ۞

وَلَيْسَتِ التَّوْبَةُ لِلَّذِيْنَ يَعْمَلُوْنَ السَّيِّاٰتِ ۚ حَتّٰى اِذَا حَضَرَ اَحَدَهُمُ الْمَوْتُ قَالَ اِنِّىْ تُبْتُ الْئٰنَ وَلَا الَّذِيْنَ يَمُوْتُوْنَ وَهُمْ كُفَّارٌ ۚ اُولٰٓئِكَ اَعْتَدْنَا لَهُمْ عَذَابًا اَلِيْمًا ۞

يٰٓاَيُّهَا الَّذِيْنَ اٰمَنُوْا لَا يَحِلُّ لَكُمْ اَنْ تَرِثُوا النِّسَآءَ كَرْهًا ۚ وَلَا تَعْضُلُوْهُنَّ لِتَذْهَبُوْا بِبَعْضِ مَآ اٰتَيْتُمُوْهُنَّ اِلَّا اَنْ يَّأْتِيْنَ بِفَاحِشَةٍ مُّبَيِّنَةٍ ۚ وَعَاشِرُوْهُنَّ بِالْمَعْرُوْفِ ۚ فَاِنْ كَرِهْتُمُوْهُنَّ فَعَسٰى اَنْ تَكْرَهُوْا شَيْئًا وَّيَجْعَلَ

Allah brings about through it a great deal of good.

20. But if you decide to take one wife in place of another, even if you had given the latter a whole treasure for dower, Take not the least bit of it back: will you take it by slander and manifest wrong?

21. And how could you take it when you have gone in to each other, and they have taken from you a solemn covenant?

22. And marry not women whom your fathers married,- except what is past: it was shameful and odious,- an abominable custom indeed.

23. Prohibited to you (for marriage) are:- your mothers, daughters, sisters; father's sisters, mother's sisters; brother's daughters, sister's daughters; foster-mothers (who gave you suck), foster-sisters; your wives' mothers; your step-daughters under your guardianship, born of your wives to whom you have gone in, - no prohibition if you have not gone in; - (those who have been) wives of your sons proceeding from your loins; and two sisters in wedlock at one and the same time, except for what is past; for Allah is Oft-Forgiving, Most Merciful;-

24. Also (prohibited are) women already married, except those whom your right hands possess: thus has Allah ordained (prohi-bitions) against you: except for these, all others are lawful,

laahu feehi khayran kaseeraa.

20. Wa in arattumustib-daala zawjim-makaana zawjin wa aataytum iḥdaahunna qinṭaaran falaa taåkhuzoo minhu shay'aa; ataåkhuzoonahoo buhtaanañw-wa ismam-mubeenaa.

21. Wa kayfa taåkhuzoonahoo wa qad afḍaa ba'ḍukum ilaa ba'ḍiñw-wa akhazna minkum meesaaqan ghaleezaa.

22. Wa laa tankihoo maa nakaḥa aabaaa'ukum minan-nisaaa'i illaa maa qad salaf; innahoo kaana faaḥishatañw-wa maqtañw wa saaa'a sabeelaa.   (Section 3)

23. Ḥurrimat 'alaykum umma-haatukum wa banaatukum wa akhawaatukum wa 'ammaa-tukum wa khaalaatukum wa banaatul-akhi wa banaatul-ukhti wa ummahaatu-kumul-laateee arḍa'nakum wa akhawaatu-kum-minarraḍaa'ati wa umma-haatu nisaaa'ikum wa rabaaa'i-bukumul-laatee fee ḥujoorikum min nisaaa'ikumul-laatee dakhaltum-bihinna Fa-il-lam takoonoo dakhaltum bihinna falaa junaaḥa 'alaykum wa halaaa'ilu abnaaa'ikumul-lazeena min aṣlaabikum wa an tajma'oo baynal-ukhtayni illaa maa qad salaf; innallaaha kaana Ghafoorar-Raḥeemaa.

24. Walmuḥṣanaatu minan-nisaaa'i illaa maa malakat aymaanukum kitaabal-laahi 'alaykum; wa uḥilla lakum maa waraaa'a zaalikum

اللهَ فِيهِ خَيْرًا كَثِيرًا ۝

وَإِنْ أَرَدْتُّمُ اسْتِبْدَالَ زَوْجٍ مَّكَانَ زَوْجٍ وَّاٰتَيْتُمْ إِحْدَاهُنَّ قِنْطَارًا فَلَا تَأْخُذُوْا مِنْهُ شَيْـًٔا ۚ أَتَأْخُذُوْنَهٗ بُهْتَانًا وَّإِثْمًا مُّبِيْنًا ۝

وَكَيْفَ تَأْخُذُوْنَهٗ وَقَدْ أَفْضٰى بَعْضُكُمْ إِلٰى بَعْضٍ وَّأَخَذْنَ مِنْكُمْ مِّيْثَاقًا غَلِيْظًا ۝

وَلَا تَنْكِحُوْا مَا نَكَحَ أَبَآؤُكُمْ مِّنَ النِّسَآءِ إِلَّا مَا قَدْ سَلَفَ ۚ إِنَّهٗ كَانَ فَاحِشَةً وَّمَقْتًا ۚ وَسَآءَ سَبِيْلًا ۝

حُرِّمَتْ عَلَيْكُمْ أُمَّهٰتُكُمْ وَبَنٰتُكُمْ وَأَخَوٰتُكُمْ وَعَمّٰتُكُمْ وَخٰلٰتُكُمْ وَبَنٰتُ الْأَخِ وَبَنٰتُ الْأُخْتِ وَأُمَّهٰتُكُمُ الّٰتِيْ أَرْضَعْنَكُمْ وَأَخَوٰتُكُمْ مِّنَ الرَّضَاعَةِ وَأُمَّهٰتُ نِسَآئِكُمْ وَرَبَآئِبُكُمُ الّٰتِيْ فِيْ حُجُوْرِكُمْ مِّنْ نِّسَآئِكُمُ الّٰتِيْ دَخَلْتُمْ بِهِنَّ ۖ فَإِنْ لَّمْ تَكُوْنُوْا دَخَلْتُمْ بِهِنَّ فَلَا جُنَاحَ عَلَيْكُمْ ۖ وَحَلَآئِلُ أَبْنَآئِكُمُ الَّذِيْنَ مِنْ أَصْلَابِكُمْ ۙ وَأَنْ تَجْمَعُوْا بَيْنَ الْأُخْتَيْنِ إِلَّا مَا قَدْ سَلَفَ ۗ إِنَّ اللهَ كَانَ غَفُوْرًا رَّحِيْمًا ۝

وَالْمُحْصَنٰتُ مِنَ النِّسَآءِ إِلَّا مَا مَلَكَتْ أَيْمَانُكُمْ ۚ كِتٰبَ اللهِ عَلَيْكُمْ ۚ وَأُحِلَّ لَكُمْ مَّا وَرَآءَ ذٰلِكُمْ

provided you seek (them in marriage) with gifts from your property,- desiring chastity, not lust, seeing that you derive benefit from them, give them their dowers (at least) as prescribed; but if, after a dower is prescribed, agree mutually (to vary it), there is no blame on you, and Allah is All-knowing, All-wise.

25. If any of you have not the means wherewith to wed free believing women, they may wed believing girls from among those whom your right hands possess: and Allah has full knowledge about your faith. You are one from another: wed them with the leave of their owners, and give them their dowers, according to what is reasonable: they should be chaste, not lustful, nor taking paramours: when they are taken in wedlock, if they fall into shame, their punishment is half that for free women. This (permission) is for those among you who fear sin; but it is better for you that you practise self-restraint. And Allah is Oft-forgiving, Most Merciful.

26. Allah wishes to make clear to you and to show you the ordinances of those before you; and (He does wish to) turn to you (in Mercy): and Allah is All-knowing, All-wise.

27. Allah wishes to turn to you, but the wish of those who follow their lusts is that you should turn away (from Him),- far, far away.

28. Allah wishes to lighten your (difficulties):

an tabtaghoo bi-amwaali-kum muḥṣineena ghayra musaa-fiḥeen; famastamta‘tum bihee minhunna fa-aatoohunna ujoorahunna fareeḍah; wa laa junaaḥa ‘alaykum feemaa taraaḍaytum bihee mim-ba‘dil-fareeḍah; innal-laaha kaana ‘Aleeman Ḥakeemaa.

25. Wa mal-lam yastati‘ minkum tawlan añy-yankiḥal-muḥṣanaatil-mu’minaati famimmaa malakat aymaanukum min fatayaatikumul-mu’minaat; wallaahu a‘lamu bi-eemaani-kum; ba‘ḍukum mim ba‘ḍ; fankiḥoohunna bi-izni ahlihinna wa aatoohunna ujoorahunna bilma‘roofi muḥṣanaatin ghayra musaa-fiḥ aatiñw-wa laa muttakhizaati akhdaan; fa-izaaa uḥṣinna fa-in atayna bifaaḥi-shatin fa-‘alayhinna niṣfu maa ‘alal-muḥṣanaati minal-‘azaab; zaalika liman khashiyal-‘anata minkum; wa an taṣbiroo khayrul-lakum; wallaahu Ghafoorur-Raheem. (Section 4)

26. Yureedul-laahu liyubay-yina lakum wa yahdiyakum sunanal-lazeena min qablikum wa yatooba ‘alaykum; wallaahu ‘Aleemun Ḥakeem.

27. Wallaahu yureedu añy-yatooba ‘alaykum wa yureedul-lazeena yattabi‘oonash-shahawaati an tameeloo maylan ‘azeemaa.

28. Yureedul-laahu añy-yu-khaffifa ‘ankum;

for man was created weak (in flesh).

29. O you who believe! Eat not up your property among yourselves in vanities: but let there be among you traffic and trade by mutual good-will: nor kill (or destroy) yourselves: for verily Allah has been to you Most Merciful!

30. If any do that in rancour and injustice,- soon shall We cast them into the Fire: and easy it is for Allah.

31. If you (but) eschew the most heinous of the things which you are forbidden to do, We shall expel out of you all the evil in you, and admit you to a gate of great honour.

32. And in no wise covet those things in which Allah has bestowed His gifts more freely on some of you than on others: to men is allotted what they earn, and to women what they earn: but ask Allah of His bounty. For Allah has full knowledge of all things.

33. To (benefit) every one, We have appointed shares and heirs to property left by parents and relatives. To those, also, to whom your right hand was pledged, give their due portion. For truly Allah is witness to all things.

34. Men are the protectors and maintainers of women, because Allah has given the one more (strength) than the other, and because they support them from their means. Therefore, the righteous women are devoutly obedient, and guard in (the husband's) absence what Allah would have them guard. As to those women on whose part you fear disloyalty and ill-conduct,

wa khuliqal-insaanu ḍa'eefaa.

29. Yaaa ayyuhal-lazeena aamanoo laa taakulooo amwaalakum baynakum bilbaaṭili 'illaaa an takoona tijaaratan 'an taraaḍim minkum; wa laa taqtulooo anfusakum; innal-laaha kaana bikum Raḥeemaa.

30. Wa mañy-yaf'al zaalika 'ud-waanañw-wa zulman fasawfa nuṣleehi Naaraa; wa kaana zaalika 'alal-laahi yaseeraa.

31. In tajtaniboo kabaaa'ira maa tunhawna 'anhu nukaffir 'ankum sayyi-aatikum wa nudkhilkum mudkhalan kareemaa.

32. Wa laa tatamannaw maa faḍḍalal-laahu bihee ba'ḍakum 'alaa ba'ḍ; lirrijaali naṣeebum-mimmak-tasaboo wa linnisaaa'i naṣeebum-mimmak-tasabna; was'alullaaha min faḍlih; innal-laaha kaana bikulli shay'in 'Aleemaa.

33. Wa likullin ja'alnaa ma-waaliya mimmaa tarakal-waalidaani wal-aqraboon; wallazeena 'aqadat aymaanu-kum fa-aatoohum naṣeebahum; innal-laaha kaana 'alaa kulli shay'in Shaheedaa.   **(Section 5)**

34. Arrijaalu qawwaamoona 'alan-nisaaa'i bimaa faḍ-ḍalallaahu ba'ḍahum 'alaa ba'ḍiñw-wa bimaaa-anfaqoo min amwaalihim; faṣṣaaliḥaatu qaanitaatun ḥaafiẓaatul-lil-ghaybi bimaa ḥafiẓal-laah; wallaatee takhaafoona nushoo-zahunna

admonish them (first), (next), refuse to share their beds, (and last) beat them (lightly); but if they return to obedience, seek not against them means (of annoyance): for Allah is Most High, Great (above you all).

35. If you fear a breach between them twain, appoint (two) arbiters, one from his family, and the other from hers; if they wish for peace, Allah will cause their reconciliation: for Allah has full knowledge, and is acquainted with all things.

36. Serve Allah, and join not any partners with Him; and do good - to parents, kinsfolk, orphans, those in need, neighbours who are near, neighbours who are strangers, the companion by your side, the way-farer (you meet), and what your right hands possess: for Allah loves not the arrogant, the vainglorious.

37. (Nor) those who are niggardly or enjoin niggard-liness on others, or hide the bounties which Allah has bestowed on them; for We have prepared, for those who resist Faith, a punishment that steeps them in contempt;-

38. Nor those who spend of their substance, to be seen of men, but have no faith in Allah and the Last Day: If any take the Satan for their intimate, what a dreadful intimate he is!

39. And what burden were it on them if they had faith in Allah and in the Last Day, and they spent out of what Allah has given them for sustenance?

fa-'izoohunna wahjuroohunna fil-maḍaaji'i waḍriboohunna fa-in aṭa'nakum falaa tabghoo 'alayhinna sabeelaa; innallaaha kaana 'Aliyyan Kabeeraa.

35. Wa in khiftum shiqaaqa bayni-himaa fab'asoo ḥakamam-min ahlihee wa ḥakamam-min ahlihaa; iñy-yureedaaa iṣlaaḥ añy-yuwaffiqil-laahu baynahumaa; innal-laaha kaana 'Aleeman Khabeeraa.

36. Wa'budul-laaha wa laa tushrikoo bihee shay'añw-wa bilwaalidayni iḥsaanañw-wa biẕil-qurbaa walyataamaa walmasaakeeni waljaari ẕilqurbaa waljaaril-junubi waṣṣaaḥibi biljambi wabnis-sabeeli wa maa malakat aymaanukum; innal-laaha laa yuḥibbu man kaana mukhtaalan fakhooraa.

37. Allazeena yabkhaloona wa yaamuroonan-naasa bilbukhli wa yaktumoona maaa aataahu-mullaahu min faḍlih; wa-a'tadnaa lilkaafireena 'azaa-bam-muheenaa.

38. Wallazeena yunfiqoona amwaalahum ri'aaa'an-naasa wa laa yu'minoona billaahi wa laa bil-Yawmil-Aakhir; wa mañy-yakunish-Shayṭaanu lahoo qareenan fasaaa'a qareenaa.

39. Wa maazaa 'alayhim law aamanoo billaahi wal-Yawmil-Aakhiri wa anfaqoo mimmaa razaqahumul-

فَعِظُوهُنَّ وَاهْجُرُوهُنَّ فِى الْمَضَاجِعِ وَاضْرِبُوهُنَّ ۖ فَإِنْ أَطَعْنَكُمْ فَلَا تَبْغُوا عَلَيْهِنَّ سَبِيلًا ۗ إِنَّ اللّٰهَ كَانَ عَلِيًّا كَبِيرًا ۝

وَإِنْ خِفْتُمْ شِقَاقَ بَيْنِهِمَا فَابْعَثُوا حَكَمًا مِّنْ أَهْلِهِ وَحَكَمًا مِّنْ أَهْلِهَا ۚ إِنْ يُّرِيدَا إِصْلَاحًا يُّوَفِّقِ اللّٰهُ بَيْنَهُمَا ۗ إِنَّ اللّٰهَ كَانَ عَلِيمًا خَبِيرًا ۝

وَاعْبُدُوا اللّٰهَ وَلَا تُشْرِكُوا بِهِ شَيْئًا ۖ وَبِالْوَالِدَيْنِ إِحْسَانًا وَبِذِى الْقُرْبَىٰ وَالْيَتَامَىٰ وَالْمَسَاكِينِ وَالْجَارِ ذِى الْقُرْبَىٰ وَالْجَارِ الْجُنُبِ وَالصَّاحِبِ بِالْجَنْبِ وَابْنِ السَّبِيلِ وَمَا مَلَكَتْ أَيْمَانُكُمْ ۗ إِنَّ اللّٰهَ لَا يُحِبُّ مَنْ كَانَ مُخْتَالًا فَخُورًا ۝

الَّذِينَ يَبْخَلُونَ وَيَأْمُرُونَ النَّاسَ بِالْبُخْلِ وَيَكْتُمُونَ مَا آتَاهُمُ اللّٰهُ مِنْ فَضْلِهِ ۚ وَأَعْتَدْنَا لِلْكَافِرِينَ عَذَابًا مُّهِينًا ۝

وَالَّذِينَ يُنْفِقُونَ أَمْوَالَهُمْ رِئَاءَ النَّاسِ وَلَا يُؤْمِنُونَ بِاللّٰهِ وَلَا بِالْيَوْمِ الْآخِرِ ۗ وَمَنْ يَكُنِ الشَّيْطَانُ لَهُ قَرِينًا فَسَاءَ قَرِينًا ۝

وَمَاذَا عَلَيْهِمْ لَوْ آمَنُوا بِاللّٰهِ وَالْيَوْمِ الْآخِرِ وَأَنْفَقُوا مِمَّا رَزَقَهُمُ

For Allah has full knowledge of them.

40. Allah is never unjust in the least degree: if there is any good (done), He doubles it, and gives from His Own Presence a great reward.

41. How then if We brought from each People a witness, and We brought you as a witness against these People!

42. On that day those who reject Faith and disobey the Apostle will wish that the earth were made one with them: but never will they hide a single fact from Allah!

43. O you who believe! Approach not prayers with a mind befogged, until you can understand all that you say,- nor in a state of ceremonial impurity (except when travelling on the road), until after washing your whole body. If you are ill, or on a journey, or one of you comes from offices of nature, or you have been in contact with women, and you find no water, then take for yourselves clean sand or earth, and rub there with your faces and hands. For Allah does blot out sins and forgive again and again.

44. Have you not turned your vision to those who were given a portion of the Book? They traffic in error, and wish that you should lose the right path.

45. But Allah has full know-ledge of your enemies: Allah is enough for a Protector, and Allah is enough for a Helper.

46. Of the Jews there are those who displace

laah; wa kaanallaahu bihim 'Aleemaa.

40. Innal-laaha laa yaẓlimu misqaala zarratiñw wa in taku ḥasanatañy-yuḍaa'ifhaa wa yu'ti mil-ladunhu ajran 'aẓeemaa.

41. Fakayfa izaa ji'naa min kulli ummatim bishaheediñw-wa ji'naa bika 'alaa haaa'ulaaa'i Shaheedaa.

42. Yawma'iziny-yawad-dullazeena kafaroo wa 'aṣawur-Rasoola law tusawwaa bihimul-arḍu wa laa yaktumoonal-laaha ḥadeesaa.   **(Section 6)**

43. Yaaa ayyuhal-lazeena aamanoo laa taqrabuṣ-Ṣalaata wa antum sukaaraa ḥattaa ta'lamoo maa taqooloona wa laa junuban illaa 'aabiree sabeelin ḥattaa taghtasiloo; wa in kuntum marḍaaa aw 'alaa safarin aw jaaa'a aḥadum-minkum minal-ghaaa'iṭi aw laamastumun-nisaaa'a falam tajidoo maaa'an fatayam-mamoo ṣa'eedan ṭayyiban famsaḥoo biwujoohikum wa aydeekum; innal-laaha kaana 'Afuwwan Ghafooraa.

44. Alam tara ilal-lazeena ootoo naṣeebam-minal-Kitaabi yashtaroonaḍ-ḍalaalata wa yureedoona an taḍillus-sabeel.

45. Wallaahu a'lamu bi-a'daaa'i-kum; wa kafaa billaahi waliyyañw-wa kafaa billaahi naṣeeraa.

46. Minal-lazeena haadoo yuḥarrifoonal-

words from their (right) places, and say: "We hear and we disobey"; and "Hear what is not heard"; and "Ra'ina"; with a twist of their tongues and a slander to Faith. If only they had said: "We hear and we obey"; and "Do hear"; and "Do look at us"; it would have been better for them, and more proper; but Allah has cursed them for their Unbelief; and but few of them will believe.

47. O you People of the Book! believe in what We have (now) revealed, confirming what was (already) with you, before We change the face and fame of some (of you) beyond all recognition, and turn them hindwards, or curse them as We cursed the Sabbath-breakers, for the decision of Allah must be carried out.

48. Allah forgives not that partners should be set up with Him; but He forgives anything else, to whom He pleases; to set up partners with Allah is to devise a sin most heinous indeed.

49. Have you not turned your vision to those who claim sanctity for themselves? Nay- but Allah does sanctify whom He pleases. But never will they fail to receive justice in the least little thing.

50. See! how they invent a lie against Allah! but that by itself is a manifest sin!

51. Have you not turned your vision to those who were given a portion of the Book? They believe in sorcery and evil, and say to the Unbelievers that they are better guided in the (right) way than the Believers!

Kalima-'am-mawaadi'ihee wa yaqooloona sami'naa wa 'aṣaynaa wasma' ghayra musma'iñw-wa raa'inaa layyam bi-alsinatihim wa ṭa'nan fid-deen; wa law annahum qaaloo sami'naa wa aṭa'naa wasma' wanẓurnaa lakaana khayral-lahum wa aqwama wa laakil-la-'anahumul-laahu bikufrihim falaa yu'minoona illaa qaleela

47. Yaaa-ayyuhal-laẕeena ootul-Kitaaba aaminoo bimaa nazzalnaa muṣaddiqallimaa ma'akum min qabli an naṭmisa wujoohan fanaruddahaa 'alaaa adbaarihaaa aw nal'anahum kamaa la'annaaa Aṣḥaabas-Sabt; wa kaana amrul-laahi maf'oolaa.

48. Innal-laaha laa yaghfiru añy-yushraka bihee wa yaghfiru maa doona ẕaalika limañy-yashaaa'; wa mañy-yushrik billaahi faqadif-taraaa isman 'aẓeemaa.

49. Alam tara ilal-laẕeena yuzakkoona anfusahum; balil-laahu yuzakkee mañy-yashaaa'u wa laa yuẓlamoona fateelaa.

50. Unẓur kayfa yaftaroona 'alal-laahil-kaẕib, wa kafaa biheee iẕmam-mubeenaa.
(Section 7)

51. Alam tara-ilal-laẕeena 'ootoo naṣeebam-minal-Kitaabi yu'minoona bil-Jibti waṭ-Ṭaaghooti wa yaqooloona lillaẕeena kafaroo haaa-ulaaa'i ahdaa minal-laẕeena aamanoo sabeelaa.

52. They are (men) whom Allah has cursed: and those whom Allah has cursed, you will find, have no one to help.

53. Have they a share in dominion or power? Behold, they give not a farthing to their fellow-men.

54. Or do they envy mankind for what Allah has given them of his bounty? But We had already given the people of Abraham the Book and wisdom, and conferred upon them a great kingdom.

55. Some of them believed, and some of them averted their faces·from him: and enough is Hell for a burning fire.

56. Those who reject Our Signs, We shall soon cast (them) into the Fire: as often as their skins are roasted through, We shall change them for fresh skins, that they may taste the Chastisement: for Allah is Exalted in Power, Wise.

57. But those who believe and do deeds of righteousness, We shall soon admit (them) to Gardens, with rivers flowing beneath, - their eternal home: therein shall they have Companions pure and holy: We shall admit them to shades, cool and ever deepening.

58. Allah does command you to render back your trusts to those to whom they are due; and when you judge between man and man, that you judge with justice: verily how excellent is the teaching which He gives you! for Allah is He Who hears and sees all things.

59. O you who believe! obey Allah,

52. Ulaaa'ikal-lazeena la'ana-humul-laahu wa mañy-yal'anil-laahu falan tajida lahoo naseeraa.

53. Am lahum naseebum-minal-mulki fa-izal-laa yu'too-nan-naasa naqeeraa.

54. Am yahsudoonan-naasa 'alaa maaa aataahumul-laahu min fadlihee faqad aataynaaa Aala Ibraaheemal-Kitaaba wal-Hikmata wa aataynaahum mulkan 'azeemaa.

55. Faminhum man aamana bihee wa minhum man sadda 'anh; wa kafaa bi-Jahannama sa'eeraa.

56. Innal-lazeena kafaroo bi-Aayaatinaa sawfa nusleehim Naaran kullamaa nadijat julooduhum baddalnaahum juloodan ghayrahaa liyazooqul-'azaab; innallaaha kaana 'Azeezan Hakeemaa.

57. Wallazeena aamanoo wa 'amilus-saalihaati sanud-khiluhum Jannaatin tajree min tahtihal-anhaaru khaalideena feehaaa abadaa, lahum feehaaa azwaajum-mutahharatuñw-wa nudkhiluhum zillan zaleelaa.

58. Innal-laaha yaåmurukum an tu'addul-amaanaati ilaaa ahlihaa wa izaa hakamtum baynan-naasi an tahkumoo bil-'adl; innal-laaha ni'immaa ya'izukum bih; innal-laaha kaana Samee'am Baseeraa.

59. Yaaa-ayyuhal-lazeena aamanooo atee'ul-laaha

and obey the Apostle, and those charged with authority among you. If you differ in anything among yourselves, refer it to Allah and His Apostle, if you do believe in Allah and the Last Day: that is best, and most suitable for final determination.

60. Have you not turned your vision to those who declare that they believe in the revelations that have come to you and to those before you? Their (real) wish is to resort together for judgment (in their disputes) to the Satan, though they were ordered to reject him. But Satan's wish is to lead them astray far away (from the right).

61. When it is said to them: "Come to what Allah has revealed, and to the Apostle": you sees the Hypocrites avert their faces from you in disgust.

62. How then, when they are seized by misfortune, because of the deeds which their hands have sent forth? Then they come to you, swearing by Allah: "We meant no more than good-will and conciliation!"

63. Those men, Allah knows what is in their hearts; so keep clear of them, but admonish them, and speak to them a word to reach their very souls.

64. We sent not an Apostle, but to be obeyed, in accordance with the Will of Allah. If they had only, when they were unjust to themselves, come to you and asked Allah's forgiveness, and the Apostle had asked forgiveness for them, they would have found Allah indeed Oft-returning, Most Merciful.

wa aṭee'ur-Rasoola wa ulil-amri minkum fa-in tanaaza'tum fee shay'in faruddoohu ilal-laahi war-Rasooli in kuntum tu'minoona billaahi wal-Yawmil-Aakhir; zaalika khayruñw-wa aḥsanu taåweelaa.
(Section 8)

60. Alam tara ilal-lazeena yaz'umoona annahum aamanoo bimaa unzila ilayka wa maaa unzila min qablika yureedoona añy-yataḥaakamooo ilaṭ-Ṭaaghooti wa qad umirooo añy-yakfuroo bih, wa yureedush-Shayṭaanu añy-yuḍillahum ḍalaalam-ba'eedaa.

61. Wa izaa qeela lahum ta'aalaw ilaa maaa anzalallaahu wa ilar-Rasooli ra-aytal-munaafiqeena yaṣuddoona 'anka ṣudoodaa.

62. Fakayfa izaaa aṣaabathum muṣeebatum bimaa qaddamat aydeehim summa jaaa'ooka yaḥlifoona billaahi in aradnaaa illaaa iḥsaanañw-wa tawfeeqaa.

63. Ulaaa'ikal-lazeena ya'lamullaahu maa fee quloobihim fa-a'riḍ 'anhum wa 'iẓhum wa qul lahum feee anfusihim qawlam-baleeghaa.

64. Wa maaa arsalnaa mir-Rasoolin illaa liyuṭaa'a bi-iznillaah; wa law annahum 'iz ẓalamooo anfusahum jaaa'ooka fastaghfarul-laaha wastaghfara lahumur-Rasoolu la-wajadul-laaha Tawwaabar-Raḥeemaa.

65. But no, by your Lord, they can have no (real) Faith, until they make you judge in all disputes between them, and find in their souls no resistance against your decisions, but accept them with the fullest conviction.

66. If We had ordered them to sacrifice their lives or to leave their homes, very few of them would have done it: but if they had done what they were (actually) told, it would have been best for them, and would have gone farthest to strengthen their (faith);

67. And We would then have given them from Our Presence a great reward;

68. And We would have shown them the Straight Way.

69. All who obey Allah and the Apostle are in the company of those on whom is the Grace of Allah, - of the Prophets (who teach), the Sincere (lovers of Truth), the Witnesses (who testify), and the Righteous (who do good): ah! what a beautiful Fellowship!

70. Such is the bounty from Allah: and sufficient is it that Allah knows all.

71. O you who believe! take your precautions, and either go forth in parties or go forth all together.

72. There are certainly among you men who would tarry behind: if a misfortune befalls you, they say: "Allah did favour us in that we were not present among them."

73. But if good fortune comes to you from Allah, they would be sure to say - as if there had never been ties of affection between you and them - "Oh! I wish I had been with them; a fine thing should I then have made of it!"

65. Falaa wa Rabbika laa yu'minoona ḥattaa yuḥak-kimooka fe-emaa shajara baynahum summa laa yajidoo feee anfusihim ḥarajam-mimmaa qaḍayta wa yusal-limoo tasleemaa.

66. Wa law annaa katabnaa 'alayhim aniq-tulooo anfu-sakum awikh-rujoo min diyaarikum maa fa'aloohu illaa qaleelum-minhum wa law annahum fa'aloo maa yoo'aẓoona bihee lakaana khayral-lahum wa ashadda tasbeetaa.

67. Wa-izal-la-aataynaahum mil-ladunnaaa-ajran 'aẓeemaa.

68. Wa lahadaynaahum Ṣiraa-ṭam-Mustaqeemaa.

69. Wa mañy-yuṭi'i'il-laaha war-Rasoola fa-ulaaa'ika ma'al-lazeena an'amal-laahu 'alayhim minan-Nabiyyeena waṣṣid-deeqeena washshuhadaaa'i waṣṣaaliḥeen; wa ḥasuna ulaaa'ika rafeeqaa.

70. Zaalikal-faḍlu minal-laah; wa kafaa billaahi 'Aleemaa.

(Section 9)

71. Yaaa-ayyuhal-lazeena aamanoo khuzoo ḥizrakum fanfiroo ṣubaatin awin-firoo jamee'aa.

72. Wa inna minkum lamal-la-yubaṭṭi'anna fa-in aṣaabatkum muṣeebatun qaala qad an'amal-laahu 'alayya iz lam akum-ma'ahum shaheedaa.

73. Wa la'in aṣaabakum faḍlum-minal-laahi la-yaqoolanna ka-al-lam takum-baynakum wa baynahoo mawaddatuñy-yaa laytanee kuntu ma'ahum fa-afooza fawzan 'aẓeemaa.

74. Let those fight in the cause of Allah Who sell the life of this world for the Hereafter. To him who fights in the cause of Allah,- whether he is slain or gets victory - soon shall We give him a reward of great (value).

75. And why should you not fight in the cause of Allah and of those who, being weak, are ill-treated (and oppressed)?- men, women, and children, whose cry is: "Our Lord! Rescue us from this town, whose people are oppressors; and raise for us from You one who will protect; and raise for us from You one who will help!"

76. Those who believe fight in the cause of Allah, and those who reject Faith fight in the cause of Evil: so fight you against the friends of Satan: feeble indeed is the cunning of Satan.

77. Have you not turned your vision to those who were told to hold back their hands (from fight) but establish regular prayers and spend in regular charity? When (at length) the order for fighting was issued to them, behold! a section of them feared men as - or even more than - they should have feared Allah: they said: "Our Lord! Why have You ordered us to fight? Would You not Grant us respite to our (natural) term, near (enough)?" Say: "Short is the enjoyment of this world: the Hereafter is the best for those who do right: never will you be dealt with unjustly in the very least!

78. "Wherever you are, death will find you out, even if you are in towers built up strong and high!" If some good befalls them, they say, "This is from

74. Falyuqaatil fee sabeelil-laahil-lazeena yashroonal-ḥayaatad-dunyaa bil-Aakhirah; wa mañy-yuqaatil fee sabeelil-laahi fa-yuqtal aw yaghlib fasawfa nu'teehi ajran 'azeemaa.

75. Wa maa lakum laa tuqaatiloona fee sabeelil-laahi walmustaḍ'afeena minar-rijaali wannisaaa'i walwildaanil-lazeena yaqooloona Rabbanaaa akhrijnaa min haazihil-qarya-tiz-zaalimi ahluhaa waj'al-lanaa mil-ladunka waliyyañw-waj'al-lanaa mil-ladunka naseeraa.

76. Allazeena aamanoo yuqaatiloona fee sabeelil-laahi wallazeena kafaroo yuqaati-loona fee sabeeliṭ-Ṭaaghoot faqaatilooo awliyaaa'ash-Shayṭaan; inna kaydash-Shay-ṭaani kaana ḍa'eefaa. **(Section 10)**

77. Alam tara ilal-lazeena qeela lahum kuffooo aydiyakum wa aqeemuṣ-Ṣalaata wa aatuz-Zakaata falammaa kutiba 'alayhimul-qitaalu izaa faree-qum-minhum yakhshawnan-naasa kakhashyatil-laahi aw ashadda khashyah; wa qaaloo Rabbanaa lima katabta 'alaynal-qitaala law laaa akhkhartanaaa ilaa ajalin qareeb; qul mataa'ud-dunyaa qaleeluñw wal-Aakhiratu khayrul-limanit-taqaa wa laa tuẓlamoona fateelaa.

78. Aynamaa takoonoo yudrikkumul-mawtu wa law kuntum fee buroojim-mushay-yadah; wa in tusibhum ḥasa-natuñy-yaqooloo haazihee min

Allah"; but if evil, they say, "This is from you" (O Prophet). Say: "All things are from Allah." But what have come to these people, that they fail to understand a single fact?

79. Whatever good, (O man!) happens to you is from Allah; but whatever evil happens to you, is from your (own) soul. and We have sent you as an Apostle to (instruct) mankind. And enough is Allah for a Witness.

80. He who obeys the Apostle, obeys Allah: but if any turn away, We have not sent you to watch over their (evil deeds).

81. They have "Obedience" on their lips; but when they leave you, a section of them meditate all night on things very different from what you tell them. But Allah records their nightly (plots): so keep clear of them, and put your trust in Allah, and enough is Allah as a disposer of affairs.

82. Do they not consider the Qur'an (with care)? Had it been from other than Allah, they would surely have found therein much discrepancy.

83. When there comes to them some matter touching (public) safety or fear, they divulge it. If they had only referred it to the Apostle, or to those charged with authority among them, the proper investigators would have tested it from them (direct). Were it not for the Grace and Mercy of Allah unto you, all but a few of you would have fallen into the clutches of Satan.

84. Then fight in Allah's cause - you are held responsible only

'indil-laahi wa in tuṣibhum sayyi'atuñy-yaqooloo haazihee min 'indik; qul kullum-min 'indillaahi famaa lihaaaa-'ulaaa'il-qawmi laa yakaadoona yafqahoona ḥadeesaa.

79. Maaa aṣaabaka min ḥasanatin faminal-laahi wa maaa aṣaabaka min sayyi'atin famin-nafsik; wa arsalnaaka linnaasi Rasoolaa; wa kafaa billaahi Shaheedaa.

80. Man yuṭi'ir-Rasoola faqad aṭaa'al-laaha wa man tawallaa famaaa arsalnaaka 'alayhim ḥafeeẓaa.

81. Wa yaqooloona ṭaa'atun fa-iẓaa barazoo min 'indika bayyata ṭaaa'ifatum-minhum ghayral-lazee taqoolu wallaahu yaktubu maa yubayyitoona fa-a'riḍ 'anhum wa tawakkal 'alal-laah; wa kafaa billaahi Wakeelaa.

82. Afalaa yatadabbaroonal-Qur'aan; wa law kaana min 'indi ghayril-laahi la-wajadoo fee-hikh-tilaafan kaseeraa.

83. Wa izaa jaaa'ahum amrum-minal-amni awil-khawfi azaa'oo bihee wa law raddoohu ilar-Rasooli wa ilaaa ulil-amri minhum la'alimahul-lazeena yastambiṭoonahoo minhum; wa law laa faḍlul-laahi 'alaykum wa raḥmatuhoo lattaba'tu-mush-Shayṭaana illaa qaleelaa.

84. Faqaatil fee sabeelil-laahi laa tukallafu illaa

for yourself - and motivate the Believers. It may be that Allah will restrain the fury of the Unbelievers; for Allah is the strongest in might and in punishment.

85. Whoever recommends and helps a good cause becomes a partner therein: and whoever recommends and helps an evil cause, shares in its burden: and Allah has power over all things.

86. When a (courteous) greeting is offered you, meet it with a greeting still more courteous, or (at least) of equal courtesy. Allah takes careful account of all things.

87. Allah! There is no god but He: of a surety He will gather you together against the Day of Judgment, about which there is no doubt. And whose word can be truer than Allah's?

88. Why should you be divided into two parties about the Hypocrites? Allah has upset them for their (evil) deeds. Would you guide those whom Allah has thrown out of the Way? For those whom Allah has thrown out of the Way, never shall you find the Way.

89. They but wish that you should reject Faith, as they do, and thus be on the same footing (as they): but take not friends from their ranks until they flee in the way of Allah (from what is forbidden). But if they turn renegades, seize them and slay them wherever you find them; and (in any case) take no friends or helpers from their ranks;-

90. Except those who join a group between whom and you there is a treaty (of peace), or those who approach you with hearts restraining them from fighting

nafsaka wa ḥarriḍil-mu'mineena 'asallaahu añy-yakuffa baåsallazeena kafaroo; wallaahu ashaddu baåsañw-wa ashaddu tankeelaa.

85. Mañy-yashfa' shafaa'atan ḥasanatañy-yakul-lahoo naṣeebum-minhaa wa mañy-yashfa' shafaa'atan sayyi'atañy-yakul-lahoo kiflum-minhaa; wa kaanal-laahu 'alaa kulli shay'im-Muqeetaa.

86. Wa izaa ḥuyyeetum bitaḥiy-yatin faḥayyoo bi-aḥsana minhaaa aw ruddoohaa; innal-laahu kaana 'alaa kulli shay'in Ḥaseebaa.

87. Allaahu laaa ilaaha illaa huwa la-yajma'annakum ilaa Yawmil-Qiyaamati laa rayba feeh; wa man aṣdaqu minallaahi ḥadeesaa. **(Section 11)**

88. Famaa lakum filmuna-afiqeena fi'atayni wallaahu arkasahum bimaa kasaboo; atureedoona an tahdoo man aḍallal-laahu wa mañy-yuḍlilil-laahu falan tajida lahoo sabeelaa.

89. Wadoo law takfuroona kamaa kafaroo fatakoonoona sawaaa'an falaa tattakhizoo minhum awliyaaa'a ḥattaa yuhaajiroo fee sabeelil-laah; fa-in tawallaw fa-khuzoohum waqtuloohum ḥaysu wajat-tumoohum wa laa tattakhizoo minhum waliyyañw wa laa naṣeeraa.

90. Illal-lazeena yaṣiloona ilaa qawmim-baynakum wa baynahum meesaaqun aw jaaa'ookum ḥaṣirat ṣudooru-hum añy-yuqaatilookum

you as well as fighting their own people. If Allah had pleased, He could have given them power over you, and they would have fought you: therefore if they withdraw from you but fight you not, and (instead) send you (guarantees of) peace, then Allah has opened no way for you (to war against them).

91. Others you will find that wish to gain your confidence as well as that of their people: every time they are sent back to temptation, they succumb thereto: if they withdraw not from you nor give you (guarantees) of peace besides restraining their hands, seize them and slay them wherever you get them: in their case We have provided you with a clear argument against them.

92. Never should a believer kill a believer; but (if it so happens) by mistake, (compensation is due): if one (so) kills a believer, it is ordained that he should free a believing slave, and pay compensation to the deceased's family, unless they remit it freely. If the deceased belonged to a people at war with you, and he was a believer, the freeing of a believing slave (is enough). If he belonged to a people with whom you have treaty of mutual alliance, compensation should be paid to his family, and a believing slave be freed. For those who find this beyond their means, (is prescribed) a fast for two months running: by way of repentance to Allah: for Allah has all knowledge and all wisdom.

93. If a man kills a Believer intentionally, his recompense is

---

aw yuqaatiloo qawmahum, wa law shaaa'al-laahu lasallaṭahum 'alaykum falaqaatalookum; fa-ini'-tazalookum falam yuqaati-lookum wa alqaw ilaykumus-salama famaa ja'alal-laahu lakum 'alayhim sabeelaa.

91. Satajidoona aakhareena yureedoona añy-yaåmanookum wa yaåmanoo qawmahum kullamaa ruddooo ilal-fitnati urkisoo feehaa; fa-il-lam ya'tazilookum wa yulqooo ilay-kumus-salama wa yakuffooo aydiyahum fakhuzoohum waqtuloohum ḥayṣu ṣaqif-tumoohum; wa ulaaa'ikum ja'alnaa lakum 'alayhim sulṭaanam-mubeenaa.

(Section 12)

92. Wa maa kaana limu'minin añy-yaqtula mu'minan illaa khaṭa'aa; waman qatala mu'minan khaṭa'an fataḥreeru raqabatim-mu'minatiñw-wa diyatum-musallamatun ilaaa ahliheee illaaa añy-yaṣṣad-daqoo; fa-in kaana min qawmin 'aduwwil-lakum wa huwa mu'minun fataḥreeru raqa-batim mu'minah; wa in kaana min qawmim baynakum wa baynahum meesaaqun fadiyatum-musallamatun ilaaa ahlihee wa taḥreeru raqabatim-mu'minatin famal-lam yajid fa-Ṣiyaamu shahrayni muta-taabi'ayni tawbatam-minal-laah; wa kaanal-laahu 'Aleeman Ḥakeemaa.

93. Wa mañy-yaqtul mu'minam-muta'ammidan fajazaaa'uhoo

Hell, to abide therein (for ever): and the wrath and the curse of Allah are upon him, and a dreadful Chastisement is prepared for him.

94. O you who believe! When you go abroad in the cause of Allah, investigate carefully, and say not to any one who offers you a salutation: "you are not a Believer!" coveting the perishable goods of this life: with Allah are profits and spoils abundant. Even thus were you yourselves before, till Allah conferred on you His favours: therefore carefully investigate. For Allah is well aware of all that you do.

95. Not equal are those believers who sit (at home) and receive no hurt, and those who strive and fight in the cause of Allah with their goods and their persons. Allah has granted a grade higher to those who strive and fight with their goods and persons than to those who sit (at home). Unto all (in Faith) has Allah promised good: but those who strive and fight He has distinguished above those who sit (at home) by a special reward,-

96. Ranks specially bestowed by Him, and Forgiveness and Mercy. For Allah is Oft-forgiving, Most Merciful.

97. When angels take the souls of those who die in sin against their souls, they say: "In what (plight) were you?" They reply: "Weak and oppressed were we in the earth." They say: "Was not the earth of Allah spacious enough for you to move yourselves away (from evil)?" Such men will find their abode in Hell, - What an evil refuge! -

Jahannamu khaalidan feehaa wa ghaḍibal-laahu 'alayhi wa la'anahoo wa a'adda lahoo 'azaaban 'azeemaa.

94. Yaaa-ayyuhal-lazeena aamanooo izaa ḍarabtum fee sabeelil-laahi fatabayyanoo wa laa taqooloo liman alqaaa ilaykumus-salaama lasta mu'minan tabtaghoona 'araḍal-ḥayaatid-dunyaa fa'indal-laahi maghaanimu kaseerah; kazaalika kuntum min qablu famannal-laahu 'alaykum fatabayyanoo; innallaaha kaana bimaa ta'maloona Khabeeraa.

95. Laa yastawil-qaa'idoona Minal-mu'mineena ghayru uliḍ-ḍarari walmujaahidoona fee sabeelil-laahi bi-amwaali-him wa anfusihim; faḍḍalal-laahul-mujaahideena bi-amwaalihim wa anfusihim 'alal-qaa'ideena darajah; wa kullaňw wa'adal-laahul-ḥusnaa; wa faḍḍalal-laahul-mujaahideena 'alal-qaa'ideena ajran 'azeemaa.

96. Darajaatim-minhu wa maghfirataňw-wa raḥmah; wa kaanal-laahu Ghafoorar-Raḥeemaa.   (Section 13)

97. Innal-lazeena tawaffaa-humul-malaaa'ikatu zaalimeee-anfusihim qaaloo feema kuntum qaaloo kunnaa mustaḍ'afeena fil-arḍ; qaalooo alam takun arḍul-laahi waasi'atan fatuhaajiroo feehaa; fa-ulaaa'ika maåwaahum Ja-hannamu wa saaa'at maṣeeraa.

98. Except those who are (really) weak and oppressed - men, women, and children - who have no means in their power, nor (a guide-post) to their way.

99. For these, there is hope that Allah will forgive: for Allah blots out (sins) and forgive again and again.

100. He who forsakes his home in the cause of Allah, finds in the earth many a refuge, wide and spacious: should he die as a refugee from home for Allah and His Apostle, His reward becomes due and sure with Allah: And Allah is Oft-forgiving, Most Merciful.

101. When you travel through the earth, there is no blame on you if you shorten your prayers, for fear the Unbelievers may attack you: for the Unbelievers are open enemies to you.

102. When you (O Apostle) are with them, and stand to lead them in prayer, let one party of them stand up (in prayer) with you, taking their arms with them: when they finish their prostrations, let them take their position in the rear. And let the other party come up which has not yet prayed - and let them pray with you, taking all precaution, and bearing arms: the Unbelievers wish, if you were negligent of your arms and your baggage, to assault you in a single rush. But there is no blame

98. Illal-mustaḍ'afeena minar-rijaali wannisaaa'i walwildaani laa yastatee'oona heelatañw-wa laa yahtadoona sabeelaa.

99. Fa-ulaaa'ika 'asal-laahu añy-ya'fuwa 'anhum; wa kaanal-laahu 'Afuwwan Ghafooraa.

100. Wa mañy-yuhaajir fee sabeelil-laahi yajid fil-arḍi muraaghaman kaseerañw-wa sa'ah; wa mañy-yakhruj mim-baytihee muhaajiran ilal-laahi wa Rasoolihee summa yudrik-hul-mawtu faqad waqa'a ajruhoo 'alal-laah; wa kaanal-laahu Ghafoorar-Raḥeemaa.

(Section 14)

101. Wa izaa ḍarabtum fil-arḍi falaysa 'alaykum junaaḥun an taqṣuroo minaṣ-Ṣalaati in khiftum añy-yaftinakumul-lazeena kafarooo; innal-kaafireena kaanoo lakum aduwwam-mubeenaa.

102. Wa izaa kunta feehim fa-aqamta lahumuṣ-Ṣalaata faltaqum ṭaaa'ifatum-minhum ma'aka walyaåkhuzooo asliḥatahum fa-izaa sajadoo fal-yakoonoo miñw-waraaa'ikum waltaåti ṭaaa'ifatun ukhraa lam yuṣalloo falyuṣalloo ma'aka walyaåkhuzoo ḥizrahum wa asliḥatahum; waddal-lazeena kafaroo law taghfuloona 'an asliḥatikum wa amti'atikum fa-yameeloona 'alaykum maylatañw-waaḥidah; wa laa junaaḥa

on you if you put away your arms because of the inconvenience of rain or because you are ill; but take (every) precaution for your-selves. For the Unbelievers Allah has prepared a humiliating punishment.

103. When you pass (congregational) prayers, celebrate Allah's praises, standing, sitting down, or lying down on your sides; but when you are free from danger, set up regular Prayers: for such prayers are enjoined on Believers at stated times.

104. And slacken not in following up the enemy: if you are suffering hardships, they are suffering similar hardships; but you have hope from Allah, while they have none. And Allah is full of knowledge and wisdom.

105. We have sent down to you the Book in truth, that you might judge between men, as guided by Allah: so be not (used) as an advocate by those who betray their trust;

106. But seek the forgiveness of Allah; for Allah is Oft-forgiving, Most Merciful.

107. Contend not on behalf of such as betray their own souls; for Allah loves not one given to perfidy and crime:

108. They may hide (their crimes) from men, but they cannot hide (them) from Allah, seeing that He is in their midst when they plot by night, in words that He cannot approve: And Allah does compass round all that they do.

'alaykum in kaana bikum azam-mimmaṭarin aw kuntum marḍaaa an taḍa'ooo asliḥatakum wa khuzoo ḥizrakum; innal-laaha a'adda lilkaafireena 'azaabam-muheenaa.

103. Fa-izaa qaḍaytumuṣ-Ṣalaata fazkurul-laaha qiyaa-mañw-wa qu'oodañw-wa 'alaa junoobikum; fa-izaṭ-maa-nantum fa-aqeemuṣ-Ṣalaah; innaṣ-Ṣalaata kaanat 'alal-mu'mineena kitaabam-mawqootaa.

104. Wa laa tahinoo fibtighaaa'il-qawmi in takoonoo taalamoona fa-innahum yaa-lamoona kamaa taalamoona wa tarjoona minal-laahi maa laa yarjoon; wa kaanal-laahu 'Aleeman Ḥakeemaa.   (Sec. 15)

105. Innaaa anzalnaaa ilaykal-Kitaaba bilḥaqqi litaḥkuma baynan-naasi bimaaa araakal-laah; wa laa takul-lilkhaaa'i-neena khaṣeemaa.

106. Wastaghfiril-laaha innallaaha kaana Ghafoorar-Raḥeemaa.

107. Wa laa tujaadil 'anil-lazeena yakhtaanoona anfusa-hum; innal-laaha laa yuḥibbu man kaana khawwaanan aseemaa.

108. Yastakhfoona minannaasi wa laa yastakh-foona minal-laahi wa huwa ma'ahum iz yubayyitoona maa laa yarḍaa minal-qawl; wa kaanal-laahu bimaa ya'maloona muḥeeṭaa.

109. Ah! These are the sort of men on whose behalf you may contend in this world; but who will contend with Allah on their behalf on the Day of Judgment, or who will carry their affairs through?

110. If any one does evil or wrongs his own soul but afterwards seeks Allah's forgiveness, he will find Allah Oft-forgiving, Most Merciful.

111. And if any one earns sin, he earns it against his own soul: for Allah is full of knowledge and wisdom.

112. But if any one earns a fault or a sin and throws it on to one that is innocent, he carries (on himself) (both) a falsehood and a flagrant sin.

113. But for the Grace of Allah to you and His Mercy, a party of them would certainly have plotted to lead you astray. But (in fact) they will only lead their own souls astray, and to you they can do no harm in the least. For Allah has sent down to you the Book and wisdom and taught you what you knew not (before): and great is the Grace of Allah unto you.

114. In most of their secret talks there is no good: but if one exhorts to a deed of charity or justice or conciliation between men, (secrecy is permissible): to him who does this, seeking the good pleasure of Allah, We shall soon give a reward of the highest (value).

115. If anyone contends with the Apostle even after

109. Haaa-antum haaa'ulaaa'i jaadaltum 'anhum fil-ḥayaatid-dunyaa famañy-yujaadilul-laaha 'anhum Yawmal-Qiyaamati am mañy-yakoonu 'alayhim wakeelaa.

110. Wa mañy-ya'mal sooo'an aw yaẓlim nafsahoo ṣumma yastaghfiril-laaha yajidil-laaha Ghafoorar-Raḥeemaa.

111. Wa mañy-yaksib iṣman fa-innamaa yaksibuhoo 'alaa nafsih; wa kaanal-laahu 'Aleeman Ḥakeemaa.

112. Wa mañy-yaksib kha-ṭee'atan aw iṣman ṣumma yarmi bihee baree'an faqadiḥ-tamala buhtaanañw-wa iṣmam-mubeenaa. **(Section 16)**

113. Wa law laa faḍlul-laahi 'alayka wa raḥmatuhoo lahammaṭ-ṭaaa'ifatum minhum añy-yuḍillooka wa maa yuḍilloona illaaa anfusahum wa maa yaḍurroonaka min shay'; wa anzalal-laahu 'alaykal-Kitaaba wal-Ḥikmata wa 'allamaka maa lam takun ta'lam; wa kaana faḍlul-laahi 'alayka 'aẓeemaa.

114. Laa khayra fee kaseerim-min najwaahum illaa man amara biṣadaqatin aw ma'roo-fin aw iṣlaaḥim-baynan-naas; wa mañy-yaf'al zaalikab-tighaaa'a marḍaatil-laahi fa-sawfa nu'teehi ajran 'aẓeemaa.

115. Wa mañy-yushaaqiqir-Rasoola mim-ba'di

guidance has been plainly conveyed to him, and follows a path other than that becoming to men of Faith, We shall leave him in the path he has chosen, and land him in Hell, - what an evil refuge!

116. Allah forgives not (the sin of) joining other gods with Him; but He forgives whom He pleases other sins than this: one who joins other gods with Allah has strayed far, far away (from the Right).

117. (The Pagans), leaving Him, call but upon female deities: they call but upon Satan the persistent rebel!

118. Allah did curse him, but he said: "I will take of Your servants a portion marked off;

119. "I will mislead them, and I will create in them false desires; I will order them to slit the ears of cattle, and to deface the (fair) nature created by Allah." Whoever, forsaking Allah, takes Satan for a friend, has of a surety suffered a loss that is manifest.

120. Satan makes them promises, and creates in them false desires; but Satan's promises are nothing but deception.

121. They (his dupes) will have their dwelling in Hell, and from it they will find no way of escape.

122. But those who believe and do deeds of righteousness, - We shall soon admit them to Gardens, with rivers flowing beneath, - to dwell therein for ever. Allah's promise is the truth, and whose word can be truer than Allah's?

123. Not your desires, nor those of the People of

---

maa tabayyana lahul-hudaa wa yattabi' ghayra sabeelil-mu'mineena nuwallihee maa tawallaa wa nuṣlihee Jahannama wa saaa'at maṣeeraa.

(Section 17)

116. Innal-laaha laa yaghfiru añy-yushraka bihee wayaghfiru maa doona ẕaalika limâñy yashaaa'; wa mâñy-yushrik billaahi faqad ḍalla ḍalaalam-ba'eedaa.

117. Iñy-yad'oona min doonihee illaaa inaaṣañw wa iñy-yad'oona illaa Shayṭaanam-mareedaa.

118. La'anahul-laah; wa qaala la-attakhiẕanna min 'ibaadika naṣeebam-mafrooḍaa.

119. Wa la-uḍillannahum wa la-umanniyannahum wa la-aamurannahum fala-yubat-tikunna aaẕaanal-an'aami wa la-aamurannahum fala-yughay-yirunna khalqal-laah; wa mâñy-yattakhiẕish-Shayṭaana waliy-yam-min doonil-laahi faqad khasira khusraanam-mubeenaa.

120. Ya'iduhum wa yuman-neehim wa maa ya'iduhumush-Shayṭaanu illaa ghurooraa.

121. Ulaaa'ika maåwaahum Jahannamu wa laa yajidoona 'anhaa maḥeeṣaa.

122. Wallaẕeena aamanoo wa 'amiluṣ-ṣaaliḥaati sanud-khiluhum Jannaatin tajree min taḥtihal-anhaaru khaalideena feehaaa abadaa; wa'dal-laahi ḥaqqaa; wa man aṣdaqu minal-laahi qeelaa.

123. Laysa bi-amaaniyyikum wa laaa amaaniyyi Ahlil-

the Book (can prevail): whoever works evil, will be requited accordingly. Nor will he find, besides Allah any protector or helper.

124. If any do deeds of righteousness,- be they male or female - and have faith, they will enter Heaven, and not the least injustice will be done to them.

125. Who can be better in religion than one who submits his whole self to Allah, does good, and follows the way of Abraham the true in faith? For Allah did take Abraham for a friend.

126. But to Allah belong all things in the heavens and on earth: and He it is that encompasses all things.

127. They ask your instruction concerning the Women. Say: Allah does instruct you about them: and (remember) what has been rehearsed unto you in the Book, concerning the orphans of women to whom you give not the portions prescribed, and yet whom you desire to marry, as also concerning the children who are weak and oppressed: that you stand firm for justice to orphans. There is not a good deed which you do, but Allah is well-acquainted therewith.

128. If a wife fears cruelty or desertion on her husband's part, there is no blame on them if they arrange an amicable settlement between themselves; and such settlement is best; even though men's souls are

Kitaab; mañy-ya'mal sooo'añy-yujza bihee wa laa yajid lahoo min doonil-laahi waliyyañw-wa laa naseeraa.

124. Wa mañy-ya'mal minas-saaliḥaati min zakarin aw unsaa wa huwa mu'minun fa-ulaaa'ika yadkhuloonal-Jannata wa laa yuẓlamoona naqeeraa.

125. Wa man aḥsanu deenam-mimman aslama wajhahoo lillaahi wa huwa muḥsinuñw-wattaba'a Millata Ibraaheema Ḥaneefaa; wattakhazal-laahu Ibraaheema khaleelaa.

126. Wa lillaahi maa fis-samaa-waati wa maa fil-arḍ; wa kaanal-laahu bikulli shay'im-muḥeeṭaa.
(Section 18)

127. Wa yastaftoonaka finni-saaa'i qulil-laahu yufteekum feehinna wa maa yutlaa 'alaykum fil-Kitaabi fee yataaman-nisaaa'il-laatee laa tu'toonahunna maa kutiba lahunna wa targhaboona an tankiḥoohunna wal-mustaḍ'a-feena minal-wildaani wa an taqoomoo lilyataamaa bilqist; wa maa taf'aloo min khayrin fa-innal-laaha kaana bihee 'Alee-maa.

128. Wa inimra-atun khaafat mim ba'lihaa nushoozan aw i'raaḍan falaa junaaḥa 'alayhi-maaa añy-yuṣliḥaa baynahumaa ṣulḥaa; waṣṣulḥu khayr; wa uḥḍiratil-anfusush-

swayed by greed. But if you do good and practise self-restraint, Allah is well-acquainted with all that you do.

129. You are never able to be fair and just as between women, even if it is your ardent desire: but turn not away (from a woman) altogether, so as to leave her (as it were) hanging (in the air). If you come to a friendly understanding, and practise self-restraint, Allah is Oft-forgiving, Most Merciful.

130. But if they disagree (and must part), Allah will provide abundance for all from His all-reaching bounty: for Allah is He that cares for all and is Wise.

131. To Allah belong all things in the heavens and on earth. Verily We have directed the People of the Book before you, and you (O Muslims) to fear Allah. But if you deny Him, lo! to Allah belong all things in the heavens and on earth, and Allah is free of all wants, worthy of all praise.

132. Yes, to Allah belong all things in the heavens and on earth, and enough is Allah to carry through all affairs.

133. If it were His Will, He could destroy you, O mankind, and create another race; for Allah has power to do this.

134. If any one desires a reward in this life, in Allah's (gift) is the reward (both) of this life and of the hereafter: for Allah is He that hears and sees (all things).

135. O you who believe! stand out firmly for justice, as witnesses to Allah, even as against yourselves, or your parents, or your kin,

shuḥḥ; wa in tuḥsinoo wa tattaqoo fa-innal-laaha kaana bimaa ta'maloona Khabeeraa.

129. Wa lan tastatee'ooo an ta'diloo baynan-nisaaa'i wa law ḥaraṣtum falaa tameeloo kullal-mayli fatazaroohaa kalmu'al-laqah; wa in tuṣliḥoo wa tattaqoo fa-innal-laaha kaana Ghafoorar-Raḥeemaa.

130. Wa iñy-yatafarraqaa yugh-nil-laahu kullam-min sa'atih; wa kaanal-laahu Waasi'an Ḥakeemaa.

131. Wa lillaahi maafis-sa-maawaati wa maa fil-arḍ; wa laqad waṣṣaynal-lazeena ootul-Kitaaba min qablikum wa iyyaakum anit-taqul-laah; wa in takfuroo fa-inna lillaahi maa fis-samaawaati wa maa fil-arḍ; wa kaanal-laahu Ghaniyyan Ḥameedaa.

132. Wa lillaahi maa fis-sa-maawaati wa maa fil-arḍ; wa kafaa billaahi Wakeelaa.

133. Iñy-yashaaa yuzhibkum ayyuhan-naasu wa yaâti bi-aakhareen; wa kaanal-laahu 'alaa zaalika Qadeeraa.

134. Man kaana yureedu sawaabad-dunyaa fa'indallaahi sawaabud-dunyaa wal-Aakhi-rah; wa kaanal-laahu Samee-'am-Baṣeeraa. **(Section 19)**

135. Yaaa-ayyuhal-lazeena aamanoo koonoo qawwa-ameena bilqisti shuhadaaa'a lillaahi wa law 'alaaa anfusikum awil-waalidayni wal-aqrabeen;

الشُّحَّ ۚ وَإِن تُحْسِنُوا وَتَتَّقُوا فَإِنَّ اللَّهَ كَانَ بِمَا تَعْمَلُونَ خَبِيرًا ۝

وَلَن تَسْتَطِيعُوٓا أَن تَعْدِلُوا بَيْنَ النِّسَآءِ وَلَوْ حَرَصْتُمْ فَلَا تَمِيلُوا كُلَّ الْمَيْلِ فَتَذَرُوهَا كَالْمُعَلَّقَةِ ۚ وَإِن تُصْلِحُوا وَتَتَّقُوا فَإِنَّ اللَّهَ كَانَ غَفُورًا رَّحِيمًا ۝

وَإِن يَتَفَرَّقَا يُغْنِ اللَّهُ كُلًّا مِّن سَعَتِهِ ۚ وَكَانَ اللَّهُ وَاسِعًا حَكِيمًا ۝

وَلِلَّهِ مَا فِي السَّمَوَٰتِ وَمَا فِي الْأَرْضِ ۗ وَلَقَدْ وَصَّيْنَا الَّذِينَ أُوتُوا الْكِتَٰبَ مِن قَبْلِكُمْ وَإِيَّاكُمْ أَنِ اتَّقُوا اللَّهَ ۚ وَإِن تَكْفُرُوا فَإِنَّ لِلَّهِ مَا فِي السَّمَوَٰتِ وَمَا فِي الْأَرْضِ ۚ وَكَانَ اللَّهُ غَنِيًّا حَمِيدًا ۝

وَلِلَّهِ مَا فِي السَّمَوَٰتِ وَمَا فِي الْأَرْضِ ۚ وَكَفَىٰ بِاللَّهِ وَكِيلًا ۝

إِن يَشَأْ يُذْهِبْكُمْ أَيُّهَا النَّاسُ وَيَأْتِ بِآخَرِينَ ۚ وَكَانَ اللَّهُ عَلَىٰ ذَٰلِكَ قَدِيرًا ۝

مَّن كَانَ يُرِيدُ ثَوَابَ الدُّنْيَا فَعِندَ اللَّهِ ثَوَابُ الدُّنْيَا وَالْآخِرَةِ ۚ وَكَانَ اللَّهُ سَمِيعًا بَصِيرًا ۝

يَٰٓأَيُّهَا الَّذِينَ آمَنُوا كُونُوا قَوَّٰمِينَ بِالْقِسْطِ شُهَدَآءَ لِلَّهِ وَلَوْ عَلَىٰٓ أَنفُسِكُمْ أَوِ الْوَٰلِدَيْنِ وَالْأَقْرَبِينَ ۚ

and whether it be (against) rich or poor: for Allah can best protect both. Follow not the lusts (of your hearts), lest you swerve, and if you distort (justice) or decline to do justice, verily Allah is well- acquainted with all that you do.

136. O you who believe! Believe in Allah and His Apostle, and the scripture which He has sent to His Apostle and the scripture which He sent to those before (him). Any who denies Allah, His Angels, His Books, His Apostles, and the Day of Judgment, has gone far, far astray.

137. Those who believe, then reject faith, then believe (again) and (again) reject faith, and go on increasing in unbelief, - Allah will not forgive them nor guide them on the Way.

138. To the Hypocrites give the glad tidings that there is for them (but) a grievous Chastisement.

139. Yes, to those who take for friends Unbelievers rather than Believers: is it honour they seek among them? No,- all honour is with Allah.

140. Already has He sent you Word in the Book, that when you hear the signs of Allah held in defiance and ridicule, you are not to sit with them unless they turn to a different theme: if you did, you would be like them. For Allah will collect the hypocrites and those who defy Faith - all in Hell:-

141. (These are) the ones who wait and watch about you: if

iñy-yakun ghaniyyan aw faqeeran fallaahu awlaa bihimaa falaaa tattabi'ul hawaaa an ta'diloo; wa in talwooo aw tu'riḍoo fa-innallaaha kaana bimaa ta'maloona Khabeeraa.

136. Yaaa-ayyuhal-lazeena aamanooo aaminoo billaahi wa Rasoolihee wal-Kitaabil-lazee nazzala 'alaa Rasoolihee wal-Kitaabil-lazeee anzala min qabl; wa mañy-yakfur billaahi wa Malaaa'ikatihee wa Kutubihee wa Rusulihee wal-Yawmil-Aakhiri faqad ḍalla ḍalaalam-ba'eedaa.

137. Innal-lazeena aamanoo summa kafaroo summa aamanoo summa kafaroo summaz-daadoo kufral-lam yakunil-laahu liyaghfira lahum wa laa liyahdiyahum sabeelaa.

138. Bashshiril-munaafiqeena bi-anna lahum 'azaaban aleemaa.

139. Allazeena yattakhizoonal-kaafireena awliyaaa'a min doonil-mu'mineen; a-yabtaghoona 'indahumul-'izzata fa-innal-'izzata lillaahi jamee'aa.

140. Wa qad nazzala 'alaykum fil-Kitaabi an izaa sami'tum Aayaatil-laahi yukfaru bihaa wa yustahza-u bihaa falaa taq'udoo ma'ahum ḥattaa yakhooḍoo fee ḥadeesin ghayrih; innakum izam-misluhum; innal-laaha jaami'ul-munaafiqeena wal-kaafireena fee Jahannama jamee'aa.

141. Allazeena yatarabbaṣoona bikum fa-in kaana

you do gain a victory from Allah, they say: "Were we not with you?"- but if the Unbelievers gain a success, they say (to them): "Did we not gain an advantage over you, and did we not guard you from the Believers?" But Allah will judge between you on the Day of Judgment. And never will Allah grant to the Unbelievers a way (to triumphs) over the Believers.

142. The Hypocrites - they think they are over-reaching Allah, but He will over- reach them: when they stand up to prayer, they stand without earnestness, to be seen of men, but little do they hold Allah in remembrance;

143. (They are) distracted in mind even in the midst of it,- being (sincerely) for neither one group nor for another. Whom Allah leaves straying,- never will you find for him the Way.

144. O you who believe! Take not for friends Unbelievers rather than Believers: do you wish to offer Allah an open proof against yourselves?

145. The Hypocrites will be in the lowest depths of the Fire: no helper will you find for them;-

146. Except for those who repent, mend (their lives) hold fast to Allah, and purify their religion as in Allah's sight: if so they will be (numbered) with the believers. And soon will Allah grant to the believers a reward of immense value.

147. What can Allah gain by your punishment, if you are grateful and you believe? No, it is Allah that recogniseth (all good), and knows all things.

148. Allah does not love that evil should be noised

lakum fatḥum-minal-laahi qaalooo alam nakum ma'akum wa in kaana lilkaafireena naṣeebun qaalooo alam nastaḥ-wiz 'alaykum wa namna'kum minal-mu'mineen; fallaahu yaḥkumu baynakum Yawmal-Qiyaamah; wa lañy-yaj'alal-laahu lilkaafireena 'alal-mu'mineena sabeelaa.

(Section 20)

142. Innal-munaafiqeena yu-khaadi'oonal-laaha wa huwa khaadi'uhum wa iza qaamooo ilaṣ-Ṣalaati qaamoo kusaalaa yuraaa'oonan-naasa wa laa yazkuroonal-laaha illaa qaleelaa.

143. Muzabzabeena bayna zaalika laaa ilaa haaa'ulaaa'i wa laaa ilaa haaa'ulaaa'; wa mañy-yuḍlilil-laahu falan tajida lahoo sabeelaa.

144. Yaaa-ayyuhal-lazeena aamanoo laa tattakhizul-kaafireena awliyaaa'a min doonil-mu'mineen; atureedoona an taj'aloo lillaahi 'alaykum sulṭaanam-mubee-naa.

145. Innal-munaafiqeena fid-darkil-asfali minan-Naari wa lan tajida lahum naṣeeraa.

146. Illal-lazeena taaboo wa aṣlaḥoo wa'taṣamoo billaahi wa akhlaṣoo deenahum lillaahi faulaaa'ika ma'al-mu'mineena wa sawfa yu'til-laahul-mu'mineena ajran 'aẓeemaa.

147. Maa yafa'lul-laahu bi-'azaabikum in shakartum wa aamantum; wa kaanal-laahu Shaakiran 'Aleemaa.

148. Laa yuḥibbullaahul-jahra bis-sooo'i

abroad in public speech, except where injustice has been done; for Allah is He who hears and knows all things.

149. Whether you publish a good deed or conceal it or cover evil with pardon, verily Allah blots out (sins) and has power (in the judgment of values).

150. Those who deny Allah and His apostles, and (those who) wish to separate Allah from His apostles, saying: "We believe in some but reject others": And (those who) wish to take a course midway,-

151. They are in truth (equally) unbelievers; and we have prepared for Unbelievers a humiliating punishment.

152. To those who believe in Allah and His apostles and make no distinction between any of the apostles, we shall soon give their (due) rewards: for Allah is Oft- forgiving, Most Merciful.

153. The people of the Book ask you to cause a book to descend to them from heaven: Indeed they asked Moses for an even greater (miracle), for they said: "Show us Allah in public," but they were dazed for their presumption, with thunder and lightning. Yet they worshipped the calf even after clear signs had come to them; even so we forgave them; and gave Moses manifest proofs of authority.

154. And for their Covenant we raised over them (the towering height) of Mount (Sinai); and (on another occasion) we said:"Enter the gate with humility"; and (once again) we commanded them: "Transgress not in the matter of the Sabbath."

minal-qawli illaa man zulim; wa kaanallaahu Samee'an 'Alee-maa.

149. In tubdoo khayran aw tukhfoohu aw ta'foo 'an sooo'in fa-innal-laaha kaana 'Afuwwan Qadeeraa.

150. Innal-lazeena yakfuroona billaahi wa Rusulihee wa yureedoona añy-yufarriqoo baynal-laahi wa Rusulihee wa yaqooloona nu'minu biba'diñw-wa nakfuru biba'diñw-wa yureedoona añy-yattakhizoo bayna zaalika sabeelaa.

151. Ulaaa'ika humul-kaafi-roona haqqaa; wa a'tadnaa lilkaafireena 'azaabam-mu-heenaa.

152. Wallazeena aamanoo billaahi wa Rusulihee wa lam yufarriqoo bayna ahadim-minhum ulaaa'ika sawfa yu'teehim ujoorahum; wa kaanal-laahu Ghafoorar-Raheemaa.   (Section 21)

153. Yas'aluka Ahlul-Kitaabi an tunazzila 'alayhim Kitaabam-minas-samaaa'i faqad sa-aloo Moosaaa-akbara min zaalika faqaalooo arinal-laaha jahratan fa-akhazat-humus-saa'iqatu bizulmihim; summat-takhazul-'ijla mim ba'di maa jaa'at-humul-bayyinaatu fa'afawnaa 'an zaalik; wa aataynaa Moosaa sultaanam-mubeenaa.

154. Wa rafa'naa fawqahumut-Toora bimeesaaqihim wa qulnaa lahumud-khulul-baaba sujjadaňw-wa qulnaa lahum laa ta'doo fis-Sabti

And We took from them a solemn Covenant.

155. (They have incurred divine displeasure): In that they broke their Covenant; that they rejected the signs of Allah; that they slew the Messengers in defiance of right; that they said, "Our hearts are the wrappings (which preserve Allah's Word; We need no more)";- No, Allah has set the seal on their hearts for their blasphemy, and little is it they believe;-

156. That they rejected Faith; that they uttered against Mary a grave false charge;

157. That they said (in boast), "We killed Christ Jesus the son of Mary, the Apostle of Allah";- but they killed him not, nor crucified him, but so it was made to appear to them, and those who differ therein are full of doubts, with no (certain) knowledge, but only conjecture to follow, for of a surety they killed him not:-

158. No, Allah raised him up unto Himself; and Allah is Exalted in Power, Wise;-

159. And there is none of the People of the Book but must believe in him before his death; and on the Day of Judgment he will be a witness against them;-

160. For the iniquity of the Jews We made unlawful for them certain (foods) good and wholesome which had been lawful for them;- in that they hindered many from Allah's Way;-

161. That they took interest, though they were forbidden; and that they devoured men's substance wrongfully;- we have prepared for those among them who reject Faith a grievous punishment.

wa akhaznaa minhum meesaaqan ghaleezaa.

155. Fabimaa naqdihim meesaaqahum wa kufrihim bi-Aayaatil-laahi wa qatlihimul-Ambiyaaa'a bighayri ḥaqqiñw-wa qawlihim quloobunaa ghulf; bal ṭaba'al-laahu 'alayhaa bikufrihim falaa yu'minoona illaa qaleelaa.

156. Wa bikufrihim wa qawli-him 'alaa Maryama buh-taanan 'azeemaa.

157. Wa qawlihim innaa qatal-nal-Maseeḥa 'Eesab-na-Maryama Rasoolal-laahi wa maa qataloohu wa maa ṣalaboohu wa laakin shubbiha lahum; wa innal-lazeenakh-talafoo feehi lafee shakkim-minh; maa lahum bihee min 'ilmin illat-tibaa'az-ẓann; wa maa qataloohu yaqeenaa.

158. Bar-rafa'ahul-laahu ilayh; wa kaanal-laahu 'Azee-zan Hakeemaa.

159. Wa im-min Ahlil-Kitaabi illaa layu'minanna bihee qabla mawtihee wa Yawmal-Qiyaamati yakoonu 'alayhim shaheedaa.

160. Fabiẓulmim-minal-lazeena haadoo ḥarramnaa 'alayhim ṭayyibaatin uḥillat lahum wa biṣaddihim 'an sabeelil-laahi kaseeraa.

161. Wa akhzihimur-ribaa wa qad nuhoo 'anhu wa aklihim amwaalan-naasi bilbaaṭil; wa a'tadnaa lilkaafireena minhum 'azaaban aleemaa.

162. But those among them who are well-grounded in knowledge, and the believers, believe in what has been revealed to you and what was revealed before you: And (especially) those who establish regular prayer and practise regular charity and believe in Allah and in the Last Day: To them shall We soon give a great reward.

162. Laakinir-raasikhoona fil'ilmi minhum walmu'minoona yu'minoona bimaaa unzila ilayka wa maaa unzila min qablika walmuqeemeenaṣ-Ṣalaata walmu'toonaz-Zakaata walmu'minoona billaahi wal-Yawmil-Aakhir; ulaaa'ika sanu'teehim ajran 'aẓeemaa.

(Section 22)

163. We have sent you inspiration, as We sent it to Noah and the Messengers after him: we sent inspiration to Abraham, Isma'il, Isaac, Jacob and the Tribes, to Jesus, Job, Jonah, Aaron, and solomon, and to David We gave the Psalms.

163. Innaaa awḥaynaaa ilayka kamaaa awḥaynaaa ilaa Nooḥiñw-wan-Nabiyyeena mim ba'dih; wa awḥaynaaa ilaaa Ibraaheema wa Ismaa'eela wa Isḥaaqa wa Ya'qooba wal-Asbaaṭi wa 'Eesaa wa Ayyooba wa Yoonusa wa Haaroona wa Sulaymaan; wa aataynaa Daawooda Zabooraa.

164. Of some apostles We have already told you the story; of others We have not;- and to Moses Allah spoke direct;-

164. Wa Rusulan qad qaṣaṣnaahum 'alayka min qablu wa Rusulal-lam naqṣuṣhum 'alayk; wa kallamallaahu Moosaa takleemaa.

165. Apostles who gave good news as well as warning, that mankind, after (the coming) of the Apostles, should have no plea against Allah: For Allah is Exalted in Power, Wise.

165. Rusulam-mubashshireena wa munẕireena li'allaa yakoona linnaasi 'alal-laahi ḥujjatum ba'dar-Rusul; wa kaanallaahu 'Azeezan Ḥakeemaa.

166. But Allah hears witness that what He has sent unto you He has sent from His (own) knowledge, and the Angels bear witness: But enough is Allah for a witness.

166. Laakinil-laahu yashhadu bimaaa anzala ilayka anzalahoo bi'ilmihee wal-malaaa'ikatu yashhadoon; wa kafaa billaahi Shaheedaa.

167. Those who reject Faith and keep off (men) from the way of Allah, have verily strayed far, far away from the Path.

167. Innal-laẕeena kafaroo wa ṣaddoo 'an sabeelil-laahi qad ḍalloo ḍalaalam-ba'eedaa.

168. Those who reject Faith and do wrong,- Allah will not forgive them nor guide them to any way-

168. Innal-laẕeena kafaroo wa ẓalamoo lam yakunillaahu liyaghfira lahum wa laa liyahdiyahum ṭareeqaa.

لٰكِنِ الرّٰسِخُوْنَ فِى الْعِلْمِ مِنْهُمْ وَالْمُؤْمِنُوْنَ يُؤْمِنُوْنَ بِمَاۤ اُنْزِلَ اِلَيْكَ وَمَاۤ اُنْزِلَ مِنْ قَبْلِكَ وَ الْمُقِيْمِيْنَ الصَّلٰوةَ وَالْمُؤْتُوْنَ الزَّكٰوةَ وَالْمُؤْمِنُوْنَ بِاللّٰهِ وَالْيَوْمِ الْاٰخِرِ ؕ اُولٰٓئِكَ سَنُؤْتِيْهِمْ اَجْرًا عَظِيْمًا ۟

اِنَّاۤ اَوْحَيْنَاۤ اِلَيْكَ كَمَاۤ اَوْحَيْنَاۤ اِلٰى نُوْحٍ وَّ النَّبِيّٖنَ مِنْ بَعْدِهٖۚ وَاَوْحَيْنَاۤ اِلٰۤى اِبْرٰهِيْمَ وَاِسْمٰعِيْلَ وَاِسْحٰقَ وَيَعْقُوْبَ وَالْاَسْبَاطِ وَعِيْسٰى وَاَيُّوْبَ وَيُوْنُسَ وَهٰرُوْنَ وَسُلَيْمٰنَۚ وَاٰتَيْنَا دَاوٗدَ زَبُوْرًا ۟

وَرُسُلًا قَدْ قَصَصْنٰهُمْ عَلَيْكَ مِنْ قَبْلُ وَرُسُلًا لَّمْ نَقْصُصْهُمْ عَلَيْكَۚ وَكَلَّمَ اللّٰهُ مُوْسٰى تَكْلِيْمًا ۟

رُسُلًا مُّبَشِّرِيْنَ وَمُنْذِرِيْنَ لِئَلَّا يَكُوْنَ لِلنَّاسِ عَلَى اللّٰهِ حُجَّةٌۢ بَعْدَ الرُّسُلِؕ وَكَانَ اللّٰهُ عَزِيْزًا حَكِيْمًا ۟

لٰكِنِ اللّٰهُ يَشْهَدُ بِمَاۤ اَنْزَلَ اِلَيْكَ اَنْزَلَهٗ بِعِلْمِهٖۚ وَالْمَلٰٓئِكَةُ يَشْهَدُوْنَؕ وَكَفٰى بِاللّٰهِ شَهِيْدًا ۟

اِنَّ الَّذِيْنَ كَفَرُوْا وَصَدُّوْا عَنْ سَبِيْلِ اللّٰهِ قَدْ ضَلُّوْا ضَلٰلًاۢ بَعِيْدًا ۟

اِنَّ الَّذِيْنَ كَفَرُوْا وَظَلَمُوْا لَمْ يَكُنِ اللّٰهُ لِيَغْفِرَ لَهُمْ وَلَا لِيَهْدِيَهُمْ طَرِيْقًا ۟

169. Except the way of Hell, to dwell therein for ever. And this to Allah is easy.

170. O mankind! The Apostle has come to you in truth from Allah: believe in him: It is best for you. But if you reject Faith, to Allah belong all things in the heavens and on earth: And Allah is All-knowing, All-wise.

171. O People of the Book! commit no excesses in your religion: Nor say of Allah anything but the truth. Christ Jesus the son of Mary was (no more than) an Apostle of Allah, and His Word, which He bestowed on Mary, and a spirit proceeding from Him: so believe in Allah and His Apostles. Say not "Trinity" desist: it will be better for you: for Allah is one Allah: Glory be to Him: (far exalted is He) above having a son. To Him belong all things in the heavens and on earth. And enough is Allah as a Disposer of affairs.

172. Christ does not disdain to serve and worship Allah, nor do the angels, those nearest (to Allah): those who disdain His worship and are arrogant,-He will gather them all together unto Himself to (answer).

173. But to those who believe and do deeds of righteousness, He will give their (due) rewards,- and more, out of His bounty: But those who are disdainful and arrogant, He will punish with a grievous Chastisement; Nor will they find, besides Allah, any to protect or help them.

169. Illaa ṭareeqa Jahannama khaalideena feehaaa abadaa; wa kaana zaalika 'alal-laahi yaseeraa.

170. Yaaa ayyuhan-naasu qad jaaa'akumur-Rasoolu bilḥaqqi mir-Rabbikum fa-aaminoo khayral-lakum; wa in takfuroo fainna lillaahi maa fis-samaawaati wal-arḍ; wa kaanal-laahu 'Aleeman Ḥakeemaa.

171. Yaaa Ahlal-Kitaabi laa taghloo fee deenikum wa laa taqooloo 'alal-laahi illalḥaqq; innamal-Maseeḥu 'Eesab-nu-Maryama Rasoolul-laahi wa Kalimatuhooo alqaahaaa ilaa Maryama wa rooḥum-minhu fa-aaminoo billaahi wa Rusulihee wa laa taqooloo salaasah; intahoo khayrallakum; innamal-laahu Ilaahuñw-Waaḥid, Subḥaanahooo añy-yakoona lahoo walad; lahoo maa fis-samaawaati wa maa fil-arḍ; wa kafaa billaahi Wakeelaa.

(Section 23)

172. Lañy-yastankifal-Maseeḥu añy-yakoona 'abdal-lillaahi wa lal-malaaa'ikatul-muqarraboon; wa mañy-yastankif 'an 'ibaadatihee wa yastakbir fasa-yaḥshuruhum ilayhi jamee'aa.

173. Fa-ammal-lazeena aamanoo wa 'amiluṣ-ṣaaliḥaati fa-yuwaffeehim ujoorahum wa yazeeduhum-min faḍlihee wa ammal-lazeenas-tankafoo wastakbaroo fa-yu'azzibuhum 'azaaban aleemañw-wa laa yajidoona lahum min doonil-laahi waliyyañw-wa laa naṣeeraa.

174. O mankind! verily there has come to you a convincing proof from your Lord: For We have sent unto you a light (that is) manifest.

175. Then those who believe in Allah, and hold fast to Him,- soon will He admit them to mercy and grace from Himself, and guide them to Himself by a straight way.

176. They ask you for a legal decision. Say: Allah directs (thus) about those who leave no descendants or ascendants as heirs. If it is a man that dies, leaving a sister but no child, she shall have half the inheritance: If (such a deceased was) a woman, who left no child, Her brother takes her inheritance: If there are two sisters, they shall have two-thirds of the inheritance (between them): if there are brothers and sisters, (they share), the male having twice the share of the female. Thus does Allah make clear to you (His law), lest you err. And Allah has knowledge of all things.

5. The Table Spread
In the name of Allah, Most Gracious, Most Merciful.

1. O you who believe! fulfil (all) obligations. Lawful to you (for food) are all four-footed animals, with the exceptions named: But animals of the chase are forbidden while you are in the sacred precincts or in pilgrim garb: for Allah does command according to His will and plan.

2. O you who believe! violate not the sanctity of the symbols of Allah, nor of the Sacred Month, nor of the animals brought for sacrifice, nor the Garlands that mark out such animals, nor the people resorting to the Sacred House, seeking of the bounty and good pleasure of their Lord.

174. Yaaa-ayyuhan-naasu qad jaaa'akum burhaanum-mir-Rabbikum wa anzalnaaa ilaykum Nooram-Mubeenaa.

175. Fa-ammal-lazeena aamanoo billaahi wa'taṣamoo bihee fasa-yudkhiluhum fee raḥ-matim-minhu wa faḍliñw-wa yahdeehim ilayhi Ṣiraaṭam-Mustaqeema.

176. Yastaftoonaka qulillaahu yufteekum fil-kalaalah; inim-ru'un halaka laysa lahoo waladuñw-wa lahooo ukhtun falahaa niṣfu maa tarak; wa huwa yariṣuhaaa il-lam yakul-lahaa walad; fa-in kaanatas-natayni falahumaṣ-ṣuluṣaani mimmaa tarak; wa in kaanooo ikhwatar-rijaalañw-wa nisaaa'an faliz-zakari miṣlu ḥazzil-unṣayayn; yubayyinullaahu lakum an taḍilloo; wallaahu bikulli shay'in 'Aleem.

(Section 24)

Sûrat al-Mâ'idah–5
(Revealed at Madinah)
Bismillaahir Raḥmaanir Raḥeem

1. Yaaa-ayyuhal-lazeena aamanooo awfoo bil'uqood; uḥillat lakum baheematul-an'aami illaa maa yutlaa 'alaykum ghayra muḥilliṣ-ṣaydi wa antum ḥurum; innal-laaha yaḥkumu maa yureed.

2. Yaaa ayyuhal-lazeena aamanoo laa tuḥilloo sha'aaa-'iral-laahi wa lash-Shahral-Ḥaraama wa lal-hadya wa lal-qalaaa'ida wa laaa aaammee-nal-Baytal-Ḥaraama yabta-ghoona faḍlam-mir-Rabbihim wa riḍwaanaa;

But when you are clear of the Sacred precincts and of pilgrim garb, you may hunt and let not the hatred of some people in (once) shutting you out of the Sacred Mosque lead you to transgression (and hostility on your part). Help you one another in righteousness and piety, but help you not one another in sin and rancour: fear Allah: for Allah is strict in punishment.

3. Forbidden to you (for food) are: dead meat, blood, the flesh of swine, and that on which has been invoked the name of other than Allah; that which has been killed by strangling, or by a violent blow, or by a headlong fall, or by being gored to death; that which has been (partly) eaten by a wild animal; unless you are able to slaughter it (in due form); that which is sacrificed on stone (altars); (forbidden) also is the division (of meat) by raffling with arrows: that is impiety. This day have those who reject faith given up all hopes of your religion: yet fear them not but fear Me. This day have I perfected your religion for you, completed My favour upon you, and have chosen for you Islam as your religion. But if any is forced by hunger, with no inclination to transgression, Allah is indeed Oft-forgiving, Most Merciful.

4. They ask you what is lawful to them (as food). Say: lawful unto you are (all) things good and pure: and what you have taught your trained hunting animals (to catch) in the manner directed to you by Allah: eat what they catch for you, but pronounce the name of Allah over it: and fear Allah; for Allah is swift in taking account.

5. This day are (all) things good and pure made lawful for you. The food of the People of the Book is lawful for you and

wa izaa ḥalaltum faṣṭaadoo; wa laa yajrimannakum shana-aanu qawmin an ṣaddookum 'anil-Masjidil-Ḥaraami an ta'tadoo; wa ta'aawanoo 'alalbirri wattaqwaa; wa laa ta'aawanoo 'alal-ismi wal'udwaan; wattaqul-laah; innal-laaha shadeedul-'iqaab.

3 Ḥurrimat 'alaykumul-maytatu waddamu wa laḥmul-khinzeeri wa maaa uhilla lighayril-laahi bihee walmunkhani-qatu walmawqoozatu walmutarad-diyatu wanna-ṭeeḥatu wa maaa akalas-sabu'u illaa maa zakkaytum wa maa zubiḥa 'alan-nuṣubi wa an tastaqsimoo bil-azlaam; zaalikum fisq; alyawma ya'isal-lazeena kafaroo min deenikum falaa takhshawhum wakh-shawn; alyawma akmaltu lakum deenakum wa atmamtu 'alaykum ni'matee wa raḍeetu lakumul-Islaama deenaa; famaniḍṭurra fee makhmaṣatin ghayra mutajaanifil-li-iṣmin fa-innallaaha Ghafoorur Raḥeem.

4. Yas'aloonaka maazaaa uhilla lahum; qul uhilla lakumuṭ-ṭayyibaatu wa maa 'allamtum minal-jawaariḥi mukallibeena tu'allimoonahunna mimmaa 'allamakumul-laahu fakuloo mimmaaa amsakna 'alaykum wazkurus-mal-laahi 'alayh; wattaqul-laah; innal-laaha saree'ul-ḥisaab.

5. Alyawma uhilla lakumuṭ-ṭayyibaatu wa ṭa'aamul-lazeena ootul-Kitaaba ḥillul-lakum wa

yours is lawful to them. (Lawful to you in marriage) are (not only) chaste women who are believers, but chaste women among the People of the Book, revealed before your time,- when you give them their due dowers, and desire chastity, not lewdness, nor secret intrigues if any one rejects faith, fruitless is his work, and in the Hereafter he will be in the ranks of those who have lost (all spiritual good).

6. O you who believe! when you prepare for prayer, wash your faces, and your hands (and arms) to the elbows; rub your heads (with water); and (wash) your feet to the ankles. If you are in a state of ceremonial impurity, bathe your whole body. But if you are ill, or on a journey, or one of you comes from offices of nature, or you have been in contact with women, and you find no water, then take for yourselves clean sand or earth, and rub therewith your faces and hands, Allah does not wish to place you in a difficulty, but to make you clean, and to complete his favour to you, that you may be grateful.

7. And call in remembrance the favour of Allah to you, and His Covenant, which He ratified with you, when you said: "We hear and we obey": And fear Allah, for Allah knows well the secrets of your hearts.

8. O you who believe! stand out firmly for Allah, as witnesses to fair dealing, and let not the hatred of others to you make you swerve to wrong and depart from justice. Be just:

ta'aamukum ḥillul-lahum wal-muḥsanaatu minal-mu'minaati walmuḥsanaatu minal-lazeena ootul-Kitaaba min qablikum izaaa aataytumoohunna ujoorahunna muḥsineena ghayra musaafiḥeena wa laa mutta-khizeee akhdaan; wa mañy-yakfur bil-eemaani faqad ḥabiṭa 'amaluhoo wa huwa fil-Aakhirati minal-khaasireen.

(Section 1)

6. Yaaa-ayyuhal-lazeena aamanooo izaa qumtum-ilaṣ-Ṣalaati faghsiloo wujoohakum wa Aydiyakum ilal maraafiqi wamsaḥoo biru'oosikum wa arjulakum ilal-ka'bayn; wa in kuntum junuban faṭṭahharoo; wain kuntum marḍaaa aw 'alaa safarin aw jaaa'a aḥadum-minkum minal-ghaaa'iṭi aw laamastumunnisaaa'a falam tajidoo maaa'an fatayamma-moo ṣa'eedan ṭayyiban famsaḥoo biwujoohikum wa aydee-kum-minh; maa yureedul-laahu liyaj'ala 'alaykum min ḥarajiñw-wa laakiñy-yureedu liyuṭahhirakum wa liyutimma ni'matahoo 'alaykum la'allakum tashkuroon.

7. Wazkuroo ni'matal-laahi 'alaykum wa meesaaqahul-lazee waasaqakum biheee iz qultum sami'naa wa aṭa'naa wattaqul-laah; innal-laaha 'aleemum-bizaatiṣ-ṣudoor.

8. Yaaa ayyuhal-lazeena aamanoo koonoo qawwaa-meena lillaahi shuhadaaa'a bilqist, wa laa yajrimannakum shana-aanu qawmin 'alaaa allaa ta'diloo; i'diloo;

that is next to piety: and fear Allah. For Allah is well-acquainted with all that you do.

9. To those who believe and do deeds of righteousness has Allah promised forgiveness and a great reward.

10. Those who reject faith and deny our signs will be companions of Hell-fire.

11. O you who believe! call in remembrance the favour of Allah unto you when certain men formed the design to stretch out their hands against you, but (Allah) held back their hands from you: so fear Allah. And on Allah let Believers put (all) their trust.

12. Allah did (aforetime) take a Covenant from the Children of Israel, and we appointed twelve captains among them. And Allah said: "I am with you: if you (but) establish regular prayers, practise regular charity, believe in my Apostles, honour and assist them, and loan to Allah a beautiful loan, verily I will wipe out from you your evils, and admit you to gardens with rivers flowing beneath; but if any of you, after this, resists faith, he has truly wandered from the path of rectitude."

13. But because of their breach of their Covenant, We cursed them, and made their hearts grow hard; they change the words from their (right) places and forget a good part of the message that was sent them, nor will you cease to find them-barring a few - ever bent on (new) deceits:

huwa aqrabu littaqwaa wattaqul-laah; innal-laaha khabeerum-bimaa ta'maloon.

9. Wa'adal-laahul-lazeena aamanoo wa 'amilus-saalihaati lahum maghfiratuñw-wa ajrun 'azeem.

10. Wallazeena kafaroo wa kaz-zaboo bi-Aayaatinaaa ulaaa'ika Ashaabul-Jaheem.

11. Yaaa ayyuhal-lazeena aamanuz-kuroo ni'matallaahi 'alaykum iz hamma qawmun añy-yabsutooo ilaykum aydiyahum fakaffa aydiyahum 'ankum wattaqullaah; wa 'alal-laahi fal-yatawakkalil-mu'minoon. **(Section 2)**

12. Wa laqad akhazal-laahu meesaaqa Banee Israaa'eela wa ba'asnaa minhumus-nay 'ashara naqeebañw wa qaalal-laahu innee ma'akum la'in aqamtumus-Salaata wa aataytu-muz-Zakaata wa aamantum bi-Rusulee wa 'azzartumoohum wa aqradtumul-laaha qardan hasanal-la-ukaffiranna 'ankum sayyi-aatikum wa la-udkhilan-nakum Jannaatin tajree min tahtihal-anhaar; faman kafara ba'da zaalika minkum faqad dalla sawaaa'as-Sabeel.

13. Fabimaa naqdihim meesaa-qahum la'annaahum wa ja'al-naa quloobahum qaasiyatañy yuharrifoonal-kalima 'am-mawaadi'ihee wa nasoo hazzam-mimmaa zukkiroo bih; wa laa tazaalu tattali'u 'alaa khaaa'inatim-minhum illaa qaleelam-minhum

but forgive them, and overlook (their misdeeds): for Allah loves those who are kind.

14. From those, too, who call themselves Christians, We did take a Covenant, but they forgot a good part of the message that was sent them: so we estranged them, with enmity and hatred between the one and the other, to the Day of judgment. And soon will Allah show them what it is they have done.

15. O people of the Book! there has come to you our Apostle, revealing to you much that you used to hide in the Book, and passing over much (that is now unnecessary). There has come to you from Allah a (new) light and a perspicuous Book,

16. Wherewith Allah guides all who seek His good pleasure to ways of peace and safety, and leads them out of darkness, by His will, unto the light,- guides them to a path that is straight.

17. In blasphemy indeed are those that say that Allah is Christ the son of Mary. Say: "Who then has the least power against Allah, if His will were to destroy Christ the son of Mary, his mother, and all every - one that is on the earth? For to Allah belongs the dominion of the heavens and the earth, and all that is between. He creates what He pleases. For Allah has power over all things."

18. (Both) the Jews and the Christians say: "We are sons of Allah, and His beloved." Say: "Why then does He punish you for your sins? Nay, you are but men,- of the men he has created: He forgives whom He pleases, and He punishes

fa'fu 'anhum wasfah; innal-laaha yuhibbul-muhsineen.

14. Wa minal-lazeena qaalooo innaa Nasaaraaa akhaznaa meesaaqahum fanasoo hazzam-mimmaa zukkiroo bihee fa-aghraynaa baynahumul-'adaawata walbaghdaaa'a ilaa Yawmil-Qiyaamah; wa sawfa yunabbi'uhumul-laahu bimaa kaanoo yasna'oon.

15. Yaaa Ahlal-Kitaabi qad jaaa'akum Rasoolunaa yubay-yinu lakum kaseeram-mimmaa kuntum tukhfoona minal-Kitaabi wa ya'foo 'an kaseer; qad jaaa'akum minal-laahi nooruñw-wa Kitaabum-Mubeen.

16. Yahdee bihil-laahu manit-taba'a ridwaanahoo subulas-salaami wa yukhrijuhum minaz-zulumaati ilan-noori bi-iznihee wa yahdeehim ilaa Siraatim-Mustaqeem.

17. Laqad kafaral-lazeena qaalooo innal-laaha Huwal-Maseehub-nu-Maryam; qul famañy-yamliku minal-laahi shay'an in araada añy-yuhlikal Maseeh ab-na-Maryama wa ummahoo wa man fil-ardi jamee'aa; wa lillaahi mulkus-samaawaati wal-ardi wa maa baynahumaa; yakhluqu maa-Yashaaa'; wallaahu 'alaa kulli shay'in Qadeer.

18. Wa qaalatil-Yahoodu wan-Nasaaraa nahnu abnaaa'ul-laahi wa ahibbaaa'uh; qul falima yu'azzibukum bizunoobikum bal antum basharum-mimman khalaq; yaghfiru limañy-yashaaa'u wa yu'azzibu

فَاعْفُ عَنْهُمْ وَاصْفَحْ ۚ إِنَّ اللّٰهَ

يُحِبُّ الْمُحْسِنِينَ ۝

وَمِنَ الَّذِينَ قَالُوٓا إِنَّا نَصَارَىٰٓ أَخَذْنَا

مِيثَاقَهُمْ فَنَسُوا حَظًّا مِّمَّا ذُكِّرُوا بِهِۦ

فَأَغْرَيْنَا بَيْنَهُمُ الْعَدَاوَةَ وَالْبَغْضَآءَ

إِلَىٰ يَوْمِ الْقِيَامَةِ ۚ وَسَوْفَ يُنَبِّئُهُمُ اللّٰهُ

بِمَا كَانُوا يَصْنَعُونَ ۝

يَٰٓأَهْلَ الْكِتَابِ قَدْ جَآءَكُمْ رَسُولُنَا

يُبَيِّنُ لَكُمْ كَثِيرًا مِّمَّا كُنتُمْ تُخْفُونَ

مِنَ الْكِتَابِ وَيَعْفُوا عَن كَثِيرٍ ۚ قَدْ

جَآءَكُم مِّنَ اللّٰهِ نُورٌ وَكِتَابٌ مُّبِينٌ ۝

يَهْدِي بِهِ اللّٰهُ مَنِ اتَّبَعَ رِضْوَانَهُۥ

سُبُلَ السَّلَامِ وَيُخْرِجُهُم مِّنَ

الظُّلُمَاتِ إِلَى النُّورِ بِإِذْنِهِۦ وَيَهْدِيهِمْ

إِلَىٰ صِرَاطٍ مُّسْتَقِيمٍ ۝

لَّقَدْ كَفَرَ الَّذِينَ قَالُوٓا إِنَّ اللّٰهَ هُوَ

الْمَسِيحُ ابْنُ مَرْيَمَ ۚ قُلْ فَمَن يَمْلِكُ

مِنَ اللّٰهِ شَيْئًا إِنْ أَرَادَ أَن يُهْلِكَ

الْمَسِيحَ ابْنَ مَرْيَمَ وَأُمَّهُ وَمَن فِي

الْأَرْضِ جَمِيعًا ۗ وَلِلّٰهِ مُلْكُ السَّمَاوَاتِ

وَالْأَرْضِ وَمَا بَيْنَهُمَا ۚ يَخْلُقُ

مَا يَشَآءُ ۚ وَاللّٰهُ عَلَىٰ كُلِّ شَيْءٍ قَدِيرٌ ۝

وَقَالَتِ الْيَهُودُ وَالنَّصَارَىٰ نَحْنُ أَبْنَاؤُا

اللّٰهِ وَأَحِبَّاؤُهُ ۚ قُلْ فَلِمَ يُعَذِّبُكُم

بِذُنُوبِكُم ۖ بَلْ أَنتُم بَشَرٌ مِّمَّنْ

خَلَقَ ۚ يَغْفِرُ لِمَن يَشَآءُ وَيُعَذِّبُ

whom He pleases: and to Allah belongs the dominion of the heavens and the earth, and all that is between: and unto Him is the final goal (of all)".

19. O People of the Book! now has come to you, making (things) clear to you, Our Apostle, after the break in (the series of) Our apostles, lest you should say: "There came unto us no bringer of glad tidings and no warner (from evil)": But now has come unto you a bringer of glad tidings and a warner (from evil). And Allah has power over all things.

20. Remember Moses said to his people: "O my people! call in remembrance the favour of Allah to you, when He produced prophets among you, made you kings, and gave you what He had not given to any other among the people.

21. "O my people! Enter the holy land which Allah has assigned unto you, and turn not back ignominiously, for then will you be overthrown, to your own ruin."

22. They said: "O Moses! In this land are a people of exceeding strength: Never shall we enter it until they leave it: if (once) they leave, then shall we enter."

23. (But) among (their) Allah-fearing men were two on whom Allah had bestowed His grace: They said: "Assault them at the (proper) gate: when once you are in, victory will be yours; But on Allah put your trust if you have faith."

24. They said: "O Moses! while they remain there, never shall we be able to enter, to the end of time. Go you,

mañy-yashaaa'; wa lillaahi mulkus-samaawaati wal-ardi wa maa baynahumaa wa ilayhil-maseer.

19. Yaaa Ahlal-Kitaabi qad jaaa'akum Rasoolunaa yubayyinu lakum 'alaa fatra-tim-minar-Rusuli an taqooloo maa jaaa'anaa mim basheeriñw-wa laa nazeerin faqad jaaa'akum basheeruñw-wa nazeer; wallaahu 'alaa kulli shay'in Qadeer. **(Section 3)**

20. Wa iz qaala Moosaa liqawmihee yaa-qawmiz-kuroo ni'matal-laahi 'alaykum iz ja'ala feekum ambiyaaa'a wa ja'alakum mulookañw-wa aataakum maa lam yu'ti ahadam-minal-'aalameen.

21. Yaa qawmid-khulul-Ardal-Muqaddasatal-latee katabal-laahu lakum wa laa tartaddoo 'alaaa adbaarikum fatanqaliboo khaasireen.

22. Qaaloo yaa Moosaaa inna feehaa qawman jabbaareena wa innaa lan nadkhulahaa hattaa yakhrujoo minhaa fa-iñy-yakhrujoo minhaa fa-innaa daakhiloon.

23. Qaala rajulaani minal-lazeena yakhaafoona an'am-allaahu 'alayhimad-khuloo 'alayhimul-baab, fa-izaa dakhaltumoohu fa-innakum ghaaliboon; wa 'alal-laahi fatawakkalooo in kuntum mu'mineen.

24. Qaaloo yaa Moosaaa innaa lan nadkhulahaaa abadam-maa daamoo feehaa fazhab anta

and your Lord, and fight you two, while we sit here (and watch)."

25. He said: "O my Lord! I have power only over myself and my brother: so separate us from this rebellious people!"

26. Allah said: "Therefore the land will be out of their reach for forty years: In distraction they will wander through the land: But you dont grieve over these rebellious people.

27. Recite to them the truth of the story of the two sons of Adam. Behold! they each presented a sacrifice (to Allah): It was accepted from one, but not from the other. Said the latter: "Be sure I will slay you." "Surely," said the former, "Allah accepts of the sacrifice of those who are righteous.

28. "If you do stretch your hand against me, to slay me, it is not for me to stretch my hand against you to slay you: for I do fear Allah, the Cherisher of the worlds.

29. "For me, I intend to let you draw on yourself my sin as well as yours, for you will be among the companions of the fire, and that is the reward of those who do wrong."

30. The (selfish) soul of the other led him to the murder of his brother: he murdered him, and became (himself) one of the lost ones.

31. Then Allah sent a raven, who scratched the ground, to show him how to hide the shame of his brother. "Woe is me!" said he; "Was I not even able to be as this raven, and to hide the shame of my brother?" then he became full of regrets-

32. On that account: We ordained for the Children of

Wa Rabbuka faqaatilaaa innaa haahunaa qaa'idoon.

25. Qaala Rabbi innee laaa amliku illaa nafsee wa akhee fafruq baynanaa wa baynal-qawmil-faasiqeen.

26. Qaala fa-innahaa muḥar-ramatun 'alayhim arba'eena sanah; yateehoona fil-arḍ; falaa taāsa 'alal-qawmil-faasiqeen.
(Section 4)

27. Watlu 'alayhim naba-abnay Aadama bilḥaqq; iz qarrabaa qurbaanan fatuqubbila min aḥadihimaa wa lam yutaqabbal minal-aakhari qaala la-aqtulannaka qaala innamaa yataqabbalul-laahu minal-muttaqeen.

28. La'im basatta ilayya yadaka litaqtulanee maaa ana bibaasiṭiñy-yadiya ilayka li-aqtulaka inneee akhaaful-laaha Rabbal-'aalameen.

29. Ineee ureedu an tabooo'a bi-ismee wa ismika fatakoona min Asḥaabin-Naar; wa zaalika jazaaa'uẓ-ẓaalimeen.

30. Faṭawwa'at lahoo nafsu-hoo qatla akheehi faqatalahoo fa-aṣbaḥa minal-khaasireen.

31. Faba'aṣal-laahu ghu-raabañy-yabḥaṣu fil-arḍi liyuri-yahoo kayfa yuwaaree sawata akheeh; qaala yaa waylataaa a'ajaztu an akoona miṣla haazal-ghuraabi fa-uwaariya saw-ata akhee fa-aṣbaḥa minan-naadimeen.

32. Min ajli zaalika katabnaa 'alaa Baneee

Israel that if any one slew a person - unless it be for murder or for spreading mischief in the land - it would be as if he slew the whole people: and if any one saved a life, it would be as if he saved the life of the whole people. Then although there came to them our apostles with clear signs, yet, even after that, many of them continued to commit excesses in the land.

33. The punishment of those who wage war against Allah and His Apostle, and strive with might and main for mischief through the land is: execution, or crucifixion, or the cutting off of hands and feet from opposite sides, or exile from the land: that is their disgrace in this world, and a heavy punishment is theirs in the Hereafter;

34. Except for those who repent before they fall into your power: in that case, know that Allah is Oft-forgiving, Most Merciful.

35. O you who believe! Do your duty to Allah, seek the means of approach unto Him, and strive with might and main in his cause: that you may prosper.

36. As to those who reject Faith,- if they had everything on earth, and twice repeated, to give as ransom for the Chastisement of the Day of Judgment, it would never be accepted of them, theirs would be a grievous Chastisement.

37. Their wish will be to get out of the Fire, but never will they get out therefrom: their

Israaa'eela annahoo man qatala nafsam bighayri nafsin aw fasaadin fil-arḍi faka-annamaa qatalan-naasa jamee'añw wa man aḥyaahaa faka-annamaaa aḥyan-naasa jamee'aa; wa laqad jaaa'at-hum Rusulunaa bilbayyinaati summa inna kaseeram-minhum ba'da zaalika fil-arḍi lamusrifoon.

33. Innamaa jazaaa'ul-lazeena yuḥaariboonal-laaha wa Rasoolahoo wa yas'awna fil-arḍi fasaadan añy-yuqattalooo aw yuṣallabooo aw tuqaṭṭa'a aydeehim wa arjuluhum min khilaafin aw yunfaw minalarḍ; zaalika lahum khizyun fiddunyaa wa lahum fil-Aakhirati 'azaabun 'azeem.

34. Illal-lazeena taaboo min qabli an taqdiroo 'alayhim fa'lamooo annal-laaha Ghafoorur-Raḥeem.   **(Section 5)**

35. Yaaa ayyuhal-lazeena aamanut-taqul-laaha wabtaghooo ilayhil-waseelata wa jaahidoo fee sabeelihee la'allakum tufliḥoon.

36. Innal-lazeena kafaroo law anna lahum maa fil-arḍi jamee'añw-wa mislahoo ma'ahoo liyaftadoo bihee min 'azaabi Yawmil-Qiyaamati maa tuqubbila minhum wa lahum 'azaabun aleem.

37. Yureedoona añy-yakhrujoo minan-Naari wa maa hum bikhaarijeena minhaa wa lahum

Chastisement will be one that endures.

38. As to the thief, male or female, cut off his or her hands: a punishment by way of example, from Allah, for their crime: and Allah is Exalted in power.

39. But if the thief repents after his crime, and amends his conduct, Allah turns to him in forgiveness; for Allah is Oft-forgiving, Most Merciful.

40. Do you not know that to Allah (alone) belongs the dominion of the heavens and the earth? He punishes whom He pleases, and He forgives whom He pleases: and Allah has power over all things.

41. O Apostle! let not those grieve you, who race each other into unbelief: (whether it be) among those who say "We believe" with their lips but whose hearts have no faith; or it be among the Jews,- men who will listen to any lie,- will listen even to others who have never so much as come to you. They change the words from their (right) times and places: they say, "If you are given this, take it, but if not, beware!" If any one's trial is intended by Allah you have no authority in the least for him against Allah. For such - it is not Allah's will to purify their hearts. For them there is disgrace in this world, and in the Hereafter a heavy punishment.

42. (They are fond of) listening to falsehood, of devouring anything forbidden.

'azaabum-muqeem.

38. Wassaariqu wassaariqatu faqta'ooo aydiyahumaa jazaaa-'am-bimaa kasabaa nakaalam-minal-laah; wallaahu 'Azeezun Ḥakeem.

39. Faman taaba mim ba'di zulmihee wa aṣlaḥa fa-innal-laaha yatoobu 'alayh; innal-laaha Ghafoorur-Raḥeem.

40. Alam ta'lam annal-laaha lahoo mulkus-samaawaati wal-arḍi yu'az-zibu mañy-yashaa'u wa yaghfiru limañy-yashaaa'; wallaahu 'alaa kulli shay'in Qadeer.

41. Yaaa-ayyuhar-Rasoolu laa yaḥzunkal-lazeena yusaari'oona fil-kufri minal-lazeena qaalooo aamannaa bi-afwaahi-him wa lam tu'min quloobu-hum; wa minal-lazeena haadoo sammaa'oona lilkazibi sammaa'oona liqawmin aakhareena lam yaatooka yuḥarrifoonal-kalima mim ba'di mawaaḍi'i-hee yaqooloona in ooteetum haazaa fakhuzoohu wa il-lam tu'tawhu faḥzaroo; wa mañy-yuridil-laahu fitnatahoo falan tamlika lahoo minal-laahi shay'aa; ulaaa'ikal-lazeena lam yuridil-laahu añy-yuṭahhira quloobahum; lahum fid-dunyaa khizyuñw-wa lahum fil-Aakhirati 'azaabun 'azeem.

42. Sammaa'oona lilkazibi akkaaloona lissuḥt;

If they do come to you, either judge between them, or decline to interfere. If you decline, they cannot hurt you in the least. If you judge, judge in equity between them. For Allah loves those who judge in equity.

Fa-in jaaa'ooka faḥkum baynahum aw a'riḍ 'anhum wa in tu'riḍ 'anhum falañy-yaḍurrooka shay'añw wa in ḥakamta faḥkum baynahum bilqisṭ; innal-laaha yuḥibbul-muqsiṭeen.

فَإِن جَآءُوكَ فَٱحْكُم بَيْنَهُمْ أَوْ أَعْرِضْ عَنْهُمْ وَإِن تُعْرِضْ عَنْهُمْ فَلَن يَضُرُّوكَ شَيْئًا وَإِنْ حَكَمْتَ فَٱحْكُم بَيْنَهُم بِٱلْقِسْطِ إِنَّ ٱللَّهَ يُحِبُّ ٱلْمُقْسِطِينَ ۝

43. But why do they come to you for decision, when they have (their own) law before them?- therein is the (plain) command of Allah; yet even after that, they would turn away. For they are not (really) People of Faith.

43. Wa kayfa yuḥakkimoo-naka wa 'indahumut-Tawraatu feehaa ḥukmul-laahi summa yatawallawna mim ba'di zaalik; wa maaa ulaaa'ika bilmu'mineen. **(Section 6)**

وَكَيْفَ يُحَكِّمُونَكَ وَعِندَهُمُ ٱلتَّوْرَىٰةُ فِيهَا حُكْمُ ٱللَّهِ ثُمَّ يَتَوَلَّوْنَ مِنۢ بَعْدِ ذَٰلِكَ وَمَآ أُو۟لَٰٓئِكَ بِٱلْمُؤْمِنِينَ ۝

44. It was We who revealed the law (to Moses): therein was guidance and light. By its standard have been judged the Jews, by the prophets who bowed (as in Islam) to Allah's will, by the rabbis and the doctors of law: for to them was entrusted the protection of Allah's book, and they were witnesses there to: therefore fear not men, but fear me, and sell not my signs for a miserable price. If any do fail to judge by (the light of) what Allah has revealed, they are (no better than) Unbelievers.

44. Innaaa anzalnat Tawraata feehaa hudañw-wa noor; yaḥkumu bihan-Nabiyyoonal-lazeena aslamoo lillazeena haadoo war-rabbaaniyyoona wal-aḥbaaru bimas-tuḥfizoo min Kitaabil-laahi wa kaanoo 'alayhi shuhadaaa'; falaa takhshawun-naasa wakhshawni wa laa tashtaroo bi-Aayaatee samanan qaleelaa; wa mal-lam yaḥkum bimaaa anzalal-laahu fa-ulaaa'ika humul-kaafiroon.

إِنَّآ أَنزَلْنَا ٱلتَّوْرَىٰةَ فِيهَا هُدًى وَنُورٌ يَحْكُمُ بِهَا ٱلنَّبِيُّونَ ٱلَّذِينَ أَسْلَمُوا۟ لِلَّذِينَ هَادُوا۟ وَٱلرَّبَّٰنِيُّونَ وَٱلْأَحْبَارُ بِمَا ٱسْتُحْفِظُوا۟ مِن كِتَٰبِ ٱللَّهِ وَكَانُوا۟ عَلَيْهِ شُهَدَآءَ فَلَا تَخْشَوُا۟ ٱلنَّاسَ وَٱخْشَوْنِ وَلَا تَشْتَرُوا۟ بِـَٔايَٰتِى ثَمَنًا قَلِيلًا وَمَن لَّمْ يَحْكُم بِمَآ أَنزَلَ ٱللَّهُ فَأُو۟لَٰٓئِكَ هُمُ ٱلْكَٰفِرُونَ ۝

45. We ordained therein for them: "Life for life, eye for eye, nose for nose, ear for ear, tooth for tooth, and wounds equal for equal." But if any one remits the retaliation by way of charity, it is an act of atonement for himself. And if any fail to judge by (the light of) what Allah has revealed, they are (no better than) wrong-doers.

45. Wa katabnaa 'alayhim feehaaa annan-nafsa binnafsi wal'ayna bil'ayni wal-anfa bilanfi wal-uzuna bil-uzuni wassinna bissinni waljurooḥa qiṣaaṣ; faman taṣaddaqa bihee fahuwa kaffaaratul-lah; wa mal-lam yaḥkum bimaaa anzalal-laahu fa-ulaaa'ika humuẓ-ẓalimoon.

وَكَتَبْنَا عَلَيْهِمْ فِيهَآ أَنَّ ٱلنَّفْسَ بِٱلنَّفْسِ وَٱلْعَيْنَ بِٱلْعَيْنِ وَٱلْأَنفَ بِٱلْأَنفِ وَٱلْأُذُنَ بِٱلْأُذُنِ وَٱلسِّنَّ بِٱلسِّنِّ وَٱلْجُرُوحَ قِصَاصٌ فَمَن تَصَدَّقَ بِهِۦ فَهُوَ كَفَّارَةٌ لَّهُۥ وَمَن لَّمْ يَحْكُم بِمَآ أَنزَلَ ٱللَّهُ فَأُو۟لَٰٓئِكَ هُمُ ٱلظَّٰلِمُونَ ۝

46. And in their footsteps We sent Jesus the son of

46. Wa qaffaynaa 'alaaa aaṣaarihim bi-'Eesab-ni-

وَقَفَّيْنَا عَلَىٰٓ ءَاثَٰرِهِم بِعِيسَى ٱبْنِ

Mary, confirming the Law that had come before him: We sent him the Gospel: therein was guidance and light, and confirmation of the Law that had come before him: a guidance and an admonition to those who fear Allah.

47. Let the people of the Gospel judge by what Allah has revealed therein. If any do fail to judge by (the light of) what Allah has revealed, they are (no better than) those who rebel.

48. To you We sent the Scripture in truth, confirming the scripture that came before it, and guarding it in safety: so judge between them by what Allah has revealed, and follow not their vain desires, diverging from the Truth that has come to you. To each among you we have prescribed a law and an open way. If Allah had so willed, He would have made you a single people, but (His plan is) to test you in what He have given you: so strive as in a race in all virtues. The goal of you all is to Allah; it is He that will show you the truth of the matters in which you dispute;

49. And this (He commands): Judge you between them by what Allah has revealed, and follow not their vain desires, but beware of them lest they beguile you from any of that (teaching) which Allah has sent down to you. And if they turn away, be assured that for some of their crime it is Allah's purpose to punish them. And truly most men are rebellious.

Maryama muṣaddiqal-limaa bayna yadayhi minat-Tawraati wa aataynaahul-Injeela feehi hudanw-wa nooruñw-wa muṣaddiqal-limaa bayna yadayhi minat-Tawraati wa hudanw-wa mawʻiẓatal-lilmuttaqeen.

47. Walyaḥkum Ahlul-Injeeli bimaaa anzalal-laahu feeh; wa mal-lam yaḥkum bimaaa anzalal-laahu fa-ulaaa'ika humul-faasiqoon.

48. Wa anzalnaaa ilaykal-Kitaaba bilḥaqqi muṣaddiqallimaa bayna yadayhi minal-Kitaabi wa muhayminan ʻalayhi faḥkum baynahum bimaaa anzalal-laahu wa laa tattabiʻ ahwaaa'ahum ʻammaa jaaa'aka minal-ḥaqq; likullin jaʻalnaa minkum shirʻatañw-wa minhaajaa; wa law shaaa'al-laahu lajaʻalakum ummatañw-waaḥidatañw-wa laakil-liyabluwakum fee maaa aataakum fastabiqul-khayraat; ilal-laahi marjiʻukum jameeʻan fayunab-biʻukum bimaa kuntum feehi takhtalifoon.

49. Wa aniḥ-kum baynahum bimaaa anzalal-laahu wa laa tattabiʻ ahwaaa'ahum waḥzar-hum añy-yaftinooka ʻam baʻḍi maaa anzalal-laahu ilayka fa-in tawallaw faʻlam annamaa yureedul-laahu añy-yuṣeebahum biba'ḍi ẓunoobihim; wa inna kaseeram-minan-naasi lafaa-siqoon.

50. Do they then seek after a judgment of (the days of) ignorance? But who, for a people whose faith is assured, can give better judgment than Allah?

51. O you who believe! take not the Jews and the Christians for your friends and protectors: they are but friends and protectors to each other. And he amongst you that turns to them (for friendship) is of them. Verily Allah guides not a people unjust.

52. Those in whose hearts is a disease - you see how eagerly they run about amongst them, saying: "We do fear lest a change of fortune bring us disaster." Ah! perhaps Allah will give (thee) victory, or a decision according to His will. Then will they repent of the thoughts which they secretly harboured in their hearts.

53. And those who believe will say: "Are these the men who swore their strongest oaths by Allah, that they were with you?" All that they do will be in vain, and they will fall into (nothing but) ruin.

54. O you who believe! if any from among you turn back from his Faith, soon will Allah produce a people whom He will love as they will love Him,- lowly with the believers, mighty against the rejecters, fighting in the way of Allah, and never afraid of the reproaches of such as find fault. That is the grace of Allah, which He will bestow on whom He pleases. And Allah encompasses all, and He knows all things.

50. Afaḥukmal-Jaahiliyyati yabghoon; wa man aḥsanu minal-laahi ḥukmal-liqawmiñy-yooqinoon. **(Section 7)**

51. Yaaa-ayyuhal-lazeena aamanoo laa tattakhizul-Yahooda wan-Naṣaaraaa awliyaaa'; ba'ḍuhum-awliyaaa'u ba'ḍ; wa mañy-yatawallahum minkum fa-innahoo minhum; innal-laaha laa yahdil-qawmaz-zaalimeen.

52. Fataral-lazeena fee quloobihim maraḍuñy-yusaari'oona feehim yaqooloona nakhshaaa-an tuṣeebanaa daaa'irah; fa'asallaahu-añy-yaåtiya bilfatḥi aw amrim-min 'indihee fa-yuṣbiḥoo 'alaa maaa asarroo feee anfusihim naadimeen.

53. Wa yaqoolul-lazeena aamanooo ahaaa'ulaaa'il-lazeena aqsamoo billaahi jahda aymaanihim innahum lama-'akum; ḥabiṭat a'maaluhum fa-aṣbaḥoo khaasireen.

54. Yaaa ayyuhal-lazeena aamanoo mañy-yartadda minkum 'an deenihee fasawfa yaåtil-laahu biqawmiñy-yuḥibbuhum wa yuḥibboonahooo azillatin 'alal-mu'mineena a'izzatin 'alal-kaafireena yujaahidoona fee sabeelil-laahi wa laa yakhaafoona lawmata laaa'im; zaalika faḍlul-laahi yu'teehi mañy-yashaaa'; wallaahu Waasi'un 'Aleem.

55. Your (real) friends are (no less than) Allah, His Apostle, and the (fellowship of) Believers,- those who establish regular prayers and regular charity, and they bow down humbly (in worship).

56. As to those who turn (for friendship) to Allah, His Apostle, and the (fellowship of) Believers,- it is the fellowship of Allah that must certainly triumph.

57. O you who believe! take not for friends and protectors those who take your religion for a mockery or sport,- whether among those who received the Scripture before you, or among those who reject Faith; but fear you Allah, if you have Faith (indeed).

58. When you proclaim your call to prayer, they take it (but) as mockery and sport; that is because they are a people without understanding.

59. Say: "O people of the Book! Do you disapprove of us for no other reason than that we believe in Allah, and the revelation that has come to us and that which came before (us), and (perhaps) that most of you are rebellious and disobedient?"

60. Say: "Shall I point out to you something much worse than this, (as judged) by the treatment it received from Allah? those who incurred the curse of Allah and His wrath, those of whom some He transformed into apes and swine, those who worshipped evil;- these are (many times) worse in rank, and far more astray from the even path!"

61. When they come to you, they say: "We believe": but in fact they enter with a mind against Faith, and they go out with the same. But Allah knows fully all that they hide.

---

55. Innamaa waliyyukumul-laahu wa Rasooluhoo wal-lazeena aamanul-lazeena yu-qeemoonas-Salaata wa yu'too-naz-Zakaata wa hum raaki'oon.

56. Wa mañy-yatawallal-laaha wa Rasoolahoo wallazeena aamanoo fa-inna ḥizbal-laahi humul-ghaaliboon. (Section 8)

57. Yaaa ayyuhal-lazeena aamanoo laa tattakhizul-lazeenat-takhazoo deenakum huzuwañw-wa la'ibam-minal-lazeena ootul-Kitaaba min qablikum walkuffaara awliyaaa'; wattaqul-laaha in kuntum mu'mineen.

58. Wa izaa naadaytum ilaṣ-Ṣalaatit-takhazoohaa huzu-wañw-wa la'ibaa; zaalika bi-annahum qawmul-laa ya'qiloon.

59. Qul yaaa Ahlal-Kitaabi hal tanqimoona minnaaa illaaa an aamannaa billaahi wa maaa unzila ilaynaa wa maaa unzila min qablu wa anna aksarakum faasiqoon.

60. Qul hal unabbi'ukum bisharrim-min zaalika masoo-batan 'indal-laah; malla'ana-hul-laahu wa ghaḍiba 'alayhi wa ja'ala minhumul-qiradata wal-khanaazeera wa 'abadaṭ-Ṭaaghoot; ulaaa'ika sharrum-makaanañw-wa aḍallu 'an Sawaaa'is-Sabeel.

61. Wa-izaa jaaa'ookum qaalooo aamannaa wa qad dakhaloo bilkufri wa hum qad kharajoo bih; wallaahu a'lamu bimaa kaanoo yaktumoon.

---

62. You see many of them, racing each other in sin and rancour, and their eating of things forbidden. Evil indeed are the things that they do.

62. Wa taraa kaseeram-minhum yusaari'oona fil-ismi wal'udwaani wa aklihimus-suht; labi'sa maa kaanoo ya'maloon.

وَتَرَىٰ كَثِيرًا مِّنْهُمْ يُسَارِعُونَ فِى الْإِثْمِ وَالْعُدْوَانِ وَأَكْلِهِمُ السُّحْتَ لَبِئْسَ مَا كَانُوا يَعْمَلُونَ ۞

63. Why do not the rabbis and the doctors of Law forbid them from their (habit of) uttering sinful words and eating things forbidden? Evil indeed are their works.

63. Law laa yanhaahumur-rabbaaniyyoona wal-aḥbaaru 'an qawlihimul-isma wa aklihimus-suht; labi'sa maa kaanoo yaṣna'oon.

لَوْلَا يَنْهَاهُمُ الرَّبَّانِيُّونَ وَالْأَحْبَارُ عَنْ قَوْلِهِمُ الْإِثْمَ وَأَكْلِهِمُ السُّحْتَ لَبِئْسَ مَا كَانُوا يَصْنَعُونَ ۞

64. The Jews say: "Allah's hand is tied up." Be their hands tied up and be they accursed for the (blasphemy) they utter. No, both His hands are widely outstretched: He gives and spends (of His bounty) as He pleases. But the revelation that comes to you from Allah increases in most of them their obstinate rebellion and blasphemy. Amongst them we have placed enmity and hatred till the Day of Judgment. Every time they kindle the fire of war, Allah does extinguish it; but they (ever) strive to do mischief on earth. And Allah loves not those who do mischief.

64. Wa qaalatil-Yahoodu Yadullaahi maghloolah; ghullat aydeehim wa lu'inoo bimaa qaaloo; bal Yadaahu mabsoo-ṭaṭaani yunfiqu kayfa yashaaa'; wa la-yazeedanna kaseeram-minhum-maaa unzila ilayka mir-Rabbika ṭughyaananw-wa kufraa; wa alqaynaa bayna-humul-'adaawata wal-bagh-ḍaaa-a' ilaa Yawmil-Qiyaamah; kullamaaa awqadoo naaral-lilḥarbi aṭfa-ahal-laah; wa yas'awna fil-arḍi fasaadaa; wal-laahu laa yuḥibbul-mufsideen.

وَقَالَتِ الْيَهُودُ يَدُ اللّٰهِ مَغْلُولَةٌ ۚ غُلَّتْ أَيْدِيهِمْ وَلُعِنُوا بِمَا قَالُوا ۘ بَلْ يَدَاهُ مَبْسُوطَتَانِ يُنفِقُ كَيْفَ يَشَاءُ ۚ وَلَيَزِيدَنَّ كَثِيرًا مِّنْهُم مَّا أُنزِلَ إِلَيْكَ مِن رَّبِّكَ طُغْيَانًا وَكُفْرًا ۚ وَأَلْقَيْنَا بَيْنَهُمُ الْعَدَاوَةَ وَالْبَغْضَاءَ إِلَىٰ يَوْمِ الْقِيَامَةِ ۚ كُلَّمَا أَوْقَدُوا نَارًا لِّلْحَرْبِ أَطْفَأَهَا اللّٰهُ ۚ وَيَسْعَوْنَ فِى الْأَرْضِ فَسَادًا ۚ وَاللّٰهُ لَا يُحِبُّ الْمُفْسِدِينَ ۞

65. If only the People of the Book had believed and been righteous, We should indeed have blotted out their iniquities and admitted them to gardens of bliss.

65. Wa law anna Ahlal-Kitaabi aamanoo wattaqaw lakaffarnaa 'anhum sayyi-aatihim wa la-adkhalnaahum Jannaatin-Na'eem.

وَلَوْ أَنَّ أَهْلَ الْكِتَابِ آمَنُوا وَاتَّقَوْا لَكَفَّرْنَا عَنْهُمْ سَيِّئَاتِهِمْ وَلَأَدْخَلْنَاهُمْ جَنَّاتِ النَّعِيمِ ۞

66. If only they had stood fast by the Law, the Gospel, and all the revelation that was sent to them from their Lord, they would have enjoyed happiness from every side. There is from among them a party on the right course: but many of them follow a course that is evil.

(Section 9)

66. Wa law annahum aqaa-mut-Tawraata wal-Injeela wa maaa unzila ilayhim-mir-Rabbihim la-akaloo min fawqi-him wa min taḥti arjulihim; minhum ummatum-muqta-ṣidatuňw wa kaseerum-minhum saaa'a maa ya'maloon.

وَلَوْ أَنَّهُمْ أَقَامُوا التَّوْرَاةَ وَالْإِنجِيلَ وَمَا أُنزِلَ إِلَيْهِم مِّن رَّبِّهِمْ لَأَكَلُوا مِن فَوْقِهِمْ وَمِن تَحْتِ أَرْجُلِهِم ۚ مِّنْهُمْ أُمَّةٌ مُّقْتَصِدَةٌ ۖ وَكَثِيرٌ مِّنْهُمْ سَاءَ مَا يَعْمَلُونَ ۞

67. O Apostle! proclaim the (message) which has been sent to you from your Lord. If you did not, you would not have fulfilled and proclaimed

67. Yaaa ayyuhar-Rasoolu balligh maaa unzila ilayka mir-Rabbika wa il-lam taf'al famaa ballaghta

يَا أَيُّهَا الرَّسُولُ بَلِّغْ مَا أُنزِلَ إِلَيْكَ مِن رَّبِّكَ ۖ وَإِن لَّمْ تَفْعَلْ فَمَا بَلَّغْتَ

His mission. And Allah will defend you from men (who mean mischief). For Allah guides not those who reject Faith.

68. Say: "O People of the Book! you have no ground to stand upon unless you stand fast by the Law, the Gospel, and all the revelation that has come to you from your Lord." It is the revelation that comes to you from your Lord, that increases in most of them their obstinate rebellion and blasphemy. But you do not grieve over (these) people without Faith.

69. Those who believe (in the Qur'an), those who follow the Jewish (scriptures), and the Sabians and the Christians,- any who believe in Allah and the Last Day, and work righteousness,- on them shall be no fear, nor shall they grieve.

70. We took the Covenant of the Children of Israel and sent them Apostles, every time, there came to them an Apostle with what they themselves desired not - some (of these) they called impostors, and some they (go so far as to) slay.

71. They thought there would be no trial (or punishment); so they became blind and deaf; yet Allah (in mercy) turned to them; yet again many of them became blind and deaf. But Allah sees well all that they do.

72. They do blaspheme who say: "Allah is Christ the son of Mary." But Christ said: "O Children of Israel! worship Allah, my Lord and your Lord." Whoever joins other gods with Allah,- Allah will forbid

Risaalatah; wallaahu ya'şimuka minan-naas; innal-laaha laa yahdil-qawmal-kaafireen.

68. Qul yaaa Ahlal-Kitaabi lastum 'alaa shay'in ḥattaa tuqeemut-Tawraata wal-Injeela wa maaa unzila ilaykum-mir-Rabbikum; wa layazeedanna kaseeram-minhum-maaa unzila ilayka mir-Rabbika ṭugh-yaananw-wa kufran falaa taåsa 'alal-qawmil-kaafireen.

69. Innal-lazeena aamanoo wallazeena haadoo waṣ-Ṣaabi'oona wan-Naṣaaraa man aamana billaahi wal-Yawmil-Aakhiri wa 'amila ṣaaliḥan falaa khawfun 'alayhim wa laa hum yaḥzanoon.

70. Laqad akhaznaa meesaaqa Baneee Israaa'eela wa arsal-naaa ilayhim Rusulan kullamaa jaaa'ahum Rasoolum-bimaa laa tahwaaa anfusuhum fareeqan kazzaboo wa fareeqañy-yaqtuloon.

71. Wa ḥasibooo allaa takoona fitnatun fa'amoo wa ṣammoo summa taabal-laahu 'alayhim summa 'amoo wa ṣammoo kaseerum-minhum; wallaahu baṣeerum-bimaa ya'maloon.

72. Laqad kafaral-lazeena qaalooo innal-laaha Huwal-Maseeḥub-nu-Maryama wa qaalal-Maseeḥu yaa Baneee Israaa'eela'-budul-laaha Rabbee wa Rabbakum innahoo mañy-yushrik billaahi faqad ḥarramal-laahu

him the Garden, and the Fire will be his abode. There will for the wrong-doers be no one to help.

73. They do blaspheme who say: Allah is one of three in a Trinity; for there is no Allah except One Allah. If they desist not from their word (of blasphemy), verily a grievous Chastisement will befall the blasphemers among them.

74. Why turn they not to Allah, and seek His forgiveness? For Allah is Oftforgiving, Most Merciful.

75. Christ the son of Mary was no more than an Apostle; many were the Apostles that passed away before him. His mother was a woman of truth. They had both to eat their (daily) food. See how Allah does make His signs clear to them; yet see in what ways they are deluded away from the truth!

76. Say: "Will you worship, besides Allah, something which has no power either to harm or benefit you? But Allah,- He it is that hears and knows all things."

77. Say: "O people of the Book! exceed not in your religion the bounds (of what is proper), trespassing beyond the truth, nor follow the vain desires of people who went wrong in times gone by,- who misled many, and strayed (themselves) from the even way.

78. Curses were pronounced on those among the Children of Israel who rejected Faith, by the tongue of David and of Jesus the son of Mary: because they disobeyed and persisted in excesses.

79. Nor did they (usually) forbid one another the iniquities

'alayhil-Jannata wa maåwaahun-Naaru wa maa liẓẓaalimeena min anṣaar.

73. Laqad kafaral-lazeena qaalooo innal-laaha saalisu salaasah; wa maa min ilaahin illaaa Ilaahuñw-Waaḥid; wa illam yantahoo 'ammaa yaqooloona layamas-sannal-lazeena kafaroo minhum 'azaabun aleem.

74. Afalaa-yatooboona ilallaahi wa yastaghfiroonah; wallaahu Ghafoorur- Raḥeem.

75. Mal-Maseeḥub-nu-Maryama illaa Rasoolun qad khalat min qablihir-Rusulu wa ummuhoo ṣiddeeqatun kaanaa yaåkulaaniṭ-ṭa'aam; unẓur kayfa nubayyinu lahumul-Aayaati summan-ẓur annaa yu'fakoon.

76. Qul ata'budoona min ḍoonil-laahi maa laa yamliku lakum ḍarrañw-wa laa naf'aa; wallaahu Huwas-Samee'ul 'Aleem.

77. Qul yaaa Ahlal-Kitaabi laa taghloo fee deenikum ghayral-ḥaqqi wa laa tattabi-'ooo ahwaaa'a qawmin qad ḍalloo min qablu wa aḍalloo kaseerañw-wa ḍalloo 'an Sawaaa'is-Sabeel. **(Section 10)**

78. Lu'inal-lazeena kafaroo mim Baneee Israaa'eela 'alaa lisaani Daawooda wa 'Eesabni-Maryam; zaalika bimaa 'aṣaw wa kaanoo ya'tadoon.

79. Kaanoo laa yatanaahawna 'am-munkarin

which they committed: Evil indeed were the deeds which they did.

80. You see many of them turning in friendship to the Unbelievers. Evil indeed are (the works) which their souls have sent forward before them (with the result), that Allah's wrath is on them, and in torment will they abide.

81. If only they had believed in Allah, in the Apostle, and in what has been revealed to him, never would they have taken them for friends and protectors, but most of them are rebellious wrong-doers.

82. Strongest among men in enmity to the believers will you find the Jews and Pagans; and nearest among them in love to the believers will you find those who say, "We are Christians": because among these are men devoted to learning and men who have renounced the world, and they are not arrogant.

83. And when they listen to the revelation received by the Apostle, you will see their eyes overflowing with tears, for they recognise the truth: they pray: "Our Lord! we believe; write us down among the witnesses.

84. "What cause can we have not to believe in Allah and the truth which has come to us, seeing that we long for our Lord to admit us to the company of the righteous?"

85. And for this their prayer has Allah rewarded them with gardens, with rivers flowing underneath,- their eternal home. Such is the recompense of those who do good.

86. But those who reject Faith and belie our Signs,-

fa'aluhoo; labi'sa maa kaanoo yafa'loon.

80. Taraa kaseeram-minhum yatawallawnal-lazeena kafaroo; labi'sa maa qaddamat lahum anfusuhum an sakhiṭallaahu 'alayhim wa fil-'azaabi hum khaalidoon.

81. Wa law kaanoo yu'minoona billaahi wan-Nabiyyi wa maaa unzila ilayhi mattakhazoohum awliyaaa'a wa laakinna kaseeram-minhum faasiqoon.

82. Latajidanna ashad-dannaasi 'adaawatal-lillazeena aamanul-Yahooda wallazeena ashrakoo wa latajidanna aqrabahum-mawaddatal-lillazeena aamanul-lazeena qaaloo innaa Naṣaaraa; zaalika bianna minhum qisseeseena wa ruhbaanañw-wa annahum laa yastakbiroon.

83. Wa izaa sami'oo maaa unzila ilar-Rasooli taraaa a'yunahum tafeeḍu minaddam'i mimmaa 'arafoo minalḥaqq; yaqooloona Rabbanaaa aamannaa faktubnaa ma'ash-shaahideen.

84. Wa maa lanaa laa nu'minu billaahi wa maa jaaa'anaa minal-ḥaqqi wa naṭma'u añy-yudkhilanaa Rabbunaa ma'alqawmiṣ-ṣaaliḥeen.

85. Fa-asaabahumul-laahu bimaa qaaloo Jannaatin tajree min taḥtihal-anhaaru khaalideena feehaa; wa zaalika jazaaa'ul-muḥsineen.

86. Wallazeena kafaroo wa kaz-zaboo bi-Aayaatinaaa

فَعَلُوهُ ۚ لَبِئْسَ مَا كَانُوا يَفْعَلُونَ ۞

تَرَىٰ كَثِيرًا مِّنْهُمْ يَتَوَلَّوْنَ الَّذِينَ كَفَرُوا ۚ لَبِئْسَ مَا قَدَّمَتْ لَهُمْ أَنفُسُهُمْ أَن سَخِطَ اللَّهُ عَلَيْهِمْ وَفِي الْعَذَابِ هُمْ خَالِدُونَ ۞

وَلَوْ كَانُوا يُؤْمِنُونَ بِاللَّهِ وَالنَّبِيِّ وَمَا أُنزِلَ إِلَيْهِ مَا اتَّخَذُوهُمْ أَوْلِيَاءَ وَلَٰكِنَّ كَثِيرًا مِّنْهُمْ فَاسِقُونَ ۞

لَتَجِدَنَّ أَشَدَّ النَّاسِ عَدَاوَةً لِّلَّذِينَ آمَنُوا الْيَهُودَ وَالَّذِينَ أَشْرَكُوا ۖ وَلَتَجِدَنَّ أَقْرَبَهُم مَّوَدَّةً لِّلَّذِينَ آمَنُوا الَّذِينَ قَالُوا إِنَّا نَصَارَىٰ ۚ ذَٰلِكَ بِأَنَّ مِنْهُمْ قِسِّيسِينَ وَرُهْبَانًا وَأَنَّهُمْ لَا يَسْتَكْبِرُونَ ۞

وَإِذَا سَمِعُوا مَا أُنزِلَ إِلَى الرَّسُولِ تَرَىٰ أَعْيُنَهُمْ تَفِيضُ مِنَ الدَّمْعِ مِمَّا عَرَفُوا مِنَ الْحَقِّ ۖ يَقُولُونَ رَبَّنَا آمَنَّا فَاكْتُبْنَا مَعَ الشَّاهِدِينَ ۞

وَمَا لَنَا لَا نُؤْمِنُ بِاللَّهِ وَمَا جَاءَنَا مِنَ الْحَقِّ وَنَطْمَعُ أَن يُدْخِلَنَا رَبُّنَا مَعَ الْقَوْمِ الصَّالِحِينَ ۞

فَأَثَابَهُمُ اللَّهُ بِمَا قَالُوا جَنَّاتٍ تَجْرِي مِن تَحْتِهَا الْأَنْهَارُ خَالِدِينَ فِيهَا ۚ وَذَٰلِكَ جَزَاءُ الْمُحْسِنِينَ ۞

وَالَّذِينَ كَفَرُوا وَكَذَّبُوا بِآيَاتِنَا

they shall be Companions of Hell-fire.

87. O you who believe! make not unlawful the good things which Allah has made lawful for you, but commit no excess: for Allah loves not those given to excess.

88. Eat of the things which Allah has provided for you, lawful and good; but fear Allah, in Whom you believe.

89. Allah will not call you to account for what is futile in your oaths, but He will call you to account for your deliberate oaths: for expiation, feed ten indigent persons, on a scale of the average for the food of your families; or clothe them; or give a slave his freedom. If that is beyond your means, fast for three days. That is the expiation for the oaths you have sworn. But keep to your oaths. Thus Allah makes clear to you His Signs, that you may be grateful.

90. O you who believe! Intoxicants and gambling, (dedication of) stones, and (divination by) arrows, are an abomination,- of Satan's handwork: eschew such (abomination), that you may prosper.

91. Satan's plan is (but) to excite enmity and hatred between you, with intoxicants and gambling, and hinder you from the remembrance of Allah, and from prayer: will you not then abstain?

92. Obey Allah, and obey the Apostle, and beware (of evil): if you do turn back, you should know that it is Our Apostle's duty to proclaim (the message) in the clearest manner.

ulaaa'ika Aṣḥaabul-Jaḥeem.

(Section 11)

87. Yaaa ayyuhal-lazeena aamanoo laa tuḥarrimoo ṭayyibaati maaa aḥallal-laahu lakum wa laa ta'tadooo; innal-laaha laa yuḥibbul-mu'tadeen.

88. Wa kuloo mimmaa razaqakumul-laahu ḥalaalan ṭayyibaa; wattaqul-laahallazeee antum bihee mu'minoon.

89. Laa yu'aakhizukumul-laahu billaghwi feee aymaanikum wa laakiñy-yu'aakhizukum bimaa 'aqqattumul-aymaana fakaff-faaratuhooo iṭ'aamu 'asharati masaakeena min awsaṭi maa tuṭ'imoona ahleekum aw kiswatuhum aw taḥreeru raqabatin famallam yajid fa-Ṣiyaamu ṣalaaṣati ayyaam; zaalika kaffaaratu aymaanikum izaa ḥalaftum; waḥfazooo aymaanakum; kazaalika yubayyi-nul-laahu lakum Aayaatihee la'allakum tashkuroon.

90. Yaaa ayyuhal-lazeena aamanooo innamal-khamru walmaysiru wal-anṣaabu wal-azlaamu rijsum-min 'amalish-shayṭaani fajtaniboohu la'al-lakum tufliḥoon.

91. Innamaa yureedush-Shay-ṭaanu añy-yooqi'a baynakumul-'adaawata wal-baghḍaaa'a fil-khamri walmaysiri wa yaṣud-dakum 'an zikril-laahi wa 'aniṣ-Ṣalaati fahal antum muntahoon.

92. Wa aṭee'ul-laaha wa aṭee'ur-Rasoola waḥzaroo; fa-in tawal-laytum fa'lamooo annamaa 'alaa Rasoolinal-balaaghul-mubeen.

93. On those who believe and do deeds of righteousness there is no blame for what they ate (in the past), when they guard themselves from evil, and believe, and do deeds of righteousness,- (or) again, guard themselves from evil and believe,- (or) again, guard them-selves from evil and do good. For Allah loves those who do good.

94. O you who believe! Allah makes a trial of you in a little matter of game well within reach of your hands and your lances, that He may test who fears Him unseen: and who transgress thereafter, will have a grievous Chastisement.

95. O you who believe! kill game while in the Sacred precincts or in pilgrim garb. If any of you does so intentionally, the compensation is an offering, brought to the Ka'ba, of a domestic animal equivalent to the one he killed, as adjudged by two just men among you; or by way of atonement, the feeding of the indigent; or its equivalent in fasts: that he may taste of the Chastisement of his deed. Allah forgives what is past: for repetition Allah will exact from him the Chastisement. For Allah is Exalted, and Lord of Retribution.

96. Lawful to you is the pursuit of water-game and its use for food,- for the benefit of your-selves and those who travel; but forbidden is the pursuit of land-game;- as long as you are in the Sacred Precincts or in pilgrim garb. And fear Allah, to Whom you shall be gathered back.

97. Allah made the Ka'ba, the Sacred House, an asylum of security for men, as also the Sacred Months, the animals for offerings, and the garlands that mark them: that you may know that Allah

93. Laysa 'alal-lazeena aamanoo wa 'amilus-saalihaati junaahun feemaa ta'imooo izaa mat-taqaw wa aamanoo wa 'amilus-saalihaati summat-taqaw wa aamanoo summat-taqaw wa ahsanoo; wallaahu yuhibbul-muhsineen.

94. Yaaa ayyuhal-lazeena aamanoo la-yabluwannakumul-laahu bishay'im-minas-saydi tanaaluhooo aydeekum wa rimaahukum liya'lamal-laahu many-yakhaafuhoo bilghayb; famani'-tadaa ba'da zaalika falahoo 'azaabun aleem.

(Section 12)

95. Yaaa ayyuhal-lazeena aamanoo laa taqtulus-sayda wa antum hurum; wa man qatalahoo minkum muta'am-midan fajazaaa'um mislu maa qatala minanna'ami yahkumu bihee zawaa 'adlim-minkum hadyam baalighal-Ka'bati aw kaffaaratun ta'aamu masaa-keena aw 'adlu zaalika Siyaamal-liyazooqa wabaala amrih; 'afal-laahu 'ammaa salaf; wa man 'aada fayanta-qimul-laahu minh; wallaahu 'azeezun zuntiqaam.

96. Uhilla lakum saydul-bahri wa ta'aamuhoo mataa'al-lakum wa lissayyaarati wa hurrima 'alaykum saydul-barri maa dumtum hurumaa; wattaqul-laahal-lazeee ilayhi tuhsharoon.

97. Ja'alal-laahul-Ka'batal-Baytal-Haraama qiyaamal-linnaasi wash-Shahral-Haraa-ma walhadya walqalaaa'id; zaalika lita'lamooo annal-laaha

has knowledge of what is in the heavens and on earth and that Allah is well acquainted with all things.

98. You should know that Allah is strict in punishment and that Allah is Oft-forgiving, Most Merciful.

99. The Apostle's duty is but to proclaim (the message). But Allah knows all that you reveal and all that you conceal.

100. Say: "Not equal are things that are bad and things that are good, even though the abundance of the bad may dazzle you; so fear Allah, O you that understand; that (so) you may prosper."

101. O you who believe! do not ask questions about things which, if made plain to you, may cause you trouble. But if you ask about things when the Qur'an is being revealed, they will be made plain to you, Allah will forgive those: for Allah is Oft-forgiving, Most Forbearing.

102. Some people before you did ask such questions, and on that account lost their faith.

103. It was not Allah who instituted (superstitions like those of) a slit-ear she- camel, or a she-camel let loose for free pasture, or idol sacrifices for twin-births in animals, or stallion-camels freed from work: It is blasphemers who invent a lie against Allah; but most of them lack wisdom.

104. When it is said to them: "Come to what Allah has revealed; come to the Apostle": they say: "Enough for us are the ways we found our fathers following." what! even though their fathers were void of knowledge and guidance?

105. O you who believe! Guard your own souls:

ya'lamu maa fis-samaawaati wa maa fil-arḍi wa annal-laaha bikulli shay'in 'Aleem.

98. I'lamoo annal-laaha sha-deedul-'iqaabi wa annal-laaha Ghafoorur-Raheem.

99. Maa 'alar-Rasooli illal-balaagh; wallaahu ya'lamu maa tubdoona wa maa taktumoon.

100. Qul laa yastawil-khabeesu waṭṭayyibu wa law a'jabaka kaṣratul-khabeeṣ; fattaqul-laaha yaaa-ulil-albaabi la'alla-kum tufliḥoon.　　**(Section 13)**

101. Yaaa ayyuhal-lazeena aamanoo laa tas'aloo 'an ashyaaa'a in tubda lakum tasu'kum; wa in tas'aloo 'anhaa heena yunazzalul-Qur'aanu tubda lakum; 'afallaahu 'anhaa; wallaahu Ghafoorun Ḥaleem.

102. Qad sa-alahaa qawmum min qablikum summa aṣbaḥoo bihaa kaafireen.

103. Maa ja'alal-laahu mim baheeratiñw-wa laa saaa'iba-tiñw-wa laa waṣeelatiñw-wa laa ḥaamiñw wa laakinnal-lazeena kafaroo yaftaroona 'alallaahil-kazib; wa akṣaruhum laa ya'qiloon.

104. Wa izaa qeela lahum ta'aalaw ilaa maaa anzalallaahu wa ilar-Rasooli qaaloo has-bunaa maa wajadnaa 'alayhi aabaaa'anaa; awa law kaana aabaaa'uhum laa ya'lamoona shay'añw-wa laa yahtadoon.

105. Yaaa ayyuhal-lazeena aamanoo 'alaykum anfusakum

if you follow (right) guidance, no hurt can come to you from those who stray. The goal of you all is to Allah: it is He that will show you the truth of all that you do.

106. O you who believe! When death approaches any of you, (take) witnesses among your-selves when making bequests,- two just men of your own (brotherhood) or others from outside if you are jour-neying through the earth, and the chance of death befalls you (thus). If you doubt (their truth), detain them both after prayer, and let them both swear by Allah: "We wish not in this for any worldly gain, even though the (beneficiary) be our near relation: we shall hide not the evidence before Allah: if we do, then behold! the sin be upon us!"

107. But if it gets known that these two were guilty of the sin (of perjury), let two others stand forth in their places,- nearest in kin from among those who claim a lawful right: let them swear by Allah: "We affirm that our witness is truer than that of those two, and that we have not trespassed (beyond the truth): if we did, behold! the wrong be upon us!"

108. That is most suitable: that they may give the evidence in its true nature and shape, or else they would fear that other oaths would be taken after their oaths. But fear Allah, and listen (to His counsel): for Allah guides not a rebellious people!

109. One day will Allah gather the apostles together, and ask: "What was the response you received (from men to your teaching)?" They will say: "We have no knowledge: it is you Who knows in full all that is hidden."

110. Then will Allah say: "O Jesus the son of Mary! recount My favour to you and to your mother.

laa yaḍurrukum man ḍalla izḥ-tadaytum; ilal-laahi marji'ukum jamee'an fayunabbi'ukum bimaa kuntum ta'maloon.

106. Yaaa ayyuhal-lazeena aamanoo shahaadatu baynikum izaa ḥaḍara aḥadakumul-mawtu ḥeenal-waṣiyyatis-naani zawaa 'adlim-minkum aw aakharaani min ghayrikum in antum ḍarabtum fil-arḍi fa-aṣaabat-kum-muṣeebatul-mawt; taḥbi-soonahumaa mim-ba'diṣ-Ṣalaati fa-yuqsimaani billaahi inirtabtum laa nashtaree bihee ṣamanaňw-wa law kaana zaa qurbaa wa laa naktumu shahaadatal-laahi innaaa izal-laminal-aasimeen.

107. Fa-in 'usira 'alaaa annahumas-tahaqqaaa isman fa-aakharaani yaqoomaani maqaamahumaa minal-lazeenas-taḥaqqa 'alayhimul-awlayaani fa-yuqsimaani billaahi lashahaadatunaaa aḥaqqu min shahaadatihimaa wa ma'taydaynaaa innaaa izal-laminaẓ-ẓaalimeen.

108. Zaalika adnaaa aňy-yaátoo bishshahaadati 'alaa wajhihaaa aw yakhaafooo an turadda aymaanum ba'da aymaanihim; wattaqul-laaha wasma'oo; wallaahu laa yahdil-qawmal-faasiqeen. **(Section 14)**

109. Yawma yajma'ul-laahur-Rusula fa-yaqoolu maazaaa ujibtum qaaloo laa 'ilma lanaa innaka Anta 'Allaamul-Ghuyoob.

110. Iz qaalal-laahu yaa 'Eesab-na-Maryamaz-kur ni'matee 'alayka wa 'alaa waalidatik;

لَا يَضُرُّكُم مَّن ضَلَّ إِذَا اهْتَدَيْتُمْ إِلَى اللَّهِ مَرْجِعُكُمْ جَمِيعًا فَيُنَبِّئُكُم بِمَا كُنتُمْ تَعْمَلُونَ ۝

يَٰٓأَيُّهَا الَّذِينَ ءَامَنُوا شَهَٰدَةُ بَيْنِكُمْ إِذَا حَضَرَ أَحَدَكُمُ الْمَوْتُ حِينَ الْوَصِيَّةِ اثْنَانِ ذَوَا عَدْلٍ مِّنكُمْ أَوْ ءَاخَرَانِ مِنْ غَيْرِكُمْ إِنْ أَنتُمْ ضَرَبْتُمْ فِى الْأَرْضِ فَأَصَٰبَتْكُم مُّصِيبَةُ الْمَوْتِ تَحْبِسُونَهُمَا مِنۢ بَعْدِ الصَّلَوٰةِ فَيُقْسِمَانِ بِاللَّهِ إِنِ ارْتَبْتُمْ لَا نَشْتَرِى بِهِۦ ثَمَنًا وَلَوْ كَانَ ذَا قُرْبَىٰ وَلَا نَكْتُمُ شَهَٰدَةَ اللَّهِ إِنَّا إِذًا لَّمِنَ الْءَاثِمِينَ ۝

فَإِنْ عُثِرَ عَلَىٰٓ أَنَّهُمَا اسْتَحَقَّآ إِثْمًا فَءَاخَرَانِ يَقُومَانِ مَقَامَهُمَا مِنَ الَّذِينَ اسْتَحَقَّ عَلَيْهِمُ الْأَوْلَيَٰنِ فَيُقْسِمَانِ بِاللَّهِ لَشَهَٰدَتُنَآ أَحَقُّ مِن شَهَٰدَتِهِمَا وَمَا اعْتَدَيْنَآ إِنَّآ إِذًا لَّمِنَ الظَّٰلِمِينَ ۝

ذَٰلِكَ أَدْنَىٰٓ أَن يَأْتُوا بِالشَّهَٰدَةِ عَلَىٰ وَجْهِهَآ أَوْ يَخَافُوٓا أَن تُرَدَّ أَيْمَٰنٌۢ بَعْدَ أَيْمَٰنِهِمْ وَاتَّقُوا اللَّهَ وَاسْمَعُوا وَاللَّهُ لَا يَهْدِى الْقَوْمَ الْفَٰسِقِينَ ۝

يَوْمَ يَجْمَعُ اللَّهُ الرُّسُلَ فَيَقُولُ مَاذَآ أُجِبْتُمْ قَالُوا لَا عِلْمَ لَنَآ إِنَّكَ أَنتَ عَلَّٰمُ الْغُيُوبِ ۝

إِذْ قَالَ اللَّهُ يَٰعِيسَى ابْنَ مَرْيَمَ اذْكُرْ نِعْمَتِى عَلَيْكَ وَعَلَىٰ وَالِدَتِكَ

Behold! I strengthened you with the holy spirit, so that you did speak to the people in childhood and in maturity. Behold! I taught you the Book and Wisdom, the Law and the Gospel and behold! you made out of clay, as it were, the figure of a bird, by My leave, and you breathed into it and it became a bird by My leave, and you healed those born blind, and the lepers, by My leave. And behold ! you brought forth the dead by My leave. And behold! I did restrain the Children of Israel from (violence to) you when you showed them the Clear Signs, and the unbelievers among them said: 'This is nothing but evident magic.'

111. "And behold! I inspired the Disciples to have faith in Me and Mine Apostle: they said, 'We have faith, and You bear witness that we bow to Allah as Muslims'".

112. Behold! the disciples, said: "O Jesus the son of Mary! can your Lord send down to us a table set (with viands) from heaven?" Said Jesus: "Fear Allah, if you have faith."

113. They said: "We only wish to eat thereof and satisfy our hearts, and to know that you have indeed told us the truth; and that we ourselves may be witnesses to the miracle."

114. Jesus the son of Mary said: "O Allah our Lord! send us from heaven a table set (with viands), that there may be for us - for the first and the last of us - a solemn festival and a sign from You; and provide for our sustenance, for You are the best Sustainer (of our needs)."

115. Allah said: "I will send it down unto you: But if any

iz ayyattuka bi-Roohil-Qudusi tukallimun-naasa fil-mahdi wa kahlañw wa iz 'allamtukal-Kitaaba wal-Ḥikmata wat-Tawraata wal-Injeela wa iz Takhluqu minaṭ-ṭeeni kahay'atiṭ-ṭayri bi-iznee fatanfukhu feehaa fatakoonu ṭayram-bi-iznee wa tubri'ul-akmaha wal-abraṣa bi-iznee wa iz tukhrijul-mawtaa bi-iznee wa iz kafaftu Banee Israaa'eela 'anka iz ji'tahum bil-bayyinaati fa-qaalal-lazeena kafaroo minhum in haazaaa illaa siḥrum-mubeen.

111. Wa iz awḥaytu ilal-Ḥawaariyyeena an aaminoo bee wa bi-Rasoolee qaalooo aamannaa washhad bi-annanaa muslimoon.

112. Iz qaalal-Ḥawaariyyoona yaa 'Eesab-na-Maryama hal yastaṭe'u Rabbuka añy-yunazzila 'alaynaa maaa'idatam-minas-samaaa'i qaalat-taqul-laaha in kuntum mu'mineen.

113. Qaaloo nureedu an naåkula minhaa wa taṭma'inna quloo-bunaa wa na'lama an qad ṣadaqtanaa wa nakoona 'alayhaa minash-shaahideen.

114. Qaala 'Eesab-nu-Marya-mal-laahumma Rabbanaaa anzil 'alaynaa maaa'idatam-minas-samaaa'i takoonu lanaa 'eedal-li-awwalinaa wa aakhi-rinaa wa Aayatam-minka warzuqnaa wa Anta khayrur-raaziqeen.

115. Qaalal-laahu innee munaz-ziluhaa 'alaykum faman

of you after that resists faith, I will punish him with a Chastisement such as I have not inflicted on any one among all the peoples."

116. And behold! Allah will say: "O Jesus the son of Mary! Did you say to men, worship me and my mother as gods in derogation of Allah'?" He will say: "Glory to You! never could I say what I had no right (to say). Had I said such a thing, you would indeed have known it. You know what is in my heart, though I dont know what is in Yours. For You know in full all that is hidden.

117. "Never said I to them anything except what You commanded me to say, to wit, 'Worship Allah, my Lord and your Lord'; and I was a witness over them while I dwelt amongst them; when You took me up, You were the Watcher over them, and You are a Witness to all things.

118. "If You punish them, they are Your servant: If You forgive them, You are the Exalted in power, the Wise."

119. Allah will say: "This is a day on which the truthful will profit from their truth: theirs are Gardens, with rivers flowing beneath,- their eternal home: Allah well-pleased with them, and they with Allah: that is the great salvation, (the fulfilment of all desires).

120. To Allah belongs the dominion of the heavens and the earth, and all that is therein, and it is He Who has power over all things.

yakfur ba'du minkum fa-inneee u'azzibuhoo 'azaabal-laaa u'azzibuhooo ahadam-minal-'aalameen. **(Section 15)**

116. Wa iz qaalal-laahu yaa 'Eesab-na-Maryama 'a-anta qulta linnaasit-takhizoonee wa ummiya ilaahayni min doonil-laahi qaala Subhaanaka maa yakoonu leee an aqoola maa laysa lee bihaqq; in kuntu qultuhoo faqad 'alimtah; ta'lamu maa fee nafsee wa laaa a'lamu maa fee nafsik; innaka Anta 'Allaamul-Ghuyoob.

117. Maa qultu lahum illaa maaa amartanee bihee ani'budul-laaha Rabbeee wa Rabbakum; wa kuntu 'alayhim shaheedam-maa dumtu feehim falammaa tawaffaytanee kunta Antar-Raqeeba 'alayhim; wa Anta 'alaa kulli shay'in Shaheed.

118. In tu'azzibhum fa-inna-hum 'ibaaduka wa in taghfir lahum fa-innaka Antal-'Azeezul-Hakeem.

119. Qaalal-laahu haazaa Yawmu yanfa'us-saadiqeena sidquhum; lahum Jannaatun tajree min tahtihal-anhaaru khaalideena feehaaa abadaa; radiyal-laahu 'anhum wa radoo 'anh; zaalikal-fawzul-'azeem.

120. Lillaahi mulkus-samaa-waati wal-ardi wa maa feehinn; wa Huwa 'alaa kulli shay'in Qadeer. **(Section 16)**

---

6. The Cattle In the name of Allah, Most Gracious, Most Merciful	**Sûrat al-An'âm–6** (Revealed at Makkah) **Bismillaahir Rahmaanir Raheem**
1. Praise be to Allah, Who created the heavens and	**1.** Alhamdu lillaahil-lazee khalaqas-samaawaati wal-

the earth, and made the darkness and the light. Yet those who reject Faith hold (others) as equal, with their Guardian-Lord.

2. He it is who created you from clay, and then decreed a stated term (for you). And there is in His presence another determined term; yet you doubt within yourselves!

3. And He is Allah in the heavens and on earth. He knows what you hide, and what you reveal, and He knows the (recompense) which you earn (by your deeds).

4. But never did a single one of the Signs of their Lord reach them, but they turned away therefrom.

5. And now they reject the truth when it reaches them: but soon shall they learn the reality of what they used to mock at.

6. Don't they see how many of those before them We destroyed?- generations We had established on the earth, in strength such as We have not given to you - for whom We poured out rain from the skies in abundance, and gave (fertile) streams flowing beneath their (feet): yet for their sins We destroyed them, and raised in their wake fresh generations (to succeed them).

7. If We had sent to you a written (message) on parchment, so that they could touch it with their hands, the Unbelievers would have been sure to say: "This is nothing but obvious magic!"

8. They say: "Why is not an angel sent down to him?" If we sent down an angel, the matter would be settled at once, and no respite would be granted them.

---

arḍa wa ja'alaẓ-ẓulumaati wannoor; summal-lazeena kafaroo bi-Rabbihim ya'iloon.

2. Huwal-lazee khalaqakum min ṭeenin summa qaḍaaa ajalañw wa ajalum musamman 'indahoo summa antum tamtaroon.

3. Wa Huwal-laahu fissamaa- waati wa fil-arḍi ya'lamu sirrakum wa jahrakum wa ya'lamu maa taksiboon.

4. Wa maa taåteehim min Aaya- tim-min Aayaati Rabbihim illaa kaanoo 'anhaa mu'riḍeen.

5. Faqad kazzaboo bilḥaqqi lammaa jaaa'ahum fasawfa yaåteehim ambaaa'u maa kaanoo bihee yastahzi'oon.

6. Alam yaraw kam ahlaknaa min qablihim min qarnim- makkannaahum fil-arḍi maa lam numakkil-lakum wa arsalnas-samaaa'a 'alayhim midraarañw-wa ja'alnal-anhaara tajree min taḥtihim fa-ahlak- naahum bizunoobihim wa anshaånaa mim-ba'dihim qarnan aakhareen.

7. Wa law nazzalnaa 'alayka Kitaaban fee qirṭaasin falamasoohu bi-aydeehim laqaalal-lazeena kafaroo in haazaaa illaa siḥrum-mubeen.

8. Wa qaaloo law laaa unzila 'alayhi malakuñw wa law anzalna malakal-laquḍiyal- amru summa laa yunẓaroon.

الْأَرْضَ وَجَعَلَ الظُّلُمَٰتِ وَالنُّورَ ۖ ثُمَّ الَّذِينَ كَفَرُوا بِرَبِّهِمْ يَعْدِلُونَ ۝

هُوَ الَّذِى خَلَقَكُم مِّن طِينٍ ثُمَّ قَضَىٰ أَجَلًا ۖ وَأَجَلٌ مُّسَمًّى عِندَهُ ۖ ثُمَّ أَنتُمْ تَمْتَرُونَ ۝

وَهُوَ اللَّهُ فِى السَّمَٰوَٰتِ وَفِى الْأَرْضِ ۖ يَعْلَمُ سِرَّكُمْ وَجَهْرَكُمْ وَيَعْلَمُ مَا تَكْسِبُونَ ۝

وَمَا تَأْتِيهِم مِّنْ ءَايَةٍ مِّنْ ءَايَٰتِ رَبِّهِمْ إِلَّا كَانُوا عَنْهَا مُعْرِضِينَ ۝

فَقَدْ كَذَّبُوا بِالْحَقِّ لَمَّا جَآءَهُمْ ۖ فَسَوْفَ يَأْتِيهِمْ أَنۢبَٰٓؤُا۟ مَا كَانُوا بِهِ يَسْتَهْزِءُونَ ۝

أَلَمْ يَرَوْا كَمْ أَهْلَكْنَا مِن قَبْلِهِم مِّن قَرْنٍ مَّكَّنَّٰهُمْ فِى الْأَرْضِ مَا لَمْ نُمَكِّن لَّكُمْ وَأَرْسَلْنَا السَّمَآءَ عَلَيْهِم مِّدْرَارًا وَجَعَلْنَا الْأَنْهَٰرَ تَجْرِى مِن تَحْتِهِمْ فَأَهْلَكْنَٰهُم بِذُنُوبِهِمْ وَأَنشَأْنَا مِنۢ بَعْدِهِمْ قَرْنًا ءَاخَرِينَ ۝

وَلَوْ نَزَّلْنَا عَلَيْكَ كِتَٰبًا فِى قِرْطَاسٍ فَلَمَسُوهُ بِأَيْدِيهِمْ لَقَالَ الَّذِينَ كَفَرُوا إِنْ هَٰذَا إِلَّا سِحْرٌ مُّبِينٌ ۝

وَقَالُوا لَوْلَا أُنزِلَ عَلَيْهِ مَلَكٌ ۖ وَلَوْ أَنزَلْنَا مَلَكًا لَّقُضِىَ الْأَمْرُ ثُمَّ لَا يُنظَرُونَ ۝

9. If We had made it an angel, We should have sent him as a man, and We should certainly have caused them confusion in a matter which they have already covered with confusion.

10. Mocked were (many) Apostles before you; but their scoffers were hemmed in by the thing that they mocked.

11. Say: "Travel through the earth and see what was the end of those who rejected Truth."

12. Say: "To whom belongs all that is in the heavens and on earth?" Say: "To Allah. He has inscribed for Himself (the rule of) Mercy. That He will gather you together for the Day of Judgment, there is no doubt whatever. It is they who have lost their own souls, that will not believe.

13. To him belongs all that dwells (or lurks) in the Night and the Day. For He is the One Who hears and knows all things."

14. Say: "Shall I take for my protector any other than Allah, the Maker of the heavens and the earth? And He it is that feeds but is not fed." Say: "Nay! but I am commanded to be the first of those who bow to Allah (in Islam), and be not of the company of those who join gods with Allah."

15. Say: "I would, if I disobeyed my Lord, indeed have fear of the Chastisement of a Mighty Day.

16. "On that day, if the Chastisement is averted from any, it is due to Allah's mercy; And that would be (Salvation), the obvious fulfilment of all desire.

17. "If Allah touch you with affliction, none can remove it but He; if He touch you with happiness, He has power over all things.

9. Wa law ja'alnaahu mala-kal-laja'alnaahu rajulañw-wa lalabasnaa 'alayhim maa yalbisoon.

10. Wa laqadis-tuhzi'a bi-Rusulim-min qablika fahaaqa billazeena sakhiroo minhum maa kaanoo bihee yastahzi'oon.
(Section 1)

11. Qul seeroo fil-ardi summan-zuroo kayfa kaana 'aaqibatul-mukazzibeen.

12. Qul limam-maa fis-samaawaati wal-ardi qul lillaah; kataba 'alaa nafsihir-rahmah; la-yajma'annakum ilaa Yawmil-Qiyaamati laa rayba feeh; allazeena khasiroo anfusahum fahum laa yu'minoon.

13. Wa lahoo maa sakana fillayli wannahaar; wa Huwas-Samee'ul-'Aleem.

14. Qul aghayral-laahi atta-khizu waliyyan faatiris-samaawaati wal-ardi wa Huwa yut'imu wa laa yut'am; qul ineee umirtu an akoona awwala man aslama wa laa takoonanna minal-mushrikeen.

15. Qul ineee akhaafu in 'asaytu Rabbee 'azaaba Yawmin 'Azeem.

16. Mañy-yusraf 'anhu Yawma'izin faqad rahimah; wa zaalikal-fawzul-mubeen.

17. Wa iñy-yamsaskal-laahu bidurrin falaaa kaashifa lahooo illaa Huwa wa iñy-yamsaska bikhayrin fa-Huwa 'alaa kulli shay'in Qadeer.

18. "He is the irresistible, (watching) from above over His worshippers; and He is the Wise, acquainted with all things."

19. Say: "What thing is most weighty in evidence?" Say: "Allah is witness between me and you; This Qur'an has been revealed to me by inspiration, that I may warn you and all whom it reaches. Can you possibly bear witness that besides Allah there is another God?" Say: "Nay! I cannot bear witness!" Say: "But in truth He is the one Allah, and I truly am innocent of (your blasphemy of) joining others with Him."

20. Those to whom We have given the Book know this as they know their own sons. Those who have lost their own souls refuse therefore to believe.

21. Who does more wrong than he who invents a lie against Allah or rejects His signs? But verily the wrong-doers never shall prosper.

22. One day We shall gather them all together: We shall say to those who ascribed partners (to Us): "Where are the partners whom you (invented and) talked about?"

23. There will then be (left) no subterfuge for them but to say: "By Allah, our Lord, we were not those who joined gods with Allah."

24. Behold! how they lie against their own souls! But the (lie) which they invented will leave them in the lurch.

25. Of them there are some who (pretend to) listen to you; but We have thrown veils on their hearts, So they do not understand it, and deafness in their ears; if they saw every one of the signs, they will not believe in them; in so much that when they come to you,

18. Wa Huwal-qaahiru fawqa 'ibaadih; wa Huwal-Ḥakeemul-Khabeer.

19. Qul ayyu shay'in akbaru shahaadatan qulil-laahu shaheedum baynee wa baynakum; wa ooḥiya ilayya haaẓal-Qur'aanu li-unẓirakum bihee wa mam-balagh; a'innakum latashhadoona anna ma'al-laahi aalihatan ukhraa; qul laaa ashhad; qul innamaa Huwa Ilaahuñw-Waaḥiduñw-wa innanee bareee'um-mimmaa tushrikoon.

20. Allaẓeena aataynaa-humul-Kitaaba ya'rifoonahoo kamaa ya'rifoona abnaaa'ahum; allaẓeena khasirooo anfusahum fahum laa yu'minoon. **(Section 2)**

21. Wa man aẓlamu mim-manif-taraa 'alal-laahi kaẓiban aw kazzaba bi-Aayaatih; innahoo laa yufliḥuẓ-ẓaalimoon.

22. Wa Yawma naḥshuruhum jamee'an ṣumma naqoolu lillaẓeena ashrakooo ayna shurakaaa'ukumul-laẓeena kuntum taz'umoon.

23. Ṣumma lam takun fitnatuhum illaaa an qaaloo wallaahi Rabbinaa maa kunnaa mushrikeen.

24. Unẓur kayfa kaẓaboo 'alaaa anfusihim, wa ḍalla 'anhum maa kaanoo yaftaroon.

25. Wa minhum mañy-yastami'u ilayka wa ja'alnaa 'alaa quloobihim akinnatan añy-yafqahoohu wa feee aazaani-him waqraa; wa iñy-yaraw kulla Aayatil-laa yu'minoo bihaa; ḥattaaa iẓaa jaaa'ooka

وَهُوَ الْقَاهِرُ فَوْقَ عِبَادِهِ ۖ وَهُوَ الْحَكِيمُ الْخَبِيرُ ۝

قُلْ أَيُّ شَيْءٍ أَكْبَرُ شَهَادَةً ۖ قُلِ اللَّهُ ۖ شَهِيدٌ بَيْنِي وَبَيْنَكُمْ ۚ وَأُوحِيَ إِلَيَّ هَٰذَا الْقُرْآنُ لِأُنذِرَكُم بِهِ وَمَن بَلَغَ ۚ أَئِنَّكُمْ لَتَشْهَدُونَ أَنَّ مَعَ اللَّهِ آلِهَةً أُخْرَىٰ ۚ قُل لَّا أَشْهَدُ ۚ قُلْ إِنَّمَا هُوَ إِلَٰهٌ وَاحِدٌ وَإِنَّنِي بَرِيءٌ مِّمَّا تُشْرِكُونَ ۝

الَّذِينَ آتَيْنَاهُمُ الْكِتَابَ يَعْرِفُونَهُ كَمَا يَعْرِفُونَ أَبْنَاءَهُمُ ۘ الَّذِينَ خَسِرُوا أَنفُسَهُمْ فَهُمْ لَا يُؤْمِنُونَ ۝

وَمَنْ أَظْلَمُ مِمَّنِ افْتَرَىٰ عَلَى اللَّهِ كَذِبًا أَوْ كَذَّبَ بِآيَاتِهِ ۗ إِنَّهُ لَا يُفْلِحُ الظَّالِمُونَ ۝

وَيَوْمَ نَحْشُرُهُمْ جَمِيعًا ثُمَّ نَقُولُ لِلَّذِينَ أَشْرَكُوا أَيْنَ شُرَكَاؤُكُمُ الَّذِينَ كُنتُمْ تَزْعُمُونَ ۝

ثُمَّ لَمْ تَكُن فِتْنَتُهُمْ إِلَّا أَن قَالُوا وَاللَّهِ رَبِّنَا مَا كُنَّا مُشْرِكِينَ ۝

انظُرْ كَيْفَ كَذَبُوا عَلَىٰ أَنفُسِهِمْ ۚ وَضَلَّ عَنْهُم مَّا كَانُوا يَفْتَرُونَ ۝

وَمِنْهُم مَّن يَسْتَمِعُ إِلَيْكَ ۖ وَجَعَلْنَا عَلَىٰ قُلُوبِهِمْ أَكِنَّةً أَن يَفْقَهُوهُ وَفِي آذَانِهِمْ وَقْرًا ۚ وَإِن يَرَوْا كُلَّ آيَةٍ لَّا يُؤْمِنُوا بِهَا ۚ حَتَّىٰ إِذَا جَاءُوكَ

they (but) dispute with you; the Unbelievers say: "These are nothing but tales of the ancients."

26. Others they keep away from it, and themselves they keep away; but they only destroy their own souls, and they do not perceive it.

27. If you could but see when they are confronted with the Fire! They will say: "Would that we were but sent back! Then would we not reject the signs of our Lord, but would be amongst those who believe!"

28. Yes, in their own (eyes) will become manifest what before they concealed. But if they were returned, they would certainly relapse to the things they were forbidden, for they are indeed liars.

29. And they (sometimes) say: "There is nothing except our life on this earth, and never shall we be raised up again."

30. If you could but see when they are confronted with their Lord! He will say: "Is not this the truth?" They will say: "Yes, by our Lord!" He will say: "You then test the Chastisement, because you rejected Faith."

31. Lost indeed are they who treat it as a falsehood that they must meet Allah,- until on a sudden the hour is on them, and they say: "Ah! woe unto us that we took no thought of it"; for they bear their burdens on their backs, and evil indeed are the burdens that they bear?

32. What is the life of this world but play and amusement? But best is the Home in the Hereafter, for those who are righteous. Will you not then understand?

33. We know indeed the grief which

yujaadiloonaka yaqoolul-lazeena kafarooo in haazaaa illaaa asaateerul-awwaleen.

26. Wa hum yanhawna 'anhu wa yan'awna 'anhu wa iñy-yuhlikoona illaaa anfusahum wa maa yash'uroon.

27. Wa law taraaa iz wuqifoo 'alan-Naari faqaaloo yaa laytanaa nuraddu wa laa nukaz-ziba bi-Aayaati Rabbinaa wa nakoona minal-mu'mineen.

28. Bal badaa lahum maa kaanoo yukhfoona min qablu wa law ruddoo la'aadoo limaa nuhoo 'anhu wa innahum lakaaziboon.

29. Wa qaalooo in hiya illaa hayaatunad-dunyaa wa maa nahnu bimab'ooseen.

30. Wa law taraaa iz wuqifoo 'alaa Rabbihim; qaala alaysa haazaa bilhaqq; qaaloo balaa wa Rabbinaa; qaala fazooqul-'azaaba bimaa kuntum takfuroon.   (Section 3)

31. Qad khasiral-lazeena kaz-zaboo biliqaaa'il-laahi hattaaa izaa jaaa'at-humus-Saa'atu baghtatan qaaloo yaa hasra-tanaa 'alaa maa farratnaa feehaa wa hum yahmiloona awzaarahum 'alaa zuhoorihim; alaa saaa'a maa yaziroon.

32. Wa mal-hayaatud-dun-yaaa illaa la'ibuñw-wa lahwuñw wa lad-Daarul-Aakhiratu kahyrul-lillazeena yattaqoon; afalaa ta'qiloon.

33. Qad na'lamu innahoo layahzunukal-lazee

their words do cause you: It is not you they reject: it is the Signs of Allah, which the wicked disdain.

34. Rejected were the Apostles before you: with patience and constancy they bore their rejection and their wrongs, until Our aid reached them: there is none that can alter the words (and decrees) of Allah. Already you have received some account of those apostles.

35. If their spurning is hard on your mind, yet if you were able to seek a tunnel in the ground or a ladder in the skies and bring them a Sign,- (what good?). If it were Allah's will, He could gather them together unto true guidance: so you be not amongst those who are swayed by ignorance (and impatience)!

36. Those who listen (in truth), be sure, will accept: as to the dead, Allah will raise them up; then will they be turned unto Him.

37. They say: "Why is not a Sign sent down to him from his Lord?" Say: "Allah has certainly power to send down a Sign: but most of them do not understand.

38. There is not an animal (that lives) on the earth, nor a being that flies on its wings, but (forms part of) communities like you. Nothing have we omitted from the Book, and they (all) shall be gathered to their Lord in the end.

39. Those who reject Our Signs are deaf and dumb,- in the midst of darkness profound: whom Allah wills, He leaves to wander: whom He wills, He places on the Way that is Straight.

40. Say: "You think to your-selves, if there come upon you the wrath of Allah, or the Hour (that you dread), would you then call upon other than Allah?-

yaqooloona fa-innahum laa yukazziboonaka wa laakinnaz-zaalimeena bi-Aayaatil-laahi yajhadoon.

34. Wa laqad kuzzibat Rusu-lum-min qablika faṣabaroo 'alaa maa kuzziboo wa oozoo ḥattaaa ataahum naṣrunaa; wa laa mubaddila li-Kalimaatil-laah; wa laqad jaaa'aka min naba'il-mursaleen.

35. Wa in kaana kabura 'alay-ka i'raaḍuhum fa-inistaṭa'ta an tabtaghiya nafaqan fil-arḍi aw sullaman fis-samaaa'i fataå-tiyahum bi-Aayah; wa law shaaa'al-laahu lajama'ahum 'alal-hudaa; falaa takoonanna minal-jaahileen.

36. Innamaa yastajeebul-lazeena yasma'oon; walmawtaa yab'asuhumul-laahu summa ilayhi yurja'oon.

37. Wa qaaloo law laa nuzzila 'alayhi Aayatum-mir-Rabbih; qul innal-laaha qaadirun 'alaaa añy-yunazzila 'Aayataňw-wa laakinna aksarahum laa ya'lamoon.

38. Wa maa min daaabbatin fil-arḍi wa laa ṭaaa'iriñy-yaṭeeru bijanaaḥayhi illaaa umamun amsaalukum; maa farraṭnaa fil-Kitaabi min shay'in summa ilaa Rabbihim yuḥsharoon.

39. Wallazeena kazzaboo bi-Aayaatinaa summuñw-wa buk-mun fiẓ-ẓulumaat; mañy-yasha-il-laahu yuḍlilh; wa mañy-yashaå yaj'alhu 'alaa Ṣiraaṭim-Mustaqeem.

40. Qul ara'aytakum in ataakum 'azaabul-laahi aw atatkumus-Saa'atu a-ghayral-laahi tad'oona

(reply) if you are truthful!

41. "Nay,- On Him would you call, and if it be His will, He would remove (the distress) which occasioned your call upon Him, and you would forget (the false gods) which you join with Him!"

42. Before you We sent (Apostles) to many nations, and We afflicted the nations with suffering and adversity, that they might learn humility.

43. When the suffering reached them from Us, why then did they not learn humility? On the contrary their hearts became hardened, and Satan made their (sinful) acts seem alluring to them.

44. But when they forgot the warning they had received, We opened to them the gates of all (good) things, until, in the midst of their enjoyment of Our gifts, on a sudden, We called them to account, when lo! they were plunged in despair!

45. Of the wrong-doers the last remnant was cut off. Praise be to Allah, the Cherisher of the worlds.

46. Say: "Do you think, if Allah took away your hearing and your sight, and sealed up your hearts, who - a god other than Allah - could restore them to you?" See how We explain the Signs by various (symbols); yet they turn aside.

47. Say: "Do you think, if the punishment of Allah comes to you, whether suddenly or openly, will any be destroyed except those who do wrong?

48. We send the Apostles only to give good news and to warn: so those who believe and mend (their lives),- upon them shall be no fear, nor shall they grieve.

---

in kuntum ṣaadiqeen.

41. Bal iyyaahu tad'oona fa-yakshifu maa tad'oona ilayhi in shaaa'a wa tansawna maa tushrikoon. **(Section 4)**

42. Wa laqad arsalnaaa ilaa umamim min qablika fa-akhaznaahum bilbaåsaaa'i waḍḍarraaa'i la'allahum yataḍarra'oon.

43. Falaw laaa iz jaaa'ahum baåsunaa taḍarra'oo wa laakin qasat quloobuhum wa zayyana lahumush-Shayṭaanu maa kaanoo ya'maloon.

44. Falammaa nasoo maa zukkiroo bihee fataḥnaa 'alayhim abwaaba kulli shay'in ḥattaaa izaa fariḥoo bimaaa ootooo akhaznaahum baghtatan fa-izaa hum mublisoon.

45. Faquṭi'a daabirul-qawmil-lazeena ẓalamoo; walḥamdu lillaahi Rabbil-'aalameen.

46. Qul ara'aytum in akhazal-laahu sam'akum wa abṣaara-kum wa khatama 'alaa quloobikum man ilaahun ghay-rul-laahi yaåteekum bih; unẓur kayfa nuṣarriful-Aayaati summa hum yaṣdifoon.

47. Qul ara'aytakum in ataakum 'azaabul-laahi baghtatan aw jahratan hal yuhlaku illal-qawmuẓ-ẓaalimoon.

48. Wa maa nursilul-mursaleena illaa mubashshireena wa munzireena faman aamana wa aṣlaḥa falaa khawfun 'alayhim wa laa hum yaḥzanoon.

49. But those who reject our Signs,- punishment shall touch them, for that they ceased not from transgressing.

50. Say: "I tell you not that with me are the treasures of Allah, nor do I know what is hidden, nor do I tell you I am an angel. I but follow what is revealed to me." Say: "can the blind be held equal to the seeing?" Will you then not consider?

51. Give this warning to those in whose (hearts) is the fear that they will be brought (to judgment) before their Lord: except for Him they will have no protector nor intercessor: that they may guard (against evil).

52. Do not send away those who call on their Lord morning and evening, seeking His Face. In nothing are you accountable for them, and in nothing are they accountable for you, that you should turn them away, and thus be (one) of the unjust.

53. Thus did We try some of them by comparison with others that they should say: "Is it these then that Allah has favoured from amongst us?" Does not Allah know best those who are grateful?

54. When those come to you who believe in Our Signs, Say: "Peace be on you: Your Lord has inscribed for Himself (the rule of) mercy: verily, if any of you did evil in ignorance, and thereafter repented, and amended (his conduct), lo! He is Oft-forgiving, Most Merciful.

55. Thus do We explain the Signs in detail: so that

49. Wallazeena kazzaboo bi-Aayaatinaa yamassuhumul-'azaabu bimaa kaanoo yafsuqoon.

50. Qul laaa aqoolu lakum 'indee khazaaa'inul-laahi wa laaa a'lamul-ghayba wa laaa aqoolu lakum innee malakun in attabi'u illaa maa yoohaaa ilayy; qul hal yastawil-a'maa walbaseer; afalaa tatafak-karoon. (Section 5)

51. Wa anzir bihil-lazeena yakhaafoona añy-yuhsharooo ilaa Rabbihim laysa lahum min doonihee waliyyuñw-wa laa shafee'ul-la'allahum yatta-qoon.

52. Wa laa tatrudil-lazeena yad'oona Rabbahum bilgha-daati wal'ashiyyi yureedoona Wajhahoo maa 'alayka min hisaabihim min shay'iñw-wa maa min hisaabika 'alayhim min shay'in fatatrudahum fata-koona minaz-zaalimeen.

53. Wa kazaalika fatannaa ba'dahum biba'dil-liyaqoolooo ahaaa'ulaaa'i mannal-laahu 'alayhim mim bayninaa; alaysal-laahu bi-a'lama bish-shaakireen.

54. Wa izaa jaaa'akal-lazeena yu'minoona bi-Aayaatinaa faqul salaamun 'alaykum kataba Rabbukum 'alaa nafsihir-rahmata annahoo man 'amila minkum sooo'am bijahaalatin summa taaba mim ba'dihee wa aslaha fa-annahoo Ghafoorur-Raheem.

55. Wa kazaalika nufassilul-Aayaati wa litastabeena

وَالَّذِيْنَ كَذَّبُوْا بِاٰيٰتِنَا يَمَسُّهُمُ الْعَذَابُ بِمَا كَانُوْا يَفْسُقُوْنَ ۝

قُلْ لَّآ اَقُوْلُ لَكُمْ عِنْدِيْ خَزَآئِنُ اللّٰهِ وَلَآ اَعْلَمُ الْغَيْبَ وَلَآ اَقُوْلُ لَكُمْ اِنِّيْ مَلَكٌ ۚ اِنْ اَتَّبِعُ اِلَّا مَا يُوْحٰۤى اِلَيَّ ۚ قُلْ هَلْ يَسْتَوِى الْاَعْمٰى وَالْبَصِيْرُ ؕ اَفَلَا تَتَفَكَّرُوْنَ ۝

وَاَنْذِرْ بِهِ الَّذِيْنَ يَخَافُوْنَ اَنْ يُّحْشَرُوْۤا اِلٰى رَبِّهِمْ لَيْسَ لَهُمْ مِّنْ دُوْنِهٖ وَلِيٌّ وَّلَا شَفِيْعٌ لَّعَلَّهُمْ يَتَّقُوْنَ ۝

وَلَا تَطْرُدِ الَّذِيْنَ يَدْعُوْنَ رَبَّهُمْ بِالْغَدٰوةِ وَالْعَشِيِّ يُرِيْدُوْنَ وَجْهَهٗ ؕ مَا عَلَيْكَ مِنْ حِسَابِهِمْ مِّنْ شَيْءٍ وَّمَا مِنْ حِسَابِكَ عَلَيْهِمْ مِّنْ شَيْءٍ فَتَطْرُدَهُمْ فَتَكُوْنَ مِنَ الظّٰلِمِيْنَ ۝

وَكَذٰلِكَ فَتَنَّا بَعْضَهُمْ بِبَعْضٍ لِّيَقُوْلُوْۤا اَهٰٓؤُلَآءِ مَنَّ اللّٰهُ عَلَيْهِمْ مِّنْ بَيْنِنَا ؕ اَلَيْسَ اللّٰهُ بِاَعْلَمَ بِالشّٰكِرِيْنَ ۝

وَاِذَا جَآءَكَ الَّذِيْنَ يُؤْمِنُوْنَ بِاٰيٰتِنَا فَقُلْ سَلٰمٌ عَلَيْكُمْ كَتَبَ رَبُّكُمْ عَلٰى نَفْسِهِ الرَّحْمَةَ ۙ اَنَّهٗ مَنْ عَمِلَ مِنْكُمْ سُوْٓءًا بِجَهَالَةٍ ثُمَّ تَابَ مِنْ بَعْدِهٖ وَاَصْلَحَ فَاَنَّهٗ غَفُوْرٌ رَّحِيْمٌ ۝

وَكَذٰلِكَ نُفَصِّلُ الْاٰيٰتِ وَلِتَسْتَبِيْنَ

the way of the sinners may be shown up.

56. Say: "I am forbidden to worship those - other than Allah- whom you call upon." Say: "I will not follow your vain desires: If I did, I would stray from the path, and be not of the company of those who receive guidance."

57. Say: "For me, I (work) on a clear Sign from my Lord, but you reject Him. What you wish to see hastened, is not in my power. The Command rests with none but Allah: He declares the Truth, and He is the best of judges."

58. Say: "If what you would see hastened were in my power, the matter would be settled at once between you and me. But Allah knows best those who do wrong."

59. With Him are the keys of the Unseen, the treasures that none knows but He. He knows whatever there is on the earth and in the sea. Not a leaf falls but with His knowledge: there is not a grain in the darkness (or depths) of the earth, nor anything fresh or dry (green or withered), but is (inscribed) in a Record clear (to those who can read).

60. It is He who takes your souls by night, and has knowledge of all that you have done by day: by day He raises you up again; that a term appointed be fulfilled; In the end unto Him will be your return; then will He show you the truth of all that you did.

61. He is the irresistible, (watching) from above over His worshippers, and He sets guardians over you. At length, when death approaches one of you, Our angels take his soul,

sabeelul-mujrimeen. **(Section 6)**

56. Qul innee nuheetu an a'budal-lazeena tad'oona min doonil-laah; qul laaa attabi'u ahwaaa'akum qad dalaltu izanw-wa maaa ana minal-muhtadeen.

57. Qul innee 'alaa bayyi-natim-mir-Rabbee wa kaz-zabtum bih; maa 'indee maa tasta'iloona bih; inil-hukmu illaa lillaahi yaqussul-haqqa wa Huwa khayrul-faasileen.

58. Qul law anna 'indee maa tasta'iloona bihee laqudiyal-amru baynee wa baynakum; wallaahu a'lamu bizzaalimeen.

59. Wa 'indahoo mafaatihul-ghaybi laa ya'lamuhaaa illaa Hoo; wa ya'lamu maa fil-barri walbahr; wa maa tasqutu minw-waraqatin illaa ya'lamuhaa wa laa habbatin fee zulumaatil-ardi wa laa ratbinw-wa laa yaabisin illaa fee Kitaabim-Mubeen.

60. Wa Huwal-lazee yatawaf-faakum billayli wa ya'lamu maa jarahtum binnahaari summa yab'asukum feehi liyuqdaaa ajalum-musamman summa ilayhi marji'ukum summa yunabbi'ukum bimaa kuntum ta'maloon. **(Section 7)**

61. Wa Huwal-qaahiru fawqa 'ibaadihee wa yursilu 'alaykum hafazatan hattaaa izaa jaaa'a ahadakumul-mawtu tawaffat-hu rusulunaa

and they never fail in their duty.

62. Then men are returned unto Allah, their protector, the (only) reality: Is not His the command? and He is the swiftest in taking account.

63. Say: "Who is it that deliveres you from the dark recesses of land and sea, when you call upon Him in humility and silent terror: 'If He only delivers us from these (dangers), (we vow) we shall truly show our gratitude'.?"

64. Say "It is Allah that delivers you from these and all (other) distresses: and yet you worship false gods!"

65. Say: "He has power to send calamities on you, from above and below, or to cover you with confusion in party strife, giving you a taste of mutual vengeance-each from the other." See how We explain the Signs by various (symbols); that they may understand.

66. But your people reject this, though it is the truth. Say: "Not mine is the responsibility for arranging your affairs;

67. For every Message is a limit of time, and soon shall you know it."

68. When you see men engaged in vain discourse about Our Signs, turn away from them unless they turn to a different theme. If Satan ever makes you forget, then after recollection, do not sit in the company of those who do wrong.

69. On their account no responsibility falls on the righteous, but (their duty) is to remind them, that they may (learn to) fear Allah.

70. Leave alone those who take their religion to be mere play

wa hum laa yufarriṭoon.

62. Ṣumma ruddooo ilallaahi mawlaahumul-ḥaqq; alaa lahul-ḥukmu wa Huwa asra'ul-ḥaasibeen.

63. Qul mañy-yunajjeekum min ẓulumaatil-barri walbaḥri tad'oonahoo taḍarru'añw-wa khufyatan la'in anjaanaa min haaẕihee lanakoonanna minash-shaakireen.

64. Qulil-laahu yunajjeekum minhaa wa min kulli karbin ṣumma antum tushrikoon.

65. Qul Huwal-Qaadiru 'alaaa añy-yab'aṣa 'alaykum 'aẕaa-bam-min fawqikum aw min taḥti arjulikum aw yalbisakum shiya'añw-wa yuẕeeqa ba'ḍa-kum baåsa ba'ḍ; unẓur kayfa nuṣarriful-Aayaati la'allahum yafqahoon.

66. Wa kaẕ-ẕaba bihee qawmuka wa huwal-ḥaqq; qul lastu 'alaykum biwakeel.

67. Likulli naba-im-mustaqar-ruñw-wa sawfa ta'lamoon.

68. Wa iẕaa ra-aytal-laẕeena yakhooḍoona feee Aayaatinaa fa-a'riḍ 'anhum ḥattaa yakhoo-ḍoo fee ḥadeeṣin ghayrih; wa immaa yunsiyannakash-Shayṭaanu falaa taq'ud ba'daẕ-ẕikraa ma'al-qawmiẕ-ẓaali-meen.

69. Wa maa 'alal-laẕeena yattaqoona min ḥisaabihim min shay'iñw-wa laakin ẕikraa la'allahum yattaqoon.

70. Wa ẕaril-laẕeenat-takhaẕoo deenahum la'ibañw-

وَهُمْ لَا يُفَرِّطُونَ ۞

ثُمَّ رُدُّوٓا۟ إِلَى ٱللَّهِ مَوْلَىٰهُمُ ٱلْحَقِّ ۚ أَلَا لَهُ ٱلْحُكْمُ وَهُوَ أَسْرَعُ ٱلْحَٰسِبِينَ ۞

قُلْ مَن يُنَجِّيكُم مِّن ظُلُمَٰتِ ٱلْبَرِّ وَٱلْبَحْرِ تَدْعُونَهُۥ تَضَرُّعًا وَخُفْيَةً لَّئِنْ أَنجَىٰنَا مِنْ هَٰذِهِۦ لَنَكُونَنَّ مِنَ ٱلشَّٰكِرِينَ ۞

قُلِ ٱللَّهُ يُنَجِّيكُم مِّنْهَا وَمِن كُلِّ كَرْبٍ ثُمَّ أَنتُمْ تُشْرِكُونَ ۞

قُلْ هُوَ ٱلْقَادِرُ عَلَىٰٓ أَن يَبْعَثَ عَلَيْكُمْ عَذَابًا مِّن فَوْقِكُمْ أَوْ مِن تَحْتِ أَرْجُلِكُمْ أَوْ يَلْبِسَكُمْ شِيَعًا وَيُذِيقَ بَعْضَكُم بَأْسَ بَعْضٍ ۗ ٱنظُرْ كَيْفَ نُصَرِّفُ ٱلْءَايَٰتِ لَعَلَّهُمْ يَفْقَهُونَ ۞

وَكَذَّبَ بِهِۦ قَوْمُكَ وَهُوَ ٱلْحَقُّ ۚ قُل لَّسْتُ عَلَيْكُم بِوَكِيلٍ ۞

لِّكُلِّ نَبَإٍ مُّسْتَقَرٌّ ۚ وَسَوْفَ تَعْلَمُونَ ۞

وَإِذَا رَأَيْتَ ٱلَّذِينَ يَخُوضُونَ فِىٓ ءَايَٰتِنَا فَأَعْرِضْ عَنْهُمْ حَتَّىٰ يَخُوضُوا۟ فِى حَدِيثٍ غَيْرِهِۦ ۚ وَإِمَّا يُنسِيَنَّكَ ٱلشَّيْطَٰنُ فَلَا تَقْعُدْ بَعْدَ ٱلذِّكْرَىٰ مَعَ ٱلْقَوْمِ ٱلظَّٰلِمِينَ ۞

وَمَا عَلَى ٱلَّذِينَ يَتَّقُونَ مِنْ حِسَابِهِم مِّن شَىْءٍ وَلَٰكِن ذِكْرَىٰ لَعَلَّهُمْ يَتَّقُونَ ۞

وَذَرِ ٱلَّذِينَ ٱتَّخَذُوا۟ دِينَهُمْ لَعِبًا

and amusement, and are deceived by the life of this world. But proclaim (to them) this (truth): that every soul delivers itself to ruin by its own acts: it will find for itself no protector or intercessor except Allah: if it offered every ransom, (or reparation), none will be accepted: such is (the end of) those who deliver themselves to ruin by their own acts: they will have for drink (only) boiling water, and for punishment, one most grievous: for they persisted in rejecting Allah.

71. Say: "Shall we indeed call on others besides Allah,- things that can do us neither good nor harm,- and turn on our heels after receiving guidance from Allah? - like one whom the evil ones have made into a fool, wandering bewildered through the earth, his friends calling, 'Come to us', (vainly) guiding him to the path." Say: "Allah's guidance is the (only) guidance, and we have been directed to submit ourselves to the Lord of the worlds;-

72. "To establish regular prayers and to fear Allah for it is to Him that we shall be gathered together."

73. It is He who created the heavens and the earth in true (proportions): the day He says, "Be," Behold! it is. His word is the Truth. His will be the dominion the day the trumpet will be blown. He knows the Unseen as well as that which is open. For He is the Wise, well acquainted (with all things).

74. Lo! Abraham said to his father Azar: "Do you take idols for gods? For I see you and your people in manifest error."

75. So also did We show Abraham the power and the laws of

wa lahwañw-wa gharrat-humul-ḥa-yaatud-dunyaa; wa zakkir biheee an tubsala nafsum bimaa kasabat laysa lahaa min doonil-laahi waliyyuñw-wa laa shafee'uñw wa in ta'dil kulla 'adlil-laa yu'khaz minhaa; ulaaa'ikal-lazeena ubsiloo bimaa kasaboo lahum sharaa-bum-min ḥameemiñw-wa 'azaabun aleemum bimaa kaanoo yakfuroon. **(Section 8)**

71. Qul anad'oo min doonil-laahi maa laa yanfa'unaa wa laa yaḍurrunaa wa nuraddu 'alaaa a'qaabinaa ba'da iz hadaanal-laahu kallazis-tahwat-hush-Shayaaṭeenu fil-arḍi ḥayraana lahoo aṣḥaabuñy-yad'oo-nahooo ilal-huda'-tinaa; qul inna hudal-laahi huwal-hudaa wa umirnaa linuslima li-Rabbil-'aalameen.

72. Wa an aqeemuṣ-Ṣalaata wattaqooh; wa Huwal-lazeee ilayhi tuḥsharoon.

73. Wa Huwal-lazee khala-qas-samaawaati wal-arḍa bilḥaqq; wa Yawma yaqoolu kun fa-yakoon; Qawluhul-haqq; wa lahul-mulku Yawma yunfakhu fiṣ-Ṣoor; 'Aalimul-Ghaybi wash-shahaadah; wa Huwal-Ḥakeemul-Khabeer.

74. Wa iz qaala Ibraaheemu li-abeehi Aazara a-tattakhizu aṣnaaman aalihatan inneee araaka wa qawmaka fee ḍalaalim-mubeen.

75. Wa kazaalika nureee Ibraaheema malakootas-

the heavens and the earth, that he might (with understanding) have certitude.

76. When the night covered him over, He saw a star: He said: "This is my Lord." But when it set, He said: "I love not those that set."

77. When he saw the moon rising in splendour, he said: "This is my Lord." But when the moon set, He said: "unless my Lord guide me, I shall surely be among those who go astray."

78. When he saw the sun rising in splendour, he said: "This is my Lord; this is the greatest (of all)." But when the sun set, he said: "O my people! I am indeed free from your (guilt) of giving partners to Allah."

79. "For me, I have set my face, firmly and truly, towards Him Who created the heavens and the earth, and never shall I give partners to Allah."

80. His people disputed with him. He said: "Do you (come) to dispute with me, about Allah, when He (Himself) has guided me? I fear not (the beings) you associate with Allah: Unless my Lord wills, (nothing can happen). My Lord comprehends in His knowledge all things. Will you not (yourselves) be admonished?

81. "How should I fear (the beings) you associate with Allah, when you fear not to give partners to Allah without any warrant having been given to you? Which of (us) two parties has more right to security? (Tell me) if you know.

82. "It is those who believe and confuse not their beliefs with wrong - that are (truly) in security, for they are

samaawaati wal-ardi wa liyakoona minal-mooqineen.

76. Falammaa janna 'alayhil-laylu ra-aa kawkaban qaala haazaa Rabbee falammaaa afala qaala laaa uhibbul-aafileen.

77. Falammaa ra-al-qamara baazighan qaala haazaa Rabbee falammaaa afala qaala la'il-lam yahdinee Rabbee la-akoonanna minal-qawmid-daalleen.

78. Falammaa ra-ash-shamsa baazighatan qaala haazaa Rabbee haazaaa akbaru falammaaa afalat qaala yaa qawmi innee baree'um-mimmaa tushrikoon.

79. Innee wajjahtu wajhiya lillazee fataras-samaawaati wal-arda Haneefanw-wa maaa ana minal-mushrikeen.

80. Wa haaajjahoo qawmuh; qaala a-tuh aaajjoonnee fillaahi wa qad hadaan; wa laaa akhaafu maa tushrikoona biheee illaaa any-yashaaa'a Rabbee shay'anw wasi'a Rabbee kulla shay'in 'ilman afalaa tatazakkaroon.

81. Wa kayfa akhaafu maaa ashraktum wa laa takhaafoona annakum ashraktum billaahi maa lam yunazzil bihee 'alaykum sultaanaa; fa-ayyul-fareeqayni ahaqqu bil-amni in kuntum ta'lamoon.

82. Allazeena aamanoo wa lam yalbisooo eemaanahum bizulmin ulaaa'ika lahumul-amnu wa hum

السَّمٰوٰتِ وَالْأَرْضِ وَلِيَكُوْنَ
مِنَ الْمُوْقِنِيْنَ ۞
فَلَمَّا جَنَّ عَلَيْهِ الَّيْلُ رَاٰ كَوْكَبًا ۚ
قَالَ هٰذَا رَبِّيْ ۚ فَلَمَّا أَفَلَ قَالَ
لَا أُحِبُّ الْاٰفِلِيْنَ ۞
فَلَمَّا رَاَ الْقَمَرَ بَازِغًا قَالَ هٰذَا رَبِّيْ ۚ
فَلَمَّا أَفَلَ قَالَ لَئِنْ لَّمْ يَهْدِنِيْ
رَبِّيْ لَأَكُوْنَنَّ مِنَ الْقَوْمِ الضَّآلِّيْنَ ۞
فَلَمَّا رَاَ الشَّمْسَ بَازِغَةً قَالَ هٰذَا
رَبِّيْ هٰذَآ أَكْبَرُ ۚ فَلَمَّا أَفَلَتْ قَالَ
يٰقَوْمِ إِنِّيْ بَرِيْٓءٌ مِّمَّا تُشْرِكُوْنَ ۞
إِنِّيْ وَجَّهْتُ وَجْهِيَ لِلَّذِيْ فَطَرَ
السَّمٰوٰتِ وَالْأَرْضَ حَنِيْفًا وَّمَآ أَنَا
مِنَ الْمُشْرِكِيْنَ ۞
وَحَآجَّهٗ قَوْمُهٗ ۚ قَالَ أَتُحَآجُّوْٓنِّيْ
فِي اللّٰهِ وَقَدْ هَدٰنِ ۚ وَلَآ أَخَافُ
مَا تُشْرِكُوْنَ بِهٖٓ إِلَّآ أَنْ يَّشَآءَ
رَبِّيْ شَيْئًا ۚ وَسِعَ رَبِّيْ كُلَّ شَيْءٍ
عِلْمًا ۚ أَفَلَا تَتَذَكَّرُوْنَ ۞
وَكَيْفَ أَخَافُ مَآ أَشْرَكْتُمْ وَلَا
تَخَافُوْنَ أَنَّكُمْ أَشْرَكْتُمْ بِاللّٰهِ
مَا لَمْ يُنَزِّلْ بِهٖ عَلَيْكُمْ سُلْطٰنًا ۚ
فَأَيُّ الْفَرِيْقَيْنِ أَحَقُّ بِالْأَمْنِ ۚ
إِنْ كُنْتُمْ تَعْلَمُوْنَ ۞
الَّذِيْنَ اٰمَنُوْا وَلَمْ يَلْبِسُوْٓا إِيْمَانَهُمْ
بِظُلْمٍ أُولٰٓئِكَ لَهُمُ الْأَمْنُ وَهُمْ

on (right) guidance."

83. That was the reasoning about Us, which We gave to Abraham (to use) against his people: We raise whom We will, degree after degree: for your Lord is full of wisdom and knowledge.

84. We gave him Isaac and Jacob: all (three) guided: and before him, We guided Noah, and among his progeny, David, Solomon, Job, Joseph, Moses, and Aaron: thus do We reward those who do good:

85. And Zakariya and John, and Jesus and Elias: all in the ranks of the righteous:

86. And Isma'il and Elisha, and Jonas, and Lot: and to all We gave favour above the nations:

87. (To them) and to their fathers, and progeny and brethren: We chose them, and we guided them to a straight way.

88. This is the guidance of Allah: He gives that guidance to whom He pleases, of His worshippers. If they were to join other Allah's with Him, all that they did would be vain for them.

89. These were the men to whom We gave the Book, and authority, and prophethood: if these (their descendants) reject them, Behold! We shall entrust their charge to a new people who reject them not.

90. Those were the (prophets) who received Allah's guidance: follow the guidance they received; Say: "No reward for this do I ask of you: This is no less than a message for the nations."

muhtadoon.   **(Section 9)**

83. Wa tilka ḥujjatunaaa aataynaahaaa Ibraaheema 'alaa qawmih; narfa'u darajaatim-man nashaaa'; inna Rabbaka Ḥakeemun 'Aleem.

84. Wa wahabnaa lahooo Isḥaaqa wa ya'qoob; kullan hadaynaa; wa Nooḥan hadaynaa min qablu wa min zurriyyatihee Daawooda wa Sulaymaana wa Ayyooba wa Yoosufa wa Moosaa wa Haaroon; wa kazaalika najzil-muḥsineen.

85. Wa Zakariyyaa wa Yaḥyaa wa 'Eesaa wa Ilyaasa kullum-minaṣ-ṣaaliḥeen.

86. Wa Ismaa'eela wal-Yasa'a wa Yoonusa wa Looṭaa; wa kullan faḍḍalnaa 'alal-'aalameen.

87. Wa min aabaaa'ihim wa zurriyyaatihim wa ikhwaanihim wajtabaynaahum wa hadaynaahum ilaa Ṣiraaṭim-Mustaqeem.

88. Zaalika hudal-laahi yahdee bihee mañy-yashaaa'u min 'ibaadih; wa law ashrakoo laḥabiṭa 'anhum maa kaanoo ya'maloon.

89. Ulaaa'ikal-lazeena aataynaahumul-Kitaaba wal-ḥukma wan-Nubuwwah; fa-iny-yakfur bihaa haaa'ulaaa'i faqad wakkalnaa bihaa qawmal-laysoo bihaa bikaafireen.

90. Ulaaa'ikal-lazeena hadal-laahu fabihudaahumuq-tadih; qul laaa as'alukum 'alayhi ajran in huwa illaa zikraa lil-'aalameen.   **(Section 10)**

91. No just estimate of Allah do they make when they say: "Nothing does Allah send down to man (by way of revelation)" Say: "Who then sent down the Book which Moses brought?- a light and guidance to man: but you make it into (separate) sheets for show, while you conceal much (of its contents): therein were you taught that which you knew not- neither you nor your fathers." Say: "Allah (sent it down)": then leave them to plunge in vain discourse and trifling.

92. And this is a Book which We have sent down, bringing blessings, and confirming (the revelations) which came before it: that you may warn the mother of cities and all around her. Those who believe in the Hereafter believe in this (Book), and they are constant in guarding their prayers.

93. Who can be more wicked than one who invents a lie against Allah, or says, "I have received inspiration," when he has received none, or (again) who says, "I can reveal the like of what Allah has revealed"? If you could but see how the wicked (do fare) in the flood of confusion at death! - the angels stretch forth their hands, (saying),"Yield up your souls: this day shall you receive your reward,- a Chastisement of shame, for that you used to tell lies against Allah, and scornfully to reject of His Signs!"

94. "And behold! you come to us bare and alone as We created you for the first time: you have left behind you all (the favours) which We bestowed on you: We see not with you your intercessors whom you thought to be partners in your affairs: so now all relations between you have been cut off, and your (pet) fancies have left you in the lurch!"

91. Wa maa qadarul-laaha ḥaqqa qadriheee iz qaaloo maaa anzalal-laahu 'alaa basharim-min shay'; qul man anzalal-Kitaabal-lazee jaaa'a bihee Moosaa nooranw-wa hudal-linnaasi taj'aloonahoo qaraa-ṭeesa tubdoonahaa wa tukh-foona kaseeranw wa 'ullimtum maa lam ta'lamoo antum wa laaa aabaaa'ukum qulil-laahu summa zarhum fee khawḍihim yal'aboon

92. Wa haazaa Kitaabun anzalnaahu Mubaarakum-muṣaddiqul-lazee bayna yaday-hi wa litunzira Ummal-Quraa wa man ḥawlahaa; wallazeena yu'minoona bil-Aakhirati yu'minoona bihee wa hum 'alaa Ṣalaatihim yuḥaafizoon.

93. Wa man aẓlamu mimmanif-taraa 'alal-laahi kaziban aw qaala ooḥiya ilayya wa lam yooḥa ilayhi shay'uñw-wa man qaala sa-unzilu misla maaa anzalal-laah; wa law taraaa iziz-ẓaalimoona fee ghamaraatil-mawti walmalaaa'ikatu baasiṭoo aydeehim akhrijooo anfusakum; al-yawma tujzawna 'azaabal-hooni bimaa kuntum taqooloona 'alal-laahi ghayral-ḥaqqi wa kuntum 'an Aayaati-hee tastakbiroon.

94. Wa laqad ji'tumoonaa furaadaa kamaa khalaqnaakum awwala marratiñw-wa taraktum maa khawwalnaakum waraaa'a ẓuhoorikum wa maa naraa ma'akum shufa'aaa'akumul-lazeena za-'amtum annahum feekum shurakaaa'; laqat-taqaṭṭa'a baynakum wa ḍalla 'ankum maa kuntum taz'umoon.

(Section 11)

وَمَا قَدَرُوا اللهَ حَقَّ قَدْرِهِ إِذْ قَالُوا مَا أَنْزَلَ اللهُ عَلَى بَشَرٍ مِنْ شَيْءٍ ۗ قُلْ مَنْ أَنْزَلَ الْكِتَابَ الَّذِي جَاءَ بِهِ مُوسَى نُورًا وَهُدًى لِلنَّاسِ ۖ تَجْعَلُونَهُ قَرَاطِيسَ تُبْدُونَهَا وَتُخْفُونَ كَثِيرًا ۖ وَعُلِّمْتُمْ مَا لَمْ تَعْلَمُوا أَنْتُمْ وَلَا آبَاؤُكُمْ ۖ قُلِ اللهُ ۖ ثُمَّ ذَرْهُمْ فِي خَوْضِهِمْ يَلْعَبُونَ ۝

وَهَذَا كِتَابٌ أَنْزَلْنَاهُ مُبَارَكٌ مُصَدِّقُ الَّذِي بَيْنَ يَدَيْهِ وَلِتُنْذِرَ أُمَّ الْقُرَى وَمَنْ حَوْلَهَا ۚ وَالَّذِينَ يُؤْمِنُونَ بِالْآخِرَةِ يُؤْمِنُونَ بِهِ ۖ وَهُمْ عَلَى صَلَاتِهِمْ يُحَافِظُونَ ۝

وَمَنْ أَظْلَمُ مِمَّنِ افْتَرَى عَلَى اللهِ كَذِبًا أَوْ قَالَ أُوحِيَ إِلَيَّ وَلَمْ يُوحَ إِلَيْهِ شَيْءٌ وَمَنْ قَالَ سَأُنْزِلُ مِثْلَ مَا أَنْزَلَ اللهُ ۗ وَلَوْ تَرَى إِذِ الظَّالِمُونَ فِي غَمَرَاتِ الْمَوْتِ وَالْمَلَائِكَةُ بَاسِطُوا أَيْدِيهِمْ أَخْرِجُوا أَنْفُسَكُمُ ۖ الْيَوْمَ تُجْزَوْنَ عَذَابَ الْهُونِ بِمَا كُنْتُمْ تَقُولُونَ عَلَى اللهِ غَيْرَ الْحَقِّ وَكُنْتُمْ عَنْ آيَاتِهِ تَسْتَكْبِرُونَ ۝

وَلَقَدْ جِئْتُمُونَا فُرَادَى كَمَا خَلَقْنَاكُمْ أَوَّلَ مَرَّةٍ وَتَرَكْتُمْ مَا خَوَّلْنَاكُمْ وَرَاءَ ظُهُورِكُمْ ۖ وَمَا نَرَى مَعَكُمْ شُفَعَاءَكُمُ الَّذِينَ زَعَمْتُمْ أَنَّهُمْ فِيكُمْ شُرَكَاءُ ۚ لَقَدْ تَقَطَّعَ بَيْنَكُمْ وَضَلَّ عَنْكُمْ مَا كُنْتُمْ تَزْعُمُونَ ۝

95. It is Allah Who causes the seed-grain and the date-stone to split and sprout. He causes the living to issue from the dead, and He is the one to cause the dead to issue from the living. That is Allah: then how are you deluded away from the truth?

96. He it is that cleaves the day-break (from the dark): He makes the night for rest and tranquillity, and the sun and moon for the reckoning (of time): Such is the judgment and ordering of (Him), the Exalted in Power, the Omniscient.

97. It is He Who makes the stars (as beacons) for you, that you may guide yourselves, with their help, through the dark spaces of land and sea: We detail Our Signs for people who know.

98. It is He Who has produced you from a single person: here is a place of sojourn and a place of departure: We detail Our Signs for people who understand.

99. It is He Who sends down rain from the skies: with it We produce vegetation of all kinds: from some We produce green (crops), out of which We produce grain, heaped up (at harvest); out of the date-palm and its sheaths (or spathes) (come) clusters of dates hanging low and near: and (then there are) gardens of grapes, and olives, and pomegranates, each similar (in kind) yet different (in variety): when they begin to bear fruit, feast your eyes with the fruit and the ripeness thereof. Behold! in these things there are signs for people who believe.

100. Yet they make the Jinns equals with Allah, though Allah did create the Jinns; and they falsely, having no knowledge, attribute to Him sons and daughters. Praise and glory be to Him! (for He is) above what they attribute to Him!

101. To Him is due the primal origin of the heavens and the earth: how can He have a son when He has no consort? He created all things, and He has full knowledge of all things.

95. Innal-laaha faaliqul-ḥabbi wannawaa yukhrijul-ḥayya minal-mayyiti wa mukhrijul-mayyiti minal-ḥayy; zaalikumul-laahu fa-annaa tu'fakoon.

96. Faaliqul-iṣbaaḥi wa ja-'alal-layla sakanaṅw-wash-shamsa walqamara ḥusbaanaa; zaalika taqdeerul-'Azeezil-'Aleem.

97. Wa Huwal-lazee ja'ala lakumun-nujooma litahtadoo bihaa fee ẓulumaatil-barri walbaḥr; qad faṣṣalnal-Aayaati liqawminỹ-ya'lamoon.

98. Wa Huwal-lazeee ansha-akum min nafsiṅw-waaḥidatin famustaqarruṅw-wa mustawda'; qad faṣṣalnal-Aayaati liqaw-miñy-yafqahoon.

99. Wa Huwal-lazeee anzala minas-samaaa'i maaa'an fa-akhrajnaa bihee nabaata kulli shay'in fa-akhrajnaa minhu khaḍiran-nukhriju minhu ḥabbam-mutaraakibaṅw wa minan-nakhli min ṭal'ihaa qinwaanun daaniyatuṅw-wa jannaatim-min a'naabiṅw-wazzaytoona warrummaana mushtabihaṅw-wa ghayra mutashaabih; unẓurooo ilaa samariheee izaaa asmara wa yan'ih; inna fee zaalikum la-Aayaatil-liqawminỹ-yu'minoon.

100. Wa ja'aloo lillaahi shura-kaaa'al-jinna wa khalaqa hum wa kharaqoo lahoo baneena wa banaatim bighayri 'ilm; Subḥaanahoo wa Ta'aalaa 'ammaa yaṣifoon. **(Section 12)**

101. Badee'us-samaawaati wal-arḍi annaa yakoonu lahoo waladuṅw-wa lam takul-lahoo ṣaaḥibatuṅw wa khalaqa kulla shay'iṅw wa Huwa bikulli shay'in 'Aleem.

102. That is Allah, your Lord! there is no Allah but He, the Creator of all things: then worship Him: and He has power to dispose of all affairs.

103. No vision can grasp Him, but His grasp is over all vision: He is above all comprehension, yet is acquainted with all things.

104. "Now have come to you, from your Lord, proofs (to open your eyes): if any will see, it will be for (the good of) his own soul; if any will be blind, it will be to his own (harm): I am not (here) to watch over your doings."

105. Thus do we explain the signs by various (symbols): that they may say, "You have taught (us) diligently," and that We may make the matter clear to those who know.

106. Follow what you are taught by inspiration from your Lord: there is no god but He: and turn aside from those who join gods with Allah.

107. If it had been Allah's plan, they would not have taken false Allah's: but We made you not one to watch over their doings, nor are you set over them to dispose of their affairs.

108. Revile not those whom they call upon besides Allah, lest they out of spite revile Allah in their ignorance. Thus have We made alluring to each people its own doings. In the end will they return to their Lord, and We shall then tell them the truth of all that they did.

109. They swear their strongest oaths by Allah, that if a (special) sign came to them, by it they would believe. Say: "Certainly (all) Signs are in the power of Allah: but what he wishes you (Muslims) realise that (even) if (special) signs came, they will not believe."?

110. We (too) shall turn to (confusion) their hearts and their eyes, even as they refused to believe in this in the first instance: We shall leave them

102. Zaalikumul-laahu Rabbukum laaa ilaaha illaa Huwa khaaliqu kulli shay'in fa'budooh; wa Huwa 'alaa kulli shay'inw-Wakeel.

103. Laa tudrikuhul-abşaaru wa Huwa yudrikul-abşaara wa Huwal-Lateeful-Khabeer.

104. Qad jaaa'akum başaaa'iru mir-Rabbikum faman abşara falinafsihee wa man 'amiya fa'alayhaa; wa maaa ana 'alaykum biḥafeez.

105. Wa kazaalika nuşarriful-Aayaati wa liyaqooloo darasta wa linubayyinahoo liqawmiñy-ya'lamoon.

106. Ittabi' maaa oohiya ilayka mir-Rabbika laaa ilaaha illaa Huwa wa a'riḍ 'anil-mush-rikeen.

107. Wa law shaaa'al-laahu maaa ashrakoo; wa maa ja'alnaaka 'alayhim ḥafeezañw wa maaa anta 'alayhim biwakeel.

108. Wa laa tasubbul-lazeena yad'oona min doonil-laahi fa-yasubbul-laaha 'adwam bighayri 'ilm; kazaalika zayyannaa likulli ummatin 'amalahum ṣumma ilaa Rabbihim marji'uhum fa-yunabbi'uhum bimaa kaanoo ya'maloon.

109. Wa aqsamoo billaahi jahda aymaanihim la'in jaaa'at-hum Aayaatul-la-yu'minunna bihaa; qul innamal-Aayaatu 'indal-laahi wa maa yush'irukum annahaaa izaa jaaa'at laa yu'minoon.

110. Wa nuqallibu af'idatahum wa abşaarahum kamaa lam yu'minoo bihee awwala marratinwa-wa nazaruhum fee

in their trespasses, to wander in distraction.

ṭughyaanihim ya'mahoon.

(Section 13)

طُغْيَانِهِمْ يَعْمَهُونَ ۝

111. Even if We sent angels to them, and the dead spoke to them, and We gathered together all things before their very eyes, they are not the ones to believe, unless it is in Allah's plan. But most of them ignore (the truth).

111. Wa law annanaa nazzalnaaa ilayhimul-malaaa'ikata wa kallamahumul-mawtaa wa ḥasharnaa 'alayhim kulla shay'in qubulam-maa kaanoo liyu'minooo illaaa añy-yashaaa'al-laahu wa laakinna akṣarahum yajhaloon.

وَلَوْ أَنَّنَا نَزَّلْنَا إِلَيْهِمُ الْمَلَٰئِكَةَ وَكَلَّمَهُمُ الْمَوْتَىٰ وَحَشَرْنَا عَلَيْهِمْ كُلَّ شَىْءٍ قُبُلًا مَّا كَانُوا لِيُؤْمِنُوٓا إِلَّا أَن يَشَاءَ اللَّهُ وَلَٰكِنَّ أَكْثَرَهُمْ يَجْهَلُونَ ۝

112. Likewise, We made for every Messenger an enemy, Satan among men and jinns, inspiring each other with flowery discourses by way of deception. If your Lord had so planned, they would not have done it: so leave them and their inventions alone.

112. Wa kazaalika ja'alnaa likulli Nabiyyin 'aduwwan Shayaaṭeenal-insi waljinni yooḥee ba'ḍuhum ilaa ba'ḍin zukhrufal-qawli ghurooraa; wa law shaaa'a Rabbuka maa fa'aloohu fazarhum wa maa yaftaroon.

وَكَذَٰلِكَ جَعَلْنَا لِكُلِّ نَبِىٍّ عَدُوًّا شَيَٰطِينَ الْإِنسِ وَالْجِنِّ يُوحِى بَعْضُهُمْ إِلَىٰ بَعْضٍ زُخْرُفَ الْقَوْلِ غُرُورًا وَلَوْ شَاءَ رَبُّكَ مَا فَعَلُوهُ فَذَرْهُمْ وَمَا يَفْتَرُونَ ۝

113. To such (deceit) let the hearts of those incline, who have no faith in the Hereafter: let them delight in it, and let them earn from it what they may.

113. Wa litaṣghaaa ilayhi af'idatul-lazeena laa yu'minoona bil-Aakhirati wa liyarḍawhu wa liyaqtarifoo maa hum muqtarifoon.

وَلِتَصْغَىٰ إِلَيْهِ أَفْـِٔدَةُ الَّذِينَ لَا يُؤْمِنُونَ بِالْءَاخِرَةِ وَلِيَرْضَوْهُ وَلِيَقْتَرِفُوا مَا هُم مُّقْتَرِفُونَ ۝

114. Say: "Shall I seek for judge other than Allah? - when He it is Who has sent unto you the Book, explained in detail." They know full well, to whom We have given the Book, that it has been sent down from your Lord in truth. Never be then of those who doubt.

114. Afaghayral-laahi abtaghee ḥakamañw-wa Huwal-lazee anzala ilaykumul-Kitaaba mufaṣṣalaa; wallazeena aataynaahumul-Kitaaba ya'lamoona annahoo munazzalum-mir-Rabbika bilḥaqqi falaa takoonanna minal-mumtareen.

أَفَغَيْرَ اللَّهِ أَبْتَغِى حَكَمًا وَهُوَ الَّذِىٓ أَنزَلَ إِلَيْكُمُ الْكِتَٰبَ مُفَصَّلًا وَالَّذِينَ ءَاتَيْنَٰهُمُ الْكِتَٰبَ يَعْلَمُونَ أَنَّهُ مُنَزَّلٌ مِّن رَّبِّكَ بِالْحَقِّ فَلَا تَكُونَنَّ مِنَ الْمُمْتَرِينَ ۝

115. The Word of your Lord finds its fulfilment in truth and in justice: None can change His Words: for He is the one who hears and knows all.

115. Wa tammat Kalimatu Rabbika ṣidqañw-wa 'adlaa; laa mubaddila li-Kalimaatih; wa Huwas-Samee'ul-'Aleem.

وَتَمَّتْ كَلِمَتُ رَبِّكَ صِدْقًا وَعَدْلًا لَّا مُبَدِّلَ لِكَلِمَٰتِهِ وَهُوَ السَّمِيعُ الْعَلِيمُ ۝

116. Were you to follow the common run of those on earth, they will lead you away from the Way of Allah. They follow nothing but conjecture: they do nothing but lie.

116. Wa in tuṭi' aksara man fil-arḍi yuḍillooka 'an sabeelil-laah; iñy-yattabi'oona illaz-zanna wa in hum illaa yakhruṣoon.

وَإِن تُطِعْ أَكْثَرَ مَن فِى الْأَرْضِ يُضِلُّوكَ عَن سَبِيلِ اللَّهِ إِن يَتَّبِعُونَ إِلَّا الظَّنَّ وَإِنْ هُمْ إِلَّا يَخْرُصُونَ ۝

117. Your Lord knows best who strays

117. Inna Rabbaka Huwa a'lamu mañy-yaḍillu

إِنَّ رَبَّكَ هُوَ أَعْلَمُ مَن يَضِلُّ

from His Way: He knows best who they are that receive His guidance.

118. So eat of (meats) on which Allah's name has been pronounced, if you have faith in His Signs.

119. Why should you not eat of (meats) on which Allah's name has been pronounced, when He has explained to you in detail what is forbidden to you - except under compulsion of necessity? But many do mislead (men) by their appetites unchecked by knowledge. Your Lord knows best those who transgress.

120. Eschew all sin, open or secret: those who earn sin will get due recompense for their "earnings."

121. Do not eat of (meats) on which Allah's name has not been pronounced: that would be impiety. But the evil ones ever inspire their friends to contend with you if you were to obey them, you would indeed be Pagans.

122. Can he who was dead, to whom We gave life, and a light whereby he can walk amongst men, be like him who is in the depths of darkness, from which he can never come out? Thus to those without Faith their own deeds seem pleasing.

123. Thus have We placed leaders in every town, its wicked men, to plot (and burrow) therein: but they only plot against their own souls, and they do not perceive it.

124. When there comes to them a Sign (from Allah), they say: "We shall not believe until we receive one (exactly) like those received by Allah's apostles."

'an sabeelihee wa Huwa a'lamu bilmuhtadeen.

118. Fakuloo mimmaa zukirasmul-laahi 'alayhi in kuntum bi-Aayaatihee mu'mineen.

119. Wa maa lakum allaa taå-kuloo mimmaa zukirasmul-laahi 'alayhi wa qad fassala lakum maa harrama 'alaykum illaa mad-turirtum ilayh; wa inna kaseeral-la-yudilloona bi-ahwaaa'ihim bighayri 'ilm; inna Rabbaka Huwa a'lamu bilmu'tadeen.

120. Wa zaroo zaahiral-ismi wa baatinah; innal-lazeena yaksiboonal-isma sa-yujzawna bimaa kaanoo yaqtarifoon.

121. Wa laa taåkuloo mimmaa lam yuzkaris-mullaahi 'alayhi wa innahoo lafisq; wa innash-Shayaateena la-yoohoona ilaaa awliyaaa'ihim liyujaadilookum wa in ata'tumoohum innakum lamushrikoon. **(Section 14)**

122. Awa man kaana maytan fa-ahyaynaahu wa ja'alnaa lahoo noorañy-yamshee bihee fin-naasi kamam-masaluhoo fiz-zulumaati laysa bikhaarijim-minhaa; kazaalika zuyyina lilkaafireena maa kaanoo ya'maloon.

123. Wa kazaalika ja'alnaa fee kulli qaryatin akaabira mujrimeehaa liyamkuroo feehaa wa maa yamkuroona illaa bi-anfusihim wa maa yash'uroon.

124. Wa izaa jaaa'athum Aayatun qaaloo lan nu'mina hattaa nu'taa misla maaa ootiya Rusulul-laah;

Allah knows best where (and how) to carry out His mission. Soon will the wicked be overtaken by humiliation before Allah, and a severe punishment, for all their plots.

125. Those whom Allah (in His Plan) wills to guide,- He opens their breast to Islam; those whom He wills to leave straying,- He makes their breast close and constricted, as if they had to climb up to the skies: thus Allah (heaps) the Chastisement on those who refuse to believe.

126. This is the Way of your Lord, leading straight: We have detailed the Signs for those who receive admonition.

127. For them will be a Home of peace in the presence of their Lord: He will be their friend, because they practised (righteousness).

128. One day He will gather them all together, (and say): "O you assembly of Jinns! much (toll) did you take of men." Their friends amongst men will say: "Our Lord! we made profit from each other: but (alas!) we reached our term - which you appointed for us." He will say: "The Fire be your dwelling-place: you will dwell therein for ever, except as Allah wills." for your Lord is full of wisdom and knowledge.

129. Thus do we make the wrong-doers turn to each other, because of what they earn.

130. "O you assembly of Jinns and men! did not the Messengers come to you from amongst you, setting forth unto you My Signs, and warning you of the meeting of this Day of yours?"

Allaahu a'lamu ḥaysu yaj'alu Risaalatah; sa-yuṣeebul-lazeena ajramoo ṣaghaarun 'indal-laahi wa 'azaabun shadeedum bimaa kaanoo yamkuroon.

125. Famañy-yuridil-laahu añy-yahdiyahoo yashraḥ ṣadrahoo lil-Islaami wa mañy-yurid añy-yuḍillahoo yaj'al ṣadrahoo ḍayyiqan ḥarajan ka-annamaa yaṣṣa-'-'adu fis-samaaa'; kazaalika yaj'alul-laahur-rijsa 'alal-lazeena laa yu'minoon.

126. Wa haazaa Ṣiraaṭu Rabbika Mustaqeemaa; qad faṣṣalnal-Aayaati liqawmiñy-yazzakkaroon.

127. Lahum daarus-salaami 'inda Rabbihim wa Huwa waliyyuhum bimaa kaanoo ya'maloon.

128. Wa Yamwa yaḥshuruhum jamee'añy yaa ma'sharal-jinni qadistaksartum minal-insi wa qaala awliyaaa'uhum minal-insi Rabbanas-tamta'a ba'ḍunaa biba'ḍiñw-wa balagh-naaa ajalanal-lazee ajjalta lanaa; qaalan-Naaru maswaa-kum khaalideena feehaaa illaa maa shaaa'allaah; inna Rabbaka Ḥakeemun 'Aleem.

129. Wa kazaalika nuwallee ba'aẓ-ẓaalimeena ba'am bimaa kaanoo yaksiboon.

(Section 15)

130. Yaa ma'sharal-jinni wal-insi alam yaātikum Rusulum-minkum yaqussoona 'alaykum Aayaatee wa yunziroonakum liqaaa'a Yawmikum

They will say: "We bear witness against ourselves." It was the life of this world that deceived them. So against themselves will they bear witness that they rejected Faith.

131. (The apostles were sent) thus, for your Lord would not destroy for their wrong-doing men's habitations whilst their occupants were unwarned.

132. To all are degrees (or ranks) according to their deeds: for your Lord is not unmindful of anything that they do.

133. Your Lord is Self-sufficient, full of Mercy: if it were His will, He could destroy you, and in your place appoint whom He will as your successors, even as He raised you up from the posterity of other people.

134. All that has been promised unto you will come to pass: nor can you frustrate it (in the least bit).

135. Say: "O my people! Do whatever you can: I will do (my part): soon will you know who it is whose end will be (best) in the Hereafter: certain it is that the wrong-doers will not prosper."

136. Out of what Allah has produced in abundance in tilth and in cattle, they assigned Him a share: they say, according to their fancies: "This is for Allah, and this" - for our "partners"! but the share of their "partners" does not reach Allah, whilst the share of Allah reaches their "partners"! evil (and unjust) is their assignment!

137. Even so, in the eyes of most of the pagans, their "partners" made alluring the slaughter of their children, in order to lead them to their own destruction, and cause confusion in their religion. If Allah had willed,

haazaa; qaaloo shahidnaa 'alaaa anfusinaa wa gharrat-humul-hayaatud-dunyaa wa shahidoo 'alaaa anfusihim annahum kaanoo kaafireen.

131. Zaalika al-lam yakur-Rabbuka muhlikal-quraa bizulmiñw-wa ahluhaa ghaa-filoon.

132. Wa likullin darajaatum-mimmaa 'amiloo; wa maa Rabbuka bighaafilin 'ammaa ya'maloon.

133. Wa Rabbukal-ghaniyyu zur-rahmah; iñy-yashaå yuz-hibkum wa yastakhlif mim ba'dikum maa yashaaa'u kamaaa ansha-akum min zurriyyati qawmin aakhareen.

134. Inna maa too'adoona la-aatiñw-wa maaa antum bimu'jizeen.

135. Qul yaa qawmi'-maloo 'alaa makaanatikum innee 'aamilun fasawfa ta'lamoona man takoonu lahoo 'aaqibatud-daar; innahoo laa yuflihuz-zaalimoon.

136. Wa ja'aloo lillaahi mimmaa zara-a minal-harsi walan'aami naseeban faqaaloo haazaa lillaahi biza'mihim wa haazaa lishurakaaa'inaa famaa kaana lishurakaaa'ihim falaa yasilu ilal-laahi wa maa kaana lillaahi fahuwa yasilu ilaa shurakaaa'ihim; saaa'a maa yahkumoon.

137. Wa kazaalika zayyana likaseerim-minal-mushrikeena qatla awlaadihim shura-kaaa'uhum liyurdoohum wa liyalbisoo 'alayhim deenahum wa law shaaa-'al-

they would not have done so: But leave them and their inventions alone.

138. And they say that such and such cattle and crops are taboo, and none should eat of them except those whom - so they say - We wish; further, there are cattle forbidden to yoke or burden, and cattle on which, (at slaughter), the name of Allah is not pronounced; - inventions against Allah's name: soon will He requite them for their inventions.

139. They say: "What is in the wombs of such and such cattle is specially reserved (for food) for our men, and forbidden to our women; but if it is still-born, then all have shares therein. For their (false) attribution (of superstitions to Allah), He will soon punish them: for He is full of wisdom and knowledge.

140. Lost are those who slay their children, from folly, without knowledge, and forbid food which Allah has provided for them, inventing (lies) against Allah. They have indeed gone astray and heeded no guidance.

141. It is He Who produces gardens, with trellises and without, and dates, and tilth with produce of all kinds, and olives and pomegranates, similar (in kind) and different (in variety): eat of their fruit in their season, but render the dues that are proper on the day that the harvest is gathered. But waste not by excess: for Allah does not loves the wasters.

142. Of the cattle are some for burden and some for meat: eat what Allah has provided for you, and follow not the footsteps of Satan: for he is to you an avowed enemy.

143. (Take) eight (head of cattle) in (four) pairs: of sheep a pair, and of goats a pair; say, has He forbidden the two males,

laahu maa fa'aloohu fazarhum wa maa yaftaroon.

138. Wa qaaloo haaziheee an'aamuñw-wa harsun hijrun laa yat'amuhaaa illaa man nashaaa'u biza'mihim wa an'aamun hurrimat zuhooruhaa wa an'aamul-laa yazkuroonas-mal-laahi 'alayhaf-tiraaa'an 'alayh; sa-yajzeehim bimaa kaanoo yaftaroon.

139. Wa qaaloo maa fee butooni haazihil-an'aami khaalisatul-lizukoorinaa wa muharramun 'alaaa azwaajinaa wa iñy-yakum maytatan fahum feehi shurakaaa'; sa-yajzeehim wasfahum; innahoo Hakeemun 'Aleem.

140. Qad khasiral-lazeena qatalooo awlaadahum safaham bighayri 'ilmiñw-wa harramoo maa razaqahumul-laahuf-tiraaa'an 'alal-laah; qad dalloo wa maa kaanoo muhtadeen. **(Section 16)**

141. Wa Huwal-lazeee ansha-a jannaatim-ma'rooshaatiñw-wa ghayra ma'rooshaatiñw-wan-nakhla wazzar'a mukhtalifan ukuluhoo wazzaytoona warrum-maana mutashaabihañw-wa ghayra mutashaabih; kuloo min samariheee izaaa asmara wa aatoo haqqahoo yawma hasaa-dihee wa laa tusrifoo; innahoo laa yuhibbul-musrifeen.

142. Wa minal-an'aami hamoolatañw-wa farshaa; kuloo mimmaa razaqakumul-laahu wa laa tattabi'oo khutuwaatish-Shaytaan; innahoo lakum 'aduwwum-mubeen.

143. Samaaniyata azwaaj(im) minad-daanis-nayni wa minal-ma'zis-nayn; qul 'aaazzaka-rayni

اللهُ مَا فَعَلُوهُ فَذَرْهُمْ وَمَا يَفْتَرُونَ ﴿١٣٧﴾

وَقَالُوا هَٰذِهِ أَنْعَامٌ وَحَرْثٌ حِجْرٌ لَّا يَطْعَمُهَا إِلَّا مَن نَّشَاءُ بِزَعْمِهِمْ وَأَنْعَامٌ حُرِّمَتْ ظُهُورُهَا وَأَنْعَامٌ لَّا يَذْكُرُونَ اسْمَ اللهِ عَلَيْهَا افْتِرَاءً عَلَيْهِ ۚ سَيَجْزِيهِم بِمَا كَانُوا يَفْتَرُونَ ﴿١٣٨﴾

وَقَالُوا مَا فِي بُطُونِ هَٰذِهِ الْأَنْعَامِ خَالِصَةٌ لِّذُكُورِنَا وَمُحَرَّمٌ عَلَىٰ أَزْوَاجِنَا ۖ وَإِن يَكُن مَّيْتَةً فَهُمْ فِيهِ شُرَكَاءُ ۚ سَيَجْزِيهِمْ وَصْفَهُمْ ۚ إِنَّهُ حَكِيمٌ عَلِيمٌ ﴿١٣٩﴾

قَدْ خَسِرَ الَّذِينَ قَتَلُوا أَوْلَادَهُمْ سَفَهًا بِغَيْرِ عِلْمٍ وَحَرَّمُوا مَا رَزَقَهُمُ اللهُ افْتِرَاءً عَلَى اللهِ ۚ قَدْ ضَلُّوا وَمَا كَانُوا مُهْتَدِينَ ﴿١٤٠﴾

وَهُوَ الَّذِي أَنشَأَ جَنَّاتٍ مَّعْرُوشَاتٍ وَغَيْرَ مَعْرُوشَاتٍ وَالنَّخْلَ وَالزَّرْعَ مُخْتَلِفًا أُكُلُهُ وَالزَّيْتُونَ وَالرُّمَّانَ مُتَشَابِهًا وَغَيْرَ مُتَشَابِهٍ ۚ كُلُوا مِن ثَمَرِهِ إِذَا أَثْمَرَ وَآتُوا حَقَّهُ يَوْمَ حَصَادِهِ ۖ وَلَا تُسْرِفُوا ۚ إِنَّهُ لَا يُحِبُّ الْمُسْرِفِينَ ﴿١٤١﴾

وَمِنَ الْأَنْعَامِ حَمُولَةً وَفَرْشًا ۚ كُلُوا مِمَّا رَزَقَكُمُ اللهُ وَلَا تَتَّبِعُوا خُطُوَاتِ الشَّيْطَانِ ۚ إِنَّهُ لَكُمْ عَدُوٌّ مُّبِينٌ ﴿١٤٢﴾

ثَمَانِيَةَ أَزْوَاجٍ ۖ مِّنَ الضَّأْنِ اثْنَيْنِ وَمِنَ الْمَعْزِ اثْنَيْنِ ۗ قُلْ آلذَّكَرَيْنِ

or the two females, or (the young) which the wombs of the two females enclose? Tell me with knowledge if you are truthful:

144. Of camels a pair, and oxen a pair; say, has He forbidden the two males, or the two females, or (the young) which the wombs of the two females enclose? - Were you present when Allah ordered you such a thing? But who does more wrong than one who invents a lie against Allah, to lead astray men without knowledge? For Allah guides not people who do wrong.

145. Say: "I do not find in the Message received by me by inspiration any (meat) forbidden to be eaten by one who wishes to eat it, unless it be dead meat, or blood poured forth, or the flesh of swine,- for it is an abomination - or, what is impious, (meat) on which a name has been invoked, other than Allah's". But (even so), if a person is forced by necessity, without wilful disobedience, nor transgressing due limits,- your Lord is Oft-forgiving, Most Merciful.

146. For those who followed the Jewish Law, We forbade every (animal) with undivided hoof, and We forbade them that fat of the ox and the sheep, except what adheres to their backs or their entrails, or is mixed up with a bone: this in recompense for their wilful disobedience: for We are true (in Our ordinances).

147. If they accuse you of falsehood, say: "Your Lord is full of mercy all- embracing; but from people in guilt never will His wrath be turned back."

ḥarrama amil-unṣayayni ammash-tamalat 'alayhi arḥaamul-unṣayayni nabbi-'oonee bi'ilmin in kuntum ṣaadiqeen.

144. Wa minal-ibilis-nayni wa minal-baqaris-nayn; qul 'aaazzakarayni ḥarrama amil-unṣayayni ammash-tamalat 'alayhi arḥaamul-unṣayayni am kuntum shuhadaaa'a iz waṣṣaakumul-laahu bihaazaa; faman aẓlamu mimmanif-taraa 'alal-laahi kaziba-liyuḍillan-naasa bighayri 'ilm; innal-laaha laa yahdil-qawmaẓ-ẓaalimeen.
(Section 17)

145. Qul laaa ajidu fee maaa oohiya ilayya muḥarraman 'alaa ṭaa'imiñy-yaṭ'amuhooo illaaa añy-yakoona maytatan aw damam-masfoohan aw laḥma khinzeerin fa-innahoo rijsun aw fisqan uhilla lighayril-laahi bih; famaniḍ-ṭurra ghayra baaghiñw-wa laa 'aadin fa-inna Rabbaka Ghafoorur-Raḥeem.

146. Wa 'alal-lazeena haadoo ḥarramnaa kulla zee ẓufuriñw wa minal-baqari walghanami ḥarramnaa 'alayhim shu-hoomahumaaa illaa maa ḥamalat ẓuhooruhumaaa awil-ḥawaayaaa aw makhlaṭa bi'aẓm; zaalika jazaynaahum bibaghyihim wa innaa laṣaa-diqoon.

147. Fa-in kazzabooka faqur-Rabbukum zoo rahmatiñw-waasi'atiñw wa laa yuraddu baåsuhoo 'anil-qawmil-mujri-meen.

حَرَّمَ أَمِ الْأُنْثَيَيْنِ أَمَّا اشْتَمَلَتْ عَلَيْهِ أَرْحَامُ الْأُنْثَيَيْنِ ۖ نَبِّئُونِي بِعِلْمٍ إِن كُنتُمْ صَادِقِينَ ۝

وَمِنَ الْإِبِلِ اثْنَيْنِ وَمِنَ الْبَقَرِ اثْنَيْنِ ۗ قُلْ ءَالذَّكَرَيْنِ حَرَّمَ أَمِ الْأُنْثَيَيْنِ أَمَّا اشْتَمَلَتْ عَلَيْهِ أَرْحَامُ الْأُنْثَيَيْنِ ۖ أَمْ كُنتُمْ شُهَدَاءَ إِذْ وَصَّاكُمُ اللَّهُ بِهَٰذَا ۚ فَمَنْ أَظْلَمُ مِمَّنِ افْتَرَىٰ عَلَى اللَّهِ كَذِبًا لِّيُضِلَّ النَّاسَ بِغَيْرِ عِلْمٍ ۗ إِنَّ اللَّهَ لَا يَهْدِي الْقَوْمَ الظَّالِمِينَ ۝

قُل لَّا أَجِدُ فِي مَا أُوحِيَ إِلَيَّ مُحَرَّمًا عَلَىٰ طَاعِمٍ يَطْعَمُهُ إِلَّا أَن يَكُونَ مَيْتَةً أَوْ دَمًا مَّسْفُوحًا أَوْ لَحْمَ خِنزِيرٍ فَإِنَّهُ رِجْسٌ أَوْ فِسْقًا أُهِلَّ لِغَيْرِ اللَّهِ بِهِ ۚ فَمَنِ اضْطُرَّ غَيْرَ بَاغٍ وَلَا عَادٍ فَإِنَّ رَبَّكَ غَفُورٌ رَّحِيمٌ ۝

وَعَلَى الَّذِينَ هَادُوا حَرَّمْنَا كُلَّ ذِي ظُفُرٍ ۖ وَمِنَ الْبَقَرِ وَالْغَنَمِ حَرَّمْنَا عَلَيْهِمْ شُحُومَهُمَا إِلَّا مَا حَمَلَتْ ظُهُورُهُمَا أَوِ الْحَوَايَا أَوْ مَا اخْتَلَطَ بِعَظْمٍ ۚ ذَٰلِكَ جَزَيْنَاهُم بِبَغْيِهِمْ ۖ وَإِنَّا لَصَادِقُونَ ۝

فَإِن كَذَّبُوكَ فَقُل رَّبُّكُمْ ذُو رَحْمَةٍ وَاسِعَةٍ وَلَا يُرَدُّ بَأْسُهُ عَنِ الْقَوْمِ الْمُجْرِمِينَ ۝

148. Those who give partners (to Allah) will say: "If Allah had wished, we should not have given partners to Him nor would our fathers; nor should we have had any taboos." So did their ancestors argue falsely, until they tasted of Our wrath. Say: "Have you any (certain) knowledge? If so, produce it before us. You follow nothing but conjecture: you do nothing but lie."

149. Say: "With Allah is the argument that reaches home: if it had been His will, He could indeed have guided you all."

150. Say: "Bring forward your witnesses to prove that Allah forbade you so and so." If they bring such witnesses, you should not be amongst them: nor you should follow the vain desires of such as treat our Signs as falsehoods, and such as do not believe in the Hereafter: for they hold others as equal with their Guardian-Lord.

151. Say: "Come, I will rehearse what Allah has (really) prohibited you from": Join not anything as equal with Him; be good to your parents; kill not your children on a plea of want;- We provide sustenance for you and for them;- do not come near to shameful deeds. Whether open or secret; take not life, which Allah has made sacred, except by way of justice and law: thus does He command you, that you may learn wisdom.

152. And come not near to the orphan's property, except to improve it, until he attain the age of full strength; give measure and weight with (full) justice;-

148. Sayaqoolul-lazeena ashrakoo law shaaa'al-laahu maaa ashraknaa wa laaa aabaaa'unaa wa laa ḥarramnaa min shay'; kazaalika kazzabal-lazeena min qablihim ḥattaa zaaqoo baasanaa; qul hal 'indakum min 'ilmin fatukhrijoohu lanaa in tattabi'oona illaz-zanna wa in antum illaa takhruṣoon.

149. Qul falillaahil-ḥujjatul-baalighatu falaw shaaa'a lahadaakum ajma'een.

150. Qul halumma shuhadaaa'akumul-lazeena yash-hadoona annal-laaha ḥarrama haazaa fa-in shahidoo falaa tashhad ma'ahum; wa laa tattabi' ahwaaa'al-lazeena kazzaboo bi-Aayaatinaa wallazeena laa yu'minoona bil-Aakhirati wa hum bi-Rabbihim ya'diloon. **(Section 18)**

151. Qul ta'aalaw atlu maa ḥarrama Rabbukum 'alaykum allaa tushrikoo bihee shay'añw-wa bilwaalidayni iḥsaanañw-wa laa taqtulooo awlaadakum min imlaaq; naḥnu narzuqukum wa iyyaahum wa laa taqrabul-fawaaḥisha maa zahara minhaa wa maa baṭana wa laa taqtulun-nafsal-latee ḥarramal-laahu illaa bilḥaqq; zaalikum waṣṣaakum bihee la'allakum ta'qiloon.

152. Wa laa taqraboo maalal-yateemi illaa billatee hiya aḥsanu ḥattaa yablugha ashuddahoo wa awful-kayla walmeezaana bilqisṭi

no burden do We place on any soul, but that which it can bear;- whenever you speak, speak justly, even if a near relative is concerned; and fulfil the Covenant of Allah: thus He commands you, that you may remember.

153. Verily, this is My Way, leading straight: follow it: do not follow (other) paths: they will scatter you about from His (great) path: thus He commands you that you may be righteous.

154. Moreover, We gave Moses the Book, completing (Our favour) to those who would do right, and explained all things in detail,- and a guide and a mercy, that they might believe in the meeting with their Lord.

155. And this is a Book which We have revealed as a blessing: so follow it and be righteous, that you may receive mercy:

156. Lest you should say: "The Book was sent down to two Peoples before us, and for our part, we remained unacquainted with all that they learned by assiduous study:"

157. Or lest you should say: "If the Book had only been sent down to us, we should have followed its guidance better than they." Now then has come unto you a Clear (Sign) from your Lord,- and a guide and a mercy: then who could do more wrong than one who rejects Allah's Signs, and turns away therefrom? In good time shall We requite those who turn away from Our Signs, with a dreadful Chastisement, for their turning away.

158. Are they waiting to see if the angels come to them, or your Lord (Himself), or

---

laa nukallifu nafsan illaa wus'ahaa wa izaa qultum fa'diloo wa law kaana zaa qurbaa wa bi-'Ahdil-laahi awfoo; zaalikum waṣṣaakum bihee la'allakum tazakkaroon.

153. Wa anna haazaa Ṣiraaṭee Mustaqeeman fattabi'oohu wa laa tattabi'us-subula fatafarraqa bikum 'an sabeelih; zaalikum waṣṣaakum bihee la'allakum tattaqoon.

154. Ṣumma aataynaa Moosal-Kitaaba tamaaman 'alal-lazeee aḥsana wa tafṣeelal-likulli shay'iñw-wa hudañw-wa raḥmatal-la'allahum biliqaaa'i Rabbihim yu'minoon.
(Section 19)

155. Wa haazaa Kitaabun anzalnaahu Mubaarakun fattabi'oohu wattaqoo la'al-lakum turḥamoon.

156. An taqoolooo innamaaa unzilal-Kitaabu 'alaa ṭaaa'ifatayni min qablinaa wa in kunnaa 'an diraasatihim laghaafileen.

157. Aw taqoolooo law annaaa unzila 'alaynal-Kitaabu lakunnaaa ahdaa minhum; faqad jaaa'akum bayyinatum-mir-Rabbikum wa hudañw-wa raḥmah; faman aẓlamu mimman kazzaba bi-Aayaatil-laahi wa ṣadafa 'anhaa; sanajzil-lazeena yaṣdifoona 'an Aayaatinaa sooo'al-'azaabi bimaa kaanoo yaṣdifoon.

158. Hal yanẓuroona illaaa an taåtiyahumul-malaaa'ikatu aw yaåtiya Rabbuka aw yaåtiya

certain of the Signs of your Lord! the day that certain of the Signs of your Lord do come, no good will it do to a soul to believe in them then, if it believed not before nor earned righteousness through its faith. Say: "Wait you: we too are waiting."

ba'du Aayaati Rabbik; Yawma yaåtee ba'du Aayaati Rabbika laa yanfa'u nafsan eemaanuhaa lam takun aamanat min qablu aw kasabat feee eemaanihaa khayraa; qulin-taziroo innaa muntaziroon.

159. As for those who divide their religion and break up into sects, you have no part in them in the least: their affair is with Allah: He will in the end tell them the truth of all that they did.

159. Innal-lazeena farraqoo deenahum wa kaanoo shiya'allasta minhum fee shay'; innamaaa amruhum ilallaahi summa yunabbi'uhum bimaa kaanoo yaf'aloon.

160. He that does good shall have ten times as much to his credit: He that does evil shall only be recompensed according to his evil: no wrong shall be done to (any of) them.

160. Man jaaa'a bilhasanati falahoo 'ashru amsaalihaa wa man jaaa'a bissayyi'ati falaa yujzaaa illaa mislahaa wa hum laa yuzlamoon.

161. Say: "Verily, my Lord has guided me to a way that is straight,- a religion of right,- the path (trod) by Abraham, the true in faith, and he (certainly) did not join gods with Allah."

161. Qul innanee hadaanee Rabbeee ilaa Siraatim-Mustaqeemin deenan qiyamam-Millata Ibraaheema Haneefaa; wa maa kaana minal-mushrikeen.

162. Say: "Truly, my prayer and my service of sacrifice, my life and my death, are (all) for Allah, the Cherisher of the Worlds:

162. Qul inna Salaatee wa nusukee wa mahyaaya wa mamaatee lillaahi Rabbil 'aalameen.

163. No partner has He: this I am commanded, and I am the first of those who bow to His Will.

163. Laa shareeka lahoo wa bizaalika umirtu wa ana awwalul-muslimeen.

164. Say: "Shall I seek for (my) Cherisher other than Allah, when He is the Cherisher of all things (that exist)? Every soul draws the meed of its acts on none but itself: no bearer of burdens can bear the burden of another. Your goal in the end is towards Allah: He will tell you the truth of the things wherein you disputed."

164. Qul aghayral-laahi abghee Rabbanw-wa Huwa Rabbu kulli shay'; wa laa taksibu kullu nafsin illaa 'alayhaa; wa laa taziru waaziratuñw-wizra ukhraa; summa ilaa Rabbikum marji'ukum fa-yunabbi'ukum bimaa kuntum feehi takhtalifoon.

165. It is He Who has made you (His) agents, inheritors of the earth: He has raised you in ranks, some above others:

165. Wa Huwal-lazee ja'alakum khalaaa'ifal-ardi wa rafa'a ba'dakum fawqa ba'din darajaatil-

that He may try you in the gifts He has given you: for your Lord is quick in punishment: He is indeed Oft-forgiving, Most Merciful.

7. The Heights
In the name of Allah, Most Gracious, Most Merciful.

1. *Alif-Lam-Mim-Sad.*

2. A Book revealed unto you,- So let your heart be oppressed no more by any difficulty on that account,- that with it you might warn (the erring) and teach the Believers).

3. Follow (O men!) the revelation given unto you from your Lord, and follow not, as friends or protectors, other than Him. Little it is you remember of admonition.

4. How many towns have We destroyed (for their sins)? Our punishment took them on a sudden by night or while they slept for their afternoon rest.

5. When (thus) Our punishment took them, no cry did they utter but this: "Indeed we did wrong."

6. Then shall we question those to whom Our message was sent and those by whom We sent it.

7. And verily, We shall recount their whole story with knowledge, for We were never absent (at any time or place).

8. The balance that day will be true (to a nicety): those whose scale (of good) will be heavy, will prosper:

9. Those whose scale will be light, will find their souls in perdition, for that they wrongfully treated Our Signs.

10. It is We Who have placed you with authority on earth, and

---

liyabluwakum fee maaa aataakum; inna Rabbaka saree'ul-'iqaab; wa innahoo la-Ghafoorur-Raḥeem. (Section 20)

Sûrat al-A'râf–7
(Revealed at Makkah)
Bismillaahir Raḥmaanir Raḥeem

1. Alif-Laaam-Meeem-Ṣaaad.

2. Kitaabun unzila ilayka falaa yakun fee ṣadrika ḥarajum-minhu litunẕira bihee wa ẕikraa lilmu'mineen.

3. Ittabi'oo maaa unzila 'ilaykum mir-Rabbikum wa laa tattabi'oo min dooniheee awliyaaa'; qaleelam-maa tazakkaroon.

4. Wa kam min qaryatin ahlaknaahaa fajaaa'ahaa baå-sunaa bayaatan aw hum qaaa'iloon.

5. Famaa kaana da'waahum iz jaaa'ahum baåsunaaa illaaa an qaalooo innaa kunnaa zaalimeen.

6. Falanas'alannal-lazeena ursila ilayhim wa lanas'alannal-mursaleen.

7. Falanaquṣṣanna 'alayhim bi'ilmiñw-wa maa kunnaa ghaaa'ibeen.

8. Walwaznu Yawma'izinil-ḥaqq; faman saqulat mawaa-zeenuhoo fa-ulaaa'ika humul-mufliḥoon.

9. Wa man khaffat mawaa-zeenuhoo fa-ulaaa'ikal-lazeena khasirooo anfusahum bimaa kaanoo bi-Aayaatinaa yazli-moon.

10. Wa laqad makkannaakum fil-arḍi wa

provided you therein with means for the fulfilment of your life: small are the thanks that you give!

11. It is We Who created you and gave you shape; then We said the angels bow down to Adam, and they bowed down; not so Iblis; He refused to be of those who bow down.

12. (Allah) said: "What prevented you from bowing down when I commanded you?" He said: "I am better than he: you created me from fire, and him from clay."

13. (Allah) said: "Get you down from here: it is not for you to be arrogant here: get out, for you are of the meanest(of creatures)."

14. He said: "Give me respite till the day they are raised up."

15. (Allah) said: "Be you among those who have respite."

16. He said: "Because You have thrown me out of the way, I will lie in wait for them on Your Straight Way:

17. "Then I will assault them from before them and behind them, from their right and their left: Nor will You find, in most of them, gratitude (for Your mercies)."

18. (Allah) said: "Get out from this, disgraced and expelled. If any of them follow you,- I will fill Hell with you all.

19. "O Adam! You and your wife dwell in the Garden, and enjoy (its good things) as you wish: but do not approach this tree, or you run into harm and transgression."

20. Then began Satan to whisper suggestions to them, in order to reveal to them

ja'alnaa lakum feehaa ma'aayish; qaleelam maa tashkuroon.   **(Section 1)**

11. Wa laqad khalaqnaakum summa sawwarnaakum summa qulnaa lilmalaa'ikatis-judoo li-Aadama fa-sajadooo illaaa Ibleesa lam yakum-minas-saajideen.

12. Qaala maa mana'aka allaa tasjuda iz amartuka qaala ana khayrum-minhu khalaqtanee min naariñw-wa khalaqtahoo min teen.

13. Qaala fahbit minhaa famaa yakoonu laka an tatakabbara feehaa fakhruj innaka minas-saaghireen.

14. Qaala anzirneee ilaa Yawmi yub'asoon.

15. Qaala innaka minal-munzareen.

16. Qaala fabimaaa aghway-tanee la-aq'udanna lahum Siraatakal-Mustaqeem

17. Summa la-aatiyannahum mim bayni aydeehim wa min khalfihim wa 'an aymaanihim wa 'an shamaaa'ilihim wa laa tajidu aksarahum shaakireen.

18. Qaalakh-ruj minhaa maz'oomam-madhooraa; laman tabi'aka minhum la-amla'anna Jahannama minkum ajma'een.

19. Wa yaaa Aadamus-kun anta wa zawjukal-Jannata fakulaa min haysu shi'tumaa wa laa taqrabaa haazihish-shajarata fatakoonaa minaz-zaalimeen.

20. Fawaswasa lahumash-Shaytaanu liyubdiya lahumaa

their shame that was hidden from them (before): he said: "Your Lord only forbade you this tree, lest you should become angels or such beings as live for ever."

21. And he swore to them both, that he was their sincere adviser.

22. So by deceit he brought about their fall: when they tasted of the tree, their shame became manifest to them, and they began to sew together the leaves of the Garden over their bodies. And their Lord called unto them: "Did I not forbid you that tree, and tell you that Satan was an avowed enemy to you?"

23. They said: "Our Lord! We have wronged our own souls: If You do not forgive us and bestow not upon us Your Mercy, we shall certainly be lost."

24. (Allah) said: "Get you down. With enmity between yourselves. On earth will be your dwelling-place and your means of livelihood,- for a time."

25. He said: "Therein you shall live, and therein you shall die; but from it you shall be taken out (at last)."

26. O you Children of Adam! We have bestowed raiment upon you to cover your shame, as well as to be an adornment to you. But the raiment of righteousness,- that is the best. Such are among the Signs of Allah, that they may receive admonition!

27. O you Children of Adam! Let not Satan seduce you, in the same manner as He got your parents out of the Garden, stripping them of their raiment, to expose their shame:

maa wooriya 'anhumaa min saw-aatihimaa wa qaala maa nahaakumaa Rabbukumaa 'an haazihish-shajarati illaa an takoonaa malakayni aw takoonaa minal-khaalideen.

21. Wa qaasamahumaaa innee lakumaa laminan-naasiheen.

22. Fadallaahumaa bighuroor; falammaa zaaqash-shajarata badat lahumaa saw-aatuhumaa wa tafiqaa yakhsi-faani 'alayhimaa miñw-waraqil-jannati wa naadaahumaa Rabbuhumaaa alam anhakumaa 'an tilkumash-shajarati wa aqul lakumaaa innash-Shaytaana lakumaa 'aduwwum-mubeen.

23. Qaalaa Rabbanaa zalam-naaa anfusanaa wa illam taghfir lanaa wa tarhamnaa lanakoo-nanna minal-khaasireen.

24. Qaalah-bitoo ba'dukum liba'din 'aduwwuñw-wa lakum fil-ardi mustaqarruñw-wa mataa'un ilaa heen.

25. Qaala feehaa tahyawna wa feehaa tamootoona wa minhaa tukhrajoon. (Section 2)

26. Yaa Banee Aadama qad anzalnaa 'alaykum libaasañy-yuwaaree saw-aatikum wa reeshañw wa libaasut-taqwaa zaalika khayr; zaalika min Aayaatil-laahi la'allahum yaz-zakkaroon.

27. Yaa Baneee Aadama laa yaftinannakumush-Shaytaanu kamaaa akhraja abawaykum minal-Jannati yanzi'u 'anhumaa libaasahumaa liyuriyahumaa saw-aatihimaaa;

for he and his tribe watch you from a position where you cannot see them: We made the Satan friends (only) to those without Faith.

28. When they do anything that is shameful, they say: "We found our fathers doing so"; and "Allah commanded us thus": Say: "Nay, Allah never commands what is shameful: do you say of Allah what you do not know?"

29. Say: "My Lord has commanded justice; and that you set your whole selves (to Him) at every time and place of prayer, and call upon Him, making your devotion sincere as in His sight: such as He created you in the beginning, so shall you return."

30. Some He has guided: Others have (by their choice) deserved the loss of their way; in that they took the Satan, in preference to Allah, for their friends and protectors, and think that they receive guidance.

31. O Children of Adam! wear your beautiful apparel at every time and place of prayer: eat and drink: but do not waste by excess, for Allah does not loves the wasters.

32. Say: Who has forbidden the beautiful (gifts) of Allah, which He has produced for His servants, and the things, clean and pure, which (He has provided) for sustenance? Say: They are, in the life of this world, for those who believe, (and) purely for them on the Day of Judgment. Thus do We explain the Signs in detail for those who understand.

33. Say: The things that my Lord has indeed forbidden are: shameful deeds, whether open or secret; sins and trespasses against truth or reason; assigning of partners to Allah,

innahoo yaraakum huwa wa qabeeluhoo min ḥaysu laa tarawnahum; innaa ja'alnash-Shayaaṭeena awliyaaa'a lillazeena laa yu'minoon.

28. Wa izaa fa'aloo faaḥishatan qaaloo wajadnaa 'alayhaaa aabaaa'anaa wallaahu amaranaa bihaa; qul innal-laaha laa yaamuru bilfaḥshaaa'i a-taqooloona 'alal-laahi maa laa ta'lamoon.

29. Qul amara Rabbee bilqisṭi wa aqeemoo wujoohakum 'inda kulli masjidiñw-wad'oohu mukhliṣeena lahud-deen; kamaa bada-akum ta'oodoon.

30. Fareeqan hadaa wa fareeqan ḥaqqa 'alayhimud-ḍalaalah; innahumut-takhazush-Shayaaṭeena awliyaaa'a min doonil-laahi wa yaḥsaboona annahum muhtadoon.

31. Yaa Baneee Adama khuzoo zeenatakum 'inda kulli masji-diñw-wa kuloo washraboo wa laa tusrifoo; innahoo laa yuḥibbul-musrifeen. **(Section 3)**

32. Qul man ḥarrama zeenatal-laahil-lateee akhraja li'ibaa-dihee waṭṭayyibaati minar-rizq; qul hiya lillazeena aamanoo fil-ḥayaatid-dunyaa khaaliṣatañy-Yawmal Qiyaamah; kazaalika nufaṣṣilul-Aayaati liqawmiñy-ya'lamoon.

33. Qul innamaa ḥarrama Rabbiyal-fawaaḥisha maa zahara minhaa wa maa baṭana wal-isma walbaghya bighayril-ḥaqqi wa an tushrikoo billaahi maa lam

for which He has given no authority; and saying things about Allah of which you have no knowledge.

34. To every people is a term appointed: when their term is reached, not an hour can they cause delay, nor (an hour) can they advance (it in anticipation).

35. O you Children of Adam! whenever there come to you Apostles from amongst you, rehearsing My Signs to you,- those who are righteous and mend (their lives),- on them shall be no fear nor shall they grieve.

36. But those who reject Our Signs and treat them with arrogance,- they are Companions of the Fire, to dwell therein (for ever).

37. Who is more unjust than one who invents a lie against Allah or rejects His Signs? For such, their portion appointed must reach them from the Book (of decrees): until, when our messengers (of death) arrive and take their souls, they say: "Where are the things that you used to invoke besides Allah?" They will reply, "They have left us in the lurch," and they will bear witness against themselves, that they had rejected Allah.

38. He will say: "You enter in the company of the peoples who passed away before you - men and jinns, - into the Fire." Every time a new people enters, it curses its sister-people (that went before), until they follow each other, all into the Fire. Says the last about the first: "Our Lord! it is these that misled us: so give them a double Chastisement in the Fire." He will say: "Doubled for all" : but

yunazzil bihee sulṭaananw-wa an taqooloo 'alal-laahi maa laa ta'lamoon.

34. Wa likulli ummatin ajalun fa-izaa jaaa'a ajaluhum laa yastaåkhiroona saa'atanw-wa laa yastaqdimoon.

35. Yaa Baneee Aadama immaa yaåtiyannakum Rusulum-minkum yaquṣṣoona 'alaykum Aayaatee famanit-taqaa wa aṣlaḥa falaa khawfun 'alayhim wa laa hum yaḥzanoon.

36. Wallazeena kazzaboo bi-Aayaatinaa wastakbaroo 'anhaaa ulaaa'ika Aṣḥaabun Naari hum feehaa khaalidoon.

37. Faman aẓlamu mimman-iftaraa 'alal-laahi kaziban aw kazzaba bi-Aayaatih; ulaaa'ika yanaaluhum naṣeebuhum minal-Kitaab; ḥattaaa izaa jaaa'at-hum rusulunaa yatawaf-fawnahum qaalooo ayna maa kuntum tad'oona min doonil-laahi qaaloo ḍalloo 'annaa wa shahidoo 'alaaa anfusihim annahum kaanoo kaafireen.

38. Qaalad-khuloo feee umamin qad khalat min qablikum minal-jinni wal-insi fin-Naari kullamaa dakhalat ummatul-la'anat ukhtahaa ḥattaaa izad-daarakoo feehaa jamee'an qaalat ukhraahum li-oolaahum Rabbanaa haaa'u-laaa'i aḍalloonaa fa-aatihim 'azaaban ḍi'fam-minan-Naari qaala likullin ḍi'fuñw-wa laakil

this you do not understand.

39. Then the first will say to the last: "See then! You do not have any advantage over us; so you taste of the Chastisement for all that you did."

40. To those who reject Our Signs and treat them with arrogance, no opening will there be of the gates of heaven, nor will they enter the Garden, until the camel can pass through the eye of the needle: such is Our reward for those in sin.

41. For them there is Hell, as a couch (below) and folds of covering above: such is Our requital of those who do wrong.

42. But those who believe and work righteousness,- no burden do We place on any soul, but that which it can bear,-they will be Companions of the Garden, therein to dwell (for ever).

43. And We shall remove from their hearts any lurking sense of injury;- beneath them there will be rivers flowing;- and they shall say: "Praise be to Allah, who has guided us to this (felicity): never could we have found guidance, had it not been for the guidance of Allah: indeed it was the truth, that the Apostles of our Lord brought to us." And they shall hear the cry: "Behold! the Garden before you! You have been made its inheritors, for your deeds (of righteousness)."

44. The Companions of the Garden will call out to the Companions of the Fire: "We have indeed found the promises of our Lord to us true: Have you also found Your Lord's promises true?" They shall say, "Yes"; But a

laa ta'lamoon.

39. Wa qaalat oolaahum li-ukhraahum famaa kaana lakum 'alaynaa min faḍlin fazooqul-azaaba bimaa kuntum taksiboon. **(Section 4)**

40. Innal-lazeena kazzaboo bi-Aayaatinaa wastakbaroo 'anhaa laa tufattaḥu lahum abwaabus-samaaa'i wa laa yadkhuloonal-jannata ḥattaa yalijal-jamalu fee sammil-khiyaaṭ; wa kazaalika najzil-mujrimeen.

41. Lahum min jahannama mihaaduñw-wa min fawqihim ghawaash; wa kazaalika najziz-zaalimeen.

42. Wallazeena aamanoo wa 'amiluṣ-ṣaaliḥaati laa nukallifu nafsan illaa wus'ahaaa ulaaa'ika Aṣḥaabul-jannati hum feehaa khaalidoon.

43. Wa naza'naa maa fee ṣudoorihim min ghillin tajree min taḥtihimul-anhaaru wa qaalul-ḥamdu lillaahil-lazee hadaanaa lihaazaa wa maa kunnaa linahtadiya law laaa an hadaanal-laahu laqad jaaa'at Rusulu Rabbinaa bilḥaqq; wa noodooo an tilkumul-jannatu ooristumoohaa bimaa kuntum ta'maloon.

44. Wa naadaaa Aṣḥaabul-jannati Aṣḥaaban-Naari an qad wajadnaa maa wa'adanaa Rabbunaa ḥaqqan fahal wajattum maa wa'ada Rabbukum ḥaqqan qaaloo na'am; fa-azzana

crier shall proclaim between them: "The curse of Allah is on the wrong-doers;-

45. "Those who would hinder (men) from the path of Allah and would seek in it something crooked: they were those who denied the Hereafter."

46. Between them shall be a veil, and on the Heights will be men who would know every one by his marks: they will call out to the Companions of the Garden, "peace on you": they will not have entered, but they will have an assurance (thereof).

47. When their eyes shall be turned towards the Companions of the Fire, they will say: "Our Lord! do not send us to the company of the wrong-doers."

48. The men on the Heights will call to certain men whom they will know from their marks, saying: "Of what profit to you were your hoards and your arrogant ways?

49. "Behold! are these not the men whom you swore that Allah would never bless? with His Mercy you enter the Garden: no fear shall be on you, nor shall you grieve."

50. The Companions of the Fire will call to the Companions of the Garden: "Pour down to us water or anything that Allah provides for your sustenance." They will say: "Allah has forbidden Both these things to those who rejected Him."

51. "Such as took their religion to be mere amusement and play, and were deceived by the life of the world." That day

mu'azzinum baynahum al-la'natul-laahi 'alaz-zaalimeen.

45. Allazeena yasuddoona 'an sabeelil-laahi wa yabghoo-nahaa 'iwajañw wa hum bil-Aakhirati kaafiroon.

46. Wa baynahumaa hijaab; wa 'alal-A'raafi rijaaluñy-ya'ri-foona kullam biseemaahum; wa naadaw Ashaabal-Jannati an salaamun 'alaykum; lam yadkhuloohaa wa hum yatma'oon.

47. Wa izaa surifat absaaru-hum tilqaaa'a Ashaabin-Naari qaalo Rabbanaa laa taj'alnaa ma'al-qawmiz-zaalimeen.
      (Section 5)

48. Wa naadaaa Ashaabul-A'raafi rijaalañy-ya'rifoona-hum biseemaahum qaaloo maaa aghnaa 'ankum jam'ukum wa maa kuntum tastakbiroon.

49. A-haaa'ulaaa'il-lazeena aqsamtum laa yanaaluhumul-laahu birahmah; udkhulul-Jannata laa khawfun 'alaykum wa laaa antum tahzanoon.

50. Wa naadaaa Ashaabun-Naari Ashaabal-Jannati an afeedoo 'alaynaa minal-maaa'i aw mimmaa razaqakumul-laah; qaalooo innal-laaha harrama-humaa 'alal-kaafireen.

51. Allazeenat-takhazoo deenahum lahwañw-wa la'i-bañw-wa gharrat-humul-hayaa-tud-dunyaa; fal-Yawma

مُؤَذِّنٌۢ بَيْنَهُمْ اَنْ لَّعْنَةُ اللّٰهِ عَلَى الظّٰلِمِيْنَ ۞

الَّذِيْنَ يَصُدُّوْنَ عَنْ سَبِيْلِ اللّٰهِ وَيَبْغُوْنَهَا عِوَجًا ۚ وَهُمْ بِالْاٰخِرَةِ كٰفِرُوْنَ ۞

وَبَيْنَهُمَا حِجَابٌ ۚ وَعَلَى الْاَعْرَافِ رِجَالٌ يَّعْرِفُوْنَ كُلًّا بِسِيْمٰىهُمْ ۚ وَنَادَوْا اَصْحٰبَ الْجَنَّةِ اَنْ سَلٰمٌ عَلَيْكُمْ ۗ لَمْ يَدْخُلُوْهَا وَهُمْ يَطْمَعُوْنَ ۞

وَاِذَا صُرِفَتْ اَبْصَارُهُمْ تِلْقَآءَ اَصْحٰبِ النَّارِ ۙ قَالُوْا رَبَّنَا لَا تَجْعَلْنَا مَعَ الْقَوْمِ الظّٰلِمِيْنَ ۞

وَنَادٰٓى اَصْحٰبُ الْاَعْرَافِ رِجَالًا يَّعْرِفُوْنَهُمْ بِسِيْمٰىهُمْ قَالُوْا مَاۤ اَغْنٰى عَنْكُمْ جَمْعُكُمْ وَمَا كُنْتُمْ تَسْتَكْبِرُوْنَ ۞

اَهٰٓؤُلَآءِ الَّذِيْنَ اَقْسَمْتُمْ لَا يَنَالُهُمُ اللّٰهُ بِرَحْمَةٍ ۗ اُدْخُلُوا الْجَنَّةَ لَا خَوْفٌ عَلَيْكُمْ وَلَاۤ اَنْتُمْ تَحْزَنُوْنَ ۞

وَنَادٰٓى اَصْحٰبُ النَّارِ اَصْحٰبَ الْجَنَّةِ اَنْ اَفِيْضُوْا عَلَيْنَا مِنَ الْمَآءِ اَوْ مِمَّا رَزَقَكُمُ اللّٰهُ ۗ قَالُوْۤا اِنَّ اللّٰهَ حَرَّمَهُمَا عَلَى الْكٰفِرِيْنَ ۞

الَّذِيْنَ اتَّخَذُوْا دِيْنَهُمْ لَهْوًا وَّلَعِبًا وَّغَرَّتْهُمُ الْحَيٰوةُ الدُّنْيَا ۚ فَالْيَوْمَ

We shall forget them as they forgot the meeting of this day of theirs, and as they were wont to reject Our Signs.

52. For We had certainly sent to them a Book, based on knowledge, which We explained in detail,- a guide and a mercy to all who believe.

53. Do they just wait for the final fulfilment of the event? On the day the event is finally fulfilled, those who disregarded it before will say: "The Apostles of our Lord did indeed bring true (tidings). Have we no intercessors now to intercede on our behalf? Or could we be sent back? Then should we behave differently from our behaviour in the past." In fact they will have lost their souls, and the things they invented will leave them in the lurch.

54. Your Guardian-Lord is Allah, Who created the heavens and the earth in six Days, and is firmly established on the Throne (of authority): He draws the night as a veil over the day, each seeking the other in rapid succession: He created the sun, the moon, and the stars, (all) governed by laws under His Command. Is it not His to create and to govern? Blessed be Allah, the Cherisher and Sustainer of the Worlds.

55. Call on your Lord with humility and in private: for Allah does not loves those who trespass beyond bounds.

56. Do no mischief on the earth, after it has been set in order, but call on Him with fear and longing (in your hearts): for the Mercy of Allah is (always) near to those who do good.

57. It is He Who sends the winds like heralds of glad tidings, going before His mercy: when

nansaahum kamaa nasoo liqaaa‘a Yawmihim haazaa wa maa kaanoo bi-Aayaatinaa yajhadoon.

52. Wa laqad ji'naahum bi-Kitaabin fassalnaahu ‘alaa ‘ilmin hudanw-wa rahmatal-liqawmiñy-yu'minoon.

53. Hal yanzuroona illaa taa-weelah; Yawma yaåtee taa-weeluhoo yaqoolul-lazeena nasoohu min qablu qad jaaa'at Rusulu Rabbinaa bilhaqq; fahal lanaa min shufa‘aaa‘a fa-yashfa‘oo lanaaa aw nuraddu fana‘mala ghayral-lazee kunnaa na‘mal; qad khasirooo anfusahum wa dalla ‘anhum maa kaanoo yaftaroon.

(Section 6)

54. Inna Rabbakumul-laahul-lazee khalaqas-samaawaati walarda fee sittati ayyaamin summas-tawaa ‘alal-‘arshi yughshil-laylan-nahaara yatlu-buhoo haseesañw-washshamsa walqamara wannujooma musakhkharaatim bi-amrih; alaa lahul-khalqu wal-amr; tabaarakal-laahu Rabbul-‘aala-meen.

55. Ud‘oo Rabbakum tadar-ru‘añw-wa khufyah; innahoo laa yuhibbul-mu‘tadeen.

56. Wa laa tufsidoo fil-ardi ba‘da islaahihaa wad‘oohu khawfañw-wa tama‘aa; inna rahmatal-laahi qareebum-minal-muhsineen.

57. Wa Huwal-lazee yursilur-riyaaha bushram bayna yaday rahmatihee hattaaa izaa

they have carried the heavy-laden clouds, We drive them to a land that is dead, make rain to descend thereon, and produce every kind of harvest therewith: thus shall We raise up the dead: perchance you may remember.

58. From the land that is clean and good, by the will of its Cherisher, springs up produce, (rich) after its kind: but from the land that is bad, springs up nothing but that which is niggardly: thus do we explain the Signs by various (symbols) to those who are grateful.

59. We sent Noah to his people. He said: "O my people! worship Allah! you have no other god but Him. I fear for you the punishment of a dreadful Day!

60. The leaders of his people said: "Ah! we see you evidently wandering (in mind)."

61. He said: "O my people! no wandering is there in my (mind): on the contrary I am an apostle from the Lord and Cherisher of the Worlds!

62. "I but fulfil towards you the duties of my Lord's mission: sincere is my advice to you, and I know from Allah something that you do not know.

63. "Do you wonder that there has come to you a message from your Lord, through a man of your own people, to warn you,-so that you may fear Allah and haply receive His Mercy?"

64. But they rejected him, and We delivered him, and those with him, in the Ark: but We overwhelmed in the Flood those who rejected Our Signs. They were indeed a blind people!

65. To the 'Ad people, (We sent) Hud, one of their (own) brethren: He said:

aqallat saḥaaban ṣiqaalan suqnaahu libaladim-mayyitin fa-anzalnaa bihil-maaa'a fa-akhrajnaa bihee min kullis-samaraat; kazaalika nukhrijul-mawtaa la'allakum tazak-karoon.

58. Walbaladuṭ-ṭayyibu yakhruju nabaatuhoo bi-izni Rabbihee wallazee khabuṣa laa yakhruju illaa nakidaa; kazaalika nuṣarriful-Aayaati liqawmiñy-yashkuroon.

(Section 7)

59. Laqad arsalnaa Noohan ilaa qawmihee faqaala yaa qawmi-'budul-laaha maa lakum min ilaahin ghayruhoo ineee akhaafu 'alaykum 'azaaba Yawmin 'Azeem.

60. Qaalal-mala-u min qaw-miheee innaa lanaraaka fee ḍalaalim-mubeen.

61. Qaala yaa qawmi laysa bee ḍalaalatuñw-wa laakinnee Rasoolum-mir-Rabbil-'aala-meen.

62. Uballighukum Risaalaati Rabbee wa anṣaḥu lakum wa a'lamu minal-laahi maa laa ta'lamoon.

63. Awa 'ajibtum an jaaa'akum zikrum-mir-Rabbikum 'alaa rajulim-minkum liyunzirakum wa litattaqoo wa la'allakum turḥamoon.

64. Fakazzaboohu fa-anjay-naahu wallazeena ma'ahoo fil-fulki wa aghraqnal-lazeena kaz-zaboo bi-Aayaatinaa; innahum kaanoo qawman 'ameen.

(Section 8)

65. Wa ilaa 'Aadin akhaahum Hoodaa; qaala

O my people! worship Allah! you have no other god but Him, will you not fear (Allah)?"

66. The leaders of the Unbelievers among his people said: "Ah! we see you are an imbecile!" and "We think you are a liar!"

67. He said: "O my people! I am no imbecile, but (I am) an Apostle from the Lord and Cherisher of the worlds!

68. "I but fulfil towards you the duties of my Lord's mission: I am to you a sincere and trustworthy adviser.

69. "Do you wonder that there has come to you a message from your Lord through a man of your own people, to warn you? Call in remembrance that He made you inheritors after the people of Noah, and gave you a stature tall among the nations. Call in remembrance the benefits (you have received) from Allah: that so you may prosper."

70. They said: "Do you come to us saying, that we may worship Allah alone, and give up the cult of our fathers? Bring us what you threaten us with, if so be that you tell the truth!"

71. He said: "Punishment and wrath have already come upon you from your Lord: do you dispute with me over names which you have devised - you and your fathers,- without authority from Allah? Then wait: I am amongst you, also waiting."

72. We saved him and those who adhered to him,

yaa qawmi'-budul-laaha maa lakum min ilaahin ghayruh; afalaa tattaqoon.

66. Qaalal-mala-ul-lazeena kafaroo min qawmiheee innaa lanaraaka fee safaahatiñw-wa innaa lanazunnuka minal-kaazibeen.

67. Qaala yaa qawmi laysa bee safaahatuñw-wa laakinnee Rasoolum-mir-Rabbil-'aala-meen.

68. Uballighukum Risaalaati Rabbee wa ana lakum naasihun ameen.

69. Awa 'ajibtum an jaaa'akum zikrum-mir-Rabbikum 'alaa rajulim-minkum liyunzirakum; wazkurooo iz ja'alakum khulafaaa'a mim ba'di qawmi Noohiñw-wa zaadakum filkhal-qi bastatan fazkurooo aalaaa'al-laahi la'allakum tuflihoon.

70. Qaalooo aji'tanaa lina'bu-dal-laaha wahdahoo wa nazara maa kaana ya'budu aabaaa'u-naa faåtinaa bimaa ta'idunaaa in kunta minas-saadiqeen.

71. Qaala qad waqa'a alaykum-mir-Rabbikum rijsuñw-wa ghadab, atujaadiloonanee feee asmaaa'in sammaytumoohaaa antum wa aabaaa'ukum maa nazzalal-laahu bihaa min sultaan; fantazirooo innee ma'akum minal-muntazireen.

72. Fa-anjaynaahu wallazeena ma'ahoo birahmatim-

يٰقَوْمِ اعْبُدُوا اللّٰهَ وَاللّٰهُ مَا لَكُمْ مِّنْ اِلٰهٍ غَيْرُهٗ ؕ اَفَلَا تَتَّقُوْنَ ۝

قَالَ الْمَلَاُ الَّذِيْنَ كَفَرُوْا مِنْ قَوْمِهٖۤ اِنَّا لَنَرٰىكَ فِيْ سَفَاهَةٍ وَّ اِنَّا لَنَظُنُّكَ مِنَ الْكٰذِبِيْنَ ۝

قَالَ يٰقَوْمِ لَيْسَ بِيْ سَفَاهَةٌ وَّ لٰكِنِّيْ رَسُوْلٌ مِّنْ رَّبِّ الْعٰلَمِيْنَ ۝

اُبَلِّغُكُمْ رِسٰلٰتِ رَبِّيْ وَ اَنَا لَكُمْ نَاصِحٌ اَمِيْنٌ ۝

اَوَعَجِبْتُمْ اَنْ جَآءَكُمْ ذِكْرٌ مِّنْ رَّبِّكُمْ عَلٰى رَجُلٍ مِّنْكُمْ لِيُنْذِرَكُمْ وَاذْكُرُوْۤا اِذْ جَعَلَكُمْ خُلَفَآءَ مِنْۢ بَعْدِ قَوْمِ نُوْحٍ وَّ زَادَكُمْ فِي الْخَلْقِ بَصْۜطَةً ۚ فَاذْكُرُوْۤا اٰلَآءَ اللّٰهِ لَعَلَّكُمْ تُفْلِحُوْنَ ۝

قَالُوْۤا اَجِئْتَنَا لِنَعْبُدَ اللّٰهَ وَحْدَهٗ وَنَذَرَ مَا كَانَ يَعْبُدُ اٰبَآؤُنَا ۚ فَاْتِنَا بِمَا تَعِدُنَاۤ اِنْ كُنْتَ مِنَ الصّٰدِقِيْنَ ۝

قَالَ قَدْ وَقَعَ عَلَيْكُمْ مِّنْ رَّبِّكُمْ رِجْسٌ وَّ غَضَبٌ ؕ اَتُجَادِلُوْنَنِيْ فِيْۤ اَسْمَآءٍ سَمَّيْتُمُوْهَاۤ اَنْتُمْ وَ اٰبَآؤُكُمْ مَّا نَزَّلَ اللّٰهُ بِهَا مِنْ سُلْطٰنٍ ؕ فَانْتَظِرُوْۤا اِنِّيْ مَعَكُمْ مِّنَ الْمُنْتَظِرِيْنَ ۝

فَاَنْجَيْنٰهُ وَالَّذِيْنَ مَعَهٗ بِرَحْمَةٍ

by Our Mercy, and We cut off the roots of those who rejected Our Signs and did not believe.

73. To the Thamud people (We sent) Salih, one of their own brethren: He said: "O my people! worship Allah: you have no other god but Him. Now has come to you a clear (Sign) from your Lord! This she-camel of Allah is a Sign for you: So leave her to graze in Allah's earth, and let her come to no harm, or you shall be seized with a grievous punishment.

74. "And remember how He made you inheritors after the 'Ad people and gave you habitations in the land: you build for yourselves palaces and castles in (open) plains, and carve out homes in the mountains; so bring to remembrance the benefits (you have received) from Allah, and refrain from evil and mischief on the earth."

75. The leaders of the arrogant party among his people said to those who were reckoned powerless - those among them who believed: "Do you know indeed that Salih is an Apostle from his Lord?" They said: "We do indeed believe in the revelation which has been sent through him."

76. The Arrogant party said: "For our part, we reject what you believe in."

77. Then they ham-strung the she-camel, and insolently defied the order of their Lord, saying: "O Salih! bring about your threats, if you are an Apostle (of Allah)!"

78. So the earthquake took them unawares, and they lay

minnaa wa qaṭa'naa daabiral-lazeena kazzaboo bi-Aayaati-naa wa maa kaanoo mu'mineen.
(Section 9)

73. Wa ilaa Samooda akhaahum Ṣaaliḥaa; qaala yaa qawmi'-budul-laaha maa lakum min ilaahin ghayruhoo qad jaaa'atkum bayyinatum-mir-Rabbikum haazihee naaqatul-laahi lakum Aayatan fazaroohaa taåkul feee arḍil-laahi wa laa tamassoohaa bisooo'in fa-yaåkhuzakum 'azaabun aleem.

74. Wazkurooo iz ja'alakum khulafaaa'a mim ba'di 'Aadiñw-wa bawwa-akum fil-arḍi tattakhizoona min suhoolihaa quṣooranw-wa tanḥitoonal-jibaala buyootan fazkurooo aalaaa'al-laahi wa laa ta'saw fil-arḍi mufsideen.

75. Qaalal-mala-ul-lazeenas-takbaroo min qawmihee lillazeenas-tuḍ'ifoo liman aamana minhum ata'lamoona anna Ṣaaliḥam-mursalum-mir-Rabbih; qaalooo innaa bimaaa ursila bihee mu'minoon.

76. Qaalal-lazeenas-takbarooo innaa billazeee aamantum bihee kaafiroon.

77. Fa'aqarun-naaqata wa 'ataw 'an amri Rabbihim wa qaaloo yaa Ṣaaliḥu'-tinaa bimaa ta'idunaaa in kunta minal-mursaleen.

78. Fa-akhazat-humur-rajfatu fa-aṣbaḥoo fee

prostrate in their homes in the morning!

79. So Salih left them, saying: "O my people! I did indeed convey to you the message for which I was sent by my Lord: I gave you good counsel, but you do not love good counsellors!"

80. We also (sent) Lut: He said to his people: "Do you commit lewdness such as no people in creation (ever) committed before you?

81. "For you practise your lusts on men in preference to women : you are indeed a people transgressing beyond bounds."

82. And his people gave no answer but this: they said, "Drive them out of your city: these are indeed men who want to be clean and pure!"

83. But we saved him and his family, except his wife: she was of those who lagged behind.

84. And we rained down on them a shower (of brimstone): then see what was the end of those who indulged in sin and crime!

85. To the Madyan people We sent Shu'aib, one of their own brethren: he said: "O my people! worship Allah; You have no other god but Him. Now has come unto you a clear (Sign) from your Lord! so give just measure and weight, nor withhold from the people the things that are their due; and do no mischief on the earth after it has been set in order: that will be best for you, if you have Faith.

86. "And do not squat on every road, breathing threats, hindering from the path of Allah those who believe in Him, and seeking in it something crooked;

daarihim jaasimeen.

79. Fa-tawallaa 'anhum wa qaala yaa qawmi laqad ablaghtukum Risaalata Rabbee wa naṣaḥtu lakum wa laakil-laa tuḥibboonan-naaṣiḥeen.

80. Wa Lootan iz qaala liqawmiheee ataåtoonal-faaḥishata maa sabaqakum bihaa min aḥadim-minal-'aalameen.

81. Innakum lataåtoonar-rijaala shahwatam-min dooninnisaaa'; bal antum qawmum-musrifoon.

82. Wa maa kaana jawaaba qawmiheee illaa an qaalooo akhrijoohum min qaryatikum innahum unaasuñy-yataṭah-haroon.

83. Fa-anjaynaahu wa ahla-hooo illam-ra-atahoo kaanat minal-ghaabireen.

84. Wa 'amṭarnaa 'alayhim maṭaran fanzur kayfa kaana aaqibatul-mujrimeen.
(Section 10)

85. Wa ilaa Madyana akhaa-hum Shu'aybaa; qaala yaa qawmi'-budul-laaha maa lakum min ilaahin ghayruhoo qad jaaa'atkum bayyinatum-mir-Rabbikum fa-awful-kayla walmeezaana wa laa tabkhasun-naasa ashyaaa'ahum wa laa tufsidoo fil-arḍi ba'da iṣlaaḥi-haa; zaalikum khayrul-lakum in kuntum mu'mineen.

86. Wa laa taq'udoo bikulli ṣiraaṭin too'idoona wa taṣud-doona 'an sabeelil-laahi man aamana bihee wa tabghoonahaa 'iwajaa; waz-

But remember how you were small in numbers, and He gave you increase. And hold in your mind's eye what was the end of those who did mischief.

87. "And if there is a party among you who believes in the message with which I have been sent, and a party which does not believe, hold yourselves in patience until Allah decides between us: for He is the best to decide.

88. The leaders, the arrogant party among his people, said: "O Shu'aib! we shall certainly drive you out of our city - (you) and those who believe with you; or else you (and they) shall have to return to our ways and religion." He said: "What! even though we do detest (them)?

89. "We should indeed invent a lie against Allah, if we returned to your ways after Allah has rescued us therefrom; nor could we by any manner of means return thereto unless it be as in the will and plan of Allah, Our Lord. Our Lord can reach out to the utmost recesses of things by His knowledge. In Allah is our trust. Our Lord! You decide between us and our people in truth, for you are the best to decide."

90. The leaders, the unbelievers among his people, said: "If you follow Shu'aib, be sure then you are ruined!"

91. But the earthquake took them unawares, and they lay prostrate in their homes before the morning!

92. The men who rejected Shu'aib became as if they had never been in the homes where they had flourished: the men who rejected Shu'aib - it was they who were ruined!

93. So Shu'aib left them, saying: "O my people! I did indeed

kuroo iz kuntum qaleelan fakassarakum wanzuroo kayfa kaana 'aaqibatul-mufsideen.

87. Wa in kaana ṭaaa'ifatum-minkum aamanoo billazeee ursiltu bihee wa ṭaaa'ifatul-lam yu'minoo faṣbiroo ḥattaa yaḥkumal-laahu baynanaa; wa Huwa khayrul-ḥaakimeen.

88. Qaalal-mala-ul-lazeenas-takbaroo min qawmihee lanukhrijannaka yaa Shu'aybu wallazeena aamanoo ma'aka min qaryatinaaa aw lata'oo-dunna fee millatinaa; qaala awa law kunnaa kaariheen.

89. Qadif-taraynaa 'alal-laahi kaziban in 'udnaa fee millatikum ba'da iz najjaanal-laahu minhaa; wa maa yakoonu lanaaa an na'ooda feehaaa illaaa añy-yashaaa'al-laahu Rabbunaa; wasi'a Rabbunaa kulla shay'in 'ilmaa; 'alal-laahi tawakkalnaa; Rabbanaf-taḥ baynanaa wa bayna qawminaa bilḥaqqi wa Anta khayrul-faatiḥeen.

90. Wa qaalal-mala-ul-lazeena kafaroo min qawmihee la'init-taba'tum Shu'ayban innakum izal-lakhaasiroon.

91. Fa-akhazat-humur-rajfatu fa-aṣbaḥoo fee daarihim jaasimeen.

92. Allazeena kazzaboo Shu'ayban ka-al-lam yaghnaw feehaa; allazeena kazzaboo Shu'ayban kaanoo humul-khaasireen.

93. Fatawallaa 'anhum wa qaala yaa qawmi laqad

convey to you the Messages for which I was sent by my Lord: I gave you good counsel, but how shall I lament over a people who refuse to believe!"

94. Whenever We sent a prophet to a town, We took up its people in suffering and adversity, in order that they might learn humility.

95. Then We changed their suffering into prosperity, until they grew and multiplied, and began to say: "Our fathers (too) were touched by suffering and affluence" ... Behold! We called them to account of a sudden, while they did not realised (their peril).

96. If the people of the towns had but believed and feared Allah, We should indeed have opened out to them (All kinds of) blessings from heaven and earth; but they rejected (the truth), and We brought them to book for their misdeeds.

97. Did the people of the towns feel secure against the coming of Our wrath by night while they were asleep?

98. Or else did they feel secure against its coming in broad daylight while they played about (care-free)?

99. Did they then feel secure against the Plan of Allah?- but no one can feel secure from the Plan of Allah, except those (doomed) to ruin!

100. To those who inherit the earth in succession to its (previous) possessors, is it not a guiding, (lesson) that, if We so willed, We could punish them (too) for their sins, and seal up their hearts so that they could not hear?

101. Such were the towns whose story We (thus) relate unto you: there came indeed to them their Apostles with clear (Signs): But they would not believe what

ablaghtukum Risaalaati Rabbee wa naṣaḥtu lakum fakayfa aasaa 'alaa qawmin kaafireen.
(Section 11)

94. Wa maaa arsalnaa fee qaryatim-min-Nabiyyin illaaa akhaznaaa ahlahaa bil-baåsaaa'i waḍḍarraaa'i la'allahum yaḍḍarra'oon.

95. Summa baddalnaa makaa-nas-sayyi'atil-ḥasanata ḥattaa 'afaw wa qaaloo qad massa aabaaa'anaḍ-ḍarraaa'u wassar-raaa'u fa-akhaznaahum baghta-tañw-wa hum laa yash'uroon.

96. Wa law anna ahlal-quraaa aamanoo wattaqaw lafataḥnaa 'alayhim barakaatim-minas-samaaa'i wal-arḍi wa laakin kazzaboo fa-akhaznaahum bimaa kaanoo yaksiboon.

97. Afa-amina ahlul-quraaa añy-yaåtiyahum baåsunaa bayaatañw-wa hum naaa'imoon.

98. Awa amina ahlul-quraaa añy-yaåtiyahum baåsunaa ḍuḥañw-wa hum yal'aboon.

99. Afa-aminoo makral-laah; falaa yaåmanu makral-laahi illal-qawmul-khaasiroon.
(Section 12)

100. Awa lam yahdi lillazeena yariṣoonal-arḍa mim ba'di ahlihaaa al-law nashaaa'u aṣabnaahum bizunoobihim; wa naṭba'u 'alaa quloobihim fahum laa yasma'oon.

101. Tilkal-quraa naquṣṣu 'alayka min ambaaa'ihaa; wa laqad jaaa'at-hum Rusuluhum bilbayyinaati famaa kaanoo liyu'minoo bimaa

they had rejected before. Thus does Allah seal up the hearts of those who reject faith.

102. Most of the men We did not find (true) to their covenant: but most of them We found rebellious and disobedient.

103. Then after them We sent Moses with Our Signs to Pharaoh and his chiefs, but they wrongfully rejected them: So see what was the end of those who made mischief.

104. Moses said: "O Pharaoh! I am an Apostle from the Lord of the worlds,-

105. One for whom it is right to say nothing but truth about Allah. Now I have come to you (people), from your Lord, with a clear (Sign): So let the Children of Israel depart along with me."

106. (Pharaoh) said: "If indeed you have come with a Sign, show it forth,- if you are telling the truth."

107. Then (Moses) threw his rod, and behold! it was a serpent, plain (for all to see)!

108. And he drew out his hand, and behold! it was white to all beholders!

109. Said the Chiefs of the people of Pharaoh: "This is indeed a sorcerer well-versed.

110. "His plan is to get you out of your land: then what is it you counsel?"

111. They said: "Keep him and his brother in suspense (for a while); and send to the cities men to collect-

112. And bring up to you all (our) sorcerers well-versed."

113. So there came the sorcerers to Pharaoh: They said, "of course we shall have a (suitable) reward if we win!"

114. He said: "Yes, (and more),- for you shall in that case be (raised to posts) nearest (to my person)."

---

kazzaboo min qabl; kazaalika yatba'ul-laahu 'alaa quloobil-kaafireen.

102. Wa maa wajadnaa li-aksarihim min 'ahd; wa iñw-wajadnaaa aksarahum lafaasi-qeen.

103. Summa ba'asnaa mim ba'dihim Moosaa bi-Aayaa-tinaaa ilaa Fir'awna wa mala-i-hee fazalamoo bihaa fanzur kayfa kaana 'aaqibatul-mufsideen.

104. Wa qaala Moosaa yaa Fir'awnu innee Rasoolum-mir-Rabbil-'aalameen.

105. Haqeequn 'alaaa al-laaa aqoola 'alal-laahi illal-haqq; qad ji'tukum bibayyinatim-mir-Rabbikum fa-arsil ma'iya Baneee Israaa'eel.

106. Qaala in kunta ji'ta bi-Aayatin faati bihaaa in kunta minas-saadiqeen.

107. Fa-alqaa 'asaahu fa-izaa hiya su'baanum-mubeen.

108. Wa naza'a yadahoo fa-izaa hiya baydaaa'u linnaazireen.

109. Qaalal-mala-u min qawmi Fir'awna inna haazaa lasaa-hirun 'aleem.

110. Yureedu añy-yukhrijakum min ardikum famaazaa taa-muroon.

111. Qaaloo arjih wa akhaahu wa arsil filmadaaa'ini haashi-reen.

112. Yaatooka bikulli saahirin 'aleem.

113. Wa jaaa'as-saharatu Fir-'awna qaaloo inna lanaa la-ajran in kunnaa nahnul-ghaalibeen.

114. Qaala na'am wa innakum laminal-muqarrabeen.

115. They said: "O Moses! will you throw (first), or shall we have the (first) throw?"

116. Said Moses: "You throw (first)." So when they threw, they bewitched the eyes of the people, and struck terror into them: for they showed a great (feat of) magic.

117. We put it into Moses's mind by inspiration: "Throw (now) your rod":and behold! it swallows up straight away all the falsehoods which they fake!

118. Thus truth was confirmed, and all that they did was made of no effect.

119. So the (great ones) were vanquished there and then, and were made to look small.

120. But the sorcerers fell down prostrate in adoration.

121. Saying: "We believe in the Lord of the Worlds,-

122. "The Lord of Moses and Aaron."

123. Said Pharaoh: "Do you believe in Him before I give you permission? Surely this is a trick which you have planned in the city to drive out its people: but soon you shall know (the consequences).

124. "Be sure I will cut off your hands and your feet on opposite sides, and I will cause you all to die on the cross."

125. They said: "For us, We are but sent back to our Lord:

126. "But you wreak your vengeance on us simply because we believed in the Signs of our Lord when they reached us! Our Lord! pour out on us patience and constancy, and take our souls unto You as Muslims (who bow to Your Will)!

127. Said the chiefs of Pharaoh's people:" Will you leave Moses and his people, to spread mischief in the land, and to abandon you and your gods?" He said:

115. Qaaloo yaa Moosaaa immaaa an tulqiya wa immaaa an nakoona naḥnul-mulqeen.

116. Qaala alqoo falam-maaa alqaw saharooo a'yunannaasi wastarhaboohum wa jaaa'oo bisiḥrin 'aẓeem.

117. Wa awḥaynaaa ilaa Moosaaa an alqi 'aṣaaka fa-izaa hiya talqafu maa yaåfikoon.

118. Fawaqa'al-ḥaqqu wa baṭala maa kaanoo ya'maloon.

119. Faghuliboo hunaalika wanqalaboo ṣaaghireen.

120. Wa ulqiyas-saḥaratu saajideen.

121. Qaalooo aamannaa bi-Rabbil-'aalameen.

122. Rabbi Moosaa wa Haaroon.

123. Qaala Fir'awnu aamantum bihee qabla an aazana lakum; inna haazaa lamakrum-makartumoohu filmadeenati litukhrijoo minhaaa ahlahaa fasawfa ta'lamoon.

124. La-uqaṭṭi'anna aydiyakum wa arjulakum min khilaafin summa la-uṣallibannakum ajma'een.

125. Qaalooo innaaa ilaa Rabbinaa munqaliboon.

126. Wa maa tanqimu minnaaa illaaa an aamannaa bi-Aayaati Rabbinaa lammaa jaaa'atnaa; Rabbanaaa afrigh 'alaynaa ṣabrañw-wa tawaffanaa muslimeen. **(Section 14)**

127. Wa qaalal-mala-u min qawmi Fir'awna atazaru Moosaa wa qawmahoo liyufsidoo fil-arḍi wa yazaraka wa aalihatak; qaala

قَالُوا يَٰمُوسَىٰٓ إِمَّآ أَن تُلْقِىَ وَإِمَّآ أَن نَّكُونَ نَحْنُ الْمُلْقِينَ ۝

قَالَ أَلْقُوا ۖ فَلَمَّآ أَلْقَوْا سَحَرُوٓا أَعْيُنَ النَّاسِ وَاسْتَرْهَبُوهُمْ وَجَآءُو بِسِحْرٍ عَظِيمٍ ۝

وَأَوْحَيْنَآ إِلَىٰ مُوسَىٰٓ أَنْ أَلْقِ عَصَاكَ ۖ فَإِذَا هِىَ تَلْقَفُ مَا يَأْفِكُونَ ۝

فَوَقَعَ الْحَقُّ وَبَطَلَ مَا كَانُوا يَعْمَلُونَ ۝

فَغُلِبُوا هُنَالِكَ وَانقَلَبُوا صَاغِرِينَ ۝

وَأُلْقِىَ السَّحَرَةُ سَٰجِدِينَ ۝

قَالُوٓا آمَنَّا بِرَبِّ الْعَٰلَمِينَ ۝

رَبِّ مُوسَىٰ وَهَٰرُونَ ۝

قَالَ فِرْعَوْنُ آمَنتُم بِهِ قَبْلَ أَنْ آذَنَ لَكُمْ ۖ إِنَّ هَٰذَا لَمَكْرٌ مَّكَرْتُمُوهُ فِى الْمَدِينَةِ لِتُخْرِجُوا مِنْهَآ أَهْلَهَا ۖ فَسَوْفَ تَعْلَمُونَ ۝

لَأُقَطِّعَنَّ أَيْدِيَكُمْ وَأَرْجُلَكُم مِّنْ خِلَافٍ ثُمَّ لَأُصَلِّبَنَّكُمْ أَجْمَعِينَ ۝

قَالُوٓا إِنَّآ إِلَىٰ رَبِّنَا مُنقَلِبُونَ ۝

وَمَا تَنقِمُ مِنَّآ إِلَّآ أَنْ آمَنَّا بِآيَٰتِ رَبِّنَا لَمَّا جَآءَتْنَا ۚ رَبَّنَآ أَفْرِغْ عَلَيْنَا صَبْرًا وَتَوَفَّنَا مُسْلِمِينَ ۝

وَقَالَ الْمَلَأُ مِن قَوْمِ فِرْعَوْنَ أَتَذَرُ مُوسَىٰ وَقَوْمَهُ لِيُفْسِدُوا فِى الْأَرْضِ وَيَذَرَكَ وَآلِهَتَكَ ۚ قَالَ

"We will slay their male children; we will save alive (only) their females; and we have irresistible power over them."

128. Moses said to his people: "Pray for help from Allah, and (wait) in patience and constancy: for the earth is Allah's, to give as a heritage to such of His servants as He pleases; and the end is (best) for the righteous.

129. They said: "We have had (nothing but) trouble, both before and after you came to us." He said: "It may be that your Lord will destroy your enemy and make you inheritors in the earth; that so He may try you by your deeds."

130. We punished the people of Pharaoh with years (of droughts) and shortness of crops; that they might receive admonition.

131. But when good (times) came, they said, "This is due to us;" when gripped by calamity, they ascribed it to evil omens connected with Moses and those with him! Behold! in truth the omens of evil are theirs in Allah's sight, but most of them do not understand!

132. They said (to Moses): "Whatever be the Signs you bring, to work therewith your sorcery on us, we shall never believe in you.

133. So We sent (plagues) on them: wholesale Death, Locusts, Lice, Frogs, and Blood: Signs openly self-explained: but they were steeped in arrogance,- a people given to sin.

134. Every time the Chastisement fell on them, they said: "O Moses!

sanuqattilu abnaaa'ahum wa nastaḥyee nisaaa'ahum wa innaa fawqahum qaahiroon.

128. Qaala Moosaa liqawmihis-ta'eenoo billaahi waṣbiroo innal-arḍa lillaahi yoorisuhaa mañy-yashaaa'u min 'ibaadihee wal'aaqibatu lilmuttaqeen.

129. Qaalooo oozeenaa min qabli an taåtiyanaa wa mim ba'di maa ji'tanaa; qaala 'asaa Rabbukum añy-yuhlika 'aduwwakum wa yastakhlifakum fil-arḍi fayanẓura kayfa ta'maloon. **(Section 15)**

130. Wa laqad akhaznaaa Aala Fir'awna bis-sineena wa naqṣim-minas-ṣamaraati la'allahum yazzakkaroon.

131. Fa-izaa jaaa'at-humulḥasanatu qaaloo lanaa haazihee wa in tuṣibhum sayyi'atuñy-yaṭṭayyaroo bi Moosaa wa mam-ma'ah; alaaa innamaa ṭaaa'iruhum 'indal-laahi wa laakinna aksarahum laa ya'lamoon.

132. Wa qaaloo mahmaa taåtinaa bihee min Aayaatil-litasharanaa bihaa famaa naḥnu laka bimu'mineen.

133. Fa-arsalnaa 'alayhimuṭ-ṭoofaana waljaraada walqummala waddafaadi'a waddama Aayaatim-mufaṣṣalaatin fastakbaroo wa kaanoo qawmam-mujrimeen.

134. Wa lammaa waqa'a 'alayhimur-rijzu qaaloo yaa Moosad-

on our behalf call on your Lord in virtue of his promise to you: If you will remove the Chastisement from us, we shall truly believe in you, and we shall send away the Children of Israel with you."

135. But every time We removed the plague from them according to a fixed term which they had to fulfil,- Behold! they broke their word!

136. So We exacted retribution from them: We drowned them in the sea, because they rejected Our Signs and failed to take warning from them.

137. And We made a people, considered weak (and of no account), inheritors of lands in both East and West, - lands whereon We sent down Our blessings. The fair promise of your Lord was fulfilled for the Children of Israel, because they had patience and constancy, and We levelled to the ground the great works and fine buildings which Pharaoh and his people erected (with such pride).

138. We took the Children of Israel (with safety) across the sea. They came upon a people devoted entirely to some idols they had. They said: "O Moses! fashion for us a god like the gods they have." He said: "Surely you are a people without knowledge.

139. "As to these folks,- the cult they are in is (but) a fragment of a ruin, and vain is the (worship) which they practise."

140. He said: "Shall I seek for you a god other than the (true) God, when it is Allah who has endowed you with gifts above the nations?"

141. And remember We rescued you from Pharaoh's people, who afflicted you with the worst of penalties, Who slew

'u lanaa rabbaka bimaa 'ahida 'indaka la'in kashafta 'annar-rijza lanu'minanna laka wa lanursilanna ma'aka Baneee Israaa'eel.

135. Falammaa kashafnaa 'anhumur-rijza ilaa ajalin hum baalighoohu izaa hum yankusoon.

136. Fantaqamnaa minhum fa-aghraqnaahum fil-yammi bi-annahum kazzaboo bi-Aayaatinaa wa kaanoo 'anhaa ghaafileen.

137. Wa awrasnal-qawmal-lazeena kaanoo yustaḍ'afoona mashaariqal-arḍi wa maghaari-bahal-latee baaraknaa feehaa wa tammat Kalimatu Rabbikal-ḥusnaa 'alaa Baneee Israaa'eela bimaa ṣabaroo wa dammarnaa maa kaana yaṣna'u Fir'awnu wa qawmuhoo wa maa kaanoo ya'rishoon.

138. Wa jaawaznaa bi-Baneee Israaa'eelal-baḥra fa-ataw 'alaa qawminy-ya'kufoona 'alaaa aṣnaamil-lahum; qaaloo yaa Moosaj'al-lanaaa ilaahan kamaa lahum aalihah; qaala innakum qawmun tajhaloon.

139. Inna haaaulaaa'i mutab-barum-maa hum feehi wa baaṭilum-maa kaanoo ya'maloon.

140. Qaala a-ghayral-laahi abgheekum ilaahañw-wa Huwa faḍḍalakum 'alal-'aalameen.

141. Wa iz anjaynaakum min Aali Fir'awna yasoomoo-nakum sooo'al-'azaab, yuqat-tiloona

your male children and saved alive your females: in that was a momentous trial from your Lord.

142. We appointed for Moses thirty nights, and completed (the period) with ten (more): thus was completed the term (of communion) with his Lord, forty nights. And Moses had charged his brother Aaron (before he went up): "Act for me amongst my people: do right, and follow not the way of those who do mischief."

143. When Moses came to the place appointed by Us, and his Lord addressed him, He said: "O my Lord! show (Yourself) to me, that I may look upon You." Allah said: "By no means can you see Me (direct); But look upon the mount; if it abide in its place, then shall you see Me." When his Lord manifested His glory on the Mount, He made it as dust, and Moses fell down in a swoon. When he recovered his senses he said: "Glory be to You! to You I turn in repentance, and I am the first to believe."

144. (Allah) said: "O Moses! I have chosen you above (other) men, by the mission I (have given you) and the words I (have spoken to you): take then the (revelation) which I give you, and be of those who give thanks."

145. And We ordained laws for him in the tablets in all matters, both commanding and explaining all things, (and said): "Take and hold these with firmness, and enjoin your people to hold fast by the best in the precepts: soon shall I show you the homes of the wicked,- (How they lie desolate)."

146. Those who behave arrogantly on the earth in defiance of right - I will turn them away from My Signs: Even if they see all the Signs, they will not believe in them;

abnaaa'akum wa yastaḥyoona nisaaa'akum; wa fee zaalikum balaaa'um-mir-Rabbikum 'azeem. **(Section 16)**

142. Wa waa'adnaa Moosaa salaaseena laylatañw-wa at-mamnaahaa bi'ashrin fatamma meeqaatu Rabbiheee arba'eena laylah; wa qaala Moosaa liakheehi Haaroonakh-luf-nee fee qawmee wa aşliḥ wa laa tattabi' sabeelal-mufsideen.

143. Wa lammaa jaaa'a Moosaa limeeqaatinaa wa kallamahoo Rabbuhoo qaala Rabbi arineee anzur ilayk; qaala lan taraanee wa laakininzur ilal-jabali fa-instaqarra makaanahoo fasawfa taraanee; falammaa tajallaa Rabbuhoo liljabali ja'alahoo dakkañw-wa kharra Moosaa şa'iqaa; falammaaa afaaqa qaala Subḥaanaka tubtu ilayka wa ana awwalul-mu'mineen.

144. Qaala yaa Moosaaa inniş-ţafaytuka 'alan-naasi bi-Risaalaatee wa bi-Kalaamee fakhuz maaa aataytuka wa kum-minash-shaakireen.

145. Wa katabnaa lahoo fil-alwaaḥi min kulli shay'im-maw'izatañw-wa tafşeelal-likulli shay'in fakhuzhaa biquwwatiñw-waåmur qawmaka yaåkhuzoo bi-aḥsanihaa; sa-ooreekum daaral-faasiqeen.

146.Sa-aşrifu 'an Aayaatiyal-lazeena yatakabbaroona fil-arḍi bighayril-ḥaqq; wa iñy-yaraw kulla Aayatil-laa yu'minoo bihaa

and if they see the way of right conduct, they will not adopt it as the way; but if they see the way of error, that is the way they will adopt. For they have rejected Our Signs, and failed to take warning from them.

147. Those who reject Our Signs and the Meeting in the Hereafter,- vain are their deeds: can they expect to be rewarded except as they have wrought?

148. The people of Moses made, in his absence, out of their ornaments, the image of a calf, (for worship) having lowing sound. Did they not see that it could neither speak to them, nor show them the way? They took it for worship and they did wrong.

149. When they repented, and saw that they had erred, they said: "If our Lord have not mercy upon us and forgive us, we shall indeed be of those who perish."

150. When Moses came back to his people, angry and grieved, he said: "Evil it is that you have done in my place in my absence: did you make haste to bring on the judgment of your Lord?" He put down the Tablets, seized his brother by (the hair of) his head, and dragged him to him. Aaron said: "Son of my mother! The people did indeed reckon me as nothing, and went near to slaying me! Make not the enemies rejoice over my misfortune, nor count you me amongst the people of sin."

151. Moses prayed: "O my Lord! forgive me and my brother! Admit us to Your mercy! for You are the Most Merciful of those who show mercy!"

152. Those who took the calf (for worship) will indeed be

wa iñy-yaraw sabeelar-rushdi laa yattakhizoohu sabeelañw wa iñy-yaraw sabeelal-ghayyi yatta-khizoohu sabeelaa; zaalika bi-annahum kazzaboo bi-Aayaatinaa wa kaanoo 'anhaa ghaafileen.

147. Wallazeena kazzaboo bi-Aayaatinaa wa liqaaa'il-Aakhirati habitat 'amaaluhum; hal yujzawna illaa maa kaanoo ya'maloon. **(Section 17)**

148. Wattakhaza qawmu Moosaa mim ba'dihee min huliyyihim 'ijlan jasadal-lahoo khuwaar; alam yaraw annahoo laa yukallimuhum wa laa yahdeehim sabeelaa; ittakha-zoohu wa kaanoo zaalimeen.

149. Wa lammaa suqita feee aydeehim wa ra-aw annahum qad dalloo qaaloo la'il-lam yarhamnaa Rabbunaa wa yaghfir lanaa lanakoonanna minal-khaasireen.

150. Wa lammaa raja'a Moosaaa ilaa qawmihee ghad-baana asifan qaala bi'samaa khalaftumoonee mim ba'dee a-'ajiltum amra Rabbikum wa alqal-alwaaha wa akhaza biraåsi akheehi yajurruhooo ilayh; qaalab-na-umma innal-qawmas tad'afoonee wa kaadoo yaqtu-loonanee; falaa tushmit biyal-a'daaa'a wa laa taj'alnee ma'al-qawmiz-zaalimeen.

151. Qaala Rabbigh-fir lee wa li-akhee wa adkhilnaa fee rahmatika wa Anta arhamur-raahimeen. **(Section 18)**

152 Innal-lazeenat-takhazul-'ijla sa-yanaaluhum

overwhelmed with wrath from their Lord, and with shame in this life: thus do We recompense those who invent (falsehoods).

ghaḍabum-mir-Rabbihim wa zillatun fil-ḥayaatid-dunyaa; wa kazaalika najzil-muftareen.

غَضَبٌ مِّنْ رَّبِّهِمْ وَذِلَّةٌ فِي الْحَيَوةِ الدُّنْيَا ۚ وَكَذَٰلِكَ نَجْزِى الْمُفْتَرِيْنَ ۝

153. But those who do wrong but repent thereafter and (truly) believe,- verily your Lord is thereafter Oft-Forgiving, Most Merciful.

153. Wallazeena 'amilus-sayyi-aati ṣumma taaboo mim ba'dihaa wa aamanooo inna Rabbaka mim ba'dihaa la-Ghafoorur-Raḥeem.

وَالَّذِيْنَ عَمِلُوا السَّيِّئَاتِ ثُمَّ تَابُوْا مِنْ بَعْدِهَا وَاٰمَنُوْۤا ۙ إِنَّ رَبَّكَ مِنْ بَعْدِهَا لَغَفُوْرٌ رَّحِيْمٌ ۝

154. When the anger of Moses was appeased, he took up the Tablets: in the writing thereon was Guidance and Mercy for such as fear their Lord.

154. Wa lammaa sakata 'am-Moosal-ghaḍabu akhazal-al-waaḥa wa fee nuskhatihaa hudañw-wa raḥmatul-lillazeena hum li-Rabbihim yarhaboon.

وَلَمَّا سَكَتَ عَنْ مُّوسَى الْغَضَبُ أَخَذَ الْأَلْوَاحَ ۖ وَفِيْ نُسْخَتِهَا هُدًى وَّرَحْمَةٌ لِّلَّذِيْنَ هُمْ لِرَبِّهِمْ يَرْهَبُوْنَ ۝

155. And Moses chose seventy of his people for Our place of meeting: when they were seized with violent quaking, he prayed: "O my Lord! if it had been Your will You could have destroyed, long before, both them and me: would You destroy us for the deeds of the foolish ones among us? this is no more than trial from You by it. You cause whom You will to stray, and You lead whom You will into the right path. You are our Protector: so forgive us and give us Your mercy; for You are the best of those who forgive.

155. Wakhtaara Moosaa qawmahoo sab'eena rajulal-limeeqaatinaa falammaaa akhazat-humur-rajfatu qaala Rabbi law shi'ta ahlaktahum min qablu wa iyyaaya atuhlikunaa bimaa fa'alas-sufahaaa'u minnaa in hiya illaa fitnatuka tuḍillu bihaa man tashaaa'u wa tahdee man tashaaaa'u Anta waliyyunaa faghfir lanaa warḥamnaa wa Anta khayrul-ghaafireen.

وَاخْتَارَ مُوسَى قَوْمَهُ سَبْعِيْنَ رَجُلًا لِّمِيْقَاتِنَا ۚ فَلَمَّا أَخَذَتْهُمُ الرَّجْفَةُ قَالَ رَبِّ لَوْ شِئْتَ أَهْلَكْتَهُمْ مِّنْ قَبْلُ وَإِيَّايَ ۖ أَتُهْلِكُنَا بِمَا فَعَلَ السُّفَهَاءُ مِنَّا ۚ إِنْ هِيَ إِلَّا فِتْنَتُكَ ۖ تُضِلُّ بِهَا مَنْ تَشَاءُ وَتَهْدِيْ مَنْ تَشَاءُ ۚ أَنْتَ وَلِيُّنَا فَاغْفِرْ لَنَا وَارْحَمْنَا ۖ وَأَنْتَ خَيْرُ الْغَافِرِيْنَ ۝

156. "And ordain for us that which is good, in this life and in the Hereafter: for we have turned unto You." He said: "With My punishment I visit whom I will; but My mercy extends to all things. That (mercy) I shall ordain for those who do right, and pay Zakat, and those who believe in Our Signs;-

156. Waktub lanaa fee haazi-hid-dunyaa ḥasanataῆw-wa fil-Aakhirati innaa hudnaaa ilayk; qaala 'azaabeee uṣeebu bihee man ashaaa'u wa raḥmatee wasi'at kulla shay'; fasa-aktubuhaa lillazeena yatta-qoona wa yu'toonaz-Zakaata wallazeena hum bi-Aayaatinaa yu'minoon.

وَاكْتُبْ لَنَا فِيْ هَٰذِهِ الدُّنْيَا حَسَنَةً وَّفِي الْأَخِرَةِ إِنَّا هُدْنَاۤ إِلَيْكَ ۚ قَالَ عَذَابِيْ أُصِيْبُ بِهِ مَنْ أَشَاءُ ۖ وَرَحْمَتِيْ وَسِعَتْ كُلَّ شَيْءٍ ۚ فَسَأَكْتُبُهَا لِلَّذِيْنَ يَتَّقُوْنَ وَيُؤْتُوْنَ الزَّكَوةَ وَالَّذِيْنَ هُمْ بِاٰيٰتِنَا يُؤْمِنُوْنَ ۝

157. "Those who follow the Apostle, the unlettered Prophet,

157. Allazeena yattabi'oonar-Rasoolan-Nabiyyal-

الَّذِيْنَ يَتَّبِعُوْنَ الرَّسُوْلَ النَّبِيَّ

whom they find mentioned in their own (scriptures),- in the Torah and the Gospel;- for he commands them what is just and forbids them what is evil; he allows them as lawful what is good (and pure) and prohibits them from what is bad (and impure); He releases them from their heavy burdens and from the yokes that are upon them. So it is those who believe in him, honour him, help him, and follow the light which is sent down with him,- it is they who will prosper."

158. Say: "O men! I am sent unto you all, as the Apostle of Allah, to Whom belongs the dominion of the heavens and the earth: there is no god but He: it is He that gives both life and death. So believe in Allah and His Apostle, the unlettered Prophet, who believes in Allah and His Words: follow him that (so) you may be guided."

159. Of the people of Moses there is a section who guide and do justice in the light of truth.

160. We divided them into twelve tribes or nations. We directed Moses by inspiration, when his (thirsty) people asked him for water: "Strike the rock with your staff": out of it there gushed forth twelve springs: each group knew its own place for water. We gave them the shade of clouds, and sent down to them manna and quails, (saying): "Eat of the good things We have provided for you": (but they rebelled); to Us they did no harm,

ummiyyal-lazee yajidoonahoo maktooban 'indahum fit-Tawraati wal-Injeeli yaâ-muruhum bilma'roofi wa yanhaahum 'anil-munkari wa yuḥillu lahumuṭ-ṭayyibaati wa yuḥarrimu 'alayhimul-kha-baaa'iṣa wa yaḍa'u 'anhum iṣrahum wal-aghlaalal-latee kaanat 'alayhim; fallazeena aamanoo bihee wa 'azzaroohu wa naṣaroohu wattaba'un-noor-alazeee unzila ma'ahooo ulaaa'ika humul-mufliḥoon.

(Section 19)

158. Qul yaaa ayyuhan-naasu innee Rasoolul-laahi ilaykum jamee'anil-lazee lahoo mulkus-samaawaati wal-arḍi laaa ilaaha illaa Huwa yuḥyee wa yumeetu fa-aaminoo billaahi wa Rasoolihin-Nabiyyil-ummiy-yil-lazee yu'minu billaahi wa Kalimaatihee wattabi'oohu la'allakum tahtadoon.

159. Wa min qawmi Moosaaa ummatuñy-yahdoona bilḥaqqi wa bihee ya'diloon.

160. Wa qaṭṭa'naahumuṣ-natay 'ashrata asbaaṭan umamaa; wa awḥaynaaa ilaa Moosaaa iẕis-tasqaahu qawmuhooo aniḍ-rib bi'aṣaakal-ḥajara fambajasat minhuṣ-nataa 'ashrata 'aynan qad 'alima kullu unaasim-mashrabahum; wa zallalnaa 'alayhimul-ghamaama wa anzalnaa 'alayhimul-Manna was-Salwaa kuloo min ṭayyi-baati maa razaqnaakum; wa maa zalamoonaa

الْأُمِّيَّ الَّذِى يَجِدُونَهُ مَكْتُوبًا عِنْدَهُمْ فِى التَّوْرَاةِ وَالْإِنْجِيلِ يَأْمُرُهُمْ بِالْمَعْرُوفِ وَيَنْهَاهُمْ عَنِ الْمُنْكَرِ وَيُحِلُّ لَهُمُ الطَّيِّبَاتِ وَيُحَرِّمُ عَلَيْهِمُ الْخَبَائِثَ وَيَضَعُ عَنْهُمْ إِصْرَهُمْ وَالْأَغْلَالَ الَّتِى كَانَتْ عَلَيْهِمْ فَالَّذِينَ آمَنُوا بِهِ وَعَزَّرُوهُ وَنَصَرُوهُ وَاتَّبَعُوا النُّورَ الَّذِى أُنْزِلَ مَعَهُ أُولَئِكَ هُمُ الْمُفْلِحُونَ ۞

قُلْ يَا أَيُّهَا النَّاسُ إِنِّى رَسُولُ اللَّهِ إِلَيْكُمْ جَمِيعًا الَّذِى لَهُ مُلْكُ السَّمَاوَاتِ وَالْأَرْضِ لَا إِلَهَ إِلَّا هُوَ يُحْيِى وَيُمِيتُ فَآمِنُوا بِاللَّهِ وَرَسُولِهِ النَّبِيِّ الْأُمِّيِّ الَّذِى يُؤْمِنُ بِاللَّهِ وَكَلِمَاتِهِ وَاتَّبِعُوهُ لَعَلَّكُمْ تَهْتَدُونَ ۞

وَمِنْ قَوْمِ مُوسَى أُمَّةٌ يَهْدُونَ بِالْحَقِّ وَبِهِ يَعْدِلُونَ ۞

وَقَطَّعْنَاهُمُ اثْنَتَىْ عَشْرَةَ أَسْبَاطًا أُمَمًا وَأَوْحَيْنَا إِلَى مُوسَى إِذِ اسْتَسْقَاهُ قَوْمُهُ أَنِ اضْرِبْ بِعَصَاكَ الْحَجَرَ فَانْبَجَسَتْ مِنْهُ اثْنَتَا عَشْرَةَ عَيْنًا قَدْ عَلِمَ كُلُّ أُنَاسٍ مَشْرَبَهُمْ وَظَلَّلْنَا عَلَيْهِمُ الْغَمَامَ وَأَنْزَلْنَا عَلَيْهِمُ الْمَنَّ وَالسَّلْوَى كُلُوا مِنْ طَيِّبَاتِ مَا رَزَقْنَاكُمْ وَمَا ظَلَمُونَا

but they harmed their own souls.

161. And remember it was said to them: "Dwell in this town and eat therein as you wish, but say the word of humility and enter the gate in a posture of humility: We shall forgive you your faults; We shall increase (the portion of) those who do good."

162. But the transgressors among them changed the word from that which had been given them so We sent on them a plague from heaven. For that they repeatedly transgressed.

163. Ask them concerning the town standing close by the sea. Behold! they transgressed in the matter of the Sabbath. For on the day of their Sabbath their fish did come to them, openly holding up their heads, but on the day they had no Sabbath, they came not: thus did We make a trial of them, for they were given to transgression.

164. When some of them said: "Why do you preach to a people whom Allah will destroy or visit with a terrible punishment?"—said the preachers:" To discharge our duty to your Lord, and perchance they may fear Him."

165. When they disregarded the warnings that had been given them, We rescued those who forbade Evil; but We visited the wrong-doers with a grievous punishment because they were given to transgression.

166. When in their insolence they transgressed (all) prohibitions, We said to them: "Be you apes, despised and rejected."

167. Behold! Your Lord did declare that He would send against them, to the Day of Judgment, those who would afflict them with

wa laakin kaanooo anfusahum yazlimoon.

161. Wa iz qeela lahumuskunoo haazihil-qaryata wa kuloo minhaa haysu shi'tum wa qooloo hittatuñw-wadkhulul-baaba sujjadan naghfir lakum khatee'aatikum; sanazeedul-muhsineen.

162. Fabaddalal-lazeena zalamoo minhum qawlan ghayral-lazee qeela lahum faarsalnaa 'alayhim rijzamminas-samaaa'i bimaa kaanoo yazlimoon.   (Section 20)

163. Was'alhum 'anil-qaryatillatee kaanat haadiratal-bahri iz ya'doona fis-Sabti iz taåteehim heetaanuhum yawma Sabtihim shurra'añw-wa yawma laa yasbitoona laa taåteehim; kazaalika nabloohum bimaa kaanoo yafsuqoon.

164. Wa iz qaalat ummatumminhum lima ta'izoona qawmanil-laahu muhlikuhum aw mu'azzibuhum 'azaaban shadeedan qaaloo ma'ziratan ilaa Rabbikum wa la'allahum yattaqoon.

165. Falammaa nasoo maa zukkiroo bihee anjaynallazeena yanhawna 'anis-sooo'i wa akhaznal-lazeena zalamoo bi'azaabim ba'eesim bimaa kaanoo yafsuqoon.

166. Falammaa 'ataw 'ammaa nuhoo 'anhu qulnaa lahum koonoo qiradatan khaasi'een.

167. Wa iz ta-azzana Rabbuka la-yab'asanna 'alayhim ilaa Yawmil-Qiyaamati mañy-yasoomuhum

grievous chastisement. Your Lord is quick in retribution, but He is also Oft-forgiving, Most Merciful.

168. We broke them up into sections on this earth. There are among them some that are the righteous, and some that are the opposite. We have tried them with both prosperity and adversity: in order that they might turn (to us).

169. After them succeeded an (evil) generation: they inherited the Book, but they chose (for themselves) the vanities of this world, saying (for excuse): "(Everything) will be forgiven us." (Even so), if similar vanities came their way, they would (again) seize them. Was not the covenant of the Book taken from them, that they would not ascribe to Allah anything but the truth? And they study what is in the Book. But best for the righteous is the home in the Hereafter. Will you not understand?

170. As to those who hold fast by the Book and establish regular prayer,- never shall We suffer the reward of the righteous to perish.

171. When We raised the Mount over them, as if it had been a canopy, and they thought it was going to fall on them (We said): "Hold firmly to what We have given you, and bring (ever) to remembrance what is therein; perchance you may fear Allah."

172. When your Lord drew forth from the Children of Adam- from their loins - their descendants, and made them testify concerning themselves, (saying): "Am I not your Lord (who cherishes and sustains you)?"- They said: "Yes! We do testify!" (This), lest you should say on the Day of Judgment: "Of this we were never mindful":

sooo'al-'azaab; inna Rabbaka lasaree'ul-'iqaab, wa innahoo la-Ghafoorur-Raheem.

168. Wa qatta'naahum fil-ardi umamam minhumus-saalihoona wa minhum doona zaalika wa balawnaahum bilhasanaati wassayyi-aati la'allahum yarji'oon.

169. Fakhalafa mim ba'dihim khalfuñw-warisul-Kitaaba yaa-khuzoona 'arada haazal-adnaa wa yaqooloona sayughfaru lanaa wa iñy-yaatihim 'aradum-misluhoo yaakhuzooh; alam yu'khaz 'alayhim meesaaqul-Kitaabi al-laa yaqooloo 'alal-laahi illal-haqqa wa darasoo maa feeh; wad-Daarul-Aakhiratu khayrul-lillazeena yattaqoon; afalaa ta'qiloon.

170. Wallazeena yumas-sikoona bil-Kitaabi wa aqaamus-Salaata innaa laa nudee'u ajral-musliheen.

171. Wa iz nataqnal-jabala fawqahum ka-annahoo zulla-tuñw-wa zannooo annahoo waaqi'um bihim khuzoo maaa aataynaakum biquwwatiñw-wazkuroo maa feehi la'allakum tattaqoon. **(Section 21)**

172. Wa iz akhaza Rabbuka mim Baneee Aadama min zuhoorihim zurriyyatahum wa ash-hadahum 'alaaa anfusihim alastu bi-Rabbikum qaaloo balaa shahidnaaa; an taqooloo Yawmal-Qiyaamati innaa kunnaa 'an haazaa ghaafileen.

سُوٓءُ الْعَذَابِ ۗ إِنَّ رَبَّكَ لَسَرِيعُ الْعِقَابِ ۖ وَإِنَّهُ لَغَفُورٌ رَّحِيمٌ ۝

وَقَطَّعْنَاهُمْ فِى الْأَرْضِ أُمَمًا ۖ مِنْهُمُ الصّٰلِحُونَ وَمِنْهُمْ دُونَ ذَٰلِكَ ۖ وَبَلَوْنَاهُمْ بِالْحَسَنَاتِ وَالسَّيِّئَاتِ لَعَلَّهُمْ يَرْجِعُونَ ۝

فَخَلَفَ مِنۢ بَعْدِهِمْ خَلْفٌ وَرِثُوا الْكِتَابَ يَأْخُذُونَ عَرَضَ هٰذَا الْأَدْنٰى وَيَقُولُونَ سَيُغْفَرُ لَنَا ۚ وَإِن يَأْتِهِمْ عَرَضٌ مِثْلُهُ يَأْخُذُوهُ ۚ أَلَمْ يُؤْخَذْ عَلَيْهِمْ مِيثَاقُ الْكِتَابِ أَن لَّا يَقُولُوا عَلَى اللّٰهِ إِلَّا الْحَقَّ وَدَرَسُوا مَا فِيهِ ۗ وَالدَّارُ الْأَخِرَةُ خَيْرٌ لِّلَّذِينَ يَتَّقُونَ ۗ أَفَلَا تَعْقِلُونَ ۝

وَالَّذِينَ يُمَسِّكُونَ بِالْكِتَابِ وَأَقَامُوا الصَّلٰوةَ ۚ إِنَّا لَا نُضِيعُ أَجْرَ الْمُصْلِحِينَ ۝

وَإِذْ نَتَقْنَا الْجَبَلَ فَوْقَهُمْ كَأَنَّهُ ظُلَّةٌ وَظَنُّوا أَنَّهُ وَاقِعٌ بِهِمْ ۚ خُذُوا مَا آتَيْنَاكُم بِقُوَّةٍ وَاذْكُرُوا مَا فِيهِ لَعَلَّكُمْ تَتَّقُونَ ۝

وَإِذْ أَخَذَ رَبُّكَ مِنۢ بَنِىٓ آدَمَ مِن ظُهُورِهِمْ ذُرِّيَّتَهُمْ وَأَشْهَدَهُمْ عَلَىٰٓ أَنفُسِهِمْ أَلَسْتُ بِرَبِّكُمْ ۖ قَالُوا بَلَىٰ ۛ شَهِدْنَا ۛ أَن تَقُولُوا يَوْمَ الْقِيَامَةِ إِنَّا كُنَّا عَنْ هٰذَا غَافِلِينَ ۝

173. Or lest you should say: "Our fathers before us may have taken false Allah's, but we are (their) descendants after them: will you then destroy us because of the deeds of men who followed falsehood?"

174. Thus do We explain the signs in detail; and perchance they may turn (unto Us).

175. Relate to them the story of the man to whom We sent Our signs, but he passed them by: so Satan followed him up, and he went astray.

176. If it had been Our will, We should have elevated him with Our signs; but he inclined to the earth, and followed his own vain desires. His similitude is that of a dog: if you attack him, he lolls out his tongue, or if you leave him alone, he (still) lolls out his tongue. That is the similitude of those who reject Our signs; so relate the story; perchance they may reflect.

177. Evil as an example are people who reject Our signs and wrong their own souls.

178. Whom Allah does guide,- he is on the right path: whom He rejects from His guidance,- such are the persons who perish.

179. Many are the Jinns and men we have made for Hell: they have hearts wherewith they do not understand, eyes wherewith they do not see, and ears wherewith they do not hear. They are like cattle,- nay more misguided: for they are heedless (of warning).

173. Aw taqoolooo innamaaa ashraka aabaaa'unaa min qablu wa kunnaa zurriyyatam-mim ba'dihim afatuhlikunaa bimaa fa'alal-mubṭiloon.

174. Wa kazaalika nufaṣṣilul-Aayaati wa la'allahum yar-ji'oon.

175. Watlu 'alayhim naba-al-lazeee aataynaahu Aayaatinaa fansalakha minhaa fa-atba'a-hush-Shayṭaanu fakaana minal-ghaaween.

176. Wa law shi'naa lara-fa'naahu bihaa wa laakin-nahooo akhlada ilal-arḍi watta-ba'a hawaah; famasaluhoo kamasalil-kalb; in taḥmil 'alayhi yalhas aw tatruk-hu yalhas; zaalika masalul-qawmil-lazeena kazzaboo bi-Aayaatinaa; faqṣuṣil-qaṣaṣa la'allahum yatafakkaroon.

177. Saaa'a maṣalanil-qaw-mul-lazeena kazzaboo bi-Aayaatinaa wa anfusahum kaanoo yaẓlimoon.

178. Mañy-yahdil-laahu fa-huwal-muhtadee wa mañy-yuḍlil fa-ulaaa'ika humul-khaasiroon.

179. Wa laqad zaraånaa li-Jahannama kaseeram-minal-jinni wal-insi lahum quloobul-laa yafqahoona bihaa wa lahum a'yunul-laa yubṣiroona bihaa wa lahum aazaanul-laa yas-ma'oona bihaa; ulaaa'ika kal-an'aami bal hum aḍall; ulaaa'ika humul-ghaafiloon.

180. The most beautiful names belong to Allah: so call on Him by them; but shun such men as use profanity in His names: for what they do, they will soon be requited.

181. Of those We have created are people who direct (others) with truth. And dispense justice therewith.

182. Those who reject Our Signs, We will lead them step by step to ruin while they know not;

183. Respite will I grant unto them: for My scheme is strong (and unfailing).

184. Do they not reflect? Their companion is not seized with madness: he is but a perspicuous warner.

185. Do they see nothing in the kingdom of the heavens and the earth and all that Allah has created? (Do they not see) that it may well be that their terms is drawing to an end? In what message after this will they then believe?

186. To such as Allah rejects from His guidance, there can be no guide: He will leave them in their trespasses, wandering in distraction.

187. They ask you about the (final) Hour - when will be its appointed time? Say: "The knowledge thereof is with my Lord (alone): none but He can reveal as to when it will occur. Heavy were its burden through the heavens and the earth. Only, all of a sudden will it come to you." They ask you as if you were eager in search thereof: say: "The knowledge thereof is with Allah (alone), but most men know not."

188. Say: "I have no power over any good or harm to myself

180. Wa lillaahil-Asmaaa'ul-Ḥusnaa fad'oohu bihaa wa zarul-lazeena yulḥidoona feee Asmaaa'ih; sa-yujzawna maa kaanoo ya'maloon.

181. Wa mimman khalaqnaaa ummatuñy-yahdoona bilḥaqqi wa bihee ya'diloon.   **(Section 22)**

182. Wallazeena kazzaboo bi-Aayaatinaa sanastadrijuhum min ḥaysu laa ya'lamoon.

183. Wa umlee lahum; inna kaydee mateen.

184. Awalam yatafakkaroo maa biṣaaḥibihim min jinnah; in huwa illaa nazeerum-mubeen.

185. Awalam yanzuroo fee malakootis-samaawaati wal-arḍi wa maa khalaqal-laahu min shay'iñw-wa an 'asaaa añy-yakoona qadiqtaraba ajaluhum fabi-ayyi ḥadeesim ba'dahoo yu'minoon.

186. Mañy-yuḍlilil-laahu falaa haadiya lah; wa yazaruhum fee ṭughyaanihim ya'mahoon.

187. Yas'aloonaka 'anis-Saa'ati ayyaana mursaahaa qul inna-maa 'ilmuhaa 'inda Rabbee laa yujalleehaa liwaqtihaaa illaa Hoo; saqulat fis-samaawaati wal-arḍ; laa taåteekum illaa baghtah; yas'aloonaka ka-annaka ḥafiyyun 'anhaa qul innamaa 'ilmuhaa 'indal-laahi wa laakinna aksaran-naasi laa ya'lamoon.

188. Qul laaa amliku linafsee naf'añw-wa laa ḍarran

except as Allah wills. If I had knowledge of the unseen, I should have multiplied all good, and no evil should have touched me: I am but a warner, and a bringer of glad tidings to those who have faith."

illaa maa shaaaa'al-laah; wa law kuntu a'lamul-ghayba lastaksartu minal-khayri wa maa massaniyas-soo'; in ana illaa nazeeruñw-wa basheerul-liqawmiñy-yu'minoon.

(Section 23)

إِلَّا مَا شَاءَ اللّٰهُ ۚ وَلَوْ كُنْتُ أَعْلَمُ الْغَيْبَ لَاسْتَكْثَرْتُ مِنَ الْخَيْرِ ۖ وَمَا مَسَّنِيَ السُّوٓءُ ۚ إِنْ أَنَا إِلَّا نَذِيرٌ وَّبَشِيرٌ لِّقَوْمٍ يُّؤْمِنُوْنَ ۝

189. It is He Who created you from a single person, and made his mate of like nature, in order that he might dwell with her (in love). When they are united, she bears a light burden and carries it about (unnoticed). When she grows heavy, they both pray to Allah their Lord, (saying): "If you give us a goodly child, we vow we shall (ever) be grateful."

189. Huwal-lazee khalaqakum min nafsiñw-waahidatiñw-wa ja'ala minhaa zawjahaa liyaskuna ilayhaa falammaa taghashshaahaa hamalat hamlan khafeefan famarrat bihee falammaaa asqalad-da'awallaaha Rabbahumaa la'in aataytanaa saalihal-lanakoonanna minash-shaakireen.

هُوَ الَّذِيْ خَلَقَكُمْ مِّنْ نَّفْسٍ وَّاحِدَةٍ وَّجَعَلَ مِنْهَا زَوْجَهَا لِيَسْكُنَ إِلَيْهَا ۖ فَلَمَّا تَغَشّٰىهَا حَمَلَتْ حَمْلًا خَفِيْفًا فَمَرَّتْ بِهٖ ۖ فَلَمَّا أَثْقَلَتْ دَّعَوَا اللّٰهَ رَبَّهُمَا لَئِنْ اٰتَيْتَنَا صَالِحًا لَّنَكُوْنَنَّ مِنَ الشَّاكِرِيْنَ ۝

190. But when He gives them a goodly child, they ascribe to others a share in the gift they have received: but Allah is exalted high above the partners they ascribe to Him.

190. Falammaaa aataahumaa saalihan ja'alaa lahoo shurakaaa'a feemaaa aataahumaa; fata'aalal-laahu 'ammaa yushrikoon.

فَلَمَّا اٰتٰىهُمَا صَالِحًا جَعَلَا لَهٗ شُرَكَآءَ فِيْمَا اٰتٰىهُمَا ۚ فَتَعٰلَى اللّٰهُ عَمَّا يُشْرِكُوْنَ ۝

191. Do they indeed ascribe to Him as partners things that can create nothing, but are themselves created?

191. A yushrikoona maa laa yakhluqu shay'añw-wa hum yukhlaqoon.

أَيُشْرِكُوْنَ مَا لَا يَخْلُقُ شَيْئًا وَّهُمْ يُخْلَقُوْنَ ۝

192. No aid can they give them, nor can they aid themselves!

192. Wa laa yastatee'oona lahum nasrañw-wa laaa anfusahum yansuroon

وَلَا يَسْتَطِيْعُوْنَ لَهُمْ نَصْرًا وَّلَا أَنْفُسَهُمْ يَنْصُرُوْنَ ۝

193. If you call them to guidance, they will not obey: For you it is the same whether you call them or you hold your peace!

193. Wa in tad'oohum ilalhudaa laa yattabi'ookum; sawaaa'un 'alaykum a-da'awtumoohum am antum saamitoon.

وَإِنْ تَدْعُوْهُمْ إِلَى الْهُدٰى لَا يَتَّبِعُوْكُمْ ۚ سَوَآءٌ عَلَيْكُمْ أَدَعَوْتُمُوْهُمْ أَمْ أَنْتُمْ صَامِتُوْنَ ۝

194. Verily those whom you call upon besides Allah are servants like unto you: call upon them, and let them listen to your prayer, if you are (indeed) truthful!

194. Innal-lazeena tad'oona min doonil-laahi 'ibaadun amsaalukum fad'oohum falyastajeeboo lakum in kuntum saadiqeen.

إِنَّ الَّذِيْنَ تَدْعُوْنَ مِنْ دُوْنِ اللّٰهِ عِبَادٌ أَمْثَالُكُمْ فَادْعُوْهُمْ فَلْيَسْتَجِيْبُوْا لَكُمْ إِنْ كُنْتُمْ صَادِقِيْنَ ۝

195. Have they feet to walk with? Or

195. A-lahum arjuluñy-yamshoona bihaaa am lahum

أَلَهُمْ أَرْجُلٌ يَّمْشُوْنَ بِهَآ ۖ أَمْ لَهُمْ

hands to lay hold with? Or eyes to see with? Or ears to hear with? Say: "Call your 'Allah-partners', scheme (your worst) against me, and give me no respite!

196. "For my Protector is Allah, Who revealed the Book (from time to time), and He will choose and befriend the righteous.

197. "But those you call upon besides Him, are unable to help you, and indeed to help themselves."

198. If you call them to guidance, they do not hear. You will see them looking at you, but they do not see.

199. Hold to forgiveness; command what is right; but turn away from the ignorant.

200. If a suggestion from Satan assail your (mind), seek refuge with Allah; for He hears and knows (all things).

201. Those who fear Allah, when a thought of evil from Satan assaults them, bring Allah to remembrance, when lo! they see (aright)!

202. But their brethren (the evil ones) plunge them deeper into error, and never relax (their efforts).

203. If you bring them not a revelation, they say: "Why have you not got it together?" Say: "I but follow what is revealed to me from my Lord: this is (nothing but) lights from your Lord, and Guidance, and Mercy, for any who have faith."

aydiñy-yabṭishoona bihaaa am lahum a'yunuñy-yubṣiroona bihaaa am lahum aazaanuñy-yasma'oona bihaa; qulid-'oo shurakaaa'akum ṣumma keedooni falaa tunẓiroon.

196. Inna waliyyiyal-laahul-lazee nazzalal-Kitaaba wa Huwa yatawallaṣ-ṣaaliḥeen.

197. Wallazeena tad'oona min doonihee laa yastaṭee'oona naṣrakum wa laaa anfusahum yanṣuroon.

198. Wa in tad'oohum ilal-hudaa laa yasma'oo wa taraahum yanẓuroona ilayka wa hum laa yubṣiroon.

199. Khuzil-'afwa waåmur bil'urfi wa a'riḍ 'anil-jaahileen.

200. Wa immaa yanzaghannaka minash-Shayṭaani nazghun fasta'iz billaah; innahoo Samee'un 'Aleem.

201. Innal-lazeenat-taqaw izaa massahum ṭaaa'ifum minash-Shayṭaani tazakkaroo fa-izaa hum mubṣiroon.

202. Wa ikhwaanuhum yamud-doonahum fil-ghayyi ṣumma laa yuqṣiroon.

203. Wa izaa lam taåtihim bi-Aayatin qaaloo law lajtabay-tahaa; qul innamaaa attabi'u maa yooḥaaa ilayya mir-Rabbee; haazaa baṣaaa'iru mir-Rabbikum wa hudañw-wa raḥmatul-liqawmiñy-yu'minoon.

204. When the Qur'an is read, listen to it with attention, and hold your peace: that you may receive Mercy.

205. And you (O reader!) bring your Lord to remembrance in your (very) soul, with humility and in reverence, without loudness in words, in the mornings and evenings; and be not you of those who are unheedful.

206. Those who are near to your Lord, disdain not to do Him worship: they celebrate His praises, and bow down before Him.

204. Wa izaa quri'al-Qur-aanu fastami'oo lahoo wa anşitoo la'allakum turḥamoon.

205. Wazkur Rabbaka fee nafsika taḍarru'añw-wa khee-fataňw-wa doonal-jahri minal-qawli bilghuduwwi wal-aaşaali wa laa takum minal-ghaafileen.

206. Innal-lazeena 'inda Rabbika laa yastakbiroona 'an 'ibaadatihee wa yusab-biḥoonahoo wa lahoo yasju-doon. 🕋   (Section 24)

8. The Spoil of War
In the name of Allah, Most Gracious, Most Merciful.

Sûrat al-Anfâl–8
(Revealed at Madinah)
Bismillaahir Raḥmaanir Raḥeem

1. They ask you concerning (things taken as) spoils of war. Say: "(Such) spoils are at the disposal of Allah and the Apostle: so fear Allah, and keep straight the relations between yourselves: obey Allah and His Apostle, if you do believe."

2. For, Believers are those who, when Allah is mentioned, feel a tremor in their hearts, and when they hear His Signs rehearsed, find their faith strengthened, and put (all) their trust in their Lord;

3. Who establish regular prayers and spend (freely) out of the gifts We have given them for sustenance:

4. Such in truth are the Believers: they have grades of dignity with their Lord, and forgiveness, and generous sustenance:

5. Just as your Lord ordered you out of your house in truth, even though a party among the Believers

1. Yas'aloonaka 'anil-anfaali qulil-anfaalu lillaahi war-Rasooli fattaqul-laaha wa aşliḥoo zaata baynikum wa aţee'ul-laaha wa Rasoolahooo in kuntum mu'mineen.

2. Innamal-mu'minoonal-lazeena izaa zukiral-laahu wajilat quloobuhum wa izaa tuliyat 'alayhim Aayaatuhoo zaadat-hum eemaanañw-wa 'alaa Rabbihim yatawakkaloon.

3. Allazeena yuqeemoonaş-Şalaata wa mimmaa razaq-naahum yunfiqoon.

4. Ulaaa'ika humul-mu'mi-noona ḥaqqaa; lahum darajaa-tun 'inda Rabbihim wa magh-firatuňw-wa rizqun kareem.

5. Kamaaa akhrajaka Rabbuka mim baytika bilḥaqq, wa inna fareeqam-minal-mu'mineena

disliked it.

6. Disputing with you concerning the truth after it was made manifest, as if they were being driven to death and they (actually) saw it.

7. Behold! Allah promised you one of the two (enemy) parties, that it should be yours: you wished that the one unarmed should be yours, but Allah willed to justify the Truth according to His words and to cut off the roots of the Unbelievers;-

8. That He might justify Truth and prove Falsehood false, distasteful though it be to those in guilt.

9. Remember you implored the assistance of your Lord, and He answered you: "I will assist you with a thousand of the angels, ranks on ranks."

10. Allah made it but a message of hope, and an assurance to your hearts: (in any case) there is no help except from Allah: and Allah is Exalted in Power, Wise.

11. Remember He covered you with a sort of drowsiness, to give you calm as from Himself, and He caused rain to descend on you from heaven, to clean you therewith, to remove from you the stain of Satan, to strengthen your hearts, and to plant your feet firmly therewith.

12. Remember your Lord inspired the angels (with the message): "I am with you: give firmness to the Believers: I will instil terror into the hearts of the Unbelievers: smite you above their necks

lakaarihoon.

6. Yujaadiloonaka fil-ḥaqqi ba'da maa tabayyana ka-annamaa yusaaqoona ilal-mawti wa hum yanẓuroon.

7. Wa iz ya'idukumul-laahu iḥdaṭ-ṭaaa'ifatayni annahaa lakum wa tawaddoona anna ghayra zaatish-shawkati takoonu lakum wa yureedul-laahu añy-yuḥiqqal-ḥaqqa bikalimaatihee wa yaqṭa'a daabiral-kaafireen.

8. Liyuḥiqqal-ḥaqqa wa yubṭilal-baaṭila wa law karihal-mujrimoon.

9. Iz tastagheeṣoona Rabba-kum fastajaaba lakum annee mumiddukum bi-alfim-minal-malaaa'ikati murdifeen.

10. Wa maa ja'alahul-laahu illaa bushraa wa litaṭma'inna bihee quloobukum; wa man-naṣru-illaa min 'indil-laah; innal-laaha Azeezun Ḥakeem.
    (Section 1)

11. Iz yughashsheekumun-nu'aasa amanatam-minhu wa yunazzilu 'alaykum minas-samaaa'i maaa'al-liyuṭah-hirakum bihee wa yuzhiba 'ankum rijzash-Shayṭaani wa liyarbiṭa 'ala quloobikum wa yuṣabbita bihil-aqdaam.

12. Iz yooḥee Rabbuka ilal-malaaa'ikati annee ma'akum faṣabbitul-lazeena aamanoo; sa-ulqee fee quloobil-lazeena kafarur-ru'ba faḍriboo fawqal-a'naaqi

لَكَارِهُوْنَ ۞

يُجَادِلُوْنَكَ فِى الْحَقِّ بَعْدَ مَا تَبَيَّنَ كَاَنَّمَا يُسَاقُوْنَ اِلَى الْمَوْتِ وَهُمْ يَنْظُرُوْنَ ۞

وَاِذْ يَعِدُكُمُ اللهُ اِحْدَى الطَّآئِفَتَيْنِ اَنَّهَا لَكُمْ وَتَوَدُّوْنَ اَنَّ غَيْرَ ذَاتِ الشَّوْكَةِ تَكُوْنُ لَكُمْ وَيُرِيْدُ اللهُ اَنْ يُّحِقَّ الْحَقَّ بِكَلِمَاتِهٖ وَيَقْطَعَ دَابِرَ الْكَافِرِيْنَ ۞

لِيُحِقَّ الْحَقَّ وَيُبْطِلَ الْبَاطِلَ وَلَوْ كَرِهَ الْمُجْرِمُوْنَ ۞

اِذْ تَسْتَغِيْثُوْنَ رَبَّكُمْ فَاسْتَجَابَ لَكُمْ اَنِّيْ مُمِدُّكُمْ بِاَلْفٍ مِّنَ الْمَلٰٓئِكَةِ مُرْدِفِيْنَ ۞

وَمَا جَعَلَهُ اللهُ اِلَّا بُشْرٰى وَلِتَطْمَئِنَّ بِهٖ قُلُوْبُكُمْ وَمَا النَّصْرُ اِلَّا مِنْ عِنْدِ اللهِ اِنَّ اللهَ عَزِيْزٌ حَكِيْمٌ ۞

اِذْ يُغَشِّيْكُمُ النُّعَاسَ اَمَنَةً مِّنْهُ وَيُنَزِّلُ عَلَيْكُمْ مِّنَ السَّمَآءِ مَآءً لِّيُطَهِّرَكُمْ بِهٖ وَيُذْهِبَ عَنْكُمْ رِجْزَ الشَّيْطٰنِ وَلِيَرْبِطَ عَلٰى قُلُوْبِكُمْ وَيُثَبِّتَ بِهِ الْاَقْدَامَ ۞

اِذْ يُوْحِيْ رَبُّكَ اِلَى الْمَلٰٓئِكَةِ اَنِّيْ مَعَكُمْ فَثَبِّتُوا الَّذِيْنَ اٰمَنُوْا سَاُلْقِيْ فِيْ قُلُوْبِ الَّذِيْنَ كَفَرُوا الرُّعْبَ فَاضْرِبُوْا فَوْقَ الْاَعْنَاقِ

and smite all their finger-tips off them."

13. This because they contended against Allah and His Apostle: if any contend against Allah and His Apostle, Allah is strict in punishment.

14. Thus (will it be said): "You taste then of the (punishment): for those who resist Allah, is the Chastisement of the Fire."

15. O you who believe! when you meet the Unbelievers in hostile array, never turn your backs to them.

16. If any do turn his back to them on such a day - unless it be in a stratagem of war, or to retreat to a troop (of his own) - he draws on himself the wrath of Allah, and his abode is Hell,- an evil refuge (indeed)!

17. It is not you who slew them; it was Allah: when you threwest (a handful of dust), it was not your act, but Allah's: in order that He might test the Believers by a gracious trial from Himself: for Allah is He Who heareth and knoweth (all things).

18. That, and also because Allah is He Who makes feeble the plans and stratagem of the Unbelievers.

19. (O Unbelievers!) if you prayed for victory and judgment, now has the judgment come to you: if you desist (from wrong), it will be best for you: if you return (to the attack), so shall We. Not the least good will your forces be to you even if they were multiplied: for verily Allah is with those who believe!

20. O you who believe! Obey Allah and His Apostle, and do not turn away from him when you

waḍriboo minhum kulla banaan.

13. Zaalika bi-annahum shaaaqqul-laaha wa Rasoolah; wa mañy-yushaqiqil-laaha wa Rasoolahoo fa-innal-laaha shadeedul-'iqaab.

14. Zaalikum faẓooqoohu wa anna lilkaafireena 'azaaban-Naar.

15. Yaaa ayyuhal-lazeena aamanooo izaa laqeetumul-lazeena kafaroo zaḥfan falaa tuwalloohumul-adbaar.

16. Wa mañy-yuwallihim yawma'izin duburahooo illaa mutaḥarrifal-liqitaalin aw mutaḥayyizan ilaa fi'atin faqad baaa'a bighaḍabim-minal-laahi wa maåwaahu Jahannamu wa bi'sal-maṣeer.

17. Falam taqtuloohum wa laakinnal-laaha qatalahum; wa maa ramayta iz ramayta wa laakinnal-laaha ramaa; wa liyubliyal-mu'mineena minhu balaaa'an ḥasanaa; innal-laaha Samee'un 'Aleem.

18. Zaalikum wa annal-laaha moohinu kaydil-kaafireen.

19. In tastaftiḥoo faqad jaaa'akumul-fatḥu wa in tantahoo fahuwa khayrul-lakum wa in ta'oodoo na'ud wa lan tughniya 'ankum fi'atukum shay'añw-wa law kaṣurat wa annal-laaha ma'al-mu'mineen.
(Section 2)

20. Yaaa ayyuhal-lazeena aamanooo aṭee'ul-laaha wa Rasoolahoo wa laa tawallaw 'anhu wa antum

hear (him speak).

21. Nor be like those who say, "We hear," but listen not.

22. For the worst of beasts in the sight of Allah are the deaf and the dumb,- those who do not understand.

23. If Allah had found in them any good, He would indeed have made them listen: (As it is), if He had made them listen, they would but have turned back and declined (Faith).

24. O you who believe! give your response to Allah and His Apostle, when He calls you to that which will give you life; and know that Allah comes in between a man and his heart, and that it is He to Whom you shall (all) be gathered.

25. And fear tumult or oppression, which affects not in particular (only) those of you who do wrong: and know that Allah is strict in punishment.

26. Call to mind when you were a small (band), deemed weak through the land, and afraid that men might despoil and kidnap you; but He provided a safe asylum for you, strengthened you with His aid, and gave you good things for sustenance: that you might be grateful.

27. O you that believe! do not betray the trust of Allah and the Apostle, nor misappropriate knowingly things entrusted to you.

28. And know you that your possessions and your progeny are but a trial; and that it is Allah with Whom lies your highest reward.

29. O you who believe! if you fear Allah, He will grant you a Criterion (to judge between right and wrong), remove from you (all) evil (that may afflict) you, and forgive you: for Allah

tasma'oon.

21. Wa laa takoonoo kal-lazeena qaaloo sami'naa wa hum laa yasma'oon.

22. Inna sharrad-dawaaabbi 'indal-laahiṣ-ṣummul-bukmul-lazeena laa ya'qiloon.

23. Wa law 'alimal-laahu feehim khayral-la-asma'ahum; wa law asma'ahum latawallaw wa hum mu'riḍoon.

24. Yaaa ayyuhal-lazeena aamanus-tajeeboo lillaahi wa lir-Rasooli izaa da'aakum limaa yuhyeekum wa'lamoo annal-laaha yahoolu baynal-mar'i wa qalbihee wa annahooo ilayhi tuḥsharoon.

25. Wattaqoo fitnatal-laa tuṣeebannal-lazeena ẓalamoo minkum khaaaṣṣataňw wa'la-mooo annal-laaha shadeedul-'iqaab.

26. Wazkurooo iz antum qaleelum-mustaḍ'afoona fil-arḍi takhaafoona aňy-yatakhaṭ-ṭafakumun-naasu fa-aawaakum wa ayyadakum binaṣrihee wa razaqakum minaṭ-ṭayyibaati la'allakum tashkuroon.

27. Yaaa ayyuhal-lazeena aamanoo laa takhoonul-laaha war-Rasoola wa takhoonooo amaanaatikum wa antum ta'lamoon.

28. Wa'lamooo annamaaa amwaalukum wa awlaadukum fitnatuňw-wa annal-laaha 'indahooo ajrun aẓeem. (Sec. 3)

29. Yaaa ayyuhal-lazeena aamanooo in tattaqul-laaha yaj'al lakum furqaanaňw-wa yukaffir 'ankum sayyi-aatikum wa yaghfir lakum; wallaahu

is the Lord of grace unbounded.

ẕul-faḍlil-'aẓeem.

ذُوالْفَضْلِ الْعَظِيْمِ ۝

30. Remember how the Unbelievers plotted against you, to keep you in bonds, or slay you, or get you out (of your home). They plot and plan, and Allah too plans, but the best of planners is Allah.

30. Wa iẕ yamkuru bikal-laẕeena kafaroo liyus̱bitooka aw yaqtulooka aw yukhrijook; wa yamkuroona wa yamkurul-laahu wallaahu khayrul-maakireen.

وَاِذْ يَمْكُرُ بِكَ الَّذِيْنَ كَفَرُوْا لِيُثْبِتُوْكَ اَوْ يَقْتُلُوْكَ اَوْ يُخْرِجُوْكَ ۚ وَاللّٰهُ وَاللّٰهُ خَيْرُ الْمَاكِرِيْنَ ۝

31. When Our Signs are rehearsed to them, they say: "We have heard this (before): if we wished, we could say (words) like these: these are nothing but tales of the ancients."

31. Wa iẕaa tutlaa 'alayhim Aayaatunaa qaaloo qad sami'-naa law nashaaa'u laqulnaa mis̱la haaẕaaa in haaẕaaa illaaa asaaṭeerul-awwaleen.

وَاِذَا تُتْلٰى عَلَيْهِمْ اٰيٰتُنَا قَالُوْا قَدْ سَمِعْنَا لَوْ نَشَاۤءُ لَقُلْنَا مِثْلَ هٰذَا ۙ اِنْ هٰذَا اِلَّآ اَسَاطِيْرُ الْاَوَّلِيْنَ ۝

32. Remember how they said: "O Allah if this is indeed the Truth from You, rain down on us a shower of stones form the sky, or send us a grievous Chastisement."

32. Wa iẕ qaalul-laahumma in kaana haaẕaa huwal-ḥaqqa min 'indika fa-amṭir 'alaynaa ḥijaaratam-minas-samaaa'i awi-ṭinaa bi'aẕaabin aleem.

وَاِذْ قَالُوا اللّٰهُمَّ اِنْ كَانَ هٰذَا هُوَ الْحَقَّ مِنْ عِنْدِكَ فَاَمْطِرْ عَلَيْنَا حِجَارَةً مِّنَ السَّمَاۤءِ اَوِ ائْتِنَا بِعَذَابٍ اَلِيْمٍ ۝

33. But Allah was not going to send them a Chastisement whilst you were amongst them; nor was He going to send it whilst they could ask for pardon.

33. Wa maa kanal-laahu liyu'aẕ-ẕibahum wa anta feehim; wa maa kaanal-laahu mu'aẕ-ẕibahum wa hum yastagh-firoon.

وَمَا كَانَ اللّٰهُ لِيُعَذِّبَهُمْ وَاَنْتَ فِيْهِمْ ۚ وَمَا كَانَ اللّٰهُ مُعَذِّبَهُمْ وَهُمْ يَسْتَغْفِرُوْنَ ۝

34. But what plea have they that Allah should not punish them, when they keep out (men) from the Sacred Mosque - and they are not its guardians? No men can be its guardians except the righteous; but most of them do not understand.

34. Wa maa lahum allaa yu'aẕ-ẕibahumul-laahu wa hum yaṣuddoona 'anil-Masjidil-Ḥaraami wa maa kaanooo awliyaaa'ah; in awliyaaa'uhooo illal-muttaqoona wa laakinna aks̱arahum laa ya'lamoon.

وَمَا لَهُمْ اَلَّا يُعَذِّبَهُمُ اللّٰهُ وَهُمْ يَصُدُّوْنَ عَنِ الْمَسْجِدِ الْحَرَامِ وَمَا كَانُوْۤا اَوْلِيَاۤءَهٗ ۚ اِنْ اَوْلِيَاۤؤُهٗۤ اِلَّا الْمُتَّقُوْنَ وَلٰكِنَّ اَكْثَرَهُمْ لَا يَعْلَمُوْنَ ۝

35. Their prayer at the House (of Allah) is nothing but whistling and clapping of hands: (its only answer can be), "You taste the Chastisement because you blasphemed."

35. Wa maa kaana Ṣalaatuhum 'indal-Bayti illaa mukaaa'añw-wa taṣdiyah; faẕooqul-'aẕaaba bimaa kuntum takfuroon.

وَمَا كَانَ صَلَاتُهُمْ عِنْدَ الْبَيْتِ اِلَّا مُكَاۤءً وَّتَصْدِيَةً ۚ فَذُوْقُوا الْعَذَابَ بِمَا كُنْتُمْ تَكْفُرُوْنَ ۝

36. The Unbelievers spend their wealth to hinder (man) from the path of Allah, and so will they continue to spend; but in the end they will have (only) regrets and sighs; at length they will be overcome: and the

36. Innal-laẕeena kafaroo yunfiqoona amwaalahum liyaṣuddoo 'an sabeelil-laah; fasayunfiqoonahaa s̱umma takoonu 'alayhim ḥasratan s̱umma yughlaboon; wal-laẕeena

اِنَّ الَّذِيْنَ كَفَرُوْا يُنْفِقُوْنَ اَمْوَالَهُمْ لِيَصُدُّوْا عَنْ سَبِيْلِ اللّٰهِ ۗ فَسَيُنْفِقُوْنَهَا ثُمَّ تَكُوْنُ عَلَيْهِمْ حَسْرَةً ثُمَّ يُغْلَبُوْنَ ۗ وَالَّذِيْنَ

Unbelievers will be gathered together to Hell;

37. In order that Allah may separate the impure from the pure, put the impure, one on another, heap them together, and cast them into Hell. They will be the ones to have lost.

38. Say to the Unbelievers, if (now) they desist (from Unbelief), their past would be forgiven them; but if they persist, the punishment of those before them is already (a matter of warning for them).

39. And fight them on until there is no more tumult or oppression, and religion becomes Allah's in its entirety, but if they cease, surely Allah sees all that they do.

40. If they refuse, be sure that Allah is your Protector - the Best to protect and the best to help.

41. And know that out of all the booty that you may acquire (in war), a fifth share is assigned to Allah,- and to the Apostle, and to near relatives, orphans, the needy, and the wayfarer,- if you do believe in Allah and in the revelation We sent down to Our Servant on the Day of discrimination,- the Day of the meeting of the two forces. For Allah has power over all things.

42. Remember you were on the hither side of the valley, and they on the farther side, and the caravan on lower ground than you. Even if you had made a mutual appointment to meet, you would certainly have failed in the appointment: but (thus you met), that Allah might accomplish a matter already decided; that those who died might die after a clear Sign (had been given), and those who lived might live after

kafarooo ilaa Jahannama yuḥsharoona.

37. Liyameezal-laahul khabeesa minaṭ-ṭayyibi wa yaj'alalkhabeesa ba'ḍahoo 'ala ba'din fayarkumahoo jamee'an fayaj'alahoo fee Jahannam; ulaaa'ika humul-khaasiroon.
(Section 4)

38. Qul-lillaẓeena kafarooo iny-yantahoo yughfar lahum maa qad salafa wa iny-ya'oodoo faqad maḍat sunnatul-awwaleen.

39. Wa qaatiloohum ḥattaa laa takoona fitnatuñw-wa yakoo-naddeenu kulluhoo lillaah; fa-in-tahaw fa-innallaaha bimaa ya'maloona Baṣeer.

40. Wa in tawallaw fa'lamooo annal-laaha mawlaakum; ni'mal-mawlaa wa ni'man-naṣeer.

41. Wa'lamooo annamaa ghanimtum min shay'in fa-anna lillaahi khumusahoo wa lir-Rasooli wa liẓil-qurbaa walyataamaa walmasaakeeni wabnissabeeli in kuntum aamantum billaahi wa maaa anzalnaa 'ala 'abdinaa yawmal-Furqaani yawmaltaqal-jam'aan; wallaahu 'alaa kulli shay'in Qadeer.

42. Iẓ antum bil'udwatiddunyaa wa hum bil'udwatilquṣwaa warrakbu asfala minkum; wa law tawaa'attum lakhtalaftum fil-mee'aadi wa laakil-liyaqḍiyal-laahu amran kaana maf'oolal liyahlika man halaka 'am bayyinatiñw-wa yahyaa man ḥayya 'am

a Clear Sign (had been given). And verily Allah is He Who hears and knows (all things).

43. Remember in your dream Allah showed them to you as few: if He had shown them to you as many, you would surely have been discouraged, and you would surely have disputed in (your) decision; but Allah saved (you): for He knows well the (secrets) of (all) hearts.

44. And remember when you met, He showed them to you as few in your eyes, and He made you appear as contemptible in their eyes: that Allah might accomplish a matter already decided. For to Allah do all questions go back (for decision).

45. O you who believe! When you meet a force, be firm, and call Allah in remembrance much (and often); that you may prosper:

46. And obey Allah and His Apostle; and fall into no disputes, lest you lose heart and your power depart; and be patient and persevering: for Allah is with those who patiently persevere:

47. And be not like those who started from their homes insolently and to be seen of men, and to hinder (men) from the path of Allah: for Allah compasses round about all that they do.

48. Remember Satan made their (sinful) acts seem alluring to them, and said: "No one among men can overcome you this day, while I am near to you": But when the two forces came in sight of each other, he turned on his heels, and said: "Lo! I am clear of you; Lo! I see what you see not; Lo! I fear Allah: for Allah is strict in punishment."

bayyinah; wa innal-laaha la-Samee'un 'Aleem.

43. Iz yureekahumul-laahu fee manaamika qaleela(ñw-) wa law araakahum kaseeral-lafashil-tum wa latanaaza'tum fil-amri wa laakinnal-laaha sallam; innahoo 'aleemum bizaatiṣ-ṣudoor.

44. Wa iz yureekumoohum izil-taqaytum feee a'yunikum qaleelañw-wa yuqallilukum feee a'yunihim liyaqḍiyal-laahu amran kaana maf'oolaa; wa ilal-laahi turja'ul-umoor. **(Section 5)**

45. Yaaa ayyuhal-lazeena aamanooo izaa laqeetum fi'atan faṣbutoo wazkurul-laaha kaseeral-la'allakum tuflihoon.

46. Wa aṭee'ul-laaha wa Rasoolahoo wa laa tanaaza'oo fatafshaloo wa tazhaba reehu-kum waṣbiroo; innal-laaha ma'aṣ-ṣaabireen.

47. Wa laa takoonoo kallazeena kharajoo min diyaarihim baṭarañw-wa ri'aaa'an-naasi wa yaṣuddoona 'an sabeelil-laah; wallaahu bimaa ya'maloona muheeṭ.

48. Wa iz-zayyana lahumush-Shayṭaanu a'ma-alahum wa qaala laa ghaaliba lakumul yawma minan-naasi wa innee jaarul-lakum falammaa taraaa'atil-fi'ataani nakaṣa 'alaa aqibayhi wa qaala innee bareee'um-minkum innee araa maa laa tarawna inneee akhaaful-laah; wallaahu sha-deedul-'iqaab. **(Section 6)**

49. Lo! the hypocrites say, and those in whose hearts is a disease: "These people,- their religion has misled them." But if any trust in Allah, behold! Allah is Exalted in might, Wise.

50. If you could see, when the angels take the souls of the Unbelievers (at death), (How) they smite their faces and their backs, (saying): "Taste the Chastisement of the blazing Fire-

51. "Because of (the deeds) which your (own) hands sent forth; for Allah is never unjust to His servants:

52. "(Deeds) after the manner of the people of Pharaoh and of those before them: they rejected the Signs of Allah, and Allah punished them for their crimes: for Allah is Strong, and Strict in punishment:

53. "Because Allah will never change the grace which He has bestowed on a people until they change what is in their (own) souls, and surely Allah is He Who hears and knows (all things)."

54. "(Deeds) after the manner of the people of Pharaoh and those before them": they treated as false the Signs of their Lord, so We destroyed them for their crimes, and We drowned the people of Pharaoh: for they were all oppressors and wrong-doers.

55. For the worst of beasts in the sight of Allah are those who reject Him: they will not believe.

56. They are those with whom you made a covenant, but

49. Iz yaqoolul-munaafiqoona wallazeena fee quloobihim maradun gharra haaa'ulaaa'i deenuhum; wa many-yatawak-kal 'alal-laahi fa-innal-laaha 'Azee-zun Ḥakeem.

50. Wa law taraaa iz yatawaf-fal-lazeena kafarul malaaa'ikatu yaḍriboona wujoohahum wa adbaarahum wa zooqoo 'azaa-bal-ḥareeq.

51. Zaalika bimaa qaddamat aydeekum wa annal-laaha laysa biẓallaamil-lil'abeed.

52. Kadaabi Aali Fir'awna wal-lazeena min qablihim; kafaroo bi-Aayaatil-laahi fa-akhazahu-mul-laahu bizunoobihim; innal-laaha qawiyyun shadeedul-'iqaab.

53. Zaalika bi-annal-laaha lam yaku mughayyiran-ni'matan an'amahaa 'alaa qawmin ḥattaa yughayyiroo maa bianfusihim wa annallaaha Samee'un 'Aleem.

54. Kadaabi Aali Fir'awna wallazeena min qablihim; kaz-zaboo bi-Aayaati Rabbihim fa-ahlaknaahum bizunoobihim wa aghraqnaaa Aala Fir'awn; wa kullun kaanoo zaalimeen.

55. Inna sharrad-dawaaabbi 'indal-laahil-lazeena kafaroo fahum laa yu'minoon.

56. Allazeena 'aahatta min-hum summa

إِذْ يَقُولُ الْمُنَافِقُونَ وَالَّذِينَ فِى قُلُوبِهِم مَّرَضٌ غَرَّ هَؤُلَاءِ دِينُهُمْ ۗ وَمَن يَتَوَكَّلْ عَلَى اللَّهِ فَإِنَّ اللَّهَ عَزِيزٌ حَكِيمٌ ۝

وَلَوْ تَرَىٰ إِذْ يَتَوَفَّى الَّذِينَ كَفَرُوا ۙ الْمَلَائِكَةُ يَضْرِبُونَ وُجُوهَهُمْ وَأَدْبَارَهُمْ ۖ وَذُوقُوا عَذَابَ الْحَرِيقِ ۝

ذَٰلِكَ بِمَا قَدَّمَتْ أَيْدِيكُمْ وَأَنَّ اللَّهَ لَيْسَ بِظَلَّامٍ لِّلْعَبِيدِ ۝

كَدَأْبِ آلِ فِرْعَوْنَ ۙ وَالَّذِينَ مِن قَبْلِهِمْ ۚ كَفَرُوا بِآيَاتِ اللَّهِ فَأَخَذَهُمُ اللَّهُ بِذُنُوبِهِمْ ۗ إِنَّ اللَّهَ قَوِيٌّ شَدِيدُ الْعِقَابِ ۝

ذَٰلِكَ بِأَنَّ اللَّهَ لَمْ يَكُ مُغَيِّرًا نِّعْمَةً أَنْعَمَهَا عَلَىٰ قَوْمٍ حَتَّىٰ يُغَيِّرُوا مَا بِأَنفُسِهِمْ ۙ وَأَنَّ اللَّهَ سَمِيعٌ عَلِيمٌ ۝

كَدَأْبِ آلِ فِرْعَوْنَ ۙ وَالَّذِينَ مِن قَبْلِهِمْ ۚ كَذَّبُوا بِآيَاتِ رَبِّهِمْ فَأَهْلَكْنَاهُم بِذُنُوبِهِمْ وَأَغْرَقْنَا آلَ فِرْعَوْنَ ۚ وَكُلٌّ كَانُوا ظَالِمِينَ ۝

إِنَّ شَرَّ الدَّوَابِّ عِندَ اللَّهِ الَّذِينَ كَفَرُوا فَهُمْ لَا يُؤْمِنُونَ ۝

الَّذِينَ عَاهَدتَّ مِنْهُمْ ثُمَّ

they break their covenant every time, and they do not have the fear (of Allah).

57. If you encounter them in a battle deal severely with them so as to put terror in those who follow them, that they may remember.

58. If you fear treachery from any group, throw back (their covenant) to them, (so as to be) on equal terms: for Allah does not love the treacherous.

59. Let not the Unbelievers think that they can get the better (of the godly): they will never frustrate (them).

60. Against them make ready your strength to the utmost of your power, including steeds of war, to strike terror into (the hearts of) the enemies, of Allah and your enemies, and others besides, whom you may not know, but whom Allah knows. Whatever you shall spend in the Cause of Allah, shall be repaid to you, and you shall not be treated unjustly.

61. But if the enemy incline towards peace, do you (also) incline towards peace, and trust in Allah: for He is One that hears and knows (all things).

62. Should they intend to deceive you,- verily Allah suffices you: He it is That has strengthened you with His aid and with (the company of) the Believers;

63. And (moreover) He has put affection between their hearts: not if you had spent all that is in the earth, could you have produced that affection, but Allah has done it: for He is Exalted in might, Wise.

---

yanquḍoona 'ahdahum fee kulli marratiñw-wa hum laa yattaqoon.

57. Fa-immaa taṣqafannahum fil-ḥarbi fasharrid bihim man khalfahum la'allahum yaz-zakkaroon.

58. Wa immaa takhaafanna min qawmin khiyaanatan fambiz ilayhim 'alaa sawaaa'; innal-laaha laa yuḥibbul-khaaa'ineen.
(Section 7)

59. Wa laa yaḥsabannal-lazeena kafaroo sabaqooo; innahum laa yu'jizoon.

60. Wa a'iddoo lahum mas-taṭa'tum min quwwatiñw-wa mirribaaṭil-khayli turhiboona bihee 'aduwwal-laahi wa 'aduwwakum wa-aakhareena min doonihim laa ta'lamoo-nahum Allaahu ya'lamuhum; wa maa tunfiqoo min shay'in fee sabeelil-laahi yuwaf-failaykum wa antum laa tuẓla-moon.

61. Wa in janaḥoo lissalmi fajnaḥ lahaa wa tawakkal 'alal-laah; innahoo Huwas-Samee-'ul-'Aleem.

62. Wa iñy-yureedooo añy-yakhda'ooka fainna ḥasbakal-laah; Huwal-lazee ayyadaka binaṣrihee wa bilmu'mineen.

63. Wa allafa bayna quloobi-him; law-anfaqta maa fil-arḍi jamee'am-maaa-allafta bayna quloobihim wa laakinnallaaha allafa baynahum; innahoo 'Azeezun Ḥakeem.

64. O Apostle! sufficient to you is Allah,- (to you) and to those who follow you among the Believers.

65. O Apostle! rouse the Believers to the fight. If there are twenty amongst you, patient and persevering, they will vanquish two hundred: if a hundred, they will vanquish a thousand of the Unbelievers: for these are a people without understanding.

66. For the present, Allah has lightened your (task), for He knows that there is a weak spot in you: but (even so), if there are a hundred of you, patient and persevering, they will vanquish two hundred, and if a thousand, they will vanquish two thousand, with the leave of Allah: for Allah is with those who patiently persevere.

67. It is not fitting for an Apostle that he should have prisoners of war until he has thoroughly subdued the land. You look for the temporal goods of this world; but Allah looks to the Hereafter: and Allah is Exalted in might, Wise.

68. Had it not been for a previous ordainment from Allah, a severe penalty would have reached you for the (ransom) that you took.

69. But (now) enjoy what you took in war, lawful and good: but fear Allah: for Allah is Oft-forgiving, Most Merciful.

70. O Apostle! say to those who are captives in your hands: "If Allah finds any good in your hearts, He will give you something better than what has been taken from you, and He will forgive you: for Allah is Oft-forgiving, Most Merciful."

---

64. Yaaa ayyuhan-Nabiyyu ḥasbukal-laahu wa manittaba‘aka minal-mu’mineen.
    (Section 8)

65. Yaaa ayyuhan-Nabiyyu ḥarriḍil-mu’mineena ‘alal-qitaal; iñy-yakum-minkum ‘ishroona ṣaabiroona yaghliboo mi’atayn; wa iñy-yakum-minkum mi’atuñy-yaghliboo alfam-minal-lazeena kafaroo bi-annahum qawmul-laa yafqahoon.

66. Al’aana khaffafal-laahu ‘ankum wa ‘alima anna feekum ḍa‘faa; fa-iñy-yakum-minkum mi’atun ṣaabiratuñy-yaghliboo mi’atayn; wa iñy-yakum-minkum alfuñy-yaghliboo alfayni bi-iznil-laah; wallaahu ma‘aṣ-ṣaabireen.

67. Maa kaana li-Nabiyyin añy-yakoona lahoo asraa ḥattaa yuskhina fil-arḍ; tureedoona-araḍ ad-dunyaa wallaahu yureedul-Aakhirah; wallaahu ‘Azeezun Ḥakeem.

68. Law laa Kitaabum-minallaahi sabaqa lamassakum feemaaa akhaztum ‘azaabun ‘azeem.

69. Fakuloo mimmaa ghanimtum ḥalaalan ṭayyibaa; wattaqullaah; innal-laaha Ghafoorur-Raḥeem.   **(Section 9)**

70. Yaaa ayyuhan-Nabiyyu qul liman feee aydeekum minal-asraaa iñy-ya‘lamillaahu fee quloobikum khayrañy-yu’tikum khayram-mimmaaa ukhiza minkum wa yaghfir lakum; wallaahu Ghafoorur-Raḥeem.

يَآأَيُّهَا النَّبِيُّ حَسْبُكَ اللهُ وَمَنِ اتَّبَعَكَ مِنَ الْمُؤْمِنِينَ ۞

يَآأَيُّهَا النَّبِيُّ حَرِّضِ الْمُؤْمِنِينَ عَلَى الْقِتَالِ ۗ إِن يَكُن مِّنكُمْ عِشْرُونَ صَابِرُونَ يَغْلِبُوا مِائَتَيْنِ ۚ وَإِن يَكُن مِّنكُم مِّائَةٌ يَغْلِبُوٓا أَلْفًا مِّنَ الَّذِينَ كَفَرُوا بِأَنَّهُمْ قَوْمٌ لَّا يَفْقَهُونَ ۞

الْـٰٔنَ خَفَّفَ اللهُ عَنكُمْ وَعَلِمَ أَنَّ فِيكُمْ ضَعْفًا ۚ فَإِن يَكُن مِّنكُم مِّائَةٌ صَابِرَةٌ يَغْلِبُوا مِائَتَيْنِ ۚ وَإِن يَكُن مِّنكُمْ أَلْفٌ يَغْلِبُوٓا أَلْفَيْنِ بِإِذْنِ اللهِ ۗ وَاللهُ مَعَ الصَّابِرِينَ ۞

مَا كَانَ لِنَبِيٍّ أَن يَكُونَ لَهُ أَسْرَىٰ حَتَّىٰ يُثْخِنَ فِي الْأَرْضِ ۚ تُرِيدُونَ عَرَضَ الدُّنْيَا وَاللهُ يُرِيدُ الْآخِرَةَ ۗ وَاللهُ عَزِيزٌ حَكِيمٌ ۞

لَّوْلَا كِتَابٌ مِّنَ اللهِ سَبَقَ لَمَسَّكُمْ فِيمَآ أَخَذْتُمْ عَذَابٌ عَظِيمٌ ۞

فَكُلُوا مِمَّا غَنِمْتُمْ حَلَالًا طَيِّبًا ۚ وَاتَّقُوا اللهَ ۚ إِنَّ اللهَ غَفُورٌ رَّحِيمٌ ۞

يَآأَيُّهَا النَّبِيُّ قُل لِّمَن فِي أَيْدِيكُم مِّنَ الْأَسْرَىٰ إِن يَعْلَمِ اللهُ فِي قُلُوبِكُمْ خَيْرًا يُؤْتِكُمْ خَيْرًا مِّمَّا أُخِذَ مِنكُمْ وَيَغْفِرْ لَكُمْ ۗ وَاللهُ غَفُورٌ رَّحِيمٌ ۞

71. But if they have treacherous designs against you,(O Apostle!), they have already been in treason against Allah, and so has He given (you) power over them. And Allah is He Who has (full) knowledge and wisdom.

72. Those who believed, and adopted exile, and fought for the Faith, with their property and their persons, in the cause of Allah, as well as those who gave (them) asylum and aid,- these are (all) friends and protectors, one of another. As to those who believed but came not into exile, you owe no duty of protection to them until they come into exile; but if they seek your aid in religion, it is your duty to help them, except against a people with whom you have a treaty of mutual alliance. And (remember) Allah sees all that you do.

73. The Unbelievers are protectors, one of another: unless you do this, (protect each other), there would be tumult and oppression on earth, and great mischief.

74. Those who believe, and adopt exile, and fight for the Faith, in the cause of Allah as well as those who give (them) asylum and aid,- these are (all) in very truth the Believers: for them is the forgiveness of sins and a provision most generous.

75. And those who accept Faith subsequently, and adopt exile, and fight for the Faith in your company,- they are of you. But kindred by blood have prior rights against each other in the Book of Allah. Verily Allah is well-acquainted with all things.

71. Wa iñy-yureedoo khiyaanataka faqad khaanullaaha min qablu fa-amkana minhum; wallaahu 'Aleemun Ḥakeem.

72. Innal-lazeena aamanoo wa haajaroo wa jaahadoo bi-amwaalihim wa anfusihim fee sabeelil-laahi wallazeena aawaw wa naṣarooo ulaaa'ika ba'ḍuhum awliyaaa'u ba'ḍ; wallazeena aamanoo wa lam yuhaajiroo maa lakum miñw-walaayatihim min shay'in ḥattaa yuhaajiroo; wa inistanṣarookum fid-deeni fa'alayku-munnaṣru illaa 'alaa qawmim baynakum wa baynahum meeṣaaq; wallaahu bimaa ta'maloona Baṣeer.

73. Wallazeena kafaroo ba'ḍuhum awliyaaa'u ba'ḍ; illaa taf'aloohu takun fitnatun fil-arḍi wa fasaadun kabeer.

74. Wallazeena aamanoo wa haajaroo wa jaahadoo fee sabeelil-laahi wallazeena aawaw wa naṣarooo ulaaa'ika humul-mu'minoona ḥaqqaa; lahum maghfiratuñw-wa rizqun kareem.

75. Wallazeena aamanoo mim ba'du wa haajaroo wa jaahadoo ma'akum faulaaa'ika minkum; wa ulul-arḥaami baḍuhum awlaa biba'ḍin fee Kitaabil-laah; innal-laaha bikulli shay'in 'Aleem. **(Section 10)**

9. Repentance or Immunity

Sûrat al-Taubah/Barâ'at –9
(Revealed at Madinah)

1. A (declaration) of immunity from Allah and His Apostle, to those of the Pagans with whom you have contracted mutual alliances:-

2. You go, then, for four months, backwards and forwards, (as you will), throughout the land, but know that you cannot frustrate Allah (by your falsehood) but that Allah will cover with shame those who reject Him.

3. And an announcement from Allah and His Apostle, to the people (assembled) on the day of the Great Pilgrimage,- that Allah and His Apostle dissolve (treaty) obligations with the Pagans. If then, you repent, it were best for you; but if you turn away, you (should) know that you cannot frustrate Allah. And proclaim a grievous Chastisement to those who reject Faith.

4. (But the treaties are) not dissolved with those Pagans with whom you have entered into alliance and who have not subsequently failed you in any thing, nor aided any one against you. So fulfil your agreements with them to the end of their term: for Allah loves the righteous.

5. But when the forbidden months are past, then fight and slay the Pagans wherever you find them, and seize them, beleaguer them, and lie in wait for them in every stratagem (of war); but if they repent, and establish regular prayers and practise regular charity, then open the way for them: for Allah is Oft-forgiving, Most Merciful.

6. If one amongst the Pagans ask you for asylum, grant it to him, so that he may hear the Word of Allah; and then escort him to where he can be secure. This is because they are

1. Baraaa'atum-minal-laahi wa Rasooliheee ilal-lazeena 'aahattum-minal-mushrikeen.

2. Faseehoo fil-ardi arba'ata ashhuriñw-wa'lamooo annakum ghayru mu'jizil-laahi wa annal-laaha mukhzil-kaafireen.

3. Wa azaanum-minal-laahi wa Rasooliheee ilan-naasi yawmal-Hajjil-Akbari annal-laaha bareee'um-minal-mush-rikeena wa Rasooluh; fa-in tubtum fahuwa khayrullakum wa in tawallaytum fa'lamooo annakum ghayru mu'jizil-laah; wa bashshiril-lazeena kafaroo biazaabin aleem.

4. Illal-lazeena 'aahattum minal-mushrikeena summa lam yanqusookum shay'añw-wa lam yuzaahiroo 'alaykum ahadan fa-atimmooo ilayhim 'ahdahum ilaa muddatihim; innal-laaha yuhibbul-muttaqeen.

5. Fa-izansalakhal Ash-hurul Hurumu faqtulul-mushrikeena haysu wajattumoohum wa khuzoohum wahsuroohum waq'udoo lahum kulla marsad; fa-in taaboo wa aqaamus-Salaata wa aatawuz-Zakaata fakhalloo sabeelahum; innal-laaha Ghafoorur-Raheem.

6. Wa in ahadum-minal-mushrikeenas-tajaaraka fa-ajirhu hattaa yasma'a Kalaa-mal-laahi summa ablighhu maå-manah; zaalika bi-annahum

men without knowledge.

qawmul-laa ya'lamoon.
(Section 1)

قَوْمٌ لَّا يَعْلَمُوْنَ ۟

7. How can there be a league, before Allah and His Apostle, with the Pagans, except those with whom you made a treaty near the Sacred Mosque? As long as these stand true to you, you stand true to them: for Allah loves the righteous.

7. Kayfa yakoonu lilmush-rikeena 'ahdun 'indallaahi wa 'inda Rasooliheee illal-lazeena 'aahattum 'indal-Masjidil-Haraami famas-taqaamoo lakum fastaqeemoo lahum; innallaaha yuhibbul-muttaqeen.

كَيْفَ يَكُوْنُ لِلْمُشْرِكِيْنَ عَهْدٌ عِنْدَ اللهِ وَعِنْدَ رَسُوْلِهٖ اِلَّا الَّذِيْنَ عَاهَدْتُّمْ عِنْدَ الْمَسْجِدِ الْحَرَامِ ۚ فَمَا اسْتَقَامُوْا لَكُمْ فَاسْتَقِيْمُوْا لَهُمْ ؕ اِنَّ اللهَ يُحِبُّ الْمُتَّقِيْنَ ۟

8. How (can there be such a league), seeing that if they get an advantage over you, they do not respect in you the ties either of kinship or of covenant? With (fair words from) their mouths they please you, but their hearts are averse from you; and most of them are rebellious and wicked.

8. Kayfa wa iny-yazharoo 'alaykum laa yarquboo feekum illanw-wa laa zimmah; yurdoo-nakum biafwaahihim wa taåbaa quloobuhum wa aksaruhum faasiqoon.

كَيْفَ وَاِنْ يَّظْهَرُوْا عَلَيْكُمْ لَا يَرْقُبُوْا فِيْكُمْ اِلًّا وَّلَا ذِمَّةً ؕ يُرْضُوْنَكُمْ بِاَفْوَاهِهِمْ وَتَاْبٰى قُلُوْبُهُمْ ۚ وَاَكْثَرُهُمْ فٰسِقُوْنَ ۟

9. The Signs of Allah have they sold for a miserable price, and (many) have they hindered from His Way: evil indeed are the deeds they have done.

9. Ishtaraw bi-Aaayaatil-laahi samanan qaleelan fasaddoo'an sabeelih; innahum saaa'a maa kaanoo ya'maloon.

اِشْتَرَوْا بِاٰيٰتِ اللهِ ثَمَنًا قَلِيْلًا فَصَدُّوْا عَنْ سَبِيْلِهٖ ؕ اِنَّهُمْ سَآءَ مَا كَانُوْا يَعْمَلُوْنَ ۟

10. In a Believer they do not respect the ties either of kinship or of covenant! It is they who have transgressed all bounds.

10. Laa yarquboona fee mu'-minin illanw-wa laa zimmah; wa ulaaa'ika humulmu'ta-doon.

لَا يَرْقُبُوْنَ فِيْ مُؤْمِنٍ اِلًّا وَّلَا ذِمَّةً ؕ وَاُولٰٓئِكَ هُمُ الْمُعْتَدُوْنَ ۟

11. But (even so), if they repent, establish regular prayers, and practise regular charity,- then they are your brethren in Faith: (thus) do We explain the Signs in detail, for those who understand.

11. Fa-in taaboo wa aqaamus-Salaata wa aatawuz-Zakaata fa-ikhwaanukum fid-deen; wa nufassilul-Aaayaati liqawminy-ya'lamoon.

فَاِنْ تَابُوْا وَاَقَامُوا الصَّلٰوةَ وَاٰتَوُا الزَّكٰوةَ فَاِخْوَانُكُمْ فِى الدِّيْنِ ؕ وَنُفَصِّلُ الْاٰيٰتِ لِقَوْمٍ يَّعْلَمُوْنَ ۟

12. But if they violate their oaths after their covenant, and taunt you for your Faith,- you fight the chiefs of Unfaith: for their oaths are nothing to them: that thus they may be restrained.

12. Wa in nakasooo aymaana-hum mim ba'di-'ahdihim wa ta'anoo fee deenikum faqaati-looo a'immatal-kufri innahum laaa aymaana lahum la'allahum yantahoon.

وَاِنْ نَّكَثُوْا اَيْمَانَهُمْ مِّنْ بَعْدِ عَهْدِهِمْ وَطَعَنُوْا فِيْ دِيْنِكُمْ فَقَاتِلُوْا اَئِمَّةَ الْكُفْرِ ۙ اِنَّهُمْ لَا اَيْمَانَ لَهُمْ لَعَلَّهُمْ يَنْتَهُوْنَ ۟

13. Will you not fight people who violated their oaths, plotted to expel the Apostle, and took the aggressive by being the first (to assault) you? Do you fear them? Nay, it is Allah Whom you should more justly fear, if you

13. Alaa tuqaatiloona qaw-man nakasooo aymaanahum wa hammoo bi-ikhraajir-Rasooli wa hum bada'ookum awwala marrah; atakhshawnahum; fallaahu ahaqqu an takhshawhu in kuntum

اَلَا تُقَاتِلُوْنَ قَوْمًا نَّكَثُوْا اَيْمَانَهُمْ وَهَمُّوْا بِاِخْرَاجِ الرَّسُوْلِ وَهُمْ بَدَءُوْكُمْ اَوَّلَ مَرَّةٍ ؕ اَتَخْشَوْنَهُمْ ۚ فَاللهُ اَحَقُّ اَنْ تَخْشَوْهُ اِنْ كُنْتُمْ

believe!

14. Fight them, and Allah will punish them by your hands, cover them with shame, help you (to victory) over them, heal the breasts of Believers,

15. And still the indignation of their hearts. For Allah will turn (in mercy) to whom He will; and Allah is All-Knowing, All-Wise.

16. On do you think that you shall be abandoned, as though Allah did not know those among you who strive with might and main, and take none for friends and protectors except Allah, His Apostle, and the (community of) Believers? But Allah is well-acquainted with (all) that you do.

17. It is not for such as join gods with Allah, to visit or maintain the mosques of Allah while they witness against their own souls to infidelity. The works of such bear no fruit: In Fire shall they dwell.

18. The mosques of Allah shall be visited and maintained by such as believe in Allah and the Last Day, establish regular prayers, and practise regular charity, and fear none (at all) except Allah. It is they who are expected to be on true guidance.

19. Do you make the giving of drink to pilgrims, or the maintenance of the Sacred Mosque, equal to (the pious service of) those who believe in Allah and the Last Day, and strive with might and main in the cause of Allah? They are not comparable in the sight of Allah: and Allah does not guides those who do wrong.

mu'mineen.

14. Qaatiloohum yu'az-zib-humul-laahu bi-aydeekum wa yukhzihim wa yanṣurkum 'alayhim wa yashfi ṣudoora qawmim mu'mineen.

15. Wa yuzhib ghayẓa quloo-bihim; wa yatoobullaahi 'alaa mañy-yashaaa'; wallaahu 'Aleemun Ḥakeem.

16. Am ḥasibtum an tutrakoo wa lammaa ya'lamil-laahul-lazeena jaahadoo minkum wa lam yattakhizoo min doonil-laahi wa laa Rasoolihee wa lalmu'mineena waleejah; wallaahu-khabeerum bimaa ta'maloon.   (Section 2)

17. Maa kaana lilmushrikeena añy-ya'muroo masaajidal-laahi shaahideena 'alaaa anfusihim bilkufr; ulaaa'ika ḥabiṭat a'maaluhum wa fin-Naari hum khaalidoon.

18. Innamaa ya'muru masaa-jidal-laahi man aamana billaahi wal-Yawmil-Aakhiri wa aqaa-maṣ-Ṣalaata wa aataz-Zakaata wa lam yakhsha illal-laaha fa'asaaa ulaaa'ika añy-yakoo-noo minal-muhtadeen.

19. Aja'altum siqaayatal-ḥaaajji wa 'imaaratal-Masjidil-Ḥaraami kaman aamana billaahi wal-Yawmil-Aakhiri wa jaahada fee sabeelil-laah; laa yastawoona 'indal-laah; wallaahu laa yahdil-qawmaz-ẓaalimeen.

مُّؤْمِنِيْنَ ۞

قَاتِلُوْهُمْ يُعَذِّبْهُمُ اللّٰهُ بِاَيْدِيْكُمْ وَيُخْزِهِمْ وَيَنْصُرْكُمْ عَلَيْهِمْ وَيَشْفِ صُدُوْرَ قَوْمٍ مُّؤْمِنِيْنَ ۞

وَيُذْهِبْ غَيْظَ قُلُوْبِهِمْ ۖ وَيَتُوْبُ اللّٰهُ عَلٰى مَنْ يَّشَآءُ ۗ وَاللّٰهُ عَلِيْمٌ حَكِيْمٌ ۞

اَمْ حَسِبْتُمْ اَنْ تُتْرَكُوْا وَلَمَّا يَعْلَمِ اللّٰهُ الَّذِيْنَ جَاهَدُوْا مِنْكُمْ وَلَمْ يَتَّخِذُوْا مِنْ دُوْنِ اللّٰهِ وَلَا رَسُوْلِهٖ وَلَا الْمُؤْمِنِيْنَ وَلِيْجَةً ۚ وَاللّٰهُ خَبِيْرٌۢ بِمَا تَعْمَلُوْنَ ۞

مَا كَانَ لِلْمُشْرِكِيْنَ اَنْ يَّعْمُرُوْا مَسٰجِدَ اللّٰهِ شٰهِدِيْنَ عَلٰٓى اَنْفُسِهِمْ بِالْكُفْرِ ۚ اُولٰٓئِكَ حَبِطَتْ اَعْمَالُهُمْ ۚ وَفِي النَّارِ هُمْ خٰلِدُوْنَ ۞

اِنَّمَا يَعْمُرُ مَسٰجِدَ اللّٰهِ مَنْ اٰمَنَ بِاللّٰهِ وَالْيَوْمِ الْاٰخِرِ وَاَقَامَ الصَّلٰوةَ وَاٰتَى الزَّكٰوةَ وَلَمْ يَخْشَ اِلَّا اللّٰهَ ۖ فَعَسٰٓى اُولٰٓئِكَ اَنْ يَّكُوْنُوْا مِنَ الْمُهْتَدِيْنَ ۞

اَجَعَلْتُمْ سِقَايَةَ الْحَاجِّ وَعِمَارَةَ الْمَسْجِدِ الْحَرَامِ كَمَنْ اٰمَنَ بِاللّٰهِ وَالْيَوْمِ الْاٰخِرِ وَجَاهَدَ فِيْ سَبِيْلِ اللّٰهِ ۗ لَا يَسْتَوُوْنَ عِنْدَ اللّٰهِ ۗ وَاللّٰهُ لَا يَهْدِى الْقَوْمَ الظّٰلِمِيْنَ ۞

20. Those who believe, and suffer exile and strive with might and main, in Allah's cause, with their goods and their persons, have the highest rank in the sight of Allah: they are the people who will achieve (salvation).

21. Their Lord gives them glad tidings of a Mercy from Himself, of His good pleasure, and of gardens for them, wherein are delights that endure:

22. They will dwell therein for ever. Verily in Allah's presence is a reward, the greatest (of all).

23. O you who believe! Do not take for protectors your fathers and your brothers if they love infidelity above Faith: if any of you do so, they do wrong.

24. Say: If it be that your fathers, your sons, your brothers, your mates, or your kindred; the wealth that you have gained; the commerce in which you fear a decline: or the dwellings in which you delight - are dearer to you than Allah, or His Apostle, or the striving in His cause;- then wait until Allah brings about His Decision: and Allah does not guides the rebellious.

25. Assuredly Allah did help you in many battle-fields and on the day of Hunain: Behold! your great numbers elated you, but they availed you nothing: the land, for all that it is wide,

20. Allazeena aamanoo wa haajaroo wa jaahadoo fee sabeelil-laahi bi-amwaalihim wa anfusihim a'zamu darajatan 'indal-laah; wa ulaaa'ika humul-faaa'izoon.

21. Yubashshiruhum Rabbu-hum biraḥmatim-minhu wa riḍwaaniñw-wa Jannaatil-lahum feehaa na'eemum-muqeem.

22. Khaalideena feehaaa aba-daa; innal-laaha 'indahooo ajrun 'azeem.

23. Yaaa ayyuhal-lazeena aa-manoo laa tattakhizooo aabaaa-'akum wa ikhwaanakum awliyaaa'a inis-taḥabbul-kufra 'alal-eemaan; wa mañy-yata-wal-lahum minkum fa-ulaaa'ika humuz-zaalimoon.

24. Qul in kaana aabaa-aa'ukum wa abnaaa'ukum wa ikhwaanukum wa azwaajukum wa 'asheeratukum wa amwaa-luniq-taraftumoohaa wa tijaa-ratun takhshawna kasaadahaa wa masaakinu tarḍawnahaaa aḥabba ilaykum minal-laahi wa Rasoolihee wa Jihaadin fee Sabeelihee fatarabbaṣoo ḥattaa yaåtiyallaahu bi-amrih; wallaahu laa yahdil-qawmal-faasiqeen.

(Section 3)

25. Laqad naṣarakumul-laahu fee mawaatina kaṣeeratiñw-wa yawma Ḥunaynin iz a'jabatkum kasratukum falam tughni 'ankum shay'añw-wa ḍaaqat 'alaykumul-arḍu bimaa

did constrain you, and you turned back in retreat.

26. But Allah poured His calm on the Apostle and on the Believers, and sent down forces which you did not see: He punished the Unbelievers; thus does He reward those without Faith.

27. Again will Allah, after this, turn (in mercy) to whom He will: for Allah is Oft- forgiving, Most Merciful.

28. O you who believe! Truly the Pagans are unclean; so let them not, after this year of theirs, approach the Sacred Mosque. And if you fear poverty, soon will Allah enrich you, if He wills, out of His bounty, for Allah is All-Knowing, All-Wise.

29. Fight those who did not believe in Allah nor the Last Day, nor hold that forbidden which has been forbidden by Allah and His Apostle, nor acknowledge the Religion of Truth, (even if they are) of the People of the Book, until they pay the Jizya with willing submission, and feel themselves subdued.

30. The Jews call 'Uzair a son of Allah, and the Christians call Christ the son of Allah. That is a saying from their mouth;(in this) they but imitate what the Unbelievers of old used to say. Allah's curse be on them: how they are deluded away from the Truth!

31. They take their priests and their anchorites to be their lords in derogation of Allah, and (they take as their Lord) Christ the son of

rahubat summa wallaytum mudbireen.

26. Summa anzalal-laahu sakeenatahoo 'alaa Rasoolihee wa 'alalmu'mineena wa anzala junoodal-lam tarawhaa wa azzabal-lazeena kafaroo; wa zaalika jazaaa'ul-kaafireen.

27. Summa yatoobul-laahu mim ba'di zaalika 'alaa mañy-yashaaa'; wallaahu Ghafoorur-Raheem.

28. Yaaa ayyuhal-lazeena aamanooo innamal-mushrikoona najasun falaa yaqrabul-Masjidal-Haraama ba'da 'aami-him haazaa; wa in khiftum 'aylatan fasawfa yughnee-kumul-laahu min fadliheee in shaaa'; innallaaha 'Aleemun Hakeem.

29. Qaatilul-lazeena laa yu'mi-noona billaahi wa laa bil-Yawmil-Aakhiri wa laa yuharri-moona maa harramal-laahu wa Rasooluhoo wa laa yadee-noona deenal-haqqi minal-lazeena ootul-Kitaaba hattaa yu'tul-jizyata 'añy-yadiñw-wa hum saaghiroon.   **(Section 4)**

30. Wa qaalatil-Yahoodu 'Uzayrunib-nul-laahi wa qaala-tin-Nasaaral-Maseehub-nul-laahi zaalika qawluhum bi-afwaahihim yudaahi'oona qawlal-lazeena kafaroo min qabl; qatalahumul-laah; annaa yu'fakoon.

31. Ittakhazooo ahbaarahum wa ruhbaanahum arbaabammin doonil-laahi wal-Maseehab-na-

Mary; yet they were commanded to worship but One God (Allah): there is no god but He. Praise and glory to Him: (Far is He) from having the partners they associate (with Him).

32. Fain would they extinguish Allah's light with their mouths, but Allah will not allow but that His Light should be perfected, even though the Unbelievers may detest (it).

33. It is He Who has sent His Apostle with guidance and the Religion of Truth, to proclaim it over all religion, even though the Pagans may detest (it).

34. O you who believe! there are indeed many among the priests and anchorites, who in falsehood devour the substance of men and hinder (them) from the Way of Allah. And there are those who bury gold and silver and do not spend it in the Way of Allah: announce to them a most grievous Chastisement-

35. On the Day when heat will be produced out of that (wealth) in the fire of Hell, and with it will be branded their foreheads, their flanks, and their backs- "This is the (treasure) which you buried for yourselves: you then taste, the (treasures) you buried!"

36. The number of months in the sight of Allah is twelve (in a year)- so ordained by Him the day He created the heavens and the earth; of them four are sacred: that is the straight usage. So do not wrong yourselves therein,

Maryama wa maaa umirooo illaa liya'budooo Ilaahañw-Waa-ḥidan laaa ilaaha illaa Hoo; Subḥaanahoo 'ammaa yushrikoon.

32. Yureedoona añy-yuṭfi'oo nooral-laahi bi-afwaahihim wa yaåballaahu illaaa añy- yutimma noorahoo wa law karihal-kaafiroon.

33. Huwal-lazeee ar-sala Rasoolahoo bilhudaa wa deenil-ḥaqqi liyuẓhirahoo 'alad-deeni kullihee wa law karihal-mushrikoon.

34. Yaaa ayyuhal-lazeena aamanooo inna kaseeramminal-aḥbaari warruhbaani la-yaå-kuloona amwaalan-naasi bil-baaṭili wa yaṣuddoona 'an sabeelil-laah; wallazeena yak-nizoonaz-zahaba walfiḍḍata wa laayunfiqoonahaa fee sabeelil-laahi fabashshirhum bi'azaabin aleem.

35. Yawma yuḥmaa 'alayhaa fee Naari Jahannama fatukwaa bihaa jibaahuhum wa junoo-buhum wa ẓuhooruhum haazaa maa kanaztum li-anfusikum fazooqoo maa kuntum takni-zoon.

36. Inna 'iddatash-shuhoori 'indal-laahis-naa 'ashara shah-ran fee Kitaabil-laahi yawma khalaqas-samaawaati wal-arḍa minhaaa arba'atun ḥurum; zaalikad-deenul-qayyim; falaa taẓlimoo feehinna anfusakum;

مَرْيَمَ ۚ وَمَآ أُمِرُوٓا إِلَّا لِيَعْبُدُوٓا إِلَٰهًا وَٰحِدًا ۖ لَّآ إِلَٰهَ إِلَّا هُوَ ۚ سُبْحَٰنَهُۥ عَمَّا يُشْرِكُونَ ۝

يُرِيدُونَ أَن يُطْفِـُٔوا نُورَ ٱللَّهِ بِأَفْوَٰهِهِمْ وَيَأْبَى ٱللَّهُ إِلَّآ أَن يُتِمَّ نُورَهُۥ وَلَوْ كَرِهَ ٱلْكَٰفِرُونَ ۝

هُوَ ٱلَّذِىٓ أَرْسَلَ رَسُولَهُۥ بِٱلْهُدَىٰ وَدِينِ ٱلْحَقِّ لِيُظْهِرَهُۥ عَلَى ٱلدِّينِ كُلِّهِۦ وَلَوْ كَرِهَ ٱلْمُشْرِكُونَ ۝

يَٰٓأَيُّهَا ٱلَّذِينَ ءَامَنُوٓا إِنَّ كَثِيرًا مِّنَ ٱلْأَحْبَارِ وَٱلرُّهْبَانِ لَيَأْكُلُونَ أَمْوَٰلَ ٱلنَّاسِ بِٱلْبَٰطِلِ وَيَصُدُّونَ عَن سَبِيلِ ٱللَّهِ ۗ وَٱلَّذِينَ يَكْنِزُونَ ٱلذَّهَبَ وَٱلْفِضَّةَ وَلَا يُنفِقُونَهَا فِى سَبِيلِ ٱللَّهِ فَبَشِّرْهُم بِعَذَابٍ أَلِيمٍ ۝

يَوْمَ يُحْمَىٰ عَلَيْهَا فِى نَارِ جَهَنَّمَ فَتُكْوَىٰ بِهَا جِبَاهُهُمْ وَجُنُوبُهُمْ وَظُهُورُهُمْ ۖ هَٰذَا مَا كَنَزْتُمْ لِأَنفُسِكُمْ فَذُوقُوا مَا كُنتُمْ تَكْنِزُونَ ۝

إِنَّ عِدَّةَ ٱلشُّهُورِ عِندَ ٱللَّهِ ٱثْنَا عَشَرَ شَهْرًا فِى كِتَٰبِ ٱللَّهِ يَوْمَ خَلَقَ ٱلسَّمَٰوَٰتِ وَٱلْأَرْضَ مِنْهَآ أَرْبَعَةٌ حُرُمٌ ۚ ذَٰلِكَ ٱلدِّينُ ٱلْقَيِّمُ ۚ فَلَا تَظْلِمُوا فِيهِنَّ أَنفُسَكُمْ

and fight the Pagans all together as they fight you all together. But know that Allah is with those who restrain themselves.

37. Verily the transposing (of a prohibited month) is an addition to Unbelief: the Unbelievers are led to wrong thereby: for they make it lawful one year, and forbidden another year, in order to adjust the number of months forbidden by Allah and make such forbidden ones lawful. The evil of their course seems pleasing to them. But Allah does not guides those who reject Faith.

38. O you who believe! what is the matter with you, that, when you are asked to go forth in the Cause of Allah, you cling heavily to the earth? Do you prefer the life of this world to the Hereafter? But little is the comfort of this life, as compared with the Hereafter.

39. Unless you go forth, He will punish you with a grievous Chastisement, and put others in your place; but Him you would not harm in the least. For Allah has power over all things.

40. If you help not (your leader), (it is no matter): for Allah did indeed help him, when the Unbelievers drove him out: he had no more than one companion; they two were in the Cave, and he said to his companion, "Have no fear, for Allah is with us": then Allah sent down His peace upon him, and strengthened him with forces which you did not see, and humbled to the depths the word of the Unbelievers. But the word of Allah is exalted to the heights: for Allah is Exalted in might, Wise.

wa qaatilul-mushrikeena kaaaf-fatan kamaa yuqaati-loonakum kaaaffah; wa'lamooo annal-laaha ma'al-muttaqeen.

37. Innaman-naseee'u ziyaa-datun filkufri yuḍallu bihil-lazeena kafaroo yuḥil-loonahoo 'aamaňw-wa yuḥar-rimoonahoo 'aamalliyu-waaṭi'oo 'iddata maa ḥarramal-laahu fayuḥilloo maa ḥarramal-laah; zuyyina lahum sooo'u a'maalihim; wallaahu laa yahdil-qawmal-kaafireen   (Section 5)

38. Yaaa ayyuhal-lazeena aamanoo maa lakum izaa qeela lakumun-firoo fee sabeelil-laahis-saaqaltum ilal-arḍ; araḍeetum bilḥayaatid-dunyaa minal-Aakhirah; famaa mataa'ul-ḥayaatiddunyaa fil-Aakhirati illaa qaleel.

39. Illaa tanfiroo yu'az-zib-kum 'azaaban aleemaňw-wa yastabdil qawman ghayrakum wa laa taḍurroohu shay'aa; wal-laahu 'alaa kulli shay'in Qadeer.

40. Illaa tanṣuroohu faqad naṣarahul-laahu iz akhrajahul-lazeena kafaroo saaniyasnayni iz humaa filghaari iz yaqoolu liṣaaḥibihee laa taḥzan innal-laaha ma'anaa fa-anzalallaahu sakeenatahoo 'alayhi wa ayyadahoo bijunoodil-lam ta-rawhaa wa ja'ala kalimatal-lazeena kafarus-suflaa; wa Kalimatul-laahi hiyal-'ulyaa; wallaahu 'Azeezun Ḥakeem.

وَقَاتِلُوا الْمُشْرِكِينَ كَآفَّةً كَمَا يُقَاتِلُونَكُمْ كَآفَّةً ۚ وَاعْلَمُوا أَنَّ اللَّهَ مَعَ الْمُتَّقِينَ ۝

إِنَّمَا النَّسِيءُ زِيَادَةٌ فِي الْكُفْرِ يُضَلُّ بِهِ الَّذِينَ كَفَرُوا يُحِلُّونَهُ عَامًا وَيُحَرِّمُونَهُ عَامًا لِّيُوَاطِئُوا عِدَّةَ مَا حَرَّمَ اللَّهُ فَيُحِلُّوا مَا حَرَّمَ اللَّهُ ۚ زُيِّنَ لَهُمْ سُوءُ أَعْمَالِهِمْ ۗ وَاللَّهُ لَا يَهْدِي الْقَوْمَ الْكَافِرِينَ ۝

يَا أَيُّهَا الَّذِينَ آمَنُوا مَا لَكُمْ إِذَا قِيلَ لَكُمُ انفِرُوا فِي سَبِيلِ اللَّهِ اثَّاقَلْتُمْ إِلَى الْأَرْضِ ۚ أَرَضِيتُم بِالْحَيَاةِ الدُّنْيَا مِنَ الْآخِرَةِ ۚ فَمَا مَتَاعُ الْحَيَاةِ الدُّنْيَا فِي الْآخِرَةِ إِلَّا قَلِيلٌ ۝

إِلَّا تَنفِرُوا يُعَذِّبْكُمْ عَذَابًا أَلِيمًا وَيَسْتَبْدِلْ قَوْمًا غَيْرَكُمْ وَلَا تَضُرُّوهُ شَيْئًا ۗ وَاللَّهُ عَلَى كُلِّ شَيْءٍ قَدِيرٌ ۝

إِلَّا تَنصُرُوهُ فَقَدْ نَصَرَهُ اللَّهُ إِذْ أَخْرَجَهُ الَّذِينَ كَفَرُوا ثَانِيَ اثْنَيْنِ إِذْ هُمَا فِي الْغَارِ إِذْ يَقُولُ لِصَاحِبِهِ لَا تَحْزَنْ إِنَّ اللَّهَ مَعَنَا ۖ فَأَنزَلَ اللَّهُ سَكِينَتَهُ عَلَيْهِ وَأَيَّدَهُ بِجُنُودٍ لَّمْ تَرَوْهَا وَجَعَلَ كَلِمَةَ الَّذِينَ كَفَرُوا السُّفْلَىٰ ۗ وَكَلِمَةُ اللَّهِ هِيَ الْعُلْيَا ۗ وَاللَّهُ عَزِيزٌ حَكِيمٌ ۝

41. You go forth, (whether equipped) lightly or heavily, and strive and struggle, with your goods and your persons, in the Cause of Allah. That is best for you, if you (but) knew.

42. If there had been immediate gain (in sight), and the journey easy, they would (all) without doubt have followed you, but the distance was long, (and weighed) on them. They would indeed swear by Allah, "If we only could, we should certainly have come out with you": they would destroy their own souls; for Allah knows that they are certainly lying.

43. Allah gave you grace! why did you grant them exemption until those who told the truth were seen by you in a clear light, and you had proved the liars?

44. Those who believe in Allah and the Last Day ask you for no exemption from fighting with their goods and persons. And Allah knows well those who do their duty.

45. Only those ask you for exemption who do not believe in Allah and the Last Day, and whose hearts are in doubt, so that they are tossed in their doubts to and fro.

46. If they had intended to come out, they would certainly have made some preparation therefor; but Allah was averse to their being sent forth; so He made them lag behind, and they were told, "You sit among those who sit (inactive)."

47. If they had come out with you, they would not have added to your (strength) but

41. Infiroo khifaafañw-wa siqaalañw-wa jaahidoo bi-amwaalikum wa anfusikum fee sabeelil-laah; zaalikum khay-rul-lakum in kuntum ta'lamoon.

42. Law kaana 'araḍan qareebañw-wa safaran qaaṣiḍal-lattaba'ooka wa laakim ba'udat 'alayhimush-shuqqah; wa sayaḥlifoona billaahi lawis-tata'naa lakharajnaa ma'akum; yuhlikoona anfusahum wal-laahu ya'lamu innahum lakaa-ziboon.   (Section 6)

43. 'Afal-laahu 'anka lima aẕinta lahum ḥattaa yatabay-yana lakal-lazeena ṣadaqoo wa ta'lamal-kaazibeen.

44. Laa yastaåẕinukal-lazeena yu'minoona billaahi wal-Yawmil-Aakhiri añy-yujaa-hidoo bi-amwaalihim wa anfusihim; wallaahu 'aleemum bilmut-taqeen.

45. Innamaa yastaåẕinukal-lazeena laa yu'minoona billaahi wal-Yawmil-Aakhiri wartaabat quloobuhum fahum fee raybi-him yataraddadoon.

46. Wa law araadul-khurooja la-a'addoo lahoo 'uddatañw-wa laakin karihal-laahum-bi'aa-sahum fasabbaṭahum wa qeelaq-'udoo ma'al-qaa'ideen.

47. Law kharajoo feekum maa zaadookum illaa

only (made for) disorder, hurrying here and there in your midst and sowing sedition among you, and there would have been some among you who would have listened to them . But Allah knows well those who do wrong.

48. Indeed they had plotted sedition before, and upset matters for you, until,- the Truth arrived, and the Decree of Allah became manifest, much to their disgust.

49. Among them is (many) a man who says: "Grant me ex-emption and do not draw me into trial." Have they not fallen into trial already? and indeed Hell surrounds the Unbelievers (on all sides).

50. If good befalls you, it grieves them; but if a misfortune befalls you, they say, "We took indeed our precautions beforehand," and they turn away rejoicing.

51. Say: "Nothing will happen to us except what Allah has decreed for us: He is our Protector": and on Allah let the Believers put their trust.

52. Say: "Can you expect for us (any fate) other than one of two glorious things- (Martyr-dom or victory)? But we can expect for you either that Allah will send His punishment from Himself, or by our hands. So wait (expectant); we too will wait with you."

53. Say: "Spend (for the Cause) willingly or unwillingly: from you it will not be accepted: for you are indeed a people rebellious and wicked."

54. The only reasons why their contributions are not

Khabaalañw-wa la-awḍa‘oo khilaalakum yabghoona-ku-mul-fitnata wa feekum sam-maa‘oona lahum; wallaahu ‘aleemum biẓ-ẓaalimeen.

48. Laqadib-taghawul-fitnata min qablu wa qallaboo lakal-umoora ḥattaa jaaa’al-ḥaqqu wa ẓahara amrul-laahi wa hum kaarihoon.

49. Wa minhum mañy-yaqoo-lu’-zal-lee wa laa taftinneee; alaa fil-fitnati saqaṭoo; wa inna Jahannama lamuḥeeṭatum bil-kaafireen.

50. In tuṣibka ḥasanatun tasu’hum; wa in tuṣibka muṣeebatuñy-yaqooloo qad akhaẕnaaa amranaa min qablu wa yatawallaw wa hum fariḥoon.

51. Qul lañy-yuṣeebanaaa illaa maa katabal-laahu lanaa Huwa mawlaanaa; wa ‘alal-laahi falyatawak-kalilmu’minoon.

52. Qul hal tarabbaṣoona binaaa illaaa iḥdal-ḥusnayayni wa naḥnu natarabbaṣu bikum añy-yuṣeebakumul-laahu bi‘aẕaa-bim-min ‘indihee aw biaydee-naa fatarabbaṣooo innaa ma‘akum mutarabbiṣoon.

53. Qul anfiqoo ṭaw‘an aw karhal-lañy-yutaqabbala min-kum innakum kuntum qawman faasiqeen.

54. Wa maa mana‘ahum an tuqbala minhum

accepted are: that they reject Allah and His Apostle; that they come to prayer without reluctantly and that they offer contributions unwillingly.

55. Let not their wealth nor their (following in) sons dazzle you: in reality Allah's plan is to punish them with these things in this life, and that their souls may perish in their (very) denial of Allah.

56. They swear by Allah that they are indeed of you; but they are not of you: yet they are afraid (to appear in their true colours).

57. If they could find a place to flee to, or caves, or a place of concealment, they would turn straightaway thereto, with an obstinate rush.

58. And among them are men who slander you in the matter of (the distribution of) the alms: if they are given part thereof, they are pleased, but if not, behold! they are indignant!

59. If only they had been content with what Allah and His Apostle gave them, and had said, "Sufficient unto us is Allah! Allah and His Apostle will soon give us of His bounty: to Allah do we turn our hopes!" (that would have been the right course).

60. Alms are for the poor and the needy, and those employed to administer the (funds); for those whose hearts have been (recently) reconciled (to Truth); for those in bondage and in debt; in the cause of Allah; and for the wayfarer: (thus is it) ordained by Allah, and Allah is full of knowledge and wisdom.

nafaqaatuhum illaaa annahum kafaroo billaahi wa bi-Rasoolihee wa laa yaåtoonaş-Şalaata illaa wa hum kusaalaa wa laa yunfiqoona illaa wa hum kaarihoon.

55. Falaa tu'jibka amwaa-luhum wa laaa awlaaduhum; innamaa yureedul-laahu liyu'az-zibahum bihaa fil-ḥayaatid-dunyaa wa tazhaqa anfusuhum wa hum kaafiroon.

56. Wa yaḥlifoona billaahi innahum laminkum wa maa hum minkum wa laakinnahum qawmuñy-yafraqoon.

57. Law yajidoona malja'an aw maghaaraatin aw mudda-khalal-lawallaw ilayhi wa hum yajmaḥoon.

58. Wa minhum mañy-yalmi-zuka fiş-şadaqaati Fa-in u'ţoo minhaa raḍoo wa illam yu'taw minhaaa izaa hum yaskhaţoon.

59. Wa law annahum raḍoo maaa aataahumul-laahu wa Rasooluhoo wa qaaloo ḥasbu-nal-laahu sayu'teenallaaha min faḍlihee wa Rasooluhooo innaaa ilallaahi raaghiboon.
(Section 7)

60. Innamaş-şadaqaatu lilfu-qaraaa'i walmasaakeeni wal-'aamileena 'alayhaa walmu'al-lafati quloobuhum wa fir-riqaabi-walghaarimeena wa fee sabeelil-laahi wabnis-sabeeli fareeḍatam-minal-laah; wal-laahu 'Aleemun Ḥakeem.

61. Among them are men who slander the Prophet and say, "He is (all) ear." Say, "He listens to what is best for you: he believes in Allah, has faith in the Believers, and is a Mercy to those of you who believe." But those who slander the Apostle will have a grievous Chastisement.

62. To you they swear by Allah, In order to please you: But it is more fitting that they should please Allah and His Apostle, if they are Believers.

63. Do they not know that for those who oppose Allah and His Apostle, is the Fire of Hell?- wherein they shall dwell. That is the supreme disgrace.

64. The Hypocrites are afraid lest a Sura should be sent down about them, showing them what is (really passing) in their hearts. Say: "Mock you! But verily Allah will bring to light all that you fear (should be revealed)."

65. If you question them, they declare (with emphasis): "We were only talking idly and in play." Say: "Was it at Allah, and His Signs, and His Apostle, that you were mocking?"

66. You do not make any excuses: you have rejected Faith after you had accepted it. If We pardon some of you, We will punish others amongst you, for that they are in sin.

67. The Hypocrites, men and women, (have an understanding) with each other: They enjoin evil, and forbid what is just, and are close

---

61. Wa minhumul-lazeena yu'zoonan-Nabiyya wa yaqooloona huwa -uzun; qul uzunu khayril-lakum yu'minu billaahi wa yu'minu lilmu'mi-neena wa rahmatul-lillazeena aamanoo minkum; wallazeena yu'zoona Rasoolal-laahi lahum 'azaabun aleem.

62. Yahlifoona billaahi lakum liyurdookum wallaahu wa Rasooluhooo ahaqqu any-yur-doohu in kaanoo mu'mineen.

63. Alam ya'lamooo annahoo mañy-yuhaadidillaaha wa Rasoolahoo faanna lahoo Naara Jahannama khaalidan feehaa; zaalikal-khizyul-'azeem.

64. Yahzarul-munaafiqoona an tunaz-zala 'alayhim Soora-tun tunabbi'uhum bimaa fee quloobihim; qulistahzi'oo innal-laaha mukhrijum-maa tahzaroon.

65. Wala'in sa-altahum-layaqoolunna innamaa kunnaa nakhoodu wa nal'ab; qul abillaahi wa 'Aayaatihee wa Rasoolihee kuntum tastah-zi'oon.

66. Laa ta'taziroo qad kafar-tum ba'da eemaanikum; in na'fu 'an taaa'ifatim-minkum nu'az-zib taaa'ifatam bi-anna-hum kaanoo mujrimeen.

(Section 8)

67. Almunaafiqoona walmu-naafiqaatu ba'duhum mim ba'd; yaamuroona bilmunkari wa yanhawna 'anil-ma'roofi wa yaqbidoona

---

with their hands. They have forgotten Allah; so He has forgotten them. Verily the Hypocrites are rebellious and perverse.

68. Allah has promised the Hypocrites men and women, and the rejecters, of Faith, the fire of Hell: therein shall they dwell: Sufficient is it for them: for them is the curse of Allah, and an enduring punishment,-

69. As in the case of those before you: they were mightier than you in power, and more flourishing in wealth and children. They had their enjoyment of their portion: and you have of yours, as did those before you; and you indulge in idle talk as they did. They!- their works are fruitless in this world and in the Hereafter, and they will lose (all spiritual good).

70. Has not the story reached them of those before them?- the People of Noah, and 'Ad, and Thamud; the People of Abraham, the men of Midian, and the cities overthrown. To them came their Apostles with Clear Signs. It is not Allah Who wrongs them, but they wrong their own souls.

71. The Believers, men and women, are protectors, one of another: they enjoin what is just, and forbid what is evil: they observe regular prayers, practise regular charity, and obey Allah and His Apostle. On them will Allah pour His mercy: for Allah is Exalted in power,

aydiyahum; nasul-laaha fanasiyahum; innal- munaafiqeena humul-faasi-qoon.

68. Wa'adal-laahul-munaafiqeena wal-munaafiqaati walkuffaara Naara Jahannama khaalideena feehaa; hiya ḥasbuhum; wa la'anahumul-laahu wa lahum 'azaabum-muqeem.

69. Kallazeena min qablikum kaanooo ashadda minkum quwwatañw-wa aksara amwaalañw-wa awlaadan fastamta'oo bikhalaaqihim fastamta'tum bikhalaaqikum kamas-tamta'allazeena min qablikum bikhalaaqihim wa khuḍtum kallazee khaaḍooo; ulaaa'ika ḥabiṭat a'maaluhum fid-dunyaa wal-Aakhirati wa ulaaa'ika humul-khaasiroon.

70. Alam yaåtihim naba-ullazeena min qablihim qawmi Nooḥiñw-wa 'Aadiñw-wa Samooda wa qawmi Ibraaheema wa aṣḥaabi Madyana walmu'tafikaat; atathum Rusuluhum bilbayyinaati famaa kaanallaahu liyaẓlimahum wa laakin kaanooo anfusahum yaẓlimoon.

71. Walmu'minoona walmu'minaatu ba'ḍuhum awliyaaa'u ba'ḍ; yaåmuroona bilma'roofi wa yanhawna 'anilmunkari wa yuqeemoonaṣ-Ṣalaata wa yu'toonaz-Zakaata wa yuṭee'oonal-laaha wa Rasoolah; ulaaa'ika sayarḥamuhumul-laah; innallaaha 'Azeezun

Wise.

Ḥakeem.

حَكِيمٌ ۞

72. Allah has promised to Believers, men and women, Gardens under which rivers flow, to dwell therein, and beautiful mansions in Gardens of everlasting bliss. But the greatest bliss is the Good pleasure of Allah: that is the supreme felicity.

72. Wa'adal-laahulmu'mineena walmu'minaati Jannaatin tajree min taḥtihal anhaaru khaalideena feehaa wa masaakina ṭayyibatan fee Jannaati 'Adn; wa riḍwaanum-minal-laahi akbar; zaalika huwal-fawzul-'aẓeem.   (Section 9)

73. O Prophet! strive hard against the unbelievers and the Hypocrites, and be firm against them, their abode is Hell,- an evil refuge indeed.

73. Yaaa-ayyuhan-Nabiyyu jaahidil-kuffaara walmunaafiqeena waghluẓ 'alayhim; wa maåwaahum Jahannamu wa bi'sal-maṣeer.

74. They swear by Allah that they said nothing (evil), but indeed they uttered blasphemy, and they did it after accepting Islam; and they meditated a plot which they were unable to carry out: this revenge of theirs was (their) only return for the bounty with which Allah and His Apostle had enriched them! If they repent, it will be best for them; but if they turn back (to their evil ways), Allah will punish them with a grievous Chastisement in this life and in the Hereafter: they shall have none on earth to protect or help them.

74. Yaḥlifoona billaahi maa qaaloo wa laqad qaaloo kalimatal-kufri wa kafaroo ba'da Islaamihim wa hammoo bimaa lam yanaaloo; wa maa naqamooo illaaa an aghnaahumullaahu wa Rasooluhoo min faḍlih; faiñy yatooboo yaku khayral-lahum wa iñy-yatawallaw yu'az-zibhumullaahu 'azaaban aleeman fiddunyaa wal-Aakhirah; wamaa lahum fil-arḍi miñw-waliyyiñw-wa laa naṣeer.

75. Amongst them are men who made a Covenant with Allah, that if He bestowed on them of His bounty, they would give (largely) in charity, and be truly amongst those who are righteous.

75. Wa minhum man 'aahadal-laaha la'in aataanaa min faḍlihee lanaṣ-ṣaddaqanna wa lanakoonanna minaṣṣaaliḥeen.

76. But when He did bestow of His bounty, they became covetous, and turned back (from their Covenant), averse (from its fulfilment).

76. Falammaaa aataahum min faḍlihee bakhiloo bihee wa tawallaw wa hum mu'riḍoon.

77. So He has put as a consequence Hypocrisy into their hearts, (to last) till the Day, whereon they shall meet Him: because they broke their

77. Fa-a'qabahum nifaaqan fee quloobihim ilaa Yawmi yalqawnahoo bimaaa akhlaful-laaha maa

Covenant with Allah, and because they lied (again and again).

78. Do they not know that Allah knows their secret (thoughts) and their secret counsels, and that Allah knows well all things unseen?

79. Those who slander such of the Believers as give themselves freely to (deeds of) charity, as well as such as can find nothing to give except the fruits of their labour,- and throw ridicule on them,- Allah will throw back their ridicule on them: and they shall have a grievous Chastisement.

80. Whether you ask for their forgiveness, or not, (their sin is unforgivable): if you ask seventy times for their forgiveness, Allah will not forgive them: because they have rejected Allah and His Apostle: and Allah does not guides those who are perversely rebellious.

81. Those who were left behind (in the Tabuk expedition) rejoiced in their inaction behind the back of the Apostle of Allah: they hated to strive and fight, with their goods and their persons, in the Cause of Allah: they said, "Do not go forth in the heat." Say, "The fire of Hell is fiercer in heat." If only they could understand!

82. Let them laugh a little: much will they weep: a recompense for the (evil) that they do.

83. If, then, Allah brings you back to any of them, and they ask your permission to come out (with you), say: "Never shall you come out with me, nor fight an enemy with me: for you preferred to sit inactive on the first occasion: then you sit (now) with those who lag behind."

84. Nor do you ever pray for any of them that dies,

wa'adoohu wa bimaa kaanoo yakziboon.

78. Alam ya'lamoo annal-laaha ya'lamu sirrahum wa najwaahum wa annal-laaha 'Allaamul-Ghuyoob.

79. Allazeena yalmizoonal-muṭ-ṭawwi'eena minalmu'mineena fiṣ-ṣadaqaati wallazeena laa yajidoona illaa juhdahum fayaskharoona minhum sakhi-ral-laahu minhum wa lahum azaabun aleem.

80. Istaghfir lahum aw laa tastaghfir lahum in tastaghfir lahum sab'eena marratan falañy-yaghfiral-laahu lahum; zaalika bi-annahum kafaroo billaahi wa Rasoolih; wallaahu laa yahdil-qawmal-faasiqeen.

(Section 10)

81. Fariḥ al-mukhallafoona bimaq'adihim khilaafa Rasoo-lil-laahi wa karihooo añy-yujaa-hidoo bi-amwaalihim wa anfu-sihim fee sabeelil-laahi wa qaaloo laa tanfiroo fil-harr; qul Naaru Jahannama ashaddu harraa; law kaanoo yafqahoon.

82. Falyaḍḥakoo qaleelañw-walyabkoo kaseeran jazaaa'am bimaa kaanoo yaksiboon.

83. Fa-ir-raja'akal-laahu ilaa ṭaaa'ifatim-minhum fastaa-zanooka lilkhurooji faqul-lan takhrujoo ma'iya abadanw-wa lan tuqaatiloo ma'iya 'aduw-wan innakum raḍeetum-bilqu'oodi awwala marratin faq'udoo ma'al-khaalifeen.

84. Wa laa tuṣalli 'alaaa aḥadim-minhum maata

nor stand at his grave; for they rejected Allah and His Apostle, and died in a state of perverse rebellion.

85. Nor let their wealth nor their children dazzle you: Allah's plan is to punish them with these things in this world, and that their souls may perish in their (very) denial of Allah.

86. When a Sura comes down, enjoining them to believe in Allah and to strive and fight along with His Apostle, those with wealth and influence among them ask you for exemption, and say: "Leave us (behind): we would be with those who sit (at home)."

87. They prefer to be with (the women), who remain behind (at home): their hearts are sealed and so they do not understand.

88. But the Apostle, and those who believe with him, strive and fight with their wealth and their persons: for them are (all) good things: and it is they who will prosper.

89. Allah has prepared for them Gardens under which rivers flow, to dwell therein: that is the supreme felicity.

(Section 11)

90. And there were, among the desert Arabs (also), men who made excuses and came to claim exemption; and those who were false to Allah and His Apostle (merely) sat inactive. Soon will a grievous Chastisement seize the Unbelievers among them.

91. There is no blame on those who are infirm, or ill, or who find no resources to spend (on the Cause), if they are sincere (in duty) to Allah and

abadañw-wa laa taqum 'alaa qabriheee innahum kafaroo billaahi wa Rasoolihee wa maatoo wa hum faasiqoon.

85. Wa laa tu'jibka amwaa-luhum wa awlaaduhum; innamaa yureedul-laahu añy-yu'az-zibahum bihaa fid-dunyaa wa tazhaqa anfusuhum wa hum kaafiroon.

86. Wa izaaa unzilat Sooratun an aaminoo billaahi wa jaahidoo ma'a Rasoolihis-taaåzanaka uluṭṭawli minhum wa qaaloo zarnaa nakum-ma'alqaa'ideen.

87. Raḍoo bi-añy-yakoonoo ma'al-khawaalifi wa ṭubi'a 'alaa quloobihim fahum laa yafqahoon.

88. Laakinir-Rasoolu wal-lazeena aamanoo ma'ahoo jaahadoo bi-amwaalihim wa anfusihim; wa ulaaa'ika lahumul-khayraatu wa ulaaa'i-ka humul-mufliḥoon.

89. A'addal-laahu lahum Jan-naatin tajree min taḥtihal-anhaaru khaalideena feehaa; zaalikal-fawzul 'aẓeem. **(Section 11)**

90. Wa jaaa'al-mu'az-ziroona minal-A'raabi liyu'zana lahum wa qa'adal-lazeena kazabul-laaha wa Rasoolah; sayuṣeebul-lazeena kafaroo minhum 'azaabun aleem.

91. Laysa 'alaḍ-ḍu'afaaa'i wa laa 'alal-marḍaa wa laa 'alal-lazeena laa yajidoona maa yunfiqoona ḥarajun izaa naṣaḥoo lillaahi wa

His Apostle: no ground (of complaint) can there be against such as do right: and Allah is Oft-forgiving, Most Merciful.

92. Nor (is there blame) on those who came to you to be provided with mounts, and when you said, "I can not find any mounts for you," they turned back, their eyes streaming with tears of grief that they had no resources wherewith to provide the expenses.

93. The ground (of complaint) is against such as claim exemption while they are rich. They prefer to stay with the (women) who remain behind: Allah has sealed their hearts; so they do not know (what they miss).

94. They will present their excuses to you when you return to them. You say: "Present no excuses: we shall not believe you: Allah has already informed us of the true state of matters concerning you: It is your actions that Allah and His Apostle will observe: in the end you will be brought back to Him Who knows what is hidden and what is open: then He will show you the truth of all that you did."

95. They will swear to you by Allah, when you return to them, that you may leave them alone. So leave them alone: For they are an abomination, and Hell is their dwelling-place,-a fitting recompense for the (evil) that they did.

96. They will swear unto you, that you may be pleased with them but if you are pleased with them, Allah is not pleased with those who disobey.

97. The Arabs of the desert are the worst in Unbelief and hypocrisy, and most fitted

Rasoolih; maa 'alal-muḥsineena min sabeel; wallaahu Ghafoorur-Raḥeem.

92. Wa laa 'alal-lazeena izaa maaa atawka litaḥmilahum qulta laaa ajidu maaa aḥmilukum 'alayhi tawallaw wa a'yunuhum tafeeḍu minad-dam'i ḥazanan allaa yajidoo maa yunfiqoon.

93. Innamas-sabeelu 'alal-lazeena yastaazinoonaka wa hum aghniyaaa'; raḍoo biany-yakoonoo ma'al-khawaalifi wa ṭaba'al-laahu 'alaa quloobihim fahum laa ya'lamoon.

94. Ya'taziroona ilaykum izaa raja'tum ilayhim; qul-laa ta'taziroo lan-nu'mina lakum qad nabba-anal-laahu min akhbaarikum; wa sa-yaral-laahu 'amalakum wa Rasooluhoo summa turaddoona ilaa 'Aali-mil-Ghaybi washshahaadati fa-yunabbi'ukum bimaa kuntum ta'maloon.

95. Sa-yaḥlifoona billaahi lakum izanqalabtum ilayhim litu'riḍoo 'anhum fa-a'riḍoo 'anhum innahum rijsuňw-wa maåwaahum Jahannamu jazaaa-'am bimaa kaanoo yaksiboon.

96. Yaḥlifoona lakum litar-ḍaw 'anhum fa-in tarḍaw 'anhum fa-innal-laaha laa yar-ḍaa 'anil-qawmil-faasiqeen.

97. Al-A'raabu ashaddu kuf-raňw-wa nifaaqaňw-wa ajdaru

to be in ignorance of the command which Allah has sent down to His Apostle: But Allah is All-knowing, All-Wise.

98. Some of the desert Arabs look upon their payments as a fine, and watch for disasters for you: on them be the disaster of evil: for Allah is He that hears and knows (all things).

99. But some of the desert Arabs believe in Allah and the Last Day, and look on their payments as pious gifts bringing them nearer to Allah and obtaining the prayers of the Apostle. Yes, indeed they bring them nearer (to Him): soon will Allah admit them to His Mercy: for Allah is Oft-forgiving, Most Merciful.

100. The vanguard (of Islam)- the first of those who forsook (their homes) and of those who gave them aid, and (also) those who follow them in (all) good deeds,- well- pleased is Allah with them, as are they with Him: for them He has prepared Gardens under which rivers flow, to dwell therein for ever: that is the supreme felicity.

101. Certain of the desert Arabs round about you are Hypocrites, as well as (desert Arabs) among the Medina folk: they are obstinate in hypocrisy: you do not know them: We know them: twice shall We punish them: and in addition they shall be sent to a grievous Chastisement.

102. Others (there are who) have acknowledged their wrong-doings: they have mixed an act that was good with another that was evil. Perhaps Allah will turn to them (in Mercy): for Allah is Oft-Forgiving, Most Merciful.

allaa ya'lamoo ḥudooda maaa anzalal-laahu 'alaa Rasoolih; wallaahu 'Aleemun Ḥakeem.

98. Wa minal-A'raabi mañy-yattakhizu maa yunfiqu maghramañw-wa yatarabbaṣu bikumud-dawaaa'ir; 'alayhim daaa'iratus-saw'; wallaahu Samee'un 'Aleem.

99. Wa minal-A'raabi mañy-yu'minu billaahi wal-Yawmil Aakhiri wa yattakhizu maa yunfiqu qurubaatin 'indal-laahi wa ṣalawaatir-Rasool; alaaa innahaa qurbatul-lahum; sa-yudkhiluhumul-laahu fee raḥmatih; innal-laaha Ghafoo-rur-Raḥeem.   (Section 12)

100. Was-saabiqoonal awwa-loona minal-Muhaajireena wal-Anṣaari wallazeenat-taba'oo-hum bi-iḥsaanir-raḍiyal-laahu 'anhum wa raḍoo 'anhu wa a'adda lahum Jannaatin tajree taḥtahal-anhaaru khaalideena feehaaa abadaa; zaalikal-fawzul-'aẓeem.

101. Wa mimman ḥawlakum minal-A'raabi munaafiqoona wa min ahlil-Madeenati maradoo 'alan-nifaaq, laa ta'lamuhum naḥnu na'lamu-hum; sanu'azzibuhum marra-tayni ṡumma yuraddoona ilaa 'azaabin 'aẓeem.

102. Wa aakharoona'-tarafoo bizunoobihim khalaṭoo 'amalan ṣaaliḥañw-wa aakhara sayyi'an 'asal-laahu añy-yatooba 'alayhim; innal-laaha Ghafoo-rur-Raḥeem.

أَلَا يَعْلَمُوٓا أَنَّ مَا وَدُوۡا وَمَاۤ أَنۡزَلَ اللّٰهُ عَلَىٰ رَسُوۡلِهِ ۚ وَاللّٰهُ عَلِيۡمٌ حَكِيۡمٌ ۞

وَمِنَ الۡأَعۡرَابِ مَنۡ يَّتَّخِذُ مَا يُنۡفِقُ مَغۡرَمًا وَّيَتَرَبَّصُ بِكُمُ الدَّوَآئِرَ ۚ عَلَيۡهِمۡ دَآئِرَةُ السَّوۡءِ ؕ وَاللّٰهُ سَمِيۡعٌ عَلِيۡمٌ ۞

وَمِنَ الۡأَعۡرَابِ مَنۡ يُّؤۡمِنُ بِاللّٰهِ وَالۡيَوۡمِ الۡأٰخِرِ وَيَتَّخِذُ مَا يُنۡفِقُ قُرُبٰتٍ عِنۡدَ اللّٰهِ وَصَلَوٰتِ الرَّسُوۡلِ ؕ أَلَاۤ إِنَّهَا قُرۡبَةٌ لَّهُمۡ ؕ سَيُدۡخِلُهُمُ اللّٰهُ فِىۡ رَحۡمَتِهٖ ؕ إِنَّ اللّٰهَ غَفُوۡرٌ رَّحِيۡمٌ ۞

وَالسّٰبِقُوۡنَ الۡأَوَّلُوۡنَ مِنَ الۡمُهٰجِرِيۡنَ وَالۡأَنۡصَارِ وَالَّذِيۡنَ اتَّبَعُوۡهُمۡ بِإِحۡسَانٍ ۙ رَّضِىَ اللّٰهُ عَنۡهُمۡ وَرَضُوۡا عَنۡهُ وَأَعَدَّ لَهُمۡ جَنّٰتٍ تَجۡرِىۡ تَحۡتَهَا الۡأَنۡهٰرُ خٰلِدِيۡنَ فِيۡهَاۤ أَبَدًا ؕ ذٰلِكَ الۡفَوۡزُ الۡعَظِيۡمُ ۞

وَمِمَّنۡ حَوۡلَكُمۡ مِّنَ الۡأَعۡرَابِ مُنٰفِقُوۡنَ ۛؕ وَمِنۡ أَهۡلِ الۡمَدِيۡنَةِ ۛ۫ مَرَدُوۡا عَلَى النِّفَاقِ ۟ لَا تَعۡلَمُهُمۡ ؕ نَحۡنُ نَعۡلَمُهُمۡ ؕ سَنُعَذِّبُهُمۡ مَّرَّتَيۡنِ ثُمَّ يُرَدُّوۡنَ إِلٰى عَذَابٍ عَظِيۡمٍ ۞

وَآخَرُوۡنَ اعۡتَرَفُوۡا بِذُنُوۡبِهِمۡ خَلَطُوۡا عَمَلًا صَالِحًا وَّآخَرَ سَيِّئًا ؕ عَسَى اللّٰهُ أَنۡ يَّتُوۡبَ عَلَيۡهِمۡ ؕ إِنَّ اللّٰهَ غَفُوۡرٌ رَّحِيۡمٌ ۞

103. Of their goods, take alms, that so you might purify and sanctify them; and pray on their behalf. Verily your prayers are a source of security for them: and Allah is One Who hears and knows.

104. Do they not know that Allah accepts repentance from His votaries and receives their gifts of charity, and that Allah is verily He, the Oft-Returning, Most Merciful.

105. And say: "Work (righteousness): soon will Allah observe your work, and His Apostle, and the Believers: soon will you be brought back to the Knower of what is hidden and what is open: then will He show you the truth of all that you did."

106. There are (yet) others, held in suspense for the command of Allah, whether He will punish them, or turn in mercy to them: and Allah is All-Knowing, Wise.

107. And there are those who put up a mosque by way of mischief and infidelity - to disunite the Believers - and in preparation for one who warred against Allah and His Apostle afore time. They will indeed swear that their intention is nothing but good ; but Allah declares that they are certainly liars.

108. You never stand forth therein. There is a mosque whose foundation was laid from the first day on piety; it is more worthy of the standing forth (for prayer) therein. In it are men who love to be purified; and Allah loves those who make themselves pure.

109. Which then is best? - he that lays his foundation on piety to Allah and His Good Pleasure? - or he

103. Khuz min amwaalihim ṣadaqtan tuṭahhiruhum wa tuzakkeehim bihaa wa ṣalli 'alayhim inna ṣalaataka sakanul-lahum; wallaahu Samee'un 'Aleem.

104. Alam ya'lamooo annal-laaha Huwa yaqbalut-tawbata 'an 'ibaadihee wa yaåkhuzuṣ-ṣadaqaati wa annal-laaha Huwat-Tawwaabur-Raḥeem.

105. Wa quli'-maloo fasa-yaral-laahu 'amalakum wa Rasooluhoo walmu'minoona wa saturaddoona ilaa 'Aalimil-Ghaybi washshahaadati fa-yunabbi'ukum bimaa kuntum ta'maloon.

106. Wa aakharoona murjawna li-amril-laahi immaa yu'az-zibuhum wa immaa yatoobu 'alayhim; wallaahu 'Aleemun Ḥakeem.

107. Wallazeenat-takhazoo masjidan ḍiraaraɴw-wa kuf-raɴw-wa tafreeqam baynal-mu'mineena wa irṣaadal-liman ḥaarabal-laaha wa Rasoolahoo min qabl; wa la-yaḥlifunna in aradnaaa illal-ḥusnaa wallaahu yash-hadu innahum lakaa-ziboon.

108. Laa taqum feehi abadaa; lamasjidun ussisa 'alat-taqwaa min awwali yawmin aḥaqqu an taqooma feeh; feehi rijaaluɴy-yuḥibboona añy-yataṭahharoo, wallaahu yuḥibbul-muṭṭah-hireen.

109. Afaman assasa bunyaa-nahoo 'alaa taqwaa minal-laahi wa riḍwaanin khayrun am-man

خُذْ مِنْ أَمْوَالِهِمْ صَدَقَةً تُطَهِّرُهُمْ وَتُزَكِّيهِم بِهَا وَصَلِّ عَلَيْهِمْ ۖ إِنَّ صَلَوٰتَكَ سَكَنٌ لَّهُمْ ۗ وَاللّٰهُ سَمِيعٌ عَلِيمٌ ۝

أَلَمْ يَعْلَمُوٓا أَنَّ اللّٰهَ هُوَ يَقْبَلُ التَّوْبَةَ عَنْ عِبَادِهِ وَيَأْخُذُ الصَّدَقٰتِ وَأَنَّ اللّٰهَ هُوَ التَّوَّابُ الرَّحِيمُ ۝

وَقُلِ اعْمَلُوا فَسَيَرَى اللّٰهُ عَمَلَكُمْ وَرَسُولُهُ وَالْمُؤْمِنُونَ ۖ وَسَتُرَدُّونَ إِلَىٰ عَالِمِ الْغَيْبِ وَالشَّهَادَةِ فَيُنَبِّئُكُم بِمَا كُنتُمْ تَعْمَلُونَ ۝

وَآخَرُونَ مُرْجَوْنَ لِأَمْرِ اللّٰهِ إِمَّا يُعَذِّبُهُمْ وَإِمَّا يَتُوبُ عَلَيْهِمْ ۗ وَاللّٰهُ عَلِيمٌ حَكِيمٌ ۝

وَالَّذِينَ اتَّخَذُوا مَسْجِدًا ضِرَارًا وَكُفْرًا وَتَفْرِيقًا بَيْنَ الْمُؤْمِنِينَ وَإِرْصَادًا لِّمَنْ حَارَبَ اللّٰهَ وَرَسُولَهُ مِن قَبْلُ ۚ وَلَيَحْلِفُنَّ إِنْ أَرَدْنَا إِلَّا الْحُسْنَىٰ ۖ وَاللّٰهُ يَشْهَدُ إِنَّهُمْ لَكَاذِبُونَ ۝

لَا تَقُمْ فِيهِ أَبَدًا ۚ لَّمَسْجِدٌ أُسِّسَ عَلَى التَّقْوَىٰ مِنْ أَوَّلِ يَوْمٍ أَحَقُّ أَن تَقُومَ فِيهِ ۚ فِيهِ رِجَالٌ يُحِبُّونَ أَن يَتَطَهَّرُوا ۚ وَاللّٰهُ يُحِبُّ الْمُطَّهِّرِينَ ۝

أَفَمَنْ أَسَّسَ بُنْيَانَهُ عَلَىٰ تَقْوَىٰ مِنَ اللّٰهِ وَرِضْوَانٍ خَيْرٌ أَم مَّنْ

that lays his foundation on an undermined sand-cliff ready to crumble to pieces? And it crumbles to pieces with him, into the fire of Hell. And Allah does not guides people that do wrong.

110. The foundation of those who so build is never free from suspicion and shakiness in their hearts, until their hearts are cut to pieces. And Allah is All-Knowing, Wise.

111. Allah has purchased of the Believers their persons and their goods; for theirs (in return) is the Garden (of Paradise): they fight in His Cause, and slay and are slain: a promise binding on Him in Truth, through the Torah, the Gospel, and the Qur 'an: and who is more faithful to his Covenant than Allah? Then rejoice in the bargain which you have concluded: that is the supreme achievement.

112. Those that turn (to Allah) in repentance; that serve Him, and praise Him; that wander in devotion to the Cause of Allah,: that bow down and prostrate themselves in prayer; that enjoin good and forbid evil; and observe the limits set by Allah;- (these do rejoice). So proclaim the glad tidings to the Believers.

113. It is not fitting, for the Prophet and those who believe, that they should pray for forgiveness for Pagans, even though they be of kin, after it is clear to them that they are companions of the Fire.

114. And Abraham prayed for his father's forgiveness only because of a promise he had made to him. But when it became clear to him that he was an enemy to Allah, he dissociated himself from him:

assasa bunyaanahoo ‘alaa shafaa jurufin haarin fanhaara bihee fee Naari Jahannam; wallaahu laa yahdil-qawmaz-zaalimeen.

110. Laa yazaalu bunyaanu-humul-lazee banaw reebatan fee quloobihim illaaa an taqatta‘a quloobuhum; wal-laahu ‘Aleemun Ḥakeem.

(Section 13)

111. Innal-laahash-taraa minal-mu’mineena anfusahum wa amwaalahum bi-anna lahumul-jannah; yuqaatiloona fee sabeelil-laahi fa-yaqtuloona wa yuqtaloona wa‘dan ‘alayhi ḥaqqan fit-Tawraati wal-Injeeli wal-Qur-aan; wa man awfaa bi‘ahdihee minal-laah; fastab-shiroo bibay‘ikumul-lazee baaya‘tum bih; wa zaalika huwal-fawzul-‘azeem.

112. At-taaa’iboonal-‘aabidoo-nal-ḥaamidoonas-saaa’iḥoo-nar-raaki‘oonas-saajidoonal-aamiroona bilma‘roofi wannaa-hoona ‘anil-munkari walḥaafi-zoona liḥudoodil-laah; wa bashshiril-mu’mineen.

113. Maa kaana lin-Nabiyyi wallazeena aamanoo añy-yastaghfiroo lilmushrikeena wa law kaanoo ulee qurbaa mim ba‘di maa tabayyana lahum annahum Aṣhaabul-jaheem.

114. Wa maa kaanas-tighfaaru Ibraaheema li-abeehi illaa ‘am-maw‘idatiñw-wa‘adahaaa iyyaahu falammaa tabayyana lahoo annahoo ‘aduwwul-lillaahi tabarra-a minh;

for Abraham was most tender-hearted, forbearing.

115. And Allah will not mislead a people after He has guided them, in order that He may make clear to them what to fear (and avoid)- for Allah has knowledge of all things.

116. To Allah belongs the dominion of the heavens and the earth. He gives life and He takes it. Except for Him you have no protector nor helper.

117. Allah turned with favour to the Prophet, the Muhajirs, and the Ansar,- who followed him in a time of distress, after that the hearts of a part of them had nearly swerved (from duty); but He turned to them (also): for He is to them Most Kind, Most Merciful.

118. (He turned in mercy also) to the three who were left behind; (they felt guilty) to such a degree that the earth seemed constrained to them, for all its spaciousness, and their (very) souls seemed straitened to them,- and they perceived that there is no fleeing from Allah (and no refuge) but to Himself. Then He turned to them, that they might repent: for Allah is Oft-Returning, Most Merciful.

119. O you who believe! Fear Allah and be with those who are true (in word and deed).

120. It was not fitting for the people of Medina and the Bedouin Arabs of the neighbourhood, to refuse to follow Allah's Apostle, nor to prefer their own lives to his: because nothing could they suffer or do, but was reckoned to their credit as a deed of righteousness, whether they suffered thirst, or fatigue, or hunger, in the Cause of Allah, or trod paths to raise the ire of

inna Ibraaheema la-awwaahun ḥaleem.

115. Wa maa kaanal-laahu liyuḍilla qawmam ba'da iz hadaahum ḥattaa yubayyina lahum-maa yattaqoon; innal-laaha bikulli shay'in 'Aleem.

116. Innal-laaha lahoo mulkus-samaawaati walarḍi yuḥyee wa yumeet; wa maa lakum-min doonil-laahi miñw-waliyyiñw-wa laa naṣeer.

117. Laqat-taabal-laahu 'alan-Nabiyyi wal-Muhaajireena wal-Anṣaaril-lazeenat-taba'oohu fee saa'atil-'usrati mim ba'di maa kaada yazeeghu quloobu fareeqim-minhum ṣumma taaba 'alayhim; innahoo bihim Ra'oofur-Raḥeem.

118. Wa 'aṣ-ṣalaaṣatil-lazee-na khullifoo ḥattaaa izaa ḍaaqat 'alayhimul-arḍu bimaa raḥubat wa ḍaaqat 'alayhim anfusuhum wa ẓannooo al-laa malja-a minal-laahi illaaa ilayhi ṣumma taaba 'alayhim liyatooboo; innal-laaha Huwat-Tawwaabur-Raḥeem. **(Section 14)**

119. Yaaa ayyuhal-lazeena aamanut-taqul-laaha wa koonoo ma'aṣ-ṣaadiqeen.

120. Maa kaana li-ahlil-Madeenati wa man ḥawlahum-minal-A'raabi añy-yatakhal-lafoo 'ar-Rasoolil-laahi wa laa yarghaboo bi-anfusihim 'an nafsih; zaalika bi-annahum laa yuṣeebuhum ẓama-uñw-wa laa naṣabuñw-wa laa makhmaṣatun fee sabeelil-laahi wa laa yaṭa-'oona mawti'añy- yagheezul-

إِنَّ إِبْرٰهِيمَ لَأَوَّاهٌ حَلِيمٌ ۝

وَمَا كَانَ اللّٰهُ لِيُضِلَّ قَوْمًا بَعْدَ إِذْ هَدٰىهُمْ حَتّٰى يُبَيِّنَ لَهُمْ مَّا يَتَّقُونَ ۚ إِنَّ اللّٰهَ بِكُلِّ شَىْءٍ عَلِيمٌ ۝

إِنَّ اللّٰهَ لَهُ مُلْكُ السَّمٰوٰتِ وَالْأَرْضِ ۚ يُحْىٖ وَيُمِيتُ ۚ وَمَا لَكُمْ مِّنْ دُونِ اللّٰهِ مِنْ وَّلِىٍّ وَّلَا نَصِيرٍ ۝

لَقَدْ تَّابَ اللّٰهُ عَلَى النَّبِيِّ وَالْمُهٰجِرِينَ وَالْأَنْصَارِ الَّذِينَ اتَّبَعُوهُ فِى سَاعَةِ الْعُسْرَةِ مِنْ بَعْدِ مَا كَادَ يَزِيغُ قُلُوبُ فَرِيقٍ مِّنْهُمْ ثُمَّ تَابَ عَلَيْهِمْ ۚ إِنَّهُ بِهِمْ رَءُوفٌ رَّحِيمٌ ۝

وَعَلَى الثَّلٰثَةِ الَّذِينَ خُلِّفُوا ۗ حَتّٰى إِذَا ضَاقَتْ عَلَيْهِمُ الْأَرْضُ بِمَا رَحُبَتْ وَضَاقَتْ عَلَيْهِمْ أَنْفُسُهُمْ وَظَنُّوا أَنْ لَّا مَلْجَأَ مِنَ اللّٰهِ إِلَّا إِلَيْهِ ۗ ثُمَّ تَابَ عَلَيْهِمْ لِيَتُوبُوا ۚ إِنَّ اللّٰهَ هُوَ التَّوَّابُ الرَّحِيمُ ۝

يٰٓأَيُّهَا الَّذِينَ اٰمَنُوا اتَّقُوا اللّٰهَ وَكُونُوا مَعَ الصّٰدِقِينَ ۝

مَا كَانَ لِأَهْلِ الْمَدِينَةِ وَمَنْ حَوْلَهُمْ مِّنَ الْأَعْرَابِ أَنْ يَّتَخَلَّفُوا عَنْ رَّسُولِ اللّٰهِ وَلَا يَرْغَبُوا بِأَنْفُسِهِمْ عَنْ نَّفْسِهِ ۚ ذٰلِكَ بِأَنَّهُمْ لَا يُصِيبُهُمْ ظَمَأٌ وَّلَا نَصَبٌ وَّلَا مَخْمَصَةٌ فِى سَبِيلِ اللّٰهِ وَلَا يَطَئُونَ مَوْطِئًا يَّغِيظُ

the Unbelievers, or received any injury whatever from an enemy: for Allah does not suffer the reward to be lost of those who do good;-

121. Nor could they spend anything (for the Cause) - small or great- nor cut across a valley, but the deed is inscribed to their credit: that Allah may requite their deed with the best (possible reward).

122. Nor should the Believers all go forth together: if a contingent from every expedition remained behind, they could devote themselves to studies in religion, and admonish the people when they return to them,- that thus they (may learn) to guard themselves (against evil).

123. O you who believe! Fight the Unbelievers who gird you about, and let them find firmness in you: and know that Allah is with those who fear Him.

124. Whenever there comes down a Sura, some of them say: "Which of you has had his faith increased by it?" Yes, those who believe,- their faith is increased and they do rejoice.

125. But those in whose hearts is a disease,- it will add doubt to their doubt, and they will die in a state of Unbelief.

126. Don't they see that they are tried every year once or twice? Yet they do not turn in repentance, and they take no heed.

kuffaara wa laa yanaaloona min 'aduwwin naylan illaa kutiba lahum bihee 'amalun ṣaaliḥ; innal-laaha laa yuḍee'u ajral-muḥsineen.

121. Wa laa yunfiqoona nafaqatan ṣagheeratañw-wa laa kabeeratañw-wa laa yaqṭa'oona waadiyan illaa kutiba lahum liyajziyahumul-laahu aḥsana maa kaanoo ya'maloon.

122. Wa maa kaanal-mu'minoona liyanfiroo kaaaffah; falaw laa nafara min kulli firqatim-minhum ṭaaa'ifatul-liyatafaqqahoo fiddeeni wa liyunziroo qawmahum izaa raja'ooo ilayhim la'allahum yaḥzaroon.　　**(Section 15)**

123. Yaaa ayyuhal-lazeena aamanoo qaatilul-lazeena yaloonakum minal-kuffaari walyajidoo feekum ghilẓah; wa'lamooo annal-laaha ma'al-muttaqeen.

124. Wa izaa maaa unzilat Sooratun faminhum mañy-yaqoolu ayyukum zaadat-hu haaziheee eemaanaa; fa-ammal-lazeena aamanoo fazaadat-hum eemaanañw-wa hum yastabshiroon.

125. Wa ammal-lazeena fee quloobihim maraḍun fazaadat-hum rijsan ilaa rijsihim wa maatoo wa hum kaafiroon.

126. Awalaa yarawna annahum yuftanoona fee kulli 'aamim marratan aw marratayni ṣumma laa yatooboona wa laa hum yazzakkaroon.

127. Whenever there comes down a Sura, they look at each other, (saying), "Does anyone see you?" Then they turn aside: Allah has turned their hearts (from the light); for they are a people that do not understand.

128. Now has come to you an Apostle from amongst yourselves: it grieves him that you should perish: he is ardently anxious over you: to the Believers he is most kind and merciful.

129. But if they turn away, say: "Allah is sufficient for me: there is no god but He: On Him is my trust,- He the Lord of the Throne (of Glory) Supreme!"

127. Wa izaa maaa unzilat Sooratun nazara ba'duhum ilaa ba'din hal yaraakum min ahadin summan-sarafoo; sarafal-laahu quloobahum bi-annahum qaw-mul-laa yafqahoon.

128. Laqad jaaa'akum Rasoo-lum-min anfusikum 'azeezun 'alayhi maa 'anittum harees un 'alaykum bilmu'mineena ra'oofur-raheem.

129. Fa-in tawallaw faqul hasbiyal-laahu laaa ilaaha illaa Huwa 'alayhi tawakkaltu wa Huwa Rabbul-'Arshil-'Azeem.

(Section 16)

10. Yunus, or Jonah
In the name of Allah, Most Gracious, Most Merciful.

Sûrat Yûnus–10
(Revealed at Makkah)
Bismillaahir Rahmaanir Raheem

1. *Alif-Lam-Ra.* These are the *ayats* of the Book of Wisdom.

2. Is it a matter of wonderment to men that We have sent Our inspiration to a man from among themselves?- that he should warn mankind (of their danger), and give the good news to the Believers that they have before their Lord, the lofty rank of Truth. (But) the Unbelievers say: "This is indeed an evident sorcerer!"

3. Verily your Lord is Allah, who created the heavens and the earth in six days, and is firmly established on the throne (of authority), regulating and governing all things. No intercessor (can plead with Him) except after His leave (has been obtained). This is Allah your Lord; you therefore serve Him: will you not receive admonition?

4. To Him will be your return- of all of you. The promise of Allah is true and sure. It is He Who begins the process of creation, and repeats it, that He may reward with justice those who believe and work righteousness;

1. Alif-Laaam-Raa; tilka Aayaatul-Kitaabil-Hakeem.

2. A kaana linnaasi 'ajaban an awhaynaaa ilaa rajulim-minhum an anzirin-naasa wa bashshiril-lazeena aamanooo anna lahum qadama sidqin 'inda Rabbihim; qaalal-kaafi-roona inna haazaa lasaahirum-mubeen.

3. Inna Rabbakumul-laahul-lazee khalaqas-samaawaati wal-arda fee sittati ayyaamin-summas-tawaa 'alal-'Arshi yudabbirul-amra maa min shafee'in illaa mim ba'di iznih; zalikumul-laahu Rabbukum fa'budooh; afalaa tazakkaroon.

4. Ilayhi marji'ukum jamee-'anw wa'dal-laahi haqqaa, innahoo yabda'ul-khalqa summa yu'eeduhoo liyajziyal-lazeena aamanoo wa 'amilus-saalihaati

but those who reject Him will have draughts of boiling fluids, and a Chastisement grievous, because they did reject Him.

5. It is He Who made the sun to be a shining glory and the moon to be a light (of beauty), and measured out stages for it, that you might know the number of years and the count (of time). Nowise did Allah create this but in truth and righteousness. (Thus) He explains His Signs in detail, for those who understand.

6. Verily, in the alternation of the night and the day, and in all that Allah has created, in the heavens and the earth, are Signs for those who fear Him.

7. Those who do not rest their hope on their meeting with Us, but are pleased and satisfied with the life of the present, and those who do not heed Our Signs,-

8. Their abode is the Fire, because of the (evil) they earned.

9. Those who believe, and work righteousness,- their Lord will guide them because of their faith: beneath them will flow rivers in Gardens of Bliss.

10. (This will be) their cry therein: "Glory to You, O Allah!" And "Peace" will be their greeting therein! and the close of their cry will be: "Praise be to Allah, the Cherisher and Sus-tainer of the Worlds!"

11. If Allah were to hasten for men the ill (they have earned) as they would fain hasten on the good, then would their respite be settled at once. But We leave those who do not rest their hope on their meeting with Us, in their trespasses, wandering in distraction to and fro.

---

bilqisṭ; wallazeena kafaroo lahum sharaabum-min ḥamee-miñw-wa ‘azaabun aleemum bimaa kaanoo yakfuroon.

5. Huwal-lazee ja‘alash-shamsa ḍiyaaa’añw-walqamara nooraäw-wa qaddarahoo manaa-zila lita‘lamoo ‘adadas-sineena walḥisaab; maa khalaqal-laahu zaalika illaa bilḥaqq; yufaṣṣilul-Aayaati liqawminy-ya‘lamoon.

6. Inna fikh-tilaafil-layli wannahaari wa maa khalaqal-laahu fis-samaawaati wal-arḍi la-Aayaatil-liqawminy-yatta-qoon.

7. Innal-lazeena laa yarjoona liqaaa’anaa wa raḍoo bilḥayaa-tid-dunyaa waṭma-annoo bihaa wallazeena hum ‘an Aayaatinaa ghaafiloon.

8. Ulaaa’ika maåwaahumun Naaru bimaa kaanoo yaksiboon.

9. Innal-lazeena aamanoo wa ‘amiluṣ-ṣaaliḥaati yahdee-him Rabbuhum bi-eemaanihim tajree min taḥtihimul-anhaaru fee Jannaatin-Na‘eem.

10. Da‘waahum feehaa Sub-ḥaanakal-laahumma wa taḥiy-yatuhum feehaa salaam; wa aakhiru da‘waahum anil-ḥamdu lillaahi Rabbil-‘aalameen.

(Section 1)

11. Wa law yu‘ajjilul-laahu linnaasish-sharras-ti‘jaalahum bilkhayri laquḍiya ilayhim ajaluhum fanazarul-lazeena laa yarjoona liqaaa’anaa fee ṭughyaanihim ya‘mahoon.

بِالْقِسْطِ ۚ وَالَّذِيْنَ كَفَرُوْا لَهُمْ شَرَابٌ مِّنْ حَمِيْمٍ وَّعَذَابٌ اَلِيْمٌ بِمَا كَانُوْا يَكْفُرُوْنَ ۞

هُوَ الَّذِيْ جَعَلَ الشَّمْسَ ضِيَآءً وَّالْقَمَرَ نُوْرًا وَّقَدَّرَهٗ مَنَازِلَ لِتَعْلَمُوْا عَدَدَ السِّنِيْنَ وَالْحِسَابَ ۚ مَا خَلَقَ اللّٰهُ ذٰلِكَ اِلَّا بِالْحَقِّ ۚ يُفَصِّلُ الْاٰيٰتِ لِقَوْمٍ يَّعْلَمُوْنَ ۞

اِنَّ فِيْ اخْتِلَافِ الَّيْلِ وَالنَّهَارِ وَمَا خَلَقَ اللّٰهُ فِي السَّمٰوٰتِ وَالْاَرْضِ لَاٰيٰتٍ لِّقَوْمٍ يَّتَّقُوْنَ ۞

اِنَّ الَّذِيْنَ لَا يَرْجُوْنَ لِقَآءَنَا وَرَضُوْا بِالْحَيٰوةِ الدُّنْيَا وَاطْمَاَنُّوْا بِهَا وَالَّذِيْنَ هُمْ عَنْ اٰيٰتِنَا غٰفِلُوْنَ ۞

اُولٰٓئِكَ مَأْوٰىهُمُ النَّارُ بِمَا كَانُوْا يَكْسِبُوْنَ ۞

اِنَّ الَّذِيْنَ اٰمَنُوْا وَعَمِلُوا الصّٰلِحٰتِ يَهْدِيْهِمْ رَبُّهُمْ بِاِيْمَانِهِمْ ۚ تَجْرِيْ مِنْ تَحْتِهِمُ الْاَنْهٰرُ فِيْ جَنّٰتِ النَّعِيْمِ ۞

دَعْوٰىهُمْ فِيْهَا سُبْحٰنَكَ اللّٰهُمَّ وَتَحِيَّتُهُمْ فِيْهَا سَلٰمٌ ۚ وَاٰخِرُ دَعْوٰىهُمْ اَنِ الْحَمْدُ لِلّٰهِ رَبِّ الْعٰلَمِيْنَ ۞

وَلَوْ يُعَجِّلُ اللّٰهُ لِلنَّاسِ الشَّرَّ اسْتِعْجَالَهُمْ بِالْخَيْرِ لَقُضِيَ اِلَيْهِمْ اَجَلُهُمْ ۚ فَنَذَرُ الَّذِيْنَ لَا يَرْجُوْنَ لِقَآءَنَا فِيْ طُغْيَانِهِمْ يَعْمَهُوْنَ ۞

12. When trouble touches a man, He cries unto Us (in all postures)- lying down on his side, or sitting, or standing. But when We have solved his trouble, he passes on his way as if he had never cried to us for a trouble that touched him! Thus do the deeds of transgressors seem fair in their eyes!

13. We destroyed generations before you when they did wrong: their Apostles came to them with Clear-Signs, but they would not believe! Thus do We requite those who sin!

14. Then We made you heirs in the land after them, to see how you would behave!

15. But when Our Clear Signs are rehearsed to them, those who do not rest their hope on their meeting with Us, Say: "Bring us a Qur'an other than this, or change this," Say: "It is not for me, of my own accord, to change it: I follow nothing but what is revealed unto me: if I were to disobey my Lord, I should myself fear the Chastisement of a Great Day (to come)."

16. Say: "If Allah had so willed, I should not have rehearsed it to you, nor would He have made it known to you. A whole life-time before this I have tarried amongst you: will you not then understand?"

17. Who does more wrong than such as forge a lie against Allah, or deny His Signs? But never will prosper those who sin.

18. They serve, besides Allah, things that do not hurt them nor profit them, and they say:

---

12. Wa izaa massal-insaanaḍ-ḍurru da'aanaa lijambiheee aw qaa'idan aw qaaa'iman falammaa kashafnaa 'anhu ḍurrahoo marra ka-al-lam yad'unaaa ilaa ḍurrim-massah; kazaalika zuyyina lilmusrifeena maa kaanoo ya'maloon.

13. Wa laqad ahlaknal-quroona min qablikum lammaa ẓalamoo wa jaaa'at-hum Rusu-luhum bil-bayyinaati wa maa kaanoo liyu'minoo; kazaalika najzil-qawmal-mujrimeen.

14. Summa ja'alnaakum kha-laaa'ifa fil-arḍi mim ba'dihim linanẓura kayfa ta'maloon.

15. Wa izaa tutlaa 'alayhim Aayaatunaa bayyinaatin qaalal-lazeena laa yarjoona liqaaa-'ana-'ti bi-Qur-aanin ghayri haazaaa aw baddilh; qul maa yakoonu leee an ubaddilahoo min tilqaaa'i nafsee in attabi'u illaa maa yoohaaa ilayya inneee akhaafu in 'aṣaytu Rabbee 'azaaba Yawmin 'Aẓeem.

16. Qul law shaaa'al-laahu maa talawtuhoo 'alaykum wa laaa adraakum bihee faqad labiṣtu feekum 'umuram-min qablih; afalaa ta'qiloon.

17. Faman aẓlamu mimma-nif-taraa 'alal-laahi kaziban aw kazzaba bi-Aayaatih; innahoo laa yuflihul-mujrimoon.

18. Wa ya'budoona min doonil-laahi maa laa yaḍur-ruhum wa laa yanfa'uhum wa yaqooloona

---

وَإِذَا مَسَّ الْإِنْسَانَ الضُّرُّ دَعَانَا لِجَنْبِهٖ أَوْ قَاعِدًا أَوْ قَآئِمًا ۚ فَلَمَّا كَشَفْنَا عَنْهُ ضُرَّهٗ مَرَّ كَأَنْ لَّمْ يَدْعُنَا إِلَىٰ ضُرٍّ مَّسَّهٗ ۚ كَذٰلِكَ زُيِّنَ لِلْمُسْرِفِينَ مَا كَانُوْا يَعْمَلُوْنَ ۝

وَلَقَدْ أَهْلَكْنَا الْقُرُوْنَ مِنْ قَبْلِكُمْ لَمَّا ظَلَمُوْا ۙ وَجَآءَتْهُمْ رُسُلُهُمْ بِالْبَيِّنَاتِ وَمَا كَانُوْا لِيُؤْمِنُوْا ۚ كَذٰلِكَ نَجْزِي الْقَوْمَ الْمُجْرِمِيْنَ ۝

ثُمَّ جَعَلْنَاكُمْ خَلَآئِفَ فِي الْأَرْضِ مِنْ بَعْدِهِمْ لِنَنْظُرَ كَيْفَ تَعْمَلُوْنَ ۝

وَإِذَا تُتْلَىٰ عَلَيْهِمْ آيَاتُنَا بَيِّنَاتٍ ۙ قَالَ الَّذِيْنَ لَا يَرْجُوْنَ لِقَآءَنَا ائْتِ بِقُرْآنٍ غَيْرِ هٰذَآ أَوْ بَدِّلْهُ ۚ قُلْ مَا يَكُوْنُ لِيْ أَنْ أُبَدِّلَهٗ مِنْ تِلْقَآئِ نَفْسِيْ ۖ إِنْ أَتَّبِعُ إِلَّا مَا يُوْحَىٰ إِلَيَّ ۖ إِنِّيْ أَخَافُ إِنْ عَصَيْتُ رَبِّيْ عَذَابَ يَوْمٍ عَظِيْمٍ ۝

قُلْ لَّوْ شَآءَ اللّٰهُ مَا تَلَوْتُهٗ عَلَيْكُمْ وَلَا أَدْرَاكُمْ بِهٖ ۖ فَقَدْ لَبِثْتُ فِيْكُمْ عُمُرًا مِّنْ قَبْلِهٖ ۚ أَفَلَا تَعْقِلُوْنَ ۝

فَمَنْ أَظْلَمُ مِمَّنِ افْتَرَىٰ عَلَى اللّٰهِ كَذِبًا أَوْ كَذَّبَ بِآيَاتِهٖ ۚ إِنَّهٗ لَا يُفْلِحُ الْمُجْرِمُوْنَ ۝

وَيَعْبُدُوْنَ مِنْ دُوْنِ اللّٰهِ مَا لَا يَضُرُّهُمْ وَلَا يَنْفَعُهُمْ وَيَقُوْلُوْنَ

"These are our intercessors with Allah." Say: "Do you indeed inform Allah of something He knows not, in the heavens or on earth?- Glory to Him! and far is He above the partners they ascribe (to Him)!"

19. Mankind was but one nation, but differed (later). Had it not been for a word that went forth before from your Lord, their differences would have been settled between them.

20. They say: "Why is not a Sign sent down to him from his Lord?" Say: "The Unseen is only for Allah (to know), Then wait you: I too will wait with you."

21. When We make mankind taste of some mercy after adversity has touched them, behold! they take to plotting against Our Signs! Say: "Swifter to plan is Allah!" Verily, Our angels record all the plots that you make.

22. He it is Who enables you to traverse through land and sea; so that you even board ships;- they sail with them with a favourable wind, and they rejoice thereat; then comes a stormy wind and the waves come to them from all sides, and they think they are being overwhelmed: they cry to Allah, sincerely offering (their) duty to Him saying, "If You deliver us from this, we shall truly show our gratitude!"

23. But when He delivers them, behold! they transgress insolently through the earth in defiance of right! O mankind! your insolence is against your own souls,- an enjoyment of the life of the present:

haaa'ulaaa'i shufa'aaa'unaa 'indal-laah; qul atunabbi'oonal-laaha bimaa laa ya'lamu fis-samaawaati wa laa fil-arḍ; Subḥaanahoo wa Ta'aalaa 'ammaa yushrikoon.

19. Wa maa kaanan-naasu illaaa ummatañw-waaḥidatan fakh-talafoo; wa law laa kalimatun sabaqat mir-Rabbika laquḍiya baynahum feemaa feehi yakhtalifoon.

20. Wa yaqooloona law laaa unzila 'alayhi Aayatum-mir-Rabbihee faqul innamal-ghaybu lillaahi fantaẓiroo innee ma'akum minal-muntaẓireen.
(Section 2)

21. Wa izaaa azaqnan-naasa raḥmatam-mim ba'di ḍarraaa'a massat-hum izaa lahum makrun feee Aayaatinaa; qulil-laahu asra'u makraa; inna rusulanaa yaktuboona maa tamkuroon.

22. Huwal-lazee yusayyi-rukum fil-barri walbaḥri ḥattaaa izaa kuntum fil-fulki wa jarayna bihim bireeḥin ṭayyibatiñw-wa fariḥoo bihaa jaaa'at-haa reeḥun 'aaṣifuñw-wa jaaa'ahumul-mawju min kulli makaaniñw-wa ẓannooo annahum uḥeeṭa bihim da'awul-laaha mukhliṣeena lahud-deena la'in anjaytanaa min haazihee lanakoonanna minash-shaakireen.

23. Falammaaa anjaahum izaa hum yabghoona fil-arḍi bighayril-ḥaqq; yaaa ayyuhan-naasu innamaa bagh-yukum 'alaaa anfusikum-mataa'al-ḥayaatid-dunyaa

in the end, to Us is your return, and We shall show you the truth of all that you did.

24. The likeness of the life of the Present is as the rain which We send down from the skies: by its mingling arises the produce of the earth- which provides food for men and animals: (It grows) till the earth is clad with its golden ornaments and is decked out (in beauty): the people to whom it belongs think they have all powers of disposal over it: there reaches it Our command by night or by day, and We make it like a harvest clean-mown, as if it had not flourished only the day before! Thus do We explain the Signs in detail for those who reflect.

25. But Allah calls to the Home of Peace: He guides those whom He pleases to a Way that is straight.

26. To those who do right is a goodly (reward)- Yes, more (than in measure)! No darkness nor shame shall cover their faces! They are companions of the Garden; they will abide therein (for ever).

27. But those who have earned evil will have a reward of like evil: ignominy will cover their (faces): no defender will they have from (the wrath of) Allah: their faces will be covered, as it were, with pieces from the depths of the darkness of Night : they are Companions of the Fire: they will abide therein (for ever)!

28. One Day We shall gather them all together. Then We shall say to those who joined gods (with Us): "To your place! you and those you joined as 'partners' We shall separate them, and their "Partners" shall say: "It was not us that you worshipped!"

summa ilaynaa marji'ukum fanunabbi'ukum bimaa kuntum ta'maloon.

24. Innamaa maṣalul-ḥayaa-tid-dunyaa kamaaa'in anzalnaa-hu minas-samaaa'i fakhtalaṭa bihee nabaatul-arḍi mimmaa yaåkulun-naasu wal-an'aam; ḥattaaa izaaa akhaẕatil-arḍu zukhrufahaa wazzayyanat wa ẓanna ahluhaaa annahum qaadiroona 'alayhaaa ataahaaa amrunaa laylan aw nahaaran faja'alnaahaa ḥaṣeedan ka-al-lam taghna bil-ams; kaẕaalika nufaṣṣilul-Aayaati liqawmiñy-yatafakkaroon.

25. Wallaahu yad'ooo ilaa daaris-salaami wa yahdee mañy-yashaaa'u ilaa Ṣiraaṭim-Mustaqeem.

26. Lillaẕeena aḥsanul-ḥus-naa wa ziyaadahtuñw wa laa yarhaqu wujoohahum qata-ruñw-wa laa ẕillah; ulaaa'ika Aṣḥaabul-jannati hum feeha khaalidoon.

27. Wallaẕeena kasabus-sayyi-aati jazaaa'u sayyi'atim bimiṣlihaa wa tarhaquhum ẕillah; maa lahum minal-laahi min 'aaṣimin ka-annamaaa ughshiyat wujoohuhum qiṭa-'am-minal-layli muẓlimaa; ulaaa'ika Aṣḥaabun-Naari hum feeha khaalidoon.

28. Wa Yawma naḥshuruhum jamee'an ṣumma naqoolu lillaẕeena ashrakoo makaa-nakum antum wa shurakaaa'u-kum; fazayyalnaa baynahum wa qaala shurakaaa'uhum maa kuntum iyyaanaa ta'budoon.

29. "Enough is Allah for a witness between us and you: we certainly knew nothing of your worship of us!"

30. There will every soul prove (the fruits of) the deeds it sent before: they will be brought back to Allah their rightful Lord, and their invented falsehoods will leave them in the lurch.

31. Say: "Who is it that sustains you (in life) from the sky and from the earth? Or who is it that has power over hearing and sight? And who is it that brings out the living from the dead and the dead from the living? And who is it that rules and regulates all affairs?" They will soon say, "Allah". Say, "Will you not then show piety (to Him)?"

32. Such is Allah, your real cherisher and sustainer; apart from Truth, what (remains) but error? How then are you turned away?

33. Thus is the Word of your Lord proved true against those who rebel: verily they will not believe.

34. Say: "Of your 'partners', can any originate creation and repeat it?" Say: "It is Allah Who originates creation and repeats it: then how are you deluded away (from the truth)?"

35. Say: "Of your 'partners' is there any that can give any guidance towards Truth?" Say: "It is Allah Who gives guidance towards Truth. Is then He Who gives guidance to truth more worthy to be followed, or he who finds not guidance (himself) unless he is guided? what then is the matter with you? How do you judge.

36. But most of them follow nothing but conjecture: truly conjecture can be of no avail against Truth.

29. Fakafaa billaahi shahee-dam-baynanaa wa baynakum in kunnaa 'an 'ibaadatikum laghaafileen.

30. Hunaalika tabloo kullu nafsim-maaa aslafat; wa ruddooo ilal-laahi mawlaahu-mul-ḥaqqi wa ḍalla 'anhum maa kaanoo yaftaroon. (Section 3)

31. Qul mañy-yarzuqukum minas-samaaa'i wal-arḍi ammañy-yamlikus-sam'a wal-abṣaara wa mañy-yukhrijul-ḥayya minal-mayyiti wa yukhrijul-mayyita minal-ḥayyi wa mañy-yudabbirul-amr; fasa-yaqooloonal-laah; faqul afalaa tattaqoon.

32. Fazaalikumul-laahu Rab-bukumul-ḥaqq; famaazaa ba'dal-ḥaqqi illaḍ-ḍalaalu fa-annaa tuṣrafoon.

33. Kazaalika ḥaqqat Kali-matu Rabbika 'alal-lazeena fasaqooo annahum laa yu'mi-noon.

34. Qul hal min shurakaaa-'ikum mañy-yabda'ul-khalqa summa yu'eeduh; qulil-laahu yabda'ul-khalqa summa yu'ee-duhoo fa-annaa tu'fakoon.

35. Qul hal min shurakaaa-'ikum mañy-yahdee ilal-ḥaqq; qulil-laahu yahdee lilḥaqq; afamañy-yahdeee ilal-ḥaqqi aḥaqqu añy-yuttaba'a ammal-laa yahiddeee illaaa añy-yuhdaa famaa lakum kayfa taḥkumoon.

36. Wa maa yattabi'u aksa-ruhum illaa ẓannaa; innaẓ-ẓanna laa yughnee minal-ḥaqqi shay'aa;

Verily Allah is well aware of all that they do.

37. This Qur'an is not such as can be produced by other than Allah; on the contrary it is a confirmation of (revelations) that went before it, and a fuller explanation of the Book - wherein there is no doubt - from the Lord of the Worlds.

38. Or do they say, "He forged it"? Say: "Bring then a Sura like it, and call (to your aid) anyone you can, besides Allah, if it be you speak the truth!"

39. Nay, they charge with falsehood that whose knowledge they cannot compass, even before the elucidation thereof has reached them: thus did those before them make charges of falsehood: but see what was the end of those who did wrong!

40. Of them there are some who believe therein, and some who do not: and your Lord knows best those who are out for mischief.

41. If they charge you with falsehood, say: "My work to me, and yours to you! you are free from responsibility for what I do, and I for what you do!"

42. Among them are some who (pretend to) listen to you: but can you make the deaf to hear,- even though they are without understanding?

43. And among them are some who look at you: but can you guide the blind,- even though they will not see?

44. Verily Allah will not deal unjustly with man in anything:

---

innal-laaha 'Aleemum bimaa yaf'aloon.

37. Wa maa kaana haazal-Qur-aanu añy-yuftaraa min doonil-laahi wa laakin taşdeeqal-lazee bayna yadayhi wa tafşeelal-Kitaabi laa rayba feehi mir-Rabbil-'aalameen.

38. Am yaqooloonaf-taraahu qul faåtoo bisooratim-mişlihee wad'oo manis-taṭa'tum-min doonil-laahi in kuntum şaadi-qeen.

39. Bal kazzaboo bimaa lam yuḥeeṭoo bi'ilmihee wa lammaa yaåtihim taåweeluh; kazaalika kazzabal-lazeena min qablihim fanzur kayfa kaana 'aaqibatuz-zaalimeen.

40. Wa minhum-mañy-yu'minu bihee wa minhum-mal-laa yu'minu bih; wa Rabbuka a'lamu bilmufsideen. **(Section 4)**

41. Wa in kazzabooka faqul lee 'amalee wa lakum 'amalukum antum bareee'oona mimmaaa a'malu wa ana bareee'um-mimmaa ta'maloon.

42. Wa minhum-mañy-yastami-'oona ilayk; afa-anta tusmi'uş-şumma wa law kaanoo laa ya'qiloon.

43. Wa minhum mañy-yanzuru ilayk; afa-anta tahdil-'umya wa law kaanoo laa yubşiroon.

44. Innal-laaha laa yaẕlimun-naasa shay'añw-

إِنَّ اللَّهَ عَلِيمٌ بِمَا يَفْعَلُونَ ۩

وَمَا كَانَ هَٰذَا الْقُرْآنُ أَن يُفْتَرَىٰ مِن دُونِ اللَّهِ وَلَٰكِن تَصْدِيقَ الَّذِي بَيْنَ يَدَيْهِ وَتَفْصِيلَ الْكِتَٰبِ لَا رَيْبَ فِيهِ مِن رَّبِّ الْعَٰلَمِينَ ۩

أَمْ يَقُولُونَ افْتَرَىٰهُ قُلْ فَأْتُوا بِسُورَةٍ مِّثْلِهِ وَادْعُوا مَنِ اسْتَطَعْتُم مِّن دُونِ اللَّهِ إِن كُنتُمْ صَٰدِقِينَ ۩

بَلْ كَذَّبُوا بِمَا لَمْ يُحِيطُوا بِعِلْمِهِ وَلَمَّا يَأْتِهِمْ تَأْوِيلُهُ كَذَٰلِكَ كَذَّبَ الَّذِينَ مِن قَبْلِهِمْ فَانظُرْ كَيْفَ كَانَ عَٰقِبَةُ الظَّٰلِمِينَ ۩

وَمِنْهُم مَّن يُؤْمِنُ بِهِ وَمِنْهُم مَّن لَّا يُؤْمِنُ بِهِ وَرَبُّكَ أَعْلَمُ بِالْمُفْسِدِينَ ۩

وَإِن كَذَّبُوكَ فَقُل لِّي عَمَلِي وَلَكُمْ عَمَلُكُمْ أَنتُم بَرِيئُونَ مِمَّا أَعْمَلُ وَأَنَا بَرِيءٌ مِّمَّا تَعْمَلُونَ ۩

وَمِنْهُم مَّن يَسْتَمِعُونَ إِلَيْكَ أَفَأَنتَ تُسْمِعُ الصُّمَّ وَلَوْ كَانُوا لَا يَعْقِلُونَ ۩

وَمِنْهُم مَّن يَنظُرُ إِلَيْكَ أَفَأَنتَ تَهْدِي الْعُمْيَ وَلَوْ كَانُوا لَا يُبْصِرُونَ ۩

إِنَّ اللَّهَ لَا يَظْلِمُ النَّاسَ شَيْئًا

It is man that wrongs his own soul.

45. One day He will gather them together: (It will be) as if they had tarried but an hour of a day: they will recognise each other: assuredly those will be lost who denied the meeting with Allah and refused to receive true guidance.

46. Whether We show you (realized in your life-time) some part of what We promise them,- or We take your soul (to Our Mercy) (before that),- in any case, to Us is their return: ultimately Allah is Witness to all that they do.

47. To every people (was sent) an Apostle: when their Apostle comes (before them), the matter will be judged between them with justice, and they will not be wronged.

48. They say: "When will this promise come to pass,- if you speak the truth?"

49. Say: "I have no power over any harm or profit to myself except as Allah wills. To every people is a term appointed: when their term is reached, not an hour can they cause delay, nor (an hour) can they advance (it in antici-pation)."

50. Say: "Do you see,- if His punishment should come to you by night or by day,- what portion of it would the Sinners wish to hasten?

51. "Would you then believe in it at last, when it actually comes to pass? (It will then be said): 'Ah! now? and you wanted (aforetime) to hasten it on!'

52. "At length will be said to the wrong-doers: 'you taste the enduring punishment! You get but the recompense of what you earned!'"

wa laakin-nannaasa anfusahum yazlimoon.

45. Wa Yawma yaḥshuruhum ka-al-lam yalbasooo illaa saa'atam-minan-nahaari yata'aarafoona baynahum; qad khasiral-lazeena kazzaboo biliqaaa'il-laahi wa maa kaanoo muhtadeen.

46. Wa imma nuriyannaka ba'ḍal-lazee na'iduhum aw natawaffayannaka fa-ilaynaa marji'uhum summal-laahu shaheedun 'alaa maa yaf'aloon.

47. Wa likulli ummatir-Rasoo-lun fa-izaa jaaa'a Rasooluhum quḍiya baynahum bilqisṭi wa hum laa yuzlamoon.

48. Wa yaqooloona mataa haazal-wa'du in kuntum ṣaadiqeen.

49. Qul laaa amliku linafsee ḍarrañw-wa laa naf'an illaa maa shaaa'al-laah; likulli ummatin ajalun izaa jaaa'a ajaluhum falaaa yastaåkhiroona saa'a-tañw-wa laa yastaqdimoon.

50. Qul ara'aytum in ataakum 'azaabuhoo bayaatan aw nahaaram-maazaa yasta'jilu minhul-mujrimoon.

51. Asumma izaa maa waqa'a aamantum bih; aaal'aana wa qad kuntum bihee tasta'jiloon.

52. Summa qeela lillazeena zalamoo zooqoo 'azaabal-khuld, hal tujzawna illaa bimaa kuntum taksiboon.

وَلَٰكِنَّ النَّاسَ أَنفُسَهُمْ يَظْلِمُونَ ٤٤

وَيَوْمَ يَحْشُرُهُمْ كَأَن لَّمْ يَلْبَثُوٓا۟ إِلَّا سَاعَةً مِّنَ النَّهَارِ يَتَعَارَفُونَ بَيْنَهُمْ ۚ قَدْ خَسِرَ الَّذِينَ كَذَّبُوا۟ بِلِقَآءِ اللَّهِ وَمَا كَانُوا۟ مُهْتَدِينَ ٤٥

وَإِمَّا نُرِيَنَّكَ بَعْضَ الَّذِى نَعِدُهُمْ أَوْ نَتَوَفَّيَنَّكَ فَإِلَيْنَا مَرْجِعُهُمْ ثُمَّ اللَّهُ شَهِيدٌ عَلَىٰ مَا يَفْعَلُونَ ٤٦

وَلِكُلِّ أُمَّةٍ رَّسُولٌ ۖ فَإِذَا جَآءَ رَسُولُهُمْ قُضِىَ بَيْنَهُم بِالْقِسْطِ وَهُمْ لَا يُظْلَمُونَ ٤٧

وَيَقُولُونَ مَتَىٰ هَٰذَا الْوَعْدُ إِن كُنتُمْ صَٰدِقِينَ ٤٨

قُل لَّآ أَمْلِكُ لِنَفْسِى ضَرًّا وَلَا نَفْعًا إِلَّا مَا شَآءَ اللَّهُ ۗ لِكُلِّ أُمَّةٍ أَجَلٌ ۚ إِذَا جَآءَ أَجَلُهُمْ فَلَا يَسْتَأْخِرُونَ سَاعَةً ۖ وَلَا يَسْتَقْدِمُونَ ٤٩

قُلْ أَرَءَيْتُمْ إِنْ أَتَىٰكُمْ عَذَابُهُۥ بَيَٰتًا أَوْ نَهَارًا مَّاذَا يَسْتَعْجِلُ مِنْهُ الْمُجْرِمُونَ ٥٠

أَثُمَّ إِذَا مَا وَقَعَ ءَامَنتُم بِهِۦٓ ۚ آلْـَٰٔنَ وَقَدْ كُنتُم بِهِۦ تَسْتَعْجِلُونَ ٥١

ثُمَّ قِيلَ لِلَّذِينَ ظَلَمُوا۟ ذُوقُوا۟ عَذَابَ الْخُلْدِ هَلْ تُجْزَوْنَ إِلَّا بِمَا كُنتُمْ تَكْسِبُونَ ٥٢

53. They seek to be informed by you: "Is that true?" Say: "Yes, by my Lord! it is the very truth and you cannot frustrat it!"

53. Wa yastambi'oonaka ahaqqun huwa qul ee wa Rabbeee innahoo lahaqq; wa maaa antum bimu'jizeen.

(Section 5)

54. Every soul that has sinned, if it possessed all that is on earth, would fain give it in ransom: they would declare (their) repentance when they see the Chastisement: but the judgment between them will be with justice, and no wrong will be done to them.

54. Wa law anna likulli nafsin zalamat maa fil-ardi laftadat bih; wa asarrun-nadaamata lammaa ra-awul-'azaab, wa qudiya baynahum bilqist; wa hum laa yuzlamoon.

55. Is it not (the case) that to Allah belongs whatever is in the heavens and on earth? Is it not (the case) that Allah's promise is assuredly true? Yet most of them understand do not.

55. Alaaa inna lillaahi maa fis-samaawaati wal-ard; alaaa inna wa'dal-laahi haqquñw-wa laakinna aksarahum laa ya'lamoon.

56. It is He Who gives life and who takes it, and to Him shall you all be brought back.

56. Huwa yuhyee wa yumeetu wa ilayhi turja'oon.

57. O mankind! there has come to you a direction from your Lord and a healing for the (diseases) in your hearts,- and for those who believe, a Guidance and a Mercy.

57. Yaaa ayyuhan-naasu qad jaaa'atkum-maw'izatum-mir-Rabbikum wa shifaaa'ul-limaa fis-sudoori wa hudañw-wa rahmatul-lilmu'mineen.

58. Say: "In the Bounty of Allah, and in His Mercy,- in that let them rejoice": that is better than the (wealth) they hoard.

58. Qul bifadlil-laahi wa birahmatihee fabizaalika falyaf-rahoo huwa khayrum-mimmaa yajma'oon.

59. Say: "Do you see what things Allah has sent down to you for sustenance? Yet you hold forbidden some things thereof and (some things) lawful." Say: "Has Allah indeed permitted you, or do you invent (things) to attribute to Allah?"

59. Qul ara'aytum-maaa anzalal-laahu lakum-mir-rizqin faja'altum-minhu haraamañw-wa halaalan qul aaallaahu azina lakum am 'alal-laahi taftaroon.

60. And what do those think who invent lies against Allah, of the Day of Judgment? Verily Allah is full of Bounty to mankind, but most of them are ungrateful.

60. Wa maa zannul-lazeena yaftaroona 'alal-laahil-kaziba Yawmal-Qiyaamah; innal-laaha lazoo fadlin 'alan-naasi wa laakinna aksarahum laa yash-kuroon.

(Section 6)

61. In whatever business you may be, and whatever portion you may be reciting

61. Wa maa takoonu fee shaániñw-wa maa tatloo

from the Qur'an,- and whatever deed you (mankind) may be doing,- We are Witnesses thereof when you are deeply engrossed therein. Nor is hidden from your Lord (so much as) the weight of an atom on the earth or in heaven. And not the least and not the greatest of these things but are recorded in a clear Record.

minhu min Qur-aaninw-wa laa ta'maloona min 'amalin illaa kunnaa 'alaykum shuhoodan iz tufeeḍoona feeh; wa maa ya'zubu 'ar-Rabbika mim-misqaali zarratin fil-arḍi wa laa fissamaaa'i wa laaa aṣghara min zaalika wa laaa akbara illaa fee Kitaabim-Mubeen.

62. Behold! verily on the friends of Allah there is no fear, nor shall they grieve;

62. Alaaa inna awliyaaa'allaahi laa khawfun 'alayhim wa laa hum yaḥzanoon.

63. Those who believe and (constantly) guard against evil;-

63. Allazeena aamanoo wa kaanoo yattaqoon.

64. For them are Glad Tidings, in the life of the Present and in the Hereafter; no change can there be in the Words of Allah. This is indeed the supreme felicity.

64. Lahumul-bushraa filḥayaatid-dunyaa wa fil Aakhirah; laa tabdeela likalimaatil-laah; zaalika huwal-fawzul-'azeem.

65. Let not their speech grieve you: for all power and honour belong to Allah: It is He Who hears and knows (all things).

65. Wa laa yaḥzunka qawluhum; innal-'izzata lillaahi jamee'aa; Huwas-Samee'ul-'Aleem.

66. Behold! verily to Allah belong all creatures, in the heavens and on earth. What do they follow who worship as His "partners" other than Allah? They follow nothing but fancy, and they do nothing but lie.

66. Alaaa inna lillaahi man fis-samaawaati wa man fil-arḍ; wa maa yattabi'ul-lazeena yad'oona min doonil-laahi shurakaaa'; iñy-yattabi'oona illaz-zanna wa in hum illaa yakhruṣoon.

67. He it is that has made for you the Night that you may rest therein, and the Day to make things visible (to you). Verily in this are Signs for those who listen (to His Message).

67. Huwal-lazee ja'ala lakumul-layla litaskunoo feehi wannahaara mubṣiraa; inna fee zaalika la-Aayaatil-liqawmiñy-yasma'oon.

68. They say: "God (Alalh) has begotten a son!" - Glory be to Him! He is self-sufficient! His are all things in the heavens and on earth! No warrant have you

68. Qaalut-takhazal-laahu waladan Subḥaanahoo Huwal-Ghaniyyu lahoo maa fissamaawaati wa maa fil-arḍ; in 'indakum-min

for this! Do you say about Allah what you do you know?

69. Say: "Those who invent a lie against Allah will never prosper."

70. A little enjoyment in this world!- and then, to Us will be their return, then shall We make them taste the severest Chastisement for their blasphemies.

71. Relate to them the story of Noah. Behold! he said to his people: "O my people, if it be hard on your (mind) that I should stay (with you) and commemorate the Signs of Allah,- yet I put my trust in Allah. You then get an agreement about your plan and among your partners, so your plan be not to you dark and dubious. Then pass your sentence on me, and give me no respite.

72. "But if you turn back, (consider): no reward have I asked of you: my reward is only due from Allah, and I have been commanded to be of those who submit to Allah's Will (in Islam)."

73. They rejected him, but We delivered him, and those with him, in the Ark, and We made them inherit (the earth), while We overwhelmed in the flood those who rejected Our Signs. Then see what was the end of those who were warned (but heeded not)!

74. Then after him We sent (many) Apostles to their peoples: they brought them Clear Signs, but they would not believe what they had already rejected beforehand. Thus do We seal the hearts of the transgressors.

sulṭaanim bihaazaaa; ataqoo-loona 'alal-laahi maa laa ta'lamoon.

69. Qul innal-lazeena yafta-roona 'alal-laahil-kaziba laa yuflihoon.

70. Mataa'un fid-dunyaa summa ilaynaa marji'uhum summa nuzeequhumul-'azaabash-shadeeda bimaa kaanoo yakfuroon. (Section 7)

71. Watlu 'alayhim naba-a Noohin iz qaala liqawmihee yaa qawmi in kaana kabura 'alaykum-maqaamee wa tazkeeree bi-Aayaatil-laahi fa'alal-laahi tawakkaltu fa-ajmi'ooo amrakum wa shura-kaaa'akum summa laa yakun amrukum 'alaykum ghumma-tan summaq-dooo ilayya wa laa tunziroon.

72. Fa-in tawallaytum famaa sa-altukum-min ajrin in ajriya illaa 'alal-laahi wa umirtu an akoona minal-muslimeen.

73. Fakazzaboohu fanaj-jaynaahu wa mamma'ahoo fil-fulki wa ja'alnaahum kha-laaa'ifa wa aghraqnal-lazeena kazzaboo bi-Aayaatinaa fan-zur kayfa kaana 'aaqibatul-munzareen.

74. Summa ba'asnaa mim ba'dihee Rusulan ilaa qawmi-him fajaaa'oohum bilbayyi-naati famaa kaanoo liyu'minoo bimaa kazzaboo bihee min qabl; kazaalika natba'u 'alaa quloobil-mu'tadeen.

75. Then after them sent We Moses and Aaron to Pharaoh and his chiefs with Our Signs. But they were arrogant: they were a people in sin.

76. When the Truth did come to them from Us, they said: "This is indeed evident sorcery!"

77. Moses said: "Did you say (this) about the Truth when it has (actually) reached you? Is sorcery (like this)? But sorcerers will not prosper."

78. They said: "Have you come to us to turn us away from the ways we found our fathers following,- in order that you and your brother may have greatness in the land? But we shall not believe in you!"

79. Pharaoh said: "Bring me every sorcerer well versed."

80. When the sorcerers came, Moses said to them: "You throw what you (wish) to throw!"

81. When they had had their throw, Moses said: "What you have brought is sorcery: Allah will surely make it of no effect: for Allah does not prosper the work of those who make mischief.

82. "And Allah by His Words proves and establishes His Truth, however much the Sinners may hate it!"

83. But none believed in Moses except some children of his people, because of the fear of Pharaoh and his chiefs, lest they should persecute them; and certainly Pharaoh was mighty on the earth and one who transgressed all bounds.

75. Summa ba'asnaa mim ba'dihim-Moosaa wa Haaroona ilaa Fir'awna wa mala'ihee bi-Aayaatinaa fastakbaroo wa kaanoo qawmam-mujrimeen.

76. Falammaa jaaa'ahumul-haqqu min 'indinaa qaalooo inna haazaa lasihrum-mubeen.

77. Qaala Moosaaa ataqooloona lilhaqqi lammaa jaaa'akum asihrun haazaa wa laa yuflihus-saahiroon.

78. Qaalooo aji'tanaa litalfitanaa 'ammaa wajadnaa 'alayhi aabaaa'anaa wa takoona lakumal-kibriyaaa'u fil-ardi wa maa nahnu lakumaa bimu'mineen.

79. Wa qaala Fir'awnu'toonee bikulli saahirin 'aleem.

80. Falammaa jaaa'assaharatu qaala lahum-Moosaaa alqoo maaa antum-mulqoon.

81. Falammaaa alqaw qaala Moosaa maa ji'tum bihis-sihru innal-laaha sa-yubtiluhoo innallaaha laa yuslihu 'amalal-mufsideen.

82. Wa yuhiqqul-laahul-haqqa bi-Kalimaatihee wa law karihal-mujrimoon. **(Section 8)**

83. Famaaa aamana li-Moosaaa illaa zurriyyatum-min qawmihee 'alaa khawfim-min Fir'awna wa mala'ihim añy-yaftinahum; wa inna Fir'awna la'aalin fil-ardi wa innahoo laminal-musrifeen.

84. Moses said: "O my people! If you do (really) believe in Allah, then in Him put your trust if you submit (your will to His)."

84. Wa qaala Moosaa yaa qawmi in kuntum aamantum billaahi fa'alayhi tawakkalooo in kuntum-muslimeen.

وَقَالَ مُوسَى يَقَوْمِ اِنْ كُنْتُمْ اٰمَنْتُمْ بِاللّٰهِ فَعَلَيْهِ تَوَكَّلُوْٓا اِنْ كُنْتُمْ مُّسْلِمِيْنَ ۝

85. They said: "In Allah do we put our trust. Our Lord! do not make us a trial for those who practise oppression;

85. Faqaaloo 'alal-laahi tawakkalnaa Rabbanaa laa taj'alnaa fitnatal-lilqawmiz-zaalimeen.

فَقَالُوْا عَلَى اللّٰهِ تَوَكَّلْنَا ۚ رَبَّنَا لَا تَجْعَلْنَا فِتْنَةً لِّلْقَوْمِ الظّٰلِمِيْنَ ۝

86. "And deliver us by Your Mercy from those who reject (You)."

86. Wa najjinaa birahmatika minal-qawmil-kaafireen.

وَنَجِّنَا بِرَحْمَتِكَ مِنَ الْقَوْمِ الْكٰفِرِيْنَ ۝

87. We inspired Moses and his brother with this Message: "Provide dwellings for your people in Egypt, make your dwellings into places of worship, and establish regular prayers: and give Glad Tidings to those who believe!"

87. Wa awhaynaaa ilaa Moosaa wa akheehi an tabaw-wa-aa liqawmikumaa bi-Misra bu-yootanw-waj'aloo bu-yoota-kum qiblatanw-wa aqeemus-Salaah; wa bashshiril-mu'mineen.

وَاَوْحَيْنَا اِلٰى مُوْسٰى وَاَخِيْهِ اَنْ تَبَوَّاٰ لِقَوْمِكُمَا بِمِصْرَ بُيُوْتًا وَّاجْعَلُوْا بُيُوْتَكُمْ قِبْلَةً وَّاَقِيْمُوا الصَّلٰوةَ ۗ وَبَشِّرِ الْمُؤْمِنِيْنَ ۝

88. Moses prayed: "Our Lord! You have indeed bestowed on Pharaoh and his Chiefs splendour and wealth in the life of the Present, and so, our Lord, they mislead (men) from Your Path. Our Lord deface, the features of their wealth, and send hardness to their hearts, so they will not believe until they see the grievous Chastisement."

88. Wa qaala Moosaa Rabba-naaa innaka aatayta Fir'awna wa mala-ahoo zeenatanw-wa amwaalan fil-hayaatid-dunyaa Rabbanaa liyudilloo 'an sabeelika Rabbanat-mis 'alaaa amwaalihim washdud 'alaa quloobihim falaa yu'minoo hattaa yarawul-'azaabal-aleem.

وَقَالَ مُوْسٰى رَبَّنَآ اِنَّكَ اٰتَيْتَ فِرْعَوْنَ وَمَلَاَهٗ زِيْنَةً وَّاَمْوَالًا فِى الْحَيٰوةِ الدُّنْيَا ۙ رَبَّنَا لِيُضِلُّوْا عَنْ سَبِيْلِكَ ۚ رَبَّنَا اطْمِسْ عَلٰٓى اَمْوَالِهِمْ وَاشْدُدْ عَلٰى قُلُوْبِهِمْ فَلَا يُؤْمِنُوْا حَتّٰى يَرَوُا الْعَذَابَ الْاَلِيْمَ ۝

89. Allah said: "Accepted is your prayer (O Moses and Aaron)! So you stand straight, and do not follow the path of those who do not know."

89. Qaala qad ujeebad-da'wa-tukumaa fastaqeemaa wa laa tattabi'aaanni sabeelal-lazeena laa ya'lamoon.

قَالَ قَدْ اُجِيْبَتْ دَّعْوَتُكُمَا فَاسْتَقِيْمَا وَلَا تَتَّبِعٰٓنِّ سَبِيْلَ الَّذِيْنَ لَا يَعْلَمُوْنَ ۝

90. We took the Children of Israel across the sea: Pharaoh and his hosts followed them in insolence and spite. At length, when overwhelmed with the flood, he said: "I believe that there is no god except Him Whom the Children of Israel believe in: I am of those who submit (to Allah in Islam)."

90. Wa jaawaznaa bi-Baneee Israaa'eelal-bahra fa-atba'a-hum Fir'awnu wa junooduhoo baghyanw-wa 'adwan hattaa izaaa adrakahul-gharaqu qaala aamantu annahoo laaa ilaaha illal-lazeee aamanat bihee Banooo Israaa'eela wa ana minal-muslimeen.

وَجٰوَزْنَا بِبَنِيْٓ اِسْرَآءِيْلَ الْبَحْرَ فَاَتْبَعَهُمْ فِرْعَوْنُ وَجُنُوْدُهٗ بَغْيًا وَّعَدْوًا ۗ حَتّٰٓى اِذَآ اَدْرَكَهُ الْغَرَقُ ۙ قَالَ اٰمَنْتُ اَنَّهٗ لَآ اِلٰهَ اِلَّا الَّذِيْٓ اٰمَنَتْ بِهٖ بَنُوْٓا اِسْرَآءِيْلَ وَاَنَا مِنَ الْمُسْلِمِيْنَ ۝

91. (It was said to him): "Ah now!- But a little while before, you were in rebellion!- and you did mischief (and violence)!

92. "This day shall We save you in the body, that you may be a Sign to those who come after you! but verily, many among mankind are heedless of Our Signs!"

93. We settled the Children of Israel in a beautiful dwelling-place, and provided for them sustenance of the best: it was after knowledge had been granted to them, that they fell into schisms. Verily Allah will judge between them as to the schisms amongst them, on the Day of Judgment.

94. If you were in doubt as to what We have revealed to you, then ask those who have been reading the Book from before you: the Truth has indeed come to you from your Lord: so be in no wise of those in doubt.

95. Nor be of those who reject the Signs of Allah, or you shall be of those who perish.

96. Those against whom the word of your Lord has been verified would not believe-

97. Even if every Sign was brought to them,- until they see (for themselves) the Chastisement grievous.

98. Why was there not a single township (among those We warned), which believed,- so its faith should have profited it,- except the people of Jonah? When they believed, We removed from them the Chastisement of ignominy in the life of the present, and permitted them to enjoy (their life) for a while.

91. Aal'aana wa qad 'aṣayta qablu wa kunta minal-mufsideen.

92. Falyawma nunajjeeka bibadanika litakoona liman khalfaka Aayah; wa inna kaṣeeram-minan-naasi 'an Aayaatinaa laghaafiloon. *(Section 9)*

93. Wa laqad bawwaảnaa Baneee Israaa'eela mubawwa-a ṣidqinw-wa razaqnaahum-minaṭ-ṭayyibaati famakh-talafoo ḥattaa jaaa'ahumul-'ilm; inna Rabbaka yaqḍee baynahum Yawmal-Qiyaamati feemaa kaanoo feehi yakhtalifoon.

94. Fa-in kunta fee shakkim-mimmaaa anzalnaaa ilayka fas'alil-laẕeena yaqra'oonal-Kitaaba min qablik; laqad jaaa'akal-ḥaqqu mir-Rabbika falaa takoonanna minal-mumtareen.

95. Wa laa takoonanna minal-laẕeena kaẕẕaboo bi-Aayaatil-laahi fatakoona minal-khaasireen.

96. Innal-laẕeena ḥaqqat 'alayhim Kalimatu Rabbika laa yu'minoon.

97. Wa law jaaa'at-hum kullu Aayatin ḥattaa yarawul-'aẕaabal-aleem.

98. Falaw laa kaanat qaryatun aamanat fanafa'ahaaa eemaa-nuhaaa illaa qawma Yoonusa lammaaa aamanoo kashafnaa 'anhum 'aẕaabal-khizyi fil-ḥayaatid-dunyaa wa matta'naa-hum ilaa ḥeen.

99. If it had been your Lord's will, they would all have believed,- all who are on earth! Will you then compel mankind, against their will, to believe!

100. No soul can believe, except by the Will of Allah, and He will place Doubt (or obscurity) on those who will not understand.

101. Say: "Behold all that is in the heavens and on earth"; but neither Signs nor Warners profit those who do not believe.

102. Do they then expect (any thing) but (what happened in) the days of the men who passed away before them? Say: "You wait then: for I, too, will wait with you."

103. In the end We deliver Our Apostles and those who believe: thus is it fitting on Our part that We should deliver those who believe!

104. Say: "O you men! If you are in doubt as to my religion, (behold!) I do not worship what you worship, other than Allah! But I worship Allah - Who will take your souls (at death): I am commanded to be (in the ranks) of the Believers,

105. "And further (thus): 'set your face towards religion with true piety, and never in any wise be of the Unbelievers;

106. "'Nor call on any, other than Allah;- Such will neither profit you nor hurt you: if you do so, behold! you shall certainly be of those who do wrong.'"

107. If Allah touches you with hurt, there is none

99. Wa law shaaa'a Rabbuka la-aamana man fil-arḍi kulluhum jamee'aa; afa-anta tukri-hun-naasa ḥattaa yakoonoo mu'mineen.

100. Wa maa kaana linafsin an tu'mina illaa bi-iznil-laah; wa yaj'alur-rijsa 'alal-lazeena laa ya'qiloon.

101. Qulin-ẓuroo maazaa fis-samaawaati wal-arḍ; wa maa tughnil-Aayaatu wannuzuru 'an qawmil-laa yu'minoon.

102. Fahal yantaẓiroona illaa misla ayyaamil-lazeena khalaw min qablihim; qul fantaẓirooo innee ma'akum minal-muntaẓireen.

103. Summa nunajjee Rus-lanaa wallazeena aamanoo; kazaalika ḥaqqan 'alaynaa nunjil-mu'mineen. (Section 10)

104. Qul yaaa ayyuhan-naasu in kuntum fee shakkim-min deenee falaaa a'budul-lazeena ta'budoona min doonil-laahi wa laakin a'budul-laahal-lazee yatawaffaakum wa umirtu an akoona minal-mu'mineen.

105. Wa an aqim wajhaka liddeeni Ḥaneefaɲw wa laa takoonanna minal-mushrikeen.

106. Wa laa tad'u min doonil-laahi maa laa yanfa'uka wa laa yaḍurruka fa-in fa'alta fa-innaka izam-minaẓ-ẓaalimeen.

107. Wa iɲy-yamsaskal-laahu biḍurrin falaa

can remove it but He: if He do design some benefit for you, there is none can keep back His favour: He causes it to reach whomsoever of His servants He pleases. And He is the Oft-Forgiving, Most Merciful.

108. Say: "O you men! Now Truth has reached you from your Lord! those who receive guidance, do so for the good of their own souls; those who stray, do so to their own loss: and I am not (set) over you to arrange your affairs."

109. You follow the inspiration sent to you, and be patient and constant, till Allah do decide: for He is the Best to decide.

كاشفا lahooo illaa Huwa wa iñy-yuridka bikhayrin falaa raaadda lifadlih; yuṣeebu bihee mañ-yashaaa'u min 'ibaadih; wa huwal-Ghafoorur-Raḥeem.

108. Qul yaaa ayyuhan-naasu qad jaaa'akumul-ḥaqqu mir-Rabbikum famanih-tadaa fa-innamaa yahtadee linafsihee wa man ḍalla fa-innamaa yaḍillu 'alayhaa wa maaa ana 'alaykum biwakeel.

109. Wattabi' maa yooḥaaa ilayka waṣbir ḥattaa yaḥkumal-laah; wa Huwa khayrul-ḥaakimeen. **(Section 11)**

---

11. Hud (The Prophet Hud)
In the name of Allah, Most Gracious, Most Merciful.

1. *Alif-Lam-Ra.* (This is) a Book, with verses basic or fundamental (of established meaning), further explained in detail,- from One Who is Wise and Well-acquainted (with all things):
2. (It teaches) that you should worship none but Allah. (Say): "Verily I am (sent) to you from Him to warn and to bring glad tidings:
3. "(And to preach thus), 'You seek the forgiveness of your Lord, and turn to Him in repentance; that He may grant you enjoyment, good (and true), for a term appointed, and bestow His abounding grace on all who abound in merit! But if you turn away , then I fear for you the Chastisement of a Great Day:
4. 'To Allah is your return, and He has power over all things."
5. Behold! they fold up their hearts, that they may lie hid from Him! Ah! even when

Sûrat Hûd–11
(Revealed at Makkah)
Bismillaahir Raḥmaanir Raḥeem

1. Alif-Laaam-Raa; Kitaa-bun uḥkimat Aayaatuhoo ṣumma fuṣṣilat mil-ladun Ḥa-keemin Khabeer.

2. Allaa ta'budooo illal-laah; innanee lakum minhu nazee-ruñw-wa basheer.

3. Wa anis-taghfiroo Rabba-kum ṣumma toobooo ilayhi yumatti'kum mataa'an ḥasanan ilaaa ajalim-musammañw-wa yu'ti kulla zee faḍlin faḍlahoo wa in tawallaw fa-innee akhaa-fu 'alaykum 'azaaba Yawmin Kabeer.

4. Ilal-laahi marji'ukum wa Huwa 'alaa kulli shay'in Qadeer.

5. Alaaa innahum yaṣnoona ṣudoorahum liyastakhfoo minh; alaa ḥeena

they cover themselves with their garments, He knows what they conceal, and what they reveal: for He knows well the (inmost secrets) of the hearts.

6. There is no moving creature on earth but its sustenance depends on Allah: He knows the time and place of its definite abode and its temporary deposit: all is in a clear Record.

7. He it is Who created the heavens and the earth in six Days - and His Throne was over the waters - that He might try you, which of you is best in conduct. But if you were to say to them, "You shall indeed be raised up after death", the Unbelievers would be sure to say, "This is nothing but obvious sorcery!"

8. If We delay the Chastisement for them for a definite term, they are sure to say, "What keeps it back?" Ah! On the day it (actually) reaches them, nothing will turn it away from them, and they will be completely encircled by that which they used to mock at!

9. If We give man a taste of Mercy from Ourselves, and then withdraw it from him, behold! he is in despair and (falls into) blasphemy.

10. But if We give him a taste of (Our) favours after adversity has touched him, he is sure to say, "All evil has departed from me:" behold! he falls into exultation and pride.

11. Not so do those who show patience and constancy, and work righteousness; for them is forgiveness (of sins) and a great reward.

12. Perchance you may (feel the inclination) to give up a part of what is revealed to you, and your heart feels straitened lest

yastaghshoona siyaabahum ya'lamu maa yusirroona wa maa yu'linoon; innahoo 'aleemum bizaatiṣ-ṣudoor.

6. Wa maa min daaabbatin fil-arḍi illaa 'alal-laahi rizquhaa wa ya'lamu mustaqarrahaa wa mustawda'ahaa; kullun fee Kitaabim-Mubeen.

7. Wa Huwal-lazee khalaqas-samaawaati wal-arḍa fee sittati ayyaamiñw-wa kaana-'Arshuhoo alal-maaa'i liyabluwakum ayyukum aḥsanu 'amalaa; wa la'in qulta innakum mab'oosoona mim ba'dil-mawti la-yaqoolannal-lazeena kafarooo in haazaaa illaa siḥrum-mubeen.

8. Wala'in akhkharnaa 'anhumul-'azaaba ilaaa ummatimma'doodatil-la-yaqoolunna maa yaḥbisuh; alaa yawma yaaa-teehim laysa maṣroofan 'anhum wa ḥaaqa bihim-maa kaanoo bihee yastahzi'oon. (Section 1)

9. Wa la'in azaqnal-insaana minnaa raḥmatan summa naza'naahaa minhu, innahoo laya'oosun kafoor.

10. Wala'in azaqnaahu na'-maaa'a ba'da ḍarraaa'a massathu la-yaqoolanna zahabassayyi-aatu 'anneee; innahoo lafariḥun fakhoor.

11. Illal-lazeena ṣabaroo wa 'amiluṣ-ṣaaliḥaati ulaaa'ika lahum-maghfiratuñw-wa ajrun kabeer.

12. Fala'allaka taarikum ba'da maa yooḥaaa ilayka wa ḍaaa'iqum-bihee ṣadruka añy-

they say, "Why is not a treasure sent down to him, or why does not an angel come down with him?" But you are there only to warn! It is Allah that arranges all affairs!

13. Or they may say, "He forged it," Say, "You then bring ten Suras forged, like unto it, and call (to your aid) whomsoever you can, other than Allah!- If you speak the truth!

14. "If then they (your false gods) do not answer your (call), you (should) know that this Revelation is sent down (replete) with the knowledge of Allah, and that there is no god but He! Will you even then not submit (to Islam)?"

15. Those who desire the life of the present and its glitter,- to them We shall pay (the price of) their deeds therein,- without diminution.

16. They are those for whom there is nothing in the Hereafter but the Fire: vain are the designs they frame therein, and of no effect and the deeds that they do!

17. Can they be (like) those who accept a Clear (Sign) from their Lord, and whom a witness from Himself teaches, as did the Book of Moses before it,- a guide and a mercy? They believe therein; but those of the Sects that reject it,- the Fire will be their promised meeting-place. Be not then in doubt thereon: for it is the Truth from your Lord: yet many among men do not believe!

18. Who does more wrong than those who invent a lie against Allah? They will be turned back to the presence of their Lord, and the witnesses will say, "These are the ones

yaqooloo law laaa unzila 'alayhi kanzun aw jaaa'a ma'ahoo malak; innamaaa anta nazeer; wallaahu 'alaa kulli shay'iñw-wakeel.

13. Am yaqooloonaf-taraahu qul faatoo bi'ashri Suwarim-mislihee muftarayaatiñw-wad'oo manis-tata'tum min doonil-laahi in kuntum saadi-qeen.

14. Fa-il-lam yastajeeboo lakum fa'lamooo annamaaa unzila bi'ilmil-laahi wa al-laaa ilaaha illaa Huwa fahal antum muslimoon.

15. Man kaana yureedul-hayaatad-dunyaa wa zeena-tahaa nuwaffi ilayhim a'maa-lahum feehaa wa hum feehaa laa yubkhasoon.

16. Ulaaa'ikal-lazeena laysa lahum fil-Aakhirati illan-Naaru wa habita maa sana'oo feehaa wa baatilum-maa kaanoo ya'maloon.

17. Afaman kaana 'alas bayyinatim-mir-Rabbihee wa yatloohu shaahidum-minhu wa min qablihee Kitaabu Moosaaa imaamañw-wa rahmah; ulaaa-'ika yu'minoona bih; wa mañy-yakfur bihee minal-Ahzaabi fan-Naaru maw'iduh; falaa taku fee miryatim-minh; innahul-haqqu mir-Rabbika wa laakinna aksaran-naasi laa yu'minoon.

18. Wa man azlamu mimma-nif-taraa 'alal-laahi kaziban; ulaaa'ika yu'radoona 'alaa Rabbihim wa yaqoolul-ashhaa-du haaa'ulaaa'il-lazeena

يَقُوْلُوْنَ لَوْلَاۤ اُنْزِلَ عَلَيْهِ كَنْزٌ اَوْ جَآءَ مَعَهٗ مَلَكٌ ۗ اِنَّمَاۤ اَنْتَ نَذِيْرٌ ۗ وَاللّٰهُ عَلٰى كُلِّ شَيْءٍ وَّكِيْلٌ ۞

اَمْ يَقُوْلُوْنَ افْتَرٰىهُ ۗ قُلْ فَأْتُوْا بِعَشْرِ سُوَرٍ مِّثْلِهٖ مُفْتَرَيٰتٍ وَّادْعُوْا مَنِ اسْتَطَعْتُمْ مِّنْ دُوْنِ اللّٰهِ اِنْ كُنْتُمْ صٰدِقِيْنَ ۞

فَاِلَّمْ يَسْتَجِيْبُوْا لَكُمْ فَاعْلَمُوْۤا اَنَّمَاۤ اُنْزِلَ بِعِلْمِ اللّٰهِ وَاَنْ لَّاۤ اِلٰهَ اِلَّا هُوَ ۚ فَهَلْ اَنْتُمْ مُّسْلِمُوْنَ ۞

مَنْ كَانَ يُرِيْدُ الْحَيٰوةَ الدُّنْيَا وَ زِيْنَتَهَا نُوَفِّ اِلَيْهِمْ اَعْمَالَهُمْ فِيْهَا وَهُمْ فِيْهَا لَا يُبْخَسُوْنَ ۞

اُولٰٓئِكَ الَّذِيْنَ لَيْسَ لَهُمْ فِى الْاٰخِرَةِ اِلَّا النَّارُ ۖ وَحَبِطَ مَا صَنَعُوْا فِيْهَا وَ بٰطِلٌ مَّا كَانُوْا يَعْمَلُوْنَ ۞

اَفَمَنْ كَانَ عَلٰى بَيِّنَةٍ مِّنْ رَّبِّهٖ وَ يَتْلُوْهُ شَاهِدٌ مِّنْهُ وَ مِنْ قَبْلِهٖ كِتٰبُ مُوْسٰۤى اِمَامًا وَّرَحْمَةً ۗ اُولٰٓئِكَ يُؤْمِنُوْنَ بِهٖ ۗ وَمَنْ يَّكْفُرْ بِهٖ مِنَ الْاَحْزَابِ فَالنَّارُ مَوْعِدُهٗ ۚ فَلَا تَكُ فِيْ مِرْيَةٍ مِّنْهُ ۗ اِنَّهُ الْحَقُّ مِنْ رَّبِّكَ وَلٰكِنَّ اَكْثَرَ النَّاسِ لَا يُؤْمِنُوْنَ ۞

وَمَنْ اَظْلَمُ مِمَّنِ افْتَرٰى عَلَى اللّٰهِ كَذِبًا ۗ اُولٰٓئِكَ يُعْرَضُوْنَ عَلٰى رَبِّهِمْ وَ يَقُوْلُ الْاَشْهَادُ هٰٓؤُلَآءِ الَّذِيْنَ

who lied against their Lord!
Behold! the Curse of Allah is on
those who do wrong!-

19. "Those who would hinder
(men) from the path of Allah
and would seek in it something
crooked: these were they who
denied the Hereafter!"

20. They will in no wise
frustrate (His design) on earth,
nor have they protectors besides
Allah! Their Chastisement will
be doubled! They lost the power
to hear, and they did not see!

21. They are the ones who
have lost their own souls: and
the (fancies) they invented have
left them in the lurch!

22. Without a doubt, these are
the very ones who will lose most
in the Hereafter!

23. But those who believe and
work righteousness, and
humble themselves before their
Lord,- they will be Companions
of the Garden, to dwell therein
for ever!

24. These two kinds (of men)
may be compared to the blind
and deaf, and those who can see
and hear well. Are they equal
when compared? Will you not
then take heed?

25. We sent Noah to his people
(with a mission): "I have come
to you with a Clear Warning:

26. "That you serve none but
Allah: Verily I do fear for you
the Chastisement of a Grievous
Day."

27. But the chiefs of the
Unbelievers among his people
said: "We see (in) you nothing
but a man like ourselves:

---

kazaboo 'alaa Rabbihim; alaa
la'natul-laahi 'alaz-zaalimeen.

19. Allazeena yaṣuddoona 'an
sabeelil-laahi wa yabghoonahaa
'iwajañw wa hum bil-Aakhirati
hum kaafiroon.

20. Ulaaa'ika lam yakoonoo
mu'jizeena fil-arḍi wa maa
kaana lahum-min doonil-laahi
min awliyaaa'; yuḍaa'afu
lahumul-'azaab; maa kaanoo
yastaṭee'oonas-sam'a wa maa
kaanoo yubṣiroon.

21. Ulaaa'ikal-lazeena khasirooo anfusahum wa ḍalla
'anhum maa kaanoo yaftaroon.

22. Laa jarama annahum fil-
Aakhirati humul-akhsaroon.

23. Innal-lazeena aamanoo
wa 'amiluṣ-ṣaaliḥaati wa akh-
batooo ilaa Rabbihim ulaaa'ika
Aṣḥaabul-Jannati hum feehaa
khaalidoon.

24. Maṣalul-fareeqayni kal-
a'maa wal-aṣammi walbaṣeeri
wassamee'; hal yastawiyaani
maṣalaa; afalaa tazakkaroon.

(Section 2)

25. Wa laqad arsalnaa Noohan
ilaa qawmihee innee lakum
nazeerum-mubeen.

26. Al-laa ta'budooo illal-
laaha inneee akhaafu 'alaykum
'azaaba Yawmin aleem.

27. Faqaalal-mala-ul-lazeena
kafaroo min qawmihee maa
naraaka illaa basharam-
miṣlanaa

nor do we see that any follow you but the meanest among us, in judgment immature: nor do we see in you (all) any merit above us: in fact we think you are liars!"

28. He said: "O my people! do you see if (it be that) I have a Clear Sign from my Lord, and that He has sent Mercy to me from His Own Presence, but that the Mercy has been obscured from your sight? Shall we compel you to accept it when you are averse to it?

29. "And O my people! I ask you for no wealth in return: my reward is from none but Allah: but I will not drive away (in contempt) those who believe: for verily they are to meet their Lord, and you, I see are the ignorant ones!

30. "And O my people! who would help me against Allah if I drove them away? Will you not then take heed?

31. "I do not tell you that with me are the Treasures of Allah, nor do I know what is hidden, nor I claim to be an angel. Nor yet do I say, of those whom your eyes do despise that Allah will not grant them (all) that is good: Allah knows best what is in their souls: I should, if I did, indeed be a wrong-doer."

32. They said: "O Noah! You have disputed with us, and much have you prolonged the dispute with us: now bring upon us what you threaten us with, if you speak the truth!?"

33. He said: "Truly, Allah will bring it on you if He wills,- and then, you will not be able to frustrate it!

34. "Of no profit will be my counsel to you, much as I desire

wa maa naraakat-taba'aka illal-lazeena hum araazilunaa baadiyar-raåyi wa maa naraa lakum 'alaynaa min faḍlim-bal naẓunnukum kaazibeen.

28. Qaala yaa qawmi ara'aytum in kuntu 'alaa bayyinatim-mir-Rabbee wa aataanee raḥmatam-min 'indihee fa'ummiyat 'alaykum anulzimukumoohaa wa antum lahaa kaarihoon.

29. Wa yaa qawmi laaa as'alukum 'alayhi maalan in ajriya illaa 'alal-laah; wa maaa ana biṭaaridil-lazeena aamanoo; innahum mulaaqoo Rabbihim wa laakinneee araakum qawman tajhaloon.

30. Wa yaa qawmi mañy-yanṣurunee minal-laahi in ṭarattuhum; afalaa tazak-karoon.

31. Wa laaa aqoolu lakum 'indee khazaa'inul-laahi wa laaa a'lamul-ghayba wa laaa aqoolu innee malakuñw-wa laaa aqoolu lillazeena tazdareee a'yunukum lañy-yu'tiyahumul-laahu khayran Allaahu a'lamu bimaa feee anfusihim inneee izal-laminaz-zaalimeen.

32. Qaaloo yaa Nooḥu qad jaadaltanaa fa-akṣarta jidaalanaa faåtinaa bimaa ta'idunaaa in kunta minaṣ-ṣaadiqeen.

33. Qaala innamaa yaåteekum bihil-laahu in shaaa'a wa maaa antum bimu'jizeen.

34. Wa laa yanfa'ukum nuṣḥee in arattu

وَمَا نَرٰىكَ اتَّبَعَكَ إِلَّا الَّذِينَ هُمْ اَرَاذِلُنَا بَادِيَ الرَّأْيِ ۚ وَمَا نَرٰى لَكُمْ عَلَيْنَا مِنْ فَضْلٍۭ بَلْ نَظُنُّكُمْ كٰذِبِينَ ۝

قَالَ يٰقَوْمِ اَرَءَيْتُمْ اِنْ كُنْتُ عَلٰى بَيِّنَةٍ مِّنْ رَّبِّي وَاٰتٰىنِي رَحْمَةً مِّنْ عِنْدِهٖ فَعُمِّيَتْ عَلَيْكُمْ ۚ اَنُلْزِمُكُمُوهَا وَاَنْتُمْ لَهَا كٰرِهُونَ ۝

وَيٰقَوْمِ لَاۤ اَسْـَٔلُكُمْ عَلَيْهِ مَالًا ۚ اِنْ اَجْرِيَ اِلَّا عَلَى اللّٰهِ وَمَاۤ اَنَا بِطَارِدِ الَّذِينَ اٰمَنُوا ۚ اِنَّهُمْ مُّلٰقُوا رَبِّهِمْ وَلٰكِنِّيۤ اَرٰىكُمْ قَوْمًا تَجْهَلُونَ ۝

وَيٰقَوْمِ مَنْ يَّنْصُرُنِي مِنَ اللّٰهِ اِنْ طَرَدْتُّهُمْ ۚ اَفَلَا تَذَكَّرُونَ ۝

وَلَاۤ اَقُوْلُ لَكُمْ عِنْدِي خَزَاۤئِنُ اللّٰهِ وَلَاۤ اَعْلَمُ الْغَيْبَ وَلَاۤ اَقُوْلُ اِنِّي مَلَكٌ وَّلَاۤ اَقُوْلُ لِلَّذِينَ تَزْدَرِيۤ اَعْيُنُكُمْ لَنْ يُّؤْتِيَهُمُ اللّٰهُ خَيْرًا ۚ اَللّٰهُ اَعْلَمُ بِمَا فِيۤ اَنْفُسِهِمْ ۚ اِنِّيۤ اِذًا لَّمِنَ الظّٰلِمِينَ ۝

قَالُوا يٰنُوْحُ قَدْ جَادَلْتَنَا فَاَكْثَرْتَ جِدَالَنَا فَاْتِنَا بِمَا تَعِدُنَاۤ اِنْ كُنْتَ مِنَ الصّٰدِقِينَ ۝

قَالَ اِنَّمَا يَاْتِيكُمْ بِهِ اللّٰهُ اِنْ شَاۤءَ وَمَاۤ اَنْتُمْ بِمُعْجِزِينَ ۝

وَلَا يَنْفَعُكُمْ نُصْحِيۤ اِنْ اَرَدْتُّ

to give you (good) counsel, if it be that Allah wills to leave you astray: He is your Lord! and to Him will you return!"

35. Or do they say, "He has forged it"? Say: "If I had forged it, on me were my sin! and I am free of the sins of which you are guilty!

36. It was revealed to Noah: "None of your people will believe except those who have believed already! So grieve no longer over their (evil) deeds.

37. "But construct an Ark under Our eyes and Our inspiration, and address Me no (further) on behalf of those who are in sin: for they are about to be overwhelmed (in the Flood)."

38. Forthwith he (starts) constructing the Ark: every time that the Chiefs of his people passed by him, they threw ridicule on him. He said: "If you ridicule us now, we (in our turn) can look down on you with ridicule likewise!

39. "But soon you will know who it is on whom will descend a Chastisement that will cover them with shame,- on whom will be unloosed a lasting Chastisement:"

40. At length, behold! there came Our Command, and the fountains of the earth gushed forth! We said: "Embark therein, of each kind two, male and female, and your family - except those against whom the Word has already gone forth,- and the Believers." But only a few believed with him.

41. So he said: "You embark on the Ark, In the name of Allah, whether it move or be at rest! For my Lord is, be sure, Oft-Forgiving, Most Merciful!"

42. So the Ark floated with them on the waves (towering) like mountains,

an anşaḥa lakum in kaanal-laahu yureedu añy-yughwi-yakum; Huwa Rabbukum wa ilayhi turja'oon.

35. Am yaqooloonaf-taraahu qul inif-taraytuhoo fa'alayya ijraamee wa ana baree'um-mimmaa tujrimoon. (Section 3)

36. Wa ooḥiya ilaa Noohin annahoo lañy-yu'mina min qawmika illaa man qad aamana falaa tabta'is bimaa kaanoo yaf'aloon.

37. Waşna'il-fulka bi-a'yuninaa wa waḥyinaa wa laa tukhaa-ṭibnee fil-lazeena zalamoo; innahum-mughraqoon.

38. Wa yaşna'ul-fulka wa kullamaa marra 'alayhi mala-um-min qawmihee sakhiroo minh; qaala in taskharoo minnaa fa-innaa naskharu minkum kamaa taskharoon.

39. Fasawfa ta'lamoona mañy-yaåteehi 'azaabuñy-yukhzeehi wa yaḥillu 'alayhi 'azaabum-muqeem.

40. Ḥattaaa izaa jaaa'a amrunaa wa faarat-tannooru qulnaḥ-mil feehaa min kullin zawjayniş-nayni wa ahlaka illaa man sabaqa 'alayhil-qawlu wa man aaman; wa maaa aamana ma'ahoo illaa qaleel.

41. Wa qaalar-kaboo feehaa bismil-laahi majrayhaa wa mursaahaa; inna Rabbee la-Ghafoorur-Raḥeem.

42. Wa hiya tajree bihim fee mawjin kaljibaali

and Noah called out to his son, who had separated himself (from the rest): "O my son! embark with us, and be not with the Unbelievers!"

43. The son replied: "I will betake myself to some mountain: it will save me from the water." Noah said: "This day nothing can save, from the Command of Allah, any but those on whom He has mercy! "And the waves came between them, and the son was among those overwhelmed in the Flood.

44. Then the word went forth: "O earth! swallow up your water, and O sky! withhold (your rain)!" And the water abated, and the matter was ended. The Ark rested on Mount Judi, and the word went forth: "Away with those who do wrong!"

45. And Noah called upon his Lord, and said: "O my Lord! surely my son is of my family! And Your promise is true, and You are the justest of Judges!"

46. He said: "O Noah! He is not of your family: for his conduct is unrighteous. So do not ask of Me that of which you have no knowledge! I give you counsel, lest you act like the ignorant!"

47. Noah said: "O my Lord! I do seek refuge with You, lest I ask You for that of which I have no knowledge. And unless You forgive me and have Mercy on me, I should indeed be lost!"

48. The word came: "O Noah! come down (from the Ark) with peace from Us, and Blessing on you and on some of the peoples (who will spring) from those with you: but (there will be other) peoples to whom We shall grant their pleasures (for a time), but in the end a grievous Chastisement will reach them from Us."

49. Such are some of the stories of the Unseen, which We have revealed

wa naadaa Noohunib-nahoo wa kaana fee ma'ziliny-yaa bunay-yarkam-ma'anaa wa laa takum ma'al-kaafireen.

43. Qaala sa-aaweee ilaa jabaliny-ya'simunee minal-maaa'; qaala laa 'aasimal-yaw-ma min amril-laahi illaa mar-rahim; wa haala baynahumal-mawju fakaana minal-mugh-raqeen.

44. Wa qeela yaaa ardubla'ee maaa'aki wa yaa samaaa'u aqli'ee wa gheedal-maaa'u wa qudiyal-amru wastawat 'alal-joodiyyi wa qeela bu'dal-lilqawmiz-zaalimeen.

45. Wa naadaa Nooh ur-Rabbahoo faqaala Rabbi innab-nee min ahlee wa inna wa'dakal-haqqu wa Anta ahkamul-haakimeen.

46. Qaala yaa Noohu innahoo laysa min ahlika innahoo 'amalun ghayru saalihin falaa tas'alni maa laysa laka bihee 'ilmun ineee a'izuka an takoona minal-jaahileen.

47. Qaala Rabbi inneee a'oozu bika an as'alaka maa laysa lee bihee 'ilmunw wa illaa taghfir lee wa tarhamneee akum-minal-khaasireen.

48. Qeela yaa Noohuh-bit bisalaamim-minnaa wa bara-kaatin 'alayka wa 'alaaa uma-mim-mimmam-ma'ak; wa umamun sanumatti'uhum summa yamassuhum-minnaa 'azaabun aleem.

49. Tilka min ambaaa'il ghaybi nooheehaaa

وَنَادَىٰ نُوحُ ابْنَهُ وَكَانَ فِى مَعْزِلٍ يَبُنَىَّ ارْكَب مَّعَنَا وَلَا تَكُن مَّعَ الْكَفِرِينَ ۝

قَالَ سَاوِىٓ إِلَىٰ جَبَلٍ يَعْصِمُنِى مِنَ الْمَآءِ قَالَ لَا عَاصِمَ الْيَوْمَ مِنْ أَمْرِ اللَّهِ إِلَّا مَن رَّحِمَ وَحَالَ بَيْنَهُمَا الْمَوْجُ فَكَانَ مِنَ الْمُغْرَقِينَ ۝

وَقِيلَ يَأَرْضُ ابْلَعِى مَآءَكِ وَيَسَمَآءُ أَقْلِعِى وَغِيضَ الْمَآءُ وَقُضِىَ الْأَمْرُ وَاسْتَوَتْ عَلَى الْجُودِىِّ وَقِيلَ بُعْدًا لِّلْقَوْمِ الظَّلِمِينَ ۝

وَنَادَىٰ نُوحُ رَّبَّهُ فَقَالَ رَبِّ إِنَّ ابْنِى مِنْ أَهْلِى وَإِنَّ وَعْدَكَ الْحَقُّ وَأَنتَ أَحْكَمُ الْحَكِمِينَ ۝

قَالَ يَنُوحُ إِنَّهُ لَيْسَ مِنْ أَهْلِكَ إِنَّهُ عَمَلٌ غَيْرُ صَلِحٍ فَلَا تَسْئَلْنِ مَا لَيْسَ لَكَ بِهِ عِلْمٌ إِنِّى أَعِظُكَ أَن تَكُونَ مِنَ الْجَهِلِينَ ۝

قَالَ رَبِّ إِنِّى أَعُوذُ بِكَ أَنْ أَسْئَلَكَ مَا لَيْسَ لِى بِهِ عِلْمٌ وَإِلَّا تَغْفِرْ لِى وَتَرْحَمْنِى أَكُن مِّنَ الْخَسِرِينَ ۝

قِيلَ يَنُوحُ اهْبِطْ بِسَلَمٍ مِّنَّا وَبَرَكَتٍ عَلَيْكَ وَعَلَىٰٓ أُمَمٍ مِّمَّن مَّعَكَ وَأُمَمٌ سَنُمَتِّعُهُمْ ثُمَّ يَمَسُّهُم مِّنَّا عَذَابٌ أَلِيمٌ ۝

تِلْكَ مِنْ أَنبَآءِ الْغَيْبِ نُوحِيهَا

to you: before this, neither you nor your people knew them. So persevere patiently: for the End is for those who are righteous.

50. To the 'Ad People (We sent) Hud, one of their own brethren. He said: "O my people! worship Allah! you have no other god but Him. (Your other gods) you do nothing but invent!

51. "O my people! I ask of you no reward for this (Message). My reward is from none but Him who created me: will you not then understand?

52. "And O my people! Ask forgiveness of your Lord, and turn to Him (in repentance): He will send you the skies pouring abundant rain, and add strength to your strength: so you do not turn back in sin!"

53. They said: "O Hud! You have brought us no Clear (Sign), and we are not the ones to desert our gods on your word! Nor shall we believe in you!

54. "We say nothing but that (perhaps) some of our gods may have seized you with imbecility." He said: "I call Allah to witness, and you do bear witness, that I am free from the sin of ascribing, to Him,

55. "Other gods as partners! So scheme (your worst) against me, all of you, and give me no respite.

56. "I put my trust in Allah, my Lord and your Lord! There is not a moving creature, but He has grasp of its fore-lock. Verily, it is my Lord that is on a straight Path.

57. "If you turn away,- I (at least) have conveyed the Message with which I was sent to you. My Lord will make another

---

ilayka maa kunta ta'lamuhaaa anta wa laa qawmuka min qabli haazaa fasbir innal-'aaqibata lilmuttaqeen. **(Section 4)**

50. Wa ilaa 'Aadin akhaahum Hoodaa; qaala yaa qawmi'-budul-laaha maa lakum min ilaahin ghayruhooo in antum illaa muftaroon.

51. Yaa qawmi laaa as'alukum 'alayhi ajran in ajriya illaa 'alal-lazee fataranee; afalaa ta'qiloon.

52. Wa yaa qawmis-taghfiroo Rabbakum summa toobooo ilayhi yursilis-samaaa'a 'alay-kum-midraarañw-wa yazidkum quwwatan ilaa quwwatikum wa laa tatawallaw mujrimeen.

53. Qaaloo yaa Hoodu maa ji'tanaa bibayyinatiñw-wa maa nahnu bitaarikeee aalihatinaa 'an qawlika wa maa nahnu laka bimu'mineen.

54. In naqoolu illaa-'taraaka ba'du aalihatinaa bisooo'; qaala inneee ushhidul-laaha wash-hadooo annee baree'um-mimmaa tushrikoon.

55. Min doonihee fakeedoonee jamee'an summa laa tunziroon.

56. Innee tawakkaltu 'alallaahi Rabbee wa Rabbikum; maa min daaabbatin illaa Huwa aakhi-zum binaasiyatihaa; inna Rabbee 'alaa Siraatim-Musta-qeem.

57. Fa-in tawallaw faqad ablaghtukum-maaa ursiltu biheee ilaykum; wa yastakhlifu Rabbee qawman

another people to succeed you, and you will not harm Him in the least. For my Lord has care and watch over all things."

58. So when Our decree issued, We saved Hud and those who believed with him, by (special) Grace from Ourselves: We saved them from a severe Chastisement.

59. Such were the 'Ad People: they rejected the Signs of their Lord and Cherisher; disobeyed His Apostles; and followed the command of every powerful, obstinate transgressor.

60. And they were pursued by a Curse in this life,- and on the Day of Judgment. Ah! Behold! For the 'Ad rejected their Lord and Cherisher! Ah! Behold! Removed (from sight) were 'Ad, the people of Hud!

61. To the Thamud People (We sent) Salih, one of their own brethren. He said: "O my people! Worship Allah: you have no other god but Him. It is He Who has produced you from the earth and settled you therein: then ask forgiveness of Him, and turn to Him (in repentance): for my Lord is (always) near, ready to answer."

62. They said: "O Salih! you have been of us!- a centre of our hopes hitherto! Do you (now) forbid us the worship of what our fathers worshipped? But we are really in suspicious (disquieting) doubt as to that to which you invite us."

63. He said: "O my people! Do you see? if I have a Clear (Sign) from my Lord and He has sent Mercy to me from Himself,- who then can help me against Allah if I were to disobey Him? What then would you add to my (portion) but perdition?

64. "And O my people! this she-camel of Allah is a symbol to

ghayrakum wa laa taḍur-roonahoo shay'aa; inna Rabbee 'alaa kulli shay'in Ḥafeez.

58. Wa lammaa jaaa'a amrunaa najjaynaa Hoodañw-wallazeena aamanoo ma'ahoo biraḥ matim-minnaa wa najjaynaahum-min 'azaabin ghaleez.

59. Wa tilka 'Aad, jaḥadoo bi-Aayaati Rabbihim wa 'aṣaw Rusulahoo wattaba'ooo amra kulli jabbaarin 'aneed.

60. Wa utbi'oo fee haazihid-dunyaa la'natañw-wa Yawmal-Qiyaamah; alaaa inna 'Aadan kafaroo Rabbahum; alaa bu'dal-li-'Aadin qawmi Hood.

(Section 5)

61. Wa ilaa Samooda akhaa-hum Ṣaaliḥaa; qaala yaa qawmi'-budul-laaha maa lakum min ilaahin ghayruhoo Huwa ansha-akum-minal-arḍi wasta'marakum feehaa fastaghfiroohu summa tooboooo ilayh; inna Rabbee Qareebum-Mujeeb.

62. Qaaloo yaa Ṣaaliḥu qad kunta feenaa marjuwwan qabla haazaaa atanhaanaaa an na'bu-da maa ya'budu aabaaa'unaa wa innanaa lafee shakkim-mimmaa tad'oonaaa ilayhi mureeb.

63. Qaala yaa qawmi ara'ay-tum in kuntu 'alaa bayyinatim-mir-Rabbee wa aataanee minhu raḥmatan famañy-yanṣurunee minal-laahi in 'aṣaytuhoo famaa tazeedoonanee ghayra takhseer.

64. Wa yaa qawmi haazihee naaqatul-laahi lakum

you: leave her to feed on Allah's (free) earth, and inflict no harm on her, or a swift Chastisement will seize you!"

65. But they hamstrung her. So he said: "Enjoy yourselves in your homes for three days: (then will be your ruin): (behold) there is a promise not to be belied!"

66. When Our Decree issued, We saved Salih and those who believed with him, by (special) Grace from Ourselves - and from the Ignominy of that Day. For your Lord - He is the Strong One, and Able to enforce His Will.

67. The (mighty) Blast overtook the wrong-doers, and they lay prostrate in their homes before the morning,-

68. As if they had never dwelt and flourished there. Ah! Behold! For the Thamud rejected their Lord and Cherisher! Ah! Behold! Removed (from sight) were the Thamud!

69. There came Our Messengers to Abraham with glad tidings. They said, "Peace!" He answered, "Peace!" and hastened to entertain them with a roasted calf.

70. But when he saw their hands did not go towards the (meal), he felt some mistrust of them, and conceived a fear of them. They said: "Fear not: we have been sent against the people of Lut."

71. And his wife was standing (there), and she laughed: but We gave her glad tidings of Isaac, and after him, of Jacob.

72. She said: "Alas for me! shall I bear a child, seeing I am an old woman, and my husband here is an old man? That would indeed be a wonderful thing!"

73. They said: "Do you wonder at Allah's decree? The Grace

Aayatan fazaroohaa taákul feee ardil-laahi wa laa tamassoohaa bisooo'in fa-yaákhuzakum azaabun qareeb.

65. Fa‘aqaroohaa faqaala tamatta‘oo fee daarikum ṣalaa-ṣata ayyaamin zaalika wa‘dun ghayru makzoob.

66. Falammaa jaaa'a amrunaa najjaynaa Ṣaaliḥ anw-wal-lazeena aamanoo ma‘ahoo biraḥmatim-minnaa wa min khizyi Yawmi'iz, inna Rab-baka Huwal-Qawiyyul-‘Azeez.

67. Wa akhazal-lazeena ẓala-muṣ-ṣayḥatu fa-aṣbaḥoo fee diyaarihim jaaṣimeena.

68. Ka-al-lam yaghnaw fee-haaa; alaaa inna Samooda kafaroo Rabbahum; alaa bu‘dal-li-Samood.   **(Section 6)**

69. Wa laqad jaaa'at Rusulu-naaa Ibraaheema bilbushraa qaaloo salaaman qaala salaa-mun famaa labiṣa an jaaa'a bi‘ijlin ḥaneez.

70. Falammaa ra-aaa aydiya-hum laa taṣilu ilayhi nakirahum wa awjasa minhum kheefah; qaaloo laa takhaf innaaa ursilnaaa ilaa qawmi Looṭ.

71. Wamra-atuhoo qaaa'imatun faḍaḥikat fabashsharnaahaa bi-Isḥaaqa wa miñw-waraaa'i Isḥaaqa Ya‘qoob.

72. Qaalat yaa waylataaa ‘a-alidu wa ana ‘ajoozuñw-wa haazaa ba‘lee shaykhan inna haazaa lashay'un ‘ajeeb.

73. Qaalooo ata‘abeena min amril-laahi raḥmatul-

اَيَةً فَذَرُوْهَا تَاْكُلْ فِىْٓ اَرْضِ

اللّٰهِ وَلَا تَمَسُّوْهَا بِسُوْٓءٍ فَيَاْخُذَكُمْ

عَذَابٌ قَرِيْبٌ ۞

فَعَقَرُوْهَا فَقَالَ تَمَتَّعُوْا فِىْ دَارِكُمْ

ثَلٰثَةَ اَيَّامٍ ذٰلِكَ وَعْدٌ غَيْرُ

مَكْذُوْبٍ ۞

فَلَمَّا جَآءَ اَمْرُنَا نَجَّيْنَا صٰلِحًا

وَّالَّذِيْنَ اٰمَنُوْا مَعَهٗ بِرَحْمَةٍ مِّنَّا

وَمِنْ خِزْيِ يَوْمِئِذٍ ؕ اِنَّ رَبَّكَ

هُوَ الْقَوِيُّ الْعَزِيْزُ ۞

وَاَخَذَ الَّذِيْنَ ظَلَمُوا الصَّيْحَةُ

فَاَصْبَحُوْا فِىْ دِيَارِهِمْ جٰثِمِيْنَ ۞

كَاَنْ لَّمْ يَغْنَوْا فِيْهَا ؕ اَلَآ اِنَّ ثَمُوْدَا۠

كَفَرُوْا رَبَّهُمْ ؕ اَلَا بُعْدًا لِّثَمُوْدَ ۞

وَلَقَدْ جَآءَتْ رُسُلُنَآ اِبْرٰهِيْمَ

بِالْبُشْرٰى قَالُوْا سَلٰمًا ؕ قَالَ سَلٰمٌ

فَمَا لَبِثَ اَنْ جَآءَ بِعِجْلٍ حَنِيْذٍ ۞

فَلَمَّا رَآٰ اَيْدِيَهُمْ لَا تَصِلُ اِلَيْهِ نَكِرَهُمْ

وَاَوْجَسَ مِنْهُمْ خِيْفَةً ؕ قَالُوْا لَا

تَخَفْ اِنَّآ اُرْسِلْنَآ اِلٰى قَوْمِ لُوْطٍ ۞

وَامْرَاَتُهٗ قَآئِمَةٌ فَضَحِكَتْ فَبَشَّرْنٰهَا

بِاِسْحٰقَ ۙ وَمِنْ وَّرَآءِ اِسْحٰقَ يَعْقُوْبَ ۞

قَالَتْ يٰوَيْلَتٰٓى ءَاَلِدُ وَاَنَا عَجُوْزٌ

وَّهٰذَا بَعْلِىْ شَيْخًا ؕ اِنَّ هٰذَا

لَشَىْءٌ عَجِيْبٌ ۞

قَالُوْٓا اَتَعْجَبِيْنَ مِنْ اَمْرِ اللّٰهِ رَحْمَتُ

of Allah and His blessings on you, O you people of the house! for He is indeed worthy of all praise, full of all glory!"

74. When fear had passed from (the mind of) Abraham and the glad tidings had reached him, he began to plead with us for Lut's people.

75. For Abraham was, without doubt, forbearing (of faults), compassionate, and given to look to Allah.

76. O Abraham! Do not seek this. The decree of your Lord has gone forth: for them there comes a Chastisement that cannot be turned back!

77. When Our Messengers came to Lut, he was grieved on their account and felt himself powerless (to protect) them. He said: "This is a distressful day."

78. And his people came rushing towards him, and they had been long in the habit of practising abominations. He said: "O my people! Here are my daughters: they are purer for you (if you marry)! Now fear Allah, and do not cover me with shame about my guests! Isn't there among you a single right-minded man?"

79. They said: "You know well we have no need of your daughters: indeed you know quite well what we want!"

80. He said: "Would that I had power to suppress you or that I could betake myself to some powerful support."

81. (The Messengers) said: "O Lut! We are Messengers from your Lord! By no means they shall reach you! Now travel with your family while yet a part of the night remains, and let not any of you look back: but your wife (will remain behind): to her will happen what happens to the people. Morning is their appointed time:

laahi wa barakaatuhoo 'alay-kum Ahlal-Bayt; innahoo Ḥameedum-Majeed.

74. Falammaa zahaba an Ibraaheemar-raw'u wa jaaa'at-hul-bushraa yujaadilunaa fee qawmi Looṭ.

75. Inna Ibraaheema laḥalee-mun awwaahum-muneeb.

76. Yaaa Ibraaheemu a'riḍ 'an haazaaa innahoo qad jaaa'a amru Rabbika wa innahum aateehim 'azaabun ghayru mardood.

77. Wa lammaa jaaa'at Rusu-lunaa Looṭan seee'a bihim wa ḍaaqa bihim zar'añw-wa qaala haazaa yawmun 'aṣeeb.

78. Wa jaaa'ahoo qawmuhoo yuhra'oona ilayhi wa min qablu kaanoo ya'maloonas-sayyi-aat; qaala yaa qawmi haaa'ulaaa'i banaatee hunna aṭharu lakum fattaqul-laaha wa laa tukhzooni fee ḍayfee alaysa minkum rajulur-rasheed.

79. Qaaloo laqad 'alimta maa lanaa fee banaatika min ḥaqq, wa innaka lata'lamu maa nureed.

80. Qaala law anna lee bikum quwwatan aw aaweee ilaa ruknin shadeed.

81. Qaaloo yaa Looṭu innaa Rusulu Rabbika lañy-yaṣilooo ilayka fa-asri bi-ahlika bi-qiṭ'im-minal-layli wa laa yaltafit minkum aḥadun illam-ra-ataka innahoo muṣeebuhaa maaa aṣaabahum; inna maw'i-dahumuṣ-ṣubḥ;

is not the morning near?"

82. When Our decree issued, We turned (the cities) upside down, and rained down on them brimstones hard as baked clay, spread, layer on layer,-

83. Marked as from your Lord: nor are they ever far from those who do wrong!

84. To the Madyan People (We sent) Shu'aib, one of their own brethren: he said: "O my people! worship Allah: You have no other god but Him. And do not give short measure or weight: I see you in prosperity, but I fear for you the Chastisement of a Day that will compass (you) all round.

85. "And O my people! give just measure and weight, nor withhold from the people the things that are their due: do not commit evil in the land with intent to do mischief.

86. "That which is left you by Allah is best for you, if you (but) believed! but I am not set over you to keep watch!"

87. They said: "O Shu'aib! Does your (religion of) prayer command you that we leave off the worship which our fathers practised, or that we leave off doing what we like with our property? truly, you are the one that forbears with faults and is right-minded!"

88. He said: "O my people! Do you see whether I have a Clear (Sign) from my Lord, and He has given me sustenance (pure and) good as from Himself? I do not wish, in opposition to you, to do that which I forbid you to do. I only desire (your) betterment to the best of my power; and my success (in my task) can only come from Allah. In Him I trust,

alaysaṣ-ṣubḥu biqareeb.

82. Falammaa jaaa'a amrunaa ja'alnaa 'aaliyahaa saafilahaa wa amṭarnaa 'alayhaa ḥijaara-tam-min sijjeelim-manḍood.

83. Musawwamatan 'inda Rabbik; wa maa hiya minaẓ-ẓaalimeena biba'eed. (Section 7)

84. Wa ilaa Madyana akhaa-hum Shu'aybaa; qaala yaa qawmi'-budul-laaha maa lakum min ilaahin ghayruhoo wa laa tanquṣul-mikyaala walmeezaan; ineee araakum bikhayriñw-wa ineee akhaafu 'alaykum 'azaaba Yawmim-muḥeeṭ.

85. Wa yaa qawmi awful-mikyaala walmeezaana bilqisṭi wa laa tabkhasun-naasa ash-yaaa'ahum wa laa ta'saw fil-arḍi mufsideen.

86. Baqiyyatul-laahi khayrul-lakum in kuntum-mu'mineen; wa maa ana 'alaykum biḥafeeẓ.

87. Qaaloo yaa Shu'aybu aṣalaatuka taåmuruka an nat-ruka maa ya'budu aabaaa'unaaa aw an naf'ala feee amwaalinaa maa nashaaa'oo innaka la-antal ḥaleemur-rasheed.

88. Qaala yaa qawmi ara'ay-tum in kuntu 'alaa bayyinatim-mir-Rabbee wa razaqanee minhu rizqan ḥasanaa; wa maaa ureedu an ukhaalifakum ilaa maaa anhaakum 'anh; in ureedu illal-iṣlaaḥa mastaṭa't; wa maa tawfeeqee illaa billaah; 'alayhi tawakkaltu

اَلَيْسَ الصُّبْحُ بِقَرِيبٍ ۝

فَلَمَّا جَآءَ اَمْرُنَا جَعَلْنَا عَالِيَهَا سَافِلَهَا وَاَمْطَرْنَا عَلَيْهَا حِجَارَةً

مِّنْ سِجِّيْلٍ ۙ۬ مَّنْضُوْدٍ ۝

مُّسَوَّمَةً عِنْدَ رَبِّكَ ۭ وَمَا هِيَ مِنَ الظّٰلِمِيْنَ بِبَعِيْدٍ ۧ ۝

وَاِلٰى مَدْيَنَ اَخَاهُمْ شُعَيْبًا ۭ قَالَ يٰقَوْمِ اعْبُدُوا اللّٰهَ مَا لَكُمْ مِّنْ اِلٰهٍ غَيْرُهٗ ۭ وَلَا تَنْقُصُوا الْمِكْيَالَ وَالْمِيْزَانَ اِنِّيْٓ اَرٰىكُمْ بِخَيْرٍ وَّاِنِّيْٓ اَخَافُ عَلَيْكُمْ عَذَابَ يَوْمٍ مُّحِيْطٍ ۝

وَيٰقَوْمِ اَوْفُوا الْمِكْيَالَ وَالْمِيْزَانَ بِالْقِسْطِ وَلَا تَبْخَسُوا النَّاسَ اَشْيَآءَهُمْ وَلَا تَعْثَوْا فِى الْاَرْضِ مُفْسِدِيْنَ ۝

بَقِيَّتُ اللّٰهِ خَيْرٌ لَّكُمْ اِنْ كُنْتُمْ مُّؤْمِنِيْنَ ۵ وَمَآ اَنَا عَلَيْكُمْ بِحَفِيْظٍ ۝

قَالُوْا يٰشُعَيْبُ اَصَلٰوتُكَ تَاْمُرُكَ اَنْ نَّتْرُكَ مَا يَعْبُدُ اٰبَآؤُنَآ اَوْ اَنْ نَّفْعَلَ فِيْٓ اَمْوَالِنَا مَا نَشٰٓؤُا ۭ اِنَّكَ لَاَنْتَ الْحَلِيْمُ الرَّشِيْدُ ۝

قَالَ يٰقَوْمِ اَرَءَيْتُمْ اِنْ كُنْتُ عَلٰى بَيِّنَةٍ مِّنْ رَّبِّيْ وَرَزَقَنِيْ مِنْهُ رِزْقًا حَسَنًا ۭ وَمَآ اُرِيْدُ اَنْ اُخَالِفَكُمْ اِلٰى مَآ اَنْهٰىكُمْ عَنْهُ ۭ اِنْ اُرِيْدُ اِلَّا الْاِصْلَاحَ مَا اسْتَطَعْتُ ۭ وَمَا تَوْفِيْقِيْٓ اِلَّا بِاللّٰهِ ۭ عَلَيْهِ تَوَكَّلْتُ

and to Him I turn.

89. "And O my people! let not my dissent (from you) cause you to sin, lest you suffer a fate similar to that of the people of Noah or of Hud or of Salih, nor are the people of Lut far off from you!

90. "But ask forgiveness of your Lord, and turn to Him (in repentance): for my Lord is indeed full of mercy and loving-kindness."

91. They said: "O Shu'aib! much of what you say we do not understand! In fact among us we see that you have no strength! Were it not for your family, we should certainly have stoned you! For you have among us no great position!"

92. He said: "O my people! is then my family of more consideration with you than Allah? For you cast Him away behind your backs (with contempt). But verily my Lord encompasses on all sides all that you do!

93. "And O my people! do whatever you can: I will do (my part): soon will you know who it is on whom descends the Chastisement of ignominy; and who is a liar! and watch you! for I too am watching with you!"

94. When Our decree issued, We saved Shu'aib and those who believed with him, by (special) Mercy from Our selves: but the (mighty) Blast seized the wrong-doers, and they lay prostrate in their homes by the morning,-

95. As if they had never dwelt and flourished there! Ah! Behold! How the Madyan were removed (from sight) as were removed the Thamud.

96. And we sent Moses, with Our Clear (Signs) and an authority manifest,

---

wa ilayhi uneeb.

89. Wa yaa qawmi laa yajri-mannakum shiqaaqeee añy-yuṣeebakum-mis̱lu maaa aṣaaba qawma Nooḥin aw qawma Hoodin aw qawma Ṣaaliḥ; wa maa qawmu Looṭim-minkum biba'eed.

90. Wastaghfiroo Rabbakum s̱umma toobooo ilayh; inna Rabbee Raḥeemuñw-Wadood.

91. Qaaloo yaa Shu'aybu maa nafqahu kas̱eeram-mimmaa taqoolu wa innaa lanaraaka feenaa ḍa'eefañw wa law laa rahṭuka larajamnaaka wa maaa anta 'alaynaa bi'azeez.

92. Qaala yaa qawmi arahṭeee a'azzu 'alaykum-minal-laahi wattakhaẕtumoohu waraaa'a-kum ẓihriyyan inna Rabbee bimaa ta'maloona muḥeet.

93. Wa yaa qawmi'-maloo 'alaa makaanatikum innee 'aamilun sawfa ta'lamoona mañy-yaåteehi 'aẕaabuñy-yukh-zeehi wa man huwa kaaẕib; wartaqibooo innee ma'akum raqeeb.

94. Wa lammaa jaaa'a amru-naa najjaynaa Shu'aybañw-wal-laẕeena aamanoo ma'ahoo biraḥmatim-minnaa wa akha-zatil-laẕeena ẓalamuṣ-ṣayḥatu fa-aṣbaḥoo fee diyaarihim jaas̱imeen.

95. Ka-al-lam yaghnaw fee-haaa; alaa bu'dal-li-Madyana kamaa ba'idat Samood.

(Section 8)

96. Wa laqad arsalnaa Moosaa bi-Aayaatinaa wa sulṭaanim-mubeen.

وَإِلَيْهِ أُنِيبُ ۝

وَيٰقَوْمِ لَا يَجْرِمَنَّكُمْ شِقَاقِيٓ أَنْ يُصِيبَكُمْ مِّثْلُ مَاۤ أَصَابَ قَوْمَ نُوحٍ أَوْ قَوْمَ هُودٍ أَوْ قَوْمَ صٰلِحٍ ۚ وَمَا قَوْمُ لُوطٍ مِّنْكُمْ بِبَعِيدٍ ۝

وَاسْتَغْفِرُوْا رَبَّكُمْ ثُمَّ تُوبُوْاۤ إِلَيْهِ ۚ إِنَّ رَبِّيْ رَحِيْمٌ وَّدُوْدٌ ۝

قَالُوْا يٰشُعَيْبُ مَا نَفْقَهُ كَثِيْرًا مِّمَّا تَقُوْلُ وَإِنَّا لَنَرٰكَ فِيْنَا ضَعِيْفًا ۚ وَلَوْلَا رَهْطُكَ لَرَجَمْنٰكَ ۖ وَمَاۤ أَنْتَ عَلَيْنَا بِعَزِيْزٍ ۝

قَالَ يٰقَوْمِ أَرَهْطِيْۤ أَعَزُّ عَلَيْكُمْ مِّنَ اللّٰهِ ۖ وَاتَّخَذْتُمُوْهُ وَرَآءَكُمْ ظِهْرِيًّا ۚ إِنَّ رَبِّيْ بِمَا تَعْمَلُوْنَ مُحِيْطٌ ۝

وَيٰقَوْمِ اعْمَلُوْا عَلٰى مَكَانَتِكُمْ إِنِّيْ عَامِلٌ ۖ سَوْفَ تَعْلَمُوْنَ ۙ مَنْ يَّأْتِيْهِ عَذَابٌ يُّخْزِيْهِ وَمَنْ هُوَ كَاذِبٌ ۗ وَارْتَقِبُوْاۤ إِنِّيْ مَعَكُمْ رَقِيْبٌ ۝

وَلَمَّا جَاۤءَ أَمْرُنَا نَجَّيْنَا شُعَيْبًا وَّالَّذِيْنَ اٰمَنُوْا مَعَهُ بِرَحْمَةٍ مِّنَّا ۚ وَأَخَذَتِ الَّذِيْنَ ظَلَمُوا الصَّيْحَةُ فَأَصْبَحُوْا فِيْ دِيَارِهِمْ جٰثِمِيْنَ ۝

كَأَنْ لَّمْ يَغْنَوْا فِيْهَا ۗ أَلَا بُعْدًا لِّمَدْيَنَ كَمَا بَعِدَتْ ثَمُوْدُ ۝

وَلَقَدْ أَرْسَلْنَا مُوْسٰى بِاٰيٰتِنَا وَسُلْطٰنٍ مُّبِيْنٍ ۝

97. Unto Pharaoh and his Chiefs: but they followed the command of Pharaoh and the command of Pharaoh was no right (guide).

98. He will go before his people on the Day of Judgment, and lead them into the Fire (as cattle are led to water): but woeful indeed will be the place to which they are led!

99. And they are followed by a curse in this (life) and on the Day of Judgment: and woeful is the gift which shall be given (to them)!

100. These are some of the stories of communities which We relate to you: of them some are standing, and some have been mown down (by the sickle of time).

101. It was not We that wronged them: they wronged their own souls: the deities, other than Allah, whom they invoked, profited them no whit when there issued the decree of your Lord: nor did they add anything (to their lot) but perdition!

102. Such is the chastisement of your Lord when He chastises communities in the midst of their wrong: grievous, indeed, and severe is His chastisement.

103. In that is a Sign for those who fear the Chastisement of the Hereafter: that is a Day for which mankind will be gathered together: that will be a Day of Testimony.

104. Nor shall We delay it but for a term appointed.

105. The day it arrives, no soul shall speak except by His leave: of those (gathered) some will be wretched and some will be blessed.

106. Those who are wretched shall be in the Fire: there will be for them therein (nothing but) the heaving of sighs and sobs:

107. They will dwell therein for all the time that the heavens and the earth endure, except as your Lord wills: for

97. Ilaa Fir‘awna wa mala’i-hee fattaba‘ooo amra Fir‘awna wa maaa amru Fir‘awna birasheed.

98. Yaqdumu qawmahoo Yawmal-Qiyaamati fa-awrada-humun-Naara wa bi’sal-wirdul-mawrood.

99. Wa utbi‘oo fee haazihee la‘natanw-wa Yawmal-Qiyaa-mah; bi’sar- rifdul-marfood.

100. Zaalika min ambaaa’il-quraa naqussuhoo ‘alayka minhaa qaaa’imunw-wa haseed.

101. Wa maa zalamnaahum wa laakin zalamooo anfusahum famaaa aghnat ‘anhum aalihatuhumul-latee yad‘oona min doonil-laahi min shay’il-lammaa jaaa’a amru Rabbika wa maa zaadoohum ghayra tatbeeb.

102. Wa kazaalika akhzu Rab-bika izaaa akhazal-quraa wa hiya zaalimah; inna akhzahooo aleemun shadeed.

103. Inna fee zaalika la-Aaya-tal-liman khaafa ‘azaabal-Aakhirah; zaalika Yawmum-majmoo‘ul-lahun-naasu wa zaalika Yawmum-mashhood.

104. Wa maa nu’akhkhiru-hooo illaa li-ajalim-ma‘dood.

105. Yawma yaåti laa takallamu nafsun illaa bi-iznih; faminhum shaqiyyunw-wa sa‘eed.

106. Fa-ammal-lazeena shaqoo fafin-Naari lahum feehaa zafeerunw-wa shaheeq.

107. Khaalideena feehaa maa daamatis-samaawaatu wal-arqu illaa maa shaaa’a Rabbuk; inna

your Lord is the (sure) Accomplisher of what He plans.

108. And those who are blessed shall be in the Garden: they will dwell therein for all the time that the heavens and the earth endure, except as your Lord willeth: a gift without break.

109. Be not then in doubt as to what these men worship. They worship nothing but what their fathers worshipped before (them): but verily We shall pay them back (in full) their portion without (the least) abatement.

110. We certainly gave the Book to Moses, but differences arose therein: had it not been that a Word had gone forth before from your Lord, the matter would have been decided between them, but they are in suspicious doubt concerning it.

111. And, of a surety, to all will your Lord pay back (in full the recompense) of their deeds: for He knows well all that they do.

112. Therefore stand firm (in the straight Path) as you are commanded,- you and those who with you turn (unto Allah); and do not transgress (from the Path): for He sees well all that you do.

113. And incline not to those who do wrong, or the Fire will seize you; and you have no protectors other than Allah, nor shall you be helped.

114. And establish regular prayers at the two ends of the day and at the approaches of the night: for those things, that are good remove those that are evil: be that the word of remembrance to those who remember (their Lord):

115. And be steadfast in patience; for verily Allah will not suffer the reward of the righteous to perish.

Rabbaka fa-'-'aalul-limaa yureed.

108. Wa ammal-lazeena su'i-doo fafil-Jannati khaalideena feehaa maa daamatis-samaawaatu wal-arḍu illaa maa shaaa'a Rabbuk; 'aṭaaa'an ghayra majzooz.

109. Falaa taku fee miryatim-mimmaa ya'budu haaa'ulaaa'; maa ya'budoona illaa kamaa ya'budu aabaaa'uhum-min qabl; wa innaa lamuwaf-foohum naṣeebahum ghayra manqooṣ. **(Section 9)**

110. Wa laqad aataynaa Moo-sal-Kitaaba fakhtulifa feeh; wa law laa Kalimatun sabaqat mir-Rabbika laquḍiya baynahum; wa innahum lafee shakkim-minhu mureeb.

111. Wa inna kullal-lammaa la-yuwaffiyannahum Rabbuka a'maalahum; innahoo bimaa ya'maloona Khabeer.

112. Fastaqim kamaaa umirta wa man taaba ma'aka wa laa taṭghaw; innahoo bimaa ta'maloona Baṣeer.

113. Wa laa tarkanooo ilal-lazeena ẓalamoo fatamassa-kumun-Naaru wa maa lakum-min doonil-laahi min awli-yaaa'a ṣumma laa tunṣaroon.

114. Wa aqimiṣ-Ṣalaata ṭara-fayin-nahaari wa zulafam-minal-layl; innal-ḥasanaati yuzhibnaṣ-sayyi-aat; zaalika zikraa lizzaakireen.

115. Waṣbir fa-innal-laaha laa yuḍee'u ajral-muḥsineen.

116. Why were there not, among the generations before you, persons possessed of balanced good sense, prohibiting (men) from mischief in the earth - except a few among them whom We saved (from harm)? But the wrong-doers pursued the enjoyment of the good things of life which were given them, and persisted in sin.

117. Nor would your Lord be the One to destroy communities for a single wrong- doing, if its members were likely to mend.

118. If your Lord had so willed, He could have made mankind one people: but they will not cease to dispute.

119. Except those on whom your Lord has bestowed His Mercy: and for this He created them: and the Word of your Lord shall be fulfilled: "I will fill Hell with (disobedient) jinns and men all together."

120. All that we relate to you of the stories of the Apostles,- with it We make firm your heart: in them there comes to you the Truth, as well as an exhortation and a message of remembrance to those who believe.

121. Say to those who do not believe: "Do whatever you can: we shall do our part;

122. "And you wait! we too shall wait."

123. To Allah do belong the unseen (secrets) of the heavens and the earth, and to Him goes back every affair (for decision): then worship Him, and put your trust in Him: and your Lord is not unmindful of anything that you do.

---

116. Falaw laa kaana minal-qurooni min qablikum ooloo baqiyyatiny-yanhawna 'anil-fasaadi fil-arḍi illaa qaleelam-mimman anjaynaa minhum; wattaba'al-lazeena ẓalamoo maaa utrifoo feehi wa kaanoo mujrimeen.

117. Wa maa kaana Rabbuka liyuhlikal-quraa biẓulminw-wa ahluhaa muṣliḥoon.

118. Wa law shaaa'a Rabbuka laja'alannaasa ummatanw-waa-ḥidatanw-wa laa yazaaloona mukhtalifeen.

119. Illaa mar-raḥima Rabbuk; wa liẓaalika khalaqahum; wa tammat Kalimatu Rabbika la-amla'anna Jahannama minal-jinnati wannaasi ajma'een.

120. Wa kullan-naquṣṣu 'alay-ka min ambaaa'ir-Rusuli maa nuṡabbitu bihee fu'aadak; wa jaaa'aka fee haaẕihil-ḥaqqu wa maw'iẓatunw-wa ẕikraa lilmu'-mineen.

121. Wa qul lillaẕeena laa yu'minoona'-maloo 'alaa ma-kaanatikum innaa 'aamiloon.

122. Wantaẓiroo innaa mun-taẓiroon.

123. Wa lillaahi ghaybus-samaawaati wal-arḍi wa ilayhi yurja'ul-amru kulluhoo fa'u-dhu wa tawakkal 'alayh; wa maa Rabbuka bighaafilin 'ammaa ta'maloon. **(Section 10)**

---

12. Yusuf or Joseph

In the name of Allah, Most Gracious, Most Merciful.

1. *Alif-Lam-Ra.* These are the symbols (or Verses) of the Perspicuous Book.

Sûrat Yûsuf–12

(Revealed at Makkah)

Bismillaahir Raḥmaanir Raḥeem

1. Alif-Laaam-Raa; tilka Aayaatul-Kitaabil-Mubeen.

2. We have sent it down as an Arabic Qur'an, in order that you may learn wisdom.

3. We do relate to you the most beautiful of stories, in that We reveal to you this (portion of the) Qur'an: before this, you too was among those who did not know it.

4. Behold! Joseph said to his father: "O my father! I saw eleven stars and the sun and the moon: I saw them prostrate themselves to me!"

5. Said (the father): "My (dear) little son! do not relate your vision to your brothers, lest they concoct a plot against you: for Satan is to man an avowed enemy!

6. "Thus will your Lord choose you and teach you the interpretation of stories (and events) and perfect His favour to you and to the posterity of Jacob - even as He perfected it to your fathers Abraham and Isaac aforetime! for Allah is full of knowledge and wisdom."

7. Verily in Joseph and his brethren are signs (or Symbols) for Seekers (after Truth).

8. They said: "Truly Joseph and his brother are loved more by our father than we: but we are a goodly body! really our father is obviously wandering (in his mind)!

9. "You slay Joseph or cast him out to some (unknown) land, that so the favour of your father may be given to you alone: (there will be time enough) for you to be righteous after that!"

10. Said one of them: "do not slay Joseph, but if you must do

2. Innaaa anzalnaahu Qur-aa-nan 'Arabiyyal-la'allakum ta'qiloon.

3. Naḥnu naquṣṣu 'alayka aḥsanal-qaṣaṣi bimaaa awḥay-naaa ilayka haazal-Qur-aana wa in kunta min qablihee laminal-ghaafileen.

4. Iz qaala Yoosufu li-abeehi yaaa abati innee ra-aytu aḥada 'ashara kawkabañw-wash-shamsa walqamara ra-aytuhum lee saajideen.

5. Qaala yaa bunayya laa taqṣuṣ ru'yaaka 'alaaa ikhwatika fa-yakeedoo laka kaydaa; innash-Shayṭaana lil-insaani 'aduw-wum-mubeen.

6. Wa kazaalika yajtabeeka Rabbuka wa yu'allimuka min taâweelil-aḥaadeeṣi wa yutim-mu ni'matahoo 'alayka wa 'alaaa Aali Ya'qooba kamaaa atammahaa 'alaaa abawayka min qablu Ibraaheema wa Isḥaaq; inna Rabbaka 'Aleemun Ḥakeem. **(Section 1)**

7. Laqad kaana fee Yoosufa wa ikhwatiheee Aayaatul-lissaaa'i-leen.

8. Iz qaaloo la-Yoosufu wa akhoohu aḥabbu ilaaa Abeenaa minnaa wa naḥnu 'uṣbah; inna abaanaa lafee ḍalaalim-mubeen.

9. Uqtuloo Yoosufa awiṭra-ḥoohu arḍañy-yakhlu lakum wajhu abeekum wa takoonoo mim ba'dihee qawman ṣaali-ḥeen.

10. Qaala qaaa'ilum-minhum laa taqtuloo Yoosufa

إِنَّآ أَنْزَلْنَهُ قُرْءَنًا عَرَبِيًّا لَّعَلَّكُمْ تَعْقِلُونَ ۝

نَحْنُ نَقُصُّ عَلَيْكَ أَحْسَنَ الْقَصَصِ بِمَآ أَوْحَيْنَآ إِلَيْكَ هَذَا الْقُرْءَانَ وَإِنْ كُنْتَ مِنْ قَبْلِهِ لَمِنَ الْغَفِلِينَ ۝

إِذْ قَالَ يُوسُفُ لِأَبِيهِ يَأَبَتِ إِنِّي رَأَيْتُ أَحَدَ عَشَرَ كَوْكَبًا وَالشَّمْسَ وَالْقَمَرَ رَأَيْتُهُمْ لِي سَجِدِينَ ۝

قَالَ يَبُنَيَّ لَا تَقْصُصْ رُءْيَاكَ عَلَى إِخْوَتِكَ فَيَكِيدُوا لَكَ كَيْدًا إِنَّ الشَّيْطَنَ لِلْإِنْسَنِ عَدُوٌّ مُّبِينٌ ۝

وَكَذَلِكَ يَجْتَبِيكَ رَبُّكَ وَيُعَلِّمُكَ مِنْ تَأْوِيلِ الْأَحَادِيثِ وَيُتِمُّ نِعْمَتَهُ عَلَيْكَ وَعَلَى آلِ يَعْقُوبَ كَمَآ أَتَمَّهَا عَلَى أَبَوَيْكَ مِنْ قَبْلُ إِبْرَهِيمَ وَإِسْحَقَ إِنَّ رَبَّكَ عَلِيمٌ حَكِيمٌ ۝

لَقَدْ كَانَ فِي يُوسُفَ وَإِخْوَتِهِ ءَايَتٌ لِّلسَّآئِلِينَ ۝

إِذْ قَالُوا لَيُوسُفُ وَأَخُوهُ أَحَبُّ إِلَى أَبِينَا مِنَّا وَنَحْنُ عُصْبَةٌ إِنَّ أَبَانَا لَفِي ضَلَلٍ مُّبِينٍ ۝

اقْتُلُوا يُوسُفَ أَوِ اطْرَحُوهُ أَرْضًا يَخْلُ لَكُمْ وَجْهُ أَبِيكُمْ وَتَكُونُوا مِنْ بَعْدِهِ قَوْمًا صَلِحِينَ ۝

قَالَ قَآئِلٌ مِّنْهُمْ لَا تَقْتُلُوا يُوسُفَ

something, throw him down to the bottom of the well: he will be picked up by some caravan of travellers."

11. They said: "O our father! why do you not trust us with Joseph,- seeing we are indeed his sincere well-wishers?

12. "Send him with us tomorrow to enjoy himself and play, and we shall take every care of him."

13. (Jacob) said: "Really it saddens me that you should take him away: I fear lest the wolf should devour him while you do not attend to him."

14. They said: "If the wolf were to devour him while we are (so large) a party, then should we indeed (first) have perished ourselves!"

15. So they took him away, and they all agreed to throw him down to the bottom of the well: and We put into his heart (this Message): 'Of a surety you shall (one day) tell them the truth of this their affair while they do not know (you)'

16. Then they came to their father in the early part of the night, weeping.

17. They said: "O our father! We went racing with one another, and left Joseph with our things; and the wolf devoured him.... But you will never believe us even though we tell the truth."

18. They stained his shirt with false blood. He said: "Nay, but your minds have made up a tale (that may pass) with you. (For me) patience is most fitting: against that which you assert, it is Allah (alone) Whose help can be sought."..

19. Then there came a caravan of travellers: they sent their water-carrier (for water), and he let down his bucket (into the well)...He said: "Ah there! Good news! Here is

wa alqoohu fee ghayaabatil-jubbi yaltaqithu baḍus-say-yaarati in kuntum faaʻileen.

11. Qaaloo yaaa abaanaa maa laka laa taʼmannaa ʻalaa Yoosufa wa innaa lahoo lanaa-ṣiḥoon.

12. Arsilhu maʻanaa ghadañy-yartaʻ wa yalʻab wa innaa lahoo laḥaafizoon.

13. Qaala innee la-yaḥzunu-neee an tazhaboo bihee wa akhaafu añy-yaʼkulahuz-zi'bu wa antum ʻanhu ghaafiloon.

14. Qaaloo la-in akalahuz-zi'bu wa naḥnu ʻuṣbatun innaaa izal-lakhaasiroon.

15. Falammaa zahaboo bihee wa ajmaʻooo añy-yajʻaloohu fee ghayaabatil-jubb; wa aw-ḥaynaaa ilayhi latunabbi-'annahum bi-amrihim haazaa wa hum laa yashʻuroon.

16. Wa jaaaʼooo abaahum ʻishaaaʼañy-yabkoon.

17. Qaaloo yaaa abaanaaa innaa zahabnaa nastabiqu wa taraknaa Yoosufa ʻinda mataaʻinaa fa-akalahuz-zi'b, wa maaa anta bimuʼminil-lanaa wa law kunnaa ṣaadiqeen.

18. Wa jaaaʼoo ʻalaa qamee-ṣihee bidamin kazib; qaala bal sawwalat lakum anfusukum amraa; faṣabrun jameel; wallaahul-mustaʻaanu ʻalaa maa taṣifoon.

19. Wa jaaaʼat sayyaaratun fa-arsaloo waaridahum fa-adlaa dalwah; qaala yaa bushraa haazaa

وَأَلْقُوهُ فِى غَيَابَتِ الْجُبِّ يَلْتَقِطْهُ بَعْضُ السَّيَّارَةِ إِنْ كُنْتُمْ فَاعِلِينَ ۞

قَالُوا يَا أَبَانَا مَا لَكَ لَا تَأْمَنَّا عَلَى يُوسُفَ وَإِنَّا لَهُ لَنَاصِحُونَ ۞

أَرْسِلْهُ مَعَنَا غَدًا يَرْتَعْ وَيَلْعَبْ وَإِنَّا لَهُ لَحَافِظُونَ ۞

قَالَ إِنِّى لَيَحْزُنُنِى أَنْ تَذْهَبُوا بِهِ وَأَخَافُ أَنْ يَأْكُلَهُ الذِّئْبُ وَأَنْتُمْ عَنْهُ غَافِلُونَ ۞

قَالُوا لَئِنْ أَكَلَهُ الذِّئْبُ وَنَحْنُ عُصْبَةٌ إِنَّا إِذًا لَخَاسِرُونَ ۞

فَلَمَّا ذَهَبُوا بِهِ وَأَجْمَعُوا أَنْ يَجْعَلُوهُ فِى غَيَابَتِ الْجُبِّ ۚ وَأَوْحَيْنَا إِلَيْهِ لَتُنَبِّئَنَّهُمْ بِأَمْرِهِمْ هَذَا وَهُمْ لَا يَشْعُرُونَ ۞

وَجَاءُوا أَبَاهُمْ عِشَاءً يَبْكُونَ ۞

قَالُوا يَا أَبَانَا إِنَّا ذَهَبْنَا نَسْتَبِقُ وَتَرَكْنَا يُوسُفَ عِنْدَ مَتَاعِنَا فَأَكَلَهُ الذِّئْبُ ۚ وَمَا أَنْتَ بِمُؤْمِنٍ لَنَا وَلَوْ كُنَّا صَادِقِينَ ۞

وَجَاءُوا عَلَى قَمِيصِهِ بِدَمٍ كَذِبٍ ۚ قَالَ بَلْ سَوَّلَتْ لَكُمْ أَنْفُسُكُمْ أَمْرًا ۖ فَصَبْرٌ جَمِيلٌ ۖ وَاللَّهُ الْمُسْتَعَانُ عَلَى مَا تَصِفُونَ ۞

وَجَاءَتْ سَيَّارَةٌ فَأَرْسَلُوا وَارِدَهُمْ فَأَدْلَى دَلْوَهُ ۖ قَالَ يَا بُشْرَى هَذَا

a (fine) young man!" So they concealed him as a treasure! But Allah knows well all that they do!

20. The (Brethren) sold him for a miserable price, for a few dirhams counted out: in such low estimation did they hold him!

21. The man in Egypt who bought him, said to his wife: "Make his stay (among us) honourable: may be he will bring us much good, or we shall adopt him as a son." Thus We established Joseph in the land, that We might teach him the interpretation of stories (and events). And Allah has full power and control over His affairs; but most among mankind do not know it.

22. When Joseph attained his full manhood, We gave him power and knowledge: thus do We reward those who do right.

23. But she in whose house he was, sought to seduce him from his (true) self: she fastened the doors, and said: "Now come, you (dear one)!" He said: "Allah forbid! truly (your husband) is my lord! he made my sojourn agreeable! truly to no good come those who do wrong!"

24. And (with passion) she desired him, and he would have desired her, but that he saw the evidence of his Lord: thus (did We order) that We might turn away from him (all) evil and shameful deeds: for he was one of Our servants, sincere and purified.

25. So they both raced each other to the door, and she tore his shirt from the back: they both found her lord near the door. She said: "What is the (fitting) punishment for one who formed an evil design against your wife, but prison or

ghulaam; wa asarroohu bi-ḍaa'ah; wallaahu 'aleemum bimaa ya'maloon.

20. Wa sharawhu biṣamanim bakhsin daraahima ma'doo-datiñw-wa kaanoo feehi minaz-zaahideen. **(Section 2)**

21. Wa qaalal-lazish-taraahu mim-Miṣra limra-atiheee akrimee maswaahu 'asaaa añy-yanfa'anaaa aw nattakhizahoo waladaa; wa kazaalika mak-kannaa li-Yoosufa fil-arḍi wa linu'allimahoo min taåweelil-aḥaadees; wallaahu ghaalibun 'alaaa amrihee wa laakinna aksaran-naasi laa ya'lamoon.

22. Wa lammaa balagha ashuddahooo aataynaahu ḥukmañw-wa 'ilmaa; wa kazaa-lika najzil-muḥsineen.

23. Wa raawadat-hul-latee huwa fee baytihaa 'an-nafsihee wa ghallaqatil-abwaaba wa qaalat hayta lak; qaala ma'aazal-laahi innahoo rabbeee aḥsana maswaay; innahoo laa yufliḥuz-ẓaalimoon.

24. Wa laqad hammat bihee wa hamma bihaa law laaa ar-ra-aa burhaana Rabbih; kazaalika linaṣrifa 'anhus-sooo'a walfa-ḥshaaa'; innahoo min 'ibaadi-nal-mukhlaṣeen.

25. Wastabaqal-baaba wa qaddat qameeṣahoo min dubu-riñw-wa alfayaa sayyidahaa ladal-baab; qaalat maa jazaaa'u man araada bi-ahlika sooo'an illaaa añy-yusjana aw

a grievous chastisement?"

26. He said: "It was she that sought to seduce me - from my (true) self." And one of her household saw (this) and bore witness, (thus):- "If it be that his shirt is rent from the front, then is her tale true, and he is a liar!

27. "But if it be that his shirt is torn from the back, then is she the liar, and he is telling the truth!"

28. So when he saw his shirt,- that it was torn at the back,- (her husband) said: "Behold! It is a snare of you women! truly, mighty is your snare!

29. "O Joseph, pass this over! (O wife), ask forgiveness for your sin, for truly you have been at fault!"

30. Ladies said in the City: "The wife of the (great) 'Aziz is seeking to seduce her slave from his (true) self: Truly has he inspired her with violent love: we see she is evidently going astray."

31. When she heard of their malicious talk, she sent for them and prepared a banquet for them: she gave each of them a knife: and she said (to Joseph), "Come out before them." When they saw him, they extolled him, and (in their amazement) cut their hands: they said, "Allah preserve us! no mortal is this! this is none other than a noble angel!"

32. She said: "There before you is the man about whom you blamed me! I sought to seduce him from his (true) self but he firmly saved himself guiltless!....

'azaabun aleem.

26. Qaala hiya raawadatnee 'an nafsee wa shahida shaahidum-min ahlihaa in kaana qameeṣuhoo qudda min qubulin faṣadaqat wa huwa minal-kaaẕibeen.

27. Wa in kaana qameeṣuhoo qudda min duburin fakaẕabat wa huwa minaṣ-ṣaadiqeen.

28. Falammaa ra-aa qameeṣahoo qudda min duburin qaala innahoo min kaydikunna inna kaydakunna 'aẕeem.

29. Yoosufu a'riḍ 'an haaẕaa wastaghfiree liẕambiki innaki kunti minal-khaaṭi'een.
(Section 3)

30. Wa qaala niswatun filma-deenatim-ra-atul-'Azeezi turaa-widu fataahaa 'an-nafsihee qad shaghafahaa ḥubbaa; innaa lana-raahaa fee ḍalaalim-mubeen.

31. Falammaa sami'at bimak-rihinna arsalat ilayhinna wa a'tadat lahunna muttaka-añw-wa aatat kulla waaḥidatim-min-hunna sikkeenañw-wa qaala-tikh-ruj 'alayhinna falammaa ra-aynahooo akbarnahoo wa qaṭṭa'na aydiyahunna wa qulna ḥaasha lillaahi maa haaẕaa basharaa; in haaẕaaa illaa malakun kareem.

32. Qaalat faẕaalikunnal-laẕee lumtunnanee feeh; wa laqad raawattuhoo 'an-nafsi-hee fasta'ṣam;

and now, if he do not my bidding, he shall certainly be cast into prison, and (what is more) be of the company of the vilest!"

33. He said: "O my Lord! the prison is more to my liking than that to which they invite me: unless You turn away their snare from me, I should (in my youthful folly) feel inclined toward them and join the ranks of the ignorant."

34. So his Lord hearkened to him (in his prayer), and turned away from him their snare: verily He hears and knows (all things).

35. Then it occurred to the men, after they had seen the Signs, (that it was best) to imprison him for a time.

36. Now with him there came into the prison two young men, said one of them: "I see myself (in a dream) pressing wine." Said the other: "I see myself (in a dream) carrying bread on my head, and birds are eating, thereof." "Tell us" (they said) "the truth and meaning thereof: for we see you are one that does good (to all)."

37. He said: "Before any food comes (in due course) to feed either of you, I will surely reveal to you the truth and meaning of this are it befall you: that is part of the (duty) which my Lord has taught me. I have (I assure you) abandoned the ways of a people that believe not in Allah and that (even) deny the Hereafter.

38. "And I follow the ways of my fathers,- Abraham, Isaac, and Jacob; and never could we attribute any partners whatever to Allah: that (comes) of the grace of Allah to us and to mankind: yet most men are not grateful.

39. "O my two companions of the prison! (I ask you): are many lords differing among Themselves

wa la'il-lam yaf'al maaa aamuruhoo la-yusjananna wa la-yakoonam-minaṣ-ṣaaghireen.

33. Qaala Rabbis-sijnu aḥabbu ilayya mimmaa yad'oonaneee ilayhi wa illaa taṣrif 'annee kaydahunna aṣbu ilayhinna wa akum-minal-jaahileen.

34. Fastajaaba lahoo Rabbuhoo faṣarafa 'anhu kaydahunn; innahoo Huwas-Samee'ul-'Aleem.

35. Summa badaa lahum-mim ba'di maa ra-awul-Aayaati layasjununnahoo ḥattaa ḥeen.

(Section 4)

36. Wa dakhala ma'ahussijna fata-yaan; qaala aḥaduhumaaa inneee araaneee a'ṣiru khamrañw wa qaalal-aakharu inneee araaneee aḥmilu fawqa raåsee khubzan taåkuluṭ-ṭayru minh; nabbi'naa bitaåweelihee innaa naraaka minal-muḥsineen.

37. Qaala laa yaåteekumaa ṭa'aamun turzaqaaniheee illaa nabbaåtukumaa bitaåweelihee qabla añy-yaåtiyakumaa; zaalikumaa mimmaa 'allamanee Rabbee; innee taraktu millata qawmil-laa yu'minoona billaahi wahum bil-Aakhirati hum kaafiroon.

38. Wattaba'tu Millata aabaaa'eee Ibraaheema wa Isḥaaqa wa Ya'qoob; maa kaana lanaaa an-nushrika billaahi min shay'; zaalikamin faḍlil-laahi 'alaynaa wa 'alan-naasi wa laakinna akṣaran-naasi laa yashkuroon.

39. Yaa ṣaaḥibayis-sijni 'a-arbaabum-mutafarriqoona

better, or the One god (Allah), Supreme and Irresistible?

40. "If not Him, you worship nothing but names which you have named,- you and your fathers,- for which Allah has sent down no authority: the Command is for none but Allah: He has commanded that you worship none but Him: that is the right religion, but most men do not understand.

41. "O my two companions of the prison! As to one of you, he will pour out the wine for his lord to drink: as for the other, he will hang from the cross, and the birds will eat from off his head. (So) has been decreed that matter whereof you twain do enquire"...

42. And of the two, to that one whom he consider about to be saved, he said: "Mention me to your lord." But Satan made him forget to mention him to his lord: and (Joseph) lingered in prison a few (more) years.

43. The king (of Egypt) said: "I do see (in a vision) seven fat kine, whom seven lean ones devour,- and seven green ears of corn, and seven (others) withered. O you chiefs! Expound to me my vision if it be that you can interpret visions."

44. They said: "A confused medley of dreams: and we are not skilled in the interpretation of dreams."

45. But the man who had been released, one of the two (who had been in prison) and who now remembered him after (so long) a space of time, said: "I will tell you the truth of its interpretation: you send me (therefore)."

46. "O Joseph!" (he said) "O man of truth! Expound to us

khayrun amil-laahul-Waahi-dul-Qahhaar.

40. Maa ta'budoona min doo-niheee illaaa asmaaa'an sammaytumoohaaa antum wa aabaaa'ukum-maaa anzalal laahu bihaa min sulṭaan; inil-ḥukmu illaa lillaah; amara allaa ta'budooo illaaa iyyaah; ẕaali-kad-deenul-qayyimu wa laakin-na akṣaran-naasi laa ya'lamoon.

41. Yaa ṣaaḥibayis-sijni am-maaa aḥadukumaa fa-yasqee rabbahoo khamraňw wa ammal-aakharu fa-yuṣlabu fataåkuluṭ-ṭayru mir-raåsih; quḍiyal-amrul-laẕee feehi tastaftiyaan.

42. Wa qaala lillaẕee ẓanna annahoo naajim-minhumaz-kurnee 'inda rabbika fa-ansaahush-Shayṭaanu ẕikra Rabbihee falabiṣa fis-sijni biḍ'a sineen. **(Section 5)**

43. Wa qaalal-maliku inneee araa sab'a baqaraatin simaaaniňy-yaåkuluhunna sab'un 'ijaafuňw-wa sab'a sumbulaatin khuḍriňw-wa ukhara yaabisaat; yaaa-ayyuhal-mala-u aftoonee fee ru'yaaya in kuntum lirru'yaa ta'buroon.

44. Qaalooo aḍghaaṣu aḥlaa-miňw wa maa naḥnu bitaåweelil-aḥlaami bi'aalimeen.

45. Wa qaalal-laẕee najaa minhumaa waddakara ba'da ummatin ana unabbi'ukum bitaåweelihee fa-arsiloon.

46. Yoosufu ayyuhaṣ-ṣiddee-qu aftinaa fee

(the dream) of seven fat kine whom seven lean ones devour, and of seven green ears of corn and (seven) others withered: that I may return to the people, and that they may understand.”

47. (Joseph) said: “For seven years you shall diligently sow as is your wont: and the harvests that you reap, you shall leave them in the ear,- except a little, of which you shall eat.

48. “Then will come after that (period) seven dreadful (years), which will devour what you shall have laid by in advance for them,- (all) except a little which you shall have (specially) guarded.

49. “Then will come after that (period) a year in which the people will have abundant water, and in which they will press (wine and oil).”

50. So the king said: “You bring him to me.” But when the messenger came to him, (Joseph) said: “You go back to your lord, and ask him, ‘What is the state of mind of the ladies who cut their hands’? For my Lord is certainly well aware of their snare.”

51. (The king) said (to the ladies): “What was your affair when you sought to seduce Joseph from his (true) self?” The ladies said: “Allah preserve us! We do not know any evil against him!” Said the ‘Aziz’s wife: “Now is the truth manifest (to all): it was I who sought to seduce him from his (true) self: he is indeed of those who are (ever) true (and virtuous).

52. “This (I say), in order that he may know that I have never been false to him in his absence, and that Allah will never guide the snare of the false ones.

53. “Nor do I absolve my own self (of blame): the (human) soul is certainly prone to evil, unless my Lord do bestow His Mercy: but surely my Lord is Oft- Forgiving, Most Merciful.”

sab‘i baqaraatin simaaniñy-yaåkuluhunna sab‘un ‘ijaafuñw-wa sab‘i sumbulaatin khuḍriñw-wa ukhara yaabisaatil-la‘allee arji‘u ilan-naasi la‘allahum ya‘lamoon.

47. Qaala tazra‘oona sab‘a sineena da-aban famaa ḥaṣattum fazaroohu fee sumbu-liheee illaa qaleelam-mimmaa taåkuloon.

48. Summa yaåtee mim-ba‘di zaalika sab‘un shidaaduñy-yaå-kulna maa qaddamtum lahunna illaa qaleelam-mimmaa tuḥṣi-noon.

49. Summa yaåtee mim ba‘di zaalika ‘aamun feehi yughaa-sun-naasu wa feehi ya‘ṣiroon.
(Section 6)

50. Wa qaalal-maliku’-toonee bihee falammaa jaaa’ahur-rasoolu qaalar-ji‘ ilaa rabbika fas’alhu maa baalun-niswatil-laatee qaṭṭa‘na aydiyahunn; inna Rabbee bikaydihinna ‘Aleem.

51. Qaala maa khaṭbukunna iz raawattunna Yoosufa ‘an-nafsih; qulna ḥaasha lillaahi maa ‘alimnaa ‘alayhi min sooo’; qaalatim-ra-atul-‘Azeezil-’aana ḥaṣhaṣal-ḥaqq, ana raawat-tuhoo ‘an-nafsihee wa innahoo laminaṣ-ṣaadiqeen.

52. Zaalika liya‘lama annee lam akhunhu bilghaybi wa annal-laaha laa yahdee kaydal-khaaa’ineen.

53. Wa maaa ubarri’u nafsee; innan-nafsa la-ammaaratum bissooo’i illaa maa raḥima Rabbee; inna Rabbee Gha-foorur-Raḥeem.

سَبْعِ بَقَرَٰتٍ سِمَانٍ يَأْكُلُهُنَّ سَبْعٌ عِجَافٌ وَّسَبْعَ سُنبُلَٰتٍ خُضْرٍ وَّ أُخَرَ يَابِسَٰتٍ لَّعَلِّىٓ أَرْجِعُ إِلَى النَّاسِ لَعَلَّهُمْ يَعْلَمُونَ ۝

قَالَ تَزْرَعُونَ سَبْعَ سِنِينَ دَأَبًا ۚ فَمَا حَصَدتُّمْ فَذَرُوهُ فِى سُنبُلِهِۦٓ إِلَّا قَلِيلًا مِّمَّا تَأْكُلُونَ ۝

ثُمَّ يَأْتِى مِنۢ بَعْدِ ذَٰلِكَ سَبْعٌ شِدَادٌ يَّأْكُلْنَ مَا قَدَّمْتُمْ لَهُنَّ إِلَّا قَلِيلًا مِّمَّا تُحْصِنُونَ ۝

ثُمَّ يَأْتِى مِنۢ بَعْدِ ذَٰلِكَ عَامٌ فِيهِ يُغَاثُ النَّاسُ وَفِيهِ يَعْصِرُونَ ۝

وَقَالَ الْمَلِكُ ائْتُونِى بِهِۦ ۖ فَلَمَّا جَآءَهُ الرَّسُولُ قَالَ ارْجِعْ إِلَىٰ رَبِّكَ فَسْـَٔلْهُ مَا بَالُ النِّسْوَةِ الَّٰتِى قَطَّعْنَ أَيْدِيَهُنَّ ۚ إِنَّ رَبِّى بِكَيْدِهِنَّ عَلِيمٌ ۝

قَالَ مَا خَطْبُكُنَّ إِذْ رَاوَدتُّنَّ يُوسُفَ عَن نَّفْسِهِۦ ۚ قُلْنَ حَٰشَ لِلَّهِ مَا عَلِمْنَا عَلَيْهِ مِن سُوٓءٍ ۚ قَالَتِ امْرَأَتُ الْعَزِيزِ الْـَٰٔنَ حَصْحَصَ الْحَقُّ أَنَا۠ رَاوَدتُّهُۥ عَن نَّفْسِهِۦ وَإِنَّهُۥ لَمِنَ الصَّٰدِقِينَ ۝

ذَٰلِكَ لِيَعْلَمَ أَنِّى لَمْ أَخُنْهُ بِالْغَيْبِ وَأَنَّ اللَّهَ لَا يَهْدِى كَيْدَ الْخَآئِنِينَ ۝

وَمَآ أُبَرِّئُ نَفْسِىٓ ۚ إِنَّ النَّفْسَ لَأَمَّارَةٌۢ بِالسُّوٓءِ إِلَّا مَا رَحِمَ رَبِّىٓ ۚ إِنَّ رَبِّى غَفُورٌ رَّحِيمٌ ۝

54. So the king said: "Bring him to me; I will take him specially to serve about my own person." Therefore when he had spoken to him, he said: "Be assured this day, you are, before our own pre-sence, with rank firmly established, and fidelity fully proved!"

55. (Joseph) said: "Set me over the store-houses of the land: I will indeed guard them, as one that knows (their importance)."

56. Thus We gave established power to Joseph in the land, to take possession therein as, when, or where he pleased. We bestow of Our Mercy on whom We please, and We suffer not, to be lost, the reward of those who do good.

57. But verily the reward of the Hereafter is the best, for those who believe, and are constant in righteousness.

58. Then came Joseph's breth-ren: they entered his presence, and he knew them, but they did not know him.

59. And when he had furni-shed them forth with provisions (suitable) for them, he said: "Bring to me a brother you have, of the same father as your-selves, (but a different mother): do you not see that I pay out full measure, and that I do provide the best hospitality?

60. "Now if you do not bring him to me, you shall have no measure (of corn) from me, nor you shall (even) come near me."

61. They said: "We shall cer-tainly seek to get our wish about him from his father: indeed we shall do it."

62. And (Joseph) told his ser-vants to put their stock-in-trade (with which they had bartered) into their saddle-bags, so they should know it only when they returned to their people, in order that they might come back.

63. Now when they returned to their father, they said: "O our father! No more measure of grain shall we get (unless we take our brother): so send

---

54. Wa qaalal-maliku'-toonee biheee astakhlishu linafsee falammaa kallamahoo qaala innakal-yawma ladaynaa makeenun ameen.

55. Qaalaj-'alnee 'alaa kha-zaaa'inil-arḍi innee ḥafeeẓun 'aleem.

56. Wa kazaalika makkannaa li-Yoosufa fil-arḍi yatabawwa-u minhaa ḥaysu yashaaa'; nuṣee-bu biraḥmatinaa man-nashaaa'u wa laa nuḍee'u ajral muḥsineen.

57. Wa la-ajrul-Aakhirati khayrul-lillaẕeena aamanoo wa kaanoo yattaqoon. **(Section 7)**

58. Wa jaaa'a ikhwatu Yoosufa fadakhaloo 'alayhi fa'arafahum wa hum lahoo munkiroon.

59. Wa lammaa jahhazahum bijahaazihim qaala'-toonee bi-akhil-lakum-min abeekum; alaa tarawna anneee oofil-kayla wa ana khayrul-munzileen.

60. Fa-il-lam taaʾtoonee bihee falaa kayla lakum 'indee wa laa taqraboon.

61. Qaaloo sanuraawidu 'an-hu abaahu wa innaa lafaa'iloon.

62. Wa qaala lifityaanihij-'aloo biḍaa'atahum fee riḥaali-him la'allahum ya'rifoonahaaa izan-qalabooo ilaaa ahlihim la'allahum yarji'oon.

63. Falammaa raja'ooo ilaaa abeehim qaaloo yaaa abaanaa muni'a minnal-kaylu fa-arsil

---

وَقَالَ الْمَلِكُ ائْتُونِي بِهِ اَسْتَخْلِصْهُ لِنَفْسِي ۚ فَلَمَّا كَلَّمَهُ قَالَ اِنَّكَ الْيَوْمَ لَدَيْنَا مَكِينٌ اَمِينٌ ۞

قَالَ اجْعَلْنِي عَلَى خَزَآئِنِ الْاَرْضِ ۚ اِنِّي حَفِيظٌ عَلِيمٌ ۞

وَكَذٰلِكَ مَكَّنَّا لِيُوسُفَ فِي الْاَرْضِ ۚ يَتَبَوَّاُ مِنْهَا حَيْثُ يَشَآءُ ۚ نُصِيبُ بِرَحْمَتِنَا مَنْ نَّشَآءُ ۖ وَلَا نُضِيعُ اَجْرَ الْمُحْسِنِينَ ۞

وَلَاَجْرُ الْاٰخِرَةِ خَيْرٌ لِّلَّذِينَ اٰمَنُوا وَكَانُوا يَتَّقُونَ ۞

وَجَآءَ اِخْوَةُ يُوسُفَ فَدَخَلُوا عَلَيْهِ فَعَرَفَهُمْ وَهُمْ لَهُ مُنْكِرُونَ ۞

وَلَمَّا جَهَّزَهُمْ بِجَهَازِهِمْ قَالَ ائْتُونِي بِاَخٍ لَّكُمْ مِّنْ اَبِيكُمْ ۚ اَلَا تَرَوْنَ اَنِّي اُوفِي الْكَيْلَ وَاَنَا خَيْرُ الْمُنْزِلِينَ ۞

فَاِنْ لَّمْ تَاْتُونِي بِهِ فَلَا كَيْلَ لَكُمْ عِنْدِي وَلَا تَقْرَبُونِ ۞

قَالُوا سَنُرَاوِدُ عَنْهُ اَبَاهُ وَاِنَّا لَفَاعِلُونَ ۞

وَقَالَ لِفِتْيَانِهِ اجْعَلُوا بِضَاعَتَهُمْ فِي رِحَالِهِمْ لَعَلَّهُمْ يَعْرِفُونَهَا اِذَا انْقَلَبُوا اِلَى اَهْلِهِمْ لَعَلَّهُمْ يَرْجِعُونَ ۞

فَلَمَّا رَجَعُوا اِلَى اَبِيهِمْ قَالُوا يَا اَبَانَا مُنِعَ مِنَّا الْكَيْلُ فَاَرْسِلْ

our brother with us, that we may get our measure; and we will indeed take every care of him."

64. He said: "Shall I trust you with him with any result other than when I trusted you with his brother aforetime? But Allah is the best to take care (of him), and He is the Most Merciful of those who show mercy!"

65. Then when they opened their baggage, they found their stock-in-trade had been returned to them. They said: "O our father! What (more) can we desire? this our stock-in-trade has been returned to us: we shall get (more) food for our family; we shall take care of our brother; and add (at the same time) a full camel's load (of grain to our provisions). This is but a small quantity.

66. (Jacob) said: "Never will I send him with you until you swear a solemn oath to me, in Allah's name, that you will be sure to bring him back to me unless you are yourselves hemmed in (and made powerless). And when they had sworn their solemn oath, he said: "Over all that we say, be Allah the Witness and Guardian!"

67. Further he said: "O my sons! enter not all by one gate: you enter by different gates. Not that I can profit you anything against Allah (with my advice): none can command except Allah: on Him do I put my trust: and let all that trust put their trust on Him."

68. And when they entered in the manner their father had enjoined, it did not profit them in the least against (the plan of) Allah: it was but a necessity of Jacob's soul, which he discharged. For he was, by Our instruction, full of knowledge (and experience): but most men do not know.

ma'anaaa akhaanaa naktal wa innaa lahoo laḥaafiẓoon

64. Qaala hal aamanukum 'alayhi illaa kamaaa amintukum 'alaaa akheehimin qabl; fallaahu khayrun ḥaafiẓañw-wa Huwa arḥamur-Raaḥimeen.

65. Wa lammaa fataḥoo mataa-'ahum wajadoo biḍaa'atahum ruddat ilayhim qaaloo yaaa abaanaa maa nabghee; haazi-hee biḍaa'atunaa ruddat ilaynaa wa nameeru ahlanaa wa naḥfaẓu akhaanaa wa nazdaadu kayla ba'eer; ẕaalika kayluñy-yaseer.

66. Qaala lan ursilahoo ma'akum ḥattaa tu'tooni mawsiqam-minal-laahis lataā-tunnanee biheee illaaa añy-yuḥaaṭa bikum falammaaa aatawhu mawsiqahum qaalal-laahu 'alaa maa naqoolu Wakeel.

67. Wa qaala yaa baniyya laa tadkhuloo mim baabiñw-waa-ḥidiñw-wadkhuloo min abwaa-bim-mutafarriqah; wa maaa ughnee 'ankum-minal-laahi min shay'i; inil-ḥukmu illaa lillaahi 'alayhi tawakkaltu wa 'alayhi fal-yatawakkalil-Mutawakki-loon.

68. Wa lammaa dakhaloo min ḥaysu amarahum aboohum-maa kaana yughnee 'anhum-minal-laahi min shay'in illaa ḥaajatan fee nafsi Ya'qooba qaḍaahaa; wa innahoo lazoo 'ilmil-limaa 'allamnaahu wa laakinna aksaran-naasi laa ya'lamoon.

(Section 8)

69. Now when they came into Joseph's presence, he received his (full) brother to stay with him. He said (to him): "Behold! I am your (own) brother; so grieve not at aught of their doings."

70. At length when he had furnished them forth with provisions (suitable) for them, he put the drinking cup into his brother's saddle-bag. Then shouted out a Crier:"O you (in) the caravan! behold! you are thieves, without doubt!"

71. They said, turning toward them:"What is it that you miss?"

72. They said: "We miss the great beaker of the King; for him who produces it, is (the reward of) a camel load; I will be bound by it."

73. (The brothers) said: "By Allah! you know well that we did not come to make mischief in the land, and we are no thieves!"

74. (The Egyptians) said: "What then shall be the penalty of this, if you are (proved) to have lied?"

75. They said: "The penalty should be that he in whose saddle-bag it is found, should be held (as bondman) to atone for the (crime). Thus it is we punish the wrong-doers!"

76. So he began (the search) with their baggage, before (he came to) the baggage of his brother: at length he brought it out of his brother's baggage. Thus did We plan for Joseph. He could not take his brother by the law of the king except that Allah willed it (so). We raise to degrees (of wisdom) whom We please: but over all endued with knowledge is One, the All-Knowing.

77. They said: "If he steals, there was a brother of his who stole before (him)." But these things Joseph kept locked in his heart, revealing not the secrets to them. He (simply) said (to himself): "You are the worse situated; and Allah knows best the truth of what you assert!"

---

69. Wa lammaa dakhaloo 'alaa Yoosufa aawaaa ilayhi akhaahu qaala inneee ana akhooka falaa tabta'is bimaa kaanoo ya'maloon.

70. Falammaa jahhazahum bijahaazihim ja'alas-siqaayata fee raḥli akheehi summa az-zana mu'azzinun ayyatuhal-'eeru innakum lasaariqoon.

71. Qaaloo wa aqbaloo 'alay-him-maazaa tafqidoon.

72. Qaaloo nafqidu ṣuwaa'al-maliki wa liman jaaa'a bihee ḥimlu ba'eeriñw-wa ana bihee za'eem.

73. Qaaloo tallaahi laqad 'alimtum-maa ji'naa linufsida fil-arḍi wa maa kunnaa saari-qeen.

74. Qaaloo famaa jazaaa'u-hooo in kuntum kaaẕibeen.

75. Qaaloo jazaaa'uhoo mañw-wujida fee raḥlihee fahuwa jazaaa'uh; kaẕaalika najziẕ-ẕaalimeen.

76. Fabada-a bi-aw'iyatihim qabla wi'aaa'i akheehi ṣummas-takhrajahaa miñw-wi'aaa'i akheeh; kaẕaalika kidnaa li-Yoosuf; maa kaana liyaakhuẕa akhaahu fee deenil-maliki illaaa añy-yashaaa'al-laah; narfa'u darajaatim-man-nashaaa'; wa fawqa kulli zee 'ilmin 'Aleem.

77. Qaalooo iñy-yasriq faqad saraqa akhul-lahoo min qabl; fa-asarrahaa Yoosufu fee nafsi-hee wa lam yubdihaa lahum; qaala antum sharrum-makaa-nañw wallaahu a'lamu bimaa taṣifoon.

وَلَمَّا دَخَلُوْا عَلٰى يُوْسُفَ اٰوٰٓى اِلَيْهِ اَخَاهُ قَالَ اِنِّىْٓ اَنَا اَخُوْكَ فَلَا تَبْتَئِسْ بِمَا كَانُوْا يَعْمَلُوْنَ ۝

فَلَمَّا جَهَّزَهُمْ بِجَهَازِهِمْ جَعَلَ السِّقَايَةَ فِىْ رَحْلِ اَخِيْهِ ثُمَّ اَذَّنَ مُؤَذِّنٌ اَيَّتُهَا الْعِيْرُ اِنَّكُمْ لَسَارِقُوْنَ ۝

قَالُوْا وَاَقْبَلُوْا عَلَيْهِمْ مَّاذَا تَفْقِدُوْنَ ۝

قَالُوْا نَفْقِدُ صُوَاعَ الْمَلِكِ وَلِمَنْ جَآءَ بِهٖ حِمْلُ بَعِيْرٍ وَّاَنَا بِهٖ زَعِيْمٌ ۝

قَالُوْا تَاللّٰهِ لَقَدْ عَلِمْتُمْ مَّا جِئْنَا لِنُفْسِدَ فِى الْاَرْضِ وَمَا كُنَّا سَارِقِيْنَ ۝

قَالُوْا فَمَا جَزَآؤُهٗٓ اِنْ كُنْتُمْ كٰذِبِيْنَ ۝

قَالُوْا جَزَآؤُهٗ مَنْ وُّجِدَ فِىْ رَحْلِهٖ فَهُوَ جَزَآؤُهٗ ۚ كَذٰلِكَ نَجْزِى الظّٰلِمِيْنَ ۝

فَبَدَاَ بِاَوْعِيَتِهِمْ قَبْلَ وِعَآءِ اَخِيْهِ ثُمَّ اسْتَخْرَجَهَا مِنْ وِّعَآءِ اَخِيْهِ ۚ كَذٰلِكَ كِدْنَا لِيُوْسُفَ ۚ مَا كَانَ لِيَاْخُذَ اَخَاهُ فِىْ دِيْنِ الْمَلِكِ اِلَّآ اَنْ يَّشَآءَ اللّٰهُ ۚ نَرْفَعُ دَرَجٰتٍ مَّنْ نَّشَآءُ ۗ وَفَوْقَ كُلِّ ذِىْ عِلْمٍ عَلِيْمٌ ۝

قَالُوْٓا اِنْ يَّسْرِقْ فَقَدْ سَرَقَ اَخٌ لَّهٗ مِنْ قَبْلُ ۚ فَاَسَرَّهَا يُوْسُفُ فِىْ نَفْسِهٖ وَلَمْ يُبْدِهَا لَهُمْ ۚ قَالَ اَنْتُمْ شَرٌّ مَّكَانًا ۚ وَاللّٰهُ اَعْلَمُ بِمَا تَصِفُوْنَ ۝

78. They said: "O exalted one! Behold! he has a father, aged and venerable, (who will grieve for him); so take one of us in his place; for we see that you are (gracious) in doing good."

79. He said: "Allah forbid that we take other than him with whom we found our property: indeed (if we did so), we should be acting wrongfully.

80. Now when they saw no hope of his (yielding), they held a conference in private. The leader among them said: "Don't you know that your father did took an oath from you in Allah's name, and how, before this, you failed in your duty with Joseph? Therefore I will not leave this land until my father permits me, or Allah commands me; and He is the best to command.

81. "You turn back to your father, and say, 'O our father! Behold! your son committed theft! we bear witness only to what we know, and we could not well guard against the unseen!

82. "'Ask at the town where we have been and the caravan in which we returned, and, (you will find) we are indeed telling the truth.'"

83. Jacob said: "Nay, but you have yourselves contrived a story (good enough) for you. So patience is most fitting (for me). May be Allah will bring them (back) all to me (in the end). For He is indeed full of knowledge and wisdom."

84. And he turned away from them, and said: "How great is my grief for Joseph!" And his eyes became white with

78. Qaaloo yaaa ayyuhal-'Azeezu inna lahooo aban shaykhan kabeeran fakhuz ahadanaa makaanahoo innaa naraaka minal-muhsineen.

79. Qaala ma'aazal-laahi an naåkhuza illaa mañw-wajadnaa mataa'anaa 'indahooo innaaa izal-lazaalimoon.   **(Section 9)**

80. Falammas-tay'asoo minhu khalasoo najiyyan qaala kabee-ruhum alam ta'lamooo anna abaakum qad akhaza 'alaykum mawsiqam-minal-laahi wa min qablu maa farrattum fee Yoosufa falan abrahal-arda hattaa yaåzana leee abeee aw yahkumal-laahu lee wa huwa khayrul-haakimeen.

81. Irji'ooo ilaaa abeekum faqooloo yaaa abaanaaa innab-naka saraq; wa maa shahidnaaa illaa bimaa 'alimnaa wa maa kunnaa lilghaybi haafizeen.

82. Was'alil-qaryatal-latee kunnaa feehaa wal'eeral-lateee aqbalnaa feehaa wa innaa lasaadiqoon.

83. Qaala bal sawwalat lakum anfusukum amran fasabrun jameelun 'asal-laahu añy-yaå-tiyanee bihim jamee'aa; inna-hoo Huwal-'Aleemul-Hakeem.

84. Wa tawallaa 'anhum wa qaala yaaa asafaa 'alaa Yoosufa wabyaddat 'aynaahu minal-

sorrow, and he fell into silent melancholy.

85. They said: "By Allah! (Never) will you cease to remember Joseph until you reach the last extremity of illness, or until you die!"

86. He said: "I only complain of my distraction and anguish to Allah, and I know from Allah that which you do not know.

87. "O my sons! you go and enquire about Joseph and his brother, and never give up hope of Allah's Soothing Mercy: truly no one despairs of Allah's Soothing Mercy, except those who have no faith."

88. Then, when they came (back) into (Joseph's) presence they said: "O exalted one! distress has seized us and our family: we have (now) brought but scanty capital: so pay us full measure, (we pray you), and treat it as charity to us: for Allah rewards the charitable."

89. He said: "Do you know how you dealt with Joseph and his brother, not knowing (what you were doing)?"

90. They said: "Are you indeed Joseph?" He said, "I am Joseph, and this is my brother: Allah has indeed been gracious to us (all): behold, he that is righteous and patient,- never will Allah suffer the reward to be lost, of those who do right."

91. They said: "By Allah! indeed Allah has preferred you above us, and we certainly have been guilty of sin!"

92. He said: "This day let no reproach be (cast) on you: Allah will forgive you, and He is the Most Merciful of those who show mercy!

93. "Go with this my shirt, and cast it

ḥuzni fahuwa kaẓeem.

85. Qaaloo tallaahi tafta'u tazkuru Yoosufa ḥattaa takoona ḥaraḍan aw takoona minal-haalikeen.

86. Qaala innamaaa ashkoo bassee wa ḥuzneee ilal-laahi wa a'lamu minal-laahi maa laa ta'lamoon.

87. Yaa baniyyaz-haboo fata-ḥassasoo miñy-Yoosufa wa akheehi wa laa tay'asoo mir-rawḥil-laahi innahoo laa yay'asu mir-rawḥil-laahi illal-qawmul-kaafiroon.

88. Falammaa dakhaloo 'alayhi qaaloo yaaa ayyuhal-'Azeezu massanaa wa ahlanaḍ-ḍurru wa ji'naa bibiḍaa'atim-muzjaatin fa-awfi lanal-kayla wa taṣaddaq 'alaynaa innal-laaha yajzil-mutaṣaddiqeen.

89. Qaala hal 'alimtum maa fa'altum bi-Yoosufa wa akhee-hi iz antum jaahiloon.

90. Qaalooo 'a-innaka la-anta Yoosufu qaala ana Yoosufu wa haazaaa akhee qad mannal-laahu 'alaynaa innahoo mañy-yattaqi wa yaṣbir fa-innal-laaha laa yuḍee'u ajral-muḥsineen.

91. Qaaloo tallaahi laqad aaṣarakal-laahu 'alaynaa wa in kunnaa lakhaaṭi'een.

92. Qaala laa taṣreeba 'alay-kumul-yawma yaghfirul-laahu lakum wa Huwa arḥamur-raaḥimeen.

93. Izhaboo biqameeṣee haa-zaa fa-alqoohu

over the face of my father: he will come to see (clearly). Then you come (here) to me together with all your family."

94. When the Caravan left (Egypt), their father said: "I do indeed scent the presence of Joseph: Nay, think me not a dotard."

95. They said: "By Allah! truly you are in your old wandering mind."

96. Then when the bearer of the good news came, He cast (the shirt) over his face, and he forthwith regained clear sight. He said: "Did I not say to you, 'I know from Allah that which you do not know?'"

97. They said: "O our father! ask for us forgiveness for our sins, for we were truly at fault."

98. He said: "Soon will I ask my Lord for forgiveness for you: for he is indeed Oft-Forgiving, Most Merciful."

99. Then when they entered the presence of Joseph, he provided a home for his parents with himself, and said: "you enter Egypt (all) in safety if it please Allah."

100. And he raised his parents high on the throne (of dignity), and they fell down in prostration, (all) before him. He said: "O my father! this is the fulfilment of my vision of old! Allah has made it come true! He was indeed good to me when He took me out of prison and brought you (all here) out of the desert, (even) after Satan had sown enmity between me and my brothers. Verily my Lord understands best the mysteries of all that He plans to do. For verily He is full of knowledge and wisdom.

'alaa wajhi abee yaåti baṣee-rañw waåtoonee bi-ahlikum ajma-'een. **(Section 10)**

94. Wa lammaa faṣalatil-'eeru qaala aboohum innee la-ajidu reeḥa Yoosufa law laaa an tufannidoon.

95. Qaaloo tallaahi innaka lafee ḍalaalikal-qadeem.

96. Falammaaa an jaaa'al-basheeru alqaahu 'alaa waj-hihee fartadda baṣeeran qaala alam aqul lakum inneee a'lamu minal-laahi maa laa ta'lamoon.

97. Qaaloo yaaa abaanas-taghfir lanaa zunoobanaaa innaa kunnaa khaaṭi'een.

98. Qaala sawfa astaghfiru lakum Rabbeee innahoo Huwal-Ghafoorur-Raḥeem.

99. Falammaa dakhaloo 'alaa Yoosufa aawaaa ilayhi abaway-hi wa qaalad-khuloo Miṣra in shaaa'al-laahu aamineen.

100. Wa rafa'a abawayhi 'alal-'arshi wa kharroo lahoo sujjadaa; wa qaala yaaa abati haazaa taåweelu ru'yaaya min qablu qad ja'alahaa Rabbee ḥaqqaa; wa qad aḥsana beee iz akhrajanee minas-sijni wa jaaa'a bikum-minal-badwi mim ba'di an nazaghash-Shayṭaanu baynee wa bayna ikhwatee; inna Rabbee laṭeeful-limaa yashaaa'; innahoo Huwal-'Aleemul-Ḥakeem.

عَلٰى وَجْهِ اَبِىْ يَاْتِ بَصِيْرًا ۚ وَاْتُوْنِىْ بِاَهْلِكُمْ اَجْمَعِيْنَ ۞

وَلَمَّا فَصَلَتِ الْعِيْرُ قَالَ اَبُوْهُمْ اِنِّىْ لَاَجِدُ رِيْحَ يُوْسُفَ لَوْلَاۤ اَنْ تُفَنِّدُوْنِ ۞

قَالُوْا تَاللّٰهِ اِنَّكَ لَفِىْ ضَلٰلِكَ الْقَدِيْمِ ۞

فَلَمَّاۤ اَنْ جَآءَ الْبَشِيْرُ اَلْقٰىهُ عَلٰى وَجْهِهٖ فَارْتَدَّ بَصِيْرًا ۚ قَالَ اَلَمْ اَقُلْ لَّكُمْ ۙ اِنِّىْۤ اَعْلَمُ مِنَ اللّٰهِ مَا لَا تَعْلَمُوْنَ ۞

قَالُوْا يٰۤاَبَانَا اسْتَغْفِرْ لَنَا ذُنُوْبَنَاۤ اِنَّا كُنَّا خٰطِئِيْنَ ۞

قَالَ سَوْفَ اَسْتَغْفِرُ لَكُمْ رَبِّىْ ؕ اِنَّهٗ هُوَ الْغَفُوْرُ الرَّحِيْمُ ۞

فَلَمَّا دَخَلُوْا عَلٰى يُوْسُفَ اٰوٰۤى اِلَيْهِ اَبَوَيْهِ وَقَالَ ادْخُلُوْا مِصْرَ اِنْ شَآءَ اللّٰهُ اٰمِنِيْنَ ۞

وَرَفَعَ اَبَوَيْهِ عَلَى الْعَرْشِ وَخَرُّوْا لَهٗ سُجَّدًا ۚ وَقَالَ يٰۤاَبَتِ هٰذَا تَاْوِيْلُ رُءْيَاىَ مِنْ قَبْلُ ۫ قَدْ جَعَلَهَا رَبِّىْ حَقًّا ؕ وَقَدْ اَحْسَنَ بِىْۤ اِذْ اَخْرَجَنِىْ مِنَ السِّجْنِ وَجَآءَ بِكُمْ مِّنَ الْبَدْوِ مِنْۢ بَعْدِ اَنْ نَّزَغَ الشَّيْطٰنُ بَيْنِىْ وَبَيْنَ اِخْوَتِىْ ؕ اِنَّ رَبِّىْ لَطِيْفٌ لِّمَا يَشَآءُ ؕ اِنَّهٗ هُوَ الْعَلِيْمُ الْحَكِيْمُ ۞

101. "O my Lord! You have indeed bestowed on me some power, and taught me something of the interpretation of dreams and events,- O you Creator of the heavens and the earth! You are my Protector in this world and in the Hereafter. You take my soul (at death) as one submitting to Your Will (as a Muslim), and unite me with the righteous."

102. Such is one of the stories of what happened unseen, which We reveal by inspiration unto you; nor were you (present) with them when they concerted their plans together in the process of weaving their plots.

103. Yet no faith will the greater part of mankind have, however ardently you do desire it.

104. And no reward do you ask of them for this: it is no less than a message for all creatures.

105. And how many Signs in the heavens and the earth do they pass by? Yet they turn (their faces) away from them!

106. And most of them do not believe in Allah without associating (others as partners) with Him!

107. Do they then feel secure from the coming against them of the covering veil of the wrath of Allah,- or of the coming against them of the (final) Hour all of a sudden while they perceive not?

108. Say you: "This is my way: I do invite to Allah,- on evidence clear as the seeing with one's eyes,- I and whoever follows me. Glory to Allah! and never will I join gods with Allah!"

109. Nor did We send before you (as Messenger) any but men, whom we inspired,- (men) living in human habitations. Do they not travel through the earth, and see what

101. Rabbi qad aataytanee minal-mulki wa 'allamtanee min taåweelil-ahaadees; faati-ras-samaawaati wal-ardi Anta waliyyee fid-dunyaa wal-Aa-khirati tawaffanee muslimañw-wa alhiqnee bissaaliheen.

102. Zaalika min ambaaa'il-ghaybi nooheehi ilayka wa maa kunta ladayhim iz ajma'ooo amrahum wa hum yamkuroon.

103. Wa maaa aksarun-naasi wa law harasta bimu'mineen.

104. Wa maa tas'aluhum 'alayhi min ajr; in huwa illaa zikrul-lil'aalameen. **(Section 11)**

105. Wa ka-ayyim-min Aayatin fis-samaawaati wal-ardi yamur-roona 'alayhaa wa hum 'anhaa mu'ridoon.

106. Wa maa yu'minu aksaru-hum billaahi illaa wa hum mushrikoon.

107. Afa-aminooo an taåtiya-hum ghaashiyatum-min 'azaa-bil-laahi aw taåtiyahumus-Saa'atu baghtatañw-wa hum laa yash'uroon.

108. Qul haazihee sabeeleee ad'ooo ilal-laah; 'alaa baseera-tin ana wa manit-taba'anee wa Subhaanal-laahi wa maaa ana minal-mushrikeen.

109. Wa maaa arsalnaa min qablika illaa rijaalan nooheee ilayhim min ahlil-quraa; afalam yaseeroo fil-ardi fa-yanzuroo kayfa

رَبِّ قَدْ اٰتَيْتَنِيْ مِنَ الْمُلْكِ وَ
عَلَّمْتَنِيْ مِنْ تَأْوِيْلِ الْاَحَادِيْثِ ۚ
فَاطِرَ السَّمٰوٰتِ وَالْاَرْضِ ۚ اَنْتَ
وَلِيِّيْ فِي الدُّنْيَا وَالْاٰخِرَةِ ۚ تَوَفَّنِيْ
مُسْلِمًا وَّاَلْحِقْنِيْ بِالصّٰلِحِيْنَ ۝

ذٰلِكَ مِنْ اَنْۢبَاءِ الْغَيْبِ نُوْحِيْهِ
اِلَيْكَ ۚ وَمَا كُنْتَ لَدَيْهِمْ اِذْ اَجْمَعُوْۤا
اَمْرَهُمْ وَهُمْ يَمْكُرُوْنَ ۝

وَمَاۤ اَكْثَرُ النَّاسِ وَلَوْ حَرَصْتَ
بِمُؤْمِنِيْنَ ۝

وَمَا تَسْـَٔلُهُمْ عَلَيْهِ مِنْ اَجْرٍ ۚ اِنْ
هُوَ اِلَّا ذِكْرٌ لِّلْعٰلَمِيْنَ ۝

وَكَاَيِّنْ مِّنْ اٰيَةٍ فِي السَّمٰوٰتِ
وَالْاَرْضِ يَمُرُّوْنَ عَلَيْهَا وَهُمْ
عَنْهَا مُعْرِضُوْنَ ۝

وَمَا يُؤْمِنُ اَكْثَرُهُمْ بِاللّٰهِ اِلَّا
وَهُمْ مُّشْرِكُوْنَ ۝

اَفَاَمِنُوْۤا اَنْ تَأْتِيَهُمْ غَاشِيَةٌ مِّنْ
عَذَابِ اللّٰهِ اَوْ تَأْتِيَهُمُ السَّاعَةُ
بَغْتَةً وَّهُمْ لَا يَشْعُرُوْنَ ۝

قُلْ هٰذِهٖ سَبِيْلِيْۤ اَدْعُوْۤا اِلَى اللّٰهِ ۚ
عَلٰى بَصِيْرَةٍ اَنَا وَمَنِ اتَّبَعَنِيْ ۚ
وَسُبْحٰنَ اللّٰهِ وَمَاۤ اَنَا مِنَ الْمُشْرِكِيْنَ ۝

وَمَاۤ اَرْسَلْنَا مِنْ قَبْلِكَ اِلَّا رِجَالًا
نُّوْحِيْۤ اِلَيْهِمْ مِّنْ اَهْلِ الْقُرٰى ۗ اَفَلَمْ
يَسِيْرُوْا فِي الْاَرْضِ فَيَنْظُرُوْا كَيْفَ

was the end of those before them? But the home of the Hereafter is best, for those who do right. Will you not then understand?

110. (Respite will be granted) until, when the messengers give up hope (of their people) and (come to) think that they were treated as liars, there reaches them Our help, and those whom We will are delivered into safety. But never will be warded off Our punishment from those who are in sin.

111. There is, in their stories, instruction for men endued with understanding. It is not a tale invented, but a confirmation of what went before it,- a detailed exposition of all things, and a Guide and a Mercy to any such as believe.

---

13. Thunder

In the name of Allah, Most Gracious, Most Merciful.

1. *Alif-Lam-Mim-Ra.* These are the Signs (or Verses) of the Book: that which has been revealed to you from your Lord is the Truth; but most men do not believe.

2. Allah is He Who raised the heavens without any pillars that you can see; is firmly established on the throne (of authority); He has subjected the sun and the moon (to His Law)! Each one runs (its course) for a term appointed. He regulates all affairs, explaining the Signs in detail, that you may believe with certainty in the meeting with your Lord.

3. And it is He Who spread out the earth, and set thereon mountains standing firm and (flowing) rivers: and fruit of every kind He made in pairs, two and two:

---

kaana 'aaqibatul-lazeena min qablihim; wa la-Daarul-Aakhirati khayrul-lillazeenat-taqaw; afalaa ta'qiloon.

110. Ḥattaaa izas-tay'asar-Rusulu wa zannooo annahum qad kuziboo jaaa'ahum naṣrunaa fanujjiya man nashaaa'u wa laa yuraddu baåsunaa 'anil-qawmil-mujrimeen.

111. Laqad kaana fee qaṣaṣihim 'ibratul-li-ulil-albaab; maa kaana ḥadeeṣañy-yuftaraa wa laakin taṣdeeqal-lazee bayna yadayhi wa tafṣeela kulli shay'iñw-wa hudañw-wa raḥmatal-liqawmiñy-yu'minoon.

(Section 12)

Sûrat ar-Ra'd–13
(Revealed at Makkah)
Bismillaahir Raḥmaanir Raḥeem

1. Alif-Laam-Meeem-Raa; tilka Aayaaul-Kitaab; wallazeee unzila ilayka mir-Rabbikal-ḥaqqu wa laakinna aksaran-naasi laa yu'minoon.

2. Allaahul-lazee rafa'as-samaawaati bighayri 'amadin tarawnahaa ṣummas-tawaa 'alal-'Arshi wa sakhkharash-shamsa walqamara kulluñy-yajree li-ajalim-musammaa; yudabbirul-amra yufaṣṣilul-Aayaati la'allakum biliqaaa'i Rabbikum tooqinoon.

3. Wa Huwal-lazee maddal-arḍa wa ja'ala feehaa rawaasiya wa anhaaraa; wa min kulliṣ-ṣamaraati ja'ala feehaa zawjaynis-nayni

---

كَانَ عَاقِبَةُ الَّذِينَ مِن قَبْلِهِمْ ۗ وَلَدَارُ الْآخِرَةِ خَيْرٌ لِّلَّذِينَ اتَّقَوْا ۗ أَفَلَا تَعْقِلُونَ ۞

حَتَّىٰ إِذَا اسْتَيْأَسَ الرُّسُلُ وَظَنُّوا أَنَّهُمْ قَدْ كُذِبُوا جَاءَهُمْ نَصْرُنَا فَنُجِّيَ مَن نَّشَاءُ ۖ وَلَا يُرَدُّ بَأْسُنَا عَنِ الْقَوْمِ الْمُجْرِمِينَ ۞

لَقَدْ كَانَ فِي قَصَصِهِمْ عِبْرَةٌ لِّأُولِي الْأَلْبَابِ ۗ مَا كَانَ حَدِيثًا يُفْتَرَىٰ وَلَٰكِن تَصْدِيقَ الَّذِي بَيْنَ يَدَيْهِ وَتَفْصِيلَ كُلِّ شَيْءٍ وَهُدًى وَرَحْمَةً لِّقَوْمٍ يُؤْمِنُونَ ۞

(١٣) سُورَةُ الرَّعْدِ مَكِّيَّةٌ (٩٦)
بِسْمِ اللَّهِ الرَّحْمَٰنِ الرَّحِيمِ

المر ۚ تِلْكَ آيَاتُ الْكِتَابِ ۗ وَالَّذِي أُنزِلَ إِلَيْكَ مِن رَّبِّكَ الْحَقُّ وَلَٰكِنَّ أَكْثَرَ النَّاسِ لَا يُؤْمِنُونَ ۞

اللَّهُ الَّذِي رَفَعَ السَّمَاوَاتِ بِغَيْرِ عَمَدٍ تَرَوْنَهَا ۖ ثُمَّ اسْتَوَىٰ عَلَى الْعَرْشِ ۖ وَسَخَّرَ الشَّمْسَ وَالْقَمَرَ ۖ كُلٌّ يَجْرِي لِأَجَلٍ مُّسَمًّى ۚ يُدَبِّرُ الْأَمْرَ يُفَصِّلُ الْآيَاتِ لَعَلَّكُم بِلِقَاءِ رَبِّكُمْ تُوقِنُونَ ۞

وَهُوَ الَّذِي مَدَّ الْأَرْضَ وَجَعَلَ فِيهَا رَوَاسِيَ وَأَنْهَارًا ۖ وَمِن كُلِّ الثَّمَرَاتِ جَعَلَ فِيهَا زَوْجَيْنِ اثْنَيْنِ

He draws the night as a veil over the day. Behold, verily in these things there are signs for those who consider!

4.   And in the earth are tracts (diverse though) neighboring, and gardens of vines and fields sown with corn, and palm-trees growing out of single roots or otherwise: watered with the same water, yet some of them We make more excellent than others to eat. Behold, verily in these things there are signs for those who understand!

5.   If you do marvel (at their want of faith), strange is their saying: "When we are (actually) dust, shall we indeed then be in a renewed creation?" They are those who deny their Lord! They are those round whose necks will be yokes (of servitude): they will be Companions of the Fire, to dwell therein (for ever)!

6.   They ask you to hasten on the evil in preference to the good: yet before them, have come to pass, (many) exemplary punishments! But verily your Lord is full of forgiveness for mankind for their wrong-doing. And verily your Lord is (also) strict in punishment.

7.   And the Unbelievers say: "Why is not a Sign sent down to him from his Lord?" But you are truly a warner, and to every people a guide.

8.   Allah knows what every female (womb) bears, by how much the wombs fall short (of their time or number) or do exceed. Every single thing is before His sight, in (due) proportion.

9.   He knows the unseen and that which is open:

Yughshil-laylan-nahaar; inna fee zaalika la-Aayaatil-liqaw-miñy-yatafakkaroon.

4.   Wa fil-arḍi qiṭa'um-muta-jaawiraatuñw-wa jannaatum-min a'naabiñw-wa zar'uñw-wa nakheelun ṣinwaanuñw-wa ghayru ṣinwaaniñy-yusqaa bimaaa'iñw-waaḥid; wa nufaḍḍilu ba'ḍahaa 'alaa ba'ḍin fil-ukul; inna fee zaalika la-Aayaatil-liqawminy-ya'qiloon.

5.   Wa in ta'jab fa'ajabun qawluhum 'a-izaa kunnaa turaaban 'a-innaa lafee khalqin jadeed; ulaaa'ikal-lazeena kafaroo bi-Rabbihim wa ulaaa'ikal-aghlaalu fee a'naaqihim wa ulaaa'ika Aṣḥaabun-Naari hum feehaa khaalidoon.

6.   Wa yasta'iloonaka bis-sayyi'ati qablal-ḥasanati wa qad khalat min qablihimul-masulaat; wa inna Rabbaka lazoo maghfiratil-linnaasi 'alaa ẓulmihim wa inna Rabbaka lashadeedul-'iqaab.

7.   Wa yaqoolul-lazeena kafaroo law laaa unzila 'alayhi Aayatum-mir-Rabbih; inna-maaa anta munziruñw-wa likulli qawmin haad.   (Section 1)

8.   Allaahu ya'lamu maa taḥmilu kullu unṣaa wa maa tagheeḍul-arḥaamu wa maa tazdaad, wa kullu shay'in 'indahoo bimiqdaar.

9.   'Aalimul-Ghaybi wash-shahaadatil-

He is the Great, the Most High.

10. It is the same (to Him) whether any of you conceal his speech or declare it openly; whether he lie hid by night or walk forth freely by day.

11. For each (such person) there are (angels) in succession, before and behind him: they guard him by command of Allah. Verily never will Allah change the condition of a people until they change it themselves (with their own souls). But when (once) Allah wills a people's punishment, there can be no turning it back, nor will they find, besides Him, any to protect.

12. It is He Who shows you the lightning, by way both of fear and of hope: it is He Who raises up the clouds, heavy with (fertilising) rain!

13. Nay, thunder repeats His praises, and so do the angels, with awe: He flings the loud-voiced thunder-bolts, and therewith He strikes whomsoever He will..Yet these (are the men) who (dare to) dispute about Allah, with the strength of His power (supreme)!

14. For Him (alone) is prayer in Truth: any others that they call upon besides Him hear them no more than if they were to stretch forth their hands for water to reach their mouths but it reaches them not: for the prayer of those without Faith is nothing but (futile) wandering (in the mind).

15. Whatever beings there are in the heavens and the earth do prostrate themselves to Allah (Acknowledging subjection),-with good-will or in spite of themselves: so do their shadows in the mornings and evenings.

16. Say: "Who is the Lord and Sustainer of the heavens and the earth?"

Kabeerul-Muta‘aal.

10. Sawaaa’um-minkum man asarral-qawla wa man jahara bihee wa man huwa mustakh-fim-billayli wa saaribum binna-haar.

11. Lahoo mu‘aqqibaatum-mim bayni yadayhi wa min khalfihee yaḥfaẓoonahoo min amril-laah; innal-laaha laa yughayyiru maa biqawmin ḥattaa yughayyiroo maa bi-anfusihim; wa izaaa araadal-laahu biqawmin sooo’an falaa maradda lah; wa maa lahum min dooniheemiñw-waal.

12. Huwal-lazee yureekumul-barqa khawfañw-wa ṭama‘añw-wa yunshi’us-saḥaabas-siqaal.

13. Wa yusabbiḥur-ra‘du biḥamdihee walmalaaa’ikatu min kheefatihee wa yursiluṣ-ṣawaa‘iqa fa-yuṣeebu bihaa mañy-yashaaa’u wa hum yujaadiloona fil-laahi wa Huwa shadeedul-miḥaal.

14. Lahoo da‘watul-ḥaqq; wallazeena yad‘oona min doonihee laa yastajeeboona lahum bishay’in illaa kabaasiṭi kaffayhi ilal-maaa’i liyablugha faahu wa maa huwa bibaa-lighih; wa maa du‘aaa’ul-kaafireena illaa fee ḍalaal.

15. Wa lillaahi yasjudu man fis-samaawaati wal-arḍi ṭaw-‘añw-wa karhañw-wa zilaalu-hum bilghuduwwi wal-aaṣaal.

16. Qul mar-Rabbus-samaa-waati wal-arḍ;

الْكَبِيْرُ الْمُتَعَالِ ۞

سَوَآءٌ مِّنْكُمْ مَّنْ اَسَرَّ الْقَوْلَ وَمَنْ جَهَرَ بِهٖ وَمَنْ هُوَ مُسْتَخْفٍ بِالَّيْلِ وَسَارِبٌ بِالنَّهَارِ ۞

لَهٗ مُعَقِّبٰتٌ مِّنْۢ بَيْنِ يَدَيْهِ وَمِنْ خَلْفِهٖ يَحْفَظُوْنَهٗ مِنْ اَمْرِ اللّٰهِ ۗ اِنَّ اللّٰهَ لَا يُغَيِّرُ مَا بِقَوْمٍ حَتّٰى يُغَيِّرُوْا مَا بِاَنْفُسِهِمْ ۗ وَاِذَآ اَرَادَ اللّٰهُ بِقَوْمٍ سُوْٓءًا فَلَا مَرَدَّ لَهٗ ۚ وَمَا لَهُمْ مِّنْ دُوْنِهٖ مِنْ وَّالٍ ۞

هُوَ الَّذِىْ يُرِيْكُمُ الْبَرْقَ خَوْفًا وَّطَمَعًا وَّيُنْشِئُ السَّحَابَ الثِّقَالَ ۚ ۞

وَيُسَبِّحُ الرَّعْدُ بِحَمْدِهٖ وَالْمَلٰٓئِكَةُ مِنْ خِيْفَتِهٖ ۚ وَيُرْسِلُ الصَّوَاعِقَ فَيُصِيْبُ بِهَا مَنْ يَّشَآءُ وَهُمْ يُجَادِلُوْنَ فِى اللّٰهِ ۚ وَهُوَ شَدِيْدُ الْمِحَالِ ۞

لَهٗ دَعْوَةُ الْحَقِّ ۗ وَالَّذِيْنَ يَدْعُوْنَ مِنْ دُوْنِهٖ لَا يَسْتَجِيْبُوْنَ لَهُمْ بِشَيْءٍ اِلَّا كَبَاسِطِ كَفَّيْهِ اِلَى الْمَآءِ لِيَبْلُغَ فَاهُ وَمَا هُوَ بِبَالِغِهٖ ۗ وَمَا دُعَآءُ الْكٰفِرِيْنَ اِلَّا فِىْ ضَلٰلٍ ۞

وَلِلّٰهِ يَسْجُدُ مَنْ فِى السَّمٰوٰتِ وَالْاَرْضِ طَوْعًا وَّكَرْهًا وَّظِلٰلُهُمْ بِالْغُدُوِّ وَالْاٰصَالِ ۞

قُلْ مَنْ رَّبُّ السَّمٰوٰتِ وَالْاَرْضِ ۗ

(Bow Down)

Say: "(It is) Allah." Say: "Do you then take (for worship) protectors other than Him, such as have no power either for good or for harm to themselves?" Say: "Are the blind equal with those who see? Or the depths of darkness equal with light?" Or do they assign to Allah partners who have created (anything) as He has created, so that the creation seemed to them similar? Say: "Allah is the Creator of all things: He is the One, the Supreme and Irresistible."

17. He sends down water from the skies, and the channels flow, each according to its measure: But the torrent bears away to foam that mounts up to the surface. Even so, from that (ore) which they heat in the fire, to make ornaments or utensils therewith, there is a scum likewise. Thus does Allah (by parables) show forth Truth and Vanity. For the scum disappears like forth cast out; while that which is for the good of mankind remains on the earth. Thus Allah sets forth parables.

18. For those who respond to their Lord, are (all) good things. But those who do not respond to Him,- even if they had all that is in the heavens and on earth, and as much more, (in vain) would they offer it for ransom. For them will the reckoning be terrible: their abode will be Hell,- what a bed of misery!

19. Is then one who knows that that which has been revealed to you from your Lord is the Truth, like one who is blind? It is those who are endued with understanding that receive admonition;-

qulillaah; qul afattakhaztum min dooniheee awliyaaa'a laa yamlikoona li-anfusihim naf-'anw-wa laa darraa; qul hal yastawil-a'maa wal-baseeru am hal tastawiz-zulumaatu wannoor; am ja'aloo lillaahi shurakaaa'a khalaqoo kakhalqihee fatashaa-bahal-khalqu 'alayhim; qulil-laahu Khaaliqu kulli shay'inw-wa Huwal-Waahidul-Qahhaar.

17. Anzala minas-samaaa'i maaa'an fasaalat awdiyatum biqadarihaa fahtamalas-saylu-zabadar-raabiyaa; wa mimmaa yooqidoona 'alayhi fin-naarib-tighaaa'a hilyatin aw mataa'in zabadum-misluh; kazaalika yadribul-laahul-haqqa wal-baatil; fa-ammaz-zabadu fa-yazhabu jufaaa'aa; wa ammaa maa yanfa'un-naasa fa-yamkusu fil-ard; kazaalika yadribul-laahul-amsaal.

18. Lillazeenas-tajaaboo li-rabbihimul-husnaa; wallazeena lam yastajeeboo lahoo law anna lahum maa fil-ardi jamee'anw-wa mislahoo ma'ahoo laftadaw bih; ulaaa'ika lahum sooo'ul-hisaab; wa maåwaahum Jahan-namu wa bi'sal-mihaad.

(Section 2)

19. Afamañy-ya'lamu anna-maaa unzila ilayka mir-Rabbikal-haqqu kaman huwa a'maa; innamaa yatazakkaru ulul-albaab.

20. Those who fulfil the covenant of Allah and do not fail in their plighted word;

21. Those who join together those things which Allah has commanded to be joined, hold their Lord in awe, and fear the terrible reckoning;

22. Those who patiently persevere, seeking the countenance of their Lord; establish regular prayers; spend, out of (the gifts) We have bestowed for their sustenance, secretly and openly; and turn off Evil with good: for such there is the final attainment of the (Eternal) Home,-

23. Gardens of perpetual bliss: they shall enter there, as well as the righteous among their fathers, their spouses, and their offspring: and angels shall enter unto them from every gate (with the salutation):

24. "Peace unto you for that you persevered in patience! Now how excellent is the final home!"

25. But those who break the Covenant of Allah, after having plighted their word thereto, and cut asunder those things which Allah has commanded to be joined, and work mischief in the land;- on them is the Curse; for them is the terrible Home!

26. Allah enlarges, or grants by (strict) measure, the sustenance (which He gives) to whomso He pleases. (The wordly) rejoice in the life of this world: But the life of this world is but little comfort in the Hereafter.

27. The Unbelievers say: "Why is not a sign sent down to him from his Lord?" Say: "Truly Allah leave to stray, whom He will; But He guides

20. Allazeena yoofoona bi'ahdil-laahi wa laa yanqu-ḍoonal-meesaaq.

21. Wallazeena yaṣiloona maaa amaral-laahu biheee an yooṣala wa yakhshawna Rabbahum wa yakhaafoona sooo'al-ḥisaab.

22. Wallazeena ṣabarub-tighaaa'a Wajhi Rabbihim wa aqaamuṣ-Ṣalaata wa anfaqoo mimmaa razaqnaahum sirrañw-wa'alaaniyatañw-wa yad-ra'oona bilḥasanatis-sayyi'ata ulaaa'ika lahum 'uqbad-daar.

23. Jannaatu 'Adniñy-yadkhu-loonahaa wa man ṣalaḥa min aabaaa'ihim wa azwaajihim wa zurriyyaatihim walmalaaa'i-katu yadkhuloona 'alayhim min kulli baab.

24. Salaamun 'alaykum bimaa ṣabartum; fani'ma 'uqbad-daar.

25. Wallazeena yanquḍoona 'Ahdal-laahi mim ba'di mee-saaqihee wa yaqṭa'oona maaa amaral-laahu biheee añy-yooṣala wa yufsidoona fil-arḍi ulaaa'ika lahumul-la'natu wa lahum sooo'ud-daar.

26. Allaahu yabsuṭur-rizqa limañy-yashaaa'u wa yaqdir; wa fariḥoo bilḥayaatid-dunyaa wa mal-ḥayaatud-dunyaa fil-Aakhirati illaa mataa'. (Section 3)

27. Wa yaqoolul-lazeena ka-faroo law laaa unzila 'alayhi Aayatum-mir-Rabbih; qul innal-laaha yuḍillu mañy-yashaaa'u wa yahdeee

to Himself those who turn to Him in penitence;

28. "Those who believe, and whose hearts find satisfaction in the remembrance of Allah: for without doubt in the remembrance of Allah do hearts find satisfaction.

29. "For those who believe and work righteousness, is (every) blessedness, and a beautiful place of (final) return."

30. Thus have we sent you amongst a People before whom (long since) have (other) Peoples (gone and) passed away; in order that you might rehearse unto them what We send down unto you by inspiration; yet they reject (Him), the Most Gracious! Say: "He is my Lord! There is no god but He! On Him is my trust, and to Him do I turn!"

31. If there were a Qur'an with which mountains were moved, or the earth were cloven asunder, or the dead were made to speak, (this would be the one!) but, truly, the command is with Allah in all things! Do not the Believers know, that, had Allah (so) willed, He could have guided all mankind (to the right)? But the Unbelievers,- never will disaster cease to seize them for their (ill) deeds, or to settle close to their homes, until the promise of Allah come to pass, for, verily, Allah will not fail in His promise.

32. Mocked were (many) Messengers before you: but I granted respite to the Unbelievers, and finally I punished them: then how (terrible) was My requital!

33. Is then He who stands over every soul (and knows) all that it does, (like any others)? And yet they ascribe partners to Allah. Say:

ilayhi man anaab.

28. Allazeena aamanoo wa taṭma'innu quloobuhum bizikril-laah; alaa bizikril-laahi taṭma'innul-quloob.

29. Allazeena aamanoo wa 'amiluṣ-ṣaaliḥaati ṭoobaa lahum wa ḥusnu ma-aab.

30. Kazaalika arsalnaaka feee ummatin qad khalat min qablihaaa umamul-litatluwa 'alayhimul-lazee awḥaynaaa ilayka wa hum yakfuroona bir-Raḥmaan; qul Huwa Rabbee laaa ilaaha illaa Huwa 'alayhi-tawakkaltu wa ilayhi mataab.

31. Wa law anna Qur-aanan suyyirat bihil-jibaalu aw quṭ-ṭi'at bihil-arḍu aw kullima bihil-mawtaa; bal lillaahil-amru ja-mee'aa; afalam yay'asil-laze-na aamanooo al-law yashaaa-'ullaahu lahadan-naasa jamee-'aa; wa laa yazaalul-lazeena kafaroo tuṣeebuhum bimaa ṣana'oo qaari'atun aw taḥullu qareebam-min daarihim ḥattaa yaātiya wa'dul-laah; innal-laaha laa yukhliful-mee'aad.
(Section 4)

32. Wa laqadis-tuhzi'a bi-Rusulim-min qablika fa-amlay-tu lillazeena kafaroo ṣumma akhaztuhum fakayfa kaana 'iqaab.

33. Afaman Huwa qaaa'imun 'alaa kulli nafsim bimaa kasabat; wa ja'aloo lillaahi shurakaaa'a qul

اِلَيْهِ مَنْ اَنَابَ ۞

اَلَّذِيْنَ اٰمَنُوْا وَتَطْمَئِنُّ قُلُوْبُهُمْ بِذِكْرِ اللّٰهِ ۗ اَلَا بِذِكْرِ اللّٰهِ تَطْمَئِنُّ الْقُلُوْبُ ۞

اَلَّذِيْنَ اٰمَنُوْا وَعَمِلُوا الصّٰلِحٰتِ طُوْبٰى لَهُمْ وَحُسْنُ مَاٰبٍ ۞

كَذٰلِكَ اَرْسَلْنٰكَ فِيْٓ اُمَّةٍ قَدْ خَلَتْ مِنْ قَبْلِهَآ اُمَمٌ لِّتَتْلُوَا۟ عَلَيْهِمُ الَّذِيْٓ اَوْحَيْنَآ اِلَيْكَ وَهُمْ يَكْفُرُوْنَ بِالرَّحْمٰنِ ۗ قُلْ هُوَ رَبِّيْ لَآ اِلٰهَ اِلَّا هُوَ ۚ عَلَيْهِ تَوَكَّلْتُ وَاِلَيْهِ مَتَابِ ۞

وَلَوْ اَنَّ قُرْاٰنًا سُيِّرَتْ بِهِ الْجِبَالُ اَوْ قُطِّعَتْ بِهِ الْاَرْضُ اَوْ كُلِّمَ بِهِ الْمَوْتٰى ۗ بَلْ لِّلّٰهِ الْاَمْرُ جَمِيْعًا ۗ اَفَلَمْ يَا۟يْـَٔسِ الَّذِيْنَ اٰمَنُوْٓا اَنْ لَّوْ يَشَآءُ اللّٰهُ لَهَدَى النَّاسَ جَمِيْعًا ۗ وَلَا يَزَالُ الَّذِيْنَ كَفَرُوْا تُصِيْبُهُمْ بِمَا صَنَعُوْا قَارِعَةٌ اَوْ تَحُلُّ قَرِيْبًا مِّنْ دَارِهِمْ حَتّٰى يَاْتِيَ وَعْدُ اللّٰهِ ۗ اِنَّ اللّٰهَ لَا يُخْلِفُ الْمِيْعَادَ ۞

وَلَقَدِ اسْتُهْزِئَ بِرُسُلٍ مِّنْ قَبْلِكَ فَاَمْلَيْتُ لِلَّذِيْنَ كَفَرُوْا ثُمَّ اَخَذْتُهُمْ ۖ فَكَيْفَ كَانَ عِقَابِ ۞

اَفَمَنْ هُوَ قَآئِمٌ عَلٰى كُلِّ نَفْسٍ بِمَا كَسَبَتْ ۚ وَجَعَلُوْا لِلّٰهِ شُرَكَآءَ ۗ قُلْ

"But name them! Is it that you will inform Him of something He does not know on earth, or is it (just) a show of words?" Nay! to those who believe not, their pretence seems pleasing, but they are kept back (thereby) from the Path. And those whom Allah leaves to stray, no one can guide.

34. For them is a Panalty in the life of this world, but harder, truly, is the Penalty of the Hereafter: and they do not have any defender against Allah.

35. The parable of the Garden which the righteous are promised!- beneath it flow rivers: perpetual is the enjoyment thereof and the shade therein: such is the End of the Righteous; and the End of Unbelievers in the Fire.

36. Those to whom We have given the Book rejoice at what has been revealed unto you: but there are among the clans those who reject a part thereof. Say: "I am commanded to worship Allah, and not to join partners with Him. To Him I call, and to Him is my return."

37. Thus have We revealed it to be a judgment of authority in Arabic. Were you to follow their (vain) desires after the knowledge which has reached you, then you would find neither protector nor defender against Allah.

38. We sent Messenger before you, and appointed for them wives and children: and it was never the part of a Messenger to bring a Sign except as Allah permitted (or commanded). For each period is a Book (revealed).

39. Allah blots out or confirms what He pleases:

sammoohum; am tunabbi'oonahoo bimaa laa ya'lamu fil-ardi; am bizaahirim-minal-qawl; bal zuyyina lillazeena kafaroo makruhum wa suddoo 'anissabeel; wa mañy-yudlilil-laahu famaa lahoo min haad.

34. Lahum 'azaabun fil-hayaatid-dunyaa wa la'azaabul-Aakhirati ashaqq, wa maa lahum minal-laahi miñw-waaq.

35. Masalul-Jannatil-latee wu'idal-muttaqoona tajree min tah tihal-anhaaru ukuluhaa daaa'imuñw-wa zilluhaa; tilka uqbal-lazeenat-taqaw wa 'uqbal-kafireenan-Naar.

36. Wallazeena aataynaahumul-Kitaaba yafrahoona bimaaa unzila ilayka wa minal-Ahzaabi mañy-yunkiru ba'dah; qul innamaaa umirtu an a'budal-laaha wa laaa ushrika bih; ilayhi ad'oo wa ilayhi maaab.

37. Wa kazaalika anzalnaahu hukman 'Arabiyyaa; wa la'inittaba'ta ahwaaa'ahum ba'da maa jaaa'aka minal-'ilmi maa laka minal-laahi miñw-waliyyiñw-wa laa waaq. (Section 5)

38. Wa laqad arsalnaa Rusulam-min qablika wa ja'alnaa lahum azwaajañw-wa zurriyyah; wa maa kaana lirasoolin añy-yaatiya bi-aayatin illaa bi-iznillaah; likulli ajalin kitaab.

39. Yamhul-laahu maa yashaaa'u wa yusbitu

with Him is the Mother of the Book.

40. Whether We shall show you (within your life-time) part of what we promised them or take to Ourselves your soul (before it is all accomplished),- your duty is to make (the Message) reach them: it is Our part to call them to account.

41. Don't they see that We gradually reduce the land (in their control) from its outlying borders? (Where) Allah commands, there is none to put back His command: and He is swift in calling to account.

42. Those before them (also) devised plots; but in all things the master-planning is Allah's, He knows the doings of every soul: and soon will the Unbelievers know who gets home in the end.

43. The Unbelievers say: "No Messenger are you." Say: "Enough for a witness between me and you is Allah, and such as have knowledge of the Book."

---

14. Abraham
In the name of Allah, Most Gracious, Most Merciful.

1. *Alif-Lam-Ra.* A Book which We have revealed to you, in order that you might lead mankind out of the depths of darkness into light - by the leave of their Lord - to the Way of (Him) the Exalted in Power, worthy of all Praise!-

2. Of Allah, to Whom do belong all things in the heavens and on earth! But alas for the Unbelievers for a terrible Penalty (their Unfaith will bring them)!-

3. Those who love the life of this world more than the Hereafter, who hinder (men) from the Path

---

wa 'indahooo Ummul-Kitaab.

40. Wa im-maa nuriyannaka ba'dal-lazee na'iduhum aw nata-waffayannaka fa-innamaa 'alaykal-balaaghu wa 'alaynal-hisaab.

41. Awalam yaraw annaa naåtil-arda nanqusuhaa min atraafihaa; wallaahu yahkumu laa mu'aqqiba lihukmih; wa Huwa saree'ul-hisaab.

42. Wa qad makaral-lazeena min qablihim falillaahil-makru jamee'aa; ya'lamu maa taksibu kullu nafs; wa sa-ya'lamul-kuffaaru liman 'uqbad-daar.

43. Wa yaqoolul-lazeena kafaroo lasta mursalaa; qul kafaa billaahi shaheedam baynee wa baynakum wa man 'indahoo 'ilmul-Kitaab. (Sec. 6)

Sûrat Ibrâhîm–14
(Revealed at Makkah)
Bismillaahir Rahmaanir Raheem

1. Alif-Laaam-Raa; Kitaabun anzalnaahu ilayka litukhrijan-naasa minaz-zulumaati ilan-noori bi-izni Rabbihim ilaa siraatil-'Azeezil-Hameed.

2. Allaahil-lazee lahoo maa fis-samaawaati wa maa fill ard; wa waylul-lilkaafireena min 'azaabin shadeed.

3. Allazeena yastahibboonal-hayaatad-dunyaa 'alal Aakhirati wa yasuddoona 'an sabeelil-

seek therein something crooked: they are astray by a long distance.

4. We did not send a Messenger except (to teach) in the language of his (own) people, in order to make (things) clear to them. Now Allah leaves straying those whom He pleases and guides whom He pleases: and He is Exalted in Power, full of Wisdom.

5. We sent Moses with Our Signs (and the command). "Bring out your people from the depths of darkness into light, and teach them to remember the Days of Allah." Verily in this there are Signs for such as are firmly patient and constant,- grateful and appreciative.

6. Remember! Moses said to his people: "Call to mind the favor of Allah to you when He delivered you from the people of Pharaoh: they set you hard tasks and punishments, slaughtered your sons, and let your women-folk live: therein was a tremendous trial from your Lord."

7. And remember! your Lord caused to be declared (publicly): "If you are grateful, I will add more (favors) to you; But if you show ingratitude, truly My punishment is terrible indeed."

8. And Moses said: "If you show ingratitude, you and all on earth together, yet is Allah free of all wants, worthy of all praise.

9. Has not the story reached you, (O people!), of those who (went) before you? - of the people of Noah, and 'Ad, and Thamud? - And of those who (came) after them? None knows them but Allah. To them came Messengers with Clear (Signs);

laahi wa yabghoonahaa 'iwajaa; ulaaa'ika fee ḍalaalim ba'eed.

4. Wa maaaa arsalnaa mir-Rasoolin illaa bilisaani qaw-mihee liyubayyina lahum fay-udillul-laahu mañy-yashaaa'u wa yahdee mañy-yashaaa'; wa Huwal-'Azeezul-Ḥakeem

5. Wa laqad arsalnaa Moosaa bi-Aayaatinaaa an akhrij qawmaka minaẓ-ẓulumaati ilan-noori wa zak-kirhum bi-ayyaamil-laah; inna fee zaalika la-Aayaatil-likulli ṣabbaarin shakoor.

6. Wa iz qaala Moosaa liqawmihiz-kuroo ni'matal-laahi 'alaykum iz anjaakum-min Aali-Fir'awna yasoomoo-nakum sooo'al-'azaabi wa yuzabbiḥoona abnaaa'akum wa yastaḥyoona nisaaa'akum; wa fee zaalikum balaaa'um-mir-Rabbikum 'aẓeem. (Section 1)

7. Wa iz ta-azzana Rabbu-kum la'in shakartum la-azee-dannakum wa la'in kafartum inna 'azaabee lashadeed.

8. Wa qaala Moosaaa in takfurooo antum wa man fil-arḍi jamee'an fa-innal-laaha la-Ghaniyyun Ḥameed.

9. Alam yaatikum naba'ul-lazeena min qablikum qawmi Nooḥiñw-wa 'Aadiñw-wa Samood, wallazeena mim ba'dihim; laa ya'lamuhum illal-laah; jaaa'at-hum Rusuluhum bilbayyinaati

but they put their hands up to their mouths, and said: "We do deny (the mission) on which you have been sent, and we are really in suspicious (disquieting) doubt as to that to which you invite us."

10. Their Messengers said: "Is there a doubt about Allah, the Creator of the heavens and the earth? It is He Who invites you, in order that He may forgive you your sins and give you respite for a term appointed!" They said: "Ah! you are no more than human, like ourselves! You wish to turn us away from the (gods) our fathers used to worship: then bring us some clear authority."

11. Their Messengers said to them: "True, we are human like yourselves, but Allah grants His grace to such of his servants as He pleases. It is not for us to bring you an authority except as Allah permits. And on Allah let all men of faith put their trust.

12. "We do not have any reason why we should not put our trust on Allah. Indeed He Has guided us to the Ways we (follow). We shall certainly bear with patience all the hurt you may cause us. For those who put their trust should put their trust on Allah."

13. And the Unbelievers said to their Messengers: "Be sure we shall drive you out of our land, or you shall return to our religion." But their Lord inspired (this Message) to them: "Verily We shall cause the wrong-doers to perish!

14. "And verily We shall cause you to abide in the land, and succeed them. This for such as fear the Time when they shall stand before My tribunal,- Such as fear

faraddooo aydiyahum feee afwaahihim wa qaalooo innaa kafarnaa bimaaa ursiltum bihee wa innaa lafee shakkim-mimmaa tad'oonanaaa ilayhi mureeb.

10. Qaalat Rusuluhum afillaahi shakkun faaṭiris-samaawaati wal-arḍi yad'ookum liyaghfira lakum-min zunoobikum wa yu'akhkhirakum ilaaa ajalim-musam-maa; qaaloo in antum illaa basharum-mislunaa tureedoona an taṣuddoonaa 'ammaa kaana ya'budu aabaaa'unaa faåtoonaa bisulṭaanim-mubeen.

11. Qaalat lahum Rusuluhum in naḥnu illaa basharummislukum wa laakinnal-laaha yamunnu 'alaa mañy-yashaaa'u min 'ibaadihee wa maa kaana lanaaa an naåtiyakum bisulṭaanin illaa bi-iznil-laah; wa 'alal-laahi falyatawakkalil-mu'minoon.

12. Wa maa lanaaa allaa natawakkala 'alal-laahi wa qad hadaanaa subulanaa; wa lanaṣbiranna 'alaa maaa aazaytumoonaa; wa 'alal-laahi falyatawakkalil-mutawakkiloon.
(Section 2)

13. Wa qaalal-lazeena kafaroo li-Rusulihim lanukhrijannakum min arḍinaaa aw lata'oodunna fee millatinaa fa-awhaaa ilayhim Rabbuhum lanuhlikannaẓ-ẓalimeen.

14 Wa lanuskinan-nakumularḍa mim ba'dihim; zaalika liman khaafa maqaamee wa khaafa

فَرَدُّوٓا أَيْدِيَهُمْ فِىٓ أَفْوَاهِهِمْ
وَقَالُوٓا إِنَّا كَفَرْنَا بِمَآ أُرْسِلْتُمْ بِهِۦ
وَإِنَّا لَفِى شَكٍّ مِّمَّا تَدْعُونَنَآ
إِلَيْهِ مُرِيبٍ ۝
قَالَتْ رُسُلُهُمْ أَفِى اللَّهِ شَكٌّ فَاطِرِ
السَّمَٰوَٰتِ وَالْأَرْضِ ۖ يَدْعُوكُمْ
لِيَغْفِرَ لَكُم مِّن ذُنُوبِكُمْ وَيُؤَخِّرَكُمْ
إِلَىٰٓ أَجَلٍ مُّسَمًّى ۚ قَالُوٓا إِنْ أَنتُمْ
إِلَّا بَشَرٌ مِّثْلُنَا تُرِيدُونَ أَن
تَصُدُّونَا عَمَّا كَانَ يَعْبُدُ ءَابَآؤُنَا
فَأْتُونَا بِسُلْطَٰنٍ مُّبِينٍ ۝
قَالَتْ لَهُمْ رُسُلُهُمْ إِن نَّحْنُ إِلَّا
بَشَرٌ مِّثْلُكُمْ وَلَٰكِنَّ اللَّهَ يَمُنُّ عَلَىٰ مَن
يَشَآءُ مِنْ عِبَادِهِۦ ۖ وَمَا كَانَ لَنَآ
أَن نَّأْتِيَكُم بِسُلْطَٰنٍ إِلَّا بِإِذْنِ اللَّهِ
وَعَلَى اللَّهِ فَلْيَتَوَكَّلِ الْمُؤْمِنُونَ ۝
وَمَا لَنَآ أَلَّا نَتَوَكَّلَ عَلَى اللَّهِ وَقَدْ
هَدَىٰنَا سُبُلَنَا ۚ وَلَنَصْبِرَنَّ عَلَىٰ مَآ
ءَاذَيْتُمُونَا ۚ وَعَلَى اللَّهِ فَلْيَتَوَكَّلِ
الْمُتَوَكِّلُونَ ۝
وَقَالَ الَّذِينَ كَفَرُوا لِرُسُلِهِمْ
لَنُخْرِجَنَّكُم مِّنْ أَرْضِنَآ أَوْ لَتَعُودُنَّ
فِى مِلَّتِنَا ۖ فَأَوْحَىٰٓ إِلَيْهِمْ رَبُّهُمْ
لَنُهْلِكَنَّ الظَّٰلِمِينَ ۝
وَلَنُسْكِنَنَّكُمُ الْأَرْضَ مِنْ بَعْدِهِمْ ۚ
ذَٰلِكَ لِمَنْ خَافَ مَقَامِى وَخَافَ

the punishment denounced."

15. But they sought victory and decision (there and then), and frustration was the lot of every powerful obstinate transgressor.

16. In front of such a one is Hell, and he is given, for drink, boiling fetid water.

17. In gulps will he sip it, but never will he be near swallowing it down his throat: death will come to him from every quarter, yet he will not die: and in front of him will be a chastisement unrelenting.

18. The parable of those who reject their Lord is that their works are as ashes, on which the wind blows furiously on a tempestuous day: no power have they over anything that they have earned: that is the straying far, far (from the goal).

19. Don't you see that Allah created the heavens and the earth in Truth? If He so will, He can remove you and put (in your place) a new Creation?

20. Nor is that for Allah any great matter.

21. They will all be marshalled before Allah together: then will the weak say to those who were arrogant, "For us, we but followed you; can you then avail us to all against the Wrath of Allah?" They will reply, "If we had received the Guidance of Allah, we should have given it to you: to us it makes no difference (now) whether we rage, or bear (these torments) with patience: for ourselves there is no way of escape."

22. And Satan will say when the matter is decided:

wa'eed.

15. Wastaftaḥoo wa khaaba kullu jabbaarin 'aneed.

16. Miñw-waraaa'ihee Jahannamu wa yusqaa mim-maaa'in ṣadeed.

17. Yatajarra'uhoo wa laa yakaadu yuseeghuhoo wa yaå-teehil-mawtu min kulli makaaniñw-wa maa huwa bimayyitiñw wa miñw-waraaa'ihee 'azaabun ghaleeẓ.

18. Maṣalul-lazeena kafaroo bi-Rabbihim a'maaluhum karamaadinish-taddat bihir-reeḥu fee yawmin 'aaṣif; laa yaqdiroona mimmaa kasaboo 'alaa shay'; zaalika huwaḍ-ḍalaalul-ba'eed.

19. Alam tara annal-laaha khalaqas-samaawaati wal arḍa bilḥaqq; iñy-yashaå yuẓhibkum wa yaåti bikhalqin jadeed.

20. Wa maa zaalika 'alal-laahi bi'azeez.

21. Wa barazoo lillaahi jamee'an faqaalaḍ-ḍu'afaaa'u lillazeenas-takbarooo innaa kunnaa lakum taba'an fahal antum mughnoona 'annaa min 'azaabil-laahi min shay'; qaaloo law hadaanal-laahu lahaday-naakum sawaaa'un 'alaynaaa ajazi'naa am ṣabarnaa maa lanaa mim-maḥeeṣ.   **(Section 3)**

22. Wa qaalash-Shayṭaanu lammaa quḍiyal-amru

"It was Allah Who gave you a promise of Truth: I too promised, but I failed in my promise to you. I had no authority over you except to call you but you listened to me: then reproach not me, but reproach your own souls. I cannot listen to your cries, nor can you listen to mine. I reject your former act in associating me with Allah. For wrong-doers there must be a grievous Penalty."

innal-laaha wa'adakum wa'dal-ḥaqqi wa wa'attukum fa-akhlaftukum wa maa kaana liya 'alaykum-min sulṭaanin illaaa an da'awtukum fastajabtum lee falaa taloomoonee wa loomooo anfusakum maaa ana bimuṣ-rikhikum wa maaa antum bimuṣrikhiyya innee kafartu bimaaa ashraktumoonee min qabl; innaẓ-ẓaalimeena lahum aẓaabun aleem.

23. But those who believe and work righteousness will be admitted to gardens beneath which rivers flow,- to dwell therein for ever with the leave of their Lord. Their greeting therein will be: "Peace!"

23. Wa udkhilal-laẓeena aamanoo wa 'amiluṣ-ṣaaliḥaati Jannaatin tajree min taḥtihal-anhaaru khaalideena feehaa bi-izni Rabbihim taḥiyyatuhum feehaa salaam.

24. Do you not see how Allah sets forth a parable? - A goodly word like a goodly tree, whose root is firmly fixed, and its branches (reach) to the heavens.

24. Alam tara kayfa ḍarabal-laahu maṣalan kalimatan ṭayyibatan kashajaratin ṭayyi-batin aṣluhaa ṣaabituňw-wa far'uhaa fis-samaaa'.

25. It brings forth its fruit at all times, by the leave of its Lord. So Allah sets forth parables for men, in order that they may receive admonition.

25. Tu'teee ukulahaa kulla ḥeenim bi-izni Rabbihaa; wa yaḍribul-laahul-amṣaala lin-naasi la'allahum yataẓak-karoon.

26. And the parable of an evil word is that of an evil tree: It is torn up by the root from the surface of the earth: it has no stability.

26. Wa maṣalu kalimatin kha-beeṣatin kashajaratin khabee-satinij-tussat min fawqil-arḍi maa lahaa min qaraar.

27. Allah will establish in strength those who believe, with the word that stands firm, in this world and in the Hereafter; but Allah will leave, to stray, those who do wrong: Allah does what He wills.

27. Yuṣabbitul-laahul-laẓeena aamanoo bilqawliṣ-ṣaabiti fil-ḥayaatid-dunyaa wa fil-Aakhirati wa yuḍillul-laahuẓ-ẓaalimeen; wa yaf'alul-laahu maa yashaaa'. **(Section 4)**

28. Have you not turned your vision to those who have exchanged the favor of Allah

28. Alam tara ilal-laẓeena baddaloo ni'matal-laahi

إِنَّ اللّٰهَ وَعَدَكُمْ وَعْدَ الْحَقِّ وَ وَعَدْتُكُمْ فَاَخْلَفْتُكُمْ ۚ وَمَا كَانَ لِىَ عَلَيْكُمْ مِّنْ سُلْطٰنٍ اِلَّا اَنْ دَعَوْتُكُمْ فَاسْتَجَبْتُمْ لِىْ ۚ فَلَا تَلُوْمُوْنِىْ وَ لُوْمُوْٓا اَنْفُسَكُمْ ۚ مَاۤ اَنَا بِمُصْرِخِكُمْ وَمَاۤ اَنْتُمْ بِمُصْرِخِىَّ ۚ اِنِّىْ كَفَرْتُ بِمَاۤ اَشْرَكْتُمُوْنِ مِنْ قَبْلُ ۗ اِنَّ الظّٰلِمِيْنَ لَهُمْ عَذَابٌ اَلِيْمٌ ۟

وَاُدْخِلَ الَّذِيْنَ اٰمَنُوْا وَ عَمِلُوا الصّٰلِحٰتِ جَنّٰتٍ تَجْرِىْ مِنْ تَحْتِهَا الْاَنْهٰرُ خٰلِدِيْنَ فِيْهَا بِاِذْنِ رَبِّهِمْ ۚ تَحِيَّتُهُمْ فِيْهَا سَلٰمٌ ۟

اَلَمْ تَرَ كَيْفَ ضَرَبَ اللّٰهُ مَثَلًا كَلِمَةً طَيِّبَةً كَشَجَرَةٍ طَيِّبَةٍ اَصْلُهَا ثَابِتٌ وَّفَرْعُهَا فِى السَّمَآءِ ۟

تُؤْتِىْ اُكُلَهَا كُلَّ حِيْنٍ بِاِذْنِ رَبِّهَا ۚ وَيَضْرِبُ اللّٰهُ الْاَمْثَالَ لِلنَّاسِ لَعَلَّهُمْ يَتَذَكَّرُوْنَ ۟

وَمَثَلُ كَلِمَةٍ خَبِيْثَةٍ كَشَجَرَةٍ خَبِيْثَةِ ۨاجْتُثَّتْ مِنْ فَوْقِ الْاَرْضِ مَا لَهَا مِنْ قَرَارٍ ۟

يُثَبِّتُ اللّٰهُ الَّذِيْنَ اٰمَنُوْا بِالْقَوْلِ الثَّابِتِ فِى الْحَيٰوةِ الدُّنْيَا وَ فِى الْاٰخِرَةِ ۚ وَيُضِلُّ اللّٰهُ الظّٰلِمِيْنَ ۙ وَيَفْعَلُ اللّٰهُ مَا يَشَآءُ ۟

اَلَمْ تَرَ اِلَى الَّذِيْنَ بَدَّلُوْا نِعْمَتَ اللّٰهِ

into blasphemy and caused their People to descend to the House of Perdition?-

29. Into Hell? They will burn therein,- an evil place to stay in!

30. And they set up (idols) as equal to Allah, to mislead (men) from the Path! Say: "Enjoy (your brief power)! But verily you are making straight way for Hell!"

31. Speak to my servants who have believed, that they may establish regular prayers, and spend (in charity) out of the sustenance we have given them, secretly and openly, before the coming of a Day in which there will be neither mutual bargaining nor befriending.

32. It is Allah Who has created the heavens and the earth and sendeth down rain from the skies, and with it bringeth out fruits wherewith to feed you; it is He Who have made the ships subject to you, that they may sail through the sea by His command; and the rivers (also) have He made subject to you.

33. And He has made subject to you the sun and the moon, both diligently pursuing their courses; and he has (also) made the Night and the Day subject to you.

34. And He gives you of all that you ask for. But if you count the favours of Allah, never will you be able to number them. Verily, man is given up to injustice and ingratitude.

35. Remember Abraham said: "O my Lord! make this city one of peace and security: and preserve me and my sons from worshipping idols.

36. "O my Lord! they have indeed led astray many among mankind; He then who follows my (ways) is of me, and he that disobeys me,- but you are indeed Oft-Forgiving, Most Merciful.

37. "O our Lord! I have made some of my offspring to dwell

kufrañw-wa aḥalloo qawmahum daaral-bawaar.

29. Jahannama yaṣlawnahaa wa bi'sal-qaraar.

30. Wa ja'aloo lillaahi andaadal-liyuḍilloo 'an sabeelih; qul tamatta'oo fa-inna maṣeerakum ilan-Naar.

31. Qul li'ibaadiyal-lazeena aamanoo yuqeemuṣ-Ṣalaata wa yunfiqoo mimmaa razaqnaahum sirrañw-wa 'alaaniyatam-min qabli añy-yaåtiya Yawmul-laa bay'un feehi wa laa khilaal.

32. Allaahul-lazee khalaqas-samaawaati wal-arḍa wa anzala minas-samaaa'i maaa'an fa-akhraja bihee minas-ṣamaraati rizqal-lakum wa sakhkhara lakumul-fulka litajriya fil-baḥri bi-amrihee wa sakhkhara lakumul-anhaar.

33. Wa sakhkhara lakumush-shamsa walqamara daaa'ibayni wa sakhkhara lakumul-layla wannahaar.

34. Wa aataakum min kulli maa sa-altumooh; wa in ta'uddoo ni'matal-laahi laa tuḥṣoohaa; innal-insaana laẓaloo-mun kaffaar.   (Section 5)

35. Wa iz qaala Ibraaheemu Rabbij-'al haazal-balada aami-nañw-wajnubnee wa baniyya an na'budal-aṣnaam.

36. Rabbi innahunna aḍlalna kaseeram-minan-naasi faman tabi'anee fa-innahoo minnee wa man 'aṣaanee fa-innaka Ghafoorur-Raḥeem.

37. Rabbanaaa inneee askantu min zurriyyatee

in a valley without cultivation, by your Sacred House; in order, O our Lord, that they may establish regular Prayer: so fill the hearts of some among men with love toward them, and feed them with fruits: so that they may give thanks.

38. "O our Lord! truly You do know what we conceal and what we reveal: for nothing whatever is hidden from Allah, whether on earth or in heaven.

39. "Praise be to Allah, Who has granted unto me in old age Isma'il and Isaac: for truly my Lord is He, the Hearer of Prayer!

40. O my Lord! make me one who establishes regular Prayer, and also (raise such) among my offspring O our Lord! and you accept my Prayer.

41. "O our Lord! cover (us) with Your Forgiveness - me, my parents, and (all) Believers, on the Day that the Reckoning will be established!

42. Think not that Allah does not heed the deeds of those who do wrong. He but gives them respite against a Day when the eyes will fixedly stare in horror,-

43. They running forward with necks outstretched, their heads uplifted, their gaze returning not toward them, and their hearts a (gaping) void!

44. So warn mankind of the Day when the Wrath will reach them: then will the wrong-doers say: "Our Lord! respite us (if only) for a short Term: we will answer Your Call, and follow the Messengers!" "What! were you not wont to swear aforetime that you should suffer no

biwaadin ghayri zee zar'in 'inda Baytikal-Muḥarrami Rabbanaa liyuqeemuṣ-Ṣalaata faj'al af'idatam-minan-naasi tahweee ilayhim warzuqhum-minas-samaraati la'allahum yashkuroon.

38. Rabbanaaa innaka ta'lamu maa nukhfee wa maa nu'lin; wa maa yakhfaa 'alal-laahi min shay'in fil-arḍi wa laa fis-samaaa'.

39. Alḥamdu lillaahil-lazee wahaba lee 'alal-kibari Ismaa-'eela wa Isḥaaq; inna Rabbee lasamee'ud-du'aaa'.

40. Rabbij-'alnee muqeemaṣ-Ṣalaati wa min zurriyyatee; Rabbanaa wa taqabbal du'aaa'.

41. Rabbanagh-fir lee wa liwaalidayya wa lilmu'mineena Yawma yaqoomul-ḥisaab.
(Section 6)

42. Wa laa taḥsabannal-laaha ghaafilan 'ammaa ya'maluz-zaalimoon; innamaa yu'akh-khiruhum li-Yawmin tashkhaṣu feehil-abṣaar.

43. Muhṭi'eena muqni'ee ru'oosihim laa yartaddu ilayhim ṭarfuhum wa af-'idatuhum hawaaa'.

44. Wa anzirin-naasa Yawma yaåteehimul-'azaabu fa-yaqoo-lul-lazeena zalamoo Rabbanaaa akhkhirnaaa ilaa ajalin qaree-bin-nujib da'wataka wa nattabi-'ir-Rusul; awalam takoonooo aqsamtum min qablu maa lakum

decline?

45. "And you dwelt in the dwellings of men who wronged their own souls; you were clearly shown how We dealt with them; and We put forth (many) Parables in your behoof!"

46. Mighty indeed were the plots which they made, but their plots were (well) within the sight of Allah, even though they were such as to shake the hills!

47. Never think that Allah would fail His Messengers in His promise: for Allah is Exalted in Power, - the Lord of Retribution.

48. One day the earth will be changed to a different Earth, and so will be the Heavens, and (men) will be marshalled forth, before Allah, the One, the Irresistible;

49. And you will see the Sinners that day bound together in fetters;-

50. Their garments of liquid pitch, and their faces covered with Fire;

51. That Allah may requite each soul according to its deserts; and verily Allah is swift in calling to account.

52. Here is a Message for mankind: let them take warning therefrom, and let them know that He is (no other than) One God (Allah): let men of under-standing take heed.

---

min zawaal.

45. Wa sakantum fee masaa-kinil-lazeena zalamooo anfusa-hum wa tabayyana lakum kayfa fa'alnaa bihim wa darabnaa lakumul-amsaal.

46. Wa qad makaroo makrahum wa 'indal-laahi makruhum wa in kaana makruhum litazoola minhul-jibaal.

47. Falaa taḥsabannal-laaha mukhlifa wa'dihee Rusulah; innal-laaha 'azeezun zunti-qaam.

48. Yawma tubaddalul-arḍu ghayral-arḍi wassamaawaatu wa barazoo lillaahil-Waaḥidil-Qahhaar.

49. Wa taral-mujrimeena Yawma'izim-muqarraneena fil-asfaad.

50. Saraabeeluhum min qati-raaniñw-wa taghshaa wujoo-hahumun-Naar.

51. Liyajziyal-laahu kulla nafsim-maa kasabat; innal-laaha saree'ul-ḥisaab.

52. Haazaa balaaghul-linnaasi wa liyunzaroo bihee wa liya'lamooo annamaa Huwa Ilaahuñw-Waaḥiduñw-wa lliyaz-zakkara ulul-albaab. (Section 7)

---

15. The Rocky Tract

In the name of Allah, Most Gracious, Most Merciful.

1. *Alif-Lam-Ra.* These are the *Ayats* of Revelation,- of a Qur'an that makes things clear.

2. Again and again will those who disbelieve, wish that

Sûrat al-Ḥijr–15

(Revealed at Makkah)

Bismillaahir Raḥmaanir Raḥeem

1. Alif-Laaam-Raa; tilka Aayaatul-Kitaabi wa Qur-aa-nim-Mubeen.

2. Rubamaa yawaddul-lazeena kafaroo law

they had bowed (to Allah's will) in Islam.

3. Leave them alone, to enjoy (the good things of this life) and to please themselves: let (false) hope amuse them: soon will knowledge (undeceive them).

4. We never destroyed a population that had not a term decreed and assigned beforehand.

5. Neither can a people anticipate its Term, nor delay it.

6. They say: "O you to whom the Message is being revealed! truly you are mad (or possessed)!

7. "Why don't you bring not angels to us if it be that you have the Truth?"

8. We don't send not the angels down except for just cause: if they came (to the ungodly), behold! no respite would they have!

9. We have, without doubt, sent down the Message; and We will assuredly guard it (from corruption).

10. We sent Messengers before you amongst the religious sects of old:

11. But never came a Messenger to them but they mocked him.

12. Even so do We let it creep into the hearts of the sinners.

13. That they should not believe in the (Message); but the ways of the ancients have passed away.

14. Even if We opened out to them a gate from heaven, and they were to continue (all day) ascending therein,

15. They would only say: "Our eyes have been intoxicated: No, we have been bewitched by sorcery."

kaanoo muslimeen.

3. Zarhum yaåkuloo wa yatamatta'oo wa yulhihimul-amalu fasawfa ya'lamoon.

4. Wa maaa ahlaknaa min qaryatin illaa wa lahaa kitaabum-ma'loom.

5. Maa tasbiqu min ummatin ajalahaa wa maa yastaåkhiroon.

6. Wa qaaloo yaaa ayyuhal-lazee nuzzila 'alayhiz-Zikru innaka lamajnoon.

7. Law maa taåteenaa bil-malaaa'ikati in kunta minaṣ-ṣaadiqeen.

8. Maa nunazzilul-malaaa'i-kata illaa bilḥaqqi wa maa kaanooo izam-munzareen.

9. Innaa Naḥnu nazalnaz-Zikra wa Innaa lahoo laḥaa-fizoon.

10. Wa laqad arsalnaa min qablika fee shiya'il-awwaleen.

11. Wa maa yaåteehim-mir-Rasoolin illaa kaanoo bihee yastahzi'oon.

12. Kazaalika naslukuhoo fee quloobil-mujrimeen.

13. Laa yu'minoona bihee wa qad khalat sunnatul-awwaleen.

14. Wa law fataḥnaa 'alayhim baabam-minas-samaaa'i fazal-loo feehi ya'rujoon.

15. Laqaalooo innamaa sukki-rat abṣaarunaa bal naḥnu qawmum-mashooroon.

(Section 1)

كَانُوْا مُسْلِمِيْنَ ۟

ذَرْهُمْ يَأْكُلُوْا وَيَتَمَتَّعُوْا وَيُلْهِهِمُ الْأَمَلُ فَسَوْفَ يَعْلَمُوْنَ ۟

وَمَاۤ اَهْلَكْنَا مِنْ قَرْيَةٍ اِلَّا وَلَهَا كِتَابٌ مَّعْلُوْمٌ ۟

مَا تَسْبِقُ مِنْ اُمَّةٍ اَجَلَهَا وَمَا يَسْتَأْخِرُوْنَ ۟

وَقَالُوْا يٰۤاَيُّهَا الَّذِىْ نُزِّلَ عَلَيْهِ الذِّكْرُ اِنَّكَ لَمَجْنُوْنٌ ۟

لَوْ مَا تَأْتِيْنَا بِالْمَلٰٓئِكَةِ اِنْ كُنْتَ مِنَ الصّٰدِقِيْنَ ۟

مَا نُنَزِّلُ الْمَلٰٓئِكَةَ اِلَّا بِالْحَقِّ وَمَا كَانُوْۤا اِذًا مُّنْظَرِيْنَ ۟

اِنَّا نَحْنُ نَزَّلْنَا الذِّكْرَ وَاِنَّا لَهٗ لَحٰفِظُوْنَ ۟

وَلَقَدْ اَرْسَلْنَا مِنْ قَبْلِكَ فِىْ شِيَعِ الْاَوَّلِيْنَ ۟

وَمَا يَأْتِيْهِمْ مِّنْ رَّسُوْلٍ اِلَّا كَانُوْا بِهٖ يَسْتَهْزِءُوْنَ ۟

كَذٰلِكَ نَسْلُكُهٗ فِىْ قُلُوْبِ الْمُجْرِمِيْنَ ۟

لَا يُؤْمِنُوْنَ بِهٖ وَقَدْ خَلَتْ سُنَّةُ الْاَوَّلِيْنَ ۟

وَلَوْ فَتَحْنَا عَلَيْهِمْ بَابًا مِّنَ السَّمَآءِ فَظَلُّوْا فِيْهِ يَعْرُجُوْنَ ۟

لَقَالُوْۤا اِنَّمَا سُكِّرَتْ اَبْصَارُنَا بَلْ نَحْنُ قَوْمٌ مَّسْحُوْرُوْنَ ۟

16. It is We Who have set out the zodiacal signs in the heavens, and made them fair-seeming to (all) beholders;

17. And (moreover) We have guarded them from every evil spirit accursed:

18. But any that gains a hearing by stealth, is pursued by a flaming fire, bright (to see).

19. And the earth We have spread out (like a carpet); set thereon mountains firm and immovable; and produced therein all kinds of things in due balance.

20. And We have provided therein means of subsistence,- for you and for those for whose sustenance you are not responsible.

21. And there is not a thing but its (sources and) treasures (inexhaustible) are with Us; but We only send down thereof in due and ascertainable measures.

22. And We send the fecundating winds, then cause the rain to descend from the sky, therewith providing you with water (in abundance), though you are not the guardians of its stores.

23. And verily, it is We Who give life, and Who give death: it is We Who remain inheritors (after all else passes away).

24. To Us are known those of you who hasten forward, and those who lag behind.

25. Assuredly it is your Lord Who will gather them together: for He is perfect in Wisdom and Knowledge.

26. We created man from sounding clay, from mud moulded into shape;

27. And the Jinn race, We had created before, from the fire of a scorching wind.

16. Wa laqad ja'alnaa fis-samaaa'i buroojañw-wa zay-yannaahaa linnaaẓireen.

17. Wa ḥafiẓnaahaa min kulli Shayṭaanir-rajeem.

18. Illaa manis-taraqas-sam'a fa-atba'ahoo shihaabum-mubeen.

19. Wal-arḍa madadnaahaa wa alqaynaa feehaa rawaasiya wa ambatnaa feehaa min kulli shay'im-mawzoon.

20. Wa ja'alnaa lakum feehaa ma'aayisha wa mal-lastum lahoo biraaziqeen.

21. Wa im-min shay'in illaa 'indanaa khazaaa'inuhoo wa maa nunazziluhooo illaa biqadarim-ma'loom.

22. Wa arsalnar-riyaaḥa la-waaqiḥa fa-anzalnaa minas-samaaa'i maaa'an fa-asqay-naakumoohu wa maaa antum lahoo bikhaazineen.

23. Wa innaa la-naḥnu nuḥyee wa numeetu wa naḥnul-waarisoon.

24. Wa la-qad 'alimnal-mus-taqdimeena minkum wa laqad 'alimnal-mustaåkhireen.

25. Wa inna Rabbaka Huwa yaḥshuruhum; innahoo Ḥakee-mun 'Aleem. **(Section 2)**

26. Wa laqad khalaqnal insaana min ṣalṣaalim-min ḥama-im-masnoon.

27. Waljaaanna khalaqnaahu min qablu min naaris-samoom.

وَلَقَدْ جَعَلْنَا فِى السَّمَآءِ بُرُوجًا ۝

وَزَيَّنَّاهَا لِلنَّاظِرِينَ ۝

وَحَفِظْنَاهَا مِن كُلِّ شَيْطَانٍ رَّجِيمٍ ۝

اِلَّا مَنِ اسْتَرَقَ السَّمْعَ فَأَتْبَعَهُ شِهَابٌ مُّبِينٌ ۝

وَالْأَرْضَ مَدَدْنَاهَا وَأَلْقَيْنَا فِيهَا رَوَاسِىَ وَأَنبَتْنَا فِيهَا مِن كُلِّ شَىْءٍ مَّوْزُونٍ ۝

وَجَعَلْنَا لَكُمْ فِيهَا مَعَايِشَ وَمَن لَّسْتُمْ لَهُ بِرَازِقِينَ ۝

وَإِن مِّن شَىْءٍ إِلَّا عِندَنَا خَزَآئِنُهُ وَمَا نُنَزِّلُهُ إِلَّا بِقَدَرٍ مَّعْلُومٍ ۝

وَأَرْسَلْنَا الرِّيَاحَ لَوَاقِحَ فَأَنزَلْنَا مِنَ السَّمَآءِ مَآءً فَأَسْقَيْنَاكُمُوهُ وَمَا أَنتُمْ لَهُ بِخَازِنِينَ ۝

وَإِنَّا لَنَحْنُ نُحْىِ وَنُمِيتُ وَنَحْنُ الْوَارِثُونَ ۝

وَلَقَدْ عَلِمْنَا الْمُسْتَقْدِمِينَ مِنكُمْ وَلَقَدْ عَلِمْنَا الْمُسْتَأْخِرِينَ ۝

وَإِنَّ رَبَّكَ هُوَ يَحْشُرُهُمْ ۚ إِنَّهُ حَكِيمٌ عَلِيمٌ ۝

وَلَقَدْ خَلَقْنَا الْإِنسَانَ مِن صَلْصَالٍ مِّنْ حَمَإٍ مَّسْنُونٍ ۝

وَالْجَآنَّ خَلَقْنَاهُ مِن قَبْلُ مِن نَّارِ السَّمُومِ ۝

28. Behold! your Lord said to the angels: "I am about to create man, from sounding clay from mud moulded into shape;

28. Wa iz qaala Rabbuka lilmalaaa'ikati innee khaaliqum basharam-min ṣalṣaalim-min ḥama-im-masnoon.

وَإِذْ قَالَ رَبُّكَ لِلْمَلَآئِكَةِ إِنِّي خَالِقٌ بَشَرًا مِّن صَلْصَالٍ مِّنْ حَمَإٍ مَّسْنُونٍ ۝

29. "When I have fashioned him (in due proportion) and breathed into him of My spirit, you fall down in obeisance to him."

29. Fa-izaa sawwaytuhoo wa nafakhtu feehi mir-rooḥee faqa'oo lahoo saajideen.

فَإِذَا سَوَّيْتُهُ وَنَفَخْتُ فِيهِ مِن رُّوحِي فَقَعُوا لَهُ سَاجِدِينَ ۝

30. So the angels prostrated themselves, all of them together:

30. Fasajadal-malaaa'ikatu kulluhum ajma'oon.

فَسَجَدَ الْمَلَآئِكَةُ كُلُّهُمْ أَجْمَعُونَ ۝

31. Not so Iblis: he refused to be among those who prostrated themselves.

31. Illaaa Ibleesa abaaa añy-yakoona ma'as-saajideen.

إِلَّا إِبْلِيسَ أَبَى أَن يَكُونَ مَعَ السَّاجِدِينَ ۝

32. (Allah) said: "O Iblis! what is your reason for not being among those who prostrated themselves?"

32. Qaala yaaa Ibleesu maa laka allaa takoona ma'as-saajideen.

قَالَ يَٰإِبْلِيسُ مَا لَكَ أَلَّا تَكُونَ مَعَ السَّاجِدِينَ ۝

33. (Iblis) said: "I am not one to prostrate myself to man, whom you created from sounding clay, from mud moulded into shape."

33. Qaala lam akul-li-asjuda libasharin khalaqtahoo min ṣalṣaalim-min ḥama-im-masnoon.

قَالَ لَمْ أَكُن لِّأَسْجُدَ لِبَشَرٍ خَلَقْتَهُ مِن صَلْصَالٍ مِّنْ حَمَإٍ مَّسْنُونٍ ۝

34. (Allah) said: "Then get out from here; for you are rejected, accursed.

34. Qaala fakhruj minhaa fa-innaka rajeem.

قَالَ فَاخْرُجْ مِنْهَا فَإِنَّكَ رَجِيمٌ ۝

35. "And the curse shall be on you till the day of Judgment."

35. Wa inna 'alaykal-la'nata ilaa Yawmid-Deen.

وَإِنَّ عَلَيْكَ اللَّعْنَةَ إِلَىٰ يَوْمِ الدِّينِ ۝

36. (Iblis) said: "O my Lord! give me then respite till the Day the (dead) are raised."

36. Qaala Rabbi fa-anzirneee ilaa Yawmi yub'asoon.

قَالَ رَبِّ فَأَنظِرْنِي إِلَىٰ يَوْمِ يُبْعَثُونَ ۝

37. (Allah) said: "Respite is granted to you,

37. Qaala fa-innaka minal-munzareen.

قَالَ فَإِنَّكَ مِنَ الْمُنظَرِينَ ۝

38. "Till the Day of the Time Appointed."

38. Ilaa Yawmil-waqtil-ma'loom.

إِلَىٰ يَوْمِ الْوَقْتِ الْمَعْلُومِ ۝

39. (Iblis) said: "O my Lord! because You have put me in the wrong, I will make (wrong) fair-seeming to them on the earth, and I will put them all in the wrong,-

39. Qaala Rabbi bimaaa aghwaytanee la-uzayyinanna lahum fil-arḍi wa la-ughwiyan-nahum ajma'een.

قَالَ رَبِّ بِمَا أَغْوَيْتَنِي لَأُزَيِّنَنَّ لَهُمْ فِي الْأَرْضِ وَلَأُغْوِيَنَّهُمْ أَجْمَعِينَ ۝

40. "Except your servants among them, sincere and purified (by your Grace)."

40. Illaa 'ibaadaka minhumul-mukhlaṣeen.

إِلَّا عِبَادَكَ مِنْهُمُ الْمُخْلَصِينَ ۝

41. (Allah) said: "This (way of My sincere servants) is indeed a Way that leads straight to Me.

41. Qaala haazaa Ṣiraaṭun 'alayya Mustaqeem.

قَالَ هَٰذَا صِرَاطٌ عَلَيَّ مُسْتَقِيمٌ ۝

42. "For over My servants no authority shall you have, except such as put themselves

42. Inna 'ibaadee laysa laka 'alayhim sulṭaanun illaa manit-taba'aka minal-

إِنَّ عِبَادِي لَيْسَ لَكَ عَلَيْهِمْ سُلْطَانٌ إِلَّا مَنِ اتَّبَعَكَ مِنَ

in the wrong and follow you."

43. And verily, Hell is the promised abode for them all!

44. To it are seven gates: for each of those gates is a (special) class (of sinners) assigned.

45. The righteous (will be) amid Gardens and fountains (of clear-flowing water).

46. (Their greeting will be): "You enter here in peace and security."

47. And We shall remove from their hearts any lurking sense of injury: (they will be) brothers (joyfully) facing each other on thrones (of dignity).

48. There no sense of fatigue shall touch them, nor shall they (ever) be asked to leave.

49. Tell My servants that I am indeed the Oft-forgiving, Most Merciful;

50. And that My Penalty will be indeed the most grievous Penalty.

51. Tell them about the guests of Abraham.

52. When they entered his presence and said, "Peace!" He said, "We feel afraid of you!"

53. They said: "Fear not! We give you glad tidings of a son endowed with wisdom."

54. He said: "Do you give me glad tidings that old age has seized me? Of what, then, is your good news?"

55. They said: "We give you glad tidings in truth: be not then in despair!"

56. He said: "And who despairs of the mercy of his Lord, but such as go astray?"

57. Abraham said: "What then is the business on which you (have come), O you messengers (of Allah)?"

58. They said: "We have been sent to a people (deep) in sin,

---

ghaaween.

43. Wa inna Jahannama lamaw'iduhum ajma'een.

44. Lahaa sab'atu abwaab; likulli baabim-minhum juz'um-maqsoom.   (Section 3)

45. Innal-muttaqeena fee Jannaatiñw-wa 'uyoon.

46. Udkhuloohaa bisalaamin aamineen.

47. Wa naza'naa maa fee sudoorihim-min ghillin ikhwaa-nan 'alaa sururim-mutaqaa-bileen.

48. Laa yamas-suhum feehaa naṣabuñw-wa maa hum-minhaa bimukhrajeen.

49. Nabbi' 'ibaadeee annee anal-Ghafoorur-Raḥeem.

50. Wa anna 'azaabee huwal-'azaabul-aleem.

51. Wa nabbi'hum 'an ḍayfi Ibraaheem.

52. Iz dakhaloo 'alayhi faqaa-loo salaaman qaala innaa minkum wajiloon.

53. Qaaloo laa tawjal innaa nubashshiruka bighulaamin 'aleem.

54. Qaala abashshartumoo-nee 'alaaa am-massaniyal-kibaru fabima tubashshiroon.

55. Qaaloo bashsharnaaka bilḥaqqi falaa takum-minal-qaaniṭeen.

56. Qaala wa mañy-yaqnaṭu mir-raḥmati Rabbiheee illaḍ-ḍaaalloon.

57. Qaala famaa khaṭbukum ayyuhal-mursaloon.

58. Qaaloo innaaa ursilnaaa ilaa qawmim-mujrimeen.

59. "Excepting the adherents of Lut: We are certainly (charged) to save them (from harm),- all -

60. "Except his wife, who, We have ascertained, will be among those who will lag behind."

61. At length when the messengers arrived among the adherents of Lut,

62. He said: "You appear to be uncommon folk."

63. They said: "Yes, we have come to you to accomplish that of which they doubt.

64. "We have brought to you that which is inevitably due, and assuredly we tell the truth.

65. "Then travel by night with your household, when a portion of the night (yet remains), and do you bring up the rear: let no one amongst you look back, but pass on whither you are ordered."

66. And We made known this decree to him, that the last remnants of those (sinners) should be cut off by the morning.

67. The inhabitants of the city came in (mad) joy (at news of the young men).

68. Lut said: "These are my guests: do not me disgrace:

69. "But fear Allah, and shame me not."

70. They said: "Did we not forbid you (to speak) for **all** and sundry?"

71. He said: "There are my daughters (to marry), if you must act (so)."

72. Verily, by your life (O Prophet), in their wild intoxication, they wander in distraction, to and fro.

73. But the (mighty) Blast overtook them before morning,

74. And We turned (the cities) upside down, and rained down on them brimstones hard as baked clay.

75. Behold! in this are Signs for those who by tokens do understand.

---

59. Illaaa Aala Looṭ; innaa lamunajjoohum ajma'een.

60. Illam-ra-atahoo qaddar-naaa innahaa laminal-ghaabi-reen. **(Section 4)**

61. Falammaa jaaa'a Aala Looṭinil-mursaloon.

62. Qaala innakum qawmum-munkaroon.

63. Qaaloo bal ji'naaka bimaa kaanoo feehi yamtaroon.

64. Wa ataynaaka bilḥaqqi wa innaa laṣaadiqoon.

65. Fa-asri bi-ahlika biqiṭ'im-minal-layli wattabi' adbaara-hum wa laa yaltafit minkum aḥaduñw-wamḍoo ḥaysu tu'ma-roon.

66. Wa qaḍaynaaa ilayhi zaalikal-amra anna daabira haaa'ulaaa'i maqṭoo'um-muṣbiḥeen.

67. Wa jaaa'a ahlul-madee-nati yastabshiroon.

68. Qaala inna haaa'ulaaa'i ḍayfee falaa tafḍaḥoon.

69. Wattaqul-laaha wa laa tukhzoon.

70. Qaalooo awalam nanhaka 'anil-'aalameen.

71. Qaala haaa'ulaaa'i banaa-teee in kuntum faa'ileen.

72. La'amruka innahum lafee sakratihim ya'mahoon.

73. Fa-akhaẕat-humuṣ-ṣay-ḥatu mushriqeen.

74. Faja'alnaa 'aaliyahaa saa-filahaa wa amṭarnaa 'alayhim ḥijaaratam-min sijjeel.

75. Inna fee zaalika la-Aayaa-til-lilmutawassimeen.

اِلَّآ اٰلَ لُوۡطٍ ؕ اِنَّا لَمُنَجُّوۡهُمۡ اَجۡمَعِیۡنَ ۙ ۵۹

اِلَّا امۡرَاَتَهٗ قَدَّرۡنَا ۙ اِنَّهَا لَمِنَ الۡغٰبِرِیۡنَ ۠ ۶۰

فَلَمَّا جَآءَ اٰلَ لُوۡطِ ۨالۡمُرۡسَلُوۡنَ ۙ ۶۱

قَالَ اِنَّکُمۡ قَوۡمٌ مُّنۡکَرُوۡنَ ۶۲

قَالُوۡا بَلۡ جِئۡنٰکَ بِمَا کَانُوۡا فِیۡهِ یَمۡتَرُوۡنَ ۶۳

وَاَتَیۡنٰکَ بِالۡحَقِّ وَاِنَّا لَصٰدِقُوۡنَ ۶۴

فَاَسۡرِ بِاَهۡلِکَ بِقِطۡعٍ مِّنَ الَّیۡلِ وَاتَّبِعۡ اَدۡبَارَهُمۡ وَلَا یَلۡتَفِتۡ مِنۡکُمۡ اَحَدٌ وَّامۡضُوۡا حَیۡثُ تُؤۡمَرُوۡنَ ۶۵

وَقَضَیۡنَاۤ اِلَیۡهِ ذٰلِکَ الۡاَمۡرَ اَنَّ دَابِرَ هٰۤؤُلَآءِ مَقۡطُوۡعٌ مُّصۡبِحِیۡنَ ۶۶

وَجَآءَ اَهۡلُ الۡمَدِیۡنَةِ یَسۡتَبۡشِرُوۡنَ ۶۷

قَالَ اِنَّ هٰۤؤُلَآءِ ضَیۡفِیۡ فَلَا تَفۡضَحُوۡنِ ۙ ۶۸

وَاتَّقُوا اللّٰهَ وَلَا تُخۡزُوۡنِ ۶۹

قَالُوۡۤا اَوَلَمۡ نَنۡهَکَ عَنِ الۡعٰلَمِیۡنَ ۷۰

قَالَ هٰۤؤُلَآءِ بَنٰتِیۡۤ اِنۡ کُنۡتُمۡ فٰعِلِیۡنَ ؕ ۷۱

لَعَمۡرُکَ اِنَّهُمۡ لَفِیۡ سَکۡرَتِهِمۡ یَعۡمَهُوۡنَ ۷۲

فَاَخَذَتۡهُمُ الصَّیۡحَةُ مُشۡرِقِیۡنَ ۙ ۷۳

فَجَعَلۡنَا عَالِیَهَا سَافِلَهَا وَاَمۡطَرۡنَا عَلَیۡهِمۡ حِجَارَةً مِّنۡ سِجِّیۡلٍ ؕ ۷۴

اِنَّ فِیۡ ذٰلِکَ لَاٰیٰتٍ لِّلۡمُتَوَسِّمِیۡنَ ۷۵

76. And the (cities were) right on the high-road.

77. Behold! in this is a Sign for those who believe!

78. And the Companions of the Wood were also wrong-doers;

79. So We exacted retribution from them. They were both on an open highway, plain to see.

80. The Companions of the Rocky Tract also rejected the Messengers:

81. We sent them Our Sings, but they persisted in turning away from them.

82. Out of the mountains did they hew (their) edifices, (feeling themselves) secure.

83. But the (mighty) Blast seized them of a morning,

84. And of no avail to them was all that they did (with such art and care)!

85. We did not create the heavens, the earth, and all between them, but for just ends. And the Hour is surely coming (when this will be manifest). So overlook (any human faults) with gracious forgiveness.

86. For verily it is your Lord Who is the Master-Creator, knowing all things.

87. And We have bestowed upon you the Seven Oft-repeated (verses) and the Grand Qur'an.

88. Do not strain your eyes (wistfully) at what We have bestowed on certain classes of them, nor grieve over them: but lower your wing (in gentleness) to the believers.

89. And say: "I am indeed he that warns openly and without ambiguity,"—

90. (Of just such wrath) as We sent down on those who divided (Scripture into arbitrary parts),-

91. (So also on such) as have made Qur'an into shreds (as they please).

92. Therefore, by the Lord, We will, of a surety, call them to account,

76. Wa innahaa labi-sabee-lim-muqeem.

77. Inna fee ẕaalika la-Aaya-tal-lilmu'mineen.

78. Wa in kaana Aṣḥaabul-Aykati laẕaalimeen.

79. Fantaqamnaa minhum wa innahumaa labi-imaamim-mubeen. **(Section 5)**

80. Wa laqad kaẕẕaba Aṣḥaa-bul-Ḥijril-mursaleen.

81. Wa aataynaahum Aayaa-tinaa fakaanoo 'anhaa mu'ri-ḍeen.

82. Wa kaanoo yanḥitoona minal-jibaali buyootan aami-neen.

83. Fa-akhaẕat-humuṣ-ṣay-ḥatu muṣbiḥeen.

84. Famaaa aghnaa 'anhum maa kaanoo yaksiboon.

85. Wa maa khalaqnas-samaawaati wal-arḍa wa maa baynahumaaa illaa bilḥaqq; wa innas-Saa'ata la-aatiyatun faṣ-faḥiṣ-ṣafḥal-jameel.

86. Inna Rabbaka Huwal-khallaaqul-'aleem.

87. Wa laqad aataynaaka sab'am-minal-maẕaanee wal-Qur-aanal-'Aẓeem.

88. Laa tamuddanna 'aynay-ka ilaa maa matta'naa bihee azwaajam-minhum wa laa taḥzan 'alayhim wakhfiḍ janaaḥaka lilmu'mineen.

89. Wa qul inneee anan-naẕeerul-mubeen.

90. Kamaaa anzalnaa 'alal-muqtasimeen.

91. Allaẕeena ja'alul-Qur-aana 'iḍeen.

92. Fawa Rabbika lanas'a-lannahum ajma'eena.

93. For all their deeds.

94. Therefore expound openly what you are commanded, and turn away from those who join false gods with Allah.

95. For sufficient are We to you against those who scoff,

96. Those who adopt, with Allah, another god: but soon will they come to know.

97. We do indeed know how your heart is distressed at what they say.

98. But celebrate the praises of your Lord, and be of those who prostrate themselves in adoration.

99. And serve your Lord until there come unto you the Hour that is Certain.

---

93. 'Ammaa kaanoo ya'maloon.

94. Faṣda' bimaa tu'maru wa a'riḍ 'anil-mushrikeen.

95. Innaa kafaynaakal-mustahzi'een.

96. Allazeena yaj'aloona ma'al-laahi ilaahan aakhar; fasawfa ya'lamoon.

97. Wa laqad na'lamu annaka yaḍeequ ṣadruka bimaa yaqooloon.

98. Fasabbiḥ biḥamdi Rabbika wa kum-minas-saajideen.

99. Wa'bud Rabbaka ḥattaa yaåtiyakal-yaqeen.   (Section 6)

---

16. The Bee
In the name of Allah, Most Gracious, Most Merciful.

1. (Inevitable) comes (to pass) the Command of Allah: seek you not then to hasten it: glory to Him, and far is He above having the partners they ascribe to Him!

2. He sends down His angels with inspiration of His Command, to such of His servants as He pleases, (saying): "Warn (Man) that there is no god but I: so do your duty unto Me."

3. He has created the heavens and the earth for just ends: far is He above having the partners they ascribe to Him!

4. He has created man from a sperm-drop; and behold this same (man) becomes an open disputer!

5. And He has created cattle for you (men): from them you derive warmth, and numerous benefits, and of their (meat) you eat.

Sûrat an-Naḥl–16
(Revealed at Makkah)
Bismillaahir Raḥmaanir Raḥeem

1. Ataaa amrul-laahi falaa tasta'jilooh; Subḥaanahoo wa Ta'aalaa 'ammaa yushrikoon.

2. Yunazzilul-malaaa'ikata bir-rooḥi min amrihee 'alaa mañy-yashaaa'u min 'ibaadiheee an anziroo annahoo laaa ilaaha illaaa ana fattaqoon.

3. Khalaqas-samaawaati wal-arḍa bilḥaqq; Ta'aalaa 'ammaa yushrikoon.

4. Khalaqal-insaana min nuṭfatin fa-izaa huwa khaṣeemum-mubeen.

5. Wal-an'aama khalaqahaa; lakum feehaa dif'uñw-wa manaafi'u wa minhaa taåku-loon.

6. And you have a sense of pride and beauty in them as you drive them home in the evening, and as you lead them forth to pasture in the morning.

7. And they carry your heavy loads to lands that you could not (otherwise) reach except with souls distressed: for your Lord is indeed Most Kind, Most Merciful,

8. And (He has created) horses, mules, and donkeys, for you to ride and use for show; and He has created (other) things of which you have no knowledge.

9. And to Allah leads straight the Way, but there are ways that turn aside: if Allah had willed, He could have guided all of you.

10. It is He who sends down rain from the sky: from it you drink, and out of it (grows) the vegetation on which you feed your cattle.

11. With it He produces for you corn, olives, date-palms, grapes and every kind of fruit: verily in this is a Sign for those who give thought.

12. He has made subject to you the Night and the Day; the Sun and the Moon; and the Stars are in subjection by His Command: verily in this are Signs for men who are wise.

13. And the things on this earth which He has multiplied in varying colours (and qualities): verily in this is a sign for men who celebrate the praises of Allah (in gratitude).

14. It is He Who has made the sea subject,

---

6. Wa lakum feehaa jamaa-lun ḥeena tureeḥoona wa ḥeena tasraḥoon.

7. Wa taḥmilu asqaalakum ilaa baladil-lam takoonoo baaligheehi illaa bishiqqil anfus; inna Rabbakum la-Ra'oofur-Raḥeem.

8. Walkhayla wal-bighaala wal-ḥameera litarkaboohaa wa zeenah; wa yakhluqu maa laa ta'lamoon.

9. Wa 'alal-laahi qaṣdus-sabeeli wa minhaa jaaa'ir; wa law shaaa'a lahadaakum ajma'een.   (Section 1)

10. Huwal-lazeee anzala minas-samaaa'i maaa'al-lakum minhu sharaabuñw-wa minhu shajarun feehi tuseemoon.

11. Yumbitu lakum bihiz-zar'a wazzaytoona wanna-kheela wal-a'naaba wa min kullis-samaraat; inna fee zaalika la-Aayatal-liqawmiñy-yatafakkaroon.

12. Wa sakhkhara lakumul-layla wannahaara wash-shamsa walqamara wannujoomu musakhkharaatum-bi-amrih; inna fee zaalika la-Aayaatil-liqawmiñy-ya'qiloon.

13. Wa maa zara-a lakum fil-arḍi mukhtalifan alwaanuh; inna fee zaalika la-Aayatal-liqawmiñy-yazzakkaroon.

14. Wa Huwal-lazee sakh-kharal-baḥra

وَلَكُمْ فِيهَا جَمَالٌ حِينَ تُرِيحُونَ وَحِينَ تَسْرَحُونَ ۝

وَتَحْمِلُ أَثْقَالَكُمْ إِلَىٰ بَلَدٍ لَّمْ تَكُونُوا بَالِغِيهِ إِلَّا بِشِقِّ الْأَنْفُسِ ۚ إِنَّ رَبَّكُمْ لَرَءُوفٌ رَّحِيمٌ ۝

وَّالْخَيْلَ وَالْبِغَالَ وَالْحَمِيرَ لِتَرْكَبُوهَا وَزِينَةً ۚ وَيَخْلُقُ مَا لَا تَعْلَمُونَ ۝

وَعَلَى اللّٰهِ قَصْدُ السَّبِيلِ وَمِنْهَا جَآئِرٌ ۚ وَلَوْ شَآءَ لَهَدَاكُمْ أَجْمَعِينَ ۝

هُوَ الَّذِيٓ أَنْزَلَ مِنَ السَّمَآءِ مَآءً لَّكُمْ مِّنْهُ شَرَابٌ وَّمِنْهُ شَجَرٌ فِيهِ تُسِيمُونَ ۝

يُنْبِتُ لَكُمْ بِهِ الزَّرْعَ وَالزَّيْتُونَ وَالنَّخِيلَ وَالْأَعْنَابَ وَمِنْ كُلِّ الثَّمَرَاتِ ۗ إِنَّ فِي ذَٰلِكَ لَآيَةً لِّقَوْمٍ يَتَفَكَّرُونَ ۝

وَسَخَّرَ لَكُمُ الَّيْلَ وَالنَّهَارَ وَالشَّمْسَ وَالْقَمَرَ وَالنُّجُومُ مُسَخَّرَاتٌ بِأَمْرِهِ ۗ إِنَّ فِي ذَٰلِكَ لَآيَٰتٍ لِّقَوْمٍ يَعْقِلُونَ ۝

وَمَا ذَرَأَ لَكُمْ فِي الْأَرْضِ مُخْتَلِفًا أَلْوَانُهُ ۚ إِنَّ فِي ذَٰلِكَ لَآيَةً لِّقَوْمٍ يَذَّكَّرُونَ ۝

وَهُوَ الَّذِي سَخَّرَ الْبَحْرَ

that you may eat thereof flesh that is fresh and tender, and that you may extract therefrom ornaments to wear; and you see the ships therein that plough the waves, that you may seek (thus) of the bounty of Allah and that you may be grateful.

15. And He has set up on the earth mountains standing firm, lest it should shake with you; and rivers and roads; that you may guide yourselves;

16. And marks and sign-posts; and by the stars (men) guide themselves.

17. Is then He Who creates like one that creates not? Will you not receive admonition?

18. If you would count up the favours of Allah, never would you be able to number them: for Allah is Oft-Forgiving, Most Merciful.

19. And Allah knows what you conceal, and what you reveal.

20. Those whom they invoke besides Allah create nothing and are themselves created.

21. (They are things) dead, lifeless: nor do they know when they will be raised up.

22. Your God (Allah) is One God (Allah): as to those who do not believe in the Hereafter, their hearts refuse to know, and they are arrogant.

23. Undoubtedly Allah knows what they conceal, and what they reveal: verily He loves not the arrogant.

24. When it is said to them, "What is it that your Lord has

litaåkuloo minhu laḥman ṭariyyañw-wa tastakhrijoo minhu ḥilyatan talbasoonahaa wa taral-fulka mawaakhira feehi wa litabtaghoo min faḍlihee wa la'allakum tashkuroon.

15. Wa alqaa fil-arḍi rawaasi-ya an tameeda bikum wa anhaarañw-wa subulal-la'alla-kum tahtadoon.

16. Wa 'alaamaat; wa bin-najmi hum yahtadoon.

17. Afamañy-yakhluqu kamal-laa yakhluq; afalaa tazak-karoon.

18. Wa in ta'uddoo ni'matal-laahi laa tuḥsoohaa; innal-laaha la-Ghafoorur-Raḥeem.

19. Wallaahu ya'lamu maa tusirroona wa maa tu'linoon.

20. Wallazeena yad'oona min doonil-laahi laa yakhluqoona shay'añw-wa hum yukhlaqoon.

21. Amwaatun ghayru aḥ-yaaa'iñw-wa maa yash'uroona ayyaana yub'asoon. **(Section 2)**

22. Ilaahukum Ilaahuñw-Waa-ḥid; fallazeena laa yu'minoona bil-Aakhirati quloobuhum-munkiratuñw-wa hum-mustak-biroon.

23. Laa jarama annal-laaha ya'lamu maa yusirroona wa maa yu'linoon; innahoo laa yuḥibbul-mustakbireen.

24. Wa izaa qeela lahum-maazaaa anzala

revealed?" they say, "Tales of the ancients!"

25. Let them bear, on the Day of Judgment, their own burdens in full, and also (something) of the burdens of those without knowledge, whom they misled. Alas, how grievous the burdens they will bear!

26. Those before them did also plot (against Allah's Way): but Allah took their structures from their foundations, and the roof fell down on them from above; and the Wrath seized them from directions they did not perceive.

27. Then, on the Day of Judgment, He will cover them with shame, and say: "Where are My 'partners' concerning whom you used to dispute (with the godly)?" Those endued with knowledge will say: "This Day, indeed, are the Unbelievers covered with Shame and Misery,-

28. "(Namely) those whose lives the angels take in a state of wrong-doing to their own souls." Then would they offer submission (with the pretence), "We did no evil (knowingly)." (The angels will reply), "Nay, but verily Allah knows all that you did;

29. "So enter the gates of Hell, to dwell therein. Thus evil indeed is the abode of the arrogant."

30. To the righteous (when) it is said, "What is it that your Lord has revealed?" they say, "All that is good." To those who do good, there is good in this world, and the Home of the Hereafter is even better and excellent indeed is the Home of the righteous,-

31. Gardens of Eternity which they will enter: beneath them

Rabbukum qaaloo asaaṭeerul-awwaleen.

25. Liyaḥmilooo awzaarahum kaamilatañy-Yawmal-Qiyaa-mati wa min awzaaril-lazeena yuḍilloonahum bighayri 'ilm; alaa saaa'a maa yaziroon.

(Section 3)

26. Qad makaral-lazeena min qablihim fa-atal-laahu bunyaa-nahum-minal-qawaa'idi fa-kharra 'alayhimus-saqfu min fawqihim wa ataahumul-'azaa-bu min ḥaysu laa yash'uroon.

27. Summa Yawmal-Qiyaa-mati yukhzeehim wa yaqoolu ayna shurakaaa'iyal-lazeena kuntum tushaaaqqoona feehim; qaalal-lazeena ootul-'ilma innal-khizyal-Yawma was-sooo'a 'alal-kaafireen.

28. Allazeena tatawaf-faahu-mul-malaaa'ikatu zaalimee anfusihim fa-alqawus-salama maa kunnaa na'malu min sooo'; balaaa innal-laaha 'aleemum bimaa kuntum ta'maloon.

29. Fadkhulooo abwaaba Jahannama khaalideena feehaa falabi'sa maswal-mutakab-bireen.

30. Wa qeela lillazeenat-taqaw maazaaa anzala Rabbu-kum; qaaloo khayraa; lillazeena aḥsanoo fee haazihid-dunyaa ḥasanah; wa la-Daarul-Aakhi-rati khayr; wa lani'ma daarul-muttaqeen.

31. Jannaatu 'Adniñy-yadkhu-loonahaa tajree

رَبُّكُمْ ۙ قَالُوْٓا اَسَاطِيْرُ الْاَوَّلِيْنَ ۞

لِيَحْمِلُوْٓا اَوْزَارَهُمْ كَامِلَةً يَّوْمَ الْقِيٰمَةِ ۙ وَمِنْ اَوْزَارِ الَّذِيْنَ يُضِلُّوْنَهُمْ بِغَيْرِ عِلْمٍ ؕ اَلَا سَآءَ مَا يَزِرُوْنَ ۞

قَدْ مَكَرَ الَّذِيْنَ مِنْ قَبْلِهِمْ فَاَتَى اللّٰهُ بُنْيَانَهُمْ مِّنَ الْقَوَاعِدِ فَخَرَّ عَلَيْهِمُ السَّقْفُ مِنْ فَوْقِهِمْ وَاَتٰىهُمُ الْعَذَابُ مِنْ حَيْثُ لَا يَشْعُرُوْنَ ۞

ثُمَّ يَوْمَ الْقِيٰمَةِ يُخْزِيْهِمْ وَيَقُوْلُ اَيْنَ شُرَكَآءِۦَ الَّذِيْنَ كُنْتُمْ تُشَآقُّوْنَ فِيْهِمْ ؕ قَالَ الَّذِيْنَ اُوْتُوا الْعِلْمَ اِنَّ الْخِزْيَ الْيَوْمَ وَالسُّوْٓءَ عَلَى الْكٰفِرِيْنَ ۞

الَّذِيْنَ تَتَوَفّٰىهُمُ الْمَلٰٓئِكَةُ ظَالِمِيْٓ اَنْفُسِهِمْ ۪ فَاَلْقَوُا السَّلَمَ مَا كُنَّا نَعْمَلُ مِنْ سُوْٓءٍ ؕ بَلٰٓى اِنَّ اللّٰهَ عَلِيْمٌ بِمَا كُنْتُمْ تَعْمَلُوْنَ ۞

فَادْخُلُوْٓا اَبْوَابَ جَهَنَّمَ خٰلِدِيْنَ فِيْهَا ؕ فَلَبِئْسَ مَثْوَى الْمُتَكَبِّرِيْنَ ۞

وَقِيْلَ لِلَّذِيْنَ اتَّقَوْا مَاذَآ اَنْزَلَ رَبُّكُمْ ؕ قَالُوْا خَيْرًا ؕ لِلَّذِيْنَ اَحْسَنُوْا فِيْ هٰذِهِ الدُّنْيَا حَسَنَةٌ ؕ وَلَدَارُ الْاٰخِرَةِ خَيْرٌ ؕ وَلَنِعْمَ دَارُ الْمُتَّقِيْنَ ۞

جَنّٰتُ عَدْنٍ يَّدْخُلُوْنَهَا تَجْرِيْ

flow (pleasant) rivers: they will have therein all that they wish: thus Allah rewards the righteous,-

32. (Namely) those whose lives the angels take in a state of purity, saying (to them), "Peace be on you; you enter the Garden, because of (the good) which you did (in the world)."

33. Do the (ungodly) wait until the angels come to them, or there comes the Command of your Lord (for their doom)? So did those who went before them. But Allah did not wrong them: nay, they wronged their own souls.

34. But the evil results of their deeds overtook them, and that very (Wrath) at which they had scoffed hemmed them in.

35. The worshippers of false gods say: "If Allah had so willed, we should not have worshipped aught but Him - neither we nor our fathers,- nor should we have prescribed prohibitions other than His." So did those who went before them. But what is the mission of Messengers but to preach the Clear Message?

36. For We assuredly sent amongst every People a Messenger, (with the Command), "Serve Allah, and eschew Evil": of the People were some whom Allah guided, and some on whom error became inevitably (established). So travel through the earth, and see what was the end of those who denied (the Truth).

37. If you are anxious for their guidance, yet Allah

min taḥtihal-anhaaru lahum feehaa maa yashaaa'oon; kazaalika yajzil-laahul-mut-taqeen.

32. Allazeena taṭawaf-faahu-mul-malaaa'ikatu ṭayyibeena yaqooloona salaamun 'alay-kumud-khulul-Jannata bimaa kuntum ta'maloon.

33. Hal yanẓuroona illaaa an taâ-tiyahumul-malaaa'ikatu aw yaâtiya amru Rabbik; kazaalika fa'alal-lazeena min qablihim; wa maa ẓalamahumul-laahu wa laakin kaanooo anfusahum yaẓlimoon.

34. Fa-aṣaabahum sayyi-aatu maa 'amiloo wa ḥaaqa bihim maa kaanoo bihee yastahzi'oon.
(Section 4)

35. Wa qaalal-lazeena ashra-koo law shaaa'al-laahu maa 'abadnaa min doonihee min shay'in-naḥnu wa laaa aabaaa-'unaa wa laa ḥarramnaa min doonihee min shay'; kazaalika fa'alal-lazeena min qablihim fahal 'alar-Rusuli illal-balaa-ghul-mubeen.

36. Wa laqad ba'asnaa fee kulli ummatir-Rasoolan ani'budul-laaha wajtanibuṭ-Ṭaaghoota faminhum man hadal-laahu wa minhum-man ḥaqqat 'alayhiḍ-ḍalaalah; faseeroo fil-arḍi fanẓuroo kayfa kaana 'aaqi-batul-mukazzibeen.

37. In taḥriṣ 'alaa hudaahum fa-innal-laaha

مِنْ تَحْتِهَا الْأَنْهَٰرُ لَهُمْ فِيهَا مَا يَشَآءُوْنَ ۚ كَذَٰلِكَ يَجْزِى اللّٰهُ الْمُتَّقِيْنَ ۞

الَّذِيْنَ تَتَوَفَّٰهُمُ الْمَلَٰٓئِكَةُ طَيِّبِيْنَ ۙ يَقُوْلُوْنَ سَلَٰمٌ عَلَيْكُمُ ۙ ادْخُلُوا الْجَنَّةَ بِمَا كُنْتُمْ تَعْمَلُوْنَ ۞

هَلْ يَنْظُرُوْنَ إِلَّآ أَنْ تَأْتِيَهُمُ الْمَلَٰٓئِكَةُ أَوْ يَأْتِيَ أَمْرُ رَبِّكَ ۚ كَذَٰلِكَ فَعَلَ الَّذِيْنَ مِنْ قَبْلِهِمْ ۚ وَمَا ظَلَمَهُمُ اللّٰهُ وَلَٰكِنْ كَانُوْۤا أَنْفُسَهُمْ يَظْلِمُوْنَ ۞

فَأَصَابَهُمْ سَيِّاٰتُ مَا عَمِلُوْا وَحَاقَ بِهِمْ مَّا كَانُوْا بِهٖ يَسْتَهْزِءُوْنَ ۞

وَقَالَ الَّذِيْنَ أَشْرَكُوْا لَوْ شَآءَ اللّٰهُ مَا عَبَدْنَا مِنْ دُوْنِهٖ مِنْ شَيْءٍ نَّحْنُ وَلَاۤ اٰبَآؤُنَا وَلَا حَرَّمْنَا مِنْ دُوْنِهٖ مِنْ شَيْءٍ ۚ كَذَٰلِكَ فَعَلَ الَّذِيْنَ مِنْ قَبْلِهِمْ ۚ فَهَلْ عَلَى الرُّسُلِ إِلَّا الْبَلَٰغُ الْمُبِيْنُ ۞

وَلَقَدْ بَعَثْنَا فِيْ كُلِّ أُمَّةٍ رَّسُوْلًا أَنِ اعْبُدُوا اللّٰهَ وَاجْتَنِبُوا الطَّاغُوْتَ ۚ فَمِنْهُمْ مَّنْ هَدَى اللّٰهُ وَمِنْهُمْ مَّنْ حَقَّتْ عَلَيْهِ الضَّلَٰلَةُ ۚ فَسِيْرُوْا فِي الْأَرْضِ فَانْظُرُوْا كَيْفَ كَانَ عَاقِبَةُ الْمُكَذِّبِيْنَ ۞

إِنْ تَحْرِصْ عَلَى هُدَٰهُمْ فَإِنَّ اللّٰهَ

does not guid (any) such as He leaves to stray, and there is none to help them.

38. They swear their strongest oaths by Allah, that Allah will not raise up those who die: nay, but it is a promise (binding) on Him in truth: but most among mankind do not realise it not.

39. (They must be raised up), in order that He may manifest to them the truth of that wherein they differ, and that the rejecters of Truth may realise that they had indeed (surrendered to) Falsehood.

40. For to anything which We have willed, We but say the Word, "Be", and it is.

41. To those who leave their homes in the cause of Allah, after suffering oppression,- We will assuredly give a goodly home in this world; but truly the reward of the Hereafter will be greater. If they only realised (this)!

42. (They are) those who persevere in patience, and put their trust on their Lord.

43. And before you also the Messengers We sent were but men, to whom We granted inspiration: if you do not realise this, ask of those who possess the Message.

44. (We sent them) with Clear Signs and Books of dark prophesies; and We have sent down to you (also) the Message; that you may explain clearly to men what is sent for them, and that they may give thought.

45. Do then those who devise evil (plots) feel secure that Allah will not cause the earth to swallow them up, or that the Wrath will not seize them from directions they little perceive?-

laa yahdee mañy-yuḍillu wa maa lahum-min-naaṣireen.

38. Wa aqsamoo billaahi jahda aymaanihim laa yab'aṣul-laahu mañy-yamoot; balaa wa'dan 'alayhi ḥaqqañw-wa laakinna akṣaran-naasi laa ya'lamoon.

39. Liyubayyina lahumul-lazee yakhtalifoona feehi wa liya'lamal-lazeena kafarooo annahum kaanoo kaaẓibeen.

40. Innamaa qawlunaa lisha-y'in iẓaa aradnaahu an-naqoola lahoo kun fa-yakoon. (Section 5)

41. Wallazeena haajaroo fil-laahi mim-ba'di maa ẓulimoo lanubawwi'annahum fid-dunyaa ḥasanatañw wa la-ajrul-Aakhirati akbar; law kaanoo ya'lamoon.

42. Allazeena ṣabaroo wa 'alaa Rabbihim yatawak-kaloon.

43. Wa maaa arsalnaa min qablika illaa rijaalan-nooḥeee ilayhim; fas'alooo ahlaz-zikri in kuntum laa ta'lamoon.

44. Bilbayyinaati waz-Zubur; wa anzalnaaa ilaykaz-Zikra litubayyina linnaasi maa nuzzila ilayhim wa la'allahum yatafakkaroon.

45. Afa-aminal-lazeena ma-karus-sayyi-aati añy-yakhsifal-laahu bihimul-arḍa aw yaå-tiyahumul-'azaabu min ḥayṡu laa yash'uroon.

46. Or that He may not call them to account in the midst of their goings to and fro, without a chance of their frustrating Him?

47. Or that He may not call them to account by a process of slow wastage - for your Lord is indeed full of kindness and mercy.

48. Do they not look at Allah's creation, (even) among (inanimate) things,- how their (very) shadows turn round, from the right and the left, prostrating themselves to Allah, and that in the humblest manner?

49. And to Allah does obeisance all that is in the heavens and on earth, whether moving (living) creatures or the angels: for none are arrogant (before their Lord).

50. They all revere their Lord, high above them, and they do all that they are commanded.

51. Allah has said: "Take not (for worship) two gods: for He is just One God (Allah): then fear Me (and Me alone)."

52. To Him belongs whatever is in the heavens and on earth, and to Him is duty due always: then will you fear other than Allah?

53. And you have no good thing but is from Allah: and moreover, when you are touched by distress, to Him you cry with groans;

54. Yet, when He removes the distress from you, behold! some of you turn to other gods to join with their Lord-

55. (As if) to show their ingratitude for the favours we have bestowed on them! then enjoy (your brief day): but soon will you know (your folly)!

56. And they (even) assign, to things they do not know, a portion out of that which We have bestowed for their sustenance! By Allah, you shall certainly be called to account for your false inventions.

(Bow Down)

---

46. Aw yaåkhuzahum fee taqallubihim famaa hum bi-mu'jizeen.

47. Aw yaåkhuzahum 'alaa takhawwuf; fa-inna Rabba-kum la-Ra'oofur-Raheem.

48. Awa lam yaraw ilaa maa khalaqal-laahu min shay'iñy-yatafayya'u zilaaluhoo 'anil-yameeni washshamaaa'ili sujjadal-lillaahi wa hum daa-khiroon.

49. Wa lillaahi yasjudu maa fis-samaawaati wa maa fil-ardi min daaabbatiñw-walma-laaa'ikatu wa hum laa yastak-biroon.

50. Yakhaafoona Rabbahum min fawqihim wa yaf'aloona maa yu'maroon. 🔼   (Section 6)

51. Wa qaalal-laahu laa tatta-khizooo ilaahaynis-nayni innamaa Huwa Ilaahuñw-Waa-hid; fa-iyyaaya farhaboon.

52. Wa lahoo maa fis-samaa-waati wal-ardi wa lahud-deenu waasibaa; afaghayral-laahi tattaqoon.

53. Wa maa bikum-min ni'matin faminal-laahi summa izaa massakumud-durru fa-ilayhi taj'aroon.

54. Summa izaa kashafad-durra 'ankum izaa fareequm-minkum bi-Rabbihim yushri-koon.

55. Liyakfuroo bimaa aatay-naahum; fatamatta'oo, fasawfa ta'lamoon.

56. Wa yaj'aloona limaa laa ya'lamoona naseebam-mim-maa razaqnaahum; tallaahi latus'alunna 'ammaa kuntum taftaroon.

57. And they assign daughters for Allah! - Glory be to Him! - and for themselves (sons,- the issue) they desire!

58. When news is brought to one of them, of (the birth of) a female (child), his face darkens, and he is filled with inward grief!

59. With shame he hides himself from his people, because of the bad news he has had! Shall he retain it on (sufferance and) contempt, or bury it in the dust? Ah! what an evil (choice) they decide on?

60. To those who believe not in the Hereafter, applies the similitude of evil: to Allah applies the highest similitude: for He is the Exalted in Power, full of Wisdom.

61. If Allah were to punish men for their wrong-doing, He would not leave, on the (earth), a single living creature: but He gives them respite for a stated Term: when their Term expires, they would not be able to delay (the punishment) for a single hour, just as they would not be able to advance it (for a single hour).

62. They attribute to Allah what they hate (for themselves), and their tongues assert the falsehood that all good things are for themselves: without doubt for them is the Fire, and they will be the first to be hastened on into it!

63. By Allah, We (also) sent (Our Messengers) to Peoples before you but Satan made, (to the wicked), their own acts seem alluring: He is also their patron today, but they shall have a most grievous Penalty.

64. And We sent down the Book to you for the express purpose, that you should make clear to them those things in which they differ,

57. Wa yaj'aloona lillaahil-banaati Subḥaanahoo wa lahum maa yashtahoon.

58. Wa izaa bushshira aḥadu-hum bil-unsaa ẓalla wajhuhoo muswaddañw-wa huwa kaẓeem.

59. Yatawaaraa minal-qawmi min sooo'i maa bushshira bih; a-yumsikuhoo 'alaa hoonin am yadussuhoo fit-turaab; alaa saaa'a maa yaḥkumoon.

60. Lillazeena laa yu'mi-noona bil-Aakhirati maṣalus-saw'i wa lillaahil-maṣalul-a'laa; wa Huwal-'Azeezul-Ḥakeem.   **(Section 7)**

61. Wa law yu'aakhizul-laahun-naasa biẓulmihim-maa taraka 'alayhaa min daaabba-tiñw-wa laakiñy-yu'akhkhiru-hum ilaaa ajalim-musamman fa-izaa jaaa'a ajaluhum laa yastaåkhiroona saa'atañw-wa laa yastaqdimoon.

62. Wa yaj'aloona lillaahi maa yakrahoona wa taṣifu alsinatuhumul-kaziba anna lahumul-ḥusnaa laa jarama anna lahumun-Naara wa annahum-mufraṭoon.

63. Tallaahi laqad arsalnaaa ilaaa umamim-min qablika fazayyana lahumush-Shay-ṭaanu a'maalahum fahuwa waliyyuhumul-yawma wa lahum 'azaabun aleem.

64. Wa maaa anzalnaa 'alay-kal-Kitaaba illaa litubayyina lahumul-lazikh-talafoo feehi

and that it should be a guide and a mercy to those who believe.

65. And Allah sends down rain from the skies, and gives therewith life to the earth after its death: verily in this is a Sign for those who listen.

66. And verily in cattle (too) will you find an instructive sign. From what is within their bodies between excretions and blood, We produce, for your drink, milk, pure and agreeable to those who drink it.

67. And from the fruit of the date-palm and the vine, you get out wholesome drink and food; behold, in this also is a Sign for those who are wise.

68. And your Lord taught the Bee to build its cells in hills, on trees, and in (men's) habitations;

69. Then to eat of all the produce (of the earth), and find with skill the spacious paths of its Lord: there issues from within their bodies a drink of varying colors, wherein is healing for men: verily in this is a Sign for those who give thought.

70. It is Allah who creates you and takes your souls at death; and of you there are some who are sent back to a feeble age, so that they know nothing after having known (much): for Allah is All-Knowing, All-Powerful.

71. Allah has bestowed His gifts of sustenance more freely

---

wa hudañw-wa raḥmatal-liqawmiñy-yu'minoon.

65. Wallaahu anzala minas-samaaa'i maaa'an fa-aḥyaa bihil-arḍa ba'da mawtihaa; inna fee zaalika la-Aayatal-liqaw-miñy-yasma'oon. (Section 8)

66. Wa inna lakum fil-an'aami la'ibrah; nusqeekum mimmaa fee buṭoonihee mim bayni farsiñw-wa damil-labanan khaaliṣan saaa'ighal-lish-shaaribeen.

67. Wa min samaraatin-nakheeli wal-a'naabi tattakhi-zoona minhu sakarañw-wa riz-qan ḥasanaa; inna fee zaalika la-Aayatal-liqawmiñy-ya'qiloon.

68. Wa awḥaa Rabbuka ilannaḥli anit-takhizee minal-jibaali buyootañw-wa minash-shajari wa mimmaa ya'rishoon.

69. Summa kulee min kullis-samaraati faslukee subula Rabbiki zululaa; yakhruju mim buṭoonihaa sharaabum-mukh-talifun alwaanuhoo feehi shifaaa'ul-linnaas, inna fee zaalika la-Aayatal-liqawmiñy-yatafakkaroon.

70. Wallaahu khalaqakum summa yatawaffaakum; wa minkum mañy-yuraddu ilaaa arzalil-'umuri likay laa ya'lama ba'da 'ilmin shay'aa; innal-laaha 'Aleemun Qadeer. (Section 9)

71. Wallaahu faḍḍala ba'ḍakum 'alaa ba'ḍin

on some of you than on others:
those more favored are not
going to throw back their gifts to
those whom their right hands
possess, so as to be equal in that
respect. Will they then deny the
favors of Allah?

72. And Allah has made for
you mates (and companions) of
your own nature, and made for
you, out of them, sons and
daughters and grandchildren,
and provided for you sustenance
of the best: will they then
believe in vain things, and be
ungrateful for Allah's favors?-

73. And worship others than
Allah,- such as have no power of
providing them, for sustenance,
with anything in heavens or
earth, and cannot possibly have
such power?

74. Do not invent similitudes
for Allah: for Allah knows, and
you do not know.

75. Allah sets forth the
Parable (of two men: one) a
slave under the dominion of
another; he has no power of any
sort; and (the other) a man on
whom We have bestowed
goodly favors from Ourselves,
and he spends thereof (freely),
privately and publicly: are the
two equal? (By no means;)
praise be to Allah. But most of
them understand not.

76. Allah sets forth (another)
Parable of two men: one of them
dumb, with no power of any
sort; a wearisome burden is he
to his master; whichever way he
directs him, he brings no good:
is such a man equal with one
who commands Justice, and is
on a Straight Way?

77. To Allah belongs the
Mystery of the heavens and the
Earth.

fir-rizq; famal-lazeena fuḍḍiloo
biraaaddee rizqihim 'alaa maa
malakat aymaanuhum fahum
feehi sawaaa'; afabini'matil-
laahi yajḥadoon.

72. Wallaahu ja'ala lakum
min anfusikum azwaajañw-wa
ja'ala lakum min azwaajikum
baneena wa ḥafadatañw-wa
razaqakum minaṭ-ṭayyibaat;
afabil-baaṭili yu'minoona wa
bini'matil-laahi hum yakfuroon.

73. Wa ya'budoona min
doonil-laahi maa laa yamliku
lahum rizqam-minas-samaa-
waati wal-arḍi shay'añw-wa laa
yastaṭee'oon.

74. Falaa taḍriboo lillaahil-
amṣaal; innal-laaha ya'lamu wa
antum laa ta'lamoon.

75. Ḍarabal-laahu maṣalan
'abdam-mamlookal-laa yaqdiru
'alaa shay'iñw-wa marraza-
qnaahu minnaa rizqan ḥasanan
fahuwa yunfiqu minhu sirrañw-
wa jahra; hal yasta-woon;
alḥamdu lillaah; bal akṣaruhum
laa ya'lamoon.

76. Wa ḍarabal-laahu maṣa-
lar-rajulayni aḥaduhumaaa
abkamu laa yaqdiru 'alaa
shay'iñw-wa huwa kallun 'alaa
mawlaahu aynamaa yuwajjihhu
laa yaåti bikhayrin hal yastawee
huwa wa mañy-yaåmuru bil-
'adli wa huwa 'alaa Ṣiraaṭim-
Mustaqeem.   (Section 10)

77. Wa lillaahi ghaybus-
samaawaati wal-arḍ;

فِي الرِّزْقِ ۚ فَمَا الَّذِينَ فُضِّلُوا
بِرَآدِّي رِزْقِهِمْ عَلٰى مَا مَلَكَتْ
اَيْمَانُهُمْ فَهُمْ فِيهِ سَوَآءٌ ۚ
اَفَبِنِعْمَةِ اللّٰهِ يَجْحَدُوْنَ ۞
وَاللّٰهُ جَعَلَ لَكُمْ مِّنْ اَنْفُسِكُمْ
اَزْوَاجًا وَّجَعَلَ لَكُمْ مِّنْ اَزْوَاجِكُمْ
بَنِيْنَ وَحَفَدَةً وَّرَزَقَكُمْ مِّنَ
الطَّيِّبٰتِ ۚ اَفَبِالْبَاطِلِ يُؤْمِنُوْنَ
وَبِنِعْمَتِ اللّٰهِ هُمْ يَكْفُرُوْنَ ۞
وَيَعْبُدُوْنَ مِنْ دُوْنِ اللّٰهِ مَا لَا
يَمْلِكُ لَهُمْ رِزْقًا مِّنَ السَّمٰوٰتِ
وَالْاَرْضِ شَيْئًا وَّلَا يَسْتَطِيْعُوْنَ ۞
فَلَا تَضْرِبُوْا لِلّٰهِ الْاَمْثَالَ ۚ اِنَّ
اللّٰهَ يَعْلَمُ وَاَنْتُمْ لَا تَعْلَمُوْنَ ۞
ضَرَبَ اللّٰهُ مَثَلًا عَبْدًا مَّمْلُوْكًا
لَّا يَقْدِرُ عَلٰى شَيْءٍ وَّمَنْ رَّزَقْنٰهُ
مِنَّا رِزْقًا حَسَنًا فَهُوَ يُنْفِقُ مِنْهُ
سِرًّا وَّجَهْرًا ۚ هَلْ يَسْتَوٗنَ ۚ اَلْحَمْدُ
لِلّٰهِ ۚ بَلْ اَكْثَرُهُمْ لَا يَعْلَمُوْنَ ۞
وَضَرَبَ اللّٰهُ مَثَلًا رَّجُلَيْنِ
اَحَدُهُمَا اَبْكَمُ لَا يَقْدِرُ عَلٰى شَيْءٍ
وَّهُوَ كَلٌّ عَلٰى مَوْلٰهُ ۙ اَيْنَمَا
يُوَجِّهْهُّ لَا يَأْتِ بِخَيْرٍ ۖ هَلْ
يَسْتَوِيْ هُوَ ۙ وَمَنْ يَّأْمُرُ بِالْعَدْلِ ۙ
وَهُوَ عَلٰى صِرَاطٍ مُّسْتَقِيْمٍ ۞
وَلِلّٰهِ غَيْبُ السَّمٰوٰتِ وَالْاَرْضِ ۚ

And the Decision of the Hour (of Judgment) is as the twinkling of an eye, or even quicker: for Allah has power over all things.

wa maaa amrus-Saa'ati illaa kalamḥil-baṣari aw huwa aqrab; innal-laaha 'alaa kulli shay'in Qadeer.

وَمَا أَمْرُ السَّاعَةِ إِلَّا كَلَمْحِ الْبَصَرِ أَوْ هُوَ أَقْرَبُ ۚ إِنَّ اللَّهَ عَلَىٰ كُلِّ شَيْءٍ قَدِيرٌ ۝

78. It is He Who brought you forth from the wombs of your mothers when you knew nothing; and He gave you hearing and sight and intelligence and affections: that you may give thanks (to Allah).

78. Wallaahu akhrajakum mim buṭooni ummahaatikum laa ta'lamoona shay'añw-wa ja'ala lakumus-sam'a wal-abṣaara wal-af'idata la'allakum tashkuroon.

وَاللَّهُ أَخْرَجَكُمْ مِّنْ بُطُونِ أُمَّهَاتِكُمْ لَا تَعْلَمُونَ شَيْئًا وَّجَعَلَ لَكُمُ السَّمْعَ وَالْأَبْصَارَ وَالْأَفْئِدَةَ ۙ لَعَلَّكُمْ تَشْكُرُونَ ۝

79. Do they not look at the birds, held poised in the midst of (the air and) the sky? Nothing holds them up but (the power of) Allah. Verily in this are signs for those who believe.

79. Alam yaraw ilaṭ-ṭayri musakhkharaatin fee jawwis-samaaa'i maa yumsikuhunna illal-laah; inna fee zaalika la-Aayaatil-liqawmiñy-yu'minoon.

أَلَمْ يَرَوْا إِلَى الطَّيْرِ مُسَخَّرَاتٍ فِي جَوِّ السَّمَاءِ ۖ مَا يُمْسِكُهُنَّ إِلَّا اللَّهُ ۗ إِنَّ فِي ذَٰلِكَ لَآيَاتٍ لِّقَوْمٍ يُؤْمِنُونَ ۝

80. It is Allah Who made your habitations homes of rest and quiet for you; and made for you, out of the skins of animals, (tents for) dwellings, which you find so light (and handy) when you travel and when you stop (in your travels); and out of their wool, and their soft fibres (between wool and hair),and their hair, rich stuff and articles of convenience (to serve you) for a time.

80. Wallaahu ja'ala lakum mim buyootikum sakanañw-wa ja'ala lakum min juloodil an'aami buyootan tastakhif-foonahaa yawma ẓa'nikum wa yawma iqaamatikum wa min aṣwaafihaa wa awbaarihaa wa ash'aarihaaa aṣaaṣañw-wa mataa'an ilaa ḥeen.

وَاللَّهُ جَعَلَ لَكُمْ مِّنْ بُيُوتِكُمْ سَكَنًا وَّجَعَلَ لَكُمْ مِّنْ جُلُودِ الْأَنْعَامِ بُيُوتًا تَسْتَخِفُّونَهَا يَوْمَ ظَعْنِكُمْ وَيَوْمَ إِقَامَتِكُمْ ۙ وَمِنْ أَصْوَافِهَا وَأَوْبَارِهَا وَأَشْعَارِهَا أَثَاثًا وَّمَتَاعًا إِلَىٰ حِينٍ ۝

81. It is Allah Who made out of the things He created, some things to give you shade; of the hills He made some for your shelter; He made you garments to protect you from heat, and coats of mail to protect you from your (mutual) violence. Thus He completes His favours on you, that you may bow to His Will (in Islam).

81. Wallaahu ja'ala lakum mimmaa khalaqa ẓilaalañw-wa ja'ala lakum-minal-jibaali aknaanañw-wa ja'ala lakum saraabeela taqeekumul-ḥarra wa saraabeela taqeekum baa'sakum; kazaalika yutimmu ni'matahoo 'alaykum la'alla-kum tuslimoon.

وَاللَّهُ جَعَلَ لَكُمْ مِّمَّا خَلَقَ ظِلَالًا وَّجَعَلَ لَكُمْ مِّنَ الْجِبَالِ أَكْنَانًا وَّجَعَلَ لَكُمْ سَرَابِيلَ تَقِيكُمُ الْحَرَّ وَسَرَابِيلَ تَقِيكُمْ بَأْسَكُمْ ۚ كَذَٰلِكَ يُتِمُّ نِعْمَتَهُ عَلَيْكُمْ لَعَلَّكُمْ تُسْلِمُونَ ۝

82. But if they turn away, your duty is only to preach the clear Message.

82. Fa-in tawallaw fa-inna-maa 'alaykal-balaaghul-mubeen.

فَإِنْ تَوَلَّوْا فَإِنَّمَا عَلَيْكَ الْبَلَاغُ الْمُبِينُ ۝

83. They recognise the favours of Allah; then they deny them;

83. Ya'rifoona ni'matal-laahi summa yunkiroonahaa

يَعْرِفُونَ نِعْمَتَ اللَّهِ ثُمَّ يُنْكِرُونَهَا

and most of them are (creatures) ungrateful.

84. One Day We shall raise from all Peoples a Witness: then will no excuse be accepted from Unbelievers, nor will they receive any favors.

85. When the wrong-doers (actually) see the Penalty, then will it in no way be mitigated, nor will they then receive respite.

86. When those who gave partners to Allah will see their "partners", they will say: "Our Lord! these are our 'partners,' those whom we used to invoke besides you." But they will throw back their word at them (and say): "Indeed you are liars!"

87. That Day they shall (openly) show (their) submission to Allah; and all their inventions shall leave them in the lurch.

88. Those who reject Allah and hinder (men) from the Path of Allah - for them will We add Penalty to Penalty; for that they used to spread mischief.

89. One day We shall raise from all Peoples a witness against them, from amongst themselves: and We shall bring you as a witness against these (your people): and We have sent down to you the Book explaining all things, a Guide, a Mercy, and Glad Tidings to Muslims.

90. Allah commands justice, the doing of good, and liberality to kith and kin, and He forbids all shameful deeds, and injustice and rebellion: He instructs you, that you may receive admonition.

91. Fulfil the Covenant of Allah when you have entered into

---

wa aksaruhumul-kaafiroon. **(Section 11)**

84. Wa yawma nab'asu min kulli ummatin shaheedan summa laa yu'zanu lillazeena kafaroo wa laa hum yusta'taboon.

85. Wa izaa ra-al-lazeena zalamul-'azaaba falaa yukhaffafu 'anhum wa laa hum yunzaroon.

86. Wa izaa ra-al-lazeena ashrakoo shurakaaa'ahum qaaloo Rabbanaa haaa'ulaaa'i shurakaaa'unal-lazeena kunnaa nad'oo min doonika fa-alqaw ilayhimul-qawla innakum lakaaziboon.

87. Wa alqaw ilal-laahi yawma'izinis-salama wa dalla 'anhum-maa kaanoo yaftaroon.

88. Allazeena kafaroo wa saddoo 'an sabeelil-laahi zidnaahum 'azaaban fawqal-'azaabi bimaa kaanoo yufsidoon.

89. Wa yawma nab'asu fee kulli ummatin shaheedan 'alayhim-min anfusihim wa ji'naa bika shaheedan 'alaa haaa'ulaaa'; wa nazzalnaa 'alaykal-Kitaaba tibyaanal-likulli shay'iñw-wa hudañw-wa rahmatañw-wa bushraa lilmuslimeen. **(Section 12)**

90. Innal-laaha yaamuru bil-'adli wal-ihsaani wa eetaaa'i zil-qurbaa wa yanhaa 'anil-fahshaaa'i walmunkari walbagh-y; ya'izukum la'allakum tazakkaroon.

91. Wa awfoo bi-Ahdil-laahi izaa 'aahattum wa laa

it, and break not your oaths after you have confirmed them; indeed you have made Allah your surety; for Allah knows all that you do.

92. And be not like a woman who breaks into untwisted strands the yarn which she has spun, after it has become strong. Nor take your oaths to practise deception between yourselves, lest one party should be more numerous than another: for Allah will test you by this; and on the Day of Judgment He will certainly make clear to you (the truth of) that wherein you disagree.

93. If Allah so willed, He could make you all one People: but He leaves straying whom He pleases, and He guides whom He pleases: but you shall certainly be called to account for all your actions.

94. And do not take your oaths, to practise deception between yourselves, with the result that someone's foot may slip after it was firmly planted, and you may have to taste the evil (consequences) of having hindered (men) from the Path of Allah, and a mighty Wrath descend on you.

95. Nor sell the Covenant of Allah for a miserable price: for with Allah is (a prize) far better for you, if you only knew.

96. What is with you must vanish: what is with Allah will endure. And We will certainly bestow, on those who patiently persevere, their reward according to the best of their actions.

97. Whoever works righteousness, man or woman, and has Faith, verily, to him will We give a new Life, a life that is good and pure and We will bestow on such

tanquḍul-aymaana ba‘da tawkeedihaa wa qad ja‘altumul-laaha ‘alaykum kafeelaa; innallaaha ya‘lamu maa taf‘aloon.

92. Wa laa takoonoo kallatee naqaḍat ghazlahaa mim ba‘di quwwatin ankaaṣaa; tattakhi-zoona aymaanakum dakhalam baynakum an takoona ummatun hiya arbaa min ummah; innamaa yablookumul-laahu bih; wa la-yubayyinanna lakum Yawmal-Qiyaamati maa kuntum feehi takhtalifoon.

93. Wa law shaaa’al-laahu laja‘alakum ummataňw-waahi-dataňw-wa laakiňy-yuḍillu maňy-yashaaa’u wa yahdee maňy-yashaaa’; wa latus’alunna ‘ammaa kuntum ta‘maloon.

94. Wa laa tattakhizooo aymaanakum dakhalam-bayna-kum fatazilla qadamum-ba‘da subootihaa wa tazooqus-sooo’a bimaa ṣadattum ‘an sabeelil-laahi wa lakum ‘azaabun ‘azeem.

95. Wa laa tashtaroo bi-‘Ahdil-laahi ṣamanan qaleelaa; inna-maa ‘indal-laahi huwa khayrul-lakum in kuntum ta‘lamoon.

96. Maa ‘indakum yanfadu wa maa ‘indal-laahi baaq; wa lanajziyannal-lazeena ṣabarooo ajrahum bi-aḥsani maa kaanoo ya‘maloon.

97. Man ‘amila saaliḥam-min zakarin aw unṣaa wa huwa mu’minun falanuḥyiyannahoo ḥayaatan ṭayyibataňw wa lanajzi-yannahum

their reward according to the best of their actions.

98. When you read the Qur'an, seek Allah's protection from Satan the rejected one.

99. No authority has he over those who believe and put their trust in their Lord.

100. His authority is over those only, who take him as patron and who join partners with Allah.

101. When We substitute one revelation for another,- and Allah knows best what He reveals (in stages),- they say, "You are but a forger": but most of them do not understand not.

102. Say, the Holy Spirit has brought the revelation from your Lord in Truth, in order to strengthen those who believe, and as a Guide and Glad Tidings to Muslims.

103. We know indeed that they say, "It is a man that teaches him." The tongue of him they wickedly point to is notably foreign, while this is Arabic, pure and clear.

104. Those who do not believe in the Signs of Allah,- Allah will not guide them, and theirs will be a grievous Penalty.

105. It is those who do not believe in the Signs of Allah, that forge falsehood: it is they who lie!

106. Any one who, after accepting faith in Allah, utters Unbelief,- except under compulsion, his heart remaining firm

ajrahum bi-aḥsani maa kaanoo ya'maloon.

98. Fa-izaa qara-tal-Qur-aana fasta'iz billaahi minash-Shay-ṭaanir-rajeem.

99. Innahoo laysa lahoo sulṭaanun 'alal-lazeena aama-noo wa 'alaa Rabbihim yata-wakkaloon.

100. Innamaa sulṭaanuhoo 'alal-lazeena yatawallawnahoo wallazeena hum bihee mushri-koon. **(Section 13)**

101. Wa izaa baddalnaaa Aaya-tam-makaana Aayatiñw-wal-laahu a'lamu bimaa yunazzilu qaalooo innamaaa anta muftar; bal akṣaruhum laa ya'lamoon.

102. Qul nazzalahoo Rooḥul-Qudusi mir-Rabbika bilḥaqqi liyuṣabbital-lazeena aamanoo wa hudañw-wa bushraa lilmus-limeen.

103. Wa laqad na'lamu anna-hum yaqooloona innamaa yu'allimuhoo bashar; lisaanul-lazee yulḥidoona ilayhi a'ja-miyyuñw-wa haazaa lisaanun 'Arabiyyum-mubeen.

104. Innal-lazeena laa yu'mi-noona bi-Aayaatil-laahi laa yahdeehimul-laahu wa lahum 'azaabun aleem.

105. Innamaa yaftaril-kazibal-lazeena laa yu'minoona bi-Aayaatil-laahi wa ulaaa'ika humul-kaaziboon.

106. Man kafara billaahi mim ba'di eemaaniheee illaa man ukriha wa qalbuhoo muṭ-ma'innum-

in Faith - but such as open their breast to Unbelief, on them is Wrath from Allah, and for them will be a dreadful Penalty.

bil-eemaani wa laakim-man sharaḥa bilkufri ṣadran fa'alayhim ghaḍabum-minallaahi wa lahum 'aẓaabun 'aẓeem.

بِالْإِيْمَانِ وَلٰكِنْ مَّنْ شَرَحَ بِالْكُفْرِ صَدْرًا فَعَلَيْهِمْ غَضَبٌ مِّنَ اللّٰهِ ، وَلَهُمْ عَذَابٌ عَظِيْمٌ ۞

107. This because they love the life of this world better than the Hereafter: and Allah will not guide those who reject Faith.

107. Zaalika bi-annahumustaḥabbul-ḥayaatad-dunyaa 'alal-Aakhirati wa annal-laaha laa yahdil-qawmal-kaafireen.

ذٰلِكَ بِأَنَّهُمُ اسْتَحَبُّوا الْحَيٰوةَ الدُّنْيَا عَلَى الْاٰخِرَةِ ۙ وَأَنَّ اللّٰهَ لَا يَهْدِى الْقَوْمَ الْكٰفِرِيْنَ ۞

108. Those are they whose hearts, ears, and eyes Allah has sealed up, and they take no heed.

108. Ulaaa'ikal-lazeena ṭaba'al-laahu 'alaa quloobihim wa sam'ihim wa abṣaarihim wa ulaaa'ika humul-ghaafiloon.

أُولٰٓئِكَ الَّذِيْنَ طَبَعَ اللّٰهُ عَلٰى قُلُوْبِهِمْ وَسَمْعِهِمْ وَأَبْصَارِهِمْ ۚ وَأُولٰٓئِكَ هُمُ الْغٰفِلُوْنَ ۞

109. Without doubt, in the Hereafter they will perish.

109. Laa jarama annahum fil-Aakhirati humul-khaasiroon.

لَا جَرَمَ أَنَّهُمْ فِى الْاٰخِرَةِ هُمُ الْخٰسِرُوْنَ ۞

110. But verily your Lord,- to those who leave their homes after trials and persecutions,- and who thereafter strive and fight for the faith and patiently persevere,- your Lord, after all this is Oft-Forgiving, Most Merciful.

110. Summa inna Rabbaka lillazeena haajaroo mim ba'di maa futinoo summa jaahadoo wa ṣabarooo inna Rabbaka mim ba'dihaa la-Ghafoorur-Raḥeem.
(Section 14)

ثُمَّ إِنَّ رَبَّكَ لِلَّذِيْنَ هَاجَرُوْا مِنْۢ بَعْدِ مَا فُتِنُوْا ثُمَّ جٰهَدُوْا وَصَبَرُوْٓا ۙ إِنَّ رَبَّكَ مِنْۢ بَعْدِهَا لَغَفُوْرٌ رَّحِيْمٌ ۞

111. One Day every soul will come up struggling for itself, and every soul will be recompensed (fully) for all its actions, and none will be unjustly dealt with.

111. Yawma taatee kullu nafsin tujaadilu 'an-nafsihaa wa tuwaffaa kullu nafsim-maa 'amilat wa hum laa yuẓlamoon.

يَوْمَ تَأْتِيْ كُلُّ نَفْسٍ تُجَادِلُ عَنْ نَّفْسِهَا وَتُوَفّٰى كُلُّ نَفْسٍ مَّا عَمِلَتْ وَهُمْ لَا يُظْلَمُوْنَ ۞

112. Allah sets forth a Parable: a city enjoying security and quiet, abundantly supplied with sustenance from every place: Yet was it ungrateful for the favors of Allah: so Allah made it taste of hunger and terror (in extremes) (closing in on it) like a garment (from every side), because of the (evil) which (its people) wrought.

112. Wa ḍarabal-laahu maṣalan qaryatan kaanat aaminatammuṭma'innataṅy-yaateehaa rizquhaa raghadam-min kulli makaanin fakafarat bi-an'umillaahi fa-azaaqahal-laahu libaasal-joo'i walkhawfi bimaa kaanoo yaṣna'oon.

وَضَرَبَ اللّٰهُ مَثَلًا قَرْيَةً كَانَتْ اٰمِنَةً مُّطْمَئِنَّةً يَّأْتِيْهَا رِزْقُهَا رَغَدًا مِّنْ كُلِّ مَكَانٍ فَكَفَرَتْ بِأَنْعُمِ اللّٰهِ فَأَذَاقَهَا اللّٰهُ لِبَاسَ الْجُوْعِ وَالْخَوْفِ بِمَا كَانُوْا يَصْنَعُوْنَ ۞

113. And there came to them a Messenger from among themselves, but they falsely rejected him; so the Wrath seized them even in the midst of their iniquities.

113. Wa laqad jaaa'ahum Rasoolum-minhum fakazzaboohu fa-akhazahumul-'azaabu wa hum ẓaalimoon.

وَلَقَدْ جَاءَهُمْ رَسُوْلٌ مِّنْهُمْ فَكَذَّبُوْهُ فَأَخَذَهُمُ الْعَذَابُ وَهُمْ ظٰلِمُوْنَ ۞

114. So eat of the sustenance which Allah has provided for you, lawful and good; and be grateful for the favors of Allah, if it is He Whom you serve.

115. He has only forbidden you dead meat, and blood, and the flesh of swine, and any (food) over which the name of other than Allah has been invoked. But if one is forced by necessity, without wilful disobedience, nor transgressing due limits,- then Allah is Oft-Forgiving, Most Merciful.

116. But say not - for any false thing that your tongues may put forth,- "This is lawful, and this is forbidden," so as to ascribe false things to Allah. For those who ascribe false things to Allah, will never prosper.

117. (In such falsehood) is but a paltry profit; but they will have a most grievous Penalty.

118. To the Jews We prohibited such things as We have mentioned to you before: We did them no wrong, but they were used to doing wrong to themselves.

119. But verily your Lord,- to those who do wrong in ignorance, but who thereafter repent and make amends,- your Lord, after all this, is Oft-Forgiving, Most Merciful.

120. Abraham was indeed a model, devoutly obedient to Allah, (and) true in Faith, and he joined not gods with Allah:

121. He showed his gratitude for the favors of Allah, who chose him, and guided him

---

114. Fakuloo mimmaa razaqa-kumul-laahu ḥalaalan ṭayyi-bañw-washkuroo ni'matal-laahi in kuntum iyyaahu ta'budoon.

115. Innamaa ḥarrma 'alay-kumul-maytata waddama wa laḥmal-khinzeeri wa maaa uhilla lighayril-laahi bihee famaniḍ-ṭurra ghayra baaghiñw-wa laa 'aadin fa-innal-laaha-Ghafoo-rur-Raḥeem.

116. Wa laa taqooloo limaa taṣifu alsinatukumul-kaziba haazaa ḥalaaluñw-wa haazaa ḥaraamul-litaftaroo 'alal-laahil-kazib; innal-lazeena yaftaroona 'alal-laahil-kaziba laa yufli-ḥoon.

117. Mataa'un qaleeluñw-wa lahum 'azaabun aleem.

118. Wa 'alal-lazeena haadoo ḥarramnaa maa qaṣaṣnaa 'alayka min qablu wa maa zalamnaahum wa laakin kaanooo anfusahum yazlimoon.

119. Summa inna Rabbaka lillazeena 'amilus-sooo'a bijahaalatin summa taaboo mim ba'di zaalika wa aṣlaḥooo inna Rabbaka mim ba'dihaa la-Ghafoorur-Raḥeem. **(Section 15)**

120. Inna Ibraaheema kaana ummatan qaanital-lillaahi Ḥaneefañw-wa lam yaku minal-mushrikeen.

121. Shaakiral-li-an'umih; ijtabaahu wa hadaahu

to a Straight Way.

122. And We gave him Good in this world, and he will be, in the Hereafter, in the ranks of the Righteous.

123. So We have taught you the inspired (message), "Follow the ways of Abraham the True in Faith, and he joined not gods with Allah."

124. The Sabbath was only made (strict) for those who disagreed (as to its observance); But Allah will judge between them on the Day of Judgment, as to their differences.

125. Invite (all) to the Way of your Lord with wisdom and beautiful preaching; and argue with them in ways that are best and most gracious: for your Lord knows best, who have strayed from His Path, and who receive guidance.

126. And if you do catch them out, catch them out no worse than they catch you out: but if you show patience, that is indeed the best (course) for those who are patient.

127. And you be patient, for your patience is with the help from Allah; nor grieve over them: and do not distress yourself because of their plots.

128. For Allah is with those who restrain themselves, and those who do good.

17. The Children of Israel
In the name of Allah, Most Gracious, Most Merciful.

1. Glory to (Allah) Who took His servant for a Journey by night

---

ilaa Ṣiraaṭim-Mustaqeem.

122. Wa aataynaahu fid-dunyaa ḥasanah; wa innahoo fil-Aakhirati laminaṣ-ṣaaliḥeen.

123. Summa awḥaynaaa ilayka anit-tabi' Millata Ibraaheema Ḥaneefaa; wa maa kaana minal-mushrikeen.

124. Innamaa ju'ilas-Sabtu 'alal-lazeenakhtalafoo feeh; wa inna Rabbaka la-yaḥkumu baynahum Yawmal-Qiyaamati feemaa kaanoo feehi yakhta-lifoon.

125. Ud'u ilaa sabeeli Rabbika bilḥikmati walmaw'iẓatil-ḥasanati wa jaadilhum billatee hiya aḥsan; inna Rabbaka Huwa a'lamu biman ḍalla 'an sabeelihee wa Huwa a'lamu bilmuhtadeen.

126. Wa in 'aaqabtum fa'aaqi-boo bimisli maa 'ooqibtum bihee wa la'in ṣabartum lahuwa khayrul-liṣṣaabireen.

127. Waṣbir wa maa ṣabruka illaa billaah; wa laa taḥzan 'alayhim wa laa taku fee ḍayqim-mimmaa yamkuroon.

128. Innal-laaha ma'al-laze-nat-taqaw wal-lazeena hum-muḥsinoon.   **(Section 16)**

Sûrat Banî Isrâ'îl—17
(Revealed at Makkah)
Bismillaahir Raḥmaanir Raḥeem

1. Subḥaanal-lazeee asraa bi'abdihee laylam-minal-

from the Sacred Mosque to the Farthest Mosque, whose precincts We did bless,- in order that We might show him some of Our Signs: for He is the One Who hears and sees (all things).

2. We gave Moses the Book, and made it a Guide to the Children of Israel, (commanding): "Do not take other than Me as Disposer of (your) affairs."

3. O you that are sprung from those whom We carried (in the Ark) with Noah! Verily he was a devotee most grateful.

4. And We gave (clear) warning to the Children of Israel in the Book, that twice would they do mischief on the earth and be elated with mighty arrogance (and twice would they be punished)!

5. When the first of the warnings came to pass, We sent against you Our servants given to terrible warfare: They entered the very inmost parts of your homes; and it was a warning (comp-letely) fulfilled.

6. Then We granted you the Return as against them: We gave you increase in resources and sons, and made you the more numerous in man-power.

7. If you did well, you did well for yourselves; if you did evil, (you did it) against yourselves. So when the second of the warnings came to pass, (We permitted your enemies) to disfigure your faces, and to enter your Temple as they had entered it before, and to visit with destruction all that fell into their power.

8. It may be that your Lord may (yet) show Mercy to you; but if you revert (to your sins), We shall revert (to Our punishments): And we have made Hell a prison for those who reject (all Faith).

9. Verily this Qur'an guides to that which is

Masjidil-Ḥaraami ilal-Masjidil-Aqṣal-lazee baaraknaa ḥawlahoo linuriyahoo min Aayaatinaa; innahoo Huwas-Samee‘ul-Baṣeer.

2. Wa aataynaa Moosal-Kitaaba wa ja‘alnaahu hudal-li-Baneee Israaa'eela allaa tat-takhizoo min doonee wakeelaa.

3. Zurriyyata man ḥamalnaa ma‘a Nooḥ; innahoo kaana ‘abdan shakooraa.

4. Wa qaḍaynaaaa ilaa Baneee Israaa'eela fil-Kitaabi-latufsidunna fil-arḍi marratayni wa lata‘lunna‘uluwwan ka-beeraa.

5. Fa-izaa jaaa'a wa‘du-oolaahumaa ba‘asnaaa ‘alykum ‘ibaadal-lanaaa ulee baåsin shadeedin fajaasoo khilaalad-diyaar; wa kaana wa‘dam-maf ‘oolaa.

6. Summa radadnaa lakumul-karrata ‘alayhim wa amdad-naakum-bi-amwaaliñw-wa baneena wa ja‘alnaakum aksara nafeeraa.

7. In aḥsantum aḥsantum li-anfusikum wa in asaåtum falahaa; fa-izaa jaaa'a wa‘dul-aakhirati liyasoooo'oo wujoo-hakum wa liyadkhulul-masjida kamaa dakhaloohu awwala marratiñw-wa liyutabbiroo maa ‘alaw tatbeeraa.

8. ‘Asaa Rabbukum añy-yarḥamakum; wa in ‘uttum ‘udnaa; wa ja‘alnaa Jahannama lilkaafireena ḥaṣeeraa.

9. Inna haazal-Qur-aana yahdee lillatee hiya

مِنَ الْمَسْجِدِ الْحَرَامِ اِلَى الْمَسْجِدِ الْاَقْصَا الَّذِیْ بٰرَكْنَا حَوْلَهٗ لِنُرِیَهٗ مِنْ اٰیٰتِنَا ؕ اِنَّهٗ هُوَ السَّمِیْعُ الْبَصِیْرُ ۝

وَاٰتَیْنَا مُوْسَى الْكِتٰبَ وَجَعَلْنٰهُ هُدًى لِّبَنِیْۤ اِسْرَآئِیْلَ اَلَّا تَتَّخِذُوْا مِنْ دُوْنِیْ وَكِیْلًا ؕ۝

ذُرِّیَّةَ مَنْ حَمَلْنَا مَعَ نُوْحٍ ؕ اِنَّهٗ كَانَ عَبْدًا شَكُوْرًا ۝

وَقَضَیْنَاۤ اِلٰى بَنِیْۤ اِسْرَآئِیْلَ فِی الْكِتٰبِ لَتُفْسِدُنَّ فِی الْاَرْضِ مَرَّتَیْنِ وَلَتَعْلُنَّ عُلُوًّا كَبِیْرًا ۝

فَاِذَا جَآءَ وَعْدُ اُوْلٰىهُمَا بَعَثْنَا عَلَیْكُمْ عِبَادًا لَّنَاۤ اُولِیْ بَاْسٍ شَدِیْدٍ فَجَاسُوْا خِلٰلَ الدِّیَارِ ؕ وَكَانَ وَعْدًا مَّفْعُوْلًا ۝

ثُمَّ رَدَدْنَا لَكُمُ الْكَرَّةَ عَلَیْهِمْ وَاَمْدَدْنٰكُمْ بِاَمْوَالٍ وَّبَنِیْنَ وَجَعَلْنٰكُمْ اَكْثَرَ نَفِیْرًا ۝

اِنْ اَحْسَنْتُمْ اَحْسَنْتُمْ لِاَنْفُسِكُمْ ۟ وَاِنْ اَسَاْتُمْ فَلَهَا ؕ فَاِذَا جَآءَ وَعْدُ الْاٰخِرَةِ لِیَسُوْٓءُوْا وُجُوْهَكُمْ وَلِیَدْخُلُوا الْمَسْجِدَ كَمَا دَخَلُوْهُ اَوَّلَ مَرَّةٍ وَّلِیُتَبِّرُوْا مَا عَلَوْا تَتْبِیْرًا ۝

عَسٰى رَبُّكُمْ اَنْ یَّرْحَمَكُمْ ۚ وَاِنْ عُدْتُّمْ عُدْنَا ۘ وَجَعَلْنَا جَهَنَّمَ لِلْكٰفِرِیْنَ حَصِیْرًا ۝

اِنَّ هٰذَا الْقُرْاٰنَ یَهْدِیْ لِلَّتِیْ هِیَ

most right (or stable), and gives the Glad Tidings to the Believers who work deeds of righteousness, that they shall have a magnificent reward;

10. And to those who do not believe in the Hereafter, (it Announces) that We have prepared for them a Penalty Grievous (indeed).

11. The prayer that man should make for good, he makes for evil; for man is given to hasty (deeds).

12. We have made the Night and the Day as two (of Our) Signs: the Sign of the Night have We made dark, while the Sign of the Day We have made to enlighten you; that you may seek bounty from your Lord, and that you may know the number and count of the years: all things have We explained in detail.

13. Every man's fate We have fastened on his own neck: On the Day of Judgment We shall bring out for him a scroll, which he will see spread open.

14. (It will be said to him:) "Read your (own) record: Sufficient is your soul this day to make out an account against you."

15. Who receives guidance, receives it for his own benefit: who goes astray does so to his own loss: no bearer of burdens can bear the burden of another: nor would We visit with Our Wrath until We had sent a Messenger (to give warning).

16. When We decide to destroy a population, We (first) send a definite order to those among them who are given the good things of this life and yet transgress; so that the word is proved true against them: then (it is) We destroy them utterly.

17. How many generations have We destroyed after Noah? And enough is your Lord to note

aqwamu wa yubashshirul-mu'mineenal-lazeena ya'maloonaṣ-ṣaaliḥaati anna lahum ajran kabeeraa.

10. Wa annal-lazeena laa yu'minoona bil-Aakhirati a'tadnaa lahum 'azaaban aleemaa.   **(Section 1)**

11. Wa yad'ul-insaanu bish-sharri du'aaa'ahoo bilkhayr; wa kaanal-insaanu 'ajoolaa.

12. Wa ja'alnal-layla wannahaara Aayatayni famaḥawnaaa Aayatal-layli wa ja'alnaaa Aayatan-nahaari mubṣiratal-litabtaghoo faḍlam-mir-Rabbikum wa lita'lamoo 'adadas-sineena walḥisaab; wa kulla shay'in faṣṣalnaahu tafṣeelaa.

13. Wa kulla insaanin alzamnaahu ṭaaa'irahoo fee 'unuqi-hee wa nukhriju lahoo Yawmal-Qiyaamati kitaabañy-yalqaahu manshooraa.

14. Iqra kitaabak kafaa binafsikal-Yawma 'alayka ḥaseebaa.

15. Manihtadaa fa-innamaa yahtadee linafsihee wa man ḍalla fa-innamaa yaḍillu 'alay-haa; wa laa taziru waaziratuñw-wizra ukhraa; wa maa kunnaa mu'azzibeena ḥattaa nab'aṣa Rasoolaa.

16. Wa izaaa aradnaaa an nuhlika qaryatan amarnaa mutrafeehaa fafasaqoo feehaa faḥaqqa 'alayhal-qawlu fadam-marnaahaa tadmeeraa.

17. Wa kam ahlaknaa minal-qurooni mim ba'di Nooḥ; wa kafaa bi-Rabbika bizunoobi

and see the sins of His servants.

18. If any do wish for the transitory things (of this life), We readily grant them - such things as We will, to such person as We will: in the end have We provided Hell for them: they will burn therein, disgraced and rejected.

19. Those who do wish for the (things of) the Hereafter, and strive therefor with all due striving, and have Faith,- they are the ones whose striving is acceptable (to Allah).

20. Of the bounties of your Lord We bestow freely on all-these as well as those: the bounties of your Lord are not closed (to anyone).

21. See how We have bestowed more on some than on others; but verily the Hereafter is more in rank and gradation and more in excellence.

22. Take not with Allah another object of worship; or you (O man!) will sit in disgrace and destitution.

23. Your Lord has decreed that you worship none but Him, and that you be kind to parents. Whether one or both of them attain old age in your life, say not to them a word of contempt, nor repel them, but address them in terms of honor.

24. And, out of kindness, lower to them the wing of humility, and say: "My Lord! bestow on them Your Mercy even as they cherished me in childhood."

25. Your Lord knows best what is in your hearts: If you do deeds of righteousness, verily He is Most Forgiving to those who turn to Him again and again (in true penitence).

26. And render to the kindred their due rights, as (also) to those in want,

---

'ibaadihee Khabeeram-Baṣee-raa.

18. Man kaana yureedul-'aajilata 'ajjalnaa lahoo feehaa maa nashaaa'u liman-nureedu summa ja'alnaa lahoo Jahan-nama yaṣlaahaa mazmoomam-mad-hooraa.

19. Wa man araadal Aakhirata wa sa'aa lahaa sa'yahaa wa huwa mu'minun fa-ulaaa'ika kaana sa'yuhum-mashkooraa.

20. Kullan-numiddu haaa-'ulaaa'i wa haaa'ulaaa'i min 'aṭaaa'i Rabbik; wa maa kaana 'aṭaaa'u Rabbika maḥzooraa.

21. Unẓur kayfa faḍḍalnaa ba'ḍahum 'alaa ba'ḍ; wa lal-Aakhiratu akbaru darajaatiñw-wa akbaru tafḍeelaa.

22. Laa taj'al ma'al-laahi ilaahan aakhara fataq'uda mazmoomam-makhzoolaa. **(Section 2)**

23. Wa qaḍaa Rabbuka allaa ta'budooo illaaa iyyaahu wa bilwaalidayni iḥsaanaa; immaa yablughanna 'indakal-kibara aḥaduhumaaa aw kilaahumaa falaa taqul-lahumaaa uffiñw-wa laa tanharhumaa wa qul-lahumaa qawlan kareemaa.

24. Wakhfiḍ lahumaa janaa-haz-zulli minar-raḥmati wa qur-Rabbir-ḥamhumaa kamaa rabbayaanee ṣagheeraa.

25. Rabbukum a'lamu bimaa fee nufoosikum; in takoonoo ṣaaliḥeena fa-innahoo kaana lil-awwaabeena Ghafoooraa.

26. Wa aati zal-qurbaa ḥaqqahoo walmiskeena

and to the wayfarer: but squander not (your wealth) in the manner of a spendthrift.

27. Verily spendthrifts are brothers of the Evil Ones; and the Evil One is to his Lord (himself) ungrateful.

28. And even if you have to turn away from them in pursuit of the Mercy from your Lord which you do expect, yet speak to them a word of easy kindness.

29. Make not your hand tied (like a miser's) to your neck, nor stretch it forth to its utmost reach, so that you become blameworthy and destitute.

30. Verily your Lord provides sustenance in abundance for whom He pleases, and He provides in a just measure. For He knows and regards all His servants.

31. Kill not your children for fear of want: We shall provide sustenance for them as well as for you. Verily the killing of them is a great sin.

32. Nor come near to adultery: for it is a shameful (deed) and an evil, opening the road (to other evils).

33. Nor take life - which Allah has made sacred - except for just cause. And if anyone is slain wrongfully, we have given his heir authority (to demand Qisas or to forgive): but let him nor exceed bounds in the matter of taking life; for he is helped (by the Law).

34. Come not near to the orphan's property except to improve it, until he attains the age of full strength; and fulfil (every) engagement, for (every) engagement will be enquired into (on the Day of Reckoning).

35. Give full measure when you measure, and weigh

wabnas-sabeeli wa laa tubazzir tabzeeraa.

27. Innal-mubazzireena kaa-nooo ikhwaanash-shayaateeni wa kaanash-Shaytaanu li-Rabbihee kafooraa.

28. Wa immaa tu'ridanna 'anhumub-tighaaa'a rahmatim-mir-Rabbika tarjoohaa faqul-lahum qawlam-maysooraa.

29. Wa laa taj'al yadaka maghlooolatan ilaa 'unuqika wa laa tabsut-haa kullal-basti fataq'uda maloomam-mah-sooraa.

30. Inna Rabbaka yabsutur-rizqa limany-yashaaa'u wa yaqdir; innahoo kaana bi'ibaa-dihee Khabeeram-Baseeraa.

(Section 3)

31. Wa laa taqtulooo awlaa-dakum khashyata imlaaq; nahnu narzuquhum wa iyyaa-kum; inna qatlahum kaana khit-an kabeeraa.

32. Wa laa taqrabuz-zinaaa innahoo kaana faahishatanw wa saaa'a sabeelaa.

33. Wa laa taqtulun-nafsal-latee harramal-laahu illaa bil-haqq; wa man qutila mazloo-man faqad ja'alnaa liwaliyyihee sultaanan falaa yusrif-fil-qatli innahoo kaana mansooraa.

34. Wa laa taqraboo maalal-yateemi illaa billatee hiya ahsa-nu hattaa yablugha ashuddah; wa awfoo bil'ahd, innal-'ahda kaana mas'oolaa.

35. Wa awful-kayla izaa kiltum wa zinoo

with a balance that is straight: that is the most fitting and the most advantageous in the final determination.

36.   And do not pursue that of which you have no knowledge; for every act of hearing, or of seeing or of (feeling in) the heart will be enquired into (on the Day of Reckoning).

37.   Nor walk on the earth with insolence: for you can not rend the earth asunder, nor reach the mountains in height.

38.   Of all such things the evil is hateful in the sight of your Lord.

39.   These are among the (precepts of) wisdom, which your Lord has revealed to you. Do not take, with Allah, another object of worship, lest you should be thrown into Hell, blameworthy and rejected.

40.   Has then your Lord (O Pagans!) preferred for you sons, and taken for Himself daughters among the angels? Truly you utter a most dreadful saying!

41.   We have explained (things) in various (ways) in this Qur'an, in order that they may receive admonition, but it only increases their flight (from the Truth)!

42.   Say: If there had been (other) gods with Him, as they say,- behold, they would certainly have sought out a way to the Lord of the Throne!

43.   Glory to Him! He is high above all that they say!- Exalted and Great (beyond measure)!

44.   The seven heavens and the earth, and all beings therein, declare His glory: there is not a thing but celebrates

bilqistaasil-mustaqeem; zaalika khayruñw-wa ahsanu taåweelaa.

36.   Wa laa taqfu maa laysa laka bihee 'ilm; innas-sam'a walbasara walfu'aada kullu ulaaa'ika kaana 'anhu mas-'oolaa.

37.   Wa laa tamshi fil-ardi marahan innaka lan takhriqal-arda wa lan tablughal-jibaala toolaa.

38.   Kullu zaalika kaana sayyi'uhoo 'inda Rabbika makroohaa.

39.   Zaalika mimmaaa awhaaa ilayka Rabbuka minal-hikmah; wa laa taj'al-ma'allaahi ilaahan aakhara fatulqaa fee Jahannama maloomam-mad-hooraa.

40.   Afa-asfaakum Rabbukum bilbaneena wattakhaza minal-malaaa'ikati inaasaa; innakum lataqooloona qawlan 'azeemaa.
(Section 4)

41.   Wa laqad sarrafnaa fee haazal-Qur-aani liyazzakkaroo wa maa yazeeduhum illaa nufooraa.

42.   Qul-law kaana ma'ahooo aalihatun kamaa yaqooloona izal-labtaghaw ilaa zil-'Arshi Sabeelaa.

43.   Subhaanahoo wa Ta'aalaa 'ammaa yaqooloona 'uluwwan kabeeraa.

44.   Tusabbihu lahus-samaa-waatus-sab'u wal-ardu wa man feehinn; wa im-min shay'in illaa yusabbihu

His praise; And yet you do not understand how they declare His glory! Verily He is Oft-Forbearing, Most Forgiving!

45. When you recite the Qur'an, We put, between you and those who do not believe in the Hereafter, an invisible veil:

46. And We put coverings over their hearts (and minds) lest they should understand the Qur'an, and deafness into their ears: when you comme-morate your Lord and Him alone in the Qur'an, they turn on their backs, fleeing (from the Truth).

47. We know best why it is they listen, when they listen to you: and when they meet in private conference, behold, the wicked say, "You follow none other than a man bewitched!"

48. See what similes they strike for you: but they have gone astray, and never can they find a way.

49. They say: "What! when we are reduced to bones and dust, should we really be raised up (to be) a new creation?"

50. Say: "(Nay!) be you stones or iron.

51. "Or any created matter which, in your minds, is hardest (to be raised up),- (Yet shall you be raised up)!" Then will they say: "Who will cause us to return?" Say: "He who created you first!" Then they will wag their heads toward you, and say, "When will that be?" Say, "May be it will be quite soon!

52. "It will be on a Day when He will call you, and you will answer (His call) with (words of) His praise, and you will think that you tarried but a little while!"

53. Say to My servants that they should (only) say those things that are

bihamdihee wa laakil-laa tafqahoona tasbeehahum; innahoo kaana Haleeman Ghafooraa.

45. Wa izaa qaraåtal-Qur-aana ja'alnaa baynaka wa baynal-lazeena laa yu'minoona bil-Aakhirati hijaabam-mastooraa.

46. Wa ja'alnaa 'alaa quloo-bihim akinnatan añy-yafqa-hoohu wa feee aazaanihim waqraa; wa izaa zakarta Rabbaka fil-Qur-aani wahda-hoo wallaw 'alaaa adbaarihim nufooraa.

47. Nahnu a'lamu bimaa yastami'oona biheee iz yas-tami'oona ilayka wa iz hum najwaaa iz yaqooluz-zaali-moona in tattabi'oona illaa rajulam-mas-hooraa.

48. Unzur kayfa daraboo lakal-amsaala fadalloo falaa yastatee'oona sabeelaa.

49. Wa qaalooo 'a-izaa kunnaa 'izaamañw-wa rufaatan 'a-innaa lamab'oosoona khalqan jadee-daa.

50. Qul koonoo hijaaratan aw hadeedaa.

51. Aw khalqam-mimmaa yakburu fee sudoorikum; fasa-yaqooloona mañy-yu'eedunaa qulil-lazee fatarakum awwala marrah; fasa-yunghidoona ilayka ru'oosahum wa yaqoo-loona mataa huwa qul 'asaaa añy-yakoona qareebaa.

52. Yawma yad'ookum fatas-tajeeboona bihamdihee wa tazunnoona il-labistum illaa qaleelaa. **(Section 5)**

53. Wa qul-li'ibaadee yaqoo-lul-latee hiya

best: for Satan does sow dissensions among them: For Satan is to man an avowed enemy.

54. It is your Lord that knows you best: If He please, He grants you mercy, or if He please, punishment: We have not sent you to be a disposer of their affairs for them.

55. And it is your Lord that knows best all beings that are in the heavens and on earth: We bestowed on some prophets more (and other) gifts than on others: and We gave to David (the gift of) the Psalms.

56. Say: "Call on those - besides Him - whom you fancy: they have neither the power to remove your troubles from you nor to change them."

57. Those whom they call upon do desire (for themselves) means of access to their Lord, - even those who are nearest: they hope for His Mercy and fear His Wrath: for the Wrath of your Lord is something to take heed of.

58. There is not a population but We shall destroy it before the Day of Judgment or punish it with a dreadful Penalty: that is written in the (eternal) Record.

59. And We refrain from sending the signs, only because the men of former generations treated them as false: We sent the she-camel to the Thamud to open their eyes, but they treated her wrongfully: We only send the Signs by way of terror (and warning from evil).

60. Behold! We told you that your Lord encompasses mankind round about: We granted the vision which We showed you, but as a trial for men,- as also the Cursed Tree

ahsan; innash-Shaytaana yanzaghu baynahum; innash-Shaytaana kaana lil-insaani 'aduwwam-mubeenaa.

54. Rabbukum a'lamu bikum iñy-yashaa yarhamkum aw iñy-yashaa yu'azzibkum; wa maaa arsalnaaka 'alayhim wakeelaa.

55. Wa Rabbuka a'lamu-biman fis-samaawaati wal-ard; wa laqad faddalnaa ba'dan-Nabiyyeena 'alaa ba'diñw-wa aataynaa Daawooda Zabooraa.

56. Qulid-'ul-lazeena za'am-tum min doonihee falaa yamlikoona kashfad-durri 'ankum wa laa tahweelaa.

57. Ulaaa'ikal-lazeena yad-'oona yabtaghoona ilaa Rabbi-himul-waseelata ayyuhum aqrabu wa yarjoona rahmatahoo wa yakhaafoona 'azaabah; inna 'azaaba Rabbika kaana mahzooraa.

58. Wa im-min qaryatin illaa Nahnu muhlikoohaa qabla Yawmil-Qiyaamati aw mu'az-ziboohaa 'azaaban shadeedaa; kaana zaalika fil-Kitaabi mas-tooraa.

59. Wa maa mana'anaaa an nursila bil-Aayaati illaaa an kazzaba bihal-awwaloon; wa aataynaa Samoodan-naaqata mubsiratan fazalamoo bihaa; wa maa nursilu bil-Aayaati illaa takhweefaa.

60. Wa iz qulnaa laka inna Rabbaka ahaata binnaas; wa maa ja'alnar-ru'yal-lateee araynaaka illaa fitnatal-linnaasi washshajaratal-mal'oonata

أَحْسَنُ ۚ إِنَّ الشَّيْطَانَ يَنْزَغُ بَيْنَهُمْ ۚ إِنَّ الشَّيْطَانَ كَانَ لِلْإِنْسَانِ عَدُوًّا مُّبِينًا ۞

رَّبُّكُمْ أَعْلَمُ بِكُمْ ۖ إِن يَشَأْ يَرْحَمْكُمْ أَوْ إِن يَشَأْ يُعَذِّبْكُمْ ۚ وَمَا أَرْسَلْنَاكَ عَلَيْهِمْ وَكِيلًا ۞

وَرَبُّكَ أَعْلَمُ بِمَن فِي السَّمَاوَاتِ وَالْأَرْضِ ۗ وَلَقَدْ فَضَّلْنَا بَعْضَ النَّبِيِّينَ عَلَىٰ بَعْضٍ ۖ وَآتَيْنَا دَاوُودَ زَبُورًا ۞

قُلِ ادْعُوا الَّذِينَ زَعَمْتُم مِّن دُونِهِ فَلَا يَمْلِكُونَ كَشْفَ الضُّرِّ عَنكُمْ وَلَا تَحْوِيلًا ۞

أُولَٰئِكَ الَّذِينَ يَدْعُونَ يَبْتَغُونَ إِلَىٰ رَبِّهِمُ الْوَسِيلَةَ أَيُّهُمْ أَقْرَبُ وَيَرْجُونَ رَحْمَتَهُ وَيَخَافُونَ عَذَابَهُ ۚ إِنَّ عَذَابَ رَبِّكَ كَانَ مَحْذُورًا ۞

وَإِن مِّن قَرْيَةٍ إِلَّا نَحْنُ مُهْلِكُوهَا قَبْلَ يَوْمِ الْقِيَامَةِ أَوْ مُعَذِّبُوهَا عَذَابًا شَدِيدًا ۚ كَانَ ذَٰلِكَ فِي الْكِتَابِ مَسْطُورًا ۞

وَمَا مَنَعَنَا أَن نُّرْسِلَ بِالْآيَاتِ إِلَّا أَن كَذَّبَ بِهَا الْأَوَّلُونَ ۚ وَآتَيْنَا ثَمُودَ النَّاقَةَ مُبْصِرَةً فَظَلَمُوا بِهَا ۚ وَمَا نُرْسِلُ بِالْآيَاتِ إِلَّا تَخْوِيفًا ۞

وَإِذْ قُلْنَا لَكَ إِنَّ رَبَّكَ أَحَاطَ بِالنَّاسِ ۚ وَمَا جَعَلْنَا الرُّؤْيَا الَّتِي أَرَيْنَاكَ إِلَّا فِتْنَةً لِّلنَّاسِ وَالشَّجَرَةَ الْمَلْعُونَةَ

(mentioned) in the Qur'an: We put terror (and warning) into them, but it only increases their inordinate transgression!

61. Behold! We said to the angels: "Bow down to Adam": They bowed down except Iblis: he said, "Shall I bow down to one whom You did create from clay?"

62. He said: "Do you see? this is the one whom You have honoured above me! If You will but respite me to the Day of Judgment, I will surely bring his descendants under my sway - all but a few!"

63. (Allah) said: "Go you away; if any of them follow you, verily Hell will be the recompense of you (all)- an ample recompense.

64. "Lead to destruction those whom you can among them, with your (seductive) voice; make assaults on them with your cavalry and your infantry; mutually share with them wealth and children; and make promises to them." But Satan promises them nothing but deceit.

65. "As for My servants, no authority shall you have over them:" Enough is your Lord for a Disposer of affairs.

66. Your Lord is He That makes the Ship go smoothly for you through the sea, in order that you may seek of His Bounty. For He is unto you most Merciful.

67. When distress seizes you at sea, those that you call upon - besides Himself - leave you in the lurch! but when He brings you back safe to land, you turn away (from Him). Most ungrateful is man!

68. Do you then feel secure that He will not cause you to be swallowed up beneath the earth when you are on land, or that He will not send against you a violent tornado (with showers of stones) so that you shall find no protector?

69. Or do you feel secure that He will not send you back a

fil-Qur-aan; wa nukhaw-wifuhum famaa yazeeduhum illaa tughyaanan kabeeraa.

(Section 6)

61. Wa iz qulnaa lilma-laaa'ikatis-judoo li-Aadama fasajadooo illaaa Ibleesa qaala 'a-asjudu liman khalaqta teenaa.

62. Qaala ara'aytaka haazal-lazee karramta 'alayya la'in akhkhartani ilaa Yawmil-Qiyaamati la-aḥtanikanna zurriyyatahooo illaa qaleelaa.

63. Qaalaz-hab faman tabi-'aka minhum fa-inna Jahanna-ma jazaaa'ukum jazaaa'am-mawfooraa.

64. Wastafziz manis-taṭa'ta minhum biṣawtika wa ajlib 'alayhim bikhaylika wa rajilika wa shaarik-hum fil-amwaali wal-awlaadi wa 'idhum; wa maa ya'iduhumush-Shayṭaanu illaa ghurooraa.

65. Inna 'ibaadee laysa laka 'alayhim sulṭaan; wa kafaa bi-Rabbika Wakeelaa.

66. Rabbukumul-lazee yuzjee lakumul-fulka fil-baḥri litab-taghoo min faḍlih; innahoo kaana bikum Raḥeemaa.

67. Wa izaa massakumuḍ-durru fil-baḥri ḍalla man tad'oona illaaa iyyaahu falam-maa najjaakum ilal-barri a'raḍtum; wa kaanal-insaanu kafooraa.

68. Afa-amintum añy-yakh-sifa bikum jaanibal-barri aw yursila 'alaykum ḥaaṣiban summa laa tajidoo lakum wakeelaa.

69. Am amintum añy-yu'eeda-kum feehi taaratan

second time to sea and send against you a heavy gale to drown you because of your ingratitude, so that you find no helper therein against Us?

70. We have honoured the sons of Adam; provided them with transport on land and sea; given them for sustenance things good and pure; and conferred on them special favours, above a great part of our creation.

71. One day We shall call together all human beings with their (respective) Imams: those who are given their record in their right hand will read it (with pleasure), and they will not be dealt with unjustly in the least.

72. But those who were blind in this world, will be blind in the Hereafter, and most astray from the Path.

73. And their purpose was to tempt you away from that which We had revealed unto you, to substitute in Our name something quite different; (in that case), behold! they would certainly have made you (their) friend!

74. And had We not given you strength, you would nearly have inclined to them a little.

75. In that case We should have made you taste double portion (of punishment) in this life, and an equal portion in death: moreover you wouldst have found none to help you against Us!

76. Their purpose was to scare you off the land, in order to expel you; but in that case they would not have stayed (therein) after you, except for a little while.

77. (This was Our) way with the Messengers We sent before you: you will find no change in Our ways.

78. Establish regular prayers at the sun's decline till the darkness of the night, and the recital of the Qur'an in morning prayer, for the recital in the morning

ukhraa fa-yursila 'alaykum qaaşifam-minar-reeḥi fa-yugh-riqakum bimaa kafartum summa laa tajidoo lakum 'alaynaa bihee tabee'aa.

70. Wa laqad karramnaa Baneee Aadama wa ḥamalnaa-hum fil-barri walbaḥri wa razaq-naahum minaṭ-ṭayyibaati wa faḍḍalnaahum 'alaa kaşeerim-mimman khalaqnaa tafḍeelaa.

(Section 7)

71. Yawma nad'oo kulla unaasim bi-imaamihim faman ootiya kitaabahoo bi-yamee-nihee fa-ulaaa'ika yaqra'oona kitaabahum wa laa yuẓlamoona fateelaa.

72. Wa man kaana fee haaẕiheee a'maa fahuwa fil-Aakhirati a'maa wa aḍallu sabeelaa.

73. Wa in kaadoo la-yafti-noonaka 'anil-laẕeee awḥay-naaa ilayka litaftariya 'alaynaa ghayrahoo wa iẕallat-takha-ẕooka khaleelaa.

74. Wa law laaa an sabbat-naaka laqad kitta tarkanu ilayhim shay'an qaleelaa.

75. Iẕal-la-aẕaqnaaka ḍi'fal-ḥayaati wa ḍi'fal-mamaati summa laa tajidu laka 'alaynaa naşeeraa.

76. Wa in kaadoo la-yastafiz-zoonaka minal-arḍi liyukhri-jooka minhaa wa iẕal-laa yalbaşoona khilaafaka illaa qaleelaa.

77. Sunnata man qad arsalnaa qablaka mir-Rusulinaa wa laa tajidu lisunnatinaa taḥweelaa.

78. Aqimiṣ-Ṣalaata liduloo-kish-shamsi ilaa ghasaqil-layli wa qur-aanal-Fajri inna qur-aa-nal-Fajri

carry (angels') testimony.

79. And as for the night keep awake a part of it as an additional prayer for you, soon will your Lord raise you to a Station of Praise and Glory!

80. Say: "O my Lord! Let my entry be by the Gate of Truth and Honour, and likewise my exit by the Gate of Truth and Honour; and grant me from Your Presence an authority to aid (me)."

81. And say: "Truth has (now) arrived, and Falsehood perished: for Falsehood is (by its nature) bound to perish."

82. We send down (stage by stage) in the Qur'an that which is a healing and a mercy to those who believe: to the unjust it causes nothing but loss after loss.

83. Yet when We bestow Our favors on man, he turns away and becomes remote on his side (instead of coming to Us), and when evil seizes him he gives himself up to despair.

84. Say: "Everyone acts according to his own disposition: but your Lord knows best who it is that is best guided on the Way."

85. They ask you concerning the Spirit (of inspiration). Say: "The Spirit (comes) by command of my Lord: of knowledge it is only a little that is communicated to you, (O men!)"

86. If it were Our Will, We could take away that which We have sent you by inspiration: then would you find none to plead your affair in that matter as against Us,-

87. Except for Mercy from your Lord: for His bounty is to you (indeed) great.

88. Say: "If the whole of mankind and Jinns were to gather

kaana mashhoodaa.

79. Wa minal-layli fatahajjad bihee naafilatal-laka 'asaaa añy-yab'asaka Rabbuka Maqaa-mam-Maḥmoodaa.

80. Wa qur-Rabbi adkhilnee mudkhala ṣidqiñw-wa akhrijnee mukhraja ṣidqiñw-waj'al lee milladunka sulṭaanan naṣeeraa.

81. Wa qul jaaa'al-ḥaqqu wa zahaqal-baaṭil; innal-baaṭila kaana zahooqaa.

82. Wa nunazzilu minal-Qur-aani maa huwa shifaaa'uñw-wa raḥmatul-lilmu'mineena wa laa yazeeduẕ-ẕaalimeena illaa khasaaraa.

83. Wa iẕaaa an'amnaa 'alal-insaani a'raḍa wa na-aa bijaani-bihee wa iẕaa massahush-sharru kaana ya'oosaa.

84. Qul kulluñy-ya'malu 'alaa shaakilatihee fa-Rabbukum a'lamu biman huwa ahdaa sabeelaa. **(Section 9)**

85. Wa yas'aloonaka 'anir-rooḥ; qulir-rooḥu min amri Rabbee wa maaa ooteetum-minal-'ilmi illaa qaleelaa.

86. Wa la'in shi'naa lanaẕ-habanna billaẕeee awḥaynaaa ilayka ṣumma laa tajidu laka bihee 'alaynaa wakeelaa.

87. Illaa raḥmatam-mir-Rabbik; inna faḍlahoo kaana 'alayka kabeeraa.

88. Qul la'inij-tama'atil-insu waljinnu

together to produce the like of this Qur'an, they could not produce the like thereof, even if they backed up each other with help and support.

89. And We have explained to man, in this Qur'an, every kind of similitude: yet the greater part of men refuse (to receive it) except with ingratitude!

90. They say: "We shall not believe in you, until you cause a spring to gush forth for us from the earth,

91. "Or (until) thou have a garden of date trees and vines, and cause rivers to gush forth in their midst, carrying abundant water;

92. "Or you cause the sky to fall in pieces, as you say (will happen), against us; or you bring Allah and the angels before (us) face to face:

93. "Or you have a house adorned with gold, or you mount a ladder right into the skies. No, we shall not even believe in your mounting until you send down to us a book that we could read." Say: "Glory to my Lord! Am I not but a man,- a Messenger?"

94. What kept men back from belief when Guidance came to them, was nothing but this: they said, "Has Allah sent a man (like us) to be (His) Messenger?"

95. Say, "If there were settled, on earth, angels walking about in peace and quiet, We should certainly have sent them down from the heavens an angel for a Messenger."

96. Say: "Enough is Allah for a witness between me and you: for He is well acquainted with His servants, and He sees (all things).

97. It is he whom Allah guides, that is on true guidance; but he whom

'alaaa añy-yaåtoo bimisli haazal-Qur-aani laa yaåtoona bimislihee wa law kaana ba'duhum liba'din zaheeraa.

89. Wa laqad sarrafnaa linnaasi fee haazal-Qur-aani min kulli masalin fa-abaaa aksarunnaasi illaa kufooraa.

90. Wa qaaloo lan-nu'mina laka hattaa tafjura lanaa minalardi yamboo'aa.

91. Aw takoona laka jannatum-min nakheeliñw-wa 'inabin fatufajjiral-anhaara khilaalahaa tafjeeraa.

92. Aw tusqitas-samaaa'a kamaa za'amta 'alaynaa kisafan aw taåtiya billaahi walmalaaa'ikati qabeelaa.

93. Aw yakoona laka baytummin zukhrufin aw tarqaa fissamaaa'i wa lan-nu'mina liruqiyyika hattaa tunazzila 'alaynaa kitaaban-naqra'uh; qul Subhaana Rabbee hal kuntu illaa basharar-Rasoolaa.

(Section 10)

94. Wa maa mana'an-naasa añy-yu'minooo iz jaaa'ahumulhudaaa illaaa an qaalooo aba-'asal-laahu basharar-Rasoolaa.

95. Qul law kaana fil-ardi malaaa'ikatuñy-yamshoona mutma'inneena lanazzalnaa 'alayhim-minas-samaaa'i malakar-Rasoolaa.

96. Qul kafaa billaahi shaheedam baynee wa baynakum; innahoo kaana bi'ibaadihee Khabeeram Baseeraa.

97. Wa mañy-yahdil-laahu fahuwal-muhtad; wa mañy-

عَلٰٓى اَنْ يَّأْتُوْا بِمِثْلِ هٰذَا الْقُرْاٰنِ لَا يَأْتُوْنَ بِمِثْلِهٖ وَلَوْ كَانَ بَعْضُهُمْ لِبَعْضٍ ظَهِيْرًا ۝

وَلَقَدْ صَرَّفْنَا لِلنَّاسِ فِيْ هٰذَا الْقُرْاٰنِ مِنْ كُلِّ مَثَلٍ ۫ فَاَبٰٓى اَكْثَرُ النَّاسِ اِلَّا كُفُوْرًا ۝

وَقَالُوْا لَنْ نُّؤْمِنَ لَكَ حَتّٰى تَفْجُرَ لَنَا مِنَ الْاَرْضِ يَنْۢبُوْعًا ۝

اَوْ تَكُوْنَ لَكَ جَنَّةٌ مِّنْ نَّخِيْلٍ وَّ عِنَبٍ فَتُفَجِّرَ الْاَنْهٰرَ خِلٰلَهَا تَفْجِيْرًا ۝

اَوْ تُسْقِطَ السَّمَآءَ كَمَا زَعَمْتَ عَلَيْنَا كِسَفًا اَوْ تَأْتِيَ بِاللّٰهِ وَالْمَلٰٓئِكَةِ قَبِيْلًا ۝

اَوْ يَكُوْنَ لَكَ بَيْتٌ مِّنْ زُخْرُفٍ اَوْ تَرْقٰى فِى السَّمَآءِ ۫ وَلَنْ نُّؤْمِنَ لِرُقِيِّكَ حَتّٰى تُنَزِّلَ عَلَيْنَا كِتٰبًا نَّقْرَؤُهٗ ۫ قُلْ سُبْحَانَ رَبِّيْ هَلْ كُنْتُ اِلَّا بَشَرًا رَّسُوْلًا ۝

وَمَا مَنَعَ النَّاسَ اَنْ يُّؤْمِنُوْٓا اِذْ جَآءَهُمُ الْهُدٰٓى اِلَّا اَنْ قَالُوْٓا اَبَعَثَ اللّٰهُ بَشَرًا رَّسُوْلًا ۝

قُلْ لَّوْ كَانَ فِى الْاَرْضِ مَلٰٓئِكَةٌ يَّمْشُوْنَ مُطْمَئِنِّيْنَ لَنَزَّلْنَا عَلَيْهِمْ مِّنَ السَّمَآءِ مَلَكًا رَّسُوْلًا ۝

قُلْ كَفٰى بِاللّٰهِ شَهِيْدًا بَيْنِيْ وَبَيْنَكُمْ ۫ اِنَّهٗ كَانَ بِعِبَادِهٖ خَبِيْرًۢا بَصِيْرًا ۝

وَمَنْ يَّهْدِ اللّٰهُ فَهُوَ الْمُهْتَدِ ۫ وَمَنْ

He leaves astray - for such will you find no protector besides Him. On the Day of Judgment We shall gather them together, prone on their faces, blind, dumb, and deaf: their abode will be Hell: every time it shows abatement, We shall increase from them the fierceness of the Fire.

98. That is their recompense, because they rejected Our Signs, and said, "When we are reduced to bones and broken dust, should we really be raised up (to be) a new Creation?"

99. Don't they see that Allah, Who created the heavens and the earth, has power to create the like of them (anew)? Only He has decreed a term appointed, of which there is no doubt. But the unjust refuse (to receive it) except with ingratitude.

100. Say: "If you had control of the Treasures of the Mercy of my Lord, behold, you would keep them back, for fear of spending them: for man is (ever) Miserly!"

101. To Moses We did give Nine Clear Sings: ask the Children of Israel: when he came to them, Pharaoh said to him: "O Moses! I consider you, indeed, to have been worked upon by sorcery!

102. Moses said, "You know well that these things have been sent down by none but the Lord of the heavens and the earth as eye-opening evidence: and I consider you indeed, O Pharaoh, to be one doomed to destruction!"

103. So he resolved to remove them from the face of the earth: but We drowned him and all who were with him.

104. And We said thereafter to the Children of Israel, "Dwell securely in the land (of promise)": but when the second of the warnings came to pass, We gathered you together in a mingled crowd.

yuḍlil falan tajida lahum awliyaaa'a min doonih; wa naḥshuruhum Yawmal-Qiyaa-mati 'alaa wujoohihim umyañw-wa bukmañw-wa ṣummaa; maa-waahum Jahannamu kullamaa khabat zidnaahum sa'eeraa.

98. Zaalika jazaaa'uhum bi-annahum kafaroo bi-Aayaa-tinaa wa qaalooo 'a-izaa kunnaa 'izaamañw-wa rufaatan 'a-innaa lamaboosoona khalqan jadee-daa.

99. Awalam yaraw annal-laahal-lazee khalaqas-samaa-waati wal-arḍa qaadirun 'alaaa añy-yakhluqa mislahum wa ja'ala lahum ajalal-laa rayba feeh; fa-abaẓ-ẓaalimoona illaa kufooraa.

100. Qul law antum tamli-koona khazaaa'ina raḥmati Rabbeee izal-la-amsaktum khash-yatal-infaaq; wa kaanal-insaanu qatooraa. **(Section 11)**

101. Wa laqad aataynaa Moosaa tis'a Aayaatim bayyi-naatin fas'al Baneee Israaa'eela iz jaaa'ahum faqaala lahoo Fir-'awnu innee la-aẓunnuka yaa Moosaa mas-hooraa.

102. Qaala laqad 'alimta maaa anzala haaa'ulaaa'i illaa Rab-bus-samaawaati wal-arḍi baṣaaa'ira wa innee la-aẓun-nuka yaa Fir'awnu masbooraa.

103. Fa-araada añy-yastafiz-zahum-minal-arḍi fa-aghraq-naahu wa mam-ma'ahoo jamee'aa.

104. Wa qulnaa mim ba'dihee li-Baneee Israaa'eelas-kunul-arḍa fa-izaa jaaa'a wa'dul-aakhirati ji'naa bikum lafeefaa.

105. We sent down the (Qur'an) in Truth, and in Truth has it descended: and We sent you but to give Glad Tidings and to warn (sinners).

106. (It is) a Qur'an which We have divided (into parts from time to time), in order that you might recite it to men at intervals: We have revealed it by stages.

107. Say: "Whether you believe in it or not, it is true that those who were given knowledge beforehand, when it is recited to them, fall down on their faces in humble prostration,

108. "And they say: 'Glory to our Lord! Truly has the promise of our Lord been fulfilled!'"

109. They fall down on their faces in tears, and it increases their (earnest) humility.

110. Say: "Call upon Allah, or call upon Rahman: by whatever name you call upon Him, (it is well): for to Him belong the Most Beautiful Names. Neither speak your Prayer aloud, nor speak it in a low tone, but seek a middle course between."

111. Say: "Praise be to Allah, Who begets no son, and has no partner in (His) dominion: nor (needs) He any to protect Him from humiliation: yes, magnify Him for His greatness and glory!

105. Wa bilḥaqqi anzalnaahu wa bilḥaqqi nazal; wa maaa arsalnaaka illaa mubash-shiranw-wa nazeeraa.

106. Wa Qur-aanan faraqnaahu litaqra-ahoo 'alan-naasi 'alaa muksinw-wa nazzalnaahu tan-zeelaa.

107. Qul aaminoo biheee aw laa tu'minoo; innal-lazeena ootul-'ilma min qabliheee izaa yutlaa 'alayhim yakhirroona lil-azqaani sujjadaa.

108. Wa yaqooloona Subḥaana Rabbinaaa in kaana wa'du Rabbinaa lamaf'oolaa.

109. Wa yakhirroona lil-azqaa-ni yabkoona wa yazeeduhum khushoo'aa. ⬆

110. Qulid-'ul-laaha awid'ur-Raḥmaana ayyam-maa tad'oo falahul-Asmaaa'ul-Ḥusnaa; wa laa tajhar bi-Ṣalaatika wa laa tukhaafit bihaa wabtaghi bayna zaalika sabeelaa.

111. Wa qulil-ḥamdu lillaahil-lazee lam yattakhiz waladanw-wa lam yakul-lahoo shareekun fil-mulki wa lam yakul-lahoo waliyyum-minaz-zulli wa kab-birhu takbeeraa.　**(Section 12)**

(Bow Down)

18. The Cave

In the name of Allah, Most Gracious, Most Merciful.

1. Praise be to Allah, Who has sent to His Servant the Book, and has allowed therein no crookedness:

2. (He has made it) Straight (and Clear) in order that He may warn (the godless) of a terrible Punishment from Him, and that He may give Glad Tidings to the Believers who work righteous Deeds, that they shall have

Sûrat al-Kahf–18

(Revealed at Makkah)

Bismillaahir Raḥmaanir Raḥeem

1. Alḥamdu lillaahil lazee anzala 'alaa 'abdihil-Kitaaba wa lam yaj'al-lahoo 'iwajaa.

2. Qayyimal-liyunzira baa-san shadeedam-mil-ladunhu wa yubashshiral-mu'mineenal-lazeena ya'maloonaṣ-ṣaaliḥaati anna lahum

a goodly Reward,

3. Wherein they shall remain for ever:

4. Further, that He may warn those (also) who say, "Allah has begotten a son":

5. They do not have any knowledge of such a thing, nor had their fathers. It is a grievous thing that issues from their mouths as a saying. What they say is nothing but falsehood!

6. You would only, perchance, fret yourself to death, following after them, in grief, if they do not believe in this Message.

7. That which is on earth we have made but as a glittering show for the earth, in order that We may test them - as to which of them are best in conduct.

8. Verily what is on earth we shall make but as dust and dry soil (without growth or herbage).

9. Or do you not reflect that the Companions of the Cave and of the Inscription were wonders among Our Signs?

10. Behold, the youths betook themselves to the Cave: they said, "Our Lord! bestow on us Mercy from Yourself, and dispose of our affair for us in the right way!"

11. Then We draw (a veil) over their ears, for a number of years, in the Cave, (so that they did not hear):

12. Then We roused them, in order to test which of the two parties was best at calculating the term of years they had tarried!

13. We relate to you their story in truth: they were youths who believed in their Lord, and We advanced them in guidance:

---

ajran ḥasanaa.

3. Maakiṣeena feehi abadaa.

4. Wa yunziral-laẕeena qaa-lut-takhaẕal-laahu waladaa.

5. Maa lahum bihee min 'ilmiñw-wa laa li-aabaaa'ihim; kaburat kalimatan takhruju min afwaahihim; iñy-yaqooloona illaa kaẕibaa.

6. Fala'allaka baakhi'un nafsaka 'alaaa aaṣaarihim illam yu'minoo bihaaẕal-ḥadeeṣi asafaa.

7. Innaa ja'alnaa maa 'alal-arḍi zeenatal-lahaa linabluwa-hum ayyuhum aḥsanu 'amalaa.

8. Wa innaa lajaa'iloona maa 'alayhaa ṣa'eedan juruzaa.

9. Am ḥasibta anna Aṣ-ḥaa-bal-Kahfi war-Raqeemi kaanoo min Aayaatinaa 'ajabaa.

10. Iz awal-fityatu ilal-Kahfi faqaaloo Rabbanaaa aatinaa mil-ladunka raḥmatañw-wa hayyi' lanaa min amrinaa rashadaa.

11. Faḍarabnaa 'alaaa aaẕaa-nihim fil-Kahfi sineena 'adadaa.

12. Ṣumma ba'aṣnaahum lina'lama ayyul-ḥizbayni aḥsaa limaa labisooo amadaa.

(Section 1)

13. Naḥnu naquṣṣu 'alayka naba-ahum bilḥaqq; innahum fityatun aamanoo bi-Rabbihim wa zidnaahum hudaa.

أَجْرًا حَسَنًا ۞

مَّاكِثِيْنَ فِيْهِ أَبَدًا ۞

وَّيُنْذِرَ الَّذِيْنَ قَالُوا اتَّخَذَ اللهُ وَلَدًا ۞

مَّالَهُمْ بِهٖ مِنْ عِلْمٍ وَّلَا لِاٰبَآئِهِمْ ۚ كَبُرَتْ كَلِمَةً تَخْرُجُ مِنْ أَفْوَاهِهِمْ ۚ إِنْ يَّقُوْلُوْنَ إِلَّا كَذِبًا ۞

فَلَعَلَّكَ بَاخِعٌ نَّفْسَكَ عَلٰٓى اٰثَارِهِمْ إِنْ لَّمْ يُؤْمِنُوْا بِهٰذَا الْحَدِيْثِ أَسَفًا ۞

إِنَّا جَعَلْنَا مَا عَلَى الْأَرْضِ زِيْنَةً لَّهَا لِنَبْلُوَهُمْ أَيُّهُمْ أَحْسَنُ عَمَلًا ۞

وَإِنَّا لَجَاعِلُوْنَ مَا عَلَيْهَا صَعِيْدًا جُرُزًا ۞

أَمْ حَسِبْتَ أَنَّ أَصْحٰبَ الْكَهْفِ وَالرَّقِيْمِ ۙ كَانُوْا مِنْ اٰيٰتِنَا عَجَبًا ۞

إِذْ أَوَى الْفِتْيَةُ إِلَى الْكَهْفِ فَقَالُوْا رَبَّنَآ اٰتِنَا مِنْ لَّدُنْكَ رَحْمَةً وَّهَيِّئْ لَنَا مِنْ أَمْرِنَا رَشَدًا ۞

فَضَرَبْنَا عَلٰٓى اٰذَانِهِمْ فِي الْكَهْفِ سِنِيْنَ عَدَدًا ۞

ثُمَّ بَعَثْنٰهُمْ لِنَعْلَمَ أَيُّ الْحِزْبَيْنِ أَحْصٰى لِمَا لَبِثُوٓا أَمَدًا ۞

نَحْنُ نَقُصُّ عَلَيْكَ نَبَأَهُمْ بِالْحَقِّ ۚ إِنَّهُمْ فِتْيَةٌ اٰمَنُوْا بِرَبِّهِمْ وَزِدْنٰهُمْ هُدًى ۞

14. We gave strength to their hearts: behold, they stood up and said: "Our Lord is the Lord of the heavens and of the earth: never shall we call upon any god other than Him: if we did, we should indeed have uttered an enormity!

15. "These our people have taken for worship gods other than Him: why do they not bring forward an authority clear (and convincing) for what they do? Who does more wrong than such as invent a falsehood against Allah?

16. "When you turn away from them and the things they worship other than Allah, betake yourselves to the Cave: your Lord will shower His mercies on you and disposes of your affair towards comfort and ease."

17. You would have seen the sun, when it rose, declining to the right from their Cave, and when it set, turning away from them to the left, while they lay in the open space in the midst of the Cave. Such are among the Signs of Allah: He whom Allah, guides is rightly guided; but he whom Allah leaves to stray,- for him will you find no protector to lead him to the Right Way.

18. You would have deemed them awake, whilst they were asleep, and We turned them on their right and on their left sides: their dog stretching forth his two fore-legs on the threshold: if you had come up on to them, you would have certainly turned back from them in flight, and would certainly have been filled with terror of them.

19. Such (being their state), we raised them up (from sleep), that they might question each other. Said one of them,

14. Wa rabaṭnaa ‘alaa quloo-bihim iz qaamoo faqaaloo Rabbunaa Rabbus-samaawaati wal-arḍi lan-nad‘uwa min dooniheee ilaahal-laqad qul-naaa izan shaṭaṭaa.

15. Haaa’ulaaa’i qawmunat-takhazoo min dooniheee aali-hatal-law laa yaåtoona ‘alayhim bisulṭaanim bayyin; faman azlamu mimmaniftaraa ‘alal-laahi kazibaa.

16. Wa izi‘tazal-tumoohum wa maa ya‘budoona illal-laaha faåwooo ilal-kahfi yanshur lakum Rabbukum-mir-raḥ-matihee wa yuhayyi’ lakum-min amrikum-mirfaqaa.

17. Wa tarash-shamsa izaa ṭala‘at-tazaawaru ‘an kahfihim zaatal-yameeni wa izaa gha-rabat taqriḍuhum zaatash-shimaali wa hum fee fajwatim-minh; zaalika min Aayaatil-laah; mañy-yahdil-laahu fahu-wal-muhtad, wa mañy-yuḍlil falan tajida lahoo waliyyam-murshidaa.   **(Section 2)**

18. Wa taḥsabuhum ayqaa-zañw-wa hum ruqood; wa nuqallibuhum zaatal-yameeni wa zaatash-shimaali wa kalbuhum baasiṭun ziraa‘ayhi bilwaṣeed; lawiṭ-ṭala‘ta ‘alayhim la-wallayta minhum firaarañw-wa lamuli’ta minhum ru‘baa.

19. Wa kazaalika ba‘asnaa-hum liyatasaaa’aloo baynahum; qaala qaaa’ilum-minhum kam

وَرَبَطْنَا عَلٰى قُلُوبِهِمْ اِذْ قَامُوْا فَقَالُوْا رَبُّنَا رَبُّ السَّمٰوٰتِ وَالْاَرْضِ لَنْ نَّدْعُوَا۟ مِنْ دُوْنِهٖ اِلٰهًا لَّقَدْ قُلْنَا اِذًا شَطَطًا ۝

هٰٓؤُلَآءِ قَوْمُنَا اتَّخَذُوْا مِنْ دُوْنِهٖٓ اٰلِهَةً ۗ لَوْلَا يَأْتُوْنَ عَلَيْهِمْ بِسُلْطٰنٍۭ بَيِّنٍ ۗ فَمَنْ اَظْلَمُ مِمَّنِ افْتَرٰى عَلَى اللّٰهِ كَذِبًا ۝

وَاِذِ اعْتَزَلْتُمُوْهُمْ وَمَا يَعْبُدُوْنَ اِلَّا اللّٰهَ فَأْوٗٓا اِلَى الْكَهْفِ يَنْشُرْ لَكُمْ رَبُّكُمْ مِّنْ رَّحْمَتِهٖ وَيُهَيِّئْ لَكُمْ مِّنْ اَمْرِكُمْ مِّرْفَقًا ۝

وَتَرَى الشَّمْسَ اِذَا طَلَعَتْ تَّزٰوَرُ عَنْ كَهْفِهِمْ ذَاتَ الْيَمِيْنِ وَاِذَا غَرَبَتْ تَّقْرِضُهُمْ ذَاتَ الشِّمَالِ وَهُمْ فِيْ فَجْوَةٍ مِّنْهُ ۗ ذٰلِكَ مِنْ اٰيٰتِ اللّٰهِ ۗ مَنْ يَّهْدِ اللّٰهُ فَهُوَ الْمُهْتَدِ ۚ وَمَنْ يُّضْلِلْ فَلَنْ تَجِدَ لَهٗ وَلِيًّا مُّرْشِدًا ۝

وَتَحْسَبُهُمْ اَيْقَاظًا وَّهُمْ رُقُوْدٌ ۖ وَّنُقَلِّبُهُمْ ذَاتَ الْيَمِيْنِ وَذَاتَ الشِّمَالِ ۖ وَكَلْبُهُمْ بَاسِطٌ ذِرَاعَيْهِ بِالْوَصِيْدِ ۚ لَوِ اطَّلَعْتَ عَلَيْهِمْ لَوَلَّيْتَ مِنْهُمْ فِرَارًا وَّلَمُلِئْتَ مِنْهُمْ رُعْبًا ۝

وَكَذٰلِكَ بَعَثْنٰهُمْ لِيَتَسَآءَلُوْا بَيْنَهُمْ ۗ قَالَ قَآئِلٌ مِّنْهُمْ كَمْ

"How long have you stayed (here)?" They said, "We have stayed (perhaps) a day, or part of a day." (At length) they (all) said, "Allah (alone) knows best how long you have stayed here.... Now you send one of you with this money of yours to the town: let him find out which is the best food (to be had) and bring some to you, that (you may) satisfy your hunger therewith: And let him behave with care and courtesy, and let him not inform anyone about you.

20. "For if they should come upon you, they would stone you or force you to return to their cult, and in that case you would never attain prosperity."

21. Thus We made their case known to the people, that they might know that the promise of Allah is true, and that there can be no doubt about the Hour of Judgment. Behold, they disputed among themselves as to their affair. (Some) said, "Construct a building over them": Their Lord knows best about them: those who prevailed over their affair said, "Let us surely build a place of worship over them."

22. (Some) say they were three, the dog being the fourth among them; (others) say they were five, the dog being the sixth,- doubtfully guessing at the unknown; (yet others) say they were seven, the dog being the eighth. You say: "My Lord knows best their number; it is but few that know their (real case)." Do not enter, therefore, into controversies concerning them, except on a matter that is clear, nor consult any of them about (the affair of) the Sleepers.

23. Nor say of anything, "I shall be sure to do

labistum qaaloo labisnaa yaw-man aw ba'da yawm; qaaloo Rabbukum a'lamu bimaa labistum fab'asooo ahadakum biwariqikum haaziheee ilal-madeenati falyanzur ayyuhaaa azkaa ta'aaman falyaatikum birizqim-minhu walyatalattaf wa laa yush'iranna bikum ahadaa.

20. Innahum iñy-yazharoo 'alaykum yarjumookum aw yu'eedookum fee millatihim wa lan tuflihooo izan abadaa.

21. Wa kazaalika a'sar-naa 'alayhim liya'lamooo anna wa'dal-laahi haqquñw-wa annas-Saa'ata laa rayba feehaa iz yatanaaza'oona baynahum amrahum faqaalub-noo 'alay-him bunyaanaa; Rabbuhum a'lamu bihim; qaalal-lazeena ghalaboo 'alaaa amrihim lanat-takhizanna 'alayhim-masjidaa.

22. Sa-yaqooloona salaasatur-raabi'uhum kalbuhum wa yaqooloona khamsatun saadisu-hum kalbuhum rajmam bilghayb; wa yaqooloona sab'a-tuñw-wa saaminuhum kalbu-hum; qur-Rabbeee a'lamu bi'iddatihim-maa ya'lamuhum illaa qaleel; falaa tumaari feehim illaa miraaa'an zaahi-rañw-wa laa tastafti feehim-minhum ahadaa.   (Section 3)

23. Wa laa taqoolanna li-shay'in inneee faa'ilun

لَبِثْتُمْ ۚ قَالُوا لَبِثْنَا يَوْمًا أَوْ بَعْضَ يَوْمٍ ۚ قَالُوا رَبُّكُمْ أَعْلَمُ بِمَا لَبِثْتُمْ فَابْعَثُوا أَحَدَكُمْ بِوَرِقِكُمْ هَٰذِهِ إِلَى الْمَدِينَةِ فَلْيَنْظُرْ أَيُّهَا أَزْكَىٰ طَعَامًا فَلْيَأْتِكُمْ بِرِزْقٍ مِنْهُ وَلْيَتَلَطَّفْ وَلَا يُشْعِرَنَّ بِكُمْ أَحَدًا ۝

إِنَّهُمْ إِنْ يَظْهَرُوا عَلَيْكُمْ يَرْجُمُوكُمْ أَوْ يُعِيدُوكُمْ فِي مِلَّتِهِمْ وَلَنْ تُفْلِحُوا إِذًا أَبَدًا ۝

وَكَذَٰلِكَ أَعْثَرْنَا عَلَيْهِمْ لِيَعْلَمُوا أَنَّ وَعْدَ اللَّهِ حَقٌّ وَأَنَّ السَّاعَةَ لَا رَيْبَ فِيهَا إِذْ يَتَنَازَعُونَ بَيْنَهُمْ أَمْرَهُمْ فَقَالُوا ابْنُوا عَلَيْهِمْ بُنْيَانًا ۖ رَبُّهُمْ أَعْلَمُ بِهِمْ ۚ قَالَ الَّذِينَ غَلَبُوا عَلَىٰ أَمْرِهِمْ لَنَتَّخِذَنَّ عَلَيْهِمْ مَسْجِدًا ۝

سَيَقُولُونَ ثَلَاثَةٌ رَابِعُهُمْ كَلْبُهُمْ وَيَقُولُونَ خَمْسَةٌ سَادِسُهُمْ كَلْبُهُمْ رَجْمًا بِالْغَيْبِ وَيَقُولُونَ سَبْعَةٌ وَثَامِنُهُمْ كَلْبُهُمْ قُلْ رَبِّي أَعْلَمُ بِعِدَّتِهِمْ مَا يَعْلَمُهُمْ إِلَّا قَلِيلٌ ۗ فَلَا تُمَارِ فِيهِمْ إِلَّا مِرَاءً ظَاهِرًا وَلَا تَسْتَفْتِ فِيهِمْ مِنْهُمْ أَحَدًا ۝

وَلَا تَقُولَنَّ لِشَيْءٍ إِنِّي فَاعِلٌ

so and so tomorrow"-

24. Without adding, "If Allah so wills" and call your Lord to mind when you forget, and say, "I hope that my Lord will guide me ever closer (even) than this to the right road."

25. So they stayed in their Cave three hundred years, and (some) add nine (more).

26. Say: "Allah knows best how long they stayed: with Him is (the knowledge of) the secrets of the heavens and the earth: how clearly He sees, how finely He hears (everything)! They have no protector other than Him; nor does He share His Command with any person whatsoever.

27. And recite (and teach) what has been revealed to you of the Book of your Lord: none can change His Words, and none will you find as a refuge other than Him.

28. And keep your soul content with those who call on their Lord morning and evening, seeking His Face; and let not your eyes pass beyond them, seeking the pomp and glitter of this Life; nor obey any whose heart We have permitted to neglect the remembrance of Us, one who follows his own desires, whose case has gone beyond all bounds.

29. Say, "The Truth is from your Lord": Let him who will believe, and let him who will, reject (it): for the wrong-doers We have prepared a Fire whose (smoke and flames), like the walls and roof of a tent, will hem them in: if they implore relief they will be granted water-like melted brass, that will scald their faces.

---

zaalika ghadaa.

24. Illaaa añy-yashaaa'al-laah; wazkur-Rabbaka izaa naseeta wa qul 'asaaa añy-yahdiyani Rabbee li-aqraba min haazaa rashadaa.

25. Wa labisoo fee kahfihim salaasa mi'atin sineena wazdaadoo tis'aa.

26. Qulil-laahu a'lamu bimaa labisoo lahoo ghaybus-samaa-waati wal-ardi absir bihee wa-asmi'; maa lahum-min doonihee miñw-waliyyiñw-wa laa yushriku fee hukmiheee ahadaa.

27. Watlu maaa oohiya ilayka min Kitaabi Rabbika laa mubaddila li-Kalimaatihee wa lan tajida min doonihee multahadaa.

28. Wasbir nafsaka ma'al-lazeena yad'oona Rabbahum bilghadaati wal'ashiyyi yuree-doona Wajhahoo wa laa ta'du 'aynaaka 'anhum tureedu zeenatal-hayaatid-dunyaa wa laa tuti' man aghfalnaa qalbahoo 'an zikrinaa wattaba'a hawaahu wa kaana amruhoo furutaa.

29. Wa qulil-haqqu mir-Rabbikum faman shaaa'a falyu'miñw-wa man shaaa'a falyakfur; innaaa a'tadnaa liz-zaalimeena Naaran ahaata bihim suraadiquhaa; wa iñy-yastagheesoo yughaasoo bi-maaa'in kalmuhli yashwil-wujooh;

how dreadful the drink! How uncomfortable a couch to recline on!

30. As to those who believe and work righteousness, verily We shall not suffer to perish the reward of any who do a (single) righteous deed.

31. For them will be Gardens of Eternity; beneath them rivers will flow; they will be adorned therein with bracelets of gold, and they will wear green garments of fine silk and heavy brocade: They will recline therein on raised thrones. How good the recompense! How beautiful a couch to recline on!

32. Set forth to them the parable of two men: for one of them We provided two gardens of grape-vines and surrounded them with date palms; in between the two We placed corn-fields.

33. Each of those gardens brought forth its produce, and did not fail in the least therein: in the midst of them We caused a river to flow.

34. (Abundant) was the produce this man had : he said to his companion, in the course of a mutual argument: "more wealth have I than you, and more honor and power in (my following of) men."

35. He went into his garden in a state (of mind) unjust to his soul: He said, "I deem not that this will ever perish,

36. "Nor do I deem that the Hour (of Judgment) will (ever) come: Even if I am brought back to my Lord, I shall surely find (there) something better in exchange."

37. His companion said to him, in the course of the argument with him: "Do you deny Him Who created you out of

bi'sash-sharaab; wa saaa'at murtafaqaa.

30. Innal-lazeena aamanoo wa 'amilus-saaliḥaati innaa laa nuḍee'u ajra man aḥsana 'amalaa.

31. Ulaaa'ika lahum Jannaatu 'Adnin tajree min taḥtihimul-anhaaru yuḥallawna feehaa min asaawira min zahabiñw-wa yalbasoona siyaaban khuḍram-min sundusiñw-wa istabraqim-muttaki'eena feehaa 'alal-araaa'ik; ni'mas-sawaab; wa ḥasunat murtafaqaa. **(Section 4)**

32. Waḍrib lahum-masalar-rajulayni ja'alnaa li-aḥadihimaa jannatayni min a'naabiñw-wa ḥafafnaahumaa binakhliñw-wa ja'alnaa baynahumaa zar'aa.

33. Kiltal-jannatayni aatat ukulahaa wa lam taẓlim-minhu shay'añw-wa fajjarnaa khi-laalahumaa naharaa.

34. Wa kaana lahoo ṣamarun faqaala liṣaaḥibihee wa huwa yuḥaawiruhooo ana aksaru minka maalañw-wa a'azzu nafaraa.

35. Wa dakhala jannatahoo wa huwa ẓaalimul-linafsihee qaala maaa aẓunnu an tabeeda haaziheee abadaa.

36. Wa maaa aẓunnus-Saa'ata qaaa'imatañw-wa la'ir-rudittu ilaa Rabbee la-ajidanna khay-ram-minhaa munqalabaa.

37. Qaala lahoo ṣaaḥibuhoo wa huwa yuḥaawiruhooo akafarta billazee khalaqaka min

dust, then out of a sperm-drop, then fashioned you into a man?

38. "But (I think) for my part that He is Allah, My Lord, and none shall I associate with my Lord.

39. "Why did you not, as you went into your garden, say: 'Allah's Will (be done)! There is no power but with Allah!' If you see me less than you in wealth and sons,

40. "It may be that my Lord will give me something better than your garden, and that He will send on your garden thunderbolts (by way of reckoning) from heaven, making it (but) slippery sand!-

41. "Or the water of the garden will run off underground so that you will never be able to find it."

42. So his fruits (and enjoyment) were encompassed (with ruin), and he remained twisting and turning his hands over what he had spent on his property, which had (now) tumbled to pieces to its very foundations, and he could only say, "Woe is me! Would I had never ascribed partners to my Lord and Cherisher!"

43. Nor had he numbers to help him against Allah, nor was he able to deliver himself.

44. There, the (only) protection comes from Allah, the True One. He is the Best to reward, and the Best to give success.

45. Set forth to them the similitude of the life of this world: It is like the rain which we send down from the skies:

turaabin summa min nuṭfatin summa sawwaaka rajulaa.

38. Laakinna Huwal-laahu Rabbee wa laaa ushriku bi-Rabbeee aḥadaa.

39. Wa law laaa iz dakhalta jannataka qulta maa shaaa'al-laahu laa quwwata illaa billaah; in tarani ana aqalla minka maalaňw-wa waladaa.

40. Fa'asaa Rabbee aňy-yu'ti-yani khayram-min jannatika wa yursila 'alayhaa ḥusbaanam-minas-samaaa'i fatuṣbiḥa ṣa'eedan zalaqaa.

41. Aw yuṣbiḥa maaa'uhaa ghawran falan tastaṭee'a lahoo ṭalabaa.

42. Wa uḥeeṭa bisamarihee fa-aṣbaḥa yuqallibu kaffayhi 'alaa maaa anfaqa feehaa wa hiya khaawiyatun 'alaa 'urooshihaa wa yaqoolu yaalaytanee lam ushrik bi-Rabbeee aḥadaa.

43. Wa lam takul-lahoo fi'atuňy-yanṣuroonahoo min doonil-laahi wa maa kaana muntaṣiraa.

44. Hunaalikal hasheeman tazroohur-Riyaaḥ; wa kaanal-laahu 'alaa kulli shay'il-walaayatu lillaahil-ḥaqq; huwa khayrun sawaabaňw-wa khayrun 'uqbaa.   **(Section 5)**

45. Waḍrib lahum-maṣalal-ḥayaatid-dunyaa kamaaa'in anzalnaahu minas-samaaa'i

The earth's vegetation absorbs it, but soon it becomes dry stubble, which the winds do scatter: it is (only) Allah who prevails over all things.

46. Wealth and sons are allurements of the life of this world: but the things that endure, Good Deeds, are best in the sight of your Lord, as rewards, and best as (the foundation for) hopes.

47. One Day We shall remove the mountains, and you will see the earth as a level stretch, and We shall gather them, all together, nor shall We leave out any one of them.

48. And they will be marshalled before your Lord in ranks, (with the announcement), "Now have you come to Us (bare) as We created you first instance; yes, you thought We shall not fulfil the appointment made to you to meet (Us)!":

49. And the Book (of Deeds) will be placed (before you); and you will see the sinful in great terror because of what is (recorded) therein; they will say, "Ah! woe to us! what a Book is this! It leaves out nothing small or great, but takes account thereof!" They will find all that they did, placed before them: And not one will your Lord treat with injustice.

50. Behold! We said to the angels, "Bow down to Adam": They bowed down except Iblis. He was one of the Jinns, and he broke the Command of his Lord. Will you then take him and his progeny as protectors rather than Me? And they are enemies to you! Evil would be the exchange for the wrong-doers!

51. I called them not to witness the creation of the heavens and the earth, nor (even) their own creation: nor

fakhtalaṭa bihee nabaatul-arḍi fa-aṣbaḥa hasheeman tazroo-hur-riyaaḥ; wa kaanal-laahu 'alaa kulli shay'im-muqtadiraa.

46. Almaalu walbanoona zeenatul-ḥayaatid-dunyaa wal-baaqiyaatuṣ-ṣaaliḥaatu khayrun 'inda Rabbika sawaabañw-wa khayrun amalaa.

47. Wa Yawma nusayyirul-jibaala wa taral-arḍa baariza-tañw-wa ḥasharnaahum falam nughaadir minhum aḥadaa.

48. Wa 'uriḍoo 'alaa Rabbika ṣaffaa, laqad ji'tumoonaa kamaa khalaqnaakum awwala marrah; bal za'amtum allan-naj'ala lakum-maw'idaa.

49. Wa wuḍi'al-kitaabu fata-ral-mujrimeena mushfiqeena mimmaa feehi wa yaqooloona yaa waylatanaa maa lihaaẓal-kitaabi laa yughaadiru ṣaghee-ratañw-wa laa kabeeratan illaa aḥṣaahaa; wa wajadoo maa 'amiloo ḥaaḍiraa; wa laa yaẓlimu Rabbuka aḥadaa.

(Section 6)

50. Wa iz qulnaa lilma-laa'ikatis-judoo li Aadama fasajadooo illaa Ibleesa kaana minal-jinni fafasaqa 'an amri Rabbih; afatattakhizoonahoo wa zurriyyatahooo awliyaaa'a min doonee wa hum lakum 'aduww; bi'sa liẓẓaalimeena badalaa.

51. Maaa ash-hattuhum khal-qas-samaawaati wal-arḍi wa laa khalqa anfusihim wa maa

فَاخْتَلَطَ بِهٖ نَبَاتُ الْأَرْضِ فَأَصْبَحَ هَشِيْمًا تَذْرُوهُ الرِّيَاحُ ۗ وَكَانَ اللّٰهُ عَلٰى كُلِّ شَيْءٍ مُّقْتَدِرًا ۝

اَلْمَالُ وَالْبَنُوْنَ زِيْنَةُ الْحَيٰوةِ الدُّنْيَا ۚ وَالْبٰقِيٰتُ الصّٰلِحٰتُ خَيْرٌ عِنْدَ رَبِّكَ ثَوَابًا وَّخَيْرٌ اَمَلًا ۝

وَيَوْمَ نُسَيِّرُ الْجِبَالَ وَتَرَى الْأَرْضَ بَارِزَةً ۙ وَّحَشَرْنٰهُمْ فَلَمْ نُغَادِرْ مِنْهُمْ اَحَدًا ۝

وَعُرِضُوْا عَلٰى رَبِّكَ صَفًّا ۗ لَقَدْ جِئْتُمُوْنَا كَمَا خَلَقْنٰكُمْ اَوَّلَ مَرَّةٍ ۢ بَلْ زَعَمْتُمْ اَلَّنْ نَّجْعَلَ لَكُمْ مَّوْعِدًا ۝

وَوُضِعَ الْكِتٰبُ فَتَرَى الْمُجْرِمِيْنَ مُشْفِقِيْنَ مِمَّا فِيْهِ وَيَقُوْلُوْنَ يٰوَيْلَتَنَا مَالِ هٰذَا الْكِتٰبِ لَا يُغَادِرُ صَغِيْرَةً وَّلَا كَبِيْرَةً اِلَّا اَحْصٰهَا ۚ وَوَجَدُوْا مَا عَمِلُوْا حَاضِرًا ۗ وَلَا يَظْلِمُ رَبُّكَ اَحَدًا ۝

وَاِذْ قُلْنَا لِلْمَلٰٓئِكَةِ اسْجُدُوْا لِاٰدَمَ فَسَجَدُوْٓا اِلَّآ اِبْلِيْسَ ۗ كَانَ مِنَ الْجِنِّ فَفَسَقَ عَنْ اَمْرِ رَبِّهٖ ۗ اَفَتَتَّخِذُوْنَهٗ وَذُرِّيَّتَهٗٓ اَوْلِيَاءَ مِنْ دُوْنِيْ وَهُمْ لَكُمْ عَدُوٌّ ۗ بِئْسَ لِلظّٰلِمِيْنَ بَدَلًا ۝

مَآ اَشْهَدْتُّهُمْ خَلْقَ السَّمٰوٰتِ وَالْأَرْضِ وَلَا خَلْقَ اَنْفُسِهِمْ ۖ وَمَا

is it for helpers such as Me to take as lead (men) astray!

52. One Day He will say, "Call on those whom you thought to be My partners," and they will call on them, but they will not listen to them; and We shall make for them a place of common perdition.

53. And the Sinful shall see the fire and apprehend that they have to fall therein: no means will they find to turn away therefrom.

54. We have explained in detail in this Qur'an, for the benefit of mankind, every kind of similitude: but man is, in most things, contentious.

55. And what is there to keep back men from believing, now that guidance has come to them, nor from praying for forgiveness from their Lord, but that (they ask that) the ways of the ancients be repeated with them, or the Wrath be brought to them face to face?

56. We only send the Messengers to give glad tidings and to give warnings; But the Unbelievers dispute with vain argument, in order therewith to weaken the Truth, and they treat My Signs as a jest as also the fact that they are warned.

57. And who does more wrong than one who is reminded of the Signs of his Lord, but turns away from them, forgetting the (deeds) which his hands have sent forth? Verily We have set veils over their hearts lest they should understand this, and over their ears, deafness, if you call them to guidance, even then will they never accept guidance.

kuntu muttakhizal-mudilleena 'adudaa.

52. Wa Yawma yaqoolu naadoo shurakaaa'i-yal-lazeena za'amtum fada'aw-hum falam yastajeeboo lahum wa ja'alnaa baynahum-mawbiqaa.

53. Wa ra-al-mujrimoonan-Naara fazannooo annahum-muwaaqi'oohaa wa lam yajidoo 'anhaa masrifaa. (Section 7)

54. Wa laqad sarrafnaa fee haazal-Qur-aani linnaasi min kulli masal; wa kaanal-insaanu aksara shay'in jadalaa.

55. Wa maa mana'an-naasa any-yu'minooo iz jaaa'ahumul-hudaa wa yastaghfiroo Rabbahum illaaa an taåtiyahum sunnatul-awwaleena aw yaå-tiyahumul-'azaabu qubulaa.

56. Wa maa nursilul-mursaleena illaa mubashshi-reena wa munzireen; wa yujaadilul-lazeena kafaroo bilbaatili liyudhidoo bihil-haqqa wattakhazooo Aayaatee wa maaa unziroo huzuwaa.

57. Wa man azlamu mimman zukkira bi-Aayaati Rabbihee fa-a'rada 'anhaa wa nasiya maa qaddamat yadaah; innaa ja'al-naa 'alaa quloobihim akinnatan any-yafqahoohu wa feee aazaanihim waqraa; wa in tad'uhum ilal-hudaa falany-yahtadooo izan abadaa.

كُنتُ مُتَّخِذَ الْمُضِلِّينَ عَضُدًا ۝

وَيَوْمَ يَقُولُ نَادُوا شُرَكَآءِىَ الَّذِينَ زَعَمْتُمْ فَدَعَوْهُمْ فَلَمْ يَسْتَجِيبُوا لَهُمْ وَجَعَلْنَا بَيْنَهُم مَّوْبِقًا ۝

وَرَءَا الْمُجْرِمُونَ النَّارَ فَظَنُّوٓا أَنَّهُم مُّوَاقِعُوهَا وَلَمْ يَجِدُوا عَنْهَا مَصْرِفًا ۝

وَلَقَدْ صَرَّفْنَا فِى هَٰذَا الْقُرْءَانِ لِلنَّاسِ مِن كُلِّ مَثَلٍ ۚ وَكَانَ الْإِنسَانُ أَكْثَرَ شَىْءٍ جَدَلًا ۝

وَمَا مَنَعَ النَّاسَ أَن يُؤْمِنُوٓا إِذْ جَآءَهُمُ الْهُدَىٰ وَيَسْتَغْفِرُوا رَبَّهُمْ إِلَّآ أَن تَأْتِيَهُمْ سُنَّةُ الْأَوَّلِينَ أَوْ يَأْتِيَهُمُ الْعَذَابُ قُبُلًا ۝

وَمَا نُرْسِلُ الْمُرْسَلِينَ إِلَّا مُبَشِّرِينَ وَمُنذِرِينَ ۚ وَيُجَٰدِلُ الَّذِينَ كَفَرُوا بِالْبَٰطِلِ لِيُدْحِضُوا بِهِ الْحَقَّ ۖ وَاتَّخَذُوٓا ءَايَٰتِى وَمَآ أُنذِرُوا هُزُوًا ۝

وَمَنْ أَظْلَمُ مِمَّن ذُكِّرَ بِـَٔايَٰتِ رَبِّهِ فَأَعْرَضَ عَنْهَا وَنَسِىَ مَا قَدَّمَتْ يَدَاهُ ۚ إِنَّا جَعَلْنَا عَلَىٰ قُلُوبِهِمْ أَكِنَّةً أَن يَفْقَهُوهُ وَفِىٓ ءَاذَانِهِمْ وَقْرًا ۖ وَإِن تَدْعُهُمْ إِلَى الْهُدَىٰ فَلَن يَهْتَدُوٓا إِذًا أَبَدًا ۝

58. But your Lord is Most forgiving, full of Mercy. If He were to call them (at once) to account for what they have earned, then surely He would have hastened their punishment: but they have their appointed time, beyond which they will find no refuge.

59. Such were the populations we destroyed when they committed iniquities; but we fixed an appointed time for their destruction.

60. Behold, Moses said to his attendant, "I will not give up until I reach the junction of the two seas or (until) I spend years and years in travel."

61. But when they reached the Junction, they forgot (about) their Fish, which took its course through the sea (straight) as in a tunnel.

62. When they had passed on (some distance), Moses said to his attendant: "Bring us our early meal; truly we have suffered much fatigue at this (stage of) our journey."

63. He replied: "Did you see (what happened) when we betook ourselves to the rock? I did indeed forget (about) the Fish: none but Satan made me forget to tell (you) about it: it took its course through the sea in a marvellous way!"

64. Moses said: "That was what we were seeking after:" so they went back on their footsteps, following (the path they had come).

65. So they found one of Our servants, on whom We had bestowed Mercy from Ourselves and whom We had taught knowledge from Our own Presence.

66. Moses said to him: "May I follow you, on the footing that you teach me something of the (Higher) Truth which you have been taught?"

58. Wa Rabbukal-Ghafooru zur-rahmati law yu'aakhi-zuhum bimaa kasaboo la'ajjala lahumul-'azaab; bal lahum maw'idul-lañy-yajidoo min doonihee maw'ilaa.

59. Wa tikal-quraaa ahlak-naahum lammaa zalamoo wa ja'alnaa limahlikihim-maw'i-daa.   **(Section 8)**

60. Wa iz qaala Moosaa lifataahu laaa abrahu hattaaa ablugha majma'al-bahrayni aw amdiya huqubaa.

61. Falammaa balaghaa maj-ma'a baynihimaa nasiyaa hootahumaa fattakhaza sabee-lahoo fil-bahri sarabaa.

62. Falammaa jaawazaa qaala lifataahu aatinaa ghadaaa'anaa laqad laqeenaa min safarinaa haazaa nasabaa.

63. Qaala ara'ayta iz away-naaa ilas-sakhrati fa-innee naseetul-hoota wa maaa ansaa-neehu illash-Shaytaanu an azkurah; wattakhaza sabeela-hoo fil-bahri 'ajabaa.

64. Qaala zaalika maa kunnaa nabgh; fartaddaa 'alaaa aasaari-himaa qasasaa.

65. Fa-wajadaa 'abdam-min 'ibaadinaaa aataynaahu Rahma-tam-min 'indinaa wa 'allamnaa-hu mil-ladunnaa 'ilmaa.

66. Qaala lahoo Moosaa hal attabi'uka 'alaaa an tu'allimani mimmaa 'ullimta rushdaa.

67. (The other) said: "Verily you will not be able to have patience with me!"

68. "And how can you have patience about things about which your understanding is not complete?"

69. Moses said: "You will find me, if Allah so will, (truly) patient: nor shall I disobey you in any matter."

70. The other said: "If then you would follow me, ask me no questions about anything until I myself speak to you concerning it."

71. So they both proceeded: until, when they were in the boat, he scuttled it. Said Moses: "Have you scuttled it in order to drown those in it? Truly a strange thing you have done!"

72. He answered: "Did I not tell you that you can have no patience with me?"

73. Moses said: "Rebuke me not for forgetting, nor grieve me by raising difficulties in my case."

74. Then they proceeded: until, when they met a young man, he slew him. Moses said: "Have you slain an innocent person who had slain none? Truly a foul (unheard of) thing have you done!"

75. He answered: "Did I not tell you that you can have no patience with me?"

76. (Moses) said: "If ever I ask you about anything after this, keep me not in your company: then would you have received (full) excuse from my side."

77. Then they proceeded: until, when they came to the inhabitants of a town, they asked them for food, but they refused them hospitality. They found there a wall on the point of falling down, but he set it up straight. (Moses) said:

67. Qaala innaka lan tasta-ṭee‘a ma‘iya ṣabraa.

68. Wa kayfa taṣbiru ‘alaa maa lam tuḥiṭ bihee khubraa.

69. Qaala satajiduneee in shaaa’al-laahu ṣaabiraňw-wa laaa a‘ṣee laka amraa.

70. Qaala fa-init-taba‘tanee falaa tas’alnee ‘an shay’in ḥattaaa uḥdiṣa laka minhu zikraa. **(Section 9)**

71. Fanṭalaqaa ḥattaaa izaa rakibaa fis-safeenati khara-qahaa qaala akharaqtahaa litughriqa ahlahaa laqad ji’ta shay’an imraa.

72. Qaala alam aqul innaka lan tastaṭee‘a ma‘iya ṣabraa.

73. Qaala laa tu’aakhiznee bimaa naseetu wa laa turhiqnee min amree ‘usraa.

74. Fanṭalaqaa ḥattaaa izaa laqiyaa ghulaaman faqatalahoo qaala aqatalta nafsan zakiy-yatam bighayri nafs; laqad ji’ta shay’an-nukraa.

75. Qaala alam aqul laka innaka lan tastaṭee‘a ma‘iya ṣabraa.

76. Qaala in sa-altuka ‘an shay’im ba‘dahaa falaa tuṣaaḥibnee qad balaghta mil-ladunnee ‘uzraa.

77. Fanṭalaqaa ḥattaaa izaaa atayaaa ahla qaryatinis-taṭ‘amaaa ahlahaa fa-abaw añy-yuḍayyifoohumaa fawajadaa feehaa jidaarañy-yureedu añy-yanqaḍḍa fa-aqaamah; qaala

"If you had wished, surely you could have exacted some recompense for it!"

78. He answered: "This is the parting between me and you: now will I tell you the interpretation of (those things) over which you were unable to hold patience.

79. "As for the boat, it belonged to certain men in dire want: they plied on the water: I but wished to render it unserviceable, for there was after them a certain king who seized on every boat by force.

80. "As for the youth, his parents were people of Faith, and we feared that he would grieve them by obstinate rebellion and ingratitude (to Allah).

81. "So we desired that their Lord would give them in exchange (a son) better in purity (of conduct) and closer in affection.

82. "As for the wall, it belonged to two youths, orphans, in the Town; there was, beneath it, a buried treasure, to which they were entitled: their father had been a righteous man: so your Lord desired that they should attain their age of full strength and get out their treasure - a mercy (and favor) from your Lord. I did it not of my own accord. Such is the interpretation of (those things) over which you were unable to hold patience."

83. They ask you concerning Zul-qarnain. Say, "I will rehearse to you something of his story."

84. Verily We established his power on earth, and We gave him the ways and the means to all ends.

85. One (such) way he followed,

86. Until, when he reached the setting of the sun, he found it set in a spring of murky water: Near it he found

---

law shi'ta lattakhazta 'alayhi ajraa.

78. Qaala haazaa firaaqu baynee wa baynik; sa-unabbi-'uka bitaåweeli maa lam tastati' 'alayhi ṣabraa.

79. Ammas-safeenatu fakaa-nat limasaakeena ya'maloona fil-baḥri fa-arattu an a'eebahaa wa kaana waraaa'ahum-malikuñy-yaåkhuzu kulla safeenatin ghaṣbaa.

80. Wa aammal-ghulaamu fakaana abawaahu mu'minayni fakhasheenaaa añy-yurhiqa-humaa ṭughyaanañw-wa kufraa.

81. Fa-aradnaaa añy-yubdila-humaa Rabbuhumaa khayram-minhu zakaatañw-wa aqraba ruḥmaa.

82. Wa ammal-jidaaru fakaa-na lighulaamayni yateemayni fil-madeenati wa kaana taḥta-hoo kanzul-lahumaa wa kaana aboohumaa ṣaaliḥan fa-araada Rabbuka añy-yablughaaa ashuddahumaa wa yastakhrijaa kanzahumaa raḥmatam-mir-Rabbik; wa maa fa'altuhoo 'an amree; zaalika taåweelu maa lam tasṭi' 'alayhi ṣabraa.

(Section 10)

83. Wa yas'aloonaka 'an Zil-Qarnayni qul sa-atloo 'alay-kum- minhu zikraa.

84. Innaa makkannaa lahoo fil-arḍi wa aataynaahu min kulli shay'in sababaa.

85. Fa-atba'a sababaa.

86. Ḥattaaa izaa balagha maghribash-shamsi wajadahaa taghrubu fee 'aynin ḥami'a-tiñw-wa wajada

a People: We said: "O Zul-qarnain! (you have authority,) either to punish them, or to treat them with kindness."

87. He said: "Whoever does wrong, him shall we punish; then shall he be sent back to his Lord; and He will punish him with a punishment unheard-of (before).

88. "But whoever believes, and works righteousness,- he shall have a goodly reward, and easy will be his task as We order it by our command."

89. Then he followed (another) way,

90. Until, when he came to the rising of the sun, he found it rising on a people for whom We had provided no covering protection against the sun.

91. (He left them) as they were: We completely understood what was before him.

92. Then he followed (another) way,

93. Until, when he reached (a tract) between two mountains, he found, beneath them, a people who scarcely understood a word.

94. They said: "O Zul-qarnain! the Gog and Magog (People) do great mischief on earth: shall we then render you tribute in order that you might erect a barrier between us and them?

95. He said: "(The power) in which my Lord has established me is better (than tribute): Help me therefore with strength (and labor): I will erect a strong barrier between you and them:

96. "Bring me blocks of iron." At length, when he had filled up the space between the two steep mountain-sides, he said, "Blow (with your bellows)"

'indahaa qawmaa; qulnaa yaa Zal-Qarnayni immaaa an tu'azziba wa immaaa an tattakhiza feehim husnaa.

87. Qaala ammaa man zalama fasawfa nu'azzibuhoo summa yuraddu ilaa Rabbihee fa-yu 'azzibuhoo 'azaaban-nukraa.

88. Wa ammaa man aamana wa 'amila saalihan falahoo jazaaa'anil-husnaa wa sanaqoolu lahoo min amrinaa yusraa.

89. Summa atba'a sababaa.

90. Hattaaa izaa balagha matli'ash-shamsi wajadahaa tatlu'u 'alaa qawmil-lam naj'allahum-min doonihaa sitraa.

91. Kazaalika wa qad ahatnaa bimaa ladayhi khubraa.

92. Summa atba'a sababaa.

93. Hattaaa izaa balagha baynas-saddayni wajada min doonihimaa qawmal-laa yakaadoona yafqahoona qawlaa.

94. Qaaloo yaa Zal-Qarnayni inna Yaâjooja wa Maâjooja-mufsidoona fil-ardi fahal naj'alu laka kharjan 'alaaa an taj'ala baynanaa wa baynahum saddaa.

95. Qaala maa makkannee feehi Rabbee khayrun faa'eenoonee biquwwatin aj'al baynakum wa baynahum radmaa.

96. Aatoonee zubaral-hadeed, hattaaa izaa saawaa baynas-sadafayni qaalan-fukhoo

Then, when he had made it (red) as fire, he said: "Bring me, that I may pour over it, molten lead."

ḥattaaa izaa ja'alahoo naaran qaala aatooneee ufrigh 'alayhi qiṭraa.

97. Thus they were made powerless to scale it or to dig through it.

97. Famas-ṭaa'ooo añy-yazha-roohu wa mastaṭaa'oo lahoo naqbaa.

98. He said: "This is a mercy from my Lord: but when the promise of my Lord comes to pass, He will make it into dust; and the promise of my Lord is true."

98. Qaala haazaa raḥmatum-mir-Rabbee fa-izaa jaaa'a wa'du Rabbee ja'alahoo dak-kaaa'a; wa kaana; wa'du Rabbee ḥaqqaa.

99. On that day We shall leave them to surge like waves on one another: the trumpet will be blown, and We shall collect them all together.

99. Wa taraknaa ba'ḍahum Yawma'iziñy-yamooju fee ba'ḍiñw-wa nufikha fiṣ-Ṣoori fajama'naahum jam'aa.

100. And We shall present Hell that day for Unbelievers to see, all spread out,-

100. Wa 'araḍnaa Jahannama Yawma'izil-lilkaafireena 'arḍaa.

101. (Unbelievers) whose eyes had been under a veil from remembrance of Me, and who had been unable even to hear.

101. Allazeena kaanat a'yunu-hum fee ghiṭaaa'in 'an-zikree wa kaanoo laa yastaṭee'oona sam'aa. **(Section 11)**

102. Do the Unbelievers think that they can take My servants as protectors besides Me? Verily We have prepared Hell for the Unbelievers for (their) enter-tainment.

102. Afaḥasibal-lazeena kafa-rooo añy-yattakhizoo 'ibaadee min doonee awliyaaa'; innaaa a'tadnaa Jahannama lilkaafi-reena nuzulaa.

103. Say: "Shall we tell you of those who lose most in respect of their deeds?-

103. Qul hal nunabbi'ukum bilakhsareena a'maalaa.

104. "Those whose efforts have been wasted in this life, while they thought that they were acquiring good by their works?"

104. Allazeena ḍalla sa'yuhum fil-ḥayaatid-dunyaa wa hum yaḥsaboona annahum yuḥsi-noona ṣun'aa.

105. They are those who deny the Signs of their Lord and the fact of their having to meet Him (in the Hereafter): vain will be their works, nor shall We, on the Day of Judgment, give them any weight.

105. Ulaaa'ikal-lazeena kafa-roo bi-Aayaati Rabbihim wa liqaaa'ihee faḥabiṭat a'maalu-hum falaa nuqeemu lahum Yawmal-Qiyaamati waznaa.

106. That is their reward, Hell, because they rejected Faith, and took My Signs and My Messengers by way of jest.

106. Zaalika jazaaa'uhum Jahannamu bimaa kafaroo wattakhazooo Aayaatee wa Rusulee huzuwaa.

107. As to those who believe and work righteous deeds, they have, for their entertainment, the Gardens of Paradise,

108. Wherein they shall dwell (for ever), no change will they wish for from them.

109. Say: "If the ocean were ink (wherewith to write out) the words of my Lord, sooner would the ocean be exhausted than would the words of my Lord, even if we added another ocean like it, for its aid."

110. Say: "I am but a man like yourselves, (but) the inspiration has come to me, that your Allah is one Allah: whoever expects to meet his Lord, let him work righteousness, and, in the worship of his Lord, admit no one as partner.

---

19. Mary

In the name of Allah, Most Gracious, Most Merciful.

1. *Kaf-Ha-Ya-Ain-Sad.*

2. (This is) a recital of the Mercy of your Lord to His servant Zakariya.

3. Behold! he cried to his Lord in secret,

4. Praying: "O my Lord! infirm indeed are my bones, and the hair of my head glistens with grey: but never am I unblest, O my Lord, in my prayer to You!

5. "Now I fear (what) my relatives (and colleagues) (will do) after me: but my wife is barren: so give me an heir as from yourself,-

6. "(One that) will (truly) represent me, and represent the posterity of Jacob; and make him, O my Lord! one with whom You are well-pleased!"

7. (His prayer was answered): "O Zakariya! We give you good news of a son: His name shall be Yahya: on none by that name have We conferred distinction before."

8. He said: "O my Lord! How shall I have a son, when

---

107. Innal-lazeena aamanoo wa 'amilus-saalihaati kaanat lahum Jannaatul-Firdawsi nuzulaa.

108. Khaalideena feehaa laa yabghoona 'anhaa hiwalaa.

109. Qul law kaanal-bahru midaadal-li-Kalimaati Rabbee lanafidal-bahru qabla an tanfada Kalimaatu Rabbee wa law ji'naa bimislihee madadaa.

110. Qul innamaaa ana basharum-mislukum yoohaaa ilayya annamaaa ilaahukum Ilaahunw-Waahid; faman kaana yarjoo liqaaa'a Rabbihee falya'mal 'amalan saalihanw-wa laa yushrik bi'ibaadati Rabbiheee ahadaa.

(Sec. 12)

Sûrat Maryam–19

(Revealed at Makkah)

Bismillaahir Rahmaanir Raheem

1. Kaaaf-Haa-Yaa-'Ayyyn-Saaad.

2. Zikru rahmati Rabbika 'abdahoo Zakariyyaa.

3. Iz naadaa Rabbahoo nidaaa'an khafiyyaa.

4. Qaala Rabbi innee wahanal-'azmu minnee washta'alar-raa-su shaybanw-wa lam akum bidu'aaa'ika Rabbi shaqiyyaa.

5. Wa innee khiftul-mawaa-liya minw-waraaa'ee wa kaana-tim-ra-atee 'aaqiran fahab lee mil-ladunka waliyyaa.

6. Yarisunee wa yarisu min aali Ya'qoob, waj'alhu Rabbi radiyyaa.

7. Yaa Zakariyyaaa innaa nubashshiruka bighulaami-nismuhoo Yahyaa lam naj'al-lahoo min qablu samiyyaa.

8. Qaala Rabbi annaa yakoo-nu lee ghulaamunw-wa

my wife is barren and I have grown quite decrepit from old age?”

9. He said: “So (it will be) your Lord says, ‘That is easy for Me: I did indeed create you before, when you had been nothing!’”

10. (Zakariya) said: “O my Lord! give me a Sign.” “your Sign,” was the answer, “Shall be that you shall speak to no man for three nights, although you are not dumb.

11. So Zakariya came out to his people from his chamber: he told them by signs to celebrate Allah’s praises in the morning and in the evening.

12. (To his son came the command):“O Yahya! take hold of the Book with might,” and We gave him Wisdom even as a youth,

13. And piety (for all creatures) as from Us, and purity: he was devout,

14. And kind to his parents, and he was not overbearing or rebellious.

15. So Peace on him the day he was born, the day that he dies, and the day that he will be raised up to life (again)!

16. Relate in the Book (the story of) Mary, when she withdrew from her family to a place in the East.

17. She placed a screen (to screen herself) from them; then We sent her Our angel, and he appeared before her as a man in all respects.

18. She said: “I seek refuge from you to (Allah) Most Gracious: (come not near) if you fear Allah.”

19. He said: “No, I am only a messenger from your Lord, (to announce) to you the gift of a holy son.

20. She said: “How shall I have a son, seeing that no man has touched me, and I am not unchaste?”

kaanatim-ra-atee aaqiranw-wa qad balaghtu minal-kibari ‘itiyyaa.

9. Qaala kazaalika qaala Rabbuka huwa ‘alayya hayyi-nunw-wa qad khalaqtuka min qablu wa lam taku shay’aa.

10. Qaala Rabbij-‘al-leee Aayah; qaala Aayatuka allaa tukalliman-naasa salaasa la-yaalin sawiyyaa.

11. Fakharaja ‘alaa qawmihee minal-mihraabi fa-awhaaa ilayhim an sabbihoo bukra-tanw- wa ‘ashiyyaa.

12. Yaa Yahyaa khuzil-Kitaa-ba biquwwatinw-wa aatay-naahul-hukma sabiyyaa.

13. Wa hanaanam-mil-ladunnaa wa zakaatanw wa kaana taqiyyaa.

14. Wa barram biwaalidayhi wa lam yakun jabbaaran ‘asiyyaa.

15. Wa salaamun ‘alayhi yaw-ma wulida wa yawma yamootu wa yawma yub‘asu hayyaa.

(Section 1)

16. Wazkur fil-Kitaabi Mar-yam; izin-tabazat min ahlihaa makaanan sharqiyyaa.

17. Fattakhazat min doonihim hijaaban fa-arsalnaaa ilayhaa roohanaa fatamassala lahaa basharan sawiyyaa.

18. Qaalat ineee a‘oozu bir-Rahmaani minka in kunta taqiyyaa.

19. Qaala innamaaa ana rasoolu Rabbiki li ahaba laki ghulaaman zakiyyaa.

20. Qaalat annaa yakoonu lee ghulaamunw-wa lam yamsas-nee basharunw-wa lam aku baghiyyaa.

21. He said: "So (it will be): your Lord says 'That is easy for Me: and (We wish) to appoint him as a Sign unto men and a Mercy from Us': It is a matter (so) decreed."

22. So she conceived him, and she retired with him to a remote place.

23. And the pains of childbirth drove her to the trunk of a palm-tree: She cried (in her anguish): "Ah! would that I had died before this! would that I had been a thing forgotten and out of sight!"

24. But (a voice) cried to her from beneath the (palm-tree): "Do not Grieve! for your Lord has provided a rivulet beneath you;

25. "And shake toward yourself the trunk of the palm-tree: it will let fall fresh ripe dates upon you.

26. "So eat and drink and cool (your) eye. And if you see any man, say, 'I have vowed a fast to (Allah) Most Gracious, and this day I will not enter into talk with any human being'"

27. At length she brought the (babe) to her people, carrying him (in her arms). They said: "O Mary! truly an amazing thing you have brought!

28. "O sister of Aaron! your father was not a man of evil, nor your mother an un-chaste woman!"

29. But she pointed to the babe. They said: "How can we talk to one who is a child in the cradle?"

30. He said: "I am indeed a servant of Allah: He has given me revelation and made me a prophet;

31. "And He has made me blessed wheresoever I be, and has enjoined on me Prayer and Charity as long as I live;

---

21. Qaala kazaaliki qaala Rabbuki huwa 'alayya hayyi-nuňw wa linaj'alahooo Aaayatal-linnaasi wa raḥmatam-minnaa; wa kaana amram-maqḍiyyaa.

22. Faḥamalat-hu fantabazat bihee makaanan qaṣiyyaa.

23. Fa-ajaaa'ahal-makhaaḍu ilaa jiz'in-nakhlati qaalat yaa laytanee mittu qabla haazaa wa kuntu nasyam-mansiyyaa.

24. Fanaadaahaa min taḥti-haaa allaa taḥzanee qad ja'ala Rabbuki taḥtaki sariyyaa.

25. Wa huzzeee ilayki bijiz-'in-nakhlati tusaaqiṭ 'alayki ruṭaban janiyyaa.

26. Fakulee washrabee wa qarree 'aynaa; fa-immaa tarayinna minal-bashari aḥadan faqooleee innee nazartu lir-Raḥmaani ṣawman falan ukallimal-yawma insiyyaa.

27. Fa-atat bihee qawmahaa taḥmiluhoo qaaloo yaa Mar-yamu laqad ji'ti shay'an fariyyaa.

28. Yaaa ukhta Haaroona maa kaana abookim-ra-a saw'iňw-wa maa kaanat ummuki baghiyyaa.

29. Fa-ashaarat ilayh; qaaloo kayfa nukallimu man kaana fil-mahdi ṣabiyyaa.

30. Qaala innee 'abdullaahi aataaniyal-Kitaaba wa ja'alanee Nabiyyaa.

31. Wa ja'alanee mubaarakan ayna maa kuntu wa awṣaanee biṣ-Ṣalaati waz-Zakaati maa dumtu ḥayyaa.

قَالَ كَذٰلِكِ ۚ قَالَ رَبُّكِ هُوَ عَلَىَّ هَيِّنٌ ۚ وَلِنَجْعَلَهُ اٰيَةً لِّلنَّاسِ وَرَحْمَةً مِّنَّا ۚ وَكَانَ اَمْرًا مَّقْضِيًّا ۞

فَحَمَلَتْهُ فَانْتَبَذَتْ بِهٖ مَكَانًا قَصِيًّا ۞

فَاَجَآءَهَا الْمَخَاضُ اِلٰى جِذْعِ النَّخْلَةِ ۚ قَالَتْ يٰلَيْتَنِيْ مِتُّ قَبْلَ هٰذَا وَكُنْتُ نَسْيًا مَّنْسِيًّا ۞

فَنَادٰىهَا مِنْ تَحْتِهَاۤ اَلَّا تَحْزَنِيْ قَدْ جَعَلَ رَبُّكِ تَحْتَكِ سَرِيًّا ۞

وَهُزِّيْۤ اِلَيْكِ بِجِذْعِ النَّخْلَةِ تُسٰقِطْ عَلَيْكِ رُطَبًا جَنِيًّا ۙ

فَكُلِيْ وَاشْرَبِيْ وَقَرِّيْ عَيْنًا ۚ فَاِمَّا تَرَيِنَّ مِنَ الْبَشَرِ اَحَدًا ۙ فَقُوْلِيْۤ اِنِّيْ نَذَرْتُ لِلرَّحْمٰنِ صَوْمًا فَلَنْ اُكَلِّمَ الْيَوْمَ اِنْسِيًّا ۞

فَاَتَتْ بِهٖ قَوْمَهَا تَحْمِلُهُ ۚ قَالُوْا يٰمَرْيَمُ لَقَدْ جِئْتِ شَيْئًا فَرِيًّا ۞

يٰۤاُخْتَ هٰرُوْنَ مَا كَانَ اَبُوْكِ امْرَاَ سَوْءٍ وَّمَا كَانَتْ اُمُّكِ بَغِيًّا ۚ

فَاَشَارَتْ اِلَيْهِ ۚ قَالُوْا كَيْفَ نُكَلِّمُ مَنْ كَانَ فِي الْمَهْدِ صَبِيًّا ۞

قَالَ اِنِّيْ عَبْدُ اللّٰهِ ۟ اٰتٰىنِيَ الْكِتٰبَ وَجَعَلَنِيْ نَبِيًّا ۙ

وَّجَعَلَنِيْ مُبٰرَكًا اَيْنَ مَا كُنْتُ ۖ وَاَوْصٰنِيْ بِالصَّلٰوةِ وَالزَّكٰوةِ مَا دُمْتُ حَيًّا ۞

32. "(He) has made me kind to my mother, and not overbearing or miserable;

33. "So peace is on me the day I was born, the day that I die, and the day that I shall be raised up to life (again)"!

34. Such (was) Jesus the son of Mary: (it is) a statement of truth, about which they (vainly) dispute.

35. It is not befitting to (the majesty of) Allah that He should beget a son. Glory be to Him! when He determines a matter, He only says to it, "Be", and it is.

36. Verily Allah is my Lord and your Lord: you, therefore serve Him: this is a Way that is straight.

37. But the sects differ among themselves: and woe to the Unbelievers because of the (coming) Judgment of a momentous Day!

38. How plainly will they see and hear, the Day that they will appear before Us! but the unjust today are in manifest error!

39. But warn them of the Day of Distress, when the matter will be determined: for (behold,) they are negligent and they do not believe!

40. It is We Who will inherit the earth, and all beings thereon: to Us will they all be returned.

41. (Also mention in the Book (the story of) Abraham: He was a man of Truth, a prophet.

42. Behold, he said to his father: "O my father! why worship that which does not hear and does not see, and can profit you nothing?

43. "O my father! to me has come knowledge which has not reached you: so follow me: I will guide you to a Way that is even and straight.

---

32. Wa barram biwaalidatee wa lam yaj'alnee jabbaaran shaqiyyaa.

33. Wassalaamu 'alayya yawma wulittu wa yawma amootu wa yawma ub'asu hayyaa.

34. Zaalika 'Eesab-nu Maryam; qawlal-haqqil-lazee feehi yamtaroon.

35. Maa kaana lillaahi añy-yattakhiza miñw-waladin Subhaanah; izaa qadaaa amran fa-innamaa yaqoolu lahoo kun fa-yakoon.

36. Wa innal-laaha Rabbee wa Rabbukum fa'budooh; haazaa Siraatum-Mustaqeem.

37. Fakhtalafal-ahzaabu mim baynihim fawaylul-lillazeena kafaroo mim-mashhadi Yaw-min 'azeem.

38. Asmi' bihim wa absir Yawma yaatoonanaa laakiniz-zaalimoonal-yawma fee dalaalim-mubeen.

39. Wa anzirhum Yawmal-hasrati iz qudiyal-amr; wa hum fee ghaflatiñw-wa hum laa yu'minoon.

40. Innaa Nahnu narisul-arda wa man 'alayhaa wa ilaynaa yurja'oon. (Section 2)

41. Wazkur fil-Kitaabi Ibraa-heem; innahoo kaana siddee-qan-Nabiyyaa.

42. Iz qaala li-abeehi yaaa abati lima ta'budu maa laa yasma'u wa laa yubsiru wa laa yughnee 'anka shay'aa.

43. Yaaa abati innee qad jaaa'anee minal-'ilmi maa lam yaatika fattabi'neee ahdika Siraatan Sawiyyaa.

44. "O my father! Do not serve Satan: for Satan is a rebel against (Allah) Most Gracious.

44. Yaaa abati laa ta'budish-Shayṭaana innash-Shayṭaana kaana lir-Raḥmaani 'aṣiyyaa.

45. "O my father! I fear lest a Penalty afflict you from (Allah) Most Gracious, so that you become a friend to Satan."

45. Yaaa abati ineee akhaafu añy-yamassaka 'aẓaabum-minar-Raḥmaani fatakoona lish-Shayṭaani waliyyaa.

46. (The father) replied: "Do you hate my gods, O Abraham? If you do not forbear, I will indeed stone you: now get away from me for a good long while!"

46. Qaala araaghibun anta 'an aalihatee yaaa Ibraaheemu la-il-lam tantahi la-arjumannaka wahjurnee maliyyaa.

47. Abraham said: "Peace be on you: I will pray to my Lord for your forgiveness: for He is to me Most Gracious.

47. Qaala salaamun 'alayka sa-astaghfiru laka Rabbeee innahoo kaana bee ḥafiyyaa.

48. "And I will turn away from you (all) and from those whom you invoke besides Allah: I will call on my Lord: perhaps, by my prayer to my Lord, I shall be not unblessed."

48. Wa a'tazilukum wa maa tad'oona min doonil-laahi wa ad'oo Rabbee 'asaaa allaaa akoona bidu'aaa'i Rabbee shaqiyyaa.

49. When he had turned away from them and from those whom they worshipped besides Allah, We bestowed on him Isaac and Jacob, and each one of them We made a prophet.

49. Falamma'-tazalahum wa maa ya'budoona min doonil-laahi wahabnaa lahoo Is-ḥaaqa wa Ya'qoob, wa kullan ja'alnaa Nabiyyaa.

50. And We bestowed of Our Mercy on them, and We granted them lofty honor on the tongue of truth.

50. Wa wahabnaa lahum-mirraḥmatinaa wa ja'alnaa lahum lisaana ṣidqin 'aliyyaa.

(Section 3)

51. Also mention in the Book (the story of) Moses: for he was specially chosen, and he was a Messenger (and) a prophet.

51. Wazkur fil-Kitaabi Moo-saaa; innahoo kaana mukhla-ṣañw-wa kaana Rasoolan-Nabiyyaa.

52. And we called him from the right side of Mount (Sinai), and made him draw near to Us, for mystic (converse).

52. Wa naadaynaahu min jaanibiṭ-Ṭooril-aymani wa qarrabnaahu najiyyaa.

53. And, out of Our Mercy, We gave him his brother Aaron, (also) a prophet.

53. Wa wahabnaa lahoo mir-raḥmatinaaa akhaahu Haaroona Nabiyyaa.

54. Also mention in the Book (the story of) Isma'il: he was (strictly) true to what he pro-mised, and he was a Messenger (and) a prophet.

54. Wazkur fil-Kitaabi Ismaa-'eel; innahoo kaana ṣaadiqal-wa'di wa kaana Rasoolan-Nabiyyaa.

55. He used to enjoin on his people Prayer and

55. Wa kaana yaåmuru ahlahoo biṣ-Ṣalaati waz-

Charity, and he was most acceptable in the sight of his Lord.

56. Also mention in the Book the case of Idris: he was a man of truth (and sincerity), (and) a prophet:

57. And We raised him to a lofty station.

58. Those were some of the prophets on whom Allah bestowed His Grace,- of the posterity of Adam, and of those who We carried (in the Ark) with Noah, and of the posterity of Abraham and Israel of those whom We guided and chose. Whenever the Signs of (Allah) Most Gracious were rehearsed to them, they would fall down in prostrate adoration and in tears.

59. But after them there followed a posterity who missed prayers and followed after lusts soon, then, will they face Destruction,-

60. Except those who repent and believe, and work righteousness: for these will enter the Garden and will not be wronged in the least,-

61. Gardens of Eternity, those which (Allah) Most Gracious has promised to His servants in the Unseen: for His promise must (necessarily) come to pass.

62. They will not hear any vain discourse, but only salutations of Peace: and therein they will have their sustenance, morning and evening.

63. Such is the Garden which We give as an inheritance to those of Our servants who guard against evil.

64. (The angels say:) "We do not descend but by command of your Lord: to Him belongs what is before us and what is behind us, and what is between us, and your Lord never forgets,-

65. "Lord of the heavens and of the earth, and of all that is between them;

zakaati wa kaana 'inda Rabbihee marḍiyyaa.

56. Wazkur fil-Kitaabi Idrees; innahoo kaana ṣiddeeqan-Nabiyyaa.

57. Wa rafa'naahu makaanan 'aliyyaa.

58. Ulaaa'ikal-lazeena an'amal-laahu 'alayhim-minan-Nabiyyeena min zurriyyati Aadama wa mimman ḥamalnaa ma'a Nooḥinw-wa min zurriyyati Ibraaheema wa Israaa'eela wa mimman hadaynaa wajtabaynaaa; izaa tutlaa 'alayhim Aayaatur-Raḥmaani kharroo sujjadanw-wa bukiyyaa.

59. Fakhalafa mim ba'dihim khalfun aḍaa'uṣ-Ṣalaata wattaba'ush-shahawaati fasawfa yalqawna ghayyaa.

60. Illaa man taaba wa aamana wa 'amila ṣaaliḥan faulaaa'ika yadkhuloonal-jannata wa laa yuẓlamoona shay'aa.

61. jannaati 'Adninil-latee wa'adar-Raḥmaanu 'ibaadahoo bilghayb; innahoo kaana wa'duhoo maåtiyyaa.

62. Laa yasma'oona feehaa laghwan illaa salaamaa; wa lahum rizquhum feehaa bukratañw-wa 'ashiyyaa.

63. Tilkal-jannatul-latee noorisu min 'ibaadinaa man kaana taqiyyaa.

64. Wa maa natanazzalu illaa bi-amri Rabbika lahoo maa bayna aydeenaa wa maa khalfanaa wa maa bayna zaalik; wa maa kaana Rabbuka nasiyyaa.

65. Rabbus-samaawaati walarḍi wa maa baynahumaa

so worship Him, and be constant and patient in His worship: do you know of any who is worthy of the same Name as He?"

66. Man says: "What! When I am dead, shall I then be raised up alive?"

67. But does not man call to mind that We created him before, out of nothing?

68. So, by your Lord, without doubt, We shall gather them together, and (also) the Evil Ones (with them); then shall We bring them forth on their knees round about Hell:

69. Then We shall certainly drag out from every sect all those who were worst in obstinate rebellion against (Allah) Most Gracious.

70. And certainly We know best those who are most worthy of being burned therein.

71. Not one of you but will pass over it: this is, with your Lord, a Decree which must be accomplished.

72. But We shall save those who guarded against evil, and We shall leave the wrong-doers therein, (humbled) to their knees.

73. When Our Clear Signs are rehearsed to them, the Unbelievers say to those who believe, "Which of the two sides is best in point of position? Which makes the best show in Council?"

74. But how many (countless) generations before them have we destroyed, who were even better in equipment and in glitter to the eye?

75. Say: "If any men go astray, (Allah) Most Gracious extends (the rope) to them, until, when they see the warning of Allah (being fulfilled) - either in punishment or in (the approach of) the Hour,- they will at length realise who is worst

fa'bud-hu waṣṭabir li'ibaadatih; hal ta'lamu lahoo samiyyaa.

(Section 4)

66. Wa yaqoolul-insaanu 'a-izaa maa mittu lasawfa ukhraju ḥayyaa.

67. Awalaa yazkurul-insaanu annaa khalaqnaahu min qablu wa lam yaku shay'aa.

68. Fawa Rabbika lanaḥshu-rannahum wash-shayaaṭeena summa lanuḥdirannahum ḥawla Jahannama jisiyyaa.

69. Summa lananzi 'anna min kulli shee'atin ayyuhum ashaddu 'alar-Raḥmaani 'itiyyaa.

70. Summa lanaḥnu a'lamu billazeena hum awlaa bihaa siliyyaa.

71. Wa im-minkum illaa waa-riduhaa; kaana 'alaa Rabbika ḥatmam-maqdiyyaa.

72. Summa nunajjil-lazeenat-taqaw wa nazaruz-zaalimeena feehaa jisiyyaa.

73. Wa izaa tutlaa 'alayhim Aayaatunaa bayyinaatin qaalal-lazeena kafaroo lillazeena aamanooo ayyul-fareeqayni khayrum-maqaamañw-wa aḥsanu nadiyyaa.

74. Wa kam ahlaknaa qabla-hum-min qarnin hum aḥsanu asaaṣañw-wa ri'yaa.

75. Qul man kaana fidda-laalati falyamdud lahur-Raḥ-maanu maddaa; ḥattaa izaa ra-aw maa yoo'adoona immal-'azaaba wa immas-Saa'ata fasa-ya'lamoona man huwa sharrum-

in position, and (who) weakest in forces!

76. "And Allah advances those in guidance who seek guidance: and the things that endure, Good Deeds, are best in the sight of your Lord, as rewards, and best in respect of (their) eventual return."

77. Have you then seen the (sort of) man who rejects Our Signs, yet says: "I shall certainly be given wealth and children?"

78. Has he penetrated to the Unseen, or has he taken a contract with (Allah) Most Gracious?

79. Nay! We shall record what he says, and We shall add and add to his punishment.

80. To Us shall return all that he talks of, and he shall appear before Us bare and alone.

81. And they have taken (for worship) gods other than Allah, to give them power and glory!

82. Instead, they shall reject their worship, and become adversaries against them.

83. Don't you see that We have set the Evil Ones on against the unbelievers, to incite them with fury?

84. So make no haste against them, for We but count out to them a (limited) number (of days).

85. The day We shall gather the righteous to (Allah) Most Gracious, like a band presented before a king for honors,

86. And We shall drive the sinners to Hell, like thirsty cattle driven down to water,-

87. None shall have the power of intercession but such a one as has received permission (or promise) from (Allah) Most Gracious.

88. They say: "(Allah) Most Gracious has begotten a son!"

89. Indeed you have put forth a thing most monstrous!

---

makaanañw-wa aḍ'afu jundaa.

76. Wa yazeedul-laahul-lazeenah-tadaw hudaa; wal-baaqiyaatuṣ-ṣaaliḥaatu khayrun 'inda Rabbika sawaabañw-wa khayrum-maraddaa.

77. Afara'aytal-lazee kafara bi-Aayaatinaa wa qaala la-oota-yanna maalañw-wa waladaa.

78. Aṭṭala'al-ghayba amitta-khaza 'indar-Raḥmaani 'ahdaa.

79. Kallaa; sanaktubu maa yaqoolu wa namuddu lahoo minal-'azaabi maddaa.

80. Wa narisuhoo maa yaqoolu wa yaåteenaa fardaa.

81. Wattakhazoo min doonil-laahi aalihatal-liyakoonoo lahum 'izzaa.

82. Kallaa; sa-yakfuroona bi'ibaadatihim wa yakoonoona 'alayhim ḍiddaa. (Section 5)

83. Alam tara annaaa arsal-nash-Shayaaṭeena 'alal-kaafi-reena ta'uzzuhum azzaa.

84. Falaa ta'jal 'alayhim innamaa na'uddu lahum 'addaa.

85. Yawma naḥshurul-mutta-qeena ilar-Raḥmaani wafdaa.

86. Wa nasooqul-mujrimeena ilaa Jahannama wirdaa.

87. Laa yamlikoonash-shafaa'ata illaa manittakhaza 'indar-Raḥmaani 'ahdaa.

88. Wa qaalut-takhazar-Raḥmaanu waladaa.

89. Laqad ji'tum shay'an iddaa.

90. At it the skies are ready to burst, the earth to split asunder, and the mountains to fall down in utter ruin,

91. That they should invoke a son for (Allah) Most Gracious.

92. For it is not consonant with the majesty of (Allah) Most Gracious that He should beget a son.

93. Not one of the beings in the heavens and the earth but must come to (Allah) Most Gracious as a servant.

94. He takes an account of them (all), and has numbered them (all) exactly.

95. And everyone of them will come to Him singly on the Day of Judgment.

96. On those who believe and work deeds of righteousness, will (Allah) Most Gracious bestow Love.

97. So We have made the (Qur'an) easy in your own tongue, that with it you may give glad ti-dings to the righteous, and warni-ngs to people given to contention

98. But how many (countless) generations before them We have destroyed? Can you find a single one of them (now) or hear (so much as) a whisper of them?

---

20. Ta-Ha
(Mystic Letters, T. H.)

In the name of Allah, Most Gracious, Most Merciful.

1. *Ta-Ha.*

2. We have not sent down the Qur'an to you to be (an occa-sion) for your distress,

3. But only as an admonition to those who fear (Allah),-

4. A revelation from Him Who created the earth and the heavens on high.

5. (Allah) Most Gracious is firmly established on the throne (of authority).

6. To Him belongs what is in the heavens and on earth, and all between them, and all beneath the soil.

7. If you pronounce the word aloud, (it is no matter): for verily He knows what is secret

---

90. Takaadus-samaawaatu yatafaṭṭarna minhu wa tanshaq-qul-arḍu wa takhirrul-jibaalu haddaa.

91. An da'aw lir-Raḥmaani waladaa.

92. Wa maa yambaghee lir-Raḥ-maani añy-yattakhiza waladaa.

93. In kullu man fis-samaa-waati wal-arḍi illaaa aatir-Raḥmaani 'abdaa.

94. Laqad aḥṣaahum wa 'addahum 'addaa.

95. Wa kulluhum aateehi Yawmal-Qiyaamati fardaa.

96. Innal-lazeena aamanoo wa 'amiluṣ-ṣaaliḥaati sa-yaj'alu lahumur-Raḥmaanu wuddaa.

97. Fa-innamaa yassarnaahu bilisaanika litubashshira bihil-muttaqeena wa tunzira bihee qawmal-luddaa.

98. Wa kam ahlaknaa qabla-hum-min qarnin hal tuḥissu minhum-min aḥadin aw tasma'u lahum rikzaa. **(Section 6)**

Sûrat Ṭâ-Hâ–20
(Revealed at Makkah)

Bismillaahir Raḥmaanir Raḥeem

1. Ṭaa-Haa.

2. Maaa anzalnaa 'alaykal-Qur-aana litashqaaa.

3. Illaa tazkiratal-limañy-yakhshaa.

4. Tanzeelam-mimman khalaqal-arḍa was-samaa-waatil-'ulaa.

5. Ar-Raḥmaanu 'alal-'Arshis-tawaa.

6. Lahoo maa fis-samaa-waati wa maa fil-arḍi wa maa baynahumaa wa maa taḥtas-saraa.

7. Wa in tajhar bilqawli fa-innahoo ya'lamus-sirra

---

and what is yet more hidden.

8. Allah! there is no god but He! To Him belong the most Beautiful Names.

9. Has the story of Moses reached you?

10. Behold, he saw a fire: so he said to his family, "you Tarry; I perceive a fire; perhaps I can bring you some burning brand therefrom, or find some guidance at the fire."

11. But when he came to the fire, a voice was heard: "O Moses!

12. "Verily I am your Lord! Therefore (in My presence) put off your shoes: you are in the sacred valley Tuwa.

13. "I have chosen you: listen, then, to the inspiration (sent to you).

14. "Verily, I am Allah: There is no god but I: so you serve Me (only), and establish regular prayer for celebrating My praise.

15. "Verily the Hour is coming My design is to keep it hidden- for every soul to receive its reward by the measure of its Endeavor.

16. "Therefore let not such as do not believe therein but follow their own lusts, divert you therefrom, lest you perish!".

17. "And what is that in your right hand, O Moses?"

18. He said, "It is my rod: on it I lean; with it I beat down fodder for my flocks; and in it I find other uses."

19. (Allah) said, "Throw it, O Moses!"

20. He threw it, and behold! it was a snake, active in motion.

21. (Allah) said, "Seize it, and fear not: We shall return it at once to its former condition"..

22. "Now draw your hand close to your side: it shall come forth white (and shining), without harm (or stain),- as another Sign,-

---

wa akhfaa.

8. Allaahu laaa ilaaha illaa Huwa lahul-Asmaaa'ul-Ḥusnaa.

9. Wa hal ataaka ḥadeesu Moosaa.

10. Iz ra-aa naaran faqaala li-ahlihim-kuṣooo inneee aanastu naaral-la'alleee aateekum minhaa biqabasin aw ajidu 'alan-naari hudaa.

11. Falammaaa ataahaa noo-diya yaa Moosaa.

12. Inneee Ana Rabbuka fakhla' na'layka innaka bilwaadil-muqaddasi Ṭuwaa.

13. Wa anakhtartuka fasta-mi' limaa yooḥaa.

14. Innaneee Anal-laahu laaa ilaaha illaaa Ana fa'budnee wa-aqimiṣ-Ṣalaata lizikree.

15. Innas-Saa'ata aatiyatun akaadu ukhfeehaa litujzaa kullu nafsim bimaa tas'aa.

16. Falaa yaṣuddannaka 'anhaa mal-laa yu'minu bihaa wattaba'a hawaahu fatardaa.

17. Wa maa tilka bi-yamee-nika yaa Moosaa.

18. Qaala hiya 'aṣaaya atawakka'u 'alayhaa wa ahushshu bihaa 'alaa ghanamee wa liya feehaa ma-aaribu ukhraa.

19. Qaala alqihaa yaa Moosaa.

20. Fa-alqaahaa fa-izaa hiya ḥayyatun tas'aa.

21. Qaala khuzhaa wa laa ta-khaf sanu'eeduhaa seeratahal-oolaa.

22. Waḍmum yadaka ilaa janaaḥika takhruj baydaaa'a min ghayri sooo'in Aayatan ukhraa.

وَأَخْفَى ۝

اللّٰهُ لَاۤ اِلٰهَ اِلَّا هُوَ لَهُ الْاَسْمَآءُ الْحُسْنٰى ۝

وَهَلْ اَتٰىكَ حَدِيْثُ مُوْسٰى ۝

اِذْ رَاٰ نَارًا فَقَالَ لِاَهْلِهِ امْكُثُوْٓا اِنِّيْٓ اٰنَسْتُ نَارًا لَّعَلِّيْٓ اٰتِيْكُمْ مِّنْهَا بِقَبَسٍ اَوْ اَجِدُ عَلَى النَّارِ هُدًى ۝

فَلَمَّاۤ اَتٰىهَا نُوْدِيَ يٰمُوْسٰى ۝

اِنِّيْٓ اَنَا رَبُّكَ فَاخْلَعْ نَعْلَيْكَ اِنَّكَ بِالْوَادِ الْمُقَدَّسِ طُوًى ۝

وَاَنَا اخْتَرْتُكَ فَاسْتَمِعْ لِمَا يُوْحٰى ۝

اِنَّنِيْٓ اَنَا اللّٰهُ لَاۤ اِلٰهَ اِلَّاۤ اَنَا فَاعْبُدْنِيْ وَاَقِمِ الصَّلٰوةَ لِذِكْرِيْ ۝

اِنَّ السَّاعَةَ اٰتِيَةٌ اَكَادُ اُخْفِيْهَا لِتُجْزٰى كُلُّ نَفْسٍۢ بِمَا تَسْعٰى ۝

فَلَا يَصُدَّنَّكَ عَنْهَا مَنْ لَّا يُؤْمِنُ بِهَا وَاتَّبَعَ هَوٰىهُ فَتَرْدٰى ۝

وَمَا تِلْكَ بِيَمِيْنِكَ يٰمُوْسٰى ۝

قَالَ هِيَ عَصَايَ اَتَوَكَّؤُا عَلَيْهَا وَاَهُشُّ بِهَا عَلٰى غَنَمِيْ وَلِيَ فِيْهَا مَاٰرِبُ اُخْرٰى ۝

قَالَ اَلْقِهَا يٰمُوْسٰى ۝

فَاَلْقٰهَا فَاِذَا هِيَ حَيَّةٌ تَسْعٰى ۝

قَالَ خُذْهَا وَلَا تَخَفْ سَنُعِيْدُهَا سِيْرَتَهَا الْاُوْلٰى ۝

وَاضْمُمْ يَدَكَ اِلٰى جَنَاحِكَ تَخْرُجْ بَيْضَآءَ مِنْ غَيْرِ سُوْٓءٍ اٰيَةً اُخْرٰى ۝

23. "In order that We may show you (two) of our Greater Signs.

24. "You go to Pharaoh, for he has indeed transgressed all bounds."

25. (Moses) said: "O my Lord! expand me my breast;

26. "Ease my task for me;

27. "And remove the impediment from my speech,

28. "So they may understand what I say:

29. "And give me a Minister from my family,

30. "Aaron, my brother;

31. "Add to my strength through him,

32. "And make him share my task:

33. "That we may celebrate Your praise without stint,

34. "And remember You without stint:

35. "For You are He that (ever) regards us."

36. (Allah) said: "Granted is your prayer, O Moses!"

37. "And indeed We conferred a favor on you another time (before).

38. "Behold! We sent to your mother, by inspiration, the message:

39. "'Throw (the child) into the chest, and throw (the chest) into the river: the river will cast him up on the bank, and he will be taken up by one who is an enemy to Me and an enemy to him': but I cast (the garment of) love over you from Me: and (this) in order that you may be reared under Mine eye.

40. "Behold! your sister goes forth and says, 'shall I show you one who will nurse and rear the (child)?' So We brought you back to your mother, that her eye might be cooled and she should not grieve. Then you slew a man, but We saved you from trouble, and We tried you in various ways. Then you tarried a number of years with the people of Midian. Then you came hither as ordained, O Moses!

---

23. Linuriyaka min Aayaa-tinal-Kubraa.

24. Izhab ilaa Fir'awna inna-hoo ṭaghaa. **(Section 1)**

25. Qaala Rabbish-raḥ lee ṣadree.

26. Wa yassir leee amree.

27. Waḥlul 'uqdatam-milli-saanee.

28. Yafqahoo qawlee.

29. Waj'al-lee wazeeram-min ahlee.

30. Haaroona akhee.

31. Ushdud biheee azree.

32. Wa ashrik-hu feee amree.

33. Kay nusabbiḥaka kaṣee-raa.

34. Wa nazkuraka kaṣeeraa.

35. Innaka kunta binaa baṣeeraa.

36. Qaala qad ooteeta su'laka yaa Moosaa.

37. Wa laqad manannaa 'alayka marratan ukhraaa.

38. Iz awḥaynaaa ilaaa ummika maa yooḥaaa.

39. Aniqzifeehi fit-Taabooti faqzifeehi fil-yammi fal-yul-qihil-yammu bis-saaḥili yaá-khuẓhu 'aduwwul-lee wa 'aduwwul-lah; wa alqaytu 'alayka maḥabbatam-minnee wa lituṣna'a 'alaa 'aynee.

40. Iz tamshee ukhtuka fataqoolu hal adullukum 'alaa mañy-yakfuluhoo faraja'naaka ilaaa ummika kay taqarra 'aynuhaa wa laa taḥzan; wa qatalta nafsan fanajjaynaaka minal-ghammi wa fatannaaka futoonaa; falabiṣta sineena feee ahli Madyana ṣumma ji'ta 'alaa qadariñy-yaa Moosaa.

41. "And I have prepared you for Myself (for service)"..

42. "Go, you and your brother, with My Signs, and slacken not, either of you, in keeping Me in remembrance.

43. "Go, both of you, to Pharaoh, for he has indeed transgressed all bounds;

44. "But speak to him mildly; perchance he may take warning or fear (Allah)."

45. They (Moses and Aaron) said: "Our Lord! We fear lest he hasten with insolence against us, or lest he transgress all bounds."

46. He said: "Do not fear: for I am with you: I hear and see (everything).

47. "So you both go to him, and say, 'Verily we are Messengers sent by your Lord: send forth, therefore, the Children of Israel with us, and afflict them not: with a Sign, indeed, have we come from your Lord! and peace to all who follow guidance!

48. "'Verily it has been revealed to us that the Chastisement (awaits) those who reject and turn away.'"

49. (When this message was delivered), (Pharaoh) said: "Who, then, O Moses, is the Lord of you two?"

50. He said: "Our Lord is He Who gave to each (created) thing its form and nature, and further, gave (it) guidance."

51. (Pharaoh) said: "What then is the condition of previous generations?"

52. He replied: "The knowledge of that is with my Lord, duly recorded: my Lord never errs, nor forgets,-

53. "He Who has, made for you the earth like a carpet spread out; has enabled you to go about therein by roads (and channels); and has sent down water from the sky." With it have We produced diverse pairs of plants each separate from the others.

---

41. Waṣṭana‘tuka linafsee.

42. Izhab anta wa akhooka bi-Aayaatee wa laa taniyaa fee zikree.

43. Izhabaaa ilaa Fir‘awna innahoo ṭaghaa.

44. Faqoolaa lahoo qawlal-layyinal-la‘allahoo yatazakkaru ‘aw yakhshaa.

45. Qaalaa Rabbanaaa inna-naa nakhaafu añy-yafruṭa ‘alaynaaa aw añy-yaṭghaa.

46. Qaala laa takhaafaaa innanee ma‘akumaaa asma‘u wa araa.

47. Faåtiyaahu faqoolaaa innaa Rasoolaa Rabbika fa-arsil ma‘anaa Baneee Israaa‘eela wa laa tu‘azzibhum qad ji’naaka bi-Aayatim-mir-Rabbika wassa-laamu ‘alaa manit-taba‘al-hudaa.

48. Innaa qad ooḥiya ilaynaaa annal-‘azaaba ‘alaa man kaz-zaba wa tawallaa.

49. Qaala famar-Rabbu-kumaa yaa Moosaa.

50. Qaala Rabbunal-lazeee a‘ṭaa kulla shay’in khalqahoo summa hadaa.

51. Qaala famaa baalul-quroonil-oolaa.

52. Qaala ‘ilmuhaa ‘inda Rabbee fee kitaab, laa yaḍillu Rabbee wa laa yansaa.

53. Allazee ja‘ala lakumul-arḍa mahdañw-wa salaka lakum feehaa subulañw-wa anzala minas-samaaa’i maaa’an fa-akhrajnaa biheee azwaajam-min-nabaatin shattaa.

54. Eat (for yourselves) and pasture your cattle: verily, in this are Signs for men endued with understanding.

55. From the (earth) We created you, and into it shall We return you, and from it shall We bring you out once again.

56. And We showed Pharaoh all Our Signs, but he rejected and refused.

57. He said: "Have you come to drive us out of our land with your magic, O Moses?

58. "But we can surely produce magic to match yours! So make a tryst between us and you, which we shall not fail to keep - neither we nor you - in a place where both shall have even chances."

59. Moses said: "Your tryst is the Day of the Festival, and let the people be assembled when the sun is well up."

60. So Pharaoh withdrew: he concerted his plan, and then came (back).

61. Moses said to him: Woe to you! You do not forge a lie against Allah, lest He destroy you (at once) utterly by chastisement: the forger must suffer frustration!"

62. So they disputed, one with another, over their affair, but they kept their talk secret.

63. They said: "These two are certainly (expert) magicians: their object is to drive you out from your land with their magic, and to do away with your most cherished institutions.

64. "Therefore concert your plan, and then assemble in (serried) ranks: he wins (all along) today who gains the upper hand."

65. They said: "O Moses! whether will you that you throw (first) or that we be the first to throw?"

54. Kuloo war‘aw an‘aama-kum; inna fee zaalika la-Aayaatil-li-ulin-nuhaa.
(Section 2)

55. Minhaa khalaqnaakum wa feehaa nu‘eedukum wa minhaa nukhrijukum taaratan ukhraa.

56. Wa laqad araynaahu Aayaatinaa kullahaa fakaz-zaba wa abaa.

57. Qaala aji’tanaa litukhri-janaa min ardinaa bisihrika yaa Moosaa.

58. Falanaåtiyannaka bisih-rim-mislihee faj‘al baynanaa wa baynaka maw‘idal-laa nukhlifuhoo naḥnu wa laaa anta makaanan suwaa.

59. Qaala maw‘idukum yaw-muz-zeenati wa añy-yuḥ-sharan-naasu ḍuhaa.

60. Fatawallaa Fir‘awnu faja-ma‘a kaydahoo summa ataa.

61. Qaala lahum-Moosaa waylakum laa taftaroo ‘alal-laahi kaziban fa-yus-ḥitakum bi ‘azaab, wa qad khaaba manif-taraa.

62. Fatanaaza‘ooo amrahum baynahum wa asarrun-najwaa.

63. Qaalooo in haazaani lasaaḥiraani yureedaani añy-yukhrijaakum min ardikum bisihrihimaa wa yazhabaa bitareeqatikumul-muslaa.

64. Fa-ajmi‘oo kaydakum summa’-too saffaa; wa qad aflaḥal-yawma manis-ta‘laa.

65. Qaaloo yaa Moosaaa immaaa an tulqiya wa immaaa an-nakoona awwala man alqaa.

66. He said, "Nay, you throw first!" Then behold their ropes and their rods-so it seemed to him on account of their magic - began to be in lively motion!

67. So Moses conceived in his mind a (sort of) fear.

68. We said: "Do not fear! for you have indeed the upper hand:

69. "Throw that which is in your right hand: quickly will it swallow up that which they have faked; what they have faked is but a magician's trick: and the magician does not thrive, (no matter) where he goes."

70. So the magicians were thrown down to prostration: they said, "We believe in the Lord of Aaron and Moses".

71. (Pharaoh) said: "Do you believe in Him before I give you permission? Surely this must be your leader, who has taught you magic! Be sure I will cut off your hands and feet on opposite sides, and I will have you crucified on trunks of palm-trees: so shall you know for certain, which of us can give the more severe and the more lasting punishment!"

72. They said: "Never shall we regard you as more than the Clear Sings that have come to us, or than Him Who created us! so decree whatever you desire to decree: for you can only decree (touching) the life of this world.

73. "For us, we have believed in our Lord: may He forgive us our faults, and the magic to which you compelled us: for Allah is Best and Most Abiding."

74. Verily he who comes to his Lord as a sinner (at Judgment),- for him is Hell: therein shall he neither die nor live.

75. But such as come to Him as Believers who have worked righteous deeds,-

66. Qaala bal alqoo fa-izaa ḥibaaluhum wa 'iṣiyyuhum yukhayyalu ilayhi min siḥrihim annahaa tas'aa.

67. Fa-awjasa fee nafsihee kheefatam-Moosaa.

68. Qulnaa laa takhaf innaka antal-a'laa.

69. Wa alqi maa fee yamee-nika talqaf maa sana'oo; innamaa ṣana'oo kaydu saaḥir; wa laa yufliḥus-saaḥiru ḥaysu ataa.

70. Fa-ulqiyas-saḥaratu suj-jadan qaalooo aamannaa bi-Rabbi Haaroona wa Moosaa.

71. Qaala aamantum lahoo qabla an aazana lakum; innahoo lakabeerukumul-lazee 'allama-kumus-siḥra fala-uqaṭṭi'anna aydiyakum wa arjulakum-min khilaafiñw-wa la-uṣallibanna-kum fee juzoo'in-nakhli wa lata'lamunna ayyunaaa ashaddu 'azaabañw-wa abqaa.

72. Qaaloo lan nu'ṣiraka 'alaa maa jaaa'anaa minal-bayyinaati wallazee faṭaranaa faqḍi maaa anta qaaḍ; innamaa taqḍee haazihil-ḥayaatad-dunyaa.

73. Innaaa aamannaa bi-Rabbinaa liyaghfira lanaa kha-ṭaayaanaa wa maaa akrahtanaa 'alayhi minas-siḥr; wallaahu khayruñw-wa abqaa.

74. Innahoo mañy-yaati Rab-bahoo mujriman fa-inna lahoo Jahannama laa yamootu feehaa wa laa yaḥyaa.

75. Wa mañy-yaåtihee mu'mi-nan qad 'amilaṣ-ṣaaliḥaati

for them are ranks exalted,-

76. Gardens of Eternity, beneath which flow rivers: they will dwell therein for ever: such is the reward of those who purify themselves (from evil).

77. We sent an inspiration to Moses: "Travel by night with My servants, and strike a dry path for them through the sea, without fear of being overtaken (by Pharaoh) and without (any other) fear."

78. Then Pharaoh pursued them with his forces, but the waters completely overwhelmed them and covered them up.

79. Pharaoh led his people astray instead of leading them aright.

80. O you Children of Israel! We delivered you from your enemy, and We made a Covenant with you on the right side of Mount (Sinai), and We sent down to you Manna and quails:

81. (Saying): "Eat of the good things We have provided for your sustenance, but commit no excess therein, lest My Wrath should justly descend on you: and those on whom descends My Wrath do perish indeed!

82. "But, without doubt, I am (also) He that forgives again and again, to those who repent, believe, and do right,- who, in fine, are ready to receive true guidance."

83. (When Moses was up on the Mount, Allah said:) "What made you hasten in advance of your people, O Moses?"

84. He replied: "Behold, they are close on my footsteps: I hastened to you, O my Lord, to please You."

85. (Allah) said: "We have tested your people in your absence: the Samiri has led them astray."

86. So Moses returned to his people in a state of indignation

---

fa-ulaaa'ika lahumud-dara-jaatul-'ulaa.

76. Jannaatu 'Adnin tajree min taḥtihal-anhaaru khaali-deena feehaa; wa zaalika jazaaa'u man tazakkaa.

(Section 3)

77. Wa laqad awḥaynaaa ilaa Moosaaa an asri bi'ibaadee faḍrib lahum ṭareeqan fil-baḥri yabasal-laa takhaafu darakañw-wa laa takhshaa.

78. Fa-atba'ahum Fir'awnu bijunoodihee faghashiyahum-minal-yammi maa ghashi-yahum.

79. Wa aḍalla Fir'awnu qaw-mahoo wa maa hadaa.

80. Yaa Banee Israaa'eela qad anjaynaakum-min 'aduw-wikum wa waa'adnaakum jaanibaṭ-Ṭooril-aymana wa nazzalnaa 'alaykumul-Manna was-Salwaa.

81. Kuloo min ṭayyibaati maa razaqnaakum wa laa taṭghaw feehi fa-yaḥilla 'alaykum ghaḍabee wa mañy-yaḥlil 'alayhi ghaḍabee faqad hawaa.

82. Wa innee la-Ghaffaarul-liman taaba wa aamana wa 'amila ṣaaliḥan summah-tadaa.

83. Wa maaa a'jalaka 'an qawmika yaa Moosaa.

84. Qaala hum ulaaa'i 'alaaa asaree wa 'ajiltu ilayka Rabbi litarḍaa.

85. Qaala fa-innaa qad fa-tannaa qawmaka mim ba'dika wa aḍallahumus-Saamiriyy.

86. Faraja'a Moosaaa ilaa qawmihee ghaḍbaana

and sorrow. He said: "O my people! did not your Lord make a handsome promise to you? Did then the promise seem to you long (in coming)? Or did you desire that Wrath should descend from your Lord on you, and so you broke your promise to me?"

87. They said: "We did not break the promise to you, as far as lay in our power: but we were made to carry the weight of the ornaments of the (whole) people, and we threw them (into the fire), and that was what the Samiri suggested.

88. "Then he brought out (of the fire) before the (people) the image of a calf: it seemed to low: so they said: This is your god, and the god of Moses, but (Moses) has forgotten!"

89. Could they not see that it could not return them a word (for answer), and that it had no power either to harm them or to do them good?

90. Aaron had already, before this said to them: "O my people! you are being tested in this: for verily your Lord is (Allah) Most Gracious; so follow me and obey my command."

91. They had said: "We will not cease to worship it, but we will devote ourselves to it until Moses returns to us."

92. (Moses) said: "O Aaron! what kept you back, when you saw them going wrong,

93. "From following me? Did you then disobey my order?"

94. (Aaron) replied: "O son of my mother! Do not seize (me) by my beard nor by (the hair of) my head! Truly I feared lest you should say, 'you has caused a division among the children of Israel, and you did not respect my word!'"

95. (Moses) said: "What then is your case, O Samiri?"

asifaa; qaala yaa qawmi alam ya'idkum Rabbukum wa'dan ḥasanaa; afaṭaala 'alaykumul-'ahdu am arattum añy-yaḥilla 'alaykum ghaḍabum-mir-Rabbikum fa-akhlaftum-maw'idee.

87. Qaaloo maaa akhlafnaa maw'idaka bimalkinaa wa laakinnaa ḥummilnaaa awzaaram-min zeenatil-qawmi faqaẓafnaahaa fakaẓaalika alqas-Saamiriyy.

88. Fa-akhraja lahum 'ijlan jasadal-lahoo khuwaarun faqaaloo haaẓaaa ilaahukum wa ilaahu Moosaa fanasee.

89. Afalaa yarawna allaa yarji'u ilayhim qawlañw-wa laa yamliku lahum ḍarrañw-wa laa naf'aa. **(Section 4)**

90. Wa laqad qaala lahum Haaroonu min qablu yaa qawmi innamaa futintum bihee wa inna Rabbakumur-Raḥmaanu fatta-bi'oonee wa aṭee'ooo amree.

91. Qaaloo lan-nabraḥa 'alayhi 'aakifeena ḥattaa yarji'a ilaynaa Moosaa.

92. Qaala yaa Haaroonu maa mana'aka iz ra-aytahum ḍaloooo.

93. Allaa tattabi'ani afa-'aṣayta amree.

94. Qaala yabna'umma laa taākhuz biliḥyatee wa laa biraā-see innee khasheetu an taqoola farraqta bayna Baneee Israaa-'eela wa lam tarqub qawlee.

95. Qaala famaa khaṭbuka yaa Saamiriyy.

96. He replied: "I saw what they did not see: so I took a handful (of dust) from the footprint of the Messenger, and threw it (into the calf)." thus did my soul suggest to me."

97. (Moses) said: "Get you gone! But your (punishment) in this life will be that you will say, 'Touch me not'; and moreover (for a future Penalty) you have a promise that will not fail: now look at your god, of whom you have become a devoted worshipper: we will certainly (melt) it in a blazing fire and scatter it broadcast in the sea!"

98. But the god of you all is the One Allah: there is no god but He: all things He comprehends in His knowledge.

99. Thus do We relate to you some stories of what happened before: for We have sent you a Message from Our own Presence.

100. If any do turn away therefrom, verily they will bear a burden on the Day of judgment;

101. They will abide in this (state): and grievous will the burden be to them on that Day,-

102. The Day when the Trumpet will be sounded: that Day, We shall gather the sinful, blear-eyed (with terror).

103. In whispers will they consult each other: "You tarried not longer than ten (Days);"

104. We know best what they will say, when their leader most eminent in conduct will say: "You did not tarry longer than a day!"

105. They ask you concerning the Mountains: say, "My Lord will uproot them and scatter them as dust;

96. Qaala baṣurtu bimaa lam yabṣuroo bihee faqabadtu qabdatam-min asharir-Rasooli fanabaztuhaa wa kazaalika sawwalat lee nafsee.

97. Qaala fazhab fa-inna laka fil-ḥayaati an taqoola laa misaasa wa inna laka maw'idal-lan tukhlafahoo wanzur ilaaa ilaahikal-lazee zalta 'alayhi 'aakifaa; lanuḥarriqannahoo summa lanansifannahoo fil-yammi nasfaa.

98. Innamaaa ilaahukumul-laahul-lazee laaa ilaaha illaa Hoo; wasi'a kulla shay'in 'ilmaa.

99. Kazaalika naquṣṣu 'alay-ka min ambaaa'i maa qad sabaq; wa qad aataynaaka mil-ladunnaa Zikraa.

100. Man a'raḍa 'anhu fa-innahoo yaḥmilu Yawmal-Qiyaamati wizraa.

101. Khaalideena feehi wa saaa'a lahum Yawmal-Qiyaamati ḥimlaa.

102. Yawma yunfakhu fiṣ-Ṣoori wa naḥshurul-mujrimeena Yawma'izin zurqaa.

103. Yatakhaafatoona bayna-hum il-labistum illaa 'ashraa.

104. Naḥnu a'lamu bimaa yaqooloona iz yaqoolu amsa-luhum ṭareeqatan illabistum illaa yawmaa. **(Section 5)**

105. Wa yas'aloonaka 'anil-jibaali faqul yansifuhaa Rabbee nasfaa.

106. "He will leave them as plains smooth and level;

107. "Nothing crooked or curved will you see in their place."

108. On that Day will they follow the Caller (straight): no crookedness (can they show) him: all sounds shall humble themselves in the Presence of (Allah) Most Gracious: nothing shall you hear but the tramp of their feet (as they march).

109. On that Day no intercession shall avail except for those for whom permission has been granted by (Allah) Most Gracious and whose word is acceptable to Him.

110. He knows what (appears to His creatures as) before or after or behind them: but they shall not compass it with their knowledge.

111. (All) faces shall be humbled before (Him) - the Living, the Self-subsisting, Eternal: hopeless indeed will be the man that carries iniquity (on his back).

112. But he who works deeds of righteousness, and has faith, will have no fear of harm nor of any curtailment (of what is his due).

113. Thus have We sent this down - an Arabic Qur'an - and explained therein in detail some of the warnings, in order that they may fear Allah, or that it may cause their remembrance (of Him).

114. High above all is Allah, the King, the Truth! Be not in haste with the Qur'an before its revelation to you is completed, but say, "O my Lord! advance me in knowledge."

115. We had already, beforehand, taken the covenant of Adam, but he forgot: and We found on his part no firm resolve.

116. When We said to the angels, "Prostrate yourselves to Adam", they prostrated themselves, but not Iblis: he refused.

117. Then We said: "O Adam! verily, this is an enemy to you and your wife: so let him not get you both out of the Garden, so that you are landed in misery.

106. Fa-yazaruhaa qaa'an ṣafṣafaa.

107. Laa taraa feehaa 'iwajañw-wa laaa amtaa.

108. Yawma'iziñy-yattabi'oo-nad-daa'iya laa 'iwaja lahoo wa khasha'atil-aṣwaatu lir-Raḥ-maani falaa tasma'u illaa hamsaa.

109. Yawma'izil-laa tanfa'ush shafaa'atu illaa man azina lahur-Raḥmaanu wa raḍiya la-hoo qawlaa.

110. Ya'lamu maa bayna aydeehim wa maa khalfa-hum wa laa yuḥeeṭoona bihee 'ilmaa.

111. Wa 'anatil-wujoohu lil-Ḥayyil-Qayyoomi wa qad khaaba man ḥamala ẓulmaa.

112. Wa mañy-ya'mal minaṣ-ṣaaliḥaati wa huwa mu'minun falaa yakhaafu ẓulmañw-wa laa haḍmaa.

113. Wa kazaalika anzalnaahu Qur-aanan 'Arabiyyañw-wa ṣarrafnaa feehi minal-wa'eedi la'allahum yattaqoona aw yuḥdiṣu lahum zikraa.

114. Fata'aalal-laahul-Malikul-Ḥaqq; wa laa ta'jal bil-Qur-aani min qabli añy-yuqḍaaa ilayka waḥyuhoo wa qur-Rabbi zidnee 'ilmaa.

115. Wa laqad 'ahidnaaa ilaa Aadama min qablu fanasiya wa lam najid lahoo 'azmaa.

(Section 6)

116. Wa iz qulnaa lilma-laaa'ikatis-judoo li Aadama fasajadooo illaaa Iblees; abaa.

117. Faqulnaa yaaa Aadamu inna haazaa 'aduwwul-laka wa lizawjika falaa yukhrijan-nakumaa minal-Jannati fatashqaa.

118. "There is therein (enough provision) for you not to go hungry nor to go naked,

119. "Nor to suffer from thirst, nor from the sun's heat."

120. But Satan whispered evil to him: he said, "O Adam! shall I lead you to the Tree of Eternity and to a kingdom that never decays?"

121. In the result, they both ate of the tree, and so their nakedness appeared to them: they began to sew together, for their covering, leaves from the Garden: thus Adam disobeyed his Lord, and allow himself to be seduced.

122. But his Lord chose him (for His Grace): He turned to him, and gave him guidance.

123. He said: "Get you down, both of you,- all together, from the Garden, with enmity one to another: but if, as is sure, there comes to you guidance from Me, whosoever follows My guidance, will not lose his way, nor fall into misery.

124. "But whosoever turns away from My Message, verily for him is a life narrowed down, and We shall raise him up blind on the Day of Judgment."

125. He will say: "O my Lord! why have you raised me up blind, while I had sight (before)?"

126. (Allah) will say: "Thus you, did when Our Signs came unto you, disregard them: so will you, this day, be disregarded."

127. And thus do We recompense him who transgresses beyond bounds and believes not in the Sings of his Lord: and the Chastisement of the Hereafter is far more grievous and more enduring.

128. Is it not a warning to such men (to call to mind) how

118. Inna laka allaa tajooʻa feeha wa laa taʻraa.

119. Wa annaka laa taẓmaʼu feehaa wa laa taḍḥaa.

120. Fa-waswasa ilayhish-Shayṭaanu qaala yaaa Aadamu hal adulluka ʻalaa shajaratil-khuldi wa mulkil-laa yablaa.

121. Fa-akalaa minhaa fabadat lahumaa saw-aatuhumaa wa ṭafiqaa yakhṣifaani ʻalayhimaa miñw-waraqil-jannah; wa ʻaṣaaa Aadamu Rabbahoo faghawaa.

122. Ṣummaj-tabaahu Rabbuhoo fataaba ʻalayhi wa hadaa.

123. Qaalah-biṭaa minhaa jameeʻam baʻḍukum liʻḍin ʻaduww; fa-immaa yaåti-yannakum-minnee hudan famanit-tabaʻa hudaaya falaa yaḍillu wa laa yashqaa.

124. Wa man aʻraḍa ʻan Zikree fa-inna lahoo maʻeeshatan ḍankañw-wa naḥshuruhoo Yawmal-Qiyaamati aʻmaa.

125. Qaala Rabbi lima ḥashartaneee aʻmaa wa qad kuntu baṣeeraa.

126. Qaala kazaalika atatka Aayaatunaa fanaseetahaa wa kazaalikal-Yawma tunsaa.

127. Wa kazaalika najzee man asrafa wa lam yuʼmim bi-Aayaati-Rabbih; wa laʻazaabul-Aakhirati ashaddu wa abqaa.

128. Afalam yahdi lahum kam ahlaknaa

many generations before them We destroyed, in whose haunts they (now) move? Verily, in this are Signs for men endued with understanding.

129. Had it not been for a Word that went forth before from your Lord, (their punishment) must necessarily have come; but there is a Term appointed (for respite).

130. Therefore be patient with what they say, and celebrate (constantly) the praises of your Lord, before the rising of the sun, and before its setting; yes, celebrate them for part of the hours of the night, and at the sides of the day: that you may have (spiritual) joy.

131. Nor strain your eyes in longing for the things We have given for enjoyment to parties of them, the splendor of the life of this world, through which We test them: but the provision of your Lord is better and more enduring.

132. Enjoin prayer on your people, and be constant therein. We ask you not to provide sustenance: We provide it for you. But the (fruit of) the Hereafter is for righteousness.

133. They say: "Why does he not bring us a sign from his Lord?" Has not a Clear Sign come to them of all that was in the former Books of revelation?

134. And if We had inflicted on them a penalty before this, they would have said: "Our Lord! If only You had sent us a Messenger, we should certainly have followed Your Signs before we were humbled and put to shame."

135. Say: "Each one (of us) is waiting: you wait, therefore, and soon shall you know who it is that is on the straight and even way, and who it is that has received guidance."

qablahum-minal-quroonī yamshoona fee masaakinihim; inna fee zaalika la-Aayaatil-li-ulinnuhaa. **(Section 7)**

129. Wa law laa Kalimatun sabaqat mir-Rabbika lakaana lizaamañw-wa ajalum-musam-maa.

130. Faṣbir 'alaa maa yaqoo-loona wa sabbiḥ biḥamdi Rabbika qabla ṭuloo'ish-shamsi wa qabla ghuroobihaa wa min aanaaa'il-layli fasabbiḥ wa aṭraafan-nahaari la'allaka tar-ḍaa.

131. Wa laa tamuddanna 'aynayka ilaa maa matta'naa biheee azwaajam-minhum zahratal-ḥayaatid-dunyaa linaftinahum feeh; wa rizqu Rabbika khayruñw-wa abqaa.

132. Waåmur ahlaka biṣ-Ṣalaati waṣṭabir 'alayhaa laa nas'aluka rizqaa; Nahnu narzuquk; wal-'aaqibatu littaqwaa.

133. Wa qaaloo law laa yaå-teenaa bi-Aayatim-mir-Rabbih; awalam taåtihim bayyinatu maa fiṣ-ṣuhufil-oolaa.

134. Wa law annaaa ahlaknaa-hum bi'azaabim-min qablihee laqaaloo Rabbanaa law laaa arsalta ilaynaa Rasoolan fanattabi'a Aayaatika min qabli an-nazilla wa nakhzaa.

135. Qul kullum-mutarabbiṣun fatarabbaṣoo fasata'lamoona man Aṣḥaabuṣ-Ṣiraaṭiṣ-Sawiyyi wa manih-tadaa. **(Section 8)**

21. The Prophets

In the name of Allah, Most Gracious, Most Merciful.

1. Closer and closer to mankind comes their Reckoning: yet they do not heed and they turn away.

2. Never comes (anything) to them of a renewed Message from their Lord, but they listen to it as in jest,-

3. Their hearts toying as with trifles. The wrong-doers conceal their private counsels, (saying), "Is this (one) more than a man like yourselves? Will you go to witchcraft with your eyes open?"

4. Say: "My Lord knows (every) word (spoken) in the heavens and on earth: He is the One that hears and knows (all things)."

5. "Nay," they say, "(these are) medleys of dreams! - Nay, he forged it! - Nay, he is (but) a poet! Let him then bring us a Sign like the ones that were sent to (Prophets) of old!"

6. (As to those) before them, not one of the populations which We destroyed believed: will these believe?

7. Before you, also, the Messengers We sent were but men, to whom We granted inspiration: if you do not realise this, ask of those who possess the Message.

8. Nor did We give them bodies that ate no food, nor were they exempt from death.

9. In the end We fulfilled to them Our Promise, and We saved them and those whom We pleased, but We destroyed those who transgressed beyond bounds.

10. We have revealed for you (O men!) a book in which is a Message for you: will you not then understand?

Sûrat al-Anbiyâ'–21
(Revealed at Makkah)

Bismillaahir Rahmaanir Raheem

1. Iqtaraba linnaasi hisaabuhum wa hum fee ghaflatim-mu'ridoon.

2. Maa yaåteehim-min zikrim-mir-Rabbihim-muhdasin illas-tama'oohu wa hum yal'aboon.

3. Laahiyatan quloobuhum; wa asarrun-najwal-lazeena zalamoo hal-haazaaa illaa basharum-mislukum afataåtoonas-sihra wa antum tubsiroon.

4. Qaala Rabbee ya'lamul-qawla fis-samaaa'i wal-ardi wa Huwas-Samee'ul-'Aleem.

5. Bal qaalooo adghaasu ahlaamim balif-taraahu bal huwa shaa'irun falyaåtinaa bi-Aayatin kamaaa ursilal-awwaloon.

6. Maaa aamanat qablahum min qaryatin ahlaknaahaaa a-fahum yu'minoon.

7. Wa maaa arsalnaa qablaka illaa rijaalan-nooheee ilayhim fas'alooo ahlaz-zikri in kuntum laa ta'lamoon.

8. Wa maa ja'alnaahum jasadal-laa yaåkuloonat-ta'aa-ma wa maa kaanoo khaalideen.

9. Summa sadaqnaahumul-wa'da fa-anjaynaahum wa man nashaaa'u wa ahlaknal-musrifeen.

10. Laqad anzalnaaa ilaykum Kitaaban feehi zikrukum afalaa ta'qiloon.

(Section 1)

11. How many were the populations We utterly destroyed because of their iniquities, setting up in their places other peoples?

12. Yet, when they felt Our Punishment (coming), behold, they (tried to) flee from it.

13. Flee not, but return to the good things of this life which were given you, and to your homes in order that you may be called to account.

14. They said: "Ah! woe to us! We were indeed wrong-doers!"

15. And that cry of theirs did not cease, till We made them as a field that is mown, as ashes silent and quenched.

16. Not for (idle) sport did We create the heavens and the earth and all that is between!

17. If it had been Our wish to take (just) a pastime, We should surely have taken it from the things nearest to Us, if We would do (such a thing)!

18. Nay, We hurl the Truth against falsehood, and it knocks out its brain, and behold, falsehood perishes! Ah! woe be to you for the (false) things you ascribe (to Us).

19. To Him belong all (creatures) in the heavens and on earth: even those who are in His (very) Presence are not too proud to serve Him, nor are they (ever) weary (of His service):

20. They celebrate His praises night and day, nor do they ever flag or intermit.

21. Or have they taken (for worship) gods from the earth who can raise (the dead)?

22. If there were, in the heavens and the earth, other gods besides Allah, there would have been confusion in both! But glory to Allah, the Lord of the Throne: (high is He) above what they attribute to Him!

11. Wa kam qaṣamnaa min qaryatin kaanat ẓaalimataňw-wa anshaånaa ba'dahaa qawman aakhareen.

12. Falammaaa aḥassoo baå-sanaaa izaa hum-minhaa yarkuḍoon.

13. Laa tarkuḍoo warji'ooo ilaa maaa utriftum feehi wa masaakinikum la'allakum tus'aloon.

14. Qaaloo yaa waylanaaa innaa kunnaa ẓaalimeen.

15. Famaa zaalat tilka da'waahum ḥattaa ja'alnaahum ḥaṣeedan khaamideen.

16. Wa maa khalaqnaṣ-samaaa'a wal-arḍa wa maa baynahumaa laa'ibeen.

17. Law aradnaaa an-nattakhiza lahwal-lat-takhaznaahu mil-ladunnaaa in kunnaa faa'ileen.

18. Bal naqzifu bilḥaqqi 'alal-baaṭili fa-yadmaghuhoo fa-izaa huwa zaahiq; wa lakumul-waylu mimmaa taṣifoon.

19. Wa lahoo man fis-samaawaati wal-arḍ; wa man 'indahoo laa yastakbiroona 'an 'ibaadatihee wa laa yastaḥsiroon.

20. Yusabbiḥoonal-layla wannahaara laa yafturoon.

21. Amit-takhazooo aalihatam-minal-arḍi hum yunshiroon.

22. Law kaana feehimaaa aalihatun illal-laahu lafasadataa; fa-Subḥaanal-laahi Rabbil-'Arshi 'ammaa yaṣifoon.

23. He cannot be questioned for His acts, but they will be questioned (for theirs).

24. Or have they taken for worship (other) gods besides Him? Say, "Bring your convincing proof: this is the Message of those with me and the Message of those before me." But most of them do not know the Truth, and so turn away.

25. Not a Messenger did We send before you without this inspiration sent by Us to him: that there is no god but I; therefore worship and serve Me.

26. And they say: "(Allah) Most Gracious has begotten offspring." Glory to Him! They are (but) servants raised to honor.

27. They do not speak before He speaks, and they act (in all things) by His Command.

28. He knows what is before them, and what is behind them, and they offer no intercession except for those who are acceptable, and they stand in awe and reverence of His (glory).

29. If any of them should say, "I am a god besides Him", such a one We should reward with Hell: thus do We reward those who do wrong.

30. Do not the Unbelievers see that the heavens and the earth were joined together (as one unit of creation), before we clove them asunder? We made from water every living thing. Will they not then believe?

31. And We have set on the earth mountains standing firm, lest it should shake with them, and We have made therein broad highways (between mountains) for them to pass through: that they may receive guidance.

32. And We have made the heavens as a canopy well guarded:

---

23. Laa yus'alu 'ammaa yaf'alu wa hum yus'aloon.

24. Amit-takhazoo min dooniheee aalihatan qul haatoo burhaanakum haazaa zikru mam-ma'iya wa zikru man qablee; bal aksaruhum laa ya'lamoonal-ḥaqqa fahum-mu'riḍoon.

25. Wa maaa arsalnaa min qablika mir-Rasoolin illaa nooḥee ilayhi annahoo laaa ilaaha illaaa Ana fa'budoon.

26. Wa qaalut-takhazar-Raḥmaanu waladan-Subḥaanah; bal 'ibaadum-mukramoon.

27. Laa yasbiqoonahoo bil-qawli wa hum bi-amrihee ya'maloon.

28. Ya'lamu maa bayna aydeehim wa maa khalfahum wa laa yashfa'oona illaa limanir-taḍaa wa hum-min khash-yatihee mushfiqoon.

29. Wa mañy-yaqul minhum ineee ilaahum-min doonihee fazaalika najzeehi Jahannam; kazaalika najziz-zaalimeen.
(Section 2)

30. Awalam yaral-lazeena kafarooo annas-samaawaati wal-arḍa kaanataa ratqan fafataqnaahumaa wa ja'alnaa minal-maaa'i kulla shay'in ḥayyin afalaa yu'minoon.

31. Wa ja'alnaa fil-arḍi rawaasiya an tameeda bihim wa ja'alnaa feehaa fijaajan subulal-la'allahum yahtadoon.

32. Wa ja'alnas-samaaa'a saqfam-maḥfoozanw-

yet do they turn away from the Signs which these things (point to)!

33. It is He Who created the Night and the Day, and the sun and the moon: all (the celestial bodies) swim along, each in its rounded course.

34. We did not grant to any man before you permanent life (here): if then you should die, would they live permanently?

35. Every soul shall have a taste of death: and We test you by evil and by good by way of trial and to Us must you return.

36. When the Unbelievers see you, they treat you not except with ridicule. "Is this," (they say), "the one who talks of your gods?" and they blaspheme at the mention of (Allah) Most Gracious!

37. Man is a creature of haste: soon (enough) will I show you My Signs; then you will not ask Me to hasten them!

38. They say: "When will this promise come to pass, if you are telling the truth?"

39. If only the Unbelievers knew (the time) when they will not be able to ward off the fire from their faces, nor yet from their backs, and (when) no help can reach them!

40. Nay, it may come to them all of a sudden and confound them: no power will they have then to avert it, nor will they (then) get respite.

41. Mocked were (many) Messenger before you; but their scoffers were hemmed in by the thing that they mocked.

wa hum 'an Aayaatihaa mu'riḍoon.

33. Wa Huwal-lazee khalaqal-layla wannahaara washshamsa walqamara kullun fee falakiñy-yasbaḥoon.

34. Wa maa ja'alnaa libasharim-min qablikal-khuld; afa-im-mitta fahumul-khaalidoon.

35. Kullu nafsin zaaa'iqatul-mawt; wa nablookum bish-sharri walkhayri fitnatañw wa ilaynaa turja'oon.

36. wa izaa ra-aakal-lazeena kafarooo iñy-yattakhizoonaka illa huzuwaa; ahaaẓal-lazee yazkuru aalihatakum wa hum bi-ẕikrir-Raḥmaani hum kaafiroon.

37. Khuliqal-insaanu min 'ajal; sa-ureekum Aayaatee falaa tasta'jiloon.

38. Wa yaqooloona mataa haazal-wa'du in kuntum ṣaadiqeen.

39. Law ya'lamul-lazeena kafaroo ḥeena laa yakuffoona 'añw-wujoohihimun-Naara wa laa 'an ẓuhoorihim wa laa hum yunṣaroon.

40. Bal taåteehim baghtatan fatabhatuhum falaa yasta-ṭee'oona raddahaa wa laa hum yunẓaroon.

41. Wa laqadis-tuhzi'a bi-Rusulim-min qablika faḥaaqa billazeena sakhiroo minhum-maa kaanoo bihee yastahzi'oon.

(Section 3)

42. Say: "Who can keep you safe by night and by day from (the Wrath of Allah) Most Gracious?" Yet they turn away from the mention of their Lord.

43. Or have they gods that can guard them from Us? They have no power to aid themselves, nor can they be defended from Us.

44. Nay, We gave the good things of this life to these men and their fathers until the period grew long for them; Do not they see that We gradually reduce the land (in their control) from its outlying borders? Is it then they who will win?

45. Say, "I do but warn you according to revelation": but the deaf will not hear the call, (even) when they are warned!

46. If but a breath of the Wrath of your Lord do touch them, they will then say, "Woe to us! we did wrong indeed!"

47. We shall set up scales of justice for the Day of Judgment, so that not a soul will be dealt with unjustly in the least, and if there be (no more than) the weight of a mustard seed, We will bring it (to account): and enough are We to take account.

48. In the past We granted to Moses and Aaron the criterion (for judgment), and a Light and a Message for those who would do right,-

49. Those who fear their Lord in their most secret thoughts, and who hold the Hour (of Judgment) in awe.

50. And this is a blessed Message which We have sent down: will you then

---

42. Qul mañy-yakla'ukum billayli wannahaari minar-Raḥmaan; bal hum 'an zikri Rabbihim-mu'riḍoon.

43. Am lahum aalihatun tamna'uhum-min dooninaa; laa yastaṭee'oona naṣra anfusihim wa laa hum-minnaa yuṣ-ḥaboon.

44. Bal matta'naa haaaa'ulaaa'i wa aabaaa'ahum ḥattaa ṭaala 'alayhimul-'umur; afalaa yarawna annaa naåtil-arḍa nanquṣuhaa min aṭraafihaa; afahumul-ghaaliboon.

45. Qul innamaaa unzirukum bilwaḥyi; wa laa yasma'uṣ-ṣummud-du'aaa'a izaa maa yunzaroon

46. Wa la'im-massat-hum nafḥatum-min 'azaabi Rabbika la-yaqoolunna yaawaylanaaa innaa kunnaa zaalimeen.

47. Wa naḍa'ul-mawaazeenal-qisṭa li-Yawmil-Qiyaamati falaa tuẓlamu nafsun shay'aa; wa in kaana misqaala ḥabba-tim-min khardalin ataynaa bihaa; wa kafaa binaa ḥaasi-been.

48. Wa laqad aataynaa Moosaa wa Haaroonal-Furqaa-na wa ḍiyaaa'añw-wa zikral-lilmuttaqeen.

49. Allazeena yakhshawna Rabbahum bilghaybi wa hum-minas-Saa'ati mushfiqoon.

50. Wa haazaa Zikrum-Mubaarakun anzalnaah; afa-antum

reject it?

51. We bestowed aforetime on Abraham his rectitude of conduct, and well were We acquainted with him.

52. Behold! he said to his father and his people, "What are these images, to which you are (so assiduously) devoted?"

53. They said, "We found our fathers worshipping them."

54. He said, "Indeed you have been in manifest error - you and your fathers."

55. They said, "Have you brought us the Truth, or are you one of those who jest?"

56. He said, "Nay, your Lord is the Lord of the heavens and the earth, He Who created them (from nothing): and I am a witness to this (truth).

57. "And by Allah, I have a plan for your idols - after you go away and turn your backs".

58. So he broke them to pieces, (all) but the biggest of them, that they might turn (and address themselves) to it.

59. They said, "Who has done this to our gods? He must indeed be some man of impiety!"

60. They said, "We heard a youth talk of them: he is called Abraham."

61. They said, "Then bring him before the eyes of the people, that they may bear witness."

62. They said, "are you the one that did this with our gods, O Abraham?"

63. He said: "Nay, this was done by - this is their biggest one!

---

lahoo munkiroon.   **(Section 4)**

51. Wa laqad aataynaaa Ibraa-heema rushdahoo min qablu wa kunnaa bihee 'aalimeen.

52. Iz qaala li-abeehi wa qawmihee maa haazihit-tamaaseelul-lateee antum lahaa 'aakifoon.

53. Qaaloo wajadnaaa aa-baaa'anaa lahaa 'aabideen.

54. Qaala laqad kuntum antum wa aabaaa'ukum fee dalaalim-mubeen.

55. Qaalooo aji'tanaa bil-haqqi am anta minal-laa'ibeen.

56. Qaala bar-Rabbukum Rabbus-samaawaati wal-ardil-lazee fatarahunna wa ana 'alaa zaalikum-minash-shaahideen.

57. Wa tallaahi la-akeedanna asnaamakum ba'da an tuwalloo mudbireen.

58. Faja'alahum juzaazan illaa kabeeral-lahum la'allahum ilayhi yarji'oon.

59. Qaaloo man fa'ala haazaa bi-aalihatinaaa innahoo lami-naz-zaalimeen.

60. Qaaloo sami'naa fatañy-yazkuruhum yuqaalu lahooo Ibraaheem.

61. Qaaloo faatoo bihee 'alaaa a'yunin-naasi la'allahum yash-hadoon.

62. Qaalooo 'a-anta fa'alta haazaa bi-aalihatinaa yaaa Ibraaheem.

63. Qaala bal fa'alahoo kabee-ruhum haazaa

ask them, if they can speak intelligently!"

64. So they turned to themselves and said, "Surely you are the ones in the wrong!"

65. Then they were confounded with shame: (they said), "you know full well that these (idols) do not speak!"

66. (Abraham) said, "Do you then worship, besides Allah, things that can neither be of any good to you nor do you harm?

67. "Fie upon you, and upon the things that you worship besides Allah! Have you no sense?".

68. They said, "Burn him and protect your gods, if you do (anything at all)!"

69. We said, "O Fire! be you cool, and (a means of) safety for Abraham!"

70. Then they planned against him: but We made them the ones that lost most!

71. But We delivered him and (his nephew) Lut (and directed them) to the land which We have blessed for the nations.

72. And We bestowed on him Isaac and, as an additional gift, (a grandson), Jacob, and We made righteous men of every one (of them).

73. And We made them leaders, guiding (men) by Our Command, and We sent them inspiration to do good deeds, to establish regular prayers, and to practise regular charity; and they constantly served Us (and Us only).

74. And to Lut, too, We gave Judgment and Knowledge, and We saved him from the town which practised abominations: truly they were

fas'aloohum in kaanoo yantiqoon.

64. Faraja'ooo ilaaa anfusi-him faqaalooo innakum antumuz-zaalimoon.

65. Summa nukisoo 'alaa ru'oosihim laqad 'alimta maa haaa'ulaaa'i yantiqoon.

66. Qaala afata'budoona min doonil-laahi maa laa yan-fa'ukum shay'añw-wa laa yadurrukum.

67. Uffil-lakum wa limaa ta'budoona min doonil-laah; afalaa ta'qiloon.

68. Qaaloo harriqoohu wan-surooo aalihatakum in kuntum faa'ileen.

69. Qulnaa yaa naaru koonee bardañw-wa salaaman 'alaaa Ibraaheem.

70. Wa araadoo bihee kaydan faja'alnaahumul-akhsareen.

71. Wa najjaynaahu wa Lootan ilal-ardil-latee baarak-naa feehaa lil-'aalameen.

72. Wa wahabnaa lahooo Is-haaq; wa Ya'qooba naafilah; wa kullan ja'alnaa saaliheen.

73. Wa ja'alnaahum a'imma-tañy-yahdoona bi-amrinaa wa awhaynaaa ilayhim fi'lal-khay-raati wa iqaamas-Salaati wa eetaaa'az-Zakaati wa kaanoo lanaa 'aabideen.

74. Wa Lootan aataynaahu hukmañw-wa 'ilmañw-wa najjaynaahu minal-qaryatil-latee kaanat-ta'malul-kha-baaa'is; innahum kaanoo

a people given to Evil, a rebellious people.

75. And We admitted him to Our Mercy: for he was one of the Righteous.

76. (Remember) Noah, when he cried (to Us) aforetime: We listened to his (prayer) and delivered him and his family from great distress.

77. We helped him against people who rejected Our Signs: truly they were a people given to Evil: so We drowned them (in the Flood) all together.

78. And remember David and Solomon, when they gave judgment in the matter of the field into which the sheep of certain people had strayed by night: We witnessed their judgment.

79. To Solomon We inspired the (right) understanding of the matter: to each (of them) We gave Judgment and Knowledge; it was Our power that made the hills and the birds celebrate Our praises, with David: it was We Who did (all these things).

80. It was We Who taught him the making of coats of mail for your benefit, to guard you from each other's violence: will you then be grateful?

81. (It was Our power that made) the violent (unruly) wind flow (tamely) for Solomon, to his order, to the land which We had blessed: for We do know all things.

82. And of the evil ones, were some who dived for him, and did other work besides; and it was We Who guarded them.

83. And (remember) Job, when He cried to his Lord, "Truly distress has seized me,

qawma saw'in faasiqeen.

75. Wa adkhalnaahu fee raḥmatinaa innahoo minaṣ-ṣaaliḥeen.   **(Section 5)**

76. Wa Nooḥan iz naadaa min qablu fastajabnaa lahoo fanajjaynaahu wa ahlahoo minal-karbil-'aẓeem.

77. Wa naṣarnaahu minal-qawmil-lazeena kazzaboo bi Aayaatinaa; innahum kaanoo qawma saw'in fa-aghraq-naahum ajma'een.

78. Wa Daawooda wa Sulay-maana iz yaḥkumaani fil-ḥarṣi iz nafashat feehi ghanamul-qawmi wa kunnaa liḥukmihim shaahideen.

79. Fafahhamnaahaa sulay-maan; wa kullan aataynaa ḥukmañw-wa 'ilmañw-wa sakh-kharnaa ma'a Daawoodal-jibaala yusabbiḥna waṭṭayr; wa kunnaa faa'ileen.

80. Wa 'allamnaahu ṣan'ata laboosil-lakum lituḥsinakum mim baåsikum fahal antum shaakiroon.

81. Wa li-Sulaymaanar-reeḥa 'aaṣifatan tajree bi-amriheee ilal-arḍil-latee baaraknaa fee-haa; wa kunnaa bikulli shay'in 'aalimeen.

82. Wa minash-Shayaaṭeeni mañy-yaghooṣoona lahoo wa ya'maloona 'amalan doona zaalika wa kunnaa lahum ḥaafiẓeen.

83. Wa Ayyooba iz naadaa Rabbahoo annee massaniyaḍ-

but you are the Most Merciful of those that are merciful."

84. So We listened to him: We removed the distress that was on him, and We restored his people to him, and doubled their number,- as a Grace from Ourselves, and a thing for commemoration, for all who serve Us.

85. And (remember) Isma'il, Idris, and Zul-kifl, all (men) of constancy and patience;

86. We admitted them to Our Mercy: for they were of the righteous ones.

87. And remember Zun-nun, when he departed in wrath: he imagined that We had no power over him! but he cried through the depths of darkness, "There is no god but You: glory to You: I was indeed wrong!"

88. So We listened to him: and delivered him from distress: and thus do We deliver those who have faith.

89. And (remember) Zakariya, when he cried to his Lord: "O my Lord! leave me not without offspring, though You are the best of inheritors."

90. So We listened to him: and We granted him Yahya: We cured his wife's (Barrenness) for him. These (three) were ever quick in emulation in good works; they used to call on Us with love and reverence, and humble themselves before Us.

91. And (remember) her who guarded her chastity: We breathed into her of Our spirit, and We made her

---

durru wa Anta arhamur-raaheemeen.

84. Fastajabnaa lahoo fakashaf-naa maa bihee min durriñw-wa-aataynaahu ahlahoo wa mislahum-ma'ahum rahmatam-min 'indinaa wa zikraa lil'aabideen.

85. Wa Ismaa'eela wa Idreesa wa Zal-Kifli kullum-minas-saabireen.

86. Wa adkhalnaahum fee rahmatinaa innahum-minas-saaliheen.

87. Wa Zan-Nooni iz zahaba mughaadiban fazaanna al-lan naqdira 'alayhi fanaadaa fiz-zulumaati al-laaa ilaaha illaaa Anta Subhaanaka innee kuntu minaz-zaalimeen.

88. Fastajabnaa lahoo wa najjaynaahu minal-ghamm; wa kazaalika nunjil-mu'mineen.

89. Wa Zakariyyaaa iz naadaa Rabbahoo Rabbi laa tazarnee fardañw-wa Anta khayrul-waariseen.

90. Fastajabnaa lahoo wa wahabnaa lahoo Yahyaa wa aslahnaa lahoo zawjah; innahum kaanoo yusaari'oona fil-khayraati wa yad'oonanaa raghabañw-wa rahabaa; wa kaanoo lanaa khaashi'een.

91. Wallateee ahsanat farja-haa fanafakhnaa feehaa mir-roohinaa wa ja'alnaahaa

---

الضُّرَّ وَأَنْتَ أَرْحَمُ الرّٰحِمِينَ ۝

فَاسْتَجَبْنَا لَهُ فَكَشَفْنَا مَا بِهِ مِنْ ضُرٍّ وَّاٰتَيْنٰهُ أَهْلَهُ وَمِثْلَهُمْ مَّعَهُمْ رَحْمَةً مِّنْ عِنْدِنَا وَذِكْرٰى لِلْعٰبِدِينَ ۝

وَإِسْمٰعِيلَ وَإِدْرِيسَ وَذَا الْكِفْلِ كُلٌّ مِّنَ الصّٰبِرِينَ ۝

وَأَدْخَلْنٰهُمْ فِي رَحْمَتِنَا إِنَّهُمْ مِّنَ الصّٰلِحِينَ ۝

وَذَا النُّونِ إِذْ ذَّهَبَ مُغَاضِبًا فَظَنَّ أَنْ لَّنْ نَّقْدِرَ عَلَيْهِ فَنَادٰى فِي الظُّلُمٰتِ أَنْ لَّا إِلٰهَ إِلَّا أَنْتَ سُبْحٰنَكَ إِنِّي كُنْتُ مِنَ الظّٰلِمِينَ ۝

فَاسْتَجَبْنَا لَهُ وَنَجَّيْنٰهُ مِنَ الْغَمِّ وَكَذٰلِكَ نُنْجِي الْمُؤْمِنِينَ ۝

وَزَكَرِيَّا إِذْ نَادٰى رَبَّهُ رَبِّ لَا تَذَرْنِي فَرْدًا وَّأَنْتَ خَيْرُ الْوٰرِثِينَ ۝

فَاسْتَجَبْنَا لَهُ وَوَهَبْنَا لَهُ يَحْيٰى وَأَصْلَحْنَا لَهُ زَوْجَهُ إِنَّهُمْ كَانُوا يُسٰرِعُونَ فِي الْخَيْرٰتِ وَ يَدْعُونَنَا رَغَبًا وَّرَهَبًا وَكَانُوا لَنَا خٰشِعِينَ ۝

وَالَّتِي أَحْصَنَتْ فَرْجَهَا فَنَفَخْنَا فِيهَا مِنْ رُّوحِنَا وَجَعَلْنٰهَا

and her son a Sign for all peoples.

92. Verily, this brotherhood of yours is a single brotherhood, and I am your Lord and Cherisher: therefore serve Me (and no other).

93. But (later generations) cut off their affair (of unity), one from another: (yet) will they all return to Us.

94. Whoever works any act of righteousness and has faith,- his endeavour will not be rejected: We shall record it in his favor.

95. But there is a ban on any population which We have destroyed: that they shall not return,

96. Until the Gog and Magog (people) are let through (their barrier), and they swiftly swarm from every hill.

97. Then will the True Promise draw near (of fulfilment): then behold! the eyes of the Unbelievers will fixedly stare in horror: "Ah! woe to us! we were indeed heedless of this; nay, we truly did wrong!"

98. Verily you, (unbelievers), and the (false) gods that you worship besides Allah, are (but) fuel for Hell! To it will you (surely) come!

99. If these had been gods, they would not have got there! but each one will abide therein.

100. There, sobbing will be their lot, nor will they there hear anything else.

101. Those for whom the good (record) from Us has gone before, will be removed far therefrom.

102. Not the slightest sound will they hear of Hell:

wabnahaaa Aayatal-lil'aalameen.

92. Inna haaziheee ummatukum ummatañw-waahidatañw-wa Ana Rabbukum fa'budoon.

93. Wa taqatta'ooo amrahum baynahum kullun ilaynaa raaji'oon. **(Section 6)**

94. Famañy-ya'mal minas-saalihaati wa huwa mu'minun falaa kufraana lisa'yihee wa-innaa lahoo kaatiboon.

95. Wa haraamun 'alaa qaryatin ahlaknaahaaa annahum laa yarji'oon.

96. Hattaaa izaa futihat Yaajooju wa Maajooju wa hum-min kulli hadabiñy-yansiloon.

97. Waqtarabal-wa'dul-haqqu fa-izaa hiya shaakhisatun absaarul-lazeena kafaroo yaa waylanaa qad kunnaa fee ghaflatim-min haazaa bal kunnaa zaalimeen.

98. Innakum wa maa ta'budoona min doonil-laahi hasabu Jahannama antum lahaa waaridoon.

99. Law kaana haaa'ulaaa'i aalihatam-maa waradoohaa wa kullun feehaa khaalidoon.

100. Lahum feehaa zafeeruñw-wa hum feehaa laa yasma'oon.

101. Innal-lazeena sabaqat lahum-minal-husnaaa ulaaa'ika 'anhaa mub'adoon.

102. Laa yasma'oona hasee-sahaa wa hum fee

what their souls desired, in that they will dwell.

103. The Great Terror will bring them no grief: but the angels will meet them (with mutual greetings): "This is your Day,- (the Day) that you were promised."

104. The Day that We roll up the heavens like a scroll rolled up for books (completed),- even as We produced the first creation, so shall We produce a new one: a promise We have undertaken: truly shall We fulfil it.

105. Before this We wrote in the Psalms, after the Message (given to Moses): My servants, the righteous, shall inherit the earth."

106. Verily in this (Qur'an) is a Message for people who would (truly) worship Allah.

107. We sent you not, but as a Mercy for all creatures.

108. Say: "What has come to me by inspiration is that your Allah is One Allah: will you therefore bow to His Will (in Islam)?"

109. But if they turn back, Say: "I have proclaimed the Message to you all alike and in truth; but I do not know whether that which you are promised is near or far.

110. "It is He Who knows what is open in speech and what you hide (in your hearts).

111. "I do not know but that it may be a trial for you, and a grant of (worldly) livelihood (to you) for a time."

112. Say: "O my Lord! judge you in truth!" "Our Lord Most Gracious is the One Whose assistance should be sought against the blasphemies you utter!

mash-tahat anfusuhum khaali-doon.

103. Laa yaḥzunuhumul-faza'ul-akbaru wa tatalaq-qaahumul-malaaa'ikatu haazaa Yawmukumul-lazee kuntum too'adoon.

104. Yawma naṭwis-samaaa'a kaṭayyis-sijilli lilkutub; kamaa badaanaaa awwala khalqin-nu'eeduh; wa'dan 'alaynaa; innaa kunnaa faa'ileen.

105. Wa laqad katabnaa fiz-Zaboori mim ba'diz-zikri annal-arḍa yarisuhaa 'ibaadi-yaṣ-ṣaaliḥoon.

106. Inna fee haazaa labalaa-ghal-liqawmin 'aabideen.

107. Wa maaa arsalnaaka illaa raḥmatal-lil'aalameen.

108. Qul innamaa yooḥaaa ilayya annamaaa ilaahukum Ilaahuñw-Waahid, fahal antum muslimoon.

109. Fa-in tawallaw faqul aazantukum 'alaa sawaaa'; wa in adreee aqareebun am ba'eedum-maa too'adoon.

110. Innahoo ya'lamul-jahra minal-qawli wa ya'lamu maa taktumoon.

111. Wa in adree la'allahoo fitnatul-lakum wa mataa'un ilaa ḥeen.

112. Qaala Rabbiḥ-kum bil-ḥaqq; wa Rabbunar-Raḥmaa-nul-musta'aanu 'alaa maa taṣifoon. (Section 7)

22. The Pilgrimage

In the name of Allah, Most Gracious, Most Merciful.

1. O mankind! fear your Lord! for the convulsion of the Hour (of Judgment) will be a thing terrible!

2. The Day you shall see it, every mother giving suck shall forget her suckling-babe, and every pregnant female shall drop her load (unformed): you shall see mankind as in a drunken riot, yet not drunk: but dreadful will be the Chastisement of Allah.

3. And yet among men there are such as dispute about Allah, without knowledge, and follow every evil one obstinate in rebellion!

4. About the (Evil One) it is decreed that whoever turns to him for friendship, he will lead him astray, and he will guide him to the Penalty of the Fire.

5. O mankind! if you have a doubt about the Resurrection, (consider) that We created you out of dust, then out of sperm, then out of a leech-like clot, then out of a morsel of flesh, partly formed and partly unformed, in order that We may manifest (Our power) to you; and We cause whom We will to rest in the wombs for an appointed term, then do We bring you out as babes, then (foster you) that you may reach your age of full strength; and some of you are called to die, and some are sent back to the feeblest old age, so that they know nothing after having known (much), and (further), you see the earth

Sûrat al-Ḥajj–22

(Revealed at Madinah)

Bismillaahir Raḥmaanir Raḥeem

1. Yaaa ayyuhan-naasuttaqoo Rabbakum; inna zalzalatas-Saa'ati shay'un 'aẓeem.

2. Yawma tarawnahaa taẓhalu kullu murḍi'atin 'ammaaa arḍa'at wa taḍa'u kullu Zaati ḥamlin ḥamlahaa wa tarannaasa sukaaraa wa maa hum bisukaaraa wa laakinna 'aẓaaballaahi shadeed.

3. Wa minan-naasi mañy-yujaadilu fil-laahi bighayri 'ilminw-wa yattabi'u kullaa shayṭaanim-mareed.

4. Kutiba 'alayhi annahoo man tawallaahu fa-annahoo yuḍilluhoo wa yahdeehi ilaa 'azaabis-sa'eer.

5. Yaaa-ayyuhan-naasu in kuntum fee raybim-minal-ba'ṣi fa-innaa khalaqnaakum-min turaabin summa min nuṭfatin ṣumma min 'alaqatin ṣumma mim-muḍghatim-mukhallaqatiñw-wa ghayri mukhallaqatil-linubayyina lakum; wa nuqirru fil-arḥaami maa nashaaa'u ilaaa ajalim-musamman ṣumma nukhrijukum ṭiflan ṣumma litablughooo ashuddakum wa minkum-mañy-yutawaffaa wa minkum-mañy-yuraddu ilaaa arẓalil-'umuri likaylaa ya'lama mim ba'di 'ilmin shay'aa; wa taral-arḍa

barren and lifeless, but when We pour down rain on it, it is stirred (to life), it swells, and it puts forth every kind of beautiful growth (in pairs).

6. This is so, because Allah is the Reality: it is He Who gives life to the dead, and it is He Who has power over all things.

7. And verily the Hour will come: there can be no doubt about it, or about (the fact) that Allah will raise up all who are in the graves.

8. Yet there is among men such a one as disputes about Allah, without knowledge, without guidance, and without a Book of Enlightenment,-

9. (Disdainfully) bending his side, in order to lead (men) astray from the Path of Allah: for him there is disgrace in this life, and on the Day of Judgment We shall make him taste the Penalty of burning (Fire).

10. (It will be said): "This is because of the deeds which your hands sent forth, for verily Allah is not unjust to His servants.

11. There are among men some who serve Allah, as it were, on the verge: if good befalls them, they are, therewith, well content; but if a trial comes to them, they turn on their faces: they lose both this world and the Hereafter: that is loss for all to see!

12. They call on such deities, besides Allah, as can neither hurt nor profit them: that is straying far indeed (from the Way)!

13. (Perhaps) they call on one whose hurt is nearer than his profit: evil, indeed, is the patron, and evil the companion (or help)!

haamidatan fa-izaaa anzalnaa 'alayhal-maaa'ah-tazzat wa rabat wa ambatat min kulli zawjim baheej.

6. Zaalika bi-annal-laaha Huwal-ḥaqqu wa annahoo yuḥyil-mawtaa wa annahoo 'alaa kulli shay'in Qadeer.

7. Wa annas-Saa'ata aatiya-tul-laa rayba feehaa wa annal-laaha yab'aṣu man fil-quboor.

8. Wa minan-naasi mañy-yujaadilu fil-laahi bighayri 'ilmiñw-wa laa hudañw-wa laa Kitaabim-Muneer.

9. Saaniya 'iṭfihee liyuḍilla 'an sabeelil-laahi lahoo fiddun-yaa khizyuñw-wa nuẓeequhoo Yawmal-Qiyaamati 'aẓaabal-ḥareeq.

10. Zaalika bimaa qaddamat yadaaka wa annal-laaha laysa biẓallaamil-lil'abeed. **(Section 1)**

11. Wa minan-naasi mañy-ya'budul-laaha 'alaa ḥarfin fa-in aṣaabahoo khayruniṭ-ma-anna bihee wa in aṣaabat-hu fitnatunin-qalaba 'alaa wajhi-hee khasirad-dunyaa wal-Aakhirah; zaalika huwal-khusraanul-mubeen.

12. Yad'oo min doonil-laahi maa laa yaḍurruhoo wa maa laa yanfa'uh; zaalika huwaḍ-ḍalaalul-ba'eed.

13. Yad'oo laman ḍarruhooo aqrabu min-naf'ih; labi'sal-mawlaa wa labi'sal-'asheer.

14. Verily Allah will admit those who believe and work righteous deeds, to Gardens, beneath which rivers flow: for Allah carries out all that He plans.

15. If any think that Allah will not help him (His Messenger) in this world and the Hereafter, let him stretch out a rope to the ceiling and cut (himself) off: then let him see whether his plan will remove that which enrages (him)!

16. Thus have We sent down Clear Sings; and verily Allah does guide whom He will!

17. Those who believe (in the Qur'an), those who follow the Jewish (scriptures), and the Sabians, Christians, Magians, and Polytheists,- Allah will judge between them on the Day of Judgment: for Allah is Witness of all things.

18. Do you not see that to Allah bow down in worship all things that are in the heavens and on earth,- the sun, the moon, the stars; the hills, the trees, the animals; and a great number among mankind? But a great number are (also) such as are fit for Punishment: and such as Allah shall disgrace,- None can raise to honor: for Allah carries out all that He wills.

19. These two antagonists dispute with each other about their Lord: but those who deny (their Lord),- for them will be cut out a garment of Fire: over their heads will be poured out boiling water.

14. Innal-laaha yudkhilul-lazeena aamanoo wa 'amiluṣ-ṣaaliḥaati Jannaatin tajree min taḥtihal-anhaar; innal-laaha yaf'alu maa yureed.

15. Man kaana yaẓunnu allañy-yanṣurahul-laahu fid-dunyaa wal-Aakhirati fal-yamdud bisa-babin ilas-samaaa'i ṣummal-yaqta' falyanẓur hal yuzhibanna kayduhoo maa yagheeẓ.

16. Wa kazaalika anzalnaahu Aayaatim bayyinaatiñw-wa annal-laaha yahdee mañy-yureed.

17. Innal-lazeena aamanoo wallazeena haadoo waṣ-Ṣaabi'eena wan-Naṣaaraa wal-Majoosa wallazeena ashrakooo innal-laaha yafṣilu baynahum Yawmal-Qiyaamah; innal-laaha 'alaa kulli shay'in Shaheed.

18. Alam tara annal-laaha yasjudu lahoo man fis-samaa-waati wa man fil-arḍi wash-shamsu walqamaru wan-nu-joomu wal-jibaalu wash-shajaru wad-dawaaabbu wa kaseerum-minan-naasi wa kaseerun ḥaqqa 'alayhil-'azaab; wa mañy-yuhinil-laahu famaa lahoo mim-mukrim; innallaaha yaf'alu maa yashaaa'.

19. Haazaani khaṣmaanikh-taṣamoo fee Rabbihim fal-lazeena kafaroo quṭṭi'at lahum siyaabum-min-naar; yuṣabbu min fawqi ru'oosihimul-ḥameem.

20. With it will be scalded what is within their bodies, as well as (their) skins.

21. In addition there will be maces of iron (to punish) them.

22. Every time they wish to get away therefrom, from anguish, they will be forced back therein, and (it will be said), "You taste the Penalty of Burning!"

23. Allah will admit those who believe and work righteous deeds, to Gardens beneath which rivers flow: they shall be adorned therein with bracelets of gold and pearls; and their garments there will be of silk.

24. For they have been guided (in this life) to the purest of speeches; they have been guided to the Path of Him Who is Worthy of (all) Praise.

25. As to those who have rejected (Allah), and would keep back (men) from the Way of Allah, and from the Sacred Mosque, which We have made (open) to (all) men - equal is the dweller there and the visitor from the country - and any whose purpose therein is profanity or wrong-doing - them will We cause to taste of a most grievous Penalty.

26. Behold! We gave the site, to Abraham, of the (Sacred) House, (saying): "Do not associate anything (in worship) with Me; and sanctify My House for those who compass it round, or stand up, or bow, or prostrate them-selves (therein in prayer).

27. "And proclaim the Pilgrimage among men: they will come to you on foot and (mounted) on every kind of camel, lean on account of journeys through deep and distant mountain highways;

28. "That they may witness the benefits (provided) for them, and celebrate

20. Yuṣharu bihee maa fee buṭoonihim waljulood.

21. Wa lahum-maqaami‘u min ḥadeed.

22. Kullamaaa araadooo añy-yakhrujoo minhaa min ghammin u‘eedoo feehaa wa zooqoo ‘azaabal-ḥareeq. (Sec. 2)

23. Innal-laaha yudkhilul-lazeena aamanoo wa ‘amiluṣ-ṣaaliḥaati Jannaatin tajree min taḥtihal-anhaaru yuḥallawna feehaa min asaawira min zahabiñw-wa lu’lu’aa; wa libaasuhum feehaa ḥareer.

24. Wa hudooo ilaṭ-ṭayyibi minal-qawli wa hudooo ilaa ṣiraaṭil-ḥameed.

25. Innal-lazeena kafaroo wa yaṣuddoona ‘an sabeelil-laahi wal-Masjidil-Ḥaraamil-lazee ja‘alnaahu linnaasi sawaaa’a-nil-‘aakifu feehi walbaad; wa mañy-yurid feehi bi-ilḥaadim biẓulmin-nuẓiqhu min ‘azaabin aleem. (Section 3)

26. Wa iz bawwaãnaa li-Ibraaheema makaanal-Bayti al-laa tushrik bee shay’añw-wa ṭahhir Baytiya liṭṭaaa’ifeena walqaaa’imeena warrukka‘is-sujood.

27. Wa azzin fin-naasi bil-Ḥajji yaãtooka rijaalañw-wa ‘alaa kulli ḍaamiriñy-yaãteena min kulli fajjin ‘ameeq.

28. Li-yashhadoo manaafi‘a lahum wa yazkurus-

the name of Allah, through the Days appointed, over the cattle which He has provided for them (for sacrifice): then you eat thereof and feed the distressed ones in want.

29. "Then let them complete the rites prescribed for them, perform their vows, and (again) circumambulate the Ancient House."

30. Such (is the Pilgrimage): whoever honors the sacred rites of Allah, for him it is good in the sight of his Lord. Lawful to you (for food in Pilgrimage) are cattle, except those men-tioned to you (as exception): but shun the abomination of idols, and shun the word that is false,-

31. Being true in faith to Allah, and never assigning partners to Him: if anyone assigns partners to Allah, he is as if he had fallen from heaven and been snatched up by birds, or the wind had swooped (like a bird on its prey) and thrown him into a far- distant place.

32. Such (is his state): and who-ever holds in honor the symbols of Allah, (in the sacrifice of animals), such (honor) should come truly from piety of heart.

33. In them you have benefits for a term appointed: in the end their place of sacrifice is near the Ancient House.

34. To every people did We appoint rites (of sacrifice), that they might celebrate the name of Allah over the sustenance He gave them from animals (fit for food). But your God is One Allah: submit then your wills to Him (in Islam): and you give the good news to those who humble themselves,-

35. To those whose hearts, when Allah is mentioned, are filled with fear, who show patient perseverance over their afflictions, keep up regular prayer,

mal-laahi feee ayyaamim-ma'loomaatin 'alaa maa razaqahum-mim baheematil-an'aami fakuloo minhaa wa aṭ'imul-baaa'isal-faqeer.

29. Summal-yaqḍoo tafaṣa-hum wal-yoofoo nuẓoorahum wal-yaṭṭawwafoo bil-Baytil-'Ateeq.

30. Ẕaalika wa mañy-yu'aẓẓim ḥurumaatil-laahi fahuwa khayrul-lahoo 'inda Rabbih; wa uḥillat lakumul-an'aamu illaa maa yutlaa 'alaykum fajtanibur-rijsa minal-awsaani wajtaniboo qawlaz-zoor.

31. Ḥunafaaa'a lillaahi ghayra mushrikeena bih; wa mañy-yushrik billaahi faka-annamaa-kharra minas-samaaa'i fatakh-ṭafuhuṭ-ṭayru aw tahwee bihir-reeḥu fee makaanin saḥeeq.

32. Ẕaalika wa mañy- yu'aẓẓim sha'aaa'iral-laahi fa-innahaa min taqwal-quloob.

33. Lakum feehaa manaafi'u ilaaa ajalim-musamman summa maḥilluhaaa ilal-Baytil-'Ateeq.
(Section 4)

34. Wa likulli ummatin ja'alnaa mansakal-liyaẕkurus-mal-laahi 'alaa maa razaqahum mim baheematil-an'aam; fa-ilaahukum Ilaahuñw-Waaḥidun falahooo aslimoo; wa bash-shiril-mukhbiteen.

35. Allaẕeena iẕaa ẕukiral-laahu wajilat quloobuhum waṣṣaabireena 'alaa maaa aṣaabahum walmuqeemiṣ-Ṣalaati

and spend (in charity) out of what We have bestowed upon them.

36. The sacrificial camels We have made for you as among the symbols from Allah: in them is (much) good for you: then pronounce the name of Allah over them as they line up (for sacrifice): when they are down on their sides (after slaughter), you eat thereof, and feed such as (beg not but) live in contentment, and such as beg with due humility: thus have We made animals subject to you, that you may be grateful.

37. It is not their meat nor their blood, that reaches Allah: it is your piety that reaches Him: He has thus made them subject to you, that you may glorify Allah for His guidance to you and proclaim the good news to all who do right.

38. Verily Allah will defend (from ill) those who believe: verily, Allah loves not any that is a traitor to faith, or show ingratitude.

39. To those against whom war is made, permission is given (to fight), because they are wronged;- and verily, Allah is most powerful for their aid;-

40. (They are) those who have been expelled from their homes in defiance of right,- (for no cause) except that they say, "Our Lord is Allah". Did not Allah check one set of people by means of another, there would surely have been pulled down monasteries, churches, synagogues, and mosques, in which the name of Allah is commemorated in abundant measure. Allah will certainly aid those who aid His (cause);- for verily Allah is full of Strength, Exalted in Might, (able to enforce His Will).

41. (They are) those who, if We establish them in the land, establish regular prayer and give regular charity,

wa mimmaa razaqnaahum yunfiqoon.

36. Walbudna ja‘alnaahaa lakum-min sha‘aaa’iril-laahi lakum feehaa khayrun fazkurusmal-laahi ‘alayhaa ṣawaaff; fa-izaa wajabat junoobuhaa fakuloo minhaa wa aṭ‘imul-qaani‘a walmu‘tarr; kazaalika sakhkharnaahaa lakum la‘allakum tashkuroon.

37. Lañy-yanaalal-laaha luḥoo-muhaa wa laa dimaaa’uhaa wa laakiñy-yanaaluhut-taqwaa minkum; kazaalika sakh-kharahaa lakum litukabbirul-laaha ‘alaa maa hadaakum; wa bashshiril-muḥsineen.

38. Innal-laaha yudaafi‘u ‘anil-lazeena aamanoo; innal-laaha laa yuḥibbu kulla khawwaanin kafoor. **(Section 5)**

39. Uzina lillazeena yuqaa-taloona bi-annahum ẓulimoo; wa innal-laaha ‘alaa naṣrihim la-Qadeer.

40. Allazeena ukhrijoo min diyaarihim bighayri ḥaqqin illaaa añy-yaqooloo Rabbunal-laah; wa law laa daf‘ul-laahin-naasa ba‘ḍahum biba‘ḍil-lahuddimat ṣawaami‘u wa biya‘uñw-wa ṣalawaatuñw-wa masaajidu yuzkaru feehasmul-laahi kaseeraa; wa layanṣuran-nal-laahu mañy-yanṣuruh; innal-laaha la-Qawiyyun ‘Azeez.

41. Allazeena im-makkan-naahum fil-arḍi aqaamuṣ-Ṣalaata wa-aatawuz-Zakaata

enjoin the right and forbid wrong: with Allah rests the end (and decision) of (all) affairs.

42. If they treat your (mission) as false so did the peoples before them (with their prophets),- the People of Noah, and 'Ad and Thamud;

43. Those of Abraham and Lut;

44. And the Companions of the Madyan People; and Moses was rejected (in the same way). But I granted respite to the Unbelievers, and (only) after that did I punish them: but how (terrible) was My rejection (of them)!

45. How many populations have We destroyed, which were given to wrong-doing? They tumbled down on their roofs. And how many wells are lying idle and neglected, and castles lofty and well-built?

46. Do they not travel through the land, so that their hearts (and minds) may thus learn wisdom and their ears may thus learn to hear? Truly it is not their eyes that are blind, but their hearts which are in their breasts.

47. Yet they ask you to hasten on the Punishment! But Allah will not fail in His Promise. Verily a Day in the sight of your Lord is like a thousand years of your reckoning.

48. And to how many populations did I give respite, which were given to wrong-doing? In the end I punished them. To me is the destination (of all).

49. Say: "O men! I am (sent) to you only to give a Clear Warning:

---

wa amaroo bilma'roofi wa nahaw 'anil-munkar; wa lillaahi 'aaqibatul-umoor.

42. Wa iñy-yukazzibooka faqad kazzabat qablahum qawmu Nooḥiñw-wa 'Aaduñw-wa Samood.

43. Wa qawmu Ibraaheema wa qawmu Loot.

44. Wa aṣ-ḥaabu Madyana wa kuzziba Moosaa fa-amlaytu lilkaafireena summa akhaztu-hum fakayfa kaana nakeer.

45. Faka-ayyim-min qaryatin ahlaknaahaa wa hiya zaali-matun fahiya khaawiyatun 'alaa 'urooshihaa wa bi'rim-mu'aṭ-ṭalatiñw-wa qaṣrim-masheed.

46. Afalam yaseeroo fil-arḍi fatakoona lahum quloobuñy-ya'qiloona bihaaa aw aazaa-nuñy-yasma'oona bihaa fa-innahaa laa ta'mal-abṣaaru wa laakin ta'mal-quloobul-latee fiṣ-ṣudoor.

47. Wa yasta'jiloonaka bil-'azaabi wa lañy-yukhlifal-laahu wa'dah; wa inna yawman 'inda-Rabbika ka-alfi sanatim-mimmaa ta'uddoon.

48. Wa ka-ayyim-min qarya-tin amlaytu lahaa wa hiya zaalimatun summa akhaztuhaa wa ilayyal-maṣeer.   (Section 6)

49. Qul yaaa ayyuhan-naasu innamaaa ana lakum nazeerum-mubeen.

50. "Those who believe and work righteousness, for them is forgiveness and a sustenance most generous.

51. "But those who strive against Our Signs, to frustrate them,- they will be Companions of the Fire."

52. Never did We send a Messenger or a prophet before you, but, when he framed a desire, Satan threw some (vanity) into his desire: but Allah will cancel anything (vain) that Satan throws in, and Allah will confirm (and establish) His Signs: for Allah is full of Knowledge and Wisdom:

53. That He may make the suggestions thrown in by Satan, but a trial for those in whose hearts is a disease and who are hardened of heart: verily the wrong-doers are in a schism far (from the Truth):

54. And that those on whom knowledge has been bestowed may learn that the (Qur'an) is the Truth from your Lord, and that they may believe therein, and their hearts may be made humbly (open) to it: for verily Allah is the Guide of those who believe, to the Straight Way.

55. Those who reject Faith will not cease to be in doubt concerning (Revelation) until the Hour (of Judgment) comes suddenly upon them, or there comes to them the Penalty of a Day of Disaster.

56. On that Day the Dominion will be that of Allah: He will judge between them: so those who believe and work righteous deeds will be in Gardens of Delight.

57. And for those who reject Faith and deny our Signs,

50. Fallaẕeena aamanoo wa 'amiluṣ-ṣaaliḥaati lahum-magh-firatuñw-wa rizqun kareem.

51. Wallaẕeena sa'aw feee Aayaatinaa mu'aajizeena ulaaa'ika Aṣ-ḥaabul-jaheem.

52. Wa maaa arsalnaa min qablika mir-Rasooliñw-wa laa Nabiyyin illaaa iẕaa tamannaaa alqash-Shayṭaanu feee umniy-yatihee fa-yansakhul-laahu maa yulqish-Shayṭaanu summa yuḥkimul-laahu Aayaatih; wallaahu 'Aleemun Ḥakeem.

53. Liyaj'ala maa yulqish-Shay-ṭaanu fitnatal-lillaẕeena fee quloobihim-maraḍuñw-walqaa-siyati quloobuhum; wa innaẓ-ẓaalimeena lafee shiqaaqim-ba'eed.

54. Wa liya'lamal-laẕeena ootul-'ilma annahul-ḥaqqu mir-Rabbika fa-yu'minoo bihee fatukhbita lahoo quloobuhum; wa innal-laaha lahaadil-laẕeena aamanooo ilaa Ṣiraaṭim-Musta-qeem.

55. Wa laa yazaalul-laẕeena kafaroo fee miryatim-minhu ḥattaa taåtiyahumus-Saa'atu baghtatan aw yaåtiyahum 'aẕaabu Yawmin 'aqeem.

56. Almulku Yawma'iẕil-lillaahi yaḥkumu baynahum; fallaẕeena aamanoo wa 'amiluṣ-ṣaaliḥaati fee Jannaa-tin-Na'eem.

57. Wallaẕeena kafaroo wa kazzaboo bi-Aayaatinaa

there will be a humiliating Punishment.

58. Those who leave their homes in the cause of Allah, and are then slain or die,- On them will Allah bestow verily a goodly Provision: truly Allah is He Who bestows the best Provision.

59. Verily He will admit them to a place with which they shall be well pleased: for Allah is All-Knowing, Most Forbearing.

60. That (is so). And if one has retaliated to no greater extent than the injury he received, and is again set upon inordinately, Allah will help him: for Allah is One that blots out (sins) and forgives (again and again).

61. That is because Allah merges night into day, and He merges day into night, and verily it is Allah Who hears and sees (all things).

62. That is because Allah - He is the Reality; and those besides Him whom they invoke,- they are but vain Falsehood: verily Allah is He, Most High, Most Great.

63. Don't you see that Allah sends down rain from the sky, and forthwith the earth becomes clothed with green? for Allah is He Who understands the finest mysteries, and is well-acquainted (with them).

64. To Him belongs all that is in the heavens and on earth: for verily Allah,- He is free of all wants, Worthy of all Praise.

65. Don't you see that Allah has made subject to you (men) all that is on the earth, and the ships that sail through the sea by His Command? He withholds the sky (rain) from failing on the earth except by His leave: for Allah is Most Kind and Most Merciful to man.

fa-ulaaa'ika lahum 'azaabum-muheen. **(Section 7)**

58. Wallazeena haajaroo fee sabeelil-laahi summa qutilooo law maatoo la-yarzuqan-nahumul-laahu rizqan ḥasanaa; wa innal-laaha la-Huwa khayrur-raaziqeen.

59. La-yudkhilan-nahum-mud-khalaáñy-yarḍawnah; wa innal-laaha la-'Aleemun Ḥaleem.

60. Zaalika wa man 'aaqaba bimisli maa 'ooqiba bihee-summa bughiya 'alayhi la-yansurannahul-laah; innal-laaha la-'Afuwwun Ghafoor.

61. Zaalika bi-annal-laaha yoolijul-layla fin-nahaari wa yoolijun-nahaara fil-layli wa annal-laaha Samee'um-Baṣeer.

62. Zaalika bi-annal-laaha Huwal-ḥaqqu wa anna maa yad'oona min doonihee huwal-baaṭilu wa annal-laaha Huwal-'Aliyyul-Kabeer.

63. Alam tara annal-laaha anzala minas-samaaa'i maaa'an fatuṣbiḥul-arḍu mukhḍarrah; innal-laaha Laṭeefun Khabeer.

64. Lahoo maa fis-samaa-waati wa maa fil-arḍ; wa innal-laaha la-Huwal-Ghaniyyul-Ḥameed. **(Section 8)**

65. Alam tara-annal-laaha sakhkhara lakum-maa fil-arḍi walfulka tajree fil-baḥri bi-amrihee wa yumsikus-samaaa'a an taqa'a 'alal-arḍi illaa bi-iznih; innal-laaha binnaasi la-Ra'oofur-Raḥeem.

66. It is He Who gave you life, will cause you to die, and will again give you life: truly man is a most ungrateful creature!

66. Wa Huwal-lazeee aḥyaa-kum ṣumma yumeetukum ṣumma yuḥyeekum; innal-insaana lakafoor.

وَهُوَ الَّذِىۤ اَحۡيَاكُمۡ ثُمَّ يُمِيۡتُكُمۡ ثُمَّ يُحۡيِيۡكُمۡ ؕ اِنَّ الۡاِنۡسَانَ لَكَفُوۡرٌ ۞

67. To every people have We appointed rites and ceremonies which they must follow: let them not then dispute with you on the matter, but do you invite (them) to your Lord: for you are assuredly on the Right Way.

67. Likulli ummatin ja'alnaa mansakan hum naasikoohu falaa yunaazi'unnaka fil-amr; wad'u ilaa Rabbika innaka la'alaa hudam-mustaqeem.

لِكُلِّ اُمَّةٍ جَعَلۡنَا مَنۡسَكًا هُمۡ نَاسِكُوۡهُ فَلَا يُنَازِعُنَّكَ فِى الۡاَمۡرِ وَادۡعُ اِلَى رَبِّكَ ؕ اِنَّكَ لَعَلٰى هُدًى مُّسۡتَقِيۡمٍ ۞

68. If they do wrangle with you, say, "Allah knows best what it is you are doing."

68. Wa in jaadalooka faqulil-laahu a'lamu bimaa ta'maloon.

وَاِنۡ جَادَلُوۡكَ فَقُلِ اللّٰهُ اَعۡلَمُ بِمَا تَعۡمَلُوۡنَ ۞

69. "Allah will judge between you on the Day of Judgment concerning the matters in which you differ."

69. Allaahu yaḥkumu bayna-kum Yawmal-Qiyaamati fee-maa kuntum feehi takhtalifoon.

اَللّٰهُ يَحۡكُمُ بَيۡنَكُمۡ يَوۡمَ الۡقِيٰمَةِ فِيۡمَا كُنۡتُمۡ فِيۡهِ تَخۡتَلِفُوۡنَ ۞

70. Don't you know that Allah knows all that is in heaven and on earth? Indeed it is all in a Record, and that is easy for Allah.

70. Alam ta'lam annal-laaha ya'lamu maa fis-samaaa'i wal-arḍ; inna zaalika fee kitaab; inna zaalika 'alal-laahi yaseer.

اَلَمۡ تَعۡلَمۡ اَنَّ اللّٰهَ يَعۡلَمُ مَا فِى السَّمَآءِ وَالۡاَرۡضِ ؕ اِنَّ ذٰلِكَ فِىۡ كِتٰبٍ ؕ اِنَّ ذٰلِكَ عَلَى اللّٰهِ يَسِيۡرٌ ۞

71. Yet they worship, besides Allah, things for which no authority has been sent down to them, and of which they have (really) no knowledge: for those that do wrong there is no helper.

71. Wa ya'budoona min doonil-laahi maa lam yunazzil bihee sulṭaananw-wa maa laysa lahum bihee 'ilm; wa maa lizzaalimeena min-naṣeer.

وَيَعۡبُدُوۡنَ مِنۡ دُوۡنِ اللّٰهِ مَا لَمۡ يُنَزِّلۡ بِهِ سُلۡطٰنًا وَّمَا لَيۡسَ لَهُمۡ بِهِ عِلۡمٌ ؕ وَمَا لِلظّٰلِمِيۡنَ مِنۡ نَّصِيۡرٍ ۞

72. When Our Clear Signs are rehearsed to them, you will notice a denial on the faces of the Unbelievers! they nearly attack with violence those who rehearse Our Signs to them. Say, "Shall I tell you of something (far) worse than these Signs? It is the Fire (of Hell)! Allah has promised it to the Unbelievers! and evil is that destination!"

72. Wa izaa tutlaa 'alayhim Aayaatunaa bayyinaatin ta'rifu fee wujoohil-lazeena kafarul-munkara yakaadoona yasṭoona bil-lazeena yatloona 'alayhim Aayaatinaa; qul afa-unab-bi'ukum bisharrim-min zaali-kum; an-Naaru wa'adahal-laahul-lazeena kafaroo wa bi'sal-maṣeer.   **(Section 9)**

وَاِذَا تُتۡلٰى عَلَيۡهِمۡ اٰيٰتُنَا بَيِّنٰتٍ تَعۡرِفُ فِىۡ وُجُوۡهِ الَّذِيۡنَ كَفَرُوا الۡمُنۡكَرَ ؕ يَكَادُوۡنَ يَسۡطُوۡنَ بِالَّذِيۡنَ يَتۡلُوۡنَ عَلَيۡهِمۡ اٰيٰتِنَا ؕ قُلۡ اَفَاُنَبِّئُكُمۡ بِشَرٍّ مِّنۡ ذٰلِكُمۡ ؕ اَلنَّارُ ؕ وَعَدَهَا اللّٰهُ الَّذِيۡنَ كَفَرُوۡا ؕ وَبِئۡسَ الۡمَصِيۡرُ ۞

73. O men! Here is a parable set forth! listen to it! Those on whom, besides Allah, you call,

73. Yaaa ayyuhan-naasu ḍuriba maṣalun fastami'oo lah; innal-lazeena tad'oona

يٰۤاَيُّهَا النَّاسُ ضُرِبَ مَثَلٌ فَاسۡتَمِعُوۡا لَهٗ ؕ اِنَّ الَّذِيۡنَ تَدۡعُوۡنَ

cannot create (even) a fly, if they all met together for the purpose! And if the fly should snatch away anything from them, they would have no power to release it from the fly. Feeble are those who petition and those whom they petition!

74. No just estimate have they made of Allah: for Allah is He Who is strong and able to Carry out His Will.

75. Allah chooses messengers from angels and from men for Allah is He Who hears and sees (all things).

76. He knows what is before them and what is behind them: and to Allah go back all questions (for decision).

77. O you who believe! Bow down, prostrate yourselves, and adore your Lord; and do good; that you may prosper.

78. And strive in His cause as you ought to strive, (with sincerity and under discipline). He has chosen you, and has imposed no difficulties on you in religion; it is the cult of your father Abraham. It is He Who has named you Muslims, both before and in this (Revelation); that the Messenger may be a witness for you, and you be witnesses for mankind! So establish regular Prayer, give regular Charity, and hold fast to Allah! He is your Protector - the Best to protect and the Best to help!

min doonil-laahi lañy-yakhlu-qoo zubaabañw-wa lawijta-ma'oo lahoo wa iñy-yaslub-humuz-zubaabu shay'al-laa yastan-qizoohu minh; da'ufat-taalibu walmatloob.

74. Maa qadarul-laaha haqqa qadrih; innal-laaha la-Qawiy-yun 'Azeez.

75. Allaahu yastafee minal-malaaa'ikati Rusulañw-wa minan-naas; innal-laaha Samee'um Baseer.

76. Ya'lamu maa bayna aydeehim wa maa khalfahum; wa ilal-laahi turja'ul-umoor.

77. Yaaa ayyuhal-lazeena aamanur-ka'oo wasjudoo wa'budoo Rabbakum waf'alul-khayra la'allakum tuflihoon. 🕌

78. Wa jaahidoo fil-laahi haqqa jihaadih; Huwaj-tabaakum wa maa ja'ala 'alaykum fid-deeni min haraj; Millata abeekum Ibraaheem; Huwa sammaakumul-muslimeena min qablu wa fee haazaa li-yakoonar-Rasoolu shaheedan 'alaykum wa takoonoo shuhadaaa'a 'alan-naas; fa-aqeemus-Salaata wa aatuz-Zakaata wa'tasimoo billaahi Huwa mawlaakum fani'mal-mawlaa wa ni'man-naseer. **(Section 10)**

---

23. The Believers
In the name of Allah, Most Gracious, Most Merciful.

1. The believers must (eventually) win through,-

Sûrat al-Mu'minûn–23
(Revealed at Makkah)
Bismillaahir Rahmaanir Raheem

1. Qad aflahal-mu'minoon.

(Bow Down)

2. Those who humble themselves in their prayers;

3. Who avoid vain talk;

4. Who are active in deeds of charity;

5. Who abstain from sex,

6. Except with those joined to them in the marriage bond, or (the captives) whom their right hands possess,- for (in their case) they are free from blame,

7. But those whose desires exceed those limits are transgressors;-

8. Those who faithfully observe their trusts and their covenants;

9. And who (strictly) guard their prayers;-

10. These will be the heirs,

11. Who will inherit Paradise: they will dwell therein (for ever).

12. We created man from a quintessence (of clay);

13. Then We placed him as (a drop of) sperm in a place of rest, firmly fixed;

14. Then We made the sperm into a clot of congealed blood; then of that clot We made a (foetus) lump; then We made out of that lump bones and clothed the bones with flesh; then We developed out of it another creature. So blessed be Allah, the best to create!

15. After that, at length you will die.

16. Again, on the Day of Judgment, will you be raised up.

---

2. Allaẕeena hum fee Ṣalaatihim khaashi'oon.

3. Wallaẕeena hum 'anil-laghwi mu'riḍoon.

4. Wallaẕeena hum liz-Zakaati faa'iloon.

5. Wallaẕeena hum lifuroo-jihim ḥaafiẕoon.

6. Illaa 'alaaa azwaajihim aw maa malakat aymaanuhum fa-innahum ghayru maloomeen.

7. Famanib-taghaa waraaa'a zaalika fa-ulaaa'ika humul-'aadoon.

8. Wallaẕeena hum li-amaanaatihim wa 'ahdihim raa'oon.

9. Wallaẕeena hum 'alaa Ṣalawaatihim yuḥaafiẕoon.

10. Ulaaa'ika humul-waari-soon.

11. Allaẕeena yariṣoonal-Firdawsa hum feehaa khaali-doon.

12. Wa laqad khalaqnal-insaana min sulaalatim-min ṭeen.

13. Summa ja'alnaahu nuṭ-fatan fee qaraarim-makeen.

14. Summa khalaqnan-nuṭfata 'alaqatan fakhalaqnal-'alaqata muḍghatan fakhalaq-nal-muḍghata 'iẕaaman fakasawnal-'iẕaama laḥman summa anshaȧnaahu khalqan aakhar; fatabaarakal-laahu aḥsanul-khaaliqeen.

15. Summa innakum ba'da zaalika la-mayyitoon.

16. Summa innakum Yaw-mal-Qiyaamati tub'aṣoon.

---

٢ اَلَّذِيْنَ هُمْ فِيْ صَلَاتِهِمْ خٰشِعُوْنَ ۙ

٣ وَالَّذِيْنَ هُمْ عَنِ اللَّغْوِ مُعْرِضُوْنَ ۙ

٤ وَالَّذِيْنَ هُمْ لِلزَّكٰوةِ فٰعِلُوْنَ ۙ

٥ وَالَّذِيْنَ هُمْ لِفُرُوْجِهِمْ حٰفِظُوْنَ ۙ

٦ اِلَّا عَلٰۤى اَزْوَاجِهِمْ اَوْ مَا مَلَكَتْ اَيْمَانُهُمْ فَاِنَّهُمْ غَيْرُ مَلُوْمِيْنَ ۚ

٧ فَمَنِ ابْتَغٰى وَرَآءَ ذٰلِكَ فَاُولٰٓئِكَ هُمُ الْعٰدُوْنَ ۚ

٨ وَالَّذِيْنَ هُمْ لِاَمٰنٰتِهِمْ وَعَهْدِهِمْ رٰعُوْنَ ۙ

٩ وَالَّذِيْنَ هُمْ عَلٰى صَلَوٰتِهِمْ يُحَافِظُوْنَ ۘ

١٠ اُولٰٓئِكَ هُمُ الْوٰرِثُوْنَ ۙ

١١ الَّذِيْنَ يَرِثُوْنَ الْفِرْدَوْسَ ؕ هُمْ فِيْهَا خٰلِدُوْنَ

١٢ وَلَقَدْ خَلَقْنَا الْاِنْسَانَ مِنْ سُلٰلَةٍ مِّنْ طِيْنٍ ۚ

١٣ ثُمَّ جَعَلْنٰهُ نُطْفَةً فِيْ قَرَارٍ مَّكِيْنٍ ۠

١٤ ثُمَّ خَلَقْنَا النُّطْفَةَ عَلَقَةً فَخَلَقْنَا الْعَلَقَةَ مُضْغَةً فَخَلَقْنَا الْمُضْغَةَ عِظٰمًا فَكَسَوْنَا الْعِظٰمَ لَحْمًا ثُمَّ اَنْشَأْنٰهُ خَلْقًا اٰخَرَ ؕ فَتَبٰرَكَ اللّٰهُ اَحْسَنُ الْخٰلِقِيْنَ ؕ

١٥ ثُمَّ اِنَّكُمْ بَعْدَ ذٰلِكَ لَمَيِّتُوْنَ ؕ

١٦ ثُمَّ اِنَّكُمْ يَوْمَ الْقِيٰمَةِ تُبْعَثُوْنَ

17. And We have made, above you, seven tracts; and We are never unmindful of (Our) Creation.

18. And We send down water from the sky according to (due) measure, and We cause it to soak in the soil; and We certainly are able to drain it off (with ease).

19. With it We grow for you gardens of date-palms and vines: in them have you abundant fruits: and of them you eat (and have enjoyment),-

20. Also a tree springing out of Mount Sinai, which produces oil, and relish for those who use it for food.

21. And in cattle (too) you have an instructive example: from within their bodies We produce (milk) for you to drink; there are, in them, (besides), numerous (other) benefits for you; and of their (meat) you eat;

22. And on them, as well as in ships, you ride.

23. We sent Noah to his people: he said, "O my people; worship Allah, you have no other god but Him. Will you not fear (Him)?"

24. The chiefs of the Unbelievers among his people said: "He is no more than a man like yourselves: his wish is to assert his superiority over you. If Allah had wished (to send Messengers), He could have sent down angels; never did we hear such a thing (as he says), among our ancestors of old."

25. (And some said): "He is only a man possessed; wait (and have patience) with him for a time."

26. (Noah) said: "O my Lord! help me: for that they accuse me of falsehood!"

27. So We inspired him (with this message): "Construct the Ark

17. Wa laqad khalaqnaa fawqakum sab'a ṭaraaa'iqa wa maa kunnaa 'anil-khalqi ghaafileen.

18. Wa anzalnaa minas-samaaa'i maaa'am biqadarin fa-askannaahu fil-arḍi wa innaa 'alaa zahaabim bihee laqaa-diroon

19. Fa-anshaånaa lakum bihee Jannaatim-min-nakheeliñw-wa a'naab; lakum feehaa fawaa-kihu kaseeratuñw-wa minhaa taåkuloon.

20. Wa shajaratan takhruju min Ṭoori Saynaaa'a tambutu bidduhni wa ṣibghil-lil-aakileen.

21. Wa inna lakum fil-an'aami la'ibrah; nusqeekum-mimmaa fee buṭoonihaa wa lakum feehaa manaafi'u kaseeratuñw-wa minhaa taåkuloon.

22. Wa 'alayhaa wa 'alal-fulki tuḥmaloon.   **(Section 1)**

23. Wa laqad arsalnaa Noohan ilaa qawmihee faqaala yaa qawmi'budul-laaha maa lakum min ilaahin ghayruhoo afalaa tattaqoon.

24. Faqaalal-mala'ul-lazeena kafaroo min qawmihee maa haazaaa illaa basharum-mislukum yureedu añy-yatafaḍḍala 'alaykum wa law shaaa'al-laahu la-anzala malaaa'ikatam-maa sami'naa bihaazaa fee aabaaa'inal-awwaleen.

25. In huwa illaa rajulum bihee jinnatun fatarabbaṣoo bihee ḥattaa ḥeen.

26. Qaala Rabbin-ṣurnee bimaa kazzaboon.

27. Fa-awḥaynaaa ilayhi anis-na'il-fulka

وَلَقَدْ خَلَقْنَا فَوْقَكُمْ سَبْعَ طَرَآئِقَ ۖ وَمَا كُنَّا عَنِ الْخَلْقِ غٰفِلِيْنَ ۞

وَاَنْزَلْنَا مِنَ السَّمَآءِ مَآءً بِقَدَرٍ فَاَسْكَنّٰهُ فِى الْاَرْضِ ۖ وَاِنَّا عَلٰى ذَهَابٍ بِهٖ لَقٰدِرُوْنَ ۞

فَاَنْشَأْنَا لَكُمْ بِهٖ جَنّٰتٍ مِّنْ نَّخِيْلٍ وَّاَعْنَابٍ ۘ لَّكُمْ فِيْهَا فَوَاكِهُ كَثِيْرَةٌ وَّمِنْهَا تَأْكُلُوْنَ ۞

وَشَجَرَةً تَخْرُجُ مِنْ طُوْرِ سَيْنَآءَ تَنْبُتُ بِالدُّهْنِ وَصِبْغٍ لِّلْاٰكِلِيْنَ ۞

وَاِنَّ لَكُمْ فِى الْاَنْعَامِ لَعِبْرَةً ۖ نُّسْقِيْكُمْ مِّمَّا فِى بُطُوْنِهَا وَلَكُمْ فِيْهَا مَنَافِعُ كَثِيْرَةٌ وَّمِنْهَا تَأْكُلُوْنَ ۞

وَعَلَيْهَا وَعَلَى الْفُلْكِ تُحْمَلُوْنَ ۞

وَلَقَدْ اَرْسَلْنَا نُوْحًا اِلٰى قَوْمِهٖ فَقَالَ يٰقَوْمِ اعْبُدُوا اللّٰهَ مَا لَكُمْ مِّنْ اِلٰهٍ غَيْرُهٗ ۚ اَفَلَا تَتَّقُوْنَ ۞

فَقَالَ الْمَلَؤُا الَّذِيْنَ كَفَرُوْا مِنْ قَوْمِهٖ مَا هٰذَا اِلَّا بَشَرٌ مِّثْلُكُمْ ۙ يُرِيْدُ اَنْ يَّتَفَضَّلَ عَلَيْكُمْ ۖ وَلَوْ شَآءَ اللّٰهُ لَاَنْزَلَ مَلٰئِكَةً ۖ مَّا سَمِعْنَا بِهٰذَا فِيْٓ اٰبَآئِنَا الْاَوَّلِيْنَ ۞

اِنْ هُوَ اِلَّا رَجُلٌ بِهٖ جِنَّةٌ فَتَرَبَّصُوْا بِهٖ حَتّٰى حِيْنٍ ۞

قَالَ رَبِّ انْصُرْنِيْ بِمَا كَذَّبُوْنِ ۞

فَاَوْحَيْنَآ اِلَيْهِ اَنِ اصْنَعِ الْفُلْكَ

within Our sight and under Our guidance: then when comes Our command, and the fountains of the earth gush forth, you take on board pairs of every species, male and female, and your family- except those of them against whom the Word has already gone forth: and do not address Me in favor of the wrong-doers; for they shall be drowned (in the Flood).

28. And when you have embarked on the Ark - you and those with you,- say: "Praise be to Allah, Who has saved us from the people who do wrong."

29. And say: "O my Lord! enable me to disembark with your blessing: for You are the Best to enable (us) to disembark."

30. Verily in this there are Signs (for men to understand); (thus) do We try (men).

31. Then We raised after them another generation.

32. And We sent to them a Messenger from among themselves, (saying), "Worship Allah! you have no other god but Him. Will you not fear (Him)?"

33. And the chiefs of his people, who disbelieved and denied the Meeting in the Hereafter, and on whom We had bestowed the good things of this life, said: "He is no more than a man like yourselves: he eats of that of which you eat, and drinks of what you drink.

34. "If you obey a man like yourselves, behold, it is certain you will be lost.

35. "Does he promise that when you die and become dust and bones, you shall be brought forth (again)?

36. "Far, very far is that which you are promised!

bi-a'yuninaa wa waḥyinaa fa-izaa jaaa'a amrunaa wa faarat-tannooru fasluk feehaa min kullin zawjaynis-nayni wa ahlaka illaa man sabaqa 'alayhil-qawlu minhum wa laa tukhaaṭibnee fil-lazeena ẓalamooo innahum-mughra-qoon.

28. Fa-izas-tawayta anta wa mam-ma'aka 'alal-fulki faqulil-ḥamdu lillaahil-lazee najjaanaa minal-qawmiẓ-ẓalimeen.

29. Wa qur-Rabbi anzilnee munzalam-mubaarakañw-wa Anta khayrul-munzileen.

30. Inna fee zaalika la-Aayaatiñw-wa in kunnaa lamubtaleen.

31. Summa anshaånaa mim ba'dihim qarnan aakhareen.

32. Fa-arsalnaa feehim Rasoolam-minhum ani'budul-laaha maa lakum-min ilaahin ghayruhoo afalaa tattaqoon.

(Section 2)

33. Wa qaalal-mala-u min qawmihil-lazeena kafaroo wa kazzaboo bi-liqaaa'il-Aakhirati wa atrafnaahum fil-ḥayaatid-dunyaa maa haazaaa illaa basharum-mislukum yaåkulu mimmaa taåkuloona minhu wa yashrabu mimmaa tashraboon.

34. Wa la'in aṭ'atum basha-ram-mislakum innakum izal-lakhaasiroon.

35. A-ya'idukum annakum izaa mittum wa kuntum turaabañw-wa izaaman anna-kum-mukhrajoon.

36. Hayhaata hayhaata limaa too'adoon.

بِأَعْيُنِنَا وَوَحْيِنَا فَإِذَا جَآءَ أَمْرُنَا وَفَارَ التَّنُّورُ فَاسْلُكْ فِيهَا مِنْ كُلٍّ زَوْجَيْنِ اثْنَيْنِ وَأَهْلَكَ إِلَّا مَنْ سَبَقَ عَلَيْهِ الْقَوْلُ مِنْهُمْ وَلَا تُخَاطِبْنِي فِي الَّذِينَ ظَلَمُوا إِنَّهُمْ مُّغْرَقُونَ ۝

فَإِذَا اسْتَوَيْتَ أَنْتَ وَمَنْ مَّعَكَ عَلَى الْفُلْكِ فَقُلِ الْحَمْدُ لِلّٰهِ الَّذِي نَجَّانَا مِنَ الْقَوْمِ الظَّالِمِينَ ۝

وَقُلْ رَّبِّ أَنْزِلْنِي مُنْزَلًا مُّبَارَكًا وَّأَنْتَ خَيْرُ الْمُنْزِلِينَ ۝

إِنَّ فِي ذَٰلِكَ لَآيَاتٍ وَّإِنْ كُنَّا لَمُبْتَلِينَ ۝

ثُمَّ أَنْشَأْنَا مِنْ بَعْدِهِمْ قَرْنًا آخَرِينَ ۝

فَأَرْسَلْنَا فِيهِمْ رَسُولًا مِّنْهُمْ أَنِ اعْبُدُوا اللّٰهَ مَا لَكُمْ مِّنْ إِلَٰهٍ غَيْرُهُ ۚ أَفَلَا تَتَّقُونَ ۝

وَقَالَ الْمَلَأُ مِنْ قَوْمِهِ الَّذِينَ كَفَرُوا وَكَذَّبُوا بِلِقَاءِ الْآخِرَةِ وَأَتْرَفْنَاهُمْ فِي الْحَيَاةِ الدُّنْيَا مَا هَٰذَا إِلَّا بَشَرٌ مِّثْلُكُمْ يَأْكُلُ مِمَّا تَأْكُلُونَ مِنْهُ وَيَشْرَبُ مِمَّا تَشْرَبُونَ ۝

وَلَئِنْ أَطَعْتُمْ بَشَرًا مِّثْلَكُمْ إِنَّكُمْ إِذًا لَّخَاسِرُونَ ۝

أَيَعِدُكُمْ أَنَّكُمْ إِذَا مِتُّمْ وَكُنْتُمْ تُرَابًا وَعِظَامًا أَنَّكُمْ مُّخْرَجُونَ ۝

هَيْهَاتَ هَيْهَاتَ لِمَا تُوعَدُونَ ۝

37. "There is nothing but our life in this world! We shall die and we live! But we shall never be raised up again!"

38. "He is only a man who invents a lie against Allah, but we are not the ones to believe in him!"

39. (The prophet) said: "O my Lord! help me: for that they accuse me of falsehood."

40. (Alalh) said: "In but a little while, they are sure to be sorry!"

41. Then the Blast overtook them with justice, and We made them as rubbish of dead leaves (floating on the stream of Time)! So away with the people who do wrong!

42. Then We raised after them other generations.

43. No people can hasten their term, nor can they delay (it).

44. Then we sent our Messengers in succession: every time there came to a people their Messenger, they accused him of falsehood: so We made them follow each other (in punishment): We made them as a tale (that is told): so away with a people that will not believe!

45. Then We sent Moses and his brother Aaron, with Our Signs and authority manifest,

46. To Pharaoh and his Chiefs: but these behaved insolently: they were an arrogant people.

47. They said: "Shall we believe in two men like ourselves? And their people are subject to us!"

48. So they (rejected) and accused them of falsehood, and they became of those who were destroyed.

49. And We gave Moses the Book, in order that they might receive guidance.

50. And We made the son of Mary and his mother as a Sign:

---

37. In hiya illaa ḥayaatunad-dunyaa namootu wa naḥyaa wa maa naḥnu bimab'ooseen.

38. In huwa illaa rajulunif-taraa 'alal-laahi kaziban̄w-wa maa naḥnu lahoo bimu'mineen.

39. Qaala Rabbin-surnee bimaa kazzaboon.

40. Qaala 'ammaa qaleelil-la-yuṣbiḥunna naadimeen.

41. Fa-akhazat-humuṣ-ṣay-ḥatu bilḥaqqi faja'alnaahum ghusaaa'aa; fabu'dal-lilqaw-miz-zaalimeen.

42. Summa anshaånaa mim ba'dihim quroonan aakhareen.

43. Maa tasbiqu min ummatin ajalahaa wa maa yastaåkhiroon.

44. Summa arsalnaa Rusu-lanaa tatraa kulla maa jaaa'a ummatar-Rasooluhaa kaz-zabooh; fa-atba'naa ba'ḍahum ba'ḍan̄w-wa ja'alnaahum aḥaadees; fabu'dal-liqawmil-laa yu'minoon.

45. Summa arsalnaa Moosaa wa akhaahu Haaroona bi Aayaatinaa wa sulṭaanim-mu-been.

46. Ilaa Fir'awna wa mala'i-hee fastakbaroo wa kaanoo qawman 'aaleen.

47. Faqaalooo anu'minu libasharayni mislinaa wa qawmuhumaa lanaa 'aabidoon.

48. Fakazzaboohumaa fa-kaanoo minal-muhlakeen.

49. Wa laqad aataynaa Moosal-Kitaaba la'allahum yahtadoon.

50. Wa ja'alnab-na-Maryama wa ummahooo Aayaatan̄w-wa

إِنْ هِيَ إِلَّا حَيَاتُنَا الدُّنْيَا نَمُوتُ وَ نَحْيَا وَمَا نَحْنُ بِمَبْعُوثِينَ ۝

إِنْ هُوَ إِلَّا رَجُلٌ افْتَرَى عَلَى اللّٰهِ كَذِبًا وَّمَا نَحْنُ لَهُ بِمُؤْمِنِينَ ۝

قَالَ رَبِّ انْصُرْنِي بِمَا كَذَّبُونِ ۝

قَالَ عَمَّا قَلِيلٍ لَّيُصْبِحُنَّ نَادِمِينَ ۝

فَأَخَذَتْهُمُ الصَّيْحَةُ بِالْحَقِّ فَجَعَلْنَاهُمْ غُثَاءً ۚ فَبُعْدًا لِّلْقَوْمِ الظَّالِمِينَ ۝

ثُمَّ أَنْشَأْنَا مِنْ بَعْدِهِمْ قُرُونًا آخَرِينَ ۝

مَا تَسْبِقُ مِنْ أُمَّةٍ أَجَلَهَا وَمَا يَسْتَأْخِرُونَ ۝

ثُمَّ أَرْسَلْنَا رُسُلَنَا تَتْرَا ۖ كُلَّمَا جَاءَ أُمَّةً رَّسُولُهَا كَذَّبُوهُ فَأَتْبَعْنَا بَعْضَهُمْ بَعْضًا وَّجَعَلْنَاهُمْ أَحَادِيثَ ۚ فَبُعْدًا لِّقَوْمٍ لَّا يُؤْمِنُونَ ۝

ثُمَّ أَرْسَلْنَا مُوسَى وَأَخَاهُ هَارُونَ ۙ بِآيَاتِنَا وَسُلْطَانٍ مُّبِينٍ ۝

إِلَى فِرْعَوْنَ وَمَلَئِهِ فَاسْتَكْبَرُوا وَكَانُوا قَوْمًا عَالِينَ ۝

فَقَالُوا أَنُؤْمِنُ لِبَشَرَيْنِ مِثْلِنَا وَقَوْمُهُمَا لَنَا عَابِدُونَ ۝

فَكَذَّبُوهُمَا فَكَانُوا مِنَ الْمُهْلَكِينَ ۝

وَلَقَدْ آتَيْنَا مُوسَى الْكِتَابَ لَعَلَّهُمْ يَهْتَدُونَ ۝

وَجَعَلْنَا ابْنَ مَرْيَمَ وَأُمَّهُ آيَةً وَّ

We gave them both shelter on high ground, affording rest and security and furnished with springs.

51. O you Messengers! enjoy (all) things good and pure, and work righteousness: for I am well-acquainted with (all) that you do.

52. And verily this Brotherhood of yours is a single Brotherhood, and I am your Lord and Cherisher: therefore fear Me (and no other).

53. But people have cut off their affair (of unity), between them, into sects: each party rejoices in that which is with itself

54. But leave them in their confused ignorance for a time.

55. Do they think that because We have granted them abundance of wealth and sons,

56. We would hasten them on in every good? Nay, they do not understand.

57. Verily those who live in awe for fear of their Lord;

58. Those who believe in the Signs of their Lord;

59. Those who do not join (in worship) partners with their Lord;

60. And those who dispense their charity with their hearts full of fear, because they will return to their Lord;-

61. It is these who hasten in every good work, and these who are foremost in them.

62. On no soul do We place a burden greater than it can bear: before Us is a record which clearly speaks the truth: they will never be wronged.

63. But their hearts are in confused ignorance of this;

aawaynaahumaaa ilaa rabwatin zaati qaraariñw-wa ma'een.
(Section 3)

51. Yaaa ayyuhar-Rusulu kuloo minat-tayyibaati wa'maloo saalihan innee bimaa ta'maloona 'Aleem.

52. Wa inna haazihee ummatukum ummatañw-waahidatañw-wa Ana Rabbukum fattaqoon.

53. Fataqatta'ooo amrahum baynahum zuburaa; kullu hizbim bimaa ladayhim farihoon.

54. Fazarhum fee ghamratihim hattaa heen.

55. A-yahsaboona annamaa numidduhum bihee mimmaaliñw-wa baneen.

56. Nusaari'u lahum fil-khayraat; bal laa yash'uroon.

57. Innal-lazeena hum-min khashyati Rabbihim-mushfiqoon.

58. Wallazeena hum bi-Aayaati Rabbihim yu'minoon.

59. Wallazeena hum bi-Rabbihim laa yushrikoon.

60. Wallazeena yu'toona maaa aataw-wa quloobuhum wajilatun annahum ilaa Rabbihim raaji'oon.

61. Ulaaa'ika yusaari'oona fil-khayraati wa hum lahaa saabiqoon.

62. Wa laa nukallifu nafsan illaa wus'ahaa wa ladaynaa kitaabuñy-yantiqu bilhaqqi wa hum laa yuzlamoon.

63. Bal quloobuhum fee ghamratim-min haazaa

and there are, besides that, deeds of theirs, which they will (continue) to do,-

64. Until, when We seize in Punishment those of them who received the good things of this world, behold, they will groan in supplication!

65. (It will be said): "Do not groan in supplication this day: for you shall certainly not be helped by Us.

66. "My Signs used to be rehearsed to you, but you used to turn back on your heels-

67. "In arrogance: talking nonsense about the (Qur'an), like one telling fables by night."

68. Do they not ponder over the Word (of Allah), or has anything (new) come to them that did not come to their fathers of old?

69. Or do they not recognise their Messenger, that they deny him?

70. Or do they say, "He is possessed"? Nay, he has brought them the Truth, but most of them hate the Truth.

71. If the Truth had been in accord with their desires, truly the heavens and the earth, and all beings therein would have been in confusion and corruption! Nay, We have sent them their admonition, but they turn away from their admonition.

72. Or is it that you ask them for some recompense? But the recompense of your Lord is best: He is the Best of those who give sustenance.

73. But verily you call them to the Straight Way;

74. And verily those who do not believe in the Hereafter are deviating from that Way.

75. If We had mercy on them and removed the distress which is on them,

wa lahum a'maalum-min dooni zaalika hum lahaa 'aamiloon.

64. Hattaaa izaaa akhznaa mutrafeehim bil'azaabi izaa hum yaj'aroon.

65. Laa taj'arul-yawma inna-kum-minnaa laa tunsaroon.

66. Qad kaanat Aayaatee tutlaa 'alaykum fakuntum 'alaaa a'qaabikum tankiṣoon.

67. Mustakbireena bihee saamiran tahjuroon.

68. Afalam yaddabbarrul-qawla am jaaa'ahum-maa lam yaati aabaaa'ahumul-awwa-leen.

69. Am lam ya'rifoo Rasoo-lahum fahum lahoo munkiroon.

70. Am yaqooloona bihee jinnah; bal jaaa'ahum bilḥaqqi wa aksaruhum lil-ḥaqqi kaarihoon.

71. Wa lawit-taba'al-ḥaqqu ahwaaa'ahum lafasadatis-samaawaatu wal-arḍu wa man feehinn; bal ataynaahum biẕikrihim fahum 'an ẕikrihim-mu'riḍoon.

72. Am tas'aluhum kharjan fakharaaju Rabbika khayrunw-wa Huwa khayrur-raaziqeen.

73. Wa innaka latad'oohum ilaa Ṣiraaṭim-Mustaqeem.

74. Wa innal-lazeena laa yu'minoona bil-Aakhirati 'aniṣ-ṣiraaṭi lanaakiboon.

75. Wa law raḥimnaahum wa kashafnaa maa bihim-min ḍurril-

they would obstinately persist in their Transgression, wandering in distraction to and fro.

76. We inflicted Punishment on them, but they did not humbled themselves to their Lord, nor do they submissively entreat (Him)!-

77. Until We open on them a gate leading to a severe Punishment: then lo! they will be plunged in despair therein!

78. It is He Who has created for you (the faculties of) hearing, sight, feeling and understanding: But little thanks it is you give!

79. And He has multiplied you through the earth, and to Him you shall be gathered back.

80. It is He Who gives life and death, and to Him (is due) the alternation of Night and Day: will you not then understand?

81. On the contrary they say things similar to what the ancients said.

82. They say: "What! when we die and become dust and bones, could we really be raised up again?

83. "Such things have been promised to us and to our fathers before! they are nothing but tales of the ancients!"

84. Say: "To whom belong the earth and all beings therein? (say) if you know!"

85. They will say, "To Allah!" say: "Yet will you not receive admonition?"

86. Say: "Who is the Lord of the seven heavens, and the Lord of the Throne (of Glory) Supreme?"

87. They will say, "(They belong) to Allah." Say: "Will you not then fear?"

88. Say: "Who is it in whose hands is the governance of all things,- who protects (all), but is not protected (of any)?

lalajjoo fee ṭughyaanihim ya'mahoon.

76. Wa laqad akhaznaahum bil'azaabi famastakaanoo li-Rabbihim wa maa yataḍar-ra'oon.

77. Ḥattaaa izaa fataḥnaa 'alayhim baaban zaa 'azaabin shadeedin izaa hum feehi mublisoon. (Section 4)

78. Wa Huwal-lazeee ansha-a-lakumus-sam'a wal-absaara wal-af'idah; qaleelam-maa tashkuroon.

79. Wa Huwal-lazee zara-akum fil-arḍi wa ilayhi tuḥsharoon.

80. Wa Huwal-lazee yuḥyee wa yumeetu wa lahukh-tilaaful-layli wannahaar; afalaa ta'qiloon.

81. Bal qaaloo misla maa qaalal-awwaloon.

82. Qaalooo 'a-izaa mitnaa wa kunnaa turaabañw-wa 'izaaman 'a-innaa lamab-'oosoon.

83. Laqad wu'idnaa naḥnu wa aabaaa'unaa haazaa min qablu in haazaaa illaaa asaaṭeerul-awwaleen.

84. Qul limanil-arḍu wa man feehaaa in kuntum ta'lamoon.

85. Sa-yaqooloona lillaah; qul afalaa tazakkaroon.

86. Qul mar-Rabbus-samaa-waatis-sab'i wa Rabbul-'Arshil-'Azeem.

87. Sa-yaqooloona lillaah; qul afalaa tattaqoon.

88. Qul mam bi-yadihee malakootu kulli shay'iñw-wa Huwa yujeeru wa laa yujaaru 'alayhi in kuntum

(say) if you know."

89. They will say, "(It belongs) to Allah." Say: "Then how are you deluded?"

90. We have sent them the Truth: but they indeed practise Falsehood!

91. No son did Allah beget, nor is there any god along with Him: (if there were many gods), behold, each god would have taken away what he had created, and some would have lorded it over others! Glory to Allah! (He is free) from the (sort of) things they attribute to Him!

92. He knows what is hidden and what is open: too high is He for the partners they attribute to Him!

93. Say: "O my Lord! if You will show me (in my lifetime) that which they are warned against,-

94. "Then, O my Lord! put me not amongst the people who do wrong!"

95. And We are certainly able to show you (in fulfilment) that against which they are warned.

96. Repel evil with that which is best: We are well acquainted with the things they say.

97. And say "O my Lord! I seek refuge with you from the suggestions of the Evil Ones.

98. "And I seek refuge with you O my Lord! lest they should come near me."

99. (In Falsehood will they be) until, when death comes to one of them, he says: "O my Lord! send me back (to life),-

100. "In order that I may work righteousness in the things I neglected." - "By no means! It is but a word he says."- Before them is a Partition till the Day they are raised up.

101. Then when the Trumpet is blown, there will be no more relationships between them that Day, nor will one ask after another!

ta'lamoon.

89. Sa-yaqooloona lillaah; qul fa-annaa tus-haroon.

90. Bal ataynaahum bil-haqqi wa innahum lakaaziboon.

91. Mat-takhazal-laahu miñw-waladiñw-wa maa kaana ma'ahoo min ilaah; izal-lazahaba kullu ilaahim bimaa khalaqa wa la'alaa ba'duhum 'alaa ba'd; Subhaanal-laahi 'ammaa yasifoon.

92. 'Aalimil-Ghaybi wash-shahaadati fata'aalaa 'ammaa yushrikoon.   **(Section 5)**

93. Qur-Rabbi immaa turi-yannee maa yoo'adoon.

94. Rabbi falaa taj'alnee fil-qawmiz-zaalimeen.

95. Wa innaa 'alaaa an-nuri-yaka maa na'iduhum laqaa-diroon.

96. Idfa' billatee hiya ahsa-nus-sayyi'ah; Nahnu a'lamu bimaa yasifoon.

97. Wa qur-Rabbi a'oozu bika min hamazaatish-Shayaateen.

98. Wa a'oozu bika Rabbi añy-yahduroon.

99. Hattaaa izaa jaaa'a ahada-humul-mawtu qaala Rabbir-ji'oon.

100. La'alleee a'malu saalihan feemaa taraktu kallaa; innahaa kalimatun huwa qaaa'iluhaa wa miñw-waraaa'ihim barzakhun ilaa Yawmi yub'asoon.

101. Fa-izaa nufikha fis-Soori falaaa ansaaba baynahum Yawma'iziñw-wa laa yata-saaa'aloon.

تَعْلَمُوْنَ ۝

سَيَقُوْلُوْنَ لِلّٰهِ ۚ قُلْ فَاَنّٰى تُسْحَرُوْنَ ۝

بَلْ اَتَيْنٰهُمْ بِالْحَقِّ وَاِنَّهُمْ لَكٰذِبُوْنَ ۝

مَا اتَّخَذَ اللّٰهُ مِنْ وَّلَدٍ وَّمَا كَانَ مَعَهٗ مِنْ اِلٰهٍ اِذًا لَّذَهَبَ كُلُّ اِلٰهٍ بِمَا خَلَقَ وَلَعَلَا بَعْضُهُمْ عَلٰى بَعْضٍ ۚ سُبْحٰنَ اللّٰهِ عَمَّا يَصِفُوْنَ ۝

عٰلِمِ الْغَيْبِ وَالشَّهَادَةِ فَتَعٰلٰى عَمَّا يُشْرِكُوْنَ ۝

قُلْ رَّبِّ اِمَّا تُرِيَنِّى مَا يُوْعَدُوْنَ ۝

رَبِّ فَلَا تَجْعَلْنِى فِى الْقَوْمِ الظّٰلِمِيْنَ ۝

وَاِنَّا عَلٰى اَنْ نُّرِيَكَ مَا نَعِدُهُمْ لَقٰدِرُوْنَ ۝

اِدْفَعْ بِالَّتِى هِىَ اَحْسَنُ السَّيِّئَةَ ۗ نَحْنُ اَعْلَمُ بِمَا يَصِفُوْنَ ۝

وَقُلْ رَّبِّ اَعُوْذُ بِكَ مِنْ هَمَزٰتِ الشَّيٰطِيْنِ ۝

وَاَعُوْذُ بِكَ رَبِّ اَنْ يَّحْضُرُوْنِ ۝

حَتّٰى اِذَا جَآءَ اَحَدَهُمُ الْمَوْتُ قَالَ رَبِّ ارْجِعُوْنِ ۝

لَعَلِّى اَعْمَلُ صَالِحًا فِيْمَا تَرَكْتُ كَلَّا ۗ اِنَّهَا كَلِمَةٌ هُوَ قَآئِلُهَا ۗ وَمِنْ وَّرَآئِهِمْ بَرْزَخٌ اِلٰى يَوْمِ يُبْعَثُوْنَ ۝

فَاِذَا نُفِخَ فِى الصُّوْرِ فَلَا اَنْسَابَ بَيْنَهُمْ يَوْمَئِذٍ وَّلَا يَتَسَآءَلُوْنَ ۝

٥ع

102. Then those whose balance (of good deeds) is heavy,- they will attain salvation:

103. But those whose balance is light, will be those who have lost their souls, in Hell will they abide.

104. The Fire will burn their faces, and they will therein grin, with their lips displaced.

105. "Were not My Signs rehearsed to you, and you but treated them as falsehoods?"

106. They will say: "Our Lord! our misfortune overwhelmed us, and we became a people astray!

107. "Our Lord! bring us out of this: if ever we return (to Evil), then shall we be wrong-doers indeed!"

108. He will say: "Be you driven into it (with ignominy)! And do not speak to Me!

109. "A part of My servants there was, who used to pray 'Our Lord! we believe; then you forgive us, and have mercy upon us: for you are the Best of those who show mercy!'

110. "But you treated them with ridicule, so much so that (ridicule of) them made you forget My Message while you were laughing at them!

111. "I have rewarded them this Day for their patience and constancy: they are indeed the ones that have achieved bliss..."

112. He will say: "What number of years did you stay on earth?"

113. They will say: "We stayed a day or part of a day: but ask those who keep account."

114. He will say: "You stayed not but a little,- if you had only known!

---

102. Faman saqulat mawaazeenuhoo fa-ulaaa'ika humulmuflihoon.

103. Wa man khaffat mawaazeenuhoo fa-ulaaa'ikal-lazeena khasirooo anfusahum fee Jahannama khaalidoon.

104. Talfahu wujoohahumun-Naaru wa hum feehaa kaalihoon.

105. Alam takun Aayaatee tutlaa 'alaykum fakuntum bihaa tukazziboon.

106. Qaaloo Rabbanaa ghalabat 'alaynaa shiqwatunaa wa kunnaa qawman daaalleen.

107. Rabbanaaa akhrijnaa minhaa fa-in 'udnaa fa-innaa zaalimoon.

108. Qaalakh-sa'oo feehaa wa laa tukallimoon.

109. Innahoo kaana fareeqummin 'ibaadee yaqooloona Rabbanaaa aamannaa faghfir lanaa warhamnaa wa Anta khayrurraahimeen.

110. Fattakhaztumoohum sikhriyyan hattaaa ansawkum zikree wa kuntum-minhum tadhakoon.

111. Innee jazaytuhumul-Yawma bimaa sabarooo annahum humul-faaa'izoon.

112. Qaala kam labistum filardi 'adada sineen.

113. Qaaloo labisnaa yawman aw ba'da yawmin fas'alil-'aaaddeen.

114. Qaala il-labistum illaa qaleelal-law annakum kuntum ta'lamoon.

فَمَنْ ثَقُلَتْ مَوَازِينُهُ فَأُولَٰئِكَ هُمُ الْمُفْلِحُونَ ۝

وَمَنْ خَفَّتْ مَوَازِينُهُ فَأُولَٰئِكَ الَّذِينَ خَسِرُوٓا أَنفُسَهُمْ فِى جَهَنَّمَ خَٰلِدُونَ ۝

تَلْفَحُ وُجُوهَهُمُ النَّارُ وَهُمْ فِيهَا كَٰلِحُونَ ۝

أَلَمْ تَكُنْ ءَايَٰتِى تُتْلَىٰ عَلَيْكُمْ فَكُنتُم بِهَا تُكَذِّبُونَ ۝

قَالُوا۟ رَبَّنَا غَلَبَتْ عَلَيْنَا شِقْوَتُنَا وَكُنَّا قَوْمًا ضَآلِّينَ ۝

رَبَّنَآ أَخْرِجْنَا مِنْهَا فَإِنْ عُدْنَا فَإِنَّا ظَٰلِمُونَ ۝

قَالَ اخْسَـُٔوا۟ فِيهَا وَلَا تُكَلِّمُونِ ۝

إِنَّهُ كَانَ فَرِيقٌ مِّنْ عِبَادِى يَقُولُونَ رَبَّنَآ ءَامَنَّا فَاغْفِرْ لَنَا وَارْحَمْنَا وَأَنتَ خَيْرُ الرَّٰحِمِينَ ۝

فَاتَّخَذْتُمُوهُمْ سِخْرِيًّا حَتَّىٰٓ أَنسَوْكُمْ ذِكْرِى وَكُنتُم مِّنْهُمْ تَضْحَكُونَ ۝

إِنِّى جَزَيْتُهُمُ الْيَوْمَ بِمَا صَبَرُوٓا أَنَّهُمْ هُمُ الْفَآئِزُونَ ۝

قُلْ كَمْ لَبِثْتُمْ فِى الْأَرْضِ عَدَدَ سِنِينَ ۝

قَالُوا۟ لَبِثْنَا يَوْمًا أَوْ بَعْضَ يَوْمٍ فَسْـَٔلِ الْعَآدِّينَ ۝

قَٰلَ إِن لَّبِثْتُمْ إِلَّا قَلِيلًا لَّوْ أَنَّكُمْ كُنتُمْ تَعْلَمُونَ ۝

115. "Did you then think that We had created you in jest, and that you would not be brought back to Us (for account)?"

116. Therefore exalted be Allah, the King, the Reality: there is no god but He, the Lord of the Throne of Honor!

117. If anyone invokes, besides Allah, Any other god, he has no authority therefor; and his reckoning will be only with his Lord! and verily the Unbelievers shall not Prosper!

118. So say: "O my Lord! Grant us forgiveness and mercy! for you are the Best of those who show mercy!"

24. The Light

In the name of Allah, Most Gracious, Most Merciful.

1. A Surah which We have sent down and which We have ordained: in it We have sent down Clear Signs, in order that you may receive admonition.

2. The woman and the man guilty of adultery or fornication,- flog each of them with a hundred stripes: let not compassion move you in their case, in a matter prescribed by Allah, if you believe in Allah and the Last Day: and let a party of the Believers witness their punishment.

3. Let no man guilty of adultery or fornication marry any but a woman similarly guilty, or an Unbeliever: nor let any but such a man or an Unbeliever marry such a woman: to the Believers such a thing is forbidden.

4. And those who launch a charge against chaste women, and produce not four witnesses (to support their allegations),- flog them with eighty stripes; and reject their evidence ever after: for such men are wicked transgressors;-

---

115. Afaḥasibtum annamaa khalaqnaakum 'abaṣañw-wa annakum ilaynaa laa turja'oon.

116. Fata'aalal-laahul-Mali-kul-Ḥaqq; laaa ilaaha illaa Huwa Rabbul-'Arshil-Kareem.

117. Wa mañy-yad'u ma'allaahi ilaahan aakhara laa burhaana lahoo bihee fa-innamaa ḥisaabuhoo 'inda Rabbih; innahoo laa yufliḥul-kaafiroon.

118. Wa qur-Rabbigh-fir warḥam wa Anta khayrur-raaḥimeen. **(Section 6)**

Sûrat an-Nûr–24
(Revealed at Madinah)
Bismillaahir Raḥmaanir Raḥeem

1. Sooratun anzalnaahaa wa faraḍnaahaa wa anzalnaa feehaaa Aayaatim-bayyinaatil-la'allakum tazakkaroon.

2. Azzaaniyatu wazzaanee fajlidoo kulla waaḥidim-minhumaa mi'ata jaldatiñw-wa laa taåkhuzkum bihimaa raå-fatun fee deenil-laahi in kuntum tu'minoona billaahi wal-Yawmil-Aakhiri wal-yashhad 'azaabahumaa ṭaaa'ifatum-minal-mu'mineen.

3. Azzaanee laa yankiḥu illaa zaaniyatan aw mushrika-tañw-wazzaaniyatu laa yanki-ḥuhaaa illaa zaanin aw mushrik; wa ḥurrima zaalika 'alal-mu'mineen.

4. Wallazeena yarmoonal-muḥsanaati summa lam yaåtoo bi-arba'ati shuhadaaa'a fajli-doohum samaaneena jaldatañw-wa laa taqbaloo lahum shahaa-datan abadaa; wa ulaaa'ika humul-faasiqoon.

5. Unless they repent thereafter and mend (their conduct); for Allah is Oft-Forgiving, Most Merciful.

6. And for those who launch a charge against their spouses, or (wives) and have (in support) no evidence but their own,- their solitary evidence (can be received) if they bear witness four times (with an oath) by Allah that they are solemnly telling the truth;

7. And the fifth (oath) (should be) that they solemnly invoke the curse of Allah on themselves if they tell a lie.

8. But it would avert the punishment from the wife, if she bears witness four times (with an oath) By Allah, that (her husband) is telling a lie;

9. And the fifth (oath) should be that she solemnly invokes the wrath of Allah on herself if (her accuser) is telling the truth.

10. If it were not for Allah's grace and mercy on you, and that Allah is Oft- Returning, full of Wisdom,- (You would be ruined indeed).

11. Those who brought forward the lie are a body among yourselves: think it not to be an evil to you; on the contrary it is good for you: to every man among them (will come the punishment) of the sin that he earned, and for him who took on himself the lead among them, will be a Penalty grievous.

12. Why did not the believers - men and women - when you heard of the affair,- thought well of their people and say, "This (charge) is an obvious lie"?

13. Why did they not bring four witnesses to prove it? When they have not brought the witnesses, such men, in the sight of Allah, (stand forth) themselves as liars!

5. Illal-lazeena taaboo mim ba'di zaalika wa aslahoo fa-innal-laaha Ghafoorur Raheem.

6. Wallazeena yarmoona azwaajahum wa lam yakul-lahum shuhadaaa'u illaaa anfusuhum fashahaadatu ahadihim arba'u shahaadaatim billaahi innahoo laminas-saadiqeen.

7. Wal-khaamisatu anna la'natal-laahi 'alayhi in kaana minal-kaazibeen.

8. Wa yadra'u anhal-'azaaba an tashhada arba'a shahaa-daatim billaahi innahoo laminal-kaazibeen.

9. Wal-khaamisata anna ghadabal-laahi 'alayhaaa in kaana minas-saadiqeen.

10. Wa law laa fadlul-laahi 'alaykum wa rahmatuhoo wa annal-laaha Tawwaabun Hakeem. **(Section 1)**

11. Innal-lazeena jaaa'oo bil-ifki 'usbatum-minkum; laa tahsaboohu sharral-lakum bal huwa khayrul-lakum; likul-limri'im-minhum-mak-tasaba minal-ism; wallazee tawallaa kibrahoo minhum lahoo 'azaabun 'azeem.

12. Law laaa iz sami'tumoohu zannal-mu'minoona walmu'-minaatu bi-anfusihim khay-rañw-wa qaaloo haazaaa ifkum-mubeen.

13. Law laa jaaa'oo 'alayhi bi-arba'ati shuhadaaa'; fa-iz lam yaatoo bishshuhadaaa'i fa-ulaaa'ika 'indal-laahi humul-kaaziboon.

14. Were it not for the grace and mercy of Allah on you, in this world and the Hereafter, a grievous Penalty would have seized you in that you rushed glibly into this affair.

15. Behold, you received it on your tongues, and said out of your mouths things of which you had no knowledge; and you thought it to be a light matter, while it was most serious in the sight of Allah.

16. And why did you not, when you heard it, say? - "It is not right of us to speak of this: Glory to Allah! this is a most serious slander!"

17. Allah admonishes you, that you may never repeat such (conduct), if you are (true) Believers.

18. And Allah makes the Signs plain to you: for Allah is full of knowledge and wisdom.

19. Those who love (to see) scandal published broadcast among the Believers, will have a grievous Penalty in this life and in the Hereafter: Allah knows, and you do not know.

20. Were it not for the grace and mercy of Allah on you, and that Allah is full of kindness and mercy, (you would be ruined indeed).

21. O you who believe! Do not follow Satan's footsteps: if any will follow the footsteps of Satan, he will (but) command what is shameful and wrong: and were it not for the grace and mercy of Allah on you, not one of you would ever have been pure: but Allah does purify whom He pleases:

14. Wa law laa faḍlul-laahi 'alaykum wa raḥmatuhoo fiddunyaa wal-Aakhirati lamassakum fee maaa afaḍtum feehi 'azaabun 'azeem.

15. Iz talaqqawnahoo bi-alsinatikum wa taqooloona bi-afwaahikum-maa laysa lakum bihee 'ilmunw-wa taḥsaboo-nahoo hayyinanw-wa huwa 'indal-laahi 'azeem.

16. Wa law laaa iz sami'tu-moohu qultum-maa yakoonu lanaaa an-natakallama bihaazaa Subḥaanaka haazaa buhtaanun 'azeem.

17. Ya'izukumul-laahu an ta'oodoo limisliheee abadan in kuntum-mu'mineen.

18. Wa yubayyinul-laahu lakumul-Aayaat; wallaahu 'Aleemun Ḥakeem.

19. Innal-lazeena yuḥibboona an tashee'al-faaḥishatu fil-lazeena aamanoo lahum 'azaabun aleemun fid-dunyaa wal-Aakhirah; wallaahu ya'la-mu wa antum laa ta'lamoon.

20. Wa law laa faḍlul-laahi 'alaykum wa raḥmatuhoo wa annal-laaha Ra'oofur-Raḥeem.
(Section 2)

21. Yaaa ayyuhal-lazeena aamanoo laa tattabi'oo khuṭuwaatish-Shayṭaan; wa many-yattabi' khuṭuwaatish-Shayṭaani fa-innahoo yaamuru bilfaḥshaaa'i walmunkar; wa law laa faḍlul-laahi 'alaykum wa raḥmatuhoo maa zakaa minkum-min aḥadin abadanw-wa laakinnal-laaha yuzakkee many-yashaaa';

and Allah is one Who hears and knows (all things).

22. Let not those among you who are endued with grace and amplitude of means resolve by oath against helping their kinsmen, those in want, and those who have left their homes in Allah's cause: let them forgive and overlook, do you not wish that Allah should forgive you? For Allah is Oft-Forgiving, Most Merciful.

23. Those who slander chaste women, indiscreet but believing, are cursed in this life and in the Hereafter: for them is a grievous Penalty,-

24. On the Day when their tongues, their hands, and their feet will bear witness against them as to their actions.

25. On that Day Allah will pay them back (all) their just dues, and they will realise that Allah is the (very) Truth, that makes all things manifest.

26. Women impure are for men impure, and men impure for women impure and women of purity are for men of purity, and men of purity are for women of purity: these are not affected by what people say: for them there is forgiveness, and a provision honorable.

27. O you who believe! Do not enter houses other than your own, until you have asked permission and saluted those in them: that is best for you, in order that you may heed (what is seemly).

28. If you find no one in the house, do not enter until permission is given to you: if

wallaahu Samee'un 'Aleem.

22. Wa laa yaåtali ulul-faḍli minkum wassa'ati añy-yu'tooo ulil-qurbaa walmasaakeena walmuhaajireena fee sabeelillaahi walya'foo walyaṣfaḥoo; alaa tuḥibboona añy-yaghfiral-laahu lakum; wallaahu Ghafoorur-Raḥeem.

23. Innal-lazeena yarmoonalmuḥ ṣanaatil-ghaafilaatilmu'minaati lu'inoo fid-dunyaa wal-Aakhirati wa lahum 'azaabun 'aẓeem.

24. Yawma tashhadu 'alayhim alsinatuhum wa aydeehim wa arjuluhum bimaa kaanoo ya'maloon.

25. Yawma'iziñy-yuwaffeehimul-laahu deenahumulḥaqqa wa ya'lamoona annallaaha Huwal-Ḥaqqul-Mubeen.

26. Alkhabeesaatu lilkhabeeseena walkhabeesoona lilkhabeesaati waṭṭayyibaatu liṭṭayyibeena waṭṭayyiboona liṭṭayyibaat; ulaaa'ika mubarra'oona mimmaa yaqooloona lahum-maghfiratuñw-wa rizqun kareem. **(Section 3)**

27. Yaaa ayyuhal-lazeena aamanoo laa tadkhuloo buyootan ghayra buyootikum ḥattaa tastaåisoo wa tusallimoo 'allaa ahlihaa; zaalikum khayrul-lakum la'allakum tazakkaroon.

28. Fa-il-lam tajidoo feehaaa aḥadan falaa tadkhuloohaa ḥattaa yu'zana lakum wa in

you are asked to go back, go back: that makes for greater purity for yourselves: and Allah knows well all that you do.

29. It is no fault on your part to enter houses not used for living in, which serve some (other) use for you: And Allah has knowledge of what you reveal and what you conceal.

30. Say to the believing men that they should lower their gaze and guard their modesty: that will make for greater purity for them: and Allah is well acquainted with all that they do.

31. And say to the believing women that they should lower their gaze and guard their modesty; that they should not display their beauty and ornaments except what (must ordinarily) appear thereof; that they should draw their veils over their bosoms and not display their beauty except to their husbands, their fathers, their husband's fathers, their sons, their husbands' sons, their brothers or their brothers' sons, or their sisters' sons, or their women, or the slaves whom their right hands possess, or male servants free of sexual urge, or small children who have no sense of the shame of sex; and that they should not strike their feet in order to draw attention to their hidden ornaments. And O you Believers! You turn all together towards Allah, that you may attain Bliss.

qeela lakumurji'oo farji'oo huwa azkaa lakum; wallaahu bimaa ta'maloona 'Aleem.

29. Laysa 'alaykum junaahun an tadkhuloo buyootan ghayra maskoonatin feehaa mataa'ul-lakum; wallaahu ya'lamu maa tubdoona wa maa taktumoon.

30. Qul lilmu'mineena yaghuddoo min absaarihim wa yahfazoo foroojahum; zaalika azkaa lahum; innallaaha khabeerum bimaa yasna'oon.

31. Wa qul lilmu'minaati yaghdudna min absaarihinna wa yahfazna foroojahunna wa laa yubdeena zeenatahunna illaa maa zahara minhaa walyadribna bikhumurihinna 'alaa juyoobihinna wa laa yubdeena zeenatahunna illaa libu'oolatihinna aw aabaaa'i-hinna aw aabaaa'i bu'oolati-hinna aw abnaaa'ihinaa aw abnaaa'i bu'oolatihinna aw ikhwaanihinna aw baneee ikhwaanihinna aw baneee akhawaatihinna aw nisaaa'i-hinna aw maa malakat aymaanuhunna awit-taabi'eena ghayri ulil-irbati minar-rijaali awit-tiflillazeena lam yazharoo 'alaa 'awraatin-nisaaa'i wa laa yadribna bi-arjulihinna liyu'lama maa yukhfeena min zeenatihinn; wa tooboo ilallaahi jamee'an ayyuhal-mu'minoona la'allakum tuflihoon.

قِيلَ لَكُمُ ارْجِعُوا فَارْجِعُوا هُوَ اَزْكَىٰ لَكُمْ ۚ وَاللّٰهُ بِمَا تَعْمَلُونَ عَلِيمٌ ۝

لَيْسَ عَلَيْكُمْ جُنَاحٌ اَنْ تَدْخُلُوا بُيُوتًا غَيْرَ مَسْكُونَةٍ فِيهَا مَتَاعٌ لَّكُمْ ۚ وَاللّٰهُ يَعْلَمُ مَا تُبْدُونَ وَمَا تَكْتُمُونَ ۝

قُلْ لِّلْمُؤْمِنِينَ يَغُضُّوا مِنْ اَبْصَارِهِمْ وَيَحْفَظُوا فُرُوجَهُمْ ۚ ذٰلِكَ اَزْكَىٰ لَهُمْ ۚ اِنَّ اللّٰهَ خَبِيرٌ بِمَا يَصْنَعُونَ ۝

وَقُلْ لِّلْمُؤْمِنَاتِ يَغْضُضْنَ مِنْ اَبْصَارِهِنَّ وَيَحْفَظْنَ فُرُوجَهُنَّ وَلَا يُبْدِينَ زِينَتَهُنَّ اِلَّا مَا ظَهَرَ مِنْهَا وَلْيَضْرِبْنَ بِخُمُرِهِنَّ عَلَىٰ جُيُوبِهِنَّ ۖ وَلَا يُبْدِينَ زِينَتَهُنَّ اِلَّا لِبُعُولَتِهِنَّ اَوْ اٰبَآئِهِنَّ اَوْ اٰبَآءِ بُعُولَتِهِنَّ اَوْ اَبْنَآئِهِنَّ اَوْ اَبْنَآءِ بُعُولَتِهِنَّ اَوْ اِخْوَانِهِنَّ اَوْ بَنِيٓ اِخْوَانِهِنَّ اَوْ بَنِيٓ اَخَوَاتِهِنَّ اَوْ نِسَآئِهِنَّ اَوْ مَا مَلَكَتْ اَيْمَانُهُنَّ اَوِ التَّابِعِينَ غَيْرِ اُولِي الْاِرْبَةِ مِنَ الرِّجَالِ اَوِ الطِّفْلِ الَّذِينَ لَمْ يَظْهَرُوا عَلَىٰ عَوْرَاتِ النِّسَآءِ ۖ وَلَا يَضْرِبْنَ بِاَرْجُلِهِنَّ لِيُعْلَمَ مَا يُخْفِينَ مِنْ زِينَتِهِنَّ ۚ وَتُوبُوٓا اِلَى اللّٰهِ جَمِيعًا اَيُّهَ الْمُؤْمِنُونَ لَعَلَّكُمْ تُفْلِحُونَ ۝

32. Marry those among you who are single, or the virtuous ones among yourselves, male or female: if they are in poverty, Allah will give them means out of His grace: for Allah encompasses all, and he knows all things.

33. Let those who find not the wherewithal for marriage keep themselves chaste, until Allah gives them means out of His grace. And if any of your slaves ask for a deed in writing (to enable them to earn their freedom for a certain sum), give them such a deed if you know any good in them: yes, give them something yourselves out of the means which Allah has given to you. But force not your maids to prostitution when they desire chastity, in order that you may make a gain in the goods of this life. But if anyone compels them, yet, after such compulsion, is Allah, Oft-Forgiving, Most Merciful (to them),

34. We have already sent down to you verses making things clear, an illustration from (the story of) people who passed away before you, and an admonition for those who fear (Allah).

35. Allah is the Light of the heavens and the earth. The parable of His Light is as if there were a Niche and within it a Lamp: the Lamp enclosed in Glass: the glass as it were a brilliant star: lit from a blessed Tree, an Olive, neither of the east nor of the west, whose oil is well-nigh Luminous, though fire scarce touched it: Light upon Light! Allah guides whom He will to His Light: Allah sets forth Parables for men: and Allah.

32. Wa ankiḥul-ayaamaa minkum waṣ-ṣaaliḥeena min 'ibaadikum wa imaa'ikum; iñy-yakoonoo fuqaraaa'a yughni-himul-laahu min faḍlih; wal-laahu Waasi'un 'Aleem.

33. Wal-yasta'fifil-lazeena laa yajidoona nikaaḥan ḥattaa yughniyahumul-laahu min faḍlih; wallazeena yabta-ghoonal-kitaaba mimmaa malakat aymaanukum fakaati-boohum in 'alimtum feehim khayrañw-wa aatoohum-mim-maalil-laahil-lazeee aataakum; wa laa tukrihoo fatayaatikum 'alal-bighaaa'i in aradna taḥaṣṣunal-litabtaghoo 'araḍal-ḥayaatid-dunyaa; wa mañy-yukrihhunna fa-innal-laaha mim ba'di ikraahihinna Ghafoorur-Raḥeem.

34. Wa laqad anzalnaaa ilaykum Aayaatim-mubay-yinaatiñw-wa maṣalam-minal-lazeena khalaw min qablikum wa maw'izatal-lilmuttaqeen.

(Section 4)

35. Allaahu noorus-samaa-waati wal-arḍ; maṣalu nooriheee kamishkaatin feehaa miṣbaaḥ; almiṣbaaḥu fee zujaajatin azzujaajatu ka-annahaa kawkabun durriyyuñy-yooqadu min shajaratim-mubaarakatin zaytoonatil-laa sharqiyyatiñw-wa laa gharbiyyatiñy-yakaadu zaytuhaa yuḍeee'u wa law lam tamsashu naar; noorun 'alaa noor; yahdil-laahu linooriheee mañy-yashaaa'; wa yaḍribul-laahul-amṣaala linnaas; wallaahu bikulli

knows all things.

36. (Lit is such a Light) in houses, which Allah has permitted to be raised to honor; for the celebration, in them, of His name: in them is He glorified in the mornings and in the evenings, (again and again),-

37. By men whom neither traffic nor merchandise can divert from the remembrance of Allah, nor from regular Prayer, nor from paying Zakat; their (only) fear is for the Day when hearts and eyes will be turned about,-

38. That Allah may reward them according to the best of their deeds, and add even more for them out of His Grace: for Allah provides for those whom He will, without measure.

39. But the Unbelievers,- their deeds are like a mirage in sandy deserts, which the man parched with thirst mistakes for water; until when he comes up to it, he finds it to be nothing: but he finds Allah (ever) with him, and Allah will pay him his account: and Allah is swift in taking account.

40. Or (the Unbelievers' state) is like the depths of darkness in a vast deep ocean, overwhelmed with billow topped by billow, topped by (dark) clouds: depths of darkness, one above another: if a man stretches out his hands, he can hardly see it! for any to whom Allah does not give light, there is no light!

41. Do not you see that it is Allah Whose praises all beings in the heavens and on earth do celebrate, and the birds (of the air) with wings outspread? Each one knows its own (mode of) prayer and praise. And Allah knows well all that they do.

shay'in 'Aleem.

36. Fee buyootin aẕinal-laahu an turfa'a wa yuzkara feehasmuhoo yusabbiḥu lahoo feehaa bilghuduwwi wal-aaṣaal.

37. Rijaalul-laa tulheehim tijaaratuñw-wa laa bay'un 'an ẕikril-laahi wa iqaamiṣ-Ṣalaati wa eetaaa'iz-Zakaati yakhaafoona Yawman tataqallabu feehil-quloobu wal-abṣaar.

38. Liyajziyahumul-laahu aḥsana maa 'amiloo wa yazeedahum-min faḍlih; wallaahu yarzuqu mañy-yashaaa'u bighayri ḥisaab.

39. Wallaẕeena kafarooo a'maaluhum kasaraabim biqee'atiñy-yaḥsabuhuẕ-ẓamaanu maaa'an ḥattaaa iẕaa jaaa'ahoo lam yajid-hu shay-'añw-wa wajadal-laaha 'indahoo fa-waffaahu ḥisaabah; wallaahu saree'ul-ḥisaab.

40. Aw kaẕulumaatin fee baḥril-lujjiyyiñy-yaghshaahu mawjum-min fawqihee mawjum-min fawqihee saḥaab; ẓulumaatum ba'ḍuhaa fawqa ba'din iẕaa akhraja yadahoo lam yakad yaraahaa wa mal-lam yaj'alil-laahu lahoo nooran famaa lahoo min-noor.

(Section 5)

41. Alam tara annal-laaha yusabbiḥu lahoo man fissamaawaati wal-arḍi waṭ-ṭayru ṣaaaffaatin kullun qad 'alima Ṣalaatahoo wa tasbeeḥah; wallaahu 'aleemum bimaa yaf'aloon.

42. Yes, to Allah belongs the dominion of the heavens and the earth; and to Allah is the final goal (of all).

42. Wa lillaahi mulkus-samaawaati wal-arḍi wa ilal-laahil-maṣeer.

وَلِلّٰهِ مُلْكُ السَّمٰوٰتِ وَالْاَرْضِ ۚ وَاِلَى اللّٰهِ الْمَصِيْرُ ۞

43. Don't you see that Allah makes the clouds move gently, then joins them together, then makes them into a heap? - then will you see rain issue forth from their midst. And He sends down from the sky mountain masses (of clouds) wherein is hail: He strikes therewith whom He pleases and He turns it away from whom He pleases, the vivid flash of His lightning well-nigh blinds the sight.

43. Alam tara annal-laaha yuzjee saḥaaban ṣumma yu'allifu baynahoo ṣumma yaj'aluhoo rukaaman fataral-wadqa yakhruju min khilaalihee wa yunazzilu minas-samaaa'i min jibaalin feehaa mim baradin fa-yuṣeebu bihee mañy-yashaaa'u wa yaṣrifuhoo 'am-mañy-yashaaa'u yakaadu sanaa barqihee yaẕhabu bil-abṣaar.

اَلَمْ تَرَ اَنَّ اللّٰهَ يُزْجِيْ سَحَابًا ثُمَّ يُؤَلِّفُ بَيْنَهٗ ثُمَّ يَجْعَلُهٗ رُكَامًا فَتَرَى الْوَدْقَ يَخْرُجُ مِنْ خِلٰلِهٖ ۚ وَيُنَزِّلُ مِنَ السَّمَاءِ مِنْ جِبَالٍ فِيْهَا مِنْ بَرَدٍ فَيُصِيْبُ بِهٖ مَنْ يَّشَاءُ وَيَصْرِفُهٗ عَنْ مَّنْ يَّشَاءُ ۗ يَكَادُ سَنَا بَرْقِهٖ يَذْهَبُ بِالْاَبْصَارِ ۞

44. It is Allah Who alternates the Night and the Day: verily in these things is an instructive example for those who have vision!

44. Yuqallibul-laahul-layla wannahaar; inna fee ẕaalika la'ibratal-li-ulil-abṣaar.

يُقَلِّبُ اللّٰهُ الَّيْلَ وَالنَّهَارَ ۚ اِنَّ فِيْ ذٰلِكَ لَعِبْرَةً لِّاُولِى الْاَبْصَارِ ۞

45. And Allah has created every animal from water: of them there are some that creep on their bellies; some that walk on two legs; and some that walk on four. Allah creates what He wills; for verily Allah has power over all things.

45. Wallaahu khalaqa kulla daaabbatim-mim-maaa'in faminhum-mañy-yamshee 'alaa baṭnihee wa minhum-mañy-yamshee 'alaa rijlayni wa minhum-mañy-yamshee 'alaaa arba'; yakhluqul-laahu maa yashaaa'; innal-laaha 'alaa kulli shay'in Qadeer.

وَاللّٰهُ خَلَقَ كُلَّ دَاۤبَّةٍ مِّنْ مَّاءٍ ۚ فَمِنْهُمْ مَّنْ يَّمْشِيْ عَلٰى بَطْنِهٖ ۚ وَمِنْهُمْ مَّنْ يَّمْشِيْ عَلٰى رِجْلَيْنِ ۚ وَمِنْهُمْ مَّنْ يَّمْشِيْ عَلٰۤى اَرْبَعٍ ۚ يَخْلُقُ اللّٰهُ مَا يَشَاءُ ۗ اِنَّ اللّٰهَ عَلٰى كُلِّ شَيْءٍ قَدِيْرٌ ۞

46. We have indeed sent down signs that make things manifest: and Allah guides whom He wills to a way that is straight.

46. Laqad anzalnaaa Aayaa-tim-mubayyinaat; wallaahu yahdee mañy-yashaaa'u ilaa Ṣiraaṭim-Mustaqeem.

لَقَدْ اَنْزَلْنَاۤ اٰيٰتٍ مُّبَيِّنٰتٍ ۗ وَاللّٰهُ يَهْدِيْ مَنْ يَّشَاءُ اِلٰى صِرَاطٍ مُّسْتَقِيْمٍ ۞

47. They say, "We believe in Allah and in the Messenger, and we obey": but even after that, some of them turn away: they are not (really) Believers.

47. Wa yaqooloona aamannaa billaahi wa bir-Rasooli wa aṭa'naa ṣumma yatawallaa fareequm-minhum-mim ba'di ẕaalik; wa maaa ulaaa'ika bilmu'mineen.

وَيَقُوْلُوْنَ اٰمَنَّا بِاللّٰهِ وَبِالرَّسُوْلِ وَاَطَعْنَا ثُمَّ يَتَوَلّٰى فَرِيْقٌ مِّنْهُمْ مِّنْ بَعْدِ ذٰلِكَ ۗ وَمَا اُولٰٓئِكَ بِالْمُؤْمِنِيْنَ ۞

48. When they are summoned to Allah and His Messenger, in order that He may judge between them, behold some of them decline (to come).

48. Wa iẕaa du'ooo ilal-laahi wa Rasoolihee li-yaḥkuma baynahum iẕaa fareequm-minhum-mu'riḍoon.

وَاِذَا دُعُوْۤا اِلَى اللّٰهِ وَرَسُوْلِهٖ لِيَحْكُمَ بَيْنَهُمْ اِذَا فَرِيْقٌ مِّنْهُمْ مُّعْرِضُوْنَ ۞

49. But if the right is on their side, they come to him with all submission.

50. Is it that there is a disease in their hearts? or do they doubt, or are they in fear, that Allah and His Messenger will deal unjustly with them? Nay, it is they themselves who do wrong.

51. The answer of the Believers, when summoned to Allah and His Messenger, in order that he may judge between them, is no other than this: they say, "We hear and we obey": it is such as these that will attain felicity.

52. It is such as obey Allah and His Messenger, and fear Allah and do right, that will win (in the end),

53. They swear their strongest oaths by Allah that, if only you would command them, they would leave (their homes). Say: "Do not swear obedience is (more) reasonable; verily, Allah is well acquainted with all that you do."

54. Say: "Obey Allah, and obey the Messenger: but if you turn away, he is only responsible for the duty placed on him and you for that placed on you. If you obey him, you shall be on right guidance. The Messenger's duty is only to preach the clear (Message).

55. Allah has promised, to those among you who believe and work righteous deeds, that He will, of a surety, grant them in the land, inheritance (of power), as He granted it to those before them; that He will establish in authority their religion - the one which He has chosen for them; and that He will change (their state), after the fear in which they (lived), to one of security and peace: 'They will worship Me (alone)

---

49. Wa iñy-yakul-lahumul-ḥaqqu yaåtoo ilayhi muẕ-'ineen.

50. Afee quloobihim-maraḍun amirtaabooo am yakhaafoona añy-yaḥeefallaahu 'alayhim wa Rasooluh; bal ulaaa'ika humuẕ-ẕaalimoon. **(Section 6)**

51. Innamaa kaana qawlal-mu'mineena iẕaa du'ooo ilal-laahi wa Rasoolihee li-yaḥkuma baynahum añy-yaqooloo sami'naa wa aṭa'naa; wa ulaaa'ika humul-mufliḥoon.

52. Wa mañy-yuṭi'il-laaha wa Rasoolahoo wa yakhshal-laaha wa yattaqhi fa-ulaaa'ika humul-faaa'izoon.

53. Wa aqsamoo billaahi jahda aymaanihim la-'in amartahum la-yakhrujunna qul laa tuqsimoo ṭaa'atum-ma'roofah innal-laaha khabee-rum bimaa ta'maloon.

54. Qul aṭee'ul-laaha wa aṭee'ur-Rasoola fa-in tawallaw fa-innamaa 'alayhi maa ḥummila wa 'alaykum-maa ḥummiltum wa in tuṭee'oohu tahtadoo; wa maa 'alar-Rasooli illal-balaaghul-mubeen.

55. Wa'adal-laahul-laẕeena aamanoo minkum wa 'amiluṣ-ṣaaliḥaati la-yastakhlifan-nahum fil-arḍi kamastakh-lafal-laẕeena min qablihim wa la-yumakkinanna lahum deenahumul-laẕir taḍaa lahum wa la-yubaddilannahum-mim ba'di khawfihim amnaa; ya'budoonanee laa

and not associate any one with Me. 'If any do reject Faith after this, they are rebellious and wicked.

56. So establish regular Prayer and give regular Charity; and obey the Messenger; that you may receive mercy.

57. You should never think that the Unbelievers are going to frustrate (Allah's Plan) on earth: their abode is the Fire,- and it is indeed an evil refuge!

58. O you who believe! Let those whom your right hands possess, and the (children) among you who have not come of age ask your permission (before they come to your presence), on three occasions: before morning prayer; the while you doff your clothes for the noonday heat; and after the late-night prayer: these are your three times of undress: outside those times it is not wrong for you or for them to move about attending to each other: Thus Allah makes clear the Signs to you: for Allah is full of knowledge and wisdom.

59. But when the children among you come of age, let them (also) ask for permission, as do those senior to them (in age): thus Allah makes clear His Signs to you: for Allah is full of knowledge and wisdom.

60. Such elderly women as are past the prospect of marriage,- there is no blame on them if they lay aside their (outer) garments, provided they make not a wanton display of their beauty: but it is best for them to be modest: and Allah is One Who sees and knows all things.

---

yushrikoona bee shay'aa; wa man kafara ba'da zaalika fa-ulaaa'ika humul-faasiqoon.

56. Wa aqeemuṣ-Ṣalaata wa aatuz-Zakaata wa aṭee'ur-Rasoola la'allakum turḥamoon.

57. Laa taḥsabannal-lazeena kafaroo mu'jizeena fil-arḍ; wa maåwaahumun-Naaru wa labi'sal-maṣeer. **(Section 7)**

58. Yaaa ayyuhal-lazeena aamanoo li-yastaåzinkumul-lazeena malakat aymaanukum wallazeena lam yablughul-ḥuluma minkum salaasa marraat; min qabli Ṣalaatil-Fajri wa ḥeena taḍa'oona siyaa-bakum-minaẓ-ẓaheerati wa mim-ba'di Ṣalaatil-'Ishaaa'; salaaṣu 'awraatil-lakum; laysa 'alaykum wa laa 'alayhim junaaḥum ba'dahunn; ṭawwaa-foona 'alaykum ba'ḍukum 'alaa ba'ḍ; kazaalika yubayyinul-laahu lakumul-Aaayaat wallaahu 'Aleemun Ḥakeem.

59. Wa izaa balaghal-aṭfaalu minkumul-ḥuluma fal-yastaå-zinoo kamas-taåzanal-lazeena min qablihim; kazaalika yubay-yinul-laahu lakum Aayaatih; wallaahu 'Aleemun Ḥakeem.

60. Walqawaa'idu minan-nisaaa'il-laatee laa yarjoona nikaaḥan falaysa 'alayhinna junaaḥun any-yaḍa'na siyaa-bahunna ghayra mutabar-rijaatim bizeenah; wa any-yasta'fifna khayrul-lahunn; wallaahu Samee'un 'Aleem.

61. It is no fault in the blind nor in one born lame, nor in one afflicted with illness, nor in yourselves, that you should eat in your own houses, or those of your fathers, or your mothers, or your brothers, or your sisters, or your father's brothers or your father's sisters, or your mohter's brothers, or your mother's sisters, or in houses of which the keys are in your possession, or in the house of a sincere friend of yours: there is no blame on you, whether you eat in company or separately. But if you enter houses, salute each other - a greeting of blessing and purity as from Allah. Thus Allah makes clear the Signs to you: that you may understand.

61. Laysa 'alal-a'maa ḥarajuñw-wa laa 'alal-a'raji ḥarajuñw-wa laa 'alal-mareeḍi ḥarajuñw-wa laa 'alaaa anfusikum an taåkuloo mim buyootikum aw buyooti aabaaa'ikum aw buyooti ummahaatikum aw buyooti ikhwaanikum aw buyooti akhawaatikum aw buyooti a'maamikum aw buyooti 'ammaatikum aw buyooti akhwaalikum aw buyooti khaalaatikum aw maa malaktum-mafaatiḥahooo aw ṣadeeqikum; laysa 'alaykum junaaḥun an taåkuloo jamee'an aw ashtaataa; fa-izaa dakhaltum buyootan fasallimoo 'alaaa anfusikum taḥiyyatam-min 'indil-laahi mubaarakatan ṭayyibah; kazaalika yubay-yinul-laahu lakumul-Aayaati la'allakum ta'qiloon. **(Section 8)**

62. Only those are believers, who believe in Allah and His Messenger: when they are with him on a matter requiring collective action, they do not depart until they have asked for his leave; those who ask for your leave are those who believe in Allah and His Messenger; so when they ask for your leave, for some business of theirs, give leave to those of them whom you will, and ask Allah for their forgiveness: for Allah is Oft-Forgiving, Most Merciful.

62. Innamal-mu'minoonallazeena aamanoo billaahi wa Rasoolihee wa izaa kaanoo ma'ahoo 'alaaa amrin jaami'illam yazhaboo ḥattaa yastaåzinooh; innal-lazeena yastaåzinoonaka ulaaa'ikal-lazeena yu'minoona billaahi wa Rasoolih; fa-izas-taåzanooka liba'ḍi shaånihim faåzal-liman shi'ta minhum wastaghfir lahumul-laah; innal-laaha Ghafoorur-Raḥeem.

63. Deem not the summons of the Messenger among yourselves

63. Laa taj'aloo du'aaa'ar-Rasooli baynakum

كَيْسَ عَلَى الْأَعْمٰى حَرَجٌ وَّلَا عَلَى الْأَعْرَجِ حَرَجٌ وَّلَا عَلَى الْمَرِيْضِ حَرَجٌ وَّلَا عَلٰٓى اَنْفُسِكُمْ اَنْ تَاْكُلُوْا مِنْۢ بُيُوْتِكُمْ اَوْ بُيُوْتِ اٰبَآئِكُمْ اَوْ بُيُوْتِ اُمَّهٰتِكُمْ اَوْ بُيُوْتِ اِخْوَانِكُمْ اَوْ بُيُوْتِ اَخَوٰتِكُمْ اَوْ بُيُوْتِ اَعْمَامِكُمْ اَوْ بُيُوْتِ عَمّٰتِكُمْ اَوْ بُيُوْتِ اَخْوَالِكُمْ اَوْ بُيُوْتِ خٰلٰتِكُمْ اَوْمَا مَلَكْتُمْ مَّفَاتِحَهٗٓ اَوْ صَدِيْقِكُمْ ۔ لَيْسَ عَلَيْكُمْ جُنَاحٌ اَنْ تَاْكُلُوْا جَمِيْعًا اَوْ اَشْتَاتًا ۔ فَاِذَا دَخَلْتُمْ بُيُوْتًا فَسَلِّمُوْا عَلٰٓى اَنْفُسِكُمْ تَحِيَّةً مِّنْ عِنْدِ اللّٰهِ مُبٰرَكَةً طَيِّبَةً ۔ كَذٰلِكَ يُبَيِّنُ اللّٰهُ لَكُمُ الْاٰيٰتِ لَعَلَّكُمْ تَعْقِلُوْنَ ۞

اِنَّمَا الْمُؤْمِنُوْنَ الَّذِيْنَ اٰمَنُوْا بِاللّٰهِ وَرَسُوْلِهٖ وَاِذَا كَانُوْا مَعَهٗ عَلٰٓى اَمْرٍ جَامِعٍ لَّمْ يَذْهَبُوْا حَتّٰى يَسْتَاْذِنُوْهُ ۔ اِنَّ الَّذِيْنَ يَسْتَاْذِنُوْنَكَ اُولٰٓئِكَ الَّذِيْنَ يُؤْمِنُوْنَ بِاللّٰهِ وَ رَسُوْلِهٖ ۚ فَاِذَا اسْتَاْذَنُوْكَ لِبَعْضِ شَاْنِهِمْ فَاْذَنْ لِّمَنْ شِئْتَ مِنْهُمْ وَاسْتَغْفِرْ لَهُمُ اللّٰهَ ۔ اِنَّ اللّٰهَ غَفُوْرٌ رَّحِيْمٌ ۞

لَا تَجْعَلُوْا دُعَآءَ الرَّسُوْلِ بَيْنَكُمْ

like the summons of one of you to another: Allah knows those of you who slip away under shelter of some excuse: then let those beware who withstand the Messenger's order, lest some trial befall them, or a grievous Penalty be inflicted on them.

64. Be quite sure that to Allah belong whatever is in the heavens and on earth. Well does He know what you are intent upon: and the day they will be brought back to Him, and He will tell them the truth of what they did: for Allah knows all things.

25. The Criterion

In the name of Allah, Most Gracious, Most Merciful.

1. Blessed is He who sent down the criterion to His servant, that it may be an admonition to all creatures;-

2. He to Whom belongs the dominion of the heavens and the earth: no son has He begotten, nor has He a partner in His dominion: it is He who created all things, and ordered them in due proportions.

3. Yet have they taken, besides him, gods that can create nothing but are themselves created; that have no control of hurt or good to themselves; nor can they control death nor life nor resurrection.

4. But the Misbelievers say: "Nothing is this but a lie which he has forged, and others have helped him at it." In truth it is they who have put forward an iniquity and a falsehood.

---

kadu-'aa'i ba‘ḍikum ba‘ḍaa; qad ya‘lamul-laahul-lazeena yatasallaloona minkum liwaazaa; fal-yaḥzaril-lazeena yukhaalifoona ‘an amriheee an tuṣeebahum fitnatun aw yuṣeebahum ‘azaabun aleem.

64. Alaaa inna lillaahi maa fis-samaawaati wal-arḍi qad ya‘lamu maaa antum ‘alayhi wa Yawma yurja‘oona ilayhi fa-yunabbi'uhum bimaa ‘amiloo; wallaahu bikulli shay'in ‘Aleem.   **(Section 9)**

Sûrat al-Furqân–25
(Revealed at Makkah)
Bismillaahir Raḥmaanir Raḥeem

1. Tabaarakal-lazee naz-zalal-Furqaana ‘alaa ‘abdihee li-yakoona lil‘aalameena nazeeraa.

2. Allazee lahoo mulkus-samaawaati wal-arḍi wa lam yattakhiz waladaɲw-wa lam yakul-lahoo shareekun fil-mulki wa khalaqa kulla shay'in faqaddarahoo taqdeeraa.

3. Wattakhazoo min dooni-heee aalihatal-laa yakhluqoona shay'aɲw-wa hum yukhlaqoona wa laa yamlikoona li-anfusihim ḍarraɲw-wa laa naf‘aɲw-wa laa yamlikoona mawtaɲw-wa laa ḥayaataɲw-wa laa nushooraa.

4. Wa qaalal-lazeena ka-farooo in haazaaa illaaa ifkunif-taraahu wa a‘aanahoo ‘alayhi qawmun aakharoona faqad jaaa‘oo zulmaɲw-wa zooraa.

5. And they say: "Tales of the ancients, which he has caused to be written: and they are dictated before him morning and evening."

6. Say: "The (Qur'an) was sent down by Him who knows the mystery (that is) in the heavens and the earth: verily He is Oft-Forgiving, Most Merciful."

7. And they say: "What sort of a Messenger is this, who eats food, and walks through the streets? Why has not an angel been sent down to him to give admonition with him?

8. "Or (Why) has not a treasure been bestowed on him, or why has he (not) a garden for enjoyment?" The wicked say: "You follow none other than a man bewitched."

9. See what kinds of comparisons they make for you! But they have gone astray, and never a way will they be able to find!

10. Blessed is He who, if that were His will, could give you better (things) than those,- Gardens beneath which rivers flow; and He could give you palaces (secure to dwell in).

11. Nay they deny the Hour (of the judgment to come): but We have prepared a blazing fire for such as deny the Hour:

12. When it sees them from a place far off, they will hear its fury and its ranging sigh.

13. And when they are cast, bound together into a constricted place therein, they will plead for destruction there and then!

14. "This day do not plead for a single destruction:

---

5. Wa qaalooo asaaṭeerul-awwaleenak-tatabahaa fahiya tumlaa 'alayhi bukratañw-wa aṣeelaa.

6. Qul anzalahul-lazee ya'lamus-sirra fis-samaawaati wal-arḍ; innahoo kaana Ghafoorar-Raḥeemaa.

7. Wa qaaloo maa li-haazar-Rasooli yaakulut-ṭa'aama wa yamshee fil-aswaaq; law laaa unzila ilayhi malakun fa-yakoona ma'ahoo nazeeraa.

8. Aw yulqaaa ilayhi kanzun aw takoonu lahoo jannatuñy-yaakulu minhaa; wa qaalaẓ-ẓaalimoona in tattabi'oona illaa rajulam-mas-ḥooraa.

9. Unẓur kayfa ḍaraboo lakal-amṣaala faḍalloo falaa yastaṭee'oona sabeelaa. (Sec. 1)

10. Tabaarakal-lazeee in shaaa'a ja'ala laka khayram-min zaalika Jannaatin tajree min taḥtihal-anhaaru wa yaj'al-laka quṣooraa.

11. Bal kazzaboo bis-Saa'ati wa a'tadnaa liman kazzaba bis-Saa'ati sa'eeraa.

12. Izaa ra-at-hum-mim-ma-kaanim ba'eedin sami'oo lahaa taghayyuẓañw-wa zafeeraa.

13. Wa izaaa ulqoo minhaa makaanan ḍayyiqam-muqar-raneena da'aw hunaalika subooraa.

14. Laa tad'ul-yawma suboo-rañw-waaḥidañw-

plead for destruction oft-repeated!"

15. Say: "Is that best, or the eternal Garden, promised to the righteous? for them, that is a reward as well as a goal (of attainment).

16. "For them there will be therein all that they wish for: they will dwell (there) for ever: A promise binding upon your Lord."

17. The day He will gather them together as well as those whom they worship besides Allah, He will ask: "Was it you who let these My servants astray, or did they stray from the Path themselves?"

18. They will say: "Glory to You! Not meet was it for us that we should take for protectors others besides You: but You did bestow, on them and their fathers, good things (in life), until they forgot the Message: for they were a people (worthless and) lost."

19. (Allah will say): "Now have they proved you liars in what you say: so you cannot avert (your Penalty) nor (get) help." And whoever among you does wrong, him shall We cause to taste of a grievous Penalty.

20. And the Messengers whom We sent before you were all (men) who ate food and walked through the streets: We have made some of you as a trial for others: will you have patience? for Allah is One Who sees (all things).

21. Such as do not fear the meeting with Us (for Judgment) say: "Why are not the angels sent down to us, or (why) do we not see

wad'oo subooran kaseeraa.

15. Qul azaalika khayrun am Jannatul-khuldil-latee wu'idal-muttaqoon; kaanat lahum jazaaa'añw-wa maseeraa.

16. Lahum feehaa maa yashaaa'oona khaalideen; kaana 'alaa Rabbika wa'dam-mas'oolaa.

17. Wa Yawma yahshuruhum wa maa ya'budoona min doonil-laahi fa-yaqoolu 'a-antum adlaltum 'ibaadee haaa'ulaaa'i am hum dallus-sabeel.

18. Qaaloo Subhaanaka maa kaana yambaghee lanaaa an-nattakhiza min doonika min awliyaaa'a wa laakim-matta'tahum wa aabaaa'ahum hattaa nasuz-zikra wa kaanoo qawmam booraa.

19. Faqad kazzabookum bimaa taqooloona famaa tastatee'oona sarfañw-wa laa nasraa; wa mañy-yazlim-minkum nuziqhu 'azaaban kabeeraa.

20. Wa maaa arsalnaa qablaka minal-mursaleena illaaa innahum la-yaâkuloonat-ta'aama wa yamshoona fil-aswaaq; wa ja'alnaa ba'dakum liba'din fitnatan atasbiroon; wa kaana Rabbuka Baseeraa.

(Section 2)

21. Wa qaalal-lazeena laa yarjoona liqaaa'anaa law laaa unzila 'alaynal-malaaa'ikatu aw naraa

our Lord?" Indeed they have an arrogant conceit of themselves, and mighty is the insolence of their impiety!

22. The Day they see the angels,- no joy will there be to the sinners that Day: The (angels) will say: "There is a barrier forbidden (to you) altogether!"

23. And We shall turn to whatever deeds they did (in this life), and We shall make such deeds as floating dust scattered about.

24. The Companions of the Garden will be well, that Day, in their abode, and have the fairest of places for repose.

25. The Day the heaven shall be rent asunder with clouds, and angels shall be sent down, descending (in ranks),-

26. That Day, the dominion as of right and truth, shall be (wholly) for (Allah) Most Merciful: it will be a Day of dire difficulty for the Misbelievers.

27. The Day that the wrong-doer will bite at his hands, he will say, "Oh! would that I had taken a (straight) path with the Messenger!

28. "Ah! woe is me! Would that I had never taken such a one for a friend!

29. "He did lead me astray from the Message (of Allah) after it had come to me! Ah! the Evil One is but a traitor to man!"

30. Then the Messenger will say: "O my Lord! Truly my people took this Qur'an for just foolish nonsense."

31. Thus have We made for every prophet an enemy among the sinners: but enough is your Lord to guide and to help.

Rabbanaa; laqadistakbaroo feee anfusihim wa 'ataw 'utuwwan kabeeraa.

22. Yawma yarawnal-malaaa-'ikata laa bushraa Yawma'izil-lilmujrimeena wa yaqooloona ḥijram-maḥjooraa.

23. Wa qadimnaaa ilaa maa 'amiloo min 'amalin faja'al-naahu habaaa'am-mansooraa.

24. Aṣ-ḥaabul-Jannati Yaw-ma'izin khayrum-mustaqar-rañw-wa aḥsanu maqeelaa.

25. Wa Yawma tashaqqaqus-samaaa'u bilghamaami wa nuzzilal-malaaa'ikatu tan-zeelaa.

26. Almulku Yawma'izinil-ḥaqqu lir-Raḥmaan; wa kaana Yawman 'alal-kaafireena 'asee-raa.

27. Wa Yawma ya'aḍḍuẓ-ẓaalimu 'alaa yadayhi yaqoolu yaa-laytanit-takhaẓtu ma'ar-Rasooli sabeelaa.

28. Yaa waylataa laytanee lam attakhiẓ fulaanan khaleelaa.

29. Laqad aḍallanee 'aniẓ-ẓikri ba'da iẓ jaaa'anee; wa kaanash-Shayṭaanu lil-insaani khaẓoolaa.

30. Wa qaalar-Rasoolu yaa Rabbi inna qawmit-takhaẓoo haaẓal-Qur-aana mahjooraa.

31. Wa kaẓaalika ja'alnaa likulli Nabiyyin 'aduwwam-minal-mujrimeen; wa kafaa bi-Rabbika haadiyañw-wa naṣeeraa.

رَبَّنَا لَقَدِ اسْتَكْبَرُوْا فِيْ اَنْفُسِهِمْ وَعَتَوْ عُتُوًّا كَبِيْرًا ۩

يَوْمَ يَرَوْنَ الْمَلٰٓئِكَةَ لَا بُشْرٰى يَوْمَئِذٍ لِّلْمُجْرِمِيْنَ وَيَقُوْلُوْنَ حِجْرًا مَّحْجُوْرًا ۩

وَقَدِمْنَاۤ اِلٰى مَا عَمِلُوْا مِنْ عَمَلٍ فَجَعَلْنٰهُ هَبَآءً مَّنْثُوْرًا ۩

اَصْحٰبُ الْجَنَّةِ يَوْمَئِذٍ خَيْرٌ مُّسْتَقَرًّا وَّاَحْسَنُ مَقِيْلًا ۩

وَيَوْمَ تَشَقَّقُ السَّمَآءُ بِالْغَمَامِ وَنُزِّلَ الْمَلٰٓئِكَةُ تَنْزِيْلًا ۩

اَلْمُلْكُ يَوْمَئِذِ نِ الْحَقُّ لِلرَّحْمٰنِ ۚ وَكَانَ يَوْمًا عَلَى الْكٰفِرِيْنَ عَسِيْرًا ۩

وَيَوْمَ يَعَضُّ الظَّالِمُ عَلٰى يَدَيْهِ يَقُوْلُ يٰلَيْتَنِى اتَّخَذْتُ مَعَ الرَّسُوْلِ سَبِيْلًا ۩

يٰوَيْلَتٰى لَيْتَنِىْ لَمْ اَتَّخِذْ فُلَانًا خَلِيْلًا ۩

لَقَدْ اَضَلَّنِىْ عَنِ الذِّكْرِ بَعْدَ اِذْ جَآءَنِىْ ۗ وَكَانَ الشَّيْطٰنُ لِلْاِنْسَانِ خَذُوْلًا ۩

وَقَالَ الرَّسُوْلُ يٰرَبِّ اِنَّ قَوْمِى اتَّخَذُوْا هٰذَا الْقُرْاٰنَ مَهْجُوْرًا ۩

وَكَذٰلِكَ جَعَلْنَا لِكُلِّ نَبِيٍّ عَدُوًّا مِّنَ الْمُجْرِمِيْنَ ۗ وَكَفٰى بِرَبِّكَ هَادِيًا وَّنَصِيْرًا ۩

32. Those who reject Faith say: "Why is not the Qur'an revealed to him all at once? Thus (is it revealed), that We may strengthen your heart thereby, and We have rehearsed it to you in slow, well-arranged stages, gradually.

33. And no question do they bring to you but We reveal to you the truth and the best explanation (thereof).

34. Those who will be gathered to Hell (prone) on their faces,- they will be in an evil plight, and, as to Path, most astray.

35. (Before this,) We sent Moses The Book, and appointed his brother Aaron with him as minister;

36. And We command: "You both go, to the people who have rejected our Signs:" and those (people) We destroyed with utter destruction.

37. And the people of Noah,- when they rejected the Messengers, We drowned them, and We made them as a Sign for mankind; and We have prepared for (all) wrong-doers a grievous Penalty;-

38. As also 'Ad and Thamud, and the Companions of the Rass, and many a generation between them.

39. To each one We set forth parables and examples; and each one We broke to utter annihilation (for their sins).

40. And the (Unbelievers) must indeed have passed by the town on which was rained a shower of evil: did they not then see it (with their own eyes)? But they do not fear the Resurrection.

41. When they see you, they treat you no otherwise than in mockery: "Is this the one whom Allah has sent as a Messenger?"

42. "He indeed would well-have misled us from our gods, had it not been that we were constant to them!" - Soon will they know,

32. Wa qaalal-lazeena kafaroo law laa nuzzila 'alayhil-Qur-aanu jumlatanw-waaḥidah; kazaalika linusabbita bihee fu'aadaka wa rattalnaahu tarteelaa.

33. Wa laa yaatoonaka bimasalin illaa ji'naaka bilḥaqqi wa aḥsana tafseeraa.

34. Allazeena yuḥsharoona 'alaa wujoohihim ilaa Jahannama ulaaa'ika sharrum-makaananw-wa aḍallu sabeelaa.

(Section 3)

35. Wa laqad aataynaa Moosal-Kitaaba wa ja'alnaa ma'ahooo akhaahu Haaroona wazeeraa.

36. Faqulnaz-habaaa ilal-qawmil-lazeena kazzaboo bi-Aayaatinaa fadammarnaahum tadmeeraa.

37. Wa qawma Nooḥil-lammaa kazzabur-Rusula aghraqnaahum wa ja'alnaahum linnaasi Aayatanw-wa a'tadnaa lizzaalimeena 'azaaban aleemaa.

38. Wa 'Aadanw-wa Samooda wa Aṣ-ḥaabar-Rassi wa quroonam bayna zaalika kaseeraa.

39. Wa kullan ḍarabnaa lahul-amsaala wa kullan tabbarnaa tatbeeraa.

40. Wa laqad ataw 'alal-qaryatil-lateee umṭirat maṭarassaw'; afalam yakoonoo yarawnahaa; bal kaanoo laa yarjoona nushooraa.

41. Wa izaa ra-awka iñy-yattakhizoonaka illaa huzuwan ahaazal-lazee ba'asal-laahu Rasoolaa.

42. In kaada la-yuḍillunaa 'an aalihatinaa law laaa an ṣabarnaa 'alayhaa; wa sawfa ya'lamoona

when they see the Penalty, who it is that is most misled in Path!

43. Do you see such a one as takes for his god his own passion (or impulse)? Could you be a disposer of affairs for him?

44. Or do you think that most of them listen or understand? They are only like cattle;- nay, they are worse astray in Path.

45. Have you not turned your vision to your Lord?- How does He prolong the shadow! If He willed, He could make it stationary! then do We make the sun its guide;

46. Then We draw it in towards Ourselves,- a contraction by easy stages.

47. And He it is Who makes the Night as a Robe for you, and Sleep as Repose, and makes the Day (as it were) a Resurrection.

48. And He it is Who sends the winds as heralds of glad tidings, going before His mercy, and We send down pure water from the sky,-

49. That with it We may give life to a dead land, and slake the thirst of things We have created,- cattle and men in great numbers.

50. And We have distributed the (water) amongst them, in order that they may celebrate (our) praises, but most men are averse (to anything) but (rank) ingratitude.

51. Had it been Our Will, We could have sent a warner to every centre of population.

52. Therefore do not listen to the Unbelievers, but strive against them with the utmost strenuousness, with the (Qur'an).

53. It is He Who has let free the two bodies of flowing water: One palatable and sweet, and the other salt and bitter; yet has He made

---

heena yarawnal-'azaaba man adallu sabeelaa.

43. Ara'ayta manit-takhaza ilaahahoo hawaahu afa-anta takoonu 'alayhi wakeelaa.

44. Am taḥsabu anna aksarahum yasma'oona aw ya'qiloon; in hum illaa kal-an'aami bal hum adallu sabeelaa.

(Section 4)

45. Alam tara ilaa Rabbika kayfa maddaz-zilla wa law shaaa'a laja'alahoo saakinan summa ja'alnash-shamsa 'alayhi daleelaa.

46. Summa qabadnaahu ilaynaa qabdañy-yaseeraa.

47. Wa Huwal-lazee ja'ala lakumul-layla libaasañw-wannawma subaatañw-wa ja'alan-nahaara nushooraa.

48. Wa Huwal-lazeee arsalar-riyaaḥa bushram bayna yaday raḥmatih; wa anzalnaa minas-samaaa'i maaa'an ṭahooraa.

49. Linuḥyiya bihee balda-tam-maytañw-wa nusqiyahoo mimmaa khalaqnaaa an'aa-mañw-wa anaasiyya kaseeraa.

50. Wa laqad ṣarrafnaahu baynahum li-yazzakkaroo fa-abaaa aksarun-naasi illaa kufooraa.

51. Wa law shi'naa laba'asnaa fee kulli qar-yatin-nazeeraa.

52. Falaa tuṭi'il-kaafireena wa jaahidhum bihee jihaadan kabeeraa.

53. Wa Huwal-lazee marajal-baḥrayni haazaa 'azbun furaatuñw-wa haazaa milḥun ujaaj; wa ja'ala

a barrier between them, a partition that is forbidden to be passed.

54. It is He Who has created man from water: then has He established relationships of lineage and marriage: for your Lord has power (over all things).

55. Yet do they worship, besides Allah, things that can neither profit them nor harm them: and the Misbeliever is a helper (of Evil), against his own Lord!

56. But you We only sent to give glad tidings and admonition.

57. Say: "No reward do I ask of you for it but this: that each one who will may take a (straight) Path to his Lord."

58. And put your trust in Him Who lives and dies not; and celebrate his praise; and enough is He to be acquainted with the faults of His servants;-

59. He Who created the heavens and the earth and all that is between, in six days, and is firmly established on the Throne (of Authority): Allah Most Gracious: ask you, then, about Him of any acquainted (with such things).

60. When it is said to them, "Adore you (Allah) Most Gracious!", they say, "And what is (Allah) Most Gracious? Shall we adore That which you command us?" And it increases their flight (from the Truth).

61. Blessed is He Who made constellations in the skies, and placed therein a Lamp and a Moon giving light;

62. And it is He Who made the Night and the Day to follow each other: for such as desire to be mindful or to show their gratitude.

63. And the servants of (Allah) Most Gracious are those who walk on the earth in humility, and when the

baynahumaa barzakhañw-wa hijram-mahjooraa.

54. Wa Huwal-lazee khalaqa minal-maaa'i basharan fa-ja'alahoo nasabañw-wa sihraa; wa kaana Rabbuka Qadeeraa.

55. Wa ya'budoona min doonil-laahi maa laa yanfa-'uhum wa laa yadurruhum; wa kaanal-kaafiru 'alaa Rabbihee zaheeraa.

56. Wa maa arsalnaaka illaa mubashshirañw-wa nazeeraa.

57. Qul maaa as'alukum 'alayhi min ajrin illaa man shaaa'a añy-yattakhiza ilaa Rabbihee sabeelaa.

58. Wa tawakkal 'alal-Hayyil-lazee laa yamootu wa sabbih bihamdih; wa kafaa bihee bizunoobi 'ibaadihee khabeeraa.

59. Allazee khalaqas-samaa-waati wal-arda wa maa baynahumaa fee sittati ayyaa-min summastawaa 'alal-'Arsh; ar-Rahmaanu fas'al bihee khabeeraa.

60. Wa izaa qeela lahumus-judoo lir-Rahmaani qaaloo wa mar-Rahmaanu anasjudu limaa taamurunaa wa zaadahum nufooraa. (Section 5)

61. Tabaarakal-lazee ja'ala fis-samaaa'i buroojañw-wa ja'ala feehaa siraajañw-wa qamaram-muneeraa.

62. Wa Huwal-lazee ja'alal-layla wannahaara khilfatal-liman araada añy-yazzakkara aw araada shukooraa.

63. Wa 'ibaadur-Rahmaanil-lazeena yamshoona 'alal-ardi hawnañw-wa izaa khaata-bahumul-

(Bow Down)

ignorant address them, they say, "Peace!";

64. Those who spend the night in adoration of their Lord prostrate and standing;

65. Those who say, "Our Lord! avert from us the Wrath of Hell, for its Wrath is indeed an affliction grievous,-

66. "Evil indeed is it as an abode, and as a place to rest in";

67. Those who, when they spend, are not extravagant and not niggardly, but hold a just (balance) between those (extremes).

68. Those who do not invoke, with Allah, any other god, nor slay such life as Allah has made sacred except for just cause, nor commit fornication; - and any that does this (not only) meets punishment.

69. (But) the Penalty on the Day of Judgment will be doubled to him, and he will dwell therein in ignominy,-

70. Unless he repents, believes, and works righteous deeds, for Allah will change the evil of such persons into good, and Allah is Oft-Forgiving, Most Merciful,

71. And whoever repents and does good has truly turned to Allah with an (acceptable) conversion;-

72. Those who witness no falsehood, and, if they pass by futility, they pass by it with honorable (avoidance);

73. Those who, when they are admonished with the Signs of their Lord, droop not down at them as if they were deaf or blind;

74. And those who pray, "Our Lord! Grant unto us wives and offspring who will be the comfort of our eyes, and

jaahiloona qaaloo salaamaa.

64. Wallazeena yabeetoona li-Rabbihim sujjadanw-wa qiyaamaa.

65. Wallazeena yaqooloona Rabbanaṣ-rif 'annaa 'azaaba Jahannama inna 'azaabahaa kaana gharaamaa.

66. Innahaa saaa'at mustaqar-ranw-wa muqaamaa.

67. Wallazeena izaaa anfaqoo lam yusrifoo wa lam yaqturoo wa kaana bayna zaalika qawaa-maa.

68. Wallazeena laa yad'oona ma'al-laahi ilaahan aakhara wa laa yaqtuloonan-nafsal-latee ḥarramal-laahu illaa bilhaqqi wa laa yaznoon; wa mañy-yaf'al zaalika yalqa asaamaa.

69. Yuḍaa'af lahul-'azaabu Yawmal-Qiyaamati wa yakhlud feehee muhaanaa.

70. Illaa man taaba wa 'aamana wa 'amila 'amalan ṣaaliḥan fa-ulaaa'ika yubad-dilul-laahu sayyi-aatihim ḥasanaat; wa kaanal-laahu Ghafoorar-Raheemaa.

71. Wa man taaba wa 'amila ṣaaliḥan fa-innahoo yatoobu ilal-laahi mataabaa.

72. Wallazeena laa yash-hadoonaz-zoora wa izaa marroo billaghwi marroo kiraamaa.

73. Wallazeena izaa zukkiroo bi-Aayaati Rabbihim lam yakhirroo 'alayhaa ṣummanw-wa 'umyaanaa.

74. Wallazeena yaqooloona Rabbanaa hab lanaa min azwaajinaa wa zurriyyaatinaa qurrata a'yuninw-waj-

give us (the grace) to lead the righteous."

75. Those are the ones who will be rewarded with the highest place in heaven, because of their patient constancy: therein shall they be met with salutations and peace,

76. Dwelling therein;- how beautiful an abode and place of rest!

77. Say (to the Rejecters): "My Lord is not uneasy because of you if you do not call on Him: but you have indeed rejected (Him), and soon will come the inevitable (punishment)!"

26. The Poets

In the name of Allah, Most Gracious, Most Merciful.

1. *Ta-Sin-Mim.*

2. These are verses of the Book that makes (things) clear.

3. It may be you will kill yourself with grief, that they do not become Believers.

4. If (such) were Our Will, We could send down to them from the sky a Sign, to which they would bend their necks in humility.

5. But there doesn't come to them a newly-revealed Message from (Allah) Most Gracious, but they turn away therefrom.

6. They have indeed rejected (the Message): so they will know soon (enough) the truth of what they mocked at!

7. Do they not look at the earth,- how many noble things of all kinds We have produced therein?

8. Verily, in this is a Sign: but most of them do not believe.

9. And verily, your Lord is He, the Exalted in Might, Most Merciful.

10. Behold, your Lord called Moses: "Go to the people of iniquity,-

'alnaa lilmuttaqeena Imaamaa.

75. Ulaaa'ika yujzawnal-ghurfata bimaa ṣabaroo wa yulaqqawna feehaa taḥiyya-tañw-wa salaamaa.

76. Khaalideena feehaa; ḥasunat mustaqarrañw-wa muqaamaa.

77. Qul maa ya'ba'u bikum Rabbee law laa du'aaa'ukum faqad kazzabtum fasawfa yakoonu lizaamaa.   (Section 6)

Sûrat ash-Shu‘arâ'-26

(Revealed at Makkah)

Bismillaahir Raḥmaanir Raḥeem

1. Ṭaa-Seeen-Meeem.

2. Tilka Aayaatul-Kitaabil-Mubeen.

3. La‘allaka baakhi‘un-naf-saka allaa yakoonoo mu'mi-neen.

4. In-nashaå nunazzil ‘alayhim minas-samaaa'i Aayatan faẓallat a‘naaquhum lahaa khaaḍi‘een.

5. Wa maa yaåteehim-min zikrim-minar-Raḥmaani muḥdasin illaa kaanoo ‘anhu mu‘riḍeen.

6. Faqad kazzaboo fasa-yaå-teehim ambaaa'u maa kaanoo bihee yastahzi'oon.

7. Awa lam yaraw ilal-arḍi kam ambatnaa feehaa min kulli zawjin kareem.

8. Inna fee zaalika la-Aayah; wa maa kaana aksaruhum mu'mineen.

9. Wa inna Rabbaka la-Huwal-‘Azeezur-Raḥeem.   (Section 1)

10. Wa iz naadaa Rabbuka Moosaaa ani'-til-qawmaẓ-ẓaalimeen.

English	Transliteration	Arabic
11. "The people of the Pharaoh: will they not fear Allah?"	11. Qawma Fir'awn; alaa yattaqoon.	قَوْمَ فِرْعَوْنَ أَلَا يَتَّقُوْنَ ۞
12. He said: "O my Lord! I do fear that they will charge me with falsehood:	12. Qaala Rabbi inneee akhaafu añy-yukazziboon.	قَالَ رَبِّ إِنِّيْ أَخَافُ أَنْ يُّكَذِّبُوْنِ ۞
13. "My breast will be straitened. And my speech may not go (smoothly): so send unto Aaron.	13. Wa yaḍeequ ṣadree wa laa yanṭaliqu lisaanee fa-arsil ilaa Haaroon.	وَيَضِيْقُ صَدْرِيْ وَلَا يَنْطَلِقُ لِسَانِيْ فَأَرْسِلْ إِلَىٰ هٰرُوْنَ ۞
14. "And (further), they have a charge of crime against me; and I fear they may slay me."	14. Wa lahum 'alayya zambun fa-akhaafu añy-yaqtuloon.	وَلَهُمْ عَلَيَّ ذَنْبٌ فَأَخَافُ أَنْ يَّقْتُلُوْنِ ۞
15. Allah said: "By no means! proceed then, both of you, with Our Signs; We are with you, and will listen (to your call).	15. Qaala kallaa fazhabaa bi-Aayaatinaaa innaa ma'akum mustami'oon.	قَالَ كَلَّا فَاذْهَبَا بِاٰيٰتِنَا إِنَّا مَعَكُمْ مُّسْتَمِعُوْنَ ۞
16. "So go forth, both of you, to Pharaoh, and say: 'We have been sent by the Lord and Cherisher of the worlds;	16. Faåtiyaa Fir'awna faqoo-laaa innaa Rasoolu Rabbil-'aalameen.	فَأْتِيَا فِرْعَوْنَ فَقُوْلَا إِنَّا رَسُوْلُ رَبِّ الْعٰلَمِيْنَ ۞
17. "'You send with us the Children of Israel.'"	17. An arsil ma'anaa Baneee Israaa'eel.	أَنْ أَرْسِلْ مَعَنَا بَنِيْ إِسْرَآءِيْلَ ۞
18. (Pharaoh) said: "Did we not cherish you as a child among us, and did you not stay in our midst many years of your life?	18. Qaala alam nurabbika feenaa waleedañw-wa labiṣta feenaa min 'umurika sineen.	قَالَ أَلَمْ نُرَبِّكَ فِيْنَا وَلِيْدًا وَّلَبِثْتَ فِيْنَا مِنْ عُمُرِكَ سِنِيْنَ ۞
19. "And you did a deed of yours which (you know) you did, and you are an ungrateful (wretch)!"	19. Wa fa'alta fa'latakal-latee fa'alta wa anta minal-kaafireen.	وَفَعَلْتَ فَعْلَتَكَ الَّتِيْ فَعَلْتَ وَأَنْتَ مِنَ الْكٰفِرِيْنَ ۞
20. Moses said: "I did it then, when I was in error.	20. Qaala fa'altuhaaa izañw-wa ana minaḍ-ḍaaalleen.	قَالَ فَعَلْتُهَا إِذًا وَّأَنَا مِنَ الضَّالِّيْنَ ۞
21. "So I fled from you (all) when I feared you; but my Lord has (since) invested me with judgment (and wisdom) and appointed me as one of the Messenger.	21. Fafarartu minkum lam-maa khiftukum fawahaba lee Rabbee ḥukmañw-wa ja'alanee minal-mursaleen.	فَفَرَرْتُ مِنْكُمْ لَمَّا خِفْتُكُمْ فَوَهَبَ لِيْ رَبِّيْ حُكْمًا وَّجَعَلَنِيْ مِنَ الْمُرْسَلِيْنَ ۞
22. "And this is the favor with which you do reproach me,- that you have enslaved the Children of Israel!"	22. Wa tilka ni'matun tamun-nuhaa 'alayya an 'abbatta Baneee Israaa'eel.	وَتِلْكَ نِعْمَةٌ تَمُنُّهَا عَلَيَّ أَنْ عَبَّدْتَّ بَنِيْ إِسْرَآءِيْلَ ۞
23. Pharaoh said: "And who is the 'Lord and Cherisher of the worlds'?"	23. Qaala Fir'awnu wa maa Rabbul-'aalameen.	قَالَ فِرْعَوْنُ وَمَا رَبُّ الْعٰلَمِيْنَ ۞
24. (Moses) said: "The Lord and Cherisher of the heavens and the earth, and all between,- if you want to be quite sure."	24. Qaala Rabbus-samaawaati wal-arḍi wa maa baynahumaa in kuntum-mooqineen.	قَالَ رَبُّ السَّمٰوٰتِ وَالْأَرْضِ وَمَا بَيْنَهُمَا إِنْ كُنْتُمْ مُّوْقِنِيْنَ ۞
25. (Pharaoh) said to those around: "Did you not listen (to what he says)?"	25. Qaala liman ḥawlahooo alaa tastami'oon.	قَالَ لِمَنْ حَوْلَهُ أَلَا تَسْتَمِعُوْنَ ۞
26. (Moses) said: "Your Lord and the Lord of your fathers from the beginning!"	26. Qaala Rabbukum wa Rabbu aabaaa'ikumul-awwaleen.	قَالَ رَبُّكُمْ وَرَبُّ اٰبَآئِكُمُ الْأَوَّلِيْنَ ۞
27. (Pharaoh) said: "Truly your Messenger who has been sent	27. Qaala inna Rasoolaku-mul-lazee ursila	قَالَ إِنَّ رَسُوْلَكُمُ الَّذِيْ أُرْسِلَ

to you is a veritable madman!"

ilaykum lamajnoon.

إِلَيْكُمْ لَمَجْنُونٌ ۝

28. (Moses) said: "Lord of the East and the West, and all between! if you only had sense!"

28. Qaala Rabbul-mashriqi walmaghribi wa maa bayna-humaa in kuntum ta'qiloon.

قَالَ رَبُّ الْمَشْرِقِ وَالْمَغْرِبِ وَمَا بَيْنَهُمَا ۖ إِنْ كُنْتُمْ تَعْقِلُونَ ۝

29. (Pharaoh) said: "If you do put forward any god other than me, I will certainly put you in prison!"

29. Qaala la'init-takhazta ilaahan ghayree la-aj'alannaka minal-masjooneen.

قَالَ لَئِنِ اتَّخَذْتَ إِلَٰهًا غَيْرِي لَأَجْعَلَنَّكَ مِنَ الْمَسْجُونِينَ ۝

30. (Moses) said: "Even if I showed you something clear (and) convincing?"

30. Qaala awalaw ji'tuka bishay'im-mubeen.

قَالَ أَوَلَوْ جِئْتُكَ بِشَيْءٍ مُبِينٍ ۝

31. (Pharaoh) said: "Show it then, if you tell the truth!"

31. Qaala faati biheee in kunta minaṣ-ṣaadiqeen.

قَالَ فَأْتِ بِهِ إِنْ كُنْتَ مِنَ الصَّادِقِينَ ۝

32. So (Moses) threw his rod, and behold, it was a serpent, plain (for all to see)!

32. Fa-alqaa 'aṣaahu fa-izaa hiya su'baanum-mubeen.

فَأَلْقَى عَصَاهُ فَإِذَا هِيَ ثُعْبَانٌ مُبِينٌ ۝

33. And he drew out his hand, and behold, it was white to all beholders!

33. Wa naza'a yadahoo fa-izaa hiya bayḍaaa'u linnaa-ẓireen.   (Section 2)

وَنَزَعَ يَدَهُ فَإِذَا هِيَ بَيْضَاءُ لِلنَّاظِرِينَ ۝

34. (Pharaoh) said to the Chiefs around him: "This is indeed a sorcerer well-versed:

34. Qaala lilmala-i ḥawlahooo inna haaẓaa lasaaḥirun 'aleem.

قَالَ لِلْمَلَإِ حَوْلَهُ إِنَّ هَٰذَا لَسَاحِرٌ عَلِيمٌ ۝

35. "His plan is to get you out of your land by his sorcery; then what is it you counsel?"

35. Yureedu añy-yukhrijakum min arḍikum bisiḥrihee famaa-zaa taåmuroon.

يُرِيدُ أَنْ يُخْرِجَكُمْ مِنْ أَرْضِكُمْ بِسِحْرِهِ فَمَاذَا تَأْمُرُونَ ۝

36. They said: "Keep him and his brother in suspense (for a while), and dispatch to the Cities heralds to collect-

36. Qaalooo arjih wa akhaahu wab'aṣ filmadaaa'ini ḥaashi-reen.

قَالُوا أَرْجِهْ وَأَخَاهُ وَابْعَثْ فِي الْمَدَائِنِ حَاشِرِينَ ۝

37. "And bring up to you all (our) sorcerers well-versed."

37. Yaåtooka bikulli saḥ-ḥaarin 'aleem.

يَأْتُوكَ بِكُلِّ سَحَّارٍ عَلِيمٍ ۝

38. So the sorcerers were got together for the appointment of a day well-known,

38. Fa-jumi'as-saḥaratu li-meeqaati Yawmim-ma'loom.

فَجُمِعَ السَّحَرَةُ لِمِيقَاتِ يَوْمٍ مَعْلُومٍ ۝

39. And the people were told: "Are you (now) assembled?-

39. Wa qeela linnaasi hal antum-mujtami'oon.

وَقِيلَ لِلنَّاسِ هَلْ أَنْتُمْ مُجْتَمِعُونَ ۝

40. "That we may follow the sorcerers (in religion) if they win?"

40. La'allanaa nattabi'us-saḥarata in kaanoo humul-ghaalibeen..

لَعَلَّنَا نَتَّبِعُ السَّحَرَةَ إِنْ كَانُوا هُمُ الْغَالِبِينَ ۝

41. So when the sorcerers arrived, they said to Pharaoh:

41. Falammaa jaaa'as-saha-ratu qaaloo li-Fir'awna

فَلَمَّا جَاءَ السَّحَرَةُ قَالُوا لِفِرْعَوْنَ

"Of course - shall we have a (suitable) reward if we win?

42. He said: "Yes, (and more),- for you shall in that case be (raised to posts) nearest (to my person)."

43. Moses said to them: "Throw you - that which you are about to throw!"

44. So they threw their ropes and their rods, and said: "By the might of Pharaoh, it is we who will certainly win!"

45. Then Moses threw his rod, when, behold, it straightway swallows up all the falsehoods which they fake!

46. Then did the sorcerers fall down, prostrate in adoration,

47. Saying: "We believe in the Lord of the Worlds,

48. "The Lord of Moses and Aaron."

49. Said (Pharaoh): "You believe in Him before I give you permission? surely he is your leader, who has taught you sorcery! but soon you shall know! "Be sure I will cut off your hands and your feet on opposite sides, and I will cause you all to die on the cross!"

50. They said: "No matter! for us, we shall but return to our Lord!

51. "Only, our desire is that our Lord will forgive us our faults, that we may become foremost among the Believers!"

52. By inspiration We told Moses: "Travel by night with my servants; for surely you shall be pursued."

53. Then Pharaoh sent heralds to (all) the Cities,

54. (Saying): "These (Israelites) are but a small band,

55. "And they are raging furiously against us;

56. "But we are a multitude amply fore-warned."

a'inna lanaa la-ajran in kunnaa nahnul-ghaalibeen.

42. Qaala na‘am wa innakum izal-laminal-muqarrabeen.

43. Qaala lahum-Moosaaa alqoo maaa antum-mulqoon.

44. Fa-alqaw hibaalahum wa ‘işiyyahum wa qaaloo bi‘izzati Fir‘awna innaa lanaḥnul-ghaaliboon.

45. Fa-alqaa Moosaa ‘aşaahu fa-izaa hiya talqafu maa yaåfikoon.

46. Fa-ulqiyas-saḥaratu saajideen.

47. Qaalooo aamannaa bi-Rabbil-‘aalameen.

48. Rabbi Moosaa wa Haaroon.

49. Qaala aamantum lahoo qabla an aazana lakum innahoo lakabeerukumul-lazee ‘allamakumus-siḥra falasawfa ta‘lamoon; la-uqaṭṭi‘anna aydiyakum wa arjulakum-min khilaafiñw-wa la-uşallibannakum ajma‘een.

50. Qaaloo laa dayra innaaa ilaa Rabbinaa munqaliboon.

51. Innaa naṭma‘u añy-yagh-fira lanaa Rabbunaa khaṭaa-yaanaaa an kunnaaa awwalal-mu'mineen. **(Section 3)**

52. Wa awḥaynaaa ilaa Moosaaa an asri bi‘ibaadeee innakum-muttaba‘oon.

53. Fa-arsala Fir‘awnu filmadaaa'ini ḥaashireen.

54. Inna haaa'ulaaa'i lashir-zimatun qaleeloon.

55. Wa innahum-lanaa la-ghaaa'izoon.

56. Wa innaa lajamee‘un ḥaaziroon.

57. So We expelled them from gardens, springs,

58. Treasures, and every kind of honorable position;

59. Thus it was, but We made the Children of Israel inheritors of such things.

60. So they pursued them at sunrise.

61. And when the two bodies saw each other, the people of Moses said: "We are sure to be overtaken."

62. (Moses) said: "By no means! my Lord is with me! soon will He guide me!"

63. Then We told Moses by inspiration: "Strike the sea with your rod." So it divided, and each separate part became like the huge, firm mass of a mountain.

64. And We made the other party approach there.

65. We delivered Moses and all who were with him;

66. But We drowned the others.

67. Verily in this is a Sign: but most of them do not believe.

68. And verily your Lord is He, the Exalted in Might, Most Merciful.

69. And rehearse to them (something of) Abraham's story.

70. Behold, he said to his father and his people: "What do you worship?"

71. They said: "We worship idols, and we remain constantly in attendance on them."

72. He said: "Do they listen to you when you call (on them),

73. Or they do you good or harm?"

74. They said: "Nay, but we found our fathers doing thus (what we do)."

75. He said: "Do you then see whom you have been worshipping,-

57. Fa-akhrajnaahum-min Jannaatiñw-wa 'uyoon.

58. Wa kunooziñw-wa ma-qaamin kareem.

59. Kazaalika wa awrasnaa-haa Baneee Israaa'eel.

60. Fa-atba'oohum-mushri-qeen.

61. Falammaa taraaa'al-jam-'aani qaala as-haabu Moosaaa innaa lamudrakoon.

62. Qaala kallaaa inna ma'iya Rabbee sa-yahdeen.

63. Fa-awhaynaaa ilaa Moo-saaa anidrib bi'asaakal-bahra fanfalaqa fakaana kullu firqin kattawdil-'azeem.

64. Wa azlafnaa sammal-aakhareen.

65. Wa anjaynaa Moosaa wa mam-ma'ahooo ajma'een.

66. Summa aghraqnal-aakha-reen.

67. Inna fee zaalika la-Aayaah; wa maa kaana aksaru-hum-mu'mineen.

68. Wa inna Rabbaka la-Huwal-'Azeezur-Raheem.
(Sec. 4)

69. Watlu 'alayhim naba-a Ibraaheem.

70. Iz qaala li-abeehi wa qawmihee maa ta'budoon.

71. Qaaloo na'budu asnaa-man fanazallu lahaa 'aakifeen.

72. Qaala hal yasma'oona-kum iz tad'oon.

73. Aw yanfa'oonakum aw yadurroon.

74. Qaaloo bal wajadnaaa aabaaa'anaa kazaalika yaf-'aloon.

75. Qaala afara'aytum-maa kuntum ta'budoon.

76. "You and your fathers before you?-

77. "For they are enemies to me; not so the Lord and Cherisher of the Worlds;

78. "Who created me, and it is He Who guides me;

79. "Who gives me food and drink,

80. "And when I am ill, it is He Who cures me;

81. "Who will cause me to die, and then to life (again);

82. "And who, I hope, will forgive me my faults on the day of Judgment.

83. "O my Lord! bestow wisdom on me, and join me with the righteous;

84. "Grant me honorable mention on the tongue of truth among the latest (generations);

85. "Make me one of the inheritors of the Garden of Bliss;

86. "Forgive my father, for that he is among those astray;

87. "And let me not be in disgrace on the Day when (men) will be raised up;-

88. "The Day whereon neither wealth nor sons will avail,

89. "But only he (will prosper) that brings to Allah a sound heart;

90. "To the righteous, the Garden will be brought near,

91. "And to those straying in Evil, the Fire will be placed in full view;

92. "And it shall be said to them: 'Where are the (gods) you worshipped-

93. "'Besides Allah? Can they help you or help themselves?'

94. "Then they will be thrown headlong into the (Fire),- they and those straying in Evil,

95. "And the whole hosts of Iblis together.

96. "They will say there in their mutual bickerings:

97. "'By Allah, we were truly in an error manifest,-

---

76. Antum wa aabaaa'ukumul-aqdamoon.

77. Fa-innahum 'aduwwulleee illaa Rabbal-'aalameen

78. Allazee khalaqanee fa-Huwa yahdeen.

79. Wallazee Huwa yuṭ'imunee wa yasqeen.

80. Wa izaa mariḍtu fahuwa yashfeen.

81. Wallazee yumeetunee summa yuḥyeen.

82. Wallazeee aṭma'u añy-yaghfira lee khaṭeee'atee Yawmad-Deen.

83. Rabbi hab lee ḥukmañw-wa alḥiqnee biṣ-ṣaaliḥeen.

84. Waj'al-lee lisaana ṣidqin fil-aakhireen.

85. Waj'alnee miñw-warasati Jannatin-Na‘eem.

86. Waghfir li-abeee innahoo kaana minḍ-ḍaaalleen.

87. Wa laa tukhzinee Yawma yub‘asoon.

88. Yawma laa yanfa‘u maaluñw-wa laa banoon.

89. Illaa man atal-laaha biqalbin saleem.

90. Wa uzlifatil-Jannatu lilmuttaqeen.

91. Wa burrizatil-Jaḥeemu lilghaaween.

92. Wa qeela lahum ayna maa kuntum ta‘budoon.

93. Min doonil-laahi hal yanṣuroonakum aw yantaṣiroon

94. Fakubkiboo feehaa hum walghaawoon.

95. Wa junoodu Ibleesa ajma‘oon.

96. Qaaloo wa hum feehaa yakhtaṣimoon.

97. Tallaahi in kunnaa lafee ḍalaalim-mubeen.

98. "'When we held you as equals with the Lord of the Worlds;

99. "'And our seducers were only those who were steeped in guilt.

100. "Now, then, we have none to intercede (for us),

101. "Nor a single friend to feel (for us).

102. "Now if we only had a chance of return we shall truly be of those who believe!"

103. Verily in this is a Sign but most of them do not believe.

104. And verily your Lord is He, the Exalted in Might, Most Merciful.

105. The people of Noah rejected the Messengers.

106. Behold, their brother Noah said to them: "Will you not fear (Allah)?

107. "I am to you a Messenger worthy of all trust:

108. "So fear Allah, and obey me.

109. "No reward do I ask of you for it: my reward is only from the Lord of the Worlds:

110. "So fear Allah, and obey me."

111. They said: "Shall we believe in you when it is the meanest that follow you?"

112. He said: "And what do I know as to what they do?

113. "Their account is only with my Lord, if you could (but) understand.

114. "I am not one to drive away those who believe.

115. "I am sent only to warn plainly in public."

116. They said: "If you desist not, O Noah! you shall be stoned (to death)."

98. Iz nusawweekum bi-Rabbil-'aalameen.

99. Wa maaa adallanaaa illal-mujrimoon.

100. Famaa lanaa min shaa-fi'een.

101. Wa laa sadeeqin hameem.

102. Falaw anna lanaa karratan fanakoona minal-mu'mineen.

103. Inna fee zaalika la-Aaya-tañw wa maa kaana aksaruhum mu'mineen.

104. Wa inna Rabbaka la-Huwal-'Azeezur-Raheem. **(Sec. 5)**

105. Kazzabat qawmu Noo-hinil-mursaleen.

106. Iz qaala lahum akhoohum Noohun alaa tattaqoon.

107. Innee lakum Rasoolun ameen.

108. Fattaqullaaha wa atee-'oon.

109. Wa maaa as'alukum 'alayhi min ajrin in ajriya illaa 'alaa Rabbil-'aalameen.

110. Fattaqul-laaha wa atee-'oon.

111. Qaalooo anu'minu laka wattaba'akal-arzaloon.

112. Qaala wa maa 'ilmee bimaa kaanoo ya'maloon.

113. In hisaabuhum illaa 'alaa Rabbee law tash'uroon.

114. Wa maaa ana bitaaridil-mu'mineen.

115. In ana illaa nazeerum-mubeen.

116. Qaaloo la'il-lam tantahi yaa Noohu latakoonanna minal-marjoomeen.

117. He said: "O my Lord! truly my people have rejected me.

118. "You judge, then, between me and them openly, and deliver me and those of the Believers who are with me."

119. So We delivered him and those with him, in the Ark filled (with all creatures).

120. Thereafter We drowned those who remained behind.

121. Verily in this is a Sign: but most of them do not believe.

122. And verily your Lord is He, the Exalted in Might, Most Merciful.

123. The 'Ad (people) rejected the Messengers.

124. Behold, their brother Hud said to them: "Will you not fear (Allah)?

125. "I am to you a Messenger worthy of all trust:

126. "So fear Allah and obey me.

127. "No reward do I ask of you for it: my reward is only from the Lord of the Worlds.

128. "Do you build a landmark on every high place to amuse yourselves?

129. "And do you get for yourselves fine buildings in the hope of living therein (for ever)?

130. "And when you strike, you strike like tyrants.

131. "Now fear Allah, and obey me.

132. "Yes, fear Him Who has bestowed on you freely all that you know.

133. "Freely has He bestowed on you cattle and sons,-

134. "And Gardens and Springs.

135. "Truly I fear for you the Penalty of a Great Day."

---

117. Qaala Rabbi inna qawmee kazzaboon.

118. Faftah baynee wa bay-nahum fat-hanw-wa najjinee wa mam-ma'iya minal-mu'mineen.

119. Fa-anjaynaahu wa mam-ma'ahoo fil-fulkil-mashhoon.

120. Summa aghraqnaa ba'dul-baaqeen.

121. Inna fee zaalika la-Aayaah; wa maa kaana aksaru-hum-mu'mineen.

122. Wa inna Rabbaka la-Huwal-'Azeezur-Raheem. (Sec. 6)

123. Kazzabat 'Aadunil-mursaleen.

124. Iz qaala lahum akhoohum Hoodun alaa tattaqoon.

125. Innee lakum Rasoolun ameen.

126. Fattaqullaaha wa atee'oon.

127. Wa maaa as'alukum 'alayhi min ajrin in ajriya illaa 'alaa Rabbil-'aalameen.

128. Atabnoona bikulli ree'in aayatan ta'basoon.

129. Wa tattakhizoona masaa-ni'a la'allakum takhludoon.

130. Wa izaa batashtum ba-tashtum jabbaareen.

131. Fattaqul-laaha wa atee-'oon.

132. Wattaqul-lazeee amad-dakum bimaa ta'lamoon.

133. Amaddakum bi-an'aa-miñw-wa baneen.

134. Wa jannaatiñw-wa 'uyoon.

135. Inneee akhaafu 'alaykum 'azaaba Yawmin 'azeem.

136. They said: "It is the same to us whether you admonish us or be not among (our) admonishers!

137. "This is no other than a customary device of the ancients,

138. "And we are not the ones to receive Pains and Penalties!"

139. So they rejected him, and We destroyed them. Verily in this is a Sign: but most of them do not believe.

140. And verily your Lord is He, the Exalted in Might, Most Merciful.

141. The Thamud (people) rejected the Messengers.

142. Behold, their brother Salih said to them: "Will you not fear (Allah)?

143. "I am to you a Messenger worthy of all trust.

144. "So fear Allah, and obey me.

145. "No reward do I ask of you for it: my reward is only from the Lord of the Worlds.

146. "Will you be left secure, in (the enjoyment of) all that you have here?-

147. "Gardens and Springs,

148. "And corn-fields and date-palms with spathes near breaking (with the weight of fruit)?

149. "And you carve houses out of (rocky) mountains with great skill.

150. "But fear Allah and obey me;

151. "And do not follow the bidding of those who are extravagant,-

152. "Who make mischief in the land, and do not mend (their ways)."

153. They said: "You are only one of those bewitched!

154. "You are no more than a mortal like us: then bring us a Sign, if you tell the truth!"

136. Qaaloo sawaaa'un 'alay-naaa awa 'azta am lam takum-minal-waa'izeen.

137. In haazaaa illaa khuluqul-awwaleen.

138. Wa maa nahnu bimu'az-zabeen.

139. Fakazzaboohu fa-ahlaknaahum; inna fee zaalika la-Aayah; wa maa kaana aksaruhum-mu'mineen.

140. Wa inna Rabbaka la-Huwal-'Azeezur-Raheem.
(Section 7)

141. Kazzabat Samoodul-mursaleen.

142. Iz qaala lahum akhoohum Saalihun alaa tattaqoon.

143. Innee lakum Rasoolun ameen.

144. Fattaqul-laaha wa atee-'oon.

145. Wa maaa as'alukum 'alayhi min ajrin in ajriya illaa 'alaa Rabbil-'aalameen.

146. Atutrakoona fee maa haahunaaa aamineen.

147. Fee jannaatinw-wa 'uyoon.

148. Wa zuroo'inw-wa nakhlin tal'uhaa hadeem.

149. Wa tanhitoona minal-jibaali buyootan faariheen.

150. Fattaqul-laaha wa atee-'oon.

151. Wa laa tutee'ooo amral-musrifeen.

152. Allazeena yufsidoona fil-ardi wa laa yuslihoon.

153. Qaaloo innamaaa anta minal-musahhareen.

154. Maaa anta illaa basharum-mislunaa faati bi-Aayatin in kunta minas-saadiqeen.

155. He said: "Here is a she-camel: she has a right of watering, and you have a right of watering, (severally) on a day appointed.

156. "Do not touch her with harm, lest the Penalty of a Great Day seize you."

157. But they ham-strung her: then did they become full of regrets.

158. But the Penalty seized them. Verily in this is a Sign: but most of them do not believe.

159. And verily your Lord is He, the Exalted in Might, Most Merciful.

160. The people of Lut rejected the Messengers.

161. Behold, their brother Lut said to them: "Will you not fear (Allah)?

162. "I am to you a Messenger worthy of all trust.

163. "So fear Allah and obey me.

164. "No reward do I ask of you for it: my reward is only from the Lord of the Worlds.

165. "Of all the creatures in the world, will you approach males,

166. "And leave those whom Allah has created for you to be your mates? Nay, you are a people transgressing (all limits)!"

167. They said: "If you do not desist, O Lut! you will assuredly be cast out!"

168. He said: "I do detest your doings."

169. "O my Lord! deliver me and my family from such things as they do!"

170. So We delivered him and his family,- all

171. Except an old woman who lingered behind,

172. But the rest We destroyed utterly.

173. We rained down on them a shower (of brimstone): and evil was the shower on those who were admonished (but heeded not)!

155. Qaala haazihee naaqatul-lahaa shirbuñw-wa lakum shirbu yawmim-ma'loom.

156. Wa laa tamassoohaa bisooo'in fa-yaåkhuzakum 'azaabu Yawmin 'Azeem.

157. Fa'aqaroohaa fa-asbahoo naadimeen.

158. Fa-akhazahumul-'azaab; inna fee zaalika la-Aayah; wa maa kaana aksaruhum-mu'mineen.

159. Wa inna Rabbaka la-Huwal-'Azeezur-Raheem. (Sec. 8)

160. Kazzabat qawmu Looti-nil-mursaleen.

161. Iz qaala lahum akhoohum Lootun alaa tattaqoon.

162. Innee lakum Rasoolun ameen.

163. Fattaqul-laaha wa atee-'oon.

164. Wa maaa as'alukum 'alayhi min ajrin in ajriya illaa 'alaa Rabbil-'aalameen.

165. Ataåtoonaz-zukraana minal-'aalameen.

166. Wa tazaroona maa khalaqa lakum Rabbukum-min azwaaji-kum; bal antum qawmun 'aadoon.

167. Qaaloo la'il-lam tantahi yaa Lootu latakoonanna minal-mukhrajeen.

168. Qaala innee li'amalikum-minal-qaaleen.

169. Rabbi najjinee wa ahlee mimmaa ya'maloon.

170. Fanajjaynaahu wa ahla-hooo ajma'een.

171. Illaa 'ajoozan filghaa-bireen.

172. Summa dammarnal-aa-khareen.

173. Wa amtarnaa 'alayhim-mataran fasaaa'a matarul-munzareen.

174. Verily in this is a Sign: but most of them do not believe.

175. And verily your Lord is He, the Exalted in Might, Most Merciful.

176. The Companions of the Wood rejected the Messengers.

177. Behold, Shu'aib said to them: "Will you not fear (Allah)?

178. "I am to you a Messenger worthy of all trust.

179. "So fear Allah and obey me.

180. "No reward do I ask of you for it: my reward is only from the Lord of the Worlds.

181. "Give just measure, and cause no loss (to others by fraud).

182. "And weigh with scales true and upright.

183. "And do not withhold things justly due to men, nor do evil in the land, working mischief.

184. "And fear Him Who created you and (Who created) the generations before (you)"

185. They said: "You are only one of those bewitched!

186. "You are no more than a mortal like us, and indeed we think you are a liar!

187. "Now cause a piece of the sky to fall on us, if you are truthful!"

188. He said: "My Lord knows best what you do."

189. But they rejected him. Then the punishment of a day of overshadowing gloom seized them, and that was the Penalty of a Great Day.

190. Verily in that is a Sign: but

174. Inna fee zaalika la-Aayah; wa maa kaana aksaruhum mu'mineen.

175. Wa inna Rabbaka la-Huwal-'Azeezur-Raheem. (Sec. 9)

176. Kazzaba As-haabul Ayka-til-mursaleen.

177. Iz qaala lahum Shu'aybun alaa tattaqoon.

178. Innee lakum Rasoolun ameen.

179. Fattaqul-laaha wa atee-'oon.

180. Wa maaa as'alukum 'alayhi min ajrin in ajriya illaa 'alaa Rabbil-'aalameen.

181. Awful-kayla wa laa ta-koonoo minal-mukhsireen.

182. Wa zinoo bilqistaasil-mustaqeem.

183. Wa laa tabkhasun-naasa ashyaaa'ahum wa laa ta'saw fil-ardi mufsideen.

184. Wattaqul-lazee khalaqa-kum waljibillatal-awwaleen.

185. Qaalooo innamaaa anta minal-musahhareen.

186. Wa maaa anta illaa basharum-mislunaa wa in-nazunnuka laminal-kaazibeen.

187. Fa-asqit 'alaynaa kisa-fam-minas-samaaa'i in kunta minas-saadiqeen.

188. Qaala Rabbeee a'lamu bimaa ta'maloon.

189. Fakazzaboohu fa-akha-zahum 'azaabu Yawmiz-zullah; innahoo kaana 'azaaba Yawmin 'Azeem.

190. Inna fee zaalika la-Aayah; wa maa kaana

most of them do not believe.

191. And verily your Lord is He, the Exalted in Might, Most Merciful.

192. Verily this is a Revelation from the Lord of the Worlds:

193. With it came down the spirit of Faith and Truth—

194. To your heart and mind, that you may admonish.

195. In the perspicuous Arabic tongue.

196. Without doubt it is (announced) in the mystic Books of former peoples.

197. Is it not a Sign to them that the Learned of the Children of Israel knew it (as true)?

198. Had We revealed it to any of the non-Arabs,

199. And had he recited it to them, they would not have believed in it.

200. Thus have We caused it to enter the hearts of the sinners.

201. They will not believe in it until they see the grievous Penalty;

202. But the (Penalty) will come to them of a sudden, while they perceive it not;

203. Then they will say: "Shall we be respited?"

204. Do they then ask for Our Penalty to be hastened on?

205. Do you see? If We do let them enjoy (this life) for a few years,

206. Yet there comes to them at length the (Punishment) which they were promised!

207. It will not profit them that they enjoyed (this life)!

208. Never did We destroy a town, but had its warners—

209. By way of reminder; and We never are unjust.

210. No evil ones have brought down this (Revelation):

211. It would neither suit them nor would they be able (to produce it).

212. Indeed they have been removed far from even (a chance of) hearing it.

aksaruhum-mu'mineen.

191. Wa inna Rabbaka la-Huwal-'Azeezur-Raheem. **(Sec. 10)**

192. Wa innahoo latanzeelu-Rabbil-'aalameen.

193. Nazala bihir-Roohul-Ameen.

194. 'Alaa qalbika litakoona minal-munzireen.

195. Bilisaanin 'Arabiyyim-mubeen.

196. Wa innahoo lafee Zuburil-awwaleen.

197. Awalam yakul-lahum Aayatan añy-ya'lamahoo 'ulamaaa'u Baneee Israaa'eel.

198. Wa law nazzalnaahu 'alaa ba'dil-a'jameen.

199. Faqara-ahoo 'alayhim maa kaanoo bihee mu'mineen.

200. Kazaalika salaknaahu fee quloobil-mujrimeen.

201. Laa yu'minoona bihee hattaa yarawul-'azaabal-aleem.

202. Fayaåtiyahum baghta-tañw-wa hum laa yash'uroon.

203. Fa-yaqooloo hal nahnu munzaroon.

204. Afabi-'azaabinaa yasta'ji-loon.

205. Afara'ayta im-matta'naa-hum sineen.

206. Summa jaaa'ahum-maa kaanoo yoo'adoon.

207. Maaa aghnaa 'anhum-maa kaanoo yumatta'oon.

208. Wa maaa ahlaknaa min qaryatin illaa lahaa munziroon.

209. Zikraa wa maa kunnaa zaalimeen.

210. Wa maa tanazzalat bihish-Shayaateen.

211. Wa maa yambaghee lahum wa maa yastatee'oon.

212. Innahum 'anis-sam'i lama'zooloon.

213. So do not call on any other god with Allah, or you will be among those under the Penalty.

214. And admonish your nearest kinsmen,

215. And lower your wing to the Believers who follow you.

216. Then if they disobey you, say: "I am free (of responsibility) for what you do!"

217. And put your trust on the Exalted in Might, the Merciful,

218. Who sees you standing forth (in prayer),

219. And your movements among those who prostrate themselves,

220. For it is He Who hears and knows all things.

221. Shall I inform you, (O people!), on whom it is that the evil ones descend?

222. They descend on every lying, wicked person,

223. (Into whose ears) they pour hearsay vanities, and most of them are liars.

224. And the Poets,- it is those straying in Evil, who follow them:

225. Don't you see that they wander distracted in every valley?-

226. And that they say what they do not practise?-

227. Except those who believe, work righteousness, engage much in the remembrance of Allah, and defend themselves only after they are unjustly attacked. And soon will the unjust assailants know what vicissitudes their affairs will take!

27. The Ants

In the name of Allah, Most Gracious, Most Merciful.

1. *Ta-Sin.* These are verses of the Qur'an,-a book that makes (things) clear;

---

213. Falaa tad'u ma'al-laahi ilaahan aakhara fatakoona minal-mu'azzabeen.

214. Wa anzir 'asheeratakal-aqrabeen.

215. Wakhfiḍ janaaḥaka lima-nit-taba'aka minal-mu'mineen.

216. Fa-in aṣawka faqul innee bareee'um-mimmaa ta'maloon.

217. Wa tawakkal alal-'Azee-zir-Raḥeem.

218. Allazee yaraaka ḥeena taqoom.

219. Wa taqallubaka fis-saaji-deen.

220. Innahoo Huwas-Samee'ul-'Aleem.

221. Hal unabbi'ukum 'alaa man tanazzalush-Shayaaṭeen.

222. Tanazzalu 'alaa kulli affaakin aseem.

223. Yulqoonas-sam'a wa aksaruhum kaaziboon.

224. Washshu'araaa'u yattabi-'uhumul-ghaawoon.

225. Alam tara annahum fee kulli waadiñy-yaheemoon.

226. Wa annahum yaqooloona maa laa yaf'aloon.

227. Illal-lazeena aamanoo wa 'amiluṣ-ṣaaliḥaati wa zakarul-laaha kaseerañw-wantaṣaroo mim ba'di maa ẓulimoo; wa sa-ya'lamul-lazeena ẓalamooo ayya munqalabiñy-yanqali-boon.   (Section 11)

Sûrat an-Naml–27

(Revealed at Makkah)

Bismillaahir Raḥmaanir Raheem

1. Ṭaa-Seeen; tilka Aayaatul-Qur-aani wa Kitaabim-Mu-been.

2. A Guide: and Glad Tidings for the Believers,-

3. Those who establish regular prayers and give in regular charity, and also have (full) assurance of the Hereafter.

4. As to those who do not believe in the Hereafter, We have made their deeds pleasing in their eyes; and so they wander about in distraction.

5. Such are they for whom a grievous Penalty is (waiting); and in the Hereafter theirs will be the greatest loss.

6. As to you, the Qur'an is bestowed upon you from the presence of One Who is Wise and All-knowing.

7. Behold! Moses said to his family: "I perceive a fire; soon will I bring you from there some information, or I will bring you a burning brand to light our fuel, that you may warm yourselves."

8. But when he came to the (fire), a voice was heard: "Blessed are those in the fire and those around: and glory to Allah, the Lord of the worlds.

9. "O Moses! Verily, I am Allah, the Exalted in Might, the Wise!.

10. "Now you throw your rod!" But when he saw it moving (of its own accord)as if it had been a snake, he turned back in retreat, and retraced not his steps: "O Moses!" (it was said), "Fear not: truly, in My presence, those called as Messenger have no fear,-

11. "But if any have done wrong and have thereafter substituted good to take the place of evil, truly, I am Oft-Forgiving, Most Merciful.

12. "Now put your hand into your bosom, and it will come forth white without stain (or harm): (these are) among the nine Signs (you wilt take) to Pharaoh and his people: for they are a people rebellious in transgression."

2. Hudañw-wa bushraa lil-mu'mineen.

3. Allaẓeena yuqeemoonaṣ-Ṣalaata wa yu'toonaz-Zakaata wa hum bil-Aakhirati hum yooqinoon.

4. Innal-laẓeena laa yu'minoona bil-Aakhirati zayyannaa lahum a'maalahum fahum ya'mahoon.

5. Ulaaa'ikal-laẓeena lahum sooo'ul-'aẓaabi wa hum fil-Aakhirati humul-akhsaroon.

6. Wa innaka latulaqqal-Qur-aana mil-ladun Ḥakeemin 'Aleem.

7. Iz qaala Moosaa li-ahli-heee inneee aanastu naaran sa-aateekum-minhaa bikhabarin aw aateekum bishihaabin qabasil-la'allakum taṣṭaloon.

8. Falammaa jaaa'ahaa noo-diya am boorika man finnaari wa man ḥawlahaa wa Sub-ḥaanal-laahi Rabbil-'aalameen.

9. Yaa Moosaaa innahooo Anal-laahul-'Azeezul-Ḥakeem.

10. Wa alqi 'aṣaak; falammaa ra-aahaa tahtazzu ka-annahaa jaaannuñw-wallaa mudbirañw-wa lam yu'aqqib; yaa Moosaa laa takhaf innee laa yakhaafu ladayyal-mursaloon.

11. Illaa man ẓalama ṣumma baddala ḥusnam ba'da sooo'in fa-innee Ghafoorur-Raḥeem.

12. Wa adkhil yaḍaka fee jaybika takhruj bayḍaaa'a min ghayri sooo'in fee tis'i Aayaatin ilaa Fir'awna wa qawmih; innahum kaanoo qawman faasiqeen.

13. But when Our Signs came to them, that should have opened their eyes, they said: "This is sorcery manifest!"

14. And they rejected those Signs in iniquity and arrogance, though their souls were convinced thereof: so see what was the end of those who acted corruptly!

15. We gave (in the past) knowledge to David and Solomon: And they both said: "Praise be to Allah, Who has favored us above many of his servants who believe!"

16. And Solomon was David's heir. He said: "O you people! we have been taught the speech of birds, and on us has been bestowed (a little) of all things: this is indeed Grace manifest (from Allah.)"

17. And before Solomon were marshalled his hosts,- of Jinns and men and birds, and they were all kept in order and ranks.

18. At length, when they came to a (lowly) valley of ants, one of the ants said: "O ants, get into your habitations, lest Solomon and his hosts crush you (under foot) without knowing it."

19. So he smiled, amused at her speech; and he said: "O my Lord! so order me that I may be grateful for Your favors, which You have bestowed on me and on my parents, and that I may work the righteousness that will please You: and admit me, by Your Grace, to the ranks of Your righteous Servants."

20. And he took a muster of the Birds; and he said: "Why is it I do not see

13. Falammaa jaaa'at-hum Aayaatunaa mubṣiratan qaaloo haazaa siḥrum-mubeen.

14. Wa jaḥadoo bihaa wastay-qanat-haaa anfusuhum ẓulmañw-wa 'uluwwaa; fanẓur kayfa kaana 'aaqibatul-muf-sideen. **(Section 1)**

15. Wa laqad aataynaa Daawooda wa Sulaymaana 'ilmaa; wa qaalal-ḥamdu lil-laahil-lazee faḍḍalanaa 'alaa kaseerim-min 'ibaadihil-mu'mineen.

16. Wa warisa Sulaymaanu Daawooda wa qaala yaaa ayyuhan-naasu 'ullimnaa manṭiqaṭ-ṭayri wa ooteenaa min kulli shay'in inna haazaa lahuwal-faḍlul-mubeen.

17. Wa ḥushira li-Sulaymaana junooduhoo minal-jinni wal-insi waṭṭayri fahum yooza'oon.

18. Ḥattaaa izaaa ataw 'alaa waadin-namli qaalat namla-tuñy-yaaa ayyuhan-namlud-khuloo masaakinakum laa yaḥṭimannakum Sulaymaanu wa junooduhoo wa hum laa yash'uroon.

19. Fatabassama ḍaaḥikam-min qawlihaa wa qaala Rabbi awzi'neee an ashkura ni'mata-kal-lateee an'amta 'alayya wa 'alaa waalidayya wa an a'mala ṣaaliḥan tarḍaahu wa adkhilnee biraḥmatika fee 'ibaadikaṣ-ṣaaliḥeen.

20. Wa tafaqqadaṭ-ṭayra faqaala maa liya laaa aral-

the Hoopoe? Or is he among the absentees?

21. "I will certainly punish him with a severe penalty, or execute him, unless he brings me a clear reason (for absence)."

22. But the Hoopoe did not tarry far: he (came up and) said: "I have compassed (territory) which you have not compassed, and I have come to you from Saba with true tidings.

23. "I found (there) a woman ruling over them and provided with every requisite; and she has a magnificent throne.

24. "I found her and her people worshipping the sun besides Allah: Satan has made their deeds seem pleasing in their eyes, and has kept them away from the Path,- so they receive no guidance,-

25. "(Kept them away from the Path), that they should not worship Allah, Who brings to light what is hidden in the heavens and the earth, and knows what you hide and what you reveal.

26. "Allah!- there is no god but He!- Lord of the Throne Supreme!"

27. (Solomon) said: "Soon shall we see whether you have told the truth or lied!

28. "You go, with this letter of mine, and deliver it to them: then draw back from them, and (wait to) see what answer they return".

29. (The queen) said: "You chiefs! here is delivered to me - a letter worthy of respect.

30. "It is from Solomon, and is (as follows): 'In the name of Allah, Most Gracious, Most Merciful:

---

hudhud, am kaana minal-ghaaa'ibeen.

21. La-u‘azzibannahoo ‘azaaban shadeedan aw la-azbahannahooo aw layaåtiyannee bisulṭaanim-mubeen.

22. Famakaṣa ghayra ba‘eedin faqaala aḥattu bimaa lam tuḥiṭ bihee wa ji'tuka min Saba-im binaba-iñy-yaqeen.

23. Innee wajattum-ra-atan tamlikuhum wa ootiyat min kulli shay'iñw-wa lahaa ‘arshun ‘azeem.

24. Wajattuhaa wa qawmahaa yasjudoona lishshamsi min doonil-laahi wa zayyana lahumush-Shayṭaanu a‘maalahum faṣaddahum ‘anis-sabeeli fahum laa yahtadoon.

25. Allaa yasjudoo lillaahil-lazee yukhrijul-khab'a fis-samaawaati wal-arḍi wa ya‘lamu maa tukhfoona wa maa tu‘linoon.

26. Allaahu laaa ilaaha illaa Huwa Rabbul-‘Arshil-‘Azeem. 📌

27. Qaala sananzuru aṣadaqta am kunta minal-kaazibeen.

28. Izhab bikitaabee haazaa fa-alqih ilayhim summa tawalla ‘anhum fanzur maazaa yarji‘oon.

29. Qaalat yaaa ayyuhal-mala'u inneee ulqiya ilayya kitaabun kareem.

30. Innahoo min Sulaymaana wa innahoo bismil-laahir-Raḥmaanir-Raḥeem.

الْهُدْهُدَ اَمْ كَانَ مِنَ الْغَآئِبِيْنَ ۞

لَاُعَذِّبَنَّهٗ عَذَابًا شَدِيْدًا اَوْ لَاَاذْبَحَنَّهٗٓ اَوْ لَيَاْتِيَنِّيْ بِسُلْطٰنٍ مُّبِيْنٍ ۞

فَمَكَثَ غَيْرَ بَعِيْدٍ فَقَالَ اَحَطْتُّ بِمَا لَمْ تُحِطْ بِهٖ وَجِئْتُكَ مِنْ سَبَاٍۭ بِنَبَاٍ يَّقِيْنٍ ۞

اِنِّيْ وَجَدْتُّ امْرَاَةً تَمْلِكُهُمْ وَاُوْتِيَتْ مِنْ كُلِّ شَيْءٍ وَّلَهَا عَرْشٌ عَظِيْمٌ ۞

وَجَدْتُّهَا وَقَوْمَهَا يَسْجُدُوْنَ لِلشَّمْسِ مِنْ دُوْنِ اللّٰهِ وَزَيَّنَ لَهُمُ الشَّيْطٰنُ اَعْمَالَهُمْ فَصَدَّهُمْ عَنِ السَّبِيْلِ فَهُمْ لَا يَهْتَدُوْنَ ۞

اَلَّا يَسْجُدُوْا لِلّٰهِ الَّذِيْ يُخْرِجُ الْخَبْءَ فِى السَّمٰوٰتِ وَالْاَرْضِ وَيَعْلَمُ مَا تُخْفُوْنَ وَمَا تُعْلِنُوْنَ ۞

اَللّٰهُ لَآ اِلٰهَ اِلَّا هُوَ رَبُّ الْعَرْشِ الْعَظِيْمِ ۩ ۞

قَالَ سَنَنْظُرُ اَصَدَقْتَ اَمْ كُنْتَ مِنَ الْكٰذِبِيْنَ ۞

اِذْهَبْ بِّكِتٰبِيْ هٰذَا فَاَلْقِهْ اِلَيْهِمْ ثُمَّ تَوَلَّ عَنْهُمْ فَانْظُرْ مَاذَا يَرْجِعُوْنَ ۞

قَالَتْ يٰٓاَيُّهَا الْمَلَؤُا اِنِّيْٓ اُلْقِيَ اِلَيَّ كِتٰبٌ كَرِيْمٌ ۞

اِنَّهٗ مِنْ سُلَيْمٰنَ وَاِنَّهٗ بِسْمِ اللّٰهِ الرَّحْمٰنِ الرَّحِيْمِ ۞

31. "'You be not arrogant against me, but come to me in submission (to the true Religion).'"

32. She said: "You chiefs! Advise me in (this) my affair: no affair have I decided except in your presence."

33. They said: "We are endued with strength, and given to vehement war: but the command is with you; so consider what you will command."

34. She said: "Kings, when they enter a country, despoil it, and make the noblest of its people its meanest, thus do they behave.

35. "But I am going to send him a present, and (wait) to see with what (answer) return (my) ambassadors."

36. Now when (the embassy) came to Solomon, he said: "Will you give me abundance in wealth? But that which Allah has given me is better than that which He has given you! Nay it is you who rejoice in your gift!

37. "Go back to them, and be sure we shall come to them with such hosts as they will never be able to meet: we shall expel them from there in disgrace, and they will feel humbled (indeed)."

38. He said (to his own men): "You Chiefs! which of you can bring me her throne before they come to me in submission?"

39. An 'Ifrit, of the Jinns said: "I will bring it to you before you rise from your Council: indeed I have full strength for the purpose, and may be trusted."

40. Said one who had knowledge of the Book: "I will bring it to you within the twinkling of

31. Allaa ta'loo 'alayya waa-toonee muslimeen. **(Section 2)**

32. Qaalat yaaa ayyuhal-mala'u aftoonee feee amree maa kuntu qaati'atan amran ḥattaa tashhadoon.

33. Qaaloo naḥnu uloo quw-watiñw-wa uloo baåsin shadee-d; wal-amru ilayki fanẓuree maazaa taåmureen.

34. Qaalat innal-mulooka izaa dakhaloo qaryatan afsadoohaa wa ja'alooo a'izzata ahlihaaa azillah; wa kazaalika yaf-'aloon.

35. Wa innee mursilatun ilayhim bihadiyyatin fanaa-ziratum bima yarji'ul-mursa-loon.

36. Falammaa jaaa'a Sulay-maana qaala atumiddoonani bimaalin famaaa aataaniyal-laahu khayrum-mimmaaa aataakum bal antum bihadi-yyatikum tafraḥoon.

37. Irji' ilayhim falanaåtiyan-nahum bijunoodil-laa qibala lahum bihaa wa lanukhri-jannahum-minhaaa azillatañw-wa hum ṣaaghiroon.

38. Qaala yaaa ayyuhal-mala'u ayyukum yaåteenee bi'arshihaa qabla añy-yaå-toonee muslimeen.

39. Qaala 'ifreetum-minal-jinni ana aateeka bihee qabla an taqooma mim-maqaamika wa innee 'alayhi laqawiyyun ameen.

40. Qaalal-lazee 'indahoo 'ilmum-minal-Kitaabi ana aateeka bihee qabla añy-yar-tadda ilayka

أَلَّا تَعْلُوا عَلَيَّ وَأْتُونِي مُسْلِمِينَ ۝

قَالَتْ يَٰٓأَيُّهَا الْمَلَؤُا۟ أَفْتُونِي فِي أَمْرِي ۚ مَا كُنتُ قَاطِعَةً أَمْرًا حَتَّىٰ تَشْهَدُونِ ۝

قَالُوا۟ نَحْنُ أُو۟لُوا قُوَّةٍ وَأُو۟لُوا بَأْسٍ شَدِيدٍ ۙ وَالْأَمْرُ إِلَيْكِ فَانظُرِي مَاذَا تَأْمُرِينَ ۝

قَالَتْ إِنَّ الْمُلُوكَ إِذَا دَخَلُوا قَرْيَةً أَفْسَدُوهَا وَجَعَلُوٓا أَعِزَّةَ أَهْلِهَا أَذِلَّةً ۖ وَكَذَٰلِكَ يَفْعَلُونَ ۝

وَإِنِّي مُرْسِلَةٌ إِلَيْهِم بِهَدِيَّةٍ فَنَاظِرَةٌ بِمَ يَرْجِعُ الْمُرْسَلُونَ ۝

فَلَمَّا جَآءَ سُلَيْمَانَ قَالَ أَتُمِدُّونَنِ بِمَالٍ فَمَآ آتَانِيَ اللَّهُ خَيْرٌ مِّمَّآ آتَاكُم بَلْ أَنتُم بِهَدِيَّتِكُمْ تَفْرَحُونَ ۝

ارْجِعْ إِلَيْهِمْ فَلَنَأْتِيَنَّهُم بِجُنُودٍ لَّا قِبَلَ لَهُم بِهَا وَلَنُخْرِجَنَّهُم مِّنْهَآ أَذِلَّةً وَّهُمْ صَاغِرُونَ ۝

قَالَ يَٰٓأَيُّهَا الْمَلَؤُا۟ أَيُّكُمْ يَأْتِينِي بِعَرْشِهَا قَبْلَ أَن يَأْتُونِي مُسْلِمِينَ ۝

قَالَ عِفْرِيتٌ مِّنَ الْجِنِّ أَنَا آتِيكَ بِهِ قَبْلَ أَن تَقُومَ مِن مَّقَامِكَ ۖ وَإِنِّي عَلَيْهِ لَقَوِيٌّ أَمِينٌ ۝

قَالَ الَّذِي عِندَهُ عِلْمٌ مِّنَ الْكِتَٰبِ أَنَا آتِيكَ بِهِ قَبْلَ أَن يَرْتَدَّ إِلَيْكَ

an eye!" Then when (Solomon) saw it placed firmly before him, he said: "This is by the Grace of my Lord!- to test me whether I am grateful or ungrateful! and if any is grateful, truly his gratitude is (a gain) for his own soul; but if any is ungrateful, truly my Lord is Free of all Needs, Supreme in Honor !"

41. He said: "Transform her throne out of all recognition by her; let us see whether she is guided (to the truth) or is one of those who receive no guidance."

42. So when she arrived, she was asked, "Is this your throne?" She said, "It was just like this; and knowledge was bestowed on us in advance of this, and we have submitted to Allah (in Islam)."

43. And he diverted her from the worship of others besides Allah: for she was (sprung) of a people that had no faith.

44. She was asked to enter the lofty Palace: but when she saw it, she thought it was a lake of water, and she (tucked up her skirts), uncovering her legs. He said: "This is but a palace paved smooth with slabs of glass." She said: "O my Lord! I have indeed wronged my soul: I do (now) submit (in Islam), with Solomon, to the Lord of the Worlds."

45. We sent (aforetime), to the Thamud, their brother Salih, saying, "Serve Allah": But behold, they became two factions quarrelling with each other.

46. He said: "O my people! why do you ask to hasten on the evil in preference to the good? If only you ask Allah for forgiveness, you may hope to receive mercy.

47. They said: "We augur ill omen do from you and those that are with you".

ṭarfuk; falammaa ra-aahu mustaqirran 'indahoo qaala haazaa min faḍli Rabbee li-yabluwaneeẹ 'a-ashkuru am akfuru wa man shakara fa-innamaa yashkuru linafsihee wa man kafara fa-inna Rabbee Ghaniyyun Kareem.

41. Qaala nakkiroo lahaa 'arshahaa nanẓur atahtadeeẹ am takoonu minal-lazeena laa yahtadoon.

42. Falammaa jaaa'at qeela ahaakazaa 'arshuki qaalat ka-annahoo hoo; wa ooteenal-'ilma min qablihaa wa kunnaa muslimeen.

43. Wa ṣaddahaa maa kaanat ta'budu min doonil-laahi innahaa kaanat min qawmin kaafireen.

44. Qeela lahad-khuliṣ-ṣarḥa falammaa ra-at-hu ḥasibat-hu lujjatañw-wa kashafat 'an saaqayhaa; qaala innahoo ṣarḥum-mumarradum-min qawaareer; qaalat Rabbi innee ẓalamtu nafsee wa aslamtu ma'a Sulaymaana lillaahi Rabbil-'aalameen.   **(Section 3)**

45. Wa laqad arsalnaaa ilaa Samooda akhaahum Ṣaaliḥan ani'-budul-lahha fa-izaa hum fareeqaani yakhtaṣimoon.

46. Qaala yaa qawmi lima tasta'jiloona bissayyi'ati qab-lal-ḥasanati law laa tas-taghfiroonal-laaha la'allakum turḥamoon.

47. Qaaluṭ-ṭayyarnaa bika wa bimam-ma'ak;

He said: "Your ill omen is with Allah; yes, you are a people under trial."

48. There were in the city nine men of a family, who made mischief in the land, and would not reform.

49. They said: "Swear a mutual oath by Allah that we shall make a secret night attack on him and his people, and that we shall then say to his heir (when he seeks vengeance): "We were not present at the slaughter of his people, and we are positively telling the truth.'"

50. They plotted and planned, but We too planned, even while they perceived it not.

51. Then see what was the end of their plot!- this, that We destroyed them and their people, all (of them).

52. Now such were their houses, - in utter ruin, - because they practised wrong-doing. Verily in this is a Sign for people of knowledge.

53. And We saved those who believed and practised righteousness.

54. (We also sent) Lut (as a Messenger): behold, he said to his people, "Do you do what is shameful though you see (its iniquity)?

55. Would you really approach men in your lusts rather than women? Nay, you are a people (grossly) ignorant!

56. But his people gave no other answer but this: they said, "Drive out the followers of Lut from your city: these are indeed men who want to be clean and pure!"

57. But We saved him and his family, except his wife;

qaala ṭaaa'irukum 'indal-laahi bal antum qawmun tuftanoon.

48. Wa kaana fil-madeenati tis'atu rahṭiny-yufsidoona fil-arḍi wa laa yuṣliḥoon.

49. Qaaloo taqaasamoo billaahi lanubayyitannahoo wa ahlahoo summa lanaqoolanna liwaliy-yihee maa shahidnaa mahlika ahlihee wa innaa laṣaadiqoon.

50. Wa makaroo makrañw-wa makarnaa makrañw-wa hum laa yash'uroon.

51. Fanzur kayfa kaana 'aaqibatu makrihim annaa dammar-naahum wa qawmahum ajma-'een.

52. Fatilka buyootuhum khaa-wiyatam bimaa ẓalamoo; inna fee ẓaalika la-Aayatal-liqaw-miñy-ya'lamoon.

53. Wa anjaynal-lazeena aamanoo wa kaanoo yattaqoon.

54. Wa Looṭan iz qaala liqawmiheee ataåtoonal-faa-ḥishata wa antum tubṣiroon.

55. A'innakum lataåtoonar-rijaala shahwatam-min doonin-nisaaa'; bal antum qawmun tajhaloon.

56. Famaa kaana jawaaba qawmiheee illaaa an qaalooo akhrijooo aala Looṭim-min qaryatikum innahum unaasuñy-yataṭahharoon.

57. Fa-anjaynaaahu wa ahla-hooo illam-ra-ataahoo

her We destined to be of those who lagged behind.

58. And We rained down on them a shower (of brimstone): and evil was the shower on those who were admonished (but heeded not)!

59. Say: Praise be to Allah, and Peace on His servants whom He has chosen (for his Message). (Who) is better?- Allah or the false gods they associate (with Him)?

60. Or, who has created the heavens and the earth, and who sends you down rain from the sky? Yes, with it We cause to grow well-planted orchards full of beauty of delight: it is not in your power to cause the growth of the trees in them. (Can there be another) god besides Allah? Nay, they are a people who swerve from justice.

61. Or, who has made the earth firm to live in; made rivers in its midst; set thereon mountains immovable; and made a separating bar between the two bodies of flowing water? (can there be another) god besides Allah? Nay, most of them do not know.

62. Or, who listens to the (soul) distressed when it calls on Him, and Who relieves its suffering, and makes you (mankind) inheritors of the earth? (Can there be another) god besides Allah? Little it is that you heed.

63. Or, who guides you through the depths of darkness on land and sea, and who sends the winds as heralds of glad tidings, going before His Mercy? (Can there be another) god besides Allah?- High is Allah above what they associate with Him!

64. Or, who originates creation, then repeats it, and who gives you sustenance from heaven and earth? (Can there be another) god besides Allah? Say, "Bring forth your argument, if

qaddarnaahaa minal-ghaa-bireen.

58. Wa amṭarnaa 'alayhim-maṭaran fasaaa'a maṭarul-munẕareen. **(Section 4)**

59. Qulil-ḥamdu lillaahi wa salaamun 'alaa 'ibaadihil-lazeenaṣ-ṭafaa; aaallaahu khayrun ammaa yushrikoon.

60. Amman khalaqas-samaa-waati wal-arḍa wa anzala lakum-minas-samaaa'i maaa'an fa-ambatnaa bihee ḥadaaa'iqa ẕaata bahjah; maa kaana lakum an tumbitoo shajarahaa; 'a-ilaahum-ma'al-laah; bal hum qawmuñy-ya'diloon.

61. Amman ja'alal-arḍa qa-raarañw-wa ja'ala khilaalahaaa anhaarañw-wa ja'ala lahaa rawaasiya wa ja'ala baynal-baḥrayni ḥaajizaa; 'a-ilaahum-ma'allaah; bal aksaruhum laa ya'lamoon.

62. Ammañy-yujeebul-muḍ-ṭarra izaa da'aahu wa yakshifus-sooo'a wa yaj'alukum khula-faaa'al-arḍi 'a-ilaahum-ma'al-laahi qaleelam-maa tazak-karoon.

63. Ammañy-yahdeekum fee ẕulumaatil-barri wal-baḥri wa mañy-yursilur-riyaaḥa bushram bayna yaday raḥmatih; 'a-ilaahum-ma'al-laah; Ta'alal-laahu 'ammaa yushrikoon.

64. Ammañy-yabda'ul-khalqa ṣumma yu'eeduhoo wa mañy-yarzuqukum-minas-samaaa'i wal-arḍ; 'a-ilaahum-ma'allaah; qul haatoo burhaanakum in

قَدَّرْنَاهَا مِنَ الْغَابِرِيْنَ ۝

وَأَمْطَرْنَا عَلَيْهِمْ مَّطَرًا ۚ فَسَآءَ مَطَرُ الْمُنْذَرِيْنَ ۝

قُلِ الْحَمْدُ لِلّٰهِ وَسَلٰمٌ عَلٰى عِبَادِهِ الَّذِيْنَ اصْطَفٰى ۗ آللّٰهُ خَيْرٌ أَمَّا يُشْرِكُوْنَ ۝

أَمَّنْ خَلَقَ السَّمٰوٰتِ وَالْأَرْضَ وَأَنْزَلَ لَكُمْ مِّنَ السَّمَآءِ مَآءً ۚ فَأَنْبَتْنَا بِهِ حَدَآئِقَ ذَاتَ بَهْجَةٍ ۚ مَا كَانَ لَكُمْ أَنْ تُنْبِتُوْا شَجَرَهَا ۗ ءَإِلٰهٌ مَّعَ اللّٰهِ ۚ بَلْ هُمْ قَوْمٌ يَّعْدِلُوْنَ ۝

أَمَّنْ جَعَلَ الْأَرْضَ قَرَارًا وَّجَعَلَ خِلٰلَهَا أَنْهَارًا وَّجَعَلَ لَهَا رَوَاسِيَ وَجَعَلَ بَيْنَ الْبَحْرَيْنِ حَاجِزًا ۗ ءَإِلٰهٌ مَّعَ اللّٰهِ ۚ بَلْ أَكْثَرُهُمْ لَا يَعْلَمُوْنَ ۝

أَمَّنْ يُّجِيْبُ الْمُضْطَرَّ إِذَا دَعَاهُ وَيَكْشِفُ السُّوْءَ وَيَجْعَلُكُمْ خُلَفَآءَ الْأَرْضِ ۗ ءَإِلٰهٌ مَّعَ اللّٰهِ ۚ قَلِيْلًا مَّا تَذَكَّرُوْنَ ۝

أَمَّنْ يَّهْدِيْكُمْ فِيْ ظُلُمٰتِ الْبَرِّ وَالْبَحْرِ وَمَنْ يُّرْسِلُ الرِّيٰحَ بُشْرًا بَيْنَ يَدَيْ رَحْمَتِهِ ۗ ءَإِلٰهٌ مَّعَ اللّٰهِ ۚ تَعٰلَى اللّٰهُ عَمَّا يُشْرِكُوْنَ ۝

أَمَّنْ يَّبْدَأُ الْخَلْقَ ثُمَّ يُعِيْدُهُ وَمَنْ يَّرْزُقُكُمْ مِّنَ السَّمَآءِ وَالْأَرْضِ ۗ ءَإِلٰهٌ مَّعَ اللّٰهِ ۚ قُلْ هَاتُوْا بُرْهَانَكُمْ إِنْ

you are telling the truth!"

kuntum ṣaadiqeen.

كُنْتُمْ صٰدِقِيْنَ ۝

65. Say: None in the heavens or on earth, except Allah, knows what is hidden: nor can they perceive when they shall be raised up (for Judgment).

65. Qul laa ya'lamu man fis-samaawaati wal-arḍil-ghayba illal-laah; wa maa yash'uroona ayyaana yub'aṣoon.

قُلْ لَّا يَعْلَمُ مَنْ فِى السَّمٰوٰتِ وَالْاَرْضِ الْغَيْبَ اِلَّا اللّٰهُ ۫ وَمَا يَشْعُرُوْنَ اَيَّانَ يُبْعَثُوْنَ ۝

66. Still less can their knowledge comprehend the Here-after; nay, they are in doubt and uncertainty threat; nay, they are blind thereunto.

66. Balid-daaraka 'ilmuhum fil-Aakhirah; bal hum fee shakkim-minhaa bal hum-minhaa 'amoon. **(Section 5)**

بَلِ ادّٰرَكَ عِلْمُهُمْ فِى الْاٰخِرَةِ ۟ بَلْ هُمْ فِىْ شَكٍّ مِّنْهَا ۫ بَلْ هُمْ مِّنْهَا عَمُوْنَ ۝

67. The Unbelievers say: "What! when we become dust,- we and our fathers,- shall we really be raised (from the dead)?

67. Wa qaalal-lazeena kafa-roo 'a-izaa kunnaa turaabañw-wa aabaaa'unaaa a'innaa lamukhrajoon.

وَقَالَ الَّذِيْنَ كَفَرُوْٓا ءَاِذَا كُنَّا تُرٰبًا وَّاٰبَآؤُنَآ اَئِنَّا لَمُخْرَجُوْنَ ۝

68. "It is true we were pro-mised this,- we and our fathers before (us): these are nothing but tales of the ancients."

68. Laqad wu'idnaa haazaa naḥnu wa aabaaa'unaa min qablu in haazaaa illaaa asaa-ṭeerul-awwaleen.

لَقَدْ وُعِدْنَا هٰذَا نَحْنُ وَاٰبَآؤُنَا مِنْ قَبْلُ ۙ اِنْ هٰذَآ اِلَّآ اَسَاطِيْرُ الْاَوَّلِيْنَ ۝

69. Say: "You go through the earth and see what has been the end of those guilty (of sin)."

69. Qul seeroo fil-arḍi fanẓu-roo kayfa kaana 'aaqibatul-mujrimeen.

قُلْ سِيْرُوْا فِى الْاَرْضِ فَانْظُرُوْا كَيْفَ كَانَ عَاقِبَةُ الْمُجْرِمِيْنَ ۝

70. But grieve not over them, nor distress yourself because of their plots.

70. Wa laa taḥzan 'alayhim wa laa takun fee ḍayqim-mimmaa yamkuroon.

وَلَا تَحْزَنْ عَلَيْهِمْ وَلَا تَكُنْ فِىْ ضَيْقٍ مِّمَّا يَمْكُرُوْنَ ۝

71. They also say: "When will this promise (come to pass)? (Say) if you are truthful."

71. Wa yaqooloona mataa haazal-wa'du in kuntum ṣaadi-qeen.

وَيَقُوْلُوْنَ مَتٰى هٰذَا الْوَعْدُ اِنْ كُنْتُمْ صٰدِقِيْنَ ۝

72. Say: "It may be that some of the events which you wish to hasten on may be (close) in your pursuit!"

72. Qul 'asaaa añy-yakoona radifa lakum ba'ḍul-lazee tasta'jiloon.

قُلْ عَسٰٓى اَنْ يَّكُوْنَ رَدِفَ لَكُمْ بَعْضُ الَّذِىْ تَسْتَعْجِلُوْنَ ۝

73. But verily your Lord is full of grace to mankind: yet most of them are ungrateful.

73. Wa inna Rabbaka lazoo faḍlin 'alan-naasi wa laakinna akṣarahum laa yashkuroon.

وَاِنَّ رَبَّكَ لَذُوْ فَضْلٍ عَلَى النَّاسِ وَلٰكِنَّ اَكْثَرَهُمْ لَا يَشْكُرُوْنَ ۝

74. And verily your Lord knows all that their hearts hide. As well as all that they reveal.

74. Wa inna Rabbaka la-ya'-lamu maa tukinnu ṣudooruhum wa maa yu'linoon.

وَاِنَّ رَبَّكَ لَيَعْلَمُ مَا تُكِنُّ صُدُوْرُهُمْ وَمَا يُعْلِنُوْنَ ۝

75. Nor is there anything of the unseen, in heaven or earth, but is (recorded) in a clear record.

75. Wa maa min ghaaa'ibatin fis-samaaa'i wal-arḍi illaa fee kitaabim-mubeen.

وَمَا مِنْ غَآئِبَةٍ فِى السَّمَآءِ وَالْاَرْضِ اِلَّا فِىْ كِتٰبٍ مُّبِيْنٍ ۝

76. Verily this Qur'an ex-plains to the Children of Israel most of the matters in which

76. Inna haazal-Qur-aana yaquṣṣu 'alaa Baneee Israaa-'eela akṣaral-lazee hum feehi

اِنَّ هٰذَا الْقُرْاٰنَ يَقُصُّ عَلٰى بَنِىْٓ اِسْرَآءِيْلَ اَكْثَرَ الَّذِىْ هُمْ فِيْهِ

they disagree.

77. And it certainly is a Guide and a Mercy to those who believe.

78. Verily your Lord will decide between them by His Decree: and He is Exalted in Might, All-Knowing.

79. So put your trust in Allah: for you are on (the path of) manifest Truth.

80. Truly you can not cause the dead to listen, nor can you cause the deaf to hear the call, (especially) when they turn back in retreat.

81. Nor can you be a guide to the Blind, (to prevent them) from straying: only those will you get to listen who believe in Our Signs, and they will bow in Islam.

82. And when the Word is fulfilled against them (the unjust), we shall produce from the earth a Beast to (face) them: he will speak to them, for that mankind did not believe with assurance in Our Signs.

83. One Day We shall gather together from every people a troop of those who reject Our Signs, and they shall be kept in ranks,-

84. Until, when they come (before the Judgment-seat), (Allah) will say: "Did you reject My Signs, though you did not comprehend them in knowledge, or what was it you did?"

85. And the Word will be fulfilled against them, because of their wrong-doing, and they will be unable to speak (in plea).

86. Do they not see that We have made the Night for them to rest in and the Day to give them light? Verily in this are Signs for any people that believe!

87. And the Day that the Trumpet will be sounded - then will be smitten with terror those who are in the heavens, and those who are on earth, except

yakhtalifoon.

77. Wa innahoo lahudañw-wa raḥmatul-lilmu'mineen.

78. Inna Rabbaka yaqḍee baynahum biḥukmih; wa Huwal-'Azeezul-'Aleem.

79. Fatawakkal 'alal-laahi innaka 'alal-ḥaqqil-mubeen.

80. Innaka laa tusmi'ul-mawtaa wa laa tusmi'uṣ-ṣummad-du'aaa'a izaa wallaw mudbireen.

81. Wa maaa anta bihaadil-'umyi 'an ḍalaalatihim in tusmi'u illaa mañy-yu'minu bi-Aayaatinaa fahum-muslimoon.

82. Wa izaa waqa'al-qawlu 'alayhim akhrajnaa lahum daaabbatam-minal-arḍi tukal-limuhum annan-naasa kaanoo bi-Aayaatinaa laa yooqinoon.

(Section 6)

83. Wa Yawma naḥshuru min kulli ummatin fawjam-mim-mañy-yukazzibu bi-Aayaa-tinaa fahum yooza'oon.

84. Ḥattaaa izaa jaaa'oo qaala akazzabtum bi-Aayaatee wa lam tuḥeeṭoo bihaa 'ilman ammaazaa kuntum ta'maloon.

85. Wa waqa'al-qawlu 'alay-him bimaa ẓalamoo fahum laa yanṭiqoon.

86. Alam yaraw annaa ja'alnal-layla li-yaskunoo feehi wannahaara mubṣiraa; inna fee zaalika la-Aayaatil-liqaw-miñy-yu'minoon.

87. Wa Yawma yunfakhu fiṣ-Ṣoori fafazi'a man fis-samaawaati wa man fil-arḍi illaa

such as Allah will please (to exempt): and all shall come to His (Presence) as beings conscious of their lowliness.

88. You see the mountains and think them firmly fixed: but they shall pass away as the clouds pass away: (such is) the artistry of Allah, who disposes of all things in perfect order: for He is well acquainted with all that you do.

89. If any do good, good will (accrue) to them therefrom; and they will be secure from terror that Day.

90. And if any do evil, their faces will be thrown headlong into the Fire: "Do you receive a reward other than that which you have earned by your deeds?"

91. For me, I have been commanded to serve the Lord of this city, Him Who has sanctified it and to Whom (belong) all things: and I am commanded to be of those who bow in Islam to Allah's Will,-

92. And to rehearse the Qur'an: and if any accept guidance, they do it for the good of their own souls, and if any stray, say: "I am only a Warner".

93. And say: "Praise be to Allah, Who will soon show you His Signs, so that you shall know them"; and your Lord is not unmindful of all that you do.

---

28. The Narration
In the name of Allah, Most Gracious, Most Merciful.

1. *Ta-Sin-Mim.*

2. These are Verses of the Book that makes (things) clear.

3. We rehearse to you some of the story of Moses and Pharaoh in Truth, for people who believe.

---

man shaaa'al-laah; wa kullun atawhu daakhireen.

88. Wa taral-jibaala taḥsabuhaa jaamidataňw-wa hiya tamurru marras-saḥaab; ṣun'allaahil-lazee atqana kulla shay'; innahoo khabeerum bimaa taf'aloon.

89. Man jaaa'a bilḥasanati falahoo khayrum-minhaa wa hum-min faza'iňy-Yawma'iẕin aaminoon.

90. Wa man jaaa'a bissayyi'ati fakubbat wujoohuhum fin-Naari hal tujzawna illaa maa kuntum ta'maloon.

91. Innamaaa umirtu an a'buda Rabba haaẕihil-baldatillazee ḥarramahaa wa lahoo kullu shay'iňw-wa umirtu an akoona minal-muslimeen.

92. Wa an atluwal-Qur-aana famanih-tadaa fa-innamaaa yahtadee linafsihee wa man ḍalla faqul innamaaa ana minal-munẕireen.

93. Wa qulil-ḥamdu lillaahi sa-yureekum Aayaatihee fata'rifoonahaa; wa maa Rabbuka bighaafilin 'ammaa ta'maloon.

(Section 7)

Sûrat al-Qaṣaṣ–28
(Revealed at Makkah)
Bismillaahir Raḥmaanir Raḥeem

1. Ṭaa-Seeen-Meeem.

2. Tilka Aayaatul-Kitaabil-mubeen.

3. Natloo 'alayka min-naba-i Moosaa wa Fir'awna bilḥaqqi liqawmiňy-yu'minoon.

4. Truly Pharaoh elated himself in the land and broke up its people into sections, depressing a small group among them: their sons he slew, but he kept alive their females: for he was indeed a maker of mischief.

5. And We wished to be Gracious to those who were being depressed in the land, to make them leaders (in Faith) and make them heirs,

6. To establish a firm place for them in the land, and to show Pharaoh, Haman, and their hosts, at their hands, the very things against which they were taking precautions.

7. So We sent this inspiration to the mother of Moses: "Suckle (your child), but when you have fears about him, cast him into the river, but fear not nor grieve: for We shall restore him to you, and We shall make him one of Our Messengers."

8. Then the people of Pharaoh picked him up (from the river): (it was intended) that (Moses) should be to them an adversary and a cause of sorrow: for Pharaoh and Haman and (all) their hosts were men of sin.

9. The wife of Pharaoh said: "(Here is) joy of the eye, for me and for you: Do not slay him. It may be that he will be use to us, or we may adopt him as a son." And they did not perceive (what they were doing)!

10. But there came to be a void in the heart of the mother of Moses: she was going almost to disclose his (case), had We not strengthened her heart (with faith), so that she might remain a (firm) believer.

11. And she said to the sister of (Moses), "Follow him". So she (the sister) watched him in the character of a stranger. And they did not know.

4. Inna Fir'awna 'alaa fil-arḍi wa ja'ala ahlahaa shiya'añy-yastaḍ'ifu ṭaaa'ifatam-minhum yuẓabbiḥu abnaaa'ahum wa yastaḥyee nisaaa'ahum; inna-hoo kaana minal-mufsideen.

5. Wa nureedu an-namunna 'alal-lazeenas-tuḍ'ifoo fil-arḍi wa naj'alahum a'immatañw-wa naj'alahumul-waariseen.

6. Wa numakkina lahum fil-arḍi wa nuriya Fir'awna wa Haamaana wa junoodahumaa minhum-maa kaanoo yaḥẓa-roon.

7. Wa awḥaynaaa ilaaa ummi Moosaaa an arḍi'eehi fa-izaa khifti 'alayhi fa-alqeehi filyammi wa laa takhaafee wa laa taḥzaneee innaa raaaddoohu ilayki wa jaa'iloohu minal-mursaleen.

8. Faltaqaṭahooo Aalu Fir-'awna li-yakoona lahum 'aduw-wañw-wa ḥazanaa; inna Fir'aw-na wa Haamaana wa junooda-humaa kaanoo khaaṭi'een.

9. Wa qaalatim-ra-atu Fir-'awna qurratu 'aynil-lee wa lak; laa taqtuloohu 'asaaa añy-yanfa'anaaa aw nattakhizahoo waladañw-wa hum laa yash-'uroon.

10. Wa aṣbaḥa fu'aadu ummi Moosaa faarighan in kaadat latubdee bihee law laaa ar-rabaṭnaa 'alaa qalbihaa lita-koona minal-mu'mineen.

11. Wa qaalat li-ukhtihee quṣ-ṣeehi fabaṣurat bihee 'an junu-biñw-wa hum laa yash'uroon.

12. And we ordained that he refused suck at first, until (His sister came up and) said: "Shall I point out to you the people of a house that will nourish and bring him up for you and be sincerely attached to him?"...

13. Thus did We restore him to his mother, that her eye might be comforted, that she might not grieve, and that she might know that the promise of Allah is true: but most of them do not understand.

14. When he reached full age, and was firmly established (in life), We bestowed on him wisdom and knowledge: for thus do We reward those who do good.

15. And he entered the city at a time when its people were not watching: and he found there two men fighting,- one of his own religion, and the other, of his foes. Now the man of his own religion appealed to him against his foe, and Moses struck him with his fist and made an end of him. He said: "This is a work of Evil (Satan): for he is an enemy that manifestly misleads!"

16. He prayed: "O my Lord! I have indeed wronged my soul! you then forgive me!" So (Allah) forgave him: for He is the Oft-Forgiving, Most Merciful.

17. He said: "O my Lord! For that You have bestowed Your Grace on me, never shall I be a help to those who sin!"

18. In the morning, he was in the City, fearful and vigilant, when he saw, the man who had, the day before, sought his help called aloud for his help (again). Moses said to him:" You are truly, it is clear, a quarrelsome fellow!"

19. Then, when he decided to lay his hands on

12. Wa ḥarramnaa 'alayhil-maraaḍi'a min qablu faqaalat hal adullukum 'alaaa ahli baytiñy-yakfuloonahoo lakum wa hum lahoo naaṣiḥoon.

13. Faradadnaahu ilaaa um-mihee kay taqarra 'aynuhaa wa laa taḥzana wa lita'lama anna wa'dal-laahi ḥaqquñw-wa laa-kinna akṣarahum laa ya'lamoon. **(Section 1)**

14. Wa lammaa balagha ashuddahoo wastawaaa aatay-naahu ḥukmañw-wa 'ilmaa; wa kazaalika najzil-muḥsineen.

15. Wa dakhalal-madeenata 'alaa ḥeeni ghaflatim-min ahlihaa fawajada feehaa raju-layni yaqtatilaani haazaa min shee'atihee wa haazaa min 'aduwwihee fastaghaaṣahul-lazee min shee'atihee 'alal-lazee min 'aduwwihee fawakazahoo Moosaa faqaḍaa 'alayhi qaala haazaa min 'amalish-Shayṭaani innahoo 'aduwwum-muḍillum-mubeen.

16. Qaala Rabbi innee ẓalam-tu nafsee faghfir lee faghafara lah; innahoo Huwal-Ghafoorur-Raḥeem.

17. Qaala Rabbi bimaaa an'amta 'alayya falan akoona ẓaheeral-lilmujrimeen.

18. Fa-aṣbaḥa fil-madeenati khaaa'ifañy-yataraqqabu fa-izal-lazis-tanṣarahoo bil-amsi yastaṣrikhuh; qaala lahoo Moosaaa innaka laghawiyyum-mubeen.

19. Falammaaa an araada añy-yabṭisha billazee

وَحَرَّمْنَا عَلَيْهِ الْمَرَاضِعَ مِنْ قَبْلُ فَقَالَتْ هَلْ أَدُلُّكُمْ عَلَىٰ أَهْلِ بَيْتٍ يَكْفُلُونَهُ لَكُمْ وَهُمْ لَهُ نَاصِحُونَ ۝

فَرَدَدْنَاهُ إِلَىٰ أُمِّهِ كَيْ تَقَرَّ عَيْنُهَا وَلَا تَحْزَنَ وَلِتَعْلَمَ أَنَّ وَعْدَ اللَّهِ حَقٌّ وَّلَٰكِنَّ أَكْثَرَهُمْ لَا يَعْلَمُونَ ۝

وَلَمَّا بَلَغَ أَشُدَّهُ وَاسْتَوَىٰ اٰتَيْنَاهُ حُكْمًا وَّعِلْمًا وَكَذَٰلِكَ نَجْزِي الْمُحْسِنِينَ ۝

وَدَخَلَ الْمَدِينَةَ عَلَىٰ حِينِ غَفْلَةٍ مِنْ أَهْلِهَا فَوَجَدَ فِيهَا رَجُلَيْنِ يَقْتَتِلَانِ هٰذَا مِنْ شِيعَتِهِ وَهٰذَا مِنْ عَدُوِّهِ فَاسْتَغَاثَهُ الَّذِي مِنْ شِيعَتِهِ عَلَى الَّذِي مِنْ عَدُوِّهِ فَوَكَزَهُ مُوسَىٰ فَقَضَىٰ عَلَيْهِ قَالَ هٰذَا مِنْ عَمَلِ الشَّيْطَانِ إِنَّهُ عَدُوٌّ مُّضِلٌّ مُّبِينٌ ۝

قَالَ رَبِّ إِنِّي ظَلَمْتُ نَفْسِي فَاغْفِرْ لِي فَغَفَرَ لَهُ إِنَّهُ هُوَ الْغَفُورُ الرَّحِيمُ ۝

قَالَ رَبِّ بِمَا أَنْعَمْتَ عَلَيَّ فَلَنْ أَكُونَ ظَهِيرًا لِّلْمُجْرِمِينَ ۝

فَأَصْبَحَ فِي الْمَدِينَةِ خَائِفًا يَتَرَقَّبُ فَإِذَا الَّذِي اسْتَنْصَرَهُ بِالْأَمْسِ يَسْتَصْرِخُهُ قَالَ لَهُ مُوسَىٰ إِنَّكَ لَغَوِيٌّ مُّبِينٌ ۝

فَلَمَّا أَنْ أَرَادَ أَنْ يَّبْطِشَ بِالَّذِي

their enemy, that man said: "O Moses! is it your intention to slay me as you slew a man yesterday? Your intention is none other than to become a powerful violent man in the land, and not to be one who sets things right!"

20. And there came a man, running, from the furthest end of the City. He said: "O Moses! the Chiefs are taking counsel together about you, to slay you: so get you away, for I do give you sincere advice."

21. He therefore got away therefrom, looking about, in a state of fear. He prayed "O my Lord! save me from people given to wrong-doing."

22. Then, when he turned his face towards (the land of) Madyan, he said: "I do hope that my Lord will show me the smooth and straight Path."

23. And when he arrived at the watering (place) in Madyan, he found there a group of men watering (their flocks), and besides them he found two women who were keeping back (their flocks). He said: "What is the matter with you?" They said: "We can not water (our flocks) until the shepherds take back (their flocks): and our father is a very old man."

24. So he watered (their flocks) for them; then he turned back to the shade, and said:"O my Lord! truly am I in (desperate) need of any good that You do send me!"

25. Afterwards one of the (damsels) came (back) to him, walking bashfully. She said: "My father invites you that he may reward you for having watered (our flocks) for us." So when he came to him and narrated the story,

huwa 'aduwwul-lahumaa qaala yaa Moosaaa atureedu an taqtulanee kamaa qatalta nafsam bil-amsi in tureedu illaaa an takoona jabbaaran fil-arḍi wa maa tureedu an takoona minal-muṣliḥeen.

20. Wa jaaa'a rajulum-min aqṣal-madeenati yas'aa qaala yaa Moosaaa innal-mala-a yaå-tamiroona bika liyaqtulooka fakhruj innee laka minan-naaṣiḥeen.

21. Fakharaja minhaa khaaa-'ifañy-yataraqqab; qaala Rabbi najjinee minal-qawmiẓ-ẓaali-meen. **(Section 2)**

22. Wa lammaa tawajjaha tilqaaa'a Madyana qaala 'asaa Rabbeee añy-yahdiyanee Sa-waaa'as-Sabeel.

23. Wa lammaa warada maaa'a Madyana wajada 'alayhi ummatam-minannaasi yasqoona wa wajada min doonihimum-ra-atayni tazoo-daani qaala maa khaṭbukumaa qaalataa laa nasqee ḥattaa yuṣdir-ri'aaa'u wa aboonaa shaykhun kabeer.

24. Fasaqaa lahumaa summa tawallaaa ilaẓ-ẓilli faqaala Rabbi innee limaaa anzalta ilayya min khayrin faqeer.

25. Fajaaa'at-hu iḥdaahumaa tamshee 'alas-tiḥyaaa'in qaalat inna abee yad'ooka li-yajziyaka ajra maa saqayta lanaa; falammaa jaaa'ahoo wa qaṣṣa 'alayhil-qaṣaṣa

he said: "you do not fear: (well) have you escaped from unjust people."

26. Said one of the (damsels): "O my (dear) father! engage him on wages: truly the best of men for you to employ is the (man) who is strong and trustworthy."

27. He said: "I intend to wed one of these my daughters to you, on condition that you serve me for eight years; but if you complete ten years, it will be (grace) from you. But I intend not to place you under a difficulty: you will find me, indeed, if Allah wills, one of the righteous."

28. He said: "Be that (the agreement) between me and you: whichever of the two terms I fulfil, let there be no ill-will to me. Be Allah a witness to what we say."

29. Now when Moses had fulfilled the term, and was travelling with his family, he perceived a fire in the direction of Mount Tur. He said to his family: "You tarry; I perceive a fire; I hope to bring you from there some information, or a burning firebrand, that you may warm yourselves."

30. But when he came to the (fire), a voice was heard from the right bank of the valley, from a tree in hallowed ground: "O Moses! Verily I am Allah, the Lord of the Worlds....

31. "Now you throw your rod!" but when he saw it moving (of its own accord) as if it had been a snake, he turned back in retreat, and did not retrace his steps: O Moses!" (It was said), "Draw near, and fear not: for you are of those who are secure.

---

qaala laa takhaf najawta minal-qawmiẓ-ẓaalimeen.

26. Qaalat iḥdaahumaa yaaa abatis-taåjirhu inna khayra manis-taåjartal-qawiyyul-ameen.

27. Qaala ineee ureedu an unkiḥaka iḥdab-natayya haatay-ni 'alaaa an taåjuranee samaa-niya ḥijaj; fa-in atmamta 'ashran famin 'indika wa maaa ureedu an ashuqqa 'alayk; satajiduneee in shaaa'al-laahu minaṣ-ṣaaliḥeen.

28. Qaala ẕaalika baynee wa baynaka ayyamal-ajalayni qaḍaytu falaa 'udwaana 'alayya wallaahu 'alaa maa naqoolu Wakeel.   (Section 3)

29. Falammaa qaḍaa Moosal-ajala wa saara bi-ahliheee aanasa min jaanibiṭ-Ṭoori naaran qaala li-ahlihim-kusooo ineee aanastu naaral-la'alleee aateekum-minhaa bikhabarin aw jazwatim-minan-naari la-'allakum taṣṭaloon.

30. Falammaaa ataahaa noo-diya min shaaṭi'il-waadil-aymani fil-buq'atil-mubaara-kati minash-shajarati any-yaa Moosaaa ineee Anal-laahu Rabbul-'aalameen.

31. Wa-an alqi 'aṣaaka falam-maa ra-aahaa tahtazzu ka-annahaa jaaannuñw-wallaa mudbirañw-wa lam yu'aqqib; yaa Moosaaa aqbil wa laa takhaf innaka minal-aamineen.

32. "Move your hand into your bosom, and it will come forth white without stain (or harm), and draw your hand close to your side (to guard) against fear. Those are the two credentials from your Lord to Pharaoh and his Chiefs: for truly they are a people rebellious and wicked."

33. He said: "O my Lord! I have slain a man among them, and I fear lest they slay me.

34. "And my brother Aaron - He is more eloquent in speech than I: so send him with me as a helper, to confirm (and strengthen) me: for I fear that they may accuse me of falsehood."

35. He said: "We will certainly strengthen your arm through your brother, and invest you both with authority, so they shall not be able to touch you: with Our Signs shall you triumph,- you two as well as those who follow you."

36. When Moses came to them with Our clear signs, they said: "This is nothing but sorcery faked up: never did we hear the like among our fathers of old!"

37. Moses said: "My Lord knows best who it is that comes with guidance from Him and whose end will be best in the Hereafter: certain it is that the wrong-doers will not prosper."

38. Pharaoh said: "O Chiefs! no god do I know for you but myself: therefore, O Haman! light me a (kiln to bake bricks) out of clay, and build me a lofty palace, that I may mount up to the god of Moses:

32. Usluk yadaka fee jaybika takhruj bayḍaaa'a min ghayri sooo'iñw-waḍmum ilayka janaaḥaka minar-rahbi faẓaanika burhaanaani mir-Rabbika ilaa Fir'awna wa mala'ih; innahum kaanoo qawman faasiqeen.

33. Qaala Rabbi innee qataltu minhum nafsan fa-akhaafu añy-yaqtuloon.

34. Wa akhee Haaroonu huwa afṣaḥu minnee lisaanan fa-arsilhu ma'iya rid-añy-yuṣaddiquneee inneee akhaafu añy-yukazziboon.

35. Qaala sanashuddu 'aḍudaka bi-akheeka wa naj'alu lakumaa sulṭaanan falaa yaṣiloona ilaykumaa; bi-Aayaatinaa antumaa wa manittaba'akumal-ghaaliboon.

36. Falammaa jaaa'ahum-Moosaa bi-Aayaatinaa bayyinaatin qaaloo maa haaẓaaa illaa siḥrum-muftarañw-wa maa sami'naa bihaaẓaa feee aabaaa-'inal-awwaleen.

37. Wa qaala Moosaa Rabbeee a'lamu biman jaaa'a bilhudaa min 'indihee wa man takoonu lahoo 'aaqibatud-daari innahoo laa yufliḥuẓ-ẓaalimoon.

38. Wa qaala Fir'awnu yaaa ayyuhal-mala-u maa 'alimtu lakum-min ilaahin ghayree fa-awqid lee yaa Haamaanu 'alaṭ-ṭeeni faj'al-lee ṣarḥal-la'alleee aṭṭali'u ilaaa ilaahi Moosaa

but as far as I am concerned, I think he (Moses) is a liar!"

39. And he was arrogant and insolent in the land, beyond reason,- he and his hosts: they thought that they would not have to return to Us!

40. So We seized him and his hosts, and We flung them into the sea: now behold what was the end of those who did wrong!

41. And we made them (but) leaders inviting to the Fire; and on the Day of Judgment no help shall they find.

42. in this world We made a curse to follow them and on the Day of Judgment they will be among the loathed (and despised).

43. We did reveal to Moses the Book after We had destroyed the earlier generations, (to give) Insight to men, and Guidance and Mercy, that they might receive admonition.

44. You were not on the Western side when We decreed the Commission to Moses, nor were you a witness (of those events).

45. But We raised up (new) generations, and long were the ages that passed over them; but you were not a dweller among the people of Madyan, rehearsing Our Signs to them; but it is We Who send Messengers (with inspiration).

46. Nor were you at the side of (the Mountain of) Tur when we called (to Moses). Yet (are you sent) as Mercy from your Lord, to give warning to a people to whom no warner had come before you: in order that they may receive admonition.

wa innee la-aẓunnuhoo minal-kaazibeen.

39. Wastakbara huwa wa junooduhoo fil-arḍi bighayril-ḥaqqi wa ẓannooo annahum ilaynaa laa yurja'oon.

40. Fa-akhaẓnaahu wa junoo-dahoo fanabaẓnaahum fil-yammi fanẓur kayfa kaana 'aaqibatuẓ-ẓaalimeen.

41. Wa ja'alnaahum a'imma-tañy-yad'oona ilan-Naari wa Yawmal-Qiyaamati laa yun-ṣaroon.

42. Wa atba'naahum fee haaẓihid-dunyaa la'natañw wa Yawmal-Qiyaamati hum-minal-maqbooḥeen. (Section 4)

43. Wa laqad aataynaa Moosal-Kitaaba mim ba'di maaa ahlaknal-quroonal-oolaa baṣaaa'ira linnaasi wa hudañw-wa raḥmatal-la'allahum yata-ẓakkaroon.

44. Wa maa kunta bijaanibil-gharbiyyi iẓ qaḍaynaaa ilaa Moosal-amra wa maa kunta minash-shaahideen.

45. Wa laakinnaaa anshaॱnaa quroonan fataṭaawala 'alay-himul-'umur; wa maa kunta ṣaawiyan feee ahli Madyana tatloo 'alayhim Aayaatinaa wa laakinnaa kunnaa mursileen.

46. Wa maa kunta bijaanibiṭ-Ṭoori iẓ naadaynaa wa laakir-raḥmatam-mir-Rabbika litun-ẓira qawmam-maaa ataahum-min-naẓeerim-min qablika la'allahum yataẓakkaroon.

47. If (We had) not (sent you to the Quraish),- in case a calamity should seize them for (the deeds) that their hands have sent forth, they might say: "Our Lord! why did You not sent us a Messenger? We should then have followed Your Signs and been amongst those who believe!"

48. But (now), when the Truth has come to them from Ourselves, they say, "Why are not (Signs) sent to him, like those which were sent to Moses?" Do they not then reject (the Signs) which were formerly sent to Moses? They say: "Two kinds of sorcery, each assisting the other!" And they say: "For us, we reject all (such things)!"

49. Say: "Then bring you a Book from Allah, which is a better guide than either of them, that I may follow it! (do), if you are truthful!"

50. But if they hearken not to you, know that they only follow their own lusts: and who is more astray than one who follow his own lusts, devoid of guidance from Allah? for Allah does not guide people given to wrong-doing.

51. Now have We caused the Word to reach them themselves, in order that they may receive admonition.

52. Those to whom We sent the Book before this,- they do believe in this (revelation):

53. And when it is recited to them, they say: "We believe therein, for it is the Truth from our Lord: indeed we have been Muslims (bowing to Allah's Will) from before this.

54. Twice will they be given their reward, for that they have persevered, that they avert Evil with Good,

47. Wa law laaa an tuṣeebahum-muṣeebatum bimaa qaddamat aydeehim fa-yaqooloo Rab-banaa law laaa arsalta ilaynaa Rasoolan fanattabi'a Aayaatika wa nakoona minal-mu'mineen.

48. Falammaa jaaa'ahumul-ḥaqqu min 'indinaa qaaloo law laaa ootiya miṣla maaa ootiya Moosaa; awalam yakfuroo bimaaa ootiya Moosaa min qablu qaaloo siḥraani taẓaa-haraa wa qaalooo innaa bikullin kaafiroon.

49. Qul faåtoo bi-Kitaabim-min 'indil-laahi huwa ahdaa minhu-maaa attabi'hu in kuntum ṣaadiqeen.

50. Fa-il-lam yastajeeboo laka fa'lam annamaa yattabi'oona ahwaaa'ahum; wa man aḍalla mimmanit-taba'a hawaahu bighayri hudam-minal-laah; innal-laaha laa yahdil-qawmaẓ-ẓaalimeen. **(Section 5)**

51. Wa laqad waṣṣalnaa lahumul-qawla la'allahum yata-zakkaroon.

52. Allaẓeena aataynaahu-mul-Kitaaba min qablihee hum bihee yu'minoon.

53. Wa iẓaa yutlaa 'alayhim qaaloo aamannaa biheee innahul-ḥaqqu mir-Rabbinaaa innaa kunnaa min qablihee muslimeen.

54. Ulaaa'ika yu'tawna ajra-hum-marratayni bimaa ṣabaroo wa yadra'oona bil-ḥasanatis-

and that they spend (in charity) out of what We have given them.

55. And when they hear vain talk, they turn away therefrom and say: "To us our deeds, and to you yours; peace be to you: we do not seek the ignorant."

56. It is true you will not be able to guide everyone, whom you love; but Allah guides those whom He will and He knows best those who receive guidance.

57. They say: "If we were to follow the guidance with you, we should be snatched away from our land." Have We not established for them a secure sanctuary, to which are brought as tribute fruits of all kinds,- a provision from Ourselves? but most of them do not understand.

58. And how many populations We destroyed, which exulted in their life (of ease and plenty)! now those habitations of theirs, after them, are deserted,- All but a (miserable) few! and We are their heirs!

59. Nor was your Lord the one to destroy a population until He had sent to its centre a Messenger, rehearsing to them Our Signs; nor are We going to destroy a population except when its members practise iniquity.

60. The (material) things which you are given are but the conveniences of this life and the glitter thereof; but that which is with Allah is better and more enduring: will you not then be wise?

61. Are (these two) alike?- one to whom We have made a goodly promise, and who is going to reach its (fulfilment), and one to whom We have given the good things of this life, but who, on the Day of Judgment,

sayyi'ata wa mimmaa razaq-naahum yunfiqoon.

55. Wa izaa sami'ul-laghwa a'radoo 'anhu wa qaaloo lanaaa a'maalunaa wa lakum a'maa-lukum salaamun 'alaykum laa nabtaghil-jaahileen.

56. Innaka laa tahdee man ahbabta wa laakinnal-laaha yahdee mañy-yashaaa'; wa Huwa a'lamu bilmuhtadeen.

57. Wa qaalooo in-nattabi'il-hudaa ma'aka nutakhattaf min ardinaa; awalam numakkil-lahum haraman aaminañy-yujbaaa ilayhi samaraatu kulli shay'ir-rizqam-mil-ladunnaa wa laakinna aksarahum laa ya'lamoon.

58. Wa kam ahlaknaa min qaryatim batirat ma'eeshatahaa fatilka masaakinuhum lam tuskam-mim ba'dihim illaa qaleelaa; wa kunnaa Nahnul-waariseen.

59. Wa maa kaana Rabbuka muhlikal-quraa hattaa yab'asa feee ummihaa Rasoolañy-yatloo 'alayhim Aayaatinaa; wa maa kunnaa muhlikil-quraaa illaa wa ahluhaa zaalimoon.

60. Wa maaa ooteetum-min shay'in famataa'ul-hayaatid-dunyaa wa zeenatuhaa; wa maa 'indal-laahi khayruñw-wa abqaa; afalaa ta'qiloon. (Sec. 6)

61. Afamañw-wa'adnaahu wa'dan hasanan fahuwa laa-qeehi kamam-matta'naahu mataa'al-hayaatid-dunyaa summa huwa Yawmal-Qiyaa-mati

is to be among those brought up (for punishment)?

62. That Day (Allah) will call to them, and say "Where are my 'partners'? - whom you imagined (to be such)?"

63. Those against whom the charge will be proved, will say: "Our Lord! These are the ones whom we led astray: we led them astray, as we were astray ourselves: we free ourselves (from them) in your presence: it was not us they worshipped."

64. It will be said (to them): "Call upon your 'partners' (for help)": they will call upon them, but they will not listen to them; and they will see the Penalty (before them); (how they will wish) 'if only they had been open to guidance!'

65. That Day (Allah) will call to them, and say: "What was the answer you gave to the Messenger?"

66. Then the (whole) story that Day will seem obscure to them (like light to the blind) and they will not be able (even) to question each other.

67. But any that (in this life) had repented, believed, and worked righteousness, haply he shall be one of the successful.

68. Your Lord creates and chooses as He pleases: no choice have they (in the matter): Glory to Allah! and far is He above the partners they ascribe (to Him)!

69. And your Lord knows all that their hearts conceal and all that they reveal.

70. And He is Allah: there is no God but He. To Him be praise, at the first and at the last: for Him is the Command, and to Him shall you (all) be brought back.

71. Say, do you see? If Allah were to make the night perpetual over you to the Day of Judgment, what

minal-muḥḍareen.

62. Wa Yawma yunaadeehim fa-yaqoolu ayna shurakaaa-'iyal-lazeena kuntum taz'u-moon.

63. Qaalal-lazeena ḥaqqa 'alayhimul-qawlu Rabbanaa haaa'ulaaa'il-lazeena aghway-naa aghwaynaahum kamaa gha-waynaa tabarraânaaa ilayka maa kaanooo iyyaanaa ya'bu-doon.

64. Wa qeelad-'oo shura-kaaa'akum fada'awhum falam yastajeeboo lahum wa ra-awul-'azaab; law annahum kaanoo yahtadoon.

65. Wa Yawma yunaadeehim fa-yaqoolu maazaaa ajabtumul-mursaleen.

66. Fa'amiyat 'alayhimul-ambaaa'u Yawma'izin fahum laa yatasaaa'aloon.

67. Fa-ammaa man taaba wa aamana wa 'amila ṣaaliḥan fa'asaaa añy-yakoona minal-mufliḥeen.

68. Wa Rabbuka yakhluqu maa yashaaa'u wa yakhtaar; maa kaana lahumul-khiyarah; Subḥaanal-laahi wa Ta'aalaa 'ammaa yushrikoon.

69. Wa Rabbuka ya'lamu maa tukinnu ṣudooruhum wa maa yu'linoon.

70. Wa Huwal-laahu laaa ilaaha illaa Huwa lahul-ḥamdu fil-oolaa wal-Aakhirati wa la-hul-ḥukmu wa ilayhi turja'oon.

71. Qul ara'aytum in ja'alal-laahu 'alaykumul-layla sarma-dan ilaa Yawmil-Qiyaamati man

مِنَ الْمُحْضَرِيْنَ ۞

وَيَوْمَ يُنَادِيْهِمْ فَيَقُوْلُ اَيْنَ شُرَكَآءِيَ الَّذِيْنَ كُنْتُمْ تَزْعُمُوْنَ ۞

قَالَ الَّذِيْنَ حَقَّ عَلَيْهِمُ الْقَوْلُ رَبَّنَا هٰٓؤُلَآءِ الَّذِيْنَ اَغْوَيْنَا ۚ اَغْوَيْنٰهُمْ كَمَا غَوَيْنَا ۚ تَبَرَّأْنَآ اِلَيْكَ ۖ مَا كَانُوْا اِيَّانَا يَعْبُدُوْنَ ۞

وَقِيْلَ ادْعُوْا شُرَكَآءَكُمْ فَدَعَوْهُمْ فَلَمْ يَسْتَجِيْبُوْا لَهُمْ وَرَاَوُا الْعَذَابَ ۚ لَوْ اَنَّهُمْ كَانُوْا يَهْتَدُوْنَ ۞

وَيَوْمَ يُنَادِيْهِمْ فَيَقُوْلُ مَاذَآ اَجَبْتُمُ الْمُرْسَلِيْنَ ۞

فَعَمِيَتْ عَلَيْهِمُ الْاَنْبَآءُ يَوْمَئِذٍ فَهُمْ لَا يَتَسَآءَلُوْنَ ۞

فَاَمَّا مَنْ تَابَ وَاٰمَنَ وَعَمِلَ صَالِحًا فَعَسٰٓى اَنْ يَّكُوْنَ مِنَ الْمُفْلِحِيْنَ ۞

وَرَبُّكَ يَخْلُقُ مَا يَشَآءُ وَيَخْتَارُ ۗ مَا كَانَ لَهُمُ الْخِيَرَةُ ۚ سُبْحٰنَ اللّٰهِ وَتَعٰلٰى عَمَّا يُشْرِكُوْنَ ۞

وَرَبُّكَ يَعْلَمُ مَا تُكِنُّ صُدُوْرُهُمْ وَمَا يُعْلِنُوْنَ ۞

وَهُوَ اللّٰهُ لَآ اِلٰهَ اِلَّا هُوَ ۖ لَهُ الْحَمْدُ فِى الْاُوْلٰى وَالْاٰخِرَةِ ۖ وَلَهُ الْحُكْمُ وَاِلَيْهِ تُرْجَعُوْنَ ۞

قُلْ اَرَءَيْتُمْ اِنْ جَعَلَ اللّٰهُ عَلَيْكُمُ الَّيْلَ سَرْمَدًا اِلٰى يَوْمِ الْقِيٰمَةِ مَنْ

god is there other than Allah, who can give you enlightenment? Will you not then hearken?

72. Say, do you see? If Allah were to make the day perpetual over you to the Day of Judgment, what god is there other than Allah, Who can give you a Night in which you can rest? Will you not then see?

73. It is out of His Mercy that He has made for you Night and Day,- that you may rest therein, and that you may seek of his Grace;- and in order that you may be grateful.

74. The Day that He will call on them, He will say: "Where are my 'partners'?- whom you imagined (to be such)?"

75. And from each people shall We draw a witness, and We shall say: "Produce your Proof": then shall they know that the Truth is in Allah (alone), and the (lies) which they invented will leave them in lurch.

76. Qarun was doubtless, of the people of Moses; but he acted insolently towards them: such were the treasures We had bestowed on him that their very keys would have been a burden to a body of strong men, behold, his people said to him: "Do not exult, for Allah does not love those who exult (in riches).

77. "But seek, with the (wealth) which Allah has bestowed on you, the Home of the Hereafter, nor forget your portion in this world: but do you good, as Allah has been good to you, and do not seek (occasions for) mischief in the land: for Allah does not love those who do mischief."

ilaahun ghayrul-laahi yaå-teekum biḍiyaaa'in afalaa tasma'oon.

72. Qul ara'aytum in ja'alal-laahu 'alaykumun-nahaara sarmadan ilaa Yawmil-Qiyaa-mati man ilaahun ghayrul-laahi yaåteekum bilaylin taskunoona feehi afalaa tubṣiroon.

73. Wa mir-raḥmatihee ja'ala lakumul-layla wannahaara litaskunoo feehi wa litabtaghoo min faḍlihee wa la'allakum tashkuroon.

74. Wa Yawma yunaadeehim fa-yaqoolu ayna shurakaaa'iyal-lazeena kuntum taz'umoon.

75. Wa naza'naa min kulli ummatin shaheedan faqulnaa haatoo burhaanakum fa'ali-mooo annal-ḥaqqa lillaahi wa ḍalla 'anhum-maa kaanoo yaftaroon. **(Section 7)**

76. Inna Qaaroona kaana min qawmi Moosaa fabaghaa 'alayhim wa aataynaahu minal-kunoozi maaa inna mafaati-ḥahoo latanooo'u bil'uṣbati ulil-quwwati iz qaala lahoo qawmuhoo laa tafraḥ innal-laaha laa yuḥibbul-fariḥeen.

77. Wabtaghi feemaaa aataa-kal-laahud-Daaral-Aakhirata wa laa tansa naṣeebaka minad-dunyaa wa aḥsin kamaaa aḥsanal-laahu ilayka wa laa tabghil-fasaada fil-arḍi innal-laaha laa yuḥibbul-mufsideen.

78. He said: "This has been given to me because of a certain knowledge which I have." Did he not know that Allah had destroyed, before him, (whole) generations,- which were superior to him in strength and greater in the amount (of riches) they had collected? but the wicked are not called (immediately) to account for their sins.

79. So he went forth among his people in the (pride of his wordly) glitter. Said those whose aim is the Life of this World: "Oh! that we had the like of what Qarun has got! for he is truly a lord of mighty good fortune!"

80. But those who had been granted (true) knowledge said: "Alas for you! The reward of Allah (in the Hereafter) is best for those who believe and work righteousness: but this none shall attain, save those who steadfastly persevere (in good)."

81. Then We caused the earth to swallow up him and his house; and he had not (the least little) party to help him against Allah, nor could he defend himself.

82. And those who had envied his position the day before began to say on the morrow: "Ah! it is indeed Allah Who enlarges the provision or restricts it, to any of His servants He pleases! Had it not been that Allah was gracious to us, He could have caused the earth to swallow us up! Ah! those who reject Allah will assuredly never prosper."

83. That Home of the Hereafter We shall give to those who do not intend high-handedness or mischief on earth:

78. Qaala innamaaa ooteetuhoo 'alaa 'ilmin 'indee; awalam ya'lam annal-laaha qad ahlaka min qablihee minal-qurooni man huwa ashaddu minhu quwwataňw-wa akṣaru jam'aa; wa laa yus'alu 'an zunoobihimul-mujrimoon.

79. Fakharaja 'alaa qawmihee fee zeenatih; qaalal-lazeena yureedoonal-ḥayaatad-dunyaa yaalayta lanaa misla maaa ootiya Qaaroonu innahoo lazoo ḥazzin 'azeem.

80. Wa qaalal-lazeena ootul-'ilma waylakum sawaabul-laahi khayrul-liman aamana wa 'amila ṣaaliḥaa; wa laa yulaqqaahaaa illaṣ-ṣaabiroon.

81. Fakhasafnaa bihee wa bidaarihil-arḍa famaa kaana lahoo min fi'atiňy-yanṣuroonahoo min doonil-laahi wa maa kaana minal-muntaṣireen.

82. Wa aṣbaḥal-lazeena tamannaw makaanahoo bil-amsi yaqooloona wayka-annal-laaha yabsuṭur-rizqa limaňy-yashaaa'u min 'ibaadihee wa yaqdiru law laaa am-mannal-laahu 'alaynaa lakhasafa binaa wayka-annahoo laa yufliḥul-kaafiroon. **(Section 8)**

83. Tilkad-Daarul-Aaakhiratu naj'aluhaa lillazeena laa yureedoona 'uluwwan fil-arḍi

and the end is (best) for the righteous.

84. If any does good, the reward to him is better than his deed; but if any does evil, the doers of evil are only punished (to the extent) of their deeds.

85. Verily He Who ordained the Qur'an for you, will bring you back to the Place of Return. Say: "My Lord knows best who it is that brings true guidance, and who is in manifest error."

86. And you had not expected that the Book would be sent to you except as a Mercy from your Lord: therefore you do not lend support in any way to those who reject (Allah's Message).

87. And let nothing keep you back from the Signs of Allah after they have been revealed to you: and invite (men) to your Lord, and be not of the company of those who join gods with Allah.

88. And call not, besides Allah, on another god. There is no god but He. Everything (that exists) will perish except His own Face. To Him belongs the Command, and to Him will you (all) be brought back.

wa laa fasaadaa; wal-'aaqibatu lilmuttaqeen.

84. Man jaaa'a bilḥasanati falahoo khayrum-minhaa wa man jaaa'a bissayyi'ati falaa yujzal-lazeena 'amilus-sayyi-aati illaa maa kaanoo ya'ma-loon.

85. Innal-lazee faraḍa 'alay-kal-Qur-aana laraaadduka ilaa ma'aad; qur-Rabbeee a'lamu man jaaa'a bil-hudaa wa man huwa fee ḍalaalim-mubeen.

86. Wa maa kunta tarjoo añy-yulqaaa ilaykal-Kitaabu illaa raḥmatam-mir-Rabbika falaa takoonanna ẓaheeral-lilkaa-fireen.

87. Wa laa yaṣuddunnaka 'an Aayaatil-laahi ba'da iz unzilat ilayka wad'u ilaa Rabbika wa laa takoonanna minal-mush-rikeen.

88. Wa laa tad'u ma'al-laahi ilaahan aakhar; laaa ilaaha illaa Hoo; kullu shay'in haalikun illaa Wajhah; lahul-ḥukmu wa ilayhi turja'oon.   (Section 9)

---

29. The Spider

In the name of Allah, Most Gracious, Most Merciful.

1. *Alif-Lam-Mim.*

2. Do men think that they will be left alone on saying, "We believe", and that they will not be tested?

3. We tested those before them, and Allah will certainly know those who are true

Sûrat al-'Ankabût–29

(Revealed at Makkah)

Bismillaahir Raḥmaanir Raḥeem

1. Alif-Laaam-Meeem.

2. Aḥasiban-naasu añy-yutra-kooo añy-yaqoolooo aamannaa wa hum laa yuftanoon.

3. Wa laqad fatannal-lazeena min qablihim fala-ya'laman-nal-laahul-lazeena ṣadaqoo

from those who are false.

4. Do those who practise evil think that they will get the better of Us? Evil is their judgment!

5. For those whose hopes are in the meeting with Allah (in the Hereafter, let them strive); for the term (appointed) by Allah is surely coming and He hears and knows (all things).

6. And if any strive (with might and main), they do so for their own souls: for Allah is free of all needs from all creation.

7. Those who believe and work righteous deeds,- from them shall We blot out all evil (that may be) in them, and We shall reward them according to the best of their deeds.

8. We have enjoined on man kindness to parents: but if they (either of them) strive (to force) you to join with Me (in worship) anything of which you have no knowledge, do not obey them. You have (all) to return to me, and I will tell you (the truth) of all that you did.

9. And those who believe and work righteous deeds,- them shall We admit to the company of the Righteous.

10. Then there are among men such as say, "We believe in Allah"; but when they suffer affliction in (the cause of) Allah, they treat men's oppression as if it were the Wrath of Allah! And if help comes (to you) from your Lord, they are sure to say, "We have (always) been with you!" Does not Allah know best all that is in the hearts of all creation?

11. And Allah most certainly knows those who believe, and as certainly those who are Hypocrites.

12. And the Unbelievers say to those who believe:

wa la-ya'lamannal-kaazibeen.

4. Am hasibal-lazeena ya-'maloonas-sayyiaati añy-yasbi-qoonaa; saaa'a maa yahku-moon.

5. Man kaana yarjoo liqaaa-'allaahi fa-inna-ajalal-laahi la-aat; wa Huwas-Samee'ul-'Aleem.

6. Wa man jaahada fa-innamaa yujaahidu linafsih; innal-laaha laghaniyyun 'anil-'aalameen.

7. Wallazeena aamanoo wa 'amilus-saalihaati lanukaf-firanna 'anhum sayyiaatihim wa lanajziyannahum ahsanal-lazee kaanoo ya'maloon.

8. Wa wassaynal-insaana biwaalidayhi husnañw wa in jaahadaaka litushrika bee maa laysa laka bihee 'ilmun falaa tuti'humaa; ilayya marji'ukum fa-unabbi'ukum bimaa kuntum ta'maloon.

9. Wallazeena aamanoo wa 'amilus-saalihaati lanudkhilan-nahum fis-saaliheen.

10. Wa minan-naasi mañy-yaqoolu aamannaa billaahi fa-izaaa ooziya fil-laahi ja'ala fitnatan-naasi ka'azaabil-laahi wa la-in jaaa'a nasrum-mir-Rabbika la-yaqoolunna innaa kunnaa ma'akum; awa laysal-laahu bi-a'lama bimaa fee sudooril-'aalameen.

11. Wa la-ya'lamannal-laahul-lazeena aamanoo wa la-ya'lamannal-munaafiqeen.

12. Wa qaalal-lazeena kafa-roo lillazeena aamanut-

"Follow our path, and we will bear (the consequences) of your faults." Never in the least will they bear their faults: in fact they are liars!

13.   They will bear their own burdens, and (other) burdens along with their own, and on the Day of Judgment they will be called to account for their falsehoods.

14.   We (once) sent Noah to his people, and he tarried among them a thousand years less fifty: but the Deluge overwhelmed them while they (persisted in) sin.

15.   But We saved him and the companions of the Ark, and We made the (Ark) a Sign for all peoples!

16.   And (We also saved) Abraham: behold, he said to his people, "Serve Allah and fear Him: that will be best for you- If you understand!

17.   "For you worship idols besides Allah, and you invent falsehood. The things that you worship besides Allah have no power to give you sustenance: then seek   sustenance from Allah, serve Him, and be grateful to Him: to Him will be your return.

18.   "And if you reject (the Message), so did generations before you: and the duty of the Messenger is only to preach publicly (and clearly)."

19.   Don't they see how Allah originates creation, then repeats it: truly that is

tabi'oo sabeelanaa walnahmil khataayaakum wa maa hum bihaamileena min khataa-yaahum-min shay'in innahum lakaaziboon.

13.   Wa la-yahmilunna asqaa-lahum wa asqaalam-ma'a asqaalihim wa la-yus'alunna Yawmal-Qiyaamati 'ammaa kaanoo yaftaroon.   (Section 1)

14.   Wa laqad arsalnaa Noohan ilaa qawmihee falabisa feehim alfa sanatin illaa khamseena 'aaman fa-akhazahumut-toofaanu wa hum zaalimoon.

15.   Fa-anjaynaahu wa as-haa-bas-safeenati wa ja'alnaahaaa Aayatal-lil'aalameen.

16.   Wa Ibraaheema iz qaala liqawmihi'-budul-laaha watta-qoohu zaalikum khayrul-lakum in kuntum ta'lamoon.

17.   Innamaa ta'budoona min doonil-laahi awsaananw-wa takhluqoona ifkaa; innal-lazeena ta'budoona min doonil-laahi laa yamlikoona lakum rizqan fabtaghoo 'indal-laahir-rizqa wa'budoohu washkuroo lahoo ilayhi turja'oon.

18.   Wa in tukazziboo faqad kazzaba umamum-min qabli-kum wa maa 'alar-Rasooli illal-balaaghul-mubeen.

19.   Awa lam yaraw kayfa yubdi'ul-laahul-khalqa summa yu'eeduh; inna zaalika

easy for Allah.

20. Say: "Travel through the earth and see how Allah did originate creation; so will Allah produce a later creation: for Allah has power over all things.

21. "He punishes whom He pleases, and He grants Mercy to whom He pleases, and towards Him are you turned.

22. "Not on earth nor in heaven will you be able (fleeing) to frustrate (His Plan), nor have you, besides Allah, any protector or helper."

23. Those who reject the Signs of Allah and the Meeting with Him (in the Hereafter),- it is they who shall despair of My Mercy: it is they who will (suffer) a most grievous Penalty.

24. So nothing was the answer of (Abraham's) people except that they said: "Slay him or burn him." But Allah saved him from the Fire. Verily in this are Signs for people who believe.

25. And he said: "For you, you have taken (for worship) idols besides Allah, out of mutual love and regard between yourselves in this life; but on the Day of Judgment you shall disown each other and curse each other: and your abode will be the Fire, and you shall have none to help."

26. But Lut had faith in Him: He said: "I will leave home for the sake of my Lord: for He is Exalted in Might, and Wise."

'alal-laahi yaseer.

20. Qul seeroo fil-arḍi fanzu-roo kayfa bada-al-khalqa summal-laahu yunshi'un-nash-atal-Aakhirah; innal-laaha 'alaa kulli shay'in Qadeer.

21. Yu‘azzibu mañy-ya-shaaa'u wa yarḥamu mañy-yashaaa', wa ilayhi tuqlaboon.

22. Wa maaa antum bimu-‘jizeena fil-arḍi wa laa fis-samaaa'i wa maa lakum-min doonil-laahi miñw-waliyyiñw-wa laa naṣeer.   **(Section 2)**

23. Wallazeena kafaroo bi-Aayaatil-laahi wa liqaaa'iheee ulaaa'ika ya'isoo mir-raḥmatee wa ulaaa'ika lahum ‘azaabun aleem.

24. Famaa kaana jawaaba qawmiheee illaaa an qaaluq-tuloohu aw ḥarriqoohu fa-anjaahul-laahu minan-naar; inna fee zaalika la-Aayaatil-liqawmiñy-yu'minoon.

25. Wa qaala innamat-takhaz-tum-min doonil-laahi awsaa-nam-mawaddata baynikum fil-ḥayaatid-dunyaa summa Yaw-mal-Qiyaamati yakfuru ba‘ḍu-kum biba‘ḍiñw-wa yal‘anu ba‘ḍukum ba‘ḍañw-wa maaa-waakumun-Naaru wa maa lakum-min-naaṣireen.

26. Fa-aamana lahoo Looṭ; wa qaala innee muhaajirun ilaa Rabbee innahoo Huwal-‘Azeezul-Ḥakeem.

27. And We gave (Abraham) Isaac and Jacob, and ordained among his progeny Prophethood and Revelation, and We granted him his reward in this life; and he will be in the Hereafter (of the company) of the Righteous.

28. And (remember) Lut: behold, he said to his people: "You commit lewdness, such as no people in Creation (ever) committed before you.

29. "Do you indeed approach men, and cut off the highway?- and practise wickedness (even) in your councils?" But his people gave no answer but this: they said: "Bring us the Wrath of Allah if you tell the truth."

30. He said: "O my Lord! You help me against people who do mischief!"

31. When Our Messengers came to Abraham with the good news, they said: "We are indeed going to destroy the people of this township: for truly they are (addicted to) crime."

32. He said: "But there is Lut there." They said: "Well do we know who is there : we will certainly save him and his followrs, except his wife: she is of those who lag behind!"

33. And when Our Messengers came to Lut, he was grieved on their account, and felt himself powerless (to protect) them: but they said: "Do not Fear, nor grieve: we

27. Wa wahabnaa lahooo Is-haaqa wa Ya'qooba wa ja'alnaa fee zurriyyatihin-Nubuwwata wal-Kitaaba wa aataynaahu ajrahoo fid-dunyaa wa innahoo fil-Aakhirati laminas-saaliheen.

28. Wa Lootan iz qaala liqawmiheee innakum lataåtoonal-faahishata maa saba-qakum-bihaa min ahadim-minal-'aalameen.

29. A'innakum lataåtoonar-rijaala wa taqta'oonas-sabeela wa taåtoona fee naadeekumul-munkara famaa kaana jawaaba qawmiheee illaaa an qaalu'-tinaa bi'azaabil-laahi in kunta minas-saadiqeen.

30. Qaala Rabbin-surnee 'alal-qawmil-mufsideen.
(Section 3)

31. Wa lammaa jaaa'at Rusu-lunaaa Ibraaheema bil-bushraa qaalooo innaa muhlikooo ahli haazihil-qaryati inna ahlahaa kaanoo zaalimeen.

32. Qaala inna feehaa Lootaa; qaaloo nahnu a'lamu biman feehaa lanunajjiyannahoo wa ahlahooo illam-ra-atahoo kaa-nat minal-ghaabireen.

33. Wa lammaaa an jaaa'at Rusulunaa Lootan seee'a bihim wa daaqa bihim zar'añw-wa qaaloo laa takhaf wa laa tahzan innaa

are (here) to save you and your kinsfolk, except your wife: she is of those who lag behind.

34. "For we are going to bring down on the people of this township a Punishment from heaven, because they have been wickedly rebellious."

35. And We have left thereof an evident Sign, for any people who (care to) understand.

36. To the Madyan (people) (We sent) their brother Shu'aib. Then he said: "O my people! serve Allah, and fear the Last Day: nor commit evil on the earth, with intent to do mischief."

37. But they rejected him: then the mighty Blast seized them, and they lay prostrate in their homes by the morning.

38. (Remember also) the 'Ad and the Thamud (people): clearly will appear to you from (the traces) of their buildings (their fate): the Evil One made their deeds alluring to them, and kept them back from the Path, though they were gifted with Intelligence and Skill.

39. (Remember also) Qarun, Pharaoh, and Haman: there came to them Moses with Clear Signs, but they behaved with insolence on the earth; yet they could not overreach (Us).

40. Each one of them We seized for his crime: of them, against some We sent a violent tornado (with showers of stones); some were caught by a (mighty) Blast; some We caused the earth to swallow up; and some We drowned (in the waters): It was not Allah

munajjooka wa ahlaka illam-ra-ataka kaanat minal-ghaabireen.

34. Innaa munziloona 'alaaa ahli haazihil-qaryati rijzam-minas-samaaa'i bimaa kaanoo yafsuqoon.

35. Wa laqat-taraknaa min-haaa Aayatam-bayyinatal-liqawminy-ya'qiloon.

36. Wa ilaa Madyana akhaa-hum Shu'ayban faqaala yaa qawmi'-budul-laaha warjul-Yawmal-Aakhira wa laa ta'saw fil-ardi mufsideen.

37. Fakazzaboohu fa-akha-zat-humur-rajfatu fa-asbahoo fee daarihim jaasimeen.

38. Wa 'Aadanw-wa Samooda wa qat-tabayyana lakum-mim-masaakinihim wa zayyana lahumush-Shaytaanu a'maala-hum fasaddahum 'anis-sabeeli wa kaanoo mustabsireen.

39. Wa Qaaroona wa Fir-'awna wa Haamaana wa laqad jaaa'ahum-Moosaa bilbay-yinaati fastakbaroo fil-ardi wa maa kaanoo saabiqeen.

40. Fakullan akhaznaa bizam-bihee faminhum-man arsalnaa 'alayhi haasibaa; wa minhum-man akhazat-hus-sayhatu wa minhum-man khasafnaa bihil-arda wa minhum-man aghraq-naa; wa maa kaanal-laahu

Who injured (or oppressed) them: they injured (or oppressed) their own souls.

li-yaẓlimahum wa laakin kaanoo anfusahum yaẓlimoon.

لِيَظْلِمَهُمْ وَلَٰكِنْ كَانُوٓا أَنْفُسَهُمْ يَظْلِمُونَ ۝

41. The parable of those who take protectors other than Allah is that of the Spider, who builds (to itself) a house; but truly the flimsiest of houses is the Spider's house;- if they but knew.

41. Maṣalul-lazeenat-takhazoo min doonil-laahi awliyaaa'a kamaṣalil-'ankaboot, ittakhazat baytaa; wa inna awhanal-buyooti la-baytul-'ankaboot; law kaanoo ya'lamoon.

مَثَلُ الَّذِينَ اتَّخَذُوا مِنْ دُونِ اللَّهِ أَوْلِيَآءَ كَمَثَلِ الْعَنْكَبُوتِ ۖ اتَّخَذَتْ بَيْتًا ۖ وَإِنَّ أَوْهَنَ الْبُيُوتِ لَبَيْتُ الْعَنْكَبُوتِ ۘ لَوْ كَانُوا يَعْلَمُونَ ۝

42. Verily Allah knows of (every thing) whatever that they call upon besides Him: and He is Exalted (in power), Wise.

42. Innal-laaha ya'lamu maa yad'oona min doonihee min shay'; wa Huwal-'Azeezul-Ḥakeem.

إِنَّ اللَّهَ يَعْلَمُ مَا يَدْعُونَ مِنْ دُونِهِ مِنْ شَيْءٍ ۚ وَهُوَ الْعَزِيزُ الْحَكِيمُ ۝

43. And such are the Parables We set forth for mankind, but only those understand them who have knowledge.

43. Wa tilkal-amṣaalu naḍribuhaa linnaasi wa maa ya'qiluhaaa illal-'aalimoon.

وَتِلْكَ الْأَمْثَالُ نَضْرِبُهَا لِلنَّاسِ ۖ وَمَا يَعْقِلُهَآ إِلَّا الْعَالِمُونَ ۝

44. Allah created the heavens and the earth in true (proportions): verily in that is a Sign for those who believe.

44. Khalaqal-laahus-samaawaati wal-arḍa bilḥaqq; inna fee zaalika la-Aayatal-lilmu'mineen. **(Section 4)**

خَلَقَ اللَّهُ السَّمَٰوَٰتِ وَالْأَرْضَ بِالْحَقِّ ۚ إِنَّ فِي ذَٰلِكَ لَآيَةً لِّلْمُؤْمِنِينَ ۝

45. Recite what is sent of the Book by inspiration to you, and establish regular Prayer: for Prayer restrains from shameful and unjust deeds; and remembrance of Allah is the greatest (thing in life) without doubt. And Allah knows the (deeds) that you do.

45. Utlu maaa ooḥiya ilayka minal-Kitaabi wa aqimiṣ-Ṣalaata innaṣ-Ṣalaata tanhaa 'anil-faḥshaaa'i wal-munkar; wa lazikrul-laahi akbar; wallaahu ya'lamu maa taṣna'oon.

اتْلُ مَآ أُوحِيَ إِلَيْكَ مِنَ الْكِتَٰبِ وَأَقِمِ الصَّلَوٰةَ ۖ إِنَّ الصَّلَوٰةَ تَنْهَىٰ عَنِ الْفَحْشَآءِ وَالْمُنْكَرِ ۗ وَلَذِكْرُ اللَّهِ أَكْبَرُ ۗ وَاللَّهُ يَعْلَمُ مَا تَصْنَعُونَ ۝

46. And you do not dispute with the People of the Book, except with means better (than mere disputation), unless it be with those of them who inflict wrong (and injury): but say, "We believe in the revelation which has come down to us and in that which came down to you; our Allah and your Allah is one; and it is to Him we bow (in Islam)."

46. Wa laa tujaadilooo Ahlal-Kitaabi illaa billatee hiya aḥsanu illal-lazeena ẓalamoo minhum wa qoolooo aamannaa billazeee unzila ilaynaa wa unzila ilaykum wa Ilaahunaa wa Ilaahukum Waaḥiduñw-wa naḥnu lahoo muslimoon.

وَلَا تُجَٰدِلُوٓا أَهْلَ الْكِتَٰبِ إِلَّا بِالَّتِي هِيَ أَحْسَنُ إِلَّا الَّذِينَ ظَلَمُوا مِنْهُمْ ۖ وَقُولُوٓا آمَنَّا بِالَّذِي أُنْزِلَ إِلَيْنَا وَأُنْزِلَ إِلَيْكُمْ وَإِلَٰهُنَا وَإِلَٰهُكُمْ وَٰاحِدٌ وَنَحْنُ لَهُ مُسْلِمُونَ ۝

47. And thus (it is) that We have sent down the Book to you. So the People of the Book believe therein,

47. Wa kazaalika anzalnaaa ilaykal-Kitaab; fallazeena aataynaahumul-Kitaaba yu'minoona bihee

وَكَذَٰلِكَ أَنْزَلْنَآ إِلَيْكَ الْكِتَٰبَ ۚ فَالَّذِينَ آتَيْنَاهُمُ الْكِتَٰبَ يُؤْمِنُونَ بِهِ

as also do some of these (pagan Arabs): and none but Unbelievers reject Our signs.

48. And you were not (able) to recite a Book before this (Book came), nor are you (able) to transcribe it with your right hand: in that case, indeed, would the talkers of vanities have doubted.

49. Nay, here are Signs self-evident in the hearts of those endowed with knowledge: and none but the unjust reject Our Signs.

50. Yet they say: "Why are not Signs sent down to him from his Lord?" Say: "The Signs are indeed with Allah: and I am indeed a clear Warner."

51. And is it not enough for them that We have sent down to you the Book which is rehearsed to them? Verily, in it is Mercy and a Reminder to those who believe.

52. Say: "Enough is Allah for a witness between me and you: He knows what is in the heavens and on earth. And it is those who believe in vanities and reject Allah, that will perish (in the end).

53. They ask you to hasten on the Punishment (for them): had it not been for a term (of respite) appointed, the Punishment would certainly have come to them: and it will certainly reach them,- of a sudden, while they perceive not!

54. They ask you to hasten on the Punishment: but, of a surety, Hell will encompass the Rejecters of Faith!-

55. On the Day that the Punish-ment shall cover them from above them and from below them, and (a Voice) shall say: "You taste (the fruits) of your deeds!"

wa min haaa'ulaaa'i many-yu'minu bih; wa maa yajḥadu bi-Aayaatinaaa illal-kaafiroon.

48. Wa maa kunta tatloo min qablihee min kitaabiñw-wa laa takhuṭṭuhoo bi-yameenika izal-lartaabal-mubṭiloon.

49. Bal huwa Aayaatum bayyinaatun fee ṣudooril-lazeena ootul-'ilm; wa maa yajḥadu bi-Aayaatinaaa illaz-zaali-moon.

50. Wa qaaloo law laaa unzila 'alayhi Aayaatum-mir-Rabbi-hee qul innamal-Aayaatu 'indal-laahi wa innamaaa ana nazee-rum-mubeen.

51. Awa lam yakfihim annaaa anzalnaa 'alaykal-Kitaaba yut-laa 'alayhim; inna fee zaalika laraḥmatañw-wa zikraa liqaw-miñy-yu'minoon. **(Section 5)**

52. Qul kafaa billaahi baynee wa baynakum shaheedaa; ya'lamu maa fis-samaawaati wal-arḍ; wallazeena aamanoo bil-baaṭili wa kafaroo billaahi ulaaa'ika humul-khaasiroon.

53. Wa yasta'iloonaka bil-'azaab; wa law laaa ajalum-mu-sammal-lajaaa'ahumul-'azaab; wa la-yaatiyannahum baghta-tañw-wa hum laa yash'uroon.

54. Yasta'iloonaka bil'azaab; wa inna Jahannama lamuḥee-ṭatum bilkaafireen.

55. Yawma yaghshaahumul-'azaabu min fawqihim wa min taḥti arjulihim wa yaqoolu zooqoo maa kuntum ta'maloon.

56. O My servants who believe! Truly, spacious is My Earth: therefore you serve Me - (and Me alone)!

57. Every soul shall have a taste of death: in the end to Us shall you be brought back.

58. But those who believe and work deeds of righteousness - to them shall We give a Home in Heaven,- lofty mansions beneath which flow rivers,- to dwell therein for ever;- an excellent reward for those who do (good)!-

59. Those who persevere in patience, and put their trust in their Lord and Cherisher.

60. How many are the creatures that carry not their own sustenance? It is Allah Who feeds (both) them and you: for He hears and knows (all things).

61. If indeed you ask them who has created the heavens and the earth and subjected the sun and the moon (to his Law), they will certainly reply, "Allah". How are they then deluded away (from the truth)?

62. Allah enlarges the sustenance (which He gives) to whichever of His servants He pleases; and He (similarly) grants by (strict) measure, (as He plea-ses): for Allah has full knowledge of all things.

63. And if indeed you ask them who it is that sends down rain from the sky, and gives life therewith to the earth after its death, they will certainly reply, "Allah!" Say, "Praise be to Allah!" But most of them do not understand.

64. What is the life of this world but amusement and play? But verily the Home in the Here-after,-

56. Yaa 'ibaadiyal-lazeena aamanooo inna arḍee waasi-'atun fa-iyyaaya fa'budoon.

57. Kullu nafsin zaaa'iqatul-mawti summa ilaynaa turja'oon.

58. Wallazeena aamanoo wa 'amiluṣ-ṣaaliḥaati la-nubawwi-'annahum-minal-Jannati ghura-fan tajree min taḥtihal-anhaaru khaalideena feehaa; ni'ma ajrul-'aamileen.

59. Allazeena ṣabaroo wa 'alaa Rabbihim yatawakkaloon.

60. Wa ka-ayyim-min daaab-batil-laa taḥmilu rizqahaa; Al-laahu yarzuquhaa wa iyyaakum; wa Huwas-Samee'ul-'Aleem.

61. Wa la'in sa-altahum-man khalaqas-samaawaati wal-arḍa wa sakhkharash-shamsa wal-qamara la-yaqoolunnal-laahu fa-annaa yu'fakoon.

62. Allaahu yabsuṭur-rizqa limañy-yashaaa'u min 'ibaadi-hee wa yaqdiru lah; innal-laaha bikulli shay'in 'Aleem.

63. Wa la'in sa-altahum-man-nazzala minas-samaaa'i maaa-'an fa-aḥyaa bihil-arḍa mim ba'di mawtihaa la-yaqoolunnal-laah; qulil-ḥamdu-lillaah; bal akṣaruhum laa ya'qiloon.

(Section 6)

64. Wa maa haazihil-ḥayaa-tud-dunyaaa illaa lahwuñw-wa la'ib; wa innad-Daaral-Aakhi-rata la-hiyal-

that is life indeed, if they but knew.

65. Now, if they embark on a boat, they call on Allah, making their devotion sincerely (and exclusively) to Him; but when He has delivered them safely to (dry) land, behold, they give a share (of their worship to others)!-

66. Disdaining ungratefully Our gifts, and giving themselves up to (worldly) enjoyment! But soon will they know.

67. Do they not then see that We have made a sanctuary secure, and that men are being snatched away from all around them? Then, do they believe in that which is vain, and reject the Grace of Allah?

68. And who does more wrong than he who invents a lie against Allah or rejects the Truth when it reaches him? Is there not a home in Hell for those who reject Faith?

69. And those who strive in Our (Cause),- We will certainly guide them to Our Paths: for verily Allah is with those who do right.

30. The Roman Empire
In the name of Allah, Most Gracious, Most Merciful.

1. *Alif-Lam-Mim.*

2. The Roman Empire has been defeated-

3. In a land close by; but they, (even) after (this) defeat of theirs, will soon be victorious-

4. Within a few years. With Allah is the Command, in the Past and in the Future: on that Day shall the Believers rejoice-

5. With the help of Allah. He gives victory to whom He will, and He is Exalted in Might, Most Merciful.

ḥa-yawaan; law kaanoo ya'la-moon.

65. Fa-izaa rakiboo fil-fulki da'awul-laaha mukhliṣeena lahud-deena falammaa najjaa-hum ilal-barri izaa hum yush-rikoon.

66. Li-yakfuroo bimaaa aa-taynaahum wa li-yatamatta'oo fasawfa ya'lamoon.

67. Awalam yaraw annaa ja'alnaa ḥaraman aaminaňw-wa yutakhaṭṭafun-naasu min ḥaw-lihim; afabil-baaṭili yu'minoo-na wa bini'matil-laahi yakfu-roon.

68. Wa man aẓlamu mimma-nif-taraa 'alal-laahi kaziban aw kazzaba bilḥaqqi lammaa jaaa'ah; alaysa fee Jahannama maswal-lil-kaafireen.

69. Wallazeena jaahadoo feenaa lanahdiyannahum subu-lanaa; wa innal-laaha lama'al-muḥsineen. (Section 7)

Sûrat ar-Rûm–30
(Revealed at Makkah)

Bismillaahir Raḥmaanir Raḥeem

1. Alif-Laaam-Meeem.

2. Ghulibatir-Room.

3. Feee adnal-arḍi wa hum-mim ba'ḍi ghalabihim sa-ya-ghliboon.

4. Fee biḍ'i sineen; lillaahil-amru min qablu wa mim ba'd; wa yawma'iziňy-yafraḥul-mu'-minoon.

5. Binaṣril-laah; yanṣuru maňy-yashaaa'u wa Huwal-'Azeezur-Raḥeem.

6. (It is) the promise of Allah. Never does Allah depart from His promise: but most men do not understand.

7. They know but the outer (things) in the life of this world: but they are heedless of the Hereafter.

8. Do they not reflect in their own minds? Not but for just ends and for a term appointed, did Allah create the heavens and the earth, and all between them: yet are there truly many among men who deny the meeting with their Lord (at the Resurrection)!

9. Do they not travel through the Earth, and see what was the end of those before them? They were superior to them in strength: they tilled the soil and populated it in greater numbers than these have done: there came to them their Messengers with Clear (Signs). (Which they rejected, to their own destruction): it was not Allah Who wronged them, but they wronged their own souls.

10. In the long run evil in the extreme will be the End of those who do evil; for that they rejected the Signs of Allah, and held them up to ridicule.

11. It is Allah Who begins (the process of) creation; then repeats it; then you shall be brought back to Him.

12. On the Day that the Hour will be established, the guilty will be struck dumb with despair.

13. No intercessor will they have among their "Partners" and they will (themselves) reject their "Partners".

14. On the Day that the Hour will be established,- that Day

6. Wa‘dal-laahi laa yukh-liful-laahu wa‘dahoo wa laakin-na aksaran-naasi laa ya‘lamoon.

7. Ya‘lamoona ẓaahiram-minal-ḥayaatid-dunyaa wa hum ‘anil-Aakhirati hum ghaafi-loon.

8. Awalam yatafakkaroo feee anfusihim; maa khalaqal-laahus-samaawaati wal-arḍa wa maa baynahumaaa illaa bil-ḥaq-qi wa ajalim-musammaa; wa inna kaseeram-minan-naasi biliqaaa’i Rabbihim lakaa-firoon.

9. Awalam yaseeroo fil-arḍi fa-yanẓuroo kayfa kaana ‘aaqibatul-lazeena min qabli-him; kaanoo ashadda minhum quwwataňw-wa asaarul-arḍa wa ‘amaroohaaa aksara mim-maa ‘amaroohaa wa jaaa’at-hum Rusuluhum bil-bayyinaati famaa kaanal-laahu li-yaẓli-mahum wa laakin kaanooo anfusahum yaẓlimoon.

10. Summa kaana ‘aaqibatal-lazeena asaaa’us-sooo-aaa an kazzaboo bi-Aayaatil-laahi wa kaanoo bihaa yastahzi’oon.

(Section 1)

11. Allaahu yabda’ul-khalqa summa yu‘eeduhoo summa ilayhi turja‘oon.

12. Wa Yawma taqoomus-Saa‘atu yublisul-mujrimoon.

13. Wa lam yakul-lahum-min shurakaaa’ihim shufa‘aaa’u wa kaanoo bishurakaaa’ihim kaafi-reen.

14. Wa Yawma taqoomus-Saa‘atu Yawma’iziiny-

shall (all men) be sorted out.

15. Then those who have believed and worked righteous deeds, shall be made happy in a Mead of Delight.

16. And those who have rejected Faith and falsely denied Our Signs and the meeting of the Hereafter,- such shall be brought forth to Punishment.

17. So (give) glory to Allah, when you reach eventide and when you rise in the morning;

18. Yes, to Him be praise, in the heavens and on earth; and in the late afternoon and when the day begins to decline.

19. It is He Who brings out the living from the dead, and brings out the dead from the living, and Who gives life to the earth after it is dead: and thus you shall be brought out (from the dead).

20. Among His Signs in this, that He created you from dust; and then,- behold, you are men scattered (far and wide)!

21. And among His Signs is this, that He created for you mates from among yourselves, that you may dwell in tranquillity with them, and He has put love and mercy between your (hearts): verily in that are Signs for those who reflect.

22. And among His Signs is the creation of the heavens and the earth, and the variations in your languages and your colors: verily in that are Signs for those who know.

23. And among His Signs is the sleep that you take by night and by day, and the quest that you (make for livelihood) out of His Bounty: verily in that are Signs for those who hearken.

24. And among His Signs, He shows you the lightning, by way both of fear

yatafarraqoon.

15. Fa-ammal-lazeena aamanoo wa 'amiluṣ-ṣaaliḥaati fa-hum fee rawḍatiñy-yuḥbaroon.

16. Wa ammal-lazeena kafaroo wa kazzaboo bi-Aayaatinaa wa liqaaa'il-Aakhirati fa-ulaaa'ika fil-'azaabi muḥḍaroon.

17. Fa-Subḥaanal-laahi ḥeena tumsoona wa ḥeena tuṣbiḥoon.

18. Wa lahul-ḥamdu fis-samaa-waati wal-arḍi wa 'ashiyyañw-wa ḥeena tuẓhiroon.

19. Yukhrijul-ḥayya minal-mayyiti wa yukhrijul-mayyita minal-ḥayyi wa yuḥyil-arḍa ba'da mawtihaa; wa kazaalika tukhrajoon. **(Section 2)**

20. Wa min Aayaatiheee an khalaqakum-min turaabin summa izaaa antum basharun tantashiroon.

21. Wa min Aayaatiheee an khalaqa lakum-min anfusikum azwaajal-litaskunooo ilayhaa wa ja'ala baynakum-mawad-datañw-wa raḥmah; inna fee zaalika la-Aayaatil-liqawmiñy-yatafakkaroon.

22. Wa min Aayaatihee khal-qus-samaawaati wal-arḍi wakhtilaafu alsinatikum wa alwaanikum; inna fee zaalika la-Aayaatil-lil-'aalimeen.

23. Wa min Aayaatihee ma-naamukum bil-layli wannahaari wabtighaaa'ukum-min faḍlih; inna fee zaalika la-Aayaatil-liqawmiñy-yasma'oon.

24. Wa min Aayaatihee yuree-kumul-barqa khawfañw-

and of hope, and He sends down rain from the sky and with it gives life to the earth after it is dead: verily in that are Signs for those who are wise.

wa ṭama'anw-wa yunazzilu minas-samaaa'i maaa'an fa-yuhyee bihil-arḍa ba'da mawtihaaa inna fee zaalika la-Aayaa-til-liqawmiñy-ya'qiloon.

وَطَمَعًا وَّيُنَزِّلُ مِنَ السَّمَآءِ مَآءً فَيُحْىٖ بِهِ الْاَرْضَ بَعْدَ مَوْتِهَا ؕ اِنَّ فِىْ ذٰلِكَ لَاٰيٰتٍ لِّقَوْمٍ يَّعْقِلُوْنَ ۞

25. And among His Signs is this, that heaven and earth stand by His Command: then when He calls you, by a single call, from the earth, behold, you (straightway) come forth.

25. Wa min Aayaatiheee an taqoomas-samaaa'u wal-arḍu bi-amrih; summa izaa da'aakum da'watam-minal-arḍi izaaa antum takhrujoon.

وَمِنْ اٰيٰتِهٖٓ اَنْ تَقُوْمَ السَّمَآءُ وَالْاَرْضُ بِاَمْرِهٖ ؕ ثُمَّ اِذَا دَعَاكُمْ دَعْوَةً ۖ مِّنَ الْاَرْضِ ۗ اِذَآ اَنْتُمْ تَخْرُجُوْنَ ۞

26. To Him belongs every being that is in the heavens and on earth: all are devoutly obedient to Him.

26. Wa lahoo man fissamaa-waati wal-arḍi kullul-lahoo qaanitoon.

وَلَهٗ مَنْ فِى السَّمٰوٰتِ وَالْاَرْضِ ؕ كُلٌّ لَّهٗ قٰنِتُوْنَ ۞

27. It is He Who begins (the process of) creation; then repeats it; and for Him it is most easy. To Him belongs the loftiest simi-litude (one can think of) in the heavens and the earth: for He is Exalted in Might, full of Wisdom.

27. Wa Huwal-lazee yab-da'ul-khalqa summa yu'eeduhoo wa huwa ahwanu 'alayh; wa lahul-masalul-a'laa fis-samaawaati wal-arḍ; wa Huwal-'Azeezul-Ḥakeem. (Section 3)

وَهُوَ الَّذِىْ يَبْدَؤُا الْخَلْقَ ثُمَّ يُعِيْدُهٗ وَهُوَ اَهْوَنُ عَلَيْهِ ؕ وَلَهُ الْمَثَلُ الْاَعْلٰى فِى السَّمٰوٰتِ وَالْاَرْضِ ۚ وَهُوَ الْعَزِيْزُ الْحَكِيْمُ ۞

28. He propounds to you a similitude from your own (experience): do you have partners among those whom your right hands possess, to share as equals in the wealth We have bestowed on you? Do you fear them as you fear each other? Thus do We explain the Signs in detail to a people that understand.

28. Ḍaraba lakum-masalam-min anfusikum hal lakum-mim-maa malakat aymaanukum-min shurakaaa'a fee maa razaq-naakum fa-antum feehi sawaaa-'un takhaafoonahum kakheefa-tikum anfusakum; kazaalika nufaṣṣilul-Aayaati liqawmiñy-ya'qiloon.

ضَرَبَ لَكُمْ مَّثَلًا مِّنْ اَنْفُسِكُمْ ؕ هَلْ لَّكُمْ مِّنْ مَّا مَلَكَتْ اَيْمَانُكُمْ مِّنْ شُرَكَآءَ فِىْ مَا رَزَقْنٰكُمْ فَاَنْتُمْ فِيْهِ سَوَآءٌ تَخَافُوْنَهُمْ كَخِيْفَتِكُمْ اَنْفُسَكُمْ ؕ كَذٰلِكَ نُفَصِّلُ الْاٰيٰتِ لِقَوْمٍ يَّعْقِلُوْنَ ۞

29. Nay, the wrong-doers (merely) follow their own lusts, being devoid of knowledge. But who will guide those whom Allah leaves astray? To them there will be no helpers.

29. Balit-taba'al-lazeena ẓa-lamooo ahwaaa'ahum bighayri 'ilmin famañy-yahdee man aḍallal-laahu wa maa lahum min-naaṣireen.

بَلِ اتَّبَعَ الَّذِيْنَ ظَلَمُوْٓا اَهْوَآءَهُمْ بِغَيْرِ عِلْمٍ ۚ فَمَنْ يَّهْدِىْ مَنْ اَضَلَّ اللّٰهُ ؕ وَمَا لَهُمْ مِّنْ نّٰصِرِيْنَ ۞

30. So you set your face stea-dily and truly to the Faith: (estab-lish) Allah's handiwork accor-ding to the pattern on which He has made mankind: no change (let there be) in the work (wrought) by Allah: that is the

30. Fa-aqim wajhaka liddeeni Ḥaneefaa; fiṭratal-laahil-latee faṭaran-naasa 'alayhaa; laa tabdeela likhalqil-laah; zaali-kad-deenul-

فَاَقِمْ وَجْهَكَ لِلدِّيْنِ حَنِيْفًا ؕ فِطْرَتَ اللّٰهِ الَّتِىْ فَطَرَ النَّاسَ عَلَيْهَا ؕ لَا تَبْدِيْلَ لِخَلْقِ اللّٰهِ ؕ ذٰلِكَ الدِّيْنُ

standard Religion: but most among mankind do not understand.

31. Turn you back in repentance to Him, and fear Him: establish regular prayers, and you be not among those who join gods with Allah,-

32. Those who split up their Religion, and become (mere) Sects,- each party rejoicing in that which is with itself!

33. When trouble touches men, they cry to their Lord, turning back to Him in repentance: but when He gives them a taste of Mercy as from Himself, behold, some of them pay part-worship to other god's besides their Lord,-

34. (As if) to show their ingratitude for the (favors) We have bestowed on them! Then enjoy (your brief day); but soon will you know (your folly)

35. Or have We sent down authority to them, which points out to them the things to which they pay part-worship?

36. When We give men a taste of Mercy, they exult thereat: and when some evil afflicts them because of what their (own) hands have sent forth, behold, they are in despair!

37. Do not they see that Allah enlarges the provision and restricts it, to whomsoever He pleases? Verily in that are Signs for those who believe.

38. So give what is due to kindred, the needy, and the wayfarer. That is best for those who seek the Countenance of Allah, and it is they who will prosper.

39. That which you lay out for increase through

qayyimu wa laakinna aksaran-naasi laa ya'lamoon.

31. Muneebeena ilayhi wat-taqoohu wa aqeemuṣ-Ṣalaata wa laa takoonoo minal-mush-rikeen.

32. Minal-lazeena farraqoo deenahum wa kaanoo shiya'an kullu ḥizbim bimaa ladayhim fariḥoon.

33. Wa izaa massan-naasa ḍurrun da'aw Rabbahum-muneebeena ilayhi ṣumma izaaa azaqahum-minhu rahmatan izaa fareequm-min-hum bi-Rabbihim yushrikoon.

34. Li-yakfuroo bimaaa aatay-naahum; fatamatta'oo fasawfa ta'lamoon.

35. Am anzalnaa 'alayhim sulṭaanan fahuwa yatakallamu bimaa kaanoo bihee yushri-koon.

36. Wa izaaa azaqnan-naasa rahmatan fariḥoo bihaa wa in tuṣibhum sayyi'atum bimaa qaddamat aydeehim izaa hum yaqnaṭoon.

37. Awalam yaraw annal-laaha yabsuṭur-rizqa limany-ya-shaaa'u wa yaqdir; inna fee zaalika la-Aayaatil-liqawmiñy-yu'minoon.

38. Fa-aati zal-qurbaa ḥaqqa-hoo walmiskeena wabnas-sabeel; zaalika khayrul-lil-lazeena yureedoona Wajhal-laahi wa ulaaa'ika humul-muf-lihoon.

39. Wa maaa aataytum-mir-ribal-li-yarbuwa feee

the property of (other) people, will have no increase with Allah: but that which you lay out for charity, seeking the Countenance of Allah, (will increase): it is these who will get a recompense multi-plied.

40. It is Allah Who has created you: further, He has provided for your sustenance; then He will cause you to die; and again He will give you life. Are there any of your (false) "Partners" who can do any single one of these things? Glory to Him! and high is He above the partners they attribute (to him)!

41. Mischief has appeared on land and sea because of (the deed) that the hands of men have earned, that (Allah) may give them a taste of some of their deeds: in order that they may turn back (from Evil).

42. Say: "Travel through the earth and see what was the end of those before (you): Most of them worshipped others besides Allah."

43. But you set your face to the right Religion, before there come from Allah the Day which there is no chance of averting: on that Day shall men be divided (in two).

44. Those who reject Faith will suffer from that rejection: and those who work righteousness will make provision for themselves (in heaven):

45. That He may reward those who believe and work righteous deeds, out of His Bounty. For He loves not those who reject Faith.

46. Among His Signs is this, that He sends the Winds, as heralds of Glad Tidings, giving you a taste of His (Grace and) Mercy,- that the ships may sail (majestically) by His Command and that you may seek of His Bounty: in order that you may be grateful.

---

amwaalin-naasi falaa yarboo 'indal-laahi wa maaa aataytum-min Zakaatin tureedoona Wajhal-laahi fa-ulaaa'ika humul-muḍ'ifoon.

40. Allaahul-lazee khalaqa-kum summa razaqakum summa yumeetukum summa yuḥyee-kum hal min shurakaaa'ikum mañy-yaf'alu min zaalikum-min shay'; Sub-ḥaanahoo wa Ta'aalaa 'ammaa yushrikoon. **(Section 4)**

41. Ẓaharal-fasaadu fil-barri wal-baḥri bimaa kasabat aydin-naasi li-yuzeeqahum ba'ḍal-lazee 'amiloo la'allahum yarji'oon.

42. Qul seeroo fil-arḍi fanẓu-roo kayfa kaana 'aaqibatul-lazeena min qabl; kaana aksaru-hum-mushrikeen.

43. Fa-aqim wajhaka lid-dee-nil-qayyimi min qabli añy-yaa-tiya Yawmul-laa maradda lahoo minal-laahi Yawma'iziñy-yaṣ-ṣadda'oon.

44. Man kafara fa'alayhi kufruhoo wa man 'amila ṣaa-liḥan fali-anfusihim yamha-doon.

45. Li-yajziyal-lazeena aama-noo wa 'amiluṣ-ṣaaliḥaati min faḍlih; innahoo laa yuḥibbul-kaafireen.

46. Wa min Aayaatiheee añy-yursilar-riyaaḥa mubashshi-raatiñw-wa li-yuzeeqakum-mir-raḥmatihee wa litajriyal-fulku bi-amrihee wa litabtaghoo min faḍlihee wa la'allakum tashkuroon.

47. We sent indeed, before you, Messengers to their (respective) peoples, and they came to them with Clear Signs: then, to those who transgressed, We meted out Retribution: and it was due from Us to aid those who believed.

48. It is Allah Who sends the Winds, and they raise the Clouds: then He spreads them in the sky as He wills, and break them into fragments, until you see rain-drops issue from the midst thereof: then when He has made them reach such of His servants as He wills behold, they do rejoice!-

49. Even though, before they received (the rain) - just before this - they were dumb with despair!

50. Then contemplate (O man!) the memorials of Allah's Mercy!- how He gives life to the earth after its death: verily the same will give life to the men who are dead: for He has power over all things.

51. And if We (but) send a Wind from which they see (their tilth) turn yellow,- behold, they become, thereafter, Ungrateful (Unbelievers)!

52. So verily you can not make the dead to hear, nor can you make the deaf to hear the call, when they show their backs and turn away.

53. Nor can you lead back the blind from their straying: only those you will make to hear, who believe in Our Signs and submit (their wills in Islam).

54. It is Allah Who created you in a state of (helpless) weakness, then gave (you) strength after weakness, then, after strength, gave (you weakness) and a hoary head:

47. Wa laqad arsalnaa min qablika Rusulan ilaa qawmihim fajaaa'oohum bil-bayyinaati fantaqamnaa minal-lazeena ajramoo wa kaana ḥaqqan 'alaynaa naṣrul-mu'mineen.

48. Allaahul-lazee yursilur-riyaaḥa fatuṣeeru saḥaaban fa-yabsuṭuhoo fis-samaaa'i kayfa yashaaa'u wa yaj'aluhoo kisa-fan fataral-wadqa yakhruju min khilaalihee fa-izaaa aṣaaba bi-hee mañy-yashaaa'u min 'ibaa-diheee izaa hum yastabshiroon.

49. Wa in kaanoo min qabli añy-yunazzala 'alayhim-min qablihee lamubliseen.

50. Fanẓur ilaaa aaṣaari raḥ-matil-laahi kayfa yuḥyil-arḍa ba'da mawtihaa; inna zaalika lamuḥyil-mawtaa wa Huwa 'alaa kulli shay'in Qadeer.

51. Wa la'in arsalnaa reeḥan fara-awhu muṣfarral-lazalloo mim ba'dihee yakfuroon.

52. Fa-innaka laa tusmi'ul-mawtaa wa laa tusmi'uṣ-ṣum-mad-du'aaa'a izaa wallaw mudbireen.

53. Wa maaa anta bihaadil-'umyi 'an ḍalaalatihim in tus-mi'u illaa mañy-yu'minu bi-Aa-yaatinaa fahum-muslimoon.

(Section 5)

54. Allaahul-lazee khalaqa-kum-min ḍu'fin ṣumma ja'ala mim ba'di ḍu'fin quwwatan ṣumma ja'ala mim ba'di quw-watin ḍu'fañw-

He creates as He wills, and it is He Who has all knowledge and power.

55. On the Day that the Hour (of Reckoning) will be established, the transgressors will swear that they did not tarry but an hour: thus were they used to being deluded!

56. But those endued with knowledge and faith will say: "Indeed you tarried, within Allah's Decree, to the Day of Resurrection, and this is the Day of Resurrection: but you were not aware!"

57. So on that Day no excuse of theirs will avail the Transgressors, nor will they be invited (then) to seek grace (by repentance).

58. Verily We have propounded for men, in this Qur'an every kind of Parable: but if you bring to them any Sign, the Unbelievers are sure to say, "You do nothing but talk vanities."

59. Thus Allah seals up the hearts of those who do not understand.

60. So patiently persevere: for verily the promise of Allah is true: nor let those shake your firmness, who have (themselves) no certainty of faith.

31. The Wise
In the name of Allah, Most Gracious, Most Merciful.

1. *Alif-Lam-Mim.*

2. These are Verses of the Wise Book,-

3. A Guide and a Mercy to the Doers of Good,-

4. Those who establish regular Prayer, and give regular Charity, and have (in their hearts)

---

wa shaybah; yakhluqu maa yashaaa'u wa Huwal-'Aleemul-Qadeer.

55. Wa Yawma taqoomus-Saa'atu yuqsimul-mujrimoona maa labisoo ghayra saa'ah; kazaalika kaanoo yu'fakoon.

56. Wa qaalal-lazeena ootul-'ilma wal-eemaana laqad labistum fee kitaabil-laahi ilaa yawmil-ba'si fahaazaa yaw-mul-ba'si wa laakinnakum kuntum laa ta'lamoon.

57. Fa-Yawma'izil-laa yanfa-'ul-lazeena zalamoo ma'ziratu-hum wa laa hum yusta'taboon.

58. Wa laqad darabnaa lin-naasi fee haazal-Qur-aani min kulli masal; wa la'in ji'tahum bi-Aayatil-la-yaqoolannal-la-zeena kafarooo in antum illaa mubtiloon.

59. Kazaalika yatba'ul-laahu 'alaa quloobil-lazeena laa ya'la-moon.

60. Fasbir inna wa'dal-laahi haqqunw-wa laa yastakhif-fannakal-lazeena laa yooqi-noon.

(Section 6)

Sûrat Luqmân–31
(Revealed at Makkah)
Bismillaahir Rahmaanir Raheem

1. Alif-Laaam-Meeem.

2. Tilka Aayaatul-Kitaabil-Hakeem.

3. Hudañw-wa rahmatal-lilmuhsineen.

4. Allazeena yuqeemoonas-Salaata wa yu'toonaz-Zakaata wa hum bil-Aakhirati hum

the assurance of the Hereafter.

5. These are on (true) guidance from their Lord: and these are the ones who will prosper.

6. But there are, among men, those who purchase idle tales, without knowledge (or meaning), to mislead (men) from the Path of Allah and throw ridicule (on the Path): for such there will be a Humiliating Penalty.

7. When Our Signs are rehearsed to such a one, he turns away in arrogance, as if he did not hear them, as if there were deaf-ness in both his ears: announce to him a grievous Penalty.

8. For those who believe and work righteous deeds, there will be Gardens of Bliss,-

9. To dwell therein. The promise of Allah is true: and He is Exalted in Power, Wise.

10. He created the heavens without any pillars that you can see; He set on the earth mountains standing firm, lest it should shake with you; and He scattered through it beasts of all kinds. We send down rain from the sky, and produce on the earth every kind of noble creature, in pairs.

11. Such is the Creation of Allah: now show Me what is there that others besides Him have created: nay, but the Transgressors are in manifest error.

12. We bestowed (in the past) Wisdom on Luqman: "Show (your) gratitude to Allah." and who is (so) grateful does so to the profit of his own soul: but if any is ungrateful, verily

---

yooqinoon.

5. Ulaaa'ika 'alaa hudam-mir-Rabbihim wa ulaaa'ika humul-mufliḥoon.

6. Wa minan-naasi mañy-yashtaree lahwal-ḥadeesi li-yuḍilla 'an sabeelil-laahi bighayri 'ilmiñw-wa yattakhizahaa huzuwaa; ulaaa'ika lahum 'azaabum-muheen.

7. Wa izaa tutlaa 'alayhi Aayaatunaa wallaa mustakbiran ka-al-lam yasma'haa ka-anna fee uzunayhi waqran fabashshirhu bi'azaabin aleem.

8. Innal-lazeena aamanoo wa 'amiluṣ-ṣaaliḥaati lahum Jannaatun-Na'eem.

9. Khaalideena feehaa wa'dallaahi ḥaqqaa; wa Huwal-'Azee-zul-Ḥakeem.

10. Khalaqas-samaawaati bighayri 'amadin tarawnahaa wa alqaa fil-arḍi rawaasiya an tameeda bikum wa bassa feehaa min kulli daaabbah; wa anzalnaa minas-samaaa'i maaa'an fa-ambatnaa feehaa min kulli zawjin kareem.

11. Haazaa khalqul-laahi fa-aroonee maazaa khalaqallazeena min doonih; baliẓ-ẓaalimoona fee ḍalaalim Mubeen.

(Section 1)

12. Wa laqad aataynaa Luqmaanal-ḥikmata anishkur lillaah; wa mañy-yashkur fa-innamaa yashkuru linafsihee wa man kafara fa-innal-

Allah is free of all wants, Worthy of all praise.

13. Behold, Luqman said to his son by way of instruction: "O my son! do not join in worship (others) with Allah: for false worship is indeed the highest wrong-doing."

14. And We have enjoined on man (to be good) to his parents: in travail upon travail his mother bore him, and in two years was his weaning: (hear the command), "Show gratitude to Me and to your parents: to Me is (your final) Goal.

15. "But if they strive to make you join in worship with Me things of which you have no knowledge, do not obey them; yet bear them company in this life with justice (and consideration), and follow the way of those who turn to Me (in love): in the end the return of you all is to Me, and I will tell you the truth (and meaning) of all that you did."

16. "O my son!" (said Luqman), "If there be (but) the weight of a mustard-seed and it were (hidden) in a rock, or (anywhere) in the heavens or on Earth, Allah will bring it forth: for Allah is Subtle and aware.

17. "O my son! establish regular prayer, enjoin what is just, and forbid what is wrong: and bear with patient constancy whatever betide you; for this is firmness (of purpose) in (the conduct of) affairs.

18. "And do not swell your cheek (for pride) at men, nor walk in insolence through the earth; for Allah does not love any arrogant boaster.

19. "And be moderate in your pace, and lower

laaha Ghaniyyun Ḥameed.

13. Wa iz qaala Luqmaanu libnihee wa huwa ya'izuhoo yaa bunayya laa tushrik billaah; innash-shirka laẓulmun 'aẓeem.

14. Wa waṣṣaynal-insaana bi-waalidayhi ḥamalat-hu ummu-hoo wahnan 'alaa wahniñw-wa fiṣaaluhoo fee 'aamayni anish-kur lee wa liwaalidayka ilayyal-maṣeer.

15. Wa in jaahadaaka 'alaaa an tushrika bee maa laysa laka bihee 'ilmun falaa tuṭi'humaa wa ṣaaḥib-humaa fid-dunyaa ma'roofañw-wattabi' sabeela man anaaba ilayy; ṡumma ilayya marji'ukum fa-unab-bi'ukum bimaa kuntum ta'maloon.

16. Yaa bunayya innahaaa in taku miṡqaala ḥabbatim-min khardalin fatakun fee ṣakhratin aw fis-samaawaati aw fil-arḍi yaåti bihal-laah; innal-laaha Laṭeefun Khabeer.

17. Yaa bunayya aqimiṣ-Ṣalaata waåmur bilma'roofi wanha 'anil-munkari waṣbir-'alaa maaa aṣaabaka inna ẓaali-ka min 'azmil-umoor.

18. Wa laa tuṣa-'ir khaddaka linnaasi wa laa tamshi fil-arḍi maraḥan innal-laaha laa yuḥib-bu kulla mukhtaalin fakhoor.

19. Waqṣid fee mashyika waghḍuḍ

your voice;for the harshest of sounds without doubt is the braying of the ass."

min ṣawtik; inna ankaral-aswaati laṣawtul-ḥameer.

(Section 2)

20. Do you not see that Allah has subjected to your (use) all things in the heavens and on earth, and has made His bounties flow to you in exceeding mea-sure, (both) seen and unseen? Yet there are among men those who dispute about Allah, with-out knowledge and without guidance, and without a Book to enlighten them!

20. Alam taraw annal-laaha sakhkhara lakum-maa fis-samaawaati wa maa fil-arḍi wa asbagha 'alaykum ni'amahoo zaahirataňw-wa baaṭinah; wa minan-naasi maňy-yujaadilu fil-laahi bighayri 'ilmiňw-wa laa hudaňw-wa laa Kitaabim-muneer.

21. When they are told to follow the (Revelation) that Allah has sent down, they say: "Nay, we shall follow the ways that we found our fathers (follo-wing). "What! even if it is Satan beckoning them to the Penalty of the (Blazing) Fire?

21. Wa izaa qeela lahumut-tabi'oo maaa anzalal-laahu qaaloo bal nattabi'u maa wajadnaa 'alayhi aabaaa'anaa; awalaw kaanash-Shayṭaanu yad'oohum ilaa 'azaabis-sa'eer.

22. Whoever submits his whole self to Allah, and is a doer of good, has grasped indeed the most trustworthy hand-hold: and to Allah shall all things return.

22. Wa maňy-yuslim wajha-hooo ilal-laahi wa huwa muḥ-sinun faqadistamsaka bil'ur-watil-wuṣqaa; wa ilal-laahi 'aaqibatul-umoor.

23. But if any reject Faith, let not his rejection grieve you: to Us is their return, and We shall tell them the truth of their deeds: for Allah knows well all that is in (men's) hearts.

23. Wa man kafara falaa yaḥzunka kufruh; ilaynaa marji'uhum fanunabbi'uhum bimaa 'amiloo; innal-laaha 'aleemum biẕaatiṣ-ṣudoor.

24. We grant them their plea-sure for a little while: in the end shall We drive them to an unrelenting chastisement.

24. Numatti'uhum qaleelan ṣumma naḍṭarruhum ilaa 'azaa-bin ghaleeẕ.

25. If you ask them, who it is that created the heavens and the earth. They will certainly say, "Allah". Say: "Praise be to Allah!" But most of them do not understand.

25. Wa la'in sa-altahum-man khalaqas-samaawaati wal-arḍa la-yaqoolunnal-laah; qulil-ḥamdu-lillaah; bal akṣaruhum laa ya'lamoon.

26. To Allah belong all things in heaven and earth: verily Allah is He (that is) free of all wants, worthy of all praise.

26. Lillaahi maa fis-samaa-waati wal-arḍ; innal-laaha Huwal-Ghaniyyul-Ḥameed.

مِنْ صَوْتِكَ ۚ إِنَّ أَنْكَرَ الْأَصْوَاتِ لَصَوْتُ الْحَمِيرِ ۝

أَلَمْ تَرَوْا أَنَّ اللّٰهَ سَخَّرَ لَكُمْ مَا فِي السَّمٰوٰتِ وَمَا فِي الْأَرْضِ وَأَسْبَغَ عَلَيْكُمْ نِعَمَهٗ ظَاهِرَةً وَّبَاطِنَةً ۚ وَمِنَ النَّاسِ مَنْ يُّجَادِلُ فِي اللّٰهِ بِغَيْرِ عِلْمٍ وَّلَا هُدًى وَّلَا كِتٰبٍ مُّنِيْرٍ ۝

وَإِذَا قِيْلَ لَهُمُ اتَّبِعُوْا مَا أَنْزَلَ اللّٰهُ قَالُوْا بَلْ نَتَّبِعُ مَا وَجَدْنَا عَلَيْهِ آبَاءَنَا ۚ أَوَلَوْ كَانَ الشَّيْطٰنُ يَدْعُوْهُمْ إِلٰى عَذَابِ السَّعِيْرِ ۝

وَمَنْ يُّسْلِمْ وَجْهَهٗ إِلَى اللّٰهِ وَهُوَ مُحْسِنٌ فَقَدِ اسْتَمْسَكَ بِالْعُرْوَةِ الْوُثْقٰى ۗ وَإِلَى اللّٰهِ عَاقِبَةُ الْأُمُوْرِ ۝

وَمَنْ كَفَرَ فَلَا يَحْزُنْكَ كُفْرُهٗ ۚ إِلَيْنَا مَرْجِعُهُمْ فَنُنَبِّئُهُمْ بِمَا عَمِلُوْا ۚ إِنَّ اللّٰهَ عَلِيْمٌ بِذَاتِ الصُّدُوْرِ ۝

نُمَتِّعُهُمْ قَلِيْلًا ثُمَّ نَضْطَرُّهُمْ إِلٰى عَذَابٍ غَلِيْظٍ ۝

وَلَئِنْ سَأَلْتَهُمْ مَّنْ خَلَقَ السَّمٰوٰتِ وَالْأَرْضَ لَيَقُوْلُنَّ اللّٰهُ ۚ قُلِ الْحَمْدُ لِلّٰهِ ۚ بَلْ أَكْثَرُهُمْ لَا يَعْلَمُوْنَ ۝

لِلّٰهِ مَا فِي السَّمٰوٰتِ وَالْأَرْضِ ۚ إِنَّ اللّٰهَ هُوَ الْغَنِيُّ الْحَمِيْدُ ۝

27. And if all the trees on earth were pens and the ocean (were ink), with seven oceans behind it to add to its (supply), yet would not the words of Allah be exhausted (in the writing): for Allah is Exalted in Power, full of Wisdom.

28. And your creation or your resurrection is in no wise but as an individual soul: for Allah is He Who hears and sees (all things).

29. Don't you see that Allah merges Night into Day and he merges Day into Night; that He has subjected the sun, and the moon (to His Law), each running its course for a term appointed; and that Allah is well-acquain-ted with all that you do?

30. That is because Allah is the (only) Reality, and because whatever else they invoke besides Him is Falsehood; and because Allah,- He is the Most High, Most Great.

31. Don't you see that the ships sail through the ocean by the Grace of Allah?- that He may show you of His Signs? Verily in this are Signs for all who constantly persevere and give thanks.

32. When a wave covers them like the canopy (of clouds), they call to Allah, offering Him sincere devotion. But when He has delivered them safely to land, there are among them those that halt between (right and wrong). But none reject Our Signs except only a perfidious ungrateful (wretch)!

33. O mankind! do your duty to your Lord, and fear (the coming of) a Day when no father can avail anything for his son, nor a son

27. Wa law annamaa fil-arḍi min shajaratin aqlaamuňw-wal baḥru yamudduhoo mim ba'di-hee sab'atu abḥurim-maa nafi-dat Kalimaatul-laah; innal-laaha 'Azeezun Ḥakeem.

28. Maa khalqukum wa laa ba'ṣukum illaa kanafsiňw-waa-ḥidah; innal-laaha Samee'um Baṣeer.

29. Alam tara annal-laaha yoolijul-layla fin-nahaari wa yoolijun-nahaara fil-layli wa sakhkharash-shamsa wal-qa-mara kulluňy-yajree ilaaa aja-lim-musammaňw-wa annal-laaha bimaa ta'maloona Kha-beer.

30. Zaalika bi-annal-laaha Huwal-Ḥaqqu wa anna maa yad'oona min doonihil-baaṭilu wa annal-laaha Huwal-'Aliy-yul-Kabeer. **(Section 3)**

31. Alam tara annal-fulka tajree fil-baḥri bini'matil-laahi li-yuriyakum-min Aayaatih; inna fee zaalika la-Aayaatil-likulli ṣabbaarin shakoor.

32. Wa izaa ghashiyahum-mawjun kazzulali da'a-wul-laaha mukhliṣeena lahud-deena fa-lammaa najjaahum ilal-barri faminhum-muqtaṣid; wa maa yajḥadu bi-Aayaatinaaa illaa kullu khattaarin kafoor.

33. Yaaa ayyuhan-naasut-taqoo Rabbakum wakhshaw Yawmal-laa yajzee waalidun 'aňw-waladihee wa laa maw-loodun huwa

avail anything for his father. Verily, the promise of Allah is true: let not then this present life deceive you, nor let the chief Deceiver deceive you about Allah.

34. Verily the knowledge of the Hour is with Allah (alone). It is He Who sends down rain, and He Who knows what is in the wombs. Nor does any one know what it is that he will earn on the morrow: Nor does any one know in what land he is to die. Verily with Allah is full knowledge and He is acquainted (with all things).

32. Adoration
In the name of Allah, Most Gracious, Most Merciful.

1. *Alif-Lam-Mim.*

2. (This is) the revelation of the Book in which there is no doubt,- from the Lord of the Worlds.

3. Or do they say, "He has forged it"? Nay, it is the Truth from your Lord, that you may admonish a people to whom no warner has come before you: in order that they may receive guidance.

4. It is Allah Who has created the heavens and the earth, and all between them, in six Days, and is firmly established on the Throne (of authority): you have none, besides Him, to protect or intercede (for you): will you not then receive admonition?

5. He rules (all) affairs from the heavens to the earth: in the end will (all affairs) go up to Him, on

---

jaazin 'añw-waalidihee shay-'aa; inna wa'dal-laahi ḥaqqun falaa taghurran-nakumul-ḥa-yaatud-dunyaa wa laa yaghur-rannakum billaahil-gharoor.

34. Innal-laaha 'indahoo 'il-mus-Saa'ati wa yunazzilul-ghaysa wa ya'lamu maa fil-arḥaami wa maa tadree nafsum-maazaa taksibu ghadaa; wa maa tadree nafsum bi-ayyi arḍin tamoot; innal-laaha 'Aleemun Khabeer.   (Section 4)

Sûrat as-Sajdah–32
(Revealed at Makkah)
Bismillaahir Raḥmaanir Raḥeem

1. Alif-Laaam-Meeem.

2. Tanzeelul-Kitaabi laa rayba feehi mir-Rabbil-'aala-meen.

3. Am yaqooloonaf-taraah; bal huwal-ḥaqqu mir-Rabbika litunzira qawmam-maaa ataa-hum-min-nazeerim-min qab-lika la'allahum yahtadoon.

4. Allaahul-lazee khalaqas-samaawaati wal-arḍa wa maa baynahumaa fee sittati ayyaa-min summas-tawaa 'alal-'Arshi maa lakum-min doonihee miñw-waliyyiñw-wa laa sha-fee'; afalaa tatazakkaroon.

5. Yudabbirul-amra minas-samaaa'i ilal-arḍi summa ya'ruju ilayhi fee

---

a Day, the space whereof will be (as) a thousand years of your reckoning.

6. Such is He, the Knower of all things, hidden and open, the Exalted (in power), the Merciful;-

7. He Who has made everything which He has created most good: He began the creation of man with (nothing more than) clay,

8. And made his progeny from a quintessence of the nature of a fluid despised:

9. But He fashioned him in due proportion, and breathed into him something of His spirit. And He gave you (the faculties of) hearing and sight and feeling (and understanding): little thanks do you give!

10. And they say: "What! when we lie, hidden and lost, in the earth, shall we indeed be in a Creation renewed? Nay, they deny the Meeting with their Lord.

11. Say: "The Angel of Death, put in charge of you, will (duly) take your souls: then you shall be brought back to your Lord."

12. If only you could see when the guilty ones will bend low their heads before their Lord, (saying:) "Our Lord! We have seen and we have heard: now then send us back (to the world): we will work righteousness: for we do indeed (now) believe."

13. If We had so willed, We could certainly have brought every soul its true guidance: but the Word from Me will come true, "I will fill Hell with Jinns and men all together."

14. "Then you taste - for you forgot the Meeting of this Day

yawmin kaana miqdaaruhooo alfa sanatim-mimmaa ta'uddoon.

6. Zaalika 'Aalimul-Ghaybi wash-shahaadatil-'Azeezur-Raheem.

7. Allazee ahsana kulla shay'in khalaqahoo wa bada-a khalqal-insaani min teen.

8. Summa ja'ala naslahoo min sulaalatim-mim-maaa'im-maheen.

9. Summa sawwaahu wa nafakha feehi mir-roohihee wa ja'ala lakumus-sam'a wal-absaara wal-af'idah; qaleelammaa tashkuroon.

10. Wa qaalooo 'a-izaa dalalnaa fil-ardi 'a-innaa lafee khalqin jadeed; bal hum biliqaaa'i Rabbihim kaafiroon.

11. Qul yatawaffaakum-Malakul-Mawtil-lazee wukkila bikum summa ilaa Rabbikum turja'oon. **(Section 1)**

12. Wa law taraaa izil-mujrimoona naakisoo ru'oosihim 'inda Rabbihim Rabbanaaa absarnaa wa sami'naa farji'naa na'mal saalihan innaa mooqinoon.

13. Wa law shi'naa la-aataynaa kulla nafsin hudaahaa wa laakin haqqal-qawlu minnee la-amla'anna Jahannama minaljinnati wannaasi ajma'een.

14. Fazooqoo bimaa naseetum liqaaa'a Yawmikum

(Bow Down)

of yours, and We too will forget you - you taste the Penalty of Eternity for your (evil) deeds!"

15. Only those believe in Our Signs, who, when these are recited to them, fall down in adoration, and celebrate the praises of their Lord, nor are they (ever) puffed up with pride.

16. Their limbs do forsake their beds of sleep, the while they call on their Lord, in Fear and Hope: and they spend (in charity) out of the sustenance which We have bestowed on them.

17. Now no person knows what delights of the eye are kept hidden (in reserve) for them - as a reward for their (good) deeds.

18. Is then the man who believes no better than the man who is rebellious and wicked? Not equal are they.

19. For those who believe and do righteous deeds are Gardens as hospitable homes, for their (good) deeds.

20. As to those who are rebellious and wicked, their abode will be the Fire: every time they wish to get away therefrom, they will be forced back thereinto, and it will be said to them: "You taste the Penalty of the Fire, the which you were wont to reject as false."

21. And indeed We will make them taste of the Penalty of this (life) prior to the supreme Penalty, in order that they may (repent and) return.

22. And who does more wrong than one to whom are recited the Signs of his Lord, and who then turns away therefrom? Verily from those

haazaa innaa naseenaakum wa zooqoo 'azaabal-khuldi bimaa kuntum ta'maloon.

15. Innamaa yu'minu bi-Aayaatinal-lazeena izaa zukkiroo bihaa kharroo sujjadanw-wa sabbahoo bihamdi Rabbi-him wa hum laa yastakbiroon. ☝

16. Tatajaafaa junoobuhum 'anil-madaaji'i yad'oona Rabba-hum khawfanw-wa tama'anw-wa mimmaa razaqnaahum yunfiqoon.

17. Falaa ta'lamu nafsum-maaa ukhfiya lahum-min qur-rati a'yunin jazaaa'am bimaa kaanoo ya'maloon.

18. Afaman kaana mu'minan kaman kaana faasiqaa; laa yasta-woon.

19. Ammal-lazeena aamanoo wa 'amilus-saalihaati falahum Jannaatul-maåwaa nuzulam bimaa kaanoo ya'maloon.

20. Wa ammal-lazeena fasa-qoo famaåwaahumun-Naaru kullamaaa araadooo any-yakh-rujoo minhaa u'eedoo feehaa wa qeela lahum zooqoo 'azaa-ban-Naaril-lazee kuntum bihee tukazziboon.

21. Wa lanuzeeqan-nahum minal-'azaabil-adnaa doonal-'azaabil-akbari la'allahum yarji'oon.

22. Wa man azlamu mimman zukkira bi-Aayaati Rabbihee summa a'rada 'anhaa; innaa minal-

who transgress We shall exact (due) Retribution.

23. We did indeed before this give the Book to Moses: be not then in doubt of its reaching (you): and We made it a guide to the Children of Israel.

24. And We appointed, from among them, leaders, giving guidance under Our command, so long as they persevered with patience and continued to have faith in Our Signs.

25. Verily your Lord will judge between them on the Day of Judgment, in the matters wherein they differ (among themselves).

26. Does it not teach them a lesson, how many generations We destroyed before them, in whose dwellings they (now) go to and fro? Verily in that are Signs: Do they not then listen?

27. And do they not see that We do drive rain to parched soil (bare of herbage), and produce therewith crops, providing food for their cattle and themselves? Have they not the vision?

28. They say: "When will this decision be, if you are telling the truth?"

29. Say: "On the Day of Decision, no profit will it be to Unbelievers if they (then) believe! nor will they be granted a respite."

30. So turn away from them, and wait: they too are waiting.

33. The Confederates
In the name of Allah, Most Gracious, Most Merciful.

1. O Prophet! Fear Allah, and do not hearken to the

---

mujrimeena muntaqimoon.

(Section 2)

23. Wa laqad aataynaa Moo-sal-Kitaaba falaa takun fee miryatim-mil-liqaaa'ihee wa ja'alnaahu hudal-li-Baneee Israaa'eel.

24. Wa ja'alnaa minhum a'immatany-yahdoona bi-amri-naa lammaa ṣabaroo wa kaanoo bi-Aayaatinaa yooqinoon.

25. Inna Rabbaka Huwa yafṣilu baynahum Yawmal-Qiyaamati feemaa kaanoo feehi yakhtalifoon.

26. Awalam yahdi lahum kam ahlaknaa min qablihim-minal-qurooni yamshoona fee masaa-kinihim; inna fee zaalika la-Aayaatin afalaa yasma'oon.

27. Awalam yaraw annaa nasooqul-maaa'a ilal-arḍil-juruzi fanukhriju bihee zar'an taåkulu minhu an'aamuhum wa anfusuhum afalaa yubṣiroon.

28. Wa yaqooloona mataa haazal-fat-ḥu in kuntum ṣaadi-qeen.

29. Qul Yawmal-fat-ḥi laa yanfa'ul-lazeena kafarooo eemaanuhum wa laa hum yunẓaroon.

30. Fa-a'riḍ 'anhum wantaẓir innahum-muntaẓiroon.

(Section 3)

Sûrat al-Aḥzâb–33
(Revealed at Madinah)
Bismillaahir Raḥmaanir Raḥeem

1. Yaaa ayyuhan-Nabiyyut-taqil-laaha wa laa tuṭi'il-

المُجرِمِينَ مُنتَقِمُونَ ۟

وَلَقَدْ اٰتَيْنَا مُوسَى الْكِتٰبَ فَلَا تَكُنْ فِي مِرْيَةٍ مِّنْ لِّقَآئِهٖ وَجَعَلْنٰهُ هُدًى لِّبَنِيْ اِسْرَآءِيْلَ ۟

وَجَعَلْنَا مِنْهُمْ اَئِمَّةً يَّهْدُوْنَ بِاَمْرِنَا لَمَّا صَبَرُوْا ۟ وَكَانُوْا بِاٰيٰتِنَا يُوْقِنُوْنَ ۟

اِنَّ رَبَّكَ هُوَ يَفْصِلُ بَيْنَهُمْ يَوْمَ الْقِيٰمَةِ فِيْمَا كَانُوْا فِيْهِ يَخْتَلِفُوْنَ ۟

اَوَلَمْ يَهْدِ لَهُمْ كَمْ اَهْلَكْنَا مِنْ قَبْلِهِمْ مِّنَ الْقُرُوْنِ يَمْشُوْنَ فِيْ مَسٰكِنِهِمْ ۟ اِنَّ فِيْ ذٰلِكَ لَاٰيٰتٍ ۟ اَفَلَا يَسْمَعُوْنَ ۟

اَوَلَمْ يَرَوْا اَنَّا نَسُوْقُ الْمَآءَ اِلَى الْاَرْضِ الْجُرُزِ فَنُخْرِجُ بِهٖ زَرْعًا تَاْكُلُ مِنْهُ اَنْعَامُهُمْ وَاَنْفُسُهُمْ ۟ اَفَلَا يُبْصِرُوْنَ ۟

وَيَقُوْلُوْنَ مَتٰى هٰذَا الْفَتْحُ اِنْ كُنْتُمْ صٰدِقِيْنَ ۟

قُلْ يَوْمَ الْفَتْحِ لَا يَنْفَعُ الَّذِيْنَ كَفَرُوْا اِيْمَانُهُمْ وَلَا هُمْ يُنْظَرُوْنَ ۟

فَاَعْرِضْ عَنْهُمْ وَانْتَظِرْ اِنَّهُمْ مُّنْتَظِرُوْنَ ۟

(٣٣) سُوْرَةُ الْاَحْزَابِ مَدَنِيَّةٌ (٩٠)

بِسْمِ اللّٰهِ الرَّحْمٰنِ الرَّحِيْمِ

يٰٓاَيُّهَا النَّبِيُّ اتَّقِ اللّٰهَ وَلَا تُطِعِ

Unbelievers and the Hypo-crites: verily Allah is full of Knowledge and Wisdom.

2.   But follow that which comes to you by inspiration from your Lord: for Allah is well acquainted with (all) that you do.

3.   And put your trust in Allah, and enough is Allah as a disposer of affairs.

4.   Allah has not made for any man two hearts in his (one) body: nor has He made your wives whom you divorce by Zihar your mothers: nor has He made your adopted sons your sons. Such is (only) your (manner of) speech by your mouths. But Allah tells (you) the Truth, and He shows the (right) Way.

5.   Call them by (the names of) their fathers: that is juster in the sight of Allah. But if you do not know their father's (names, call them) your Brothers in faith, or your *maulas*. But there is no blame on you if you make a mistake therein: (what counts is) the intention of your hearts: and Allah is Oft-Returning, Most Merciful.

6.   The Prophet is closer to the Believers than their own selves, and his wives are their mothers. Blood-relations among each other have closer personal ties, in the Decree of Allah than (the Brotherhood of) Believers and *Muhajirs*: never-theless you do what is just to your closest friends: such is the writing in the Decree (of Allah).

7.   And remember We took from the prophets their Covenant:

kaafireena wal-munaafiqeen; innal-laaha kaana 'Aleeman Ḥakeemaa.

2.   Wattabi' maa yooḥaaa ilayka mir-Rabbik; innal-laaha kaana bimaa ta'maloona Kha-beeraa.

3.   Wa tawakkal 'alal-laah; wa kafaa billaahi Wakeelaa.

4.   Maa ja'alal-laahu liraju-lim-min qalbayni fee jawfih; wa maa ja'ala azwaajakumul-laaa'ee tuẓaahiroona minhunna ummahaatikum; wa maa ja'ala ad'iyaaa'akum abnaaa'akum; ẓaalikum qawlukum bi-afwaa-hikum wallaahu yaqoolul-ḥaqqa wa Huwa yahdis-sabeel.

5.   Ud'oohum li-aabaaa'ihim huwa aqsaṭu 'indal-laah; fa-illam ta'lamooo aabaaa'ahum fa-ikhwaanukum fid-deeni wa mawaaleekum; wa laysa 'alay-kum junaaḥun feemaaa akhṭaå-tum bihee wa laakim-maa ta'ammadat quloobukum; wa kaanal-laahu Ghafoorar-Raḥee-maa.

6.   An-Nabiyyu awlaa bil-mu'mineena min anfusihim wa azwaajuhooo ummahaatuhum; wa ulul-arḥaami ba'ḍuhum awlaa biba'ḍin fee Kitaabil-laahi minal-mu'mineena wal-Muhaajireena illaaa an taf'a-looo ilaaa awliyaaa'ikum-ma'-roofaa; kaana ẓaalika fil-kitaabi masṭooraa.

7.   Wa iz akhaznaa minan-Nabiyyeena meesaaqahum

اَلْكَفِرِيْنَ وَالْمُنٰفِقِيْنَ ۚ اِنَّ اللّٰهَ كَانَ عَلِيْمًا حَكِيْمًا ۟

وَّاتَّبِعْ مَا يُوْحٰۤى اِلَيْكَ مِنْ رَّبِّكَ ۚ اِنَّ اللّٰهَ كَانَ بِمَا تَعْمَلُوْنَ خَبِيْرًا ۟

وَّتَوَكَّلْ عَلَى اللّٰهِ ۚ وَكَفٰى بِاللّٰهِ وَكِيْلًا ۟

مَا جَعَلَ اللّٰهُ لِرَجُلٍ مِّنْ قَلْبَيْنِ فِيْ جَوْفِهٖ ۚ وَمَا جَعَلَ اَزْوَاجَكُمُ الّٰٓـِٔيْ تُظٰهِرُوْنَ مِنْهُنَّ اُمَّهٰتِكُمْ ۚ وَمَا جَعَلَ اَدْعِيَاۤءَكُمْ اَبْنَاۤءَكُمْ ۚ ذٰلِكُمْ قَوْلُكُمْ بِاَفْوَاهِكُمْ ۚ وَاللّٰهُ يَقُوْلُ الْحَقَّ وَهُوَ يَهْدِى السَّبِيْلَ ۟

اُدْعُوْهُمْ لِاٰبَاۤئِهِمْ هُوَ اَقْسَطُ عِنْدَ اللّٰهِ ۚ فَاِنْ لَّمْ تَعْلَمُوْۤا اٰبَاۤءَهُمْ فَاِخْوَانُكُمْ فِى الدِّيْنِ وَمَوَالِيْكُمْ ۚ وَلَيْسَ عَلَيْكُمْ جُنَاحٌ فِيْمَاۤ اَخْطَأْتُمْ بِهٖ ۙ وَلٰكِنْ مَّا تَعَمَّدَتْ قُلُوْبُكُمْ ۚ وَكَانَ اللّٰهُ غَفُوْرًا رَّحِيْمًا ۟

اَلنَّبِيُّ اَوْلٰى بِالْمُؤْمِنِيْنَ مِنْ اَنْفُسِهِمْ وَاَزْوَاجُهٗۤ اُمَّهٰتُهُمْ ۚ وَاُولُوا الْاَرْحَامِ بَعْضُهُمْ اَوْلٰى بِبَعْضٍ فِيْ كِتٰبِ اللّٰهِ مِنَ الْمُؤْمِنِيْنَ وَالْمُهٰجِرِيْنَ اِلَّاۤ اَنْ تَفْعَلُوْۤا اِلٰۤى اَوْلِيَآئِكُمْ مَّعْرُوْفًا ۚ كَانَ ذٰلِكَ فِى الْكِتٰبِ مَسْطُوْرًا ۟

وَاِذْ اَخَذْنَا مِنَ النَّبِيّٖنَ مِيْثَاقَهُمْ

as (We did) from you: from Noah, Abraham, Moses, and Jesus the son of Mary: We took from them a solemn Covenant:

8. So that (Allah) may question the (custodians) of Truth con-cerning the Truth they (were charged with): and He has prepared for the Unbelievers a grievous Penalty.

9. O you who believe! Remember the Grace of Allah, (bestowed) on you, when there came down on you hosts (to overwhelm you): but We sent against them a hurricane and forces that you did not see: but Allah sees (clearly) all that you do.

10. Behold! They came on you from above you and from below you, and behold, the eyes became dim and the hearts gaped up to the throats, and you imagined various (vain) thoughts about Allah!

11. In that situation were the Believers tried: they were shaken as by a tremendous shaking.

12. And behold! The Hypocrites and those in whose hearts is a disease (even) say: "Allah and His Messenger promised us nothing but delusions."

13. Behold! A party among them said: "You men of Yathrib! you cannot stand (the attack)! therefore go back!" And a band of them ask for leave of the Prophet, saying, "Truly our houses are bare and exposed," though they were not exposed they intended nothing but to run away.

14. And if an entry had been effected to them from the sides of the (City), and they had been incited to sedition, they would certainly have brought it

wa minka wa min-Noohiñw-wa Ibraaheema wa Moosaa wa 'Eesab-ni-Maryama wa akhaz-naa minhum-meesaaqan gha-leezaa.

8. Liyas'alaṣ-ṣaadiqeena 'an ṣidqihim; wa a'adda lilkaa-fireena 'azaaban aleemaa.

(Section 1)

9. Yaaa ayyuhal-lazeena aamanuz-kuroo ni'matal-laahi 'alaykum iz jaaa'atkum junoo-dun fa-arsalnaa 'alayhim reeḥ añw-wa junoodal-lam tarawhaa; wa kaanal-laahu bimaa ta'maloona Baṣeeraa.

10. Iz jaaa'ookum-min fawqi-kum wa min asfala minkum wa iz zaaghatil-abṣaaru wa bala-ghatil-quloobul-ḥanaajira wa tazunnoona billaahiz-zunoo-naa.

11. Hunaalikab-tuliyal-mu'-minoona wa zulziloo zilzaalan shadeedaa.

12. Wa iz yaqoolul-munaafi-qoona wallazeena fee quloo-bihim-maraḍum-maa wa'ada-nal-laahu wa Rasooluhooo illaa ghurooraa.

13. Wa iz qaalat-ṭaaa'ifatum-minhum yaaa ahla Yaṣriba laa muqaama lakum farji'oo; wa yastaazinu fareequm-minhu-mun-Nabiyya yaqooloona inna buyootanaa 'awrah; wa maa hiya bi'awratin iñy-yureedoona illaa firaaraa.

14. Wa law dukhilat 'alayhim-min aqṭaarihaa ṣumma su'ilul-fitnata la-aatawhaa wa maa

to pass, with none but a brief delay!

15. And yet they had already covenanted with Allah not to turn their backs, and a covenant with Allah must (surely) be answered for.

16. Say: "Running away will not profit you if you are running away from death or slaughter; and even if (you do escape), no more than a brief (respite) will you be allowed to enjoy!"

17. Say: "Who is it that can screen you from Allah if it be His wish to give you punishment or to give you Mercy?" Nor will they find for themselves, besides Allah, any protector or helper.

18. Verily Allah knows those among you who keep back (men) and those who say to their brethren, "Come along to us", but come not to the fight except for just a little while.

19. Covetous over you. Then when fear comes, you will see them looking to you, their eyes revolving, like (those of) one over whom death hovers: but when the fear is past, they will smite you with sharp tongues, covetous of goods. Such men have no faith, and so Allah has made their deeds of none effect: and that is easy for Allah.

20. They think that the Confederates have not withdrawn; and if the Confederates should come (again), they would wish they were in the deserts (wandering) among the Bedouins, and seeking news about you (from a safe distance); and if they were in your midst,

talabbaṣoo bihaaa illaa yasee-raa.

15. Wa laqad kaanoo 'aahadul-laaha min qablu laa yuwal-loonal-adbaar; wa kaana 'ah-dul-laahi mas'oolaa.

16. Qul lañy-yanfa'akumul-firaaru in farartum-minal-mawti awil-qatli wa iẕal-laa tumatta'oona illaa qaleelaa.

17. Qul man ẕal-laẕee ya'ṣi-mukum-minal-laahi in araada bikum sooo'an aw araada bi-kum raḥmah; wa laa yajidoona lahum-min doonil-laahi waliy-yañw-wa laa naṣeeraa.

18. Qad ya'lamul-laahul-mu'awwiqeena minkum wal-qaaa'ileena li-ikhwaanihim halumma ilaynaa, wa laa yaå-toonal-baåsa illaa qaleelaa.

19. Ashiḥḥatan 'alaykum fa-iẕaa jaaa'al-khawfu ra-aytahum yanẕuroona ilayka tadooru a'yunuhum kallaẕee yughshaa 'alayhi minal-mawti fa-iẕaa ẕahabal-khawfu salaqookum bi-alsinatin ḥidaadin ashiḥḥatan 'alal-khayr; ulaaa'ika lam yu'minoo fa-aḥbaṭal-laahu a'maalahum; wa kaana ẕaalika 'alal-laahi yaseeraa.

20. Yaḥsaboonal-Aḥzaaba lam yaẕhaboo wa iñy-yaåtil-Aḥzaa-bu yawaddoo law annahum baadoona fil-A'raabi yas-aloona 'an ambaaa'ikum wa law kaanoo feekum

they would fight but little.

21. You have indeed in the Messenger of Allah a beautiful pattern (of conduct) for any one whose hope is in Allah and the Final Day, and who engages much in the Praise of Allah.

22. When the Believers saw the Confederate forces, they said: "This is what Allah and His Messenger had promised us, and Allah and His Messenger told us what was true." And it only added to their faith and their zeal in obedience.

23. Among the Believers are men who have been true to their covenant with Allah: of them some have completed their vow (to the extreme), and some (still) wait: but they have never changed (their determination) in the least:

24. That Allah may reward the men of Truth for their Truth, and punish the Hypocrites if that be His Will, or turn to them in Mercy: for Allah is Oft-Forgiving, Most Merciful.

25. And Allah turned back the Unbelievers for (all) their fury, no advantage did they gain; and enough is Allah for the believers in their fight. And Allah is full of Strength, able to enforce His Will.

26. And those of the People of the Book who aided them- Allah took them down from their strongholds and cast terror into their hearts, (so that) some you slew, and some you made prisoners.

27. And He made you heirs of their lands, their houses, and their goods, and of a land which you had not frequented (before). And Allah has power over all things.

maa qaatalooo illaa qaleelaa.
(Section 2)

21. Laqad kaana lakum fee Rasoolil-laahi uswatun ḥasa-natul-liman kaana yarjul-laaha wal-Yawmal-Aakhira wa za-karal-laaha kaṣeeraa.

22. Wa lammaa ra-al-mu'mi-noonal-Aḥzaaba qaaloo haazaa maa wa'adanal-laahu wa Rasooluhoo wa ṣadaqal-laahu wa Rasooluh; wa maa zaada-hum illaaa eemaanañw-wa tas-leemaa.

23. Minal-mu'mineena rijaa-lun ṣadaqoo maa 'aahadul-laaha 'alayhi faminhum-man qaḍaa naḥbahoo wa minhum-mañy-yantaẓiru wa maa baddaloo tabdeelaa.

24. Li-yajziyal-laahuṣ-ṣaadi-qeena biṣidqihim wa yu'az-zibal-munaafiqeena in shaaa'a aw yatooba 'alayhim; innal-laahu kaana Ghafoorar-Raḥee-maa.

25. Wa raddal-laahul-lazeena kafaroo bighayẓihim lam yanaaloo khayraa; wa kafal-laahul-mu'mineenal-qitaal; wa kaanal-laahu Qawiyyan 'Azee-zaa.

26. Wa anzalal-lazeena zaaha-roohum-min Ahlil-Kitaabi min ṣa-yaaṣeehim wa qazafa fee quloobihimur-ru'ba fareeqan taqtuloona wa taàsiroona faree-qaa.

27. Wa awraṣakum arḍahum wa diyaarahum wa amwaa-lahum wa arḍal-lam taṭa'oohaa; wa kaanal-laahu 'alaa kulli shay'in Qadeeraa. (Section 3)

مَا قَاتَلُوٓا إِلَّا قَلِيلًا ۝

لَقَدْ كَانَ لَكُمْ فِى رَسُولِ اللّٰهِ أُسْوَةٌ حَسَنَةٌ لِّمَن كَانَ يَرْجُوا اللّٰهَ وَالْيَوْمَ الْأٰخِرَ وَذَكَرَ اللّٰهَ كَثِيرًا ۝

وَلَمَّا رَأَ الْمُؤْمِنُونَ الْأَحْزَابَ قَالُوا هٰذَا مَا وَعَدَنَا اللّٰهُ وَرَسُولُهُ وَصَدَقَ اللّٰهُ وَرَسُولُهُ ۚ وَمَا زَادَهُمْ إِلَّا إِيمَانًا وَّتَسْلِيمًا ۝

مِنَ الْمُؤْمِنِينَ رِجَالٌ صَدَقُوا مَا عَاهَدُوا اللّٰهَ عَلَيْهِ ۖ فَمِنْهُم مَّن قَضٰى نَحْبَهُ وَمِنْهُم مَّن يَنتَظِرُ ۖ وَمَا بَدَّلُوا تَبْدِيلًا ۝

لِّيَجْزِىَ اللّٰهُ الصّٰدِقِينَ بِصِدْقِهِمْ وَيُعَذِّبَ الْمُنَافِقِينَ إِن شَاءَ أَوْ يَتُوبَ عَلَيْهِمْ ۚ إِنَّ اللّٰهَ كَانَ غَفُورًا رَّحِيمًا ۝

وَرَدَّ اللّٰهُ الَّذِينَ كَفَرُوا بِغَيْظِهِمْ لَمْ يَنَالُوا خَيْرًا ۚ وَكَفَى اللّٰهُ الْمُؤْمِنِينَ الْقِتَالَ ۚ وَكَانَ اللّٰهُ قَوِيًّا عَزِيزًا ۝

وَأَنزَلَ الَّذِينَ ظَاهَرُوهُم مِّنْ أَهْلِ الْكِتَابِ مِن صَيَاصِيهِمْ وَقَذَفَ فِى قُلُوبِهِمُ الرُّعْبَ فَرِيقًا تَقْتُلُونَ وَتَأْسِرُونَ فَرِيقًا ۝

وَأَوْرَثَكُمْ أَرْضَهُمْ وَدِيَارَهُمْ وَأَمْوَالَهُمْ وَأَرْضًا لَّمْ تَطَؤُوهَا ۚ وَكَانَ اللّٰهُ عَلَىٰ كُلِّ شَىْءٍ قَدِيرًا ۝

28. O Prophet! Say to your Consorts:"If it be that you desire the life of this World, and its glitter,- then come! I will provide for your enjoyment and set you free in a handsome manner.

29. But if you seek Allah and His Apostle, and the Home of the Hereafter, verily Allah has prepared for the well-doers amongst you a great reward.

30. O Consorts of the Prophet! If any of you were guilty of evident unseemly conduct, the Punishment would be doubled to her, and that is easy for Allah.

31. But any of you that is devout in the service of Allah and His Apostle, and works right-ousness,- to her shall We grant her reward twice: and We have prepared for her a generous Sustenance.

32. O Consorts of the Prophet! You are not like any of the (other) women: if you do fear (Allah), be not too complaisant of speech, lest one in whose heart is a disease should be moved with desire: but speak you a speech (that is) just.

33. And stay quietly in your houses, and make not a dazzling display, like that of the former Times of Ignorance; and establish regular Prayer, and give regular Charity; and obey Allah and His Apostle. And Allah only wishes to remove all abomination from you, you members of the Family, and to make you pure and spotless.

34. And recite what is rehearsed to you in your homes, of the Signs of Allah and His Wisdom: for Allah

28. Yaaa ayyuhan-Nabiyyu qul li-azwaajika in kuntunna turidnal-ḥayaatad-dunyaa wa zeenatahaa fata‘aalayna umatti‘kunna wa usarriḥkunna saraaḥan-jameelaa.

29. Wa in kuntunna turidnallaaha wa Rasoolahoo wad-Daaral-Aakhirata fa-innallaaha-a‘adda lilmuḥsinaati minkunna ajran ‘aẓeemaa.

30. Yaa nisaaa’an-Nabiyyi mañy-yaåti minkunna bifaaḥishatim-mubayyinatiñy-yuḍaa‘af lahal-‘aẓaabu ḍi‘fayn; wa kaana ẕaalika ‘alal-laahi yaseeraa.

31. Wa mañy-yaqnut minkunna lillaahi wa Rasoolihee wa ta‘mal ṣaaliḥan nu‘tihaaa ajrahaa marratayni wa a‘tadnaa lahaa rizqan kareemaa.

32. Yaa nisaaa’an-Nabiyyi lastunna ka-aḥadim minannisaaa’i init-taqaytunna falaa takhḍa‘na bilqawli fa-yaṭma‘allazee fee qalbihee maraḍuñw-wa qulna qawlam-ma‘roofaa.

33. Wa qarna fee bu-yootikunna wa laa tabarrajna tabarrujal-Jaahiliyyatil-oolaa wa aqimnaṣ-Ṣalaata wa aateenaz-Zakaata wa aṭi‘nallaaha wa Rasoolah; innamaa yureedul-laahu liyuẕhiba ‘ankumur-rijsa Ahlal-Bayti wa yuṭahhirakum taṭheeraa.

34. Waẕkurna maa yutlaa fee bu-yootikunna min Aayaatillaahi wal-Ḥikmah; innal-laahu

يَٰٓأَيُّهَا ٱلنَّبِيُّ قُل لِّأَزْوَٰجِكَ إِن كُنتُنَّ تُرِدْنَ ٱلْحَيَوٰةَ ٱلدُّنْيَا وَزِينَتَهَا فَتَعَالَيْنَ أُمَتِّعْكُنَّ وَأُسَرِّحْكُنَّ سَرَاحًا جَمِيلًا ۝

وَإِن كُنتُنَّ تُرِدْنَ ٱللَّهَ وَرَسُولَهُۥ وَٱلدَّارَ ٱلْءَاخِرَةَ فَإِنَّ ٱللَّهَ أَعَدَّ لِلْمُحْسِنَٰتِ مِنكُنَّ أَجْرًا عَظِيمًا ۝

يَٰنِسَآءَ ٱلنَّبِيِّ مَن يَأْتِ مِنكُنَّ بِفَٰحِشَةٍ مُّبَيِّنَةٍ يُضَٰعَفْ لَهَا ٱلْعَذَابُ ضِعْفَيْنِ ۚ وَكَانَ ذَٰلِكَ عَلَى ٱللَّهِ يَسِيرًا ۝

وَمَن يَقْنُتْ مِنكُنَّ لِلَّهِ وَرَسُولِهِۦ وَتَعْمَلْ صَٰلِحًا نُّؤْتِهَآ أَجْرَهَا مَرَّتَيْنِ وَأَعْتَدْنَا لَهَا رِزْقًا كَرِيمًا ۝

يَٰنِسَآءَ ٱلنَّبِيِّ لَسْتُنَّ كَأَحَدٍ مِّنَ ٱلنِّسَآءِ ۚ إِنِ ٱتَّقَيْتُنَّ فَلَا تَخْضَعْنَ بِٱلْقَوْلِ فَيَطْمَعَ ٱلَّذِى فِى قَلْبِهِۦ مَرَضٌ وَقُلْنَ قَوْلًا مَّعْرُوفًا ۝

وَقَرْنَ فِى بُيُوتِكُنَّ وَلَا تَبَرَّجْنَ تَبَرُّجَ ٱلْجَٰهِلِيَّةِ ٱلْأُولَىٰ ۖ وَأَقِمْنَ ٱلصَّلَوٰةَ وَءَاتِينَ ٱلزَّكَوٰةَ وَأَطِعْنَ ٱللَّهَ وَرَسُولَهُۥٓ ۚ إِنَّمَا يُرِيدُ ٱللَّهُ لِيُذْهِبَ عَنكُمُ ٱلرِّجْسَ أَهْلَ ٱلْبَيْتِ وَيُطَهِّرَكُمْ تَطْهِيرًا ۝

وَٱذْكُرْنَ مَا يُتْلَىٰ فِى بُيُوتِكُنَّ مِنْ ءَايَٰتِ ٱللَّهِ وَٱلْحِكْمَةِ ۚ إِنَّ ٱللَّهَ

understands the finest mysteries and is well-acquainted (with them).

35. For Muslim men and women, - for believing men and women, for devout men and women, for true men and women who are patient and constant, for men and women who humble themselves, for men and women who give in Charity, for men and women who fast (and deny themselves), for men and women who guard their chastity, and for men and women who engage much in Allah's praise, - for them Allah has prepared forgiveness and great reward.

36. It is not fitting for a Believer, man or woman, when a matter has been decided by Allah and His Apostle, to have any option about their decision: if any one disobeys Allah and His Apostle, he is indeed on a clearly wrong Path.

37. Behold! You did say to one who had received the grace of Allah and your favour: "You (in wedlock) your wife, and fear Allah." But you retain hid in your heart that which Allah was about to make manifest: you feared the people, but it is more fitting that you should fear Allah. Then when Zaid had dissolved (his marriage) with her, with the necessary (formality), We joined her in marriage to you: in order that (in future) there may be no difficulty to the Believers in (the matter of) marriage with the wives of their adopted sons, when the latter have dissolved with the necessary (formality) (their marriage) with them. And Allah's command must be fulfilled.

38. There can be no difficulty to the Prophet in what Allah has indicated to him as a duty. It was the practice (approved) of Allah amongst

kaana Laṭeefan Khabeeraa.
(Section 4)

35. Innal-muslimeena wal-muslimaati walmu'mineena walmu'minaati walqaaniteena walqaanitaati waṣṣaadiqeena waṣṣaadiqaati waṣṣaabireena waṣṣaabiraati walkhaashi'eena walkhaashi'aati walmutaṣad-diqeena walmutaṣaddiqaati waṣṣaaa'imeena waṣṣaaa'i-maati walḥaafiẓeena furooja-hum walḥaafiẓaati waz-zaaki-reenal-laaha kaseeranw-waz-zaakiraati a'addal-laahu lahum-maghfiratanw-wa ajran 'aẓee-maa.

36. Wa maa kaana limu'mi-niñw-wa laa mu'minatin izaa qaḍal-laahu wa Rasooluhooo amran añy-yakoona lahumul-khiyaratu min amrihim; wa mañy-ya'ṣil-laaha wa Rasoo-lahoo faqad ḍalla ḍalaalam-mubeenaa.

37. Wa iz taqoolu lillazeee an'amal-laahu 'alayhi wa an'amta 'alayhi amsik 'alayka zawjaka wattaqil-laaha wa tukhfee fee nafsika mal-laahu mubdeehi wa takhshan-naasa wallaahu aḥaqqu an takhshaah; falammaa qaḍaa Zaydum-minhaa waṭaran zawwajnaa-kahaa likay laa yakoona 'alal-mu'mineena ḥarajun feee azwaaji ad'iyaaa'ihim izaa qaḍaw minhunna waṭaraa; wa kaana amrul-laahi maf'oolaa.

38. Maa kaana 'alan-Nabiyyi min ḥarajin feemaa faraḍal-laahu lahoo sunnatal-laahi fil-

كَانَ لَطِيْفًا خَبِيْرًا ۝

اِنَّ الْمُسْلِمِيْنَ وَالْمُسْلِمٰتِ وَالْمُؤْمِنِيْنَ وَالْمُؤْمِنٰتِ وَالْقٰنِتِيْنَ وَالْقٰنِتٰتِ وَالصّٰدِقِيْنَ وَالصّٰدِقٰتِ وَالصّٰبِرِيْنَ وَالصّٰبِرٰتِ وَالْخٰشِعِيْنَ وَالْخٰشِعٰتِ وَالْمُتَصَدِّقِيْنَ وَالْمُتَصَدِّقٰتِ وَالصَّآئِمِيْنَ وَالصّٰٓئِمٰتِ وَالْحٰفِظِيْنَ فُرُوْجَهُمْ وَالْحٰفِظٰتِ وَالذّٰكِرِيْنَ اللّٰهَ كَثِيْرًا وَّالذّٰكِرٰتِ ۙ اَعَدَّ اللّٰهُ لَهُمْ مَّغْفِرَةً وَّاَجْرًا عَظِيْمًا ۝

وَمَا كَانَ لِمُؤْمِنٍ وَّلَا مُؤْمِنَةٍ اِذَا قَضَى اللّٰهُ وَرَسُوْلُهٗٓ اَمْرًا اَنْ يَّكُوْنَ لَهُمُ الْخِيَرَةُ مِنْ اَمْرِهِمْ ۗ وَمَنْ يَّعْصِ اللّٰهَ وَرَسُوْلَهٗ فَقَدْ ضَلَّ ضَلٰلًا مُّبِيْنًا ۝

وَاِذْ تَقُوْلُ لِلَّذِيْٓ اَنْعَمَ اللّٰهُ عَلَيْهِ وَاَنْعَمْتَ عَلَيْهِ اَمْسِكْ عَلَيْكَ زَوْجَكَ وَاتَّقِ اللّٰهَ وَتُخْفِيْ فِيْ نَفْسِكَ مَا اللّٰهُ مُبْدِيْهِ وَتَخْشَى النَّاسَ ۚ وَاللّٰهُ اَحَقُّ اَنْ تَخْشٰهُ ۗ فَلَمَّا قَضٰى زَيْدٌ مِّنْهَا وَطَرًا زَوَّجْنٰكَهَا لِكَيْ لَا يَكُوْنَ عَلَى الْمُؤْمِنِيْنَ حَرَجٌ فِيْٓ اَزْوَاجِ اَدْعِيَآئِهِمْ اِذَا قَضَوْا مِنْهُنَّ وَطَرًا ۗ وَكَانَ اَمْرُ اللّٰهِ مَفْعُوْلًا ۝

مَا كَانَ عَلَى النَّبِيِّ مِنْ حَرَجٍ فِيْمَا فَرَضَ اللّٰهُ لَهٗ ۗ سُنَّةَ اللّٰهِ فِي

those of old that have passed away. And the command of Allah is a decree determined.

39. (It is the practice of those) who preach the Messages of Allah, and fear Him, and fear none but Allah. And enough is Allah to call (men) to account.

40. Muhammad is not the father of any of your men, but (he is) the Apostle of Allah, and the Seal of the Prophets: and Allah has full knowledge of all things.

41. O you who believe! Celebrate the praises of Allah, and do this often;

42. And glorify Him morning and evening.

43. He it is Who sends blessings on you, as do His angels, that He may bring you out from the depths of Darkness into Light: and He is Full of Mercy to the Believers.

44. Their salutation on the Day they meet Him will be "Peace!"; and He has prepared for them a generous Reward.

45. O Prophet! Truly We have sent you as a Witness, a Bearer of Glad Tidings, and a Warner,-

46. And as one who invites to Allah's (Grace) by His leave, and as a lamp spreading light.

47. Then give the glad tidings to the Believers, that they shall have from Allah a very great Bounty.

48. And do not obey (the behests) of the Unbelievers and the Hypocrites, and heed not their annoyances, but put your Trust in Allah. For enough is Allah as a Disposer of affairs.

49. O you who believe! When you marry

lazeena khalaw min qabl; wa kaana amrul-laahi qadaram-maqdooraa.

39. Allazeena yuballighoona Risaalaatil-laahi wa yakhshaw-nahoo wa laa yakhshawna ahadan illal-laah; wa kafaa billaahi Ḥaseebaa.

40. Maa kaana Muḥammadun abaaa ahadim-mir-rijaalikum wa laakir-Rasoolal-laahi wa Khaataman-Nabiyyeen; wa kaanal-laahu bikulli shay'in 'Aleemaa. **(Section 5)**

41. Yaaa ayyuhal-lazeena aamanuz-kurul-laaha zikran kaseeraa.

42. Wa sabbiḥoohu bukra-tañw-wa aṣeelaa.

43. Huwal-lazee yuṣallee 'alaykum wa malaaa'ikatuhoo liyukhrijakum-minaẓẓulumaati ilan-noor; wa kaana bilmu'-mineena Raḥeemaa.

44. Taḥiyyatuhum Yawma yalqawnahoo salaamuñw-wa a'adda lahum ajran kareemaa.

45. Yaaa ayyuhan-Nabiyyu innaaa arsalnaaka shaahidañw-wa mubashshirañw-wa naẓee-raa.

46. Wa daa'iyan ilal-laahi bi-iznihee wa siraajam-muneeraa.

47. Wa bashshiril-mu'mi-neena bi-anna lahum-minal-laahi faḍlan kabeeraa.

48. Wa laa tuṭi'il-kaafireena walmunaafiqeena wa da' azaahum wa tawakkal 'alallaah; wa kafaa billaahi Wakeelaa.

49. Yaaa ayyuhal-lazeena aamanooo izaa nakaḥtumul-

believing women, and then divorce them before you have touched them, no period of 'Iddat have you to count in respect of them: so give them a present, and set them free in a handsome manner.

50. O Prophet! We have made lawful to you your wives to whom you have paid their dowers; and those whom your right hand possesses out of the prisoners of war whom Allah has assigned to you; and daughters of your paternal uncles and aunts, and daughters of your maternal uncles and aunts, who migrated (from Makkah) with you; and any believing woman who dedicates her soul to the Prophet if the Prophet wishes to wed her;- this only for you, and not for the Believers (at large); We know what We have appointed for them as to their wives and the captives whom their right hands possess;- in order that there should be no difficulty for you. And Allah is Oft-Forgiving, Most Merciful.

51. You may defer (the turn of) any of them that you please, and you may receive any you please: and there is no blame on you if you invite one whose (turn) you had set aside. This were nearer to the cooling of their eyes, the prevention of their grief, and their satisfaction - that of all of them - with that which you have to give them: and Allah knows (all) that is in your hearts: and Allah is All-Knowing, Most Forbearing.

52. It is not lawful for you (to marry more) women after this, nor to change them for (other) wives, even though

mu'minaati summa ṭallaqtumoohunna min qabli an tamassoohunna famaa lakum 'alayhinna min 'iddatin ta'taddoonahaa famatti'oohunna wa sarriḥoohunna saraaḥan jameelaa.

50. Yaaa ayyuhan-Nabiyyu innaaa aḥlalnaa laka azwaajakal-laateee aatayta ujoorahunna wa maa malakat yameenuka mimmaaa afaaa'al-laahu 'alayka wa banaati 'ammika wa banaati 'ammaatika wa banaati khaalika wa banaati khaalaatikal-laatee haajarna ma'aka wamra-atam-mu'minatan iñwwahabat nafsahaa lin-Nabiyyi in araadan-Nabiyyu añy-yastankiḥahaa khaaliṣatal-laka min doonil-mu'mineen; qad 'alimnaa maa faraḍnaa 'alayhim feee azwaajihim wa maa malakat aymaanuhum likaylaa yakoona 'alayka ḥaraj; wa kaanal-laahu Ghafoorar-Raḥeemaa.

51. Turjee man tashaaa'u minhunna wa tu'weee ilayka man tashaaa'u wa manibtaghayta mimman 'azalta falaa junaaḥa 'alayk; zaalika adnaaa an taqarra a'yunuhunna wa laa yaḥzanna wa yarḍayna bimaaa aataytahunna kulluhunn; wallaahu ya'lamu maa fee quloobikum; wa kaanal-laahu 'Aleeman Ḥaleemaa.

52. Laa yaḥillu lakan-nisaaa'u mim ba'du wa laaa an tabaddala bihinna min azwaajiñw-wa law

الْمُؤْمِنٰتِ ثُمَّ طَلَّقْتُمُوْهُنَّ مِنْ قَبْلِ اَنْ تَمَسُّوْهُنَّ فَمَا لَكُمْ عَلَيْهِنَّ مِنْ عِدَّةٍ تَعْتَدُّوْنَهَا ۚ فَمَتِّعُوْهُنَّ وَسَرِّحُوْهُنَّ سَرَاحًا جَمِيْلًا ۞

يٰۤاَيُّهَا النَّبِيُّ اِنَّاۤ اَحْلَلْنَا لَكَ اَزْوَاجَكَ الّٰتِيْۤ اٰتَيْتَ اُجُوْرَهُنَّ وَمَا مَلَكَتْ يَمِيْنُكَ مِمَّاۤ اَفَآءَ اللّٰهُ عَلَيْكَ وَبَنٰتِ عَمِّكَ وَبَنٰتِ عَمّٰتِكَ وَبَنٰتِ خَالِكَ وَبَنٰتِ خٰلٰتِكَ الّٰتِيْ هَاجَرْنَ مَعَكَ ۫ وَامْرَاَةً مُّؤْمِنَةً اِنْ وَّهَبَتْ نَفْسَهَا لِلنَّبِيِّ اِنْ اَرَادَ النَّبِيُّ اَنْ يَّسْتَنْكِحَهَا ۗ خَالِصَةً لَّكَ مِنْ دُوْنِ الْمُؤْمِنِيْنَ ۗ قَدْ عَلِمْنَا مَا فَرَضْنَا عَلَيْهِمْ فِيْۤ اَزْوَاجِهِمْ وَمَا مَلَكَتْ اَيْمَانُهُمْ لِكَيْلَا يَكُوْنَ عَلَيْكَ حَرَجٌ ۗ وَكَانَ اللّٰهُ غَفُوْرًا رَّحِيْمًا ۞

تُرْجِيْ مَنْ تَشَآءُ مِنْهُنَّ وَتُـٔوِيْۤ اِلَيْكَ مَنْ تَشَآءُ ۗ وَمَنِ ابْتَغَيْتَ مِمَّنْ عَزَلْتَ فَلَا جُنَاحَ عَلَيْكَ ۚ ذٰلِكَ اَدْنٰۤى اَنْ تَقَرَّ اَعْيُنُهُنَّ وَلَا يَحْزَنَّ وَيَرْضَيْنَ بِمَاۤ اٰتَيْتَهُنَّ كُلُّهُنَّ ۗ وَاللّٰهُ يَعْلَمُ مَا فِيْ قُلُوْبِكُمْ ۗ وَكَانَ اللّٰهُ عَلِيْمًا حَلِيْمًا ۞

لَا يَحِلُّ لَكَ النِّسَآءُ مِنْۢ بَعْدُ وَلَاۤ اَنْ تَبَدَّلَ بِهِنَّ مِنْ اَزْوَاجٍ وَّلَوْ

their beauty attract you, except any your right hand should possess (as handmaidens): and Allah watches over all things.

53. O you who believe! Do not enter the Prophet's houses,- until leave is given you,- for a meal, (and then) not (so early as) to wait for its preparation: but when you are invited, enter; and when you have taken your meal, disperse, without seeking familiar talk. Such (behaviour) annoys the Prophet: he is ashamed to dismiss you, but Allah is not ashamed (to tell you) the truth. And when you ask (his ladies) for anything you want, ask them from before a screen: that makes for greater purity for your hearts and for theirs. Nor is it right for you that you should annoy Allah's Apostle, or that you should marry his widows after him at any time. Truly such a thing is in Allah's sight an enormity.

54. Whether you reveal anything or conceal it, verily Allah has full knowledge of all things.

55. There is no blame (on these ladies if they appear) before their fathers or their sons, their brothers, or their brother's sons, or their sisters' sons, or their women, or the (slaves) whom their right hands possess. And (ladies), fear Allah; for Allah is Witness to all things.

56. Allah and His angels send blessings on the Prophet: O you that believe! You send blessings

a'jabaka ḥusnuhunna illaa maa malakat yameenuk; wa kaanallaahu 'alaa kulli shay'ir-Raqeebaa. **(Section 6)**

53. Yaaa ayyuhal-lazeena aamanoo laa tadkhuloo bu-yoo-tan-Nabiyyi illaaa añy-yu'zana lakum ilaa ṭa'aamin ghayra naaẓireena inaahu wa laakin izaa du'eetum fadkhuloo fa-izaa ṭa'imtum fantashiroo wa laa mustaåniseena liḥadees; inna zaalikum kaana yu'zin-Nabiyya fa-yastaḥyee minkum wallaahu laa yastaḥyee minal-ḥaqq; wa izaa sa-altumoohunna mataa'an fas'aloohunna miñw-waraaa'i ḥijaab; zaalikum aṭharu liquloobikum wa quloobihinn; wa maa kaana lakum an tu'zoo Rasoolal-laahi wa laaa an tankiḥooo azwaajahoo mim ba'diheee abadaa; inna zaalikum kaana 'indal-laahi 'aẓeemaa.

54. In tubdoo shay'an aw tukhfoohu fa-innal-laaha kaana bikulli shay'in 'Aleemaa.

55. Laa junaaḥa 'alayhinna feee aabaaa'ihinna wa laaa abnaaa'ihinna wa laaa ikhwaani-hinna wa laaa abnaaa'i ikhwaanihinna wa laaa abnaaa'i akhawaatihinna wa laa nisaaa'i-hinna wa laa Maa malakat aymaanuhunn; wattaqeenal-laah; innal-laaha kaana 'alaa kulli shay'in Shaheedaa.

56. Innal-laaha wa malaaa'i-katahoo yuṣalloona 'alan-Nabiyy; yaaa ayyuhal-lazeena aamanoo ṣalloo

أَعْجَبَكَ حُسْنُهُنَّ إِلَّا مَا مَلَكَتْ يَمِينُكَ ۗ وَكَانَ اللَّهُ عَلَىٰ كُلِّ شَيْءٍ رَّقِيبًا ۝

يَٰٓأَيُّهَا الَّذِينَ ءَامَنُوا لَا تَدْخُلُوا بُيُوتَ النَّبِيِّ إِلَّآ أَن يُؤْذَنَ لَكُمْ إِلَىٰ طَعَامٍ غَيْرَ نَٰظِرِينَ إِنَىٰهُ وَلَٰكِنْ إِذَا دُعِيتُمْ فَٱدْخُلُوا فَإِذَا طَعِمْتُمْ فَٱنتَشِرُوا وَلَا مُسْتَأْنِسِينَ لِحَدِيثٍ ۚ إِنَّ ذَٰلِكُمْ كَانَ يُؤْذِي النَّبِيَّ فَيَسْتَحْىِۦ مِنكُمْ ۖ وَٱللَّهُ لَا يَسْتَحْىِۦ مِنَ ٱلْحَقِّ ۚ وَإِذَا سَأَلْتُمُوهُنَّ مَتَٰعًا فَسْـَٔلُوهُنَّ مِن وَرَآءِ حِجَابٍ ۚ ذَٰلِكُمْ أَطْهَرُ لِقُلُوبِكُمْ وَقُلُوبِهِنَّ ۚ وَمَا كَانَ لَكُمْ أَن تُؤْذُوا رَسُولَ اللَّهِ وَلَآ أَن تَنكِحُوٓا أَزْوَٰجَهُۥ مِنۢ بَعْدِهِۦٓ أَبَدًا ۚ إِنَّ ذَٰلِكُمْ كَانَ عِندَ اللَّهِ عَظِيمًا ۝

إِن تُبْدُوا شَيْـًٔا أَوْ تُخْفُوهُ فَإِنَّ اللَّهَ كَانَ بِكُلِّ شَيْءٍ عَلِيمًا ۝

لَّا جُنَاحَ عَلَيْهِنَّ فِىٓ ءَابَآئِهِنَّ وَلَآ أَبْنَآئِهِنَّ وَلَآ إِخْوَٰنِهِنَّ وَلَآ أَبْنَآءِ إِخْوَٰنِهِنَّ وَلَآ أَبْنَآءِ أَخَوَٰتِهِنَّ وَلَا نِسَآئِهِنَّ وَلَا مَا مَلَكَتْ أَيْمَٰنُهُنَّ ۗ وَٱتَّقِينَ اللَّهَ ۚ إِنَّ اللَّهَ كَانَ عَلَىٰ كُلِّ شَيْءٍ شَهِيدًا ۝

إِنَّ اللَّهَ وَمَلَٰٓئِكَتَهُۥ يُصَلُّونَ عَلَى النَّبِيِّ ۚ يَٰٓأَيُّهَا الَّذِينَ ءَامَنُوا صَلُّوا

on him, and salute him with all respect.

57. Those who annoy Allah and His Apostle - Allah has cursed them in this World and in the Hereafter, and has prepared for them a humiliating Punishment.

58. And those who annoy believing men and women undeservedly, bear (on themselves) a calumny and a glaring sin.

59. O Prophet! Tell your wives and daughters, and the believing women, that they should cast their outer garments over their persons (when abroad): that is most convenient, that they should be known (as such) and not molested. And Allah is Oft-Forgiving, Most Merciful.

60. Truly, if the Hypocrites, and those in whose hearts is a disease, and those who stir up sedition in the City, desist not, We shall certainly stir you up against them: then will they not be able to stay in it as your neighbours for any length of time:

61. They shall have a curse on them: whenever they are found, they shall be seized and slain (without mercy).

62. (Such was) the practice (approved) of Allah among those who lived aforetime: no change will you find in the practice (approved) of Allah.

63. Men ask you concerning the Hour: Say, "The knowledge thereof is with Allah (alone)": and what will make you understand?- perchance the Hour is near!

64. Verily Allah has cursed the Unbelievers and prepared for them a Blazing Fire.

65. To dwell therein for ever: no protector will they find,

‘alayhi wa ṣallimoo tasleemaa.

57. Innal-lazeena yu’zoonal-laaha wa Rasoolahoo la‘ana-humul-laahu fid-dunyaa wal-Aakhirati wa a‘adda lahum ‘azaabam-muheenaa.

58. Wallazeena yu’zoonal-mu’mineena walmu’minaati bighayri mak-tasaboo faqadiḥ-tamaloo buhtaanañw-wa iṣ-mam-mubeenaa. **(Section 7)**

59. Yaaa ayyuhan-Nabiyyu qul li-azwaajika wa banaatika wa nisaaa’il-mu’mineena yud-neena ‘alayhinna min jalaabee-bihinn; zaalika adnaaa añy-yu‘rafna falaa yu’zayn; wa kaanal-laahu Ghafoorar-Raḥee-maa.

60. La’il-lam yantahil-munaa-fiqoona wallazeena fee quloo-bihim-maraḍ uñw-walmur-jifoona fil-madeenati lanughri-yannaka bihim ṣumma laa yujaawiroonaka feehaaa illaa qaleelaa.

61. Mal‘ooneena aynamaa suqifooo ukhizoo wa quttiloo taqteelaa.

62. Sunnatal-laahi fil-lazeena khalaw min qablu wa lan tajida lisunnatil-laahi tabdeelaa.

63. Yas’alukan-naasu ‘anis-Saa‘ati qul innamaa ‘ilmuhaa ‘indal-laah; wa maa yudreeka la‘allas-Saa‘ata takoonu qaree-baa.

64. Innal-laaha la‘anal-kaafi-reena wa a‘adda lahum sa‘ee-raa.

65. Khaalideena feehaaa aba-daa, laa yajidoona waliyyañw-

عَلَيْهِ وَسَلِّمُوا تَسْلِيمًا ۝

٥٧ إِنَّ الَّذِينَ يُؤْذُونَ اللَّهَ وَرَسُولَهُ لَعَنَهُمُ اللَّهُ فِي الدُّنْيَا وَالْآخِرَةِ وَأَعَدَّ لَهُمْ عَذَابًا مُهِينًا ۝

٥٨ وَالَّذِينَ يُؤْذُونَ الْمُؤْمِنِينَ وَالْمُؤْمِنَاتِ بِغَيْرِ مَا اكْتَسَبُوا فَقَدِ احْتَمَلُوا بُهْتَانًا وَإِثْمًا مُبِينًا ۝

٥٩ يَا أَيُّهَا النَّبِيُّ قُلْ لِأَزْوَاجِكَ وَبَنَاتِكَ وَنِسَاءِ الْمُؤْمِنِينَ يُدْنِينَ عَلَيْهِنَّ مِنْ جَلَابِيبِهِنَّ ۚ ذَٰلِكَ أَدْنَى أَنْ يُعْرَفْنَ فَلَا يُؤْذَيْنَ ۗ وَكَانَ اللَّهُ غَفُورًا رَحِيمًا ۝

٦٠ لَئِنْ لَمْ يَنْتَهِ الْمُنَافِقُونَ وَالَّذِينَ فِي قُلُوبِهِمْ مَرَضٌ وَالْمُرْجِفُونَ فِي الْمَدِينَةِ لَنُغْرِيَنَّكَ بِهِمْ ثُمَّ لَا يُجَاوِرُونَكَ فِيهَا إِلَّا قَلِيلًا ۝

٦١ مَلْعُونِينَ ۖ أَيْنَمَا ثُقِفُوا أُخِذُوا وَقُتِّلُوا تَقْتِيلًا ۝

٦٢ سُنَّةَ اللَّهِ فِي الَّذِينَ خَلَوْا مِنْ قَبْلُ ۖ وَلَنْ تَجِدَ لِسُنَّةِ اللَّهِ تَبْدِيلًا ۝

٦٣ يَسْأَلُكَ النَّاسُ عَنِ السَّاعَةِ ۖ قُلْ إِنَّمَا عِلْمُهَا عِنْدَ اللَّهِ ۚ وَمَا يُدْرِيكَ لَعَلَّ السَّاعَةَ تَكُونُ قَرِيبًا ۝

٦٤ إِنَّ اللَّهَ لَعَنَ الْكَافِرِينَ وَأَعَدَّ لَهُمْ سَعِيرًا ۝

٦٥ خَالِدِينَ فِيهَا أَبَدًا ۖ لَا يَجِدُونَ وَلِيًّا

nor helper.

66. The Day that their faces will be turned upside down in the Fire, they will say: "Woe to us! would that we had obeyed Allah and obeyed the Apostle!"

67. And they would say: "Our Lord! We obeyed our chiefs and our great ones, and they misled us as to the (right) Path.

68. "Our Lord! Give them double Chastisement and curse them with a very great Curse!"

69. O you who believe! You do not be like those who vexed and insulted Moses, but Allah cleared him of the (calumnies) they had uttered: and he was honourable in Allah's sight.

70. O you who believe! Fear Allah, and (always) say a word directed to the Right:

71. That He may make your conduct whole and sound and forgive you your sins: he that obeys Allah and His Apostle, has already attained the highest Achievement.

72. We did indeed offer the Trust to the Heavens and the Earth and the Mountains; but they refused to undertake it, being afraid thereof: but man undertook it;- he was indeed unjust and foolish;

73. (With the result) that Allah has to punish the Hypocrites, men and women, and the Unbelievers, men and women, and Allah turns in Mercy to the Believers, men and women: for Allah is Oft-Forgiving, Most Merciful.

34. The City of Saba
In the name of Allah, Most Gracious, Most Merciful.

1. Praise be to Allah, to Whom belong all things in the heavens

---

wa laa naṣeeraa.

66. Yawma tuqallabu wujoo-huhum fin-Naari yaqooloona yaa laytanaaa aṭa'nal-laaha wa aṭa'nar-Rasoolaa.

67. Wa qaaloo Rabbanaaa innaaa aṭa'naa saadatanaa wa kubaraaa'anaa fa-aḍalloonas-sabeelaa.

68. Rabbanaaa aatihim ḍi'fay-ni minal-'azaabi wal'anhum la'nan kabeeraa. **(Section 8)**

69. Yaaa ayyuhal-lazeena aamanoo laa takoonoo kalla-zeena aazaw Moosaa fa-barra-ahul-laahu mimmaa qaaloo; wa kaana 'indal-laahi wajeehaa.

70. Yaaa ayyuhal-lazeena aamanut-taqul-laaha wa qooloo qawlan sadeedaa.

71. Yuṣliḥ lakum a'maalakum wa yaghfir lakum zunoobakum; wa mañy-yuṭi'il-laaha wa Rasoolahoo faqad faaza fawzan 'azeemaa.

72. Innaa 'araḍnal-amaanata 'alas-samaawaati walarḍi wal-jibaali fa-abayna añy-yaḥmil-nahaa wa ashfaqna minhaa wa ḥamalahal-insaanu innahoo kaana zalooman jahoolaa.

73. Liyu'azzibal-laahul-munaafiqeena walmunaafiqaati walmushrikeena walmush-rikaati wa yatoobal-laahu 'alal-mu'mineena walmu'minaat; wa kaanal-laahu Ghafoorar-Raheema. **(Section 9)**

Sûrat Saba'–34
(Revealed at Makkah)
Bismillaahir Raḥmaanir Raḥeem

1. Alḥamdu lillaahil-lazee lahoo maa fis-samaawaati

and on earth: to Him be Praise in the Hereafter: and He is Full of Wisdom, acquainted with all things.

2. He knows all that goes into the earth, and all that comes out thereof; and all that comes down from the sky and all that ascends thereto and He is the Most Merciful, the Oft-Forgiving.

3. The Unbelievers say, "Never to us will come the Hour": Say, "Nay! but most surely, by my Lord, it will come upon you;- by Him Who knows the unseen,- from Whom is not hidden the least little atom in the heavens or on earth: nor is there anything less than that, or greater, but is in the Record Perspicuous.

4. That He may reward those who believe and work deeds of righteousness: for such is Forgiveness and a Sustenance Most Generous."

5. But those who strive against Our Signs, to frustrate them,- for such will be a Chastisement,- a Punishment most humiliating.

6. And those to whom knowledge has come see that the (Revelation) sent down to you from your Lord - that is the Truth, and that it guides to the Path of the Exalted (in might), Worthy of all praise.

7. The Unbelievers say (in ridicule): "Shall we point out to you a man that will tell you, when' you are all scattered to pieces in disintegration, that you shall (then be raised) in a New Creation?

8. "Has he invented a falsehood against Allah, or has a spirit (seized) him?"- no, it is those who do not believe in the Hereafter, that are in (real) Chastisement, and in farthest error.

9. See they not what is before them and

wa maa fil-arḍi wa lahul-ḥamdu fil-Aakhirah; wa Huwal-Ḥakeemul-Khabeer.

2. Ya‘lamu maa yaliju fil-arḍi wa maa yakhruju minhaa wa maa yanzilu minas-samaaa’i wa maa ya‘ruju feehaa; wa Huwar-Raḥeemul-Ghafoor.

3. Wa qaalal-lazeena kafaroo laa taåteenas-Saa‘ah; qul balaa wa Rabbee lataåtiyannakum ‘Aalimil-Ghayb; laa ya‘zubu ‘anhu misqaalu zarratin fis-samaawaati wa laa fil-arḍi wa laaa aṣgharu min zaalika wa laaa akbaru illaa fee kitaabim-mubeen.

4. Liyajziyal-lazeena aamanoo wa ‘amiluṣ-ṣaaliḥaat; ulaaa’ika lahum-maghfiratuñw-wa rizqun kareem.

5. Wallazeena sa‘aw feee Aayaatinaa mu‘aajizeena ulaaa’ika lahum ‘azaabum-mir-rijzin aleem.

6. Wa yaral-lazeena utul-‘Ilmal-lazeee unzila ilayka mir-Rabbika huwal-ḥaqqa wa yahdeee ilaa ṣiraaṭil-‘Azeezil-Ḥameed.

7. Wa qaalal-lazeena kafaroo hal nadullukum ‘alaa rajuliñy-yunabbi’ukum izaa muzziqtum kulla mumazzaqin innakum lafee khalqin jadeed.

8. Aftaraa ‘alal-laahi kaziban am bihee jinnah; balil-lazeena laa yu’minoona bil-Aakhirati fil-‘azaabi waḍḍa-laalil-ba‘eed.

9. Afalam yaraw ilaa maa bayna aydeehim wa maa

وَمَا فِي الْأَرْضِ وَلَهُ الْحَمْدُ فِي الْأَخِرَةِ ۚ وَهُوَ الْحَكِيمُ الْخَبِيرُ ۞

يَعْلَمُ مَا يَلِجُ فِي الْأَرْضِ وَمَا يَخْرُجُ مِنْهَا وَمَا يَنْزِلُ مِنَ السَّمَاءِ وَمَا يَعْرُجُ فِيهَا ۚ وَهُوَ الرَّحِيمُ الْغَفُورُ ۞

وَقَالَ الَّذِينَ كَفَرُوا لَا تَأْتِينَا السَّاعَةُ ۖ قُلْ بَلَىٰ وَرَبِّي لَتَأْتِيَنَّكُمْ عَالِمِ الْغَيْبِ ۖ لَا يَعْزُبُ عَنْهُ مِثْقَالُ ذَرَّةٍ فِي السَّمَاوَاتِ وَلَا فِي الْأَرْضِ وَلَا أَصْغَرُ مِنْ ذَٰلِكَ وَلَا أَكْبَرُ إِلَّا فِي كِتَابٍ مُبِينٍ ۞

لِيَجْزِيَ الَّذِينَ آمَنُوا وَعَمِلُوا الصَّالِحَاتِ ۚ أُولَٰئِكَ لَهُمْ مَغْفِرَةٌ وَرِزْقٌ كَرِيمٌ ۞

وَالَّذِينَ سَعَوْا فِي آيَاتِنَا مُعَاجِزِينَ أُولَٰئِكَ لَهُمْ عَذَابٌ مِنْ رِجْزٍ أَلِيمٌ ۞

وَيَرَى الَّذِينَ أُوتُوا الْعِلْمَ الَّذِي أُنْزِلَ إِلَيْكَ مِنْ رَبِّكَ هُوَ الْحَقَّ وَيَهْدِي إِلَىٰ صِرَاطِ الْعَزِيزِ الْحَمِيدِ ۞

وَقَالَ الَّذِينَ كَفَرُوا هَلْ نَدُلُّكُمْ عَلَىٰ رَجُلٍ يُنَبِّئُكُمْ إِذَا مُزِّقْتُمْ كُلَّ مُمَزَّقٍ إِنَّكُمْ لَفِي خَلْقٍ جَدِيدٍ ۞

أَفْتَرَىٰ عَلَى اللَّهِ كَذِبًا أَمْ بِهِ جِنَّةٌ ۗ بَلِ الَّذِينَ لَا يُؤْمِنُونَ بِالْأَخِرَةِ فِي الْعَذَابِ وَالضَّلَالِ الْبَعِيدِ ۞

أَفَلَمْ يَرَوْا إِلَىٰ مَا بَيْنَ أَيْدِيهِمْ وَمَا

behind them, of the sky and the earth? If We wished, We could cause the earth to swallow them up, or cause a piece of the sky to fall upon them. Verily in this is a Sign for every devotee that turns to Allah (in repentance).

10. We bestowed Grace aforetime on David from ourselves: "O you Mountains! You sing back the Praises of Allah with him! and you birds (also)! And We made the iron soft for him;-

11. (Commanding), "You make coats of mail, balancing well the rings of chain armour, and you work righteousness; for be sure I see (clearly) all that you do."

12. And to Solomon (We made) the Wind (obedient): its early morning (stride) was a month's (journey), and its evening (stride) was a month's (journey); and We made a Font of molten brass to flow for him; and there were Jinns that wor-ked in front of him, by the leave of his Lord, and if any of them turned aside from Our command, We made him taste of the Chastisement of the Blazing Fire.

13. They worked for him as he desired, (making) Arches, Images, Basins as large as Reservoirs, and (cooking) Cauldrons fixed (in their places): "You work, sons of David, with thanks! but few of My servants are grateful!"

14. Then, when We decreed (Solomon's) death, nothing showed them his death except a little worm of the earth, which kept (slowly) gnawing away at his staff: so when he fell down, the Jinns saw plainly that if they had known the unseen, they would not have tarried in the humiliating Chastisement (of their Task).

15. There was, for Saba, aforetime, a Sign in their home-land - two Gardens to the right and to the left. "Eat

---

khalfahum-minas-samaaa'i wal-arḍ; in-nashaa nakhsif bihimul-arḍa aw nusqiṭ 'alay-him kisafam-minas-samaaa'; inna fee ẕaalika la-Aayatal-likulli 'abdim-muneeb.

(Section 1)

10. Wa laqad aataynaa Daawooda minnaa faḍlañy yaa jibaalu awwibee ma'ahoo waṭṭayra wa alannaa lahul-ḥadeed.

11. Ani'mal saabighaatiñw-wa qaddir fis-sardi wa'maloo ṣaa-liḥan innee bimaa ta'maloona Baṣeer.

12. Wa li-Sulaymaanar-reeḥa ghuduwwuhaa shahruñw-wa ra-waaḥuhaa shahruñw wa asal-naa lahoo 'aynal-qiṭr; wa minal-jinni mañy-ya'malu bayna ya-dayhi bi-izni Rabbih; wa mañy-yazigh minhum 'an amrinaa nuẕiqhu min 'aẕaabis-sa'eer.

13. Ya'maloona lahoo maa yashaaa'u mim-maḥaareeba wa tamaaseela wa jifaanin kal-jawaabi wa qudoorir-raasiyaat; i'malooo aala Daawooda shukraa; wa qaleelum-min 'ibaadiyash-shakoor.

14. Falammaa qaḍaynaa 'alayhil-mawta maa dallahum 'alaa mawtiheee illaa daaab-batul-arḍi taåkulu minsa-atahoo falammaa kharra tabayyanatil-jinnu al-law kaanoo ya'la-moonal-ghayba maa labisoo fil-'aẕaabil-muheen.

15. Laqad kaana li-Saba-in fee maskanihim Aayatun janna-taani 'añy-yameeniñw-wa shimaalin kuloo

of the Sustenance (provided) by your Lord, and be grateful to Him: a territory fair and happy, and a Lord Oft-Forgiving!

16. But they turned away (from Allah), and We sent against them the flood (released) from the Dams, and We converted their two gardens (rows) into "two gardens" producing bitter fruit, and tamarisks, and some few (stunted) Lote-trees.

17. That was the Requital We gave them because they ungratefully rejected Faith: and never do We give (such) requital except to such as are ungrateful rejecters.

18. Between them and the Cities on which We had poured Our blessings, We had placed Cities in prominent positions, and between them We had appointed stages of journey in due proportion: "Travel therein, secure, by night and by day."

19. But they said: "Our Lord! Place longer distances between our journey-stages": but they wronged themselves (therein). At le-ngth We made them as a tale (that is told), and We dispersed them all in scattered fragments. Verily in this are Signs for every (soul that is) patiently constant and grateful.

20. And on them did Satan prove true his idea, and they followed him, all but a party that believed.

21. But he had no authority over them,- except that We might test the man who believes in the Hereafter from him who is in doubt concerning it: and your Lord watches over all things.

22. Say: "Call upon other (gods) whom you fancy, besides Allah: they have no power,- not the weight of an atom,- in the heavens or on earth: no (sort of) share have they therein, nor is any of them

mir-rizq Rabbikum washkuroo lah; baldatun ṭayyibatuñw-wa Rabbun Ghafoor.

16. Fa-a'raḍoo fa-arsalnaa 'alayhim Saylal-'Arimi wa baddalnaahum bijannatayhim jannatayni zawaatay ukulin khamṭiñw-wa asliñw-wa shay-'im-min sidrin qaleel.

17. Zaalika jazaynaahum bimaa kafaroo wa hal nujaazeee illal-kafoor.

18. Wa ja'alnaa baynahum wa baynal-qural-latee baaraknaa feehaa quran ẓaahiratañw-wa qaddarnaa feehas-sayr; seeroo feehaa la-yaaliya wa ayyaaman aamineen.

19. Faqaaloo Rabbanaa baa-'id bayna asfaarinaa wa ẓalamooo anfusahum faja'al-naahum ahaadeesa wa mazzaq-naahum kulla mumazzaq; inna fee zaalika la-Aayaatil-likulli ṣabbaarin shakoor.

20. Wa laqad ṣaddaqa 'alayhim Ibleesu ẓannahoo fatta-ba'oohu illaa fareeqam-minal-mu'mineen.

21. Wa maa kaana lahoo 'alayhim-min sulṭaanin illaa lina'lama mañy-yu'minu bil-Aakhirati mimman huwa minhaa fee shakk; wa Rabbuka 'alaa kulli shay'in Ḥafeeẓ.

(Section 2)

22. Qulid-'ul-laẓeena za'am-tum-min doonil-laahi laa yamli-koona misqaala ẓarratin fis-samaawaati wa laa fil-arḍi wa maa lahum feehimaa min shirkiñw-wa maa lahoo min-hum-

مِن رِّزْقِ رَبِّكُمْ وَاشْكُرُوا لَهُ ۚ بَلْدَةٌ طَيِّبَةٌ وَّرَبٌّ غَفُورٌ ۞

فَأَعْرَضُوا فَأَرْسَلْنَا عَلَيْهِمْ سَيْلَ الْعَرِمِ وَبَدَّلْنَاهُم بِجَنَّتَيْهِمْ جَنَّتَيْنِ ذَوَاتَيْ أُكُلٍ خَمْطٍ وَّأَثْلٍ وَّشَيْءٍ مِّن سِدْرٍ قَلِيلٍ ۞

ذَٰلِكَ جَزَيْنَاهُم بِمَا كَفَرُوا ۖ وَهَلْ نُجَازِي إِلَّا الْكَفُورَ ۞

وَجَعَلْنَا بَيْنَهُمْ وَبَيْنَ الْقُرَى الَّتِي بَارَكْنَا فِيهَا قُرًى ظَاهِرَةً وَّقَدَّرْنَا فِيهَا السَّيْرَ ۖ سِيرُوا فِيهَا لَيَالِيَ وَأَيَّامًا آمِنِينَ ۞

فَقَالُوا رَبَّنَا بَاعِدْ بَيْنَ أَسْفَارِنَا وَظَلَمُوا أَنفُسَهُمْ فَجَعَلْنَاهُمْ أَحَادِيثَ وَمَزَّقْنَاهُمْ كُلَّ مُمَزَّقٍ ۚ إِنَّ فِي ذَٰلِكَ لَآيَاتٍ لِّكُلِّ صَبَّارٍ شَكُورٍ ۞

وَلَقَدْ صَدَّقَ عَلَيْهِمْ إِبْلِيسُ ظَنَّهُ فَاتَّبَعُوهُ إِلَّا فَرِيقًا مِّنَ الْمُؤْمِنِينَ ۞

وَمَا كَانَ لَهُ عَلَيْهِم مِّن سُلْطَانٍ إِلَّا لِنَعْلَمَ مَن يُؤْمِنُ بِالْآخِرَةِ مِمَّنْ هُوَ مِنْهَا فِي شَكٍّ ۗ وَرَبُّكَ عَلَىٰ كُلِّ شَيْءٍ حَفِيظٌ ۞

قُلِ ادْعُوا الَّذِينَ زَعَمْتُم مِّن دُونِ اللَّهِ ۖ لَا يَمْلِكُونَ مِثْقَالَ ذَرَّةٍ فِي السَّمَاوَاتِ وَلَا فِي الْأَرْضِ وَمَا لَهُمْ فِيهِمَا مِن شِرْكٍ وَمَا لَهُ مِنْهُم

a helper to Allah.

23. "No intercession can avail in His Presence, except for those for whom He has granted permission. So far (is this the case) that, when terror is removed from their hearts (at the Day of Judgment, then) they will say, 'What is it that your Lord commanded?' They will say, 'That which is true and just; and He is the Most High, Most Great'."

24. Say: "Who gives you sustenance, from the heavens and the earth?" Say: "It is Allah; and certain it is that either we or you are on right guidance or in manifest error!"

25. Say: "You shall not be questioned as to our sins, nor shall we be questioned as to what you do."

26. Say: "Our Lord will gather us together and will in the end decide the matter between us (and you) in truth and justice: and He is the one to decide, the One Who knows all."

27. Say: "Show me those whom you have joined with Him as partners: by no means (can you). Nay, He is Allah, the Exalted in Power, the Wise."

28. We have not sent you but as a universal (Messenger) to men, giving them glad tidings, and warning them (against sin), but most men understand not.

29. They say: "When will this promise (come to pass) if you are telling the truth?"

30. Say: "The appointment to you is for a Day, which you cannot put back for an hour nor put forward."

31. The Unbelievers say: "We shall neither believe in this scripture nor in (any) that (came) before it." Could you but see when the wrong-doers will be made to stand before their Lord, throwing back the word (of blame) on one another! Those who had been despised will say

min ẓaheer.

23. Wa laa tanfa'ush-sha-faa'atu 'indahooo illaa liman aẓina lah; ḥattaaa iẓaa fuzzi'a 'an quloobihim qaaloo maaẓaa qaala Rabbukum; qaalul-ḥaqq, wa Huwal-'Aliyyul-Kabeer.

24. Qul mañy-yarzuqukum-minas-samaawaati wal-arḍi qulil-laahu wa innaaa aw iyyaakum la'alaa hudan aw fee ḍalaalim-mubeen.

25. Qul laa tus'aloona 'am-maaa ajramnaa wa laa nus'alu 'ammaa ta'maloon.

26. Qul yajma'u baynanaa Rabbunaa ṣumma yaftaḥu baynanaa bilḥaqq; wa Huwal-Fattaaḥul-'Aleem.

27. Qul arooniyal-laẓeena alḥaqtum bihee shurakaaa'a kallaa; bal Huwal-laahul-'Azeezul-Ḥakeem.

28. Wa maaa arsalnaaka illaa kaaaffatal-linnaasi basheerañw-wa naẓeerañw-wa laakinna akṣaran-naasi laa ya'lamoon.

29. Wa yaqooloona mataa haaẓal-wa'du in kuntum ṣaadiqeen.

30. Qul lakum-mee'aadu Yawmil-laa tastaåkhiroona 'anhu saa'atañw-wa laa tastaq-dimoon. **(Section 3)**

31. Wa qaalal-laẓeena ka-faroo lan-nu'mina bihaaẓal-Qur-aani wa laa billaẓee bayna yadayh; wa law taraaa iẓiẓ-ẓaalimoona mawqoofoona 'inda Rabbihim yarji'u ba'ḍuhum ilaa ba'ḍinil-qawla yaqoolul-laẓeenas-tuḍ'ifoo

to the arrogant ones: "Had it not been for you, we should certainly have been believers!"

lillazeenas-takbaroo law laaa antum lakunnaa mu'mineen.

32. The arrogant ones will say to those who had been despised: "Was it we who kept you back from Guidance after it reached you? Nay, rather, it was you who transgressed.

32. Qaalal-lazeenas-takbaroo lillazeenas-tuḍ'ifooo anaḥnu ṣadadnaakum 'anil-hudaa ba'da iz jaaa'akum bal kuntum-mujrimeen.

33. Those who had been despised will say to the arrogant ones: "Nay! it was a plot (of yours) by day and by night: behold! you (constantly) ordered us to be ungrateful to Allah and to attribute equals to Him!" They will declare (their) repentance when they see the Chastisement: We shall put yokes on the necks of the Unbelievers: it would only be a requital for their (ill) Deeds.

33. Wa qaalal-lazeenastuḍ-'ifoo lillazeenas-takbaroo bal makrul-layli wannahaari iz taa-muroonanaaa an-nakfura bil-laahi wa naj'ala lahooo andaa-daa; wa asarrun-nadaamata lammaa ra-awul-'azaab; wa ja'alnal-aghlaala fee a'naaqil-lazeena kafaroo; hal yujzawna illaa maa kaanoo ya'maloon.

34. Never did We send a Warner to a population, but the wealthy ones among them said: "We do not believe in the (Message) with which you have been sent."

34. Wa maaa arsalnaa fee qaryatim-min-nazeerin illaa qaala mutrafoohaaa innaa bimaaa ursiltum bihee kaafiroon.

35. They said: "We have more in wealth and in sons, and we cannot be punished."

35. Wa qaaloo naḥnu aksaru amwaalañw-wa awlaadañw-wa maa naḥnu bimu'azzabeen.

36. Say: "Verily my Lord enlarges and restricts the Provision to whom He pleases, but most men do not understand."

36. Qul inna Rabbee yabsu-ṭur-rizqa limañy-yashaaa'u wa yaqdiru wa laakinna aksaran-naasi laa ya'lamoon. **(Section 4)**

37. It is not your wealth nor your sons, that will bring you nearer to Us in degree: but only those who believe and work righteousness - these are the ones for whom there is a multiplied Reward for their deeds, while secure they (reside) in the dwellings on high!

37. Wa maaa amwaalukum wa laaa awlaadukum billatee tuqarribukum 'indanaa zulfaaa illaa man aamana wa 'amila ṣaaliḥan fa-ulaaa'ika lahum jazaaa'uḍ-ḍi'fi bimaa 'amiloo wa hum fil-ghurufaati aaminoon.

38. Those who strive against Our Signs, to frustrate them, will be given over into Punishment.

39. Say: "Verily my Lord enlarges and restricts the Sustenance to such of his servants as He pleases: and nothing do you spend in the least (in His Cause) but He replaces it: for He is the Best of those who grant Sustenance.

40. One Day He will gather them all together, and say to the angels, "Were it you that these men used to worship?"

41. They will say, "Glory to You! our (tie) is with You - as Protector - not with them. Nay, but they worshipped the Jinns: most of them believed in them."

42. So on that Day no power shall they have over each other, for profit or harm: and We shall say to the wrong-doers, "You taste the Chastisement of the Fire,- the which you were wont to deny!"

43. When Our Clear Signs are rehearsed to them, they say, "This is only a man who wishes to hinder you from the (worship) which your fathers practised." And they say, "This is only a falsehood invented!" And the Unbelievers say of the Truth when it comes to them, "This is nothing but evident magic!"

44. But We had not given them Books which they could study, nor sent Apostles to them before you as Warners.

45. And their predecessors rejected (the Truth); these have not

---

38. Wallazeena yas'awna feee Aayaatinaa mu'aajizeena ulaaa'ika fil-'azaabi muḥḍaroon.

39. Qul inna Rabbee yabsuṭur-rizqa limañy-yashaaa'u min 'ibaadihee wa yaqdiru lah; wa maaaa anfaqtum-min shay'in fahuwa yukhlifuhoo wa Huwa khayrur-raaziqeen.

40. Wa Yawma yaḥshuruhum jamee'an summa yaqoolu lilmalaaa'ikati a-haaa'ulaaa'i iyyaakum kaanoo ya'budoon.

41. Qaaloo Subḥaanaka Anta waliyyunaa min doonihim bal kaanoo ya'budoonal-jinna aksaruhum bihim-mu'minoon.

42. Fal-Yawma laa yamliku ba'ḍukum liba'ḍin-naf'añw-wa laa ḍarraa; wa naqoolu lillzeena ẓalamoo zooqoo 'azaaban-Naaril-latee kuntum bihaa tukazziboon.

43. Wa izaa tutlaa 'alayhim Aayaatunaa bayyinaatin qaaloo maa haazaaa illaa rajuluñy-yureedu añy-yaṣuddakum 'ammaa kaana ya'budu aabaaa'ukum wa qaaloo maa haazaaa illaaa ifkum-muftaraa; wa qaalal-lazeena kafaroo lilḥaqqi lammaa jaaa'ahum in haazaaa illaa siḥrum-mubeen.

44. Wa maaaa aataynaahum min Kutubiñy-yadrusoonahaa wa maaaa arsalnaaaa ilayhim qablaka min-nazeer.

45. Wa kazzabal-lazeena min qablihim wa maa

received a tenth of what We had granted to those: yet when they rejected My Apostles, how (terrible) was My rejection (of them)!

46. Say: "I do admonish you on one point: that you do stand up before Allah,- (It may be) in pairs, or (it may be) singly,- and reflect (within yourselves): your Companion is not possessed: he is no less than a Warner to you, in face of a terrible Chastisement."

47. Say: "No reward do I ask of you: it is (all) in your interest: my reward is only due from Allah: and He is witness to all things."

48. Say: "Verily my Lord casts the (mantle of) Truth (over His servants),- He that has full knowledge of (all) that is hidden."

49. Say: "The Truth has arrived, and Falsehood neither creates anything new, nor restores anything."

50. Say: "If I am astray, I only stray to the loss of my own soul: but if I receive guidance, it is because of the inspiration of my Lord to me: it is He Who hears all things, and is (ever) near."

51. If you could but see when they will quake with terror; but then there will be no escape (for them), and they will be seized from a position (quite) near.

52. And they will say, "We do believe (now) in the (Truth)"; but how could they receive (Faith) from a position (so far off),-

53. Seeing that they did reject Faith (entirely) before, and that they (continually) cast (slanders) on the Unseen from a position far off?

54. And between them and their desires, is placed a barrier, as was done in the past with their partisans: for they were indeed in suspicious (disquieting) doubt.

balaghoo mi'shaara maaa aataynaahum fakazzaboo Rusulee; fakayfa kaana nakeer.

(Section 5)

46. Qul innamaaa a'izukum biwaahidatin an taqoomoo lillaahi masnaa wa furaadaa summa tatafakkaroo; maa bisaahibikum-min jinnah; in huwa illaa nazeerul-lakum bayna yaday 'azaabin shadeed.

47. Qul maa sa-altukum-min ajrin fahuwa lakum in ajriya illaa 'alal-laahi wa Huwa 'alaa kulli shay'in Shaheed.

48. Qul inna Rabbee yaqzifu bilhaqq, 'Allaamul-Ghuyoob.

49. Qul jaaa'al-haqqu wa maa yubdi'ul-baatilu wa maa yu'eed.

50. Qul in dalaltu fainnamaaa adillu 'alaa nafsee wa inih-tadaytu fabimaa yooheee ilayya Rabbee; innahoo Samee'un Qareeb.

51. Wa law taraaa iz fazi'oo falaa fawta wa ukhizoo mim-makaanin qareeb.

52. Wa qaaloo aamannaa bihee wa annaa lahumut-tanaawushu mim-makaanim ba'eed.

53. Wa qad kafaroo bihee min qablu wa yaqzifoona bilghaybi mim-makaanim ba'eed.

54. Wa heela baynahum wa bayna maa yashtahoona kamaa fu'ila bi-ashyaa'ihim-min qabl; innahum kaanoo fee shakkim-mureeb.

(Section 6)

بَلَغُوْا مِعْشَارَ مَاۤ اٰتَيْنٰهُمْ فَكَذَّبُوْا رُسُلِيْ فَكَيْفَ كَانَ نَكِيْرِ ۞

قُلْ اِنَّمَاۤ اَعِظُكُمْ بِوَاحِدَةٍ اَنْ تَقُوْمُوْا لِلّٰهِ مَثْنٰى وَفُرَادٰى ثُمَّ تَتَفَكَّرُوْا مَا بِصَاحِبِكُمْ مِّنْ جِنَّةٍ اِنْ هُوَ اِلَّا نَذِيْرٌ لَّكُمْ بَيْنَ يَدَيْ عَذَابٍ شَدِيْدٍ ۞

قُلْ مَا سَاَلْتُكُمْ مِّنْ اَجْرٍ فَهُوَ لَكُمْ اِنْ اَجْرِيَ اِلَّا عَلَى اللّٰهِ وَهُوَ عَلٰى كُلِّ شَيْءٍ شَهِيْدٌ ۞

قُلْ اِنَّ رَبِّيْ يَقْذِفُ بِالْحَقِّ عَلَّامُ الْغُيُوْبِ ۞

قُلْ جَاۤءَ الْحَقُّ وَمَا يُبْدِئُ الْبَاطِلُ وَمَا يُعِيْدُ ۞

قُلْ اِنْ ضَلَلْتُ فَاِنَّمَاۤ اَضِلُّ عَلٰى نَفْسِيْ وَاِنِ اهْتَدَيْتُ فَبِمَا يُوْحِيْ اِلَيَّ رَبِّيْ اِنَّهٗ سَمِيْعٌ قَرِيْبٌ ۞

وَلَوْ تَرٰۤى اِذْ فَزِعُوْا فَلَا فَوْتَ وَاُخِذُوْا مِنْ مَّكَانٍ قَرِيْبٍ ۞

وَّقَالُوْۤا اٰمَنَّا بِهٖ وَاَنّٰى لَهُمُ التَّنَاوُشُ مِنْ مَّكَانٍ بَعِيْدٍ ۞

وَّقَدْ كَفَرُوْا بِهٖ مِنْ قَبْلُ وَيَقْذِفُوْنَ بِالْغَيْبِ مِنْ مَّكَانٍ بَعِيْدٍ ۞

وَحِيْلَ بَيْنَهُمْ وَبَيْنَ مَا يَشْتَهُوْنَ كَمَا فُعِلَ بِاَشْيَاعِهِمْ مِّنْ قَبْلُ اِنَّهُمْ كَانُوْا فِيْ شَكٍّ مُّرِيْبٍ ۞

35. The Originator of Creation

In the name of Allah, Most Gracious, Most Merciful.

1. Praise be to Allah, Who created (out of nothing) the heavens and the earth, Who made the angels, messengers with wings,- two, or three, or four (pairs): He adds to Creation as He pleases: for Allah has power over all things.

2. What Allah out of His Mercy bestows on mankind there is none can withhold: what He withholds, there is none can grant, apart from Him: and He is the Exalted in Power, full of Wisdom.

3. O men! Call to mind the grace of Allah unto you! Is there a creator, other than Allah, to give you sustenance from heaven or earth? There is no god but He: how then are you deluded away from the Truth?

4. And if they reject you, so were Apostles rejected before you: to Allah go back for decision all affairs.

5. O men! Certainly the promise of Allah is true. Let not then this present life deceive you, nor let the Chief Deceiver deceive you about Allah.

6. Verily Satan is an enemy to you: so treat him as an enemy. He only invites his adherents, that they may become companions of the Blazing Fire.

7. For those who reject Allah, is a terrible Chastisement: but for those who believe and work righteous deeds, is Forgiveness, and a magnificent Reward.

Sûrat Fâtir–35
(Revealed at Makkah)

Bismillaahir Rahmaanir Raheem

1. Alḥamdu lillaahi faaṭiris-samaawaati wal-arḍi jaa‘ilil-malaaa’ikati rusulan uleee ajniḥatim-maṣnaa wa ṣulaaṣa wa rubaa‘; yazeedu fil-khalqi maa yashaaa’; innal-laaha ‘alaa kulli shay’in Qadeer.

2. Maa yaftaḥil-laahu lin-naasi mir-raḥmatin falaa mumsika lahaa wa maa yumsik falaa mursila lahoo mimba‘dih; wa Huwal-‘Azeezul-Ḥakeem.

3. Yaaa ayyuhan-naasuz-kuroo ni‘matal-laahi ‘alaykum; hal min khaaliqin ghayrul-laahi yarzuqukum-minas-samaaa’i wal-arḍ; laaa ilaaha illaa Huwa fa-annaa tu’fakoon.

4. Wa iñy-yukazzibooka faqad kuzzibat Rusulum-min qablik; wa ilal-laahi turja‘ul-umoor.

5. Yaaa ayyuhan-naasu inna wa‘dal-laahi ḥaqqun falaa taghurrannakumul-ḥayaatud-dunyaa: wa laa yaghurran-nakum billaahil-gharoor.

6. Innash-Shayṭaana lakum ‘aduwwun fattakhizoohu ‘aduwwaa; innamaa yad‘oo ḥizbahoo liyakoonoo min aṣḥaabis-sa‘eer.

7. Allazeena kafaroo lahum ‘azaabun shadeed; wallazeena aamanoo wa ‘amiluṣ-ṣaaliḥaati lahum-maghfiratuñw-wa ajrun kabeer. **(Section 1)**

8. Is he, then, to whom the evil of his conduct is made alluring, so that he looks upon it as good, (equal to one who is rightly guided)? For Allah leaves to stray whom He wills, and guides whom He wills. So let not your soul go out in (vainly) sighing after them: for Allah knows well all that they do!

8. Afaman zuyyina lahoo sooo'u 'amalihee fara-aahu ḥasanaa; fa-innal-laaha yuḍillu mañy-yashaaa'u wa yahdee mañy-yashaaa'u falaa tazhab nafsuka 'alayhim ḥasaraat; innal-laaha 'aleemum bimaa yaṣna'oon.

9. It is Allah Who sends forth the Winds, so that they raise up the Clouds, and We drive them to a land that is dead, and revive the earth therewith after its death: even so (will be) the Resurrection!

9. Wallaahul-lazeee arsalar-riyaaḥa fatuseeru saḥaaban fasuqnaahu ilaa baladim-mayyitin fa-aḥyaynaa bihil-arḍa ba'da mawtihaa; kazaa-likan-nushoor.

10. If any do seek for glory and power,- to Allah belong all glory and power. To Him mount up (all) Words of Purity: it is He Who exalts each Deed of Righteousness. Those that lay Plots of Evil,- for them is a terrible penalty; and the plotting of such will be void (of result).

10. Man kaana yureedul 'izzata falillaahil-'izzatu jamee'aa; ilayhi yaṣ'adul-kalimuṭ-ṭayyibu wal'amaluṣ-ṣaaliḥu yarfa'uh; wallazeena yamkuroonas-sayyiaati lahum 'azaabun shadeed; wa makru ulaaa'ika huwa yaboor.

11. And Allah created you from dust; then from a sperm-drop; then He made you in pairs. And no female conceives, or lays down (her load), but with His knowledge. Nor is a man long-lived granted length of days, nor is a part cut off from his life, but is in a Decree (ordained). All this is easy to Allah.

11. Wallaahu khalaqakum-min turaabin ṣumma min-nuṭfatin ṣumma ja'alakum azwaajaa; wa maa taḥmilu min unṣaa wa laa taḍa'u illaa bi'ilmih; wa maa yu'ammaru mim-mu'ammariñw-wa laa yunqaṣu min 'umuriheee illaa fee kitaab; inna zaalika 'alal-laahi yaseer.

12. Nor are the two bodies of flowing water alike,- the one palatable, sweet, and pleasant to drink, and the other, salt and bitter. Yet from each (kind of water) you eat flesh fresh and tender, and you extract ornaments to wear; and you see the ships therein that plough the waves, that you may seek

12. Wa maa yastawil-baḥraani haazaa 'azbun furaatun saaa'ighun sharaabuhoo wa haazaa milḥun ujaaj; wa min kullin taåkuloona laḥman ṭariyyyañw-wa tastakhrijoona ḥilyatan talbasoonahaa wa taral-fulka feehi mawaakhira litabtaghoo

(thus) of the Bounty of Allah that you may be grateful.

13. He merges Night into Day, and He merges Day into Night, and He has subjected the sun and the moon (to His Law): each one runs its course for a term appointed. Such is Allah your Lord: to Him belongs all Dominion. And those whom you invoke besides Him have not the least power.

14. If you invoke them, they will not listen to your call, and if they were to listen, they cannot answer your (prayer). On the Day of Judgment they will reject your "Partnership". And none, (O man!) can tell you (the Truth) like the One Who is acquainted with all things.

15. O you men! It is you that have need of Allah: but Allah is the One Free of all wants, worthy of all praise.

16. If He so pleased, He could blot you out and bring in a New Creation.

17. Nor is that (at all) difficult for Allah.

18. Nor can a bearer of burdens bear another's burden. If one heavily laden should call another to (bear) his load, not the least portion of it can be carried (by the other), even though he be nearly related. You can but admonish such as fear their Lord unseen and establish regular Prayer. And whoever purifies himself does so for the benefit of his own soul; and the destination (of all) is to Allah.

19. The blind and the seeing are not alike;

20. Nor are the depths of Darkness and the Light;

21. Nor are the (chilly) shade and the (genial) heat of the sun:

min faḍlihee wa la'allakum tashkuroon.

13. Yoolijul-layla fin-nahaari wa yoolijun-nahaara fil-layli wa sakhkharash-shamsa wal-qamara kulluny-yajree li-aja-lim-musammaa; zaalikumul-laahu Rabbukum lahul-mulk; wallazeena tad'oona min doonihee maa yamlikoona min qiṭmeer.

14. In tad'oohum laa yas-ma'oo du'aaa'akum wa law sami'oo mas-tajaaboo lakum; wa Yawmal-Qiyaamati yakfu-roona bishirkikum; wa laa yunabbi'uka mislu khabeer.

(Section 2)

15. Yaaa ayyuhan-naasu antumul-fuqaraaa'u ilallaahi wallaahu Huwal-Ghaniyyul-Ḥameed.

16. Iñy-yashaå yuzhibkum wa yaåti bikhalqin jadeed.

17. Wa maa zaalika 'alal-laahi bi'azeez.

18. Wa laa taziru waaziratuñw-wizra ukhraa; wa in tad'u musqalatun ilaa ḥimlihaa laa yuḥmal minhu shay'uñw-wa law kaana zaa qurbaa; innamaa tunzirul-lazeena yakhshawna Rabbahum bilghaybi wa aqaamuṣ-Ṣalaah; wa man tazakkaa fa-innamaa yatazakkaa linaf-sih; wa ilal-laahil-maṣeer.

19. Wa maa yastawil-a'maa wal-baṣeer.

20. Wa laz-zulumaatu wa lannoor.

21. Wa laz-zillu wa lal-haroor.

22. Nor are alike those that are living and those that are dead. Allah can make any that He wills to hear; but you cannot make those to hear who are (buried) in graves.

23. You are no other than a warner.

24. Verily We have sent you in truth, as a bearer of glad tidings, and as a warner: and there never was a people, without a warner having lived among them (in the past).

25. And if they reject you, so did their predecessors, to whom came their Apostles with Clear Signs, Books of dark prophecies, and the Book of Enlightenment.

26. In the end did I punish those who rejected Faith: and how (terrible) was My rejection (of them)!

27. Do you not see that Allah sends down rain from the sky? With it We then bring out produce of various colours. And in the mountains are tracts white and red, of various shades of colour, and black intense in hue.

28. And so amongst men and crawling creatures and cattle, they are of various colours. Those truly fear Allah, among His servants, who have knowledge: for Allah is Exalted in Might, Oft-Forgiving.

29. Those who rehearse the Book of Allah, establish regular Prayer, and spend (in charity) out of what We have provided for them, secretly and openly, hope for a commerce that will never fail:

30. For He will pay them their meed, nay, He will give them (even) more out of His Bounty: for He is Oft-Forgiving, Most Ready to appreciate (service).

31. That which We have revealed to thee of the Book

---

22. Wa maa yastawil-aḥyaaa-'u wa lal-amwaat; innal-laaha yusmi'u mañy-yashaaa'u wa maaa anta bimusmi'im-man fil-quboor.

23. In anta illaa nazeer.

24. Innaaa arsalnaaka bil-ḥaqqi basheerañw-wa nazeeraa; wa im-min ummatin illaa khalaa feehaa nazeer.

25. Wa iñy-yukazzibooka faqad kazzabal-lazeena min qablihim jaaa'at-hum Rusuluhum bilbayyinaati wa biz-Zuburi wa bil-Kitaabil-Muneer.

26. Summa akhaztul-lazeena kafaroo fakayfa kaana nakeer.

(Section 3)

27. Alam tara annal-laaha anzala minas-samaaa'i maaa'an fa-akhrajnaa bihee samaraatim-mukhtalifan alwaanuhaa; wa minal-jibaali judadum bee-ḍuñw-wa ḥumrum-mukhtali-fun alwaanuhaa wa gharaa-beebu sood.

28. Wa minan-naasi wadda-waaabbi wal-an'aami mukh-talifun alwaanuhoo kazalik; innamaa yakhshal-laaha min 'ibaadihil-'ulamaaa'; innal-laaha 'Azeezun Ghafoor.

29. Innal-lazeena yatloona Kitaabal-laahi wa aqaamuṣ-Ṣalaata wa anfaqoo mimmaa razaqnaahum sirrañw-wa 'alaa-niyataññy-yarjoona tijaaratal-lan taboor.

30. Liyuwaffiyahum ujoo-rahum wa yazeedahum-min faḍlih; innahoo Ghafoorun Shakoor.

31. Wallazeee awḥaynaaa ilayka minal-Kitaabi

وَمَا يَسْتَوِي الْأَحْيَاءُ وَلَا الْأَمْوَاتُ ۚ إِنَّ اللّٰهَ يُسْمِعُ مَنْ يَشَاءُ ۖ وَمَا أَنْتَ بِمُسْمِعٍ مَنْ فِي الْقُبُورِ ۞

إِنْ أَنْتَ إِلَّا نَذِيرٌ ۞

إِنَّا أَرْسَلْنَاكَ بِالْحَقِّ بَشِيرًا وَنَذِيرًا ۚ وَإِنْ مِنْ أُمَّةٍ إِلَّا خَلَا فِيهَا نَذِيرٌ ۞

وَإِنْ يُكَذِّبُوكَ فَقَدْ كَذَّبَ الَّذِينَ مِنْ قَبْلِهِمْ جَاءَتْهُمْ رُسُلُهُمْ بِالْبَيِّنَاتِ وَبِالزُّبُرِ وَبِالْكِتَابِ الْمُنِيرِ ۞

ثُمَّ أَخَذْتُ الَّذِينَ كَفَرُوا فَكَيْفَ كَانَ نَكِيرِ ۞

أَلَمْ تَرَ أَنَّ اللّٰهَ أَنْزَلَ مِنَ السَّمَاءِ مَاءً فَأَخْرَجْنَا بِهِ ثَمَرَاتٍ مُخْتَلِفًا أَلْوَانُهَا ۚ وَمِنَ الْجِبَالِ جُدَدٌ بِيضٌ وَحُمْرٌ مُخْتَلِفٌ أَلْوَانُهَا وَغَرَابِيبُ سُودٌ ۞

وَمِنَ النَّاسِ وَالدَّوَابِّ وَالْأَنْعَامِ مُخْتَلِفٌ أَلْوَانُهُ كَذَلِكَ ۗ إِنَّمَا يَخْشَى اللّٰهَ مِنْ عِبَادِهِ الْعُلَمَاءُ ۗ إِنَّ اللّٰهَ عَزِيزٌ غَفُورٌ ۞

إِنَّ الَّذِينَ يَتْلُونَ كِتَابَ اللّٰهِ وَأَقَامُوا الصَّلَاةَ وَأَنْفَقُوا مِمَّا رَزَقْنَاهُمْ سِرًّا وَعَلَانِيَةً يَرْجُونَ تِجَارَةً لَنْ تَبُورَ ۞

لِيُوَفِّيَهُمْ أُجُورَهُمْ وَيَزِيدَهُمْ مِنْ فَضْلِهِ ۚ إِنَّهُ غَفُورٌ شَكُورٌ ۞

وَالَّذِي أَوْحَيْنَا إِلَيْكَ مِنَ الْكِتَابِ

is the Truth,- confirming what was (revealed) before it: for Allah is assuredly- with respect to His servants - well acquainted and fully Observant.

32. Then We have given the Book for inheritance to such of Our Servants as We have chosen: but there are among them some who wrong their own souls; some who follow a middle course; and some who are, by Allah's leave, foremost in good deeds; that is the highest Grace.

33. Gardens of Eternity will they enter: therein they will be adorned with bracelets of gold and pearls; and their garments there will be of silk.

34. And they will say: "Praise be to Allah, Who has removed from us (all) sorrow: for our Lord is indeed Oft-Forgiving ready to appreciate (service):

35. "Who has, out of His Bounty, settled us in a Home that will last: no toil nor sense of weariness shall touch us therein."

36. But those who reject (Allah) - for them will be the Fire of Hell: No term shall be determined for them, so they should die, nor shall its Chastisement be lightened for them. Thus do We reward every ungrateful one!

37. Therein will they cry aloud (for assistance): "Our Lord! Bring us out: we shall work righteousness, not the (deeds) we used to do!" "Did We not give you long enough life so that he that would should receive admonition? And (moreover) the warner came to you. So you taste (the fruits of your deeds): for the wrong-doers there is no helper."

38. Verily Allah knows (all) the hidden things of the heavens and the earth: verily He has full knowledge of all that is in (men's) hearts.

huwal-ḥaqqu muṣaddiqal-limaa bayna yadayh; innal-laaha bi'ibaadihee la-Khabeerum Baṣeer.

32. Summa awraṣnal-Kitaaballazeenaṣ-ṭafaynaa min 'ibaadinaa faminhum ẓaalimul-linafsihee wa minhum-muqtaṣid, wa minhum saabiqum bilkhayraati bi-iznillaah; zaalika huwal-faḍlulkabeer.

33. Jannaatu 'Adniny-yadkhuloonahaa yuḥallawna feehaa min asaawira min zahabiñw-wa lu'lu'añw wa libaasuhum feehaa ḥareer.

34. Wa qaalul-ḥamdu lillaahil-lazee azhaba 'annal-ḥazan; inna Rabbanaa la-Ghafoorun Shakoor.

35. Allazee aḥallanaa daaralmuqaamati min faḍlihee laa yamassunaa feehaa naṣabuñw-wa laa yamassunaa feehaa lughoob.

36. Wallazeena kafaroo lahum Naaru Jahannama laa yuqḍaa 'alayhim fa-yamootoo wa laa yukhaffafu 'anhum-min 'azaabihaa; kazaalika najzee kulla kafoor.

37. Wa hum yaṣṭarikhoona feehaa Rabbanaaa akhrijnaa na'mal ṣaaliḥan ghayral-lazee kunnaa na'mal; awa lam nu'ammirkum-maa yatazakkaru feehi man tazakkara wa jaaa'akumun-nazeeru fazooqoo famaa lizẓaalimeena min naṣeer.   **(Section 4)**

38. Innal-laaha 'aalimu ghaybis-samaawaati wal-arḍ; innahoo 'aleemum bizaatiṣ-ṣudoor.

هُوَالْحَقُّ مُصَدِّقٌ لِّمَا بَيْنَ يَدَيْهِ ۚ إِنَّ اللّٰهَ بِعِبَادِهٖ لَخَبِيْرٌۢ بَصِيْرٌ ۞

ثُمَّ اَوْرَثْنَا الْكِتٰبَ الَّذِيْنَ اصْطَفَيْنَا مِنْ عِبَادِنَا ۚ فَمِنْهُمْ ظَالِمٌ لِّنَفْسِهٖ ۚ وَمِنْهُمْ مُّقْتَصِدٌ ۚ وَمِنْهُمْ سَابِقٌۢ بِالْخَيْرٰتِ بِاِذْنِ اللّٰهِ ؕ ذٰلِكَ هُوَ الْفَضْلُ الْكَبِيْرُ ۞

جَنّٰتُ عَدْنٍ يَّدْخُلُوْنَهَا يُحَلَّوْنَ فِيْهَا مِنْ اَسَاوِرَ مِنْ ذَهَبٍ وَّلُؤْلُؤًا ۚ وَلِبَاسُهُمْ فِيْهَا حَرِيْرٌ ۞

وَقَالُوا الْحَمْدُ لِلّٰهِ الَّذِيْٓ اَذْهَبَ عَنَّا الْحَزَنَ ؕ إِنَّ رَبَّنَا لَغَفُوْرٌ شَكُوْرُۨ ۞

الَّذِيْٓ اَحَلَّنَا دَارَ الْمُقَامَةِ مِنْ فَضْلِهٖ ۚ لَا يَمَسُّنَا فِيْهَا نَصَبٌ وَّلَا يَمَسُّنَا فِيْهَا لُغُوْبٌ ۞

وَالَّذِيْنَ كَفَرُوْا لَهُمْ نَارُ جَهَنَّمَ ۚ لَا يُقْضٰى عَلَيْهِمْ فَيَمُوْتُوْا وَلَا يُخَفَّفُ عَنْهُمْ مِّنْ عَذَابِهَا ؕ كَذٰلِكَ نَجْزِيْ كُلَّ كَفُوْرٍ ۞

وَهُمْ يَصْطَرِخُوْنَ فِيْهَا ۚ رَبَّنَآ اَخْرِجْنَا نَعْمَلْ صَالِحًا غَيْرَ الَّذِيْ كُنَّا نَعْمَلُ ؕ اَوَلَمْ نُعَمِّرْكُمْ مَّا يَتَذَكَّرُ فِيْهِ مَنْ تَذَكَّرَ وَجَآءَكُمُ النَّذِيْرُ ؕ فَذُوْقُوْا فَمَا لِلظّٰلِمِيْنَ مِنْ نَصِيْرٍ ۞

إِنَّ اللّٰهَ عٰلِمُ غَيْبِ السَّمٰوٰتِ وَالْاَرْضِ ؕ إِنَّهٗ عَلِيْمٌۢ بِذَاتِ الصُّدُوْرِ ۞

39. He it is that has made you inheritors in the earth: if, then, any do reject (Allah), their rejection (works) against themselves: their rejection but adds to the odium for the Unbelievers in the sight of their Lord: their rejection but adds to (their own) undoing.

40. Say: "Have you seen (these) 'Partners' of yours whom you call upon besides Allah? Show Me what it is they have created in the (wide) earth. Or have they a share in the heavens? Or have We given them a Book from which they (can derive) clear (evidence)?- Nay, the wrong-doers promise each other nothing but delusions.

41. It is Allah Who sustains the heavens and the earth, lest they cease (to function): and if they should fail, there is none - not one - can sustain them thereafter: Verily He is Most Forbearing, Oft-Forgiving.

42. They swore their strongest oaths by Allah that if a warner came to them, they would follow his guidance better than any (other) of the Peoples: but when a warner came to them, it has only increased their flight (from righteousness),-

43. On account of their arrogance in the land and their plotting of Evil. But the plotting of Evil will hem in only the authors thereof. Now are they but looking for the way the ancients were dealt with? But no change will you find in Allah's way (of dealing): no turning off will you find in Allah's way (of dealing).

44. Do they not travel through the earth, and see what was the End of those

39. Huwal-lazee ja'alakum khalaaa'ifa fil-arḍ; faman kafara fa'alayhi kufruhoo; wa laa yazeedul-kaafireena kufruhum 'inda Rabbihim illaa maqtañw wa laa yazeedul-kaafireena kufruhum illaa khasaaraa.

40. Qul ara'aytum shura-kaaa'a kumul-lazeena tad'oona min doonil-laah; aroonee maazaa khalaqoo minal-arḍi am lahum shirkun fis-samaawaati am aataynaahum Kitaaban fahum 'alaa bayyinatim-minh; bal iñy-ya'iduẓ-ẓaalimoona ba'ḍuhum ba'ḍan illaa ghuroo-raa.

41. Innal-laaha yumsikus-samaawaati wal-arḍa an tazoo-laa; wa la'in zaalataaa in amsa-kahumaa min aḥadim-mim ba'dih; innahoo kaana Ḥalee-man Ghafooraa.

42. Wa aqsamoo billaahi jahda aymaanihim la'in jaaa'a-hum naẓeerul-layakoonunna ahdaa min iḥdal-umami falam-maa jaaa'ahum naẓeerum-maa zaadahum illaa nufooraa.

43. Istikbaaran fil-arḍi wa makras-sayyi'; wa laa yaḥee-qul-makrus-sayyi'u illaa bi-ahlih; fahal yanẓuroona illaa sunnatal-awwaleen; falan tajida lisunnatil-laahi tabdeelañw wa lan tajida lisunnatil-laahi taḥ-weelaa.

44. Awalam yaseeroo fil-arḍi fa-yanẓuroo kayfa kaana 'aaqibatul-lazeena min

before them,- though they were superior to them in strength? Nor is Allah to be frustrated by anything what-ever in the heavens or on earth: for He is All-Knowing. All-Powerful.

45. If Allah were to punish men according to what they deserve. He would not leave on the back of the (earth) a single living creature: but He gives them respite for a stated Term: when their Term expires, verily Allah has in His sight all His servants.

36. Ya-Sin
In the name of Allah, Most Gracious, Most Merciful.

1. *Ya-Sin.*

2. By the Qur'an, full of Wisdom,-

3. You are indeed one of the Apostles,

4. On a Straight Way.

5. It is a Revelation sent down by (Him), the Exalted in Might, Most Merciful.

6. In order that you may admonish a people, whose fathers had received no admonition, and who therefore remain heedless (of the Signs of Allah).

7. The Word is proved true against the greater part of them: for they do not believe.

8. We have put yokes round their necks right up to their chins, so that their heads are forced up (and they cannot see).

9. And We have put a bar in front of them and a bar behind them, and further, We have covered them up; so that they cannot see.

10. The same is it to them whether you admonish them or you do not

qablihim wa kaanooo ashadda minhum quwwah; wa maa kaanal-laahu liyu'jizahoo min shay'in fis-samaawaati wa laa fil-arḍ; innahoo kaana 'Alee-man Qadeeraa.

45. Wa law yu'aakhizul-laahun-naasa bimaa kasaboo maa taraka 'alaa ẓahrihaa min daaabbatiñw-wa laakiñy-yu'akhkhiruhum ilaaa ajalim-musamman fa-izaa jaaa'a ajaluhum fa-innal-laaha kaana bi'ibaadihee Baṣeeraa.

(Section 5)

Sûrat Yâ-Sîn—36
(Revealed at Makkah)
Bismillaahir Raḥmaanir Raḥeem

1. Yaa-Seeen.

2. Wal-Qur-aanil-Ḥakeem.

3. Innaka laminal-mursaleen.

4. 'Alaa Ṣiraaṭim-Musta-qeem.

5. Tanzeelal-'Azeezir-Ra-ḥeem.

6. Litunzira qawmam-maaa unzira aabaaa'uhum fahum ghaafiloon.

7. Laqad ḥaqqal-qawlu 'alaaa aksarihim fahum laa yu'minoon.

8. Innaa ja'alnaa feee a'naa-qihim aghlaalan fahiya ilal-azqaani fahum-muqmaḥoon.

9. Wa ja'alnaa mim bayni aydeehim saddañw-wa min khalfihim saddan fa-aghshay-naahum fahum laa yubṣiroon.

10. Wa sawaaa'un 'alayhim 'a-anzartahum am lam

admonish them: they will not believe.

11. You can but admonish such a one as follows the Message and fears the (Lord) Most Gracious, unseen: give such a one, therefore, good tidings of Forgiveness and a Reward most generous.

12. Verily We shall give life to the dead, and We record that which they send before and that which they leave behind, and of all things have We taken account in a clear Book (of evidence).

13. Set forth to them, by way of a parable, the (story of) the Companions of the City. Behold! there came Apostles to it.

14. When We (first) sent to them two Apostles, they rejected them: but We strengthened them with a third: they said, "Truly, we have been sent on a mission to you."

15. The (people) said: "You are only men like ourselves; and (Allah) Most Gracious sends no sort of revelation: you do nothing but lie."

16. They said: "Our Lord knows that we have been sent on a mission to you:

17. "And our duty is only to proclaim the clear Message."

18. The (people) said: "For us, we augur an evil omen from you: if you desist not, we will certainly stone you. And a grievous punishment indeed will be inflicted on you by us."

19. They said: "Your evil omens are with yourselves: (you deem this an evil omen), if you are admonished: Nay, but you are a people transgressing all bounds!"

20. Then there came running from the farthest part of the City, a man, saying, "O my people! Obey the Apostles:

21. "Obey those who ask no reward of you (for themselves), and who have themselves received Guidance.

tunzirhum laa yu'minoon.

11. Innamaa tunziru manittaba'az-Zikra wa khashiyar-Rahmaana bilghayb, fabashshirhu bimaghfiratiñw-wa ajrin kareem.

12. Innaa Nahnu nuhyil-mawtaa wa naktubu maa qaddamoo wa aasaarahum; wa kulla shay'in ahsaynaahu feee Imaamim-Mubeen. **(Section 1)**

13. Wadrib lahum-masalan Ashaabal-Qaryatih; iz jaaa'a-hal-mursaloon.

14. Iz arsalnaaa ilayhimusnayni fakazzaboohumaa fa'azzaznaa bisaalisin faqaalooo innaaa ilaykum-mursaloon.

15. Qaaloo maaa antum illaa basharum-mislunaa wa maaa anzalar-Rahmaanu min shay'in in antum illaa takziboon.

16. Qaaloo Rabbunaa ya'lamu innaaa ilaykum lamursaloon.

17. Wa maa 'alaynaaa illalbalaaghul-mubeen.

18. Qaalooo innaa tatayyarnaa bikum la'il-lam tantahoo lanarjumannakum wa la-yamassannakum-minnaa 'azaabun aleem.

19. Qaaloo taaa'irukummma'akum; a'in zukkirtum; bal antum qawmum-musrifoon.

20. Wa jaaa'a min aqsalmadeenati rajuluñy-yas'aa qaala yaa qawmit-tabi'ul-mursaleen.

21. Ittabi'oo mal-laa yas'alukum ajrañw-wa hum-muhtadoon.

22. "It would not be reasonable in me if I did not serve Him Who created me, and to Whom you shall (all) be brought back.

23. "Shall I take (other) gods besides Him? If (Allah) Most Gracious should intend some adversity for me, of no use whatever will be their intercession for me, nor can they deliver me.

24. "I would indeed, if I were to do so, be in manifest Error.

25. "For me, I have faith in the Lord of you (all): listen, then, to me!"

26. It was said: "You enter you the Garden." He said: "Ah me! Would that my People knew (what I know)!-

27. "For that my Lord has granted me Forgiveness and has enrolled me among those held in honour!"

28. And We did not send down against his People, after him, any hosts from heaven, nor was it needful for Us so to do.

29. It was no more than a single mighty Blast, and behold! they were (like ashes) quenched and silent.

30. Ah! Alas for (My) servants! There comes not an Apostle to them but they mock him!

31. Don't they see how many generations before them We destroyed? Not to them will they return:

32. But each one of them all - will be brought before Us (for judgment).

33. A Sign for them is the earth that is dead: We do give it life, and produce grain therefrom, of which you do eat.

34. And We produce therein orchards with date-palms and vines, and We cause springs to gush forth therein:

35. That they may enjoy the fruits of this (artistry): it was not

---

22. Wa maa liya laaa a'budul-lazee faṭaranee wa ilayhi turja'oon.

23. 'A-attakhizu min dooni-heee aalihatan iñy-yuridnir-Raḥmaanu biḍurril-laa tughni 'annee shafaa'atuhum shay-'añw-wa laa yunqizoon.

24. Inneee izal-lafee ḍalaa-lim-mubeen.

25. Inneee aamantu bi-Rabbikum fasma'oon.

26. Qeelad-khulil-Jannah; qaala yaa layta qawmee ya'lamoon.

27. Bimaa ghafara lee Rabbee wa ja'alanee minal-mukra-meen.

28. Wa maaa anzalnaa 'alaa qawmihee mim ba'dihee min jundim-minas-samaaa'i wa maa kunnaa munzileen.

29. In kaanat illaa ṣayḥatañw-waaḥidatan fa-izaa hum khaamidoon.

30. Yaa ḥasratan 'alal-'ibaad; maa yaåteehim-mir Rasoolin illaa kaanoo bihee yastahzi'oon.

31. Alam yaraw kam ahlak-naa qablahum-minal-quroonee annahum ilayhim laa yarji'oon.

32. Wa in kullul-lammaa jamee'ul-ladaynaa muḥḍaroon.
(Section 2)

33. Wa Aayatul-lahumul-arḍul-maytatu aḥyaynaahaa wa akhrajnaa minhaa ḥabban faminhu yaåkuloon.

34. Wa ja'alnaa feehaa jannaatim-min nakheeliñw-wa a'naabiñw-wa fajjarnaa feehaa minal-'uyoon.

35. Liyaåkuloo min samari-hee wa maa 'amilat-hu

وَمَا لِيَ لَاۤ اَعْبُدُ الَّذِيْ فَطَرَنِيْ وَاِلَيْهِ تُرْجَعُوْنَ ۞

ءَاَتَّخِذُ مِنْ دُوْنِهٖۤ اٰلِهَةً اِنْ يُّرِدْنِ الرَّحْمٰنُ بِضُرٍّ لَّا تُغْنِ عَنِّيْ شَفَاعَتُهُمْ شَيْـًٔا وَّلَا يُنْقِذُوْنَ ۞

اِنِّيْۤ اِذًا لَّفِيْ ضَلٰلٍ مُّبِيْنٍ ۞

اِنِّيْۤ اٰمَنْتُ بِرَبِّكُمْ فَاسْمَعُوْنِ ۞

قِيْلَ ادْخُلِ الْجَنَّةَ ۖ قَالَ يٰلَيْتَ قَوْمِيْ يَعْلَمُوْنَ ۞

بِمَا غَفَرَ لِيْ رَبِّيْ وَجَعَلَنِيْ مِنَ الْمُكْرَمِيْنَ ۞

وَمَاۤ اَنْزَلْنَا عَلٰى قَوْمِهٖ مِنْ بَعْدِهٖ مِنْ جُنْدٍ مِّنَ السَّمَاۤءِ وَمَا كُنَّا مُنْزِلِيْنَ ۞

اِنْ كَانَتْ اِلَّا صَيْحَةً وَّاحِدَةً فَاِذَا هُمْ خٰمِدُوْنَ ۞

يٰحَسْرَةً عَلَى الْعِبَادِ ۚ مَا يَأْتِيْهِمْ مِّنْ رَّسُوْلٍ اِلَّا كَانُوْا بِهٖ يَسْتَهْزِءُوْنَ ۞

اَلَمْ يَرَوْا كَمْ اَهْلَكْنَا قَبْلَهُمْ مِّنَ الْقُرُوْنِ اَنَّهُمْ اِلَيْهِمْ لَا يَرْجِعُوْنَ ۞

وَاِنْ كُلٌّ لَّمَّا جَمِيْعٌ لَّدَيْنَا مُحْضَرُوْنَ ۞

وَاٰيَةٌ لَّهُمُ الْاَرْضُ الْمَيْتَةُ ۖ اَحْيَيْنٰهَا وَاَخْرَجْنَا مِنْهَا حَبًّا فَمِنْهُ يَأْكُلُوْنَ ۞

وَجَعَلْنَا فِيْهَا جَنّٰتٍ مِّنْ نَّخِيْلٍ وَّاَعْنَابٍ وَّفَجَّرْنَا فِيْهَا مِنَ الْعُيُوْنِ ۞

لِيَأْكُلُوْا مِنْ ثَمَرِهٖ ۙ وَمَا عَمِلَتْهُ

their hands that made this: will they not then give thanks?

36. Glory to Allah, Who created in pairs all things that the earth produces, as well as their own (human) kind and (other) things of which they have no knowledge.

37. And a Sign for them is the Night: We withdraw therefrom the Day, and behold they are plunged in darkness;

38. And the sun runs his course for a period determined for him: that is the decree of (Him), the Exalted in Might, the All-Know-ing.

39. And the Moon,- We have measured for her mansions (to traverse) till she returns like the old (and withered) lower part of a date-stalk.

40. It is not permitted to the Sun to catch up the Moon, nor can the Night outstrip the Day: each (just) swims along in (its own) orbit (according to Law).

41. And a Sign for them is that We bore their race (through the Flood) in the loaded Ark;

42. And We have created for them similar (vessels) on which they ride.

43. If it were Our Will, We could drown them: then would there be no helper (to hear their cry), nor could they be delivered,

44. Except by way of Mercy from Us, and by way of (worldly) convenience (to serve them) for a time.

45. When they are told, "You fear that which is before you and that which will be after you, in order that you may receive Mercy," (they turn back).

46. Not a Sign comes to them from among the Signs of their Lord, but they turn away there-from.

47. And when they are told, "You spend of (the bounties) with which Allah has provided you," the Unbelievers say to those who believe:

aydeehim; afalaa yashkuroon.

36. Sabḥaanal-lazee khalaqal-azwaaja kullahaa mimmaa tumbitul-arḍu wa min anfusi-him wa mimmaa laa ya'lamoon.

37. Wa Aayatul-lahumul-laylu naslakhu minhun-nahaara fa-izaa hum-muẓlimoon.

38. Wash-shamsu tajree limustaqarril-lahaa; zaalika taqdeerul-'Azeezil-'Aleem.

39. Walqamara qaddarnaahu manaazila ḥattaa 'aada kal'ur-joonil-qadeem.

40. Lash-shamsu yambaghee lahaaa an tudrikal-qamara wa lal-laylu saabiqun-nahaar; wa kullun fee falakiñy-yasbaḥoon.

41. Wa Aayatul-lahum-annaa ḥamalnaa zurriyyatahum fil-fulkil-mashḥoon.

42. Wa khalaqnaa lahum-mim-mislihee maa yarkaboon.

43. Wa in nashaå nughriqhum falaa ṣareekha lahum wa laa hum yunqazoon.

44. Illaa raḥmatam-minnaa wa mataa'an ilaa ḥeen.

45. Wa izaa qeela lahumut-taqoo maa bayna aydeekum wa maa khalfakum la'allakum turḥamoon.

46. Wa maa taåteehim-min Aayatim-min Aayaati Rabbi-him illaa kaanoo 'anhaa mu'ri-ḍeen.

47. Wa izaa qeela lahum anfiqoo mimmaa razaqakumul-laahu qaalal-lazeena kafaroo lillazeena aamanooo

"Shall we then feed those whom, if Allah had so willed, He would have fed, (Himself)?- you are in nothing but manifest error."

48. Further, they say, "When will this promise (come to pass), if what you say is true?"

49. They will not (have to) wait for anything but a single Blast: it will seize them while they are yet disputing among themselves!

50. No (chance) will they then have, by will, to dispose (of their affairs), nor to return to their own people!

51. The trumpet shall be sounded, when behold! from the sepulchres (men) will rush forth to their Lord!

52. They will say: "Ah! woe unto us! Who has raised us up from our beds of repose?"... (A voice will say:) "This is what (Allah) Most Gracious had promised. And true was the word of the Apostles!"

53. It will be no more than a single Blast, when lo! they will all be brought up before Us!

54. Then, on that Day, not a soul will be wronged in the least, and you shall but be repaid the meeds of your past Deeds.

55. Verily the Companions of the Garden shall that Day have joy in all that they do;

56. They and their associates will be in groves of (cool) shade, reclining on Thrones (of dignity);

57. (Every) fruit (enjoyment) will be there for them; they shall have whatever they call for;

58. "Peace!"-a Word (of salutation) from a Lord, Most Merciful!

59. "And O you in sin! You get apart this Day!

60. "Did I not enjoin on you, O you children of Adam,

anuṭ'imu mal-law yashaaa'ul-laahu aṭ'amahooo in antum illaa fee ḍalaalim-mubeen.

48. Wa yaqooloona mataa haazal-wa'du in kuntum ṣaadiqeen.

49. Maa yanẓuroona illaa ṣayḥatañw-waaḥidatan taåkhuzuhum wa hum yakhiṣṣimoon.

50. Falaa yastaṭee'oona tawṣiyatañw-wa laaa ilaaa ahlihim yarji'oon.   (Section 3)

51. Wa nufikha fiṣ-Ṣoori fa-izaa hum-minal-ajdaasi ilaa Rabbihim yansiloon.

52. Qaaloo yaa waylanaa mam ba'asanaa mim-marqadinaa; haazaa maa wa'adar-Raḥmaanu wa ṣadaqal-mursaloon.

53. In kaanat illaa ṣayḥatañw-waaḥidatan fa-izaa hum jamee'ul-ladaynaa muḥḍaroon.

54. Fal-Yawma laa tuẓlamu nafsun shay'añw-wa laa tujzawna illaa maa kuntum ta'maloon.

55. Inna Aṣḥaabal-Jannatil-Yawma fee shughulin faaki-hoon.

56. Hum wa azwaajuhum fee ẓilaalin 'alal-araaa'iki mutta-ki'oon.

57. Lahum feehaa faakiha-tuñw-wa lahum-maa yadda'oon.

58. Salaamun qawlam-mir-Rabbir-Raḥeem.

59. Wamtaazul-Yawma ayyu-hal-mujrimoon.

60. Alam a'had ilaykum yaa Baneee Aadama

that you should not worship Satan; for that he was to you an enemy avowed?-

al-laa ta'budush-Shayṭaana innahoo lakum 'aduwwum-mubeen.

اَنْ لَّا تَعْبُدُوا الشَّيْطٰنَ ۚ اِنَّهٗ لَكُمْ عَدُوٌّ مُّبِيْنٌ ۟

61. "And that you should worship Me, (for that) this was the Straight Way?

61. Wa ani'-budoonee; haazaa Ṣiraaṭum-Mustaqeem.

وَّاَنِ اعْبُدُوْنِيْ ۚ هٰذَا صِرَاطٌ مُّسْتَقِيْمٌ ۟

62. "But he did lead astray a great multitude of you. Did you not, then, understand?

62. Wa laqad aḍalla minkum jibillan kaseeraa; afalam takoonoo ta'qiloon.

وَلَقَدْ اَضَلَّ مِنْكُمْ جِبِلًّا كَثِيْرًا ۗ اَفَلَمْ تَكُوْنُوْا تَعْقِلُوْنَ ۟

63. "This is the Hell of which you were (repeatedly) warned!

63. Haazihee Jahannamul-latee kuntum too'adoon.

هٰذِهٖ جَهَنَّمُ الَّتِيْ كُنْتُمْ تُوْعَدُوْنَ ۟

64. "You embrace the (fire) this Day, for that you (persistently) rejected (Truth)."

64. Iṣlawhal-Yawma bimaa kuntum takfuroon.

اِصْلَوْهَا الْيَوْمَ بِمَا كُنْتُمْ تَكْفُرُوْنَ ۟

65. That Day We shall set a seal on their mouths. But their hands will speak to Us, and their feet bear witness, to all that they did.

65. Al-Yawma nakhtimu 'alaa afwaahihim wa tukallimunaaa aydeehim wa tashhadu arjulu-hum bimaa kaanoo yaksiboon.

الْيَوْمَ نَخْتِمُ عَلٰۤى اَفْوَاهِهِمْ وَ تُكَلِّمُنَاۤ اَيْدِيْهِمْ وَتَشْهَدُ اَرْجُلُهُمْ بِمَا كَانُوْا يَكْسِبُوْنَ ۟

66. If it had been Our Will, We could surely have blotted out their eyes; then should they have run about groping for the Path, but how could they have seen?

66. Wa law nashaaa'u laṭa-masnaa 'alaaa a'yunihim fasta-baquṣ-ṣiraaṭa fa-annaa yubṣi-roon.

وَلَوْ نَشَاۤءُ لَطَمَسْنَا عَلٰۤى اَعْيُنِهِمْ فَاسْتَبَقُوا الصِّرَاطَ فَاَنّٰى يُبْصِرُوْنَ ۟

67. And if it had been Our Will, We could have transformed them (to remain) in their places; then they should have been unable to move about, nor could they have returned (after error).

67. Wa law nashaaa'u lamasakh-naahum 'alaa makaanatihim famas-taṭaa'oo muḍiyyañw-wa laa yarji'oon. (Section 4)

وَلَوْ نَشَاۤءُ لَمَسَخْنٰهُمْ عَلٰى مَكَانَتِهِمْ فَمَا اسْتَطَاعُوْا مُضِيًّا وَّلَا يَرْجِعُوْنَ ۟

68. If We grant long life to any, We cause him to be reversed in nature: will they not then understand?

68. Wa man-nu'ammirhu nunakkishu fil-khalq; afalaa ya'qiloon.

وَمَنْ نُّعَمِّرْهُ نُنَكِّسْهُ فِى الْخَلْقِ ۗ اَفَلَا يَعْقِلُوْنَ ۟

69. We have not instructed the (Prophet) in Poetry, nor is it meet for him: this is no less than a Message and a Qur'an making things clear:

69. Wa maa 'allamnaahush-shi'ra wa maa yambaghee lah; in huwa illaa zikruñw-wa Qur-aa-num-Mubeen.

وَمَا عَلَّمْنٰهُ الشِّعْرَ وَمَا يَنْۢبَغِيْ لَهٗ ۗ اِنْ هُوَ اِلَّا ذِكْرٌ وَّقُرْاٰنٌ مُّبِيْنٌ ۟

70. That it may give admonition to any (who are) alive, and that the charge may be proved against those who reject (Truth).

70. Liyunzira man kaana ḥayyañw-wa yaḥiqqal-qawlu 'alal-kaafireen.

لِّيُنْذِرَ مَنْ كَانَ حَيًّا وَّيَحِقَّ الْقَوْلُ عَلَى الْكٰفِرِيْنَ ۟

71. Don't they See that it is We Who have created for them - among the things which Our hands have fashioned - cattle, which are under their dominion?-

71. Awalam yaraw annaa khalaqnaa lahum-mimmaa 'amilat aydeenaaa an'aaman fahum lahaa maalikoon.

اَوَلَمْ يَرَوْا اَنَّا خَلَقْنَا لَهُمْ مِّمَّا عَمِلَتْ اَيْدِيْنَاۤ اَنْعَامًا فَهُمْ لَهَا مٰلِكُوْنَ ۟

72. And that We have subjected them to their (use)? of them some do carry them and some they eat:

72. Wa zallalnaahaa lahum faminhaa rakoobuhum wa minhaa yaåkuloon.

وَذَلَّلْنٰهَا لَهُمْ فَمِنْهَا رَكُوْبُهُمْ وَمِنْهَا يَاْكُلُوْنَ ۟

73. And they have (other) profits from them (besides), and they get (milk) to drink. Will they not then be grateful?

74. Yet they take (for worship) gods other than Allah, (hoping) that they might be helped!

75. They have not the power to help them: but they will be brought up (before Our Judgment-seat) as a troop (to be condemned).

76. Let not their speech, then, grieve you. Verily We know what they hide as well as what they disclose.

77. Does not man see that it is We Who created him from sperm? Yet behold! he (stands forth) as an open adversary!

78. And he makes comparisons for Us, and forgets his own (origin and) Creation: he says, "Who can give life to (dry) bones and decomposed ones (at that)?"

79. Say, "He will give them life Who created them for the first time! for He is Well-versed in every kind of creation!-

80. "The same Who produces for you fire out of the green tree, when behold! you kindle therewith (your own fires)!

81. "Is not He Who created the heavens and the earth able to create the like thereof?" - yes, indeed! for He is the Creator Supreme, of skill and knowledge (infinite)!

82. Verily, when He intends a thing, His Command is, "Be", and it is!

83. So glory to Him in Whose hands is the dominion of all things: and to Him will you be all brought back.

---

37. Those ranged in Ranks
In the name of Allah, Most Gracious, Most Merciful.

1. By those who range themselves in ranks,

---

73. Wa lahum feehaa manaafi-'u wa mashaarib; afalaa yash-kuroon.

74. Wattakhazoo min doonil-laahi aalihatal-la'allahum yun-ṣaroon.

75. Laa yastaṭee'oona naṣra-hum wa hum lahum jundum-muḥḍaroon.

76. Falaa yaḥzunka qawlu-hum; innaa na'lamu maa yusir-roona wa maa yu'linoon.

77. Awalam yaral-insaanu annaa khalaqnaahu min-nuṭfatin fa-izaa huwa khaṣee-mum-mubeen.

78. Wa ḍaraba lanaa maṣa-lanw-wa nasiya khalqahoo qaala many-yuḥyil-'iẓaama wa hiya rameem.

79. Qul yuḥyeehal-lazee ansha-ahaaa awwala marrah; wa Huwa bikulli khalqin 'Aleem.

80. Allazee ja'ala lakum-minash-shajaril-akhḍari naaran fa-izaaa antum-minhu tooqi-doon.

81. Awa laysal-lazee khala-qas-samaawaati wal-arḍa bi-qaadirin 'alaaa any-yakhluqa miṣlahum; balaa wa Huwal-Khallaaqul-'Aleem.

82. Innamaaa amruhooo izaaa araada shay'an any-yaqoola lahoo kun fa-yakoon.

83. Fa-Subḥaanal-lazee biya-dihee malakootu kulli shay-'inw-wa ilayhi turja'oon. (Sec. 5)

Sûrat aṣ-Ṣâffât–37
(Revealed at Makkah)
Bismillaahir Raḥmaanir Raḥeem

1. Waṣṣaaaffaati ṣaffaa.

2. And so are strong in repelling (evil),

3. And thus proclaim the Message (of Allah)!

4. Verily, verily, your God (Allah) is One!-

5. Lord of the heavens and of the earth and all between them, and Lord of every point at the rising of the sun!

6. We have indeed decked the lower heaven with beauty (in) the stars,-

7. (For beauty) and for guard against all obstinate rebellious evil spirits,

8. (So) they should not strain their ears in the direction of the Exalted Assembly but be cast away from every side,

9. Repulsed, for they are under a perpetual Chastisement,

10. Except such as snatch away something by stealth, and they are pursued by a flaming Fire, of piercing brightness.

11. Just ask their opinion: are they the more difficult to create, or the (other) beings We have created? We have created them out of a sticky clay!

12. Truly you marvel, while they ridicule,-

13. And, when they are admonished, pay no heed,-

14. And, when they see a Sign, turn it to mockery,-

15. And say, "This is nothing but evident sorcery!

16. "What! when we die, and become dust and bones, shall we (then) be raised up (again)

17. "And also our fathers of old?"

18. Say you: "Yes, and you shall then be humiliated (on account of your evil)."

19. Then it will be a single (compelling) cry; and behold, they will begin to see!

---

2. Fazzaajiraati zajraa.

3. Fattaaliyaati Ẕikraa.

4. Inna Ilaahakum la-Waaḥid.

5. Rabbus-samaawaati wal-arḍi wa maa baynahumaa wa Rabbul-mashaariq.

6. Innaa zayyannas-samaaa-'ad-dunyaa bizeenatinil-kawaakib.

7. Wa ḥifẓam-min kulli Shayṭaanim-maarid.

8. Laa yassamma'oona ilal-mala-il-a'laa wa yuqzafoona min kulli jaanib.

9. Duḥooranw-wa lahum 'aẕaabuñw-waaṣib.

10. Illaa man khaṭifal-khaṭfata fa-atba'ahoo shihaabun ṣaaqib.

11. Fastaftihim ahum ashaddu khalqan am-man khalaqnaa; innaa khalaqnaahum-min ṭeenil-laazib.

12. Bal 'ajibta wa yaskharoon.

13. Wa iẕaa ẕukkiroo laa yaẕkuroon.

14. Wa iẕaa ra-aw Aayataññw-yastaskhiroon.

15. Wa qaalooo in haaẕaaa illaa siḥrum-mubeen.

16. 'A-iẕaa mitnaa wa kunnaa turaabañw-wa 'iẕaaman 'a-innaa lamab'oosoon.

17. Awa aabaaa'unal-awwaloon.

18. Qul na'am wa antum daakhiroon.

19. Fa-innamaa hiya zajratuñw-waaḥidatun fa-iẕaa hum yanẓuroon.

20. They will say, "Ah! woe to us! this is the Day of Judgment!"

21. (A voice will say,) "This is the Day of Sorting Out, whose Truth you (once) denied!"

22. "Bring you up", it shall be said, "The wrong-doers and their wives, and the things they worshipped-

23. "Besides Allah, and lead them to the Way to the (Fierce) Fire.

24. "But stop them, for they must be asked:

25. "'What is the matter with you that you do not help each other?'"

26. Nay, but that day they shall submit (to Judgment);

27. And they will turn to one another, and question one another.

28. They will say: "It was you who used to come to us from the right hand (of power and authority)!"

29. They will reply: "Nay, you yourselves had no Faith!

30. "Nor had we any authority over you. Nay, it was you who were a people in obstinate rebellion!

31. "So now has been proved true, against us, the Word of our Lord that we shall indeed (have to) taste (the punishment of our sins).

32. "We led you astray: for truly we were ourselves astray."

33. Truly, that Day, they will (all) share in the Chastisement.

34. Verily that is how We shall deal with sinners.

35. For they, when they were told that there is no god except Allah, would puff themselves up with pride,

36. And say: "What! shall we give up our gods for the sake of a Poet possessed?"

37. Nay! he has come with the (very) Truth, and he confirms (the Message of) the Apostles (before him).

20. Wa qaaloo yaa waylanaa haazaa Yawmud-Deen.

21. Haazaa Yawmul-Faṣlil-lazee kuntum bihee tukaz-ziboon.   **(Section 1)**

22. Uḥshurul-lazeena ẓala-moo wa azwaajahum wa maa kaanoo ya'budoon.

23. Min doonil-laahi fahdoo-hum ilaa ṣiraaṭil-Jaḥeem.

24. Wa qifoohum innahum-mas'ooloon.

25. Maa lakum laa tanaaṣa-roon.

26. Bal humul-Yawma mus-taslimoon.

27. Wa aqbala ba'ḍuhum 'alaa ba'ḍiny-yatasaaa'aloon.

28. Qaalooo innakum kuntum taåtoonanaa 'anil-yameen.

29. Qaaloo bal lam takoonoo mu'mineen.

30. Wa maa kaana lanaa 'alaykum-min sulṭaanim bal kuntum qawman ṭaagheen.

31. Faḥaqqa 'alaynaa qawlu Rabbinaaa innaa lazaaa'iqoon.

32. Fa-aghwaynaakum innaa kunnaa ghaaween.

33. Fa-innahum Yawma'izin fil-'azaabi mushtarikoon.

34. Innaa kazaalika naf'alu bil-mujrimeen.

35. Innahum kaanooo izaa qeela lahum laaa ilaaha illal-laahu yastakbiroon.

36. Wa yaqooloona a'innaa lataarikooo aalihatinaa lishaa'i-rim-majnoon.

37. Bal jaaa'a bilḥaqqi wa ṣaddaqal-mursaleen.

38. You shall indeed taste of the grievous Chastisement;-

39. But it will be no more than the retribution of (the Evil) that you have wrought;-

40. But the sincere (and devoted) Servants of Allah,-

41. For them is a Sustenance determined,

42. Fruits (Delights); and they (shall enjoy) honour and dignity,

43. In Gardens of Felicity,

44. Facing each other on Thrones (of dignity):

45. Round will be passed to them a cup from a clear-flowing fountain,

46. Crystal-white, of a taste delicious to those who drink (thereof),

47. Free from headiness; nor will they suffer intoxication therefrom.

48. And besides them will be chaste women, restraining their glances, with big eyes (of wonder and beauty).

49. As if they were (delicate) eggs closely guarded.

50. Then they will turn to one another and question one another.

51. One of them will start the talk and say: "I had an intimate companion (on the earth),

52. Who used to say, "What! are you among those who bear witness to the truth (of the Message)?"

53. "'When we die and become dust and bones, shall we indeed receive rewards and punish-ments?'"

54. (A voice) said: "Would you like to look down?"

55. He looked down and saw him in the midst of the Fire.

56. He said: "By Allah! you were little short of bringing me to perdition!

57. "Had it not been for the Grace of my Lord, I should certainly have been among those brought (there)!

58. "Is it (the case) that we shall not die,

59. "Except our first death, and that we shall not

---

38. Innakum lazaaa'iqul-'azaabil-aleem.

39. Wa maa tujzawna illaa maa kuntum ta'maloon.

40. Illaa 'ibaadal-laahil-mukhlaṣeen.

41. Ulaaa'ika lahum rizqum-ma'loom.

42. Fa waakihu wa hum-mukramoon.

43. Fee Jannaatin-Na'eem.

44. 'Alaa sururim-mutaqaa-bileen.

45. Yuṭaafu 'alayhim bikaå-sim-mim-ma'een.

46. Bayḍaaa'a laz-zatil-lish-shaaribeen.

47. Laa feehaa ghawluñw-wa laa hum 'anhaa yunzafoon.

48. Wa 'indahum qaaṣiraatuṭ-ṭarfi 'een.

49. Ka-annahunna bayḍum-maknoon.

50. Fa-aqbala ba'ḍuhum 'alaa baḍiñy-yatasaaa'aloon.

51. Qaala qaaa'ilum-minhum innee kaana lee qareen.

52. Yaqoolu a'innaka laminal-muṣaddiqeen.

53. 'A-izaa mitnaa wa kunnaa turaabañw-wa 'izaaman 'a-innaa lamadeenoon.

54. Qaala hal antum-muṭṭali'oon.

55. Faṭṭala'a fara-aahu fee sawaaa'il-Jaheem.

56. Qaala tallaahi in kitta laturdeen.

57. Wa law laa ni'matu Rabbee lakuntu minal-muḥḍareen.

58. Afamaa naḥnu bimayyi-teen.

59. Illa mawtatanal-oolaa wa maa naḥnu

---

be punished?"

bimu'azzabeen.

60. Verily this is the supreme achievement!

60. Inna haazaa lahuwal-fawzul-'azeem.

61. For the like of this let all strive, who wish to strive.

61. Limisli haazaa falya'ma-lil-'aamiloon.

62. Is that the better entertainment or the Tree of Zaqqum?

62. Azaalika khayrun-nuzu-lan am shajaratuz-Zaqqoom.

63. For We have truly made it (as) a trial for the wrong-doers.

63. Innaa ja'alnaahaa fitnatal-lizzaalimeen.

64. For it is a tree that springs out of the bottom of Hell-fire:

64. Innahaa shajaratun takh-ruju feee aṣlil-Jaheem.

65. The shoots of its fruit-stalks are like the heads of devils:

65. Ṭal'uhaa ka-annahoo ru'oosush-Shayaaṭeen.

66. Truly they will eat thereof and fill their bellies therewith.

66. Fa-innahum la-aakiloona minhaa famaali'oona minhal-buṭoon.

67. Then on top of that they will be given a mixture made of boiling water.

67. Summa inna lahum 'alay-haa lashawbam-min ḥameem.

68. Then shall their return be to the (Blazing) Fire.

68. Summa inna marji'ahum la-ilal-Jaheem.

69. Truly they found their fathers on the wrong Path;

69. Innahum alfaw aabaaa'a-hum ḍaalleen.

70. So they (too) were rushed down on their footsteps!

70. Fahum 'alaaa aaṣaarihim yuhra'oon.

71. And truly before them, many of the ancients went astray,

71. Wa laqad ḍalla qablahum aksarul-awwaleen.

72. But We sent aforetime, among them, (Apostles) to admonish them;-

72. Wa laqad arsalnaa feehim-munzireen.

73. Then see what was the end of those who were admonished (but heeded not),

73. Fanzur kayfa kaana 'aaqi-batul-munzareen.

74. Except the sincere (and devoted) Servants of Allah.

74. Illaa 'ibaadal-laahil-mukhlaṣeen. **(Section 2)**

75. (In the days of old), Noah cried to Us, and We are the best to hear prayer.

75. Wa laqad naadaanaa Noohun falani'mal-mujeeboon.

76. And We delivered him and his people from the Great Calamity,

76. Wa najjaynaahu wa ahla-hoo minal-karbil-'azeem.

77. And made his progeny to endure (on this earth)

77. Wa ja'alnaa zurriyyatahoo humul-baaqeen.

78. And We left (this blessing) for him among generations to come in later times:

78. Wa taraknaa 'alayhi fil-aakhireen.

79. "Peace and salutation to Noah among the nations!"

79. Salaamun 'alaa Noohin fil-'aalameen.

80. Thus indeed do We reward those who do right.

81. For he was one of Our believing Servants.

82. Then the rest We overwhelmed in the Flood.

83. Verily among those who followed his Way was Abraham.

84. Behold! he approached his Lord with a sound heart.

85. Behold! he said to his father and to his people, "What is that which you worship?

86. "Is it a falsehood - gods other than Allah- that you desire?

87. "Then what is your idea about the Lord of the Worlds?"

88. Then did he cast a glance at the Stars.

89. And he said, "I am indeed sick (at heart)!"

90. So they turned away from him, and departed.

91. Then did he turn to their gods and said, "Will you not eat (of the offerings before you)?...

92. "What is the matter with you that you speak not (intelligently)?"

93. Then did he turn upon them, striking (them) with the right hand.

94. Then came (the worshippers) with hurried steps, and faced (him).

95. He said: "Do you worship that which you have (yourselves) carved?

96. "But Allah has created you and your handiwork!"

97. They said, "Build him a furnace, and throw him into the blazing fire!"

98. (This failing), they then sought a strategem against him, but We made them the ones most humiliated!

99. He said: "I will go to my Lord! He will surely guide me!

100. "O my Lord! Grant me a righteous (son)!"

---

80. Innaa kazaalika najzil-muhsineen.

81. Innahoo min 'ibaadinal-mu'mineen.

82. Summa aghraqnal-aakhareen.

83. Wa inna min shee'atihee la-Ibraaheem.

84. Iz jaa'a Rabbahoo bi-qalbin saleem.

85. Iz qaala li-abeehi wa qawmihee maazaa ta'budoon.

86. A'ifkan aalihatan doonal-laahi tureedoon.

87. Famaa zannukum bi-Rabbil-'aalameen.

88. Fanazara nazratan finnujoom.

89. Faqaala innee saqeem.

90. Fatawallaw 'anhu mudbireen.

91. Faraagha ilaa aalihatihim faqaala alaa taåkuloon.

92. Maa lakum laa tantiqoon.

93. Faraagha 'alayhim darbam bilyameen.

94. Fa-aqbalooo ilayhi yazif-foon.

95. Qaala ata'budoona maa tanhitoon.

96. Wallaahu khalaqakum wa maa ta'maloon.

97. Qaalub-noo lahoo bun-yaanan fa-alqoohu fil-jaheem.

98. Fa-araadoo bihee kaydan faja'alnaahumul-asfaleen.

99. Wa qaala innee zaahibun ilaa Rabbee sa-yahdeen.

100. Rabbi hab lee minaṣ-ṣaaliheen.

101. So We gave him the good news of a boy ready to suffer and forbear.

102. Then, when (the son) reached (the age of) (serious) work with him, he said: "O my son! I see in vision that I offer you in sacrifice: now say what is your view!" (The son) said: "O my father! Do as you are commanded: you will find me, if Allah so wills, one practising patience and constancy!"

103. So when they had both submitted their wills (to Allah), and he had laid him prostrate on his forehead (for sacrifice),

104. We called out to him "O Abraham!

105. "You have already fulfilled the vision!" - thus indeed do We reward those who do right.

106. For this was obviously a trial,-

107. And We ransomed him with a momentous sacrifice:

108. And We left (this blessing) for him among generations (to come) in later times:

109. "Peace and salutation to Abraham!"

110. Thus indeed do We reward those who do right.

111. For he was one of Our believing Servants.

112. And We gave him the good news of Isaac - a prophet,- one of the Righteous.

113. We blessed him and Isaac: but of their progeny are (some) that do right, and (some) that obviously do wrong, to their own souls.

114. Again (of old) We bestowed Our favour on Moses and Aaron,

115. And We delivered them and their people from (their) Great Calamity;

116. And We helped them, so they overcame (their troubles);

117. And We gave them the Book which helps to make things clear;

101. Fabashsharnaahu bighu-laamin ḥaleem.

102. Falammaa balagha ma‘a-hus-sa‘ya qaala yaa bunayya ineee araa fil-manaami anneee azbaḥuka fanẓur maaẓaa taraa; qaala yaaa abatif-‘al maa tu’maru satajiduneee in shaaa’-allaahu minaṣ-ṣaabireen.

103. Falammaaa aslamaa wa tallahoo liljabeen.

104. Wa naadaynaahu añy-yaaa Ibraaheem.

105. Qad ṣaddaqtar-ru’yaa; innaa kaẓaalika najzil-muḥsi-neen.

106. Inna haaẓaa lahuwal-balaaa’ul-mubeen

107. Wa fadaynaahu biẓibḥin ‘aẓeem.

108. Wa taraknaa ‘alayhi fil-aakhireen.

109. Salaamun ‘alaaa Ibraaheem.

110. Kaẓaalika najzil-muḥ-sineen.

111. Innahoo min ‘ibaadinal-mu’mineen.

112. Wa bashsharnaahu bi-Isḥaaqa Nabiyyam-minaṣ-ṣaaliheen.

113. Wa baaraknaa ‘alayhi wa ‘alaaa Isḥaaq; wa min ẓurriyya-tihimaa muḥsinuñw-wa ẓaali-mul-linafsihee mubeen.

(Section 3)

114. Wa laqad manannaa ‘alaa Moosaa wa Haaroon.

115. Wa najjaynaahumaa wa qawmahumaa minal-karbil-‘aẓeem.

116. Wa naṣarnaahum fakaanoo humul-ghaalibeen.

117. Wa aataynaahumal-Ki-taabal-mustabeen.

118. And We guided them to the Straight Way.

119. And We left (this blessing) for them among generations (to come) in later times:

120. "Peace and salutation to Moses and Aaron!"

121. Thus indeed do We reward those who do right.

122. For they were two of Our believing Servants.

123. So also was Elias among those sent (by Us).

124. Behold, he said to his people, "Will you not fear (Allah)?

125. "Will you call upon Baal and forsake the Best of Creators,

126. "Allah, your Lord and Cherisher and the Lord and Cherisher of your fathers of old?"

127. But they rejected him, and they will certainly be called up (for punishment),-

128. Except the sincere and devoted Servants of Allah (among them).

129. And We left (this blessing) for him among generations (to come) in later times:

130. "Peace and salutation to such as Elias!"

131. Thus indeed do We reward those who do right.

132. For he was one of Our believing Servants.

133. So also was Lut among those sent (by Us).

134. Behold, We delivered him and his adherents, all;

135. Except an old woman who was among those who lagged behind:

136. Then We destroyed the rest.

137. Verily, you pass by their (sites), by day-

138. And by night: will you not understand?

139. So also was Jonah among those sent (by Us).

140. When he ran away (like a slave from captivity) to the ship (fully) laden,

141. He (agreed to) cast lots, and he was condemned:

142. Then the big fish swallowed him, and he had done acts worthy of blame.

---

118. Wa hadaynaahumuṣ-Ṣiraaṭal-Mustaqeem.

119. Wa taraknaa 'alayhimaa fil-aakhireen.

120. Salaamun 'alaa Moosaa wa Haaroon.

121. Innaa kazaalika najzil-muḥsineen.

122. Innahumaa min 'ibaadi-nal-mu'mineen.

123. Wa inna Ilyaasa laminal-mursaleen.

124. Iz qaala liqawmiheee alaa tattaqoon.

125. Atad'oona Ba'lanw-wa tazaroona aḥsanal-khaaliqeen.

126. Allaaha Rabbakum wa Rabba aabaaa'ikumul-awwaleen.

127. Fakazzaboohu fa-inna hum lamuḥḍaroon.

128. Illaa 'ibaadal-laahil-mukhlaṣeen.

129. Wa taraknaa 'alayhi fil-aakhireen.

130. Salaamun 'alaaa Ilyaaseen.

131. Innaa kazaalika najzil-muḥsineen.

132. Innahoo min 'ibaadinal-mu'mineen.

133. Wa inna Looṭal-laminal-mursaleen.

134. Iz najjaynaahu wa ahla-hooo ajma'een.

135. Illaa 'ajoozan fil-ghaa-bireen.

136. Summa dammarnal-aa-khareen.

137. Wa innakum latamurroona 'alayhim-muṣbiḥeen.

138. Wa billayl; afalaa ta'qi-loon.   **(Section 4)**

139. Wa inna Yoonusa laminal-mursaleen.

140. Iz abaqa ilal-fulkil-mash-ḥoon.

141. Fasaahama fakaana minal-mudḥaḍeen.

142. Faltaqamahul-ḥootu wa huwa muleem.

143. Had it not been that he (repented and) glorified Allah,

144. He would certainly have remained inside the fish till the Day of Resurrection.

145. But We cast him forth on the naked shore in a state of sickness,

146. And We caused to grow, over him, a spreading plant of

147. And We sent him (on a mission) to a hundred thousand (men) or more.

148. And they believe; so We permitted them to enjoy (their life) for a while.

149. Now ask them their opinion: is it that your Lord has (only) daughters, and they have sons?-

150. Or that We created the angels female, and they are witnesses (thereto)?

151. Is it not, that they say, from their own invention,

152. "Allah has begotten children"? But they are liars!

153. Did He (then) choose daughters rather than sons?

154. What is the matter with you? How do you judge?

155. Will you not then receive admonition.

156. Or do you have an authority manifest?

157. Then you bring your Book (of authority) if you be truthful!

158. And they have invented a blood-relationship between Him and the Jinns: but the Jinns know (quite well) that they have indeed to appear (before His Judgment-seat)!

159. Glory to Allah! (He is free) from the things they ascribe (to Him)!

160. Not (so do) the Servants of Allah, sincere and devoted.

161. For, verily, neither you nor those you worship-

162. Can lead (any) into temptation concerning Allah,

163. Except such as are (themselves) going to the blazing Fire!

164. (Those ranged in ranks say): "Not one of us but has a place appointed;

---

143. Falaw laaa annahoo kaana minal-musabbiheen.

144. Lalabisa fee batniheee ilaa Yawmi yub'asoon.

145. Fanabaznaahu bil'araaa'i wa huwa saqeem.

146. Wa ambatnaa 'alayhi shajaratam-miny-yaqteen.

147. Wa arsalnaahu ilaa mi'ati alfin aw yazeedoon.

148. Fa-aamanoo famatta'-naahum ilaa heen.

149. Fastaftihim ali-Rabbikal-banaatu wa lahumul-banoon.

150. Am khalaqnal-malaaa'ikata inaasanw-wa hum shaahidoon.

151. Alaaa innahum-min ifkihim la-yaqooloon.

152. Waladal-laahu wa innahum lakaaziboon.

153. Astafal-banaati 'alal-baneen.

154. Maa lakum kayfa tahkumoon.

155. Afalaa tazakkaroon.

156. Am lakum sultaanum-mubeen.

157. Faåtoo bi-Kitaabikum in kuntum saadiqeen.

158. Wa ja'aloo baynahoo wa baynal-jinnati nasabaa; wa laqad 'alimatil-jinnatu innahum lamuhdaroon.

159. Subhaanal-laahi 'ammaa yasifoon.

160. Illaa 'ibaadal-laahil-mukhlaseen.

161. Fa-innakum wa maa ta'budoon.

162. Maaa antum 'alayhi bifaatineen.

163. Illaa man huwa saalil-Jaheem.

164. Wa maa minnaaa illaa lahoo maqaamum-ma'loom.

165. "And we are verily ranged in ranks (for service);

166. "And we are verily those who declare (Allah's) glory!"

167. And there were those who said,

168. "If only we had had before us a Message from those of old,

169. "We should certainly have been Servants of Allah, sincere (and devoted)!"

170. But (now that the Qur'an has come), they reject it: but soon will they know!

171. Already has Our Word been passed before (this) to Our Servants sent (by Us),

172. That they would certainly be assisted,

173. And that Our forces,- they surely must conquer.

174. So you turn away from them for a little while,

175. And watch them (how they fare), and they soon shall see (how you fare)!

176. Do they wish (indeed) to hurry on our Punishment?

177. But when if descends into the open space before them, evil will be the morning for those who were warned (and heeded not)!

178. So you turn away from them for a little while,

179. And watch (how they fare) and they soon shall see (how you fare)!

180. Glory to your Lord, the Lord of Honor and Power! (He is free) from what they ascribe (to Him)!

181. And Peace on the Apostles!

182. And praise to Allah, the Lord and cherisher of the Worlds!

---

165. Wa innaa lanaḥnuṣ-ṣaaaffoon.

166. Wa innaa lanaḥnul-musabbiḥoon.

167. Wa in kaanoo la-yaqoo-loon.

168. Law anna 'indanaa zikram-minal-awwaleen.

169. Lakunnaa 'ibaadal-laahil-mukhlaṣeen.

170. Fakafaroo bihee fasawfa ya'lamoon.

171. Wa laqad sabaqat Kalimatunaa li'ibaadinal-mursa-leen.

172. Innahum lahumul-man-ṣooroon.

173. Wa inna jundanaa lahu-mul-ghaaliboon.

174. Fatawalla 'anhum ḥatta heen.

175. Wa abṣirhum fasawfa yubṣiroon.

176. Afabi'azaabinaa yas-ta'jiloon.

177. Fa-izaa nazala bisaaḥa-tihim fasaaa'a ṣabaaḥul-munzareen.

178. Wa tawalla 'anhum ḥattaa heen.

179. Wa abṣir fasawfa yubṣi-roon.

180. Subḥaana Rabbika Rab-bil-'izzati 'ammaa yaṣifoon.

181. Wa salaamun 'alal-mursaleen.

182. Walḥamdu lillaahi Rabbil-'aalameen.

(Section 5)

---

38. Saad

In the name of Allah, Most Gracious, Most Merciful.

1. *Saad*: by the Qur'an, Full of Admonition: (this is the Truth).

2. But the Unbelievers (are steeped) in Self-glory and Separatism.

3. How many generations before them did We destroy?

Sûrat Ṣâd–38

(Revealed at Makkah)

Bismillaahir Raḥmaanir Raḥeem

1. Ṣaaad; wal-Qur-aani ziz-zikr.

2. Balil-lazeena kafaroo fee 'izzatiñw-wa shiqaaq.

3. Kam ahlaknaa min qabli-him-min qarnin

In the end they cried (for mercy)- when there was no longer time for being saved!

4. So they wonder that a Warner has come to them from among themselves! and the Unbelievers say, "This is a sorce-rer telling lies!

5. "Has he made the gods (all) into one God (Allah)? Truly this is a wonderful thing!"

6. And the leader among them go away (impatiently), (saying), "Walk you away, and remain constant to your gods! For this is truly a thing designed (against you)!

7. "We never heard (the like) of this among the people of these latter days: this is nothing but a made-up tale!"

8. "What! has the Message been sent to him - (of all persons) among us?"...But they are in doubt concerning My (Own) Message! Nay, they have not yet tasted My Punishment!

9. Or have they the Treasures of the Mercy of your Lord,- the Exalted in Power, the Grantor of Bounties without measure?

10. Or have they the dominion of the heavens and the earth and all between? If so, let them mount up with the ropes and means (to reach that end)!

11. But there - will be put to flight even a host of confede-rates.

12. Before them (were many who) rejected Apostles,- the People of Noah, and 'Ad, and Pharaoh, the Lord of Stakes,

13. And Thamud, and the people of Lut, and the Compa-nions of the Wood; - such were the Confederates.

14. Not one (of them) but rejected the Apostles, but My Punishment came justly and inevitably (on them).

15. These (today) only wait for a single mighty Blast,

fanaadaw wa laata ḥeena manaaṣ.

4. Wa 'ajibooo an jaaa'a-hum-munẕirum-minhum wa qaalal-kaafiroona haaẕaa saaḥi-run kaẕẕaab.

5. Aja'alal-aalihata Ilaahañw-Waaḥidan inna haaẕaa lashay-'un 'ujaab.

6. Wanṭalaqal-mala-u min-hum anim-shoo waṣbiroo 'alaaa aalihatikum inna haaẕaa lashay'uñy-yuraad.

7. Maa sami'naa bihaaẕaa fil-millatil-aakhirati in haaẕaaa illakh-tilaaq.

8. 'A-unzila 'alayhiẕ-ẕikru mim bayninaa; bal hum fee shakkim-min Ẕikree bal lammaa yaẕooqoo 'aẕaab.

9. Am 'indahum khazaaa'inu raḥmati Rabbikal-'Azeezil-Wahhaab.

10. Am lahum-mulkus-samaa-waati wal-arḍi wa maa bayna-humaa falyartaqoo fil-asbaab.

11. Jundum-maa hunaalika mahzoomum-minal-Aḥzaab.

12. Kaẕẕabat qablahum qaw-mu Nooḥiñw-wa 'Aaduñw-wa Fir'awnu ẕul-awtaad.

13. Wa Ṣamoodu wa qawmu Looṭiñw-wa Aṣḥaabul-'Aykah; ulaaa'ikal-Aḥzaab.

14. In kullun illaa kaẕẕabar-Rusula faḥaqqa 'iqaab.

(Section 1)

15. Wa maa yanzuru haaa-ulaaa'i illaa ṣayḥatañw-

فَنَادَوْا وَّلَاتَ حِيْنَ مَنَاصٍ ۝

وَعَجِبُوْٓا اَنْ جَآءَهُمْ مُّنْذِرٌ مِّنْهُمْ ۖ وَقَالَ الْكٰفِرُوْنَ هٰذَا سٰحِرٌ كَذَّابٌ ۝

اَجَعَلَ الْاٰلِهَةَ اِلٰهًا وَّاحِدًا ۖ اِنَّ هٰذَا لَشَيْءٌ عُجَابٌ ۝

وَانْطَلَقَ الْمَلَاُ مِنْهُمْ اَنِ امْشُوْا وَاصْبِرُوْا عَلٰٓى اٰلِهَتِكُمْ ۖ اِنَّ هٰذَا لَشَيْءٌ يُّرَادُ ۝

مَا سَمِعْنَا بِهٰذَا فِي الْمِلَّةِ الْاٰخِرَةِ ۖ اِنْ هٰذَآ اِلَّا اخْتِلَاقٌ ۝

ءَاُنْزِلَ عَلَيْهِ الذِّكْرُ مِنْ بَيْنِنَا ۖ بَلْ هُمْ فِيْ شَكٍّ مِّنْ ذِكْرِيْ ۖ بَلْ لَّمَّا يَذُوْقُوْا عَذَابِ ۝

اَمْ عِنْدَهُمْ خَزَآئِنُ رَحْمَةِ رَبِّكَ الْعَزِيْزِ الْوَهَّابِ ۝

اَمْ لَهُمْ مُّلْكُ السَّمٰوٰتِ وَالْاَرْضِ وَمَا بَيْنَهُمَا ۖ فَلْيَرْتَقُوْا فِي الْاَسْبَابِ ۝

جُنْدٌ مَّا هُنَالِكَ مَهْزُوْمٌ مِّنَ الْاَحْزَابِ ۝

كَذَّبَتْ قَبْلَهُمْ قَوْمُ نُوْحٍ وَّعَادٌ وَّفِرْعَوْنُ ذُو الْاَوْتَادِ ۝

وَثَمُوْدُ وَقَوْمُ لُوْطٍ وَّاَصْحٰبُ لْئَيْكَةِ ۖ اُولٰٓئِكَ الْاَحْزَابُ ۝

اِنْ كُلٌّ اِلَّا كَذَّبَ الرُّسُلَ فَحَقَّ عِقَابِ ۝

وَمَا يَنْظُرُ هٰٓؤُلَآءِ اِلَّا صَيْحَةً

which (when it comes) will brook no delay.

16. They say: "Our Lord! hasten to us our sentence (even) before the Day of Account!"

17. Have patience at what they say, and remember Our Servant David, the man of strength: for he ever turned (to Allah).

18. It was We that made the hills declare, in unison with him, Our praises, at eventide and at break of day,

19. And the birds gathered (in assemblies): all with him turned (to Allah).

20. We strengthened his kingdom, and gave him wisdom and sound judgment in speech and decision.

21. Has the story of the Disputants reached you? Behold, they climbed over the wall of the private chamber;

22. When they entered the presence of David, and he was terrified of them, they said: "Fear not: we are two disputants, one of whom has wronged the other: Decide now between us with truth, and treat us not with injustice, but guide us to the even Path.

23. "This man is my brother: he has nine and ninety ewes, and I have (but) one: yet he says, 'Commit her to my care,' and is (moreover) harsh to me in speech."

24. (David) said: "He has undoubtedly wronged you in demanding your (single) ewe to be added to his (flock of) ewes: truly many are the partners (in business) who wrong each other: not so do those who believe and work deeds of righteousness, and how few are they?"... and David gathered that We had tried him: he asked forgiveness of his Lord, fell down, bowing (in prostration), and turned (to Allah in repentance).

25. So We forgave him this (lapse): he enjoyed, indeed, a Near Approach to Us,

(Bow Down)

waaḥidatam-maa lahaa min fawaaq.

16. Wa qaaloo Rabbanaa 'ajjil lanaa qiṭṭanaa qabla Yawmil-Ḥisaab.

17. Iṣbir 'alaa maa yaqooloona wazkur 'abdanaa Daawooda zal-aydi innahooo awwaab.

18. Innaa sakhkharnal-jibaala ma'ahoo yusabbiḥna bil'ashiyyi wal-ishraaq.

19. Waṭṭayra maḥshoorah; kullul-lahooo awwaab.

20. Wa shadadnaa mulkahoo wa aataynaahul-Ḥikmata wa faṣlal-khiṭaab.

21. Wa hal ataaka naba'ul-khaṣm; iz tasawwarul-miḥraab.

22. Iz dakhaloo 'alaa Daawooda fafazi'a minhum qaaloo laa takhaf khaṣmaani baghaa ba'ḍunaa 'alaa ba'ḍin faḥkum baynanaa bilḥaqqi wa laa tushṭiṭ wahdinaaa ilaa Sawaaa'iṣ-Ṣiraaṭ.

23. Inna haazaaa akhee lahoo tis'uñw-wa tis'oona na'jatañw-wa liya na'jatuñw-waaḥidah; faqaala akfilneehaa wa 'azzanee filkhiṭaab.

24. Qaala laqad ẓalamaka bisu'aali na'jatika ilaa ni'aajihee wa inna kaseeram-minal-khulaṭaaa'i la-yabghee ba'ḍuhum 'alaa ba'ḍin illal-lazeena aamanoo wa 'amiluṣ-ṣaaliḥaati wa qaleelum-maa hum; wa ẓanna Daawoodu annamaa fatannaahu fastaghfara Rabbahoo wa kharra raaki'añw-wa anaab. 🔺

25. Faghafarnaa lahoo zaalik; wa inna lahoo 'indanaa

قَاضِ الرَّحْمٰن

السَّجْدَة (١٠٦)

Manzil 6

and a beautiful Place of (Final) Return.

26. O David! We did indeed make you a vicegerent on earth: so you judge between men in truth (and justice): nor do you follow the lusts (of your heart), for they will mislead you from the Path of Allah: for those who wander astray from the Path of Allah, is a Chastisement Grievous, for that they forget the Day of Account.

27. Not without purpose did We create heaven and earth and all between! that were the thought of Unbelievers! but woe to the Unbelievers because of the Fire (of Hell)!

28. Shall We treat those who believe and work deeds of righteousness, the same as those who do mischief on earth? Shall We treat those who guard against evil, the same as those who turn aside from the right?

29. (Here is) a Book which We have sent down unto you, full of blessings, that they may meditate on its Signs, and that men of under-standing may receive admonition.

30. To David We gave Solomon (for a son),- how excellent in Our service! Ever did he turn (to Us).

31. Behold, there were brought before him, at eventide coursers of the highest breeding, and swift of foot;

32. And he said, "Truly do I love the love of good, with a view to the glory of my Lord," until (the sun) was hidden in the veil (of Night):

33. "Bring them back to me." Then he began to pass his hand over (their) legs and their necks.

34. And We did try Solomon: We placed on his throne a body (without life); but he turned (to Us in true devotion):

lazulfaa wa ḥusna ma-aab.

26. Yaa Daawoodu innaa ja'alnaaka khaleefatan fil-arḍi faḥkum baynan-naasi bilḥaqqi wa laa tattabi'il-hawaa fa-yuḍillaka 'an sabeelil-laah; innal-lazeena yaḍilloona 'an sabeelil-laah; lahum 'azaabun shadeedum bimaa nasoo Yawmal-Ḥisaab. **(Section 2)**

27. Wa maa khalaqnas-samaaa'a wal-arḍa wa maa baynahumaa baaṭilaa; zaalika zannul-lazeena kafaroo; fawaylul-lillazeena kafaroo minan-Naar.

28. Am naj'alul-lazeena aamanoo wa 'amiluṣ-ṣaaliḥaati kalmufsideena fil-arḍi am naj'alul-muttaqeena kalfujjaar.

29. Kitaabun anzalnaahu ilayka mubaarakul-liyaddabbarooo Aayaatihee wa liyatazakkara ulul-albaab.

30. Wa wahabnaa li-Daawooda Sulaymaan; ni'mal-'abd; innahooo awwaab.

31. Iz 'uriḍa 'alayhi bil'ashiy-yiṣ-ṣaafinaatul-jiyaad.

32. Faqaala ineee aḥbabtu ḥubbal-khayri 'an zikri Rabbee ḥattaa tawaarat bilḥijaab.

33. Ruddoohaa 'alayya faṭafiqa masḥam bissooqi wal-a'naaq.

34. Wa laqad fatannaa Sulaymaana wa alqaynaa 'alaa kursiyyihee jasadan ṣumma anaab.

35. He said, "O my Lord! Forgive me, and grant me a kingdom which, (it may be), does not suit another after me: for You are the Grantor of Bounties (without measure)."

36. Then We subjected the wind to his power, to flow gently to his order, whithersoever he willed,-

37. As also the evil ones, (including) every kind of builder and diver,-

38. As also others bound together in fetters.

39. "Such are Our Bounties: whether you bestow them (on others) or withhold them, no account will be asked."

40. And he enjoyed, indeed, a Near Approach to Us, and a beautiful Place of (Final) Return.

41. Commemorate Our Servant Job. Behold! he cried to his Lord: "The Evil has afflicted me with distress and suffering!"

42. (The command was given:) "Strike with your foot: here is (water) wherein to wash, cool and refreshing, and (water) to drink."

43. And We gave him (back) his people, and doubled their number, - as a Grace from Ourselves, and a thing for commemoration, for all who have Understanding.

44. "And take in your hand a little grass, and strike therewith: and do not break (your oath)." Truly We found him full of patience and constancy. How excellent in Our service! ever did he turn (to Us)!

45. And commemorate Our Servants Abraham, Isaac, and Jacob, possessors of Power and Vision.

46. Verily We did choose them for a special (purpose)- proclaiming the Message of the Hereafter.

47. They were, in Our sight, truly, of the company of the Elect

35. Qaala Rabbigh-fir lee wa hab lee mulkal-laa yambaghee li-aḥadim-mim ba'dee innaka Antal-Wahhaab.

36. Fasakhkharnaa lahur-reeḥa tajree bi-amrihee rukhaaa'an ḥaysu aṣaab.

37. Wash-Shayaaṭeena kulla bannaaa'iñw-wa ghawwaaṣ.

38. Wa aakhareena muqarraneena fil-aṣfaad.

39. Haazaa 'aṭaaa'unaa famnun aw amsik bighayri ḥisaab.

40. Wa inna lahoo 'indanaa lazulfaa wa ḥusna ma-aab.

(Section 3)

41. Wazkur 'abdanaaa Ayyoob; iz naadaa Rabbahooo annee massaniyash-Shayṭaanu binuṣbiñw-wa 'azaab.

42. Urkuḍ birijlika haazaa mughtasalum baariduñw-wa sharaab.

43. Wa wahabnaa lahooo ahlahoo wa mislahum-ma'ahum raḥmatam-minnaa wa zikraa li-ulil-albaab.

44. Wa khuz biyadika ḍighṣan faḍrib bihee wa laa taḥnas, innaa wajadnaahu ṣaabiraa; ni'mal-'abd; innahooo awwaab.

45. Wazkur 'ibaadanaaa Ibraaheema wa Is-ḥaaqa wa Ya'qooba ulil-aydee wal-abṣaar.

46. Innaaa akhlaṣnaahum bi-khaaliṣatin zikrad-daar.

47. Wa innahum 'indanaa laminal-muṣṭafaynal-

and the Good.

48. And commemorate Ismail, Elisha, and Zul-Kifl: each of them was of the company of the Good.

49. This is a Message (of admonition): and verily, for the Righteous, is a beautiful place of (final) Return,-

50. Gardens of Eternity, whose doors will (ever) be open to them;

51. Therein will they recline (at ease): therein can they call (at pleasure) for fruit in abundance, and (delicious) drink;

52. And beside them will be chaste women restraining their glances, (companions) of equal age.

53. Such is the Promise made, to you for the Day of Account!

54. Truly such will be Our Bounty (to you); it will never fail;-

55. Yes, such! but - for the wrong-doers will be an evil place of (final) Return!-

56. Hell!- They will burn therein,- an evil bed (indeed, to lie on)!-

57. Yes, such!- Then shall they taste it, - a boiling fluid, and a fluid darkm murky, intensely cold!-

58. And other penalties of a similar kind, to match them!

59. Here is a troop rushing headlong with you! No welcome for them! truly, they shall burn in the Fire!

60. (Then followers shall cry to the misleaders:) "Nay, you (too)! No welcome for you! It is you who have brought this upon us! Now evil is (this) place to stay in!"

61. They will say: "Our Lord! Whoever brought this upon us,- Add to him a double Chastisement in the Fire!"

62. And they will say: "What has happened to us that we do not see men whom we used to number among the bad ones?

63. "Did we treat them (as such) in ridicule, or have (our) eyes failed to perceive them?"

64. Truly that is just and fitting,- the mutual recriminations of the People of the Fire!

---

akhyaar.

48. Wazkur Ismaa'eela wal-Yasa'a wa Zal-Kifli wa kullum-minal-akhyaar.

49. Haazaa zikr; wa inna lilmuttaqeena laḥusna ma-aab.

50. Jannaati 'Adnim-mufat-taḥatal-lahumul-abwaab.

51. Muttaqi'eena feehaa yad-'oona feehaa bifaakihatin kaseeratiñw-wa sharaab.

52. Wa 'indahum qaaṣiraatut-ṭarfi atraab.

53. Haazaa maa too'adoona li-Yawmil-Ḥisaab.

54. Inna haazaa larizqunaa maa lahoo min-nafaad.

55. Haazaa; wa inna liṭṭaa-gheena lasharra ma-aab.

56. Jahannama yaṣlawnahaa fabi'sal-mihaad.

57. Haazaa falyazooqoohu ḥameemuñw-wa ghassaaq.

58. Wa aakharu min shak-liheee azwaaj.

59. Haazaa fawjum-muqta-ḥimum-ma'akum laa marḥabam bihim; innahum ṣaalun-Naar.

60. Qaaloo bal antum laa mar-ḥabam bikum; antum qad-damtumoohu lanaa fabi'sal-qaraar.

61. Qaaloo Rabbanaa man qaddama lanaa haazaa fazidhu 'azaaban ḍi'fan fin-Naar.

62. Wa qaaloo maa lanaa laa naraa rijaalan kunnaa na'udduhum-minal-ashraar.

63. Attakhaznaahum sikh-riyyan am zaaghat 'anhumul-abṣaar.

64. Inna zaalika lahaqqun takhaaṣumu Ahlin-Naar. (Sec. 4)

الْأَخْيَارِۜ

وَاذْكُرْ إِسْمَاعِيلَ وَالْيَسَعَ وَذَا الْكِفْلِۖ وَكُلٌّ مِّنَ الْأَخْيَارِۜ

هَٰذَا ذِكْرٌۚ وَإِنَّ لِلْمُتَّقِينَ لَحُسْنَ مَآبٍ

جَنَّاتِ عَدْنٍ مُّفَتَّحَةً لَّهُمُ الْأَبْوَابُ

مُّتَّكِئِينَ فِيهَا يَدْعُونَ فِيهَا بِفَاكِهَةٍ كَثِيرَةٍ وَشَرَابٍ

وَعِندَهُمْ قَاصِرَاتُ الطَّرْفِ أَتْرَابٌ

هَٰذَا مَا تُوعَدُونَ لِيَوْمِ الْحِسَابِ

إِنَّ هَٰذَا لَرِزْقُنَا مَا لَهُ مِن نَّفَادٍ

هَٰذَاۚ وَإِنَّ لِلطَّاغِينَ لَشَرَّ مَآبٍ

جَهَنَّمَ يَصْلَوْنَهَا فَبِئْسَ الْمِهَادُ

هَٰذَا فَلْيَذُوقُوهُ حَمِيمٌ وَغَسَّاقٌ

وَآخَرُ مِن شَكْلِهِ أَزْوَاجٌ

هَٰذَا فَوْجٌ مُّقْتَحِمٌ مَّعَكُمْ لَا مَرْحَبًا بِهِمْۚ إِنَّهُمْ صَالُوا النَّارِ

قَالُوا بَلْ أَنتُمْ لَا مَرْحَبًا بِكُمْۖ أَنتُمْ قَدَّمْتُمُوهُ لَنَاۖ فَبِئْسَ الْقَرَارُ

قَالُوا رَبَّنَا مَن قَدَّمَ لَنَا هَٰذَا فَزِدْهُ عَذَابًا ضِعْفًا فِي النَّارِ

وَقَالُوا مَا لَنَا لَا نَرَىٰ رِجَالًا كُنَّا نَعُدُّهُم مِّنَ الْأَشْرَارِ

أَتَّخَذْنَاهُمْ سِخْرِيًّا أَمْ زَاغَتْ عَنْهُمُ الْأَبْصَارُ

إِنَّ ذَٰلِكَ لَحَقٌّ تَخَاصُمُ أَهْلِ النَّارِ

65. Say: "Truly am I a Warner: no god is there but the One God (Allah), Supreme and Irresistible,-

66. The Lord of the heavens and the earth, and all between,- Exalted in Might, able to enforce His Will, forgiving again and again."

67. Sat: "That is a Message Supreme (above all)-

68. "From which you do turn away!

69. "No knowledge have I of the chiefs on high, when they discuss (matters) among themselves.

70. 'Only this has been revealed to me: that I am to give warning plainly and publicly."

71. Behold, your Lord said to the angels: "I am about to create man from clay:

72. "When I have fashioned him (in due proportion) and breathed into him of My spirit, you fall down in obeisance to him."

73. So the angels prostrated themselves, all of them together.

74. Not so Iblis: he was haughty, and became one of those who reject Faith.

75. (Allah) said: "O Iblis! What prevents you from prostrating yourself to one whom I have created with My hands? Are you haughty? Or are you one of the high (and mighty) ones?"

76. (Iblis) said: "I am better than he: You created me from fire, and him You created from clay."

77. (Allah) said: "Then you get out from here: for you are rejected, accursed.

78. "And My Curse shall be on you till the Day of Judgment."

79. (Iblis) said: "O my Lord! Give me then respite till the Day the (dead) are raised."

---

65. Qul innamaaa ana munzi-ruñw-wa maa min ilaahin illal-laahul-Waaḥidul-Qahhaar.

66. Rabbus-samaawaati wal-arḍi wa maa baynahumal-'Azeezul-Ghaffaar.

67. Qul huwa naba'un 'aẓeem.

68. Antum 'anhu mu'riḍoon.

69. Maa kaana liya min 'ilmim bilmala-il-a'laaa iz yakhtaṣimoon.

70. Iñy-yoohaaa ilayya illaaa annamaaa ana naẓeerum-mubeen.

71. Iz qaala Rabbuka lilmalaaa'ikati innee khaaliqum basharam-min ṭeen.

72. Fa-izaa sawwaytuhoo wa nafakhtu feehi mir-rooḥee faqa'oo lahoo saajideen.

73. Fasajadal-malaaa'ikatu kulluhum ajma'oon.

74. Illaaa Iblees; istakbara wa kaana minal-kaafireen.

75. Qaala yaaa Ibleesu maa mana'aka an tasjuda limaa khalaqtu biyadayy; astakbarta am kunta minal-'aaleen.

76. Qaala ana khayrum-minh; khalaqtanee min-naariñw-wa khalaqtahoo min ṭeen.

77. Qaala fakhruj minhaa fa-innaka rajeem.

78. Wa inna 'alayka la'neteee ilaa Yawmid-Deen.

79. Qaala Rabbi fa-anẓirnee ilaa Yawmi yub'asoon.

80. (Allah) said: "Respite then is granted you-
81. "Till the Day of the Time Appointed."
82. (Iblis) said: "Then, by Your Power, I will put them all in the wrong,-
83. "Except Your Servants amongst them, sincere and purified (by Your grace).
84. (Allah) said: "Then it is just and fitting - and I say what is just and fitting-
85. "That I will certainly fill Hell with you and those that follow you,- every one."
86. Say: "No reward do I ask of you for this (Qur'an), nor I am a pretender.

87. "This is no less than a Message to (all) the Worlds.
88. "And you shall certainly know the truth of it (all) after a while."

39. The Crowds
In the name of Allah, Most Gracious, Most Merciful.

1. The revelation of this Book is from Allah, the Exalted in Power, full of Wisdom.

2. Verily it is We Who have revealed the Book to you in Truth: so serve Allah, offering Him sincere devotion.

3. Is it not to Allah that sincere devotion is due? But those who take for protectors other than Allah (say): "We only serve them in order that they may bring us nearer to Allah." Truly Allah will judge between them in that wherein they differ. But Allah does not guides such as are false and ungrateful.

4. Had Allah wished to take to Himself a son, He could have chosen whom He pleased out of those whom He creates: but Glory be to Him! (He is above such things.) He is Allah, the One, the Irresistible.

80. Qaala fa-innaka minal-munzareen.
81. Ilaa Yawmil-waqtil-ma'loom.
82. Qaala fabi'izzatika la-ughwiyannahum ajma'een.
83. Illaa 'ibaadaka minhumul-mukhlaseen.
84. Qaala falhaqq, walhaqqa aqool.
85. La-amla'anna Jahannama minka wa mimman tabi'aka minhum ajma'een.
86. Qul maaa as'alukum 'alayhi min ajriñw-wa maaa ana minal-mutakallifeen.

87. In huwa illaa zikrul-lil'aalameen.
88. Wa lata'lamunna naba-ahoo ba'da heen.   (Section 5)

Sûrat az-Zumar–39
(Revealed at Makkah)
Bismillaahir Rahmaanir Raheem

1. Tanzeelul-Kitaabi minal-laahil-'Azeezil-Hakeem.

2. Innaaa anzalnaaa ilaykal-Kitaaba bilhaqqi fa'budil-laaha mukhlisal-lahud-deen.

3. Alaa lillaahid-deenul-khaalis; wallazeenat-takhazoo min doonihee awliyaaa'a maa na'buduhum illaa liyuqar-riboonaaa ilal-laahi zulfaa; innal-laaha yahkumu bayna-hum fee maa hum feehi yakhtalifoon; innal-laaha laa yahdee man huwa kaazibun kaffaar.

4. Law araadal-laahu añy-yattakhiza waladal-lastafaa mimmaa yakhluqu maa yashaaa'; Subhaanahoo Huwal-laahul-Waahidul-Qahhaar.

5. He created the heavens and the earth in true (proportions): He makes the Night overlap the Day, and the Day overlap the Night: He has subjected the sun and the moon (to His law): each one follows a course for a time appointed. Is not He the Exalted in Power - He Who forgives again and again?

6. He created you (all) from a single Person: then created, of like nature, his mate; and He sent down for you eight head of cattle in pairs: He makes you, in the wombs of your mothers, in stages, one after another, in three veils of darkness. such is Allah, your Lord and Cherisher: to Him belongs (all) dominion. There is no god but He: then how are you turned away (from your true Centre)?

7. If you reject (Allah), Truly Allah has no need of you; but He does not like ingratitude from His servants: if you are grateful, He is pleased with you. No bearer of burdens can bear the burden of another. In the End, to your Lord is your Return, when He will tell you the truth of all that you did (in this life). For He knows well all that is in (men's) hearts.

8. When some trouble touches man, he cries unto his Lord, turning to Him in repentance: but when He bestows a favour upon him as from Himself, (man) forgets what he cried and prayed for before, and he sets up rivals to Allah, thus misleading others from Allah's Path. Say, "Enjoy your blasphemy for a little while: verily you are (one) of the Companions of the Fire!"

9. Is one who worships devoutly during the hours of the night prostrating himself or standing (in adoration), who takes heed of the Hereafter, And who places his hope in

5. Khalaqas-samaawaati wal-arḍa bilḥaqq; yukawwirul-layla 'alan-nahaari wa yukaw-wirun-nahaara 'alaal-layli wa sakhkharash-shamsa walqa-mara kulluny-yajree li-ajalim-musammaa; alaa Huwal-'Azeezul-Ghaffaar.

6. Khalaqakum-min nafsinw-waaḥidatin ṣumma ja'ala minhaa zawjahaa wa anzala lakum-minal-an'aami ṣamaani-yata azwaaj; yakhluqukum fee buṭooni ummahaatikum khal-qam-mim ba'di khalqin fee ẓulumaatin ṣalaaṣ; ẓaalikumul-laahu Rabbukum lahul-mulk; laaa ilaaha illaa Huwa fa-annaa tuṣrafoon.

7. In takfuroo fa-innal-laaha ghaniyyun 'ankum; wa laa yarḍaa li'ibaadihil-kufra wa in tashkuroo yarḍahu lakum; wa laa taziru waaziratuñw-wizra ukhraa; ṣumma ilaa Rabbikum marji'ukum fa-yunabbi'ukum bimaa kuntum ta'maloon; innahoo 'aleemum biẓaatiṣ-ṣudoor.

8. Wa iẓaa massal-insaana ḍurrun da'aa Rabbahoo munee-ban ilayhi ṣumma iẓaa khawwalahoo ni'matam-minhu nasiya maa kaana yad'ooo ilayhi min qablu wa ja'ala lillaahi andaadal-liyuḍilla 'an sabeelih; qul tamatta' bikufrika qaleelan innaka min Aṣḥaabin-Naar.

9. Amman huwa qaanitun aanaaa'al-layli saajidañw-wa qaaa'imañy-yaḥẓarul-Aakhirata wa yarjoo

the Mercy of his Lord - (like one who does not)? Say: "Are those equal, those who know and those who do not know? It is those who are endued with understanding that receive admonition.

10. Say: "O you my servants who believe! Fear your Lord. Good is (the reward) for those who do good in this world. Spacious is Allah's earth! those who patiently persevere will truly receive a reward without measure!"

11. Say: "Verily, I am commanded to serve Allah with sincere devotion;

12. "And I am commanded to be the first of those who bow to Allah in Islam."

13. Say: "I would, if I disobeyed my Lord, indeed have fear of the Penalty of a Mighty Day."

14. Say: "It is Allah I serve, with my sincere (and exclusive) devotion:

15. "You serve what you will besides Him." Say: "Truly, those in loss are those who lose their own souls and their People on the Day of Judgment: Ah! that is indeed the (real and) evident Loss!

16. They shall have layers of Fire above them, and layers (of Fire) below them: with this Allah warns off His servants: "O My Servants! then fear you Me!"

17. Those who eschew Evil,- and do not fall into its worship,- and turn to Allah (in repentance),- for them is Good News: so announce the Good News to My Servants,-

18. Those who listen to the Word, and follow the best (meaning) in it: those are the ones whom Allah has guided,

rahmata Rabbih; qul hal yastawil-lazeena ya'lamoona wallazeena laa ya'lamoon; innamaa yatazakkaru ulul-albaab. **(Section 1)**

10. Qul yaa 'ibaadil-lazeena aamanut-taqoo Rabbakum; lillazeena ahsanoo fee haazihid-dunyaa hasanah; wa ardul-laahi waasi'ah; innamaa yuwaffas-saabiroona ajrahum bighayri hisaab.

11. Qul inneee umirtu an a'budal-laaha mukhlisal-lahud-deen.

12. Wa umirtu li-an akoona awwalal-muslimeen.

13. Qul inneee akhaafu in 'asaytu Rabbee 'azaaba Yawmin 'azeem.

14. Qulil-laaha a'budu mukhlisal-lahoo deenee.

15. Fa'budoo maa shi'tum-min doonih; qul innal-khaasireenal-lazeena khasirooo anfusahum wa ahleehim Yawmal-Qiyaamah; alaa zaalika huwal-khusraanul-mubeen.

16. Lahum-min fawqihim zulalum-minan-Naari wa min tahtihim zulal; zaalika yukhaw-wiful-laahu bihee 'ibaadah; yaa 'ibaadi fattaqoon.

17. Wallazeenaj-tanabut-Taaghoota añy-ya'budoohaa wa anaabooo ilal-laahi lahumul-bushraa; fabashshir 'ibaad.

18. Allazeena yastami'oonal-qawla fa-yattabi'oona ahsanah; ulaaa'ikal-lazeena hadaahumul-

and those are the ones endued with understanding.

19. Is, then, one against whom the decree of Punishment is justly due (equal to one who eschews Evil)? Would you, then, deliver one (who is) in the Fire?

20. But it is for those who fear their Lord, that lofty mansions, one above another, have been built: beneath them flow rivers (of delight): (such is) the Promise of Allah: never does Allah fail in (His) promise.

21. Do you see not that Allah sends down rain from the sky, and leads it through springs in the earth? Then He causes to grow, therewith, produce of various colours: then it withers; you will see it grow yellow; then He makes it dry up and crumble away. Truly, in this, is a Message of remembrance to men of understanding.

22. Is one whose heart Allah has opened to Islam, so that he has received enlightenment from Allah, (no better than one hard-hearted)? Woe to those whose hearts are hardened against celebrating the praises of Allah! They are manifestly wandering (in error)!

23. Allah has revealed (from time to time) the most beautiful Message in the form of a Book, consistent with itself, (yet) repeating (its teaching in various aspects): the skins of those who fear their Lord tremble thereat; then their skins and their hearts do soften to the celebration of Allah's praises. Such is the guidance of Allah: He guides therewith whom He pleases, but such as Allah leaves to stray, can have none to guide.

24. Is, then, one who has to fear the brunt of the Chastisement on the Day of Judgment (and receive it) on his face, (like one guarded therefrom)? It will be said to the wrong-doers: "You taste (the fruits of)

laahu wa ulaaa'ika hum ulul-albaab.

19. Afaman ḥaqqa 'alayhi kalimatul-'azaab; afa-anta tunqizu man fin-Naar.

20. Laakinil-lazeenat-taqaw Rabbahum lahum ghurafum-min fawqihaa ghurafum-mabniyyatun tajree min taḥti-hal-anhaar; wa'dal-laah; laa yukhliful-laahul-mee'aad.

21. Alam tara annal-laaha anzala minas-samaaa'i maaa'an fasalakahoo yanaabee'a fil-arḍi ṣumma yukhriju bihee zar'am-mukhtalifan alwaanuhoo ṣumma yaheeju fataraahu muṣfarran ṣumma yaj'aluhoo ḥuṭaamaa; inna fee zaalika lazikraa li-ulil-albaab. **(Section 2)**

22. Afaman sharaḥal-laahu ṣadrahoo lil-Islaami fahuwa 'alaa noorim-mir-Rabbih; fa-waylul-lilqaasiyati quloobu-hum-min zikril-laah; ulaaa'ika fee ḍalaalim-mubeen.

23. Allaahu nazzala aḥsanal-ḥadeeṣi Kitaabam-mutashaa-biham-maṣaaniya taqsha'irru minhu juloodul-lazeena yakh-shawna Rabbahum ṣumma taleenu julooduhum wa quloo-buhum ilaa zikril-laah; zaalika hudal-laahi yahdee bihee mañy-yashaaa'; wa mañy-yuḍlilil-laahu famaa lahoo min haad.

24. Afamañy-yattaqee biwaj-hihee sooo'al-'azaabi Yawmal-Qiyaamah; wa qeela lizzaali-meena zooqoo

what you earned!"

25. Those before them (also) rejected (revelation), and so the Punishment came to them from directions they did not perceive.

26. So Allah gave them a taste of humiliation in the present life, but greater is the punishment of the Hereafter, if they only knew!

27. We have put forth for men, in this Qur'an every kind of Parable, in order that they may receive admonition.

28. (It is) a Qur'an in Arabic, without any crookedness (therein): in order that they may guard against Evil.

29. Allah puts forth a Parable - a man belonging to many partners at variance with each other, and a man belonging entirely to one master: are those two equal in comparison? Praise be to Allah! but most of them have no know-ledge.

30. Truly you will die (one day), and truly they (too) will die (one day).

31. In the End you will (all), on the Day of Judgment, settle your disputes in the presence of your Lord.

32. Who, then, does more wrong than one who utters a lie concerning Allah, and rejects the Truth when it comes to him; is there not in Hell an abode for blasphemers?

33. And he who brings the Truth and he who confirms (and supports) it - such are the men who do right.

34. They shall have all that they wish for, in the presence of their Lord: such is the reward of those who do good;

35. So that Allah will turn off from them (even) the worst in their deeds

maa kuntum taksiboon.

25. Kazzabal-lazeena min qablihim fa-ataahumul-'azaabu min hay̲su laa yash'uroon.

26. Fa-azaaqahumul-laahul-khizya fil-hayaatid-dunyaa wa la'azaabul-Aakhirati akbar; law kaanoo ya'lamoon.

27. Wa laqad darabnaa lin-naasi fee haazal-Qur-aani min kulli masalil-la'allahum yata-zakkaroon.

28. Qur-aanan 'Arabiyyan ghayra zee 'iwajil-la'allahum yattaqoon.

29. Darabal-laahu masalar-rajulan feehi shurakaaa'u mutashaakisoona wa rajulan salamal-lirajulin hal yastawi-yaani masalaa; alhamdu lillaah; bal aksaruhum laa ya'lamoon.

30. Innaka mayyituñw-wa inna hum-mayyitoon.

31. Summa innakum Yaw-mal-Qiyaamati 'inda Rabbikum takhtasimoon.   **(Section 3)**

32. Faman azlamu mimman kazaba 'alal-laahi wa kazzaba bissidqi iz jaaa'ah; alaysa fee Jahannama maswal-lilkaafireen.

33. Wallazee jaaa'a bissidqi wa saddaqa biheee ulaaa'ika humul-muttaqoon.

34. Lahum-maa yashaaa'oona 'inda Rabbihim; zaalika jazaaa'ul-muhsineen.

35. Liyukaffiral-laahu 'anhum aswa-allazee 'amiloo

and give them their reward according to the best of what they have done.

wa yajziyahum ajrahum bi-aḥsanil-lazee kaanoo ya'maloon.

وَيَجْزِيَهُمْ أَجْرَهُم بِأَحْسَنِ الَّذِي كَانُوا يَعْمَلُونَ ۝

36. Is not Allah enough for his Servant? But they try to frighten you with other (gods) besides Him! for such as Allah leaves to stray, there can be no guide.

36. Alaysal-laahu bikaafin 'abdahoo wa yukhawwifoonaka billazeena min doonih; wa mañy-yuḍlilil-laahu famaa lahoo min haad.

أَلَيْسَ اللَّهُ بِكَافٍ عَبْدَهُ وَيُخَوِّفُونَكَ بِالَّذِينَ مِن دُونِهِ وَمَن يُضْلِلِ اللَّهُ فَمَا لَهُ مِنْ هَادٍ ۝

37. And such as Allah does guide there can be none to lead astray. Is not Allah Exalted in Power, (Able to enforce His Will), Lord of Retribution?

37. Wa mañy-yahdil-laahu famaa lahoo mim-muḍill; alaysal-laahu bi'azeezin zin-tiqaam.

وَمَن يَهْدِ اللَّهُ فَمَا لَهُ مِن مُضِلٍّ أَلَيْسَ اللَّهُ بِعَزِيزٍ ذِي انتِقَامٍ ۝

38. If indeed you ask them who it is that created the heavens and the earth, they would be sure to say, "Allah". Say: "See you then? the things that you invoke besides Allah,- can they, if Allah wills some Penalty for me, remove His Penalty?- Or if He wills some Grace for me, can they keep back His Grace?" Say: "Sufficient is Allah for me! In Him trust those who put their trust."

38. Wa la'in sa-altahum man khalaqas-samaawaati wal-arḍa la-yaqoolunnal-laah; qul afara'aytum maa tad'oona min doonil-laahi in araadaniyal-laahu biḍurrin hal hunna kaashifaatu ḍurriheee aw araadanee biraḥmatin hal hunna mumsikaatu raḥmatih; qul ḥasbiyal-laahu 'alayhi yatawakkalul-mutawakkiloon.

وَلَئِن سَأَلْتَهُم مَّنْ خَلَقَ السَّمَاوَاتِ وَالْأَرْضَ لَيَقُولُنَّ اللَّهُ قُلْ أَفَرَأَيْتُم مَّا تَدْعُونَ مِن دُونِ اللَّهِ إِنْ أَرَادَنِيَ اللَّهُ بِضُرٍّ هَلْ هُنَّ كَاشِفَاتُ ضُرِّهِ أَوْ أَرَادَنِي بِرَحْمَةٍ هَلْ هُنَّ مُمْسِكَاتُ رَحْمَتِهِ قُلْ حَسْبِيَ اللَّهُ عَلَيْهِ يَتَوَكَّلُ الْمُتَوَكِّلُونَ ۝

39. Say: "O my People! Do whatever you can: I will do (my part): but soon will you know-

39. Qul yaa qawmi'-maloo 'alaa makaanatikum innee 'aamilun fasawfa ta'lamoon.

قُلْ يَا قَوْمِ اعْمَلُوا عَلَى مَكَانَتِكُمْ إِنِّي عَامِلٌ فَسَوْفَ تَعْلَمُونَ ۝

40. "Who it is to whom comes a Chastisement of ignominy, and on whom descends a Penalty that abides."

40. Mañy-yaåteehi 'azaabuñy-yukhzeehi wa yaḥillu 'alayhi 'azaabum-muqeem.

مَن يَأْتِيهِ عَذَابٌ يُخْزِيهِ وَيَحِلُّ عَلَيْهِ عَذَابٌ مُّقِيمٌ ۝

41. Verily We have revealed the Book to you in Truth, for (instructing) mankind. He, then, that receives guidance benefits his own soul: but he that strays injures his own soul. Nor you are set over them to dispose of their affairs.

41. Innaaa anzalnaa 'alaykal-Kitaaba linnaasi bilḥaqq, famanih-tadaa falinafsihee wa man ḍalla fa-innamaa yaḍillu 'alayhaa wa maaa anta 'alayhim biwakeel.　(Section 4)

إِنَّا أَنزَلْنَا عَلَيْكَ الْكِتَابَ لِلنَّاسِ بِالْحَقِّ فَمَنِ اهْتَدَى فَلِنَفْسِهِ وَمَن ضَلَّ فَإِنَّمَا يَضِلُّ عَلَيْهَا وَمَا أَنتَ عَلَيْهِم بِوَكِيلٍ ۝

42. It is Allah that takes the souls (of men) at death; and those that die not (He takes) during their sleep: those on whom He has passed the decree of death, He keeps back (from returning to life), but the rest He sends (to their bodies) for a term appointed verily in

42. Allaahu yatawaffal-anfusa ḥeena mawtihaa wallatee lam tamut fee manaamihaa fa-yumsikul-latee qaḍaa 'alayhal-mawta wa yursilul-ukhraaa ilaaa ajalim-musammaa; inna fee

اللَّهُ يَتَوَفَّى الْأَنفُسَ حِينَ مَوْتِهَا وَالَّتِي لَمْ تَمُتْ فِي مَنَامِهَا فَيُمْسِكُ الَّتِي قَضَى عَلَيْهَا الْمَوْتَ وَيُرْسِلُ الْأُخْرَى إِلَى أَجَلٍ مُّسَمًّى إِنَّ فِي

this are Signs for those who reflect.

43. What! Do they take for intercessors others besides Allah? Say: "Even if they have no power whatever and no intelligence?"

44. Say: "To Allah belongs exclusively (the right to grant) intercession: to Him belongs the dominion of the heavens and the earth: In the End, it is to Him that you shall be brought back."

45. When Allah, the One and Only, is mentioned, the hearts of those who believe not in the Hereafter are filled with disgust and horror; but when (gods) other than He are mentioned, behold, they are filled with joy!

46. Say: "O Allah! Creator of the heavens and the earth! Knower of all that is hidden and open! it is You that will judge between Your Servants in those matters about which they have differed."

47. Even if the wrong-doers had all that there is on earth, and as much more, (in vain) would they offer it for ransom from the pain of the Chastisement on the Day of Judgment: but something will confront them from Allah, which they could never have counted upon!

48. For the evils of their Deeds will confront them, and they will be (completely) encircled by that which they used to mock at!

49. Now, when trouble touches man, he cries to Us: But when We bestow a favour upon him as from Ourselves, he says, "This has been given to me because of a certain knowledge (I have)!" No, but this is but a trial, but most of them understand not !

50. Thus did the (generations) before them say! But all that they did was of no profit to them.

51. No, the evil results of their Deeds overtook them.

zaalika la-Aayaatil-liqawmiñy-yatafakkaroon.

43. Amit-takhazoo min doo-nillaahi shufa‘aaa'; qul awa-law kaanoo laa yamlikoona shay'añw- wa laa ya‘qiloon.

44. Qul lillaahish-shafaa‘atu jamee‘aa; lahoo mulkus-samaa-waati wal-arḍi ṣumma ilayhi turja‘oon.

45. Wa izaa zukiral-laahu waḥdahush-ma-azzat quloobul-lazeena laa yu'minoona bil-Aakhirati wa izaa zukiral-lazeena min dooniheee izaa hum yastabshiroon.

46. Qulil-laahumma faaṭiras-samaawaati wal-arḍi ‘Aalimal-Ghaybi washshahaadati Anta taḥkumu bayna ‘ibaadika fee maa kaanoo feehi yakhtalifoon.

47. Wa law anna lillazeena ẓalamoo maa fil-arḍi jamee‘añw- wa mislahoo ma‘ahoo laftadaw bihee min soooo'il-‘azaabi Yawmal-Qiyaamah; wa badaa lahum minal-laahi maa lam yakoonoo yaḥtasiboon.

48. Wa badaa lahum sayyi-aatu maa kasaboo wa ḥaaqa bihim maa kaanoo bihee yastahzi'oon.

49. Fa-izaa massal-insaana ḍurrun da‘aanaa ṣumma izaa khawwalnaahu ni‘matam-minnaa qaala innamaaa ootee-tuhoo ‘alaa ‘ilm; bal hiya fitna-tuñw-wa laakinna aksarahum laa ya‘lamoon.

50. Qad qaalahal-lazeena min qablihim famaaa aghnaa ‘an-hum maa kaanoo yaksiboon.

51. Fa-aṣaabahum sayyi-aatu maa kasaboo; wallazeena

And the wrong-doers of this (generation)- the evil results of their Deeds will soon overtake them (too), and they shall never escape.

52. Do they not know that Allah enlarges the provision or restricts it, for any He pleases? Verily, in this are Signs for those who believe!

53. Say: "O my Servants who have transgressed against their souls! Despair not of the Mercy of Allah: for Allah forgives all sins: for He is Oft-Forgiving, Most Merciful.

54. "Turn you to your Lord (in repentance) and bow to His (Will), before the Chastisement comes on you: after that you shall not be helped.

55. "And follow the best of (the courses) revealed to you from your Lord, before the Chastisement comes on you - of a sudden while ye perceive not!-

56. "Lest the soul should (then) say: 'Ah! Woe is me!- In that I neglected (my duty) towards Allah, and was but among those who mocked!'-

57. "Or (lest) it should say: 'If only Allah had guided me, I should certainly have been among the righteous!'

58. "Or (lest) it should say when it (actually) sees the Chastisement: 'If only I had another chance, I should certainly be among those who do good!'

59. "(The reply will be:) 'No, but there came to you My Signs, and you did reject them: You were Haughty, and became one of those who reject faith!'

60. On the Day of Judgment will you see those who told lies against Allah;- their faces will be turned black; Is there not in

ẓalamoo min haaa'ulaaa'i sa-yu-ṣeebuhum sayyi-aatu maa kasa-boo wa maa hum bimu'jizeen.

52. Awalam ya'lamooo annal-laaha yabsuṭur-rizqa limañy-yashaaa'u wa yaqdir; inna fee zaalika la-Aayaatil-liqawmiñy-yu'minoon. (Section 5)

53. Qul yaa 'ibaadiyal-lazeena asrafoo 'alaaa anfusihim laa taqnaṭoo mirraḥmatil-laah; innal-laaha yaghfiruz-zunooba jamee'aa; innahoo Huwal-Ghafoorur-Raḥeem.

54. Wa aneebooo ilaa Rabbi-kum wa aslimoo lahoo min qabli añy-yaåtiyakumul-'azaabu summa laa tunṣaroon.

55. Wattabi'ooo aḥsana maaa unzila ilaykum mir-Rabbikum min qabli añy-yaåtiyakumul-'azaabu baghtatañw-wa antum laa tash'uroon.

56. An taqoola nafsuñy-yaa ḥasrataa 'alaa maa farraṭtu fee jambil-laahi wa in kuntu laminas-saakhireen.

57. Aw taqoola law annal-laaha hadaanee lakuntu minal-muttaqeen.

58. Aw taqoola ḥeena taral-'azaaba law anna lee karratan fa-akoona minal-muḥsineen.

59. Balaa qad jaaa'atka Aa-yaatee fakazzabta bihaa wastak-barta wa kunta minal-kaafireen.

60. Wa Yawmal-Qiyaamati taral-lazeena kazaboo 'alallaahi wujoohuhum muswaddah; alaysa fee

Hell an abode for the Haughty?

61. But Allah will deliver the righteous to their place of salvation: no evil shall touch them, nor shall they grieve.

62. Allah is the Creator of all things, and He is the Guardian and Disposer of all affairs.

63. To Him belong the keys of the heavens and the earth: and those who reject the Signs of Allah,- it is they who will be in loss.

64. Say: "Is it someone other than Allah that you order me to worship, O you ignorant ones?"

65. But it has already been revealed to you,- as it was to those before you,- "If you were to join (gods with Allah), truly fruitless will be your work (in life), and you will surely be in the ranks of those who lose (all spiritual good)".

66. No, but worship Allah, and be of those who give thanks.

67. No just estimate have they made of Allah, such as is due to Him: On the Day of Judgment the whole of the earth will be but His handful, and the heavens will be rolled up in His right hand: Glory to Him! High is He above the Partners they attribute to Him!

68. The Trumpet will (just) be sounded, when all that are in the heavens and on earth will swoon, except such as it will please Allah (to exempt). Then will a second one be sounded, when, behold, they will be standing and looking on!

69. And the Earth will shine with the Glory of its Lord: the Record (of Deeds) will be placed (open); the prophets and the witnesses will be brought forward; and a just decision pronounced between them; and they will not be wronged (in the least).

70. And to every soul will be paid in full (the fruit) of its Deeds; and (Allah) knows best all that they do.

Jahannama maswal-lilmuta-kabbireen.

61. Wa yunajjil-laahul-lazee-nat-taqaw bimafaazatihim laa yamassuhumus-sooo'u wa laa hum yaḥzanoon.

62. Allaahu khaaliqu kulli shay'iñw-wa Huwa 'alaa kulli shay'iñw-Wakeel.

63. Lahoo maqaaleedus-sa-maawaati wal-arḍ; wallazeena kafaroo bi-Aayaatil-laahi ulaa-a'ika humul-khaasiroon. (Sec. 2)

64. Qul afaghayral-laahi taa-murooonneee a'budu ayyuhal-jaahiloon.

65. Wa laqad ooḥiya ilayka wa ilal-lazeena min qablika la-in ashrakta la-yaḥbaṭanna 'amalu-ka wa latakoonanna minal-khaasireen.

66. Balil-laaha fa'bud wa kum-minash-shaakireen.

67. Wa maa qadarul-laaha ḥaqqa qadrihee wal-arḍu jamee-'an qabḍatuhoo Yawmal-Qiyaamati wassamaawaatu maṭwiyyaatum biyameenih; Subḥaanahoo wa Ta'aalaa 'ammaa yushrikoon.

68. Wa nufikha fiṣ-Ṣoori faṣa'iqa man fis-samaawaati wa man fil-arḍi illaa man shaaa'al-laahu ṣumma nufikha feehi ukhraa fa-izaa hum qiyaamuñy-yanẓuroon.

69. Wa ashraqatil-arḍu binoori Rabbihaa wa wuḍi'al-Kitaabu wa jeee'a bin-Nabiyyeena wash-shuhadaaa'i wa quḍiya baynahum bilḥaqqi wa hum laa yuẓlamoon.

70. Wa wuffiyat kullu nafsim maa 'amilat wa Huwa a'lamu bimaa yaf'aloon. (Section 7)

جَهَنَّمُ مَثْوًى لِّلْمُتَكَبِّرِيْنَ ۞

وَيُنَجِّى اللهُ الَّذِيْنَ اتَّقَوْا بِمَفَازَتِهِمْ

لَا يَمَسُّهُمُ السُّوْٓءُ وَلَا هُمْ يَحْزَنُوْنَ ۞

اللهُ خَالِقُ كُلِّ شَيْءٍ ۖ وَّهُوَ عَلٰى كُلِّ

شَيْءٍ وَّكِيْلٌ ۞

لَهٗ مَقَالِيْدُ السَّمٰوٰتِ وَالْأَرْضِ ۗ وَالَّذِيْنَ

كَفَرُوْا بِاٰيٰتِ اللهِ أُولٰٓئِكَ هُمُ الْخٰسِرُوْنَ ۞

قُلْ أَفَغَيْرَ اللهِ تَأْمُرُوْٓنِّيْٓ أَعْبُدُ أَيُّهَا

الْجٰهِلُوْنَ ۞

وَلَقَدْ أُوْحِيَ إِلَيْكَ وَإِلَى الَّذِيْنَ مِنْ

قَبْلِكَ ۚ لَئِنْ أَشْرَكْتَ لَيَحْبَطَنَّ عَمَلُكَ

وَلَتَكُوْنَنَّ مِنَ الْخٰسِرِيْنَ ۞

بَلِ اللهَ فَاعْبُدْ وَكُنْ مِّنَ الشّٰكِرِيْنَ ۞

وَمَا قَدَرُوا اللهَ حَقَّ قَدْرِهٖ ۗ وَالْأَرْضُ

جَمِيْعًا قَبْضَتُهٗ يَوْمَ الْقِيٰمَةِ وَ

السَّمٰوٰتُ مَطْوِيّٰتٌ بِيَمِيْنِهٖ ۚ سُبْحٰنَهٗ

وَتَعٰلٰى عَمَّا يُشْرِكُوْنَ ۞

وَنُفِخَ فِى الصُّوْرِ فَصَعِقَ مَنْ فِى

السَّمٰوٰتِ وَمَنْ فِى الْأَرْضِ إِلَّا مَنْ

شَاءَ اللهُ ۖ ثُمَّ نُفِخَ فِيْهِ أُخْرٰى فَإِذَا

هُمْ قِيَامٌ يَّنْظُرُوْنَ ۞

وَأَشْرَقَتِ الْأَرْضُ بِنُوْرِ رَبِّهَا وَوُضِعَ

الْكِتٰبُ وَجِاْيٓءَ بِالنَّبِيّٖنَ وَالشُّهَدَآءِ

وَقُضِيَ بَيْنَهُمْ بِالْحَقِّ وَهُمْ لَا يُظْلَمُوْنَ ۞

وَوُفِّيَتْ كُلُّ نَفْسٍ مَّا عَمِلَتْ وَهُوَ

أَعْلَمُ بِمَا يَفْعَلُوْنَ ۞

71. The Unbelievers will be led to Hell in crowd: until, when they arrive, there, its gates will be opened. And its keepers will say, "Did not apostles come to you from among yourselves, rehearsing to you the Signs of your Lord, and warning you of the Meeting of This Day of yours?" The answer will be: "True: but the Decree of Punishment has been proved true against the Unbelievers!"

72. (To them) will be said: "Enter you the gates of Hell, to dwell therein: and evil is (this) Abode of the Arrogant!"

73. And those who feared their Lord will be led to the Garden in crowds: until behold, they arrive there; its gates will be opened; and its keepers will say: "Peace be upon you! well have you done! enter you here, to dwell therein."

74. They will say: "Praise be to Allah, Who has truly fulfilled His Promise to us, and has given us (this) land in heritage: We can dwell in the Garden as we will: how excellent a reward for those who work (righteousness)!"

75. And you will see the angels surrounding the Throne (Divine) on all sides, singing Glory and Praise to their Lord. The Decision between them (at Judgment) will be in (perfect) justice, and the cry (on all sides) will be, "Praise be to Allah, the Lord of the Worlds!"

40. The Believer
In the name of Allah, Most Gracious, Most Merciful.

1. *Ha-Mim.*

2. The revelation of this Book is from Allah, Exalted in Power, Full of Knowledge,-

---

71. Wa seeqal-lazeena kafa-rooo ilaa Jahannama zumaran ḥattaaa izaa jaaa'oohaa futiḥat abwaabuhaa wa qaala lahum khazanatuhaaa alam yaåtikum Rusulum-minkum yatloona 'alaykum Aayaati Rabbikum wa yunziroonakum liqaaa'a Yawmikum haazaa; qaaloo balaa wa laakin ḥaqqat kali-matul-'azaabi 'alal-kaafireen.

72. Qeelad-khuloooo abwaaba Jahannama khaalideena feehaa fabi'sa maṣwal-mutakabbireen.

73. Wa seeqal-lazeenat-taqaw Rabbahum ilal-Jannati zumaran ḥattaaa izaa jaaa'oohaa wa futiḥat abwaabuhaa wa qaala lahum khazanatuhaa salaamun 'alaykum ṭibtum fadkhuloohaa khaalideen.

74. Wa qaalull-ḥamdulillaa-hil-lazee ṣadaqanaa wa'dahoo wa awraṣanal-arḍa natabaw-wa-u minal-Jannati ḥaysu na-shaaa'u fani'ma ajrul-'aami-leen.

75. Wa taral-malaaa'ikata ḥaaaffeena min ḥawlil-'Arshi yusabbiḥoona biḥamdi Rabbi-him wa quḍiya baynahum bilḥaqqi wa qeelal-ḥamdu lillaahi Rabbil-'aalameen.

(Section 8)

Sûrat al-Mu'min–40
(Revealed at Makkah)
Bismillaahir Raḥmaanir Raheem

1. Ḥaa-Meeem.

2. Tanzeelul-Kitaabi minal-laahil-Azeezil-'Aleem.

3. Who forgives sin, accepteth repentance, is strict in punishment, and hath a long reach (in all things). There is no god but He: to Him is the final goal.

4. None can dispute about the Signs of Allah but the Unbelievers. Let not, then, their strutting about through the land deceive you!

5. But (there were people) before them, who denied (the Signs),- the People of Noah, and the Confederates (of Evil) after them; and every People plotted against their prophet, to seize him, and disputed by means of vanities, therewith to condemn the Truth; but it was I that seized them! and how (terrible) was My Requital!

6. Thus was the Decree of your Lord proved true against the Unbelievers; that truly they are Companions of the Fire!

7. Those who sustain the Throne (of Allah) and those around it Sing Glory and Praise to their Lord; believe in Him; and implore Forgiveness for those who believe: "Our Lord! your Reach is over all things, in Mercy and Knowledge. Forgive, then, those who turn in Repentance, and follow Your Path; and preserve them from the Chastisement of the Blazing Fire!

8. "And grant, our Lord! that they enter the Gardens of Eternity, which You have promised to them, and to the righteous among their fathers, their wives, and their posterity! For You are (He), the Exalted in Might, Full of Wisdom.

9. "And preserve them from (all) ills; and any whom You does preserve from (all) ills that Day,- on them will You have bestowed Mercy indeed: and that will be truly (for them) the highest Achievement".

3. Ghaafiriz-zambi wa qaa-bilit-tawbi shadeedil-'iqaabi zit-tawli laaa ilaaha illaa Huwa ilayhil-maseer.

4. Maa yujaadilu feee Aa-yaatil-laahi illal-lazeena kafaroo falaa yaghrurka taqallubuhum fil-bilaad.

5. Kazzabat qablahum qawmu Nooh-iñw-wal-Ahzaabu mim ba'dihim wa hammat kullu ummatim bi-Rasoolihim liyaå-khuzoohu wa jaadaloo bilbaatili liyudhidoo bihil-haqqa fa-akhaztuhum fakayfa kaana 'iqaab.

6. Wa kazaalika haqqat Kalimatu Rabbika 'alal-lazeena kafarooo annahum Ashaabun-Naar.

7. Allazeena yahmiloonal-'Arsha wa man hawlahoo yusabbihoona bihamdi Rabbihim wa yu'minoona bihee wa yastaghfiroona lillazeena aamanoo Rabbanaa wasi'ta kulla shay'ir-rahmatañw wa 'ilman faghfir lillazeena taaboo wattaba'oo sabeelaka wa qihim 'azaabal-Jaheem.

8. Rabbanaa wa adkhilhum Jannaati 'Adninil-latee wa'atta-hum wa man salaha min aabaaa-'ihim wa azwaajihim wa zurriy-yaatihim; innaka Antal-'Azeezul-Hakeem.

9. Wa qihimus-sayyi-aat; wa man taqis-sayyi-aati Yawma'izin faqad rahimtah; wa zaalika huwal-fawzul-'azeem. **(Section 1)**

10. The Unbelievers will be addressed: "Greater was the aversion of Allah to you than (is) your aversion to yourselves, seeing that you were called to the Faith and you used to refuse."

11. They will say: "Our Lord! twice have You made us without life, and twice have You given us Life! Now that have we recognised our sins: Is there any way out (of this)?"

12. (The answer will be:) "This is because, when Allah was invoked as the Only (object of worship), you did reject Faith, but when partners were joined to Him, you believed! the Command is with Allah, Most High, Most Great!"

13. He it is Who shows you His Signs, and sends down sustenance for you from the sky: but only those receive admonition who turn (to Allah).

14. Call you, then, upon Allah with sincere devotion to Him, even though the Unbelievers may detest it.

15. Raised high above ranks (or degrees), (He is) the Lord of the Throne (of Authority): by His Command doth He send the Spirit (of inspiration) to any of His servants He pleases, that it may warn (men) of the Day of Mutual Meeting,-

16. The Day whereon they will (all) come forth: not a single thing concerning them is hidden from Allah. Whose will be the dominion that Day?" That of Allah, the One the Irresistible!

17. That Day will every soul be requited for what it earned; no injustice will there be that Day, for Allah is Swift in taking account.

18. Warn them of the Day that is (ever) drawing near, when the hearts will (come) right up to the throats to choke (them); No intimate friend nor intercessor will the wrong-doers have,

10. Innal-lazeena kafaroo yunaadawna lamaqtul-laahi akbaru mim-maqtikum anfusakum iz tud'awna ilal-eemaani fatakfuroon.

11. Qaaloo Rabbanaaa amattanasnatayni wa ahyaytanasnatayni fa'tarafnaa bizunoobinaa fahal ilaa khuroojim-min sabeel.

12. Zaalikum bi-annahooo izaa du'iyal-laahu wahdahoo kafartum wa iny-yushrak bihee tu'minoo; falhukmu lillaahil 'Aliyyil-Kabeer.

13. Huwal-lazee yureekum Aayaatihee wa yunazzilu lakum minas-samaaa'i rizqaa; wa maa yatazakkaru illaa many-yuneeb.

14. Fad'ul-laaha mukhliseena lahud-deena wa law karihal-kaafiroon.

15. Rafee'ud-darajaati zul-'Arshi yulqir-rooha min amrihee 'alaa many-yashaaa'u min 'ibaadihee liyunzira yawmat-talaaq.

16. Yawma hum baarizoona laa yakhfaa 'alal-laahi minhum shay'; limanil-mulkul-Yawma lillaahil-Waahidil-Qahhaar.

17. Al-Yawma tujzaa kullu nafsim bimaa kasabat; laa zulmal-Yawm; innal-laaha saree'ul-hisaab.

18. Wa anzirhum yawmal-aazifati izil-quloobu ladal-hanaajiri kaazimeen; maa lizzaalimeena min hameeminw-wa laa shafee'iny-

who could be listened to.

19. (Allah) knows of (the tricks) that deceive with the eyes, and all that the hearts (of men) conceal.

20. And Allah will judge with (justice and) Truth: but those whom (men) invoke besides Him, will not (be in a position) to judge at all. Verily it is Allah (alone) Who hears and sees (all things).

21. Do they not travel through the earth and see what was the End of those before them? They were even superior to them in strength, and in the traces (they have left) in the land: but Allah did call them to account for their sins, and none had they to defend them against Allah.

22. That was because there came to them their apostles with Clear (Signs), but they rejected them: So Allah called them to account: for He is Full of Strength, Strict in Punishment.

23. Of old We sent Moses, with Our Signs and an authority manifest,

24. To Pharaoh, Haman, and Qarun; but they called (him)" a sorcerer telling lies!"...

25. Now, when he came to them in Truth, from Us, they said, "Slay the sons of those who believe with him, and keep alive their females," but the plots of Unbelievers (end) in nothing but errors (and delusions)!...

26. Said Pharaoh: "Leave me to slay Moses; and let him call on his Lord! What I fear is lest he should change your religion, or lest he should cause

---

yutaa'.

19. Ya'lamu khaaa'inatala-'yuni wa maa tukhfiṣ-ṣudoor.

20. Wallaahu yaqḍee bilḥaqq, wallazeena yad'oona min doonihee laa yaqḍoona bishay'; innal-laaha Huwas-Samee'ul-Baṣeer. **(Section 2)**

21. Awalam yaseeroo fil-arḍi fa-yanẓuroo kayfa kaana 'aaqibatul-lazeena kaanoo min qablihim; kaanoo hum ashadda minhum quwwataňw-wa aaṣaaran fil-arḍi fa-akhaẕahumul-laahu bizunoobihim wa maa kaana lahum minal-laahi miñw-waaq.

22. Zaalika bi-annahum kaa-nat taåteehim Rusuluhum bilbayyinaati fakafaroo fa-akhaẕahumul-laah; innahoo qawiyyun shadeedul-'iqaab.

23. Wa laqad arsalnaa Moosaa bi-Aayaatinaa wa sulṭaanim-mubeen.

24. Ilaa Fir'awna wa Haamaa-na wa Qaaroona faqaaloo saaḥirun kazzaab.

25. Falamma jaaa'ahum-bil-ḥaqqi min 'indinaa qaaluq-tulooo abnaaa'al-lazeena aamanoo ma'ahoo wastaḥyoo nisaaa'ahum; wa maa kaydul-kaafireena illaa fee ḍalaal.

26. Wa qaala Fir'awnu zaroo-neee aqtul Moosaa walyad'u Rabbahoo ineee akhaafu añy-yubaddila deenakum aw añy-yuẕhira fil-

---

يُطَاعُ ۩

يَعْلَمُ خَآئِنَةَ الْأَعْيُنِ وَمَا تُخْفِي الصُّدُوْرُ ۝

وَاللّٰهُ يَقْضِىْ بِالْحَقِّ ۖ وَالَّذِيْنَ يَدْعُوْنَ مِنْ دُوْنِهٖ لَا يَقْضُوْنَ بِشَىْءٍ ۗ اِنَّ اللّٰهَ هُوَ السَّمِيْعُ الْبَصِيْرُ ۝

اَوَلَمْ يَسِيْرُوْا فِى الْأَرْضِ فَيَنْظُرُوْا كَيْفَ كَانَ عَاقِبَةُ الَّذِيْنَ كَانُوْا مِنْ قَبْلِهِمْ ۚ كَانُوْا هُمْ اَشَدَّ مِنْهُمْ قُوَّةً وَّاٰثَارًا فِى الْأَرْضِ فَاَخَذَهُمُ اللّٰهُ بِذُنُوْبِهِمْ ۗ وَمَا كَانَ لَهُمْ مِّنَ اللّٰهِ مِنْ وَّاقٍ ۝

ذٰلِكَ بِاَنَّهُمْ كَانَتْ تَّأْتِيْهِمْ رُسُلُهُمْ بِالْبَيِّنٰتِ فَكَفَرُوْا فَاَخَذَهُمُ اللّٰهُ ۗ اِنَّهٗ قَوِىٌّ شَدِيْدُ الْعِقَابِ ۝

وَلَقَدْ اَرْسَلْنَا مُوْسٰى بِاٰيٰتِنَا وَ سُلْطٰنٍ مُّبِيْنٍ ۝

اِلٰى فِرْعَوْنَ وَهَامٰنَ وَقَارُوْنَ فَقَالُوْا سٰحِرٌ كَذَّابٌ ۝

فَلَمَّا جَآءَهُمْ بِالْحَقِّ مِنْ عِنْدِنَا قَالُوا اقْتُلُوْۤا اَبْنَآءَ الَّذِيْنَ اٰمَنُوْا مَعَهٗ وَاسْتَحْيُوْا نِسَآءَهُمْ ۗ وَمَا كَيْدُ الْكٰفِرِيْنَ اِلَّا فِىْ ضَلٰلٍ ۝

وَقَالَ فِرْعَوْنُ ذَرُوْنِىْۤ اَقْتُلْ مُوْسٰى وَلْيَدْعُ رَبَّهٗ ۚ اِنِّىْۤ اَخَافُ اَنْ يُّبَدِّلَ دِيْنَكُمْ اَوْ اَنْ يُّظْهِرَ فِى

mischief to appear in the land!"

27. Moses said: "I have indeed called upon my Lord and your Lord (for protection) from every arrogant one who believes not in the Day of Account!"

28. A believer, a man from among the people of Pharaoh, who had concealed his faith, said: "Will you slay a man because he says, 'My Lord is Allah'?- when he has indeed come to you with Clear (Signs) from your Lord? and if he be a liar, on him is (the sin of) his lie: but, if he is telling the Truth, then will fall on you something of the (calamity) of which he warns you: Truly Allah guides not one who transgresses and lies!

29. "O my People! Yours is the dominion this day: You have the upper hand in the land: but who will help us from the Punishment of Allah, should it befall us?" Pharaoh said: "I but point out to you that which I see (myself); Nor do I guide you but to the Path of Right!"

30. Then said the man who believed: "O my people! Truly I do fear for you something like the Day (of disaster) of the Confederates (in sin)!-

31. "Something like the fate of the People of Noah, the 'Ad, and the Thamud, and those who came after them: but Allah never wishes injustice to His Servants.

32. "And O my people! I fear for you a Day when there will be Mutual calling (and wailing),-

33. "A Day when you shall turn your backs and flee: No defender shall you have from Allah: Any whom Allah leaves to stray,

ardil-fasaad.

27. Wa qaala Moosaaa innee-'uztu bi-Rabbee wa Rabbikum min kulli mutakabbiril-laa yu'minu bi-Yawmil-Ḥisaab. **(Section 3)**

28. Wa qaala rajulum mu'mi-num-min Aali Fir'awna yaktumu eemaanahooo ataqtu-loona rajulan any-yaqoola Rabbi-yal-laahu wa qad jaaa'akum bil-bayyinaati mir-Rabbikum wa iny-yaku kaaziban fa'alayhi kazi-buhoo wa iny-yaku saadiqany-yusibkum ba'dul-lazee ya'idu-kum innal-laaha laa yahdee man huwa musrifun kazzaab.

29. Yaa qawmi lakumul-mulkul-yawma zaahireena fil ardi famany-yansurunaa mim baåsil-laahi in jaaa'anaa; qaala Fir'awnu maaa ureekum illaa maaa araa wa maaa ahdeekum illaa sabeelar-rashaad.

30. Wa qaalal-lazeee aamana yaa qawmi inneee akhaafu 'alaykum misla yawmil-Aḥzaab.

31. Misla daåbi qawmi Noo-hiñw-wa 'Aadiñw-wa Samooda wallazeena mim ba'dihim; wa mal-laahu yureedu zulmal-lil-'ibaad.

32. Wa yaa qawmi inneee akhaafu 'alaykum yawmat-tanaad.

33. Yawma tuwalloona mud-bireena maa lakum minal-laahi min 'aasim; wa many-yudlilil-laahu

there is none to guide...

فَمَا لَهُ مِنْ هَادٍ ۞

34. "And to you there came Joseph in times gone by, with Clear Signs, but you ceased not to doubt of the (Mission) for which he had come: At length, when he died, you said: 'No apostle will Allah send after him.' thus does Allah leave to stray such as transgress and live in doubt,-

34. Wa laqad jaaa'akum Yoosufu min qablu bil-bayyinaati famaa ziltum fee shakkim-mimmaa jaaa'akum bihee ḥattaaa izaa halaka qultum lañy-yab'aṣal-laahu mim ba'dihee Rasoolaa; kazaalika yuḍillul-laahu man huwa Musrifum-murtaab.

وَلَقَدْ جَآءَكُمْ يُوسُفُ مِنْ قَبْلُ بِالْبَيِّنَتِ فَمَا زِلْتُمْ فِيْ شَكٍّ مِّمَّا جَآءَكُمْ بِهِ ۗ حَتّٰى إِذَا هَلَكَ قُلْتُمْ لَنْ يَّبْعَثَ اللّٰهُ مِنْ بَعْدِهِ رَسُوْلًا ۗ كَذٰلِكَ يُضِلُّ اللّٰهُ مَنْ هُوَ مُسْرِفٌ مُّرْتَابٌ ۞

35. "(Such) as dispute about the Signs of Allah, without any authority that has reached them, grievous and odious (is such conduct) in the sight of Allah and of the Believers. Thus does Allah, seal up every heart of arrogant and obstinate Transgressors."

35. Allazeena yujaadiloona fee Aaayaatil-laahi bighayri sulṭaanin ataahum kabura maqtan 'indal-laahi wa 'indal-lazeena aamanoo; kazaalika yaṭba'ul-laahu 'alaa kulli qalbi mutakabbirin jabbaar.

الَّذِيْنَ يُجَادِلُوْنَ فِيْ اٰيٰتِ اللّٰهِ بِغَيْرِ سُلْطٰنٍ اَتٰىهُمْ ۗ كَبُرَ مَقْتًا عِنْدَ اللّٰهِ وَعِنْدَ الَّذِيْنَ اٰمَنُوْا ۗ كَذٰلِكَ يَطْبَعُ اللّٰهُ عَلٰى كُلِّ قَلْبِ مُتَكَبِّرٍ جَبَّارٍ ۞

36. Pharaoh said: "O Haman! Build me a lofty palace, that I may attain the ways and means,-

36. Wa qaala Fir'awnu yaa Haamaanub-ni lee ṣarḥal-la'alleee ablughul-asbaab.

وَقَالَ فِرْعَوْنُ يٰهَامٰنُ ابْنِ لِيْ صَرْحًا لَّعَلِّيْ أَبْلُغُ الْأَسْبَابَ ۞

37. "The ways and means of (reaching) the heavens, and that I may mount up to the Allah of Moses: But as far as I am concerned, I think (Moses) is a liar!" Thus was made alluring, in Pharaoh's eyes, the evil of his deeds, and he was hindered from the Path; and the plot of Pharaoh led to nothing but perdition (for him).

37. Asbaabas-samaawaati fa-aṭṭali'a ilaaa ilaahi Moosaa wa innee la-azunnuhoo kaazibaa; wa kazaalika zuyyina li-Fir-'awna sooo'u 'amalihee wa ṣudda 'anis-sabeel; wa maa kaydu Fir'awna illaa fee tabaab. **(Section 4)**

أَسْبَابَ السَّمٰوٰتِ فَأَطَّلِعَ إِلٰى إِلٰهِ مُوْسٰى وَإِنِّيْ لَأَظُنُّهُ كَاذِبًا ۗ وَكَذٰلِكَ زُيِّنَ لِفِرْعَوْنَ سُوْءُ عَمَلِهِ وَصُدَّ عَنِ السَّبِيْلِ ۗ وَمَا كَيْدُ فِرْعَوْنَ إِلَّا فِيْ تَبَابٍ ۞

38. The man who believed said further: "O my people! Follow me: I will lead you to the Path of Right.

38. Wa qaalal-lazeee aamana yaa qawmit-tabi'ooni ahdikum sabeelar-rashaad.

وَقَالَ الَّذِيْ اٰمَنَ يٰقَوْمِ اتَّبِعُوْنِ أَهْدِكُمْ سَبِيْلَ الرَّشَادِ ۞

39. "O my people! This life of the present is nothing but (temporary) convenience: It is the Hereafter that is the Home that will last.

39. Yaa qawmi innamaa haazihil-ḥayaatud-dunyaa mataa'uñw-wa innal-Aakhirata hiya daarul-qaraar.

يٰقَوْمِ إِنَّمَا هٰذِهِ الْحَيٰوةُ الدُّنْيَا مَتَاعٌ ۖ وَإِنَّ الْاٰخِرَةَ هِيَ دَارُ الْقَرَارِ ۞

40. "He that works evil will not be requited but by the like thereof: and he that works a righteous deed - whether man or woman - and is a Believer- such

40. Man 'amila sayyi'atan falaa yujzaaa illaa mislahaa wa man 'amila ṣaaliḥam-min zakarin aw unṣaa wa huwa mu'minun fa-ulaaa'ika

مَنْ عَمِلَ سَيِّئَةً فَلَا يُجْزٰى إِلَّا مِثْلَهَا ۖ وَمَنْ عَمِلَ صَالِحًا مِّنْ ذَكَرٍ أَوْ أُنْثٰى وَهُوَ مُؤْمِنٌ فَأُولٰٓئِكَ

will enter the Garden (of Bliss):"Taste you (the fruits of) what you earned!"Therein will they have abundance without measure.

41. "And O my people! How (strange) it is for me to call you to Salvation while you call me to the Fire!

42. "You do call upon me to blaspheme against Allah, and to join with Him partners of whom I have no knowledge; and I call you to the Exalted in Power, Who forgives again and again!"

43. "Without doubt you do call me to one who is not fit to be called to, whether in this world, or in the Hereafter; our return will be to Allah; and the Transgressors will be Companions of the Fire!

44. "Soon will you remember what I say to you (now), My (own) affair I commit to Allah: for Allah (ever) watches over His Servants."

45. Then Allah saved him from (every) ill that they plotted (against him), but the burnt of the Penalty encompassed on all sides the People of Pharaoh.

46. In front of the Fire will they be brought, morning and evening: And (the sentence will be) on the Day that Judgment will be established: "Cast you the People of Pharaoh into the severest Chastisement!"

47. Behold, they will dispute with each other in the Fire! The weak ones (who followed) will say to those who had been arrogant, "We but followed you: Can you then take (on your-selves) from us some share of the Fire?

48. Those who had been arrogant will say: "We are all in this (Fire)! Truly, Allah has judged between (His) Servants!"

49. Those in the Fire will say to the Keepers of

yadkhuloonal-Jannata yurza-qoona feehaa bighayri ḥisaab.

41. Wa yaa qawmi maa leee ad'ookum ilan-najaati wa tad'oonaneee ilan-Naar.

42. Tad'oonanee li-akfura billaahi wa ushrika bihee maa laysa lee bihee 'ilmunw-wa ana ad'ookum ilal'Azeezil-Ghaf-faar.

43. Laa jarama annamaa tad'oonaneee ilayhi laysa lahoo da'watun fid-dunyaa wa laa fil-Aakhirati wa anna maraddanaaa ilal-laahi wa annal-musrifeena hum Aṣḥaabun-Naar.

44. Fasatazkuroona maaa aqoolu lakum; wa ufawwiḍu amreee ilal-laah; innallaaha baṣeerum bil'ibaad.

45. Fa-waqaahul-laahu sayyi-aati maa makaroo wa ḥaaqa bi-Aali-Fir'awna sooo'ul-'azaab.

46. An-Naaru yu'raḍoona 'alayhaa ghuduwwañw-wa 'ashiyyañw wa Yawma taqoo-mus-Saa'atu adkhilooo Aala Fir'awna ashaddal-'azaab.

47. Wa iz yataḥaaajjoona fin Naari fa-yaqooluḍ-ḍu'afaaa'u lillazeenas-takbarooo innaa kunnaa lakum taba'an fahal antum mughnoona 'annaa naṣeebam-minan-Naar.

48. Qaalal-lazeenas-takba-rooo innaa kullun feehaaa innal-laaha qad ḥakama baynal-'ibaad.

49. Wa qaalal-lazena fin-Naari likhazanati

Hell: "Pray to your Lord to lighten us the Penalty for a day (at least)!"

50. They will say: "Did there not come to you your apostles with Clear Signs?" They will say, "Yes". They will reply, "Then pray (as you like)! But the prayer of those without Faith is nothing but (futile wandering) in (mazes of) error!"

51. We will, without doubt, help Our apostles and those who believe, (both) in this world's life and on the Day when the Witnesses will stand forth,

52. The Day when no profit will it be to Wrong-doers to present their excuses, but they will (only) have the Curse and the Home of Misery.

53. We did aforetime give Moses the (Book of) Guidance, and We gave the book in inheritance to the Children of Israel,-

54. A Guide and a Message to men of Understanding.

55. Patiently, then, persevere: for the Promise of Allah is true: and ask forgiveness for your fault, and celebrate the Praises of thy Lord in the evening and in the morning.

56. Those who dispute about the signs of Allah without any authority bestowed on them,- there is nothing in their breasts but (the quest of) greatness, which they shall never attain to: seek refuge, then, in Allah: It is He Who hears and sees (all things).

57. Assuredly the creation of the heavens and the earth is a greater (matter) than the creation of men: Yet most men understand not.

58. Not equal are the blind and those who (clearly) see: Nor are (equal) those who believe and work deeds of righteousness, and those who do evil. Little do you learn by admonition!

Jahannamad-'oo Rabbakum yukhaffif 'annaa yawmam-minal-'azaab.

50. Qaalooo awalam taku taa-teekum Rusulukum bilbayyi-naati qaaloo balaa; qaaloo fad'oo; wa maa du'aaa'ul-kaafireena illaa fee dalaal. (Sec. 5)

51. Innaa lananşuru Rusu-lanaa wallazeena aamanoo fil-hayaatid-dunyaa wa Yawma yaqoomul-ashhaad.

52. Yawma laa yanfa'uz-zaalimeena ma'ziratuhum wa lahumul-la'natu wa lahum sooo'ud-daar.

53. Wa laqad aataynaa Moosal-hudaa wa awrasnaa Baneee Israaa'eelal-Kitaab.

54. Hudañw-wa zikraa li-ulil-albaab.

55. Faşbir inna wa'dal-laahi haqquñw-wastaghfir lizambika wa sabbiḥ biḥamdi Rabbika bil'ashiyyi wal-ibkaar.

56. Innal-lazeena yujaadi-loona feee Aayaatil-laahi bighayri sulţaanin ataahum in fee şudoorihim illaa kibrum-maa hum bibaaligheeh; fasta'iz billaahi innahoo Huwas-Samee'ul-Başeer.

57. Lakhalqus-samaawaati wal-ardi akbaru min khalqin-naasi wa laakinna aksaran-naasi laa ya'lamoon.

58. Wa maa yastawil-a'maa walbaşeeru wallazeena aama-noo wa 'amiluş-şaaliḥaati wa lal-museee'; qaleelam-maa tatazakkaroon.

59. The Hour will certainly come: Therein is no doubt: Yet most men believe not.

60. And your Lord says: "Call on Me; I will answer your (Prayer): but those who are too arrogant to serve Me will surely find themselves in Hell - in humiliation!"

61. It is Allah Who has made the Night for you, that ye may rest therein, and the days as that which helps (you) to see. Verily Allah is full of Grace and Bounty to men: yet most men give no thanks.

62. Such is Allah, your Lord, the Creator of all things, there is no Allah but He: Then how you are deluded away from the Truth!

63. Thus are deluded those who are wont to reject the Signs of Allah.

64. It is Allah Who has made for you the earth as a resting place, and the sky as a canopy, and has given you shape- and made your shapes beautiful,- and has provided for you Sustenance, of things pure and good;- such is Allah your Lord. So Glory to Allah, the Lord of the Worlds!

65. He is the Living (One): There is no god but He: Call upon Him, giving Him sincere devotion. Praise be to Allah, Lord of the Worlds!

66. Say: "I have been forbidden to invoke those whom you invoke besides Allah,- seeing that the Clear Sings have come to me from my Lord; and I have been commanded to submit (in Islam) to the Lord of the Worlds."

67. It is He Who has created you from dust then

59. Innas-Saa'ata la-aatiyatul-laa rayba feehaa wa laakinna aksaran-naasi laa yu'minoon.

60. Wa qaala Rabbukumud-'ooneee astajib lakum; innallazeena yastakbiroona an 'ibaadatee sa-yadkhuloona Jahannama daakhireen. (Sec. 6)

61. Allaahul-lazee ja'ala lakumul-layla litaskunoo feehi wannahaara mubṣiraa; innallaaha lazoo faḍlin 'alan-naasi wa laakinna aksaran-naasi laa yashkuroon.

62. Zaalikumul-laahu Rabbu-kum khaaliqu kulli shay'; laaa ilaaha illaa Huwa fa-annaa tu'fakoon.

63. Kazaalika yu'fakul-lazee-na kaanoo bi-Aayaatil-laahi yajḥadoon.

64. Allaahul-lazee ja'ala laku-mul-arḍa qaraaranw-wassa-maaa'a binaaa'anw-wa ṣawwara-kum fa-aḥsana ṣuwarakum wa razaqakum minaṭ-ṭayyibaat; zaalikumul-laahu Rabbukum fatabaarakal-laahu Rabbul-'aalameen.

65. Huwal-Ḥayyu laaa ilaaha illaa Huwa fad'oohu mukh-liṣeena lahud-deen; alḥamdu lillaahi Rabbil-'aalameen.

66. Qul innee nuheetu an a'budal-lazeena tad'oona min doonil-laahi lammaa jaaa'a-niyal-bayyinaatu mir-Rabbee wa umirtu an uslima li-Rabbil-'aalameen.

67. Huwal-lazee khalaqakum min turaabin ṣumma

from a sperm-drop, then from a leech-like clot; then does He get you out (into the light) as a child: then lets you (grow and) reach your age of full strength; then lets you become old,- though of you there are some who die before;- and lets you reach a Term appointed; in order that ye may learn wisdom.

min nuṭfatin ṣumma min 'alaqatin ṣumma yukhrijukum ṭiflan ṣumma litablughooo ashuddakum ṣumma litakoonoo shuyookhaa; wa minkum mañy-yutawaffaa min qablu wa litablughooo ajalam-musam-mañw-wa la'allakum ta'qiloon.

68. It is He Who gives Life and Death; and when He decides upon an affair, He says to it, "Be", and it is.

68. Huwal-lazee yuḥyee wa yumeetu fa-izaa qaḍaaa amran fa-innamaa yaqoolu lahoo kun fa-yakoon. **(Section 7)**

69. Do you see not those that dispute concerning the Sings of Allah? How are they turned away (from Reality)?-

69. Alam tara ilal-lazeena yujaadiloona feee Aayaatil-laahi annaa yuṣrafoon.

70. Those who reject the Book and the (revelations) with which We sent Our apostles: but soon shall they know,-

70. Allazeena kazzaboo bil-Kitaabi wa bimaaa arsalnaa bihee Rusulanaa fasawfa ya'lamoon.

71. When the yokes (shall be) round their necks, and the chains; they shall be dragged along-

71. Izil-aghlaalu feee a'naaqi-him wassalaasilu yuṣḥaboon.

72. In the boiling fetid fluid: then in the Fire shall they be burned;

72. Fil-ḥameemi ṣumma fin-Naari yusjaroon.

73. Then shall it be said to them: "Where are the (deities) to which you gave part- worship-

73. Ṣumma qeela lahum ayna maa kuntum tushrikoon.

74. "Besides Allah?" They will reply: "They have left us in the lurch: No, we invoked not, of old, anything (that had real existence)." Thus does Allah leave the Unbelievers to stray.

74. Min doonil-laahi qaaloo ḍalloo 'annaa bal-lam nakun nad'oo min qablu shay'aa; kazaalika yuḍillul-laahul-kaafireen.

75. "That was because you were wont to rejoice on the earth in things other than the Truth, and that you were wont to be insolent.

75. Zaalikum bimaa kuntum tafraḥoona fil-arḍi bighayril-ḥaqqi wa bimaa kuntum tamraḥoon.

76. "Enter you the gates of Hell, to dwell therein: and evil is (this) abode of the arrogant!"

76. Udkhulooo abwaaba Jahannama khaalideena feehaa fabi'sa maṣwal-mutakabbireen.

77. So persevere in patience; for the Promise of Allah is true: and whether

77. Faṣbir inna wa'dal-laahi ḥaqq; fa-immaa

We show thee (in this life) some part of what We promise them,- or We take your soul (to Our Mercy) (before that),-(in any case) it is to Us that they shall (all) return.

78. We did aforetime send apostles before you: of them there are some whose story We have related to you, and some whose story We have not related to you. It was not (possible) for any apostle to bring a sign except by the leave of Allah: but when the Command of Allah issued, the matter was decided in truth and justice, and there perished, there and then those who stood on Falsehoods.

79. It is Allah Who made cattle for you, that ye may use some for riding and some for food;

80. And there are (other) advantages in them for you (besides); that you may through them attain to any need (there may be) in your hearts; and on them and on ships you are carried.

81. And He shows you (always) His Signs: then which of the Signs of Allah will you deny?

82. Do they not travel through the earth and see what was the End of those before them? They were more numerous than these and superior in strength and in the traces (they have left) in the land: Yet all that they accomplished was of no profit to them.

83. For when their apostles came to them with Clear Signs, they exulted in such knowledge (and skill) as they had;but that very (wrath) at which they were wont to scoff hemmed them in.

84. But when they saw Our Punishment, they said: "We believe in Allah,- the one Allah - and we reject the partners we used to join with Him."

85. But their professing the Faith when they (actually) saw

nuriyannaka ba'dal-lazee na'i-duhum aw natawaffayannaka fa-ilaynaa yurja'oon.

78. Wa laqad arsalnaa Rusulam-min qablika minhum man qaṣaṣnaa 'alayka wa minhum mal-lam naqṣuṣ 'alayk; wa maa kaana li-Rasoolin añy-yaåtiya bi-Aayatin illaa bi-iznil-laah; fa-izaa jaaa'a amrul-laahi qudiya bilḥaqqi wa khasira hunaaalikal-mubṭiloon.   **(Section 8)**

79. Allaahul-lazee ja'ala lakumul-an'aama litarkaboo minhaa wa minhaa taåkuloon.

80. Wa lakum feehaa manaafi'u wa litablughoo 'alayhaa ḥaajatan fee ṣudoorikum wa 'alayhaa wa 'alal-fulki tuḥma-loon.

81. Wa yureekum Aayaatihee fa-ayya Aayaatil-laahi tunki-roon.

82. Afalam yaseeroo fil-ardi fa-yanẓuroo kayfa kaana 'aaqibatul-lazeena min qabli-him; kaanooo akṣara minhum wa ashadda quwwatañw-wa aaṣaaran fil-ardi famaaa aghnaa 'anhum maa kaanoo yaksiboon.

83. Falammaa jaaa'at-hum Rusuluhum bilbayyinaati fariḥoo bimaa 'indahum minal-'ilmi wa ḥaaqa bihim maa kaanoo bihee yastahzi'oon.

84. Falammaa ra-aw baåsanaa qaalooo aamannaa billaahi waḥdahoo wa kafarnaa bimaa kunnaa bihee mushrikeen.

85. Falam yaku yanfa'uhum eemaanuhum lammaa ra-aw

Our Punishment was not going to profit them. (Such has been) Allah's Way of dealing with His Servants (from the most ancient times). And even thus did the Rejecters of Allah perish (utterly)!

41. Ha Mim Sajda
In the name of Allah, Most Gracious, Most Merciful.

1. *Ha-Mim.*

2. A Revelation from (Allah), Most Gracious, Most Merciful;-

3. A Book, whereof the verses are explained in detail;- a Qur'an in Arabic, for people who understand;-

4. Giving good news and admonition: yet most of them turn away, and so they hear not.

5. They say: "Our hearts are under veils, (concealed) from that to which you does invite us, and in our ears is a deafness, and between us and you is a screen: so do you (what you will); for us, we shall do (what we will!)"

6. Say thou: "I am but a man like you: It is revealed to me by Inspiration, that your Allah is one Allah: so stand true to Him, and ask for His Forgiveness." And woe to those who join gods with Allah,-

7. Those who practise not regular Charity, and who even deny the Hereafter.

8. For those who believe and work deeds of righteousness is a reward that will never fail.

9. Say: Is it that you deny Him Who created the earth in two Days? And do you join equals with Him? He is the Lord of (all) the Worlds.

baåsanaa sunnatal-laahil-latee qad khalat fee 'ibaadihee wa khasira hunaalikal-kaafiroon.

(Section 9)

Sûrat Ḥâ Mîm as-Sajdah–41
(Revealed at Makkah)

Bismillaahir Raḥmaanir Raḥeem

1. Ḥaa-Meeem.

2. Tanzeelum Minar-Raḥ-maanir-Raḥeem.

3. Kitaabun fuṣṣilat Aayaa-tuhoo Qur-aanan 'Arabiyyal-liqawmiñy-ya'lamoon.

4. Basheerañw-wa naẓeeran fa-a'raḍa akṣaruhum fahum laa yasma'oon.

5. Wa qaaloo quloobunaa feee akinnatim-mimmaa tad'oonaaa ilayhi wa feee aazaaninaa waqruñw-wa mim bayninaa wa baynika ḥijaabun fa'mal innaaa 'aamiloon.

6. Qul innamaaa ana basha-rum-miṣlukum yooḥaaa ilayya annamaaa ilaahukum Ilaahuñw-Waaḥidun fastaqeemooo ilayhi wastaghfirooh; wa waylul-lil-mushrikeen.

7. Allazeena laa yu'toonaz-Zakaata wa hum bil-Aakhirati hum kaafiroon.

8. Innal-lazeena aamanoo wa 'amiluṣ-ṣaaliḥaati lahum ajrun ghayru mamnoon. **(Section 1)**

9. Qul a'innakum latak-furoona billazee khalaqal-arḍa fee yawmayni wa taj'aloona lahooo andaadaa; zaalika Rabbul-'aalameen.

10. He set on the (earth), mountains standing firm, high above it, and bestowed blessings on the earth, and measure therein its sustenance in four Days, alike for (all) who ask.

11. Moreover He comprehended in His design the sky, and it had been (as) smoke: He said to it and to the earth: "Come you together, willingly or unwillingly." They said: "We do come (together), in willing obedience."

12. So He completed them as seven firmaments in two Days, and He assigned to each heaven its duty and command. And We adorned the lower heaven with lights, and (provided it) with guard. Such is the Decree of (Him) the Exalted in Might, Full of Knowledge.

13. But if they turn away, say you: "I have warned you of a stunning Punishment (as of thunder and lightning) like that which (overtook) the 'Ad and the Thamud!"

14. Behold, the apostles came to them, from before them and behind them, (preaching): "Serve none but Allah." They said, "If our Lord had so pleased, He would certainly have sent down angels (to preach). Now we reject your mission (altogether)."

15. Now the 'Ad behaved arrogantly through the land, against (all) truth and reason, and said: "Who is superior to us in strength?" What! did they not see that Allah, Who created them, was superior to them in strength? But they continued to reject Our Signs!

16. So We sent against them a **furious Wind through days of disaster,** that We might give them a taste of a Chastisement of humiliation in this life;

10. Wa ja'ala feehaa rawaa-siya min fawqihaa wa baaraka feehaa wa qaddara feehaaa aqwaatahaa feee arba'ati ayyaa-min sawaaa'al-lissaaa'ileen.

11. Summas-tawaaa ilas-samaaa'i wa hiya dukhaanun faqaala lahaa wa lil-arḍi'-tiyaa ṭaw'an aw karhan qaalataaa ataynaa ṭaaa'i'een.

12. Faqaḍaahunna sab'a samaawaatin fee yawmayni wa awḥaa fee kulli samaaa'in amrahaa; wa zayyannassa-maaa'ad-dunyaa bimaṣaabeeḥa wa ḥifẓaa; zaalika taqdeerul-'Azeezil-'Aleem.

13. Fa-in a'raḍoo faqul anzar-tukum ṣaa'iqatam-misla ṣaa'iqati 'Aadiñw-wa Samood.

14. Iz jaaa'at-humur-Rusulu mim bayni aydeehim wa min khalfihim allaa ta'budooo illal-laaha qaaloo law shaaa'a Rab-bunaa la-anzala malaaa'ikatan fa-innaa bimaaa ursiltum bihee kaafiroon.

15. Fa-ammaa 'Aadun fastak-baroo fil-arḍi bighayril-ḥaqqi wa qaaloo man ashaddu minnaa quwwatan awalam yaraw annal-laahal-lazee khalaqahum Huwa ashaddu minhum quw-watañw-wa kaanoo bi-Aayaati-naa yajḥadoon.

16. Fa-arsalnaa 'alayhim reeḥan ṣarṣaran feee ayyaamin naḥisaatil-linuzeeqahum 'azaa-bal-khizyi fil-ḥayaatid-dunyaa wa

وَجَعَلَ فِيهَا رَوَاسِيَ مِن فَوْقِهَا وَبَارَكَ فِيهَا وَقَدَّرَ فِيهَآ أَقْوَاتَهَا فِىٓ أَرْبَعَةِ أَيَّامٍ سَوَآءً لِّلسَّآئِلِينَ ۞

ثُمَّ اسْتَوَىٰٓ إِلَى السَّمَآءِ وَهِىَ دُخَانٌ فَقَالَ لَهَا وَلِلْأَرْضِ ائْتِيَا طَوْعًا أَوْ كَرْهًا قَالَتَآ أَتَيْنَا طَآئِعِينَ ۞

فَقَضَاهُنَّ سَبْعَ سَمَاوَاتٍ فِى يَوْمَيْنِ وَأَوْحَىٰ فِى كُلِّ سَمَآءٍ أَمْرَهَا وَزَيَّنَّا السَّمَآءَ الدُّنْيَا بِمَصَابِيحَ وَحِفْظًا ذَٰلِكَ تَقْدِيرُ الْعَزِيزِ الْعَلِيمِ ۞

فَإِنْ أَعْرَضُوا فَقُلْ أَنذَرْتُكُمْ صَٰعِقَةً مِّثْلَ صَٰعِقَةِ عَادٍ وَّثَمُودَ ۞

إِذْ جَآءَتْهُمُ الرُّسُلُ مِن بَيْنِ أَيْدِيهِمْ وَمِنْ خَلْفِهِمْ أَلَّا تَعْبُدُوٓا إِلَّا اللَّهَ قَالُوا لَوْ شَآءَ رَبُّنَا لَأَنزَلَ مَلَٰٓئِكَةً فَإِنَّا بِمَآ أُرْسِلْتُم بِهِ كَٰفِرُونَ ۞

فَأَمَّا عَادٌ فَاسْتَكْبَرُوا فِى الْأَرْضِ بِغَيْرِ الْحَقِّ وَقَالُوا مَنْ أَشَدُّ مِنَّا قُوَّةً أَوَلَمْ يَرَوْا أَنَّ اللَّهَ الَّذِى خَلَقَهُمْ هُوَ أَشَدُّ مِنْهُمْ قُوَّةً وَكَانُوا بِـَٔايَٰتِنَا يَجْحَدُونَ ۞

فَأَرْسَلْنَا عَلَيْهِمْ رِيحًا صَرْصَرًا فِىٓ أَيَّامٍ نَّحِسَاتٍ لِّنُذِيقَهُمْ عَذَابَ الْخِزْىِ فِى الْحَيَوٰةِ الدُّنْيَا وَ

but the Chastisement of a Hereafter will be more humiliating still: and they will find no help.

17. As to the Thamud, We gave them Guidance, but they preferred blindness (of heart) to Guidance: so the stunning Punishment of humiliation seized them, because of what they had earned.

18. But We delivered those who believed and practised righteousness.

19. On the Day that the enemies of Allah will be gathered together to the Fire, they will be marched in ranks.

20. At length, when they reach the (Fire), their hearing, their sight, and their skins will bear witness against them, as to (all) their deeds.

21. They will say to their skins: "Why bear you witness against us?" They will say: "Allah has given us speech,- (He) Who giveth speech to everything: He created you for the first time, and unto Him were you to return.

22. "You did not seek to hide yourselves, lest your hearing, your sight, and your skins should bear witness against you! But you did think that Allah knew not many of the things that you used to do!

23. "But this thought of yours which you did entertain concerning your Lord, has brought you to destruction, and (now) have you become of those utterly lost!"

24. If, then, they have patience, the Fire will be a home for them! and if they beg to be received into favour, into favour will they not (then) be received.

la'ẓaabul-Aakhirati akhzaa wa hum laa yunṣaroon.

17. Wa ammaa Samoodu fahadaynaahum fastaḥabbul-'amaa 'alal-hudaa fa-akhaẓat-hum ṣaa'iqatul-'aẓaabil-hooni bimaa kaanoo yaksiboon.

18. Wa najjaynal-lazeena aamanoo wa kaanoo yattaqoon.

(Section 2)

19. Wa Yawma yuḥsharu a'daaa'ul-laahi ilan-Naari fa-hum yooza'oon.

20. Ḥattaaa izaa maa jaaa'oo-haa shahida 'alayhim sam'u-hum wa abṣaaruhum wa juloo-duhum bimaa kaanoo ya'ma-loon.

21. Wa qaaloo lijuloodihim lima shahittum 'alaynaa qaalooo anṭaqanal-laahul-lazee anṭaqa kulla shay'iñw-wa Huwa khalaqakum awwala marratiñw-wa ilayhi turja'oon.

22. Wa maa kuntum tastati-roona añy-yashhada 'alaykum sam'ukum wa laaa abṣaarukum wa laa juloodukum wa laakin ẓanantum annal-laaha laa ya'lamu kaseeram-mimmaa ta'maloon.

23. Wa zaalikum ẓannuku-mul-lazee ẓanantum bi-Rabbi-kum ardaakum fa-aṣbaḥtum minal-khaasireen.

24. Fa-iñy-yaṣbiroo fan-Naaru maswal-lahum wa iñy-yasta'-taboo famaa hum minal-mu'ta-been.

25. And We have destined for them intimate companions (of like nature), who made alluring to them what was before them and behind them; and the sentence among the previous generations of Jinns and men, who have passed away, is proved against them; for they are utterly lost.

26. The Unbelievers say: "Listen not to this Qur'an, but talk at random in the midst of its (reading), that you may gain the upper hand!"

27. But We will certainly give the Unbelievers a taste of a severe Chastisement, and We will requite them for the worst of their deeds.

28. Such is the requital of the enemies of Allah,- the Fire: therein will be for them the Eternal Home: a (fit) requital, for that they were wont to reject Our Signs.

29. And the Unbelievers will say: "Our Lord! Show us those, among Jinns and men, who misled us: We shall crush them beneath our feet, so that they become the vilest (before all)."

30. In the case of those who say, "Our Lord is Allah", and, further, stand straight and steadfast, the angels descend on them (from time to time): "Fear you not!" (they suggest), "Nor grieve! but receive the Glad Tidings of the Garden (of Bliss), the which you were promised!

31. "We are your protectors in this life and in the Hereafter: therein shall you have all that your souls shall desire; therein shall you have all that you ask for!-

---

25. Wa qayyaḍnaa lahum quranaaa'a fazayyanoo lahum maa bayna aydeehim wa maa khalfahum wa ḥaqqa 'alay-himul-qawlu feee umamin qad khalat min qablihim minal-jinni wal-insi innahum kaanoo khaasireen.   (Section 3)

26. Wa qaalal-lazeena kafaroo laa tasma'oo lihaazal-Qur-aani walghaw feehi la'allakum taghliboon.

27. Falanuzeeqannal-lazeena kafaroo 'azaaban shadeedañw-wa lanajziyannahum aswa-allazee kaanoo ya'maloon.

28. Zaalika jazaaa'u a'daaa'il-laahin-Naaru lahum feehaa daarul-khuld, jazaaa'am bimaa kaanoo bi-Aayaatinaa yajḥa-doon.

29. Wa qaalal-lazeena kafaroo Rabbanaaa arinal-lazayni aḍal-laanaa minal-jinni wal-insi naj'alhumaa taḥta aqdaaminaa liyakoonaa minal-asfaleen.

30. Innal-lazeena qaaloo Rab-bunal-laahu ṣummas-taqaamoo tatanazzalu 'alayhimul-malaaa-'ikatu allaa takhaafoo wa laa taḥzanoo wa abshiroo bil-Jannatil-latee kuntum too'a-doon.

31. Naḥnu awliyaaa'ukum fil-ḥayaatid-dunyaa wa fil-Aakhi-rati wa lakum feehaa maa tashtahee anfusukum wa lakum feehaa maa tadda'oon.

32. "A hospitable gift from One Oft-Forgiving, Most Merciful!"

33. Who is better in speech than one who calls (men) to Allah, works righteousness, and says, "I am of those who bow in Islam"?

34. Nor can goodness and Evil be equal. Repel (Evil) with what is better: Then will he between whom and thee was hatred become as it were your friend and intimate!

35. And no one will be granted such goodness except those who exercise patience and self-restraint,- none but persons of the greatest good fortune.

36. And if (at any time) an incitement to discord is made to you by the Evil One, seek refuge in Allah. He is the One Who hears and knows all things.

37. Among His Signs are the Night and the Day, and the Sun and the Moon. Adore not the sun and the moon, but adore Allah, Who created them, if it is Him you wish to serve.

38. But is the (Unbelievers) are arrogant, (no matter): for in the presence of your Lord are those who celebrate His praises by night and by day. And they never flag (nor feel themselves above it).

39. And among His Signs in this: that you see the earth barren and desolate; but when We send down rain to it, it is stirred to life and yields increase. Truly, He Who gives life to the (dead) earth can surely give life to (men) who are dead. For He has power over all things.

40. Those who pervert the Truth in Our Signs are

---

32. Nuzulam-min Ghafoorir-Raḥeem.   **(Section 4)**

33. Wa man aḥsanu qawlam-mimman da‘aaa ilal-laahi wa ‘amila ṣaaliḥañw-wa qaala innanee minal-muslimeen.

34. Wa laa tastawil-ḥasanatu wa las-sayyi’ah; idfa‘ billatee hiya aḥsanu fa-izal-lazee bay-naka wa baynahoo ‘adaawatun ka-annahoo waliyyun ḥameem.

35. Wa maa yulaqqaahaaa illal-lazeena ṣabaroo wa maa yulaqqaahaaa illaa zoo ḥazzin ‘azeem.

36. Wa immaa yanzaghannaka minash-Shayṭaani nazghun fasta‘iz billaahi innahoo Huwas-Samee‘ul-‘Aleem.

37. Wa min Aayaatihil-laylu wannahaaru washshamsu walqamar; laa tasjudoo lish-shamsi wa laa lilqamari wasjudoo lillaahil-lazee khala-qahunna in kuntum iyyaahu ta‘budoon.

38. Fa-inis-takbaroo fallazee-na ‘inda Rabbika yusabbiḥoona lahoo billayli wannahaari wa hum laa yas’amoon. ☝

39. Wa min Aayaatihee annaka taral-arḍa khaashi‘atan fa-izaaa anzalnaa ‘alayhal-maaa’ah-tazzat wa rabat; innal-lazeee aḥyaahaa lamuḥyil-mawtaa; innahoo ‘alaa kulli shay’in Qadeer.

40. Innal-lazeena yulḥidoona feee Aayaatinaa

نُزُلًا مِّنْ غَفُوْرٍ رَّحِيْمٍ ۞

وَمَنْ اَحْسَنُ قَوْلًا مِّمَّنْ دَعَآ اِلَى اللّٰهِ وَعَمِلَ صَالِحًا وَّقَالَ اِنَّنِيْ مِنَ الْمُسْلِمِيْنَ ۞

وَلَا تَسْتَوِى الْحَسَنَةُ وَلَا السَّيِّئَةُ اِدْفَعْ بِالَّتِيْ هِيَ اَحْسَنُ فَاِذَا الَّذِيْ بَيْنَكَ وَبَيْنَهٗ عَدَاوَةٌ كَاَنَّهٗ وَلِيٌّ حَمِيْمٌ ۞

وَمَا يُلَقّٰىهَآ اِلَّا الَّذِيْنَ صَبَرُوْا ۚ وَمَا يُلَقّٰىهَآ اِلَّا ذُوْ حَظٍّ عَظِيْمٍ ۞

وَاِمَّا يَنْزَغَنَّكَ مِنَ الشَّيْطٰنِ نَزْغٌ فَاسْتَعِذْ بِاللّٰهِ ۚ اِنَّهٗ هُوَ السَّمِيْعُ الْعَلِيْمُ ۞

وَمِنْ اٰيٰتِهِ الَّيْلُ وَالنَّهَارُ وَالشَّمْسُ وَالْقَمَرُ ۚ لَا تَسْجُدُوْا لِلشَّمْسِ وَلَا لِلْقَمَرِ وَاسْجُدُوْا لِلّٰهِ الَّذِيْ خَلَقَهُنَّ اِنْ كُنْتُمْ اِيَّاهُ تَعْبُدُوْنَ ۩

فَاِنِ اسْتَكْبَرُوْا فَالَّذِيْنَ عِنْدَ رَبِّكَ يُسَبِّحُوْنَ لَهٗ بِالَّيْلِ وَالنَّهَارِ وَهُمْ لَا يَسْـَٔمُوْنَ ۞ ۩ السَّجْدَة

وَمِنْ اٰيٰتِهٖٓ اَنَّكَ تَرَى الْاَرْضَ خَاشِعَةً فَاِذَآ اَنْزَلْنَا عَلَيْهَا الْمَآءَ اهْتَزَّتْ وَرَبَتْ ۚ اِنَّ الَّذِيْٓ اَحْيَاهَا لَمُحْيِ الْمَوْتٰى ۚ اِنَّهٗ عَلٰى كُلِّ شَيْءٍ قَدِيْرٌ ۞

اِنَّ الَّذِيْنَ يُلْحِدُوْنَ فِيْٓ اٰيٰتِنَا

not hidden from Us. Which is better?- he that is cast into the Fire, or he that comes safe through, on the Day of Judgment? Do what you will: verily He sees (clearly) all that you do.

41. Those who reject the Message when it comes to them (are not hidden from Us). And indeed it is a Book of exalted power.

42. No falsehood can approach it from before or behind it: It is sent down by One Full of Wisdom, Worthy of all Praise.

43. Nothing is said to you that was not said to the apostles before you: that your Lord has at His Command (all) forgiveness as well as a most Grievous Chastisement.

44. Had We sent this as a Qur'an (in the language) other than Arabic, they would have said: "Why are not its verses explained in detail? What! (a Book) not in Arabic and (a Messenger an Arab?" Say: "It is a Guide and a Healing to those who believe ; and for those who believe not, there is a deafness in their ears, and it is blindness in their (eyes): They are (as it were) being called from a place far distant!"

45. We certainly gave Moses the Book aforetime: but disputes arose therein. Had it not been for a Word that went forth before from thy Lord, (their differences) would have been settled between them: but they remained in suspicious disquieting doubt thereon.

46. Whoever works righteousness benefits his own soul; whoever works evil, it is against his own soul: nor is your Lord ever unjust (in the least) to His Servants.

47. To Him is referred the Knowledge of the Hour (of Judgment: He knows all): No

laa yakhfawna 'alaynaa; afamañy-yulqaa fin-Naari khayrun am mañy-yaâtee aaminañy-Yawmal-Qiyaamah; i'maloo maa shi'tum innahoo bimaa ta'aloona Baṣeer.

41. Inna Lazeena kafaroo biz-Zikri lammaa jaa'ahum wa innahoo la-Kitaabun 'Azeez.

42. Laa yaâteehil-baaṭilu mim bayni yadayhi wa laa min khalfihee tanzeelum-min Ḥakeemin Ḥameed.

43. Maa yuqaalu laka illaa maa qad qeela lir-Rusuli min qablik; inna Rabbaka lazoo maghfira-tiñw-wa zoo 'iqaabin aleem.

44. Wa law ja'alnaahu Qur-aa-nan A'jamiyyal-laqaaloo law laa fuṣṣilat Aayaatuhoo 'a A'jamiyyuñw-wa 'Arabiyy; qul huwa lillazeena aamanoo hudañw-wa shifaaa'uñw wallazeena laa yu'minoona feee aazaanihim waqruñw-wa huwa 'alayhim 'amaa; ulaaa'ika yunaadawna mim-makaanim ba'eed.

(Section 5)

45. Wa laqad aataynaa Moosal-Kitaaba fakhtulifa feeh; wa law laa Kalimatun sabaqat mir-Rabbika laquḍiya baynahum; wa innahum lafee shakkim-minhu mureeb.

46. Man 'amila ṣaliḥan falinafsihee wa man asaaa'a fa'alayhaa; wamaa rabbuka biẓallaamil-lil-'abeed.

47. Ilayhi yuraddu 'ilmus-Saaa'ah; wa maa

date-fruit comes out of its sheath, nor does a female conceive (within her womb) nor bring forth the (young), but by His knowledge. The Day that (Allah) will propound to them the (question), "Where are the partners (you attributed to Me?" They will say, "We do assure you not one of us can bear witness!"

48. The (deities) they used to invoke aforetime will leave them in the lurch, and they will perceive that they have no way of escape.

49. Man does not weary of asking for good (things), but if ill touches him, he gives up all hope (and) is lost in despair.

50. When We give him a taste of some Mercy from Ourselves, after some adversity has touched him, he is sure to say, "This is due to my (merit): I think not that the Hour (of Judgment) will (ever) be established; but if I am brought back to my Lord, I have (much) good (stored) in His sight!" But We will show the Unbelievers the truth of all that they did, and We shall give them the taste of a severe Chastisement.

51. When We bestow favours on man, he turns away, and gets himself remote on his side (instead of coming to Us); and when evil seizes him, (he comes) full of prolonged prayer!

52. Say: "See you if the (Revelation) is (really) from Allah, and yet do you reject it? Who is more astray than one who is in a schism far (from any purpose)?"

53. Soon will We show them Our Signs in the (furthest) regions (of the earth), and in their own souls, until it becomes manifest to them that this is the Truth. Is it not enough that your Lord

takhruju min s̲amaraatim-min akmaamihaa wa maa taḥmilu min uns̲aa wa laa taḍa'u illaa bi'ilmih; wa Yawma yunaa-deehim ayna shurakaaaa'ee qaalooo aaẓannaaka maa minnaa min shaheed.

48. Wa ḍalla 'anhum maa kaanoo yad'oona min qablu wa ẓannoo maa lahum mim-maḥeeṣ.

49. Laa yas'amul-insaanu min du'aaa'il-khayri wa im-massa-hush-sharru fa-ya'oosun qanooṭ.

50. Wa la-in aẓaqnaahu raḥma-tam-minnaa mim ba'di ḍar-raaaa'a massat-hu la-yaqoolanna haaẓaa lee wa maaa aẓunnus-Saa'ata qaaa'imataṅw-wa la'in-ruji'tu ilaa Rabbeee inna lee 'indahoo lalḥusnaa; falanu-nabbi'annal-laẓeena kafaroo bimaa 'amiloo wa lanuzeeqan-nahum min 'aẓaabin ghaleeẓ.

51. Wa izaaa an'amnaa 'alal-insaani a'raḍa wa na-aa bijaani-bihee wa izaa massahush-sharru faẓoo du'aaa'in 'areeḍ.

52. Qul ara'aytum in kaana min 'indil-laahi s̲umma kafar-tum bihee man aḍalla mimman huwa fee shiqaaqim ba'eed.

53. Sanureehim Aayaatinaa fil-aafaaqi wa feee anfusihim ḥattaa yatabayyana lahum annahul-ḥaqq; awa lam yakfi bi-Rabbika annahoo

تَخْرُجُ مِن ثَمَرَٰتٍ مِّن أَكْمَامِهَا وَمَا تَحْمِلُ مِنْ أُنثَىٰ وَلَا تَضَعُ إِلَّا بِعِلْمِهِ ۚ وَيَوْمَ يُنَادِيهِمْ أَيْنَ شُرَكَآءِى قَالُوٓا۟ ءَاذَنَّٰكَ مَا مِنَّا مِن شَهِيدٍ ۝

وَضَلَّ عَنْهُم مَّا كَانُوا۟ يَدْعُونَ مِن قَبْلُ ۖ وَظَنُّوا۟ مَا لَهُم مِّن مَّحِيصٍ ۝

لَا يَسْـَٔمُ ٱلْإِنسَٰنُ مِن دُعَآءِ ٱلْخَيْرِ وَإِن مَّسَّهُ ٱلشَّرُّ فَيَـُٔوسٌ قَنُوطٌ ۝

وَلَئِنْ أَذَقْنَٰهُ رَحْمَةً مِّنَّا مِنۢ بَعْدِ ضَرَّآءَ مَسَّتْهُ لَيَقُولَنَّ هَٰذَا لِى وَمَآ أَظُنُّ ٱلسَّاعَةَ قَآئِمَةً وَلَئِن رُّجِعْتُ إِلَىٰ رَبِّىٓ إِنَّ لِى عِندَهُۥ لَلْحُسْنَىٰ ۚ فَلَنُنَبِّئَنَّ ٱلَّذِينَ كَفَرُوا۟ بِمَا عَمِلُوا۟ وَلَنُذِيقَنَّهُم مِّنْ عَذَابٍ غَلِيظٍ ۝

وَإِذَآ أَنْعَمْنَا عَلَى ٱلْإِنسَٰنِ أَعْرَضَ وَنَـَٔا بِجَانِبِهِۦ وَإِذَا مَسَّهُ ٱلشَّرُّ فَذُو دُعَآءٍ عَرِيضٍ ۝

قُلْ أَرَءَيْتُمْ إِن كَانَ مِنْ عِندِ ٱللَّهِ ثُمَّ كَفَرْتُم بِهِۦ مَنْ أَضَلُّ مِمَّنْ هُوَ فِى شِقَاقٍۭ بَعِيدٍ ۝

سَنُرِيهِمْ ءَايَٰتِنَا فِى ٱلْءَافَاقِ وَفِىٓ أَنفُسِهِمْ حَتَّىٰ يَتَبَيَّنَ لَهُمْ أَنَّهُ ٱلْحَقُّ ۗ أَوَلَمْ يَكْفِ بِرَبِّكَ أَنَّهُۥ

does witness all things?

54. Ah indeed! Are they in doubt concerning the Meeting with their Lord? Ah indeed! It is He that doth encompass all things!

42. Consultation
In the name of Allah, Most Gracious, Most Merciful.

1. *Ha-Mim.*

2. *Ain-Sin-Qaf.*

3. Thus does (He) send inspiration to you as (He did) to those before you,- Allah, Exalted in Power, Full of Wisdom.

4. To Him belongs all that is in the heavens and on earth: and He is Most High, Most Great.

5. The heavens are a lost rent asunder from above them (by Him Glory): and the angels celebrate the Praises of their Lord, and pray for forgiveness for (all) beings on earth: Behold! Verily Allah is He, the Oft-Forgiving, Most Merciful.

6. And those who take as protectors others besides Him,- Allah does watch over them; and you are not the disposer of their affairs.

7. Thus have We sent by inspiration to you an Arabic Qur'an: that you may warn the Mother of Cities and all around her,- and warn (them) of the Day of Assembly, of which there is no doubt: (when) some will be in the Garden, and some in the Blazing Fire.

8. If Allah had so willed, He could have made them a single people; but He admits whom He will

'alaa kulli shay'in Shaheed.

54. Alaaa innahum fee miryatim-mil-liqaaa'i Rabbihim; alaaa innahoo bikulli shay'im-muheet.   **(Section 6)**

Sûrat ash-Shûrâ–42
(Revealed at Makkah)

Bismillaahir Rahmaanir Raheem

1. Haa-Meeem.

2. 'Ayyyn-Seeen-Qaaaf.

3. Kazaalika yooheee ilayka wa ilal-lazeena min qablikallaahul-'Azeezul-Hakeem.

4. Lahoo maa fis-samaawaati wa maa fil-ardi wa Huwal-'Aliyyul-'Azeem.

5. Takaadus-samaawaatu yatafattarna min fawqihinn; walmalaaa'ikatu yusabbihoona bihamdi Rabbihim wa yastaghfiroona liman fil-ard; alaaa innal-laaha Huwal-Ghafoorur-Raheem.

6. Wallazeenat-takhazoo min dooniheee awliyaaa'al-laahu hafeezun 'alayhim wa maaa anta 'alayhim biwakeel.

7. Wa kazaalika awhaynaaa Ilayka Qur-aanan 'Arabiyyal-litunzira Ummal-Quraa wa man hawlahaa wa tunzira Yawmal-Jam'i laa rayba feeh; fareequn fil-Jannati wa fareequn fissa'eer.

8. Wa law shaaa'al-laahu laja'alahum ummatañw-waahidatañw-walaakiñy-yudkhilu mañy-yashaaa'u

to His Mercy; and the Wrong-doers will have no protector nor helper.

9. What! Have they taken (for worship) protectors besides Him? But it is Allah,- He is the Protector, and it is He Who gives life to the dead: It is He Who has power over all things,

10. Whatever it be wherein you differ, the decision thereof is with Allah: such is Allah my Lord: In Him I trust, and to Him I turn.

11. (He is) the Creator of the heavens and the earth: He has made for you pairs from among yourselves, and pairs among cattle: by this means does He multiply you: there is nothing whatever like unto Him, and He is the One that hears and sees (all things).

12. To Him belong the keys of the heavens and the earth: He enlarges and restricts. The Sustenance to whom He will: for He knows full well all things.

13. The same religion has He established for you as that which He enjoined on Noah - the which We have sent by inspiration to you - and that which We enjoined on Abraham, Moses, and Jesus: Namely, that you should remain steadfast in religion, and make no divisions therein: to those who worship other things than Allah, hard is the (way) to which you callest them. Allah chooses to Himself those whom He pleases, and guides to Himself those who turn (to Him).

14. And they became divided only after Knowledge reached them,- through selfish envy as between themselves. Had it not been for

fee raḥmatih; waz-ẓaalimoona maa lahum miñw-waliyyiñw-wa laa naṣeer.

9. Amit-takhazoo min dooniheee awliyaaa'a fallaahu Huwal-Waliyyu wa Huwa yuḥyil-mawtaa wa Huwa 'alaa kulli shay'in Qadeer. **(Section 1)**

10. Wa makh-talaftum feehi min shay'in faḥukmuhooo ilal-laah; zaalikumul-laahu Rabbee 'alayhi tawakkaltu wa ilayhi uneeb.

11. Faaṭirus-samaawaati wal-arḍ; ja'ala lakum min anfusi-kum azwaajañw-wa minal-an-'aami azwaajañy yazra'ukum feeh; laysa kamislihee shay'uñw wa Huwas-Samee'ul-Baṣeer.

12. Lahoo maqaaleedus-sa-maawaati wal-arḍi yabsuṭur-rizqa limañy-yashaaa'u wa yaqdir; innahoo bikulli shay'in 'Aleem.

13. Shara'a lakum minad-deeni maa waṣṣaa bihee Nooḥañw-wallazeee awḥaynaaa ilayka wa maa waṣṣaynaa biheee Ibraaheema wa Moosaa wa 'Eesaaa an aqeemud-adeena wa laa tatafarraqoo feeh; kabura 'alal-mushrikeena maa tad'oohum ilayh; Allaahu yajtabeee ilayhi mañy-yashaaa'u wa yahdeee ilayhi mañy-yuneeb.

14. Wa maa tafarraqooo illaa mim ba'di maa jaaa'ahumul-'ilmu baghyam baynahum; wa law laa

a Word that went forth before from your Lord, (tending) to a Term appo-inted, the matter would have been settled between them: But truly those who have inherited the Book after them are in suspicious (disquieting) doubt concerning it.

15. Now then, for that (reason), call (them to the Faith), and stand steadfast as you are commanded, nor follow you their vain desires; but say: "I believe in the Book which Allah has sent down; and I am commanded to judge justly between you. Allah is our Lord and your Lord: for us (is the responsibility for) our deeds, and for you for your deeds. There is no contention between us and you. Allah will bring us together, and to Him is (our) Final Goal.

16. But those who dispute concerning Allah after He has been accepted,- futile is their dispute in the Sight of their Lord: on them will be a Chastisement terrible.

17. It is Allah Who has sent down the Book in Truth, and the Balance (by which to weigh conduct). And what will make you realise that perhaps the Hour is close at hand?

18. Only those wish to hasten it who believe not in it: those who believe hold it in awe, and know that it is the Truth. Behold, verily those that dispute concerning the Hour are far astray.

19. Gracious is Allah to His servants: He gives sustenance to whom He pleases: and He is Strong, the Mighty.

20. To any that desires the tilth of the Hereafter,

Kalimatun sabaqat mir-Rabbika ilaaa ajalim musammal-laquḍiya baynahum; wa innal-lazeena ooriṣul-Kitaaba mim ba'dihim lafee shakkim minhu mureeb.

15. Falizaalika fad'u wasta-qim kamaaa umirta wa laa tattabi' ahwaaa'ahum wa qul aamantu bimaaa anzalal-laahu min Kitaab, wa umirtu li-a'dila baynakum Allaahu Rabbunaa wa Rabbukum lanaaa a'maa-lunaa wa lakum a'maalukum laa ḥujjata baynanaa wa bayna-kumul-laahu yajma'u baynanaa wa ilayhil-maṣeer.

16. Wallazeena yuḥaaajjoona fil-laahi mim ba'di mastujeeba lahoo ḥujjatuhum daaḥiḍatun 'inda Rabbihim wa 'alayhim ghaḍabuñw-wa lahum 'azaabun shadeed.

17. Allaahul-lazee anzalal-Kitaaba bilḥaqqi wal-Meezaan; wa maa yudreeka la'allas-Saa'ata qareeb.

18. Yasta'jilu bihal-lazeena laa yu'minoona bihaa walla-zeena aamanoo mushfiqoona minhaa wa ya'lamoona anna-hal-ḥaqq; alaaa innal-lazeena yumaaroona fis-Saa'ati lafee ḍalaalim ba'eed.

19. Allaahu laṭeefum bi'ibaa-dihee yarzuqu mañy-yashaaa'u wa Huwal-Qawiyyul-'Azeez.
(Section 2)

20. Man kaana yureedu ḥarṣal-Aakhirati

We give increase in his tilth, and to any that desires the tilth of this world, We grant somewhat thereof, but he has no share or lot in the Hereafter.

21. What! have they partners (in godhead), who have established for them some religion without the permission of Allah? Had it not been for the Decree of Judgment, the matter would have been decided between them (at once). But verily the Wrong-doers will have a grievous Chastisement.

22. Thou wilt see the Wrong-doers in fear on account of what they have earned, and (the burden of) that must (necessarily) fall on them. But those who believe and work righteous deeds will be in the luxuriant meads of the Gardens: they shall have, before their Lord, all that they wish for. That will indeed be the magnificent Bounty (of Allah).

23. That is (the Bounty) whereof Allah gives Glad Tidings to His Servants who believe and do righteous deeds. Say: "No reward do I ask of you for this except the love of those near of kin." And if any one earns any good, We shall give him an increase of good in respect thereof: for Allah is Oft-Forgiving, Most Ready to appreciate (service).

24. What! Do they say, "He has forged a falsehood against God"? But if Allah willed, He could seal up thy heart. And Allah blots out Vanity, and proves the Truth by His Words. For He knows well the secrets of all hearts.

25. He is the One that accepts repentance from His Servants and forgives sins: and He knows all that you do.

nazid lahoo fee ḥarsihee wa man kaana yureedu ḥarsad-dunyaa nu'tihee minhaa wa maa lahoo fil-Aakhirati min naṣeeb.

21. Am lahum shurakaaa'u shara'oo lahum minad-deeni maa lam yaåzam bihil-laah; wa law laa Kalimatul-faṣli laqu-ḍiya baynahum; wa innaz-zaalimeena lahum 'azaabun aleem.

22. Taraz-zaalimeena mushfi-qeena mimmaa kasaboo wa huwa waaqi'um bihim; walla-zeena aamanoo wa 'amiluṣ-ṣaaliḥaati fee rawḍaatil-Jannaa-ti lahum maa yashaaa'oona 'inda Rabbihim; zaalika huwal-faḍlul-kabeer.

23. Zaalikal-lazee yubash-shirul-laahu 'ibaadahul-lazeena aamanoo wa 'amiluṣ-ṣaaliḥaat; qul laaa as'alukum 'alayhi ajran illal-mawaddata fil-qurbaa; wa mañy-yaqtarif ḥasanatan nazid lahoo feehaa ḥusnaa; innal-laaha Ghafoorun Shakoor.

24. Am yaqooloonaf-tara 'alal-laahi kaziban fa-iñy-yasha-il-laahu yakhtim 'alaa qalbik; wa yamḥul-laahul-baaṭila wa yuḥiqqul-ḥaqqa bi Kalimaatih; innahoo 'Aleemum bizaatiṣ-ṣudoor.

25. Wa Huwal-lazee yaqbalut-tawbata 'an 'ibaadihee wa ya'foo 'anis-sayyi-aati wa ya'lamu maa taf'aloon.

26. And He listens to those who believe and do deeds of righteousness, and gives them increase of His Bounty: but for the Unbelievers their is a terrible Chastisement.

27. If Allah were to enlarge the provision for His Servants, they would indeed transgress beyond all bounds through the earth; but he sends (it) down in due measure as He pleases. For He is with His Servants Well-acquainted, Watchful.

28. He is the One that sends down rain (even) after (men) have given up all hope, and scatters His Mercy (far and wide). And He is the Protector, Worthy of all Praise.

29. And among His Signs is the creation of the heavens and the earth, and the living creatures that He has scattered through them: and He has power to gather them together when He wills.

30. Whatever misfortune happens to you, is because of the things your hands have wrought, and for many (a sin) He grants forgiveness.

31. Nor can you escape (aught), (fleeing) through the earth; nor have you, besides Allah, any one to protect or to help.

32. And among His Signs are the ships, smooth-running through the ocean, (tall) as mountains.

33. If it be His Will He can still the Wind: then would they become motionless on the back of the (ocean). Verily in this are Signs for everyone who patiently perseveres and is grateful.

34. Or He can cause them to perish because of the (evil) which (the men) have earned; but much does He forgive.

35. But let those know, who dispute about Our Signs, that there is for them no way of escape.

26. Wa yastajeebul-lazeena aamanoo wa 'amiluṣ-ṣaaliḥaati wa yazeeduhum min faḍlih; wal-kaafiroona lahum 'azaabun shadeed.

27. Wa law basaṭal-laahur-rizqa li'ibaadihee labaghaw fil-arḍi wa laakiny-yunazzilu biqada-rim-maa yashaaa'; innahoo bi-'ibaadihee Khabeerum Baṣeer.

28. Wa Huwal-lazee yunaz-zilul-ghaysa mim ba'di maa qanaṭoo wa yanshuru raḥmatah; wa Huwal-Waliyyul-Ḥameed.

29. Wa min Aayaatihee khal-qus-samaawaati wal-arḍi wa maa bassa feehimaa min daaabbah; wa Huwa 'alaa jam'ihim izaa yashaaa'u Qadeer. **(Section 3)**

30. Wa maaa aṣaabakum mim-muṣeebatin fabimaa kasabat aydeekum wa ya'foo 'an kaseer.

31. Wa maaa antum bimu'ji-zeena fil-arḍi wa maa lakum min doonil-laahi miñw-wa liyyiñw-wa laa naṣeer.

32. Wa min Aayaatihil-ja-waari fil-baḥri kal-a'laam.

33. Iñy-yashaaa yuskinir-reeḥa fa-yaẓlalna rawaakida 'alaa ẓahrih; inna fee ẓaalika la-Aayaatil-likulli ṣabbaarin sha-koor.

34. Aw yoobiqhunna bimaa kasaboo wa ya'fu 'an kaseer.

35. Wa ya'lamal-lazeena yujaadiloona fee Aayaatinaa maa lahum mim-maḥeeṣ.

36. Whatever you are given (here) is (but) a convenience of this life: but that which is with Allah is better and more lasting: (it is) for those who believe and put their trust in their Lord:

37. Those who avoid the greater crimes and shameful deeds, and, when they are angry even then forgive;

38. Those who hearken to their Lord, and establish regular Prayer; who (conduct) their affairs by mutual Consultation; who spend out of what We bestow on them for Sustenance;

39. And those who, when an oppressive wrong is inflicted on them, (are not cowed but) help and defend themselves.

40. The recompense for an injury is an injury equal thereto (in degree): but if a person forgives and makes reconciliation, his reward is due from Allah: for (Allah) loves not those who do wrong.

41. But indeed if any do help and defend themselves after a wrong (done) to them, against such there is no cause of blame.

42. The blame is only against those who oppress men and wrong-doing and insolently transgress beyond bounds through the land, defying right and justice: for such there will be a Chastisement grievous.

43. But indeed if any show patience and forgive, that would truly be an affair of great resolution.

44. For any whom Allah leaves astray, there is no protector thereafter. And thou wilt see the Wrong-doers, when in sight of the Penalty, Say: "Is there any way (to effect) a return?"

36. Famaaa ooteetum min shay'in famataa'ul-hayaatid-dunyaa wa maa 'indal-laahi khayrunw-wa abqaa lillazeena aamanoo wa 'alaa Rabbihim yatawakkaloon.

37. Wallazeena yajtaniboona kabaaa'iral-ismi wal-fawaa-hisha wa izaa maa ghadiboo hum yaghfiroon.

38. Wallazeenas-tajaaboo li-Rabbihim wa aqaamus-Salaata wa amruhum shooraa baynahum wa mimmaa razaqnaahum yunfiqoon.

39. Wallazeena izaaa asaa-bahumul-baghyu hum yanta-siroon.

40. Wa jazaaa'u sayyi'atin sayyi'atum-misluhaa faman 'afaa wa aslaha fa-ajruhoo 'alal-laah; innahoo laa yuhib-buz-zaalimeen.

41. Wa lamanin-tasara ba'da zulmihee fa-ulaaa'ika maa 'alayhim min sabeel.

42. Innamas-sabeelu 'alal-lazeena yazlimoonan-naasa wa yabghoona fil-ardi bighayril-haqq; ulaaa'ika lahum 'azaabun aleem.

43. Wa laman sabara wa ghafara inna zaalika lamin 'azmil-umoor. **(Section 4)**

44. Wa mañy-yudlilil-laahu famaa lahoo miñw-waliyyim-mim ba'dih; wa taraz-zaalimeena lammaa ra-awul-'azaaba yaqooloona hal ilaa maraddim-min sabeel.

45. And you will see them brought forward to the Chastisement, in a humble frame of mind because of (their) disgrace, (and) looking with a stealthy glance. And the Believers will say: "Those are indeed in loss, who have given to perdition their own selves and those belonging to them on the Day of Judgment. Behold! Truly the Wrong-doers are in a lasting Chastisement!"

46. And no protectors have they to help them, other than Allah. And for any whom Allah leaves to stray, there is no way (to the Goal).

47. Respond your Lord, before there come a Day which there will be no putting back, because of (the Ordainment of) Allah! that Day there will be for you no place of refuge nor will there be for you any room for denial (of your sins)!

48. If then they run away, We have not sent you as a guard over them. Your duty is but to convey (the Message). And truly, when We give man a taste of a Mercy from Ourselves, he does exult thereat, but when some ill happens to him, on account of the deeds which his hands have sent forth, truly then is man ungrateful!

49. To Allah belongs the dominion of the heavens and the earth. He creates what He wills (and plans). He bestows (children) male or female according to His Will (and Plan),

50. Or He bestows both males and females, and He leaves barren whom He will: for He is full of Knowledge and Power.

51. It is not fitting for a man that Allah should speak to him except by inspiration, or from behind a veil, or

45. Wa taraahum yu'raḍoona 'alayhaa khaashi'eena minaz-zulli yanẓuroona min ṭarfin khafiyy; wa qaalal-lazeena aamanooo innal-khaasireenal-lazeena khasirooo anfusahum wa ahleehim Yawmal-Qiyaa-mah; alaaa innaẓ-ẓaalimeena fee 'azaabim-muqeem.

46. Wa maa kaana lahum min awliyaaa'a yanṣuroonahum min doonil-laah; wa mañy-yuḍlilil-laahu famaa lahoo min sabeel.

47. Istajeeboo li-Rabbikum min qabli añy-yaatiya Yawmul-laa maradda lahoo minal-laah; maa lakum mim-malja-iñy-Yawma'iẕiñw-wa maa lakum min nakeer.

48. Fa-in a'raḍoo famaaa arsalnaaka 'alayhim ḥafeeẓan in 'alayka illal-balaagh; wa innaaa izaaa azaqnal-insaana minnaa raḥmatan fariḥa bihaa wa in tuṣibhum sayyi'atum bimaa qaddamat aydeehim fa-innal-insaana kafoor.

49. Lillaahi mulkus-samaa-waati wal-arḍ; yakhluqu maa yashaaa'; yahabu limañy-yashaaa'u inaaṣañw-wa yahabu limañy-yashaaa'uz-zukoor.

50. Aw yuzawwijuhum ẓukraa-nañw-wa inaaṣañw wa yaj'alu mañy-yashaaa'u 'aqeemaa; innahoo 'Aleemun Qadeer.

51. Wa maa kaana libasharin añy-yukallimahul-laahu illaa waḥyan aw miñw-waraaa'i ḥijaabin aw

by the sending of a messenger to reveal, with Allah's permission, what Allah wills: for He is Most High, Most Wise.

52. And thus have We, by Our Command, sent inspiration to you: you know not (before) what was Revelation, and what was Faith; but We have made the (Qur'an) a Light, wherewith We guide such of Our servants as We will; and verily you does guide (men) to the Straight Way,-

53. The Way of Allah, to Whom belongs whatever is in the heavens and whatever is on earth. Behold (how) all affairs tend towards Allah!

---

43. Gold Adornments
In the name of Allah, Most Gracious, Most Merciful.

1. *Ha-Mim.*

2. By the Book that makes things clear,-

3. We have made it a Qur'an in Arabic, that you may be able to understand (and learn wisdom).

4. And verily, it is in the Mother of the Book, in Our Presence, high (in dignity), full of wisdom.

5. Shall We then take away the Message from you all together for that you are a people transgressing beyond bounds?

6. But how many were the prophets We sent amongst the peoples of old?

7. And never came there a prophet to them but they mocked him.

8. So We destroyed (them)- stronger in power than these;- and (thus) has passed on the Parable of the peoples of old.

9. If you were to question them, 'Who created the heavens

---

yursila Rasoolan fa-yooḥiya bi-iznihee maa yashaaa'; innahoo 'Aliyyun Ḥakeem.

52. Wa kazaalika awḥaynaaa ilayka rooḥam-min amrinaa; maa kunta tadree mal-Kitaabu wa lal-eemaanu wa laakin ja'alnaahu nooran nahdee bihee man nashaaa'u min 'ibaadinaa; wa innaka latahdeee ilaa Ṣiraaṭim Mustaqeem.

53. Ṣiraaṭil-laahil-lazee lahoo maa fis-samaawaati wa maa fil-arḍ; alaaa ilal-laahi taṣeerul-umoor.   **(Section 5)**

Sûrat az-Zukhruf–43
(Revealed at Makkah)

Bismillaahir Raḥmaanir Raḥeem

1. Ḥaa-Meeem.

2. Wal-Kitaabil-Mubeen.

3. Innaa ja'alnaahu Qur-aa-nan 'Arabiyyal-la'allakum ta'qiloon.

4. Wa innahoo feee Ummil-Kitaabi ladaynaa la'aliyyun ḥakeem.

5. Afanaḍribu 'ankumuz-Zikra ṣafḥan an kuntum qawmam-musrifeen.

6. Wa kam arsalnaa min-Nabiyyin fil-awwaleen.

7. Wa maa yaåteehim min Nabiyyin illaa kaanoo bihee yastahzi'oon.

8. Fa-ahlaknaaa ashadda minhum baṭshaňw-wa maḍaa maṣalul-awwaleen.

9. Wa la'in sa-altahum man khalaqas-samaawaati

and the earth?' They would be sure to reply, 'they were created by (Him), the Exalted in Power, Full of Knowledge';–

10. (Yes, the same that) has made for you the earth (like a carpet) spread out, and has made for you roads (and channels) therein, in order that you may find guidance (on the way);

11. Who sends down (from time to time) rain from the sky in due measure;– and We raise to life therewith a land that is dead; even so will you be raised (from the dead);–

12. That has created pairs in all things, and has made for you ships and cattle on which you ride,

13. In order that you may sit firm and square on their backs, and when so seated, you may celebrate the (kind) favour of your Lord, and say, "Glory to Him Who has subjected these to our (use), for we could never have accomplished this (by ourselves),

14. "And to our Lord, surely, must we turn back!"

15. Yet they attribute to some of His servants a share with Him (in His godhead)! truly is man a blasphemous ingrate avowed!

16. What! has He taken daughters out of what He himself creates, and granted to you sons for choice?

17. When news is brought to one of them of (the birth of) what he sets up as a likeness to (Allah) Most Gracious, his face darkens, and he is filled with inward grief!

18. Is then one brought up among trinkets, and unable to give a clear account in a dispute (to be associated with Allah)?

19. And they make into females angels who themselves

wal-arḍa la-yaqooloonna khalaqahunnal-'Azeezul-'Aleem.

10. Allazee ja'ala lakumul-arḍa mahdanw-wa ja'ala lakum feehaa subulal-la'allakum tahtadoon.

11. Wallazee nazzala minassamaaa'i maaa'am biqadarin fa-ansharnaa bihee baldatammaytaa; kazaalika tukhrajoon.

12. Wallazee khalaqal-azwaaja kullahaa wa ja'ala lakum minalfulki wal-an'aami maa tarkaboon.

13. Litastawoo 'alaa ẓuhoorihee summa tazkuroo ni'mata Rabbikum izastawaytum 'alayhi wa taqooloo Subḥaanallazee sakhkhara lanaa haazaa wa maa kunnaa lahoo muqrineen.

14. Wa innaaa ilaa Rabbinaa lamunqaliboon.

15. Wa ja'aloo lahoo min 'ibaadihee juz'aa; innal-insaana lakafoorum-mubeen. **(Section 1)**

16. Amit-takhaza mimmaa yakhluqu banaatinw-wa aṣfaakum bilbaneen.

17. Wa izaa bushshira aḥaduhum bimaa ḍaraba lir-Raḥmaani masalan ẓalla wajhuhoo muswaddanw-wa huwa kaẓeem.

18. Awa many-yunashsha'u fil-ḥilyati wa huwa fil-khiṣaami ghayru mubeen.

19. Wa ja'alul-malaaa'ikatallazeena hum 'ibaadur-

وَالْأَرْضَ لَيَقُولُنَّ خَلَقَهُنَّ الْعَزِيزُ الْعَلِيمُۙ ٩

الَّذِيْ جَعَلَ لَكُمُ الْأَرْضَ مَهْدًا وَّجَعَلَ لَكُمْ فِيْهَا سُبُلًا لَّعَلَّكُمْ تَهْتَدُوْنَۚ ١٠

وَالَّذِيْ نَزَّلَ مِنَ السَّمَاءِ مَاءً بِقَدَرٍ فَأَنْشَرْنَا بِهٖ بَلْدَةً مَّيْتًا ۚ كَذٰلِكَ تُخْرَجُوْنَۚ ١١

وَالَّذِيْ خَلَقَ الْأَزْوَاجَ كُلَّهَا وَجَعَلَ لَكُمْ مِّنَ الْفُلْكِ وَالْأَنْعَامِ مَا تَرْكَبُوْنَۙ ١٢

لِتَسْتَوٗا عَلٰى ظُهُوْرِهٖ ثُمَّ تَذْكُرُوْا نِعْمَةَ رَبِّكُمْ إِذَا اسْتَوَيْتُمْ عَلَيْهِ وَتَقُوْلُوْا سُبْحٰنَ الَّذِيْ سَخَّرَ لَنَا هٰذَا وَمَا كُنَّا لَهٗ مُقْرِنِيْنَۙ ١٣

وَإِنَّا إِلٰى رَبِّنَا لَمُنْقَلِبُوْنَ ١٤

وَجَعَلُوْا لَهٗ مِنْ عِبَادِهٖ جُزْءًا ۚ إِنَّ الْإِنْسَانَ لَكَفُوْرٌ مُّبِيْنٌۗ ١٥

أَمِ اتَّخَذَ مِمَّا يَخْلُقُ بَنَاتٍ وَّ أَصْفٰكُمْ بِالْبَنِيْنَ ١٦

وَإِذَا بُشِّرَ أَحَدُهُمْ بِمَا ضَرَبَ لِلرَّحْمٰنِ مَثَلًا ظَلَّ وَجْهُهٗ مُسْوَدًّا وَّهُوَ كَظِيْمٌ ١٧

أَوَمَنْ يُّنَشَّؤُا فِى الْحِلْيَةِ وَهُوَ فِى الْخِصَامِ غَيْرُ مُبِيْنٍ ١٨

وَجَعَلُوا الْمَلٰٓئِكَةَ الَّذِيْنَ هُمْ عِبٰدُ

serve Allah. Did they witness their creation? Their evidence will be recorded, and they will be called to account!

20. ("Ah!") they say, "If it had been the will of (Allah) Most Gracious, we should not have worshipped such (deities)!" Of that they have no knowledge! they do nothing but lie!

21. What! have We given them a Book before this, to which they are holding fast?

22. No! they say: "We found our fathers following a certain religion, and we do guide ourselves by their footsteps."

23. Just in the same way, whenever We sent a Warner before you to any people, the wealthy ones among them said: "We found our fathers following a certain religion, and we will certainly follow in their footsteps."

24. He said: "What! Even if I brought you better guidance than that which you found your fathers following?" They said: "For us, we deny that you (prophets) are sent (on a mission at all)."

25. So We exacted retribution from them: now see what was the end of those who rejected (Truth)!

26. Behold! Abraham said to his father and his people: "I do indeed clear myself of what you worship:

27. "(I worship) only Him Who made me, and He will certainly guide me."

28. And he left it as a Word to endure among those who came after him, that they may turn back (to Allah).

29. Yes, I have given the good things of this life to these (men) and their fathers, until the Truth has come to them, and an apostle making things clear.

30. But when the Truth came to them, they said: "This is sorcery,

---

Raḥmaani inaasaa; a-shahidoo khalqahum; satuktabu shahaa-datuhum wa yus'aloon.

20. Wa qaaloo law shaaa'ar-Raḥmaanu maa 'abadnaahum; maa lahum bizaalika min 'ilmin in hum illaa yakhruṣoon.

21. Am aataynaahum Kitaa-bam-min qablihee fahum bihee mustamsikoon.

22. Bal qaalooo innaa wajad-naaa aabaaa'anaa 'alaaa ummatiñw-wa innaa 'alaaa aasaarihim muhtadoon.

23. Wa kazaalika maaa arsal-naa min qablika fee qaryatim-min nazeerin illaa qaala mutrafoohaaa innaa wajadnaaa aabaaa'anaa 'alaaa ummatiñw-wa innaa 'alaaa aasaarihim muqtadoon.

24. Qaala awa law ji'tukum bi-ahdaa mimmaa wajattum 'alayhi aabaaa'akum qaalooo innaa bimaaa ursiltum bihee kaafiroon.

25. Fantaqamnaa minhum fanzur kayfa kaana 'aaqibatul-mukazzibeen. **(Section 2)**

26. Wa iz qaala Ibraaheemu li-abeehi wa qawmiheee innanee baraaa'um-mimmaa ta'budoon.

27. Illal-lazee faṭaranee fa-innahoo sa-yahdeen.

28. Wa ja'alahaa Kalimatam baaqiyatan fee 'aqibihee la-'allahum yarji'oon.

29. Bal matta'tu haaa'ulaaa'i wa aabaaa'ahum ḥattaa jaaa'a-humul-ḥaqqu wa Rasoolum-mubeen.

30. Wa lammaa jaaa'ahumul-ḥaqqu qaaloo haazaa siḥruñw-

---

and we do reject it."

وَإِنَّا بِهٖ كٰفِرُوْنَ ۞

31. Also, they say: "Why is not this Qur'an sent down to some leading man in either of the two (chief) cities?"

31. Wa qaaloo law laa nuzzila haazal-Qur-aanu 'alaa rajulim-minal-qaryatayni 'azeem.

وَقَالُوْا لَوْلَا نُزِّلَ هٰذَا الْقُرْاٰنُ عَلٰى رَجُلٍ مِّنَ الْقَرْيَتَيْنِ عَظِيْمٍ ۞

32. Is it they who would portion out the Mercy of your Lord? It is We Who portion out between them their livelihood in the life of this world: and We raise some of them above others in ranks, so that some may command work from others. But the Mercy of your Lord is better than the (wealth) which they amass.

32. Ahum yaqsimoona raḥmata Rabbik; Naḥnu qasamnaa baynahum ma'eeshatahum fil-ḥayaatid dunyaa wa rafa'naa ba'ḍahum fawqa ba'ḍin dara-jaatil-liyattakhiza ba'ḍuhum ba'ḍan sukhriyyaa; wa raḥmatu Rabbika khayrum-mimmaa yajma'oon.

أَهُمْ يَقْسِمُوْنَ رَحْمَتَ رَبِّكَ ۚ نَحْنُ قَسَمْنَا بَيْنَهُمْ مَّعِيْشَتَهُمْ فِى الْحَيٰوةِ الدُّنْيَا وَرَفَعْنَا بَعْضَهُمْ فَوْقَ بَعْضٍ دَرَجٰتٍ لِّيَتَّخِذَ بَعْضُهُمْ بَعْضًا سُخْرِيًّا ۗ وَرَحْمَتُ رَبِّكَ خَيْرٌ مِّمَّا يَجْمَعُوْنَ ۞

33. And were it not that (all) men might become of one community, We would provide, for everyone that blasphemes against (Allah) Most Gracious, silver roofs for their houses and (silver) stair-ways on which to go up,

33. Wa law laaa añy-yakoonan-naasu ummatañw-waaḥidatal-laja'alnaa limañy-yakfuru bir-Raḥmaani libu-yootihim suqu-fam-min fiḍḍatiñw-wa ma'aarija 'alayhaa yazharoon.

وَلَوْلَا أَنْ يَّكُوْنَ النَّاسُ أُمَّةً وَّاحِدَةً لَّجَعَلْنَا لِمَنْ يَّكْفُرُ بِالرَّحْمٰنِ لِبُيُوْتِهِمْ سُقُفًا مِّنْ فِضَّةٍ وَّمَعَارِجَ عَلَيْهَا يَظْهَرُوْنَ ۞

34. And (silver) doors to their houses, and thrones (of silver) on which they could recline,

34. Wa libu-yootihim abwaa-bañw-wa sururan 'alayhaa yattaki'oon.

وَلِبُيُوْتِهِمْ أَبْوَابًا وَّسُرُرًا عَلَيْهَا يَتَّكِئُوْنَ ۞

35. And also adornments of gold. But all this were nothing but enjoyment of the present life: The Hereafter, in the sight of your Lord is for the Righteous. (Section 3)

35. Wa zukhrufaa; wa in kullu zaalika lammaa mataa'ul-ḥayaatid-dunyaa; wal-Aakhi-ratu 'inda Rabbika lilmutta-qeen.

وَزُخْرُفًا ۚ وَإِنْ كُلُّ ذٰلِكَ لَمَّا مَتَاعُ الْحَيٰوةِ الدُّنْيَا ۗ وَالْاٰخِرَةُ عِنْدَ رَبِّكَ لِلْمُتَّقِيْنَ ۞

36. If anyone withdraws himself from remembrance of (Allah) Most Gracious, We appoint for him an evil one, to be an intimate companion to him.

36. Wa mañy-ya'shu 'an zikrir-Raḥmaani nuqayyiḍ lahoo Shayṭaanan fahuwa lahoo qareen.

وَمَنْ يَّعْشُ عَنْ ذِكْرِ الرَّحْمٰنِ نُقَيِّضْ لَهٗ شَيْطٰنًا فَهُوَ لَهٗ قَرِيْنٌ ۞

37. Such (evil ones) really hinder them from the Path, but they think that they are being guided aright!

37. Wa innahum la-yaṣuddoo-nahum 'anis-sabeeli wa yaḥsa-boona annahum muhtadoon.

وَإِنَّهُمْ لَيَصُدُّوْنَهُمْ عَنِ السَّبِيْلِ وَيَحْسَبُوْنَ أَنَّهُمْ مُّهْتَدُوْنَ ۞

38. At length, when (such a one) comes to Us, he says (to his evil companion): "Would that between me and you were the distance of East and West!" Ah! evil is the companion (indeed)!

38. Ḥattaaa izaa jaaa'anaa qaala yaa laytaa baynee wa baynaka bu'dal-mashriqayni fabi'sal-qareen.

حَتّٰى إِذَا جَاءَنَا قَالَ يٰلَيْتَ بَيْنِيْ وَبَيْنَكَ بُعْدَ الْمَشْرِقَيْنِ فَبِئْسَ الْقَرِيْنُ ۞

39. When you have done wrong, it will avail you nothing, that Day, that you shall be partners in Punishment!

39. Wa lañy-yanfa'akumul-Yawma iz-zalamtum annakum fil-'azaabi mushtarikoon.

وَلَنْ يَّنْفَعَكُمُ الْيَوْمَ إِذْ ظَلَمْتُمْ أَنَّكُمْ فِى الْعَذَابِ مُشْتَرِكُوْنَ ۞

40. Can you then make the deaf to hear, or give direction to the blind or to such as (wander) in manifest error?

41. Even if We take you away, We shall be sure to exact retribution from them,

42. Or We shall show you that (accomplished) which We have promised them: for verily We shall prevail over them.

43. So hold you fast to the Revelation sent down to you; verily you are on a Straight Way.

44. The (Qur'an) is indeed the message, for you and for your people; and soon shall you (all) be brought to account.

45. And question you our apostles whom We sent before thee; did We appoint any deities other than (Allah) Most Gracious, to be worshipped?

46. We did send Moses aforetime, with Our Signs, to Pharaoh and his Chiefs: He said, "I am an apostle of the Lord of the Worlds."

47. But when he came to them with Our Signs, behold they ridiculed them.

48. We showed them Sign after Sign, each greater than its fellow, and We seized them with Punishment, in order that they might turn (to Us).

49. And they said, "O you sorcerer! Invoke your Lord for us according to His covenant with you; for we shall truly accept guidance."

50. But when We removed the Penalty from them, behold, they broke their word.

51. And Pharaoh proclaimed among his people, saying:

40. Afa-anta tusmi'us-summa aw tahdil-'umya wa man kaana fee dalaalim-mubeen.

41. Fa-immaa nazhabanna bika fa-innaa minhum muntaqimoon.

42. Aw nuriyannakal-lazee wa'adnaahum fa-innaa 'alayhim muqtadiroon.

43. Fastamsik billazeee oohiya ilayka innaka 'alaa Siraatim-Mustaqeem.

44. Wa innahoo lazikrul-laka wa liqawmika wa sawfa tus'aloon.

45. Was'al man arsalnaa min qablika mir-Rusulinaaa aja-'alnaa min doonir-Rahmaani aalihatany-yu'badoon. **(Section 4)**

46. Wa laqad arsalnaa Moosaa bi-Aayaatinaaa ilaa Fir'awna wa mala'ihee faqaala innee Rasoolu Rabbil-'aalameen.

47. Falammaa jaaa'ahum bi-Aayaatinaaa izaa hum minhaa yadhakoon.

48. Wa maa nureehim min Aayatin illaa hiya akbaru min ukhtihaa wa akhaznaahum bil'azaabi la'allahum yarji'oon.

49. Wa qaaloo yaaa ayyuhas-saahirud-'u lanaa Rabbaka bimaa 'ahida 'indaka innanaa lamuhtadoon.

50. Falammaa kashafnaa 'anhumul-'azaaba izaa hum yankusoon.

51. Wa naadaa Fir'awnu fee qawmihee qaala yaa qawmi

does not the dominion of Egypt belong to me, (witness these streams flowing underneath my (palace)? Do you not see then?

52. "Am I not better than this (Moses), who is a contemptible wretch and can scarcely express himself clearly?

53. "Then why are not gold bracelets bestowed on him, or (why) come (not) with him angels accompanying him in procession?"

54. Thus did he make fools of his people, and they obeyed him: truly were they a people rebellious (against Allah).

55. When at length they provoked Us, We exacted retribution from them, and We drowned them all.

56. And We made them (a people) of the Past and an Example to later ages.

57. When (Jesus) the son of Mary is held up as an example, behold, your people raise a clamour thereat (in ridicule)!

58. And they say, "Are our gods best, or he?" This they set forth to you, only by way of disputation: yes, they are a contentious people.

59. He was no more than a servant: We granted Our favour to him, and We made him an example to the Children of Israel

60. And if it were Our Will, We could make angels from amongst you, succeeding each other on the earth.

61. And (Jesus) shall be a Sign (for the coming of) the Hour (of Judgment): therefore have no doubt about the (Hour), but follow you Me: this is a Straight Way.

62. Let not the Evil One hinder you: for he is to you an enemy avowed.

63. When Jesus came with Clear Signs, he said: "Now have I come to you with Wisdom, and in order to make clear to you

---

alaysa lee mulku Miṣra wa haazihil-anhaaru tajree min taḥtee afalaa tubṣiroon.

52. Am ana khayrum-min haazal-lazee huwa maheenuñw-wa laa yakaadu yubeen.

53. Falaw laaa ulqiya 'alayhi aswiratum-min zahabin aw jaaa'a ma'ahul-malaaa'ikatu muqtarineen.

54. Fastakhaffa qawmahoo fa-aṭaa'ooh; innahum kaanoo qawman faasiqeen.

55. Falammaaa aasafoonan-taqamnaa minhum fa-aghraq-naahum ajma'een.

56. Faja'alnaahum salafañw-wa maṣalal-lil-aakhireen. (Section 5)

57. Wa lammaa ḍuribab-nu Maryama maṣalan izaa qawmu-ka minhu yaṣiddoon.

58. Wa qaalooo 'a-aalihatunaa khayrun am hoo; maa ḍaraboohu laka illaa jadalaa; bal hum qawmun khaṣimoon.

59. In huwa illaa 'abdun an'amnaa 'alayhi wa ja'alnaahu maṣalal-li-Baneee Israaa'eel.

60. Wa law nashaaa'u laja'al-naa minkum malaaa'ikatan fil-arḍi yakhlufoon.

61. Wa innahoo la'ilmul-lis-Saa'ati falaa tamtarunna bihaa wattabi'oon; haazaa Ṣiraaṭum-Mustaqeem.

62. Wa laa yaṣuddan-naku-mush-Shayṭaanu innahoo la-kum 'aduwwum-mubeen.

63. Wa lammaa jaaa'a 'Eesaa bilbayyinaati qaala qad ji'tu-kum bil-Ḥikmati wa li-ubay-yina lakum

---

أَلَيْسَ لِى مُلْكُ مِصْرَ وَهَٰذِهِ الْأَنْهَٰرُ تَجْرِى مِن تَحْتِى ۖ أَفَلَا تُبْصِرُونَ ۝

أَمْ أَنَا۠ خَيْرٌ مِّنْ هَٰذَا الَّذِى هُوَ مَهِينٌ ۝ وَلَا يَكَادُ يُبِينُ ۝

فَلَوْلَآ أُلْقِىَ عَلَيْهِ أَسْوِرَةٌ مِّن ذَهَبٍ أَوْ جَآءَ مَعَهُ الْمَلَٰٓئِكَةُ مُقْتَرِنِينَ ۝

فَاسْتَخَفَّ قَوْمَهُۥ فَأَطَاعُوهُ ۚ إِنَّهُمْ كَانُوا۟ قَوْمًا فَٰسِقِينَ ۝

فَلَمَّآ ءَاسَفُونَا انْتَقَمْنَا مِنْهُمْ فَأَغْرَقْنَٰهُمْ أَجْمَعِينَ ۝

فَجَعَلْنَٰهُمْ سَلَفًا وَمَثَلًا لِّلْءَاخِرِينَ ۝

وَلَمَّا ضُرِبَ ابْنُ مَرْيَمَ مَثَلًا إِذَا قَوْمُكَ مِنْهُ يَصِدُّونَ ۝

وَقَالُوٓا۟ ءَأَٰلِهَتُنَا خَيْرٌ أَمْ هُوَ ۚ مَا ضَرَبُوهُ لَكَ إِلَّا جَدَلًا ۚ بَلْ هُمْ قَوْمٌ خَصِمُونَ ۝

إِنْ هُوَ إِلَّا عَبْدٌ أَنْعَمْنَا عَلَيْهِ وَجَعَلْنَٰهُ مَثَلًا لِّبَنِىٓ إِسْرَآءِيلَ ۝

وَلَوْ نَشَآءُ لَجَعَلْنَا مِنكُم مَّلَٰٓئِكَةً فِى الْأَرْضِ يَخْلُفُونَ ۝

وَإِنَّهُۥ لَعِلْمٌ لِّلسَّاعَةِ فَلَا تَمْتَرُنَّ بِهَا وَاتَّبِعُونِ ۚ هَٰذَا صِرَٰطٌ مُّسْتَقِيمٌ ۝

وَلَا يَصُدَّنَّكُمُ الشَّيْطَٰنُ ۖ إِنَّهُۥ لَكُمْ عَدُوٌّ مُّبِينٌ ۝

وَلَمَّا جَآءَ عِيسَىٰ بِالْبَيِّنَٰتِ قَالَ قَدْ جِئْتُكُم بِالْحِكْمَةِ وَلِأُبَيِّنَ لَكُم

some of the (points) on which you dispute: therefore fear Allah and obey me.

ba'dal-lazee takhtalifoona feehi fattaqul-laaha wa atee'oon.

بَعْضَ الَّذِي تَخْتَلِفُونَ فِيهِ فَاتَّقُوا اللهَ وَأَطِيعُونِ ۝

64. "For Allah, He is my Lord and your Lord: so worship you Him: this is a Straight Way."

64. Innal-laaha Huwa Rabbee wa Rabbukum fa'budooh; haazaa Siraatum-Mustaqeem.

إِنَّ اللهَ هُوَ رَبِّي وَرَبُّكُمْ فَاعْبُدُوهُ هَذَا صِرَاطٌ مُّسْتَقِيمٌ ۝

65. But sects from among themselves fell into disagreement: then woe to the wrong-doers, from the Chastisement of a Grievous Day!

65. Fakhtalafal-ahzaabu mim baynihim fawaylul-lillazeena zalamoo min 'azaabi Yawmin aleem.

فَاخْتَلَفَ الْأَحْزَابُ مِنْ بَيْنِهِمْ فَوَيْلٌ لِّلَّذِينَ ظَلَمُوا مِنْ عَذَابِ يَوْمٍ أَلِيمٍ ۝

66. Do they only wait for the Hour - that it should come on them all of a sudden, while they perceive not?

66. Hal yanzuroona illas-Saa'ata an taàtiyahum baghta-tanw- wa hum laa yash'uroon.

هَلْ يَنْظُرُونَ إِلَّا السَّاعَةَ أَنْ تَأْتِيَهُمْ بَغْتَةً وَّهُمْ لَا يَشْعُرُونَ ۝

67. Friends on that day will be foes, one to another,- except the Righteous.

67. Al-akhillaaa'u Yawma'i-zim ba'duhum liba'din 'aduw-wun illal-muttaqeen. (Section 6)

الْأَخِلَّاءُ يَوْمَئِذٍ بَعْضُهُمْ لِبَعْضٍ عَدُوٌّ إِلَّا الْمُتَّقِينَ ۝

68. My devotees! no fear shall be on you that Day, nor shall you grieve,-

68. Yaa 'ibaadi laa khawfun 'alaykumul-Yawma wa laaa antum tahzanoon.

يَا عِبَادِ لَا خَوْفٌ عَلَيْكُمُ الْيَوْمَ وَلَا أَنْتُمْ تَحْزَنُونَ ۝

69. (Being) those who have believed in Our Signs and bowed (their wills to Ours) in Islam.

69. Allazeena aamanoo bi Aayaatinaa wa kaanoo musli-meen.

الَّذِينَ آمَنُوا بِآيَاتِنَا وَكَانُوا مُسْلِمِينَ ۝

70. Enter you the Garden, you and your wives, in (beauty and) rejoicing.

70. Udkhulul-Jannata antum wa azwaajukum tuhbaroon.

ادْخُلُوا الْجَنَّةَ أَنْتُمْ وَأَزْوَاجُكُمْ تُحْبَرُونَ ۝

71. To them will be passed round, dishes and goblets of gold: there will be there all that the souls could desire, all that their eyes could delight in: and you shall abide therein (for ever).

71. Yutaafu 'alayhim bisihaa-fim-min zahabinw-wa akwaab, wa feehaa maatashtaheehil-anfusu wa talazzul-a'yunu wa antum feehaa khaalidoon.

يُطَافُ عَلَيْهِمْ بِصِحَافٍ مِّنْ ذَهَبٍ وَأَكْوَابٍ وَفِيهَا مَا تَشْتَهِيهِ الْأَنْفُسُ وَتَلَذُّ الْأَعْيُنُ وَأَنْتُمْ فِيهَا خَالِدُونَ ۝

72. Such will be the Garden of which you are made heirs for your (good) deeds (in life).

72. Wa tilkal-Jannatul-lateee ooristumoohaa bimaa kuntum ta'maloon.

وَتِلْكَ الْجَنَّةُ الَّتِي أُورِثْتُمُوهَا بِمَا كُنْتُمْ تَعْمَلُونَ ۝

73. You shall have therein abundance of fruit, from which you shall have satisfaction.

73. Lakum feehaa faakihatun kaseeratum-minhaa taàkuloon.

لَكُمْ فِيهَا فَاكِهَةٌ كَثِيرَةٌ مِّنْهَا تَأْكُلُونَ ۝

74. The sinners will be in the Punishment of Hell,

74. Innal-mujrimeena fee 'azaabi Jahannama

إِنَّ الْمُجْرِمِينَ فِي عَذَابِ جَهَنَّمَ

to dwell therein (for ever):

75. It is not relaxed for them, and they despair therein.

76. Nowise shall We be unjust to them: but it is they who have been unjust themselves.

77. They will cry: "O Malik! would that your Lord put an end to us!" He will say, "No, but you shall abide!"

78. Verily We have brought the Truth to you: but most of you have a hatred for Truth.

79. What! have they settled some plan (among themselves)? But it is We Who settle things.

80. Or do they think that We hear not their secrets and their private counsels? Indeed (We do), and Our messengers are by them, to record.

81. Say: "If (Allah) Most Gracious had a son, I would be the first to worship."

82. Glory to the Lord of the heavens and the earth, the Lord of the Throne (of Authority)! (He is free) from the things they attribute (to him)!

83. So leave them to babble and play (with vanities) until they meet that Day of theirs, which they have been promised.

84. It is He Who is Allah in heaven and Allah on earth; and He is full of Wisdom and Knowledge.

85. And blessed is He to Whom belongs the dominion of the heavens and the earth, and all between them: with Him is the Knowledge of the Hour (of Judgment): and to Him shall you be brought back.

86. And those whom they invoke besides Allah have no power of intercession;- only he who bears witness to the Truth, and they know (him).

khaalidoon.

75. Laa yufattaru 'anhum wa hum feehi mublisoon.

76. Wa maa ẓalamnaahum wa laakin kaanoo humuẓ-ẓaa-limeen.

77. Wa naadaw yaa Maaliku liyaqḍi 'alaynaa Rabbuka qaala innakum maakisoon.

78. Laqad ji'naakum bilḥaqqi wa laakinna aksarakum lilḥaqqi kaarihoon.

79. Am abramooo amran fa-innaa mubrimoon.

80. Am yaḥsaboona annaa laa nasma'u sirrahum wa najwaahum; balaa wa Rusulunaa ladayhim yaktuboon.

81. Qul in kaana lir-Raḥmaani walad; fa-ana awwalul-'aabideen.

82. Subḥaana Rabbis-samaa-waati wal-arḍi Rabbil-'Arshi 'ammaa yaṣifoon.

83. Fazarhum yakhooḍoo wa-yal'aboo ḥattaa yulaaqoo Yawmahumul-lazee yoo'a-doon.

84. Wa Huwal-lazee fissa-maaa'i Ilaahuñw-wa fil-arḍi Ilaah; wa Huwal-Ḥakeemul-'Aleem.

85. Wa tabaarakal-lazee lahoo mulkus-samaawaati wal-arḍi wa maa baynahumaa wa 'indahoo 'ilmus-Saa'ati wa ilayhi turja'oon.

86. Wa laa yamlikul-lazeena yad'oona min doonihish-shafaa'ata illaa man shahida bilḥaqqi wa hum ya'lamoon.

خَٰلِدُونَ ۝

لَا يُفَتَّرُ عَنْهُمْ وَهُمْ فِيهِ مُبْلِسُونَ ۝

وَمَا ظَلَمْنَٰهُمْ وَلَٰكِن كَانُوا هُمُ الظَّٰلِمِينَ ۝

وَنَادَوْا يَٰمَٰلِكُ لِيَقْضِ عَلَيْنَا رَبُّكَ قَالَ إِنَّكُم مَّٰكِثُونَ ۝

لَقَدْ جِئْنَٰكُم بِالْحَقِّ وَلَٰكِنَّ أَكْثَرَكُمْ لِلْحَقِّ كَٰرِهُونَ ۝

أَمْ أَبْرَمُوٓا أَمْرًا فَإِنَّا مُبْرِمُونَ ۝

أَمْ يَحْسَبُونَ أَنَّا لَا نَسْمَعُ سِرَّهُمْ وَنَجْوَىٰهُم بَلَىٰ وَرُسُلُنَا لَدَيْهِمْ يَكْتُبُونَ ۝

قُلْ إِن كَانَ لِلرَّحْمَٰنِ وَلَدٌ فَأَنَا۠ أَوَّلُ الْعَٰبِدِينَ ۝

سُبْحَٰنَ رَبِّ السَّمَٰوَٰتِ وَالْأَرْضِ رَبِّ الْعَرْشِ عَمَّا يَصِفُونَ ۝

فَذَرْهُمْ يَخُوضُوا وَيَلْعَبُوا حَتَّىٰ يُلَٰقُوا يَوْمَهُمُ الَّذِي يُوعَدُونَ ۝

وَهُوَ الَّذِي فِي السَّمَاءِ إِلَٰهٌ وَفِي الْأَرْضِ إِلَٰهٌ وَهُوَ الْحَكِيمُ الْعَلِيمُ ۝

وَتَبَارَكَ الَّذِي لَهُ مُلْكُ السَّمَٰوَٰتِ وَالْأَرْضِ وَمَا بَيْنَهُمَا وَعِندَهُ عِلْمُ السَّاعَةِ وَإِلَيْهِ تُرْجَعُونَ ۝

وَلَا يَمْلِكُ الَّذِينَ يَدْعُونَ مِن دُونِهِ الشَّفَٰعَةَ إِلَّا مَن شَهِدَ بِالْحَقِّ وَهُمْ يَعْلَمُونَ ۝

87. If you ask them, who created them, they will certainly say, Allah: How then are they deluded away (from the Truth)?

88. (Allah has knowledge) of the (Prophet's) cry, "O my Lord! Truly these are people who will not believe!"

89. But turn away from them, and say "Peace!" But soon shall they know!

44. Smoke or Mist
In the name of Allah, Most Gracious, Most Merciful.

1. *Ha-Mim.*

2. By the Book that makes things clear;-

3. We sent it down during a Blessed Night: for We (ever) wish to warn (against Evil).

4. In the (Night) is made distinct every affair of wisdom,

5. By command, from Our Presence. For We (ever) send (revelations),

6. As Mercy from your Lord: for He hears and knows (all things);

7. The Lord of the heavens and the earth and all between them, if you (but) have an assured faith.

8. There is no god but He: It is He Who gives life and gives death,- The Lord and Cherisher to you and your earliest ancestors.

9. Yet they play about in doubt.

10. Then watch thou for the Day that the sky will bring forth a kind of smoke (or mist) plainly visible,

11. Enveloping the people: this will be a Chastisement Grievous.

12. (They will say:) "Our Lord! remove the Chastisement from us, for we do really believe!"

---

87. Wa la'in sa-altahum man khalaqahum la-yaqoolun-nallaahu fa-annaa yu'fakoon.

88. Wa qeelihee yaa Rabbi inna haaa'ulaaa'i qawmul-laa yu'minoon.

89. Faşfaḥ 'anhum wa qul salaam; fasawfa ya'lamoon.

(Section 7)

Sûrat ad-Dukhân–44
(Revealed at Makkah)
Bismillaahir Raḥmaanir Raḥeem

1. Ḥaa-Meeem.

2. Wal-Kitaabil-Mubeen.

3. Innaaa anzalnaahu fee laylatim-mubaarakah; innaa kunnaa munzireen.

4. Feehaa yufraqu kullu amrin ḥakeem.

5. Amram-min 'indinaaa; innaa kunnaa mursileen.

6. Raḥmatam-mir-Rabbik; innahoo Huwas-Samee'ul-'Aleem.

7. Rabbis-samaawaati wal-arḍi wa maa baynahumaa; in kuntum mooqineen.

8. Laaa ilaaha illaa Huwa yuḥyee wa yumeetu Rabbukum wa Rabbu aabaaa'ikumul-awwaleen.

9. Bal hum fee shakkiñy-yal'aboon.

10. Fartaqib Yawma taátis-samaaa'u bidukhaanim-mubeen.

11. Yaghshan-naasa haazaa 'azaabun aleem.

12. Rabbanak-shif 'annal-'azaaba innaa mu'minoon.

13. How shall the message be (effectual) for them, seeing that an Apostle explaining things clearly has (already) come to them,-

14. Yet they turn away from him and say: "Tutored (by others), a man possessed!"

15. We shall indeed remove the Chastisement for a while, (but) truly you will revert (to your ways).

16. One day We shall seize you with a mighty onslaught: We will indeed (then) exact Retribution!

17. We did, before them, try the people of Pharaoh: there came to them an apostle most honourable,

18. Saying: "Restore to me the Servants of Allah: I am to you an apostle worthy of all trust;

19. "And be not arrogant as against Allah: for I come to you with authority manifest.

20. "For me, I have sought safety with my Lord and your Lord, against your injuring me.

21. And if ye put no faith in me, then let me go.

22. (But they were aggressive:) then he cried to his Lord: "These are indeed a people given to sin."

23. (The reply came:) "March forth with My Servants by night: for you are sure to be pursued:

24. "And leave the sea as a furrow (divided): for they are a host (destined) to be drowned."

25. How many were the gardens and springs they left behind,

26. And corn-fields and noble buildings,

27. And pleasant things wherein they took delight!

28. Thus (was their end)! And We made other people inherit (those things)!

13. Annaa lahumuz-zikraa wa qad jaaa'ahum Rasoolum-mubeen.

14. Summa tawallaw 'anhu wa qaaloo mu'allamum-majnoon.

15. Innaa kaashiful-'azaabi qaleelaa; innakum 'aaa'idoon.

16. Yawma nabṭishul-baṭsha-tal-kubraa innaa muntaqi-moon.

17. Wa laqad fatannaa qabla-hum qawma Fir'awna wa jaaa'ahum Rasoolun kareem.

18. An addooo ilayya 'ibaa-dal-laahi innee lakum Rasoolun ameen.

19. Wa al-laa ta'loo 'alal-laahi ineee aateekum bisulṭaanim-mubeen.

20. Wa innee 'uztu bi-Rabbee wa Rabbikum an tarjumoon.

21. Wa il-lam tu'minoo lee fa'taziloon.

22. Fada'aa Rabbahooo anna haaa'ulaaa'i qawmum-mujri-moon.

23. Fa-asri bi-'ibaadee laylan innakum muttaba'oon.

24. Watrukil-baḥra rahwan innahum jundum-mughraqoon.

25. Kam tarakoo min jannaa-tiñw-wa 'uyoon.

26. Wa zuroo'iñw-wa maqaa-min kareem.

27. Wa na'matin kaanoo feehaa faakiheen.

28. Kazaalika wa awrasnaahaa qawman aakhareen.

29. And neither heaven nor earth shed a tear over them: nor were they given a respite (again).

29. Famaa bakat 'alayhimus-samaaa'u wal-arḍu wa maa kaanoo munẓareen. **(Section 1)**

فَمَا بَكَتْ عَلَيْهِمُ السَّمَآءُ وَالْأَرْضُ وَمَا كَانُوْا مُنْظَرِيْنَ ۟

30. We did deliver aforetime the Children of Israel from humiliating Punishment,

30. Wa laqad najjaynaa Baneee Israaa'eela minal-'azaabil-muheen.

وَلَقَدْ نَجَّيْنَا بَنِيْ إِسْرَآءِيْلَ مِنَ الْعَذَابِ الْمُهِيْنِ ۟

31. Inflicted by Pharaoh, for he was arrogant (even) among inordinate transgressors.

31. Min Fir'awn; innahoo kaana 'aaliyam-minal musrifeen.

مِنْ فِرْعَوْنَ ؕ إِنَّهٗ كَانَ عَالِيًا مِّنَ الْمُسْرِفِيْنَ ۟

32. And We chose them aforetime above the nations, knowingly,

32. Wa laqadikh-tarnaahum 'alaa 'ilmin 'alal-'aalameen.

وَلَقَدِ اخْتَرْنٰهُمْ عَلٰى عِلْمٍ عَلَى الْعٰلَمِيْنَ ۟

33. And granted them Signs in which there was a manifest trial.

33. Wa aataynaahum minal-Aayaati maa feehi balaaa'um-mubeen.

وَاٰتَيْنٰهُمْ مِّنَ الْاٰيٰتِ مَا فِيْهِ بَلٰٓؤٌا مُّبِيْنٌ ۟

34. As to these (Quraish), they say forsooth:

34. Inna haaa'ulaaa'i la-ya-qooloon.

إِنَّ هٰٓؤُلَآءِ لَيَقُوْلُوْنَ ۙ

35. "There is nothing beyond our first death, and we shall not be raised again.

35. In hiya illaa mawtatunaloolaa wa maa naḥnu bimunshareen.

إِنْ هِيَ إِلَّا مَوْتَتُنَا الْأُوْلٰى وَمَا نَحْنُ بِمُنْشَرِيْنَ ۟

36. "Then bring (back) our forefathers, if what you say is true!"

36. Faåtoo bi-aabaaa'inaaa in kuntum ṣaadiqeen.

فَأْتُوْا بِاٰبَآئِنَآ إِنْ كُنْتُمْ صٰدِقِيْنَ ۟

37. What! Are they better than the people of Tubba and those who were before them? We destroyed them because they were guilty of sin.

37. Ahum khayrun am qawmu Tubba'iñw-wallaẕeena min qab-lihim; ahlaknaahum innahum kaanoo mujrimeen.

أَهُمْ خَيْرٌ أَمْ قَوْمُ تُبَّعٍ ۙ وَّالَّذِيْنَ مِنْ قَبْلِهِمْ ؕ أَهْلَكْنٰهُمْ ۫ إِنَّهُمْ كَانُوْا مُجْرِمِيْنَ ۟

38. We created not the heavens, the earth, and all between them, merely in (idle) sport:

38. Wa maa khalaqnas samaawaati wal-arḍa wa maa baynahumaa laa'ibeen.

وَمَا خَلَقْنَا السَّمٰوٰتِ وَالْأَرْضَ وَمَا بَيْنَهُمَا لٰعِبِيْنَ ۟

39. We created them not except for just ends: but most of them do not understand.

39. Maa khalaqnaahumaaa illaa bilḥaqqi wa laakinna akẖarahum laa ya'lamoon.

مَا خَلَقْنٰهُمَآ إِلَّا بِالْحَقِّ وَلٰكِنَّ أَكْثَرَهُمْ لَا يَعْلَمُوْنَ ۟

40. Verily the Day of sorting out is the time appointed for all of them,-

40. Inna Yawmal-Faṣli mee-qaatuhum ajma'een.

إِنَّ يَوْمَ الْفَصْلِ مِيْقَاتُهُمْ أَجْمَعِيْنَ ۟ۙ

41. The Day when no protector can avail his client in any thing, and no help can they receive,

41. Yawma laa yughnee mawlan 'am-mawlan shay'añw-wa laa hum yunṣaroon.

يَوْمَ لَا يُغْنِيْ مَوْلًى عَنْ مَّوْلًى شَيْئًا وَّلَا هُمْ يُنْصَرُوْنَ ۟ۙ

42. Except such as receive Allah's Mercy: for He is Exalted in Might,

42. Illaa mar-raḥimal-laah; innahoo Huwal-'Azeezur-

إِلَّا مَنْ رَّحِمَ اللّٰهُ ؕ إِنَّهٗ هُوَ الْعَزِيْزُ

Most Merciful.

43. Verily the tree of Zaqqum,-

44. Will be the food of the Sinful,-

45. Like molten brass; it will boil in their insides.

46. Like the boiling of scalding water.

47. (A voice will cry: "Seize you him and drag him into the midst of the Blazing Fire!

48. "Then pour over his head the Chastisement of Boiling Water,

49. "Taste you (this)! Truly were you mighty, full of honour!

50. "Truly this is what you used to doubt!"

51. As to the Righteous (they will be) in a position of Security,

52. Among Gardens and Springs;

53. Dressed in fine silk and in rich brocade, they will face each other;

54. So; and We shall join them to Companions with beautiful, big, and lustrous eyes.

55. There can they call for every kind of fruit in peace and security;

56. Nor will they there taste Death, except the first death; and He will preserve them from the Chastisement of the Blazing Fire,

57. As a Bounty from your Lord! that will be the supreme achievement!

58. Verily, We have made this (Qur'an) easy, in your tongue, in order that they may give heed.

59. So wait you and watch; for they (too) are waiting.

Raheem.   (Section 2)

43. Inna shajarataz-Zaqqoom.

44. Ta'aamul-aseem.

45. Kalmuhli yaghlee filbu-toon.

46. Kaghalyil-hameem.

47. Khuzoohu fa'tiloohu ilaa sawaaa'il-Jaheem.

48. Summa subboo fawqa raåsihee min 'azaabil-hameem.

49. Zuq innaka antal-'azeezul-kareem.

50. Inna haazaa maa kuntum bihee tamtaroon.

51. Innal-muttaqeena fee maqaamin ameen.

52. Fee Jannaatiñw-wa 'uyoon.

53. Yalbasoona min sundusiñw-wa istbraqim-mutaqaabileen.

54. Kazaalika wa zawwajnaa-hum bihoorin 'een.

55. Yad'oona feehaa bikulli faakihatin aamineen.

56. Laa yazooqoona feehal-mawta illal-mawtatal-oolaa wa waqaahum 'azaabal-Jaheem.

57. Fadlam-mir-Rabbik; zaa-lika huwal-fawzul-'azeem.

58. Fa-innamaa yassarnaahu bilisaanika la'allahum yatazak-karoon.

59. Fartaqib innahum murta-qiboon.   (Section 3)

45. Bowing the Knee

In the name of Allah, Most Gracious, Most Merciful.

1. *Ha-Mim.*

2. The revelation of the Book is from Allah the Exalted in Power, Full of Wisdom.

3. Verily in the heavens and the earth, are Signs for those who believe.

4. And in the creation of your-selves and the fact that animals are scattered (through the earth), are Signs for those of assured Faith.

5. And in the alternation of Night and Day, and the fact that Allah sends down Sustenance from the sky, and revives there with the earth after its death, and in the change of the winds,- are Signs for those that are wise.

6. Such are the Signs of Allah, which We rehearse to you in Truth; then in what exposition will they believe after (rejecting) Allah and His Signs?

7. Woe to each sinful dealer in Falsehoods:

8. He hears the Signs of Allah rehearsed to him, yet is obstinate and lofty, as if he had not heard them: then announce to him a Chastisement Grievous!

9. And when he learns something of Our Signs, he takes them in jest: for such there will be a humiliating Penalty.

10. In front of them is Hell: and of no profit to them is anything they may have earned, nor any protectors they may have taken to themselves besides Allah:

Sûrat al-Jâsiyah–45
(Revealed at Makkah)

Bismillaahir Rahmaanir Raheem

1. Haa-Meeem.

2. Tanzeelul-Kitaabi minal-laahil-'Azeezil-Hakeem.

3. Inna fis-samaawaati wal-ardi la-Aayaatil-lilmu'mineen.

4. Wa fee khalqikum wa maa yabussu min daaabbatin Aayaatul-liqawminy-yooqinoon.

5. Wakhtilaafil-layli wanna-haari wa maaa anzalal laahu minas-samaaa'i mir-rizqin fa-ahyaa bihil-arda ba'da mawti-haa wa tasreefir-riyaahi Aayaatul-liqawminy-ya'qiloon.

6. Tilka Aayaatul-laahi nat-loohaa 'alayka bilhaqq, fabi-ayyi hadeesim ba'dal-laahi wa Aayaatihee yu'minoon.

7. Waylul-likulli affaakin aseem.

8. Yasma'u Aayaatil-laahi tutlaa 'alayhi summa yusirru mustakbiran ka-al-lam yasma'-haa fabashshirhu bi'azaabin aleem.

9. Wa izaa 'alima min Aayaatinaa shay'anit-takhaza-haa huzuwaa; ulaaa'ika lahum 'azaabum muheen.

10. Minw-waraaa'ihim Ja-hannamu wa laa yughnee 'anhum maa kasaboo shay'anw-wa laa mat-takhazoo min doonil-laahi awliyaaa'a wa

for them is a tremendous Chastisement.

11. This is (true) Guidance and for those who reject the Signs of their Lord, is a grievous Chastisement of abomination.

12. It is Allah Who has subjected the sea to you, that ships may sail through it by His command, that you may seek of His Bounty, and that you may be grateful.

13. And He has subjected to you, as from Him, all that is in the heavens and on earth: Behold, in that are Signs indeed for those who reflect.

14. Tell those who believe, to forgive those who do not look forward to the Days of Allah: It is for Him to recompense (for good or ill) each People according to what they have earned.

15. If any one does a righteous deed, it ensures to the benefit of his own soul; if he does evil, it works against (his own soul). In the end will you (all) be brought back to your Lord.

16. We did aforetime grant to the Children of Israel the Book, the Power of Command, and Prophethood; We gave them, for Sustenance, things good and pure; and We favoured them above the nations.

17. And We granted them Clear Signs in affairs (of Religion): it was only after knowledge had been granted to them that they fell into schisms, through insolent envy among themselves. Verily thy Lord will judge between them on the Day of Judgment as to those matters in which they set up differences.

18. Then We put you on the (right) Way of Religion:

lahum 'azaabun 'azeem.

11. Haazaa hudañw wallazeena kafaroo bi-Aayaati Rabbihim lahurn 'azaabum mirrijzin aleem.   **(Section 1)**

12. Allaahul-lazee sahkhara lakumul-bahra litajriyal-fulku feehi bi-amrihee wa litabtaghoo min faḍlihee wa la'allakum tashkuroon.

13. Wa sakhkhara lakum maa fis-samaawaati wa maa fil-arḍi jamee'am-minh; inna fee zaalika la-Aayaatil-liqawmiñy-yatafakkaroon.

14. Qul lillazeena aamanoo yaghfiroo lillazeena laa yarjoona ayyaamal-laahi liyajziya qawmam bimaa kaanoo yaksiboon.

15. Man 'amila ṣaaliḥan falinafsihee wa man asaaa'a fa'alayhaa ṣumma ilaa Rabbikum turja'oon.

16. Wa laqad aataynaa Baneee Israaa'eelal-Kitaaba walḥukma wan-Nubuwwata wa razaqnaahum minaṭ-ṭayyibaati wa faḍḍalnaahum 'alal-'aalameen.

17. Wa aataynaahum bayyinaatim-minal-amri famakhtalafooo illaa mim ba'di maa jaaa'ahumul-'ilmu baghyam baynahum; inna Rabbaka yaqḍee baynahum Yawmal-Qiyaamati feemaa kaanoo feehi yakhtalifoon.

18. Summa ja'alnaaka 'alaa sharee'atim-minal-amri

so follow you that (Way), and follow not the desires of those who know not.

19. They will be of no use to you in the sight of Allah: it is only Wrong-doers (that stand as) protectors, one to another: but Allah is the Protector of the Righteous.

20. These are clear evidences to men and a Guidance and Mercy to those of assured Faith.

21. What! Do those who seek after evil ways think that We shall hold them equal with those who believe and do righteous deeds,- that equal will be their life and their death? Ill is the judgment that they make.

22. Allah created the heavens and the earth for just ends, and in order that each soul may find the recompense of what it has earned, and none of them be wronged.

23. Do you see such a one as takes as his god his own vain desire? Allah has, knowing (him as such), left him astray, and sealed his hearing and his heart (and understanding), and put a cover on his sight. Who, then, will guide him after Allah (has withdrawn Guidance)? Will you not then receive admonition?

24. And they say: "What is there but our life in this world? We shall die and we live, and nothing but time can destroy us." But of that they have no knowledge: they merely conjecture:

25. And when Our Clear Signs are rehearsed to them their argument is nothing but this:

---

fattabi'haa wa laa tattabi' ahwaaa'al-lazeena laa ya'lamoon.

19. Innahum lañy-yughnoo 'anka minal-laahi shay'aa; wa innaz-zaalimeena ba'duhum awliyaaa'u ba'diñw wallaahu waliyyul-muttaqeen.

20. Haazaa basaaa'iru linnaasi wa hudañw-wa rahmatulliqawmiñy-yooqinoon.

21. Am hasibal-lazeenaj tarahus-sayyi-aati an naj'alahum kallazeena aamanoo wa 'amilus-saalihaati sawaaa'am mahyaahum wa mamaatuhum; saaa'a maa yahkumoon.

(Section 2)

22. Wa khalaqal-laahus-samaawaati wal-arda bilhaqqi wa litujzaa kullu nafsim bimaa kasabat wa hum laa yuzlamoon.

23. Afara'ayta manit-takhaza ilaahahoo hawaahu wa adallahul-laahu 'alaa 'ilmiñw-wa khatama 'alaa sam'ihee wa qalbihee wa ja'ala 'alaa basarihee ghishaawatan famañy-yahdeehi mim ba'dil-laah; afalaa tazakkaroon.

24. Wa qaaloo maa hiya illaa hayaatunad-dunyaa namootu wa nahyaa wa maa yuhlikunaaa illad-dahr; wa maa lahum bizaalika min 'ilmin in hum illaa yazunnoon.

25. Wa izaa tutlaa 'alayhim Aayaatunaa bayyinaatim-maa kaana hujjatahum illaaa an

---

فَاتَّبِعْهَا وَلَا تَتَّبِعْ أَهْوَآءَ الَّذِينَ لَا يَعْلَمُونَ ۝

إِنَّهُمْ لَنْ يُّغْنُوا عَنكَ مِنَ اللّٰهِ شَيْـًٔا ۚ وَإِنَّ الظّٰلِمِينَ بَعْضُهُمْ أَوْلِيَآءُ بَعْضٍ ۚ وَاللّٰهُ وَلِيُّ الْمُتَّقِينَ ۝

هٰذَا بَصَآئِرُ لِلنَّاسِ وَهُدًى وَّرَحْمَةٌ لِّقَوْمٍ يُّوقِنُونَ ۝

أَمْ حَسِبَ الَّذِينَ اجْتَرَحُوا السَّيِّاٰتِ أَن نَّجْعَلَهُمْ كَالَّذِينَ اٰمَنُوا وَعَمِلُوا الصّٰلِحٰتِ سَوَآءً مَّحْيَاهُمْ وَمَمَاتُهُمْ ۚ سَآءَ مَا يَحْكُمُونَ ۝

وَخَلَقَ اللّٰهُ السَّمٰوٰتِ وَالْأَرْضَ بِالْحَقِّ وَلِتُجْزَىٰ كُلُّ نَفْسٍ بِمَا كَسَبَتْ وَهُمْ لَا يُظْلَمُونَ ۝

أَفَرَءَيْتَ مَنِ اتَّخَذَ إِلٰهَهُ هَوٰهُ وَأَضَلَّهُ اللّٰهُ عَلَىٰ عِلْمٍ وَّخَتَمَ عَلَىٰ سَمْعِهِ وَقَلْبِهِ وَجَعَلَ عَلَىٰ بَصَرِهِ غِشٰوَةً ۖ فَمَنْ يَّهْدِيهِ مِنْ بَعْدِ اللّٰهِ ۚ أَفَلَا تَذَكَّرُونَ ۝

وَقَالُوا مَا هِيَ إِلَّا حَيَاتُنَا الدُّنْيَا نَمُوتُ وَنَحْيَا وَمَا يُهْلِكُنَا إِلَّا الدَّهْرُ ۚ وَمَا لَهُم بِذٰلِكَ مِنْ عِلْمٍ ۖ إِنْ هُمْ إِلَّا يَظُنُّونَ ۝

وَإِذَا تُتْلَىٰ عَلَيْهِمْ اٰيَاتُنَا بَيِّنَاتٍ مَّا كَانَ حُجَّتَهُمْ إِلَّا أَن

they say, "Bring (back) our forefathers, if what you say is true!"

26. Say: "It is Allah Who gives you life, then gives you death; then He will gather you together for the Day of Judgment about which there is no doubt": But most men do not understand.

27. To Allah belongs the dominion of the heavens and the earth, and the Day that the Hour of Judgment is established,- that Day will the dealers in Falsehood perish!

28. And you will see every nation bowing the knee: Every nation will be called to its Record: "This Day shall you be recompensed for all that you did!

29. "This Our Record speaks about you with truth: For We were wont to put on Record all that you did."

30. Then, as to those who believed and did righteous deeds, their Lord will admit them to His Mercy that will be the achievement for all to see.

31. But as to those who rejected Allah, (to them will be said): "Were not Our Signs rehearsed to you? But you were arrogant, and were a people given to sin!

32. "And when it was said that the promise of Allah was true, and that the Hour- there was no doubt about its (coming), you used to say, 'We know not what is the Hour: we only think it is an idea, and we have no firm assurance.'"

33. Then will appear to them the evil (fruits) of what they did, and they will be completely encircled

qaalu'-too bi-aabaaa'inaaa in kuntum ṣaadiqeen.

26. Qulil-laahu yuḥyeekum summa yumeetukum summa yajma'ukum ilaa Yawmil-Qiyaamati laa rayba feehi wa laakinna akṣaran-naasi laa ya'lamoon. **(Section 3)**

27. Wa lillaahi mulkus samaa-waati wal-arḍ; wa Yawma taqoomus-Saa'atu Yawma'iziñy-yakhsarul-mubṭiloon.

28. Wa taraa kulla ummatin jaasiyah; kullu ummatin tud'aaa ilaa kitaabihaa al-Yawma tuj-zawna maa kuntum ta'maloon.

29. Haazaa kitaabunaa yanṭi-qu 'alaykum bilḥaqq; innaa kunnaa nastansikhu maa kuntum ta'maloon.

30. Fa-ammal-lazeena aama-noo wa 'amiluṣ-ṣaaliḥaati fa-yudkhiluhum Rabbuhum fee raḥmatih; zaalika huwal-fawzul-mubeen.

31. Wa ammal-lazeena kafa-rooo afalam takun Aayaatee tutlaa 'alaykum fastakbartum wa kuntum qawmam-mujri-meen.

32. Wa izaa qeela inna wa'dal-laahi ḥaqquñw-was-Saa'atu laa rayba feehaa qultum maa nadree mas-Saa'atu in naẓunnu illaa ẓannañw-wa maa naḥnu bimustayqineen.

33. Wa badaa lahum sayyi-aatu maa 'amiloo wa ḥaaqa

by that which they used to mock at!

34. It will also be said: "This Day We will forget you as you forgot the meeting of this Day of yours! and your abode is the Fire, and no helpers have you!

35. "This, because you used to take the Signs of Allah in jest, and the life of the world deceived you:" (From) that Day, therefore, they shall not be taken out thence, nor shall they be received into Grace.

36. Then Praise be to Allah, Lord of the heavens and Lord of the earth,- Lord and Cherisher of all the Worlds!

37. To Him be glory throughout the heavens and the earth: and He is Exalted in Power, Full of Wisdom!

46. Winding Sand-tracts
In the name of Allah, Most Gracious, Most Merciful.

1. *Ha-Mim.*

2. The Revelation of the Book is from Allah the Exalted in Power, Full of Wisdom.

3. We created not the heavens and the earth and all between them but for just ends, and for a Term Appointed. But those who reject Faith turn away from that whereof they are warned.

4. Say: "Do you see what it is you invoke besides Allah? Show me what it is they have created on earth, or have they a share in the heavens, bring me a book (revealed) before this, or any remnant of knowledge (you may have), if you are telling the truth!

---

bihim maa kaanoo bihee yastahzi'oon.

34. Wa qeelal-Yawma nansaakum kamaa naseetum liqaaa'a Yawmikum haazaa wa maåwaakumun-Naaru wa maa lakum min naaṣireen.

35. Zaalikum bi-annakumuttakhaztum Aayaatil-laahi huzuwañw-wa gharratkumulḥayaatud-dunyaa; fal-Yawma laa yukhrajoona minhaa wa laa hum yusta‘taboon.

36. Falillaahil-ḥamdu Rabbissamaawaati wa Rabbil-arḍi Rabbil-‘aalameen.

37. Wa lahul-kibriyaaa'u fissamaawaati wal-arḍi wa Huwal-‘Azeezul-Ḥakeem.
(Section 4)

Sûrat al-Aḥqâf–46
(Revealed at Makkah)
Bismillaahir Raḥmaanir Raḥeem

1. Ḥaa-Meeem.

2. Tanzeelul-Kitaabi minallaahil-‘Azeezil-Ḥakeem.

3. Maa khalaqnas-samaawaati wal-arḍa wa maa baynahumaaa illaa bilḥaqqi wa ajalim-musammaa; wallazeena kafaroo ‘ammaaa unziroo mu‘riḍoon.

4. Qul ara'aytum maa tad‘oona min doonil-laahi aroonee maazaa khalaqoo minal-arḍi am lahum shirkun fis-samaawaati eetoonee biKitaabim-min qabli haazaaa aw aṣaaratim min ‘ilmin in kuntum ṣaadiqeen.

5. And who is more astray than one who invokes besides Allah, such as will not answer him to the Day of Judgment, and who (in fact) are unconscious of their call (to them)?

6. And when mankind are gathered together (at the Resurrection), they will be hostile to them and reject their worship (altogether)!

7. When Our Clear Signs are rehearsed to them, the Unbelievers say, of the Truth when it comes to them: "This is evident sorcery!"

8. Or do they say, "He has forged it"? Say: "Had I forged it, then you will not at all be able to save me from the wrath of Allah. He knows best of that whereof you talk (so glibly)! Enough is He for a witness between me and you! And He is Oft-Forgiving, Most Merciful."

9. Say: "I am no bringer of new-fangled doctrine among the apostles, nor do I know what will be done with me or with you. I follow but that which is revealed to me by inspiration; I am but a Warner open and clear."

10. Say: "See you? If (this teaching) be from Allah, and you reject it, and a witness from among the Children of Israel testifies to its similarity (with earlier scripture), and has believed while you are arrogant, (how unjust you are!) truly, Allah guides not a people unjust."

11. The Unbelievers say of those who believe: "If (this Message) were a good thing, (such men) would not have gone to it first, before us!" And seeing that they guide not themselves thereby, they will say,

---

5. Wa man aḍallu mimmañy-yad‘oo min doonil-laahi mallaa yastajeebu lahooo ilaa Yawmil-Qiyaamati wa hum ‘an du‘aaa’i-him ghaafiloon.

6. Wa izaa ḥushiran-naasu kaanoo lahum a‘daaa’añw-wa kaanoo bi‘ibaadatihim kaafi-reen.

7. Wa izaa tutlaa ‘alayhim Aayaatunaa bayyinaatin qaalal-lazeena kafaroo lilḥaqqi lam-maa jaaa’ahum haazaa siḥrum-mubeen.

8. Am yaqooloonaf-taraahu qul inif-taraytuhoo falaa tamlikoona lee minal-laahi shay’an Huwa a‘lamu bimaa tufeeḍoona feehi kafaa bihee shaheedam baynee wa baynakum wa Huwal-Ghafoorur-Raḥeem.

9. Qul maa kuntu bid‘am-minar-Rusuli wa maaa adree maa yuf‘alu bee wa laa bikum in attabi‘u illaa maa yooḥaaa ilayya wa maaa ana illaa nazeerum-mubeen.

10. Qul ara’aytum in kaana min ‘indil-laahi wa kafartum bihee wa shahida shaahidum-mim-Baneee Israaa’eela ‘alaa mislihee fa-aamana wastak-bartum innal-laaha laa yahdil-qawmaz-zaalimeen. (Section 1)

11. Wa qaalal-lazeena kafa-roo lillazeena aamanoo law kaana khayram-maa sabaqoo-naaa ilayh; wa iz lam yahtadoo bihee fasa-yaqooloona

---

"this is an (old,) falsehood!"

12. And before this, was the Book of Moses as a guide and a mercy: And this Book confirms (it) in the Arabic tongue; to admonish the unjust, and as glad tidings to those who do right.

13. Verily those who say, "Our Lord is Allah," and remain firm (on that Path),- on them shall be no fear, nor shall they grieve.

14. Such shall be Companions of the Gardens, dwelling therein (for ever): a recompense for their (good) deeds.

15. We have enjoined on man kindness to his parents: In pain did his mother bear him, and in pain did she give him birth. The carrying of the (child) to his weaning is (a period of) thirty months. At length, when he reaches the age of full strength and attains forty years, he says, "O my Lord! Grant me that I may be grateful for Your favour which You has bestowed upon me, and upon both my parents, and that I may work righteousness such as You may approve; and be gracious to me in my issue. Truly have I turned to You and truly do I bow (to You) in Islam."

16. Such are they from whom We shall accept the best of their deeds and pass by their ill deeds: (They shall be) among the Companions of the Garden: a promise! of truth, which was made to them (in this life).

17. But (there is one) who says to his parents, "Fie on you! Do you hold out the promise to me that I shall be raised up,

haazaaa ifkun qadeem.

12. Wa min qablihee Kitaabu Moosaaa imaamanw-wa rahmah; wa haazaa Kitaabum-musaddiqul-lisaanan 'Arabiyyalliyunzical-lazeena zalamoo wa bushraa lilmuhsineen.

13. Innal-lazeena qaaloo Rabbunal-laahu summas-taqaamoo falaa khawfun 'alayhim wa laa hum yahzanoon.

14. Ulaaa'ika Aṣḥaabul-Jannati khaalideena feehaa jazaaa'am bimaa kaanoo ya'maloon.

15. Wa waṣṣaynal-insaana biwaalidayhi iḥsaanan ḥamalathu ummuhoo kurhaṅw-wa waḍa-'at-hu kurhaṅw wa ḥamluhoo wa fiṣaaluhoo salaasoona shahraa; ḥattaaa izaa balagha ashuddahoo wa balagha arba-'eena sanatan qaala Rabbi awzi'neee an ashkura ni'matakal-lateee an'amta 'alayya wa 'alaa waalidayya wa an a'mala ṣaaliḥan tarḍaahu wa aṣliḥ lee fee zurriyyatee innee tubtu ilayka wa innee minal-muslimeen.

16. Ulaaa'ikal-lazeena nataqabbalu 'anhum aḥsana maa 'amiloo wa natajaawazu 'an sayyi-aatihim feee Aṣḥaabil-Jannati wa'daṣ-ṣidqil-lazee kaanoo yoo'adoon.

17. Wallazee qaala liwaalidayhi uffil-lakumaaa ata'i-daanineee an ukhraja wa qad khalatil-

هٰذَآ إِفْكٌ قَدِيمٌ ۝

وَمِنْ قَبْلِهِ كِتٰبُ مُوسٰى إِمَامًا وَّرَحْمَةً ۚ وَهٰذَا كِتٰبٌ مُّصَدِّقٌ لِّسَانًا عَرَبِيًّا لِّيُنْذِرَ الَّذِينَ ظَلَمُوا ۖ وَبُشْرٰى لِلْمُحْسِنِينَ ۝

إِنَّ الَّذِينَ قَالُوا رَبُّنَا اللّٰهُ ثُمَّ اسْتَقَامُوا فَلَا خَوْفٌ عَلَيْهِمْ وَلَا هُمْ يَحْزَنُونَ ۝

أُولٰٓئِكَ أَصْحٰبُ الْجَنَّةِ خٰلِدِينَ فِيهَا ۚ جَزَآءً بِمَا كَانُوا يَعْمَلُونَ ۝

وَوَصَّيْنَا الْإِنْسَانَ بِوَالِدَيْهِ إِحْسَانًا ۖ حَمَلَتْهُ أُمُّهُ كُرْهًا وَّوَضَعَتْهُ كُرْهًا ۖ وَحَمْلُهُ وَفِصٰلُهُ ثَلٰثُونَ شَهْرًا ۚ حَتّٰى إِذَا بَلَغَ أَشُدَّهُ وَبَلَغَ أَرْبَعِينَ سَنَةً ۙ قَالَ رَبِّ أَوْزِعْنِي أَنْ أَشْكُرَ نِعْمَتَكَ الَّتِي أَنْعَمْتَ عَلَيَّ وَعَلٰى وَالِدَيَّ وَأَنْ أَعْمَلَ صَالِحًا تَرْضٰهُ وَأَصْلِحْ لِي فِي ذُرِّيَّتِي ۖ إِنِّي تُبْتُ إِلَيْكَ وَإِنِّي مِنَ الْمُسْلِمِينَ ۝

أُولٰٓئِكَ الَّذِينَ نَتَقَبَّلُ عَنْهُمْ أَحْسَنَ مَا عَمِلُوا وَنَتَجَاوَزُ عَنْ سَيِّئَاتِهِمْ فِي أَصْحٰبِ الْجَنَّةِ ۖ وَعْدَ الصِّدْقِ الَّذِي كَانُوا يُوعَدُونَ ۝

وَالَّذِي قَالَ لِوَالِدَيْهِ أُفٍّ لَّكُمَا أَتَعِدَانِنِي أَنْ أُخْرَجَ وَقَدْ خَلَتِ

even though generations have passed before me (without rising again)?" And they two seek Allah's aid, (and rebuke the son): "Woe to thee! Have faith! for the promise of Allah is true." But he says, "This is nothing but tales of the ancients!"

18. Such are they against whom is proved the sentence among the previous generations of Jinns and men, that have passed away; for they will be (utterly) lost.

19. And to all are (assigned) degrees according to the deeds which they (have done), and in order that (Allah) may recompense their deeds, and no injustice be done to them.

20. And on the Day that the Unbelievers will be placed before the Fire, (It will be said to them): "You received your good things in the life of the world, and you took your pleasure out of them: but today shall you be recompensed with a Chastisement of humiliation: for that you were arrogant on earth without just cause, and that you (ever) transgressed."

21. Mention (Hud) one of 'Ad's (own) brethren: behold, he warned his people about the winding Sand-tracts: but there have been warners before him and after him: "Worship you none other than Allah: Truly I fear for you the Chastisement of a Mighty Day."

22. They said: "Have you come in order to turn us aside from our gods? Then bring upon us the (calamity) with which you dost threaten us, if you are telling the truth?"

23. He said: "The Knowledge (of when it will come) is only with Allah: I proclaim to you the mission on which I have been sent: But I see that you are a people in ignorance!"..

quroonu min qablee wa humaa yastagheesaanil-laaha waylaka aamin inna wa'dal-laahi ḥaqq, fa-yaqoolu maa haazaaa illaaa asaaṭeerul-awwaleen.

18. Ulaaa'ikal-lazeena ḥaqqa 'alayhimul-qawlu feee umamin qad khalat min qablihim minal-jinni wal-insi innahum kaanoo khaasireen.

19. Wa likullin darajaatum mimmaa 'amiloo wa liyuwaf-fiyahum a'maalahum wa hum laa yuẓlamoon.

20. Wa Yawma yu'raḍul-lazeena kafaroo 'alan-Naari aẓhabtum ṭayyibaatikum fee ḥayaatikumud-dunyaa wastam-ta'tum bihaa fal-Yawma tujzawna 'azaabal-hooni bimaa kuntum tastakbiroona fil-arḍi bighayril-ḥaqqi wa bimaa kuntum tafsuqoon. **(Section 2)**

21. Wazkur akhaa 'Aad, iz anzara qawmahoo bil-Aḥqaafi wa qad khalatin-nuzuru mim bayni yadayhi wa min khalfiheee allaa ta'budooo illal-laaha inneee akhaafu 'alaykum 'azaaba Yawmin 'aẓeem.

22. Qaalooo aji'tanaa litaå-fikanaa 'an aalihatinaa faåtinaa bimaa ta'idunaaa in kunta minaṣ-ṣaadiqeen.

23. Qaala innamal-'ilmu 'indal-laahi wa uballighukum maaa ursiltu bihee wa laakin-neee araakum qawman tajha-loon.

القُرُونُ مِن قَبۡلِى وَهُمَا يَسۡتَغِيثٰنِ اللّٰهَ وَيۡلَكَ اٰمِنۡ إِنَّ وَعۡدَ اللّٰهِ حَقٌّ ۖ فَيَقُولُ مَا هٰذَآ إِلَّآ أَسَاطِيرُ الۡأَوَّلِينَ ۝

أُولٰٓئِكَ الَّذِينَ حَقَّ عَلَيۡهِمُ الۡقَوۡلُ فِىۡ أُمَمٍ قَدۡ خَلَتۡ مِن قَبۡلِهِم مِّنَ الۡجِنِّ وَالۡإِنسِ ۚ إِنَّهُمۡ كَانُوۡا خٰسِرِينَ ۝

وَلِكُلٍّ دَرَجٰتٌ مِّمَّا عَمِلُوا ۖ وَلِيُوَفِّيَهُمۡ أَعۡمَالَهُمۡ وَهُمۡ لَا يُظۡلَمُونَ ۝

وَيَوۡمَ يُعۡرَضُ الَّذِينَ كَفَرُوا عَلَى النَّارِ ۖ أَذۡهَبۡتُمۡ طَيِّبٰتِكُمۡ فِىۡ حَيَاتِكُمُ الدُّنۡيَا وَاسۡتَمۡتَعۡتُم بِهَا ۖ فَالۡيَوۡمَ تُجۡزَوۡنَ عَذَابَ الۡهُونِ بِمَا كُنتُمۡ تَسۡتَكۡبِرُونَ فِى الۡأَرۡضِ بِغَيۡرِ الۡحَقِّ وَبِمَا كُنتُمۡ تَفۡسُقُونَ ۝

وَاذۡكُرۡ أَخَا عَادٍ إِذۡ أَنذَرَ قَوۡمَهُ بِالۡأَحۡقَافِ وَقَدۡ خَلَتِ النُّذُرُ مِنۢ بَيۡنِ يَدَيۡهِ وَمِنۡ خَلۡفِهِ أَلَّا تَعۡبُدُوٓا إِلَّا اللّٰهَ ۖ إِنِّىۡ أَخَافُ عَلَيۡكُمۡ عَذَابَ يَوۡمٍ عَظِيمٍ ۝

قَالُوٓا أَجِئۡتَنَا لِتَأۡفِكَنَا عَنۡ اٰلِهَتِنَا فَأۡتِنَا بِمَا تَعِدُنَآ إِن كُنتَ مِنَ الصّٰدِقِينَ ۝

قَالَ إِنَّمَا الۡعِلۡمُ عِندَ اللّٰهِ وَأُبَلِّغُكُم مَّآ أُرۡسِلۡتُ بِهِ وَلٰكِنِّىٓ أَرٰىكُمۡ قَوۡمًا تَجۡهَلُونَ ۝

24. Then, when they saw a cloud advancing towards their valleys, they said, "This cloud will give us rain!" "No, it is the (Calamity) you were asking to be hastened, a wind wherein is a grievous Chastisement

25. "Everything will it destroy by the command of its Lord!" Then by the morning nothing was to be seen but (the ruins of) their houses! Thus do We recompense those given to sin!

26. And We had firmly established them in a (prosperity and) power which We have not given to you (you Quraish!) and We had endowed them with (faculties of) hearing, seeing, heart and intellect: but of no profit to them were their (faculties of) hearing, sight, and heart and intellect, when they went on rejecting the Signs of Allah; and they were (completely) encircled by that which they used to mock at!

27. We destroyed aforetime populations round about you; and We have shown the Signs in various ways, that they may turn (to Us).

28. Why then was no help forthcoming to them from those whom they worshipped as gods, besides Allah, as a means of access (to Allah)? No, they left them in the lurch: but that was their falsehood and their invention.

29. Behold, We turned towards you a company of Jinns (quietly) listening to the Qur'an: when they stood in the presence thereof, they said, "Listen in silence!" When the (reading) was finished, they returned to their people, to warn (them of their sins).

30. They said, "O our people! We have heard a Book revealed after Moses, confirming

24. Falammaa ra-awhu 'aari-ḍam-mustaqbila awdiyatihim qaaloo haazaa 'aariḍum-mumṭirunaa; bal huwa masta'jaltum bihee reeḥun feehaa 'azaabun aleem.

25. Tudammiru kulla shay'im bi-amri Rabbihaa fa-aṣbaḥoo laa yuraaa illaa masaakinuhum; kazaalika najzil-qawmal-mujri-meen.

26. Wa laqad makkannaahum feemaaa im-makkannaakum feehi wa ja'alnaa lahum sam'añw-wa abṣaarañw-wa af'idatan famaaa aghnaa 'anhum sam'u-hum wa laaa abṣaaruhum wa laaa af'idatuhum min shay'in iz kaanoo yajḥadoona bi-Aayaatil-laahi wa ḥaaqa bihim maa kaanoo bihee yastahzi'oon.
(Section 3)

27. Wa laqad ahlaknaa maa ḥawlakum minal-quraa wa ṣarrafnal-Aayaati la'allahum yarji'oon.

28. Falaw laa naṣarahumul-lazeenat-takhazoo min doonil-laahi qurbaanan aalihatam bal ḍalloo 'anhum; wa zaalika ifkuhum wa maa kaanoo yaftaroon.

29. Wa iz ṣarafnaaa ilayka nafaram-minal-jinni yastami'oo-nal-Qur-aana falammaa ḥaḍaroo-hu qaalooo anṣitoo falammaa quḍiya wallaw ilaa qawmihim munzireen.

30. Qaaloo yaa qawmanaaa innaa sami'naa Kitaaban unzila mim ba'di Moosaa muṣaddiqal-

what came before it: it guides (men) to the Truth and to a Straight Path.

31. "O our people, hearken to the one who invites (you) to Allah, and believe in him: He will forgive you your faults, and deliver you from a Chastisement Grievous.

32. "If any does not hearken to the one who invites (us) to Allah, he cannot frustrate (Allah's Plan) on earth, and no protectors can he have besides Allah: such men (wander) in manifest error."

33. See they not that Allah, Who created the heavens and the earth, and never wearied with their creation, is able to give life to the dead? Yes, verily He has power over all things.

34. And on the Day that the Unbelievers will be placed before the Fire, (they will be asked,) "Is this not the Truth?" they will say, "Yes, by our Lord!" (One will say:) "Then taste you the Chastisement, for that you were wont to deny (Truth)!"

35. Therefore patiently persevere, as did (all) apostles of inflexible purpose; and be in no haste about the (Unbelievers). On the Day that they see the (Punishment) promised them, (it will be) as if they had not tarried more than an hour in a single day. (Your but) to proclaim the Message: but shall any be destroyed except those who transgress?

47. (The Prophet) Muhammad
In the name of Allah, Most Gracious, Most Merciful.

1. Those who reject Allah and hinder (men) from the Path

limaa bayna yadayhi yahdeee ilal-ḥaqqi wa ilaa Ṭareeqim-Mustaqeem.

31. Yaa qawmanaaa ajeeboo daa'iyal-laahi wa aaminoo bihee yaghfir lakum min zunoobikum wa yujirkum min 'azaabin aleem.

32. Wa mal-laa yujib daa'iyal-laahi falaysa bimu'jizin fil-arḍi wa laysa lahoo min dooniheee awliyaaa'; ulaaa'ika fee ḍalaalimmubeen.

33. Awalam yaraw annal-laahal-lazee khalaqas-samaawaati wal-arḍa wa lam ya'ya bikhal-qihinna biqaadirin 'alaaa añy-yuḥyiyal-mawtaa; balaaa inna-hoo 'alaa kulli shay'in Qadeer.

34. Wa Yawma yu'raḍul-lazeena kafaroo 'alan-Naari alaysa haazaa bil-ḥaqq; qaaloo balaa wa Rabbinaa; qaala fazooqul-'azaaba bimaa kuntum takfuroon.

35. Faṣbir kamaa ṣabara ulul-'azmi minar-Rusuli wa laa tasta'jil-lahum; ka-annahum Yawma yarawna maa yoo'a-doona lam yalbasooo illaa saa'atam-min nahaar; balaagh; fahal yuhlaku illal-qawmul-faasiqoon.   **(Section 4)**

Sûrat Muhammad–47
(Revealed at Madinah)
Bismillaahir Raḥmaanir Raḥeem

1. Allazeena kafaroo wa ṣaddoo 'an sabeelil-

of Allah,- their deeds will Allah render astray (from their mark).

2. But those who believe and work deeds of righteousness, and believe in the (Revelation) sent down to Muhammad - for it is the Truth from their Lord,- He will remove from them their ills and improve their condition.

3. This because those who reject Allah follow falsehood, while those who believe follow the Truth from their Lord: Thus does Allah set forth for men their lessons by similitudes.

4. Therefore, when you meet the Unbelievers (in fight), smite at their necks; At length, when you have thoroughly subdued them, bind a bond firmly (on them): thereafter (is the time for) either generosity or ransom: Until the war lays down its burdens. Thus (are you commanded): but if it had been Allah's Will, He could certainly have exacted retribution from them (Himself); but (He lets you fight) in order to test you, some with others. But those who are slain in the Way of Allah,- He will never let their deeds be lost.

5. Soon will He guide them and improve their condition,

6. And admit them to the Garden which He has announced for them.

7. O you who believe! If ye will aid (the cause of) Allah, He will aid you, and plant your feet firmly.

8. But those who reject (Allah),- for them is destruction, and (Allah) will render their deeds worthless.

9. That is because they hate the Revelation of Allah; so He has made their deeds fruitless.

10. Do they not travel through the earth, and see

laahi aḍalla a'maalahum.

2. Wallaẓeena aamanoo wa 'amiluṣ-ṣaaliḥaati wa aamanoo bimaa nuzzila 'alaa Muḥam-madiñw-wa huwal-ḥaqqu mir-Rabbihim kaffara 'anhum sayyi-aatihim wa aṣlaḥa baala-hum.

3. Zaalika bi-annal-laẓeena kafarut-taba'ul-baaṭila wa annal-laẓeena aamanut-taba'ul-ḥaqqa mir-Rabbihim; kazaalika yaḍribul-laahu linnaasi amsaa-lahum.

4. Fa-iẓaa laqeetumul-laẓeena kafaroo faḍarbar-riqaab, ḥattaaa iẓaa askhan-tumoohum fashuddul-waṣaaq, fa-immaa mannam ba'du wa immaa fidaaa-an ḥattaa taḍa'al-ḥarbu awzaarahaa; zaalika wa law yashaaa-ul-laahu lantaṣara minhum wa laakil-liyabluwa ba'ḍakum biba'ḍ; wallaẓeena qutiloo fee sabeelil-laahi falañy-yuḍilla a'maalahum.

5. Sa-yahdeehim wa yuṣliḥu baalahum.

6. Wa yudkhiluhumul-Janna-ta 'arrafahaa lahum.

7. Yaaa ayyuhal-laẓeena aamanoo in tanṣurul-laaha yanṣurkum wa yuthabbit aqdaa-makum.

8. Wallaẓeena kafaroo fata'-al-lahum wa aḍalla a'maala-hum.

9. Zaalika bi-annahum kari-hoo maaa anzalal-laahu fa-aḥbaṭa a'maalahum.

10. Afalam yaseeroo fil-arḍi fayanẓuroo

اللهُ أَضَلَّ أَعْمَالَهُمْ ۝

وَالَّذِينَ ءَامَنُوا وَعَمِلُوا الصّٰلِحٰتِ وَءَامَنُوا بِمَا نُزِّلَ عَلَىٰ مُحَمَّدٍ وَهُوَ الْحَقُّ مِنْ رَّبِّهِمْ ۙ كَفَّرَ عَنْهُمْ سَيِّاٰتِهِمْ وَأَصْلَحَ بَالَهُمْ ۝

ذٰلِكَ بِأَنَّ الَّذِينَ كَفَرُوا اتَّبَعُوا الْبَاطِلَ وَأَنَّ الَّذِينَ ءَامَنُوا اتَّبَعُوا الْحَقَّ مِنْ رَّبِّهِمْ ۚ كَذٰلِكَ يَضْرِبُ اللهُ لِلنَّاسِ أَمْثَالَهُمْ ۝

فَإِذَا لَقِيتُمُ الَّذِينَ كَفَرُوا فَضَرْبَ الرِّقَابِ ۖ حَتَّىٰ إِذَا أَثْخَنْتُمُوهُمْ فَشُدُّوا الْوَثَاقَ ۖ فَإِمَّا مَنًّا بَعْدُ وَإِمَّا فِدَاءً ۚ حَتَّىٰ تَضَعَ الْحَرْبُ أَوْزَارَهَا ۚ ذٰلِكَ ۖ وَلَوْ يَشَاءُ اللهُ لَانْتَصَرَ مِنْهُمْ وَلٰكِنْ لِّيَبْلُوَا بَعْضَكُمْ بِبَعْضٍ ۗ وَالَّذِينَ قُتِلُوا فِي سَبِيلِ اللهِ فَلَنْ يُضِلَّ أَعْمَالَهُمْ ۝

سَيَهْدِيهِمْ وَيُصْلِحُ بَالَهُمْ ۝

وَيُدْخِلُهُمُ الْجَنَّةَ عَرَّفَهَا لَهُمْ ۝

يَأَيُّهَا الَّذِينَ ءَامَنُوا إِنْ تَنْصُرُوا اللهَ يَنْصُرْكُمْ وَيُثَبِّتْ أَقْدَامَكُمْ ۝

وَالَّذِينَ كَفَرُوا فَتَعْسًا لَهُمْ وَأَضَلَّ أَعْمَالَهُمْ ۝

ذٰلِكَ بِأَنَّهُمْ كَرِهُوا مَا أَنْزَلَ اللهُ فَأَحْبَطَ أَعْمَالَهُمْ ۝

أَفَلَمْ يَسِيرُوا فِي الْأَرْضِ فَيَنْظُرُوا

what was the End of those before them (who did evil)? Allah brought utter destruction on them, and similar (fates await) those who reject Allah.

11. That is because Allah is the Protector of those who believe, but those who reject Allah have no protector.

12. Verily Allah will admit those who believe and do righteous deeds, to Gardens beneath which rivers flow; while those who reject Allah will enjoy (this world) and eat as cattle eat; and the Fire will be their abode.

13. And how many cities, with more power than your city which has driven you out, have We destroyed (for their sins)? and there was none to aid them.

14. Is then one who is on a clear (Path) from his Lord, no better than one to whom the evil of his conduct seems pleasing, and such as follow their own lusts?

15. (Here is) a description of the Garden which the righteous are promised: in it are rivers of water unstaling; rivers of milk of which the taste never changes; rivers of wine, a joy to those who drink; and rivers of honey pure and clear. In it there are for them all kinds of fruits; and Grace from their Lord. (Can those in such Bliss) be compared to such as shall dwell for ever in the Fire, and be given, to drink, boiling water, so that it cuts up their bowels (to pieces)?

16. And among them are men who listen to you, but in the end, when they go out from thee, they say to those who

kayfa kaana 'aaqibatul-lazeena min qablihim; dammaral-laahu 'alayhim wa lilkaafireena amsaaluhaa.

11. Zaalika bi-annal-laaha mawlal-lazeena aamanoo wa annal-kaafireena laa mawlaa lahum. **(Section 1)**

12. Innal-laaha yudkhilul-lazeena aamanoo wa 'amiluṣ-ṣaaliḥaati Jannaatin tajree min taḥtihal-anhaaru wallazeena kafaroo yatamatta'oona wa yaåkuloona kamaa taåkulul-an'aamu wan-Naaru maswal-lahum.

13. Wa ka-ayyim-min qarya-tin hiya ashaddu quwwatam-min qaryatikal-lateee akhra-jatka ahlaknaahum falaa naaṣira lahum.

14. Afaman kaana 'alaa bayyinatim-mir-Rabbihee kaman zuyyina lahoo sooo'u 'amalihee wattaba'ooo ah-waaa'ahum.

15. Maṣalul-Jannatil-latee wu'idal-muttaqoona feehaaa anhaarum-mim-maaa'in ghayri aasiniñw wa anhaarum mil-labanil-lam yataghayyar ṭa'mu-hoo wa anhaarum-min khamril-lazzatil-lishshaaribeena wa anhaarum-min 'asalim muṣaf-fañw wa lahum feehaa min kulliṣ-ṣamaraati wa maghfi-ratum-mir-Rabbihim kaman huwa khaalidun fin-Naari wa suqoo maaa'an ḥameeman faqaṭṭa'a am'aaa'ahum.

16. Wa minhum mañy-yasta-mi'u ilayka ḥattaaa izaa kharajoo min 'indika qaaloo lilla-zeena

كَيْفَ كَانَ عَاقِبَةُ الَّذِيْنَ مِنْ قَبْلِهِمْ ۗ دَمَّرَ اللّٰهُ عَلَيْهِمْ ۖ وَلِلْكٰفِرِيْنَ اَمْثَالُهَا ۞

ذٰلِكَ بِاَنَّ اللّٰهَ مَوْلَى الَّذِيْنَ اٰمَنُوْا وَاَنَّ الْكٰفِرِيْنَ لَا مَوْلٰى لَهُمْ ۞

اِنَّ اللّٰهَ يُدْخِلُ الَّذِيْنَ اٰمَنُوْا وَعَمِلُوا الصّٰلِحٰتِ جَنّٰتٍ تَجْرِيْ مِنْ تَحْتِهَا الْاَنْهٰرُ ۗ وَالَّذِيْنَ كَفَرُوْا يَتَمَتَّعُوْنَ وَيَأْكُلُوْنَ كَمَا تَأْكُلُ الْاَنْعَامُ وَالنَّارُ مَثْوًى لَّهُمْ ۞

وَكَاَيِّنْ مِّنْ قَرْيَةٍ هِيَ اَشَدُّ قُوَّةً مِّنْ قَرْيَتِكَ الَّتِيْ اَخْرَجَتْكَ ۚ اَهْلَكْنٰهُمْ فَلَا نَاصِرَ لَهُمْ ۞

اَفَمَنْ كَانَ عَلٰى بَيِّنَةٍ مِّنْ رَّبِّهٖ كَمَنْ زُيِّنَ لَهٗ سُوْٓءُ عَمَلِهٖ وَاتَّبَعُوْٓا اَهْوَآءَهُمْ ۞

مَثَلُ الْجَنَّةِ الَّتِيْ وُعِدَ الْمُتَّقُوْنَ ۗ فِيْهَاۤ اَنْهٰرٌ مِّنْ مَّآءٍ غَيْرِ اٰسِنٍ ۚ وَاَنْهٰرٌ مِّنْ لَّبَنٍ لَّمْ يَتَغَيَّرْ طَعْمُهٗ ۚ وَاَنْهٰرٌ مِّنْ خَمْرٍ لَّذَّةٍ لِّلشّٰرِبِيْنَ ۚ وَاَنْهٰرٌ مِّنْ عَسَلٍ مُّصَفًّى ۗ وَلَهُمْ فِيْهَا مِنْ كُلِّ الثَّمَرٰتِ وَمَغْفِرَةٌ مِّنْ رَّبِّهِمْ ۗ كَمَنْ هُوَ خَالِدٌ فِي النَّارِ وَسُقُوْا مَآءً حَمِيْمًا فَقَطَّعَ اَمْعَآءَهُمْ ۞

وَمِنْهُمْ مَّنْ يَّسْتَمِعُ اِلَيْكَ ۚ حَتّٰى اِذَا خَرَجُوْا مِنْ عِنْدِكَ قَالُوْا لِلَّذِيْنَ

have received Knowledge, "What is it he said just then?" Such are men whose hearts Allah has sealed, and who follow their own lusts.

17. But to those who receive Guidance, He increases the (light of) Guidance, and bestows on them their Piety and Restraint (from evil).

18. Do they then only wait for the Hour,- that it should come on them of a sudden? But already have come some tokens thereof, and when it (actually) is on them, how can they benefit then by their admonition?

19. Know, therefore, that there is no god but Allah, and ask forgiveness for your fault, and for the men and women who believe: for Allah knows how you move about and how you dwell in your homes.

20. Those who believe say, "Why is not a sura sent down (for us)?" But when a sura of basic or categorical meaning is revealed, and fighting is mentioned therein, you will see those in whose hearts is a disease looking at you with a look of one in swoon at the approach of death. But more fitting for them-

21. Were it to obey and say what is just, and when a matter is resolved on, it were best for them if they were true to Allah.

22. Then, is it to be expected of you, if you were put in authority, that you will do mischief in the land, and break your ties of kith and kin?

23. Such are the men whom Allah has cursed for He has made them deaf and blinded their sight.

24. Do they not then earnestly seek to understand the Qur'an, Or are their

ootul-'ilma maazaa qaala aanifaa; ulaaa'ikal-lazeena ṭaba'al-laahu 'alaa quloobihim wattaba'ooo ahwaaa'ahum.

17. Wallazeenah-tadaw zaadahum hudañw-wa aataahum taqwaahum.

18. Fahal yanzuroona illas-Saa'ata an taátiyahum baghtatan faqad jaaa'a ashraaṭuhaa; fa-annaa lahum izaa jaaa'at-hum zikraahum.

19. Fa'lam annahoo laaa ilaaha illal-laahu wastaghfir lizambika wa lilmu'mineena walmu'minaat; wallaahu ya'lamu mutaqallabakum wa maswaakum.
(Section 2)

20. Wa yaqoolul-lazeena aamanoo law laa nuzzilat Sooratun fa-izaaa unzilat Sooratum-Muḥkamatuñw-wa zukira feehal-qitaalu ra-aytal-lazeena fee quloobihim maraḍuñy-yanzuroona ilayka nazaral-maghshiyyi 'alayhi minal-mawti fa-awlaa lahum.

21. Ṭaa'atuñw-wa qawlumma'roof; fa-izaa 'azamal-amru falaw ṣadaqul-laaha lakaana khayral-lahum.

22. Fahal 'asaytum in tawallaytum an tufsidoo fil-arḍi wa tuqaṭṭi'ooo arḥaamakum.

23. Ulaaa'ikal-lazeena la'anahumul-laahu fa-aṣammahum wa a'maaa abṣaarahum.

24. Afalaa yatadabbaroonal-Qur-aana am 'alaa

hearts locked up by them?

25. Those who turn back as apostates after Guidance was clearly shown to them,- the Evil One has instigated them and buoyed them up with false hopes.

26. This, because they said to those who hate what Allah has revealed, "We will obey you in part of (this) matter"; but Allah knows their (inner) secrets.

27. But how (will it be) when the angels take their souls at death, and smite their faces and their backs?

28. This because they followed that which called forth the Wrath of Allah, and they hated Allah's good pleasure; so He made their deeds of no effect.

29. Or do those in whose hearts is a disease, think that Allah will not bring to light all their rancour?

30. Had We so willed, We could have shown them up to you, and you should have known them by their marks: but surely you will know them by the tone of their speech! And Allah knows all that you do.

31. And We shall try you until We test those among you who strive their utmost and persevere in patience; and We shall try your reported (mettle).

32. Those who reject Allah, hinder (men) from the Path of Allah, and resist the Apostle, after Guidance has been clearly shown to them, will not injure Allah in the least, but He will make their deeds of no effect.

33. O you who believe! Obey Allah, and

---

quloobin aqfaaluhaa.

25. Innal-lazeenar-taddoo 'alaaa adbaarihim mim ba'di maa tabayyana lahumul-hudash-Shayṭaanu sawwala lahum wa amlaa lahum.

26. Zaalika bi-annahum qaaloo lillazeena karihoo maa nazzalal-laahu sanuṭee'ukum fee ba'ḍil-amri wallaahu ya'lamu israarahum.

27. Fakayfa izaa tawaffat-humul-malaaa'ikatu yaḍri-boona wujoohahum wa adbaa-rahum.

28. Zaalika bi-annahumut taba'oo maaa askhaṭal-laaha wa karihoo riḍwaanahoo fa-aḥbaṭa a'maalahum. (Section 3)

29. Am ḥasibal-lazeena fee quloobihim maraḍun al-lan yukhrijal-laahu aḍghaanahum.

30. Wa law nashaaa'u la-aray-naakahum fala-'araftahum bi-seemaahum; wa lata'rifan-nahum fee laḥnil-qawl; wallaahu ya'lamu a'maalakum.

31. Wa lanabluwannakum ḥattaa na'lamal-mujaahideena minkum waṣṣaabireena wa nabluwa akhbaarakum.

32. Innal-lazeena kafaroo wa ṣaddoo 'an sabeelil-laahi wa shaaaqqur-Rasoola mim ba'di maa tabayyana lahumul-hudaa lañy-yaḍurrul-laaha shay'añw wa sa-yuḥbiṭu a'maalahum.

33. Yaaa ayyuhal-lazeena aamanooo aṭee'ul-laaha

قُلُوْبٌ اَقْفَالُهَا ۞

اِنَّ الَّذِيْنَ ارْتَدُّوْا عَلٰٓى اَدْبَارِهِمْ مِّنْ بَعْدِ مَا تَبَيَّنَ لَهُمُ الْهُدَى الشَّيْطٰنُ سَوَّلَ لَهُمْ ۗ وَاَمْلٰى لَهُمْ ۞

ذٰلِكَ بِاَنَّهُمْ قَالُوْا لِلَّذِيْنَ كَرِهُوْا مَا نَزَّلَ اللّٰهُ سَنُطِيْعُكُمْ فِيْ بَعْضِ الْاَمْرِ ۚ وَاللّٰهُ يَعْلَمُ اِسْرَارَهُمْ ۞

فَكَيْفَ اِذَا تَوَفَّتْهُمُ الْمَلٰٓئِكَةُ يَضْرِبُوْنَ وُجُوْهَهُمْ وَاَدْبَارَهُمْ ۞

ذٰلِكَ بِاَنَّهُمُ اتَّبَعُوْا مَآ اَسْخَطَ اللّٰهَ وَكَرِهُوْا رِضْوَانَهٗ فَاَحْبَطَ اَعْمَالَهُمْ ۞

اَمْ حَسِبَ الَّذِيْنَ فِيْ قُلُوْبِهِمْ مَّرَضٌ اَنْ لَّنْ يُّخْرِجَ اللّٰهُ اَضْغَانَهُمْ ۞

وَلَوْ نَشَآءُ لَاَرَيْنٰكَهُمْ فَلَعَرَفْتَهُمْ بِسِيْمٰهُمْ ۗ وَلَتَعْرِفَنَّهُمْ فِيْ لَحْنِ الْقَوْلِ ۚ وَاللّٰهُ يَعْلَمُ اَعْمَالَكُمْ ۞

وَلَنَبْلُوَنَّكُمْ حَتّٰى نَعْلَمَ الْمُجٰهِدِيْنَ مِنْكُمْ وَالصّٰبِرِيْنَ ۙ وَنَبْلُوَا اَخْبَارَكُمْ ۞

اِنَّ الَّذِيْنَ كَفَرُوْا وَصَدُّوْا عَنْ سَبِيْلِ اللّٰهِ وَشَآقُّوا الرَّسُوْلَ مِنْ بَعْدِ مَا تَبَيَّنَ لَهُمُ الْهُدَى ۙ لَنْ يَّضُرُّوا اللّٰهَ شَيْئًا ۗ وَسَيُحْبِطُ اَعْمَالَهُمْ ۞

يٰٓاَيُّهَا الَّذِيْنَ اٰمَنُوْٓا اَطِيْعُوا اللّٰهَ

obey the apostle, and make not vain your deeds!

34. Those who reject Allah, and hinder (men) from the Path of Allah, then die rejecting Allah,- Allah will not forgive them.

35. Be not weary and faint-hearted, crying for peace, when you should be uppermost: for Allah is with you, and will never put you in loss for your (good) deeds.

36. The life of this world is but play and amusement: and if you believe and guard against Evil, He will grant you your recompense, and will not ask you (to give up) your possessions.

37. If He were to ask you for all of them, and press you, you would covetously withhold, and He would bring out all your ill-feeling.

38. Behold, you are those invited to spend (of your substance) in the Way of Allah: But among you are some that are niggardly. But any who are niggardly are so at the expense of their own souls. But Allah is free of all wants, and it is you that are needy. If you turn back (from the Path), He will substitute in your stead another people; then they would not be like you!

---

48. Victory
In the name of Allah, Most Gracious, Most Merciful.

1. Verily We have granted you a manifest Victory:

2. That Allah may forgive you your faults of the past and those to follow; fulfil His favour to you; and guide you on the Straight Way;

3. And that Allah may help you with powerful help.

---

wa aṭee'ur-Rasoola wa laa tubṭilooo a'maalakum.

34. Innal-lazeena kafaroo wa ṣaddoo 'an sabeelil-laahi ṣumma maatoo wa hum kuffaarun falany-yaghfirallaahu lahum.

35. Falaa tahinoo wa tad'ooo ilas-salmi wa antumul-a'lawna wallaahu ma'akum wa lany-yatirakum a'maalakum.

36. Innamal-ḥayaatud-dunyaa la'ibunw-wa lahw; wa in to'minoo wa tattaqoo yu'tikum ujoorakum wa laa yas'alkum am-waalakum.

37. Iny-yas'alkumoohaa fa-yuḥfikum ṭabkhaloo wa yukhrij aḍghaanakum.

38. Haaa antum haaa'ulaaa'i tud'awna litunfiqoo fee sabee-lillaahi faminkum many-yab-khalu wa many-yabkhal fa-innamaa yabkhalu 'an nafsih; wallaahul-Ghaniyyu wa antu-mul-fuqaraaa'; wa in tatawal-law yastabdil qawman ghayra-kum ṣumma laa yakoonooo amṣaalakum.

(Section 4)

Sûrat al-Fatḥ–48
(Revealed at Madinah)
Bismillaahir Raḥmaanir Raḥeem

1. Innaa fataḥnaa laka Fat-ḥam-Mubeenaa.

2. Liyaghfira lakal-laahu maa taqaddama min zambika wa maa ta-akhkhara wa yutimma ni'matahoo 'alayka wa yahdi-yaka Ṣiraaṭam Mustaqeemaa.

3. Wa yanṣurakal-laahu naṣran 'azeezaa.

4. It is He Who sent down tranquillity into the hearts of the Believers, that they may add faith to their faith;- for to Allah belong the Forces of the heavens and the earth; and Allah is Full of Knowledge and Wisdom;-

4. Huwal-lazeee anzalas-sakeenata fee quloobil-mu'mineena liyazdaadooo eemaanamma'a eemaanihim; wa lillaahi junoodus-samaawaati wal-arḍ; wa kaanal-laahu 'Aleeman Ḥakeemaa.

هُوَ الَّذِىٓ اَنْزَلَ السَّكِيْنَةَ فِىْ قُلُوْبِ الْمُؤْمِنِيْنَ لِيَزْدَادُوْٓا اِيْمَانًا مَّعَ اِيْمَانِهِمْ ۭ وَ لِلّٰهِ جُنُوْدُ السَّمٰوٰتِ وَالْاَرْضِ ۭ وَكَانَ اللّٰهُ عَلِيْمًا حَكِيْمًا ۟

5. That He may admit the men and women who believe, to Gardens beneath which rivers flow, to dwell therein for ever, and remove their ills from them;- and that is, in the sight of Allah, the highest achievement (for man),-

5. Liyudkhilal-mu'mineena walmu'minaati Jannaatin tajree min taḥtihal-anhaaru khaalideena feehaa wa yukaffira 'anhum sayyi-aatihim; wa kaana zaalika 'indal-laahi fawzan 'aẓeemaa.

لِيُدْخِلَ الْمُؤْمِنِيْنَ وَالْمُؤْمِنٰتِ جَنّٰتٍ تَجْرِىْ مِنْ تَحْتِهَا الْاَنْهٰرُ خٰلِدِيْنَ فِيْهَا وَيُكَفِّرَ عَنْهُمْ سَيِّاٰتِهِمْ ۭ وَكَانَ ذٰلِكَ عِنْدَ اللّٰهِ فَوْزًا عَظِيْمًا ۟

6. And that He may punish the Hypocrites, men and women, and the Polytheists, men and women, who imagine an evil opinion of Allah. On them is a round of Evil: the Wrath of Allah is on them: He has cursed them and got Hell ready for them: and evil is it for a destination.

6. Wa yu'azzibal-munaafiqeena walmunaafiqaati walmushrikeena walmushrikaatiẓ-ẓaaanneena billaahi ẓannassaw'; 'alayhim daaa'iratus-saw'i wa ghaḍibal-laahu 'alayhim wa la'anahum wa a'adda lahum Jahannama wa saaa'at maṣeeraa.

وَيُعَذِّبَ الْمُنٰفِقِيْنَ وَالْمُنٰفِقٰتِ وَالْمُشْرِكِيْنَ وَالْمُشْرِكٰتِ الظَّآنِّيْنَ بِاللّٰهِ ظَنَّ السَّوْءِ ۭ عَلَيْهِمْ دَآئِرَةُ السَّوْءِ ۚ وَغَضِبَ اللّٰهُ عَلَيْهِمْ وَلَعَنَهُمْ وَاَعَدَّ لَهُمْ جَهَنَّمَ ۭ وَسَاۗءَتْ مَصِيْرًا ۟

7. For to Allah belong the Forces of the heavens and the earth; and Allah is Exalted in Power, Full of Wisdom.

7. Wa lillaahi junoodus-samaawaati wal-arḍ; wa kaanal-laahu 'Azeezan Ḥakeemaa.

وَلِلّٰهِ جُنُوْدُ السَّمٰوٰتِ وَالْاَرْضِ ۭ وَكَانَ اللّٰهُ عَزِيْزًا حَكِيْمًا ۟

8. We have truly sent you as a witness, as a bringer of Glad Tidings, and as a Warner:

8. Innaaa arsalnaaka shaahidaňw-wa mubashshiraňw-wa nazeeraa.

اِنَّآ اَرْسَلْنٰكَ شَاهِدًا وَّمُبَشِّرًا وَّنَذِيْرًا ۟

9. In order that you (O men) may believe in Allah and His Apostle, that you may assist and honour Him, and celebrate His praise morning and evening.

9. Litu'minoo billaahi wa Rasoolihee wa tu'azziroohu watuwaqqiroohu watusabbiḥoohu bukrataňw-wa aṣeelaa.

لِتُؤْمِنُوْا بِاللّٰهِ وَرَسُوْلِهٖ وَتُعَزِّرُوْهُ وَتُوَقِّرُوْهُ ۭ وَتُسَبِّحُوْهُ بُكْرَةً وَّاَصِيْلًا ۟

10. Verily those who plight their fealty to you do no less than plight their fealty to Allah: the Hand of Allah is over their hands: then any one who violates his oath, does so to the harm of his own soul, and any one who fulfils what he has covenanted with Allah,-

10. Innal-lazeena yubaayi'oonaka innamaa yubaayi'oonal-laaha Yadul-laahi fawqa aydeehim; faman nakaṣa fa-innamaa yankuṣu 'alaa nafsihee wa man awfaa bimaa 'aahada 'alayhul-

اِنَّ الَّذِيْنَ يُبَايِعُوْنَكَ اِنَّمَا يُبَايِعُوْنَ اللّٰهَ ۭ يَدُ اللّٰهِ فَوْقَ اَيْدِيْهِمْ ۚ فَمَنْ نَّكَثَ فَاِنَّمَا يَنْكُثُ عَلٰى نَفْسِهٖ ۚ وَمَنْ اَوْفٰى بِمَا عٰهَدَ عَلَيْهُ

Allah will soon grant him a great Reward.

11. The desert Arabs who lagged behind will say to you: "We were engaged in (looking after) our flocks and herds, and our families: do you then ask forgiveness for us." They say with their tongues what is not in their hearts. Say: "Who then has any power at all (to intervene) on your behalf with Allah, if His Will is to give you some loss or to give you some profit? But Allah is well acquainted with all that you do.

12. "No, you thought that the Apostle and the Believers would never return to their families; this seemed pleasing in your hearts, and you conceived an evil thought, for you are a people lost (in wickedness)."

13. And if any believe not in Allah and His Apostle, We have prepared, for those who reject Allah, a Blazing Fire!

14. To Allah belongs the dominion of the heavens and the earth: He forgives whom He wills, and He punishes whom He wills: but Allah is Oft-Forgiving, Most Merciful.

15. Those who lagged behind (will say), when ye (are free to) march and take booty (in war): "Permit us to follow you." They wish to change Allah's decree: Say: "Not thus will you follow us: Allah has already declared (this) beforehand": then they will say, "But you are jealous of us." No, but little do they understand (such things).

16. Say to the desert Arabs who lagged behind:

laaha fasa-yu'teehi ajran 'azee-maa.   **(Section 1)**

11. Sa-yaqoolu lakal-mukhal-lafoona minal-A'raabi sha-ghalatnaaa amwaalunaa wa ahloonaa fastaghfir lanaa; yaqooloona bi-alsinatihim maa laysa fee quloobihim; qul famañy-yamliku lakum-minal-laahi shay'an in araada bikum darran aw araada bikum naf'aa; bal kaanal-laahu bimaa ta'ma-loona Khabeeraa.

12. Bal zanantum al-lañy-yanqalibar-Rasoolu walmu'mi-noona ilaaa ahleehim abadañw-wa zuyyina zaalika fee quloobikum wa zanantum zannas-saw'i wa kuntum qawmam-booraa.

13. Wa mal-lam yu'mim-billaahi wa Rasoolihee fa-innaaa a'tadnaa lilkaafireena sa'eeraa.

14. Wa lillaahi mulkus samaa-waati wal-ard; yaghfiru limañy-yashaaa'u wa yu'azzibu mañy-yashaaa'; wa kaanal-laahu Ghafoorar-Raheemaa.

15. Sa-yaqoolul-mukhalla-foona izan-talaqtum ilaa maghaanima litaakhuzoohaa zaroonaa nattabi'kum yuree-doona añy-yubaddiloo Kalaamal-laah; qul lan tattabi'oonaa kazaalikum qaalal-laahu min qablu fasa-yaqooloona bal tahsudoonanaa; bal kaanoo laa yafqahoona illaa qaleelaa.

16. Qul lilmukhallafeena minal-A'raabi

"You shall be summoned (to fight) against a people given to vehement war: then shall you fight, or they shall submit. Then if you show obedience, Allah will grant you a goodly reward, but if you turn back as you did before, He will punish you with a grievous Chastisement."

17. No blame is there on the blind, nor is there blame on the lame, nor on one ill (if he joins not the war): But he that obeys Allah and His Apostle,- (Allah) will admit him to Gardens beneath which rivers flow; and he who turns back, (Allah) will punish him with a grievous Chastisement.

18. Allah's Good Pleasure was on the Believers when they swore Fealty to you under the Tree: He knew what was in their hearts, and He sent down Tranquillity to them; and He rewarded them with a speedy Victory;

19. And many gains will they acquire (besides): and Allah is Exalted in Power, Full of Wisdom.

20. Allah has promised you many gains that you shall acquire, and He has given you these beforehand; and He has restrained the hands of men from you; that it may be a Sign for the Believers, and that He may guide you to a Straight Path;

21. And other gains (there are), which are not within your power, but which Allah has compassed and Allah has power over all things.

22. If the Unbelievers should fight you, they would certainly

satud'awna ilaa qawmin ulee baåsin shadeedin tuqaati-loonahum aw yuslimoona fa-in tutee'oo yu'tikumul-laaha ajran ḥasanañw wa in tatawallaw kamaa tawallaytum min qablu yu'azzibkum 'azaaban aleemaa.

17. Laysa 'alal-a'maa ḥara-juñw-wa laa 'alal-a'raji ḥara-juñw-wa laa 'alal-mareeḍi ḥaraj; wa mañy-yuṭi'il-laaha wa Rasoolahoo yudkhilhu Jannaa-tin tajree min taḥtihal-anhaaru wa mañy-yatawalla yu'azzib-hu 'azaaban aleemaa. **(Section 2)**

18. Laqad raḍiyal-laahu 'anil-mu'mineena iz yubaayi'oonaka taḥtash-shajarati fa'alima maa fee quloobihim fa-anzalas-sakeenata 'alayhim wa asaa-bahum fat-ḥan qareebaa.

19. Wa maghaanima kaseera-tañy-yaåkhuzoonahaa; wa kaanal-laahu 'Azeezan Ḥakeemaa.

20. Wa'adakumul-laahu ma-ghaanima kaseeratan taåkhuzoo-nahaa fa'ajjala lakum haazihee wa kaffa aydiyan-naasi 'ankum wa litakoona Aayatal-lilmu'mi-neena wa yahdiyakum Ṣiraaṭam-Mustaqeemaa.

21. Wa ukhraa lam taqdiroo 'alayhaa qad aḥaaṭal-laahu bihaa; wa kaanal-laahu 'alaa kulli shay'in Qadeeraa.

22. Wa law qaatalakumul-lazeena kafaroo la-wallawul-

turn their backs; then would they find neither protector nor helper.

23. (Such has been) the practice (approved) of Allah already in the past: no change will you find in the practice (approved) of Allah.

24. And it is He Who has restrained their hands from you and your hands from them in the midst of Makka, after that He gave you the victory over them. And Allah sees well all that you do.

25. They are the ones who denied Revelation and hindered you from the Sacred Mosque and obstructed the sacrificial animals, detained from reaching their place of sacrifice. Had there not been believing men and believing women whom you did not know that you were trampling down and on whose account a crime would have accrued to you without (your) knowledge, (Allah would have allowed you to force your way, but He held back your hands) that He may admit to His Mercy whom He will. If they had been apart, We should certainly have punished the Unbelievers among them with a grievous Punishment.

26. While the Unbelievers got up in their hearts heat and cant - the heat and cant of ignorance,- Allah sent down His Tranquillity to His Apostle and to the Believers, and made them stick close to the command of self-restraint; and well were they entitled to it and worthy of it. And Allah has full knowledge of all things.

27. Truly did Allah fulfil the vision for His Apostle: you shall enter the Sacred Mosque,

adbaara ṣumma laa yajidoona waliyyaňw-wa laa naṣeeraa.

23. Sunnatal-laahil-latee qad khalat min qablu wa lan tajida lisunnatil-laahi tabdeelaa.

24. Wa Huwal-laẓee kaffa aydiyahum 'ankum wa aydiyakum 'anhum bibaṭni Makkata mim ba'di an aẓfarakum 'alayhim; wa kaanal-laahu bimaa ta'maloona Baṣeeraa.

25. Humul-laẓeena kafaroo wa ṣaddookum 'anil-Masjidil-Ḥaraami walhadya ma'koofan aňy-yablugha maḥillah; wa law laa rijaalum-mu'minoona wa nisaaa'um-mu'minaatul-lam ta'lamoohum an taṭa'oohum fatuṣeebakum minhum ma'ar-ratum bighayri 'ilmin liyud-khilal-laahu fee raḥmatihee maňy-yashaaa'; law tazayyaloo la'azzabnal-laẓeena kafaroo minhum 'aẓaaban aleemaa.

26. Iz ja'alal-laẓeena kafaroo fee quloobihimul-ḥamiyyata ḥamiyyatal-Jaahiliyyati fa-anzalal-laahu sakeenatahoo 'alaa Rasoolihee wa 'alal-mu'mineena wa alzamahum kalimatat-taqwaa wa kaanooo aḥaqqa bihaa wa ahlahaa; wa kaanal-laahu bikulli shay'in 'Aleemaa. **(Section 3)**

27. Laqad ṣadaqal-laahu Rasoolahur-ru'yaa bilḥaqq, latadkhulunnal-Masjidal-Ḥaraama

الْأَدْبَارَ ثُمَّ لَا يَجِدُونَ وَلِيًّا وَلَا نَصِيرًا ۝

سُنَّةَ اللهِ الَّتِي قَدْ خَلَتْ مِنْ قَبْلُ ۖ وَلَنْ تَجِدَ لِسُنَّةِ اللهِ تَبْدِيلًا ۝

وَهُوَ الَّذِي كَفَّ أَيْدِيَهُمْ عَنْكُمْ وَأَيْدِيَكُمْ عَنْهُمْ بِبَطْنِ مَكَّةَ مِنْ بَعْدِ أَنْ أَظْفَرَكُمْ عَلَيْهِمْ ۚ وَكَانَ اللهُ بِمَا تَعْمَلُونَ بَصِيرًا ۝

هُمُ الَّذِينَ كَفَرُوا وَصَدُّوكُمْ عَنِ الْمَسْجِدِ الْحَرَامِ وَالْهَدْيَ مَعْكُوفًا أَنْ يَبْلُغَ مَحِلَّهُ ۚ وَلَوْلَا رِجَالٌ مُؤْمِنُونَ وَنِسَاءٌ مُؤْمِنَاتٌ لَمْ تَعْلَمُوهُمْ أَنْ تَطَئُوهُمْ فَتُصِيبَكُمْ مِنْهُمْ مَعَرَّةٌ بِغَيْرِ عِلْمٍ ۖ لِيُدْخِلَ اللهُ فِي رَحْمَتِهِ مَنْ يَشَاءُ ۚ لَوْ تَزَيَّلُوا لَعَذَّبْنَا الَّذِينَ كَفَرُوا مِنْهُمْ عَذَابًا أَلِيمًا ۝

إِذْ جَعَلَ الَّذِينَ كَفَرُوا فِي قُلُوبِهِمُ الْحَمِيَّةَ حَمِيَّةَ الْجَاهِلِيَّةِ فَأَنْزَلَ اللهُ سَكِينَتَهُ عَلَى رَسُولِهِ وَعَلَى الْمُؤْمِنِينَ وَأَلْزَمَهُمْ كَلِمَةَ التَّقْوَى وَكَانُوا أَحَقَّ بِهَا وَأَهْلَهَا ۚ وَكَانَ اللهُ بِكُلِّ شَيْءٍ عَلِيمًا ۝

لَقَدْ صَدَقَ اللهُ رَسُولَهُ الرُّؤْيَا بِالْحَقِّ ۖ لَتَدْخُلُنَّ الْمَسْجِدَ الْحَرَامَ

if Allah wills, with minds secure, heads shaved, hair cut short, and without fear. For He knew what you knew not, and He granted, besides this, a speedy victory.

28. It is He Who has sent His Apostle with Guidance and the Religion of Truth, to proclaim it over all religion: and enough is Allah for a Witness.

29. Muhammad is the apostle of Allah; and those who are with him are strong against Unbelievers, (but) compassionate amongst each other. you will see them bow and prostrate themselves (in prayer), seeking Grace from Allah and (His) Good Pleasure. On their faces are their marks, (being) the traces of their prostration. This is their similitude in the Taurat; and their similitude in the Gospel is: like a seed which sends forth its blade, then makes it strong; it then becomes thick, and it stands on its own stem, (filling) the sowers with wonder and delight. As a result, it fills the Unbelievers with rage at them. Allah has promised those among them who believe and do righteous deeds forgiveness, and a great Reward.

---

49. The Inner Apartments
In the name of Allah, Most Gracious, Most Merciful.

1. O You who believe! Put not yourselves forward before Allah and His Apostle; but fear Allah: for Allah is He Who hears and knows all things.

2. O you who believe! Raise not your voices above the voice of the Prophet, nor speak aloud to him in talk,

---

in shaaa'al-laahu aamineena muhalliqeena ru'oosakum wa muqaṣṣireena laa takhaafoona fa'alima maa lam ta'lamoo faja'ala min dooni zaalika fat-ḥan qareebaa.

28. Huwal-lazeee arsala Rasoolahoo bilhudaa wa deenil-ḥaqqi liyuẓhirahoo 'alad-deeni kullih; wa kafaa billaahi Shaheedaa.

29. Muhammadur-Rasoolul-laah; wallazeena ma'ahooo ashiddaaa'u 'alal-kuffaari ruḥa-maaa'u baynahum taraahum rukka'an sujjadañy-yabtaghoona faḍlam-minal-laahi wa riḍwaa-nan seemaahum fee wujoohi-him min aṣaris-sujood; zaalika maṣaluhum fit-Tawraah; wa maṣaluhum fil-Injeeli kazar'in akhraja shaṭ-'ahoo fa-'aaza-rahoo fastaghlaẓa fastawaa 'alaa sooqihee yu'jibuz-zurraa'a liyagheeẓa bihimul-kuffaar; wa'adal-laahul-lazeena aamanoo wa 'amiluṣ-ṣaaliḥaati minhum maghfiratañw-wa ajran 'aẓeemaa.   **(Section 4)**

Sûrat al-Ḥujurât–49
(Revealed at Madinah)
Bismillaahir Raḥmaanir Raḥeem

1. Yaa ayyuhal-lazeena aamanoo laa tuqaddimoo bayna yada-yil-laahi wa Rasoolihee wattaqul-laah; innal-laaha Samee'un 'Aleem.

2. Yaaa ayyuhal-lazeena aamanoo laa tarfa'ooo aṣwaa-takum fawqa ṣawtin Nabiyyi wa laa

as you may speak aloud to one another, lest your deeds become vain and you perceive not.

tajharoo lahoo bilqawli kajahri ba'dikum liba'din an taḥbaṭa a'maalukum wa antum laa tash'uroon.

تَجْهَرُوْا لَهٗ بِالْقَوْلِ كَجَهْرِ بَعْضِكُمْ لِبَعْضٍ اَنْ تَحْبَطَ اَعْمَالُكُمْ وَاَنْتُمْ لَا تَشْعُرُوْنَ ۞

3. Those that lower their voices in the presence of Allah's Apostle,- their hearts has Allah tested for piety: for them is Forgiveness and a great Reward.

3. Innal-laẕeena yaghuḍḍoona aṣwaatahum 'inda Rasoolil-laahi ulaaa'ikal-laẕeenam-taḥanal-laahu quloobahum littaqwaa; lahum-maghfiratuñw-wa ajrun 'aẕeem.

اِنَّ الَّذِيْنَ يَغُضُّوْنَ اَصْوَاتَهُمْ عِنْدَ رَسُوْلِ اللّٰهِ اُولٰٓئِكَ الَّذِيْنَ امْتَحَنَ اللّٰهُ قُلُوْبَهُمْ لِلتَّقْوٰى ۙ لَهُمْ مَّغْفِرَةٌ وَّاَجْرٌ عَظِيْمٌ ۞

4. Those who shout out to you from without the inner apartments - most of them lack understanding.

4. Innal-laẕeena yunaadoo-naka miñw-waraaa'il-ḥujuraati aksaruhum laa ya'qiloon.

اِنَّ الَّذِيْنَ يُنَادُوْنَكَ مِنْ وَّرَآءِ الْحُجُرٰتِ اَكْثَرُهُمْ لَا يَعْقِلُوْنَ ۞

5. If only they had patience until you couldst come out to them, it would be best for them: but Allah is Oft-Forgiving, Most Merciful.

5. Wa law annahum ṣabaroo ḥattaa takhruja ilayhim lakaana khayral-lahum; wallaahu Gha-foorur-Raḥeem.

وَلَوْ اَنَّهُمْ صَبَرُوْا حَتّٰى تَخْرُجَ اِلَيْهِمْ لَكَانَ خَيْرًا لَّهُمْ ۚ وَاللّٰهُ غَفُوْرٌ رَّحِيْمٌ ۞

6. O you who believe! If a wicked person comes to you with any news, ascertain the truth, lest you harm people unwittingly, and afterwards become full of repentance for what you have done.

6. Yaaa ayyuhal-laẕeena aamanooo in jaaa'akum faasi-qum binaba-in fatabayyanooo an tuṣeeboo qawmam bija-haalatin fatuṣbiḥoo 'alaa maa fa'altum naadimeen.

يٰٓاَيُّهَا الَّذِيْنَ اٰمَنُوْٓا اِنْ جَآءَكُمْ فَاسِقٌ بِنَبَاٍ فَتَبَيَّنُوْٓا اَنْ تُصِيْبُوْا قَوْمًا بِجَهَالَةٍ فَتُصْبِحُوْا عَلٰى مَا فَعَلْتُمْ نٰدِمِيْنَ ۞

7. And know that among you is Allah's Apostle: were he, in many matters, to follow your (wishes), you would certainly fall into misfortune: But Allah has endeared the Faith to you, and has made it beautiful in your hearts, and He has made hateful to you Unbelief, wickedness, and rebellion: such indeed are those who walk in righteous-ness;-

7. Wa'lamooo anna feekum Rasoolal-laah; law yuṭee'ukum fee kaseerim-minal-amri la'anittum wa laakinnal-laaha ḥabbaba ilaykumul-eemaana wa zayyanahoo fee quloobikum wa karraha ilaykumul-kufra walfusooqa wal'iṣyaan; ulaaa'ika humur-raashidoon.

وَاعْلَمُوْٓا اَنَّ فِيْكُمْ رَسُوْلَ اللّٰهِ ۚ لَوْ يُطِيْعُكُمْ فِيْ كَثِيْرٍ مِّنَ الْاَمْرِ لَعَنِتُّمْ وَلٰكِنَّ اللّٰهَ حَبَّبَ اِلَيْكُمُ الْاِيْمَانَ وَزَيَّنَهٗ فِيْ قُلُوْبِكُمْ وَكَرَّهَ اِلَيْكُمُ الْكُفْرَ وَالْفُسُوْقَ وَالْعِصْيَانَ ۚ اُولٰٓئِكَ هُمُ الرّٰشِدُوْنَ ۞

8. A Grace and Favour from Allah; and Allah is full of Knowledge and Wisdom.

8. Faḍlam-minal-laahi wa ni'mah; wallaahu 'Aleemun Ḥakeem.

فَضْلًا مِّنَ اللّٰهِ وَنِعْمَةً ۚ وَاللّٰهُ عَلِيْمٌ حَكِيْمٌ ۞

9. If two parties among the Believers fall into a quarrel, make you peace between them: but if

9. Wa in ṭaaa'ifataani minal-mu'mineenaq-tataloo fa-aṣliḥoo baynahumaa fa-im-

وَاِنْ طَآئِفَتٰنِ مِنَ الْمُؤْمِنِيْنَ اقْتَتَلُوْا فَاَصْلِحُوْا بَيْنَهُمَا ۚ فَاِنْ

one of them transgresses beyond bounds against the other, then fight you (all) against the one that transgresses until it complies with the command of Allah; But if it complies, then make peace between them with justice, and be fair: For Allah loves those who are fair (and just).

10. The Believers are but a single Brotherhood: So make peace and reconciliation between your two (contending) brothers; and fear Allah, that you may receive Mercy.

11. O you who believe! Let not some men among you laugh at others: It may be that the (latter) are better than the (former): Nor let some women laugh at others: It may be that the (latter are better than the (former): Nor defame nor be sarcastic to each other, nor call each other by (offensive) nicknames: Ill-seeming is a name connoting wickedness, (to be used of one) after he has believed: And those who do not desist are (indeed) doing wrong.

12. O you who believe! Avoid suspicion as much (as possible): for suspicion in some cases is a sin: And spy not on each other behind their backs. Would any of you like to eat the flesh of his dead brother? No, you would abhor it...But fear Allah: For Allah is Oft-Returning, Most Merciful.

13. O mankind! We created you from a single (pair) of a male and a female, and made you into nations and tribes, that you may know each other (not that you may despise (each other). Verily the most honoured of you in the sight of

baghat iḥdaahumaa 'alal-ukhraa faqaatilul-latee tabghee ḥattaa tafeee'a ilaa amril-laah; fa-in faaa'at fa-aṣliḥoo bay-nahumaa bil'adli wa aqsiṭoo innal-laaha yuḥibbul-muq-siṭeen.

10. Innamal-mu'minoona ikhwatun fa-aṣliḥoo bayna akhawaykum wattaqul-laaha la'allakum turḥamoon.

(Section 1)

11. Yaaa ayyuhal-lazeena aamanoo laa yaskhar qawmum min qawmin 'asaaa añy-yakoonoo khayram minhum wa laa nisaaa'um min nisaaa'in 'Asaaa añy-Yakunna khayram-minhunna wa laa talmizooo anfusakum wa laa tanaabazoo bil-alqaab; bi'sal-ismul-fusooqu ba'dal-eemaan; wa mal-lam yatub fa-ulaaa'ika humuz-zaalimoon.

12. Yaaa ayyuhal-lazeena aamanuj-taniboo kaseeram-minaz-zanni inna ba'daz-zanni ismuñw-wa laa tajassasoo wa la yaghtab ba'dukum ba'daa; a yuḥibbu aḥadukum añy-yaäkula laḥma akheehi maytan fakarih-tumooh; wattaqul-laah; innal-laaha Tawwaabur-Raḥeem.

13. Yaaa ayyuhan-naasu innaa khalaqnaakum min zakariñw-wa unṣaa wa ja'alnaakum shu'oobañw-wa qabaaa'ila lita'aarafoo inna akramakum

Allah is (he who Is) the most righteous of you. And Allah has full knowledge and is well acquainted (with all things).

14. The desert Arabs say, "We believe." Say, "You have no faith; but you (only) say, 'We have submitted our wills to Allah,' For not yet has Faith entered your hearts. But if ye obey Allah and His Apostle, He will not belittle any of your deeds: for Allah is Oft-Forgiving, Most Merciful."

15. Only those are Believers who have believed in Allah and His Apostle, and have never since doubted, but have striven with their belongings and their persons in the Cause of Allah: Such are the sincere ones.

16. Say: "What! Will you instruct Allah about your religion? But Allah knows all that is in the heavens and on earth: He has full knowledge of all things.

17. They impress on you as a favour that they have embraced Islam. Say, "Count not your Islam as a favour upon me: No, Allah has conferred a favour upon you that He has guided you to the faith, if you be true and sincere.

18. "Verily Allah knows the secrets of the heavens and the earth: and Allah Sees well all that you do."

50. Qaf
In the name of Allah, Most Gracious, Most Merciful.

1. *Qaf.* By the Glorious Qur'an (Thou art God's Apostle).

2. But they wonder that there has come to them a Warner

'indal-laahi atqaakum innal-laaha 'Aleemun khabeer

14. Qaalatil-A'raabu aamannaa qul lam tu'minoo wa laakin qoolooo aslamnaa wa lamma yadkhulil-eemaanu fee quloobikum wa in tutee'ul-laaha wa Rasoolahoo laa yalitkum min a'maalikum shay'aa; innal-laaha Ghafoorur-Raheem.

15. Innamal-mu'minoonal-lazeena aamanoo billaahi wa Rasoolihee summa lam yartaaboo wa jaahadoo bi-amwaalihim wa anfusihim fee sabeelil-laah; ulaaa'ika humus-saadiqoon.

16. Qul atu'allimoonal-laaha bideenikum wallaahu ya'lamu maa fis-samaawaati wa maa fil-ard; wallaahu bikulli shay'in 'Aleem.

17. Yamunnoona 'alayka an aslamoo qul laa tamunnoo 'alayya Islaamakum balillaahu yamunnu 'alaykum an hadaakum lil-eemaani in kuntum saadiqeen.

18. Innal-laaha ya'lamu ghaybas-samaawaati wal-ard; wallaahu baseerum bimaa ta'maloon.　　(Section 2)

Sûrat Qâf–50
(Revealed at Makkah)
Bismillaahir Rahmaanir Raheem

1. Qaaaf; wal-Qur-aanil-Majeed.

2. Bal 'ajibooo an jaaa'ahum munzirum-

from among themselves. So the Unbelievers say: "This is a wonderful thing

3. "What! When we die and become dust, (shall we live again?) That is a (sort of) return far (from our understanding)."

4. We already know how much of them the earth takes away: With Us is a record guarding (the full account).

5. But they deny the Truth when it comes to them: so they are in a confused state.

6. Do they not look at the sky above them?- How We have made it and adorned it, and there are no flaws in it?

7. And the earth- We have spread it out, and set thereon mountains standing firm, and produced therein every kind of beautiful growth (in pairs)-

8. To be observed and commemorated by every devotee turning (to Allah).

9. And We send down from the sky rain charted with blessing, and We produce therewith gardens and Grain for harvests;

10. And tall (and stately) palm-trees, with shoots of fruit-stalks, piled one over another;-

11. As sustenance for (Allah's) Servants;- and We give (new) life therewith to land that is dead: Thus will be the Resurrection.

12. Before them was denied (the Hereafter) by the People of Noah, the Companions of the Rass, the Thamud,

13. The 'Ad, Pharaoh, the brethren of Lut,

14. The Companions of the Wood, and the People of Tubba'; each one (of them) rejected the apostles, and My warning was duly fulfilled (in them).

---

minhum faqaalal-kaafiroona haazaa shay'un 'ajeeb.

3. 'A-izaa mitnaa wa kunnaa turaaban zaalika raj'um ba'eed.

4. Qad 'alimnaa maa tanqu-sul-ardu minhum wa 'indanaa Kitaabun Ḥafeez.

5. Bal kazzaboo bilḥaqqi lammaa jaaa'ahum fahum feee amrim-mareej.

6. Afalam yanzurooo ilas-samaaa'i fawqahum kayfa banaynaahaa wa zayyannaahaa wa maa lahaa min furooj.

7. Wal-arda madadnaahaa wa alqaynaa feehaa rawaasiya wa ambatnaa feehaa min kulli zawjim baheej.

8. Tabṣirataňw-wa zikraa likulli 'abdim-muneeb.

9. Wa nazzalnaa minas-samaaa'i maaa'am mubaarakan fa-ambatnaa bihee jannaatiňw-wa ḥabbal-ḥaṣeed.

10. Wannakhla baasiqaatil-lahaa ṭal'un-nadeed.

11. Rizqal-lil'ibaad, wa aḥ-yaynaa bihee baldatam-maytaa; kazaalikal-khurooj.

12. Kazzabat qablahum qaw-mu Nooḥiňw-wa Aṣḥaabur-Rassi wa Ṣamood.

13. Wa 'Aaduňw-wa Fir'awnu wa ikhwaanu Looṭ.

14. Wa Aṣḥaabul-Aykati wa qawmu Tubba'; kullun kaz-zabar-Rusula faḥaqqa wa'eed.

15. Were We then weary with the first Creation, that they should be in confused doubt about a new Creation?

16. It was We Who created man, and We know what dark suggestions his soul makes to him: for We are nearer to him than (his) jugular vein.

17. Behold, two (guardian angels) appointed to learn (his doings) learn (and noted them), one sitting on the right and one on the left,

18. Not a word does he utter but there is a sentinel by him, ready (to note it).

19. And the stupor of death will bring Truth (before his eyes): "This was the thing which thou wast trying to escape!"

20. And the Trumpet shall be blown: that will be the Day whereof Warning (had been given).

21. And there will come forth every soul: with each will be an (angel) to drive, and an (angel) to bear witness.

22. (It will be said:) "You were heedless of this; now have We removed your veil, and sharp is your sight this Day!"

23. And his Companion will say: "Here is (his Record) ready with me!"

24. (The sentence will be:) "Throw, both of you into Hell every contumacious Rejecter (of Allah)!-

25. "Who forbade what was good, transgressed all bounds, cast doubts and suspicions;

26. "Who set up another god beside Allah: Throw him into a severe Chastisement."

27. His Companion will say: "Our Lord! I did not make him

15. Afa'a-yeenaa bilkhalqil-awwal; bal hum fee labsim-min khalqin jadeed. (Section 1)

16. Wa laqad khalaqnal-insaana wa na'lamu maa tuwaswisu bihee nafsuhoo wa Naḥnu aqrabu ilayhi min ḥablil-wareed.

17. 'Iz yatalaqqal-mutalaqqi-yaani 'anil-yameeni wa 'anish-shimaali qa'eed.

18. Maa yalfiẓu min qawlin illaa ladayhi raqeebun 'ateed.

19. Wa jaaa'at sakratul-mawti bilḥaqq; zaalika maa kunta minhu taḥeed.

20. Wa nufikha fiṣ-Ṣoor; zaalika yawmul-wa'eed.

21. Wa jaaa'at kullu nafsim-ma'ahaa saaa'iquñw-wa shaheed.

22. Laqad kunta fee ghaf-latim-min haazaa fakashafnaa 'anka ghiṭaaa'aka fabaṣarukal-Yawma ḥadeed.

23. Wa qaala qareenuhoo haazaa maa ladayya 'ateed.

24. Alqiyaa fee Jahannama kulla kaffaarin 'aneed.

25. Mannaa'il-lilkhayri mu'-tadim-mureeb.

26. Allazee ja'ala ma'al-laahi ilaahan aakhara fa-alqiyaahu fil-'azaabish-shadeed.

27. Qaala qareenuhoo Rab-banaa maaa aṭghaytuhoo

transgress, but he was (himself) far astray."

28. He will say: "Dispute not with each other in My Presence: I had already in advance sent you Warning.

29. "The Word changes not before Me, and I do not the least injustice to My Servants."

30. That Day We will ask Hell, "Are you filled to the full?" It will say, "Are there any more (to come)?"

31. And the Garden will be brought near to the Righteous,- no more a thing distant.

32. (A voice will say:) "This is what was promised for you,- for every one who turned (to Allah) in sincere repentance, who kept (His Law),

33. "Who feared (Allah) Most Gracious Unseen, and brought a heart turned in devotion (to Him):

34. "Enter you therein in Peace and Security; this is a Day of Eternal Life!"

35. There will be for them therein all that they wish,- and more besides in Our Presence.

36. But how many generations before them did We destroy (for their sins),- stronger in power than they? Then did they wander through the land: was there any place of escape (for them)?

37. Verily in this is a Message for any that has a heart and understanding or who gives ear and earnestly witnesses (the truth).

38. We created the heavens and the earth and all between them in Six Days, nor did any sense of weariness touch Us.

39. Bear, then, with patience, all that they say, and celebrate the praises of your Lord, before the rising of the sun

wa laakin kaana fee ḍalaalim ba'eed.

28. Qaala laa takhtaṣimoo ladayya wa qad qaddamtu ilaykum bilwa'eed.

29. Maa yubaddalul-qawlu ladayya wa maaa ana biẓal-laamil-lil'abeed. *(Section 2)*

30. Yawma naqoolu li-Jahannama halim-talaâti wa taqoolu hal mim-mazeed.

31. Wa uzlifatil-Jannatu lil-muttaqeena ghayra ba'eed.

32. Haazaa maa too'adoona likulli awwaabin ḥafeeẓ.

33. Man khashiyar-Raḥmaana bilghaybi wa jaaa'a biqalbim-muneeb.

34. Udkhuloohaa bisalaamin zaalika yawmul-khulood.

35. Lahum maa yashaaa'oona feehaa wa ladaynaa mazeed.

36. Wa kam ahlaknaa qabla-hum min qarnin hum ashaddu minhum baṭshan fanaqqaboo fil-bilaad, hal mim-maḥeeṣ.

37. Inna fee zaalika lazikraa liman kaana lahoo qalbun aw alqas-sam'a wa huwa shaheed.

38. Wa laqad khalaqnas-samaawaati wal-arḍa wa maa baynahumaa fee sittati ayyaa-miñw-wa maa massanaa mil-lughoob.

39. Faṣbir 'alaa maa yaqoo-loona wa sabbiḥ biḥamdi Rabbika qabla ṭuloo'ish-shamsi

and before (its) setting.

wa qablal-ghuroob.

وَقَبْلَ الْغُرُوبِ ۩

40. And during part of the night, (also,) celebrate His praises, and (so likewise) after the postures of adoration.

40. Wa minal-layli fasabbiḥ-hu wa adbaaras-sujood.

وَمِنَ الَّيْلِ فَسَبِّحْهُ وَاَدْبَارَ السُّجُودِ ۩

41. And listen for the Day when the Caller will call out from a place quiet near,-

41. Wastami‘ Yawma yunaa-dil-munaadi mim-makaanin qareeb.

وَاسْتَمِعْ يَوْمَ يُنَادِ الْمُنَادِ مِنْ مَّكَانٍ قَرِيبٍ ۩

42. The Day when they will hear a (mighty) Blast in (very) truth: that will be the Day of Resurrection.

42. Yawma yasmaoonaṣ-ṣay-ḥata bilḥaqq; zaalika yawmul-khurooj.

يَوْمَ يَسْمَعُونَ الصَّيْحَةَ بِالْحَقِّ ط ذٰلِكَ يَوْمُ الْخُرُوجِ ۩

43. Verily it is We Who give Life and Death; and to Us is the Final Goal-

43. Innaa Naḥnu nuḥyee wa numeetu wa ilaynal-maṣeer.

اِنَّا نَحْنُ نُحْىٖ وَنُمِيتُ وَاِلَيْنَا الْمَصِيرُ ۩

44. The Day when the Earth will be rent asunder, from (men) hurrying out: that will be a gathering together,- quite easy for Us.

44. Yawma tashaqqaqul-arḍu ‘anhum siraa‘aa; zaalika ḥash-run ‘alaynaa yaseer.

يَوْمَ تَشَقَّقُ الْاَرْضُ عَنْهُمْ سِرَاعًا ط ذٰلِكَ حَشْرٌ عَلَيْنَا يَسِيرٌ ۩

45. We know best what they say; and you are not one to overawe them by force. So admonish with the Qur'an such as fear My Warning!

45. Naḥnu a‘lamu bimaa yaqooloona wa maaa anta ‘alayhim bijabbaarin fazakkir bil-Qur-aani mañy-yakhaafu wa‘eed.   (Section 3)

نَحْنُ اَعْلَمُ بِمَا يَقُولُونَ وَمَا اَنْتَ عَلَيْهِمْ بِجَبَّارٍ فَذَكِّرْ بِالْقُرْاٰنِ مَنْ يَّخَافُ وَعِيدِ ۩

51. The Winds that Scatter
In the name of Allah, Most Gracious, Most Merciful.

Sûrat az-Zâriyât–51
(Revealed at Makkah)
Bismillaahir Raḥmaanir Raḥeem

(٥١) سُورَةُ الذَّارِيٰتِ مَكِّيَّةٌ (٦٠)
بِسْمِ اللهِ الرَّحْمٰنِ الرَّحِيمِ

1. By the (Winds) that scatter broadcast;

1. Waz-zaariyaati zarwaa.

وَالذَّارِيٰتِ ذَرْوًا ۩

2. And those that lift and bear away heavy weights;

2. Falḥaamilaati wiqraa.

فَالْحٰمِلٰتِ وِقْرًا ۩

3. And those that flow with ease and gentleness;

3. Faljaariyaati yusraa.

فَالْجٰرِيٰتِ يُسْرًا ۩

4. And those that distribute and apportion by Command;

4. Falmuqassimaati amraa.

فَالْمُقَسِّمٰتِ اَمْرًا ۩

5. Verily that which you are promised is true;

5. Innamaa too‘adoona la-ṣaadiq.

اِنَّمَا تُوعَدُونَ لَصَادِقٌ ۩

6. And verily Judgment and Justice must indeed come to pass.

6. Wa innad-deena la-waaqi‘:

وَاِنَّ الدِّينَ لَوَاقِعٌ ط ۩

7. By the Sky with (its) numerous Paths,

7. Wassamaaa'i zaatil-ḥu-buk.

وَالسَّمَاءِ ذَاتِ الْحُبُكِ ۩

8. Truly you are in a doctrine discordant,

8. Innakum lafee qawlim-mukhtalif.

اِنَّكُمْ لَفِى قَوْلٍ مُّخْتَلِفٍ ۩

9. Through which are deluded (away from the Truth) such as would be deluded.

9. Yu'faku ‘anhu man ufik.

يُؤْفَكُ عَنْهُ مَنْ اُفِكَ ۩

10. Woe to the falsehood-mongers,-

10. Qutilal-kharraaṣoon.

قُتِلَ الْخَرَّاصُونَ ۩

11. Those who (flounder) heedless in a flood of confusion:

12. They ask, "When will be the Day of Judgment and Justice?"

13. (It will be) a Day when they will be tried (and tested) over the Fire!

14. "Taste you your trial! This is what you used to ask to be hastened!"

15. As to the Righteous, they will be in the midst of Gardens and Springs,

16. Taking joy in the things which their Lord gives them, because, before then, they lived a good life.

17. They were in the habit of sleeping but little by night,

18. And in the hour of early dawn, they (were found) praying for Forgiveness;

19. And in their wealth the beggar and the outcast had due share.

20. On the earth are signs for those of assured Faith,

21. As also in your own selves: Will you not then see?

22. And in heaven is your Sustenance, as (also) that which you are promised.

23. Then, by the Lord of heaven and earth, this is the very Truth, as much as the fact that you can speak intelligently to each other.

24. Has the story reached thee, of the honoured guests of Abraham?

25. Behold, they entered his presence, and said: "Peace!" He said, "Peace!" (and thought, "These seem) unusual people."

26. Then he turned quickly to his household, brought out a fatted calf,

27. And placed it before them.. he said, "Will you not eat?"

28. (When they did not eat), He conceived a fear of them. They said, "Fear not," and they gave him glad tidings of a son endowed with knowledge.

29. But his wife came forward (laughing) aloud: she smote

---

11. Allazeena hum fee ghamratin saahoon.

12. Yas'aloona ayyaana Yawmud-Deen

13. Yawma hum 'alan-Naari yuftanoon.

14. Zooqoo fitnatakum haazal-lazee kuntum bihee tasta'jiloon.

15. Innal-muttaqeena fee Jannaatiñw-wa 'uyoon.

16. Aakhizeena maaa aataahum Rabbuhum; innahum kaanoo qabla zaalika muhsineen.

17. Kaanoo qaleelam-minal-layli maa yahja'oon.

18. Wa bil-ashaari hum yastaghfiroon.

19. Wa fee amwaalihim haqqul-lissaaa'ili walmahroom.

20. Wa fil-ardi Aayaatul-lil-mooqineen.

21. Wa feee anfusikum; afalaa tubsiroon.

22. Wa fis-samaaa'i rizqukum wa maa too'adoon.

23. Fawa-Rabbis-samaaa'i wal-ardi innahoo lahaqqum-misla maaa annakum tantiqoon.

(Section 1)

24. Hal ataaka hadeesu dayfi Ibraaheemal-mukrameen.

25. Iz dakhaloo 'alayhi faqaaloo salaaman qaala salaamun qawmum-munkaroon.

26. Faraagha ilaaa ahlihee fajaaa'a bi'ijlin sameen.

27. Faqarrabahooo ilayhim qaala alaa taakuloon.

28. Fa-awjasa minhum kheefatan qaaloo laa takhaf wa bashsharoohu bighulaamin 'aleem.

29. Fa-aqbalatim-ra-atuhoo fee sarratin fasakkat

forehead and said: "A barren old woman!"

30. They said, "Even so has your Lord spoken: and He is full of Wisdom and Knowledge."

31. (Abraham) said: "And what, O you Messengers, is your errand (now)?"

32. They said, "We have been sent to a people (deep) in sin;-

33. "To bring on, on them, (a shower of) stones of clay (brimstone),

34. "Marked as from your Lord for those who trespass beyond bounds."

35. Then We evacuated those of the Believers who were there,

36. But We found not there any just (Muslim) persons except in one house:

37. And We left there a Sign for such as fear the Grievous Chastisement.

38. And in Moses (was another Sign): Behold, We sent him to Pharaoh, with authority manifest.

39. But (Pharaoh) turned back with his Chiefs, and said, "A sorcerer, or one possessed!"

40. So We took him and his forces, and threw them into the sea; and his was the cursed.

41. And in the 'Ad (people) (was another Sign): Behold, We sent against them the devastating Wind:

42. It left nothing whatever that it came up against, but reduced it to ruin and rottenness.

43. And in the Thamud (was another Sign): Behold, they were told, "Enjoy (your brief day) for a little while!"

44. But they insolently defied the Command of their Lord: So the stunning noise (of an

wajhahaa wa qaalat 'ajoozun 'aqeem.

30. Qaaloo kazaaliki qaala Rabbuki innahoo Huwal-Ḥakeemul-'Aleem.

31. Qaala famaa khaṭbukum ayyuhal-mursaloon.

32. Qaalooo innaaa ursilnaaa ilaa qawmim-mujrimeen.

33. Linursila 'alayhim ḥijaa-ratam-min ṭeen.

34. Musawwamatan 'inda Rabbika lilmusrifeen.

35. Fa-akhrajnaa man kaana feehaa minal-mu'mineen.

36. Famaa wajadnaa feehaa ghayra baytim-minal-musli-meen.

37. Wa taraknaa feehaaa Aayatal-lillazeena yakhaafoo-nal-'azaabal-aleem.

38. Wa fee Moosaaa iz arsal-naahu ilaa Fir'awna bisulṭaa-nim-mubeen.

39. Fatawallaa biruknihee wa qaala saaḥirun aw majnoon.

40. Fa-akhaznaahu wa junoo-dahoo fanabaznaahum fil-yammi wa huwa muleem.

41. Wa fee 'Aadin iz arsalnaa 'alayhimur-reeḥal-'aqeem.

42. Maa tazaru min shay'in atat 'alayhi illaa ja'alat-hu karmeem.

43. Wa fee Samooda iz qeela lahum tamatta'oo ḥattaa ḥeen.

44. Fa'ataw 'an amri Rabbi-him fa-akhazat-humuṣ-

وَجْهَهَا وَقَالَتْ عَجُوزٌ عَقِيمٌ ۝

قَالُوا كَذَٰلِكِ قَالَ رَبُّكِ ۚ إِنَّهُ هُوَ الْحَكِيمُ الْعَلِيمُ ۝

قَالَ فَمَا خَطْبُكُمْ أَيُّهَا الْمُرْسَلُونَ ۝

قَالُوا إِنَّا أُرْسِلْنَا إِلَىٰ قَوْمٍ مُّجْرِمِينَ ۝

لِنُرْسِلَ عَلَيْهِمْ حِجَارَةً مِّن طِينٍ ۝

مُّسَوَّمَةً عِندَ رَبِّكَ لِلْمُسْرِفِينَ ۝

فَأَخْرَجْنَا مَن كَانَ فِيهَا مِنَ الْمُؤْمِنِينَ ۝

فَمَا وَجَدْنَا فِيهَا غَيْرَ بَيْتٍ مِّنَ الْمُسْلِمِينَ ۝

وَتَرَكْنَا فِيهَا آيَةً لِّلَّذِينَ يَخَافُونَ الْعَذَابَ الْأَلِيمَ ۝

وَفِي مُوسَىٰ إِذْ أَرْسَلْنَاهُ إِلَىٰ فِرْعَوْنَ بِسُلْطَانٍ مُّبِينٍ ۝

فَتَوَلَّىٰ بِرُكْنِهِ وَقَالَ سَاحِرٌ أَوْ مَجْنُونٌ ۝

فَأَخَذْنَاهُ وَجُنُودَهُ فَنَبَذْنَاهُمْ فِي الْيَمِّ وَهُوَ مُلِيمٌ ۝

وَفِي عَادٍ إِذْ أَرْسَلْنَا عَلَيْهِمُ الرِّيحَ الْعَقِيمَ ۝

مَا تَذَرُ مِن شَيْءٍ أَتَتْ عَلَيْهِ إِلَّا جَعَلَتْهُ كَالرَّمِيمِ ۝

وَفِي ثَمُودَ إِذْ قِيلَ لَهُمْ تَمَتَّعُوا حَتَّىٰ حِينٍ ۝

فَعَتَوْا عَنْ أَمْرِ رَبِّهِمْ فَأَخَذَتْهُمُ

earthquake) seized them, even while they were looking on.

45. Then they could not even stand (on their feet), nor could they help themselves.

46. So were the People of Noah before them for they wickedly transgressed.

47. With power and skill did We construct the Firmament: for it is We Who create the vastness of pace.

48. And We have spread out the (spacious) earth: How excellently We do spread out!

49. And of every thing We have created pairs: That you may receive instruction.

50. Then you Hasten (at once) to Allah: I am from Him a Warner to you, clear and open!

51. And make not another an object of worship with Allah: I am from Him a Warner to you, clear and open!

52. Similarly, no apostle came to the Peoples before them, but they said (of him) in like manner, "A sorcerer, or one possessed"!

53. Is this the legacy they have transmitted, one to another? No, they are themselves a people transgressing beyond bounds!

54. So turn away from them: not blame on you.

55. But teach (your Message) for teaching benefits the Believers.

56. I have only created Jinns and men, that they may serve Me.

57. No Sustenance do I require of them, nor do I require that they should feed Me.

58. For Allah is He Who gives (all) Sustenance,- Lord of Power,- Steadfast (for ever)!

59. For the Wrong-doers, their portion is like unto the portion of their fellows (of earlier generations): then let them not ask Me to hasten (that portion)!

60. Woe, then, to the Unbelievers, on account of that Day of theirs

---

șaa'iqatu wa hum yanzuroon.

45. Famas-tataa'oo min qi-yaaminw-wa maa kaanoo muntaṣireen.

46. Wa qawma Nooḥim-min qablu innahum kaanoo qawman faasiqeen. **(Section 2)**

47. Wassamaaa'a banaynaa-haa bi-aydinw-wa innaa lamoo-si'oon.

48. Wal-arḍa farashnaahaa fani'mal-maaḥidoon.

49. Wa min kulli shay'in khalaqnaa zawjayni la'allakum tazakkaroon.

50. Fafirrooo ilal-laahi innee lakum minhu nazeerum-mubeen.

51. Wa laa taj'aloo ma'al-laahi ilaahan aakhara innee lakum minhu nazeerum mubeen.

52. Kazaalika maaa atal-lazeena min qablihim-mir-Rasoolin illaa qaaloo saaḥirun aw majnoon.

53. Atawaaṣaw bih; bal hum qawmun ṭaaghoon.

54. Fatawalla 'anhum famaaa anta bimaloom.

55. Wa zakkir fa-innaz-zikraa tanfa'ul-mu'mineen.

56. Wa maa khalaqtul-jinna wal-insa illaa liya'budoon.

57. Maaa ureedu minhum mir-rizqinw-wa maaa ureedu añy-yuṭ'imoon.

58. Innal-laaha Huwar-Raz-zaaqu Zul-Quwwatil-Mateen.

59. Fa-inna lillazeena ẓalamoo zanoobam-misla zanoobi aṣḥaabihim falaa yasta'jiloon.

60. Fawaylul-lillazeena kafa-roo miñy-Yawmihimul-

which they have been promised!

52. The Mount
In the name of Allah, Most Gracious, Most Merciful.

1. By the Mount (of Revelation);

2. By a Decree inscribed;

3. In a Scroll unfolded;

4. By the much-frequented Fane;

5. By the Canopy Raised High;

6. And by the Ocean filled with Swell;-

7. Verily, the Doom of thy Lord will indeed come to pass;-

8. There is none can avert it;-

9. On the Day when the firmament will be in dreadful commotion.

10. And the mountains will fly hither and thither.

11. Then woe that Day to those that treat (Truth) as Falsehood;-

12. That play (and paddle) in shallow trifles.

13. That Day shall they be thrust down to the Fire of Hell, irresistibly.

14. "This:, it will be said, "Is the Fire,- which you were wont to deny!

15. "Is this then a fake, or is it you that do not see?

16. "Burn you therein: the same is it to you whether you bear it with patience, or not: You but receive the recompense of your (own) deeds."

17. As to the Righteous, they will be in Gardens, and in Happiness,-

18. Enjoying the (Bliss) which their Lord has bestowed on them, and their Lord shall deliver them from the Chastisement of the Fire.

19. (To them will be said:) "Eat and drink you, with good pleasure, because of your

---

lazee yoo'adoon.   (Section 3)

Sûrat aṭ-Ṭûr–52
(Revealed at Makkah)
Bismillaahir Raḥmaanir Raḥeem

1. Waṭ-Ṭoor.

2. Wa Kitaabim-masṭoor.

3. Fee raqqim-manshoor.

4. Wal-Baytil-Ma'moor.

5. Wassaqfil-marfoo'.

6. Wal-baḥril-masjoor.

7. Inna 'azaaba Rabbika lawaaqi'.

8. Maa lahoo min daafi'.

9. Yawma tamoorus-samaaa'u mawraa.

10. Wa taseerul-jibaalu sayraa.

11. Fawayluñy-Yawma'izil-lil-mukazzibeen.

12. Allazeena hum fee khawḍiñy-yal'aboon.

13. Yawma yuda'-'oona ilaa Naari Jahannama da'-'aa.

14. Haazihin-Naarul-latee kuntum bihaa tukazziboon.

15. Afasiḥrun haazaaa am antum laa tubṣiroon.

16. Iṣlawhaa faṣbirooo aw laa taṣbiroo sawaaa'un 'alaykum innamaa tujzawna maa kuntum ta'maloon.

17. Innal-muttaqeena fee Jannaatiñw-wa na'eem.

18. Faakiheena bimaaa aataa-hum Rabbuhum wa waqaahum Rabbuhum 'azaabal-Jaḥeem.

19. Kuloo washraboo haneee-'am bimaa kuntum

الَّذِى يُوعَدُونَ ۝

(٥٢) سُورَةُ الطُّورِ مَكِّيَّةٌ (٤٦)

بِسْمِ اللهِ الرَّحْمٰنِ الرَّحِيمِ

وَالطُّورِ ۝

وَكِتٰبٍ مَّسْطُورٍ ۝

فِى رَقٍّ مَّنْشُورٍ ۝

وَّالْبَيْتِ الْمَعْمُورِ ۝

وَالسَّقْفِ الْمَرْفُوعِ ۝

وَالْبَحْرِ الْمَسْجُورِ ۝

إِنَّ عَذَابَ رَبِّكَ لَوَاقِعٌ ۝

مَّا لَهُ مِنْ دَافِعٍ ۝

يَّوْمَ تَمُورُ السَّمَاءُ مَوْرًا ۝

وَّتَسِيرُ الْجِبَالُ سَيْرًا ۝

فَوَيْلٌ يَّوْمَئِذٍ لِّلْمُكَذِّبِينَ ۝

الَّذِينَ هُمْ فِى خَوْضٍ يَّلْعَبُونَ ۝

يَوْمَ يُدَعُّونَ إِلَى نَارِ جَهَنَّمَ دَعًّا ۝

هٰذِهِ النَّارُ الَّتِى كُنْتُمْ بِهَا تُكَذِّبُونَ ۝

أَفَسِحْرٌ هٰذَا أَمْ أَنْتُمْ لَا تُبْصِرُونَ ۝

إِصْلَوْهَا فَاصْبِرُوا أَوْ لَا تَصْبِرُوا سَوَاءٌ عَلَيْكُمْ إِنَّمَا تُجْزَوْنَ مَا كُنْتُمْ تَعْمَلُونَ ۝

إِنَّ الْمُتَّقِينَ فِى جَنّٰتٍ وَّنَعِيمٍ ۝

فٰكِهِينَ بِمَا آتٰهُمْ رَبُّهُمْ وَوَقٰهُمْ رَبُّهُمْ عَذَابَ الْجَحِيمِ ۝

كُلُوا وَاشْرَبُوا هَنِيئًا بِمَا كُنْتُمْ

(good) deeds."

20. They will recline (with ease) on Thrones (of dignity) arranged in ranks; and We shall join them to Companions, with beautiful big and lustrous eyes.

21. And those who believe and whose families follow them in Faith,- to them shall We join their families: Nor shall We deprive them (of the fruit) of any of their works: (Yet) is each individual in pledge for his deeds.

22. And We shall bestow on them, of fruit and meat, anything they shall desire.

23. They shall there exchange, one with another, a (loving) cup free of frivolity, free of all taint of ill.

24. Round about them will serve, (devoted) to them, youths (handsome) as Pearls well-guarded.

25. They will advance to each other, engaging in mutual enquiry.

26. They will say: "Aforetime, we were not without fear for the sake of our people.

27. "But Allah has been good to us, and has delivered us from the Penalty of the Scorching Wind.

28. "Truly, we did call unto Him from of old: truly it is He, the Beneficent, the Merciful!"

29. Therefore proclaim you the praises (of your Lord): for by the Grace of your Lord, thou art no (vulgar) soothsayer, nor are you one possessed.

30. Or do they say:- "A Poet! we await for him some calamity (hatched) by Time!"

31. Say: "Await you!- I too will wait

ta'maloon.

20. Muttaki'eena 'alaa suru-rim-maṣfoofatiñw wa zawwaj-naahum biḥoorin 'een.

21. Wallazeena aamanoo wat-taba'at-hum zurriyyatuhum bi-eemaanin alḥaqnaa bihim zur-riyyatahum wa maaa alatnaa-hum min 'amalihim min shay'; kullum-ri'im bimaa kasaba raheen.

22. Wa amdadnaahum bifaa-kihatiñw-wa laḥmim-mimmaa yashtahoon.

23. Yatanaaza'oona feehaa kaåsal-laa laghwun feehaa wa laa taåseem.

24. Wa yaṭoofu 'alayhim ghilmaanul-lahum ka-annahum lu'lu'um-maknoon.

25. Wa aqbala ba'ḍuhum 'alaa ba'ḍiñy-yatasaaa'aloon.

26. Qaalooo innaa kunnaa qablu feee ahlinaa mushfiqeen.

27. Famannal-laahu 'alaynaa wa waqaanaa 'azaabas-sa-moom.

28. Innaa kunnaa min qablu nad'oohu innahoo Huwal-Barrur-Raḥeem. **(Section 1)**

29. Fazakkir famaaa anta bini'mati Rabbika bikaahiniñw-wa laa majnoon.

30. Am yaqooloona shaa'irun natarabbaṣu bihee raybal-manoon.

31. Qul tarabbaṣoo fa-innee ma'akum minal-

along with you!"

32. Is it that their faculties of understanding urge them to this, or are they but a people transgressing beyond bounds?

33. Or do they say, "He fabricated the (Message)"? No, they have no faith!

34. Let them then produce a recital like unto it,- If (it be) they speak the truth!

35. Were they created of nothing, or were they themselves the creators?

36. Or did they create the heavens and the earth? No, they have no firm belief.

37. Or are the Treasures of your Lord with them, or are they the managers (of affairs)?

38. Or have they a ladder, by which they can (climb up to heaven and) listen (to its secrets)? Then let (such a) listener of theirs produce a manifest proof.

39. Or has He only daughters and you have sons?

40. Or is it that you does ask for a reward, so that they are burdened with a load of debt?-

41. Or that the Unseen is in their hands, and they write it down?

42. Or do they intend a plot (against you)? But those who defy Allah are themselves involved in a Plot!

43. Or have they a god other than Allah? Exalted is Allah far above the things they associate with Him!

44. Were they to see a piece of the sky falling (on them), they would (only) say: "Clouds gathered in heaps!"

45. So leave them alone until they encounter that Day of theirs, wherein they shall (perforce) swoon (with terror),-

mutarabbiṣeen.

32. Am taåmuruhum aḥlaamuhum bihaazaaa am hum qawmun ṭaaghoon.

33. Am yaqooloona taqawwalah; bal laa yu'minoon.

34. Falyaåtoo biḥadeesimmisliheee in kaanoo ṣaadiqeen.

35. Am khuliqoo min ghayri shay'in am humul-khaaliqoon.

36. Am khalaqus-samaawaati wal-arḍ; bal laa yooqinoon.

37. Am 'indahum khazaaa'inu Rabbika am humul-musayṭiroon.

38. Am lahum sullamuñy-yastami'oona feehi falyaåti mustami'uhum bisulṭaanim-mubeen.

39. Am lahul-banaatu wa lakumul-banoon.

40. Am tas'aluhum ajran fahum mim-maghramim-musqaloon.

41. Am 'indahumul-ghaybu fahum yaktuboon.

42. Am yureedoona kaydan fallazeena kafaroo humul-makeedoon.

43. Am lahum ilaahun ghayrul-laah; Subḥaanal-laahi 'ammaa yushrikoon.

44. Wa iñy-yaraw kisfamminas-samaaa'i saaqiṭañy-yaqooloo saḥaabum-markoom.

45. Fazarhum ḥattaa yulaaqoo Yawmahumul-lazee feehi yuṣ'aqoon.

46. The Day when their plotting will avail them nothing and no help shall be given them.

47. And verily, for those who do wrong, there is another punishment besides this: But most of them understand not.

48. Now await in patience the command of your Lord: for verily you are in Our eyes: and celebrate the praises of your Lord the while you stand forth,

49. And for part of the night also praise you Him,- and at the retreat of the stars!

53. The Star
In the name of Allah, Most Gracious, Most Merciful.

1. By the Star when it goes down,-

2. Your Companion is neither astray nor being misled.

3. Nor does he say (anything) of (his own) Desire.

4. It is no less than inspiration sent down to him:

5. He was taught by one Mighty in Power,

6. Endued with Wisdom: for he appeared (in stately form);

7. While he was in the highest part of the horizon:

8. Then he approached and came closer,

9. And was at a distance of but two bow-lengths or (even) nearer;

10. So did (Allah) convey the inspiration to His Servant (conveyed) what He (meant) to convey.

11. The (Prophet's) (mind and) heart in no way falsified that which he saw.

12. Will you then dispute with him concerning what he saw?

13. For indeed he saw him at a second descent,

14. Near the Lote-tree beyond which none may pass:

15. Near it is the Garden of Abode.

16. Behold, the Lote-tree was shrouded (in mystery unspeakable!)

17. (His) sight never swerved, nor did it go wrong!

46. Yawma laa yughnee 'anhum kayduhum shay'añw-wa laa hum yunsaroon.

47. Wa inna lillazeena zalamoo 'azaaban doona zaalika wa laakinna aksarahum laa ya'lamoon.

48. Wasbir lihukmi Rabbika fa-innaka bi-a'yuninaa wa sabbih bihamdi Rabbika heena taqoom.

49. Wa minal-layli fasabbihhu wa idbaaran-nujoom. (Section 2)

Sûrat an-Najm–53
(Revealed at Makkah)
Bismillaahir Rahmaanir Raheem

1. Wannajmi izaa hawaa.

2. Maa dalla saahibukum wa maa ghawaa.

3. Wa maa yantiqu 'anil-hawaaa.

4. In huwa illaa Wahyuñy-yoohaa.

5. 'Allamahoo shadeedul-quwaa.

6. Zoo mirratin fastawaa.

7. Wa huwa bil-ufuqil-a'laa.

8. Summa danaa fatadallaa.

9. Fakaana qaaba qawsayni aw adnaa.

10. Fa-awhaaa ilaa 'abdihee maaa awhaa.

11. Maa kazabal-fu'aadu maa ra-aa.

12. Afatumaaroonahoo 'alaa maa yaraa.

13. Wa laqad ra-aahu nazlatan ukhraa.

14. 'Inda Sidratil-Muntahaa.

15. 'Indahaa Jannatul-Maåwaa.

16. Iz yaghshas-Sidrata maa yaghshaa.

17. Maa zaaghal-basaru wa maa taghaa.

18. For truly did he see, of the Signs of his Lord, the Greatest!

19. Have you seen Lat and 'Uzza,

20. And another, the third (goddess), Manat?

21. What! for you the male sex, and for Him, the female?

22. Behold, such would be indeed a division most unfair!

23. These are nothing but names which you have devised,- you and your fathers,- for which Allah has sent down no authority (whatever). They follow nothing but conjecture and what their own souls desire!- Even though there has already come to them Guidance from their Lord!

24. No, shall man have (just) anything he hankers after?

25. But it is to Allah that the End and the Beginning (of all things) belong.

26. How many-so-ever be the angels in the heavens, their intercession will avail nothing except after Allah has given leave for whom He pleases and that he is acceptable to Him.

27. Those who believe not in the Hereafter, name the angels with female names.

28. But they have no knowledge therein. They follow nothing but conjecture; and conjecture avails nothing against Truth.

29. Therefore shun those who turn away from Our Message and desire nothing but the life of this world.

30. That is as far as knowledge will reach them. Verily your Lord knows best those who stray from His Path, and He knoweth best those who receive guidance.

31. Yes, to Allah belongs all that is in the heavens and on earth:

18. Laqad ra-aa min Aayaati Rabbihil-Kubraaa.

19. Afara'aytumul-Laata wal-'Uzzaa.

20. Wa Manaatas-saalisatal-ukhraa.

21. A-lakumuz-zakaru wa lahul-unsaa.

22. Tilka izan qismatun deezaa.

23. In hiya illaaa asmaaa'un sammaytumoohaaa antum wa aabaaa'ukum maaa anzalal-laahu bihaa min sultaan; iñy-yattabi'oona illaz-zanna wa maa tahwal-anfusu wa laqad jaaa'ahum-mir-Rabbihimul-hudaa.

24. Am lil-insaani maa taman-naa.

25. Falillaahil-Aakhiratu wal-oolaa.   **(Section 1)**

26. Wa kam mim-malakin fis-samaawaati laa tughnee shafaa'atuhum shay'an illaa mim ba'di añy-yaåzanal-laahu limañy-yashaaa'u wa yardaa.

27. Innal-lazeena laa yu'minoona bil-Aakhirati la-yusam-moonal-malaaa'ikata tasmi-yatal-unsaa.

28. Wa maa lahum bihee min 'ilmin iñy-yattabi'oona illaz-zanna wa innaz-zanna laa yughnee minal-haqqi shay'aa.

29. Fa-a'riḍ 'am-man tawallaa 'an zikrinaa wa lam yurid illal-hayaatad-dunyaa.

30. Zalika mablaghuhum mi-nal-'ilm; inna Rabbaka Huwa a'lamu biman ḍalla 'an sabee-lihee wa Huwa a'lamu bimanih-tadaa.

31. Wa lillaahi maa fis-samaawaati wa maa fil-arḍi

so that He rewards those who do evil, according to their deeds, and He rewards those who do good, with what is best.

32. Those who avoid great sins and shameful deeds, only (falling into) small faults,- verily your Lord is ample in forgiveness. He knows you well when He brings you out of the earth, and when you are hidden in your mothers' wombs. Therefore, justify not yourselves: He knows best who it is that guards against evil.

33. Do you see one who turns back,

34. Gives a little, then hardens (his heart)?

35. What! Has he knowledge of the Unseen so that he can see?

36. Or hath he not bad news of what is in books of Moses.

37. And of Abraham who fulfilled his engagements?-

38. That no laden one shall bear another's load.

39. That man can have nothing but what he strives for;

40. That (the fruit of) his striving will soon come in sight:

41. Then will he be rewarded with a reward complete;

42. That to your Lord is the final Goal;

43. That it is He Who grants Laughter and Tears;

44. That it is He Who grants Death and Life;

45. That He did create in pairs,- male and female,

46. From a seed when lodged (in its place);

47. That He has promised a Second Creation (Raising of the Dead);

48. That it is He Who gives wealth and satisfaction;

49. That He is the Lord of Sirius (the Mighty Star);

liyajziyal-lazeena asaaa'oo bimaa 'amiloo wa yajziyal-lazeena ahsanoo bilhusnaa.

32. Allazeena yajtaniboona kabaaa'iral-ismi walfawaa-hisha illal-lamam; inna Rabbaka waasi'ul-maghfirah; Huwa a'lamu bikum iz ansha-akum minal-ardi wa iz antum ajinnatun fee butooni umma-haatikum falaa tuzakkooo anfu-sakum Huwa a'lamu bimanit-taqaa.   (Section 2)

33. Afara'aytal-lazee tawallaa.

34. Wa a'taa qaleelanw-wa akdaa.

35. A'indahoo 'ilmul-ghaybi fahuwa yaraa.

36. Am lam yunabbaå bimaa fee Suhufi Moosaa.

37. Wa Ibraaheemal-lazee waffaaa.

38. Allaa taziru waaziratuñw-wizra ukhraa.

39. Wa al-laysa lil-insaani illaa maa sa'aa.

40. Wa anna sa'yahoo sawfa yuraa.

41. Summa yujzaahul-jazaaa'al-awfaa.

42. Wa anna ilaa Rabbikal-muntahaa.

43. Wa annahoo Huwa adhaka wa abkaa.

44. Wa annahoo Huwa amaata wa ahyaa.

45. Wa annahoo khalaqaz-zawjayniz-zakara wal-unsaa.

46. Min nutfatin izaa tumnaa.

47. Wa anna 'alayhin-nash-atal-ukhraa.

48. Wa annahoo Huwa aghnaa wa aqnaa.

49. Wa annahoo Huwa Rabbush-Shi'raa.

(Bow Down)

50. And that He destroyed the former (tribe of) 'Aad,

51. And the Thamud, nor gave them a lease of perpetual life.

52. And before them, the people of Noah, for that they were (all) most unjust and most insolent transgressors,

53. And Al-Mu'tafikah He destroyed..

54. So that (ruins unknown) have covered them up.

55. Then which of the gifts of your Lord, (O man,) will you dispute about?

56. This is a Warner, of the (series of) Warners of old!

57. The (Judgment) ever approaching draws closer:

58. No (soul) but Allah can lay it bare.

59. Do you then wonder at this recital?

60. And will you laugh and not weep,-

61. Wasting your time in vanities?

62. But fall down in prostration to Allah, and adore (Him)

---

54. The Moon

In the name of Allah, Most Gracious, Most Merciful.

1. The Hour drew nigh and the moon was rent in twain.

2. But if they see a Sign, they turn away, and say, "This is (but) transient magic."

3. They reject (the warning) and follow their (own) lusts but every matter has its appointed time.

4. There have already come to them such tidings as contain a deterrent–

5. Effective wisdom; but warnings avail not.

6. Therefore, (O Prophet,) turn away from them. The Day that the Caller will call (them) to a terrible affair,

---

50. Wa annahooo ahlaka 'Aadanil-oolaa.

51. Wa Samooda famaaa abqaa.

52. Wa qawma Noohim-min qablu innahum kaanoo hum azlama wa atghaa.

53. Wal-mu'tafikata ahwaa.

54. Faghashshaahaa maa ghashshaa.

55. Fabi-ayyi aalaaa'i Rabbika tatamaaraa.

56. Haazaa nazeerum-minan-nuzuril-oolaa.

57. Azifatil-aazifah.

58. Laysa lahaa min doonil-laahi kaashifah.

59. Afamin haazal-hadeesi ta'jaboon.

60. Wa tadhakoona wa laa tabkoon.

61. Wa antum saamidoon.

62. Fasjudoo lillaahi wa'-budoo. 🕮 (Section 3)

Sûrat al-Qamar–54
(Revealed at Makkah)
Bismillaahir Rahmaanir Raheem

1. Iqtarabatis-Saa'atu wan-shaqqal-qamar.

2. Wa iny-yaraw Aayatany-yu'ridoo wa yaqooloo sihrum-mustamirr.

3. Wa kazzaboo wattaba'ooo ahwaaa'ahum; wa kullu am-rim-mustaqirr.

4. Wa laqad jaaa'ahum minal-ambaaa'i maa feehi muzdajar.

5. Hikmatum baalighatun famaa tughnin-nuzur.

6. Fatawalla 'anhum; Yawma yad'ud-daa'i ilaa shay'in nukur.

7. They will come forth,- their eyes humbled - from (their) graves, (torpid) like locusts scattered abroad,

8. Hastening, with eyes transfixed, towards the Caller!- "Hard is this Day!", the Unbelievers will say.

9. Before them the People of Noah rejected (their apostle): they rejected Our servant, and said, "Here is one possessed!", and he was driven out.

10. Then he called on his Lord: "I am one overcome: do You then help (me)!"

11. So We opened the gates of heaven, with water pouring forth.

12. And We caused the earth to gush forth with springs, so the waters met (and rose) to the extent decreed.

13. And We carried him upon a thing of planks and nails,

14. She floats under our eyes (and care): a recompense to one who had been rejected (with scorn)!

15. And We have left this as a Sign (for all time): then is there any that will receive admonition?

16. But how (terrible) was My Chastisement and My Warning?

17. And We have indeed made the Qur'an easy to understand and remember: then is there any that will receive admonition?

18. The 'Ad (people) (too) rejected (Truth): then how terrible was My Chastisement and My Warning?

19. For We sent against them a furious wind, on a Day of violent Disaster,

20. Plucking out men as if they were roots of palm-trees torn up (from the ground).

21. Yes, how (terrible) was My Chastisement and My Warning!

22. But We have indeed made the Qur'an easy to understand and remember:

7. Khushsha'an abṣaaruhum yakhrujoona minal-ajdaaṣi ka-annahum jaraadum-muntashir.

8. Muhṭi'eena ilad-daa'i yaqoolul-kaafiroona haazaa yawmun 'asir.

9. Kazzabat qablahum qawmu Nooḥin fakazzaboo 'abdanaa wa qaaloo majnoo-nuñw-wazdujir.

10. Fada'aa Rabbahooo annee maghloobun fantaṣir.

11. Fafataḥnaaa abwaabas-samaaa'i bimaaa'im-munhamir.

12. Wa fajjarnal-arḍa 'uyoo-nan-faltaqal-maaa'u 'alaaa amrin qad qudir.

13. Wa ḥamalnaahu 'alaa zaati alwaaḥiñw-wa dusur.

14. Tajree bi-a'yuninaa jazaaa-'al-liman kaana kufir.

15. Wa laqat-taraknaahaaa Aayatan fahal mim-muddakir.

16. Fakayfa kaana 'azaabee wa nuzur.

17. Wa laqad yassarnal-Qur-aana liz-zikri fahal mim-muddakir.

18. kazzabat 'Aadun fakayfa kaana 'azaabee wa nuzur.

19. Innaaa arsalnaa 'alayhim reeḥan ṣarṣaran fee Yawmi naḥsim-mustamirr.

20. Tanzi'un-naasa ka-annahum a'jaazu nakhlim-munqa'ir.

21. Fakayfa kaana 'azaabee wa nuzur.

22. wa laqad yassarnal-Qur-aana liz-zikri

then is there any that will receive admonition?

23. The Thamud (also) rejected (their) Warners.

24. For they said: "What! a man! a Solitary one from among ourselves! shall we follow such a one? Truly should we then be straying in mind, and mad!

25. "Is it that the Message is sent to him, of all people amongst us? No, he is a liar, an insolent one!"

26. Ah! they will know on the morrow, which is the liar, the insolent one!

27. For We will send the she-camel by way of trial for them. So watch them, (O Salih), and possess yourself in patience!

28. And inform them that the water is to be shared between (her and) them. Every drinking will be witnessed.

29. But they called to their companion, and he took a sword in hand, and hamstrung (her).

30. Ah! how (terrible) was My Chastisement and My Warning!

31. For We sent against them a single Mighty Blast, and they became like the dry stubble used by one who pens cattle.

32. And We have indeed made the Qur'an easy to understand and remember: then is there any that will receive admonition?

33. The people of Lut rejected (his) warning.

34. We sent against them a violent Tornado with showers of stones, (which destroyed them), except Lut's household: them We delivered by early Dawn,-

35. As a Grace from Us: thus do We reward those who give thanks.

36. And (Lut) did warn them of Our Punishment, but they disputed about the Warning.

37. And they even sought to snatch away his guests from him, but We blinded their eyes. (They heard:) "Now taste you My Wrath and My Warning."

fahal mim-muddakir.   **(Section 1)**

23. Kazzabat Samoodu binnuzur.

24. Faqaalooo a-basharam-minnaa waahidan natta-bi'uhooo innaaa izal-lafee dalaaliñw-wa su'ur.

25. 'A-ulqiyaz-zikru 'alayhi mim bayninaa bal huwa kaz-zaabun ashir.

26. Sa-ya'lamoona ghadam-manil-kazzaabul-ashir.

27. Innaa mursilun-naaqati fitnatal-lahum fartaqibhum wastabir.

28. Wa nabbi'hum annal-maaa'a qismatum baynahum kullu shirbim-muhtadar.

29. Fanaadaw saahibahum fata'aataa fa'aqar.

30. Fakayfa kaana 'azaabee wa nuzur.

31. Innaaa arsalnaa 'alayhim sayhatañw-waahidatan fakaanoo kahasheemil-muhtazir.

32. Wa laqad yassarnal-Qur-aana liz-zikri fahal mim-muddakir.

33. Kazzabat qawmu Lootim binnuzur.

34. Innaaa arsalnaa 'alayhim haasiban illaaa aala Loot, najjaynaahum bisahar.

35. Ni'matam-min 'indinaa; kazaalika najzee man shakar.

36. Wa laqad anzarahum bat-shatanaa fatamaaraw binnuzur.

37. Wa laqad raawadoohu 'an dayfihee fatamasnaaa a'yu-nahum fazooqoo 'azaabee wa nuzur.

38. Early on the morrow an abiding Punishment seized them:

39. "So taste you My Wrath and My Warning."

40. And We have indeed made the Qur'an easy to understand and remember: then is there any that will receive admonition?

41. To the People of Pharaoh, too, aforetime, came Warners (from Allah).

42. The (people) rejected all Our Signs; but We seized them with such Chastisement (as comes) from One Exalted in Power, able to carry out His Will.

43. Are your Unbelievers, (O Quraish), better than they? Or have you an immunity in the Sacred Books?

44. Or do they say: "We acting together can defend ourselves"?

45. The hosts will all be routed and will turn and flee.

46. No, the Hour (of Judgment) is the time promised them (for their full recompense): And that Hour will be most grievous and most bitter.

47. Truly those in sin are the ones straying in mind, and mad.

48. The Day they will be dragged through the Fire on their faces, (they will hear:) "Taste you the touch of Hell!"

49. Lo! We have created every thing by measure.

50. And Our Command is but a single (Act),- like the twinkling of an eye.

51. And (oft) in the past, have We destroyed gangs like unto you: then is there any that will receive admonition?

52. All that they do is noted in (their) Books (of Deeds):

53. Every matter, small and great, is on record.

54. As to the Righteous, they will be in the midst of Gardens and Rivers,

55. In an Assembly of Truth, in the Presence of a Sovereign Omnipotent.

---

38. Wa laqad ṣabbaḥahum bukratan 'azaabum-mustaqirr.

39. Fazooqoo 'azaabee wa nuzur.

40. Wa laqad yassarnal-Qur-aana liz-zikri fahal mim-muddakir. **(Section 2)**

41. Wa laqad jaaa'a Aala Fir-'awnan-nuzur.

42. Kazzaboo bi-Aayaatinaa kullihaa fa-akhaznaahum akhza 'azeezim-muqtadir.

43. Akuffaarukum khayrum-min ulaaa'ikum am lakum baraaa'atun fiz-Zubur.

44. Am yaqooloona naḥnu jamee'um-muntaṣir.

45. Sa-yuhzamul-jam'u wa yuwalloonad-dubur.

46. Balis-Saa'atu maw'iduhum was-Saa'atu adhaa wa amarr.

47. Innal-mujrimeena fee ḍalaaliñw-wa su'ur.

48. Yawma yus-ḥaboona fin-Naari 'alaa wujoohihim zooqoo massa saqar.

49. Innaa kulla shay'in kha-laqnaahu biqadar.

50. Wa maaa amrunaaa illaa waaḥidatun kalamḥim bilbaṣar.

51. Wa laqad ahlaknaaa ash-yaa'akum fahal mim-muddakir.

52. Wa kullu shay'in fa'aloo-hu fiz-Zubur.

53. Wa kullu sagheeriñw-wa kabeerim-mustaṭar.

54. Innal-muttaqeena fee Jannaatiñw-wa nahar.

55. Fee maq'adi ṣidqin 'inda Maleekim-Muqtadir. **(Section 3)**

55. Allah, Most Gracious In the name of Allah, Most Gracious, Most Merciful.	**Sûrat ar-Raḥmân–55** (Revealed at Madinah) **Bismillaahir Raḥmaanir Raḥeem**	(٥٥) سُوْرَةُ الرَّحمٰنِ مَدَنِيَّةٌ (٩٧) بِسۡمِ اللهِ الرَّحمٰنِ الرَّحِيۡمِ

1. (Allah) Most Gracious!

1. Ar-Raḥmaan.

الرَّحۡمٰنُ ۚ

2. It is He Who has taught the Qur'an.

2. 'Allamal-Qur-aan.

عَلَّمَ الۡقُرۡاٰنَ ؕ

3. He has created man:

3. Khalaqal-insaan.

خَلَقَ الۡاِنۡسَانَ ۙ

4. He has taught him speech (and intelligence).

4. 'Allamahul-ba-yaan.

عَلَّمَهُ الۡبَيَانَ ۝

5. The sun and the moon follow courses (exactly) computed;

5. Ashshamsu walqamaru biḥusbaan.

الشَّمۡسُ وَ الۡقَمَرُ بِحُسۡبَانٍ ۙ

6. The stars and the trees adore.

6. Wannajmu washshajaru yasjudaan.

وَّالنَّجۡمُ وَ الشَّجَرُ يَسۡجُدٰنِ ۙ

7. And the sky He hath uplifted; and He hath set the measure.

7. Wassamaaa'a rafa'ahaa wa waḍa'al-Meezaan.

وَالسَّمَاۤءَ رَفَعَهَا وَوَضَعَ الۡمِيۡزَانَ ۙ

8. In order that ye may not transgress (due) balance.

8. Allaa taṭghaw fil-meezaan.

اَلَّا تَطۡغَوۡا فِى الۡمِيۡزَانِ ۝

9. So establish weight with justice and fall not short in the balance.

9. Wa aqeemul-wazna bil-qisṭi wa laa tukhsirul-meezaan.

وَاَقِيۡمُوا الۡوَزۡنَ بِالۡقِسۡطِ وَلَا تُخۡسِرُوا الۡمِيۡزَانَ ۝

10. It is He Who has spread out the earth for (His) creatures:

10. Wal-arḍa waḍa'ahaa lil-anaam.

وَالۡاَرۡضَ وَضَعَهَا لِلۡاَنَامِ ۙ

11. Therein is fruit and date-palms, producing spathes (enclosing dates);

11. Feehaa faakihatuñw-wan-nakhlu zaatul-akmaam.

فِيۡهَا فَاكِهَةٌ ۖ وَّالنَّخۡلُ ذَاتُ الۡاَكۡمَامِ ۙ

12. Husked grain and scented herb.

12. Walḥabbu zul-'aṣfi war-Rayḥaan.

وَالۡحَبُّ ذُو الۡعَصۡفِ وَالرَّيۡحَانُ ۚ

13. Then which of the favours of your Lord will you deny?

13. Fabi-ayyi aalaaa'i Rabbi-kumaa tukazzibaan.

فَبِاَيِّ اٰلَاۤءِ رَبِّكُمَا تُكَذِّبٰنِ ۝

14. He created man from sounding clay like unto pottery,

14. Khalaqal-insaana min ṣalṣaalin kalfakhkhaar.

خَلَقَ الۡاِنۡسَانَ مِنۡ صَلۡصَالٍ كَالۡفَخَّارِ ۙ

15. And He created Jinns from fire free of smoke:

15. Wa khalaqal-jaaanna mim-maarijim-min-Naar.

وَخَلَقَ الۡجَاۤنَّ مِنۡ مَّارِجٍ مِّنۡ نَّارٍ ۚ

16. Then which of the favours of your Lord will you deny?

16. Fabi-ayyi aalaaa'i Rabbi-kumaa tukazzibaan.

فَبِاَيِّ اٰلَاۤءِ رَبِّكُمَا تُكَذِّبٰنِ ۝

17. (He is) Lord of the two Easts and Lord of the two Wests:

17. Rabbul-mashriqayni wa Rabbul-maghribayn.

رَبُّ الۡمَشۡرِقَيۡنِ وَرَبُّ الۡمَغۡرِبَيۡنِ ۚ

18. Then which of the favours of your Lord will you deny?

18. Fabi-ayyi aalaaa'i Rabbi-kumaa tukazzibaan.

فَبِاَيِّ اٰلَاۤءِ رَبِّكُمَا تُكَذِّبٰنِ ۝

19. He hath loosed the two seas. They meet.

19. Marajal-baḥrayni yalta-qiyaan.

مَرَجَ الۡبَحۡرَيۡنِ يَلۡتَقِيٰنِ ۙ

20. Between them is a Barrier which they do not transgress:

20. Baynahumaa barzakhul-laa yabghiyaan.

بَيۡنَهُمَا بَرۡزَخٌ لَّا يَبۡغِيٰنِ ۝

21. Then which of the favours of your Lord will you deny?

21. Fabi-ayyi aalaaa'i Rabbi-kumaa tukazzibaan.

فَبِاَيِّ اٰلَاۤءِ رَبِّكُمَا تُكَذِّبٰنِ ۝

22. Out of them come Pearls and Coral:	22. Yakhruju minhumal-lu'lu'u wal-marjaan.	يَخْرُجُ مِنْهُمَا اللُّؤْلُؤُ وَالْمَرْجَانُ ۞
23. Then which of the favours of your Lord will you deny?	23. Fabi-ayyi aalaaa'i Rabbi-kumaa tukazzibaan.	فَبِأَيِّ الَاءِ رَبِّكُمَا تُكَذِّبَانِ ۞
24. And His are the Ships sailing smoothly through the seas, lofty as mountains:	24. Wa lahul-jawaaril-mun-sha'aatu fil-baḥri kal-a'laam.	وَلَهُ الْجَوَارِ الْمُنْشَئَاتُ فِي الْبَحْرِ كَالْأَعْلَامِ ۞
25. Then which of the favours of your Lord will you deny?	25. Fabi-ayyi aalaaa'i Rabbi-kumaa tukazzibaan. (Section 1)	فَبِأَيِّ الَاءِ رَبِّكُمَا تُكَذِّبَانِ ۞
26. All that is on earth will perish:	26. Kullu man 'alayhaa faan.	كُلُّ مَنْ عَلَيْهَا فَانٍ ۞
27. But will abide (for ever) the Face of your Lord,- full of Majesty, Bounty and Honour.	27. Wa yabqaa Wajhu Rabbika Zul-Jalaali wal-Ikraam.	وَّيَبْقَى وَجْهُ رَبِّكَ ذُو الْجَلَلِ وَالْإِكْرَامِ ۞
28. Then which of the favours of your Lord will you deny?	28. Fabi-ayyi aalaaa'i Rabbi-kumaa tukazzibaan.	فَبِأَيِّ الَاءِ رَبِّكُمَا تُكَذِّبَانِ ۞
29. Of Him seeks (its need) every creature in the heavens and on earth: every day in (new) Splendour does He (shine)!	29. Yas'aluhoo man fis-samaawaati walarḍ; kulla yawmin Huwa fee shaan.	يَسْأَلُهُ مَنْ فِي السَّمَوَاتِ وَالْأَرْضِ كُلَّ يَوْمٍ هُوَ فِي شَأْنٍ ۞
30. Then which of the favours of your Lord will you deny?	30. Fabi-ayyi aalaaa'i Rabbi-kumaa tukazzibaan.	فَبِأَيِّ الَاءِ رَبِّكُمَا تُكَذِّبَانِ ۞
31. Soon shall We settle your affairs, O burden of the world.	31. Sanafrughu lakum ayyu-has-saqalaan.	سَنَفْرُغُ لَكُمْ أَيُّهَ الثَّقَلَانِ ۞
32. Then which of the favours of your Lord will you deny?	32. Fabi-ayyi aalaaa'i Rabbi-kumaa tukazzibaan.	فَبِأَيِّ الَاءِ رَبِّكُمَا تُكَذِّبَانِ ۞
33. O you assembly of Jinns and men! If it be you can pass beyond the zones of the heavens and the earth, pass you! not without authority shall you be able to pass!	33. Yaa ma'sharal-jinni wal-insi inis-taṭa'tum an tanfuzoo min aqṭaaris-samaawaati wal-arḍi fanfuzoo; laa tanfuzoona illaa bisulṭaan.	يَمَعْشَرَ الْجِنِّ وَالْإِنْسِ إِنِ اسْتَطَعْتُمْ أَنْ تَنْفُذُوا مِنْ أَقْطَارِ السَّمَوَاتِ وَالْأَرْضِ فَانْفُذُوا لَا تَنْفُذُونَ إِلَّا بِسُلْطَانٍ ۞
34. Then which of the favours of your Lord will you deny?	34. Fabi-ayyi aalaaa'i Rabbi-kumaa tukazzibaan.	فَبِأَيِّ الَاءِ رَبِّكُمَا تُكَذِّبَانِ ۞
35. On you will be sent (O you evil ones twain) a flame of fire (to burn) and a smoke (to choke): no defence will you have:	35. Yursalu 'alaykumaa shu-waazum-min naariñw-wa nu-ḥaasun falaa tantaṣiraan.	يُرْسَلُ عَلَيْكُمَا شُوَاظٌ مِنْ نَارٍ وَنُحَاسٌ فَلَا تَنْتَصِرَانِ ۞
36. Then which of the favours of your Lord will you deny?	36. Fabi-ayyi aalaaa'i Rabbi-kumaa tukazzibaan.	فَبِأَيِّ الَاءِ رَبِّكُمَا تُكَذِّبَانِ ۞
37. When the sky is rent asunder, and it becomes red like ointment:	37. Fa-izan shaqqatis-samaaa'u fakaanat wardatan kaddihaan.	فَإِذَا انْشَقَّتِ السَّمَاءُ فَكَانَتْ وَرْدَةً كَالدِّهَانِ ۞
38. Then which of the favours of your Lord will you deny?	38. Fabi-ayyi aalaaa'i Rabbi-kumaa tukazzibaan.	فَبِأَيِّ الَاءِ رَبِّكُمَا تُكَذِّبَانِ ۞
39. On that Day no question will be asked of man	39. Fa-yawma'izil-laa yus'alu 'an zambiheee insuñw-	فَيَوْمَئِذٍ لَا يُسْأَلُ عَنْ ذَنْبِهِ إِنْسٌ ۞

or Jinn as to his sin.

40. Then which of the favours of your Lord will you deny?

41. (For) the sinners will be known by their marks: and they will be seized by their forelocks and their feet.

42. Then which of the favours of your Lord will you deny?

43. This is the Hell which the Sinners deny:

44. In its midst and in the midst of boiling hot water will they wander round!

45. Then which of the favours of your Lord will you deny?

46. But for him who feareth the standing before his Lord there are two gardens.

47. Then which of the favours of your Lord will you deny?-

48. Containing all kinds (of trees and delights);-

49. Then which of the favours of your Lord will you deny?-

50. In them (each) will be two Springs flowing (free);

51. Then which of the favours of your Lord will you deny?-

52. In them will be Fruits of every kind, two and two.

53. Then which of the favours of your Lord will you deny?

54. Reclining upon couches lined with silk brocade, the fruit of both gardens near to hand..

55. Then which of the favours of your Lord will you deny?

56. In them will be (Maidens), chaste, restraining their glances, whom no man or Jinn before them has touched;-

57. Then which of the favours of your Lord will you deny?-

58. Like unto Rubies and coral.

59. Then which of the favours of your Lord will you deny?

60. Is there any Reward for Good - other than Good?

wa laa jaaann.

40. Fabi-ayyi aalaaa'i Rabbikumaa tukazzibaan.

41. Yu'raful-mujrimoona biseemaahum fa-yu'khazu binnawaaşi wal-aqdaam.

42. Fabi-ayyi aalaaa'i Rabbikumaa tukazzibaan.

43. Haazihee Jahannamullatee yukazzibu bihal-mujrimoon.

44. Yaṭoofoona baynahaa wa bayna ḥameemin aan.

45. Fabi-ayyi aalaaa'i Rabbikumaa tukazzibaan.   (Section 2)

46. Wa liman khaafa maqaama Rabbihee Jannataan.

47. Fabi-ayyi aalaaa'i Rabbikumaa tukazzibaan.

48. Zawaataaa afnaan.

49. Fabi-ayyi aalaaa'i Rabbikumaa tukazzibaan.

50. Feehimaa 'aynaani tajriyaan.

51. Fabi-ayyi aalaaa'i Rabbikumaa tukazzibaan.

52. Feehimaa min kulli faakihatin zawjaan.

53. Fabi-ayyi aalaaa'i Rabbikumaa tukazzibaan.

54. Muttaki'eena 'alaa furushim baṭaaa'inuhaa min istabraq; wa janal-jannatayni daan.

55. Fabi-ayyi aalaaa'i Rabbikumaa tukazzibaan.

56. Feehinna qaaşiratuṭ-ṭarfi lam yaṭmishunna insun qablahum wa laa jaaann.

57. Fabi-ayyi aalaaa'i Rabbikumaa tukazzibaan.

58. Ka-annahunnal-yaaqootu wal-marjaan.

59. Fabi-ayyi aalaaa'i Rabbikumaa tukazzibaan.

60. Hal jazaaa'ul-ihsaani illalihsaan.

61. Then which of the favours of your Lord will you deny?

62. And besides these two, there are two other Gardens,-

63. Then which of the favours of your Lord will you deny?-

64. Dark-green in colour (from plentiful watering).

65. Then which of the favours of your Lord will you deny?

66. Wherein are two abundant spring.

67. Then which of the favours of your Lord will you deny?

68. In them will be Fruits, and dates and pomegranates:

69. Then which of the favours of your Lord will you deny?

70. In them will be fair (Companions), good, beautiful;-

71. Then which of the favours of your Lord will you deny?-

72. Fair ones, close-guarded in pavilions–

73. Then which of the favours of your Lord will you deny?-

74. Whom no man or Jinn before them has touched;-

75. Then which of the favours of your Lord will you deny?-

76. Reclining on green Cushions and rich Carpets of beauty.

77. Then which of the favours of your Lord will you deny?

78. Blessed be the name of thy Lord, Mighty and Glorious!

61. Fabi-ayyi aalaaa'i Rabbi-kumaa tukazzibaan.

62. Wa min doonihimaa Jannataan.

63. Fabi-ayyi aalaaa'i Rabbi-kumaa tukazzibaan.

64. Mudhaaammataan.

65. Fabi-ayyi aalaaa'i Rabbi-kumaa tukazzibaan.

66. Feehimaa 'aynaani naḍ-ḍaakhataan.

67. Fabi-ayyi aalaaa'i Rabbi-kumaa tukazzibaan.

68. Feehimaa faakihatuñw-wa nakhluñw-wa rummaan.

69. Fabi-ayyi aalaaa'i Rabbi-kumaa tukazzibaan.

70. Feehinna khayraatun ḥisaan.

71. Fabi-ayyi aalaaa'i Rabbi-kumaa tukazzibaan.

72. Hoorum-maqṣooraatun fil-khiyaam.

73. Fabi-ayyi aalaaa'i Rabbi-kumaa tukazzibaan.

74. Lam yaṭmis-hunna insun qablahum wa laa jaaann.

75. Fabi-ayyi aalaaa'i Rabbi-kumaa tukazzibaan.

76. Muttaki'eena 'alaa rafrafin khuḍriñw-wa 'abqariyyin ḥisaan.

77. Fabi-ayyi aalaaa'i Rabbi-kumaa tukazzibaan.

78. Tabaarakasmu Rabbika Zil-Jalaali wal-Ikraam.

(Section 3)

---

56. The Inevitable Event
In the name of Allah, Most Gracious, Most Merciful.

1. When the inevitable event comes to pass,

2. Then will no (soul) deny its coming.

3. (Many) will it bring low; (many) will it exalt;

4. When the Earth shall be shaken to its depths,

Sûrat al-Wâqi'ah–56
(Revealed at Makkah)
Bismillaahir Raḥmaanir Raḥeem

1. Izaa waqa'atil-waaqi'ah.

2. Laysa liwaq'atihaa kaazi-bah.

3. Khaafiḍatur-raafi'ah.

4. Izaa rujjatil-arḍu rajjaa.

5. And the mountains shall be crumbled to atoms,

6. Becoming dust scattered abroad,

7. And you shall be sorted out into three classes.

8. Then (there will be) the People of the Right Hand;– What will be the People of the Right Hand?

9. And the People of the Left Hand,–what will be the People of the Left Hand?

10. And the foremost in the race, the foremost in the race:

11. These will be those Nearest to Allah:

12. In Gardens of Bliss:

13. A number of people from those of old,

14. And a few from those of later times.

15. On lined couches,

16. Reclining on them, facing each other.

17. There wait on them immortal youths.

18. With goblets, (shining) beakers, and cups (filled) out of clear-flowing fountains:

19. No after-ache will they receive therefrom, nor will they suffer intoxication:

20. And with fruits, any that they may select:

21. And the flesh of fowls, any that they may desire.

22. And (there are) fair ones with wide, lovely eyes,

23. Like unto Pearls well-guarded.

24. A Reward for the deeds of their past (life).

25. Not frivolity will they hear therein, nor any taint of ill,–

26. Only the saying, "Peace! Peace".

27. The Companions of the Right Hand,- what will be the Companions of

5. Wa bussatil-jibaalu bassaa.

6. Fakaanat habaaa'am-mumbassaa.

7. Wa kuntum azwaajan salaasah.

8. Fa-Aṣ-ḥaabul-Maymanati maaa Aṣ-ḥaabul-Maymanah.

9. Wa Aṣ-ḥaabul-Mash'amati maaa Aṣ-ḥaabul-Mash'amah.

10. Wassaabiqoonas-saabiqoon.

11. Ulaaa'ikal-muqarraboon.

12. Fee Jannaatin-Na'eem.

13. Sullatum-minal-awwaleen.

14. Wa qaleelum-minal-aakhireen.

15. 'Alaa sururim-mawḍoonah.

16. Muttaki'eena 'alayhaa mutaqaabileen.

17. Yaṭoofu 'alayhim wildaanum-mukhalladoon.

18. Bi-akwaabiñw-wa abaareeq, wa kaåsim-mim-ma'een.

19. Laa yuṣadda'oona 'anhaa wa laa yunzifoon.

20. Wa faakihatim-mimmaa yatakhayyaroon.

21. Wa laḥmi ṭayrim-mimmaa yashtahoon.

22. Wa ḥoorun 'een.

23. Ka-amsaalil-lu'lu'il-maknoon.

24. Jazaaa'am bimaa kaanoo ya'maloon.

25. Laa yasma'oona feehaa laghwañw-wa laa taåseemaa.

26. Illaa qeelan salaaman salaamaa.

27. Wa Aṣ-ḥaabul-Yameeni maaa Aṣ-ḥaabul-

the Right Hand?

Yameen.

الْيَمِينِ ۞

28. (They will be) among Lote-trees without thorns,

28. Fee sidrim-makhdood.

فِىْ سِدْرٍ مَّخْضُوْدٍ ۞

29. And clustered plantains,

29. Wa talhim-mandood.

وَّطَلْحٍ مَّنْضُوْدٍ ۞

30. In shade long-extended,

30. Wa zillim-mamdood.

وَّظِلٍّ مَّمْدُوْدٍ ۞

31. And water gushing,

31. Wa maaa'im-maskoob.

وَّمَآءٍ مَّسْكُوْبٍ ۞

32. And fruit in abundance.

32. Wa faakihatin kaseerah.

وَّفَاكِهَةٍ كَثِيْرَةٍ ۞

33. Whose season is not limited, nor (supply) forbidden,

33. Laa maqtoo'atiñw-wa laa mamnoo'ah.

لَّا مَقْطُوْعَةٍ وَّلَا مَمْنُوْعَةٍ ۞

34. And on Thrones (of Dignity), raised high.

34. Wa furushim-marfoo'ah.

وَّفُرُشٍ مَّرْفُوْعَةٍ ۞

35. Lo! We have created them a (new) creation.

35. Innaaa anshaånaahunna inshaaa'aa.

اِنَّآ اَنْشَأْنٰهُنَّ اِنْشَآءً ۞

36. And made them virgins,

36. Faja'alnaahunna abkaaraa.

فَجَعَلْنٰهُنَّ اَبْكَارًا ۞

37. Lovers, friends,

37. 'Uruban atraabaa.

عُرُبًا اَتْرَابًا ۞

38. For the Companions of the Right Hand.

38. Li-As-haabil-Yameen. (Section 1)

لِّاَصْحٰبِ الْيَمِيْنِ ۞

39. A (goodly) number from those of old,

39. Sullatum-minal-awwa-leen.

ثُلَّةٌ مِّنَ الْاَوَّلِيْنَ ۞

40. And a (goodly) number from those of later times.

40. Wa sullatum-minal-aakhi-reen.

وَثُلَّةٌ مِّنَ الْاٰخِرِيْنَ ۞

41. The Companions of the Left Hand,- what will be the Companions of the Left Hand?

41. Wa As-haabush-Shimaali maaa As-haabush-Shimaal.

وَاَصْحٰبُ الشِّمَالِ ۥ مَآ اَصْحٰبُ الشِّمَالِ ۞

42. In scorching wind and scalding water.

42. Fee samoomiñw-wa ha-meem.

فِىْ سَمُوْمٍ وَّحَمِيْمٍ ۞

43. And in the shades of Black Smoke:

43. Wa zillim-miñy-yahmoom.

وَّظِلٍّ مِّنْ يَّحْمُوْمٍ ۞

44. Nothing (will there be) to refresh, nor to please:

44. Laa baaridiñw-wa laa kareem.

لَّا بَارِدٍ وَّلَا كَرِيْمٍ ۞

45. Lo! hereto fore they were effete with luxury.

45. Innahum kaanoo qabla zaalika mutrafeen.

اِنَّهُمْ كَانُوْا قَبْلَ ذٰلِكَ مُتْرَفِيْنَ ۞

46. And persisted obstinately in wickedness supreme!

46. Wa kaanoo yusirroona 'Alal-hinsil-'azeem.

وَكَانُوْا يُصِرُّوْنَ عَلَى الْحِنْثِ الْعَظِيْمِ ۞

47. And they used to say, "What! when we die and become dust and bones, shall we then indeed be raised up again?-

47. Wa kaanoo yaqooloona a'izaa mitnaa wa kunnaa turaabañw-wa 'izaaman 'a-innaa lamab'oosoon.

وَكَانُوْا يَقُوْلُوْنَ ۥ اَئِذَا مِتْنَا وَكُنَّا تُرَابًا وَّعِظَامًا ءَاِنَّا لَمَبْعُوْثُوْنَ ۞

48. "(We) and our fathers of old?"

48. Awa aabaaa'unal-awwa-loon.

اَوَ اٰبَآؤُنَا الْاَوَّلُوْنَ ۞

49. Say: "Yes, those of old and those of later times,

49. Qul innal-awwaleena wal-aakhireen.

قُلْ اِنَّ الْاَوَّلِيْنَ وَالْاٰخِرِيْنَ ۞

50. "All will certainly be gathered together for the meeting appointed for a Day well-known.

51. Then lo! Ye, the erring, the deniers,

52. "You will surely taste of the Tree of Zaqqum.

53. "Then will you fill your insides therewith,

54. "And drink Boiling Water on top of it:

55. Drinking even as the camel drinketh.

56. This will be their welcome on the Day of Judgment.

57. We created you. Will ye then admit the truth?

58. Have you seen that which ye emit?

59. Is it you who create it, or are We the Creators?

60. We have decreed Death to be your common lot, and We are not to be frustrated-

61. from changing your Forms and creating you (again) in (forms) that you know not.

62. And you certainly know already the first form of creation: why then do you not celebrate His praises?

63. See you the seed that you sow in the ground?

64. Is it you that cause it to grow, or are We the Cause?

65. If We willed, We verily could make it chaff, then would ye cease not to exclaim.

66. (Saying), "We are indeed left with debts (for nothing):

67. "Indeed are we shut out (of the fruits of our labour)"

68. See you the water which you drink?

69. Do you bring it down (in rain) from the cloud or do We?

50. Lamajmoo'oona ilaa meeqaati Yawmim-ma'loom.

51. Summa innakum ayyuhaḍ-ḍaaalloonal-mukaẓẓiboon.

52. La-aakiloona min shajarim-min Zaqqoom.

53. Famaali'oona minhal-butoon.

54. Fashaariboona 'alayhi minal-ḥameem.

55. Fashaariboona shurbal-heem.

56. Haaẓaa nuzuluhum Yawmad-Deen.

57. Naḥnu khalaqnaakum fa-law laa tuṣaddiqoon.

58. Afara'aytum maa tumnoon.

59. 'A-antum takhluqoonahooo am Naḥnul-khaaliqoon.

60. Naḥnu qaddarnaa bayna-kumul-mawta wa maa Naḥnu bimasbooqeen.

61. 'Alaaa an nubaddila amṣaalakum wa nunshi'akum fee maa laa ta'lamoon.

62. Wa laqad 'alimtumun-nash-atal-oolaa falaw laa taẓakkaroon.

63. Afara'aytum maa taḥru-soon.

64. 'A-antum tazra'oonahooo am Naḥnuz-zaari'oon.

65. Law nashaaa'u laja'al-naahu ḥuṭaaman faẓaltum tafakkahoon.

66. Innaa lamughramoon.

67. Bal naḥnu maḥroomoon.

68. Afara'aytumul-maaa'al-laẓee tashraboon.

69. 'A-antum anzaltumoohu minal-muzni am Naḥnul-munziloon.

70. Were it Our Will, We could make it salt (and unpalatable): then why do you not give thanks?

71. See you the Fire which you kindle?

72. Is it you who grow the tree which feeds the fire, or do We grow it?

73. We have made it a memorial (of Our handiwork), and an article of comfort and convenience for the denizens of deserts.

74. Then celebrate with praises the name of your Lord, the Supreme!

75. Furthermore I call to witness the setting of the Stars,-

76. And lo! That verily is a tremendous oath, if ye but knew—

77. That this is indeed a qur'an Most Honourable,

78. In Book well-guarded,

79. Which none shall touch but those who are clean:

80. A Revelation from the Lord of the Worlds.

81. Is it such a Message that you would hold in light esteem?

82. And make denial thereof your livelihood?

83. Why, then, when (the soul) cometh up to the throat (of the dying)

84. And you the while (sit) looking on,-

85. But We are nearer to him than you, and yet see not,-

86. Why then, if ye are not in bondage (unto Us),

87. Do ye not force it back, if ye are truthful?

88. Thus, then, if he be of those Nearest to Allah,

89. Then breath of life, and plenty, and a Garden of delight.

90. And if he be of the Companions of the Right Hand,

91. (For him is the salutation), "Peace be unto you", from the Companions of the Right Hand.

70. Law nashaaa'u ja‘alnaahu ujaajan falaw laa tashkuroon.

71. Afara'aytumun-naaral-latee tooroon.

72. 'A-antum anshaâtum shajaratahaaa am Naḥnul-munshi'oon.

73. Naḥnu ja‘alnaahaa tazkira-tañw-wa mataa‘al-lilmuqween.

74. Fasabbiḥ bismi-Rabbikal-‘aẓeem. **(Section 2)**

75. Falaaa uqsimu bimawaa-qi‘in-nujoom.

76. Wa innahoo laqasamul-law ta‘lamoona ‘aẓeem.

77. Innahoo la-Qur-aanun Kareem.

78. Fee kitaabim-maknoon.

79. Laa yamassuhooo illal-muṭahharoon.

80. Tanzeelum-mir-Rabbil-‘aalameen.

81. Afabihaazal-ḥadeesi an-tum mudhinoon.

82. Wa taj‘aloona rizqakum annakum tukazziboon.

83. Falaw laaa izaa balaghatil-ḥulqoom.

84. Wa antum ḥeena'izin tanzuroon.

85. Wa Naḥnu aqrabu ilayhi minkum wa laakil-laa tubṣi-roon.

86. Falaw laaa in kuntum ghayra madeeneen.

87. Tarji‘oonahaaa in kuntum ṣaadiqeen.

88. Fa-ammaaa in kaana minal-muqarrabeen.

89. Farawḥuñw-wa rayḥaa-nuñw-wa Jannatu Na‘eem.

90. Wa ammaaa in kaana min Aṣ-ḥaabil-Yameen.

91. Fasalaamul-laka min Aṣ-ḥaabil-Yameen.

92. And if he be of those who treat (Truth) as Falsehood, who go wrong,

93. For him is Entertainment with Boiling Water.

94. And burning in Hell-Fire.

95. Verily, this is the very Truth of assured certainty.

96. So celebrate with praises the name of thy Lord, the Supreme.

57. Iron

In the name of Allah, Most Gracious, Most Merciful.

1. All that is in the heavens and the earth glorifieth Allah; and He is the Mighty, the Wise.

2. His is the Sovereignty of the heavens and the earth; He quickeneth and He giveth death; and He is Able to do all things.

3. He is the First and the Last, the Evident and the Hidden: and He has full knowledge of all things.

4. He it is Who created the heavens and the earth in Six Days, and is moreover firmly established on the Throne (of Authority). He knows what enters within the earth and what comes forth out of it, what comes down from heaven and what mounts up to it. And He is with you wheresoever you may be. And Allah sees well all that you do.

5. To Him belongs the dominion of the heavens and the earth: and all affairs are referred back to Allah.

6. He merges Night into Day, and He merges Day into Night; and He has full knowledge of the secrets of (all) hearts.

92. Wa ammaaa in kaana minal-mukazzibeenaḍ-ḍaaalleen.

93. Fanuzulum-min ḥameem.

94. Wa taṣliyatu Jaḥeem.

95. Inna haazaa lahuwa ḥaqqul-yaqeen.

96. Fasabbiḥ bismi Rabbikal-'aẓeem.   (Section 3)

Sûrat al-Ḥadîd–57

(Revealed at Madinah)

Bismillaahir Raḥmaanir Raḥeem

1. Sabbaḥa lillaahi maa fissamaawaati wal-arḍi wa Huwal-'Azeezul-Ḥakeem.

2. Lahoo mulkus-samaawaati wal-arḍi yuḥyee wa yumeetu wa Huwa 'alaa kulli shay'in Qadeer.

3. Huwal-Awwalu wal-Aakhiru waẓ-Ẓaahiru wal-Baaṭinu wa Huwa bikulli shay'in 'Aleem.

4. Huwal-lazee khalaqassamaawaati wal-arḍa fee sittati ayyaamin summas-tawaa 'alal-'Arsh; ya'lamu maa yaliju fil-arḍi wa maa yakhruju minhaa wa maa yanzilu minas-samaaa'i wa maa ya'ruju feehaa wa Huwa ma'akum ayna maa kuntum; wallaahu bimaa ta'maloona Baṣeer.

5. Lahoo mulkus-samaawaati wal-arḍ; wa ilal-laahi turja'ul-umoor.

6. Yoolijul-layla fin-nahaari wa yoolijun-nahaara fil-layl; wa Huwa 'Aleemum bizaatiṣ-ṣudoor.

7. Believe in Allah and His apostle, and spend (in charity) out of the (substance) whereof He has made you heirs. For, those of you who believe and spend (in charity),- for them is a great Reward.

8. What cause have you why you should not believe in Allah?- and the Apostle invites you to believe in your Lord, and has indeed taken your Covenant, if you are men of Faith.

9. He is the One Who sends to His Servant Manifest Signs, that He may lead you from the depths of Darkness into the Light and verily Allah is to you most kind and Merciful.

10. And what cause have you why you should not spend in the cause of Allah? For to Allah belongs the heritage of the heavens and the earth. Not equal among you are those who spent (freely) and fought, before the Victory, (with those who did so later). Those are higher in rank than those who spent (freely) and fought afterwards. But to all has Allah promised a goodly (reward). And Allah is well acquainted with all that you do.

11. Who is he that will Loan to Allah a beautiful loan? for (Allah) will increase it manifold to his credit, and he will have (besides) a liberal Reward.

12. One Day shall you see the believing men and the believing women- how their Light runs forward before them and by their right hands: (their greeting will be): "Good News for you this Day! Gardens beneath which flow rivers to dwell therein for ever! This is indeed the highest Achievement!"

7. Aaminoo billaahi wa Rasoolihee wa anfiqoo mim-maa ja'alakum mustakh-lafeena feehi fallazeena aamanoo minkum wa anfaqoo lahum ajrun kabeer.

8. Wa maa lakum laa tu'minoona billaahi war-Rasoolu yad'ookum litu'minoo bi-Rabbikum wa qad akhaza meesaaqakum in kuntum mu'mineen.

9. Huwal-lazee yunazzilu 'alaa 'abdihee Aayaatim bayyinaatil-liyukhrijakum minaz-zulumaati ilan-noor; wa innal-laaha bikum la-Ra'oofur-Raheem.

10. Wa maa lakum allaa tunfiqoo fee sabeelil-laahi wa lillaahi meeraasus-samaawaati wal-ard; laa yastawee minkum man anfaqa min qablil-Fat-ḥi wa qaatal; ulaaa'ika a'zamu darajatam-minal-lazeena an-faqoo mim ba'du wa qaataloo; wa kullanw-wa'adallaahul-ḥusnaa; wallaahu bimaa ta'maloona Khabeer. (Section 1)

11. Man zal-lazee yuqriḍul-laaha qarḍan ḥasanan fa-yu-ḍaa'ifahoo lahoo wa lahooo ajrun kareem.

12. Yawma taral-mu'mineena walmu'minaati yas'aa nooru-hum bayna aydeehim wa bi-aymaanihim bushraakumul-Yawma Jannaatun tajree min taḥtihal-anhaaru khaalideena feehaa; zaalika huwal-fawzul-'azeem.

13. One Day will the Hypocrites- men and women - say to the Believers: "Wait for us! Let us borrow (a Light) from your Light!" It will be said: "Turn you back to your rear! then seek a Light (where you can)!" So a wall will be put up between them, with a gate therein. Within it will be Mercy throughout, and without it, all alongside, will be (Wrath and) Punishment!

14. (Those without) will call out, "Were we not with you?" (The others) will reply, "True! but you led yourselves into temptation; you looked forward (to our ruin); you doubted (Allah's Promise); and (your false) desires deceived you; until there issued the Command of Allah. And the Deceiver deceived you in respect of Allah.

15. "This Day shall no ransom be accepted of you, nor of those who rejected Allah." Your abode is the Fire: that is the proper place to claim you: and an evil refuge it is!"

16. Has not the Time arrived for the Believers that their hearts in all humility should engage in the remembrance of Allah and of the Truth which has been revealed (to them), and that they should not become like those to whom was given Revelation aforetime, but long ages passed over them and their hearts grew hard? For many among them are rebellious transgressors.

17. Know you (all) that Allah giveth life to the earth after its death! already have We shown the Signs plainly to you, that you may learn wisdom.

18. For those who give in Charity, men and women, and loan to Allah a Beautiful Loan, it shall be increased manifold (to their credit), and they shall have (besides) a liberal reward.

13. Yawma yaqoolul-munaafiqoona walmunaafiqaatu lillazeena aamanun-zuroonaa naqtabis min noorikum qeelarji'oo waraaa'akum faltamisoo nooran faduriba baynahum bisooril-lahoo baab, baatinuhoo feehir-rahmatu wa zaahiruhoo min qibalihil-'azaab.

14. Yunaadoonahum alam nakum-ma'akum qaaloo balaa wa laakinnakum fatantum anfusakum wa tarabbastum wartabtum wa gharratkumulamaaniyyu hattaa jaaa'a amrullaahi wa gharrakum billaahilgharoor.

15. Fal-Yawma laa yu'khazu minkum fidyatuñw-wa laa minal-lazeena kafaroo; maawaakumun-Naaru hiya mawlaakum wa bi'sal-maseer.

16. Alam yaáni lillazeena aamanooo an takhsha'a quloobuhum lizikril-laahi wa maa nazala minal-haqqi wa laa yakoonoo kallazeena ootul-Kitaaba min qablu fataala 'alayhimul-amadu faqasat quloobuhum wa kaseerumminhum faasiqoon.

17. I'lamooo annal-laaha yuhyil-arda ba'da mawtihaa; qad bayyannaa lakumul-Aayaati la'allakum ta'qiloon.

18. Innal-mussaddiqeena walmussaddiqaati wa aqradullaaha qardan hasanañy-yudaa'afu lahum wa lahum ajrun kareem.

يَوْمَ يَقُوْلُ الْمُنٰفِقُوْنَ وَالْمُنٰفِقٰتُ لِلَّذِيْنَ اٰمَنُوا انْظُرُوْنَا نَقْتَبِسْ مِنْ نُّوْرِكُمْ قِيْلَ ارْجِعُوْا وَرَآءَكُمْ فَالْتَمِسُوْا نُوْرًا ۖ فَضُرِبَ بَيْنَهُمْ بِسُوْرٍ لَّهٗ بَابٌ ۖ بَاطِنُهٗ فِيْهِ الرَّحْمَةُ وَظَاهِرُهٗ مِنْ قِبَلِهِ الْعَذَابُ ۞

يُنَادُوْنَهُمْ اَلَمْ نَكُنْ مَّعَكُمْ ۖ قَالُوْا بَلٰى وَلٰكِنَّكُمْ فَتَنْتُمْ اَنْفُسَكُمْ وَتَرَبَّصْتُمْ وَارْتَبْتُمْ وَغَرَّتْكُمُ الْاَمَانِيُّ حَتّٰى جَآءَ اَمْرُ اللّٰهِ وَغَرَّكُمْ بِاللّٰهِ الْغَرُوْرُ ۞

فَالْيَوْمَ لَا يُؤْخَذُ مِنْكُمْ فِدْيَةٌ وَّلَا مِنَ الَّذِيْنَ كَفَرُوْا ۖ مَأْوٰىكُمُ النَّارُ ۖ هِيَ مَوْلٰىكُمْ ۖ وَبِئْسَ الْمَصِيْرُ ۞

اَلَمْ يَأْنِ لِلَّذِيْنَ اٰمَنُوْا اَنْ تَخْشَعَ قُلُوْبُهُمْ لِذِكْرِ اللّٰهِ وَمَا نَزَلَ مِنَ الْحَقِّ ۖ وَلَا يَكُوْنُوْا كَالَّذِيْنَ اُوْتُوا الْكِتٰبَ مِنْ قَبْلُ فَطَالَ عَلَيْهِمُ الْاَمَدُ فَقَسَتْ قُلُوْبُهُمْ ۖ وَكَثِيْرٌ مِّنْهُمْ فٰسِقُوْنَ ۞

اِعْلَمُوْا اَنَّ اللّٰهَ يُحْيِ الْاَرْضَ بَعْدَ مَوْتِهَا ۖ قَدْ بَيَّنَّا لَكُمُ الْاٰيٰتِ لَعَلَّكُمْ تَعْقِلُوْنَ ۞

اِنَّ الْمُصَّدِّقِيْنَ وَالْمُصَّدِّقٰتِ وَاَقْرَضُوا اللّٰهَ قَرْضًا حَسَنًا يُّضٰعَفُ لَهُمْ وَلَهُمْ اَجْرٌ كَرِيْمٌ ۞

19. And those who believe in Allah and His apostles- they are the Sincere (lovers of Truth), and the witnesses (who testify), in the eyes of their Lord: They shall have their Reward and their Light. But those who reject Allah and deny Our Signs,- they are the Companions of Hell-Fire.

20. Know you (all), that the life of this world is but play and amusement, pomp and mutual boasting and multiplying, (in rivalry) among yourselves, riches and children. Here is a similitude: How rain and the growth which it brings forth, delight (the hearts of) the tillers; soon it withers; you will see it grow yellow; then it becomes dry and crumbles away. But in the Hereafter is a Chastisement severe (for the devotees of wrong). And Forgiveness from Allah and (His) Good Pleasure (for the devotees of Allah). And what is the life of this world, but goods and chattels of deception?

21. Be you foremost (in seeking) Forgiveness from your Lord, and a Garden (of Bliss), the width whereof is as the width of heaven and earth, prepared for those who believe in Allah and His apostles: that is the Grace of Allah, which He bestows on whom he pleases: and Allah is the Lord of Grace abounding.

22. No misfortune can happen on earth or in your souls but is recorded in a decree before We bring it into existence: That is truly easy for Allah:

23. In order that you may not despair over matters that pass you by, nor exult over favours bestowed upon you. For Allah

19. Wallażeena aamanoo bil-laahi wa Rusuliheee ulaaa'ika humuṣ-ṣiddeeqoona wash-shuhadaaa'u 'inda Rabbihim lahum ajruhum wa nooruhum wallażeena kafaroo wa każ-żaboo bi-Aayaatinaaa ulaaa'ika Aṣ-ḥaabul-Jaḥeem. (Section 2)

20. I'lamooo annamal-ḥayaa-tud-dunyaa la'ibuñw-wa lahwuñw-wa zeenatuñw-wa tafaakhurum baynakum wa takaaṣurun fil-amwaali wal-awlaad, kamaṣali ghaysin a'jabal-kuffaara nabaatuhoo ṣumma yaheeju fataraahu muṣfarran ṣumma yakoonu ḥuṭaamaa; wa fil-Aakhirati 'ażaabun shadeeduñw-wa magh-firatum-minal-laahi wa riḍ-waan; wa mal-ḥayaa-tuddun-yaaa illaa mataa'ul-ghuroor.

21. Saabiqooo ilaa magh-firatim-mir-Rabbikum wa Jannatin 'arḍuhaa ka-'arḍis-samaaa'i wal-arḍi u'iddat lillażeena aamanoo billaahi wa Rusulih; żaalika faḍlul-laahi yu'teehi mañy-yashaaa'; wal-laahu żul-faḍlil-'ażeem.

22. Maaa aṣaaba mim-muṣee-batin fil-arḍi wa laa feee anfusi-kum illaa fee kitaabim-min qabli an nabra-ahaa; inna żaalika 'alal-laahi yaseer.

23. Likaylaa taåsaw 'alaa maa faatakum wa laa tafraḥoo bimaaa aataakum; wallaahu

loves not any vainglorious boaster,-

24. Such persons as are covetous and commend covetousness to men. And if any turn back (from Allah's Way), verily Allah is Free of all Needs, Worthy of all Praise.

25. We sent aforetime our apostles with Clear Signs and sent down with them the Book and the Balance (of Right and Wrong), that men may stand forth in justice; and We sent down Iron, in which is (material for) mighty war, as well as many benefits for mankind, that Allah may test who it is that will help, Unseen, Him and His apostles: For Allah is Full of Strength, Exalted in Might (and able to enforce His Will).

26. And We sent Noah and Abraham, and established in their line Prophethood and Revelation: and some among their progeny were on right guidance. But many of them became rebellious transgressors.

27. Then, in their wake, We followed them up with (others of) Our apostles: We sent after them Jesus the son of Mary, and bestowed on him the Gospel; and We ordained in the hearts of those who followed him Compassion and Mercy. But the Monasticism which they invented for themselves, We did not prescribe for them: (We commanded) only the seeking for the Good Pleasure of Allah; but that they did not foster as they should have done. Yet We bestowed, on those among them who believed, their (due) reward, but many of them are rebellious transgressors.

28. O you that believe! Fear Allah, and believe in His Apostle, and He will bestow on you a double portion

laa yuḥibbu kulla mukhtaalin fakhoor.

24. Allazeena yabkhaloona wa yaåmuroonan-naasa bilbukhl; wa mañy-yatawalla fa-innal-laaha Huwal-Ghaniyyul-Ḥameed.

25. Laqad arsalnaa Rusulanaa bilbayyinaati wa anzalnaa ma'ahumul-Kitaaba wal-Meezaana liyaqooman-naasu bilqisṭ, wa anzalnal-ḥadeeda feehi baåsun shadeeduñw-wa manaafi'u linnaasi wa liya'lamal-laahu mañy-yanṣuruhoo wa Rusulahoo bilghayb; innallaaha Qawiyyun 'Azeez. **(Section 3)**

26. Wa laqad arsalnaa Noo-ḥañw-wa Ibraaheema wa ja'alnaa fee zurriyyatihiman-Nubuwwata wal-Kitaaba faminhum muhtad; wa kaseerum-minhum faasiqoon.

27. Summa qaffaynaa 'alaaa aasaarihim bi-Rusulinaa wa qaffaynaa bi-'Eesab-ni-Maryama wa aataynaahul-Injeela wa ja'alnaa fee quloobil-lazeenattaba'oohu raåfatañw-wa raḥmatañw wa rahbaaniyyatanibtada'oohaa maa katabnaahaa 'alayhim illab-tighaaa'a riḍwaanil-laahi famaa ra'awhaa ḥaqqa ri'aayatihaa fa-aataynallazeena aamanoo minhum ajrahum wa kaseerum-minhum faasiqoon.

28. Yaaa ayyuhal-lazeena aamanut-taqullaaha wa aaminoo bi-Rasoolihee yu'tikum kiflayni

لَا يُحِبُّ كُلَّ مُخْتَالٍ فَخُورٍۨ ۝

ٱلَّذِينَ يَبْخَلُونَ وَيَأْمُرُونَ النَّاسَ بِالْبُخْلِ ۗ وَمَنْ يَتَوَلَّ فَإِنَّ اللّٰهَ هُوَ الْغَنِيُّ الْحَمِيدُ ۝

لَقَدْ أَرْسَلْنَا رُسُلَنَا بِالْبَيِّنَٰتِ وَأَنزَلْنَا مَعَهُمُ الْكِتَٰبَ وَالْمِيزَانَ لِيَقُومَ النَّاسُ بِالْقِسْطِ ۖ وَأَنزَلْنَا الْحَدِيدَ فِيهِ بَأْسٌ شَدِيدٌ وَمَنَٰفِعُ لِلنَّاسِ وَلِيَعْلَمَ اللّٰهُ مَن يَنصُرُهُۥ وَرُسُلَهُۥ بِالْغَيْبِ ۚ إِنَّ اللّٰهَ قَوِيٌّ عَزِيزٌ ۝

وَلَقَدْ أَرْسَلْنَا نُوحًا وَإِبْرَٰهِيمَ وَجَعَلْنَا فِي ذُرِّيَّتِهِمَا النُّبُوَّةَ وَالْكِتَٰبَ ۖ فَمِنْهُم مُّهْتَدٍ ۖ وَكَثِيرٌ مِّنْهُمْ فَٰسِقُونَ ۝

ثُمَّ قَفَّيْنَا عَلَىٰ آثَٰرِهِم بِرُسُلِنَا وَقَفَّيْنَا بِعِيسَى ابْنِ مَرْيَمَ وَآتَيْنَٰهُ الْإِنجِيلَ ۖ وَجَعَلْنَا فِي قُلُوبِ الَّذِينَ اتَّبَعُوهُ رَأْفَةً وَرَحْمَةً وَرَهْبَانِيَّةً ابْتَدَعُوهَا مَا كَتَبْنَٰهَا عَلَيْهِمْ إِلَّا ابْتِغَآءَ رِضْوَٰنِ اللّٰهِ فَمَا رَعَوْهَا حَقَّ رِعَايَتِهَا ۖ فَآتَيْنَا الَّذِينَ آمَنُوا مِنْهُمْ أَجْرَهُمْ ۖ وَكَثِيرٌ مِّنْهُمْ فَٰسِقُونَ ۝

يَٰٓأَيُّهَا الَّذِينَ آمَنُوا اتَّقُوا اللّٰهَ وَآمِنُوا بِرَسُولِهِۦ يُؤْتِكُمْ كِفْلَيْنِ

of His Mercy: He will provide for you a Light by which you shall walk (straight in your path), and He will forgive you (your past): for Allah is Oft-Forgiving, Most Merciful.

29. That the People of the Book may know that they have no power whatever over the Grace of Allah, that (His) Grace is (entirely) in His Hand, to bestow it on whomsoever He wills. For Allah is the Lord of Grace abounding.

58. The Woman Who Pleads
In the name of Allah, Most Gracious, Most Merciful.

1. Allah has indeed heard (and accepted) the statement of the woman who pleads with thee concerning her husband and carries her complaint (in prayer) to Allah: and Allah (always) heard the arguments between both sides among you: for Allah hears and sees (all things).

2. If any men among you divorce their wives by Zihar (calling them mothers), they cannot be their mothers: None can be their mothers except those who gave them birth. And in fact they use words (both) iniquitous and false: but truly Allah is one that blots out (sins), and forgives (again and again).

3. But those who divorce their wives by Zihar, then wish to go back on the words they uttered,- (It is ordained that such a one) should free a slave before they touch each other: Thus are you admonished to perform: and Allah is well-acquainted with (all) that you do.

4. And if any has not (the wherewithal), he should fast for two months consecutively before they touch each other. But if any is unable to do so, he should feed sixty indigent ones, this, that you may show your faith in Allah and His Apostle.

mir raḥmatihee wa yaj‘al lakum nooran tamshoona bihee wa yaghfir lakum; wallaahu Ghafoorur-Raḥeem.

29. Li’allaa ya‘lama Ahlul-kitaabi allaa yaqdiroona ‘alaa shay’im-min faḍlil-laahi wa annal-faḍla bi-Yadil-laahi yu’teehi mañy-yashaaa’; wallaahu Zul-faḍlil-‘aẓeem.
(Section 4)

Sûrat al-Mujâdilah–58
(Revealed at Madinah)
Bismillaahir Raḥmaanir Raḥeem

1. Qad sami‘al-laahu qawlal-latee tujaadiluka fee zawjihaa wa tashtakee ilal-laahi wallaa-hu yasma‘u taḥaawurakumaa; innal-laaha Samee‘um Baṣeer.

2. Allażeena yuẓaahiroona minkum min nisaaa’ihim maa hunna ummahaatihim in ummahaatuhum illal-laaa’ee waladnahum; wa innahum la-yaqooloona munkaram-minal-qawli wa zooraa; wa innal-laaha la-‘Afuwwun Ghafoor.

3. Wallażeena yuẓaahiroona min nisaaa’ihim summa ya‘oodoona limaa qaaloo fataḥreeru raqabatim-min qabli añy-yatamaaassaa; zaalikum too‘aẓoona bih; wallaahu bimaa ta‘maloona Khabeer.

4. Famal-lam yajid fa-Ṣiyaa-mu shahrayni mutataabi‘ayni min qabli any-yatamaaassaa famal-lam yastaṭi‘ fa-iṭ‘aamu sitteena miskeenaa; zaalika litu’minoo billaahi wa Rasoolih;

Those are limits (set by) Allah. For those who reject (Him), there is a grievous Chastisement.

5. Those who resist Allah and His Apostle will be humbled to dust, as were those before them: for We have already sent down Clear Signs. And the Unbelievers (will have) a humiliating Chastisement,-

6. On the Day that Allah will raise them all up (again) and show them the Truth (and meaning) of their conduct. Allah has reckoned its (value), though they may have forgotten it, for Allah is Witness to all things.

7. Do you see not that Allah does know (all) that is in the heavens and on earth? There is not a secret consultation between three, but He makes the fourth among them, - Nor between five but He makes the sixth,- nor between fewer nor more, but He is in their midst, wheresoever they be: In the end will He tell them the truth of their conduct, on the Day of Judgment. For Allah has full knowledge of all things.

8. Turnest you not your sight towards those who were forbidden secret counsels yet revert to that which they were forbidden (to do)? And they hold secret counsels among themselves for iniquity and hostility, and disobedience to the Apostle. And when they come to thee, they salute you, not as Allah salutes thee, (but in crooked ways): And they say to themselves, "Why does not Allah punish us for our words?" Enough for them is Hell: In it will they burn, and evil is that destination!

9. O you who believe! When you hold secret counsel, do it not for iniquity and hostility, and disobedience to the Prophet; but do it for righteousness

wa tilka ḥudoodul-laah; wa lilkaafireena 'azaabun aleem.

5. Innal-lazeena yuḥaaad-doonal-laaha wa Rasoolahoo kubitoo kamaa kubital-lazeena min qablihim; wa qad anzalnaaa Aayaatim bayyinaat; wa lilkaa-fireena 'azaabum-muheen.

6. Yawma yab'asuhumul-laahu jamee'an fa-yunabbi'u-hum bimaa 'amiloo; aḥsaahul-laahu wa nasooh; wallaahu 'alaa kulli shay'in Shaheed. **(Section 1)**

7. Alam tara annal-laaha ya'lamu maa fis-samaawaati wa maa fil-arḍi maa yakoonu min najwaa salaasatin illaa Huwa raabi'uhum wa laa khamsatin illaa Huwa saadisuhum wa laaa adnaa min zaalika wa laaa aksara illaa Huwa ma'ahum ayna maa kaanoo summa yunabbi'uhum bimaa 'amiloo Yawmal-Qiyaamah; innal-laaha bikulli shay'in 'Aleem.

8. Alam tara ilal-lazeena nuhoo 'anin-najwaa summa ya'oodoona limaa nuhoo 'anhu wa yatanaajawna bil-ismi wal'udwaani wa ma'ṣiyatir-Rasooli wa izaa jaaa'ooka ḥayyawka bimaa lam yuḥay-yika bihil-laahu wa yaqooloona feee anfusihim law laa yu'az-zibunal-laahu bimaa naqool; ḥasbuhum Jahannamu yaṣlaw-nahaa fabi'sal-maṣeer.

9. Yaaa ayyuhal-lazeena aamanooo izaa tanaajaytum falaa tatanaajaw bil-ismi wal-'udwaani wa ma'ṣiyatir-Rasooli wa tanaajaw bil-birri

and self-restraint; Whom you shall be brought back.

wattaqwaa wattaqul-laahal-lazeee ilayhi tuḥsharoon.

10. Secret counsels are only (inspired) by the Evil One, in order that he may cause grief to the Believers; but he cannot harm them in the least, except as Allah permits; and on Allah let the Believers put their trust.

10. Innaman-najwaa minash-Shayṭaani liyaḥzunal-lazeena aamanoo wa laysa biḍaaarrihim shay'an illaa bi-iznil-laah; wa 'alal-laahi falyatawakkalil-mu'minoon.

11. O you who believe! When you are told to make room in the assemblies, (spread out and) make room: (ample) room will Allah provide for you. And when you are told to rise up, rise up, Allah will raise up, to (suitable) ranks (and degrees) those of you who believe and who have been granted (mystic) Knowledge. And Allah is well-acquainted with all you do.

11. Yaaa ayyuhal-lazeena aamanooo izaa qeela lakum tafassaḥoo fil-majaalisi fafsaḥoo yafsaḥil-laahu lakum wa izaa qeelan-shuzoo fanshuzoo yarfa'il-laahul-lazeena aamanoo minkum wallazeena ootul-'ilma darajaat; wallaahu bimaa ta'maloona Khabeer.

12. O you who believe! When you consult the Apostle in private, spend something in charity before your private consultation. That will be best for you, and most conducive to purity (of conduct). But if you find not (the wherewithal), Allah is Oft-Forgiving, Most Merciful.

12. Yaaa-ayyuhal-lazeena aamanooo izaa naajaytumur-Rasoola faqaddimoo bayna yaday najwaakum ṣadaqah; zaalika khayrul-lakum wa aṭhar; fa-il-lam tajidoo fa-innal-laaha Ghafoorur-Raḥeem.

13. Is it that you are afraid of spending sums in charity before your private consultation (with him)? If, then, you do not so, and Allah forgives you, then (at least) establish regular prayer; practise regular charity; and obey Allah and His Apostle. And Allah is well-acquainted with all that you do.

13. 'A-ashfaqtum an tuqad-dimoo bayna yaday najwaakum ṣadaqaat; fa-iz lam taf'aloo wa taabal-laahu 'alaykum fa-aqeemuṣ-Ṣalaata wa aatuz-Zakaata wa aṭee'ul-laaha wa Rasoolah; wallaahu khabeerum bimaa ta'maloon.   (Section 2)

14. Turnest you not your attention to those who turn (in friendship) to such as have the Wrath of Allah upon them? They are neither of you nor of them, and they swear to falsehood knowingly.

14. Alam tara ilal-lazeena tawallaw qawman ghaḍibal-laahu 'alayhim maa hum minkum wa laa minhum wa yaḥlifoona 'alal-kazibi wa hum ya'lamoon.

15. Allah has prepared for them a severe Chastisement: evil indeed are their deeds.

16. They have made their oaths a screen (for their misdeeds): thus they obstruct (men) from the Path of Allah: therefore shall they have a humiliating Chastisement.

17. Of no profit whatever to them, against Allah, will be their riches nor their sons: they will be Companions of the Fire, to dwell therein (for ever)!

18. One day will Allah raise them all up (for Judgment): then will they swear to Him as they swear to you: And they think that they have something (to stand upon). No, indeed! they are but liars!

19. The Evil One has got the better of them: so he has made them lose the remembrance of Allah. They are the Party of the Evil One. Truly, it is the Party of the Satan that will perish!

20. Those who resist Allah and His Apostle will be among those most humiliated.

21. Allah has decreed: "It is I and My apostles who must prevail": For Allah is One full of strength, able to enforce His Will.

22. You will not find any people who believe in Allah and the Last Day, loving those who resist Allah and His Apostle, even though they were their fathers or their sons, or their brothers, or their kindred. For such He has written Faith in their hearts, and strengthened them with a spirit from Himself. And He will admit them to Gardens beneath which Rivers flow, to dwell therein (for ever). Allah will be well pleased with them, and they with Him. They are the Party of

15. A'addal-laahu lahum-'azaaban shadeedan innahum saaa'a maa kaanoo ya'maloon.

16. Ittakhazooo aymaanahum junnatan fasaddoo 'an sabeelil-laahi falahum 'azaabum-muheen.

17. Lan tughniya 'anhum amwaaluhum wa laaa awladuhum minal-laahi shay'aa; ulaaa'ika As-haabun-Naari hum feehaa khaalidoon.

18. Yawma yab'asuhumul-laahu jamee'an fa-yahlifoona lahoo kamaa yahlifoona lakum wa yahsaboona annahum 'Alaa shay'; alaaa innahum humul-kaaziboon.

19. Istahwaza 'alayhimush-Shaytaanu fa-ansaahum zikral-laah; ulaaa'ika hizbush-Shaytaan; alaaa inna hizbash-Shay-taani humul-khaasiroon.

20. Innal-lazeena yuhaaad-doonal-laaha wa Rasoolahooo ulaaa'ika fil-azalleen.

21. Katabal-laahu la-aghli-banna ana wa Rusulee; innal-laaha Qawiyyun 'Azeez.

22. Laa tajidu qawmany-yu'mi-noona billaahi wal-Yawmil-Aakhiri yuwaaaddoona man haaaddal-laaha wa Rasoolahoo wa law kaanooo aabaaa'ahum aw abnaaa'ahum aw ikhwaa-nahum aw 'asheeratahum; ulaaa'ika kataba fee quloobihi-mul-eemaana wa ayyadahum biroohim-minhu wa yudkhilu-hum Jannaatin tajree min tahtihal-anhaaru khaalideena feehaa; radiyal-laahu 'anhum wa radoo 'anh; ulaaa'ika hizbul-

اَعَدَّ اللّٰهُ لَهُمْ عَذَابًا شَدِيدًا ۖ اِنَّهُمْ سَآءَ مَا كَانُوْا يَعْمَلُوْنَ ۞

اِتَّخَذُوْۤا اَيْمَانَهُمْ جُنَّةً فَصَدُّوْا عَنْ سَبِيْلِ اللّٰهِ فَلَهُمْ عَذَابٌ مُّهِيْنٌ ۞

لَنْ تُغْنِيَ عَنْهُمْ اَمْوَالُهُمْ وَلَاۤ اَوْلَادُهُمْ مِّنَ اللّٰهِ شَيْئًا ۚ اُولٰٓئِكَ اَصْحَابُ النَّارِ ۚ هُمْ فِيْهَا خٰلِدُوْنَ ۞

يَوْمَ يَبْعَثُهُمُ اللّٰهُ جَمِيْعًا فَيَحْلِفُوْنَ لَهٗ كَمَا يَحْلِفُوْنَ لَكُمْ وَ يَحْسَبُوْنَ اَنَّهُمْ عَلٰى شَيْءٍ ۚ اَلَاۤ اِنَّهُمْ هُمُ الْكٰذِبُوْنَ ۞

اِسْتَحْوَذَ عَلَيْهِمُ الشَّيْطٰنُ فَاَنْسٰهُمْ ذِكْرَ اللّٰهِ ۚ اُولٰٓئِكَ حِزْبُ الشَّيْطٰنِ ۚ اَلَاۤ اِنَّ حِزْبَ الشَّيْطٰنِ هُمُ الْخٰسِرُوْنَ ۞

اِنَّ الَّذِيْنَ يُحَآدُّوْنَ اللّٰهَ وَرَسُوْلَهٗۤ اُولٰٓئِكَ فِى الْاَذَلِّيْنَ ۞

كَتَبَ اللّٰهُ لَاَغْلِبَنَّ اَنَا وَرُسُلِيْ ۚ اِنَّ اللّٰهَ قَوِيٌّ عَزِيْزٌ ۞

لَا تَجِدُ قَوْمًا يُّؤْمِنُوْنَ بِاللّٰهِ وَالْيَوْمِ الْاٰخِرِ يُوَآدُّوْنَ مَنْ حَآدَّ اللّٰهَ وَ رَسُوْلَهٗ وَلَوْ كَانُوْۤا اٰبَآءَهُمْ اَوْ اَبْنَآءَهُمْ اَوْ اِخْوَانَهُمْ اَوْ عَشِيْرَتَهُمْ ۚ اُولٰٓئِكَ كَتَبَ فِيْ قُلُوْبِهِمُ الْاِيْمَانَ وَاَيَّدَهُمْ بِرُوْحٍ مِّنْهُ ۚ وَيُدْخِلُهُمْ جَنّٰتٍ تَجْرِيْ مِنْ تَحْتِهَا الْاَنْهٰرُ خٰلِدِيْنَ فِيْهَا ۚ رَضِيَ اللّٰهُ عَنْهُمْ وَرَضُوْا عَنْهُ ۚ اُولٰٓئِكَ حِزْبُ

Allah. Truly it is the Party of Allah that will achieve Felicity.

59. The Gathering
In the name of Allah, Most Gracious, Most Merciful.

1. Whatever is in the heavens and on earth, let it declare the Praises and Glory of Allah: for He is the Exalted in Might, the Wise.

2. It is He Who got out the Unbelievers among the People of the Book from their homes at the first gathering (of the forces). Little did you think that they would get out: And they thought that their fortresses would defend them from Allah! But the (Wrath of) Allah came to them from quarters from which they little expected (it), and cast terror into their hearts, so that they destroyed their dwellings by their own hands and the hands of the Believers, take warning, then, O you with eyes (to see)!

3. And had it not been that Allah had decreed banishment for them, He would certainly have punished them in this world: And in the Hereafter they shall (certainly) have the Punishment of the Fire.

4. That is because they resisted Allah and His Apostle: and if any one resists Allah, verily Allah is severe in Punishment.

5. Whether you cut down (O you Muslim!) The tender palm-trees, or you left them standing on their roots, it was by leave of Allah, and in order that He might cover with shame the rebellious transgressors.

6. What Allah has bestowed on His Apostle (and taken away) from them - for this you made no expedition with either cavalry or camelry: but Allah gives power to His apostles over any He pleases: and Allah has power over all things.

---

laah; alaaa inna ḥizbal-laahi humul-mufliḥoon.   (Section 3)

Sûrat al-Ḥashr–59
(Revealed at Madinah)
Bismillaahir Raḥmaanir Raḥeem

1. Sabbaḥa lillaahi maa fis-samaawaati wa maa fil-arḍi wa Huwal-'Azeezul-Ḥakeem.

2. Huwal-lazee akhrajal-lazeena kafaroo min Ahlil-Kitaabi min diyaarihim li-awwalil-Ḥashr; maa ẓanantum añy-yakhrujoo wa ẓannooo anna-hum maa ni'atuhum ḥuṣoonu-hum minal-laahi fa-ataahumul-laahu min ḥayṡu lam yaḥtasiboo wa qazafa fee quloobihimur-ru'ba yukhriboona bu-yootahum bi-aydeehim wa aydil-mu'mineena fa'tabiroo yaaa ulil-abṣaar.

3. Wa law laaa an katabal-laahu 'alayhimul-jalaaa'a la'az-zabahum fid-dunyaa wa lahum fil-Aakhirati 'azaabun-Naar.

4. Zaalika bi-annahum shaaq-qul-laaha wa Rasoolahoo wa mañy-yushaaaqqil-laaha fa-innal-laaha shadeedul-'iqaab.

5. Maa qaṭa'tum mil-leenatin aw taraktumoohaa qaaa'imatan 'alaaa uṣoolihaa fabi-iznil-laahi wa liyukhziyal-faasiqeen.

6. Wa maaa afaaa'al-laahu 'alaa Rasoolihee minhum famaaa awjaftum 'alayhi min khayliñw-wa laa rikaabiñw-wa laakinnal-laaha yusalliṭu Rusula-hoo 'alaa mañy-yashaaa'; wallaa-hu 'alaa kulli shay'in Qadeer.

7. What Allah has bestowed on His Apostle (and taken away) from the people of the townships,- belongs to Allah,- to His Apostle and to kindred and orphans, the needy and the wayfarer; In order that it may not (merely) make a circuit between the wealthy among you. So take what the Apostle assigns to you, and deny yourselves that which he withholds from you. And fear Allah; for Allah is strict in Punishment.

8. (Some part is due) to the indigent Muhajirs, those who were expelled from their homes and their property, while seeking Grace from Allah and (His) Good Pleasure, and aiding Allah and His Apostle: such are indeed the sincere ones:-

9. But those who before them, had homes (in Medina) and had adopted the Faith,- show their affection to such as came to them for refuge, and entertain no desire in their hearts for things given to the (latter), but give them preference over themselves, even though poverty was their (own lot). And those saved from the covetousness of their own souls,- they are the ones that achieve prosperity.

10. And those who came after them say: "Our Lord! Forgive us, and our brethren who came before us into the Faith, and leave not, in our hearts, rancour (or sense of injury) against those who have believed. Our Lord! You are indeed Full of Kindness, Most Merciful."

11. Have you not observed the Hypocrites say to their misbelieving brethren among the

7. Maaa afaaa'al-laahu 'alaa Rasoolihee min ahlil-quraa falillaahi wa lir-Rasooli wa liẕil-qurbaa wal-yataamaa walmasaakeeni wabnis-sabeeli kay laa yakoona doolatam baynal-aghniyaaa'i minkum; wa maaa aataakumur-Rasoolu fakhuẕoohu wa maa nahaakum 'anhu fantahoo; wattaqul-laaha innal-laaha shadeedul-'iqaab.

8. Lilfuqaraaa'il-Muhaajireenal-laẕeena ukhrijoo min diyaarihim wa amwaalihim yabtaghoona faḍlam-minal-laahi wa riḍwaananw-wa yanṣuroonal-laaha wa Rasoolah; ulaaa'ika humuṣ-ṣaadiqoon.

9. Wallaẕeena tabawwa'ud-daara wal-eemaana min qablihim yuḥibboona man haajara ilayhim wa laa yajidoona fee ṣudoorihim ḥaajatam-mimmaaa ootoo wa yu'siroona 'alaa anfusihim wa law kaana bihim khaṣaaṣah; wa mañy-yooqa shuḥḥa nafsihee fa-ulaaa'ika humul-mufliḥoon.

10. Wallaẕeena Jaaa'oo min ba'dihim yaqooloona Rabbanagh-fir lanaa wa li-ikhwaaninal-laẕeena sabaqoonaa bileemaani wa laa taj'al fee quloobinaa ghillallil-laẕeena aamanoo Rabbanaaa innaka Ra'oofur-Raḥeem. **(Section 1)**

11. Alam tara ilal-laẕeena naafaqoo yaqooloona li-ikhwaanihimul-laẕeena kafaroo min

People of the Book? - "If you are expelled, we too will go out with you, and we will never hearken to any one in your affair; and if you are attacked (in fight) you will help you". But Allah is witness that they are indeed liars.

12. If they are expelled, never will they go out with them; and if they are attacked (in fight), they will never help them; and if they do help them, they will turn their backs; so they will receive no help.

13. Of a truth you are stronger (than they) because of the terror in their hearts, (sent) by Allah. This is because they are men devoid of understanding.

14. They will not fight you (even) together, except in fortified townships, or from behind walls. Strong is their fighting (spirit) amongst themselves: you would think they were united, but their hearts are divided: that is because they are a people devoid of wisdom.

15. Like those who lately preceded them, they have tasted the evil result of their conduct; and (in the Hereafter there is) for them a grievous Chastisement;-

16. (Their allies deceived them), like the Evil One, when he says to man, "Deny Allah": but when (man) denies Allah, (the Evil One) says, "I am free of you: I do fear Allah, the Lord of the Worlds!"

17. The end of both will be that they will go into the Fire, dwelling therein for ever. Such is the reward of the wrong-doers.

18. O you who believe! Fear Allah, and let every soul look to what (provision) he has sent forth for the morrow. Yes, fear Allah: for Allah is well-acquainted with (all)

Ahlil-Kitaabi la'in ukhrijtum lanakhrujanna ma'akum wa laa nutee'u feekum aḥadan abadañw-wa in qootiltum lananṣuran-nakum wallaahu yashhadu innahum lakaaziboon.

12. La'in ukhrijoo laa yakhru-joona ma'ahum wa la'in qoo-tiloo laa yanṣuroonahum wa la'in naṣaroohum la-yuwallun-nal-adbaara summa laa yunṣa-roon.

13. La-antum ashaddu rahba-tan fee ṣudoorihim minal-laah; zaalika bi-annahum qawmul-laa yafqahoon.

14. Laa yuqaatiloonakum ja-mee'an illaa fee quram-muḥaṣ-ṣanatin aw miñw-waraaa'i judur; baåsuhum baynahum shadeed; taḥsabuhum jamee'añw-wa qu-loobuhum shattaa; zaalika bi-annahum qawmul-laa ya'qi-loon.

15. Kamaṣalil-lazeena min qablihim qareeban zaaqoo wabaala amrihim wa lahum 'azaabun aleem.

16. Kamaṣalish-Shayṭaani iz qaala lil-insaanik-fur falammaa kafara qaala innee baree'um-minka ineee akhaaful-laaha Rabbal-'aalameen.

17. Fakaana 'aaqibatahumaaa annahumaa fin-Naari khaali-dayni feehaa; wa zaalika jazaaa-'uz-zaalimeen.   (Section 2)

18. Yaaa ayyuhal-lazeena aamanut-taqul-laaha waltanzur nafsum-maa qaddamat lighad, wattaqul-laah; innal-laaha Khabeerum bimaa

that you do.

19. And be you not like those who forgot Allah; and He made them forget their own souls! Such are the rebellious transgressors!

20. Not equal are the Companions of the Fire and the Companions of the Garden: it is the Companions of the Garden, that will achieve Felicity.

21. Had We sent down this Qur'an on a mountain, verily, thou wouldst have seen it humble itself and cleave asunder for fear of Allah. Such are the similitudes which We propound to men, that they may reflect.

22. Allah is He, than Whom there is no other god;- Who knows (all things) both secret and open; He, Most Gracious, Most Merciful.

23. Allah is He, other than Whom there is no other god;- the Sovereign, the Holy One, the Source of Peace (and Perfection), the Guardian of Faith, the Preserver of Safety, the Exalted in Might, the Irresistible, the Supreme: Glory to Allah! (High is He) above the partners they attribute to Him.

24. He is Allah, the Creator, the Evolver, the Fashioner, the Bestower of Forms (or Colours). To Him belong the Most Beautiful Names: whatever is in the heavens and on earth, does declare His Praises and Glory: and He is the Exalted in Might, the Wise.

60. The Woman to be Examined
In the name of Allah, Most Gracious, Most Merciful.

1. O you who believe! Take not my enemies and yours as friends (or protectors),- offering them (your) love, even though they have rejected the Truth that has come to you, and have (on the contrary) driven out

ta'maloon.

19. Wa laa takoonoo kalla-zeena nasul-laaha fa-ansaahum anfusahum; ulaaa'ika humul-faasiqoon.

20. Laa yastawee Aṣ-ḥaabun-Naari wa Aṣ-ḥaabul-Jannah; Aṣ-ḥaabul-Jannati humul-faaa'izoon.

21. Law anzalnaa haazal-Qur-aana 'alaa jabalil-lara-aytahoo khaashi'am-mutaṣaddi'am-min khashyatillaah; wa tilkal-amṣaalu naḍribuhaa linnaasi la'allahum yatafakkaroon.

22. Huwal-laahul-lazee laaa Ilaaha illaa Huwa 'Aalimul-Ghaybi wash-shahaadati Huwar-Raḥmaanur-Raḥeem.

23. Huwal-laahul-lazee laaa Ilaaha illaa Huwa al-Malikul-Quddoosus-Salaamul-Mu'mi-nul-Muhayminul-'Azeezul-Jabbaarul-Mutakabbir; Subḥaa-nal-laahi 'Ammaa yushrikoon.

24. Huwal-laahul-Khaaliqul-Baari'ul-Muṣawwiru lahul-Asmaaa'ul-Ḥusnaa; yusabbiḥu lahoo maa fis-samaawaati wal-arḍi wa Huwal-'Azeezul-Ḥakeem.   **(Section 3)**

Sûrat al-Mumtaḥanah–60
(Revealed at Madinah)
Bismillaahir Raḥmaanir Raḥeem

1. Yaaa ayyuhal-lazeena aamanoo laa tattakhizoo 'aduwwee wa 'aduwwakum awliyaaa'a tulqoona ilayhim bilmawaddati wa qad kafaroo bimaa jaaa'akum minal-ḥaqq, yukhrijoonar-

the Prophet and yourselves (from your homes), (simply) because ye believe in Allah your Lord! If you have come out to strive in My Way and to seek My Good Pleasure, (take them not as friends), holding secret conclave of love (and friendship) with them: for I know full well all that you conceal and all that you reveal. And any of you that does this has strayed from the Straight Path.

2. If they were to get the better of you, they would behave to you as enemies, and stretch forth their hands and their tongues against you for evil: and they desire that you should reject the Truth.

3. Of no profit to you will be your relatives and your children on the Day of Judgment: He will judge between you: for Allah sees well all that you do.

4. There is for you an excellent example (to follow) in Abraham and those with him, when they said to their people: "We are clear of you and of whatever ye worship besides Allah: we have rejected you, and there has arisen, between us and you, enmity and hatred for ever,- unless you believe in Allah and Him alone": But not when Abraham said to his father: "I will pray for forgiveness for you, though I have no power (to get) aught on your behalf from Allah." (They prayed): "Our Lord! in You do we trust, and to You do we turn in repentance: to Thee is (our) Final Goal.

5. "Our Lord! Make us not a (test and) trial for the Unbelievers, but forgive us, our Lord! for You are the Exalted in Might, the Wise."

6. There was indeed in them an excellent example for you to follow,-

Rasoola wa iyyaakum an tu'minoo billaahi Rabbikum in kuntum kharajtum jihaadan fee sabeelee wabtighaaa'a marḍaatee; tusirroona ilayhim bilmawaddati wa ana a'lamu bimaaa akhfaytum wa maaa a'lantum; wa mañy-yaf'alhu minkum faqad ḍalla Sawaaa'as-Sabeel.

2. Iñy-yasqafookum yakoonoo lakum a'daaa'añw-wa yabsuṭooo ilaykum aydiyahum wa alsinatahum bissooo'i wa waddoo law takfuroon.

3. Lan tanfa'akum arḥaamukum wa laaa awlaadukum; Yawmal-Qiyaamati yafṣilu baynakum; wallaahu bimaa ta'maloona Baṣeer.

4. Qad kaanat lakum uswatun ḥasanatun feee Ibraaheema wallazeena ma'ahoo iz qaaloo liqawmihim innaa bura'aaa'u minkum wa mimmaa ta'budoona min doonil-laahi kafarnaa bikum wa badaa baynanaa wa baynakumul-'adaawatu wal-baghḍaaa'u abadan ḥattaa tu'minoo billaahi waḥdahooo illaa qawla Ibraheema li-abeehi la-astaghfiranna laka wa maaa amliku laka minal-laahi min shay'; Rabbanaa 'alayka tawakkalnaa wa ilayka anabnaa wa ilaykal-maṣeer.

5. Rabbanaa laa taj'alnaa fitnatal-lillazeena kafaroo waghfir lanaa Rabbanaa innaka Antal-'Azeezul-Ḥakeem.

6. Laqad kaana lakum feehim uswatun

for those whose hope is in Allah and in the Last Day. But if any turn away, truly Allah is Free of all Wants, Worthy of all Praise.

7. It may be that Allah will grant love (and friendship) between you and those whom you (now) hold as enemies. For Allah has power (over all things); And Allah is Oft-Forgiving, Most Merciful.

8. Allah forbids you not, with regard to those who fight you not for (your) Faith nor drive you out of your homes, from dealing kindly and justly with them: for Allah loves those who are just.

9. Allah only forbids you, with regard to those who fight you for (your) Faith, and drive you out of your homes, and support (others) in driving you out, from turning to them (for friendship and protection). It is such as turn to them (in these circumstances), that do wrong.

10. O you who believe! When there come to you believing women refugees, examine (and test) them: Allah knows best as to their Faith: if you ascertain that they are Believers, then send them not back to the Unbelievers. They are not lawful (wives) for the Unbelievers, nor are the (Unbelievers) lawful (husbands) for them. But pay the Unbelievers what they have spent (on their dower), and there will be no blame on you if you marry them on payment of their dower to them. But hold not to the guardianship of unbelieving women: ask for what you have spent on their dowers, and let the (Unbelievers) ask for what they have spent (on the dowers of women who come over to you). Such is the command of Allah: He judges (with justice) between you. And Allah is Full of Knowledge and Wisdom.

ḥasanatul-liman kaana yarjul-laaha wal-Yawmal-Aakhir; wa mañy-yatawalla fa-innal-laaha Huwal-Ghaniyyul-Ḥameed.

(Section 1)

7. 'Asal-laahu añy-yaj'ala baynakum wa baynal-lazeena 'aadaytum minhum mawaddah; wallahu Qadeer; wallahu Ghafoorur-Raḥeem.

8. Laa yanhaakumul-laahu 'anil-lazeena lam yuqaati-lookum fid-deeni wa lam yukhrijookum-min diyaarikum an tabarroohum wa tuqsiṭooo ilayhim; innal-laaha yuḥibbul-muqsiṭeen.

9. Innamaa yanhaakumul-laahu 'anil-lazeena qaataloo-kum fid-deeni wa akhrajookum min diyaarikum wa ẕaaharoo 'alaa ikhraajikum an tawallaw-hum; wa mañy-yatawallahum fa-ulaaa'ika humuẕ-ẕaalimoon.

10. Yaaa ayyuhal-lazeena aamanoo izaa jaaa'akumul-mu'minaatu muhaajiraatin famtaḥinoohunna Allaahu a'lamu bi-eemaanihinna fa-in 'alimtumoohunna mu'mi-naatin falaa tarji'oohunna ilal-kuffaar; laa hunna ḥillul-lahum wa laa hum yaḥilloona lahunna wa aatoohum maa anfaqoo wa laa junaaḥa 'alaykum an tankiḥoohunna izaaa aatay-tumoohunna ujoorahunn; wa laa tumsikoo bi-'iṣamil-kawaafiri was'aloo maaa anfaqtum walyas'aloo maaa anfaqoo zaalikum ḥukmul-laahi yaḥ-kumu baynakum wallaahu 'Aleemun Ḥakeem.

حَسَنَةٌ لِّمَنْ كَانَ يَرْجُو اللّٰهَ وَ الْيَوْمَ الْاٰخِرَ وَمَنْ يَّتَوَلَّ فَاِنَّ اللّٰهَ هُوَ الْغَنِيُّ الْحَمِيْدُ ۞

عَسَى اللّٰهُ اَنْ يَّجْعَلَ بَيْنَكُمْ وَبَيْنَ الَّذِيْنَ عَادَيْتُمْ مِّنْهُمْ مَّوَدَّةً ۗ وَ اللّٰهُ قَدِيْرٌ ۗ وَاللّٰهُ غَفُوْرٌ رَّحِيْمٌ ۞

لَا يَنْهٰكُمُ اللّٰهُ عَنِ الَّذِيْنَ لَمْ يُقَاتِلُوْكُمْ فِى الدِّيْنِ وَلَمْ يُخْرِجُوْكُمْ مِّنْ دِيَارِكُمْ اَنْ تَبَرُّوْهُمْ وَتُقْسِطُوْۤا اِلَيْهِمْ ۗ اِنَّ اللّٰهَ يُحِبُّ الْمُقْسِطِيْنَ ۞

اِنَّمَا يَنْهٰكُمُ اللّٰهُ عَنِ الَّذِيْنَ قَاتَلُوْكُمْ فِى الدِّيْنِ وَاَخْرَجُوْكُمْ مِّنْ دِيَارِكُمْ وَظَاهَرُوْا عَلٰۤى اِخْرَاجِكُمْ اَنْ تَوَلَّوْهُمْ ۚ وَمَنْ يَّتَوَلَّهُمْ فَاُولٰٓئِكَ هُمُ الظّٰلِمُوْنَ ۞

يٰۤاَيُّهَا الَّذِيْنَ اٰمَنُوْۤا اِذَا جَآءَكُمُ الْمُؤْمِنٰتُ مُهٰجِرٰتٍ فَامْتَحِنُوْهُنَّ ۗ اَللّٰهُ اَعْلَمُ بِاِيْمَانِهِنَّ ۚ فَاِنْ عَلِمْتُمُوْهُنَّ مُؤْمِنٰتٍ فَلَا تَرْجِعُوْهُنَّ اِلَى الْكُفَّارِ ۗ لَا هُنَّ حِلٌّ لَّهُمْ وَلَا هُمْ يَحِلُّوْنَ لَهُنَّ ۖ وَاٰتُوْهُمْ مَّاۤ اَنْفَقُوْا ۚ وَلَا جُنَاحَ عَلَيْكُمْ اَنْ تَنْكِحُوْهُنَّ اِذَاۤ اٰتَيْتُمُوْهُنَّ اُجُوْرَهُنَّ ۗ وَلَا تُمْسِكُوْا بِعِصَمِ الْكَوَافِرِ وَسْـَٔلُوْا مَاۤ اَنْفَقْتُمْ وَلْيَسْـَٔلُوْا مَاۤ اَنْفَقُوْا ۚ ذٰلِكُمْ حُكْمُ اللّٰهِ ۗ يَحْكُمُ بَيْنَكُمْ ۗ وَاللّٰهُ عَلِيْمٌ حَكِيْمٌ ۞

11. And if any of your wives deserts you to the Unbelievers, and ye have an accession (by the coming over of a woman from the other side), then pay to those whose wives have deserted the equivalent of what they had spent (on their dower). And fear Allah, in Whom ye believe.

12. O Prophet! When believing women come to you to take the oath of fealty to you, that they will not associate in worship any other thing whatever with Allah, that they will not steal, that they will not commit adultery (or fornication), that they will not kill their children, that they will not utter slander, intentionally forging falsehood, and that they will not disobey thee in any just matter,- then do you receive their fealty, and pray to Allah for the forgiveness (of their sins): for Allah is Oft-Forgiving, Most Merciful.

13. O you who believe! Turn not (for friendship) to people on whom is the Wrath of Allah, of the Hereafter they are already in despair, just as the Unbelievers are in despair about those (buried) in graves.

61. Battle Array
In the name of Allah, Most Gracious, Most Merciful.

1. Whatever is in the heavens and on earth, let it declare the Praises and Glory of Allah: for He is the Exalted in Might, the Wise.

2. O you who believe, why say you that which you do not?

3. Grievously odious is it in the sight of Allah that you say that which you do not.

4. Truly Allah loves those who fight

11. Wa in faatakum shay'um-min azwaajikum ilal-kuffaari fa'aaqabtum fa-aatul-lazeena zahabat azwaajuhum misla maaa anfaqoo; wattaqul-laahal-lazeee antum bihee mu'minoon.

12. Yaaa ayyuhan-Nabiyyu izaa jaaa'akal-mu'minaatu yubaayi'naka 'alaaa allaa yushrikna billaahi shay'anw-wa laa yasriqna wa laa yazneena wa laa yaqtulna awlaadahunna wa laa yaåteena bibuhtaaniñy-yaftareenahoo bayna aydeehinna wa arjulihinna wa laa ya'ṣeenaka fee ma'roofin fabaayi'hunna wastaghfir lahunnal-laaha innal-laaha Ghafoorur Raḥeem.

13. Yaaa ayyuhal-lazeena amanoo laa tatawallaw qawman ghaḍibal-laahu 'alayhim qad ya'isoo minal-Aakhirati kamaa ya'isal-kuffaaru min aṣ-ḥaabil-quboor. *(Section 2)*

Sûrat aṣ-Ṣaff–61
(Revealed at Madinah)
Bismillaahir Raḥmaanir Raḥeem

1. Sabbaḥa lillaahi maa fissamaawaati wa maa fil-arḍi wa Huwal-'Azeezul-Ḥakeem.

2. Yaa ayyuhal-lazeena aamanoo lima taqooloona maa laa taf'aloon.

3. Kabura maqtan 'indal-laahi an taqooloo maa laa taf'aloon.

4. Innal-laaha yuḥibbul-lazeena yuqaatiloona

in His Cause in battle array, as if they were a solid cemented structure.

5. And remember, Moses said to his people: "O my people! why do you vex and insult me, though you know that I am the apostle of Allah (sent) to you?" Then when they went wrong, Allah let their hearts go wrong. For Allah guides not those who are rebellious transgressors.

6. And remember, Jesus, the son of Mary, said: "O Children of Israel! I am the apostle of Allah (sent) to you, confirming the Law (which came) before me, and giving Glad Tidings of an Apostle to come after me, whose name shall be Ahmad." But when he came to them with Clear Signs, they said, "this is evident sorcery!"

7. Who does greater wrong than one who invents falsehood against Allah, even as he is being invited to Islam? And Allah guides not those who do wrong.

8. Their intention is to extinguish Allah's Light (by blowing) with their mouths: But Allah will complete (the revelation of) His Light, even though the Unbelievers may detest (it).

9. It is He Who has sent His Apostle with Guidance and the Religion of Truth, that he may proclaim it over all religion, even though the Pagans may detest (it).

10. O you who believe! Shall I lead you to a bargain that will save you from a grievous Chastisement?-

11. That you believe in Allah and His Apostle, and that you strive (your utmost) in the Cause of Allah, with your property and your persons:

---

fee sabeelihee ṣaffan ka-annahum bunyaanum-marṣooṣ.

5. Wa iz qaala Moosaa li-qawmihee yaa qawmi lima tu'zoonanee wa qat-ta'lamoona annee Rasoolul-laahi ilaykum falammaa zaaghooo azaaghal-laahu quloobahum; wallaahu laa yahdil-qawmal-faasiqeen.

6. Wa iz qaala 'Eesab-nu-Mayama yaa Baneee Israaa-'eela innee Rasoolul-laahi ilaykum-muṣaddiqal-limaa bayna yadayya minat-Tawraati wa mubashshiram bi-Rasooliñy-yaåtee mim ba'dis-muhooo Aḥmad; falammaa jaaa'ahum bil-bayyinaati qaaloo haazaa siḥrum mubeen.

7. Wa man aẓlamu mimma-nif-taraa 'alal-laahil-kaziba wa huwa yad'aaa ilal-Islaam; wallaahu laa yahdil-qawmaẓ-ẓaalimeen.

8. Yureedoona liyuṭfi'oo nooral-laahi bi-afwaahihim wallaahu mutimmu noorihee wa law karihal-kaafiroon.

9. Huwal-lazee arsala Rasoo-lahoo bilhudaa wa deenil-ḥaqqi liyuẓhirahoo 'alad-deeni kulli-hee wa law karihal-mushrikoon.
(Section 1)

10. Yaaa ayyahal-lazeena aammanoo hal adullukum 'alaa tijaaratin tunjeekum min 'azaa-bin aleem.

11. Tu'minoona billaahi wa Rasoolihee wa tujaahidoona fee sabeelil-laahi bi-amwaalikum wa anfusikum;

فِىْ سَبِيْلِهٖ صَفًّا كَاَنَّهُمْ بُنْيَانٌ
مَّرْصُوْصٌ ۞

وَاِذْ قَالَ مُوْسٰى لِقَوْمِهٖ يٰقَوْمِ لِمَ
تُؤْذُوْنَنِىْ وَقَدْ تَّعْلَمُوْنَ اَنِّىْ رَسُوْلُ
اللّٰهِ اِلَيْكُمْ ۗ فَلَمَّا زَاغُوْۤا اَزَاغَ اللّٰهُ
قُلُوْبَهُمْ ۗ وَاللّٰهُ لَا يَهْدِى الْقَوْمَ
الْفٰسِقِيْنَ ۞

وَاِذْ قَالَ عِيْسَى ابْنُ مَرْيَمَ يٰبَنِىْۤ
اِسْرَآءِيْلَ اِنِّىْ رَسُوْلُ اللّٰهِ اِلَيْكُمْ
مُّصَدِّقًا لِّمَا بَيْنَ يَدَىَّ مِنَ
التَّوْرٰىةِ وَمُبَشِّرًا بِرَسُوْلٍ يَّأْتِىْ مِنْ
بَعْدِى اسْمُهٗۤ اَحْمَدُ ۗ فَلَمَّا جَآءَهُمْ
بِالْبَيِّنٰتِ قَالُوْا هٰذَا سِحْرٌ مُّبِيْنٌ ۞

وَمَنْ اَظْلَمُ مِمَّنِ افْتَرٰى عَلَى اللّٰهِ
الْكَذِبَ وَهُوَ يُدْعٰۤى اِلَى الْاِسْلَامِ ۗ
وَاللّٰهُ لَا يَهْدِى الْقَوْمَ الظّٰلِمِيْنَ ۞

يُرِيْدُوْنَ لِيُطْفِـُٔوْا نُوْرَ اللّٰهِ
بِاَفْوَاهِهِمْ ۗ وَاللّٰهُ مُتِمُّ نُوْرِهٖ
وَلَوْ كَرِهَ الْكٰفِرُوْنَ ۞

هُوَ الَّذِىْۤ اَرْسَلَ رَسُوْلَهٗ بِالْهُدٰى
وَدِيْنِ الْحَقِّ لِيُظْهِرَهٗ عَلَى الدِّيْنِ
كُلِّهٖ وَلَوْ كَرِهَ الْمُشْرِكُوْنَ ۞

يٰۤاَيُّهَا الَّذِيْنَ اٰمَنُوْا هَلْ اَدُلُّكُمْ عَلٰى
تِجَارَةٍ تُنْجِيْكُمْ مِّنْ عَذَابٍ اَلِيْمٍ ۞

تُؤْمِنُوْنَ بِاللّٰهِ وَرَسُوْلِهٖ وَتُجَاهِدُوْنَ
فِىْ سَبِيْلِ اللّٰهِ بِاَمْوَالِكُمْ وَاَنْفُسِكُمْ

that will be best for you, if you but knew!

12. He will forgive you your sins, and admit you to Gardens beneath which Rivers flow, and to beautiful mansions in Gardens of Eternity: that is indeed the Supreme Achievement.

13. And another (favour will He bestow,) which you do love,- help from Allah and a speedy victory. So give the Glad Tidings to the Believers.

14. O you who believe! Be you helpers of Allah: As said Jesus the son of Mary to the Disciples, "Who will be my helpers to (the work of) Allah?" Said the disciples, "We are Allah's helpers!" then a portion of the Children of Israel believed, and a portion disbelieved: But We gave power to those who believed, against their enemies, and they became the ones that prevailed.

62. The Assembly–Friday Prayer
In the name of Allah, Most Gracious, Most Merciful.

1. Whatever is in the heavens and on earth, doth declare the Praises and Glory of Allah,- the Sovereign, the Holy One, the Exalted in Might, the Wise.

2. It is He Who has sent amongst the Unlettered an apostle from among themselves, to rehearse to them His Signs, to purify them, and to instruct them in Scripture and Wisdom,- although they had been, before, in manifest error;-

3. As well as (to confer all these benefits upon) others of them, who have not already joined them: And He is Exalted in Might, Wise.

4. Such is the Bounty of Allah, which He bestows on whom He will:

---

zaalikum khayrul-lakum in kuntum ta'lamoon.

12. Yaghfir lakum zunoobakum wa yudkhilkum Jannaatin tajree min taḥtihal-anhaaru wa masaakina ṭayyibatan fee Jannaati 'Adn; zaalikal-fawzul-'azeem.

13. Wa ukhraa tuḥibboonahaa naṣrum-minal-laahi wa fat-ḥun qareeb; wa bashshiril-mu'mineen.

14. Yaaa ayyuhal-lazeena aamanoo koonooo anṣaarallaahi kamaa qaala 'Eesab-nu Maryama lil-Ḥawaariyyeena man anṣaaree ilal-laah; qaalal-Ḥawaariyyoona naḥnu anṣaarul-laahi fa-aamanaṭ-ṭaaa'ifatum-mim Bannee Israaa'eela wa kafaraṭ-ṭaaa'ifatun faayyadnal-lazeena aammanoo 'alaa 'aduwwihim fa-aṣbaḥoo zaahireen.   (Section 2)

Sûrat al-Jumu'ah–62
(Revealed at Madinah)
Bismillaahir Raḥmaanir Raḥeem.

1. Yusabbiḥu lilaahi maa fissamaawaati wa maa fil-arḍilMalikil-Quddoosil-'AzeezilḤakeem.

2. Huwal-lazee ba'aṣa filummiyyeena Rasoolam-minhum yatloo 'alayhim Aayaatihee wa yuzakkeehim wa yu'allimuhumul-Kitaaba walḤikmata wa in kaanoo min qablu lafee ḍalaalim-Mubeen.

3. Wa aakhareena minhum lammaa yalḥaqoo bihim wa Huwal-'Azeezul-Ḥakeem.

4. Zaalika faḍlul-laahi yu'teehi mañy-yashaaa';

and Allah is the Lord of the highest bounty.

5. The similitude of those who were charged with the (obligations of the) Mosaic Law, but who subsequently failed in those (obligations), is that of a donkey which carries huge tomes (but understands them not). Evil is the similitude of people who falsify the Signs of Allah: and Allah guides not people who do wrong.

6. Say: "O you that stand on Judaism! If you think that you are friends to Allah, to the exclusion of (other) men, then express your desire for Death, if you are truthful!"

7. But never will they express their desire (for Death), because of the (deeds) their hands have sent on before them! and Allah knows well those that do wrong!

8. Say: "The Death from which you flee will truly overtake you: then will you be sent back to the Knower of things secret and open: and He will tell you (the truth of) the things that you did!"

9. O you who believe! When the call is proclaimed to prayer on Friday (the Day of Assembly), hasten earnestly to the Remembrance of Allah, and leave off business (and traffic): That is best for you if you but knew!

10. And when the Prayer is finished, then may you disperse through the land, and seek of the Bounty of Allah: and celebrate the Praises of Allah often (and without stint): that you may prosper.

11. But when they see some bargain or some amusement, they disperse headlong to it, and leave you standing. Say: "The (blessing) from the Presence of Allah is better than any amusement or

---

wallaahu Zul-fadlil-'azeem.

5. Masalul-lazeena hum-milut-Tawraata summa lam yahmiloohaa kamasalil-himaari yahmilu asfaaraa; bi'sa masalul-qawmil-lazeena kazzaboo bi-Aayaatil-laah; wallaahu laa yahdil-qawmaz-zaalimeen.

6. Qul yaaa ayyuhal-lazeena haadooo in za'amtum annakum awliyaaa'u lilaahi min doonin-naasi fatamannawul-mawta in kuntum saadiqeen.

7. Wa laa yatamannaw-nahooo abadam bimaa qaddamat aydeehim; wallaahu 'Alee-mum biz-zaalimeen.

8. Qul innal-mawtal-lazee tafirroona minhu fa-innahoo mulaaqeekum summa turad-doona ilaa 'Aalimil-Ghaybi wash-shahaadati fa-yunabbi'ukum bimaa kuntum ta'maloon.

(Section 1)

9. Yaaa ayyuhal-lazeena aamanooo izaa noodiya lis-Salaati miny-yawmil-Jumu'ati fas'aw ilaa zikril-laahi wa zarul-bay'; zaalikum khayrul-lakum in kuntum ta'lamoon.

10. Fa-izaa qudiyatis-Salaatu fantashiroo fil-ardi wabtaghoo min fadlil-laahi wazkurul-laaha kaseeral-la'allakum tuflihoon.

11. Wa izaa ra-aw tijaaratan aw lahwanin-faddooo ilayhaa wa tarakooka qaaa'imaa; qul maa 'indal-laahi khayrum-minal-lahwi wa minat-

---

وَٱللّٰهُ ذُو ٱلْفَضْلِ ٱلْعَظِيمِ ۞

مَثَلُ ٱلَّذِينَ حُمِّلُوا ٱلتَّوْرَىٰةَ ثُمَّ لَمْ يَحْمِلُوهَا كَمَثَلِ ٱلْحِمَارِ يَحْمِلُ أَسْفَارًا ۚ بِئْسَ مَثَلُ ٱلْقَوْمِ ٱلَّذِينَ كَذَّبُوا بِـَٔايَـٰتِ ٱللّٰهِ ۚ وَٱللّٰهُ لَا يَهْدِى ٱلْقَوْمَ ٱلظَّـٰلِمِينَ ۞

قُلْ يَـٰٓأَيُّهَا ٱلَّذِينَ هَادُوٓا إِن زَعَمْتُمْ أَنَّكُمْ أَوْلِيَآءُ لِلّٰهِ مِن دُونِ ٱلنَّاسِ فَتَمَنَّوُا ٱلْمَوْتَ إِن كُنتُمْ صَـٰدِقِينَ ۞

وَلَا يَتَمَنَّوْنَهُۥٓ أَبَدًۢا بِمَا قَدَّمَتْ أَيْدِيهِمْ ۚ وَٱللّٰهُ عَلِيمٌۢ بِٱلظَّـٰلِمِينَ ۞

قُلْ إِنَّ ٱلْمَوْتَ ٱلَّذِى تَفِرُّونَ مِنْهُ فَإِنَّهُۥ مُلَـٰقِيكُمْ ۖ ثُمَّ تُرَدُّونَ إِلَىٰ عَـٰلِمِ ٱلْغَيْبِ وَٱلشَّهَـٰدَةِ فَيُنَبِّئُكُم بِمَا كُنتُمْ تَعْمَلُونَ ۞

يَـٰٓأَيُّهَا ٱلَّذِينَ ءَامَنُوٓا إِذَا نُودِىَ لِلصَّلَوٰةِ مِن يَوْمِ ٱلْجُمُعَةِ فَٱسْعَوْا إِلَىٰ ذِكْرِ ٱللّٰهِ وَذَرُوا ٱلْبَيْعَ ۚ ذَٰلِكُمْ خَيْرٌ لَّكُمْ إِن كُنتُمْ تَعْلَمُونَ ۞

فَإِذَا قُضِيَتِ ٱلصَّلَوٰةُ فَٱنتَشِرُوا فِى ٱلْأَرْضِ وَٱبْتَغُوا مِن فَضْلِ ٱللّٰهِ وَٱذْكُرُوا ٱللّٰهَ كَثِيرًا لَّعَلَّكُمْ تُفْلِحُونَ ۞

وَإِذَا رَأَوْا تِجَـٰرَةً أَوْ لَهْوًا ٱنفَضُّوٓا إِلَيْهَا وَتَرَكُوكَ قَآئِمًا ۚ قُلْ مَا عِندَ ٱللّٰهِ خَيْرٌ مِّنَ ٱللَّهْوِ وَمِنَ

bargain! and Allah is the Best to provide (for all needs)."

63. The Hypocrites
In the name of Allah, Most Gracious, Most Merciful.

1. When the Hypocrites come to you, they say, "We bear witness that you are indeed the Apostle of Allah." Yes, Allah knoweth that you are indeed His Apostle, and Allah bears witness that the Hypocrites are indeed liars.

2. They have made their oaths a screen (for their misdeeds): thus they obstruct (men) from the Path of Allah: truly evil are their deeds.

3. That is because they believed, then they rejected Faith: So a seal was set on their hearts: therefore they understand not.

4. When you look at them, their exteriors please thee; and when they speak, you listened to their words. They are as (worthless as hollow) pieces of timber propped up, (unable to stand on their own). They think that every cry is against them. They are the enemies; so beware of them. The curse of Allah be on them! How are they deluded (away from the Truth)!

5. And when it is said to them, "Come, the Apostle of Allah will pray for your forgiveness", they turn aside their heads, and you would see them turning away their faces in arrogance.

6. It is equal to them whether thou pray for their forgiveness or not. Allah will not forgive them. Truly Allah guides not rebellious transgressors.

7. They are the ones who say, "Spend nothing on those who are with Allah's Apostle, to the end that they may disperse

tijaarah; wallaahu khayrur-raaziqeen.　　(Section 2)

Sûrat al-Munâfiqûn–63
(Revealed at Madinah)

Bismillaahir Rahmaanir Raheem

1. Izaa jaaa'akal-munaafi-qoona qaaloo nashhadu innaka la-Rasoolul-laah; wallaahu ya'lamu innaka la-Rasooluhoo wallaahu yashhadu innal-munaafiqeena lakaaziboon.

2. Ittakhazooo aymaanahum junnatan fasaddoo 'an sabeelil-laah; innahum saaa'a maa kaanoo ya'maloon.

3. Zaalika bi-annahum aama-noo summa kafaroo fatubi'a 'alaa quloobihim fahum laa yafqahoon.

4. Wa izaa ra-aytahum tu'ji-buka ajsaamuhum wa-iñy-yaqooloo tasma' liqawlihim ka-annahum khushubum musannadah; yahsaboona kulla sayhatin 'alayhim; humul-'aduwwu fah-zarhum; qaatalahumul-laahu annaa yu'fakoon.

5. Wa izaa qeela lahum ta'aalaw yastaghfir lakum Rasoolul-laahi lawwaw ru'oo-sahum wa ra-aytahum yasud-doona wa hum mustakbiroon.

6. Sawaaa'un 'alayhim as-taghfarta lahum am lam tastaghfir lahum lañy-yaghfiral-laahu lahum; innal-laaha laa yahdil-qawmal-faasiqeen.

7. Humul-lazeena yaqoo-loona laa tunfiqoo 'alaa man 'inda Rasoolil-laahi hattaa yanfaddoo;

(and quit Medina)." But to Allah belong the treasures of the heavens and the earth; but the Hypocrites understand not.

8. They say, "If we return to Medina, surely the more honourable (element) will expel therefrom the meaner." But honour belongs to Allah and His Apostle, and the Believers; but the Hypocrites know not.

9. O you who believe! Let not your riches or your children divert you from the remembrance of Allah. If any act thus, the loss is their own.

10. And spend something (in charity) out of the substance which We have bestowed on you, before Death should come to any of you and he should say, "O my Lord! why did You not give me respite for a little while? I should then have given (largely) in charity, and I should have been one of the doers of good".

11. But to no soul will Allah grant respite when the time appointed (for it) has come; and Allah is well acquainted with (all) that you do.

wa lillaahi khazaaa'inus-samaawaati wal-ardi wa laakinnal-munaafiqeena laa yafqahoon.

8. Yaqooloona la'ir-raja'naaa ilal-Madeenati la-yukhrijannal-a'azzu minhal-azall; wa lillaahil-'izzatu wa li-Rasoolihee wa lilmu'mineena wa laakinnal-munaafiqeena laa ya'lamoon. **(Section 1)**

9. Yaaa ayyuhal-lazeena aamanoo laa tulhikum amwaalukum wa laaa awlaadukum 'an zikril-laah; wa mañy-yaf'al-zaalika fa-ulaaa'ika humul-khaasiroon.

10. Wa anfiqoo mim-maa razaqnaakum min qabli añy-yaatiya ahadakumul-mawtu fa-yaqoola Rabbi law laaa akh-khartaneee ilaa ajalin qareebin fa-assaddaqa wa akum-minas-saaliheen.

11. Wa lañy-yu'akhkhiral-laahu nafsan izaa jaaa'a ajaluhaa; wallaahu khabeerum bimaa ta'maloon. **(Section 2)**

وَلِلّٰهِ خَزَآئِنُ السَّمٰوٰتِ وَالْأَرْضِ ۖ وَلٰكِنَّ الْمُنٰفِقِيْنَ لَا يَفْقَهُوْنَ ۞

يَقُوْلُوْنَ لَئِنْ رَّجَعْنَآ إِلَى الْمَدِيْنَةِ لَيُخْرِجَنَّ الْأَعَزُّ مِنْهَا الْأَذَلَّ ۚ وَ لِلّٰهِ الْعِزَّةُ وَلِرَسُوْلِهٖ وَلِلْمُؤْمِنِيْنَ وَلٰكِنَّ الْمُنٰفِقِيْنَ لَا يَعْلَمُوْنَ ۞

يٰٓأَيُّهَا الَّذِيْنَ اٰمَنُوْا لَا تُلْهِكُمْ أَمْوَالُكُمْ وَلَا أَوْلَادُكُمْ عَنْ ذِكْرِ اللّٰهِ ۚ وَمَنْ يَّفْعَلْ ذٰلِكَ فَأُولٰٓئِكَ هُمُ الْخٰسِرُوْنَ ۞

وَأَنْفِقُوْا مِنْ مَّا رَزَقْنٰكُمْ مِّنْ قَبْلِ أَنْ يَّأْتِيَ أَحَدَكُمُ الْمَوْتُ فَيَقُوْلَ رَبِّ لَوْلَآ أَخَّرْتَنِيْ إِلَى أَجَلٍ قَرِيْبٍ ۙ فَأَصَّدَّقَ وَأَكُنْ مِّنَ الصّٰلِحِيْنَ ۞

وَلَنْ يُّؤَخِّرَ اللّٰهُ نَفْسًا إِذَا جَآءَ أَجَلُهَا ۚ وَاللّٰهُ خَبِيْرٌۢ بِمَا تَعْمَلُوْنَ ۞

64. Mutual Loss and Gain
In the name of Allah, Most Gracious, Most Merciful.

1. Whatever is in the heavens and on earth, doth declare the Praises and Glory of Allah: to Him belongs dominion, and to Him belongs praise: and He has power over all things.

2. It is He Who has created you; and of you are some that are Unbelievers, and some that are Believers: and Allah sees well all that you do.

3. He has created the heavens and the earth in just proportions,

Sûrat at-Taghâbun–64
(Revealed at Madinah)
Bismillaahir Rahmaanir Raheem

1. Yusabbihu lillaahi maa fis-samaawaati wa maa fil-ardi lahul-mulku wa lahul-hamd, wa Huwa 'alaa kulli shay'in Qadeer.

2. Huwal-lazee khalaqakum faminkum kaafiruñw-wa min-kum mu'min; wallaahu bimaa ta'maloona Baseer.

3. Khalaqas-samaawaati wal-arda bilhaqqi

(٦٤) سُوْرَةُ التَّغَابُنِ مَدَنِيَّةٌ (١٠٨)

بِسْمِ اللّٰهِ الرَّحْمٰنِ الرَّحِيْمِ

يُسَبِّحُ لِلّٰهِ مَا فِي السَّمٰوٰتِ وَمَا فِي الْأَرْضِ ۖ لَهُ الْمُلْكُ وَلَهُ الْحَمْدُ ۖ وَهُوَ عَلٰى كُلِّ شَيْءٍ قَدِيْرٌ ۞

هُوَ الَّذِيْ خَلَقَكُمْ فَمِنْكُمْ كَافِرٌ وَّمِنْكُمْ مُّؤْمِنٌ ۚ وَاللّٰهُ بِمَا تَعْمَلُوْنَ بَصِيْرٌ ۞

خَلَقَ السَّمٰوٰتِ وَالْأَرْضَ بِالْحَقِّ

and has given you shape, and made your shapes beautiful: and to Him is the final Goal.

4. He knows what is in the heavens and on earth; and He knows what you conceal and what you reveal: yes, Allah knows well the (secrets) of (all) hearts.

5. Has not the story reached you, of those who rejected Faith aforetime? So they tasted the evil result of their conduct; and they had a grievous Chastisement.

6. That was because there came to them apostles with Clear Signs, but they said: "Shall (mere) human beings direct us?" So they rejected (the Message) and turned away. But Allah can do without (them): and Allah is free of all needs, worthy of all praise.

7. The Unbelievers think that they will not be raised up (for Judgment). Say: "Yes, By my Lord, You shall surely be raised up: then shall you be told (the truth) of all that you did. And that is easy for Allah."

8. Believe, therefore, in Allah and His Apostle, and in the Light which We have sent down. And Allah is well acquainted with all that you do.

9. The Day that He assembles you (all) for a Day of Assembly,- that will be a Day of mutual loss and gain (among you), and those who believe in Allah and work righteousness,- He will remove from them their ills, and He will admit them to Gardens beneath which Rivers flow, to dwell therein for ever: that will be the Supreme Achievement.

10. But those who reject Faith and treat Our Signs as falsehoods, they will be Companions of the Fire, to dwell therein for ever: and evil is that Goal.

---

wa ṣawwarakum fa-aḥsana ṣuwarakum wa ilayhil-maṣeer.

4. Ya'lamu maa fis-samaawaati wal-arḍi wa ya'lamu maa tusirroona wa maa tu'linoon; wallaahu 'Aleemum bizaatiṣ-ṣudoor.

5. Alam yaåtikum naba'ul-lazeena kafaroo min qablu fazaaqoo wabaala amrihim wa lahum 'azaabun aleem.

6. Zaalika bi-annahoo kaanat taåteehim Rusuluhum bilbayyi-naati faqaalooo a-basharuñy-yahdoonanaa fakafaroo wa tawallaw; wastaghnal-laah; wallaahu Ghaniyyun Ḥameed.

7. Za'amal-lazeena kafarooo al-lañy-yub'aṣoo; qul balaa wa Rabbee latub'aṣunna ṣumma latunabba'unna bimaa 'amiltum; wa zaalika 'alal-laahi yaseer.

8. Fa-aaminoo billaahi wa Rasoolihee wannooril-lazeee anzalnaa; wallaahu bimaa ta'maloona Khabeer.

9. Yawma yajma'ukum li-yawmil-jam'i zaalika yawmut-taghaabun; wa mañy-yu'mim billaahi wa ya'mal ṣaaliḥañy-yukaffir 'anhu sayyi-aatihee wa yudkhilhu Jannaatin tajree min taḥtihal-anhaaru khaalideena feehaaa abadaa; zaalikal-fawzul-'aẓeem.

10. Wallazeena kafaroo wa kaz-zaboo bi-Aayaatinaaa ulaaa'ika Aṣ-ḥaabun-Naari khaalideena feehaa wa bi'sal-maṣeer.

(Section 1)

وَصَوَّرَكُمْ فَأَحْسَنَ صُوَرَكُمْ ۖ وَإِلَيْهِ الْمَصِيرُ ۝

يَعْلَمُ مَا فِي السَّمَوَاتِ وَالْأَرْضِ وَيَعْلَمُ مَا تُسِرُّوْنَ وَمَا تُعْلِنُوْنَ ۚ وَاللّٰهُ عَلِيْمٌۢ بِذَاتِ الصُّدُوْرِ ۝

اَلَمْ يَأْتِكُمْ نَبَؤُا الَّذِيْنَ كَفَرُوْا مِنْ قَبْلُ ۫ فَذَاقُوْا وَبَالَ اَمْرِهِمْ وَلَهُمْ عَذَابٌ اَلِيْمٌ ۝

ذٰلِكَ بِاَنَّهٗ كَانَتْ تَّأْتِيْهِمْ رُسُلُهُمْ بِالْبَيِّنٰتِ فَقَالُوْٓا اَبَشَرٌ يَّهْدُوْنَنَا ۫ فَكَفَرُوْا وَتَوَلَّوْا وَّاسْتَغْنَى اللّٰهُ ۚ وَاللّٰهُ غَنِيٌّ حَمِيْدٌ ۝

زَعَمَ الَّذِيْنَ كَفَرُوْٓا اَنْ لَّنْ يُّبْعَثُوْا ۚ قُلْ بَلٰى وَرَبِّيْ لَتُبْعَثُنَّ ثُمَّ لَتُنَبَّؤُنَّ بِمَا عَمِلْتُمْ ۚ وَذٰلِكَ عَلَى اللّٰهِ يَسِيْرٌ ۝

فَاٰمِنُوْا بِاللّٰهِ وَرَسُوْلِهٖ وَالنُّوْرِ الَّذِيْٓ اَنْزَلْنَا ۚ وَاللّٰهُ بِمَا تَعْمَلُوْنَ خَبِيْرٌ ۝

يَوْمَ يَجْمَعُكُمْ لِيَوْمِ الْجَمْعِ ذٰلِكَ يَوْمُ التَّغَابُنِ ۗ وَمَنْ يُّؤْمِنْ بِاللّٰهِ وَيَعْمَلْ صَالِحًا يُّكَفِّرْ عَنْهُ سَيِّاٰتِهٖ وَيُدْخِلْهُ جَنّٰتٍ تَجْرِيْ مِنْ تَحْتِهَا الْاَنْهٰرُ خٰلِدِيْنَ فِيْهَا اَبَدًا ۚ ذٰلِكَ الْفَوْزُ الْعَظِيْمُ ۝

وَالَّذِيْنَ كَفَرُوْا وَكَذَّبُوْا بِاٰيٰتِنَا اُولٰٓئِكَ اَصْحٰبُ النَّارِ خٰلِدِيْنَ فِيْهَا ۚ وَبِئْسَ الْمَصِيْرُ ۝

11. No kind of calamity can occur, except by the leave of Allah: and if any one believes in Allah, (Allah) guides his heart (aright): for Allah knows all things.

12. So obey Allah, and obey His Apostle: but if you turn back, the duty of Our Apostle is but to proclaim (the Message) clearly and openly.

13. Allah! There is no god but He: and on Allah, therefore, let the Believers put their trust.

14. O you who believe! Truly, among your wives and your children are (some that are) enemies to yourselves: so beware of them! But if you forgive and overlook, and cover up (their faults), verily Allah is Oft-Forgiving, Most Merciful.

15. Your riches and your children may be but a trial: but in the Presence of Allah, is the highest Reward.

16. So fear Allah as much as you can; listen and obey and spend in charity for the benefit of your own soul and those saved from the covetousness of their own souls,- they are the ones that achieve prosperity.

17. If you loan to Allah, a beautiful loan, He will double it to your (credit), and He will grant you Forgiveness: for Allah is most Ready to appreciate (service), Most Forbearing,-

18. Knower of what is hidden and what is open, Exalted in Might, Full of Wisdom.

11. Maaa aṣaaba mim-muṣee-batin illaa bi-iznil-laah; wa mañy-yu'mim billaahi yahdi qalbah; wallaahu bikulli shay'in 'Aleem.

12. Wa aṭee'ul-laaha wa aṭee-'ur-Rasool; fa-in tawallaytum fa-innamaa 'alaa Rasoolinal-balaaghul-mubeen.

13. Allaahu laaa ilaaha illaa Hoo; wa 'alal-laahi falyata-wakkalil-mu'minoon.

14. Yaaa ayyuhal-lazeena aamanooo inna min azwaaji-kum wa awlaadikum 'aduwwal-lakum faḥzaroohum; wa in ta'foo wa taṣfaḥoo wa taghfiroo fa-innal-laaha Ghafoorur-Raheem.

15. Innamaaa amwaalukum wa awlaadukum fitnah; wallaahu 'indahooo ajrun 'aẓeem.

16. Fattaqul-laaha mastaṭa'-tum wasma'oo wa aṭee'oo wa-anfiqoo khayral li-anfusikum; wa mañy-yooqa shuḥḥa nafsihee fa-ulaaa'ika humul-mufliḥoon.

17. In tuqriḍul-laaha qarḍan ḥasanañy-yuḍaa'ifhu lakum wa yaghfir lakum; wallaahu Shakoorun Ḥaleem.

18. 'Aalimul-Ghaybi wash-shahaadatil-'Azeezul-Ḥakeem.

(Section 2)

---

65. Divorce
In the name of Allah, Most Gracious, Most Merciful.

1. O Prophet! When you do divorce women,

Sûrat aṭ-Ṭalâq–65
(Revealed at Madinah)
Bismillaahir Raḥmaanir Raheem

1. Yaaa ayyuhan-Nabiyyu izaa ṭallaqtumun-nisaaa'a

divorce them at their prescribed periods, and count (accurately), their prescribed periods: And fear Allah your Lord: and turn them not out of their houses, nor shall they (themselves) leave, except in case they are guilty of some open lewdness, those are limits set by Allah: and any who trans-gresses the limits of Allah, does verily wrong his (own) soul: you know not if perchance Allah will bring about thereafter some new situation.

2. Thus when they fulfil their term appointed, either take them back on equitable terms or part with them on equitable terms; and take for witness two persons from among you, endued with justice, and establish the evidence (as) before Allah. Such is the admonition given to him who believes in Allah and the Last Day. And for those who fear Allah, He (ever) prepares a way out,

3. And He provides for him from (sources) he never could imagine. And if any one puts his trust in Allah, sufficient is (Allah) for him. For Allah will surely accomplish his purpose: verily, for all things has Allah appointed a due proportion.

4. Such of your women as have passed the age of monthly courses, for them the prescribed period, if you have any doubts, is three months, and for those who have no courses (it is the same): for those who carry (life within their wombs), their period is until they deliver their burdens: and for those who fear Allah, He will make their path easy.

5. That is the Command of Allah, which He has sent down to you: and if any one

faṭalliqoohunna li‘iddatihinna wa aḥsul-‘iddata; wattaqul-laaha Rabbakum laa tukhri-joohunna mim bu-yootihinna wa laa yakhrujna illaaa añy-yaateena bifaaḥishatim-mubay-yinah; wa tilka ḥudoodul-laah; wa mañy-yata‘adda ḥudoodal-laahi faqad ẓalama nafsah; laa tadree la‘allal-laaha yuḥdisu ba‘da zaalika amraa.

2. Fa-izaa balaghna ajala-hunna fa-amsikoohunna bima‘-roofin aw faariqoohunna bima‘roofiñw-wa ashhidoo zaway ‘adlim-minkum wa aqeemush-shahaadata lillaah; zaalikum yoo‘aẓu bihee man kaana yu’minu billaahi wal-Yawmil-Aakhir; wa mañy-yattaqil-laaha yaj‘al lahoo makhrajaa.

3. Wa yarzuqhu min ḥaysu laa yaḥtasib; wa mañy-yatawakkal ‘alal-laahi fahuwa ḥasbuh; innal-laaha baalighu amrih; qad ja‘alal-laahu likulli shay’in qadraa.

4. Wallaaa’ee ya’isna minal-maheeḍi min nisaaa’ikum inir-tabtum fa‘iddatuhunna salaasatu ashhuriñw-wallaaa’ee lam yaḥiḍn; wa ulaatul-aḥmaali ajaluhunna añy-yaḍa‘na ḥamlahunn; wa mañy-yattaqil-laaha yaj‘al-lahoo min armrihee yusraa.

5. Zaalika amrul-laahi anzalahoo ilaykum; wa mañy-

fears Allah, He will remove his ills, from him, and will enlarge his reward.

6. Let the women live (in 'iddat) in the same style as you live, according to your means: Annoy them not, so as to restrict them. And if they carry (life in their wombs), then spend (your substance) on them until they deliver their burden: and if they suckle your (offspring), give them their recompense: and take mutual counsel together, according to what is just and reasonable. And if you find yourselves in difficulties, let another woman suckle (the child) on the (father's) behalf.

7. Let the man of means spend according to his means: and the man whose resources are restricted, let him spend according to what Allah has given him. Allah puts no burden on any person beyond what He has given him. After a difficulty, Allah will soon grant relief.

8. How many populations that insolently opposed the Command of their Lord and of His apostles, did We not then call to account,- to severe account?- and We imposed on them an exemplary Punishment.

9. Then did they taste the evil result of their conduct, and the End of their conduct was Perdition.

10. Allah has prepared for them a severe Punishment (in the Hereafter). Therefore fear Allah, O you men of understanding - who have believed!- for Allah has indeed sent down to you a Message,-

11. An Apostle, who rehearses to you the Signs of Allah containing clear explanations, that he may lead forth those who believe

---

yattaqil-laaha yukaffir 'anhu sayyi-aatihee wa yu'zim lahoo ajraa.

6. Askinoohunna min haysu sakantum miñw-wujdikum wa laa tudaaarroohunna lituḍayyiqoo 'alayhinn; wa in kunna ulaati hamlin fa-anfiqoo 'alayhinna hattaa yaḍa'na hamlahunn; fa-in arḍa'na lakum fa-aatoohunna ujoorahunna waåtamiroo baynakum bima'roofiñw wa in ta'aasartum fasaturḍi'u lahooo ukhraa.

7. Liyunfiq zoo sa'atim-min sa'atihee wa man qudira 'alayhi rizquhoo falyunfiq mimmaaa aataahul-laah; laa yukalliful-laahu nafsan illaa maaa aataahaa; sa-yaj'alul-laahu ba'da 'usriñy-yusraa.

(Section 1)

8. Wa ka-ayyim-min qaryatin 'atat 'an amri Rabbihaa wa Rusulihee faḥaasabnaahaa hisaaban shadeedañw-wa 'azzabnaahaa 'azaaban nukraa.

9. Fazaaqat wabaala amrihaa wa kaana 'aaqibatu amrihaa khusraa.

10. A'addal-laahu lahum 'azaaban shadeedan fattaqullaaha yaaa ulil-albaab, allazeena aammanoo; qad anzalal-laahu ilaykum zikraa.

11. Rasoolañy-yatloo 'alaykum Aayaatil-laahi mubayyinaatil-liyukhrijal-lazeena aamanoo

and do righteous deeds from the depths of Darkness into Light. And those who believe in Allah and work righteousness, He will admit to Gardens beneath which Rivers flow, to dwell therein for ever: Allah has indeed granted for them a most excellent Provision.

12. Allah is He Who created seven Firmaments and of the earth a similar number. Through the midst of them (all) descends His Command: that you may know that Allah has power over all things, and that Allah comprehends, all things in (His) Knowledge.

66. Holding - something - to be Forbidden
In the name of Allah, Most Gracious, Most Merciful.

1. O Prophet! Why hold you to be forbidden that which Allah has made lawful to thee? You seekest to please thy consorts. But Allah is Oft-Forgiving, Most Merciful.

2. Allah has already ordained for you, (O men), the absolution of your oaths (in some cases): and Allah is your Protector, and He is Full of Knowledge and Wisdom.

3. When the Prophet disclosed a matter in confidence to one of his consorts, and she then divulged it (to another), and Allah made it known to him, he confirmed part thereof and repudiated a part. Then when he told her thereof, she said, "Who told you this? "He said, "He told me Who knows and is Well-acquainted (with all things)."

4. If you two turn in repentance to Him, your

---

wa ‘amiluṣ-ṣaaliḥaati minaẓ-ẓulumaati ilan-noor; wa mañy-yu’mim billaahi wa ya‘mal ṣaaliḥañy-yudkhilhu Jannaatin tajree min taḥtihal-anhaaru khaalideena feehaa abadan qad aḥsanal-laahu lahoo rizqaa.

12. Allaahul-lazee khalaqa Sab‘a Samaawaatiñw-wa minal-arḍi mislahunna yatanazzalul-amru baynahunna lita‘lamooo annal-laaha ‘alaa kulli shay’in Qadeeruñw-wa annal-laaha qad aḥaaṭa bikulli shay’in ‘ilmaa.

(Section 2)

Sûrat at-Taḥrîm—66
(Revealed at Madinah)
Bismillaahir Raḥmaanir Raḥeem

1. Yaaa ayyuhan-Nabiyyu lima tuḥarrimu maaa-aḥallal-laahu laka tabtaghee marḍaata azwaajik; wallaahu Ghafoorur-Raḥeem.

2. Qad faraḍal-laahu lakum taḥillata aymaanikum; wallaahu mawlaakum wa Huwal-‘Aleemul-Ḥakeem.

3. Wa iz asarran-Nabiyyu ilaa ba‘ḍi azwaajihee ḥadeesan falammaa nabba-at bihee wa aẓharahul-laahu ‘alayhi ‘arrafa ba‘ḍahoo wa a‘raḍa ‘am ba‘ḍin falammaa nabba-ahaa bihee qaalat man amba-aka haazaa qaala nabba-aniyal-‘Aleemul-Khabeer.

4. In tatoobaaa ilal-laahi faqad ṣaghat

hearts are indeed so inclined; But if you back up each other against him, truly Allah is his Protector, and Gabriel, and (every) righteous one among those who believe,- and furthermore, the angels - will back (him) up.

5. It may be, if he divorced you (all), that Allah will give him in exchange consorts better than you,- who submit (their wills), who believe, who are devout, who turn to Allah in repentance, who worship (in humility), who travel (for Faith) and fast, - previously married or virgins.

6. O you who believe! save yourselves and your families from a Fire whose fuel is Men and Stones, over which are (appointed) angels stern (and) severe, who flinch not (from executing) the Commands they receive from Allah, but do (precisely) what they are commanded.

7. (They will say), "O you Unbelievers! Make no excuses this Day! You are being but requited for all that ye did!"

8. O you who believe! Turn to Allah with sincere repentance: In the hope that your Lord will remove from you your ills and admit you to Gardens beneath which Rivers flow,- the Day that Allah will not permit to be humiliated the Prophet and those who believe with him. Their Light will run forward before them and by their right hands, while they say, "Our Lord! Perfect our Light for us, and grant us Forgiveness: for You have power over all things."

quloobukumaa wa in tazaaharaa 'alayhi fa-innal-laaha Huwa mawlaahu wa Jibreelu wa saalihul-mu'mineen; walma-laaa'ikatu ba'da zaalika zaheer.

5. 'Asaa Rabbuhooo in tal-laqakunna añy-yubdilahooo azwaajan khayram-minkunna muslimaatim-mu'minaatin qaa-nitaatin taaa'ibaatin 'aabidaatin saaa'ihaatin sayyibaatiñw-wa abkaaraa.

6. Yaaa ayyuhal-lazeena aamanoo Qooo anfusakum wa ahleekum Naaraññw-waqoodu-han-naasu wal-hijaaratu 'alay-haa malaaa'ikatun ghilaazun shidaadul-laa ya'soonal-laaha maaa amarahum wa yaf'aloona maa yu'maroon.

7. Yaaa ayyuhal-lazeena kafaroo laa ta'taziril-Yawma innamaa tujzawna maa kuntum ta'maloon. (Section 1)

8. Yaaa ayyuhal-lazeena aammanoo toobooo ilal-laahi tawbatan-nasoohan 'asaa Rabbukum añy-yukaffira 'ankum sayyi-aatikum wa yudkhilakum Jannaatin tajree min tahtihal-anhaaru Yawma laa yukhzil-laahun-Nabiyya wallazeena aamanoo ma'ahoo nooruhum yas'aa bayna aydeehim wa bi-aymaanihim yaqooloona Rab-banaaa atmim lanaa nooranaa waghfir lanaa innaka 'alaa kulli shay'in Qadeer.

9. O Prophet! Strive hard against the Unbelievers and the Hypocrites, and be firm against them. Their abode is Hell,- an evil refuge (indeed).

10. Allah sets forth, for an example to the Unbelievers, the wife of Noah and the wife of Lut: they were (respectively) under two of our righteous servants, but they were false to their (husbands), and they profited nothing before Allah on their account, but were told: "Enter you the Fire along with (others) that enter!"

11. And Allah sets forth, as an example to those who believe the wife of Pharaoh: Behold she said: "O my Lord! Build for me, in nearness to you, a mansion in the Garden, and save me from Pharaoh and his doings, and save me from those that do wrong"

12. And Mary the daughter of 'Imran, who guarded her chastity; and We breathed into (her body) of Our spirit; and she testified to the truth of the words of her Lord and of His Revelations, and was one of the devout (servants).

67. Dominion
In the name of Allah, Most Gracious, Most Merciful.

1. Blessed be He in Whose hands is Dominion; and He over all things hath Power;-

2. He Who created Death and Life, that He may try which of you is best in deed: and He is the Exalted in Might, Oft-Forgiving;-

3. He Who created the seven heavens one above another: No

---

9. Yaaa ayyuhan-Nabiyyu jaahidil-kuffaara walmunaa-fiqeena waghluz 'alayhim; wa maåwaahum Jahannamu wa bi'sal-maşeer.

10. Ḍarabal-laahu maṣalal-lillazeena kafarum-ra-ata Noo-ḥiñw-wamra-ata Looṭ, kaanataa taḥta 'abdayni min 'ibaadinaa ṣaaliḥayni fakhaanataahumaa falam yughniyaa 'anhumaa minal-laahi shay'añw-wa qeelad-khulan-Naara ma'ad-Daakhi-leen.

11. Wa ḍarabal-laahu maṣa-lal-lillazeena aamanumra-ata Fir'awn; iz qaalat Rabbibni lee 'indaka baytan fil-Jannati wa najjinee min Fir'awna wa 'amalihee wa najjinee minal-qawmiẓ-ẓaalimeen.

12. Wa Maryamab-nata 'Imraanal-lateee aḥ ṣanat farjahaa fanafakhnaa feehi mir-rooḥinaa wa ṣaddaqat bikali-maati Rabbihaa wa Kutubihee wa kaanat minal-qaaniteen.
(Section 2)

Sûrat al-Mulk–67
(Revealed at Makkah)
Bismillaahir Raḥmaanir Raḥeem

1. Tabaarakal-lazee biyadi-hil-mulku wa Huwa 'alaa kulli shay'in Qadeer.

2. Allazee khalaqal-mawta walḥayaata liyabluwakum ayyukum aḥsanu 'amalaa; wa Huwal-'Azeezul-Ghafoor.

3. Allazee khalaqa Sab'a samaawaatin ṭibaaqam-maa

want of proportion wilt thou see in the Creation of (Allah) Most Gracious. So turn thy vision again: do you see any flaw?

4. Again turn your vision a second time: (thy) vision will come back to you dull and discomfited, in a state worn out.

5. And We have, (from of old), adorned the lowest heaven with Lamps, and We have made such (Lamps) (as) missiles to drive away the Evil Ones, and have prepared for them the Chastisement of the Blazing Fire.

6. For those who reject their Lord (and Cherisher) is the Penalty of Hell: and evil is (such), Destination.

7. When they are cast therein, they will hear the (terrible) drawing in of its breath even as it blazes forth,

8. Almost bursting with fury: Every time a Group is cast therein, its Keepers will ask, "Did no Warner come to you?"

9. They will say: "Yes indeed; a Warner did come to us, but we rejected him and said, 'Allah never sent down any (Message): ye are nothing but an egregious delusion!'"

10. They will further say: "Had we but listened or used our intelligence, we should not (now) be among the Companions of the Blazing Fire!"

11. They will then confess their sins: but far will be (Forgiveness) from the Companions of the Blazing Fire!

12. As for those who fear their Lord unseen, for them is Forgiveness and a great Reward.

13. And whether you hide your word or publish it, He certainly has (full) knowledge, of the secrets of (all) hearts.

14. Should He not know,- He that created? and He is the One

taraa fee khalqir-Rahmaani min tafaawutin farji'il-basara hal taraa min futoor.

4. Summar-ji'il-basara karratayni yanqalib ilaykal-basaru khaasi'anw-wa huwa haseer.

5. Wa laqad zayyannas-samaaa'ad-dunyaa bimasaa-beeha wa ja'alnaahaa rujoomal-lish-Shayaateeni wa a'tadnaa lahum 'azaabas-sa'eer.

6. Wa lillazeena kafaroo bi-Rabbihim 'azaabu Jahannama wa bi'sal-maseer.

7. Izaaa ulqoo feehaa sami-'oo lahaa shaheeqanw-wa hiya tafoor.

8. Takaadu tamayyazu minal-ghayzi kullamaaa ulqiya feehaa fawjun sa-alahum khazanatuhaaa alam yaatikum nazeer.

9. Qaaloo balaa qad jaaa'anaa nazeerun fakazzab-naa wa qulnaa maa nazzalal-laahu min shay'in in antum illaa fee dalaalin kabeer.

10. Wa qaaloo law kunnaa nasma'u aw na'qilu maa kunnaa feee as-haabis-sa'eer.

11. Fa'tarafoo bizambihim fasuhqal-li-as-haabis-sa'eer.

12. Innal-lazeena yakh-shawna Rabbahum bilghaybi lahum maghfiratuñw-wa ajrun kabeer.

13. Wa asirroo qawlakum awijharoo bihee innahoo 'Aleemum bizaatis-sudoor.

14. Alaa ya'lamu man khalaq, wa Huwal-Lateeful-

تَرَىٰ فِيْ خَلْقِ الرَّحْمٰنِ مِنْ تَفٰوُتٍ ۖ فَارْجِعِ الْبَصَرَ ۖ هَلْ تَرٰى مِنْ فُطُوْرٍ ۝

ثُمَّ ارْجِعِ الْبَصَرَ كَرَّتَيْنِ يَنْقَلِبْ اِلَيْكَ الْبَصَرُ خَاسِئًا وَّهُوَ حَسِيْرٌ ۝

وَلَقَدْ زَيَّنَّا السَّمَاءَ الدُّنْيَا بِمَصَابِيْحَ وَجَعَلْنٰهَا رُجُوْمًا لِّلشَّيٰطِيْنِ وَاَعْتَدْنَا لَهُمْ عَذَابَ السَّعِيْرِ ۝

وَلِلَّذِيْنَ كَفَرُوْا بِرَبِّهِمْ عَذَابُ جَهَنَّمَ ۖ وَبِئْسَ الْمَصِيْرُ ۝

اِذَاۤ اُلْقُوْا فِيْهَا سَمِعُوْا لَهَا شَهِيْقًا وَّهِيَ تَفُوْرُ ۝

تَكَادُ تَمَيَّزُ مِنَ الْغَيْظِ ۖ كُلَّمَاۤ اُلْقِيَ فِيْهَا فَوْجٌ سَاَلَهُمْ خَزَنَتُهَاۤ اَلَمْ يَاْتِكُمْ نَذِيْرٌ ۝

قَالُوْا بَلٰى قَدْ جَاۤءَنَا نَذِيْرٌ ە فَكَذَّبْنَا وَقُلْنَا مَا نَزَّلَ اللّٰهُ مِنْ شَيْءٍ ۙ اِنْ اَنْتُمْ اِلَّا فِيْ ضَلٰلٍ كَبِيْرٍ ۝

وَقَالُوْا لَوْ كُنَّا نَسْمَعُ اَوْ نَعْقِلُ مَا كُنَّا فِيْۤ اَصْحٰبِ السَّعِيْرِ ۝

فَاعْتَرَفُوْا بِذَنْۢبِهِمْ ۚ فَسُحْقًا لِّاَصْحٰبِ السَّعِيْرِ ۝

اِنَّ الَّذِيْنَ يَخْشَوْنَ رَبَّهُمْ بِالْغَيْبِ لَهُمْ مَّغْفِرَةٌ وَّاَجْرٌ كَبِيْرٌ ۝

وَاَسِرُّوْا قَوْلَكُمْ اَوِ اجْهَرُوْا بِهٖ ۗ اِنَّهٗ عَلِيْمٌۢ بِذَاتِ الصُّدُوْرِ ۝

اَلَا يَعْلَمُ مَنْ خَلَقَ ۗ وَهُوَ اللَّطِيْفُ

well-acquainted (with them).

15. It is He Who has made the earth manageable for you, so traverse you through its tracts and enjoy of the Sustenance which He furnishes: but unto Him is the Resurrection.

16. Do you feel secure that He Who is in heaven will not cause you to be swallowed up by the earth even it shakes (as in an earthquake)?

17. Or do you feel secure that He Who is in Heaven will not send against you a violent tornado (with showers of stones), so that you shall know how (terrible) was My warning?

18. But indeed men before them rejected (My warning): then how (terrible) was My rejection (of them)?

19. Do they not observe the birds above them, spreading their wings and folding them in? None can uphold them except (Allah) Most Gracious: Truly it is He that watches over all things.

20. No, who is there that can help you, (even as) an army, besides (Allah) Most Merciful? In nothing but delusion are the Unbelievers.

21. Or who is there that can provide you with Sustenance if He were to withhold His provision? No, they obstinately persist in insolent impiety and flight (from the Truth).

22. Is then one who walks headlong, with his face grovelling, better guided,- or one who walks evenly on a Straight Way?

23. Say: "It is He Who has created you (and made you grow), and made for you the faculties of hearing, seeing, feeling and understanding: little thanks it is you give.

24. Say: "It is He Who has multiplied you through the earth,

Khabeer. **(Section 1)**

15. Huwal-lazee ja'ala lakumul-arḍa zaloolan famshoo fee manaakibihaa wa kuloo mir-rizqihee wa ilayhin-nushoor.

16. 'A-amintum man fis-samaaa'i añy-yakhsifa bikumul-arḍa fa-izaa hiya tamoor.

17. Am amintum man fis-samaaa'i añy-yursila 'alaykum ḥaaṣiban fasata'lamoona kayfa naẕeer.

18. Wa laqad kazzabal-lazeena min qablihim fakayfa kaana nakeer.

19. Awalam yaraw ilaṭ-ṭayri fawqahum ṣaaaffaatiñw-wa yaqbiḍn; maa yumsikuhunna illaar-Raḥmaan; innahoo bikulli shay'im Baṣeer.

20. Amman haazal-lazee huwa jundul-lakum yanṣurukum min doonir-Raḥmaan; inil-kaafiroona illaa fee ghuroor.

21. Amman haazal-lazee yarzuqukum in amsaka rizqah; bal lajjoo fee 'utuwwiñw-wa nufoor.

22. Afamañy-yamshee mukibban 'alaa wajhiheee ahdaaa ammañy-yamshee sawiyyan 'alaa Ṣiraṭim-Mustaqeem.

23. Qul Huwal-lazee anshaakum wa ja'ala lakumus-sam'a wal-abṣaara wal-af'idata qaleelam-maa tashkuroon.

24. Qul Huwal-lazee zaraakum fil-arḍi

and to Him shall you be gathered together."

25. They ask: When will this promise be (fulfilled)? - If you are telling the truth.

26. Say: "As to the knowledge of the time, it is with Allah alone: I am (sent) only to warn plainly in public."

27. At length, when they see it close at hand, grieved will be the faces of the Unbelievers, and it will be said (to them): "This is (the promise fulfilled), which you were calling for!"

28. Say: "See you?- If Allah were to destroy me, and those with me, or if He bestows His Mercy on us,- yet who can deliver the Unbelievers from a grievous Chastisement?"

29. Say: "He is (Allah) Most Gracious: We have believed in Him, and on Him have we put our trust: So, soon will you know which (of us) it is that is in manifest error."

30. Say: "Don 't you see?- If your stream be some morning lost (in the underground earth), who then can supply you with clear-flowing water?"

68. The Pen
In the name of Allah, Most Gracious, Most Merciful.

1. *Nun.* By the Pen and the (Record) which (men) write,-

2. You are not, by the Grace of your Lord, mad or possessed.

3. No, verily for thee is a Reward unfailing:

4. And thou (standest) on an exalted standard of character.

5. Soon will you see, and they will see,

6. Which of you is afflicted with madness.

7. Verily it is your Lord that knows best, which (among men) hath strayed from His Path: and He knows best those who receive (true) Guidance.

---

wa ilayhi tuḥsharoon.

25. Wa yaqooloona mataa haazal-wa‘du in kuntum ṣaadiqeen.

26. Qul innamal-‘ilmu ‘indal-laahi wa innamaaa ana nazee-rum-mubeen.

27. Falaammaa ra-awhu zulfatan seee’at wujoohul-lazeena kafaroo wa qeela haazal-lazee kuntum bihee tadda‘oon.

28. Qul ara’aytum in ahlaka-niyal-laahu wa mam-ma‘iya aw raḥimanaa famañy-yujeerul-kaafireena min ‘azaabin aleem.

29. Qul Huwar-Raḥmaanu aamannaa bihee wa ‘alayhi tawakkalnaa fasata‘lamoona man huwa fee ḍalaalim-mubeen.

30. Qul ara’aytum in aṣbaḥa maaa’ukum ghawran famañy-yaåteekum bimaaa’im-ma‘een.

(Section 2)

Sûrat al-Qalam–68
(Revealed at Makkah)
Bismillaahir Raḥmaanir Raḥeem

1. Noon; walqalami wa maa yasṭuroon.

2. Maa anta bini‘mati Rabbi-ka bimajnoon.

3. Wa inna laka la-ajran ghayra mamnoon.

4. Wa innaka la-‘alaa khu-luqin ‘aẓeem.

5. Fasatubṣiru wa yubṣiroon.

6. Bi-ayyikumul-maftoon.

7. Inna Rabbaka Huwa a‘la-mu biman ḍalla ‘an sabeelihee wa Huwa a‘lamu bilmuhtadeen.

8. So hearken not to those who deny (the Truth).

9. Their desire is that thou shouldst be pliant: so would they be pliant.

10. Do not obey every mean swearer;

11. A slanderer, going about with calumnies,

12. (Habitually) hindering (all) good, transgressing beyond bounds, deep in sin,

13. Violent (and cruel),- with all that, base-born,-

14. Because he possesses wealth and (numerous) sons.

15. When to him are rehearsed Our Signs, "Tales of the ancients", he cries!

16. Soon shall We brand (the beast) on the snout!

17. Verily We have tried them as We tried the People of the Garden, when they resolved to gather the fruits of the (garden) in the morning.

18. But made no reservation, ("If it be Allah's Will").

19. Then there came on the (garden) a visitation from thy Lord, (which swept away) all around, while they were asleep.

20. And in the morning it was as if plucked.

21. As the morning broke, they called out, one to another,-

22. "Go you to your tilth (betimes) in the morning, if you would gather the fruits."

23. So they departed, conversing in secret low tones, (saying)-

24. "Let not a single indigent person break in upon you into the (garden) this day."

25. And they opened the morning, strong in an (unjust) resolve.

26. But when they saw the (garden), they said: "We have surely lost our way:

27. "Indeed we are shut out (of the fruits of our labour)!"

28. Said one of them, more just (than the rest): "Did I not say to you,

8. Falaa tuṭi'il-mukazzibeen.

9. Waddoo law tudhinu fa-yudhinoon.

10. Wa laa tuṭi' kulla ḥallaa-fim-maheen.

11. Hammaazim mash-shaaa'im binameem.

12. Mannaa'il-lilkhayri mu'-tadin aseem.

13. 'Utullim ba'da zaalika zaneem.

14. An kaana zaa maaliñw-wa baneen.

15. Izaa tutlaa 'alayhi Aayaatunaa qaala asaaṭeerul-awwaleen.

16. Sanasimuhoo 'alal-khur-ṭoom.

17. Innaa balawnaahum ka-maa balawnaaa Aṣ-ḥaabal jannati iz 'aqsamoo la-yaṣri munnahaa muṣbiḥeen.

18. Wa laa yastasnoon.

19. Faṭaafa 'alayhaa ṭaaa'i-fum-mir-Rabbika wa hum naaa'imoon.

20. Fa-aṣbaḥat kaṣṣareem.

21. Fatanaadaw muṣbiḥeen.

22. Anighdoo 'alaa ḥarsikum in kuntum ṣaarimeen.

23. Fanṭalaqoo wa hum yata-khaafatoon.

24. Al-laa yadkhulannahal-yawma 'alaykum-miskeen.

25. Wa ghadaw 'alaa ḥardin qaadireen.

26. Falammaa ra-awhaa qaa-loo innaa laḍaaalloon.

27. Bal naḥnu maḥroomoon.

28. Qaala awsaṭuhum alam aqul lakum

فَلَا تُطِعِ الْمُكَذِّبِيْنَ ۞

وَدُّوْا لَوْ تُدْهِنُ فَيُدْهِنُوْنَ ۞

وَلَا تُطِعْ كُلَّ حَلَّافٍ مَّهِيْنٍ ۙ

هَمَّازٍ مَّشَّآءٍ بِنَمِيْمٍ ۙ

مَّنَّاعٍ لِّلْخَيْرِ مُعْتَدٍ اَثِيْمٍ ۙ

عُتُلٍّ بَعْدَ ذٰلِكَ زَنِيْمٍ ۗ

اَنْ كَانَ ذَا مَالٍ وَّبَنِيْنَ ۗ

اِذَا تُتْلٰى عَلَيْهِ اٰيٰتُنَا قَالَ اَسَاطِيْرُ الْاَوَّلِيْنَ ۞

سَنَسِمُهٗ عَلَى الْخُرْطُوْمِ ۞

اِنَّا بَلَوْنٰهُمْ كَمَا بَلَوْنَاۤ اَصْحٰبَ الْجَنَّةِ ۚ اِذْ اَقْسَمُوْا لَيَصْرِمُنَّهَا مُصْبِحِيْنَ ۙ

وَلَا يَسْتَثْنُوْنَ ۞

فَطَافَ عَلَيْهَا طَآئِفٌ مِّنْ رَّبِّكَ وَهُمْ نَآئِمُوْنَ ۞

فَاَصْبَحَتْ كَالصَّرِيْمِ ۙ

فَتَنَادَوْا مُصْبِحِيْنَ ۙ

اَنِ اغْدُوْا عَلٰى حَرْثِكُمْ اِنْ كُنْتُمْ صٰرِمِيْنَ ۞

فَانْطَلَقُوْا وَهُمْ يَتَخَافَتُوْنَ ۙ

اَنْ لَّا يَدْخُلَنَّهَا الْيَوْمَ عَلَيْكُمْ مِّسْكِيْنٌ ۙ

وَّغَدَوْا عَلٰى حَرْدٍ قٰدِرِيْنَ ۞

فَلَمَّا رَاَوْهَا قَالُوْۤا اِنَّا لَضَآلُّوْنَ ۙ

بَلْ نَحْنُ مَحْرُوْمُوْنَ ۞

قَالَ اَوْسَطُهُمْ اَلَمْ اَقُلْ لَّكُمْ

"Why not glorify (Allah)?"

law laa tusabbiḥoon.

لَوْلَا تُسَبِّحُوْنَ ۝

29. They said: "Glory to our Lord! Verily we have been doing wrong!"

29. Qaaloo Subḥaana Rabbinaaa innaa kunnaa ẓaalimeen.

قَالُوْا سُبْحٰنَ رَبِّنَاۤ اِنَّا كُنَّا ظٰلِمِيْنَ ۝

30. Then they turned, one against another, in reproach.

30. Fa-aqbala ba'ḍuhum 'alaa ba'ḍiñy-yatalaawamoon.

فَاَقْبَلَ بَعْضُهُمْ عَلٰى بَعْضٍ يَّتَلَاوَمُوْنَ ۝

31. They said: "Alas for us! We have indeed transgressed!"

31. Qaaloo yaa waylanaaa innaa kunnaa ṭaagheen.

قَالُوْا يٰوَيْلَنَاۤ اِنَّا كُنَّا طٰغِيْنَ ۝

32. "It may be that our Lord will give us in exchange a better (garden) than this: for we do turn to Him (in repentance)!"

32. 'Asaa Rabbunaaa añy-yubdilanaa khayram-minhaaa innaaa ilaa Rabbinaa raaghiboon.

عَسٰى رَبُّنَاۤ اَنْ يُّبْدِلَنَا خَيْرًا مِّنْهَاۤ اِنَّاۤ اِلٰى رَبِّنَا رٰغِبُوْنَ ۝

33. Such is the Punishment (in this life); but greater is the Punishment in the Hereafter,- if only they knew!

33. Kazaalikal-azaab, wa la-'azaabul-Aakhirati akbar; law kaanoo ya'lamoon. (Section 1)

كَذٰلِكَ الْعَذَابُ ۖ وَلَعَذَابُ الْاٰخِرَةِ اَكْبَرُ ۘ لَوْ كَانُوْا يَعْلَمُوْنَ ۝

34. Verily, for the Righteous, are Gardens of Delight, in the Presence of their Lord.

34. Inna lilmuttaqeena 'inda Rabbihim Jannaatin-Na'eem.

اِنَّ لِلْمُتَّقِيْنَ عِنْدَ رَبِّهِمْ جَنّٰتِ النَّعِيْمِ ۝

35. Shall We then treat the People of Faith like the People of Sin?

35. Afanaj'alul-muslimeena kalmujrimeen.

اَفَنَجْعَلُ الْمُسْلِمِيْنَ كَالْمُجْرِمِيْنَ ۝

36. What is the matter with you? How judge you?

36. Maa lakum kayfa taḥkumoon.

مَا لَكُمْ ۣ كَيْفَ تَحْكُمُوْنَ ۝

37. Or have you a book through which you learn-

37. Am lakum kitaabun feehi tadrusoon.

اَمْ لَكُمْ كِتٰبٌ فِيْهِ تَدْرُسُوْنَ ۝

38. That you shall have, through it whatever you choose?

38. Inna lakum feehi lamaa takhayyaroon.

اِنَّ لَكُمْ فِيْهِ لَمَا تَخَيَّرُوْنَ ۝

39. Or have you Covenants with Us to oath, reaching to the Day of Judgment, (providing) that you shall have whatever you shall demand?

39. Am lakum aymaanun 'alaynaa baalighatun ilaa Yawmil-Qiyaamati inna lakum lamaa taḥkumoon.

اَمْ لَكُمْ اَيْمَانٌ عَلَيْنَا بَالِغَةٌ اِلٰى يَوْمِ الْقِيٰمَةِ ۙ اِنَّ لَكُمْ لَمَا تَحْكُمُوْنَ ۝

40. Ask you of them, which of them will stand surety for that!

40. Salhum ayyuhum bizaalika za'eem.

سَلْهُمْ اَيُّهُمْ بِذٰلِكَ زَعِيْمٌ ۝

41. Or have they some "Partners" (in Godhead)? Then let them produce their "partners", if they are truthful!

41. Am lahum shurakaaa'u falyaåtoo bishurakaaa'ihim in kaanoo ṣaadiqeen.

اَمْ لَهُمْ شُرَكَاۤءُ ۚ فَلْيَاْتُوْا بِشُرَكَاۤئِهِمْ اِنْ كَانُوْا صٰدِقِيْنَ ۝

42. The Day that the shin shall be laid bare, and they shall be summoned to bow in adoration, but they shall not be able,-

42. Yawma yukshafu 'an saaqiñw-wa yud'awna ilassujoodi falaa yastaṭee'oon.

يَوْمَ يُكْشَفُ عَنْ سَاقٍ وَّيُدْعَوْنَ اِلَى السُّجُوْدِ فَلَا يَسْتَطِيْعُوْنَ ۝

43. Their eyes will be cast down,- ignominy will cover them; seeing that they had been summoned aforetime to bow in adoration, while they were hale and healthy, (and had refused).

43. Khaashi'atan abṣaaruhum tarhaquhum zillatuñw wa qad kaanoo yud'awna ilassujoodi wa hum saalimoon.

خَاشِعَةً اَبْصَارُهُمْ تَرْهَقُهُمْ ذِلَّةٌ ۖ وَقَدْ كَانُوْا يُدْعَوْنَ اِلَى السُّجُوْدِ وَهُمْ سٰلِمُوْنَ ۝

44. Then leave Me alone with such as reject this Message: by degrees shall We punish them from directions they perceive not.

44. Fazarnee wa mañy-yukazzibu bihaazal-ḥadeesi sanastadrijuhum min ḥaysu laa ya'lamoon.

فَذَرْنِيْ وَمَنْ يُّكَذِّبُ بِهٰذَا الْحَدِيْثِ ۖ سَنَسْتَدْرِجُهُمْ مِّنْ حَيْثُ لَا يَعْلَمُوْنَ ۝

45. Yet I bear with them, for lo! My scheme is firm.

46. Or is it that you does ask them for a reward, so that they are burdened with a load of debt?-

47. Or that the Unseen is in their hands, so that they can write it down?

48. So wait with patience for the Command of your Lord, and be not like the Companion of the Fish,- when he cried out in agony.

49. Had not Grace from his Lord reached him, he would indeed have been cast off on the naked shore, in disgrace.

50. Thus did his Lord choose him and make him of the Company of the Righteous.

51. And the Unbelievers would almost trip you up with their eyes when they hear the Message; and they say: "Surely he is possessed!"

52. But it is nothing less than a Message to all the worlds.

69. The Sure Reality
In the name of Allah, Most Gracious, Most Merciful.

1. The Sure Reality!

2. What is the Sure Reality?

3. And what will make you realise what the Sure Reality is?

4. The Thamûd and the 'Ad People (branded) as false the Stunning Calamity!

5. As for Thamûd, they were destroyed by the lightning.

6. And the 'Ad, they were destroyed by a furious Wind, exceedingly violent;

7. He made it rage against them seven nights and eight days in succession: so that you could see the (whole) people lying

---

45. Wa umlee lahum; inna kaydee mateen.

46. Am tas'aluhum ajran fahum mim-maghramim musqaloon.

47. Am 'indahumul-ghaybu fahum yaktuboon.

48. Faṣbir liḥukmi Rabbika wa laa takun kaṣaaḥibil-ḥoot; iz naadaa wa huwa makzoom.

49. Law laaa an tadaara-kahoo ni'matum-mir-Rabbihee lanubiza bil-'araaa'i wa huwa mazmoom.

50. Fajtabaahu Rabbuhoo faja'alahoo minaṣ-ṣaaliḥeen.

51. Wa iñy-yakaadul-lazeena kafaroo la-yuzliqoonaka bi-abṣaarihim lammaa sami'uz-Zikra wa yaqooloona innahoo lamajnoon.

52. Wa maa huwa illaa zikrul-lil'aalameen. (Section 2)

Sûrat al-Ḥâqqah–69
(Revealed at Makkah)
Bismillaahir Raḥmaanir Raḥeem

1. Al-ḥaaaqqah.

2. Mal-ḥaaaqqah.

3. Wa maaa adraaka mal-ḥaaaqqah.

4. Kazzabat Samoodu wa 'Aadum bil-qaari'ah.

5. Fa-ammaa Samoodu fa-uhlikoo biṭṭaaghiyah.

6. Wa ammaa 'Aadun fa-uh-likoo bireeḥin ṣarṣarin 'aatiyah.

7. Sakhkharahaa 'alayhim sab'a la-yaaliñw-wa samaaniyata ayyaamin ḥusooman fataral-qawma feehaa

prostrate in its (path), as they had been roots of hollow palm-trees tumbled down!

8. Then do you see any of them left surviving?

9. And Pharaoh, and those before him, and the Cities Over-thrown, committed habitual Sin.

10. And disobeyed (each) the apostle of their Lord; so He punished them with an abundant Chastisement.

11. We, when the water (of Noah's Flood) overflowed beyond its limits, carried you (mankind), in the floating (Ark),

12. That We might make it a Message unto you, and that ears (that should hear the tale and) retain its memory should bear its (lessons) in remembrance.

13. Then, when one blast is sounded on the Trumpet,

14. And the earth is moved, and its mountains, and they are crushed to powder at one stroke,-

15. On that Day shall the (Great) Event come to pass.

16. And the sky will be rent asunder, for it will that Day be flimsy,

17. And the angels will be on its sides, and eight will, that Day, bear the Throne of your Lord above them.

18. On that day ye will be exposed; not a secret of you will be hidden.

19. Then he that will be given his Record in his right hand will say: "Ah here! Read you my Record!

20. "I did really understand that my Account would (One Day) reach me!"

21. And he will be in a life of Bliss,

22. In a Garden on high,

23. The Fruits whereof (will hang in bunches) low and near.

şar‘aa ka-annahum a‘jaazu nakhlin khaawiyah.

8. Fahal taraa lahum mim baaqiyah.

9. Wa jaaa'a Fir‘awnu wa man qablahoo wal-mu'tafikaatu bilkhaaṭi'ah.

10. Fa‘aşaw Rasoola Rabbihim fa-akhazahum akhzatar-raabiyah.

11. Innaa lammaa ṭaghal-maaa'u ḥamalnaakum fil-jaariyah.

12. Linaj‘alahaa lakum tazki-ratañw-wa ta‘iyahaaa uzunuñw-waa‘iyah.

13. Fa-izaa nufikha fiṣ-Ṣoori nafkhatuñw-waaḥidah.

14. Wa ḥumilatil-arḍu wal-jibaalu fadukkataa dakkatañw-waaḥidah.

15. Fa-yawma'iẕiñw-waqa-‘atil-waaqi‘ah.

16. Wanshaqqatis-samaaa'u fahiya Yawma'iẕiñw-waahiyah.

17. Wal-malaku ‘alaaa ar-jaaa'ihaa; wa yaḥmilu ‘Arsha Rabbika fawqahum Yawma'i-ẕin samaaniyah.

18. Yawma'iẕin tu‘raḍoona laa takhfaa minkum khaafiyah.

19. Fa-ammaa man ootiya kitaabahoo biyameenihee fa-yaqoolu haaa'umuq-ra'oo ki-taabiyah.

20. Innee ẓanantu annee mu-laaqin ḥisaabiyah.

21. Fahuwa fee ‘eeshatir-raa-ḍiyah.

22. Fee Jannatin ‘aaliyah.

23. Quṭoofuhaa daaniyah.

صَرْعٰى كَاَنَّهُمْ اَعْجَازُ نَخْلٍ خَاوِيَةٍ ۝

فَهَلْ تَرٰى لَهُمْ مِّنْ بَاقِيَةٍ ۝

وَجَآءَ فِرْعَوْنُ وَمَنْ قَبْلَهٗ وَالْمُؤْتَفِكٰتُ بِالْخَاطِئَةِ ۚ ۝

فَعَصَوْا رَسُوْلَ رَبِّهِمْ فَاَخَذَهُمْ اَخْذَةً رَّابِيَةً ۝

اِنَّا لَمَّا طَغَا الْمَآءُ حَمَلْنٰكُمْ فِى الْجَارِيَةِ ۝

لِنَجْعَلَهَا لَكُمْ تَذْكِرَةً وَّتَعِيَهَآ اُذُنٌ وَّاعِيَةٌ ۝

فَاِذَا نُفِخَ فِى الصُّوْرِ نَفْخَةٌ وَّاحِدَةٌ ۝

وَّحُمِلَتِ الْاَرْضُ وَالْجِبَالُ فَدُكَّتَا دَكَّةً وَّاحِدَةً ۝

فَيَوْمَئِذٍ وَّقَعَتِ الْوَاقِعَةُ ۝

وَانْشَقَّتِ السَّمَآءُ فَهِيَ يَوْمَئِذٍ وَّاهِيَةٌ ۝

وَّالْمَلَكُ عَلٰى اَرْجَآئِهَا ۚ وَيَحْمِلُ عَرْشَ رَبِّكَ فَوْقَهُمْ يَوْمَئِذٍ ثَمٰنِيَةٌ ۝

يَوْمَئِذٍ تُعْرَضُوْنَ لَا تَخْفٰى مِنْكُمْ خَافِيَةٌ ۝

فَاَمَّا مَنْ اُوْتِيَ كِتٰبَهٗ بِيَمِيْنِهٖ ۙ فَيَقُوْلُ هَآؤُمُ اقْرَءُوْا كِتٰبِيَهْ ۝

اِنِّيْ ظَنَنْتُ اَنِّيْ مُلٰقٍ حِسَابِيَهْ ۝

فَهُوَ فِيْ عِيْشَةٍ رَّاضِيَةٍ ۝

فِيْ جَنَّةٍ عَالِيَةٍ ۝

قُطُوْفُهَا دَانِيَةٌ ۝

24. "Eat you and drink you, with full satisfaction; because of the (good) that you sent before you, in the days that are gone!"

25. And he that will be given his Record in his left hand, will say: "Ah! Would that my Record had not been given to me!

26. "And that I had never realised how my account (stood)!

27. "Ah! Would that (Death) had made an end of me!

28. "Of no profit to me has been my wealth!

29. "My power has perished from me!"...

30. (The stern command will say): "Seize you him, and bind you him,

31. "And burn you him in the Blazing Fire.

32. "Further, make him march in a chain, whereof the length is seventy cubits!

33. "This was he that would not believe in Allah Most High.

34. "And would not encourage the feeding of the indigent!

35. "So no friend hath he here this Day.

36. "Nor hath he any food except the corruption from the washing of wounds,

37. "Which none do eat but those in sin."

38. So I do call to witness what you see,

39. And what you see not,

40. That this is verily the word of an honoured apostle;

41. It is not the word of a poet: little it is you believe!

42. Nor is it the word of a soothsayer: little admonition it is you receive.

43. (This is) a Message sent down from the Lord of the Worlds.

44. And if the apostle were to invent any sayings in Our name,

---

24. Kuloo washraboo haneee-'am bimaaa aslaftum fil-ayyaamil-khaaliyah.

25. Wa ammaa man ootiya kitaabahoo bishimaalihee fa-yaqoolu yaalaytanee lam oota kitaabiyah.

26. Wa lam adri maa ḥisaa-biyah.

27. Yaa laytahaa kaanatil-qaaḍiyah.

28. Maaa aghnaa 'annee maaliyah.

29. Halaka 'annee sulṭaa-niyah.

30. Khuẕoohu faghullooh.

31. Summal-Jaḥeema ṣallooh.

32. Summa fee silsilatin zar-'uhaa sab'oona ziraa'an faslu-kooh.

33. Innahoo kaana laa yu'mi-nu billaahil-'Aẓeem.

34. Wa laa yaḥuḍḍu 'alaa ṭa'aamil-miskeen.

35. Falaysa lahul-Yawma haahunaa ḥameem.

36. Wa laa ṭa'aamun illaa min ghisleen.

37. Laa yaàkuluhooo illal-khaaṭi'oon. (Section 1)

38. Falaaa uqsimu bimaa tubṣiroon

39. Wa maa laa tubṣiroon.

40. Innahoo laqawlu Rasoo-lin kareem.

41. Wa maa huwa biqawli shaa'ir; qaleelam-maa tu'mi-noon.

42. Wa laa biqawli kaahin; qaleelam-maa tazakkaroon.

43. Tanzeelum-mir-Rabbil-'aalameen.

44. Wa law taqawwala 'alay-naa ba'ḍal-aqaaweel.

45. We should certainly seize him by his right hand,

46. And then severed his life-artry,

47. Nor could any of you withhold him (from Our wrath).

48. But verily this is a Message for the God-fearing.

49. And lo! We know that some among you will deny (it).

50. And lo! It is indeed an anguish for the disbelievers.

51. But verily it is Truth of assured certainty.

52. So glorify the name of your Lord Most High.

70. The Ways of Ascent
In the name of Allah, Most Gracious, Most Merciful.

1. A questioner asked about a Chastisement to befall-

2. The Unbelievers, the which there is none to ward off,-

3. (A Penalty) from Allah, Lord of the Ways of Ascent.

4. The angels and the spirit ascend unto him in a Day the measure whereof is (as) fifty thousand years:

5. But be patient (O Muhammad) with a patience fair to see.

6. They see the (Day) indeed as a far-off (event):

7. But We see it (quite) near.

8. The Day that the sky will be like molten brass,

9. And the mountains will be like wool,

10. And no friend will ask after a friend,

11. Though they will be given sight of them. The guilty man will long to be able to ransom himself from the punishment of that day at the price of his children.

12. His wife and his brother,

13. His kindred who sheltered him,

45. La-akhaznaa minhu bilya-meen.

46. Summa laqata'naa min-hul-wateen.

47. Famaa minkum min ahadin 'anhu haajizeen.

48. Wa innahoo latazkiratul-lilmuttaqeen.

49. Wa inna lana'lamu anna minkum mukazzibeen.

50. Wa innahu lahasratun 'alal-kaafireen

51. Wa innahoo lahaqqul-yaqeen.

52. Fasabbih bismi Rabbikal-'Azeem.   (Section 2)

Sûrat al-Ma'ârij–70
(Revealed at Makkah)
Bismillaahir Rahmaanir Raheem

1. Sa-ala saaa'ilum bi'azaa-biñw-waaqi'.

2. Lilkaafireena laysa lahoo daafi'.

3. Minal-laahi zil-ma'aarij.

4. Ta'rujul-malaaa'ikatu war-Roohu ilayhi fee yawmin kaana miqdaaruhoo khamseena alfa sanah.

5. Fasbir sabran jameelaa.

6. Inaahum yarawnahoo ba'eedaa.

7. Wa naraahu qareebaa.

8. Yawma takoonus-samaaa-'u kalmuhl.

9. Wa takoonul-jibaalu kal-'ihn.

10. Wa laa yas'alu hameemun hameemaa.

11. Yubassaroonahum; ya-wad-dul-mujrimu law yaftadee min 'azaabi Yawma'izim bibaneeh.

12. Wa saahibatihee wa akheeh.

13. Wa faseelatihil-latee tu'-weeh.

14. And all, all that is on earth,- so it could deliver him:

15. By no means! for it would be the Fire of Hell!-

16. Plucking out (his being) right to the skull!-

17. It calleth him who turned and fled (from truth),

18. And collect (wealth) and hide it (from use)!

19. Truly man was created very impatient;-

20. Fretful when evil touches him;

21. And niggardly when good reaches him;-

22. Not so those devoted to Prayer;-

23. Those who remain steadfast to their prayer;

24. And those in whose wealth is a recognised right.

25. For the beggar and the destitute;

26. And those who hold to the truth of the Day of Judgment;

27. And those who fear the displeasure of their Lord,-

28. For their Lord's displeasure is the opposite of Peace and Tranquillity;-

29. And those who guard their chastity,

30. Except with their wives and the (captives) whom their right hands possess,- for (then) they are not to be blamed,

31. But those who trespass beyond this are transgressors;

32. And those who respect their trusts and covenants;

33. And those who stand firm in their testimonies;

34. And those who guard (the sacredness) of their worship;-

14. Wa man fil-arḍi jamee'an summa yunjeeh.

15. kallaa innahaa laẓaa.

16. Nazzaa'atal-lishshawaa.

17. Tad'oo man adbara wa tawallaa.

18. Wa jama'a fa-aw'aa.

19. Innal-insaana khuliqa haloo'aa.

20. Izaa massahush-sharru jazoo'aa.

21. Wa izaa massahul-khayru manoo'aa.

22. Illal-muṣalleen.

23. Allazeena hum 'alaa Ṣalaatihim daaa'imoon.

24. Wallazeena feee amwaalihim ḥaqqum-ma'loom.

25. Lissaaa'ili walmaḥroom.

26. Wallazeena yuṣaddiqoona bi-Yawmid-Deen.

27. Wallazeena hum min 'azaabi Rabbihim mushfiqoon.

28. Inna 'azaaba Rabbihim ghayru maâmoon.

29. Wallazeena hum lifuroojihim ḥaafiẓoon.

30. Illaa 'alaaa azwaajihim aw maa malakat aymaanuhum fa-innahum ghayru maloomeen.

31. Famanib-taghaa waraaa'a zaalika fa-ulaaa'ika humul-'aadoon.

32. Wallazeena hum li-amaanaatihim wa 'ahdihim raa'oon.

33. wallazeena hum bishahaadaatihim qaaa'imoon.

34. Wallazeena hum 'alaa Ṣalaatihim yuḥaafiẓoon.

35. Such will be the honoured ones in the Gardens (of Bliss).

36. Now what is the matter with the Unbelievers that they rush madly before you–

37. From the right and from the left, in crowds?

38. Does every man of them long to enter the Garden of Bliss?

39. By no means! For We have created them out of the (base matter) they know about.

40. Now I do call to witness the Lord of all points in the East and the West that We can certainly-

41. Substitute for them better (men) than they; And We are not to be defeated (in Our Plan).

42. So leave them to plunge in vain talk and play about, until they encounter that Day of theirs which they have been promised!-

43. The day when they come forth from the graves in haste, as racing to a goal.

44. Their eyes lowered in dejection,- ignominy covering them (all over)! such is the Day the which they are promised!

35. Ulaaa'ika fee Jannaatim-mukramoon. (Section 1)

36. Famaa lil-lazeena kafa-roo qibalaka muhti'een.

37. 'Anil-yameeni wa 'anish-shimaali 'izeen.

38. Ayaṭma'u kullum-ri'im minhum añy-yudkhala jannata Na'eem.

39. Kallaaa innaa khalaq-naahum-mimmaa ya'lamoon.

40. Falaaa uqsimu bi-Rabbil-mashaariqi wal-maghaaribi innaa laqaadiroon.

41. 'Alaaa an nubaddila khayram-minhum wa maa Naḥnu bimasbooqeen.

42. Fazarhum yakhooḍoo wa yal'aboo ḥattaa yulaaqoo Yaw-mahumul-lazee yoo'adoon.

43. Yawma yakhrujoona minal-ajdaaṣi siraa'an ka-annahum ilaa nuṣubiñy-yoofiḍoon.

44. Khaashi'atan abṣaaru-hum tarhaquhum zillah; zaa-likal-Yawmul-lazee kaanoo yoo'adoon. (Section 2)

---

71. Noah - The Prophet
In the name of Allah, Most Gracious, Most Merciful.

1. We sent Noah to his People (with the Command): "Do thou warn your People before there comes to them a grievous Chastisement."

2. He said: O my People! Lo! I am a plain warner unto you

3. "That you should worship Allah, fear Him and obey me:

4. "So that He may forgive you your sins and give you respite for a stated Term: for when the Term given by Allah is

Sûrat Nûḥ–71
(Revealed at Makkah)
Bismillaahir Raḥmaanir Raḥeem

1. Innaaa arsalnaa Noohan ilaa qawmiheee an anzir qawmaka min qabli añy-yaåtiya-hum 'azaabun aleem.

2. Qaala yaa qawmi innee lakum nazeerum-mubeen.

3. Ani'-budul-laaha watta-qoohu wa aṭee'oon.

4. Yaghfir lakum min zu-noobikum wa yu'akhkhirkum ilaaa ajalim-musammaa; inna ajalal-laahi izaa

accomplished, it cannot be put forward: if you only knew."

5. He said: "O my Lord! I have called to my People night and day:

6. But all my calling doth but add to their repugnance;

7. "And every time I have called to them, that you mightest forgive them, they have (only) thrust their fingers into their ears, covered themselves up with their garments, grown obstinate, and given themselves up to arrogance.

8. "So I have called to them aloud;

9. "Further I have spoken to them in public and secretly in private,

10. "Saying, 'Ask forgiveness from your Lord; for He is Oft-Forgiving;

11. "'He will send rain to you in abundance;

12. "'Give you increase in wealth and sons; and bestow on you gardens and bestow on you rivers (of flowing water).

13. What aileth you that ye hope not toward Allah for dignity,

14. When He created you by (diverse) stages?

15. 'See you not how Allah has created the seven heavens one above another,

16. "'And made the moon a light in their midst, and made the sun as a (Glorious) Lamp?

17. "'And Allah has produced you from the earth growing (gradually),

18. "'And in the End He will return you into the (earth), and raise you forth (again at the Resurrection)?

19. And Allah hath made the earth a wide expanse for you.

jaaa'a laa yu'akhkhar; law kuntum ta'lamoon.

5. Qaala Rabbi innee da'awtu qawmee laylanw-wa naharaa.

6. Falam yazid-hum du'aaa-'eee illaa firaaraa.

7. Wa innee kullamaa da-'awtuhum litaghfira lahum ja'a-looo asaabi'ahum feee aazaanihim wastaghshaw siyaabahum wa asarroo wastakbarus-tik-baaraa.

8. Summa innee da'aw-tuhum jihaaraa.

9. Summa inneee a'lantu lahum wa asrartu lahum israaraa.

10. Faqultus-taghfiroo Rab-bakam innahoo kaana Ghaf-faaraa.

11. Yursilis-samaaa'a 'alay-kum midraaraa.

12. Wa yumdidkum bi-am-waaliñw-wa baneena wa yaj'al lakum Jannaatiñw-wa yaj'al lakum anhaaraa.

13. Maa lakum laa tarjoona lillaahi waqaaraa.

14. Wa qad khalaqakum at-waaraa.

15. Alam taraw kayfa khala-qal-laahu sab'a samaawaatin-tibaaqaa.

16. Wa ja'alal-qamara fee-hinna nooraňw-wa ja'alash shamsa siraajaa.

17. Wallaahu ambatakum minal-ardi nabaataa.

18. Summa yu'eedukum fee-haa wa yukhrijukum ikhraajaa.

19. Wallaahu ja'ala lakumul-arda bisaataa.

قَالَ رَبِّ إِنِّي دَعَوْتُ قَوْمِي لَيْلًا وَّنَهَارًا ۞

فَلَمْ يَزِدْهُمْ دُعَآئِيْ إِلَّا فِرَارًا ۞

وَإِنِّي كُلَّمَا دَعَوْتُهُمْ لِتَغْفِرَ لَهُمْ جَعَلُوْا أَصَابِعَهُمْ فِيْ آذَانِهِمْ وَاسْتَغْشَوْا ثِيَابَهُمْ وَأَصَرُّوْا وَاسْتَكْبَرُوا اسْتِكْبَارًا ۞

ثُمَّ إِنِّي دَعَوْتُهُمْ جِهَارًا ۞

ثُمَّ إِنِّي أَعْلَنْتُ لَهُمْ وَأَسْرَرْتُ لَهُمْ إِسْرَارًا ۞

فَقُلْتُ اسْتَغْفِرُوْا رَبَّكُمْ إِنَّهُ كَانَ غَفَّارًا ۞

يُرْسِلِ السَّمَآءَ عَلَيْكُمْ مِّدْرَارًا ۞

وَّيُمْدِدْكُمْ بِأَمْوَالٍ وَّبَنِيْنَ وَيَجْعَلْ لَكُمْ جَنَّاتٍ وَّيَجْعَلْ لَّكُمْ أَنْهَارًا ۞

مَا لَكُمْ لَا تَرْجُوْنَ لِلّٰهِ وَقَارًا ۞

وَقَدْ خَلَقَكُمْ أَطْوَارًا ۞

أَلَمْ تَرَوْا كَيْفَ خَلَقَ اللّٰهُ سَبْعَ سَمٰوَاتٍ طِبَاقًا ۞

وَّجَعَلَ الْقَمَرَ فِيْهِنَّ نُوْرًا وَّجَعَلَ الشَّمْسَ سِرَاجًا ۞

وَاللّٰهُ أَنْبَتَكُمْ مِّنَ الْأَرْضِ نَبَاتًا ۞

ثُمَّ يُعِيْدُكُمْ فِيْهَا وَيُخْرِجُكُمْ إِخْرَاجًا ۞

وَاللّٰهُ جَعَلَ لَكُمُ الْأَرْضَ بِسَاطًا ۞

20. 'That you may go about therein, in spacious roads.'

21. Noah said: "O my Lord! They have disobeyed me, but they follow (men) whose wealth and children give them no increase but only Loss.

22. "And they have devised a tremendous Plot.

23. "And they have said (to each other), 'Abandon not your gods: Abandon neither Wadd nor Suwa', neither Yaguth nor Ya'uq, nor Nasr';-

24. "They have already misled many; and grant you no increase to the wrong-doers but in straying (from their mark)."

25. Because of their sins they were drowned (in the flood), and were made to enter the Fire (of Punishment): and they found- in lieu of Allah- none to help them.

26. And Noah, said: "O my Lord! Leave not of the Unbelievers, a single one on earth!

27. If Thou shouldst leave them, they will mislead Thy slaves and will beget none save lewd ingrates.

28. "O my Lord! Forgive me, my parents, all who enter my house in Faith, and (all) believing men and believing women: and to the wrong-doers grant You no increase but in perdition!"

---

20. Litaslukoo minhaa subulan fijaajaa. *(Section 1)*

21. Qaala Noohur-Robbi innahum 'aşawnee wattaba'oo mal-lam yazid-hu maaluhoo wa waladuhooo illaa khasaaraa.

22. Wa makaroo makran kubbaaraa.

23. Wa qaaloo laa tazarunna aalihatakum wa laa tazarunna Waddañw-wa laa Suwaa'añw-wa laa Yaghoosa wa Ya'ooqa wa Nasraa.

24. Wa qad aḍalloo kaseerañw-wa laa tazidiz-zaalimeena ḍalaalaa.

25. Mimmaa khaṭee'aatihim ughriqoo fa-udkhiloo Naaran falam yajidoo lahum min doonil-laahi anşaaraa.

26. Wa qaala Noohur-Rabbi laa tazar 'alal-arḍi minal-kaafireena dayyaaraa.

27. Innaka in tazarhum yuḍilloo 'ibaadaka wa laa yalidooo illaa faajiran kaffaaraa.

28. Rabbigh-fir lee wa liwaalidayya wa liman dakhala baytiya mu'minañw-wa lil-mu'mineena wal-mu'minaati wa laa tazidiz-zaalimeena illaa tabaaraa. *(Section 2)*

---

1. Say: It has been revealed to me that a company of Jinns listened (to the Qur'an). They said, 'We have really heard a wonderful Recital!

Sûrat al-Jinn–72
(Revealed at Makkah)
Bismillaahir Raḥmaanir Raḥeem

1. Qul oohiya ilayya annahus-tama'a nafarum-minaljinni faqaalooo innaa sami'naa Qur-aanan 'ajabaa.

---

2. 'It gives guidance to the Right, and we have believed therein: we shall not join (in worship) any (gods) with our Lord.

3. 'And Exalted is the Majesty of our Lord: He has taken neither a wife nor a son.

4. 'There were some foolish ones among us, who used to utter extravagant lies against Allah;

5. 'But we do think that no man or spirit should say anything that untrue against Allah.

6. 'True, there were persons among mankind who took shelter with persons among the Jinns, but they increased them in folly.

7. 'And they (came to) think as you thought, that Allah would not raise up any one (to Judgment).

8. 'And we pried into the secrets of heaven; but we found it filled with stern guards and flaming fires.

9. 'We used, indeed, to sit there in (hidden) stations, to (steal) a hearing; but any who listen now will find a flaming fire watching him in ambush.

10. And we know not whether harm is boded unto all who are in the earth, or whether their Lord intendeth guidance for them.

11. 'There are among us some that are righteous, and some the contrary: we follow divergent paths.

12. 'But we think that we can by no means frustrate Allah throughout the earth, nor can we frustrate Him by flight.

13. 'And as for us, since we have listened to the Guidance, we have accepted it: and any who believes in his Lord has no fear,

2. Yahdeee ilar-rushdi fa-aamannaa bihee wa lan nushrika bi-Rabbinaaaa aḥadaa.

3. Wa annahoo Ta‘aalaa jaddu Rabbinaa mat-takhaza ṣaaḥibatañw-wa laa waladaa.

4. Wa annahoo kaana ya-qoolu safeehunaa ‘alal-laahi shaṭaṭaa

5. Wa annaa ẓanannaaaa al-lan taqoolal-insu wal-jinnu ‘alal-laahi kazibaa.

6. Wa annahoo kaana rijaa-lum-minal-insi ya‘oozoona birijaalim-minal-jinni fazaa-doohum rahaqaa.

7. Wa annahum ẓannoo kamaa ẓanantum al-lañy-yab-‘aṣal-laahu aḥadaa.

8. Wa annaa lamasnas-sa-maaa‘a fa-wajadnaahaa muli’at ḥarasan shadeedañw-wa shuhu-baa.

9. Wa annaa kunnaa naq-‘udu minhaa maqaa‘ida lis-sam‘i famañy-yastami‘il-aana yajid lahoo shihaabar-raṣadaa.

10. Wa annaa laa nadree asharrun ureeda biman fil-arḍi am araada bihim Rabbuhum rashadaa.

11. Wa annaa minnaṣ-ṣaali-ḥoona wa minnaa doona zaalika kunnaa ṭaraaa’iqa qidadaa.

12. Wa annaa ẓanannaaaa al-lan nu‘jizal-laaha fil-arḍi wa lan nu‘jizahoo harabaa.

13. Wa annaa lammaa sami‘-nal-hudaaaa aamannaa bihee famañy-yu’mim bi-Rabbihee falaa yakhaafu

يَهْدِىٓ اِلَى الرُّشْدِ فَاٰمَنَّا بِهٖ ۖ

وَلَنْ نُّشْرِكَ بِرَبِّنَآ اَحَدًا ۙ

وَّاَنَّهٗ تَعٰلٰى جَدُّ رَبِّنَا مَا اتَّخَذَ

صَاحِبَةً وَّلَا وَلَدًا ۙ

وَّاَنَّهٗ كَانَ يَقُوْلُ سَفِيْهُنَا عَلَى

اللهِ شَطَطًا ۙ

وَّاَنَّا ظَنَنَّآ اَنْ لَّنْ تَقُوْلَ الْاِنْسُ

وَالْجِنُّ عَلَى اللهِ كَذِبًا ۙ

وَّاَنَّهٗ كَانَ رِجَالٌ مِّنَ الْاِنْسِ

يَعُوْذُوْنَ بِرِجَالٍ مِّنَ الْجِنِّ

فَزَادُوْهُمْ رَهَقًا ۙ

وَّاَنَّهُمْ ظَنُّوْا كَمَا ظَنَنْتُمْ اَنْ لَّنْ

يَّبْعَثَ اللهُ اَحَدًا ۙ

وَّاَنَّا لَمَسْنَا السَّمَآءَ فَوَجَدْنٰهَا مُلِئَتْ

حَرَسًا شَدِيْدًا وَّشُهُبًا ۙ

وَّاَنَّا كُنَّا نَقْعُدُ مِنْهَا مَقَاعِدَ

لِلسَّمْعِ ۖ فَمَنْ يَّسْتَمِعِ الْاٰنَ يَجِدْ

لَهٗ شِهَابًا رَّصَدًا ۙ

وَّاَنَّا لَا نَدْرِىٓ اَشَرٌّ اُرِيْدَ بِمَنْ فِى

الْاَرْضِ اَمْ اَرَادَ بِهِمْ رَبُّهُمْ رَشَدًا ۙ

وَّاَنَّا مِنَّا الصّٰلِحُوْنَ وَمِنَّا دُوْنَ

ذٰلِكَ ۖ كُنَّا طَرَآئِقَ قِدَدًا ۙ

وَّاَنَّا ظَنَنَّآ اَنْ لَّنْ نُّعْجِزَ اللهَ فِى

الْاَرْضِ وَلَنْ نُّعْجِزَهٗ هَرَبًا ۙ

وَّاَنَّا لَمَّا سَمِعْنَا الْهُدٰىٓ اٰمَنَّا بِهٖ ۖ

فَمَنْ يُّؤْمِنْۢ بِرَبِّهٖ فَلَا يَخَافُ

either of a short (account) or of any injustice.

14. 'Amongst us are some that submit their wills (to Allah), and some that swerve from justice. Now those who submit their wills - they have sought out (the path) of right conduct:

15. 'But those who swerve,- they are (but) fuel for Hell-fire'-

16. If they (the idolaters) tread the right path, We shall give them to drink of water in abundance.

17. "That We might try them by that (means). But if any turns away from the remembrance of his Lord, He will cause him to undergo a severe Chastisement.

18. "And the places of worship are for Allah (alone): So invoke not any one along with Allah;

19. "Yet when the Devotee of Allah stands forth to invoke Him, they just make round him a dense crowd."

20. Say: "I do no more than invoke my Lord, and I join not with Him any (false god)."

21. Say: "It is not in my power to cause you harm, or to bring you to right conduct."

22. Say: "No one can deliver me from Allah (If I were to disobey Him), nor should I find refuge except in Him,

23. "Unless I proclaim what I receive from Allah and His Messages: for any that disobey Allah and His Apostle,- for them is Hell: they shall dwell therein for ever."

24. At length, when they see (with their own eyes) that which they are promised,- then will they know who it is that is weakest in (his) helper and least important in point of numbers.

25. Say: "I know not whether the (Punishment) which you are promised is near,

bakhsanw-wa laa rahaqaa.

14. Wa annaa minnal-mus-limoona wa minnal-qaasitoona faman aslama fa-ulaaa'ika taharraw rashadaa.

15. Wa ammal-qaasitoona fa-kaanoo li-Jahannama hatabaa.

16. Wa alla-wis-taqaamoo 'alat-tareeqati la-asqaynaahum maa-'an ghadaqaa.

17. Linaftinahum feeh; wa mañy-yu'rid 'an zikri Rabbihee yasluk-hu 'azaaban sa'adaa.

18. Wa annal-masaajida lillaahi falaa tad'oo ma'al-laahi ahadaa.

19. Wa annahoo lammaa qaama 'abdul-laahi yad'oohu kaadoo yakoonoona 'alayhi libadaa. **(Section 1)**

20. Qul innamaaa ad'oo Rabbee wa laaa ushriku biheee ahadaa.

21. Qul innee laaa amliku lakum darranw-wa laa rashadaa.

22. Qul innee lañy-yujeera-nee minal-laahi ahad, wa lan ajida min doonihee multahadaa.

23. Illaa balaagham-minal-laahi wa Risaalaatih; wa mañy-ya'sil-laaha wa Rasoolahoo fa-inna lahoo Naara Jahannama khaalideena feehaaa abadaa.

24. Hattaaa izaa ra-aw maa yoo'adoona fasa-ya'lamoona man ad'afu naasiranw-wa aqallu 'adadaa.

25. Qul in adreee a-qareebum-maa too'adoona

بَخْسًا وَّلَا رَهَقًا ۖ

وَّاَنَّا مِنَّا الْمُسْلِمُوْنَ وَمِنَّا الْقٰسِطُوْنَ ۖ فَمَنْ اَسْلَمَ فَاُولٰٓئِكَ تَحَرَّوْا رَشَدًا ۖ

وَاَمَّا الْقٰسِطُوْنَ فَكَانُوْا لِجَهَنَّمَ حَطَبًا ۖ

وَّاَنْ لَّوِ اسْتَقَامُوْا عَلَى الطَّرِيْقَةِ لَاَسْقَيْنٰهُمْ مَّاءً غَدَقًا ۖ

لِنَفْتِنَهُمْ فِيْهِ ۖ وَمَنْ يُّعْرِضْ عَنْ ذِكْرِ رَبِّهٖ يَسْلُكْهُ عَذَابًا صَعَدًا ۖ

وَّاَنَّ الْمَسٰجِدَ لِلّٰهِ فَلَا تَدْعُوْا مَعَ اللّٰهِ اَحَدًا ۖ

وَّاَنَّهٗ لَمَّا قَامَ عَبْدُ اللّٰهِ يَدْعُوْهُ كَادُوْا يَكُوْنُوْنَ عَلَيْهِ لِبَدًا ۖ

قُلْ اِنَّمَاۤ اَدْعُوْا رَبِّيْ وَلَاۤ اُشْرِكُ بِهٖۤ اَحَدًا ۖ

قُلْ اِنِّيْ لَاۤ اَمْلِكُ لَكُمْ ضَرًّا وَّلَا رَشَدًا ۖ

قُلْ اِنِّيْ لَنْ يُّجِيْرَنِيْ مِنَ اللّٰهِ اَحَدٌ ۖ وَّلَنْ اَجِدَ مِنْ دُوْنِهٖ مُلْتَحَدًا ۖ

اِلَّا بَلٰغًا مِّنَ اللّٰهِ وَرِسٰلٰتِهٖ ۖ وَمَنْ يَّعْصِ اللّٰهَ وَرَسُوْلَهٗ فَاِنَّ لَهٗ نَارَ جَهَنَّمَ خٰلِدِيْنَ فِيْهَاۤ اَبَدًا ۖ

حَتّٰى اِذَا رَاَوْا مَا يُوْعَدُوْنَ فَسَيَعْلَمُوْنَ مَنْ اَضْعَفُ نَاصِرًا وَّاَقَلُّ عَدَدًا ۖ

قُلْ اِنْ اَدْرِيْۤ اَقَرِيْبٌ مَّا تُوْعَدُوْنَ

or whether my Lord will appoint for it a distant term.

26. "He (alone) knows the Unseen, nor does He make any one acquainted with His Mysteries,-

27. "Except an apostle whom He has chosen: and then He makes a band of watchers march before him and behind him,

28. That He may know that they have indeed conveyed the messages of their Lord. He surroundeth all their doings, and He keepeth count of all things.

am yaj'alu lahooRabbeee amadaa.

26. 'Aalimul-Ghaybi falaa yuzhiru alaa ghaybiheee ahadaa.

27. Illaa manir-tadaa mir Rasoolin fa-innahoo yasluku mim bayni yadayhi wa min khalfihee rasadaa.

28. Liya'lama an qad ablaghoo Risaalaati Rabbihim wa ahaata bima ladayhim wa ahsaa Kulla shay'in 'adadaa. **(Section 2)**

73. Folded in Garments
In the name of Allah, Most Gracious, Most Merciful.

1. O you folded in garments!
2. Stand (to prayer) by night, but not all night,-
3. Half of it,- or a little less,
4. Or add (a little) thereto — and chant the Qur'an in measure.
5. Soon shall We send down to thee a weighty Message.
6. Lo! The vigil of the night is (a time) when impression is more keen and speech more certain.
7. Lo! Thou hast by day a chain of business.
8. But keep in remembrance the name of your Lord and devote thyself to Him wholeheartedly.
9. (He is) Lord of the East and the West: there is no god but He: take Him therefore for (thy) Disposer of Affairs.
10. And have patience with what they say, and leave them with noble (dignity).
11. And leave Me (alone to deal with) those in possession of the good things of life,

Sûrat al-Muzzammil–73
(Revealed at Makkah)
Bismillaahir Rahmaanir Raheem

1. Yaw ayyuhal-muzzammil.
2. Qumil-layla illaa qaleelaa.
3. Nisfahooo awinqus minhu qaleelaa.
4. Aw zid 'alayhi wa rattilil-Qur'aana tarteelaa.
5. Innaa sanulqee 'alayka qawalan saqeelaa.
6. Inna naashi'atal-layli hiya ashaddu wat-anw-wa aqwamu-qeelaa.
7. Inna laka fin-nahaari sabhan taweelaa.
8. Wazkuris-ma Rabbika wa tabattal ilayhi tabteelaa.
9. Rabbul-mashriqi wal-maghribi laaa ilaaha illaa Huwa fattakhizhu Wakeelaa.
10. Wasbir 'alaa maa yaqooloona wahjurhum hajran jameelaa.
11. Wa zarnee walmukaz zibeena ulin-na'mati

who (yet) deny the Truth; and bear with them for a little while.

12. Lo! With Us are heavy fetters and a raging fire.

13. And a Food that chokes, and a Chastisement Grievous.

14. On the Day when the earth and the hills rock, and the hills become a heap of running sand.

15. We have sent to you, (O men!) an apostle, to be a witness concerning you, even as We sent an apostle to Pharaoh.

16. But Pharaoh disobeyed the apostle; so We seized him with a heavy Punishment.

17. Then how shall you, if you deny (Allah), guard yourselves against a Day that will make children hoary-headed?-

18. Whereon the sky will be cleft asunder? His Promise needs must be accomplished.

19. Verily this is an Admonition: therefore, whoso will, let him take a (straight) path to his Lord!

20. Thy Lord does know that thou stands forth (to prayer) nearly two-thirds of the night, or half the night, or a third of the night, and so does a party of those with you. But Allah does appoint night and day in due measure He knoweth that you are unable to keep count thereof. So He has turned to you (in mercy): read you, therefore, of the Qur'an as much as may be easy for you. He knows that there may be (some) among you in ill-health; others travelling through the land, seeking of Allah's bounty ; yet others fighting in Allah's Cause, read ye, therefore,

---

wa mahhilhum qaleelaa.

12. Inna ladaynaaa ankaalañw-wa Jaheemaa.

13. Wa ta'aaman zaa ghussa-tiñw-wa 'azaaban aleemaa.

14. Yawma tarjuful-ardu waljibaalu wa kaanatil-jibaalu kaseebam-maheelaa.

15. Innaaa arsalnaaa ilaykum Rasoolan shaahidan 'alaykum kamaaa arsalnaaa ilaa Fir'awna Rasoolaa.

16. Fa'asaa Fir'awnur-Rasoo-la fa-akhaznaahu akhzañw-wabeelaa.

17. Fakayfa tattaqoona in kafartum Yawmañy-yaj'alul-wildaana sheebaa.

18. Assamaaa'u munfatirum bih; kaana wa'duhoo maf-'oolaa.

19. Inna haazihee tazkiratun fa-man shaaa'at-takhaza ilaa Rabbihee sabeelaa. (Section 1)

20. Inna Rabbaka ya'lamu annaka taqoomu-adnaa min sulusa-yil-layli wa nisfahoo wa sulusahoo wa taaa'ifatum-minal-lazeena ma'ak; wal-laahu yuqaddirul-layla wanna-haar; 'alima al-lan tuhsoohu fataaba 'alaykum faqra'oo maa tayassara minal-Qur-aan; 'alima an sa-yakoonu minkum mardaa wa aakharoona yadri-boona fil-ardi yabtaghoona min fadlil-laahi wa aakharoona yu-qaatiloona fee sabeelil-laahi faqra'oo

---

وَمَهِّلْهُمْ قَلِيلًا ۝

اِنَّ لَدَيْنَاۤ اَنْكَالًا وَّجَحِيمًا ۝

وَّطَعَامًا ذَا غُصَّةٍ وَّعَذَابًا اَلِيمًا ۝

يَوْمَ تَرْجُفُ الْاَرْضُ وَالْجِبَالُ وَكَانَتِ الْجِبَالُ كَثِيبًا مَّهِيلًا ۝

اِنَّاۤ اَرْسَلْنَاۤ اِلَيْكُمْ رَسُوْلًا ۙ شَاهِدًا عَلَيْكُمْ كَمَاۤ اَرْسَلْنَاۤ اِلٰى فِرْعَوْنَ رَسُوْلًا ۝

فَعَصٰى فِرْعَوْنُ الرَّسُوْلَ فَاَخَذْنٰهُ اَخْذًا وَّبِيْلًا ۝

فَكَيْفَ تَتَّقُوْنَ اِنْ كَفَرْتُمْ يَوْمًا يَّجْعَلُ الْوِلْدَانَ شِيْبًا ۝

السَّمَاۤءُ مُنْفَطِرٌ بِهٖ ۗ كَانَ وَعْدُهٗ مَفْعُوْلًا ۝

اِنَّ هٰذِهٖ تَذْكِرَةٌ ۚ فَمَنْ شَاۤءَ اتَّخَذَ اِلٰى رَبِّهٖ سَبِيْلًا ۝

اِنَّ رَبَّكَ يَعْلَمُ اَنَّكَ تَقُوْمُ اَدْنٰى مِنْ ثُلُثَيِ الَّيْلِ وَنِصْفَهٗ وَثُلُثَهٗ وَطَاۤئِفَةٌ مِّنَ الَّذِيْنَ مَعَكَ ۗ وَاللّٰهُ يُقَدِّرُ الَّيْلَ وَالنَّهَارَ ۗ عَلِمَ اَنْ لَّنْ تُحْصُوْهُ فَتَابَ عَلَيْكُمْ فَاقْرَءُوْا مَا تَيَسَّرَ مِنَ الْقُرْاٰنِ ۗ عَلِمَ اَنْ سَيَكُوْنُ مِنْكُمْ مَّرْضٰى ۙ وَاٰخَرُوْنَ يَضْرِبُوْنَ فِى الْاَرْضِ يَبْتَغُوْنَ مِنْ فَضْلِ اللّٰهِ وَاٰخَرُوْنَ يُقَاتِلُوْنَ فِىْ سَبِيْلِ اللّٰهِ ۖ فَاقْرَءُوْا

as much of the Qur'an as may be easy (for you); and establish regular Prayer and give regular Charity; and loan to Allah a Beautiful Loan. And whatever good you send forth for your souls you shall find it in Allah's Presence,- yes, better and greater, in Reward and seek you the Grace of Allah: for Allah is Oft-Forgiving, Most Merciful.

maa tayassara minhu wa aqeemuṣ-Ṣalaata wa aatuz-Zakaata wa aqriḍul-laaha qarḍan ḥasanaa; wa maa tuqaddimoo li-anfusikum min khayrin tajidoohu 'indal-laahi huwa khayrañw-wa a'ẓama ajraa; wastaghfirul-laaha innal-laaha Ghafoorur-Raḥeem.   (Section 2)

74. The One Wrapped Up
In the name of Allah, Most Gracious, Most Merciful.

Sûrat al-Muddaṣṣir–74
(Revealed at Makkah)
Bismillaahir Raḥmaanir Raḥeem

1.   O you wrapped up (in the mantle)!

2.   Arise and deliver thy warning!

3.   And your Lord do thou magnify!

4.   And thy garments keep free from stain!

5.   And all abomination shun!

6.   Nor expect, in giving, any increase (for yourself)!

7.   But, for your Lord's (Cause), be patient and constant!

8.   Finally, when the Trumpet is sounded,

9.   That will be- that Day - a Day of Distress,-

10.   Far from easy for those without Faith.

11.   Leave me (to deal) with him whom I created lonely,

12.   To whom I granted resources in abundance,

13.   And sons to be by his side!-

14.   To whom I made (life) smooth and comfortable!

15.   Yet is he greedy-that I should add (yet more);-

16.   By no means! For to Our Signs he has been refractory!

17.   Soon will I visit him with a mount of calamities!

18.   For he thought and he plotted;-

1.   Yaaa ayyuhal-muddaṣṣir.

2.   Qum fa-anẕir.

3.   Wa Rabbaka fakabbir.

4.   Wa ṣiyaabaka faṭahhir.

5.   Warrujza fahjur.

6.   Wa laa tamnun tastaksir.

7.   Wa li-Rabbika faṣbir.

8.   Fa-iẕaa nuqira fin-naaqoor.

9.   Fazaalika Yawma'iẕiñy-yawmun 'aseer.

10.   'Alal-kaafireena ghayru yaseer.

11.   Zarnee wa man khalaqtu waḥeedaa.

12.   Wa ja'altu lahoo maalam-mamdoodaa.

13.   Wa baneena shuhoodaa.

14.   Wa mahhattu lahoo tamheedaa.

15.   Ṣumma yaṭma'u an azeed.

16.   Kallaaa innahoo kaana li-Aayaatinaa 'aneedaa.

17.   Sa-urhiquhoo ṣa'oodaa.

18.   Innahoo fakkara wa qaddar.

19. And woe to him! How he plotted!-

20. Yes, Woe to him; How he plotted!-

21. Then he looked round;

22. Then he frowned and he scowled;

23. Then he turned back and was haughty;

24. And said: This is naught else than magic from of old;

25. "This is nothing but the word of a mortal!"

26. Soon will I cast him into Hell-Fire!

27. And what will explain to thee what Hell-Fire is?

28. It leaveth naught; it spareth naught.

29. Darkening and changing the colour of man!

30. Over it are Nineteen.

31. And We have set none but angels as Guardians of the Fire; and We have fixed their number only as a trial for Unbelievers,- in order that the People of the Book may arrive at certainty, and the Believers may increase in Faith,- and that no doubts may be left for the People of the Book and the Believers, and that those in whose hearts is a disease and the Unbelievers may say, "What symbol does Allah intend by this ?" Thus does Allah leave to stray whom He pleases, and guide whom He pleases: and none can know the forces of thy Lord, except He and this is no other than a warning to mankind.

32. No, verily: By the Moon,

33. And by the Night as it retreateth,

19. Faqutila kayfa qaddar.

20. Summa qutila kayfa qaddar.

21. Summa nazar.

22. Summa 'abasa wa basar.

23. Summa adbara wastakbar.

24. Faqaala in haazaaa illaa sihruny-yu'sar.

25. In haazaaa illaa qawlul-bashar.

26. Sa-usleehi saqar.

27. Wa maaa adraaka maa saqar.

28. Laa tubqee wa laa tazar.

29. Lawwaahatul-lilbashar.

30. 'Alayhaa tis'ata 'ashar.

31. Wa maa ja'alnaaa Ashaaban-Naari illaa malaaa'ikatanw-wa maa ja'alnaa 'iddatahum illaa fitnatal-lillazeena kafaroo liyastayqinal-lazeena ootul-Kitaaba wa yazdaadal-lazeena aamanoooo eemaananw-wa laa yartaabal-lazeena ootul-Kitaaba walmu'minoona wa liyaqoolal-lazeena fee quloobihim maraduñw-walkaafiroona maazaaa araadal-laahu bihaazaa masalaa; kazaalika yudillul-laahu mañy-yashaaa'u wa yahdee mañy-yashaaa'; wa maa ya'lamu junooda Rabbika illaa Hoo; wa maa hiya illaa zikraa lil-bashar.

(Section 1)

32. Kallaa walqamar.

33. Wallayli iz adbar.

34. And by the Dawn as it shines forth,-

35. This is but one of the mighty (portents),

36. A warning to mankind,-

37. To any of you that chooses to press forward, or to follow behind;-

38. Every soul will be (held) in pledge for its deeds.

39. Except the Companions of the Right Hand.

40. In garden they will ask one another,

41. And (ask) of the Sinners:

42. "What led you into Hell Fire?"

43. They will say: "We were not of those who prayed;

44. "Nor were we of those who fed the indigent;

45. "But we used to talk vanities with vain talkers;

46. "And we used to deny the Day of Judgment,

47. "Until there came to us (the Hour) that is certain."

48. The mediation of no mediators will avail them then.

49. Why now turn they away from the Admonishment,

50. As if they were affrighted asses,

51. Fleeing from a lion!

52. Forsooth, each one of them wants to be given scrolls (of revelation) spread out!

53. By no means! But they fear not the Hereafter,

54. No, this surely is an admonition:

55. Let any who will, keep it in remembrance!

56. But none will keep it in remembrance except as Allah wills: He is the Lord of Righteousness, and the Lord of Forgiveness.

34. Waṣṣub-ḥi izaaa asfar.

35. Innahaa la-iḥdal-kubar.

36. Nazeeral-lilbashar.

37. Liman shaaa'a minkum añy-yataqaddama aw yata-akhkhar.

38. Kullu nafsim bimaa kasabat raheenah.

39. Illaaa Aṣ-ḥaabal-Yameen.

40. Fee Jannaatiñy yata-saaa'aloon.

41. 'Anil-mujrimeen.

42. Maa salakakum fee saqar.

43. Qaaloo lam naku minal-muṣalleen.

44. Wa lam naku nuṭ'imul-miskeen.

45. Wa kunnaa nakhooḍu ma'al-khaaa'iḍeen.

46. Wa kunnaa nukazzibu bi-Yawmid-Deen.

47. Ḥattaaa ataanal-yaqeen.

48. Famaa tanfa'uhum sha-faa'atush-shaafi'een.

49. Famaa lahum 'anit-tazkirati mu'riḍeen.

50. Ka-annahum ḥumurum-mustanfirah.

51. Farrat min qaswarah.

52. Bal yureedu kullum-ri-'im-minhum añy-yu'taa ṣuḥufam-munashsharah.

53. Kallaa bal laa yakhaa-foonal-aakhirah.

54. Kallaaa innahoo tazkirah.

55. Fa-man shaaa'a zakarah.

56. Wa maa yazkuroona illaaa añy-yashaaa'al-laah; Huwa ahlut-taqwaa wa ahlul-magh-firah. **(Section 2)**

75. The Resurrection
In the name of Allah, Most Gracious, Most Merciful.

Sûrat al-Qiyâmah–75
(Revealed at Makkah)

Bismillaahir Rahmaanir Raheem

سُوْرَةُ الْقِيٰمَةِ مَكِّيَّةٌ (٣١) (٧٥)

بِسْمِ اللهِ الرَّحْمٰنِ الرَّحِيْمِ

1. I do call to witness the Resurrection Day;

1. Laaa uqsimu bi-Yawmil-Qiyaamah.

لَاۤ اُقْسِمُ بِيَوْمِ الْقِيٰمَةِ

2. And I do call to witness the self-reproaching spirit: (eschew Evil).

2. We laaa uqsimu bin-nafsil-lawwaamah.

وَلَاۤ اُقْسِمُ بِالنَّفْسِ اللَّوَّامَةِ

3. Does man think that We cannot assemble his bones?

3. Ayahsabul-insaanu al-lan najma'a 'izaamah.

اَيَحْسَبُ الْاِنْسَانُ اَلَّنْ نَّجْمَعَ عِظَامَهٗ

4. Yea, verily. Yea, We are able to restore his very fingers!

4. Balaa qaadireena 'alaaa an nusawwiya banaanah.

بَلٰى قٰدِرِيْنَ عَلٰۤى اَنْ نُّسَوِّيَ بَنَانَهٗ

5. But man would fain deny what is before him.

5. Bal yureedul-insaanu liyafjura amaamah.

بَلْ يُرِيْدُ الْاِنْسَانُ لِيَفْجُرَ اَمَامَهٗ

6. He questions: "When is the Day of Resurrection?"

6. Yas'alu ayyaana Yawmul-Qiyaamah.

يَسْئَلُ اَيَّانَ يَوْمُ الْقِيٰمَةِ

7. At length, when the sight is dazed,

7. Fa-izaa bariqal-basar.

فَاِذَا بَرِقَ الْبَصَرُ

8. And the moon is buried in darkness.

8. We khasafal-qamar.

وَخَسَفَ الْقَمَرُ

9. And the sun and moon are joined together,-

9. Wa jumi'ash-shamsu wal-qamar.

وَجُمِعَ الشَّمْسُ وَالْقَمَرُ

10. That Day will Man say: "Where is the refuge?"

10. Yaqoolul-insaanu Yawma'izin aynal-mafarr.

يَقُوْلُ الْاِنْسَانُ يَوْمَئِذٍ اَيْنَ الْمَفَرُّ

11. By no means! No place of safety!

11. Kallaa laa wazar.

كَلَّا لَا وَزَرَ

12. Before your Lord (alone), that Day will be the place of rest.

12. Ilaa Rabbika Yawma-'izinil-mustaqarr.

اِلٰى رَبِّكَ يَوْمَئِذٍ الْمُسْتَقَرُّ

13. That Day will Man be told (all) that he put forward, and all that he put back.

13. Yunabba'ul-insaanu Yawma'izim bimaa qaddama wa akhkhar.

يُنَبَّؤُا الْاِنْسَانُ يَوْمَئِذٍ بِمَا قَدَّمَ وَاَخَّرَ

14. No, man will be evidence against himself,

14. Balil-insaanu 'alaa naf-sihee baseerah.

بَلِ الْاِنْسَانُ عَلٰى نَفْسِهٖ بَصِيْرَةٌ

15. Even though he were to put up his excuses.

15. Wa law alqaa ma'aazee-rah.

وَلَوْ اَلْقٰى مَعَاذِيْرَهٗ

16. Stir not thy tongue here with to hasten it.

16. Laa tuharrik bihee lisaa-naka lita'jala bih.

لَا تُحَرِّكْ بِهٖ لِسَانَكَ لِتَعْجَلَ بِهٖ

17. It is for Us to collect it and to promulgate it:

17. Inna 'alaynaa jam'ahoo wa qur-aanah.

اِنَّ عَلَيْنَا جَمْعَهٗ وَقُرْاٰنَهٗ

18. And when We read it, follow thou the reading;

18. Fa-izaa qaraanaahu fatta-bi' qur-aanah.

فَاِذَا قَرَاْنَاهُ فَاتَّبِعْ قُرْاٰنَهٗ

19. No more, it is for Us to explain it (and make it clear):

19. Summa inna 'alaynaa bayaanah.

ثُمَّ اِنَّ عَلَيْنَا بَيَانَهٗ

20. No, (you men!) but ye love the fleeting life,

20. Kallaa bal tuhibboonal-'aajilah.

كَلَّا بَلْ تُحِبُّوْنَ الْعَاجِلَةَ

21. And leave alone the Hereafter.

21. Wa tazaroonal-Aakhirah.

وَتَذَرُوْنَ الْاٰخِرَةَ

22. Some faces, that Day, will beam (in brightness and beauty);-

22. Wujoohuny-Yawma'izin naadirah.

وُجُوْهٌ يَوْمَئِذٍ نَّاضِرَةٌ

23. Looking towards their Lord;

24. And some faces, that Day, will be sad and dismal,

25. Thou wilt know that some great disaster is about to fall on them.

26. Nay, but when the life cometh up to the throat.

27. And men say: Where is the wizard (who can save him now)?

28. And he will conclude that it was (the Time) of Parting;

29. And one leg will be joined with another;

30. That Day the Drive will be (all) to your Lord!

31. So he gave nothing in charity, nor did he pray!-

32. But on the contrary, he rejected Truth and turned away!

33. Then did he stalk to his family in full conceit!

34. Woe to you, (O men!), yes, woe!

35. Again, Woe to thee, (O men!), yes, woe!

36. Thinketh man that he is to be left aimless?

37. Was he not a drop of sperm emitted (in lowly form)?

38. Then he became a clot; then (Allah) shaped and fashioned,

39. And of him He made two sexes, male and female.

40. Has not He, (the same), the power to give life to the dead.

23. Ilaa Rabbihaa naaẓirah.

24. Wa wujoohuñy-Yawma'izim baasirah.

25. Taẓunnu añy-yuf'ala bihaa faaqirah.

26. Kallaaa iẓaa balaghatit-taraaqee.

27. Wa qeela man raaq.

28. Wa ẓanna annahul-firaaq.

29. Waltaffatis-saaqu bissaaq.

30. Ilaa Rabbika Yawma'izinil-masaaq. **(Section 1)**

31. Falaa ṣaddaqa wa laa ṣallaa.

32. Wa laakin kazzaba wa tawallaa.

33. Ṣumma zahaba ilaaa ahlihee yatamaṭṭaa.

34. Awlaa laka fa-awlaa.

35. Ṣumma awlaa laka fa-awlaa.

36. Ayaḥsabul-insaanu añy-yutraka sudaa.

37. Alam yaku nuṭfatam-mim-maniyyiñy-yumnaa.

38. Ṣumma kaana 'alaqatan fakhalaqa fasawwaa.

39. Faja'ala minhuz-zawjayniz-zakara wal-unṣaa.

40. Alaysa zaalika biqaadirin 'alaaa añy-yuḥyiyal-mawtaa. **(Section 2)**

---

76. Time; or Man
In the name of Allah, Most Gracious, Most Merciful.

1. Has there not been over Man a long period of Time, when he was nothing - (not even) mentioned?

2. Verily We created Man from a drop of mingled sperm, in order to try him: So We gave him (the gifts), of Hearing and

Sûrat ad-Dahr; al-Insân–76
(Revealed at Madinah)
Bismillaahir Raḥmaanir Raḥeem

1. Hal ataa 'alal-insaani ḥeenum-minad-dahri lam yakun shay'am maẓkooraa.

2. Innaa khalaqnal-insaana min-nuṭfatin amshaajin nabta-leehi faja'alnaahu samee'am-

Sight.

3. We showed him the Way: whether he be grateful or ungrateful (rests on his will).

4. For the Rejecters We have prepared chains, yokes, and a blazing Fire.

5. As to the Righteous, they shall drink of a Cup (of Wine) mixed with Kafur,-

6. A Fountain where the Devotees of Allah do drink, making it flow in unstinted abundance.

7. They perform (their) vows, and they fear a Day whose evil flies far and wide.

8. And they feed, for the love of Allah, the indigent, the orphan, and the captive,-

9. (Saying),"We feed you for the sake of Allah alone: no reward do we desire from you, nor thanks.

10. "We only fear a Day of distressful Wrath from the side of our Lord."

11. But Allah will deliver them from the evil of that Day, and will shed over them a Light of Beauty and (blissful) Joy.

12. And hath awarded them for all that they endured, a Garden and silk attire;

13. Reclining in the (Garden) on raised thrones, they will see there neither the sun's (excessive heat) nor (the moon's) excessive cold.

14. And the shades of the (Garden) will come low over them, and the bunch (of fruit), there, will hang low in humility.

15. And amongst them will be passed round vessels of silver and goblets of crystal,-

---

baseeraa.

3. Innaa hadaynaahus-sabeela immaa shaakirañw-wa immaa kafooraa.

4. Innaaa a'tadnaa lilkaa-fireena salaasila wa aghlaalañw-wa sa'eeraa.

5. Innal-abraara yashraboona min kaåsin kaana mizaajuhaa kaafooraa.

6. 'Aynañy-yashrabu bihaa 'ibaadul-laahi yufajjiroonahaa tafjeeraa.

7. Yoofoona binnazri wa yakhaafoona yawman kaana sharruhoo mustateeraa.

8. Wa yut'imoonat-ta'aama 'alaa hubbihee miskeenañw-wa yateemañw-wa aseeraa.

9. Innamaa nut'imukum li-wajhil-laahi laa nureedu minkum jazaaa'añw-wa laa shukooraa.

10. Innaa nakhaafu mir-Rabbinaa Yawman 'aboosan qamtareeraa.

11. Fa-waqaahumul-laahu sharra zaalikal-Yawmi wa laqqaahum nadratañw-wa surooraa.

12. Wa jazaahum bimaa sabaroo Jannatañw-wa hareeraa.

13. Muttaki'eena feehaa 'alal-araaa'iki laa yarawna fee-haa shamsañw-wa laa zamha-reeraa.

14. Wa daaniyatan 'alayhim zilaaluhaa wa zullilat qutoofu-haa tazleelaa.

15. Wa yutaafu 'alayhim bi-aaniyatim-min fiddatiñw-wa akwaabin kaanat qawaareeraa.

16. Crystal-clear, made of silver: they will determine the measure thereof (according to their wishes).

17. And they will be given to drink there of a Cup (of Wine) mixed with Zanjabil,-

18. A fountain there, called Salsabil.

19. And round about them will (serve) youths of perpetual (freshness): If you see them, you would think them scattered Pearls.

20. And when you look, it is there you will see a Bliss and a Realm Magnificent.

21. Upon them will be green Garments of fine silk and heavy brocade, and they will be adorned with Bracelets of silver; and their Lord will give to them to drink of a Wine Pure and Holy.

22. "Verily this is a Reward for you, and your Endeavour is accepted and recognised."

23. It is We Who have sent down the Qur'an to you by stages.

24. Therefore, be patient with constancy to the Command of your Lord, and hearken not to the sinner or the ingrate among them.

25. And celebrate the name of your Lord morning and evening,

26. And part of the night, prostrate yourself to Him; and glorify Him a long night through.

27. As to these, they love the fleeting life, and put away behind them a Day (that will be) hard.

28. It is We Who created them, and We have made their joints strong; but, when We will, We can substitute the like of them by a complete change.

16. Qawaareera min fiḍḍatin qaddaroohaa taqdeeraa.

17. Wa yusqawna feehaa kaå-san kaana mizaajuhaa zanja-beelaa.

18. 'Aynan feehaa tusammaa salsabeelaa.

19. Wa yaṭoofu 'alayhim wildaanum-mukhalladoona izaa ra-aytahum ḥasibtahum lu'lu'am-mansooraa.

20. Wa izaa ra-ayta ṣumma ra-ayta na'eemaảnw-wa mulkan kabeeraa.

21. 'Aaliyahum ṣiyaabu sun-dusin khuḍruňw-wa istabraq, wa ḥullooo asaawira min fiḍḍatiňw wa saqaahum Rab-buhum sharaaban ṭahooraa.

22. Inna haazaa kaana lakum jazaaa'aňw-wa kaana sa'yukum mashkooraa.   (Section 1)

23. Innaa Naḥnu nazzalnaa 'alaykal-Qur-aana tanzeelaa.

24. Faṣbir liḥukmi Rabbika wa laa tuṭi' minhum aaṣiman aw kafooraa.

25. Wazkuris-ma Rabbika bukrataňw-wa aṣeelaa.

26. Wa minal-layli fasjud lahoo wa sabbiḥhu laylan ṭaweelaa.

27. Inna haaa'ulaaa'i yuḥib-boonal-'aajilata wa yazaroona waraaa'ahum Yawman saqee-laa.

28. Naḥnu khalaqnaahum wa shadadnaaa asrahum wa izaa shi'naa baddalnaaa amsaala-hum tabdeelaa.

29. This is an admonition: Whosoever will, let him take a (straight) Path to his Lord.

30. But you will not, except as Allah wills; for Allah is full of Knowledge and Wisdom.

31. He will admit to His Mercy whom He will; But the wrong-doers,- for them has He prepared a grievous Chastisement.

77. Those Sent Forth
In the name of Allah, Most Gracious, Most Merciful.

1. By the emissary winds, (sent) one after another

2. Which then blow violently in tempestuous Gusts,

3. And scatter (things) far and wide;

4. Then separate them, one from another,

5. Then spread abroad a Message,

6. Whether of Justification or of Warning;-

7. Assuredly, what you are promised must come to pass.

8. Then when the stars become dim;

9. When the heaven is cleft asunder;

10. When the mountains are scattered (to the winds) as dust;

11. And when the time fixed for the gathering of all Apostles comes.

12. For what Day are these (portents) deferred?

13. For the Day of Sorting out.

14. And what will explain to you what is the Day of Sorting out?

15. Ah woe, that Day, to the Rejecters of Truth!

16. Did We not destroy the men of old (for their evil)?

17. So shall We make later (generations) follow them.

18. Thus do We deal with men of sin.

---

29. Inna haazihee tazkiratun fa-man shaaa'at-takhaza ilaa Rabbihee sabeelaa.

30. Wa maa tashaaa'oona illaaa añy-yashaaa'al-laah; innal-laaha kaana 'Aleeman Hakeemaa.

31. Yudkhilu mañy-yashaaa'u fee rahmatih; wazzaalimeena a'adda lahum 'azaaban aleemaa. (Section 2)

Sûrat al-Mursalât–77
(Revealed at Makkah)
Bismillaahir Rahmaanir Raheem

1. Wal-mursalaati 'urfaa.

2. Fal-'aasifaati 'asfaa.

3. Wannaashiraati nashraa.

4. Falfaariqaati farqaa.

5. Falmulqiyaati zikraa.

6. 'Uzran aw nuzraa.

7. Innamaa too'adoona la-waaqi'.

8. Fa-izan-nujoomu tumisat.

9. Wa izas-samaaa'u furijat.

10. Wa izal-jibaalu nusifat.

11. Wa izar-Rusulu uqqitat.

12. Li-ayyi Yawmin ujjilat.

13. Li-Yawmil-Fasl.

14. Wa maaa adraaka maa Yawmul-Fasl.

15. Wayluñy-Yawma'izil-lilmukazzibeen.

16. Alam nuhlikil-awwaleen.

17. Summa nutbi'uhumul-aakhireen.

18. Kazaalika naf'alu bilmuj-rimeen.

19. Ah, woe that Day, to the Rejecters of Truth!

20. Have We not created you from a fluid (held) despicable?

21. The which We placed in a place of rest, firmly fixed,

22. For a period (of gestation), determined (according to need)?

23. For We do determine (according to need); for We are the Best to determine (things).

24. Ah woe, that Day! to the Rejecters of Truth!

25. Have we not made the earth a receptacle.

26. The living and the dead,

27. And made therein mountains standing firm, lofty (in stature); and provided for you water sweet (and wholesome)?

28. Ah woe, that Day, to the Rejecters of Truth!

29. (It will be said:) "Depart you to that which you used to reject as false!

30. Depart unto the shadow falling threefold.

31. (Which yet is) no relief nor shelter from the flame.

32. "Indeed it throws about sparks (huge) as Forts,

33. (Or) as it might be camels of bright yellow hue.

34. Ah woe, that Day, to the Rejecters of Truth!

35. That will be a Day when they shall not be able to speak.

36. Nor will it be open to them to put forth pleas.

37. Ah woe, that Day, to the Rejecters of Truth!

38. That will be a Day of Sorting out! We shall gather you together and those before (you)!

39. Now, if you have a trick (or plot), use it against Me!

40. Ah woe, that Day, to the Rejecters of Truth!

41. Lo! Those who kept their duty are amid shade and fountains,

42. And (they shall have) fruits,- all they desire.

---

19. Wayluñy-Yawma'izil-lil-mukazzibeen.

20. Alam nakhlukkum mim-maaa'im-maheen.

21. Faja'alnaahu fee qaraa-rim-makeen.

22. Ilaa qadarim-ma'loom.

23. Faqadarnaa fani'mal-qaadiroon.

24. Wayluñy-Yawma'izil-lilmukazzibeen.

25. Alam naj'alil-arḍa kifaataa.

26. Aḥyaaa'añw-wa amwaataa.

27. Wa ja'alnaa feehaa ra-waasiya shaamikhaatiñw-wa asqaynaakum maaa'an furaataa.

28. Wayluñy-Yawma'izil-lilmukazzibeen.

29. Inṭaliqooo ilaa maa kuntum bihee tukazziboon.

30. Inṭaliqooo ilaa ẓillin zee salaaṣi shu'ab.

31. Laa ẓaleeliñw-wa laa yughnee minal-lahab.

32. Innahaa tarmee bishararin kalqaṣr.

33. Ka-annahoo jimaalatun ṣufr.

34. Wayluñy-Yawma'izil-lilmukazzibeen.

35. Haazaa Yawmu laa yanṭi-qoon.

36. Wa laa yu'zanu lahum fa-ya'taziroon.

37. Wayluñy-Yawma'izil-lilmukazzibeen.

38. Haazaa Yawmul-Faṣli jama'naakum wal-awwaleen.

39. Fa-in kaana lakum kay-dun fakeedoon.

40. Wayluñy-Yawma'izil-lilmukazzibeen. **(Section 1)**

41. Innal-muttaqeena fee ẓilaaliñw-wa 'uyoon.

42. Wa fawaakiha mimmaa yashtahoon.

43. "Eat ye and drink ye to your heart's content: for that you worked (Righteousness).

44. Thus do We certainly reward the Doers of Good.

45. Ah woe, that Day, to the Rejecters of Truth!

46. (O you unjust!) Eat ye and enjoy yourselves (but) a little while, for that ye are Sinners.

47. Ah woe, that Day, to the Rejecters of Truth!

48. When it is said unto them: Bow down, they bow not down!

49. Ah woe, that Day, to the Rejecters of Truth!

50. Then what Message, after that, will they believe in?

78. The (Great) News
In the name of Allah, Most Gracious, Most Merciful.

1. Concerning what are they disputing?

2. Concerning the Great News,

3. About which they cannot agree.

4. Verily, they shall soon (come to) know!

5. Verily, verily they shall soon (come to) know!

6. Have We not made the earth as a wide expanse,

7. And the mountains as pegs?

8. And (have We not) created you in pairs,

9. And made your sleep for rest,

10. And made the night as a covering,

11. And made the day as a means of subsistence?

12. And (have We not) built over you the seven firmaments,

13. And placed (therein) a Light of Splendour?

14. And do We not send down from the clouds water in abundance,

---

43. Kuloo washraboo haneee-'am bimaa kuntum ta'maloon.

44. Innaa kazaalika najzil-muḥsineen.

45. Wayluñy-Yawma'izil-lilmukazzibeen.

46. Kuloo wa tamatta'oo qaleelan innakum mujrimoon.

47. Waylunñy-Yawma'izil-lilmukazzibeen.

48. Wa izaa qeela lahumur-ka'oo laa yarka'oon.

49. Waylunñy-Yawma'izil-lilmukazzibeen.

50. Fabi-ayyi ḥadeesim ba'-dahoo yu'minoon. (Section 2)

Sûrat an-Naba'—78
(Revealed at Makkah)

Bismillaahir Raḥmaanir Raḥeem

1. 'Amma yatasaaa'aloon.

2. 'Anin-naba-il-'aẓeem.

3. Allazee hum feehi mukh-talifoon.

4. Kallaa sa-ya'lamoon.

5. Summa kallaa sa-ya'la-moon.

6. Alam naj'alil-arḍa mi-haadaa.

7. Wal-jibaala awtaadaa.

8. Wa khalaqnaakum az-waajaa.

9. Wa ja'alnaa nawmakum subaataa.

10. Wa ja'alnal-layla libaa-saa.

11. Wa ja'alnan-nahaara ma'aashaa.

12. Wa banaynaa fawqakum sab'an shidaadaa.

13. Wa ja'alnaa siraajañw-wahhaajaa.

14. Wa anzalnaa minal-mu'-ṣiraati maaa'an sajjaajaa.

15. That We may produce therewith corn and vegetables,

16. And gardens of luxurious growth?

17. Verily the Day of Sorting out is a thing appointed,

18. The Day that the Trumpet shall be sounded, and you will come forth in crowds;

19. And the heavens shall be opened as if there were doors,

20. And the mountains shall vanish, as if they were a mirage.

21. Truly Hell is as a place of ambush,

22. For the transgressors a place of destination:

23. They will dwell therein for ages.

24. Nothing cool shall they taste therein, nor any drink,

25. Save boiling water and a paralysing cold:

26. A fitting recompense (for them).

27. For lo! They looked not for a reckoning.

28. But they (impudently) treated Our Signs as false.

29. And all things have We preserved on record.

30. So taste (of that which ye have earned). No increase do We give you save of torment.

31. Lo! For the duteous is achievement—

32. Gardens enclosed, and grapevines;

33. Companions of equal age;

34. And a cup full (to the brim).

35. No loose talk shall they hear therein, nor Untruth:-

36. Recompense from your Lord, a gift, (amply) sufficient,

37. Lord of the heavens and the earth, and (all) that is between them, the Beneficent; with Whom none can converse.

38. The Day that the Spirit and the angels will stand forth in ranks,

---

15. Linukhrija bihee ḥabbañw-wa nabaataa.

16. Wa jannaatin alfaafaa.

17. Inna Yawmal-Faṣli kaana meeqaataa.

18. Yawma yunfakhu fiṣ-Ṣoori fataåtoona afwaajaa.

19. Wa futiḥatis-samaaa'u fakaanat abwaabaa.

20. Wa suyyiratil-jibaalu fakaanat saraabaa.

21. Inna Jahannama kaanat mirṣaadaa.

22. Liṭṭaagheena ma-aabaa.

23. Laabiṣeena feehaaa aḥqaabaa.

24. Laa yazooqoona feehaa bardañw-wa laa sharaabaa.

25. Illaa ḥameemañw-wa ghassaaqaa.

26. Jazaaa'añw-wifaaqaa.

27. Innahum kaanoo laa yarjoona ḥisaabaa.

28. Wa kazzaboo bi-Aayaatinaa kizzaabaa.

29. Wa kulla shay'in aḥṣaynaahu kitaabaa.

30. Fazooqoo falan nazeedakum illaa 'azaabaa. **(Section 1)**

31. Inna lilmuttaqeena mafaazaa.

32. Ḥadaaa'iqa wa a'naabaa.

33. Wa kawaa'iba atraabaa.

34. Wa kaåsan dihaaqaa.

35. Laa yasma'oona feehaa laghwañw-wa laa kizzaabaa.

36. Jazaaa'am-mir-Rabbika 'aṭaaa'an ḥisaabaa.

37. Rabbis-samaawaati wal-arḍi wa maa baynahumar-Raḥmaani laa yamlikoona minhu khiṭaabaa.

38. Yawma yaqoomur-Roo-ḥu wal-malaaa'ikatu ṣaffal-

لِنُخْرِجَ بِهٖ حَبًّا وَّنَبَاتًا ۙ

وَّجَنّٰتٍ اَلْفَافًا ۗ

اِنَّ يَوْمَ الْفَصْلِ كَانَ مِيْقَاتًا ۙ

يَّوْمَ يُنْفَخُ فِى الصُّوْرِ فَتَأْتُوْنَ اَفْوَاجًا ۙ

وَّفُتِحَتِ السَّمَآءُ فَكَانَتْ اَبْوَابًا ۙ

وَّسُيِّرَتِ الْجِبَالُ فَكَانَتْ سَرَابًا ۗ

اِنَّ جَهَنَّمَ كَانَتْ مِرْصَادًا ۙ

لِّلطَّاغِيْنَ مَاٰبًا ۙ

لّٰبِثِيْنَ فِيْهَاۤ اَحْقَابًا ۚ

لَا يَذُوْقُوْنَ فِيْهَا بَرْدًا وَّلَا شَرَابًا ۙ

اِلَّا حَمِيْمًا وَّغَسَّاقًا ۙ

جَزَآءً وِّفَاقًا ۗ

اِنَّهُمْ كَانُوْا لَا يَرْجُوْنَ حِسَابًا ۙ

وَّكَذَّبُوْا بِاٰيٰتِنَا كِذَّابًا ۗ

وَكُلَّ شَيْءٍ اَحْصَيْنٰهُ كِتٰبًا ۙ

فَذُوْقُوْا فَلَنْ نَّزِيْدَكُمْ اِلَّا عَذَابًا ۧ

اِنَّ لِلْمُتَّقِيْنَ مَفَازًا ۙ

حَدَآئِقَ وَاَعْنَابًا ۙ

وَّكَوَاعِبَ اَتْرَابًا ۙ

وَّكَأْسًا دِهَاقًا ۗ

لَا يَسْمَعُوْنَ فِيْهَا لَغْوًا وَّلَا كِذّٰبًا ۚ

جَزَآءً مِّنْ رَّبِّكَ عَطَآءً حِسَابًا ۙ

رَّبِّ السَّمٰوٰتِ وَالْاَرْضِ وَمَا بَيْنَهُمَا الرَّحْمٰنِ لَا يَمْلِكُوْنَ مِنْهُ خِطَابًا ۚ

يَوْمَ يَقُوْمُ الرُّوْحُ وَالْمَلٰٓئِكَةُ صَفًّا ۗ

none shall speak except any who is permitted by (Allah) Most Gracious, and He will say what is right.

39. That Day will be the sure Reality: Therefore, whoso will, let him take a (straight) return to his Lord!

40. Verily, We have warned you of a Chastisement near, the Day when man will see (the deeds) which his hands have sent forth, and the Unbeliever will say, "Woe unto me! Would that I were (mere) dust!

79. Those Who Tear Out
In the name of Allah, Most Gracious, Most Merciful.

1. By those who drag forth to destruction.

2. By those who gently draw out (the souls of the blessed);

3. And by those who glide along (on errands of mercy),

4. Then press forward as in a race,

5. Then arrange to do (the Commands of their Lord),

6. On the day when the first trumpet resoundeth.

7. Followed by oft-repeated (commotions):

8. Hearts that Day will be in agitation;

9. Cast down will be (their owners') eyes.

10. They say (now): "What! shall we indeed be returned to (our) former state?

11. "What! - when we shall have become rotten bones?"

12. They say: "It would, in that case, be a return with loss!"

13. But verily, it will be but a single (Compelling) Cry,

14. And lo! They will be awakened.

15. Has the story of Moses reached you?

16. Behold, your Lord did call to him in the sacred valley of Tuwa:-

laa yatakallamoona illaa man azina lahur-Raḥmaanu wa qaala ṣawaabaa.

39. Zaalikal-Yawmul-Ḥaqq, faman shaaa’at-takhaza ilaa Rabbihee ma-aabaa.

40. Innaaa anzarnaakum ‘azaaban qareebaňy-Yawma yanzurul-mar’u maa qaddamat yadaahu wa yaqoolul-kaafiru yaa laytanee kuntu turaabaa.
(Section 2)

Sûrat an-Nâzi‘ât—79
(Revealed at Makkah)

Bismillaahir Raḥmaanir Raḥeem

1. Wannaazi‘aati gharqaa.

2. Wannaashiṭaati nashṭaa.

3. Wassaabiḥaati sabḥaa.

4. Fassaabiqaati sabqaa.

5. Falmudabbiraati amraa.

6. Yawma tarjufur-raajifah.

7. Tatba‘uhar-raadifah.

8. Quloobuňy-Yawma’iziñw-waajifah.

9. Abṣaaruhaa khaashi‘ah.

10. Yaqooloona ‘a-innaa la-mardoodoona fil-ḥaafirah.

11. ‘A-izaa kunnaa ‘izaaman nakhirah.

12. Qaaloo tilka izan karra-tun khaasirah.

13. Fa-innamaa hiya zajratuñw-waaḥidah.

14. Fa-izaa hum bissaahirah.

15. Hal ataaka ḥadeesu Moosaa.

16. Iz naadaahu Rabbuhoo bil-waadil-muqaddasi Ṭuwaa.

17. (Saying:) Go thou unto Pharaoh—Lo! He hath rebelled—

18. "And say to him, 'do you wish to be purified (from sin)?-

19. Then I will guide thee to thy Lord and thou shalt fear (Him).

20. Then did (Moses) show him the Great Sign.

21. But (Pharaoh) rejected it and disobeyed (guidance);

22. Then turned he away in haste,

23. Then he collected (his men) and made a proclamation,

24. Saying, "I am your Lord, Most High".

25. But Allah did punish him, (and made an) example of him, - in the Hereafter, as in this life.

26. Lo! Herein is indeed a lesson for him who feareth.

27. Are ye the harder to create, or is the heaven that He built?

28. He raised the height thereof and ordered it;

29. Its night does He endow with darkness, and its splendour doth He bring out (with light).

30. And after that He spread the earth,

31. He draws out therefrom its moisture and its pasture;

32. And the mountains has He firmly fixed;-

33. A provision for you and your cattle.

34. But when the great disaster cometh,

35. The day when man will call to mind his (whole) endeavour,

36. And hell will stand forth visible to him who seeth,

37. Then, for such as had transgressed all bounds,

38. And had preferred the life of this world,

39. The Abode will be Hell-Fire;

40. And for such as had entertained the fear of standing before their Lord's (tribunal) and had restrained (their) soul from lower desires,

---

17. Izhab ilaa Fir'awna innahoo ṭaghaa.

18. Faqul hal laka ilaaa an tazakkaa.

19. Wa ahdiyaka ilaa Rabbika fatakhshaa.

20. Fa-araahul-Aayatal-Kubraa.

21. Fakazzaba wa 'aṣaa.

22. Summa adbara yas'aa.

23. Faḥashara fanaadaa.

24. Faqaala Ana Rabbukumul-A'laa.

25. Fa-akhazahul-laahu nakaalal-Aakhirati wal-oolaaa.

26. Inna fee zaalika la'ibratal-limany- yakhshaa. (Sec. 1)

27. 'A-antum ashaddu khalqan amis-samaaa'; banaahaa.

28. Rafa'a samkahaa fasawwaahaa.

29. Wa aghṭasha laylahaa wa akhraja ḍuḥaahaa.

30. Wal-arḍa ba'da zaalika daḥaahaa.

31. Akhraja minhaa maaa'ahaa wa mar'aahaa.

32. Wal-jibaala arsaahaa.

33. Mataa'al-lakum wa li-an'aamikum.

34. Fa-izaa jaaa'atiṭ-ṭaaammatul-kubraa.

35. Yawma yatazakkarul-insaanu maa sa'aa.

36. Wa burrizatil-Jaḥeemu limany-yaraa.

37. Fa-ammaa man ṭaghaa.

38. Wa aaṣaral-ḥayaatad-dunyaa.

39. Fa-innal-Jaḥeema hiyal-maawaa.

40. Wa ammaa man khaafa maqaama Rabbihee wa nahannafsa 'anil-hawaa.

41. Their abode will be the Garden.	41. Fa innal-Jannata hiyal-maåwaa.	فَاِنَّ الْجَنَّةَ هِيَ الْمَاْوٰى ۞
42. They ask thee of the Hour: When will it come to port?	42. Yas'aloonaka 'anis-Saa-'ati ayyaana mursaahaa.	يَسْئَلُوْنَكَ عَنِ السَّاعَةِ اَيَّانَ مُرْسٰهَا ۞
43. Wherein are you (concerned) with the declaration thereof?	43. Feema anta min zikraa-haa.	فِيْمَ اَنْتَ مِنْ ذِكْرٰىهَا ۞
44. With your Lord in the time fixed therefor.	44. Ilaa Rabbika muntahaa-haa.	اِلٰى رَبِّكَ مُنْتَهٰىهَا ۞
45. Thou art but a Warner for such as fear it.	45. Innamaaa anta munziru mañy-yakhshaahaa.	اِنَّمَاۤ اَنْتَ مُنْذِرُ مَنْ يَّخْشٰهَا ۞
46. The Day they see it, (It will be) as if they had tarried but a single evening, or (at most till) the following morn!	46. Ka-annahum Yawma yarawnahaa lam yalbasooo illaa 'ashiyyatan aw duhaahaa. (Section 2)	كَاَنَّهُمْ يَوْمَ يَرَوْنَهَا لَمْ يَلْبَثُوْۤا اِلَّا عَشِيَّةً اَوْ ضُحٰهَا ۞

80. He Frowned
In the name of Allah, Most Gracious, Most Merciful.

Sûrat 'Abasa—80
(Revealed at Makkah)
Bismillaahir Rahmaanir Raheem

(٨٠) سُوْرَةُ عَبَسَ مَكِّيَّةٌ (٢٣)
بِسْمِ اللهِ الرَّحْمٰنِ الرَّحِيْمِ

1. (The Prophet) frowned and turned away,	1. 'Abasa wa tawallaaa.	عَبَسَ وَتَوَلّٰى ۙ
2. Because there came to him the blind man (interrupting).	2. An jaaa'ahul-a'maa.	اَنْ جَاءَهُ الْاَعْمٰى ۚ
3. What could inform thee but that he might grow (in grace)	3. Wa maa yudreeka la'al-lahoo yazzakkaaa.	وَمَا يُدْرِيْكَ لَعَلَّهٗ يَزَّكّٰى ۙ
4. Or take heed and so the reminder might avail him?	4. Aw yazzakkaru fatanfa'ahuz-zikraa.	اَوْ يَذَّكَّرُ فَتَنْفَعَهُ الذِّكْرٰى ۭ
5. As to one who regards Himself as self-sufficient,	5. Ammaa manis-taghnaa.	اَمَّا مَنِ اسْتَغْنٰى ۙ
6. To him does you attend;	6. Fa-anta lahoo tasaddaa.	فَاَنْتَ لَهٗ تَصَدّٰى ۭ
7. Yet it is not thy concern if he grow not (in grace).	7. Wa maa 'alayka allaa yazzakkaa.	وَمَا عَلَيْكَ اَلَّا يَزَّكّٰى ۭ
8. But as to him who came to you striving earnestly,	8. Wa ammaa man jaaa'aka yas'aa.	وَاَمَّا مَنْ جَاءَكَ يَسْعٰى ۙ
9. And with fear (in his heart),	9. Wa huwa yakhshaa.	وَهُوَ يَخْشٰى ۙ
10. Of him were you unmindful.	10. Fa-anta 'anhu talahhaa.	فَاَنْتَ عَنْهُ تَلَهّٰى ۚ
11. Nay but verily it is an Admonishment,	11. Kallaaa innahaa tazkirah.	كَلَّاۤ اِنَّهَا تَذْكِرَةٌ ۚ
12. Therefore let whoso will, keep it in remembrance.	12. Faman shaaa'a zakarah.	فَمَنْ شَاءَ ذَكَرَهٗ ۘ
13. (It is) in Books held (greatly) in honour,	13. Fee suhufim-mukarramah.	فِيْ صُحُفٍ مُّكَرَّمَةٍ ۙ
14. Exalted (in dignity), kept pure and holy,	14. Marfoo'atim-mutahha-rah.	مَّرْفُوْعَةٍ مُّطَهَّرَةٍ ۭ
15. (Written) by the hands of scribes-	15. Bi-aydee safarah.	بِاَيْدِيْ سَفَرَةٍ ۙ
16. Honourable and Pious and Just.	16. Kiraamim bararah.	كِرَامٍ بَرَرَةٍ ۭ
17. Woe to man! What has made him reject Allah;	17. Qutilal-insaanu maaa akfarah.	قُتِلَ الْاِنْسَانُ مَاۤ اَكْفَرَهٗ ۭ

18. From what stuff has He created him?

19. From a drop of seed. He createth him and proportioneth him,

20. Then does He make His path smooth for him;

21. Then He causes him to die, and putteth him in his grave;

22. Then, when it is His Will, He will raise him up (again).

23. Nay, but (man) hath not done what He commanded him.

24. Then let man look at his food, (and how We provide it):

25. For that We pour forth water in abundance,

26. And We split the earth in fragments,

27. And produce therein corn,

28. And Grapes and nutritious plants,

29. And Olives and Dates,

30. And enclosed Gardens, dense with lofty trees,

31. And fruits and fodder,-

32. For use and convenience to you and your cattle.

33. At length, when there comes the Deafening Noise,-

34. That Day shall a man flee from his own brother,

35. And from his mother and his father,

36. And from his wife and his children.

37. Each one of them, that Day, will have enough concern (of his own) to make him unmindful to the others.

38. Some faces that Day will be beaming,

39. Laughing, rejoicing.

40. And other faces that Day will be dust-stained,

41. Blackness will cover them:

42. Such will be the Rejecters of Allah, the doers of iniquity.

18. Min ayyi shay'in khala-qah.

19. Min nuṭfatin khalaqahoo faqaddarah.

20. Summas-sabeela yassa-rah.

21. Summa amaatahoo fa-aqbarah.

22. Summa iẕaa shaaa'a ansharah.

23. Kallaa lammaa yaqḍi maaa amarah.

24. Falyanẕuril-insaanu ilaa ṭa'aamih.

25. Annaa ṣababnal-maaa'a ṣabbaa.

26. Summa shaqaqnal-arḍa shaqqaa.

27. Fa-ambatnaa feehaa ḥabbaa.

28. Wa 'inabañw-wa qaḍbaa.

29. Wa zaytoonañw-wa nakh-laa.

30. Wa ḥadaaa'iqa ghulbaa.

31. Wa faakihatañw-wa abbaa.

32. Mataa'al-lakum wa li-an'aamikum.

33. Fa-iẕaa jaaa'atiṣ-ṣaaakh-khah.

34. Yawma yafirrul-mar'u min akheeh.

35. Wa ummihee wa abeeh.

36. Wa ṣaaḥibatihee wa baneeh.

37. Likullim-ri-'im-minhum Yawma'iẕin shaânuñy-yughneeh.

38. Wujoohuñy-Yawma'i-zim-musfirah.

39. Ḍaaḥikatum-mustabshi-rah.

40. Wa wujoohuñy-Yawma'i-zin 'alayhaa ghabarah.

41. Tarhaquhaa qatarah.

42. Ulaaa'ika humul-kafara-tul-fajarah.

(Section 1)

مِنْ اَیِّ شَیْءٍ خَلَقَهٗ ۗ ۱۸

مِنْ نُّطْفَةٍ ۚ خَلَقَهٗ فَقَدَّرَهٗ ۙ ۱۹

ثُمَّ السَّبِیْلَ یَسَّرَهٗ ۙ ۲۰

ثُمَّ اَمَاتَهٗ فَاَقْبَرَهٗ ۙ ۲۱

ثُمَّ اِذَا شَآءَ اَنْشَرَهٗ ؕ ۲۲

کَلَّا لَمَّا یَقْضِ مَاۤ اَمَرَهٗ ؕ ۲۳

فَلْیَنْظُرِ الْاِنْسَانُ اِلٰی طَعَامِهٖۤ ۙ ۲۴

اَنَّا صَبَبْنَا الْمَآءَ صَبًّا ۙ ۲۵

ثُمَّ شَقَقْنَا الْاَرْضَ شَقًّا ۙ ۲۶

فَاَنْۢبَتْنَا فِیْهَا حَبًّا ۙ ۲۷

وَّعِنَبًا وَّقَضْبًا ۙ ۲۸

وَّزَیْتُوْنًا وَّنَخْلًا ۙ ۲۹

وَّحَدَآئِقَ غُلْبًا ۙ ۳۰

وَّفَاکِهَةً وَّاَبًّا ۙ ۳۱

مَّتَاعًا لَّکُمْ وَلِاَنْعَامِکُمْ ؕ ۳۲

فَاِذَا جَآءَتِ الصَّآخَّةُ ۫ ۳۳

یَوْمَ یَفِرُّ الْمَرْءُ مِنْ اَخِیْهِ ۙ ۳۴

وَاُمِّهٖ وَاَبِیْهِ ۙ ۳۵

وَصَاحِبَتِهٖ وَبَنِیْهِ ؕ ۳۶

لِکُلِّ امْرِئٍ مِّنْهُمْ یَوْمَئِذٍ شَاْنٌ یُّغْنِیْهِ ؕ ۳۷

وُجُوْهٌ یَّوْمَئِذٍ مُّسْفِرَةٌ ۙ ۳۸

ضَاحِکَةٌ مُّسْتَبْشِرَةٌ ۚ ۳۹

وَوُجُوْهٌ یَّوْمَئِذٍ عَلَیْهَا غَبَرَةٌ ۙ ۴۰

تَرْهَقُهَا قَتَرَةٌ ؕ ۴۱

اُولٰٓئِکَ هُمُ الْکَفَرَةُ الْفَجَرَةُ ۠ ۴۲

81. The Folding Up

In the Name of Allah, Most Gracious, Most Merciful.

1. When the sun (with its spacious light) is folded up;
2. When the stars fall, losing their lustre;
3. When the mountains vanish (like a mirage);
4. And when the camels big with young are abandoned,
5. And when the wild beasts are herded together,
6. When the oceans boil over with a swell;
7. And when souls are re-united,
8. When the female (infant), buried alive, is questioned -
9. For what crime she was killed;
10. When the scrolls are laid open;
11. When the sky is unveiled;
12. When the Blazing Fire is kindled to fierce heat;
13. And when the Garden is brought near;-
14. (Then) shall each soul know what it has put forward.
15. So verily I call to witness the planets - that recede,
16. Go straight, or hide;
17. And the Night as it dissipates;
18. And the Dawn as it breathes away the darkness;-
19. Verily this is the word of a most honourable Messenger,
20. Endued with Power, held in honour by the Lord of the Throne,
21. With authority there, (and) faithful to his trust.
22. And (O people!) your companion is not one possessed;
23. And without doubt he saw him in the clear horizon.
24. And he is not avid of the Unseen.

Sûrat at-Takwîr–81

(Revealed at Makkah)

Bismillaahir Rahmaanir Raheem

1. Izash-shamsu kuwwirat.
2. Wa izan-nujoomun-kadarat.
3. Wa izal-jibaalu suyyirat.
4. Wa izal-'ishaaru 'uttilat.
5. Wa izal-wuhooshu hushirat
6. Wa izal-bihaaru sujjirat.
7. Wa izan-nufoosu zuwwijat.
8. Wa izal-maw'oodatu su'ilat.
9. Bi-ayyi zambin qutilat.
10. Wa izas-suhufu nushirat.
11. Wa izas-samaaa'u kushitat.
12. Wa izal-Jaheemu su'-'irat.
13. Wa izal-Jannatu uzlifat.
14. 'Alimat nafsum-maaa ahdarat.
15. Falaaa uqsimu bil-khunnas.
16. Al-jawaaril-kunnas.
17. Wallayli izaa 'as'as.
18. Wassubhi izaa tanaffas.
19. Innahoo laqawlu rasoolin kareem.
20. Zee quwwatin 'inda Zil-'Arshi makeen.
21. Mutaa'in samma ameen.
22. Wa maa saahibukum bimajnoon.
23. Wa laqad ra-aahu bil-ufuqil-mubeen
24. Wa maa huwa 'alal-ghaybi-bidaneen.

25. Nor is it the word of an evil spirit accursed.

26. When whither go you?

27. Verily this is no less than a Message to (all) the Worlds:

28. (With profit) to whoever among you wills to go straight:

29. But you shall not will except as Allah wills,- the Cherisher of the Worlds.

82. The Cleaving Asunder
In the name of Allah, Most Gracious, Most Merciful.

1. When the Sky is cleft asunder;

2. When the Stars are scattered;

3. When the Oceans are suffered to burst forth;

4. And when the Graves are turned upside down;-

5. A soul will know what it hath sent before (it) and what left behind.

6. O man! What has seduced you from your Lord Most Beneficent?-

7. Who created thee, then fashioned, then proportioned thee?

8. In whatever Form He wills, does He put you together.

9. No, but you reject Right and Judgment!

10. Lo! There are above you guardians,

11. Kind and honourable,- Writing down (your deeds):

12. They know (and understand) all that you do.

13. As for the Righteous, they will be in bliss;

14. And the Wicked - they will be in the Fire,

15. Which they will enter on the Day of Judgment,

16. And they will not be able to keep away therefrom.

17. And what will explain to you what the Day of Judgment is?

25. Wa maa huwa biqawli Shayṭaanir-rajeem.

26. Fa-ayna tazhaboon.

27. In huwa illaa zikril-lil-'aalameen.

28. Liman shaaa'a minkum añy-yastaqeem.

29. Wa maa tashaaa'oona illaaa añy-yashaaa'al-laahu Rabbul-'Aalameen.
(Section 1)

Sûrat al-Infiṭâr–82
(Revealed at Makkah)
Bismillaahir Raḥmaanir Raḥeem

1. Izas-samaaa'un-faṭarat.

2. Wa izal-kawaakibun-ta-sarat.

3. Wa izal-biḥaaru fujjirat.

4. Wa izal-quboooru bu'sirat.

5. 'Alimat nafsum-maa qaddamat wa akhkharat.

6. Yaaa ayyuhal-insaaanu maa gharraka bi-Rabbikal-Kareem.

7. Allazee khalaqaka fasaw-waaka fa'adalak.

8. Feee ayye ṣooratim-maa shaaa'a rakkabak.

9. Kallaa bal tukazziboona-bid-deen.

10. Wa Inna 'alaykum laḥaa-fiẓeen.

11. Kiraaman kaatibeen.

12. Ya'lamoona ma taf'a-loon.

13. Innal-abraara lafee Na'eem.

14. Wa innal-fujjaara lafee Jaheem.

15. Yaṣlawnahaa Yawmad-Deen.

16. Wa maa hum 'anhaa bighaaa'ibeen.

17. Wa maaa adraaka maa Yawmud-Deen.

18. Again, what will explain to you what the Day of Judgment is?

19. A day on which no soul hath power at all for any (other) soul. The (absolute) command on that day is Allah's.

83. The Dealers in Fraud

In the name of Allah, Most Gracious, Most Merciful.

1. Woe to those that deal in fraud,-

2. Those who, when they have to receive by measure from men, exact full measure,

3. But when they have to give by measure or weight to men, give less than due.

4. Do they not think that they will be called to account?-

5. On a Mighty Day,

6. The day when (all) mankind stand before the Lord of the Worlds?

7. Nay but the record of the vile is in Sijjin—

8. And what will explain to thee what Sijjin is?

9. (There is) a Register (fully) inscribed.

10. Woe, that Day, to those that deny-

11. Those that deny the Day of Judgment.

12. Which none denieth save each criminal transgressor,

13. When Our Signs are rehearsed to him, he says, "Tales of the ancients!"

14. By no means! but on their hearts is the stain of the (ill) which they do!

15. Verily, from (the Light of) their Lord, that Day, will they be veiled.

16. Further, they will enter the Fire of Hell.

17. Further, it will be said to them: "This is the (reality)

18. Summa maaa adraaka maa Yawmud-Deen.

19. Yawma laa tamliku nafsul-linafsin shay'anw wal-amru Yawma'izil-lillaah. **(Sec. 1)**

Sûrat al-Muṭaffifîn–83

(Revealed at Makkah)

Bismillaahir Raḥmaanir Raḥeem

1. Waylul-lil-muṭaffifeen.

2. Allazeena izak-taaloo 'alan-naasi yastawfoon.

3. Wa izaa kaaloohum aw wazanoohum yukhsiroon.

4. Alaa yaẓunnu ulaaa'ika annahum mab'oosoon.

5. Li-Yawmin 'Aẓeem.

6. Yawma yaqoomun-naasu li-Rabbil-'aalameen.

7. Kallaaa inna kitaabal-fujjaari lafee Sijjeen.

8. Wa maa adraaka maa Sijjeen.

9. Kitaabum-marqoom.

10. Wayluñy-Yawma'izil-lil-mukazzibeen.

11. Allazeena yukazziboona bi-Yawmid-Deen.

12. Wa maa yukazzibu bi-heee illaa kullu mu'tadin aseem.

13. Izaa tutlaa 'alayhi Aayaa-tunaa qaala asaaṭeerul-awwaleen.

14. Kallaa bal raana 'alaa quloobihim maa kaanoo yaksiboon.

15. Kallaaa innahum 'ar-Rabbihim Yawma'izil-lamaḥjooboon.

16. Summa innahum laṣaa-lul-Jaḥeem.

17. Summa yuqaalu haazal-lazee kuntum biheee

وَيْلٌ لِّلْمُطَفِّفِينَ ۙ

ثُمَّ مَاۤ اَدْرٰىكَ مَا يَوْمُ الدِّيْنِ ۙ

يَوْمَ لَا تَمْلِكُ نَفْسٌ لِّنَفْسٍ شَيْئًا ؕ وَالْاَمْرُ يَوْمَئِذٍ لِّلّٰهِ ۟

سُوْرَةُ الْمُطَفِّفِيْنَ مَكِّيَّةٌ (٨٢)

بِسْمِ اللّٰهِ الرَّحْمٰنِ الرَّحِيْمِ

وَيْلٌ لِّلْمُطَفِّفِيْنَ ۙ

الَّذِيْنَ اِذَا اكْتَالُوْا عَلَى النَّاسِ يَسْتَوْفُوْنَ ۖ

وَاِذَا كَالُوْهُمْ اَوْ وَّزَنُوْهُمْ يُخْسِرُوْنَ ؕ

اَلَا يَظُنُّ اُولٰٓئِكَ اَنَّهُمْ مَّبْعُوْثُوْنَ ۙ

لِيَوْمٍ عَظِيْمٍ ۙ

يَّوْمَ يَقُوْمُ النَّاسُ لِرَبِّ الْعٰلَمِيْنَ ؕ

كَلَّا اِنَّ كِتٰبَ الْفُجَّارِ لَفِيْ سِجِّيْنٍ ؕ

وَمَاۤ اَدْرٰىكَ مَا سِجِّيْنٌ ؕ

كِتٰبٌ مَّرْقُوْمٌ ؕ

وَيْلٌ يَّوْمَئِذٍ لِّلْمُكَذِّبِيْنَ ۙ

الَّذِيْنَ يُكَذِّبُوْنَ بِيَوْمِ الدِّيْنِ ؕ

وَمَا يُكَذِّبُ بِهٖۤ اِلَّا كُلُّ مُعْتَدٍ اَثِيْمٍ ۙ

اِذَا تُتْلٰى عَلَيْهِ اٰيٰتُنَا قَالَ اَسَاطِيْرُ الْاَوَّلِيْنَ ؕ

كَلَّا بَلْ ۫ رَانَ عَلٰى قُلُوْبِهِمْ مَّا كَانُوْا يَكْسِبُوْنَ ؕ

كَلَّاۤ اِنَّهُمْ عَنْ رَّبِّهِمْ يَوْمَئِذٍ لَّمَحْجُوْبُوْنَ ؕ

ثُمَّ اِنَّهُمْ لَصَالُوا الْجَحِيْمِ ؕ

ثُمَّ يُقَالُ هٰذَا الَّذِيْ كُنْتُمْ بِهٖ

which you rejected as false!

18. Nay, but the record of the righteous is in 'Illiyin!—

19. And what will explain to you what 'Illiyun is?

20. (There is) a Register (fully) inscribed,

21. To which bear witness those Nearest (to Allah).

22. Truly the Righteous will be in Bliss:

23. On couches, gazing,

24. Thou wilt know in their faces the radiance of delight.

25. Their thirst will be slaked with Pure Wine sealed:

26. The seal thereof will be Musk: And for this let those aspire, who have aspirations:

27. With it will be (given) a mixture of Tasnim:

28. A spring whence those brought near to Allah drink.

29. Those in sin used to laugh at those who believed,

30. And wink one to another when they passed them;

31. And when they returned to their own folk, they returned jesting;

32. And whenever they saw them, they would say, "Behold! These are the people truly astray!"

33. But they had not been sent as keepers over them!

34. But on this Day the Believers will laugh at the Unbelievers:

35. On high couches, gazing.

36. Are not the disbelievers paid for what they used to do?

84. The Rending Asunder

In the name of Allah, Most Gracious, Most Merciful.

1. When the sky is rent asunder,

---

tukazziboon.

18. Kallaaa inna kitaabal-abraari lafee 'Illiyyeen.

19. Wa maaa adraaka maa 'Illiyyoon.

20. Kitaabum-marqoom.

21. Yashhadu-hul-muqarra-boon.

22. Innal-abraara lafee Na'eem.

23. 'Alal-araaa'iki yanzuroon.

24. Ta'rifu fee wujoohihim nadratan-na'eem.

25. Yusqawna mir-raheeqim-makhtoom.

26. Khitaamuhoo misk; wa fee zaalika falyatanaafasil-Mutanaafisoon.

27. Wa mizaajuhoo min Tas-neem.

28. 'Aynañy-yashrabu bihal-muqarraboon.

29. Innal-lazeena ajramoo kaanoo minal-lazeena aamanoo yadhakoon.

30. Wa izaa marroo bihim yataghaamazoon.

31. Wa izan-qalabooo ilaaa ahlihimun-qalaboo fakiheen.

32. Wa izaa ra-awhum qaa-looo inna haaa'ulaaa'i ladaaal-loon.

33. Wa maaa ursiloo 'alay-him haafizeen.

34. Fal-Yawmal-lazeena aamanoo minal-kuffaari yadha-koon.

35. 'Alal-araaa'iki yanzu-roon.

36. Hal suwwibal-kuffaaru maa kaanoo yaf'aloon. (Sec. 1)

Sûrat al-Inshiqâq–84

(Revealed at Makkah)

Bismillaahir Rahmaanir Raheem

1. Izas-samaaa'un-shaqqat.

2. And attentive to her Lord in fear,

3. And when the earth is flattened out,

4. And hath cast out all that was in her, and is empty.

5. And attentive to her Lord in fear!

6. O you man Verily you are ever toiling on towards your Lord- painfully toiling,- but you shall meet Him.

7. Then he who is given his Record in his right han,

8. Soon will his account be taken by an easy reckoning,

9. And he will turn to his people, rejoicing!

10. But he who is given his Record behind his back,-

11. Soon will he cry for perdition,

12. And he will enter a Blazing Fire.

13. Truly, did he go about among his people, rejoicing!

14. He verily deemed that he would never return (unto Allah).

15. No, no! for his Lord was (ever) watchful of him!

16. So I do call to witness the ruddy glow of Sunset;

17. The Night and its Homing;

18. And the Moon in her fullness:

19. You shall surely travel from stage to stage.

20. What then is the matter with them, that they believe not?-

21. And when the Qur'an is read to them, they fall not prostrate,

22. But on the contrary the Unbelievers reject (it).

23. And Allah knoweth best what they are hiding.

24. So announce to them a Chastisement Grievous,

25. Except to those who believe and work righteous deeds:

2. Wa azinat li-Rabbihaa wa ḥuqqat.

3. Wa izal-arḍu muddat.

4. Wa alqat maa feehaa wa takhallat.

5. Wa azinat li-Rabbihaa wa ḥuqqat.

6. Yaaa ayyuhal-insaanu innaka kaadiḥun ilaa Rabbika kad-ḥan famulaaqeeh.

7. Fa-ammaa man ootiya kitaabahoo biyameenih.

8. Fasawfa yuḥaasabu ḥisaabañy-yaseeraa.

9. Wa yanqalibu ilaaa ahli-hee masrooraa.

10. Wa ammaa man ootiya kitaabahoo waraaa'a ẓahrih.

11. Fasawfa yad'oo suboo-raa.

12. Wa yaṣlaa sa'eeraa.

13. Innahoo kaana fee ahli-hee masrooraa.

14. Innahoo ẓanna al-lañy-yaḥoor.

15. Balaaa inna Rabbahoo kaana bihee baṣeeraa.

16. Falaaa uqsimu bishsha-faq.

17. Wallayli wa maa wasaq.

18. Walqamari izat-tasaq.

19. Latarkabunna ṭabaqan 'an-ṭabaq.

20. Famaa lahum laa yu'mi-noon.

21. Wa izaa quri'a 'alayhimul-Qur-aanu laa yasjudoon. 🔲

22. Balil-lazeena kafaroo yukazziboon.

23. Wallaahu a'lamu bimaa yoo'oon.

24. Fabashshirhum bi'aẓa-bin aleem.

25. Illal-lazeena aamanoo wa 'amiluṣ-ṣaaliḥaati

وَأَذِنَتْ لِرَبِّهَا وَحُقَّتْ ۞

وَإِذَا الْأَرْضُ مُدَّتْ ۞

وَأَلْقَتْ مَا فِيهَا وَتَخَلَّتْ ۞

وَأَذِنَتْ لِرَبِّهَا وَحُقَّتْ ۞

يَا أَيُّهَا الْإِنْسَانُ إِنَّكَ كَادِحٌ إِلَى رَبِّكَ كَدْحًا فَمُلَاقِيهِ ۞

فَأَمَّا مَنْ أُوتِيَ كِتَابَهُ بِيَمِينِهِ ۞

فَسَوْفَ يُحَاسَبُ حِسَابًا يَسِيرًا ۞

وَيَنْقَلِبُ إِلَى أَهْلِهِ مَسْرُورًا ۞

وَأَمَّا مَنْ أُوتِيَ كِتَابَهُ وَرَاءَ ظَهْرِهِ ۞

فَسَوْفَ يَدْعُوا ثُبُورًا ۞

وَيَصْلَى سَعِيرًا ۞

إِنَّهُ كَانَ فِي أَهْلِهِ مَسْرُورًا ۞

إِنَّهُ ظَنَّ أَنْ لَنْ يَحُورَ ۞

بَلَى إِنَّ رَبَّهُ كَانَ بِهِ بَصِيرًا ۞

فَلَا أُقْسِمُ بِالشَّفَقِ ۞

وَالَّيْلِ وَمَا وَسَقَ ۞

وَالْقَمَرِ إِذَا اتَّسَقَ ۞

لَتَرْكَبُنَّ طَبَقًا عَنْ طَبَقٍ ۞

فَمَا لَهُمْ لَا يُؤْمِنُونَ ۞

وَإِذَا قُرِئَ عَلَيْهِمُ الْقُرْآنُ لَا ۩ يَسْجُدُونَ ۞

بَلِ الَّذِينَ كَفَرُوا يُكَذِّبُونَ ۞

وَاللَّهُ أَعْلَمُ بِمَا يُوعُونَ ۞

فَبَشِّرْهُمْ بِعَذَابٍ أَلِيمٍ ۞

إِلَّا الَّذِينَ آمَنُوا وَعَمِلُوا الصَّالِحَاتِ

(Bow Down)

for them is a Reward that will never fail.

85. The Zodiacal Signs

In the name of Allah, Most Gracious, Most Merciful.

1. By the sky, with its constellations.
2. By the promised Day (of Judgment);
3. By one that witnesses, and the subject of the witness;-
4. Woe to the makers of the pit (of fire),
5. Fire supplied (abundantly) with fuel:
6. Behold! They sat over against the (fire),
7. And they witnessed (all) that they were doing against the Believers.
8. And they ill-treated them for no other reason than that they believed in Allah, Exalted in Power, Worthy of all Praise!-
9. Him to Whom belongs the dominion of the heavens and the earth! And Allah is Witness to all things.
10. Those who persecute (or draw into temptation) the Believers, men and women, and do not turn in repentance, will have the Chastisement of Hell: They will have the Chastisement of the Burning Fire.
11. For those who believe and do righteous deeds, will be in the Gardens; beneath which rivers flow: That is the great Salvation, (the fulfilment of all desires),
12. Truly strong is the Grip (and Power) of your Lord.
13. Lo! He it is Who produceth, then reproduceth,
14. And He is the Forgiving, the Loving,
15. Lord of the Throne of Glory,
16. Doer (without let) of all that He intends.

lahum ajrun ghayru mamnoon.

(Section 1)

Sûrat al-Burûj–85

(Revealed at Makkah)

Bismillaahir Rahmaanir Raheem

1. Wassamaaa'i zaatil-burooj.
2. Wal-Yawmil-Maw'ood.
3. Wa Shaahidiñw-wa Mashhood.
4. Qutila As-haabul-Ukhdood.
5. Annaari zaatil-waqood.
6. Iz hum 'alayhaa qu'ood.
7. Wa hum 'alaa maa yaf'aloona bilmu'mineena shuhood.
8. Wa maa naqamoo minhum illaaa añy-yu'minoo billaahil-'Azeezil-Hameed.
9. Allazee lahoo mulkussamaawaati wal-ard; wallaahu 'alaa kulli shay'in Shaheed.
10. Innal-lazeena fatanulmu'mineena wal-mu'minaati summa lam yatooboo falahum 'azaabu Jahannama wa lahum 'azaabul-hareeq.
11. Innal-lazeena aamanoo wa 'amilus-saalihaati lahum Jannaatun tajree min tahtihalanhaar; zaalikal-fawzul-kabeer.
12. Inna batsha Rabbika lashadeed.
13. Innahoo Huwa yubdi'u wa yu'eed.
14. Wa Huwal-Ghafoorul-Wadood.
15. Zul-'Arshil-Majeed.
16. Fa-'aalul-limaa yureed.

17. Has the story reached you, of the forces-
18. Of Pharaoh and the Thamud?
19. And yet the Unbelievers (persist) in rejecting (the Truth)!
20. But Allah does encompass them from behind!
21. No, this is a Glorious Qur'an,
22. (Inscribed) in a Tablet Preserved.

86. The Night-Visitant
In the name of Allah, Most Gracious, Most Merciful.

1. By the Sky and the Night-Visitant (therein);-
2. And what will explain to thee what the Night-Visitant is?
3. (It is) the Star of piercing brightness;-
4. There is no soul but has a protector over it.
5. Now let man but think from what he is created!
6. He is created from a drop emitted-
7. Proceeding from between the backbone and the ribs:
8. Surely (Allah) is able to bring him back (to life)!
9. The Day that (all) things secret will be tested,
10. (Man) will have no power, and no helper.
11. By the Firmament which gives recurring rain,
12. And the earth which splitteth (with the growth of trees and plants)
13. Lo! This (Qur'an) is a conclusive word,
14. It is not a thing for amusement.
15. As for them, they are but plotting a scheme,
16. And I am planning a scheme.
17. Therefore grant a delay to the Unbelievers: Give respite to them gently (for awhile).

17. Hal ataaka ḥadeeṣul-junood.
18. Fir'awna wa Ṣamood.
19. Balil-lazeena kafaroo fee takzeeb.
20. Wallaahu miñw-waraaa'i-him-muḥeeṭ.
21. Bal huwa Qur-aanum-Majeed.
22. Fee Lawḥim-Maḥfooẓ.
(Section 1)

Sûrat aṭ-Ṭâriq–86
(Revealed at Makkah)
Bismillaahir Raḥmaanir Raḥeem

1. Wassamaaa'i waṭṭaariq.
2. Wa maaa adraaka maṭ-ṭaariq.
3. Annajmuṣ-ṣaaqib.
4. In kullu nafsil-lammaa 'alayhaa ḥaafiẓ.
5. Fal-yanẓuril-insaanu mimma khuliq.
6. Khuliqa mim-maaa'in daafiq.
7. Yakhruju mim bayniṣ-ṣulbi wat-taraaa'ib.
8. Innahoo 'alaa raj'ihee laqaadir.
9. Yawma tublas-saraaa'ir.
10. Famaa lahoo min quw-watiñw-wa laa naaṣir.
11. Wassamaaa'i zaatir-raj'.
12. Wal-arḍi zaatiṣ-ṣad'.
13. Innahoo laqawlun faṣl.
14. Wa maa huwa bil-hazl.
15. Innahum yakeedoona kaydaa.
16. Wa akeedu kaydaa.
17. Famahhilil-kaafireena amhilhum ruwaydaa. (Section 1)

Sûrah 87. Al-A'lâ
Sûrah 88. Al-Ghâshiyah
Part 30
665
الجُزْء ٣٠
الغَاشِيَة ٨٨ الأَعْلَى ٨٧

87. The Most High

In the name of Allah, Most Gracious, Most Merciful.

1. Glorify the name of thy Guardian-Lord Most High,

2. Who createth, then disposeth;

3. Who has ordained laws. And granted guidance;

4. And Who brings out the (green and luscious) pasture,

5. And then does make it (but) swarthy stubble.

6. By degrees shall We teach you to declare (the Message), so you shall not forget,

7. Except as Allah wills: For He knoweth what is manifest and what is hidden.

8. And We shall ease thy way unto the state of ease.

9. Therefore remind (men), for of use is the reminder.

10. He will heed who feareth,

11. But it will be avoided by those most unfortunate ones,

12. Who will enter the Great Fire,

13. In which they will then neither die nor live.

14. But those will prosper who purify themselves,

15. And remembereth the name of his Lord, so prayeth.

16. No, you prefer the life of this world;

17. But the Hereafter is better and more enduring.

18. And this is in the Books of the earliest (Revelation),-

19. The Books of Abraham and Moses.

88. The Overwhelming Event

In the name of Allah, Most Gracious, Most Merciful.

1. Hath there come unto thee tidings of the Overwhelming?

2. Some faces, that Day, will be humiliated,

Sûrat al-A'lâ–87
(Revealed at Makkah)

Bismillaahir Rahmaanir Raheem

1. Sabbihis-ma Rabbikal-A'laa.

2. Allazee khalaqa fasaw-waa.

3. Wallazee qaddara fahadaa.

4. Wallazeee akhrajal-mar'aa.

5. Faja'alahoo ghusaaa'an ahwaa.

6. Sanuqri'uka falaa tansaaa.

7. Illaa maa shaaa'al-laah; innahoo ya'lamul-jahra wa maa yakhfaa.

8. Wa nu-yassiruka lilyusraa.

9. Fazakkir in nafa'atiz-zikraa.

10. Sa-yazzakkaru mañy-yakhshaa.

11. Wa yatajannabuhal-ashqaa.

12. Allazee yaslan-Naaral-kubraa.

13. Summa laa yamootu feehaa wa laa yahyaa.

14. Qad aflaha man tazakkaa.

15. Wa zakaras-ma Rabbihee fasallaa.

16. Bal tu'siroonal-hayaa-tad-dunyaa.

17. Wal-Aakhiratu khayruñw-wa abqaa.

18. Inna haazaa lafis-Suhu-fil-oolaa.

19. Suhufi Ibraaheema wa Moosaa. **(Section 1)**

Sûrat al-Ghâshiyah–88
(Revealed at Makkah)

Bismillaahir Rahmaanir Raheem

1. Hal ataaka hadeesul-ghaashiyah.

2. Wujoohuñy-Yawma'izin khaashi'ah.

English	Transliteration	Arabic
3. Labouring (hard), weary,-	3. 'Aamilatun-naasibah.	عَامِلَةٌ نَّاصِبَةٌ ٣
4. The while they enter the Blazing Fire,-	4. Taşlaa Naaran Ḥaamiyah.	تَصْلَىٰ نَارًا حَامِيَةً ٤
5. The while they are given, to drink, of a boiling hot spring,	5. Tusqaa min 'aynin aaniyah.	تُسْقَىٰ مِنْ عَيْنٍ اٰنِيَةٍ ٥
6. There will be no food for them but a bitter Dhari'	6. Laysa lahum ţa'aamun illaa min đaree'.	لَيْسَ لَهُمْ طَعَامٌ إِلَّا مِنْ ضَرِيعٍ ٦
7. Which will neither nourish nor satisfy hunger.	7. Laa yusminu wa laa yughnee min joo'.	لَا يُسْمِنُ وَلَا يُغْنِي مِنْ جُوعٍ ٧
8. (Other) faces that Day will be joyful,	8. Wujoohuñy-Yawma'izin naa'imah.	وُجُوهٌ يَوْمَئِذٍ نَّاعِمَةٌ ٨
9. Pleased with their striving,-	9. Lisa'yihaa raađiyah.	لِّسَعْيِهَا رَاضِيَةٌ ٩
10. In a Garden on high,	10. Fee Jannatin 'aaliyah.	فِي جَنَّةٍ عَالِيَةٍ ١٠
11. Where they shall hear no (word) of vanity:	11. Laa tasma'u feehaa laaghiyah.	لَا تَسْمَعُ فِيهَا لَاغِيَةً ١١
12. Therein will be a bubbling spring:	12. Feehaa 'aynun jaariyah.	فِيهَا عَيْنٌ جَارِيَةٌ ١٢
13. Therein will be couches (of dignity), raised on high,	13. Feehaa sururum-marfoo'ah.	فِيهَا سُرُرٌ مَّرْفُوعَةٌ ١٣
14. Goblets placed (ready),	14. Wa akwaabum-mawđoo'ah.	وَّأَكْوَابٌ مَّوْضُوعَةٌ ١٤
15. And cushions set in rows,	15. Wa namaariqu maşfoofah.	وَّنَمَارِقُ مَصْفُوفَةٌ ١٥
16. And rich carpets (all) spread out.	16. Wa zaraabiyyu mabsoosah.	وَّزَرَابِيُّ مَبْثُوثَةٌ ١٦
17. Do they not look at the Camels, how they are made?-	17. Afalaa yanzuroona ilalibili kayfa khuliqat.	أَفَلَا يَنْظُرُونَ إِلَى الْإِبِلِ كَيْفَ خُلِقَتْ ١٧
18. And at the Sky, how it is raised high?-	18. Wa ilas-samaaa'i kayfa rufi'at.	وَإِلَى السَّمَاءِ كَيْفَ رُفِعَتْ ١٨
19. And at the Mountains, how they are fixed firm?-	19. Wa ilal-jibaali kayfa nuşibat.	وَإِلَى الْجِبَالِ كَيْفَ نُصِبَتْ ١٩
20. And at the Earth, how it is spread out?	20. Wa ilal-arđi kayfa suţiḥat.	وَإِلَى الْأَرْضِ كَيْفَ سُطِحَتْ ٢٠
21. Therefore you do give remind, for you are one to remind.	21. Fazakkir innamaa anta Muzakkir.	فَذَكِّرْ إِنَّمَا أَنْتَ مُذَكِّرٌ ٢١
22. You are not one to manage (men's) affairs.	22. Lasta 'alayhim bimuşayţir.	لَسْتَ عَلَيْهِمْ بِمُصَيْطِرٍ ٢٢
23. But if any turn away and reject Allah,-	23. Illaa man tawallaa wa kafar.	إِلَّا مَنْ تَوَلَّىٰ وَكَفَرَ ٢٣
24. Allah will punish him with a mighty Punishment,	24. Fa-yu'azzibuhul-laahul-'azaabal-akbar.	فَيُعَذِّبُهُ اللهُ الْعَذَابَ الْأَكْبَرَ ٢٤
25. For to Us will be their return;	25. Inna ilaynaaa iyaabahum.	إِنَّ إِلَيْنَا إِيَابَهُمْ ٢٥
26. Then it will be for Us to call them to account.	26. Summa inna 'alaynaa ḥisaabahum. (Section 1)	ثُمَّ إِنَّ عَلَيْنَا حِسَابَهُمْ ٢٦

89. The Break of Day
In the name of Allah, Most Gracious, Most Merciful.

1. By the break of Day;

2. By the ten Nights.

3. By the even and odd (contrasted);

4. And by the Night when it passeth away;-

5. There surely is an oath for thinking man.

6. O you not see how your Lord dealt with the 'Ad (people),

7. Of the (city of) Iram, with lofty pillars,

8. The like of which were not produced in (all) the land?

9. And with the Thamud (people), who cut out (huge) rocks in the valley?-

10. And with Pharaoh, lord of stakes?

11. (All) these transgressed beyond bounds in the lands,

12. And heaped therein mischief (on mischief).

13. Therefore did your Lord pour on them a scourge of diverse chastisements:

14. For your Lord is (as a Guardian) on a watch-tower.

15. As for man, whenever his Lord trieth him by honouring him, and is gracious unto him, he saith: My Lord honoureth me.

16. But when He tries him, restricting his subsistence for him, then says he (in despair), "My Lord has humiliated me!"

17. No, nay! but you honour not the orphans!

18. Nor do you encourage one another to feed the poor!-

19. And you devour inheritance - all with greed,

20. And you love wealth with inordinate love!

21. No! When the earth is pounded to powder,

22. And your Lord cometh, and His angels, rank upon rank,

Sûrat al-Fajr–89
(Revealed at Makkah)
Bismillaahir Raḥmaanir Raḥeem

1. Wal-Fajr.

2. Wa layaalin 'ashr.

3. Wash-shaf'i wal-watr.

4. Wallayli izaa yasr.

5. Hal fee zaalika qasamul-lizee ḥijr.

6. Alam tara kayfa fa'ala Rabbuka bi'aad.

7. Irama zaatil-'imaad.

8. Allatee lam yukhlaq misluhaa fil-bilaad.

9. Wa Samoodal-lazeena jaabuṣ-ṣakhra bil-waad.

10. Wa Fir'awna zil-awtaad.

11. Allazeena ṭaghaw fil-bilaad.

12. Fa-akṣaroo feehal-fasaad.

13. Faṣabba 'alayhim Rabbuka sawṭa 'azaab.

14. Inna Rabbaka labil-mirṣaad.

15. Fa-ammal-insaanu izaa mab-talaahu Rabbuhoo fa-akramahoo wa na'-'amahoo fa-yaqoolu Rabbeee akraman.

16. Wa ammaaa izaa mabta-laahu faqadara 'alayhi rizqahoo fa-yaqoolu Rabbeee ahaanan.

17. Kallaa bal laa tukrimoo-nal-yateem.

18. Wa laa taḥaaaḍḍoona 'alaa ṭa'aamil-miskeen.

19. Wa taåkuloonat-turaasa aklal-lammaa.

20. Wa tuḥibboonal-maala ḥubban jammaa.

21. Kallaaa izaa dukkatil-arḍu dakkan dakkaa.

22. Wa jaaa'a Rabbuka wal-malaku ṣaffan ṣaffaa.

---

23. And hell is brought near that day; on that day man will remember, but how will the remembrance (then avail him)?

24. He will say: "Ah! Would that I had sent forth (good deeds) for (this) my (Future) Life!"

25. None punisheth as He will punish on that day!

26. And His bonds will be such as none (other) can bind.

27. But ah! Thou soul at peace!

28. Return unto thy Lord, content in His good pleasure!

29. "Enter you, then, among My devotees!

30. "Yes, enter you My Heaven!

90. The City

In the name of Allah, Most Gracious, Most Merciful.

1. I do call to witness this City;-

2. And you are a freeman of this City;-

3. And (the mystic ties of) parent and child;-

4. Verily We have created man into toil and struggle.

5. Thinks he, that none has power over him?

6. And he saith: I have destroyed vast wealth:

7. Thinks he that none beholds him?

8. Have We not made for him a pair of eyes?-

9. And a tongue, and a pair of lips?-

10. And shown him the two highways?

11. But he has made no haste on the path that is steep.

12. And what will explain to you the path that is steep?-

13. (It is:) freeing the bondman;

14. Or the giving of food in a day of privation.

15. An orphan near of kin,

---

23. Wa jeee'a Yawma'izim bi-Jahannam; Yawma'iziñy-yatazakkarul-insaanu wa annaa lahuz-zikraa.

24. Yaqoolu yaa laytanee qaddamtu lihayaatee.

25. Fa-Yawma'izil-laa yu'azzibu 'azaabahooo ahad.

26. Wa laa yoosiqu wasaaqa-hooo ahad.

27. Yaaa ayyatuhan-nafsul-mutma'innah.

28. Irji'eee ilaa Rabbiki raadiyatam-mardiyyah.

29. Fadkhulee fee 'ibaadee.

30. Wadkhulee Jannatee.

(Section 1)

Sûrat al-Balad—90

(Revealed at Makkah)

Bismillaahir Rahmaanir Raheem

1. Laaa uqsimu bihaazal-balad.

2. Wa anta hillum bihaazal-balad.

3. Wa waalidiñw-wa maa walad.

4. Laqad khalaqnal-insaana fee kabad.

5. Ayahsabu al-lañy-yaqdira 'alayhi ahad.

6. Yaqoolu ahlaktu maalal-lubadaa.

7. Ayahsabu al-lam yara-hooo ahad.

8. Alam naj'al lahoo 'ay-nayn.

9. Wa lisaanañw-wa shafa-tayn.

10. Wa hadaynaahun-naj-dayn.

11. Falaq-tahamal-'aqabah.

12. Wa maaa adraaka mal-'aqabah.

13. Fakku raqabah.

14. Aw it'aamun fee yawmin zee masghabah.

15. Yateeman zaa maqrabah.

16. Or to the indigent (down) in the dust.

17. And to be of those who believe and exhort one another to perseverance and exhort one another to pity.

18. Such are the Companions of the Right Hand.

19. But those who reject Our Signs, they are the (unhappy) Companions of the Left Hand.

20. On them will be Fire vaulted over (all round).

91. The Sun
In the name of Allah, Most Gracious, Most Merciful.

1. By the Sun and his (glorious) splendour;

2. By the Moon as she follows him;

3. By the Day as it shows up (the Sun's) glory;

4. By the Night as it conceals it;

5. By the Firmament and its (wonderful) structure;

6. By the Earth and its (wide) expanse:

7. By the Soul, and the proportion and order given to it.

8. And its enlightenment as to its wrong and its right;-

9. Truly he succeeds that purifies it,

10. And he fails that corrupts it!

11. The Thamud (people) rejected (their prophet) through their inordinate wrong-doing,

12. When the basest of them broke forth.

13. But the Apostle of Allah said to them: "It is a She-camel of Allah! And (bar her not from) having her drink!"

14. Then they rejected him (as a false prophet), and they hamstrung her. So their Lord, on account of their crime, obliterated their traces and made them equal (in destruction, high and low)!

15. And for Him is no fear of its consequences.

---

16. Aw miskeenan zaa matrabah.

17. Summa kaana minallazeena aamanoo wa tawaasaw bissabri wa tawaasaw bil-marhamah.

18. Ulaaa'ika As-haabul-Maymanah.

19. Wallazeena kafaroo bi-Aayaatinaa hum As-haabul-Mash'amah.

20. 'Alayhim Naarum-mu'-sadah.   (Section 1)

Sûrat ash-Shams–91
(Revealed at Makkah)
Bismillaahir Rahmaanir Raheem

1. Wash-shamsi wa duhaa-haa.

2. Wal-qamari izaa talaa-haa.

3. Wannahaari izaa jallaa-haa.

4. Wallayli izaa yaghshaa-haa.

5. Wassamaaa'i wa maa banaahaa.

6. Wal-ardi wa maa tahaa-haa.

7. Wa nafsiñw-wa maa sawwaahaa.

8. Fa-alhamahaa fujoorahaa wa taqwaahaa.

9. Qad aflaha man zakkaa-haa.

10. Wa qad khaaba man dassaahaa.

11. Kazzabat Samoodu bi-taghwaahaaa.

12. Izim ba'asa ashqaahaa.

13. Faqaala lahum Rasoolul-laahi naaqatal-laahi wa suqyaa-haa.

14. Fakazzaboohu fa'aqa-roohaa fadamdama 'alayhim Rabbuhum bizambihim fasaw-waahaa.

15. Wa laa yakhaafu 'uqbaahaa.   (Section 1)

92. The Night

In the name of Allah, Most Gracious, Most Merciful.

1. By the Night as it conceals (the light);

2. By the Day as it appears in glory;

3. By (the mystery of) the creation of male and female;-

4. Verily, (the ends) you strive for are diverse.

5. So he who gives (in charity) and fears (Allah),

6. And (in all sincerity) testifies to the best,-

7. We will indeed make smooth for him the path to Bliss.

8. But he who is a greedy miser and thinks himself self-sufficient,

9. And gives the lie to the best,-

10. We will indeed make smooth for him the path to Misery;

11. Nor will his wealth profit him when he falls headlong (into the Pit).

12. Verily We take upon Ourselves to guide,

13. And verily unto Us (belong) the End and the Beginning.

14. Therefore do I warn you of a Fire blazing fiercely;

15. None shall reach it but those most unfortunate ones

16. Who give the lie to Truth and turn their backs.

17. But those most devoted to Allah shall be removed far from it,-

18. Those who spend their wealth for increase in self-purification,

19. And have in their minds no favour from anyone for which a reward is expected in return,

20. But only the desire to seek for the Countenance of their Lord Most High;

21. And soon will they attain (complete) satisfaction.

93. The Glorious Morning Light

In the name of Allah, Most Gracious, Most Merciful.

1. By the Glorious Morning Light,

Sûrat al-Layl–92
(Revealed at Makkah)
Bismillaahir Raḥmaanir Raḥeem

1. Wallayli iẕaa yaghshaa.

2. Wannahaari iẕaa tajallaa.

3. Wa maa khalaqaẕ-ẕakara wal-unsaaa.

4. Inna sa'yakum lashattaa.

5. Fa-ammaa man a'ṭaa wattaqaa.

6. Wa ṣaddaqa bil-ḥusnaa.

7. Fasanu-yassiruhoo lil-yusraa.

8. Wa ammaa mam bakhila wastaghnaa.

9. Wa kaẕẕaba bil-ḥusnaa.

10. Fasanu-yassiruhoo lil-'usraa.

11. Wa maa yughnee 'anhu maaluhooo iẕaa taraddaa.

12. Inna 'alaynaa lal-hudaa.

13. Wa inna lanaa lal-Aakhirata wal-oolaa.

14. Fa-anẕartukum Naaran talaẕẕaa.

15. Laa yaṣlaahaaa illal-ash-qaa.

16. Allaẕee kaẕẕaba wa tawallaa.

17. Wa sa-yujannabuhal-atqaa.

18. Allaẕee yu'tee maalahoo yatazakkaa.

19. Wa maa li-aḥadin 'inda-hoo min ni'matin tujzaaa.

20. Illab-tighaaa'a Wajhi Rabbihil-A'laa.

21. Wa lasawfa yarḍaa.
(Section 1)

Sûrat aḍ-Ḍuhâ–93
(Revealed at Makkah)
Bismillaahir Raḥmaanir Raḥeem

1. Waḍḍuhaa.

---

2. And by the Night when it is still,-

3. Your Guardian-Lord has not forsaken you, nor is He displeased.

4. And verily the Hereafter will be better for you than the present.

5. And soon will your Guardian-Lord give you (that wherewith) you shall be well-pleased.

6. Did He not find you an orphan and give you shelter (and care)?

7. And He found you wandering, and He gave you guidance.

8. And He found you in need, and made you independent.

9. Therefore, treat not the orphan with harshness,

10. Nor repulse the petitioner (unheard);

11. But the bounty of the Lord - rehearse and proclaim!

2. Wallayli izaa sajaa.

3. Maa wadda'aaka Rabbuka wa maa qalaa.

4. Wa lal-Aakhiratu khay-rul-laka minal-oolaa.

5. Wa la-sawfa yu'teeka Rabbuka fatardaa.

6. Alam yajidka yateeman fa-aawaa.

7. Wa wajadaka daaallan fahadaa.

8. Wa wajadaka 'aaa'ilan fa-aghnaa.

9. Fa-ammal-yateema falaa taqhar.

10. Wa ammas-saaa'ila falaa tanhar.

11. Wa ammaa bini'mati Rabbika fahaddis. (Section 1)

94. The Expansion
In the name of Allah, Most Gracious, Most Merciful.

1. Have We not expanded you your breast?-

2. And removed from you your burden

3. The which did gall your back?-

4. And raised high the esteem (in which) you (are held)?

5. So, verily, with every difficulty, there is relief:

6. Verily, with every difficulty there is relief.

7. Therefore, when you are free (from your immediate task), still labour hard,

8. And to your Lord turn (all) your attention.

Sûrat al-Inshirâh–94
(Revealed at Makkah)
Bismillaahir Rahmaanir Raheem

1. Alam nashrah laka sadrak.

2. Wa wada'naa 'anka wizrak.

3. Allazee anqada zahrak.

4. Wa rafa'naa laka zikrak.

5. Fa-inna ma'al-'usri yusraa.

6. Inna ma'al-'usri yusraa

7. Fa-izaa faraghta fansab.

8. Wa ilaa Rabbika farghab. (Section 1)

95. The Fig
In the name of Allah, Most Gracious, Most Merciful.

1. By the Fig and the Olive,

2. And the Mount of Sinai,

3. And this City of security,-

4. We have indeed created man in the best of

Sûrat at-Tîn–95
(Revealed at Makkah)
Bismillaahir Rahmaanir Raheem

1. Watteeni wazzaytoon.

2. Wa Toori Seeneen.

3. Wa haazal-baladil-ameen.

4. Laqad khalaqnal-insaana feee ahsani

moulds,

5. Then do We abase him (to be) the lowest of the low,-

6. Except such as believe and do righteous deeds: For they shall have a reward unfailing.

7. Then what can, after this, contradict thee, as to the judgment (to come)?

8. Is not Allah the wisest of judges?

96. The Clot of Congealed Blood

In the name of Allah, Most Gracious, Most Merciful.

1. Proclaim! (or read!) in the name of your Lord and Cherisher, Who created-

2. Created man, out of a (mere) clot of congealed blood:

3. Proclaim! And your Lord is Most Bountiful,-

4. He Who taught (the use of) the pen,-

5. Taught man that which he knew not.

6. No, but man doth transgress all bounds,

7. In that he looks upon himself as self-sufficient.

8. Verily, to your Lord is the return (of all).

9. O you see one who forbids-

10. A votary when he (turns) to pray?

11. Do you see if he is on (the road of) Guidance?-

12. Or enjoins Righteousness?

13. Do you see if he denies (Truth) and turns away?

14. Knows he not that Allah does see?

15. Let him beware! If he desist not, We will drag him by the forelock,-

16. A lying, sinful forelock!

17. Then, let him call (for help) to his council (of comrades):

18. We will call on the angels of punishment (to deal with him)!

taqweem.

5. <u>S</u>umma radadnaahu as-fala saafileen.

6. Illal-la<u>z</u>eena aamanoo wa 'amilu<u>s</u>-<u>s</u>aali<u>h</u>aati falahum ajrun ghayru mamnoon.

7. Famaa yuka<u>zz</u>ibuka ba'du bid-Deen.

8. Alaysal-laahu bi-a<u>h</u>ka-mil-<u>h</u>aakimeen. (Section 1)

Sûrat al-'Alaq–96
(Revealed at Makkah)
Bismillaahir Ra<u>h</u>maanir Ra<u>h</u>eem

1. Iqraå bismi Rabbikal-la<u>z</u>ee khalaq.

2. Khalaqal-insaana min 'alaq

3. Iqraå wa Rabbukal-Akram.

4. Alla<u>z</u>ee 'allama bil-qalam.

5. 'Allamal-insaana maa lam ya'lam.

6. Kallaaa innal-insaana la-ya<u>t</u>ghaaa.

7. Ar-ra-aahus-taghnaa.

8. Inna ilaa Rabbikar-ruj'aa.

9. Ara'aytal-la<u>z</u>ee yanhaa.

10. 'Abdan i<u>z</u>aa <u>s</u>allaa.

11. Ara'ayta in kaana 'alal-hudaaa.

12. Aw amara bitta<u>q</u>waa.

13. Ara'ayta in ka<u>zz</u>aba wa tawallaa.

14. Alam ya'lam bi-annal-laaha yaraa.

15. Kallaa la-'il-lam yantahi lanasfa'am binnaa<u>s</u>iyah.

16. Naa<u>s</u>iyatin kaa<u>z</u>ibatin khaa<u>t</u>i'ah.

17. Falyad'u naadiyah.

18. Sanad'uz-zabaaniyah.

(Bow Down)

19. No, pay no heed to him but bow down in adoration, and bring yourself the closer (to Allah)!

97. The Night of Power or Honour
In the name of Allah, Most Gracious, Most Merciful.

1. We have indeed revealed this (Message) in the Night of Power:

2. And what will explain to you what the Night of Power is?

3. The Night of Power is better than a thousand months.

4. Therein come down the angels and the Spirit by Allah's permission, on every errand:

5. Peace!...This until the rise of morn!

98. The Clear Evidence
In the name of Allah, Most Gracious, Most Merciful.

1. Those who reject (Truth), among the People of the Book and among the Polytheists, were not going to depart (from their ways) until there should come to them Clear Evidence,-

2. An apostle from Allah, rehearsing scriptures kept pure and holy:

3. Wherein are laws (or decrees) right and straight.

4. Nor did the People of the Book make schisms, until after there came to them Clear Evidence.

5. And they have been commanded no more than this: To worship Allah, offering Him sincere devotion, being true (in faith); to establish regular prayer; and to practise regular charity; and that is the Religion Right and Straight.

6. Those who reject (Truth), among the People of the Book and among the Polytheists, will be in Hell-Fire, to dwell therein (for ever). They are the worst of creatures.

7. Those who have faith and do righteous deeds,- they are the best of creatures.

19. Kallaa laa tuṭi'hu wasjud waqtarib. (Section 1)

Sûrat al-Qadr–97
(Revealed at Makkah)
Bismillaahir Raḥmaanir Raḥeem

1. Innaaa anzalnaahu fee Laylatil-Qadr.

2. Wa maaa adraaka maa Laylatul-Qadr.

3. Laylatul-Qadri khayrum-min alfi shahr.

4. Tanazzalul-malaaa'ikatu war-Rooḥu feehaa bi-izni Rabbihim min kulli amr.

5. Salaamun hiya ḥattaa maṭla'il-Fajr. (Section 1)

Sûrat al-Bayyinah–98
(Revealed at Madinah)
Bismillaahir Raḥmaanir Raḥeem

1. Lam yakunil-lazeena kafaroo min Ahlil-Kitaabi wal-mushrikeena munfakkeena ḥattaa taatiyahumul-bayyinah.

2. Rasoolum-minal-laahi yatloo ṣuḥufam-muṭahharah.

3. Feehaa kutubun qayyimah.

4. Wa maa tafarraqal-lazeena ootul-Kitaaba illaa mim ba'di maa jaaa'at-humul-bayyinah.

5. Wa maaa umirooo illaa liya'budul-laaha mukhliṣeena lahud-deena ḥunafaaa'a wa yuqeemuṣ-Ṣalaata wa yu'tuz-Zakaata wa zaalika deenul-qayyimah.

6. Innal-lazeena kafaroo min Ahlil-Kitaabi wal-mushrikeena fee Naari Jahannama khaalideena feehaa; ulaaa'ika hum sharrul-bariyyah.

7. Innal-lazeena aamanoo wa 'amiluṣ-ṣaaliḥaati ulaaa'ika hum-khayrul-bariyyah.

8. Their reward is with Allah: Gardens of Eternity, beneath which rivers flow; they will dwell therein for ever; Allah well pleased with them, and they with Him: all this for such as fear their Lord and Cherisher.

99. The Convulsion
In the name of Allah, Most Gracious, Most Merciful.

1. When the earth is shaken to her (utmost) convulsion,

2. And the earth throws up her burdens (from within),

3. And man cries (distressed): 'What is the matter with her?'-

4. On that Day will she declare her tidings:

5. For that your Lord will have given her inspiration.

6. On that Day will men proceed in companies sorted out, to be shown the deeds that they (had done).

7. Then shall anyone who has done an atom's weight of good, see it!

8. And anyone who has done an atom's weight of evil, shall see it.

100. Those that Run
In the name of Allah, Most Gracious, Most Merciful.

1. By the (Steeds) that run, with panting (breath),

2. And strike sparks of fire,

3. And push home the charge in the morning,

4. And raise the dust in clouds the while,

5. And penetrate forthwith into the midst (of the foe) en masse;-

6. Truly man is, to his Lord, ungrateful;

7. And to that (fact) he bears witness (by his deeds);

8. And violent is he in his love of wealth.

9. Does he not know,- when that which is in the

8. Jazaaa'uhum 'inda Rabbihim Jannaatu 'Adnin tajree min taḥtihal-anhaaru khaalideena feehaaa abadaa; raḍiyal-laahu 'anhum wa raḍoo 'anh; zaalika liman khashiya Rabbah.   (Section 1)

Sûrat az-Zilzâl–99
(Revealed at Madinah)
Bismillaahir Raḥmaanir Raḥeem

1. Izaa zulzilatil-arḍu zilzaa-lahaa.

2. Wa akhrajatil-arḍu asqaa-lahaa.

3. Wa qaalal-insaanu maa lahaa.

4. Yawma'izin tuḥaddiṣu akhbaarahaa.

5. Bi-anna Rabbaka awḥaa-lahaa.

6. Yawma'iziny-yaṣdurun-naasu ashtaatal-liyuraw a'maa-lahum.

7. Famañy-ya'mal miṣqaala zarratin khairañy-yarah.

8. Wa mañy-ya'mal miṣqaala zarratin sharrañy-yarah.   (Sec. 1)

Sûrat al-'Âdiyât–100
(Revealed at Makkah)
Bismillaahir Raḥmaanir Raḥeem

1. Wal-'aadiyaati ḍabḥaa.

2. Falmooriyaati qadḥaa.

3. Fal-mugheeraati ṣubḥaa.

4. Fa-aṣarna bihee naq'aa.

5. Fawasaṭna bihee jam'aa.

6. Innal-insaana li-Rabbihee lakanood.

7. Wa innahoo 'alaa zaalika lashaheed.

8. Wa innahoo liḥubbil-khayri lashadeed.

9. Afalaa ya'lamu izaa bu'-sira maa fil-

graves is scattered abroad.

10. And that which is (locked up) in (human) breasts is made manifest-

11. That their Lord had been Well-acquainted with them, (even to) that Day.?

quboor.

10. Wa ḥuṣṣila maa fiṣ-ṣudoor.

11. Inna Rabbahum bihim Yawma’izil-lakhabeer. **(Sec. 1)**

الْقُبُورُ ۝

وَحُصِّلَ مَا فِى الصُّدُورِ ۝

إِنَّ رَبَّهُمْ بِهِمْ يَوْمَئِذٍ لَّخَبِيرٌ ۝

101. The Day of Noise and Clamour
In the name of Allah, Most Gracious, Most Merciful.

Sûrat al-Qâri‘ah–101
(Revealed at Makkah)
Bismillaahir Raḥmaanir Raḥeem

سُورَةُ الْقَارِعَةِ مَكِّيَّةٌ (١٠١) (٣٠)

بِسْمِ اللهِ الرَّحْمٰنِ الرَّحِيمِ

1. The (Day) of Noise and Clamour:

2. What is the (Day) of Noise and Clamour?

3. And what will explain to you what the (Day) of Noise and Clamour is?

4. (It is) a Day whereon men will be like moths scattered about,

5. And the mountains will be like carded wool.

6. Then, he whose balance (of good deeds) will be (found) heavy,

7. Will be in a life of good pleasure and satisfaction.

8. But he whose balance (of good deeds) will be (found) light,-

9. Will have his home in a (bottomless) Pit.

10. And what will explain to you what this is?

11. (It is) a Fire Blazing fiercely!

1. Al-qaari‘ah.

2. Mal-qaari‘ah.

3. Wa maaa adraaka mal-qaari‘ah.

4. Yawma yakoonun-naasu kalfaraashil-mabsoos.

5. Wa takoonul-jibaalu kal-‘ihnil-manfoosh.

6. Fa-ammaa man saqulat mawaazeenuh.

7. Fahuwa fee ‘eeshatir-raaḍiyah.

8. Wa ammaa man khaffat mawaazeenuh.

9. Fa-ummuhoo haawiyah.

10. Wa maaa adraaka maa hiyah.

11. Naarun ḥaamiyah.
(Section 1)

الْقَارِعَةُ ۝

مَا الْقَارِعَةُ ۝

وَمَا أَدْرَاكَ مَا الْقَارِعَةُ ۝

يَوْمَ يَكُونُ النَّاسُ كَالْفَرَاشِ الْمَبْثُوثِ ۝

وَتَكُونُ الْجِبَالُ كَالْعِهْنِ الْمَنفُوشِ ۝

فَأَمَّا مَن ثَقُلَتْ مَوَازِينُهُ ۝

فَهُوَ فِى عِيشَةٍ رَّاضِيَةٍ ۝

وَأَمَّا مَنْ خَفَّتْ مَوَازِينُهُ ۝

فَأُمُّهُ هَاوِيَةٌ ۝

وَمَا أَدْرَاكَ مَا هِيَهْ ۝

نَارٌ حَامِيَةٌ ۝

102. The Piling Up
In the name of Allah, Most Gracious, Most Merciful.

Sûrat at-Takâsur–102
(Revealed at Makkah)
Bismillaahir Raḥmaanir Raḥeem

سُورَةُ التَّكَاثُرِ مَكِّيَّةٌ (١٠٢) (١٦)

بِسْمِ اللهِ الرَّحْمٰنِ الرَّحِيمِ

1. The mutual rivalry for piling up (the good things of this world) diverts you (from the more serious things),

2. Until you visit the graves.

3. But nay, you soon shall know (the reality).

4. Again, you soon shall know!

5. No, were you to know with certainty of mind, (you would beware!)

6. You shall certainly see Hell-Fire!

7. Again, you shall see it with certainty of sight!

1. Al-haakumut-takaasur.

2. Ḥattaa zurtumul-maqaabir.

3. Kallaa sawfa ta‘lamoon.

4. Summa kallaa sawfa ta‘lamoon.

5. Kallaa law ta‘lamoona ‘ilmal-yaqeen.

6. Latarawunnal-Jaheem.

7. Summa latarawunnahaa ‘aynal-yaqeen.

أَلْهَاكُمُ التَّكَاثُرُ ۝

حَتَّى زُرْتُمُ الْمَقَابِرَ ۝

كَلَّا سَوْفَ تَعْلَمُونَ ۝

ثُمَّ كَلَّا سَوْفَ تَعْلَمُونَ ۝

كَلَّا لَوْ تَعْلَمُونَ عِلْمَ الْيَقِينِ ۝

لَتَرَوُنَّ الْجَحِيمَ ۝

ثُمَّ لَتَرَوُنَّهَا عَيْنَ الْيَقِينِ ۝

8. Then, shall you be questioned that Day about the joy (you indulged in!).

8. Summa latus'alunna Yawma'izin 'anin-na'eem. (Section 1)

ثُمَّ لَتُسْـَٔلُنَّ يَوْمَىِٕذٍ عَنِ النَّعِيمِ ۝

103. Time Through the Ages
In the name of Allah, Most Gracious, Most Merciful.

1. By (the Token of) Time (through the ages),

2. Verily Man is in loss,

3. Except such as have Faith, and do righteous deeds, and (join together) in the mutual teaching of Truth, and of Patience and Constancy.

Sûrat al-'Aṣr–103
(Revealed at Makkah)
Bismillaahir Raḥmaanir Raḥeem

1. Wal-'Aṣr.

2. Innal-insaana lafee khusr.

3. Illal-lazeena aamanoo wa 'amiluṣ-ṣaaliḥaati wa tawaaṣaw bilḥaqq, wa tawaaṣaw biṣṣabr. (Section 1)

(١٠٣) سُوْرَةُ الْعَصْرِ مَكِّيَّةٌ (١٣)

بِسْمِ اللّٰهِ الرَّحْمٰنِ الرَّحِيْمِ

وَالْعَصْرِ ۝

إِنَّ الْإِنْسَانَ لَفِيْ خُسْرٍ ۝

إِلَّا الَّذِيْنَ اٰمَنُوْا وَعَمِلُوا الصّٰلِحٰتِ وَتَوَاصَوْا بِالْحَقِّ ۙ وَتَوَاصَوْا بِالصَّبْرِ ۝

104. The Scandal-monger
In the name of Allah, Most Gracious, Most Merciful.

1. Woe to every (kind of) scandal-monger and-backbiter,

2. Who piles up wealth and layeth it by,

3. Thinking that his wealth would make him last for ever!

4. By no means! He will be sure to be thrown into That which Breaks to Pieces,

5. And what will explain to you That which Breaks to Pieces?

6. (It is) the Fire of (the Wrath of) Allah kindled (to a blaze),

7. That which does mount (Right) up to the Hearts:

8. It shall be made into a vault over them,

9. In columns outstretched.

Sûrat al-Humazah–104
(Revealed at Makkah)
Bismillaahir Raḥmaanir Raḥeem

1. Waylul-likulli humazatil-lumazah.

2. Allazee jama'a maalañw-wa 'addadah.

3. Yaḥsabu anna maalahooo akhladah.

4. Kallaa la-yumbazanna fil-ḥuṭamah.

5. Wa maaa adraaka mal-ḥuṭamah.

6. Naarul-laahil-mooqadah.

7. Allatee taṭṭali'u 'alal-af'idah.

8. Innahaa 'alayhim mu'ṣadah.

9. Fee 'amadim-mumad-dadah. (Section 1)

(١٠٤) سُوْرَةُ الْهُمَزَةِ مَكِّيَّةٌ (٣٢)

بِسْمِ اللّٰهِ الرَّحْمٰنِ الرَّحِيْمِ

وَيْلٌ لِّكُلِّ هُمَزَةٍ لُّمَزَةِ ۝

الَّذِيْ جَمَعَ مَالًا وَّعَدَّدَهُ ۝

يَحْسَبُ اَنَّ مَالَهٗ اَخْلَدَهُ ۝

كَلَّا لَيُنْۢبَذَنَّ فِي الْحُطَمَةِ ۝

وَمَا اَدْرٰىكَ مَا الْحُطَمَةُ ۝

نَارُ اللّٰهِ الْمُوْقَدَةُ ۝

الَّتِيْ تَطَّلِعُ عَلَى الْاَفْـِٕدَةِ ۝

اِنَّهَا عَلَيْهِمْ مُّؤْصَدَةٌ ۝

فِيْ عَمَدٍ مُّمَدَّدَةٍ ۝

105. The Elephant
In the name of Allah, Most Gracious, Most Merciful.

1. Do you see not how your Lord dealt with the Companions of the Elephant?

2. Did He not make their treacherous plan go astray?

3. And He sent against them Flights of Birds,

4. Striking them with stones of baked clay.

5. Then did He make them like an empty field of stalks and straw, (of which the corn) has been eaten up.

Sûrat al-Fîl–105
(Revealed at Makkah)
Bismillaahir Raḥmaanir Raḥeem

1. Alam tara kayfa fa'ala Rabbuka bi-Aṣ-ḥaabil-Feel.

2. Alam yaj'al kaydahum fee taḍleel.

3. Wa arsala 'alayhim ṭayran abaabeel.

4. Tarmeehim biḥijaaratim-min sijjeel.

5. Faja'alahum ka'aṣfim-maakool. (Section 1)

(١٠٥) سُوْرَةُ الْفِيْلِ مَكِّيَّةٌ (١٩)

بِسْمِ اللّٰهِ الرَّحْمٰنِ الرَّحِيْمِ

اَلَمْ تَرَ كَيْفَ فَعَلَ رَبُّكَ بِاَصْحٰبِ الْفِيْلِ ۝

اَلَمْ يَجْعَلْ كَيْدَهُمْ فِيْ تَضْلِيْلٍ ۝

وَاَرْسَلَ عَلَيْهِمْ طَيْرًا اَبَابِيْلَ ۝

تَرْمِيْهِمْ بِحِجَارَةٍ مِّنْ سِجِّيْلٍ ۝

فَجَعَلَهُمْ كَعَصْفٍ مَّاْكُوْلٍ ۝

سُورَة قُرَيْش ١٠٦ الْمَاعُون ١٠٧ الْكَوْثَر ١٠٨ الْكَفِرُون ١٠٩

106. The Tribe of Quraish

In the name of Allah, Most Gracious, Most Merciful.

1. For the covenants (of security and safeguard enjoyed) by the Quraish,
2. Their covenants (covering safe) journeys by winter and summer,-
3. Let them adore the Lord of this House,
4. Who provides them with food against hunger, and with security against fear (of danger).

107. The Neighbourly Needs

In the name of Allah, Most Gracious, Most Merciful.

1. Did you see one who denies the Judgment (to come)?
2. Then such is the (man) who repulses the orphan (with harshness),
3. And encourages not the feeding of the indigent.
4. So woe to the worshippers,
5. Who are neglectful of their prayers,
6. Those who (want but) to be seen (of men),
7. But refuse (to supply) (even) neighbourly need

108. The Abundance

In the name of Allah, Most Gracious, Most Merciful.

1. To you have We granted the Fount (of Abundance).
2. Therefore, to your Lord turn in Prayer and Sacrifice.
3. For he who hates you, he will be cut off (from Future Hope)

109. Those who reject Faith

In the name of Allah, Most Gracious, Most Merciful.

1. Say : O you that reject Faith!
2. I worship not that which you worship,
3. Nor will you worship that which I worship.

Sûrat Quraysh–106
(Revealed at Makkah)
Bismillaahir Rahmaanir Raheem

1. Li-eelaafi Quraysh.
2. Eelaafihim rihlatash-Shitaaa'i wassayf.
3. Falya'budoo Rabba haazal-Bayt.
4. Allazee at'amahum min joo'iñw-wa aamanahum min khawf. (Section 1)

Sûrat al-Mâ'ûn–107
(Revealed at Makkah)
Bismillaahir Rahmaanir Raheem

1. Ara'aytal-lazee yukaz-zibu biddeen.
2. Fazaalikal-lazee yadu'-'ul-yateem.
3. Wa laa yahuddu 'alaa ta'aamil-miskeen.
4. Fa-waylul-lil-musalleen.
5. Allazeena hum 'an Salaa-tihim saahoon.
6. Allazeena hum yuraaa-'oon.
7. Wa yamna'oonal-maa'oon. (Section 1)

Sûrat al-Kawsar–108
(Revealed at Makkah)
Bismillaahir Rahmaanir Raheem

1. Innaaa a'taynaakal-Kawsar.
2. Fasalli li-Rabbika wanhar.
3. Inna shaani'aka huwal-abtar. (Section 1)

Sûrat al-Kâfirûn–109
(Revealed at Makkah)
Bismillaahir Rahmaanir Raheem

1. Qul yaaa ayyuhal-kaafi-roon.
2. Laaa a'budu maa ta'bu-doon.
3. Wa laaa antum 'aabidoo-na maaa a'bud.

4. And I will not worship that which you have been wont to worship,

5. Nor will you worship that which I worship.

6. To you be your Way, and to me mine.

4. Wa laaa ana 'aabidum maa 'abattum.

5. Wa laaa antum 'aabidoona maaa a'bud.

6. Lakum deenukum wa liya deen.
(Section 1)

110. The Help
In the name of Allah, Most Gracious, Most Merciful.

1. When comes the Help of Allah, and Victory,

2. And you does see the people enter Allah's Religion in crowds,

3. Celebrate the praises of your Lord, and pray for His Forgiveness: For He is Oft-Returning (in Grace and Mercy).

Sûrat an-Naṣr–110
(Revealed at Madinah)
Bismillaahir Raḥmaanir Raḥeem

1. Izaa jaaa'a naṣrul-laahi wal-Fat-ḥ.

2. Wa ra-aytan-naasa yad-khuloona fee deenil-laahi af-waajaa.

3. Fasabbiḥ biḥamdi Rabbi-ka wastaghfirh; innahoo kaana Tawwaaba.
(Section 1)

111. The Father of Flame
In the name of Allah, Most Gracious, Most Merciful.

1. Perish the hands of the Father of Flame! Perish he!

2. No benefit to him all his wealth, and all he accumulated.

3. Burnt soon will he be in a Fire of Blazing Flame!

4. His wife shall carry the (crackling) wood - as fuel!-

5. A twisted rope of palm-leaf fibre round her (own) neck!

Sûrat al-Lahab–111
(Revealed at Makkah)
Bismillaahir Raḥmaanir Raḥeem

1. Tabbat yadaaa Abee Laha-biñw-wa tabb.

2. Maaa aghnaa 'anhu maa-luhoo wa maa kasab.

3. Sa-yaṣlaa Naaran zaata lahab.

4. Wamra-atuhoo ḥammaa-latal-ḥatab.

5. Fee jeedihaa ḥablum mim masad.
(Section 1)

112. Purity (of Faith)
In the name of Allah, Most Gracious, Most Merciful.

1. Say: He is Allah, the One and Only;

2. Allah, the Eternal, Absolute;

3. He begets not, nor is He begotten;

4. And there is none like unto Him.

Sûrat al-Ikhlâs–112
(Revealed at Makkah)
Bismillaahir Raḥmaanir Raḥeem

1. Qul Huwal-laahu Aḥad.

2. Allaahuṣ-Ṣamad.

3. Lam yalid wa lam yoolad.

4. Wa lam yakul-lahoo kufu-wan aḥad.
(Section 1)

113. The Dawn
In the name of Allah, Most Gracious, Most Merciful.

1. Say: I seek refuge with the Lord of the Dawn.

Sûrat al-Falaq–113
(Revealed at Makkah)
Bismillaahir Raḥmaanir Raḥeem

1. Qul a'oozu bi Rabbil-falaq.

2. From the mischief of created things;

3. From the mischief of Darkness as it overspreads;

4. From the mischief of those who blow on knots;

5. And from the mischief of the envious one as he practises envy.

2. Min sharri maa khalaq.

3. Wa min sharri ghaasiqin izaa waqab.

4. Wa min sharrin-naffaa-saati fil-'uqad.

5. Wa min sharri ḥaasidin izaa ḥasad.   (Section 1)

مِنْ شَرِّ مَا خَلَقَ ۙ

وَمِنْ شَرِّ غَاسِقٍ إِذَا وَقَبَ ۙ

وَمِنْ شَرِّ النَّفّٰثٰتِ فِى الْعُقَدِ ۙ

وَمِنْ شَرِّ حَاسِدٍ إِذَا حَسَدَ ۟

114. Mankind
In the name of Allah, Most Gracious, Most Merciful.

Sûrat an-Nâs–114
(Revealed at Makkah)

Bismillaahir Raḥmaanir Raḥeem

سُوْرَةُ النَّاسِ مَكِّيَّةٌ (١١٤) (٢١)

بِسْمِ اللّٰهِ الرَّحْمٰنِ الرَّحِيْمِ

1. Say: I seek refuge with the Lord and Cherisher of Mankind,

2. The King (or Ruler) of Mankind,

3. The Allah (for judge) of Mankind,–

4. From the mischief of the Whisperer (of Evil), who withdraws (after his whisper),–

5. (The same) who whispers into the hearts of Mankind,–

6. Among Jinns and among men.

1. Qul a'oozu bi-Rabbin-naas.

2. Malikin-naas.

3. Ilaahin-naas.

4. Min sharril-waswaasil-khannaas.

5. Allazee yuwaswisu fee ṣudoorin-naas.

6. Minal-jinnati wannaas.   (Section 1)

قُلْ أَعُوْذُ بِرَبِّ النَّاسِ ۙ

مَلِكِ النَّاسِ ۙ

إِلٰهِ النَّاسِ ۙ

مِنْ شَرِّ الْوَسْوَاسِ ۙ الْخَنَّاسِ ۙ

الَّذِىْ يُوَسْوِسُ فِىْ صُدُوْرِ النَّاسِ ۙ

مِنَ الْجِنَّةِ وَالنَّاسِ ۟

Prayer
(To be used after reading the Holy Qur'an)

دُعَاءُ خَتْمِ الْقُرْاٰن

اللّٰهُمَّ اٰنِسْ وَحْشَتِىْ فِىْ قَبْرِىْ اللّٰهُمَّ ارْحَمْنِىْ بِالْقُرْاٰنِ الْعَظِيْمِ وَاجْعَلْهُ لِىْ إِمَامًا وَّنُوْرًا وَّ

Allahumma aanis waḥshatee fee qabree! Allahummar-ḥamnee bil-Qur-aanil-'Aẓeemi waj'alhu leee imaamaɱw-wa noorañw-wa

O Allah! Change my fear in my grave into love! O Allah! Have mercy on me in the name of the Great Qur'an; and make it for me a Guide and Light and

هُدًى وَّرَحْمَةً اللّٰهُمَّ ذَكِّرْنِىْ مِنْهُ مَا نَسِيْتُ وَعَلِّمْنِىْ مِنْهُ مَا جَهِلْتُ وَارْزُقْنِىْ تِلَاوَتَهُ اٰنَاءَ

hudañw-wa raḥmah! Allahumma zakkirnee minhu maa naseetu wa 'allimnee minhu maa jahiltu warzuqnee tilaawatahooo aanaaa'al-

O Allah! Make me remember what of it I have forgotten; and make me know of it that which have become ignorant of; and make me recite it in the hours of

الَّيْلِ وَاٰنَاءَ النَّهَارِ وَاجْعَلْهُ لِىْ حُجَّةً يَّا رَبَّ الْعٰلَمِيْنَ

layli wa aanaaa'an-nahaari waj'alhu lee ḥujjatañy-yaa Rabbal-'aalameen.

the night and the day; and make it an argument for me O Thou Sustainer of (all) the worlds!
Ameen!

الحمدُ لله نحمدُهُ ، وهو المستحقُّ للحمد والثناء، نستعين به في السَّراء والضَّراء، ونستغفره ونستهديه لما يقرّبنا إليه، ونؤمن به، ونتوكلُ عليه، في جميع حالاتنا، ونصلي ونسلم على أفضل مبعوث للعالمين، وأوّل مشفّع في يوم العرض والحساب سيّدنا محمّد ونبيّنا محمّد وعلى آله وأصحابه ومن تبع هديه إلى يوم الدِّين. اللهم يا باسطَ اليدين بالعطيّة والإجابة لعباده، وياصاحبَ المواهب والعطف والرَّأفة على خلقه، نسألكَ اللهمّ أن تصلّي وتسلم على عبدك ورسُولك محمّد، كما صلّيت على إبراهيم وعلى آل إبراهيم إنّك حميدٌ مجيدٌ. اللهمّ إنّا عبيدكَ بنو عبيدِكَ بنو إمائكَ، عدلٌ فينا قضاؤكَ، نسألُكَ بكلّ اسم هو لك، سمّيتَ به نفسكَ، أو أنزلته في كتابك، أو علّمته أحداً مِنْ خلقكَ، أو استأثرتَ به في علم الغيب عندك، يا حيُّ يا قيّوم أن تجعل القرآن العظيم ربيع قلوبنا ونور أبصارنا، وجلاء حزننا، وذهاب همّنا وغمّنا يا أرحم الرَّاحمين ، اللهُمّ يا ذاالمنّ ولايُمَنّ عليه، ياذاالجلال والإكرام، يا محيط بالليّالي والأيّام، نسألك يا أرحم الرَّاحمين، يا جار المستجيرين، يا أمان الخآئفين، أن تجعل القرآن العظيم ربيع قلوبنا ونورَ أبصارنا، وجَلاءَ حُزننا، وذَهابَ همِّنا وغمّنا. اللهُمّ إنّا نسألُكَ إيمانًا لايَرتَدُّ، ونعيماً لاينفد وقُرّةَ عينٍ لاتنقطع، ولذّةَ النَّظر إلى وجهكَ، ومرافقة نبينا مُحَمّد صلى الله عليه وسلم في جنَّات النعيم.

اللهُمَّ ارحَمْنا بترك المعاصي أبدا ماأبقيتَنا، وارحمنا أن نتكلّف فيما يُرضيك عَنّا، وارزقنا حسن النَّظر فيما يُرضيكَ عنّا. اللهُمّ بديع السَّمَوَات والأرض ذاالجلال والإكرام والعزّ ةالَّتي لاترام، نسألك يا الله يا رحمن ونور بجلالك ونور وجهكَ أن تُلزم قلوبنا حفظَ كتابك كما علّمتنا، وارزقنا أن نتلوَهُ على النَّحو الَّذي يرضيك عَنّا. اللهُمّ بديع السَّمَوَاتِ والأرضِ ذاالجلال والإكرام والعزّةِ الَّتي لاترام، نسألكَ يا الله يا رحمن ونور بجلالك ونور وجهكَ أن تنوّر بكتابك أبصارنا وأن تُطلِق به ألسنتنا وأن تُفرّج به عن قلوبنا، وأن تشرحَ به صدورنا، وأن تستعمل به أبداننا، فإنه لايُعيننا على الحَقّ غيركَ ولا يؤتيه لنا إلاّأنت ولاحول ولا قُوّةَ إلّا باللهِ العليّ العظم اللهُمّ إنّا نسألُك رحمةً من عندِك تَهدي بها قُلوبَنا، وَتجمع بها أمورنا وَتلُمّ بها شعثَنا، وتُصلِح بها غائِبَنا، وتُزكّي بها غائبَنا، وتلهمنا بها رُشدَنا وتَرُدّنا بها الألفَنَا وَتعصِمُنا بها من كلّ سوءٍ. رَبّنَا لاتؤاخِذنا إن نسينا أو أخطأنا، رَبّنَا ولاتحمل علينا إصرًا كَمَا حملتَهُ على الّذين من قبلنا، رَبّنَا ولاتُحَمِّلنا ما لا طاقة لنا به واعفُ عَنّا واغفرْ لنا وارْحَمنَا. أَنت مولانا فانصرنا على القَومِ الكَافِرِين.

اللهُمّ فارج الهَمّ، كَاشِفَ الغَمّ، مجيب دعوة المضطرّين، رحمَانَ الدُّنيا والآخِرَة ورَحيمَهُما، ارحمنا برحمةٍ تغنينا بها عن رحمة من سواك. اللهُمّ اكفنا بحلالك عن حرامك وبطاعتك عن معصيتك وأغننا بفضلك وجودك وكرمك عمن سواك. اللهُمّ إنا نسألُكَ إيمانا يباشر قلوبنا، ويقيناً صادقاً حتى نعلم أنه لايصيبُنا إلّاماكتبت لنا، واجعلنا راضين من الرّزق والعيش بما قسمت لنا، اللهُمّ إنا نسألُك موجبات رحمتك وعزائم مغفرتك، والسَّلامة من كل إثم، والغنيمة من كلّ بِرّ، ونسألُك الفوز بالجنة والنجاة من النار. اللهُمّ اقسم لنا من خشيتك ما تحول به بيننا وبين معاصيك، ومن طاعتك ما تُبَلّغنا به جنّتك. ومن اليقين ماتهوّن به مصائب الدنيا ومتّعنا اللهُمّ بأسماعنا وأبصارنا وقوّاتنا ما أحييتنا، واجعله الوارث منا. واجعل ثارنا على من ظلمنا وانصرنا على مَن عادانا. ولاتجعل مصيبتنا في ديننا، ولا تجعل الدنيا أكبر همنا. ولا مبلغ علمنا. ولا تسلّط علينا بذنوبنا من لايخافك ولا يرحمنا. وكُفّ أيدي الظّالمين عنّا، برحمتك يا أرحم الرّاحمين. اللهُمّ اجعلنا ممن سبقت لهم منك الحسنى وزيادة. اللهُمّ أغننا بالعلم. وزيّنا بالحلم. وأكرمنا بالتقوى وجملنا بالعافية. اللهُمّ علّمنا ماينفعنا وانفعنا بما علمتنا، وزدنا علماً، والحمدلله على كل حال ونعوذ باللهِ من حال أهل النار.

اللهُمّ اجعل جمعنا هذا جمعًا مرحومًا، وتفرقنا من بعده تفرقًا معصومًا، ولاتجعل فينا ولامعنا شقيًّا ولا مطرودًا ولامحرومًا برحمتك يا أرحم الرّاحمين. يا حيّ يا قيّوم برحمتك نستغيث، ومن عذابك نستجير، أصلح لنا شأننا كله، ولا تكلنا إلى أنفسنا طرفة عين. رَبّنَا لاتُزِغ قلوبنا بعد إذ هديتنا وهب لنا من لدنك رحمةً إنك أنت الوهّاب، اللهُمّ ارحمنا وارحم آباء نا وأُمّهاتنا وإخوَانَا المسلمين، الذين سبقونا بالإيمان ولاتجعل في قلوبنا غِلاًّ لِّلَّذين آمنوا ربنا إنّك رؤوف رحيم. اللهُمّ ارحمهم، وعافهم، واعف عنهم، وأكرم نُزُلهُم و وسّع مَدخَلَهُم واغسلهم بالماء والثلج والبَرَد. اللهُمّ جازهم بالحسنات إحسانًا وبالسيئات عفوًا وغفرانًا. ولَقّهم برحمتك رضاك وقِهم فتنة القبر وعذابه. اللهُمّ أوصل ثواب ماقرأناه من القرآن العظيم إليهم وضاعف رحمتك ورضوانك عليهم. اللهُمّ حل أرواحهم في محل الأبرار وتغمدهم بالرّحمة آناء الليل والنّهار برحمتك يا أرحم الراحمين. اللهُمّ انقلهم من ضيق اللحود والقبور الى سعة الدور والقصور، في سدر مخضود، وطلح منضود، وظلّ ممدود، وماءٍ مسكوب، وفاكهة كثيرة لامقطوعة ولا ممنوعة مع الذين أنعمت عليهم من النبيّين والصدّيقين والشّهدآء والصّالحين برحمتك يا أرحم الرّاحمين. اللهُمّ اجعلنا وإياهم من عبادك الذين تباهي بهم ملائكتك فى الموقف العظيم وارزقنا حسن النّظر إلى وجهك الكريم مع الذين أنعمت عليهم من النبيّين والصدّيقين والشهداء والصّالحين الذين تجري من تحتهم الأنهار في جنّات النعيم، دعواهم فيها سبحانك اللهُمّ وتحيتهم فيها سلام، وآخر دعوانا أن الحمد لله ربّ العالمين.

جمع

مدير إدارة إحياء التراث الإسلامي

خادم القرآن الكريم

عبدالله بن إبراهيم الأنصاري

Iiyit wa innaka dhuninband waj-litu fadhi iba lame riya ...
the night and the day, and of ace it an agreement you me of I hou...
cannot ...